The Parent's Desk Reference

Irene Franck and David Brownstone

Prentice Hall

New York London Toronto Sydney Tokyo Singapore

PRENTICE HALL GENERAL REFERENCE
15 Columbus Circle
New York, NY 10023

Manufactured in the United States of America

1 2 3 4 5 6 7 8 9 10

Library of Congress Cataloging-in-Publication Data

Franck, Irene M.
     The parent's desk reference / Irene Franck and David Brownstone.
          p.   cm.
     Includes bibliographical references and index.
     ISBN 0-13-650003-X (pbk.)
     1. Child rearing—United States—Handbooks, manuals, etc.
2. Parenting—United States—Handbooks, manuals, etc.
3. Children—United States—Handbooks, manuals, etc.
4. Children—Health and hygiene—United States—Handbooks,
manuals, etc.   5. Child development—United States—Handbooks,
manuals, etc.   I. Brownstone, David M.   II. Title.
[HQ769.F717   1992]
649′.1—dc20   92-2707
                                                            CIP

First Paperback Edition

Preface

The **Parent's Desk Reference** is a unique conception-to-college encyclopedia and resource book for parents, providing information, guidance, and sources of further help on a wide range of personal, educational, medical, social, and legal matters that affect parents and their children. Among the topics included are

- *pregnancy and childbirth*, including infertility treatments and prenatal screening tests, such as in vitro fertilization and amniocentesis.
- *child development*, including key skills and stages of development and suggestions for developing those skills.
- *nutrition and infant care*, including breastfeeding and proper diet.
- *genetic and other common disorders of childhood or pregnancy*, such as Down's syndrome, gestational diabetes, sudden infant death syndrome (SIDS), and chicken pox.
- *education and special education concerns*, such as learning disabilities, gifted children, the several schooling alternatives, and the multiple impacts of the Family Educational Rights and Privacy Act and other laws.
- *educational, medical, and psychological tests*, including the several general kinds of tests and such key specific tests as the Gesell Developmental Schedules, CT scans, and the California Achievement Tests.
- *family law and social services*, such as parents' rights, adoption, and the Parent Locater Service for child-support disputes.
- *key social problems relating to children*, such as drug and alcohol abuse, child abuse, and custody.

The main part of the book is an A-to-Z section consisting of over 2,500 entries on an extraordinarily wide range of matters that concern today's parents. Within each entry, words or phrases given in SMALL CAPITAL LETTERS act as cross-references, indicating that the reader can find more information under that heading.

In many of the most important entries, parents will also find descriptions of private and public organizations that will provide help and further information, as well as a sampling of recent publications on the topic. These will allow parents to tap into the now-vast network of organizations that has developed around the particular needs and interests of parents and their children—everything from mainstream groups concerned with parenting in general, such as the National Institute for Child Health and Development (NICHD), to small groups relating to very special interests, such as those for families with rare genetic disorders or single women who wish to have children by artificial insemination.

For most serious children's disorders, there is at least one major national association—often run by and for affected families—and these organizations can be lifelines for parents who need ongoing support and information as they face difficult decisions about their children's health and future. Note, however, that this is very much a book for *all* parents—for those raising children without major special problems and for those raising children *with* major special problems. For us, as for their parents, all children are "normal"; some just require more help than others.

Many of the book's A-to-Z entries are accompanied by special boxed materials, such as

- *sidelights* on what to expect, such as an explanation of the usual pattern of prenatal care or of why new parents should not worry about a baby's "funny-looking legs."
- *checklists* for possible trouble, such as signs of child abuse or observation checklists for learning disabilities or vision problems.
- *practical advice*, such as guidelines for performing the Heimlich maneuver on a choking child or for helping a child in a wheelchair.

- *evaluation guidelines*, such as what to look for in examining a child's school record or what to consider in choosing a doctor.
- *tips for parents*, on such subjects as how to make visitation work for kids and divorced parents or how to prepare for a parent–teacher conference.
- *related scientific information*, such as a description of the physiological changes that take place in a woman's body during pregnancy or the recommended immunization schedule for children.
- *other special information*, such as illustrations of basic life-support procedures or examples of the Bliss symbols used with young children unable to communicate with words.

Following the A-to-Z portion of the book is a Special Help section with even more such information, much of it too extensive to fit in the A-to-Z entries. This Special Help section will include such additional materials as

- *Hotlines, Helplines, and Helping Organizations*, a quick reference guide and index to the organizations described in the book and their hotlines and helplines, for when parents want immediate, urgent help.
- *Safety Checklist*, outlining what infants can do and how parents must protect them at various stages of development.
- *Chart of Normal Development*, outlining the development of key skills (such as motor, language, self-help, social, and cognitive skills) from birth through age six.
- *Teaching Young Children*, a section with general guidelines and teaching activities for parents of preschoolers.
- *Tips for parents on choosing a school and helping their children learn better* in various areas, such as reading, math, and test-taking.
- *Model curricula* for elementary and high school to help parents see how their own school "stacks up."
- *Help for Special Children*, including organizations and reference works to help parents assist children with special needs.
- *Parent's Bookshelf*, with works on parenting and other general topics.
- *Recommended reading lists for kids*, including prize winners and guides to children's reading, for parents seeking books for their children.

A complete listing of these Special Help sections is given on page 487.

Please note that although many health-related matters are discussed in this book, we strongly feel that no book should be used as a substitute for on-the-spot professional advice. We urge parents to quickly see their doctor, dentist, or other appropriate health professional when health problems arise.

Our thanks go to our editor, Kate Kelly, to assistant editor Susan Lauzau, and to production editor Lisa Wolff, who so capably shepherded the book through the production process. Thanks, too, to Gene Hawes for his valued counsel, and to Mary Racette for her expert typing and clerical help. As always, we also thank the staff of the Chappaqua Library and their colleagues throughout the northeastern library network, who so equably and successfully fulfilled our rather wide-ranging research needs. And here we thank, too, the scores of people in public and private organizations all over the country who so freely gave of their time and resources as we gathered information for this book.

Irene Franck
David Brownstone

abandonment In family law, deserting a child or leaving the child without effective supervision and provision for basic needs for too long a time. The age of the child, nature of the supervision (or lack of it), and the length of the unsupervised period all affect legal judgment as to whether abandonment has occurred, and state laws vary on these matters. But if a parent or parents are found to have abandoned a child, suit may be brought to terminate PARENTS' RIGHTS, after which the child may be adopted without parental permission. Stepparents or foster parents who wish to adopt a child but cannot locate the BIOLOGICAL PARENTS for permission sometimes initiate abandonment proceedings. If a child, especially an infant, is physically abandoned, as on a doorstep or in a garbage can, the parent can be liable to criminal prosecution. Such abandonment was once, and in some cultures still is, a common form of infanticide.

ABC Abbreviation for KAUFMAN ASSESSMENT BATTERY FOR CHILDREN.

ABC Inventory A type of individually administered READINESS TEST that attempts to assess the general maturity of preschoolers, ages 3½ to 6½. In the test's four different types of tasks, the child is asked to draw a man (as in the GOODENOUGH-HARRIS DRAWING TEST); answer language questions, such as "What has wings?"; answer thought questions, such as "What is ice when it melts?"; and perform motor tasks, including folding paper, copying a figure, or counting items. The test administrator then scores the results according to the test manual. The ABC Inventory is often used by schools for class placement and may also be used as a kind of DEVELOPMENTAL SCREENING TEST, to identify children who may have learning problems that require further evaluation. (For help and further information, see TESTS.)

ABC method Alternate term for PHONICS METHOD.

ability grouping Alternate term for TRACKING.

ability test A type of TEST designed to measure performance of a particular skill or skills, such as a typing test; also an alternate term for INTELLIGENCE TEST.

aborted crib death Alternate term for APPARENT LIFE-THREATENING EVENT (ALTE), referring (perhaps mistakenly) to the thought that an infant has just barely survived SUDDEN INFANT DEATH SYNDROME; sometimes called *near-miss SIDS*.

abortion Termination of a PREGNANCY, whether involuntarily or deliberately. Many abortions occur naturally, often because of GENETIC DEFECTS in the EMBRYO that are incompatible with life; medically these are called *spontaneous abortions* or MISCARRIAGES. At least 10 percent, and perhaps closer to 30 percent, of all pregnancies are thought to end in spontaneous abortions, often before the woman realizes she is pregnant.

It is the deliberate termination of a pregnancy, called *elective* or *induced abortion*, about which controversy rages. This is what those opposed to abortion often call *feticide* or *infanticide*. For a long time illegal (and still so in many parts of the world), abortions were for centuries performed in back alleys and other nonsterile settings, often by ill-trained practitioners or by the pregnant women themselves, using such dangerous tools as knitting needles and coat hangers. Such operations posed great risks to the women, including life-threatening infection or hemorrhage, especially to those too poor to travel to countries where abortions were performed legally and in hospitals or hospital-like settings. In the United States the situation changed in 1973, in *Roe v. Wade*, when the U.S. Supreme Court ruled on the issue, providing for unrestricted abortion in the first TRIMESTER (three months) of pregnancy, state regulation of abortion in the second trimester, and state regulation or prohibition of abortion in the third trimester, except where the mother's life or health was threatened (requiring a so-called *therapeutic abortion*).

After abortions became legal and widely available in the United States, millions of abortions were carried out, many at women's clinics, which offered both abortions and BIRTH-CONTROL advice. However, many people opposed abortions, arguing that life began at CONCEPTION and that the right of the fetus to life took precedence over the mother's right to choose whether or not to bear a child. Their protests placed great pressure on such clinics, and in some rural areas the nearest one might be hundreds of miles away. Various federal and state laws have also limited the use of public funds for abortion and have sometimes restricted the right of a teenage girl to have an abortion without parental consent. And in recent years, the Supreme Court has backed away somewhat from its *Roe v. Wade* position. All of these factors have limited practical access to abortions, especially to poor adolescent women in rural areas, and have put pressure on the concept of *abortion on demand*. Some women, fearing they will lose the right to legal abortion, have even formed self-help groups to perform abortions on each other.

1

But, in fact, abortions continue to be widespread. With the rise of various GENETIC SCREENING tests, such as AMNIOCENTESIS, CHORIONIC VILLUS SAMPLING, ALPHA FETOPROTEIN, and ULTRASOUND SCANS, many couples these days routinely screen their fetus for possible GENETIC DEFECTS and CHROMOSOMAL ABNORMALITIES, and many take the option of abortion if severe defects are found. Doctors may recommend therapeutic abortions in some situations, as when the mother has a condition that might become life-threatening during pregnancy, such as heart problems, kidney problems, and CANCER, especially of the BREASTS or CERVIX, or in which the mother is exposed to or carrying an infection that can seriously damage the baby, such as RUBELLA (German measles) or AIDS. Many women have also sought abortions in large numbers for their own personal, social, and economic reasons.

Abortions in the first trimester are often carried out by VACUUM EXTRACTION; sometimes this procedure is combined with *curettage*, or scraping of the lining of the UTERUS, to be sure no tissue remains from the fetus or PLACENTA, a procedure performed under general or local ANESTHESIA. Abortions in the second trimester may be performed in the same way or (especially after the 15th week) may use either a saline solution or HORMONE injection to induce CONTRACTIONS in the uterus, usually expelling the fetus in about 12 hours; the woman normally remains in a HOSPITAL for one to two days afterward. When performed under hospital or clinic conditions, the MORTALITY RATE is relatively low (less than one in 100,000 abortions in the first trimester), but it rises later in the pregnancy. In addition, multiple abortions carry an increased risk of later miscarriage or INFERTILITY.

Many couples who have decided to have no more children choose STERILIZATION, as a permanent form of birth control, rather than face the question of possible abortion later on. Parents of sexually active children, especially daughters, may want to discuss birth control as part of home SEX EDUCATION in an attempt to forestall the question of abortion. If they are not unalterably opposed to abortion for religious or other reasons, they may also want to discuss abortion openly, to open the lines of communication with their teenagers, rather than risking the possibility that they may attempt to deal with an unwanted pregnancy on their own.

For help and further information

Planned Parenthood Federation of America (PPFA), 212-541-7800. (For full group information, see BIRTH CONTROL.)

National Abortion Federation (NAF)
1436 U Street, NW, Suite 103
Washington, DC 20009
202-667-5881, toll-free hotline U.S. (except DC) 800-772-9100
Barbara Radford, Executive Director
Organization of abortion service providers, such as doctors, clinics, and women's health centers. Sets standards and guidelines; provides information and makes referrals; seeks to edu-

cate public and influence government policy; operates toll-free number; publishes various materials for professionals and public, including *Consumer's Guide to Abortion Services* (in English and Spanish).

National Abortion Rights Action League (NARAL)
1101 14th Street, NW
Washington, DC 20005
202-371-0779
Kate Michelman, Executive Director
Organization of people seeking to retain women's rights to legal abortion. Seeks to educate public and influence government policy; publishes newsletter.

Religious Coalition for Abortion Rights (RCAR)
100 Maryland Avenue, NE
Washington, DC 20002
202-543-7032
Frederick F. Hodges, Executive Director
Organization of religious groups seeking to ensure continuation of the legal right to abortion. Seeks to educate public and influence government policy; publishes various materials, including quarterly newsletter *Options* and legislative alerts and fact sheets.

National Institute of Child Health and Human Development (NICHD), 301-496-5133. (For full group information, see PREGNANCY.)

Anti-Abortion or Abortion Alternative Groups

National Right to Life Committee (NRLC)
419 Seventh Street, NW, Suite 402
Washington, DC 20004
202-626-8800
J.C. Willke, M.D., President
National organization opposing abortion and euthanasia. Seeks to educate public and influence public policy and legislation; supports alternatives to abortion, including counseling and adoption; gathers research data and maintains library; publishes biweekly *National Right to Life News* and pamphlet *Challenge to Be Pro-Life*.

Americans United for Life (AUL)
343 South Dearborn, Suite 1804
Chicago, IL 60604
312-786-9494
Edward R. Grant, Director General and Counsel
Organization devoted to protecting life, opposing abortion and euthanasia. Supports AUL Legal Defense Fund; maintains library of printed materials and legal rulings; publishes various materials, including newsletter *Lex Vitae*.

Birthright, United States of America
686 North Broad Street
Woodbury, NJ 08096

609-848-1819, Abortion Alternative Hotline 800-848-LOVE [5683] Denise Cocciolone, Executive Director
Network of independently operating, volunteer-funded, interdenominational groups aiming to persuade pregnant women to seek alternatives to abortion. Offers classes in childbirth and parenting; operates a telephone hotline; publishes various printed materials, including newsletter *Life-Guardian*.

Human Life International (HLI), 301-670-7884. (For full group information, see NATURAL FAMILY PLANNING.)

National Youth Pro-Life Coalition (NYPLC)
Jackson Avenue
Hastings-on-Hudson, NY 10706
914-478-0103
Mary Anne Hughes, Executive Director
Organization of young people, junior-high-school age and up, who oppose abortion. Seeks to educate and influence others, as through local groups; some members work summers in emergency counseling centers for pregnant women; publishes monthly *New Human*.

Other reference sources
General Works

Abortion: The Clash of Absolutes, by Laurence H. Tribe. New York: Norton, 1990.
Decoding Abortion Rhetoric: The Communication of Social Change, by Celeste M. Condit. Champaign, IL: University of Illinois Press, 1990.
Crusaders: Voices from the Abortion Front, by Marian Faux. New York: Birch Lane/Carol, 1990.
Confessing Conscience: Churched Women on Abortion, Phyllis Tickle, ed. Nashville, TN: Abingdon, 1990.
Abortion and Catholicism: The American Debate, Patricia Beattie Jung and Thomas H. Shannon, eds. Discussions by 20 leading American Catholics. New York: Crossroad, 1990.
The Abortion Question, by Hyman Rodman, Betty Sarvis, and Jay Walker Bonar. Irvington, NY: Columbia University Press, 1990.
Contested Lives: The Abortion Debate in an American Community, by Faye D. Ginsburg. Berkeley: University of California Press, 1990.
The Ethics of Abortion: Pro-Choice vs. Pro-Life, Robert M. Baird and Stuart Rosenbaum, eds. Buffalo, NY: Prometheus, 1989.
Over Our Live Bodies: Preserving Choice in America, by Shirley Radl. Dallas, TX: Steve Davis, 1989.
Mother-Love and Abortion: A Legal Interpretation, by Robert D. Goldstein. Berkeley, CA: University of California Press, 1988.
Abortion, Medicine and the Law, Dr. J. Douglas Butler and David F. Walbert, eds. New York: Facts on File, 1986.
Abortion: The Continuing Controversy, Carol C. Collins, ed. New York: Facts on File, 1984.
Abortion and the Politics of Motherhood, by Kristin Luker. Berkeley: University of California Press, 1984.
Moments on Maple Avenue: The Reality of Abortion, by Louise Kapp Howe. New York: Macmillan, 1984.

Men and Abortion: Lessons, Losses, and Love, by Arthur Shostak, Gary McLouth, and Lynn Seng. New York: Praeger, 1984.
The Law Giveth: Legal Aspects of the Abortion Controversy, by Barbara Milbauer and Bert N. Obrentz. New York: Atheneum, 1983.
Mandatory Motherhood: The True Meaning of Right to Life, by Garrett Hardin. Boston: Beacon, 1974.

For Kids

Medicine and the Law, by Neil Grauer. New York: Chelsea House, 1990. Overview of various issues including abortion. For grades 7 to 10.
Abortion, by Mandy Wharton. New York: Watts, 1989.

abruptio placentae A disorder in which the PLACENTA, which provides nourishment to a FETUS, separates prematurely from the UTERUS wall, threatening the PREGNANCY.

absence seizure In EPILEPSY, a kind of SEIZURE that involves brief periods of blankly staring unconsciousness; also called *petit mal seizure*.

absent parent A parent who does not live with a child, including a parent who has lost CUSTODY of the child, a parent who has abandoned a child (see ABANDONMENT), and a father who has never acknowledged paternity. Though absent, such parents retain the PARENTS' RESPONSIBILITY of providing support for a child, so various CHILD SUPPORT agencies spend great effort in locating them, if necessary.

ABSI Abbreviation for ADAPTIVE BEHAVIOR SCALE FOR INFANTS AND EARLY CHILDHOOD.

abused parent An adult who was subjected to abuse as a child. Such parents are considered at higher-than-normal risk of later inflicting CHILD ABUSE AND NEGLECT.

academic curriculum A type of CURRICULUM designed primarily for college-bound students.

accelerated programs In EDUCATION, programs proceeding at a faster-than-usual pace, generally meaning that a student covers course material more quickly than usual, perhaps two years' work in one year, or that a student skips a year's coursework altogether, to take more advanced courses. In decades past, skipping grades was common for GIFTED CHILDREN, but faster-paced programs, often with ENRICHMENT, are now more common. Students who finish the required high-school coursework early, as by the end of the junior year, may apply for *accelerated college entrance*. In some colleges, EARLY ADMISSION policies allow some students to enter COLLEGE without having completed secondary-school course work. The COLLEGE ENTRANCE EXAMINATION BOARD administers a special program, the Accelerated College Enrollment Program (ACE), that allows students to take college courses on campus for credit, even before they formally leave high school and enter college.

accreditation Citation that a school's program of studies meets preestablished standards set by the evaluating agency, such as a state department of education, a regional association assigned the task of evaluating educational standards, or an association that attempts to set standards in an area, as in PRESCHOOL education. Among the aspects of a school that might be examined in an accreditation evaluation are the quality of the teachers (their level of training for the subjects and ages they are teaching), the nature of the CURRICULUM, the adequacy of the school's resources (classroom and other facilities, library, laboratory equipment, and the like), the success of the school's students on STANDARDIZED TESTS, ADMISSION requirements, the STUDENT–TEACHER RATIO, and the school's general reputation. Parents who are sending their children to PRIVATE SCHOOLS or ALTERNATIVE SCHOOLS should look carefully at the school's accreditation, as some measure of the school's educational performance. (For a parent's checklist for evaluating schools, see CHOOSING A SCHOOL FOR YOUR CHILD, on page 514.) Accreditation is especially important on the COLLEGE level, because, without it, a student may not be eligible for federal financial aid or be able to transfer credits to another college, if desired.

Accutane A prescription drug whose generic name is *isotretinoin*, a synthetic derivative of VITAMIN A used to treat severe types of cystic ACNE unresponsive to other medications. Known from the time of its approval to cause BIRTH DEFECTS, Accutane continued to be used by many women who became pregnant. Often it was used in the first weeks after CONCEPTION, before the pregnancy was recognized. Among the birth defects associated with fetal exposure to Accutane are HYDROCEPHALY (increase in the amount of fluid in spaces in the BRAIN), a very small head (*microcephaly*), various ear and facial abnormalities, heart defects, and MENTAL RETARDATION. Women are advised to have a PREGNANCY TEST performed at least two weeks before starting Accutane therapy, to start the therapy on the second or third day of their next MENSTRUAL PERIOD, and to use two reliable forms of CONTRACEPTION simultaneously during therapy if they do not abstain from sexual intercourse.

For further information

March of Dimes Birth Defects Foundation, 914-428-7100 (local chapters in telephone-directory white pages). Publishes information sheet *Accutane*. (For full group information, see BIRTH DEFECTS.)

National Institute of Child Health and Human Development (NICHD), 301-496-5133. (For full group information, see PREGNANCY.)

Food and Drug Administration (FDA), 301-443-3170. (For full group information, see DRUG REACTIONS AND INTERACTIONS.)

ACE Acronym for the Accelerated College Enrollment Program. (See ACCELERATED PROGRAMS.)

achalasia A rare type of DIGESTIVE DISORDER.

achievement age Alternate term for EDUCATIONAL AGE, reflecting a student's comparative performance on an ACHIEVEMENT TEST.

achievement test A type of educational test that measures how much knowledge or what level of skills a student has gained, often after specific instruction, as opposed to an APTITUDE TEST or INTELLIGENCE TEST. Test scores are often given in comparative terms, relating a student's score to widely established norms, the result being an EDUCATIONAL AGE. Among the achievement tests commonly used in schools are the CALIFORNIA ACHIEVEMENT TESTS, IOWA TESTS OF BASIC SKILLS, METROPOLITAN ACHIEVEMENT TESTS, SRA ACHIEVEMENT SERIES, STANFORD ACHIEVEMENT TESTS, and WIDE RANGE ACHIEVEMENT TEST—REVISED. Some achievement tests are also READINESS TESTS, designed to see whether a child has learned information basic to planned new learning, such as READING. (For help and further information, see TESTS; STANDARDIZED TESTS; EDUCATIONAL AGE.)

achondroplasia A type of BONE DISORDER that leads to abnormal GROWTH of the skull and the long bones of the arms and legs, resulting in short stature, or DWARFISM, though the trunk is more nearly normal size; also called *chondrodystropy* or *fetal rickets*. In achondroplasia, the tips of the long bones, the *epiphyses*, are blocked from further growth because connecting cartilage prematurely turns to bone, in severe cases beginning during fetal development. This results in short, thick, often bowed arms and legs; protruding forehead; SPINAL DISORDERS such as LORDOSIS (swayback) and KYPHOSIS (humpback); short, stubby fingers widely separated between third and fourth fingers (called *trident fingers*); and loose joints.

Many children affected by achondroplasia die in the fetal stage or in early childhood. Those who survive have a tendency to develop EAR AND HEARING PROBLEMS from frequent ear infections, breathing problems from constriction of the chest, problems with TEETH from overcrowding, and pain and PARALYSIS in the lower body because of pressure on the spinal cord, which may require surgery. Skeletal abnormalities make the children slow to develop MOTOR SKILLS, such as WALKING and standing, but they generally have normal intelligence. They face formidable psychological problems, however, since neither the physical world nor the other people in it are geared to people of small and disproportionate body size.

Achondroplasia occurs in about one out of every 10,000 births. Many cases result from a GENETIC DISORDER of the AUTOSOMAL DOMINANT type, in which a parent with achondroplasia has a one-in-two chance of passing the defect on to his or her child. However, over 80 percent of the cases occur in children of parents without the disorder, the defect apparently resulting from a new mutation in either the egg (OVUM) or SPERM. How or why this happens is unclear, but older fathers are somewhat more likely to have children with the disorder.

Parents with achondroplasia may want to seek GENETIC COUNSELING when planning a PREGNANCY, but most cases cannot be anticipated and prevented. The condition can sometimes be diagnosed during pregnancy using ULTRASOUND. Treatment with HUMAN GROWTH HORMONE (hGH) is of little help for achondroplasia, but researchers are exploring other HORMONES that might act on the problematic cartilage cells, as well as possible gene therapy.

For help and further information

Human Growth Foundation (HGF), 301-656-7540. Publishes various materials, including quarterlies *Growth Chart* and *HGF Ink* and brochures *Growth Series*. (For full group information, see GROWTH AND GROWTH DISORDERS.)

Little People of America, 415-589-0695. Publishes newsletter *LPA Today* and booklet *My Child Is a Dwarf*. (For full group information, see GROWTH AND GROWTH DISORDERS.)

National Institute of Arthritis and Musculoskeletal and Skin Diseases (NIAMS), 301-496-8188. (For full group information, see ARTHRITIS.)

National Institute of Child Health and Human Development (NICHD), 301-496-5133. (For full group information, see PREGNANCY.)

March of Dimes Birth Defects Foundation, 914-428-7100 (local chapters in telephone-directory white pages). Publishes information sheet on achondroplasia. (For full group information, see BIRTH DEFECTS.)

acid cholesteryl ester hydrolase deficiency Alternate name for *Wolman's disease*, a type of LIPID STORAGE DISEASE.

acknowledged father Legal term for a man who has admitted or stipulated that he is the biological FATHER of a child whose BIRTH PARENTS are unmarried.

acne A type of SKIN DISORDER, often chronic and perhaps with some genetic links, involving bacterial infection and inflammation of the sebaceous (oily) glands and hair follicles, for unknown reasons. One common form of acne, *acne vulgaris*, affects primarily adolescents. A rare form, *infantile acne*, affects male infants, who are especially likely to experience acne vulgaris later on. No cures exist, but several treatments are available, including topical ointments, antibiotics, and retinoids, a class of drugs derived from VITAMIN A. Adolescent and adult women being treated for severe *cystic acne* need to be sure to anticipate any possible PREGNANCY before beginning therapy, since some medications, notably ACCUTANE, are associated with a wide range of BIRTH DEFECTS.

For help and further information

National Institute of Arthritis and Musculoskeletal and Skin Diseases (NIAMS), 301-496-8188. (For full group information, see ARTHRITIS.)

National Cancer Institute (NCI), 800-4-CANCER [422-6237]. (For full group information, see CANCER.)

Other reference sources

Overcoming Acne: The How and Why of Healthy Skin Care, by Virginia Alvin, and Robert Silverstein. New York: Morrow, 1990. For ages 12 and up.
(See also SKIN DISORDERS.)

acoustic neuroma A benign BRAIN TUMOR involving the *auditory nerve*, which transmits electrical signals from the ear to the brain; also called *eighth nerve tumor, neurinoma*, or *Schwannoma*. If detected early, the tumor can be removed without hearing damage; but if diagnosed late, acoustic neuromas (though not malignant) can be life-threatening, or surgical removal can at least involve hearing loss, disturbance of the sense of balance (related to the inner ear), and loss of feeling or PARALYSIS in the face. Symptoms associated with acoustic neuromas are hearing loss in one or both ears, HEADACHES, dizziness, ringing in the ears (TINNITUS), and numbness in the face. Acoustic neuromas are sometimes associated with the GENETIC DISORDER called NEUROFIBROMATOSIS.

For help and further information

Acoustic Neuroma Association
P.O. Box 398
Carlisle, PA 17013-0398
717-249-4783
Virginia Fickel, President
Organization of and for people with acoustic neuromas or other tumors of the cranial nerves. Encourages formation of mutual-support self-help groups; publishes various materials, including quarterly newsletter, booklet *Acoustic Neuroma*, and brochure *Acoustic Neuroma? Inside—Some Answers*.

National Institute of Neurological Disorders and Stroke (NINDS), 301-496-5751. (For full group information, see BRAIN AND BRAIN DISORDERS.)

acquired immune deficiency syndrome Full medical name of the disease better known as AIDS.

acting out A type of DEFENSE MECHANISM, in which a person expresses powerful inner feelings through behavior rather than words. When a child is troubled or in a stressful situation, acting out may seem disruptive, but it can be a way of dealing with feelings too painful or confusing to handle otherwise.

active immunization The most common form of IMMUNIZATION, in which a VACCINE is introduced into a person's system, either by injection or by mouth, triggering the formation of ANTIBODIES and the development of immunity for a limited time or a lifetime, depending on the vaccine; in contrast to PASSIVE IMMUNIZATION.

active vocabulary Words that a child can use independently in speaking or writing, as opposed to the PASSIVE VOCABULARY of words he or she can recognize or understand only in context in

READING matter. Because children, like adults, always understand much more than they can express, their passive vocabulary is much larger than their active one.

activity learning   A type of LEARNING STYLE in which the child is participating fully, using various sensory modes, as in building a model or conducting an experiment, not just sitting and listening.

acute laryngotracheobronchitis (LTB)   Medical term for CROUP.

ACYF   Initials for ADMINISTRATION FOR CHILDREN, YOUTH, AND FAMILIES, the federal arm overseeing the HEAD START program.

AD   Abbreviation for AUTOSOMAL DOMINANT, a pattern of GENETIC INHERITANCE.

adapted curriculum   Alternate term for functional CURRICULUM.

adapted education   Instruction that has been tailored to children's individual needs but, more usually, instruction modified for children who are unlikely to be able to handle a regular school program, notably students with various handicaps (see HANDICAPPED).

adaptive behavior   The skills needed to function normally in everyday settings, including SELF-HELP SKILLS, COMMUNICATION SKILLS, and SOCIAL SKILLS; a general process of development that begins in infancy as a baby makes "contact" with and begins to communicate with those around him or her and learns from them how to do all the things that will—years down the line—result in the baby becoming an independent person. In relation to DEVELOPMENTAL SCREENING TESTS and other tests for young children, such as the GESELL PRESCHOOL TESTS, the term "adaptive behavior" is often used to mean behavior indicating that a child can learn how to approach new tasks by watching how others do the tasks and then imitating them. Among children with MENTAL RETARDATION, the development of adaptive behavior is key to relatively independent functioning as an adult.

Adaptive Behavior Scale for Infants and Early Childhood (ABSI)   An individually administered test used to evaluate the development of infants and young children, from birth to age six, looking at general maturation, learning, and social adjustment. Following a standard interview and check sheet, a test administrator interviews a parent, teacher, or other adult close to the child. Among the areas covered are independent functioning (including SELF-HELP SKILLS, such as reaching and grasping, eating and drinking, toilet skills, and dressing), physical development (including both control of the body and locomotion, such as WALKING), communication skills, conceptual skills (such as awareness of quantity, shapes, or time), play (types of play performed, such as SENSORIMOTOR), self-direction (including initiative and ATTENTION SPAN), and personal responsibility and socialization (such as consideration for others and personal interaction). The level of a child's skills in various areas is compared with NORMS established on large populations. (For help and further information, see TESTS.)

ADC   Abbreviation for Aid to Dependent Children, an alternate name for AID TO FAMILIES WITH DEPENDENT CHILDREN.

ADD   Abbreviation for *attention deficit disorder*, now generally called ATTENTION DEFICIT HYPERACTIVITY DISORDER (ADHD).

Addison's disease   A condition involving a disorder of the ADRENAL GLANDS.

adenoids   Two small masses of tissue in the throat above the TONSILS, which act as filters in the *lymphatic system*, the network through which the body's IMMUNE SYSTEM operates. Situated near the back of the nose, adenoids shrink from about age five, normally disappearing by PUBERTY; but in some children they enlarge so as to obstruct the air passages, which causes snoring, a "nasal" voice, and breathing through the mouth. Sometimes they also affect the eustachian tube, resulting in EAR AND HEARING PROBLEMS. If a child has recurrent severe infections, the adenoids may be removed in an *adenoidectomy*, often at the same time as a *tonsillectomy* (see TONSILS).

adenoma   General term for a kind of TUMOR that arises from a gland, usually BENIGN but capable of causing various diseases by triggering overproduction of certain HORMONES.

ADH   Abbreviation for ANTIDIURETIC HORMONE, lack of which triggers DIABETES INSIPIDUS.

ADHD   Abbreviation for ATTENTION DEFICIT HYPERACTIVITY DISORDER.

adjustment disorder   A type of MENTAL DISORDER in which a person fails to adapt to a major stressful event in life, so that normal functioning (at home, school, or work) and social relationships are noticeably impaired. Adjustment disorders can occur at any age; among children, they often emerge around events such as parents' divorce or separation, death or serious illness in the family, loss of a job or home by a provider, and going to school. "Adjustment disorder" is a term used most often by psychiatrists for "maladaptive reactions" seen within three to six months of the onset of the stressful event but that do not primarily stem from other kinds of mental disturbances. (For help and further information, see MENTAL DISORDERS.)

Administration for Children, Youth, and Families (ACYF)   The federal arm of the Department of Health and Human Services that operates the HEAD START program. ACYF also supports social services in other areas, including CHILD CARE, ADOPTION, and placement with FOSTER PARENTS, especially focusing on children with SPECIAL NEEDS. (Address: 330 C Street, SW, Washington, DC 20201; 202-245-0354.)

administrative procedure   A method used in administering and enforcing laws in many areas, especially regarding benefits, including Social Security and many CHILD SUPPORT agencies. Administrative agencies make orders directly, such as for child support, rather than working through the court system. If individuals protest an agency's order, ruling, or decision, they can ask for an *administrative hearing*, often held before an administrative law judge, to review the case. These hearings are (perhaps deceptively) informal; witnesses may be called, but parties often have no legal representation, even though the resulting *administrative order* may have substantial effects on the persons involved. Procedure generally allows for the order to be further reviewed within the agency or in court if desired.

admission In EDUCATION, the formal acceptance of a student to enroll in a course of study at a school, after meeting the various requirements for entry, such as achieving an acceptable score on an ADMISSION TEST. At whatever level, from KINDERGARTEN to graduate school, some basic information about the student must be provided for admission, including identification and AGE (as attested by a BIRTH or BAPTISMAL CERTIFICATE). At every level beyond kindergarten, students must also provide TRANSCRIPTS of previous schoolwork. For PRIVATE SCHOOLS and for private and public COLLEGES, students also generally need to have recommendations, as from former teachers or local community leaders. In public schools, ADMISSION TESTS are normally used for SCREENING and diagnostic purposes, intended to help educators to assess where in the school the student might fit best and to see if the student has any special learning problems that need to be addressed. However, most private schools and colleges of any type base their admission decision at least partly on the student's scores on required entrance tests. Many also have students fill out applications, ranging from brief to lengthy, providing much personal information, which is also used in the admissions decision.

Admissions policies of colleges and universities vary widely. Some public colleges have an *open admissions* policy, meaning they will accept any applicant (sometimes limited by state) regardless of previous academic record, sometimes including students with a GENERAL EQUIVALENCY DIPLOMA. Such nonselective policies give many students a second chance academically, but open-admissions students often drop out at a high rate unless the colleges have special programs to help them strengthen their basic skills and unless the students themselves have strong motivation to succeed. Colleges that choose, on the basis of their particular requirements, among the students who apply are said to have *selective admissions*, while colleges that select the best qualified of the students who apply are said to have *competitive admissions*.

Normally, students applying for admissions send applications to colleges and universities by a specified date and hear the colleges' decisions in early spring, at which point the student decides which of the admission offers to accept. Under the CANDIDATES REPLY DATE AGREEMENT, sponsored by the COLLEGE ENTRANCE EXAMINATION BOARD, many colleges agree not to require students to give them a decision before May 1, by which point students will know which colleges have accepted and which have rejected them.

Some special admissions programs exist. Under the *early decision plan*, students can apply to some colleges early, usually in autumn of their senior year, and the colleges agree to respond quickly, usually in December. The student agrees to accept admission, if offered; if not offered, the student may apply to the same or other schools under the normal schedule, without prejudice. Some colleges have *rolling admissions*, under which a student's application is evaluated when received

and the decision communicated immediately, rather than on a set date.

For students in ACCELERATED PROGRAMS, some other options exist, including:

- EARLY ADMISSION to college before completing high school.
- accelerated college entrance at the end of the junior year, if all high school requirements have been met.
- the Accelerated College Enrollment Program (ACE), which allows students to take COLLEGE courses on campus for credit, even before they formally leave high school and enter college.
- ADVANCED PLACEMENT, in which students gain college credit for work done before admission, as through taking special high-school courses and passing a special examination.

(For help and further information, see EDUCATION; COLLEGE; PRESCHOOL; ADMISSION TEST.)

admission test A test required for acceptance and ADMISSION to a particular school. An acceptable score on the SCHOLASTIC APTITUDE TEST, for example, is required of many college-bound students; a good score on the GESELL PRESCHOOL TEST may be required for entrance into a selective KINDERGARTEN or PRESCHOOL. (For help and further information, see TESTS.)

adolescence The stage between childhood and adulthood; a turbulent period in which the child goes through the massive set of psychological and social problems that are the counterpart of the physical changes of PUBERTY. During this period adolescents begin to establish their own identity apart from their family and parents, to understand themselves as sexual beings with physical drives, and to begin shaping themselves as the adults they would like to be, often in imitation of local or celebrity role models.

Modern society has somewhat stacked the deck against adolescents. While in affluent Western countries, puberty is arriving sooner than in the past, adolescents are expected to postpone full adulthood ever longer, as COLLEGE is increasingly the norm. So the period during which adolescents desire and feel ready for independence extends for years, during which they remain dependent on their families, financially and to some extent emotionally. For some, the result is increasingly strong rebellion against parents, schools, and other authority figures; while at the opposite extreme others remain dependent, indecisive, and unable to move fully into adulthood.

Adolescence is often a difficult period for both parents and children. While adolescents are experimenting and trying uncertainly to discover who they are, parents are often hurt and resentful of their rebellion, sometimes seeing it as personal rejection and also frequently disapproving of the ideas, people, and styles the adolescents are "trying on." Experts in parent–adolescent relationships stress the importance of being supportive and keeping open the lines of communication, advising in particular that parents distinguish between continuing love and respect for their adolescents and possible disapproval of their behavior. Breakdown in communications can lead to escalating conflicts and, in the worst cases, to children becoming runaways or "throwaways" (see MISSING CHILDREN).

Many psychological and social problems arise during adolescence. Some, including some MENTAL DISORDERS, such as SCHIZOPHRENIA, are triggered at least partly by the physical changes of puberty; others, such as ALCOHOL ABUSE and DRUG ABUSE or ANOREXIA NERVOSA, may arise from the experimentation, uncertainty, and rebellion of the teenagers, sometimes combined with the pressure of their peers. Parents can find help in dealing with these by looking elsewhere in this book under the specific problem.

For help and further information

For or by Adolescents

Adolescence: A Guide for Teenagers and Their Parents, by Joel Engel. New York: Tor, 1990. For ages 9 and up.

Weathering the Storm: A Survival Guide for Teenagers, by Dan Clark. Latham, NY: British American, 1989.

Teenage Survival Manual, 4th edition, by H. Sam Coombs. Owls Head, NY: Discovery, 1989.

Smart Moves: How Young Adults Can Succeed in School, Sports, Career, and Life, by Dick DeVenzio. Buffalo: Prometheus, 1989.

Theo and Me: Growing Up Okay, by Malcolm-Jamal Warner with Daniel Paisner. New York: New American Library/Signet, 1989.

Teen Esteem: A Self-Direction Manual for Young Adults, by Pat Palmer with Melissa Alberti Froehner. San Luis Obispo, CA: Impact, 1989.

The Teenage Survival Book, by Sol Gordon. New York: Times Books/Random House, 1989.

Growing Up Feeling Good: A Growing Up Handbook Especially for Kids, by Ellen Rosenberg. New York: Puffin/Viking Penguin, 1989.

My Parents Are Driving Me Crazy, by Joyce L. Vedral. New York: Ballantine, 1989.

I'll Be Home Before Midnight and I Won't Get Pregnant, by Tony Wolf. New York: Vintage, 1988.

Teen Troubles: How to Keep Them from Becoming Tragedies, by Carolyn McLenahan Wesson. New York: Walker, 1988.

Thank God I'm a Teenager, revised edition, by Charles S. Mueller and Donald R. Bardill. Austin, TX: Augsburg, 1988.

Why Should I Care? Honest Answers to the Questions That Trouble Teens, by William R. Grimbol. Austin, TX: Augsburg, 1988.

Voices of Hope: Teenagers Themselves, Part III, compiled by the Glenbard East *Echo* advised by Howard Spanogle. New York: Adama, 1988. Part of a series of portraits of teenagers.

Dee Snider's Teenage Survival Guide. Garden City, NY: Doubleday, 1987.

(See also PARENT'S BOOKSHELF on page 566 for books for *parents* on adolescence and adolescent problems; also HELP AGAINST SUBSTANCE ABUSE on page 587.)

Adolescent Language Quotient (ALQ) The overall score resulting from the TEST OF ADOLESCENT LANGUAGE (TOAL).

adolescent pregnancy Pregnancies in teenage girls, of particular concern because of special problems affecting both mother and child. In the United States today, approximately one of every eight births is to an adolescent mother. Most adolescent girls become pregnant without intending to do so. Some do not wish to keep the baby and so are faced with the difficult choice of having an ABORTION or placing the child for ADOPTION. In the past, many people have emphasized that bearing the child for adoption was the better course, thinking that abortion caused both short- and long-term stress for teenage girls. Some recent studies have indicated, however, that—for at least some young girls—having an abortion may be less traumatic than giving up a baby to other parents, as well as less disruptive to their education and to their lives in general. Those who choose to bear and keep their child often fail to finish school and lack essential job skills for later in life, just as those who choose abortion are sometimes haunted by the life that might have been.

Teenagers who choose to give birth face very special health problems. They often have not yet completed their own growth, have poor NUTRITION, have used contraceptives around the time of CONCEPTION, take medications that can cause BIRTH DEFECTS (before knowing they are pregnant), and do not receive any PRENATAL CARE until after the crucial first TRIMESTER has passed, if then. They often also have habits dangerous to the baby (such as SMOKING or ALCOHOL or DRUG ABUSE). As a result, they face an increased risk of difficult LABOR and death from complications of PREGNANCY (see MATERNAL MORTALITY), and their babies are more likely to be born PREMATURE and of LOW BIRTH WEIGHT, with increased risk of MENTAL RETARDATION, various medical problems, and INFANT MORTALITY. Parents of sexually active teenagers will be wise to be sure they are well informed about the various methods of BIRTH CONTROL, through SEX EDUCATION at home as well as at school.

For help and further information

National Organization of Adolescent Pregnancy and Parenting (NOAPP)
P.O. Box 2365
Reston, VA 22090
703-435-3948
Sharon Rodine, Coordinator
For adolescents, parents, professionals, and others interested in teenage pregnancy and parenting. Aims to strengthen services available to adolescent parents and their children; seeks to influence public policy and legislation on their behalf; publishes various materials, including *Directory of Adolescent Pregnancy and Parenting Programs*.

Association of Junior Leagues (AJL)
825 Third Avenue
New York, NY 10022

212-355-4380
Deborah Seidel, Executive Director
Network of local service clubs for women 18 to 45, aiming to strengthen volunteerism in the community. Nationwide programs include Adolescent Pregnancy Child Watch, Parent Seminars on Adolescent Sexuality, and Project Lead (for training young leaders); maintains library and publishes many materials.

Children's Defense Fund (CDF), 202-628-8787. (For full group information, see INDIVIDUALIZED EDUCATION PROGRAM.)

National Urban League (NUL)
500 East 62nd Street
New York, NY 10021
212-310-9000
John E. Jacobs, President
Organization devoted to improving lives of low-income people. Works through network of individuals and community-based organizations.

Other reference sources

General Works

Teen Pregnancy and Parenting, by Annette U. Rickel. New York: Hemisphere, 1989.
T.A.P.P. Sources: A National Directory of Teenage Pregnancy Prevention Programs, by Dominique Treboux. Metuchen, NJ: Scarecrow, 1989.

For or by Teenagers

Coping with an Unplanned Pregnancy, by Carolyn Simpson. New York: Rosen, 1990.
Teen Pregnancy, by JoAnn Bren Guernsey. New York: Crestwood, 1989. Part of the Facts About Series.
Teen Guide to Pregnancy, Drugs and Smoking, by Jane Hawksley. New York: Watts, 1989.
Teenage and Pregnant: What You Can Do, by Herma Silverstein. New York: Messner, 1988.
It Won't Happen to Me: Teenagers Talk About Pregnancy, by Paula McGuire. New York: Delacorte, 1983.
What to Do If You or Someone You Know Is 18 and Pregnant, by Arlene K. Richards and Irene Willis. New York: Lothrop, 1983.

adoption Taking into one's home and raising as one's own someone born to others, the child's BIOLOGICAL parents, also called BIRTH PARENTS or NATURAL PARENTS. Formal adoption involves transfer of legal CUSTODY of a child to the adoptive parents. This makes the adoptee legally part of the new family and means that the new FATHER and/or MOTHER has PARENTS' RIGHTS and PARENTS' RESPONSIBILITIES toward the adopted child. The adopted child also then legally has certain inheritance rights, under wills and insurance; these vary widely, however, so adoptive parents need to be sure that family legal documents— especially in such references as NEXT OF KIN, descendants, heirs of the body, "born to," or issue—are changed, if necessary, to specifically include legally adopted as well as biological children.

Although historically adoption has been arranged in a variety of ways, the standard U.S. route in the late 20th century has been *sealed adoption*, in which adoptive parents and child are brought together by a neutral organization, generally a public or private adoption agency. The agency conducts an intensive HOME STUDY to assess the prospective parents' suitability to adopt a child and often provides counseling to adoptive and birth parents. Once the child has been placed for adoption, the BIRTH CERTIFICATE and other personal records are kept strictly confidential and are generally unavailable to either biological parents, adoptive parents, or adopted child except by court order. The adoptive parents, the birth parents, and the child make up what is sometimes called the *adoption triangle*.

Under sealed adoption, adoptive parents learn only very general information about birth parents, such as age, race, ethnic background, religion, educational and occupational background, general medical and psychiatric history, information on intellect and personality, and some circumstances surrounding the birth and planned adoption, including whether the child is born outside marriage. Other information may be kept from adoptive parents, such as whether one or both birth parents are imprisoned or incest is involved.

Sealed adoption is intended to provide a clean break with the past, to give the child one home and family, instead of a possibly confusing two, and to protect the identity of all involved. But the decision to seal adoption records has been a source of considerable dispute in recent decades. Some adoptees have made long, difficult searches to try to identify their birth parents; conversely, some birth parents, regretting the decision to give a child up for adoption, have sought to find their child. Though some birth parents did not want to be "found," enough birth parents and children have sought each other for organizations (see below) to spring up around the country to aid in their search. Aside from desire for personal information about family background, increasing knowledge of GENETIC DISORDERS and people's need to have detailed health information on their BLOOD RELATIVES for GENETIC COUNSELING have also spurred the drive for information about birth parents. As a result, there have been some attempts to make such information available, while still protecting the privacy of birth parents, if desired. Some states also have laws allowing adopted people, once they become adults, to obtain certain information, though sometimes only with the consent of the birth parents.

Some states gather extensive information on the medical and psychiatric backgrounds of the birth parents of an adopted child. In Wisconsin, for example, social workers must prepare reports on:

- the medical and genetic history of the birth parents, along with any available genetic information from them about other blood relatives, such as grandparents, aunts, uncles, brothers, or sisters.

- any medical exam the birth parents had within the year before the proposed TERMINATION OF PARENT'S RIGHTS.
- the child's PRENATAL care and medical condition at birth.
- any other information relevant to the child's medical and genetic history.

In addition, if either birth parent is found to have a genetically transferable disease, social workers are required to notify the child's adoptive parents, guardian, or (if over 18) the child.

Partly in response to unhappiness with traditional "closed" adoption, some parents and adoption professionals have, in recent decades, been experimenting with alternatives. The most popular of these is *open adoption*, in which birth parents and adoptive parents meet and get to know each other, often during the pregnancy. At its most open, the two sets of parents maintain full contact, as through letters, photographs, and perhaps meetings, as the child grows. In some variants, the birth and adoptive parents meet early on but with no full names, addresses, or phone numbers given and no contact later; alternatively, confidential exchanges of letters and photographs between the adoptive parents or child and the birth parents may be made through the adoption agency.

Adoption of older children is more likely to be open, as some have living relatives, such as a grandparent or sibling, with whom they want to stay in touch. Children adopted from abroad often want to keep in touch with family members in their homeland.

Critics of open adoption are concerned about the child being torn between two sets of parents and about changes of heart by birth parents, leading to disruptive attempts to reverse the adoption. They say it was precisely the defects of historically open adoption that sealed adoption was meant to remedy.

Before the 20th-century rise of social workers, adoption was done privately (as of Frank Churchill in Jane Austen's *Emma*), and many *private*, *independent*, or *direct adoptions* are still made. Often these are among relatives or friends, as when someone adopts a brother, stepdaughter, goddaughter, or nephew. In other cases, would-be adoptors may send out feelers among friends, acquaintances, doctors, or lawyers or even put personal advertisements in local newspapers, seeking a child to adopt. Such arrangements bypass traditional adoption agencies and are especially attractive to would-be adoptors who wish to shortcut the home-study and adoption-agency-evaluation procedure or who feel that some elements of their life-style would cause them difficulty in such a traditional adoption. Single people, older people, poor people, homosexuals, or people who already have large families, for example, often choose to adopt independently. Such adoptions must be registered with a court to be official.

In an independent adoption, the child is normally placed in the adoptive home directly from the hospital. For the adoptive parents, the hazard is that the birth parents may reverse their decision and remove the child during a specified period before the adoption becomes permanent. States have varying restrictions about independent or direct adoptions. The two sets of parents often deal through a lawyer, but some states forbid

intermediaries, making it mandatory for adoptive and birth parents to deal with each other directly. These legal but nontraditional adoptions are sometimes called *gray-market* adoptions.

Beyond these are illegal, or *black-market*, adoptions, which involve payment of large amounts of money to intermediaries and to the birth parents or guardians. In the late 20th century, in the wake of the *Roe v. Wade* decision on ABORTION, fewer infants have been available for adoption, so some would-be adoptors have chosen to pay money for babies, the whole process being known as *baby brokering*. Because these are illegal adoptions, they can lead to heartbreak for all involved.

Another alternative has developed for some adoptions that originate privately: *identified* or *designated adoption*. Here the prospective parents contact an adoption agency, which then handles the details of the adoption. These include making a home study, counseling the birth parents, obtaining adoption consent papers from the birth parents, and arranging for the adoptors to pay for the birth mother's living and medical expenses.

An additional alternative is *legal risk adoption* or *foster/adoption*, in which a child is placed in the home of would-be adoptors as temporary FOSTER PARENTS while the final adoption is arranged, a process that can take months or, in extreme cases, even years. This approach is designed to move children into permanent homes as quickly as possible but can be risky for parents, because they may end up losing the child if the birth mother or other relatives (once located) fail to sign the papers releasing the child for legal adoption.

In truth, there is no shortage of children to adopt, but many unplaced children are less attractive to would-be adoptors because they are older, have siblings who wish to stay together, are of minority background, or have SPECIAL NEEDS. To encourage adoption of such HARD-TO-PLACE CHILDREN, states have developed *adoption subsidies* or *adoption assistance plans*, partly funded by federal grants, to cover some of the costs incurred by parents, with no MEANS TEST involved. The Adoption Assistance and Child Welfare Act of 1980 (Public Law 96-272) describes such children as those who have "a specific factor or condition (such as ethnic background, age, membership in a minority or sibling group, or the presence of medical conditions, such as physical, mental or emotional handicaps) that make it reasonable to conclude that the child could not be placed in an adoptive family without financial assistance." Such plans may, for example, pay parents a monthly sum or cover specified medical, psychiatric, and other costs; children receiving federal adoption assistance payments are also eligible for Medicaid benefits. Since state plans vary widely, parents who have made a *subsidized adoption* can have difficulty maintaining their payments if they move from one state to another; however, some states belong to an Interstate Compact on Adoption and Medical Assistance, aimed at easing such a transition and assuring continuity of coverage.

People who wish to adopt sometimes look abroad. Such a course is long, involved, and fraught with difficulties and frustration. *The Immigration of Adopted and Prospective Adoptive Children* (published by the U.S. Immigration and Naturalization

Adoption Paperwork

Adoption involves an enormous amount of paperwork, both in connection with the initial home study and in later actual adoption applications. Most adoptions require at least the following documents, some of which can take weeks or months to obtain; since you may need multiple copies for various applications, and often at least three copies for international adoption, you should probably order multiple copies.

Basic Documents Often Needed for an Adoption Home Study and Application:

- birth certificate (certified copy)
- marriage certificate (certified copy)
- divorce record (certified copy)
- death record of former spouse, if any (certified copy)
- medical statement on physical and perhaps mental health from physician, including information on infertility (often on agency-supplied forms)
- financial statements, such as bank statements, accountant's reports, or federal income-tax returns (notarized copies)
- employment statements, including position, length of service, salary, and stability of job
- birth certificates of other children, if applicable (certified copies)
- personal autobiographies
- photographs of yourself, other children, and your home
- proof of naturalization, if applicable
- check of police files for clear police record, especially regarding child abuse (check normally performed by agency)

Other Documents Often Needed from the Adoption Agency or Birth Parents

- consent of birth parents for adoption or (if impossible) of GUARDIAN, NEXT OF KIN, NEXT FRIEND, or agency appointed by court
- medical consent giving you legal right to provide medical treatment for child

- petition for adoption, to be filed in state court
- final order of adoption from court (sometimes preceded by temporary, or interlocutory, order)
- new birth certificate for adopted child, with new name and parents

Additional Documents Often Required for Adoption from Outside United States

- translations of basic documents (above), notarized, verified, and authenticated at consulate of child's country
- I-600 petition, "Petition to Classify Orphan as an Immediate Relative," to be filed with the Immigration and Naturalization Service (INS)
- I-600A, "Application for Advance Processing of Orphan Petition," to be filed with the INS before a specific child has been identified, to speed processing
- Form FD-258, showing adoptive parents' fingerprints
- birth certificate (or other proof of age) of child (certified copy, with translation)
- death certificate of child's birth parents (certified copy, with translation)
- formal evidence of the child's surviving parent's inability to provide for child (certified copy, with translation)
- release of the child by surviving parent, formally consenting to emigration and adoption (certified copy, with translation)
- evidence of child's unconditional abandonment to an orphanage by parents (certified copy, with translation)
- adoption decree (certified copy, with translation), if child was adopted abroad
- evidence that child has met preadoption requirements of proposed state of residence, such as posting bond
- passport for child
- alien registration for child in United States
- application for readoption of child in United States
- Form N-402, "Application to File Petition for Naturalization in Behalf of Child," including under-30-day-old photographs of child, or (if both adoptive parents are U.S. citizens) Form N-600, "Application for Certificate of Citizenship"
- Form G-641, "Certification of Birth Data," to act as birth certificate

Service) outlines the conditions would-be parents must meet to complete an adoption. Beyond this are the varying conditions set in the child's country of birth and in the family's intended state of residence. So many people have taken this route, however, that organizations (see below) have been formed to pass on counsel, experience, and support.

Whether at home or abroad, the person who wishes to adopt must be prepared to handle an enormous amount of paper. ADOPTION PAPERWORK (above) summarizes the main kinds of documents that must generally be gathered, often in multiple copies. Obtaining certified copies of birth, marriage, divorce, and death certificates is not always easy; the government publication *Where to Write for Vital Records: Births, Deaths, Marriages,*

and Divorces (published by the Public Health Service, National Center for Health Statistics) tells where to start the process.

For help and further information

About Adoption in General

National Committee for Adoption (NCFA)
1930 Seventeenth Street, NW
Washington, DC 20009
202-328-1200, Hotline 202-328-8072
William L. Pierce, Executive Director

Organization for adoptees, adoptive and birth parents, and adoption professionals. Supports confidentiality of adoption and works against private, nonstandard adoptions; monitors and attempts to influence adoption legislation; maintains library and conducts research; publishes various materials for professionals and individuals, including *Adoption Factbook: United States Data, Issues, Regulations and Resources*.

North American Adoption Congress (NAAC)
P.O. Box 44040, L'Enfant Station
Washington, DC 20026
206-481-6471, Referral Service 505-296-2198
Charlotte Hood, President

Organization for adoptees, adoptive and birth parents, and adoption professionals. Gathers information on adoption; acts as national clearinghouse for public; works for adoption reform; serves as referral service; publishes various materials.

Families Adopting Children Everywhere (FACE)
P.O. Box 28058, Northwood Station
Baltimore, MD 21239
301-256-0410
Laurel Strassberger, Contact

Organization for people who have adopted or wish to do so and people and agencies involved in adoption. Provides support and information for adoptive families, as through educational course "Family Building Through Adoption"; conducts research and seeks to influence legislation; publishes newsletter and other materials, such as *They Became Part of Us*.

OURS (Organization for United Response)
3307 Highway 100 North, Suite 203
Minneapolis, MN 55422
612-535-4829

Organization of adoptive parents. Encourages sharing of personal experiences by adoptive families; publishes various materials, including bimonthly magazine.

Emergency Council of Jewish Families (ECJF)
Two Penn Plaza, Suite 1500
New York, NY 10001
212-244-3100
Mr. E.B. Wert, Contact

Organization of social workers, community leaders, and interested others, acting on behalf of poor Jewish children and their families. Helps such families obtain whatever public and private services are available; finds and supports families to act as foster or adoptive parents for Jewish children; maintains library.

Child Welfare League of America (CWLA)
440 First Street, NW
Washington, DC 20001
202-639-2952

Organization of people interested in raising the level of care for dependent children, especially those deprived, abused, or neglected. Provides information and referrals, as to adoption agencies; does research; maintains library and information service; attempts to influence legislation and policy; publishes newsletter and other materials, including *On the Frontier of Adoption: A Study of Special Needs Adoptive Families* and *The*

Adoption Resource Guide: A National Directory of Licensed Agencies.

La Leche League International (LLLI), 312-455-7730. Publishes *Nursing Your Adopted Baby* and *Helping Love Grow: Parenting Adopted Children*. (For full group information, see BREASTFEEDING.)

About Adopting Children from Abroad

Americans for International Aid and Adoption
c/o Americans for International Aid (AIA)
1370 Murdock Road
Marietta, GA 30062
404-973-5909
Jodie Darragh, Executive Director

Organization of individuals and groups, including adoptive families, interested in aiding children abroad, especially in south and east Asia, Africa, and Latin America. Assists families where appropriate or arranges for adoptions of children, including many Amerasians; publishes newsletter.

International Social Service, American Branch (ISS/AB)
95 Madison Avenue
New York, NY 10016
212-532-5858
Wells C. Klein, Executive Director

International network of social-work agencies to aid families separated by national boundaries, as by migration. Helps arrange for custody and care of children, reunion of families, access to services, and adoptions; represents interests of children in public discussion of international migration.

Latin America Parents Association (LAPA)
P.O. Box 72
Seaford, NY 11783
516-795-7427
Joseph McGough, President

Organization for parents and others concerned with adoption of children from Latin America, or who wish to, and for interested others. Provides information and support, including seminars and workshops on Latin American culture and adoption processes; publishes newsletter.

About Adoption of Children With Special Needs

National Adoption Exchange
1218 Chestnut Street
Philadelphia, PA 19107
215-925-0200
Marlene Piasecki, Contact

Adoption referral service for people who wish to adopt hard-to-place children, including older, handicapped, or minority children or siblings. Gathers information from state and private agencies and seeks to match such children with prospective parents; operates National Adoption Center; maintains library; publishes newsletter, videotapes, and other materials, including *Books on Adoption for Children and Youth* (1986).

North American Council on Adoptable Children (NACAC)
1821 University Avenue, Suite 5275
St. Paul, MN 55104
612-644-3036
Organization for groups of adoptive parents, especially those of hard-to-place children, and concerned adoption professionals. Encourages close ties between parent groups and adoption agencies; acts as clearinghouse for adoption information; holds seminars and support programs; publishes newsletter and other materials, including *Self-Awareness, Self-Selection and Success: A Parent Preparation Guidebook for Special Needs Adoptions* and *Adopting Children with Special Needs: A Sequel.*

AASK America (Aid to Adoption of Special Kids)
657 Mission Street, #601
San Francisco, CA 94105
415-543-2275, toll-free 800-23A-ASK1 [232-2751]
Diane Mahan, National Director
Network of private, no-fee, full-service adoption agencies, all with boards led by parents, focusing on adoption of children in the United States public welfare system.

Eterna International Foundation for Disabled Children (EIFDC), 312-231-4400. Arranges for adoption of handicapped infants when parents are unable to care for them. (For full group information, see HELP FOR SPECIAL CHILDREN on page 578.)

National Down's Syndrome Adoption Exchange, 914-428-1236. (For full group information, see DOWN'S SYNDROME.)

Native American Adoption Resource Exchange
c/o Council of Three Rivers American Indian Center
200 Charles Street
Dorseyville, PA 15238
412-782-4457
Organization working to place Native American children for adoption into families with documented Native American ancestry.

Spina Bifida Adoption Referral Program, 513-372-2040. (For full group information, see SPINA BIFIDA.)

Little People of America, 415-589-0695. Works through agencies to arrange for adoption of dwarf children by similar parents. (For full group information, see GROWTH AND GROWTH DISORDERS.)

About Adoption by People in Special Situations

Committee for Single Adoptive Parents (CSAP)
P.O. Box 15084
Chevy Chase, MD 20815
202-966-6367
Hope Marindin, Executive Director
Organization for single people who have adopted a child or want to do so. Provides information and makes referrals; offers support and assistance in dealing with agencies; publishes *Handbook for Single Adoptive Parents.*

Single Mothers by Choice (SMC)
Box 7788, FDR Station
New York, NY 10150
212-988-0993
Jane Mattes, Chairperson
Organization for single women having or exploring bearing or adopting children outside marriage (not for widows or divorcees). Provides for mutual support, sharing of experiences, and cooperative assistance in such areas as baby-sitting or activities groups; acts as information clearinghouse; publishes newsletter.

RESOLVE, Inc., 617-484-2424. Offers adoption services, along with infertility treatments. (For full group information, see INFERTILITY.)

Lesbian Mothers National Defense Fund (LMNDF), 206-325-2643. Provides information on adoption for would-be lesbian mothers. (For full group information, see HOMOSEXUALITY.)

Lambda Legal Defense and Education Fund, 212-995-8585. Provides legal counsel for homosexuals wishing to adopt. (For full group information, see HOMOSEXUALITY.)

National Committee on Lesbian and Gay Issues, National Association of Social Workers, 301-565-0333. Provides advice and counsel to homosexuals wishing to adopt. (For full group information, see HOMOSEXUALITY.)

About Later Relationships
Between Adoptees and Birth Parents

ALMA Society (Adoptees' Liberty Movement Association)
P.O. Box 154
Washington Bridge Station
New York, NY 10033
813-542-1342
Florence Anne Fisher, President
Organization for adopted children (over 18), adoptive parents, and natural parents. Aims to aid adoptees and birth parents in finding each other and to provide mutual support.

Concerned United Birthparents (CUB)
2000 Walker Street
Des Moines, IA 50317
319-359-4068
Carole J. Anderson, President
Organization for birth parents and other supporters of adoption reform. Aims to have birth and adoption records opened to adoptees and birth parents; supports aid to families in difficulty, seeking alternatives to family breakup and adoption; publishes newsletter and other materials.

International Soundex Reunion Registry (ISRR)
P.O. Box 2312
Carson City, NV 89702
702-882-6270
Emma May Vilardi, Executive Board Director
Organization for children (over 18) and blood relatives from whom they were separated, as through adoption or foster care. Maintains data bank of medical and genetic information, with data from other U.S. and international groups; aims to provide separated family members with confidential information on their medical and genetic background; publishes newsletter.

Origins
P.O. Box 444
East Brunswick, NJ 08816
201-257-9235
Katherine Loewenberg, Corresponding Secretary
Organization for women whose children have been given up for adoption. Provides support and assists them and other relatives in searching for information about their children; publishes newsletter.

Yesterday's Children (YC)
P.O. Box 1554
Evanston, IL 60204
312-545-6900
Donna Cullom, President
Organization for adoptees and others separated from their birth relatives, as through foster-care placement, divorce, or death in family, as well as interested others. Seeks to have adoption records opened; maintains adoption registry; aids people in searching for information on their birth families.

Birth Parent and Relative Group of Canada
5317-145 Avenue
Edmonton, Alberta, Canada T5A 4E9
403-473-4552
Organization to help reunite family members separated by adoption. Maintains registry.

Worldwide Searches (WS), 818-377-5857. Helps in searches for missing people, including adopted children. (For full group information, see MISSING CHILDREN.)

Other reference sources

General Works

Ideal Adoption: A Comprehensive Guide to Forming an Adoptive Family, by Shirley C. Samuels. New York: Penguin, 1990.
The Private Adoption Handbook: A Step-by-Step Guide to the Legal, Emotional and Practical Demands of Adopting a Baby, by Stanley B. Michelman and Meg Schneider, with Antonia Van der Meer. New York: Delacorte, 1990.
How to Raise an Adopted Child: A Guide to Help Your Child Flourish from Infancy Through Adolescence, by Judith Schaffer and Christina Lindstrom. New York: Crown, 1989.

Making Sense of Adoption, by Lois Ruskai Melina. New York: Harper & Row, 1989.
The Adoption Triangle: Sealed or Open Records: How They Affect Adoptees, Birth Parents, and Adoptive Parents, by Arthur D. Sorosky, Annette Baran, and Reuben Pannor. Austin: Texas Monthly Press, 1989.
Beating the Adoption Game, revised edition, by Cynthia D. Martin. San Diego, CA: Harcourt Brace Jovanovich, 1988.
The Adoption Resource Book, revised edition, by Lois Gilman. New York: Harper & Row, 1987.
Successful Adoption: A Guide to Finding a Child and Raising a Family, revised edition, by Jacqueline Plumez. New York: Harmony, 1987.
Adoption: Parenthood Without Pregnancy, by Charlene Canape. New York: Henry Holt, 1986.
Raising Adopted Children, by Lois Ruskai Melina. New York: Harper & Row, 1986.
The New Adoption Maze and How to Get Through It, by Fred Powledge. St. Louis, MO: C.V. Mosby, 1985.
The Penguin Adoption Handbook: A Guide to Creating Your New Family, by Edmund Blair Bolles. New York: Penguin, 1984.
The Baby Chase, by Tony Kornheiser. New York: Atheneum, 1983.
Mothers and Their Adopted Children—The Bonding Process, by Dorothy W. Smith and Laurie Nehls Sherwen. New York: Tiresias, 1983.
The Art of Adoption, by Linda Cannon Burgess. New York: Norton, 1981.
You're Our Child: A Social-Psychological Approach to Adoption, by Jerome Smith and Franklin I. Miroff. Washington, DC: University Press of America, 1981.
Beating the Adoption Game, by Cynthia Martin. San Diego: Oaktree, 1980.
Our Child: Preparation for Parenting in Adoption, by Carol Hallenbeck. Curriculum guide for adoptive parents, available from Our Child Press, 800 Maple Glen Lane, Wayne, PA 19087.

On Special Circumstances

How to Adopt from Latin America, by Jean Nelson-Erichsen and Heino R. Erichsen. Minneapolis: Dillon, 1981.
Oriental Children in American Homes: How Do They Adjust?, by Frances M. Koh. Minneapolis: East-West, 1981.
Adopting the Older Child, by Claudia Jewett. Cambridge, MA: Harvard Common, 1978.

Background Books

Encyclopedia of Adoption, by Christine Adamec. New York: Facts on File, 1990.
The Adoption Directory, Ellen Paul, ed. Detroit: Gale, 1989.
Adoption: An Annotated Bibliography and Guide, by Lois Ruskai Melina. New York: Garland, 1987.
Birth Is More Than Once: The Inner World of Adopted Children, by Hei Sook Park Wilkinson. Bloomfield Hills, MI: Sunrise Ventures, 1985.

On Open Adoption

An Open Adoption, by Lincoln Caplan. New York: Farrar, Straus & Giroux, 1990.

Children of Open Adoption, by Kathleen Silber and Patricia Martinez Dorner. San Antonio: Corona, 1990.

The Promise of Open Adoption, by Suzanne Arms. Berkeley, CA: Celestial Arts, 1989.

Open Adoption: A Caring Option, by Jeanne Warren Lindsay. Buena Park, CA: Morning Glory, 1987.

Cooperative Adoption: A Handbook, by Mary Jo Rillera and Sharon Kaplan. Westminster, CA: Triadoption, 1985.

To Love and Let Go, by Suzanne Arms. New York: Knopf, 1983.

On Later Contact Between Adoptees and Birth Parents

Birthbond: Reunions Between Birthparents and Adoptees—What Happens After . . ., by Judith S. Gediman and Linda P. Brown. Far Hills, NJ: New Horizon, 1989.

Lost and Found: The Adoption Experience, revised edition, by Betty Jean Lifton. New York: Harper & Row, 1988.

Search: A Handbook for Adoptees and Birthparents, by Jayne Askin with Bob Oskam. New York: Harper & Row, 1982.

Personal Stories

Waiting for Baby: One Couple's Journey Through Infertility to Adoption, by Mary Earle Chase. New York: McGraw-Hill, 1989.

Adoption Story: A Son Is Given, by Marguerite Ryan. New York: Rawson, 1989. About a battle between adoptive parents and the birth mother.

With Child: One Couple's Journey to Their Adopted Children, by Susan T. Viguers. San Diego: Harcourt Brace Jovanovich, 1986.

Whose Child Am I? Adults' Recollections of Being Adopted, by John Y. Powell. New York: Tiresias, 1985.

Mixed Blessing: The Dramatic True Story of a Woman's Search for Her Real Mother, by Doris McMillon with Michele Sherman. New York: St. Martin's, 1985.

Dear Birthmother: Thank You for Our Baby, by Kathleen Silber and Phylis Speedlin. San Antonio: Corona, 1983.

Patchwork Clan: How the Sweeny Family Grew, by Doris Lund. Boston: Little, Brown, 1982.

Birthmark, by Lorraine Dusky. New York: M. Evans, 1979. Birth mother's account of change of heart and long, successful search for her child.

Twice Born: Memoirs of an Adopted Daughter, by Betty Jean Lifton. New York: Penguin, 1977.

Nineteen Steps Up the Mountain: The Story of the DeBolt Family, by Joseph P. Blank. Philadelphia: Lippincott, 1976. About a family's adoption of children with special needs.

The Search for Anna Fisher, by Florence Fisher (key figure in Adoptees' Liberty Movement Association, or ALMA). New York: Arthur Fields, 1973.

For or by Kids

Growing Up Adopted, by Maxine B. Rosenberg. New York: Bradbury, 1989. For readers age 9 and up.

Adoption, by Gail B. Stewart. New York: Crestwood, 1989. Part of the Facts About Series.

Black Market Adoption and the Sale of Children, by Elaine Landau. New York: Watts, 1990.

Susan and Gordon Adopt a Baby. New York: Random House/Children's Television Workshop, 1986. From "Sesame Street," for young children.

The Adoption Experience: Stories and Commentaries, by Steven L. Nickman. New York: Julian Messner, 1985. For young adults.

Being Adopted, by Maxine B. Rosenberg. New York: Lothrop, Lee & Shepard, 1984.

How It Feels to Be Adopted, by Jill Krementz. New York: Alfred Knopf, 1983. Young people talk about being adopted.

So You're Adopted, by Fred Powledge. New York: Scribner, 1982. For young adults.

A Look at Adoption, by Margaret Sanford Pursell. Minneapolis: Lerner, 1978. For young children.

The Chosen Baby, revised edition, by Valentina P. Wasson. Philadelphia: Lippincott, 1977. For parents to read to young children.

adoption leave The equivalent of MATERNITY LEAVE for parents who are adopting a child, especially an infant; it is sometimes granted only when the child is under six months old. Parents should check with their employers early, when considering adoption, to see whether standard maternity-leave policies also apply to adoptions. If the policy is unclear, they may have time to "lobby" their personnel or human-resources department to change it to cover their adoption or to make an exception for this special case. Parents also need to see whether company and other plans automatically cover an adopted child or whether special arrangements must be made, and whether any of the expenses associated with adoption are covered.

adrenal glands A pair of small glands that sit on top of the kidneys. The outer part (the *adrenal cortex*) produces a variety of HORMONES, including STEROIDS and some male sex hormones; the inner part (*adrenal medulla*) acts as part of the NERVOUS SYSTEM, responding to STRESS by producing other hormones, including *adrenaline*, which readies the body for action. Among the disorders that may affect the adrenal gland in young people are:

- *adrenogenital syndrome (congenital adrenal hyperplasia)*, in which the adrenal glands are unable to produce sufficient hormones, resulting in FAILURE TO THRIVE and sometimes causing development of male sex attributes in female babies. It is generally treated with administration of hormones.
- TUMORS, which can cause excess production of *hydrocortisone*. This may result in *Cushing's syndrome*, which involves

wasting muscles; OBESITY; and excess male sex hormones in both sexes. In adults, these can lead to decreased fertility.

• AUTOIMMUNE DISORDERS, in which the body mistakenly attacks its own tissue in the adrenal glands, leading to *Addison's disease*, rare in children. In chronic form, this can lead to weight loss, weakness, and darkened skin, but in acute form, if untreated, it may result in confusion, COMA, and death.

Among the MEDICAL TESTS used to diagnose adrenal-gland disorders are BLOOD TESTS or URINALYSIS for determining hormone levels and various SCANS, such as a CT SCAN.

For help and further information

National Institute of Diabetes and Digestive and Kidney Diseases (NIDDK), 301-496-3583. Publishes material on various topics, such as Cushing's syndrome. (For full group information, see DIGESTIVE DISORDERS.)

National Institute of Child Health and Human Development (NICHD)
Developmental Endocrinology Branch
Building 10, Room 10N262
Bethesda, MD 20892
301-496-4686
Dr. George P. Chrousos, Contact
Federal department offering treatment of Cushing's syndrome as part of National Institutes of Health research studies.

National Cushing's Association
4620½ Van Nuys Boulevard
Sherman Oaks, CA 91403
818-788-9239
Andrea Hecht, President
Organization of Cushing's syndrome patients, their families, and interested professionals. Provides referrals; publishes various materials, including brochure *Cushing's Syndrome*; offers information packet.

adrenogenital syndrome   A condition involving a disorder of the ADRENAL GLANDS.

advanced placement   In EDUCATION, granting a student a position above that of most entrants, usually after demonstration of proficiency in some aspects of the coursework; also called *advanced standing*. In one common type of advanced placement, students receive college credit for passing set examinations, such as those offered under the ADVANCED PLACEMENT PROGRAM, COLLEGE-LEVEL EXAMINATION PROGRAM, or PROFICIENCY EXAMINATION PROGRAM. Students who transfer from one school to another receive advanced placement on the basis of their work at their previous school. Some students, though mostly returning adults, can gain either college credit or waiver of required basic courses if they have, on their own, acquired special knowledge; this is sometimes called *experiential learning* or *life-experience credit*.

Advanced Placement Program (APP)   A national program operated by the COLLEGE ENTRANCE EXAMINATION BOARD, under which HIGH SCHOOL students take college-level courses in school and, if they pass set examinations, are granted college CREDIT in those subjects.

Adverse Reaction Monitoring System (ARMS)   A program of the Food and Drug Administration (FDA) to gather, classify, interpret, and report on information about consumers' allergic reactions to FOOD ADDITIVES.

AFDC   Abbreviation for AID TO FAMILIES WITH DEPENDENT CHILDREN.

affect   A psychological term for behaviors that express felt emotion, such as sadness, euphoria, or anger. The normal affect is termed *broad*, but in some MENTAL DISORDERS, the range of facial expression, pitch of voice, and hand and body movements gradually lessens. In these, the successive stages would be termed *restricted* or *constricted affect*, *blunt affect*, and finally *flat affect*, in which the voice is a monotone and face and body are virtually immobile. In cases of abrupt mood swings, the affect is called *labile*, while behavioral expression that clashes with the situation (as when a child laughs while in great pain) is called *inappropriate affect*.

affective disorders   Alternate term for MOOD DISORDERS, such as DEPRESSION.

affective domain   One of three key categories of instructional content and learning objectives described by Benjamin Bloom, referring to feelings, emotions, values, and attitudes; the others are the COGNITIVE DOMAIN and the PSYCHOMOTOR DOMAIN. (See also DOMAINS.)

affinity   A formal term for the family relationships created by marriage, as with one's father-in-law or sister-in-law.

aflatoxin   A type of poison that often contaminates stored foods, especially peanuts and grains, produced by a mold called *Aspergillus flavus*. Aflatoxin has been shown to cause CANCER of the liver in laboratory animals and is thought to be linked to the high incidence of liver cancer in tropical Africa and Asia, though hard evidence is not available. Given the suggestion of aflatoxin's carcinogenic possibilities in humans, some parents feel it prudent to limit the amount of peanuts and peanut butter in their family's diet. (For help and further information, see FOOD ADDITIVES.)

AFP   Abbreviation for ALPHA FETOPROTEIN.

afterbirth   Popular name for the PLACENTA, the organ expelled from the UTERUS after CHILDBIRTH.

after-born   A legal designation for a child born after the death of its father; also a child born after the signing of a parent's will. Even if not specifically covered in a parent's will, an after-born child in most states is entitled to a share in that parent's property, unless the parent is shown to have intended to give the child nothing.

AGA   Abbreviation for *appropriate gestational age*. (See GESTATIONAL AGE.)

against medical advice (AMA) A designation for actions contrary to a physician's orders. In cases of possible CHILD ABUSE AND NEGLECT, an AMA action is removing a child from the hospital without medical consent. A woman with a HIGH-RISK PREGNANCY who fails to heed medical cautions about her lifestyle may also be said to be going against medical advice.

agammaglobulinemia An inherited deficiency in the IMMUNE SYSTEM.

age In the simplest terms, the number of years in a person's life, called the *chronological age*, as measured from a birthdate, often attested to on a BIRTH CERTIFICATE or other acceptable certificate. However, in education, psychology, medicine, law, statistics, and many other disciplines, a variety of other special definitions of age have emerged.

Some of these reflect laws relating to age. *Compulsory school age* refers to the starting and ending ages between which a child is required to attend school; the specific ages vary but are usually between about 6 and 16 years. The AGE OF CONSENT is the age at which a person can legally marry without obtaining consent from a parent or GUARDIAN, and *voting age* is the age at which a person can vote as a citizen. The *age of* MAJORITY is the age at which a MINOR becomes an adult for legal purposes; it again varies by law but often is around age 18.

Some other definitions of age relate to medical questions. The *age of onset* is the age at which a disease or HANDICAP first appeared or was recognized. A child's *anatomical age* is the relationship between his or her growth and the statistical average for a child of the same size; if a child of six has a degree of skeletal maturation normally seen in a seven-year-old, that child's anatomical age is seven. Similarly, a child's *grip age* would reflect his or her maturity in MOTOR SKILLS involving gripping; *dental age* would reflect the maturity of TEETH and jaw formation; and so on.

Definitions of age involving comparison of a person's growth or performance to some standard are also widely used in education. A child's EDUCATIONAL AGE (EA) reflects how the child's score relates to a wide range of other scores on an ACHIEVEMENT TEST; if a child just eight years old has a score normally achieved by children half a year older, that child's educational age will be eight years, six months. That general type of comparison is called an *age equivalent*, *age norm*, or *developmental age* and is used in many areas in education. A child's MENTAL AGE (MA) reflects comparative performance on a mental-ability or INTELLIGENCE TEST, while *reading age* reflects a child's ability on READING tests, as compared to established NORMS. The age at which a child is consistently able to correctly answer all of the items on a STANDARDIZED TEST is called the *basal age*. Sometimes a whole range of age comparisons—including educational, mental, dental, carpal (wrist), height, weight, and social comparisons—are averaged together to give a child's *organismic age*.

age-appropriate A general term describing skills, activities, toys, and behavior that are considered appropriate for a child of a certain age, sometimes referring to CHRONOLOGICAL AGE and sometimes to DEVELOPMENTAL AGE.

age-eligible A general term describing a child who is eligible to enter school on the basis of CHRONOLOGICAL AGE, measured from the birth date. With increasing use of DEVELOPMENTAL SCREENING TESTS, some children who are age-eligible are barred from school, or their parents are advised not to enter them into KINDERGARTEN, if their DEVELOPMENTAL AGE is considered too low. They will, of course, enter school in any case when they reach COMPULSORY SCHOOL AGE, but they may be placed in special READINESS classes or *transition programs*; some schools alternatively choose to enter the child with the normal class, sometimes planning to HOLD BACK the child another year. On a few occasions, parents have successfully gone to court to have their age-eligible child admitted to kindergarten over the school's protest.

age equivalent A general term for a numerical summary expressing a student's general development by comparison with average scores for other students using the same or similar tests, such as tests for EDUCATIONAL AGE, DEVELOPMENTAL AGE, or MENTAL AGE. (See also AGE.)

age norm Alternate term for EDUCATIONAL AGE.

age of consent The age (often 18) at which a person can legally marry without obtaining consent from a parent or GUARDIAN; also the age (variable by state) at which a person can legally agree to have sexual intercourse. Someone who has sex with an *under-age person*—someone under the age of consent—is liable to a charge of STATUTORY RAPE.

agnosia Partial or total inability to recognize previously familiar objects, people, or occurrences by using one's senses. Although the senses are unimpaired, the brain "short-circuits" information received from normal sense organs; the condition may result from certain kinds of brain damage, as from a BRAIN TUMOR or HEAD INJURY. If only one sense is affected, the agnosia may be labeled according to the name of the SENSORY MODE: *auditory* (hearing), *visual* (sight), *olfactory* (smell), *gustatory* (taste), or *tactile* (touch). Children with LEARNING DISABILITIES or other DEVELOPMENTAL DISORDERS often have partial agnosia involving the VISUAL SKILLS and AUDITORY SKILLS. Inability to recognize or localize parts of one's own body is called *autopagnosia*.

agoraphobia A fear of open, exposed places; a severe type of *phobic disorder*, also often associated with PANIC DISORDERS. (See PHOBIA.)

agraphia Loss of the ability to write, a form of APHASIA often resulting from damage to the brain, such as a BRAIN TUMOR or HEAD INJURY. By contrast, difficulty in writing is called DYSGRAPHIA.

AI Abbreviation for ARTIFICIAL INSEMINATION.

AID Abbreviation for artificial insemination–donor. (See ARTIFICIAL INSEMINATION.)

AIDS (acquired immune deficiency syndrome) A deadly infectious disease that drastically weakens the IMMUNE SYSTEM. AIDS is caused by the *human immunodeficiency virus*, or HIV (previously called *human T-cell lymphotropic virus III*, HTLV-III, or LAV), which attacks vital white blood cells called *helper T cells* that help produce disease-fighting ANTIBODIES. (For an explanation of how T cells work, see IMMUNE SYSTEM.) With the T cells crippled, a person becomes prey to CANCER and various opportunistic infections, so called because they spread when the body loses its normal ability to fight them off. Different strains of HIV, some stronger than others, exist; also, some other organisms (perhaps including microbes called *mycoplasmas*) may sharply increase the ability of HIV to spread.

Infection with HIV often appears first with signs of mild impairment of the immune system, such as swollen lymph nodes, skin disorders, weight loss, FEVER, DIARRHEA, common infections such as CANDIDIASIS (thrush), and increased susceptibility to other diseases such as HERPES SIMPLEX or TUBERCULOSIS. This mild condition is called *AIDS-related complex*, or ARC. As the disease progresses, full-blown AIDS develops, which often involves rare cancers such as Kaposi's sarcoma and lymphoma of the brain, infections such as TOXOPLASMOSIS and CYTOMEGALOVIRUS, and PNEUMONIA caused by a usually innocuous organism, *Pneumocystis carinii*.

If AIDS is suspected, various tests may be carried out, generally involving BLOOD TESTS for antibodies to HIV; given the nature of the disease, a positive result is often checked with a second test, and a negative result is followed up by another test some months later. Such tests are also carried out on possible blood donors and donations, to screen the AIDS virus from the blood supply.

AIDS was identified in Western countries only in the early 1980s, so much is still unknown about the disease. It is unclear whether people who show signs of antibodies to the AIDS virus will inevitably develop either ARC or AIDS or whether (as some evidence indicates) some will be able to fight off the disease altogether. It is also unclear whether ARC always progresses to fullblown AIDS or whether some people are able to stave off the deadly progression.

While researchers are exploring many possible treatments and hoping to develop a VACCINE, antiviral drugs, notably *zidovudine* (AZT), are used to slow the disease's progression. Experience shows that the earlier AIDS is recognized and treatment begun, the longer the survival and the better the quality of life. Little research has been done on the course and effects of AIDS in children, though the disease affects children somewhat differently, especially in regard to the nervous system. Medications for adults were not made available for use with children until 1990, through pressure from various organizations (see below). As of 1990, however, no cure exists. Barring discovery of a cure, the disease—once contracted in its full form— seems to have a 100-percent MORTALITY RATE.

The HIV exists in various bodily fluids, including blood, SEMEN, saliva, tears, tissue in the NERVOUS SYSTEM, breast milk, and secretions from female GENITALS. Study of the known cases indicates that it is not spread by casual contact, as in the home, office, school, or other public places. Activities such as touching, closed-mouth kissing, hugging, and *giving* blood in sterile conditions, for example, are regarded as no-risk activities. The HIV is spread by exchange of bodily fluids, apparently in just a few ways, notably by sexual intercourse, especially rough or anal intercourse; sharing of needles (in drug use or reuse of

unsterilized needles); by BLOOD TRANSFUSIONS, by SEMEN from sperm banks used in ARTIFICIAL INSEMINATION; and from mother to child by way of the PLACENTA. Testing of blood, testing of mothers before or during pregnancy, testing of sexual partners, use of condoms during sexual intercourse (so-called safe sex, better called "safer sex"), and similar measures can all reduce the risks of exposure to HIV, though complete avoidance of any of these activities is the only sure way to avoid exposure to AIDS.

Most young children with AIDS were infected by their mothers, in the UTERUS, during DELIVERY, or from later BREASTFEEDING. Not all children of infected mothers contract the disease, possibly because they are protected by antibodies from the mother. (The mothers themselves are often unaware that they carry the virus.) Some children contract AIDS from blood transfusions; this was more common before 1985, when screening tests began to be used. A few have been infected as a result of sexual abuse. Generally, few young children are exposed to AIDS, but they surely have fears about the disease, many of them based on ignorance, so parents will want to talk with children about their concerns and clarify which activities are safe and which are not.

Somewhat older children and teenagers, by contrast, are at great risk for exposure to HIV, given widespread sexual activity and DRUG ABUSE in their age groups. Parents need to be sure children understand the risks involved in sexual activity and drug use and the ways to minimize those risks. However reluctant parents may have been in the past to undertake SEX EDUCATION with their children, in the 1990s it is a lifesaving activity.

For help and further information

National AIDS Hotline, 800-342-AIDS [2437].

National AIDS Information Clearinghouse
P.O. Box 6003
Rockville, MD 20850
301-762-5111
Federal organization charged with providing the public with information on AIDS.

Pediatric AIDS Foundation (PAF)
2407 Wilshire Boulevard, Suite 613
Santa Monica, CA
Elizabeth Glaser, Chairperson
213-395-9051
Organization of people concerned with AIDS in children. Seeks to educate public and change government policy; encourages research in pediatric AIDS; supports creation of special hospital programs for children.

Mothers of AIDS Patients (MAP)
P.O. Box 3132
San Diego, CA 92103
619-544-0430
Barbara Peabody, Executive Officer
Organization for families of people with AIDS. Provides support and education; encourages formation of local self-help groups.

National Association of People with AIDS (NAPWA)
2025 I Street, NW, Suite 1118
Washington, DC 20006
202-429-2856
Michael Merdian, Executive Director
Organization of people with AIDS or related diagnoses. Seeks to educate public; works on behalf of AIDS patients; publishes various materials, including monthly newsletter.

Centers for Disease Control (CDC), 404-329-3534. (For full group information, see IMMUNIZATION.)

National Institute of Allergy and Infectious Diseases (NIAID), 301-496-5717. (For full group information, see ALLERGY.)

March of Dimes Birth Defects Foundation, 914-428-7100 (local chapters in telephone-directory white pages). Publishes information sheet *Congenital AIDS*. (For full group information, see BIRTH DEFECTS.)

National Clearinghouse for Alcohol and Drug Abuse Information (NCADI), 301-468-2600. Publishes *Acquired Immunodeficiency Syndrome and Chemical Dependency*, *AIDS and Drug Abuse*, and *Alcohol and AIDS: Update*. (For full group information, see HELP AGAINST SUBSTANCE ABUSE on page 587.)

Other reference sources

General Works

The Essential AIDS Fact Book, Columbia University Health Service. New York: Pocket, 1990.
Living with AIDS, Stephen R. Graubard, ed. Cambridge, MA: MIT Press, 1990.
Courage to Care: Responding to the Crisis of Children with AIDS, by Gary Anderson. Washington, DC: Child Welfare League, 1990.
Take These Broken Wings and Learn to Fly: The AIDS Support Book for Patients, Family and Friends, by Steven D. Dietz and M. Jane Parker Hicks, M.D. Tucson, AZ: Harbinger House, 1989.
AIDS, by Jonnie Wilson. San Diego, CA: Lucent, 1989.
The AIDS Book: Creating a Positive Approach, by Louise L. Hay. Santa Monica, CA: Hay House, 1988.

On Programs and Services

The AIDS Benefits Handbook: Everything You Need to Know to Get Social Security, Welfare, Medicaid, Medicare, Food Stamps, Housing, Drugs, and Other Benefits, by Thomas P. McCormack. New Haven, CT: Yale University Press, 1990. For people with AIDS and ARC.
Local AIDS-related Services National Directory. Available from the United States Conference of Mayors, 1620 I Street, NW, 4th Floor, Washington, DC 20006, 202-293-7330.
Health Care U.S.A., by Jean Carper. New York: Prentice Hall, 1987. Resource for general and specific health-care information; lists major AIDS clinics and programs for treatment or referral, including those for experimental treatment, and other information.

For or by Kids

What's a Virus, Anyway?: The Kid's Book about AIDS, by David Fassler and Kelly McQueen. Burlington, VT: Waterfront, 1990. For ages 3 to 6. Available in both English and Spanish.
Alex, the Kid with AIDS, by Linda Walvoord Girard. Niles, IL: Albert Whitman, 1990. For ages 7 to 10.
Know About AIDS, 2nd edition, by Margaret Hyde and Elizabeth Forsyth. New York: Walker, 1990. For ages 8 to 12.
Friends for Life, by Barbara Aiello and Jeffrey Shulman. Frederick, MD: 21st Century, 1988. Part of The Kids on the Block Book Series for readers age 8 to 12.
Children with the AIDS Virus: A Book for Children, Parents, and Teachers, by Rosemarie Hausherr. New York: Clarion, 1989; paperback, Houghton. For ages 6 to 9.
Fighting Back: What Some People Are Doing About AIDS, by Susan Kuklin. New York: Putnam, 1988.

For or by Adolescents

Risky Times: How to Be AIDS-Smart and Stay Healthy, by Jeanne Blake. New York: Workman, 1990. For teenagers, with parent's guide.
The Impact of AIDS, by Ewan Armstrong. New York: Watts/Gloucester, 1990.
AIDS: What Does It Mean to You?, 3rd edition, by Margaret Hyde and Elizabeth Forsyth, M.D. New York: Walker, 1990. For ages 12 and up.
We Have AIDS, by Elaine Landau. New York: Watts, 1990. For grades 9 to 12. About nine teenagers with AIDS.
AIDS: Trading Fears for Facts: A Guide for Teens, by Karen Hein, M.D., *et al*. New York: Consumer Reports Books, 1989.
Lynda Madaras Talks to Teens About AIDS: An Essential Guide for Parents, Teachers and Young People, by Lynda Madaras. New York: Newmarket, 1988.
AIDS, by Mary C. Turck. Mankato, MN: Crestwood, 1988.
Go Toward the Light, by Chris Oyler, with Laurie Becklund and Beth Polson. New York: Harper & Row, 1988. On children with hemophilia who contracted AIDS.
AIDS: What You Should Know, by Linda Meeks and Philip Heit. Columbus, OH: Merrill, 1987. For grades 6 to 8.

Background Works

AIDS and Schoolchildren in America's Communities, by David L. Kirp. New Brunswick, NJ: Rutgers University Press, 1990.
In the Absence of Angels: A Hollywood Family's Courageous Story, by Elizabeth Glaser and Laura Palmer. New York: Putnam, 1990. Story of a mother contracting AIDS from a blood transfusion and passing it to her child, by founder of Pediatric Aids Foundation (see above).
Children, Adolescents and AIDS, Jeffrey M. Seibert and Robert A. Olson, eds. Lincoln: University of Nebraska Press, 1989.

AIDS, Sexual Behavior, and Intravenous Drug Use. Washington, DC: National Academy Press, 1989.

The AIDS Epidemic: Private Rights and the Public Interest, Padraig O'Malley, ed. Boston: Beacon, 1989.

The Whole Truth About AIDS, by Dr. Patrick Dixon. Nashville, TN: Thomas Nelson, 1989.

AIDS: Principles, Practices and Politics, by Inge B. Corless and Mary Pittman-Lindeman. New York: Hemisphere, 1988.

Report of the Presidential Commission on the Human Immunodeficiency Virus Epidemic. Washington, DC: U.S. Government Printing Office, 1988.

(See also IMMUNE SYSTEM; SEXUALLY TRANSMITTED DISEASES; BLOOD TRANSFUSIONS.)

Aid to Dependent Children (ADC)   Alternate name for AID TO FAMILIES WITH DEPENDENT CHILDREN.

Aid to Families with Dependent Children (AFDC)   A federally provided, state-administered welfare program providing financial assistance to needy MINOR children deprived of support from one of their parents, as through death, disability, unemployment, or ABANDONMENT; sometimes called Aid to Dependent Children (ADC), established under Social Security. The assistance may go to the remaining parent or to another person who has assumed CUSTODY, such as a grandparent, stepparent, or other relative. State requirements vary. In some states, AFDC payments are made whenever need exists, even if both parents are employed but still living below the poverty level; in others, payments are made only when neither parent at home is employed. Most AFDC payments are made to women who are single parents with young children. By law the state is required to find the children's FATHER and obtain reimbursement of the CHILD SUPPORT for which he is legally responsible; in order to continue receiving payments due, the mother must help in this effort, which for unmarried mothers often includes instituting a PATERNITY SUIT to establish the legal father of the child.

AIH   Abbreviation for artificial insemination–husband (see ARTIFICIAL INSEMINATION).

Albers-Schönberg disease   Alternate name for OSTEOPETROSIS.

albinism (hypopigmentation)   A rare GENETIC DISORDER involving lack of the pigment *melanin*, because the skin cells (*melanocytes*) that normally produce melanin fail to work properly. (Another disorder, VITILIGO, involves lack of melanocytes.) Children born with albinism often have snow-white hair and skin, though these may darken slightly with age. People with albinism are subject to severe sunburn and tend to develop skin CANCER; their eyes are often extremely sensitive to bright light, and they often have other EYE AND VISION PROBLEMS, such as STRABISMUS (crossed eyes), NYSTAGMUS (jerky, involuntary movements of the eyes), and MYOPIA (nearsightedness). A genetic disorder of the AUTOSOMAL RECESSIVE type, albinism is passed on to a child only if both parents contribute the defective gene; if parents have one child with albinism, the chances are one in four that a later child will also have it.

For help and further information

National Organization for Albinism and Hypopigmentation (NOAH)
1500 Locust Street, Suite 1811
Philadelphia, PA 19102
215-471-2278 or -2265
Janice L. Knuth, President
Organization concerned with albinism and hypopigmentation. Offers support to affected individuals and their families; gathers information and disseminates it to public and health professionals; fosters research; publishes various materials, including *NOAH News* and information bulletins.

National Eye Institute (NEI), 301-496-5248. (For full group information, see EYE AND VISION PROBLEMS.) (See also SKIN DISORDERS.)

alcohol abuse   Physical and psychological dependence on alcohol, characterized by long-term excessive drinking, a felt need to continue drinking, or withdrawal symptoms on discontinuing drinking. A major social problem, long thought to be primarily an adult phenomenon, alcohol abuse has become increasingly widespread among adolescents, often in conjunction with DRUG ABUSE, a combination called *cross-addiction*.

Young children are also affected by alcohol abuse, as many of them live with a parent who is an alcoholic, the result often being CHILD ABUSE AND NEGLECT. Many babies, in fact, are affected before birth, having FETAL ALCOHOL SYNDROME as a result of their mother's drinking during PREGNANCY or inheriting a susceptibility to alcohol addiction. Drunk driving, by both adults and adolescents, is also a life-threatening hazard for many young people. (For an overview of the effects and signs of alcohol and other substance abuse, plus organizations, reference works, and recommendations for parents, see HELP AGAINST SUBSTANCE ABUSE on page 587.)

alexia (word blindness)   Inability to read, despite unimpaired vision and intelligence; an extreme form of DYSLEXIA.

alkaline phosphatase test   A kind of BLOOD TEST, often considered one of the LIVER FUNCTION TESTS, which can also indicate bone or gall bladder disorders.

alleles   Name for the two genes that make up a normal pair. (See GENETIC INHERITANCE.)

allergy   An excessive response by the IMMUNE SYSTEM to some foreign substance, called an *antigen* or, more specifically, an *allergen*. Allergy is a general term that encompasses a wide range of problems, including ASTHMA, reaction to FOOD ADDITIVES, and some kinds of FOOD INTOLERANCE (all treated in separate entries), as well as hypersensitivity to many other substances such as pollen, mold spores, insects, insect bites, animal dander, and injected drugs, such as penicillin. Why some people suffer from allergies and others do not is unclear, but some sensitivities seem to be inherited.

Allergic reactions range from the barely noticeable to the life-threatening. As the immune system mobilizes against the foreign substance, the body goes through various changes. After a chemical called *histamine* is released, blood vessels widen, tissues fill with fluid, and muscles go into spasm. (A common medication to counter allergy, *antihistamine*, is aimed at blocking just such effects.) Other parts of the body also may be involved. Common symptoms are rashes or swelling on the skin, inflammation of the breathing passages (as in asthma) and eyes, and digestive upset, including VOMITING and DIARRHEA. These are common reactions in, for example, *hay fever* or *allergic rhinitis*.

Most seriously, as in reactions to some drugs, insect venom, and foods, the body may go into anaphylactic SHOCK, a severe, life-threatening drop in BLOOD PRESSURE, which requires immediate treatment, notably injection of *epinephrine*, to counteract the effects. People who have once suffered such a severe reaction must avoid such triggering allergens, if possible, and carry with them a dose of the medication, to be injected if the reaction starts. If any family member is subject to such reactions, parents and older children should know how to give such a life-saving injection.

Sometimes the offending allergen is obvious, such as a bee sting or penicillin injection. But more often the precise substance causing the problem is unknown. Then physicians may perform a *patch test*, in which samples of various substances are taped to the skin; those that trigger the person's allergic reactions will cause the skin to be raised and red. BLOOD TESTS are also sometimes used to measure levels of antibodies to particular allergens. Once the problem allergens are known, the person should avoid them as much as possible. (Parents should see CONTROLLING THE HOME ENVIRONMENT FOR THE ASTHMATIC CHILD on page 37 for examples of how to do this.)

Where controlling the environment and taking various medications are insufficient, physicians may try *immunotherapy* (popularly called *allergy shots*). This involves injections of small, diluted doses of the allergen under the patient's skin once or twice a week, gradually increasing the size of the dose and the time between doses, over a period of three to four years, the aim being to build up tolerance to the allergen. This is a long, expensive process that requires careful monitoring, and the injections themselves can cause allergic reactions, but for some the treatment works well.

For help and further information

National Institute of Allergy and Infectious Diseases (NIAID)
9000 Rockville Pike
Building 31, Room 7A32
Bethesda, MD 20892
301-496-5717
Federal arm, one of the U.S. National Institutes of Health, sponsoring research on causes, diagnosis, prevention, and treatment of allergy and infectious diseases. Provides information to public and health professionals; maintains network of Asthma and Allergic Disease Centers; publishes various materials, including research reports for professionals and brochures on different topics, such as *Asthma, Drug Allergy, Dust Allergy, Insect Allergy, Mold Allergy, Poison Ivy Allergy, Pollen Allergy*, and *Understanding the Immune System*.

Asthma and Allergy Foundation of America (AAFA)
1717 Massachusetts Avenue, NW, Suite 305
Washington, DC 20036
202-265-0265
People and organizations concerned with allergy and asthma. Supports research; provides information; seeks to educate public; publishes various materials, including a bimonthly newspaper.

American Academy of Allergy and Immunology
611 East Wells Street
Milwaukee, WI 53202
414-272-6071
Donald MacNeil, Executive Director
Professional organization of physicians who specialize in allergy, asthma, and immunology.

Other reference sources

General Works

Conquering Your Child's Allergies, by M. Eric Gershwin, M.D., and Edwin L. Klingelhofer. Reading, MA: Addison-Wesley, 1990.

Overcoming Food Allergies, by Gwynne H. Davies. Garden City Park, NY: Avery, 1990.

Healthier Children, by Barbara Kahan. New Canaan, CT: Keats, 1990. On behavior problems resulting from environmental factors such as food sensitivity or pollution.

Living with Allergies, by Dr. T. White. New York: Watts, 1990. For young readers.

Allergies, by Edward Edelson. New York: Chelsea House, 1989.

Food Allergies, by Neil S. Orenstein and Sarah L. Bingham. New York: Putnam, 1988.

Goodbye Allergies, by Tom R. Blaine. Secaucus, NJ: Lyle Stuart, 1988.

Hidden Food Allergies: How to Find and Overcome Them, by Stephen Astor. Garden City Park, NY: Avery, 1988.

Background Works

An Alternative Approach to Allergies: The New Field of Clinical Ecology Unravels the Environmental Causes of Mental and Physical Ills, revised edition, by Theron G. Randolph and Ralph W. Moss. New York: Harper and Row, 1990.

The Allergy Discovery Diet: A Rotation Diet for Discovering Your Allergies to Food, by John E. Postley and Janet M. Barton. Garden City, NY: Doubleday, 1990.

Genetic and Environmental Factors in Clinical Allergy, David G. Marsh and Malcolm N. Blumenthal, eds. Minneapolis: University of Minnesota Press, 1990.

Migraine and the Allergy Connection: A Drug-Free Solution, by John Mansfield, M.D. Rochester, VT: Inner Traditions, 1990.

The Allergy Guide to Brand-Name Foods and Food Additives, by Stephanie Bernardo Johns. New York: New American Library, 1988.

Allergy Products Directory, 2nd edition, by the Staff of the American Allergy Association (1987). Available from Allergy Publications Group, P.O. Box 640, Menlo Park, CA 94026.

(See also ASTHMA; FOOD ADDITIVES; FOOD INTOLERANCE; IMMUNE SYSTEM.)

allogenic In medicine, a general term referring to a type of TRANSPLANT or BLOOD TRANSFUSION that comes from a donor, a person whose tissues are different from the patient's yet similar enough to be transplanted. By contrast, if the tissues or blood come from elsewhere in the person's own body, the transplant or transfusion is called AUTOLOGOUS.

alopecia Partial or total loss of hair where hair normally grows, not only as a result of the normal aging process, but also from various other causes, such as a HORMONE disorder, SKIN DISORDER, or reaction to some drugs or therapies, such as radiation therapy or chemotherapy. *Alopecia areata* is a recurring disease of unknown origin causing bald patches to appear on the body for months at a time. Hair loss of a different sort can result from compulsive hair-pulling, called trichotillomania (see IMPULSE CONTROL DISORDER).

For help and further information

National Alopecia Areata Foundation (NAAF)
714 C Street, Suite 216
San Rafael, CA 94901
415-456-4644
Vicki Kalabokes, Executive Director
Organization of people concerned about alopecia areata. Provides support; gathers and disseminates information; publishes various materials, including a bimonthly newsletter and cosmetic hints.

National Institute of Arthritis and Musculoskeletal and Skin Diseases (NIAMS), 301-496-8188. (For full group information, see ARTHRITIS.)

alphabet method Alternate term for PHONICS METHOD.

alpha fetoprotein (AFP) A protein produced in a fetus's liver that is passed into the mother's blood, where it can be sampled and tested, generally about 16 to 19 weeks into a PREGNANCY. Abnormally high AFP levels are often associated with NEURAL TUBE DEFECTS, such as SPINA BIFIDA, and with other ailments, such as KIDNEY PROBLEMS; while low levels can be linked with DOWN'S SYNDROME, so testing is done where family history warrants it. But the *maternal serum alpha-fetoprotein test* (MSAFP) is only a general screen; abnormal AFP levels do not necessarily signal abnormalities but rather the advisability of more precise GENETIC SCREENING procedures, such as AMNIOCENTESIS and ULTRASOUND. A high AFP level may also appear when a pregnant woman is carrying twins. The MSAFP test has been found somewhat unreliable in dealing with low AFP levels. (For help and further information, see GENETIC DISORDERS.)

alpha-galactosidase deficiency Alternate name for *Fabry's disease*, a type of LIPID STORAGE DISEASE.

alpha 1-antitrypsin deficiency (a_1AT) A GENETIC DISORDER that results from lack of the liver protein *alpha 1-antitrypsin*, identified by a BLOOD TEST. The deficiency affects both the liver and the lungs, causing CIRRHOSIS OF THE LIVER and emphysema (see LUNG AND BREATHING DISORDERS). No treatment currently exists, but liver TRANSPLANTS offer hope of survival to people with the deficiency.

For help and further information

American Liver Foundation (ALF), 201-857-2626 (toll-free number, U.S. except NJ, 800-223-0179). Sponsors network for parents of children with liver diseases, including alpha 1-antitrypsin deficiency; publishes information sheet *Alpha-Antitrypsin Deficiency*. (For full group information, see LIVER PROBLEMS.)

Children's Liver Foundation, 201-761-1111. Publishes *What Common Liver Deficiency Spares Some Children, Dooms Many Others? Alpha-1 Antitrypsin (a_1AT)*. (For full group information, see LIVER PROBLEMS.)

National Institute of Diabetes and Digestive and Kidney Diseases (NIDDK), 301-496-3583; **National Digestive Disease Information Clearinghouse (NNDIC)**, 301-468-6344. (For full group information, see DIGESTIVE DISORDERS.)

National Heart, Lung, and Blood Institute (NHLBI), 301-496-4236. (For full group information, see LUNG AND BREATHING DISORDERS.)

alpha-thalassemia An inherited form of ANEMIA.

ALQ Abbreviation for ADOLESCENT LANGUAGE QUOTIENT, the overall score resulting from the TEST OF ADOLESCENT LANGUAGE (TOAL).

ALS Abbreviation for amyotrophic lateral sclerosis (ALS or Lou Gehrig's disease), a type of MOTOR NEURON DISEASE.

ALTE Abbreviation for APPARENT LIFE-THREATENING EVENT.

alternative birthing center Alternate term for MATERNITY CENTER.

alternative school A school that offers nontraditional educational approaches, such as having children work primarily in small, informal groups or in UNGRADED CLASSES, rather than in the usual classrooms in a TRACKING system or in INDEPENDENT STUDY; sometimes called a SCHOOL OF CHOICE, often a type of

MAGNET SCHOOL. Though some alternative schools are public schools, most are PRIVATE SCHOOLS. Alternative schools hold attractions for many parents, but parents should make sure that the school of their choice is properly staffed and equipped and has some recognizable ACCREDITATION. The U.S. Department of Education's CHOOSING A SCHOOL FOR YOUR CHILD, excerpted on page 514, includes a checklist for evaluating schools. Some parents who are dissatisfied with schools in general opt for HOME SCHOOLING.

For help and further information

National Coalition of Alternative Community Schools (NCACS)
58 School House Road
Summertown, TN 38483
615-964-3670
Michael Traugot, National Office Coordinator
Organization of regional and local alternative schools and individuals interested in alternative education. Seeks to spread the idea of alternative education; acts as clearinghouse for information and makes referrals to existing schools; offers counsel in starting alternative schools; publishes various materials, including quarterly *National Coalition News*, semiannual journal *Skole, National Directory of Alternative Schools*, and video *Alternative School Sampler*.

National Association for Legal Support of Alternative Schools (NALSAS)
P.O. Box 2823
Santa Fe, NM 87501
505-471-6928
Ed Nagel, Coordinator
Organization of parents, educators, lawyers, nonpublic schools, and others interested in alternatives to public-school education. Gathers and provides information on legal issues and suits relating to nonpublic education; aids individuals and groups in developing workable educational alternatives; serves as accrediting agency for alternative schools; maintains library; sponsors Home Study Exchange, linking home-study students, as through pen-pal contacts; publishes semiannual *Tidbits*.

National Association of Private, Nontraditional Schools and Colleges (NAPNSC), 303-243-5441. (For full group information, see PRIVATE SCHOOLS.)
(See also EDUCATION, and specific topics highlighted in entry.)

alveolitis   Inflammation of the *alveoli*, tiny air sacs in the lungs, a kind of LUNG AND BREATHING DISORDER.

AMA   Abbreviation for AGAINST MEDICAL ADVICE.

ambidextrous   Describing a type of HANDEDNESS in which a person uses both hands with equal proficiency and skill, with neither hand having DOMINANCE over the other.

ambieyedness   A condition in which neither eye has DOMINANCE over the other.

amblyopia   A serious eye condition that may involve loss of sight in one eye. (See EYE AND VISION PROBLEMS.)

AMC   Abbreviation for ARTHROGRYPOSIS MULTIPLEX CONGENITA.

amelia   A BIRTH DEFECT that involves the absence of one or more limbs. The absence of all four limbs is called *tetramelia;* nearly absent limbs, with hands or feet attached almost directly to the body, is called *phocomelia. Amelia* is also a psychological term for the apathy and indifference sometimes associated with PSYCHOSIS.

amelogenesis imperfecta   A GENETIC DISORDER that causes the TEETH to have thin enamel, deficient in CALCIUM. A child with this disorder will have teeth that are mottled and susceptible to tooth decay and will require careful dental care.

amenorrhea   A disorder associated with MENSTRUATION.

ametropia   A condition affecting the focusing of the eye. (See EYE AND VISION PROBLEMS.)

amino acids   A group of chemical compounds that make up all PROTEINS and are therefore vital to proper NUTRITION. Approximately 20 amino acids are found in the human body, in proteins as well as elsewhere in the body, where they aid in biochemical reactions. Some amino acids can be manufactured within the body and so are termed *nonessential*; others can be obtained only from a proper diet and are called *essential*. Animal sources generally give a wider range of amino acids than do plant sources, so parents who choose a VEGETARIAN diet for themselves and their children must be especially careful that the selection of foods includes all of the essential amino acids. (For help and further information, see NUTRITION.)

aminotransferases (transaminases) test   A kind of BLOOD TEST, one of the LIVER FUNCTION TESTS, that can indicate damage to heart or liver tissues.

amniocentesis   A GENETIC SCREENING procedure that involves withdrawing AMNIOTIC FLUID from the sac surrounding the FETUS, using a needle (guided by ULTRASOUND) inserted through the abdomen. The fetal cells in the fluid can then be analyzed for many possible disorders, such as DOWN'S SYNDROME, SPINA BIFIDA, and GLYCOGEN STORAGE DISEASES; tests also show the sex of the fetus, important in assessing the risk of SEX-LINKED DISEASES. Amniocentesis is performed at about 14 to 16 weeks into the pregnancy, later than such other procedures as CHORIONIC VILLUS SAMPLING, and the laboratory analysis takes longer; it also carries some risk of MISCARRIAGE and of fetal or maternal HEMORRHAGE. Even so, it is often recommended for women over 35, for those with abnormally high ALPHA FETOPROTEIN levels, and for those whose family history indicates a higher-than-normal possibility of GENETIC DISORDERS. (For help and further information, see GENETIC DISORDERS; GENETIC SCREENING.)

amniotic fluid   The clear fluid that surrounds the FETUS in the UTERUS, held within a membrane called an *amniotic sac*, which protects the fetus against pressure from the mother's internal organs and against injury from outside. The fetus swallows the circulating fluid, absorbs it into the bloodstream, and then excretes urine into it; the developing being does not drown because the lungs are not used for breathing until after birth. Mostly water, the fluid also contains other substances, such as FATS (lipids) and waste fetal cells. It is such substances that are examined in the PRENATAL SCREENING test called AMNIOCENTESIS.

The amniotic fluid in its sac is the "bag of waters" that breaks just before, during, or after delivery of the baby. Too little amniotic fluid, called *oligohydramnios*, and too much fluid, called *hydramnios* or *polyhydramnios*, can both signal problems with and for the developing fetus. If a fetus has a problem with swallowing, as in ANENCEPHALY or ATRESIA in the esophagus, fluid will accumulate, as it may also in a woman with DIABETES MELLITUS and sometimes in MULTIPLE BIRTHS. Hydramnios is associated with higher-than-normal risk of PREMATURE delivery and abnormal FETAL PRESENTATION. On the other hand, oligohydramnios can occur if the fetus has KIDNEY AND UROLOGICAL DISORDERS, if the PLACENTA is malfunctioning, if the mother has PREECLAMPSIA or ECLAMPSIA, or if delivery is overdue (beyond about 41 weeks). Too little amniotic fluid is associated early with MISCARRIAGE and later with some physical deformities, such as CLUBFOOT. (For help and further information, see CHILDBIRTH; AMNIOCENTESIS.)

Amsterdam retardation   Alternate name for DE LANGE SYNDROME.

amyotrophic lateral sclerosis (ALS or Lou Gehrig's disease) A type of MOTOR NEURON DISEASE.

anabolic steroid   A compound related to TESTOSTERONE, the male sex hormone, liable to abuse. (See HELP AGAINST SUBSTANCE ABUSE on page 587.)

analysis-level thinking   Developing conclusions after study of the various aspects of a situation or event; from Benjamin Bloom's description of the various kinds of thinking or learning processes, the other main types being KNOWLEDGE-LEVEL THINKING, COMPREHENSION-LEVEL THINKING, APPLICATION-LEVEL THINKING, SYNTHESIS-LEVEL THINKING, and EVALUATION-LEVEL THINKING.

analytic learning   A LEARNING STYLE that focuses on the general rule or concept first, and then on the parts or supporting details.

anaphylactic shock   SHOCK induced by an allergic reaction to an injected substance, such as bee's venom or penicillin. (For help and further information, see ALLERGY.)

anaplasia   Medical term for a cell that has become less differentiated and more "primitive" in form, describing a cell that is MALIGNANT, as in CANCER. Malignant BRAIN TUMORS may be described as *anaplastic*.

anatomical age   Numerical summary of the relationship between a child's growth and the statistical average for a child of the same size and sex. If a child of six has a degree of skeletal maturation normally seen in a seven-year-old, that child's anatomical age is seven. (See also AGE.)

anemia   A condition involving deficiency of red blood cells, which contain the *hemoglobin* that carries the all-important oxygen throughout the body. Red blood cells, originally formed in

the BONE MARROW, live for about 120 days in the bloodstream, with the older ones gradually being trapped in the filtering tissues of the *lymphatic system* (see IMMUNE SYSTEM) and destroyed, often in the spleen. Anemia can result when more red blood cells are destroyed than are formed, when red blood cells self-destruct in the bloodstream (a process called *hemolysis*), when large amounts of blood have been lost (as from injury, surgery, or internal bleeding), or when blood cells themselves are defective and incapable of carrying oxygen as they should.

Anemia can range from a mild condition to a severe, life-threatening one. Symptoms include headaches, fatigue, breathing difficulty during EXERCISE, paleness, and in more severe cases dizziness from too little oxygen to the brain, pain from too little oxygen to the heart, heart palpitations, and sometimes JAUNDICE from excess of the yellow pigment *bilirubin*, formed when red blood cells are destroyed. Anemia is normally diagnosed by standard BLOOD TESTS, especially a COMPLETE BLOOD COUNT (CBC), which measures the number and proportion of the various types of blood cells in a sample of the patient's blood.

In general, treatment aims to restore the proper balance and effectiveness of the person's red blood cells, often by providing BLOOD TRANSFUSIONS and, where possible, attempting to treat the underlying cause of the anemia. How successful the treatment is depends partly on the severity of the condition, how long before it was diagnosed (and therefore how much the body was weakened or damaged), and the cause of the anemia.

Anemia can have many causes, blood being the basic "transport system" of the body and so in contact with every organ and tissue. Some of the main types of anemia found in children include:

• *iron-deficiency anemia*, by far the most widespread type of anemia, generally resulting from insufficient IRON in the diet, a key mineral needed in the synthesis of hemoglobin. Iron-deficiency anemia is uncommon in breastfed infants but often occurs if introduction of SOLID FOODS is delayed or if a toddler is allowed to subsist mostly on MILK. If children are not eating iron-bearing foods at that age, parents are advised to add an iron supplement to the diet. Young boys during their GROWTH SPURT also may need extra iron to prevent anemia, as may girls once MENSTRUATION starts, but older boys generally do not and risk having excess iron.

• *sickle-cell anemia*, a GENETIC DISORDER (of the AUTOSOMAL RECESSIVE type) in which the hemoglobin is abnormal, causing the red blood cells to be distorted into a sickle or crescent shape. These are not only less well able to carry oxygen, but their abnormal shape sometimes causes the smallest blood vessels to become clogged, a painful, potentially life-threatening condition called a *sickle-cell crisis*, which can badly damage organs involved, such as brain, kidney, liver, lungs, and spleen. Such a crisis is often treated with blood transfusions and sometimes with partial *exchange transfusions*, antibiotics to fight infection, and additional oxygen. Advances in medical treatment have increased the life expectancy of people with sickle-cell anemia, which in the past was generally fatal in early childhood; the highest MORTALITY RATE is still found among children. The sickle-cell trait is found most often among Blacks and to some extent among people whose origins are in the Mediterranean area. Children affected are those who have inherited the trait from both parents; those who inherited the trait from only one parent are CARRIERS, usually symptom free. Prospective parents with sickle-cell anemia in their family history may want to seek GENETIC COUNSELING. Various PRENATAL TESTS can tell if a FETUS has the trait.

- *thalassemia*, a genetic disorder (of the autosomal recessive type) in which the red blood cells are fragile and smaller than usual and self-destruct prematurely. Thalassemia is found most often among people of Mediterranean origin, and so it sometimes is called *Mediterranean anemia* (*thalassa* meaning "sea"), but it also occurs among people originating in Southeast Asia. Either of two chains of PROTEINS in hemoglobin may be involved, the *alpha* chain or the *beta* chain. Severity of the disorder varies from mild to life-threatening. The most severe form is *beta-thalassemia*, also called *thalassemia major* or *Cooley's anemia*. Symptoms often appear in infancy, with slow physical development and susceptibility to infections, leading to JAUNDICE; enlargement of the SPLEEN and bone marrow, which can cause abnormal bone growth; and, if undiagnosed and untreated, death in childhood or adolescence. Blood transfusions are often given but sometimes have the adverse side effect of causing excess iron to be stored in body organs (*hemosiderosis*), which can in turn cause CIRRHOSIS OF THE LIVER, DIABETES MELLITUS, and heart problems (see HEART AND HEART PROBLEMS). Approaches being explored are methods of removing excess iron from the body and the use of BONE MARROW TRANSPLANTS. Prospective parents will want to consider genetic counseling and prenatal testing.
- *megaloblastic anemia*, in which deficiency of key VITAMINS, specifically VITAMIN B_{12} and FOLIC ACID, leads to production of abnormally large, deformed red blood cells (*macrocytes*). Sometimes the deficiency results from the body's inability to absorb VITAMIN B_{12}, a condition called *pernicious anemia*. But megalobastic anemia can also result from poor NUTRITION or from MALABSORPTION, especially with disorders such as CROHN'S DISEASE or CELIAC SPRUE; it is also associated with diabetes mellitus and hypothyroidism (see THYROID GLAND). The underlying problem is treated, if possible, but beyond that, treatment may require continuing injections or supplements of the missing vitamins.
- *aplastic anemia*, in which the blood has too few blood cells of all types, because of damage to the bone marrow where the cells are produced. Though aplastic anemia can result from some kinds of viral infections, it often stems from external sources, such as anticancer therapies using RADIATION and CHEMOTHERAPY or exposure to some kinds of chemicals. A rare CONGENITAL form of aplastic anemia is *Fanconi's anemia*. In some cases aplastic anemia may be treated by bone marrow transplant. If severe and irreversible, it can be fatal.

Anemia in Pregnancy

The most common form of anemia occurs when your body does not have enough iron to build the extra red blood cells you need while you are pregnant. This form of anemia can usually be prevented by eating foods that are high in iron, including liver, red meats, dried beans, leafy green vegetables, and iron-fortified cereals.

Many doctors prescribe iron supplements during pregnancy because the amount of iron needed is greater than that contained in the average diet. When you are taking an iron supplement your bowel movements will be darker and harder, so you should increase the amounts of fluids and roughage in your diet. Be sure to keep iron-supplement tablets, like all medicine, in a safe place so children cannot accidentally eat them.

There are other, more serious forms of anemia, and if any of them are found during the early laboratory tests, your pregnancy should be followed more closely. Be sure to tell your doctor if you or any relatives are anemic or have blood diseases.

Source: *Prenatal Care* (1983). Prepared for the Public Health Service by the Health Resources and Services Administration, Bureau of Health Care Delivery and Assistance, Division of Maternal and Child Health.

Anemia can also result when a child has long-term chronic illness and when a woman is pregnant. In cases of RH INCOMPATIBILITY between mother and child, anemia may develop in the FETUS. During PRENATAL CARE and WELL-BABY EXAMINATIONS, anemia is routinely tested for so that any developing problems can be treated most effectively, before damage is done.

For help and further information

Sickle Cell Disease Branch
Division of Blood Diseases and Resources
National Heart, Lung, and Blood Institute
7550 Wisconsin Avenue, Room 504
Bethesda, MD 20892
301-496-6931

Subdivision of the National Institutes of Health. Publishes various materials, including *Adolescents with Sickle-Cell Anemia and Sickle-Cell Trait, The Family Connection*, and *Sickle-Cell Fundamentals*.

National Heart, Lung, and Blood Institute (NHLBI), 301-496-4236. (For full group information, see BLOOD AND BLOOD DISORDERS; HEART AND HEART PROBLEMS; LUNG AND BREATHING DISORDERS.)

National Association for Sickle Cell Diseases (NASCD)
4221 Wilshire Boulevard, Suite 360
Los Angeles, CA 90010

213-936-7205, toll-free number (U.S. except CA) 800-421-8453
Dorothye H. Boswell, Executive Director
Organization acting as information clearinghouse for public and
professionals regarding sickle-cell disease. Seeks to educate
public and acts as advocate for people with sickle-cell disease;
encourages formation of local chapters; publishes various
materials, including quarterly *Sickle Cell News*.

Cooley's Anemia Foundation
105 East 22nd Street, Suite 911
New York, NY 10010
212-598-0911
Teresa G. Piropato, Executive Director
Organization concerned with Cooley's anemia. Gathers and disseminates information; encourages research; supports training
of health professionals; fosters training and vocational guidance
for children with Cooley's anemia; publishes various materials,
including quarterly newsletter *Lifeline*, audiovisuals such as *A
Little Hurt* and *Precious Gift of Time*, and print works such as
*Cooley's Anemia—Prevention Through Understanding and Test-
ing* and *Cooley's Anemia—A Medical Review*.

Thalassemia Action Group (TAG)
Ralph Cazetta, President
(See Cooley's Anemia Foundation, above, for address and
phone number.)

Fanconi Anemia Support Group
2875 Baker Boulevard
Eugene, OR 97403
503-686-0434
Lynn Frohnmayer and David Frohnmayer, Contacts
Mutual-support self-help group of families of children who have
Fanconi anemia. Provides information; publishes annual *FA
Family Newsletter*.

March of Dimes Birth Defects Foundation, 914-428-7100
(local chapters in telephone-directory white pages). Publishes
fact sheets *Sickle-Cell Anemia* and *Thalassemia*. (For full group
information, see BIRTH DEFECTS; GENETIC DISORDERS.)

Other reference sources
Health Care U.S.A., by Jean Carper. New York: Prentice Hall,
   1987. Resource for general and specific health-care information; lists major sickle-cell anemia treatment or research
   centers and other information.
(See also BLOOD AND BLOOD DISORDERS; GENETIC COUNSELING;
   GENETIC DISORDERS.)

anencephaly   A BIRTH DEFECT related to SPINA BIFIDA.

anesthesia   Treatment to block the sensation of pain, as during a medical procedure; literally, absence of feeling. Anesthesia may be topical, local, regional, or general. *Topical anesthesia* is the most minimal, involving application of a sense-
deadening substance to a surface such as the skin, membrane,
or cornea of the eye. *Local anesthesia* applies to just a small

area of the body, as in dental surgery or some minor surgical
procedures, and is often administered by INJECTION, though
sometimes a surface anesthetic may be used.

A *regional anesthetic* deadens feeling in a whole area of the
body, generally by means of a *nerve block*, an injection to anesthetize the main nerve serving that area of the body. The nerve
block allows PHYSICIANS to anesthetize areas that are very large
or hard to reach directly by injection. Among the main kinds of
regional anesthetic are:

• *epidural anesthesia*, in which an anesthetic is injected into
  the spine, more precisely into the epidural space between
  the vertebrae and spinal cord, during surgery or CHILDBIRTH,
  to anesthetize the area around the pelvis, lower abdomen,
  and genitals. Often a CATHETER (thin, flexible tube) is left in
  place, so more anesthetic or *analgesics* (pain-killers) can be
  given as needed.
• *pudendal block*, in which an anesthetic is injected into the
  VAGINA wall, to anesthetize the area of the VULVA during LABOR
  (especially during FORCEPS DELIVERY) without affecting the
  contractions of the UTERUS.
• *paracervical block*, in which the anesthetic is injected into
  the CERVIX during childbirth without adversely affecting labor.
• *spinal anesthesia*, in which the anesthetic is injected
  between the vertebrae into the CEREBROSPINAL FLUID, using a
  technique similar to a LUMBAR PUNCTURE; it is used for surgery
  involving the lower limbs and abdomen, alternatively with
  epidural anesthesia.
• *caudal block*, in which an anesthetic is injected into the bottom part of the spinal cord through the sacrum (just above
  the "tail bone") during childbirth or surgery in the genital or
  rectal area; often epidural anesthesia is used instead, since
  caudal block is less reliable and, during childbirth, carries
  the risk of reducing the force of the contractions and of accidental injection of the FETUS.
• *intercostal anesthesia*, involving injection between two ribs.
• *brachial plexus anesthesia*, involving injection into the set of
  nerves that serves each arm.

Use of regional anesthesia has very much changed childbirth
(as well as many forms of surgery), allowing a woman to have
relief from pain while retaining consciousness during the birth
itself. As part of the planning for childbirth, women and their
partners will want to explore and discuss with their physician
the advantages and disadvantages of anesthesia and of the various kinds available, especially whether some forms may slow
labor by weakening contractions or may adversely affect the
baby.

Beyond regional anesthesia is *general anesthesia*, in which
the patient not only loses feeling but consciousness as well.
Still widely used in many kinds of surgery, it is rarely used
today during childbirth because it can cause breathing problems
for the baby. Before the operation, the ANESTHESIOLOGIST normally meets with the patient to assess his or her physical condition and to discuss the kind of anesthesia to be used. The
type of anesthesia used will depend on the kind and length of

procedure being performed, which might range from a 20-minute surgical BIOPSY to a many-hours-long organ TRANSPLANT.

Before leaving for the operating room, a patient is generally given an injection of a muscle relaxant and perhaps some other drugs through a vein in the hand; this is left in place for administration of other drugs later as needed. The anesthesia itself may be given by injection or by inhalation of gases, sometimes breathed in through a mask, other times (as when a muscle relaxant has been given) through breathing tubes.

Anesthesia is not risk free. A small number of people have allergic, sometimes life-threatening reactions to anesthetics, involving extremely high temperature and rigid muscles; the condition is a GENETIC DISORDER called MALIGNANT HYPERTHERMIA. If such reactions appear anywhere in a family's medical history, patients should be sure their doctor knows about them before childbirth or other kinds of treatment. On rare occasions, also, nerves can be damaged by injections of regional anesthetics, and general anesthesia can bring on dangerous and even fatal heart irregularities, breathing problems, low BLOOD PRESSURE, and other kinds of problems. Where time permits before an operation, and especially when a child is being operated on, parents should explore carefully the pros and cons of various forms of anesthesia.

For help and further information

National Institute of General Medical Sciences (NIGMS)
9000 Rockville Pike
Building 31, Room 4A52
Bethesda, MD 20892
301-496-7301
Federal arm, one of the U.S. National Institutes of Health, sponsoring research into questions of general medical concern. Provides information to public and to health professionals; publishes various materials, including technical reports for specialists and more general brochures.

Malignant Hyperthermia Association of the United States (MHAUS), 203-655-3007; Medic Alert Hotline 209-634-4917. (For full group information, see MALIGNANT HYPERTHERMIA.)

anesthesiologist (anesthetist) A medical physician who specializes in administering anesthetics, drugs to produce local or general loss of sensation, generally in preparation for some form of surgery. In some situations, a *nurse anesthetist*, a registered nurse with advanced training, may handle ANESTHESIA. If you or your child are scheduled for any procedure that may require anesthesia, you should meet with the anesthesiologist beforehand to discuss the various options and the risks and benefits of each.

anesthetist Alternate name for ANESTHESIOLOGIST.

angiogram (arteriogram) A medical test in which a contrasting material is injected into a deep artery in the body, such as in the groin or neck, and X-RAYS are taken as the material flows through the body. Angiograms can be used in many situations.

In diagnosing BRAIN TUMORS, they may help a physician to see the precise pattern of blood vessels in the brain and the amount of blood that may be feeding into a tumor. In diagnosing heart problems (see HEART AND HEART PROBLEMS), angiography often involves insertion of a CATHETER through the groin or arm to check for abnormalities in the blood vessels and in various body organs, as well as sites of blood clots or internal bleeding. In diagnosing EYE AND VISION PROBLEMS, OPHTHALMOLOGISTS sometimes use a technique called *fluorescein retinal angiography* or *eye angiography*, in which X-rays are taken of the eye, after INJECTION of the dyed fluid and use of eyedrops to dilate (open) the pupils. (For help and further information, see MEDICAL TESTS.)

angiokeratoma corporis diffusum universale Alternate name for *Fabry's disease*, a type of LIPID STORAGE DISEASE.

aniseikonia Alternate name for ANISOMETROPIA.

anisometropia (aniseikonia) A condition in which the two eyes each see an object as of a different size and shape. (See EYE AND VISION PROBLEMS.)

anomia A type of APHASIA involving the inability to recall the names of people, objects, and places.

anorexia nervosa A type of MENTAL DISORDER, psychiatrically classified as an *eating disorder*, involving self-starvation through dieting but also often through induced VOMITING and laxative abuse (characteristic of the related eating disorder BULIMIA NERVOSA). People with anorexia nervosa have not necessarily lost their appetite, as the term *anorexia* implies; they are, in fact, often obsessed with food, sometimes hoarding or concealing it, but their intense fear of gaining weight and being fat leads them to reduce their food intake drastically. They also have a distorted BODY IMAGE, imagining that they are fat even when they are emaciated, with a body weight often 15 to 25 percent under normal body weight for their age. Even before onset, only about a third of anorexics are even mildly overweight, and they rarely are obese.

The disorder can affect young children, adolescents, or adults of both sexes but is found most often among adolescent girls between 12 and 21, in whom the first sign (even before dramatic weight loss) may be cessation of the MENSTRUAL CYCLE. The drastic drop in weight and the resulting toll on the body causes a variety of other changes in the body, including lowered temperature, slowed heartbeat, lowered BLOOD PRESSURE, EDEMA, CONSTIPATION, slowing of sexual maturation (in boys and girls), loss of hair on the head, and development of LANUGO (hair like that on newborns) on the body. Often associated disorders are DEPRESSION and OBSESSIVE-COMPULSIVE DISORDER.

The causes of anorexia nervosa are unknown, but the National Institute of Child Health and Human Development (NICHD) notes, "a combination of psychological, environmental, and physiological factors are associated with development of the disorder." Psychologists note that many people with anorexia nervosa come from White middle- and upper-class families who emphasize high achievement, and that before onset of the disorder they were often good students and "model children." Some feel that the normal adolescent feelings of rebellion were suppressed and that anorexia nervosa is somehow a result of desire for independent control and perfection.

Others are researching possible physical causes. The HYPO-THALAMUS, which affects many of the body's key functions, is abnormal in people with anorexia nervosa, and researchers are exploring the possibility that malfunctions in that organ precede and help trigger the disorder.

The most important concern, once the disorder is recognized, is to get the patient to eat and gain weight; the NICHD notes the urgency: "about 10–15 percent of anorexia nervosa patients die, usually after losing at least half their normal body weight." In addition to nutritional therapy, treatment often involves both individual psychotherapy and family counseling, sometimes in the family setting but often in a hospital. If the patient is hospitalized, arrangements (called a *behavioral contract*) are made for the patient to have privileges (such as outings) in return for weight gain, which keeps control in his or her hands while he or she begins to understand the causes of the disorder. Family counseling focuses on how not to make eating become a source of family tension. Self-help groups (see below) can be helpful to both parents and anorexics, immediately and in the years that follow. Relapses sometimes occur, even after a patient has completed treatment and regained normal weight, so the NICHD recommends that follow-up therapy be maintained for three to five years. Parents should be aware that many insurance policies do not cover therapy for mental disorders, but at least one family in recent years has won a claim for coverage for the hospital care given to their daughter, which focused on physical therapy.

For help and further information

National Association of Anorexia Nervosa and Associated Disorders
P.O. Box 7
Highland Park, IL 60035
Hotline 708-831-3438
Vivian Meehan, President
Organization for anorexics and bulimics, their families, and interested others. Provides information and referrals; encourages formation of mutual-support self-help groups; seeks to educate public; supports research and fights insurance discrimination; answers personal letters and operates hotline, generally staffed by recovered anorexics or their family members; publishes various materials, including newsletter *Working Together*, fact sheets, and self-help materials.

American Anorexia Bulimia Association (AABA)
133 Cedar Lane
Teaneck, NJ 07666
201-836-1800
Linda Rothenbert, Executive Director
Network of professionally led, mutual-support self-help groups for people with eating disorders. Offers information, counseling, and referrals; links new members with recovered members; publishes various materials, such as newsletter, fact sheets, and pamphlets, including bibliography.

National Anorexic Aid Society (NAAS)
5796 Karl Road
Columbus, OH 43229
614-436-1112
Self-help organization of and for anorexics and their families. Provides information and makes referrals; linked with outpatient organization, The Center for the Treatment of Eating Disorders; publishes various materials, including quarterly *NAAS Newsletter*.

National Institute of Child Health and Human Development, 301-496-5133. Publishes *Facts About Anorexia Nervosa*. (For full group information, see PREGNANCY.)

Other reference sources

For Parents

A Parent's Guide to Anorexia and Bulimia: Understanding and Helping Self-Starvers and Binge/Purgers, by Katherine Byrne. New York: Henry Holt, 1989.

Surviving an Eating Disorder: New Perspectives and Strategies for Family and Friends, by Michele Siegel, Judith Brisman, and Margot Weinshel. New York: Harper & Row, 1988.

Health Care U.S.A., by Jean Carper. New York: Prentice Hall, 1987. Resource for general and specific health-care information. Lists major eating-disorders clinics and programs for treatment or referral, along with other information.

Background Works

Anorexia and Bulimia: Anatomy of a Social Epidemic, by Richard A. Gordon. Cambridge, MA: Basil Blackwell, 1990.

Freedom from Food: The Secret Lives of Dieters and Compulsive Eaters, by Elizabeth Hampshire. New York: Prentice Hall, 1990.

Inner Harvest: Daily Meditations for Recovery from Eating Disorders, by Elisabeth L. New York: Harper & Row/Hazelden, 1990.

Never Too Thin: Why Women Are at War with Their Bodies, by Roberta Pollack Seid. New York: Prentice Hall, 1989.

Food Trips & Traps: Coping with Eating Disorders, by Jane Claypool and Cheryl D. Nelson. Irving, CA: CompCare, 1989.

Conversations with Anorexics, by Hilde Bruch, edited by Danita Czyzewski and Melanie A. Suhr. New York: Basic, 1989.

Fasting Girls: The Emergence of Anorexia Nervosa as a Modern Disease, by Joan Jacobs Brumberg. Cambridge, MA: Harvard University Press, 1988; New York: New American Library, 1989.

When Will We Laugh Again? Living and Dealing with Anorexia Nervosa and Bulimia, by Barbara P. Kinoy, John A. Atchley, M.D., and Estelle B. Miller. New York: Columbia University Press, 1989.

Perfect Women, by Colette Dowling. New York: Summit, 1988.

The Deadly Diet: Recovering from Anorexia and Bulimia, by Terence Sandbek. Oakland, CA: New Harbinger, 1986.

Anorexia Nervosa: Finding the Life Line, by Patricia Stein and Barbara Unell. Minneapolis: CompCare, 1986.

Anorexia Nervosa: The Turning Point, by Barbara Unell. Minneapolis: CompCare, 1985.

Breaking Free from Compulsive Eating, by Geneen Roth. New York: Bobbs-Merrill, 1985.

The Anorexia Nervosa Reference Book, by Roger Slade. New York: Harper & Row, 1984.

Eating Disorders: The Facts, by Suzanne Abraham. New York: Oxford University Press, 1984.

Dear Cherry: Questions and Answers on Eating Disorders, by Cherry Boone O'Neill. New York: Continuum, 1983.

Feeding the Hungry Heart: The Experience of Compulsive Eating, by Geneen Roth. New York: Bobbs-Merrill, 1983.

The Fear of Being Fat: The Treatment of Anorexia and Bulimia, by Charles Philip Wilson, Charles C. Hogan, and Ira Mintz. New York: Jason Aronson, 1983.

Starving for Attention, by Cherry Boone O'Neill. New York: Continuum, 1982.

The Art of Starvation: A Story of Anorexia and Survival, by Sheila MacLeod. New York: Schocken, 1982.

Starving to Death in a Sea of Objects: The Anorexia Nervosa Syndrome, by John A. Sours. New York: Jason Aronson, 1980.

Anorexia Nervosa, by R.L. Palmer. New York: Penguin, 1980.

The Best Little Girl in the World, by Steven Levenkron. Chicago: Contemporary, 1978.

The Golden Cage: The Enigma of Anorexia Nervosa, by Hilde Bruch, M.D. Boston: Harvard University Press, 1977.

Eating Disorders, Obesity, Anorexia Nervosa and the Person Within, by Hilde Bruch. New York: Basic, 1973.

Professional Works

The Role of Drug Treatments for Eating Disorders, by P.E. Garfinkel and D.M. Garner. New York: Brunner/Mazel, 1986.

Handbook of Psychotherapy for Anorexia Nervosa and Bulimia, D.M. Garner and P.E. Garfinkel, eds. New York: Guilford, 1985.

Eating and Its Disorders, A.J. Stunkard and E. Stellar, eds., vol. 62, Association for Research in Nervous and Mental Disease. New York: Raven, 1984.

Anorexia Nervosa: A Multidimensional Perspective, by P.E. Garfinkel and D.M. Garner. New York: Brunner/Mazel, 1983.

Treating and Overcoming Anorexia Nervosa, by Steven Levenkron. New York: Scribner, 1982; paperback, Warner, 1983.

For Kids

Eating Habits and Disorders, by Rachel Epstein. New York: Chelsea House, 1990. For young adults.

Anorexia and Bulimia, by Dayna Wolhart. Mankato, MN: Crestwood, 1988. Part of the Facts About Series.

Why Are They Starving Themselves? Understanding Anorexia and Bulimia, by Elaine Landau. New York: Messner, 1983.

anosmia   Lack of a sense of smell; a condition that may result from certain kinds of damage to the brain, such as a BRAIN TUMOR or HEAD INJURY.

anovulation   Failure of the OVARIES to develop, mature, and release an egg (OVUM) for fertilization.

anoxia   Deficiency in or cut-off of oxygen supply to the body, as may happen during PREGNANCY, in difficult LABOR, or in some cases of high FEVER and accidents such as near-drowning. It can also result from ANEMIA in which the blood is unable to carry oxygen to body tissues or from internal toxic conditions in which the tissues are unable to absorb oxygen from the blood. However it occurs, anoxia can cause damage to affected tissues; the brain is especially susceptible, and oxygen starvation has been implicated in numerous DEVELOPMENTAL DISORDERS, such as LEARNING DISABILITIES.

antepartal care   Alternate term for PRENATAL CARE.

antibodies   Substances created by the IMMUNE SYSTEM to fight ANTIGENS, which are matter the body perceives as foreign. In IMMUNIZATION, various VACCINES are used to trigger production of antibodies, without the person actually getting and having to fight off the disease itself.

antidiuretic hormone (ADH)   A HORMONE produced by the PITUITARY GLAND, which controls how much fluid remains in the body and how much is excreted in urine. Lack of ADH can trigger DIABETES INSIPIDUS.

antigen   A substance that the body perceives as foreign and that therefore triggers a response from the IMMUNE SYSTEM, which (among other things) produces ANTIBODIES to fight it. If the antigen is involved in an ALLERGY or ASTHMA, it is often called an *allergen*.

antioxidant   A substance that works in the body to help prevent oxygen from destroying other substances. VITAMIN K is a common antioxidant in the body. As FOOD ADDITIVES, antioxidants work as preservatives, to stave off spoilage.

antisocial personality disorder   The adult form of the childhood CONDUCT DISORDER.

anus   The exit of the intestines, subject to various disorders, including ATRESIA (lack of an opening) and STENOSIS (narrowing). (See DIGESTIVE DISORDERS.)

anxiety   A feeling of uneasiness, tension, worry, and fear, often including physical changes, such as disturbed breathing, rapid heartbeat, and sweating; a common symptom in many MENTAL DISORDERS. Anxiety and AVOIDANCE behavior are especially characteristic of the disorders classified as *anxiety disorders*, including PANIC DISORDERS, *phobic disorders* (see PHOBIA), OBSESSIVE–COMPULSIVE DISORDER, SEPARATION-ANXIETY DISORDER, AVOIDANT DISORDER, and OVERANXIOUS DISORDER.

For help and further information

Anxiety Disorders Association of America (ADAA), 301-231-9350. Publishes *Breaking the Panic Cycle*. (For full group information, see MENTAL DISORDERS.)

Apgar Scoring System

Rating factor	0 points	1 point	2 points
Color	Blue or pale	Trunk pink, extremities blue	All pink
Heart rate	None	Slow (under 100 beats per minute)	Over 100 beats per minute
Muscle tone	Limp	Some movement of limbs	Active movement of limbs
Reflex irritability (on being "poked" in nose)	No response	Grimace when stimulated	Cry, cough, or sneeze
Respiratory effort	None	Irregular, with weak cry	Regular, with strong cry

Other reference services

Helping the Fearful Child: A Parent's Guide to Everyday and Problem Anxieties, by Jonathan Kellerman. New York: Norton, 1981.

The Anxiety and Phobia Workbook, by Ed Bourne. Oakland, CA: New Harbinger, 1990. Distributed by Publishers Group West.

The Nature and Treatment of Anxiety Disorders, by C. Barr Taylor and Bruce A. Arnow. New York: Free Press, 1988.

(See also MENTAL DISORDERS, PHOBIA.)

AOI Abbreviation for *apnea of infancy*; also called APNEA OF PREMATURITY. (See also SLEEP APNEA.)

α₁AT Medical abbreviation for ALPHA 1-ANTITRYPSIN DEFICIENCY.

AOP Abbreviation for APNEA OF PREMATURITY. (See also SLEEP APNEA.)

Apgar score An evaluation of the condition of a NEWBORN; a summary using a five-factor rating scale, with each factor given zero, one, or two points and a top score of 10 points. The evaluation is normally done a minute after birth and then again five minutes after birth, with both scores noted on the baby's medical record. The aim of the Apgar score is to identify as quickly as possible babies with special problems that may call for immediate treatment or transfer to a NEONATAL INTENSIVE CARE UNIT (NICU). A newborn with a score of eight to 10 is regarded as being in excellent condition (10 is rare). A score of 5 to 7 suggests some mild problems, while a lower score indicates need for immediate intervention, such as RESUSCITATION. Sometimes the second score is much higher because a problem is only temporary, as when the medical staff clears mucus from an obstructed air passage. (See chart above.)

aphasia Loss or impairment of the ability to use words and to understand language symbols in reading, writing, or speaking, usually resulting from HEAD INJURY, disease, or delayed development of the CENTRAL NERVOUS SYSTEM, called *developmental aphasia*. Impairment of language ability is also called *dysphasia*. A type of aphasia involving the inability to recall the names of people, objects, and places is called *anomia*; difficulty in producing handwriting is called DYSGRAPHIA, and total inability is *agraphia*. Children with LEARNING DISABILITIES or other DEVELOPMENTAL DISORDERS may sometimes have aphasia, and they experience great frustration at knowing what they want to say but being unable to say it.

For help and further information

National Institute of Neurological Disorders and Stroke (NINDS), 301-496-5751. (For full group information, see BRAIN AND BRAIN DISORDERS.)

Other reference sources

Sourcebook for Aphasia: A Guide to Family Activities and Community Resources, by Susan H. Brunaker. Detroit, MI: Wayne State University Press, 1982.

(See also LEARNING DISABILITIES.)

apnea of infancy (AOI) Alternate name for APNEA OF PREMATURITY (AOP).

apnea of prematurity (AOP) or **apnea of infancy (AOI)** Brief cessation of breathing, normally found in SLEEP APNEA but of special danger among PREMATURE infants and overweight children.

APP Abbreviation for ADVANCED PLACEMENT PROGRAM.

apparent death Medical phrase for the centuries-old, traditional definition of DEATH, notably lack of heartbeat and breathing as indicating cessation of life. (See BRAIN DEATH.)

apparent life-threatening event (ALTE) A frightening episode in which an observer thinks someone has died or is dying and needs RESUSCITATION; in cases of infants with pathologic SLEEP APNEA, sometimes called *aborted crib death* or *near-miss SIDS* and apparently associated with increased risk of SUDDEN INFANT DEATH SYNDROME (SIDS).

appeal In the court system, a formal request for a higher court to review the judgment of a lower court; if errors are found in the conduct of the earlier trial, the lower court may be overruled and a new trial may be granted. Outside the traditional court system, as in an ADMINISTRATIVE PROCEDURE involving EDUCATION and many family-law issues, the right of appeal was not always available, but in recent years it has been extended to many such areas. If parents disagree with a school's INDIVIDUALIZED EDUCATION PROGRAM for a child, for example, they can follow an established appeal procedure. This is often called DUE PROCESS, the constitutional right that is now being applied to noncourt areas.

appendicitis   Inflammation of the APPENDIX, a small projection off the large intestine; an acute and highly dangerous disorder that can occur at any age but is most common among children (though not infants) and young adults, especially males. Appendicitis has various causes, including obstruction by hardened feces or an undigested foreign body and infestation by parasites, leading to inflammation and infection. Early symptoms include generalized, sometimes intermittent pain around the midabdomen, gradually localizing in the lower right quarter of the abdomen; nausea and VOMITING; low-grade FEVER; increased white blood count; and decreased bowel activity and CONSTIPATION. Because these symptoms can be found with other disorders, appendicitis is not easy to diagnose. However, a child with some of these symptoms should be examined by a doctor immediately. If appendicitis is diagnosed, emergency surgery—an *appendectomy* (removal of the appendix)—is indicated. If treatment is delayed, the appendix will generally rupture, at first causing cessation of pain but quickly spreading infection to the abdominal (peritoneal) cavity. The result is *peritonitis*, a life-threatening infection that, however, is now often treatable if caught early. (For help and further information, see DIGESTIVE DISORDERS.)

appendix   A small projection off the large intestine, which contains tissue that acts as a filter in the *lymphatic system*, the network through which the body's IMMUNE SYSTEM operates. If the appendix itself becomes infected and inflamed, the resulting acute APPENDICITIS can be life-threatening and requires emergency surgery.

applanation tonometry   The basic test for *glaucoma*. (See EYE AND VISION PROBLEMS.)

application-level thinking   Use of previously learned information in a new, unfamiliar context; from Benjamin Bloom's description of the various kinds of thinking or learning processes, the other main types being KNOWLEDGE-LEVEL THINKING, COMPREHENSION-LEVEL THINKING, ANALYSIS-LEVEL THINKING, SYNTHESIS-LEVEL THINKING, and EVALUATION-LEVEL THINKING.

appropriate gestational age (AGA)   A term applied to an infant who is small and of LOW BIRTH WEIGHT but whose size and stage of development are appropriate to his or her stage of GESTATION, meaning the number of weeks since CONCEPTION; often referring to a PREMATURE baby. By contrast, an infant who is *small for gestational age* (SGA) grew more slowly than normal. (See GESTATIONAL AGE.)

apraxia   Inability to produce in sequence the movements necessary to draw shapes and figures or copy words and letters, because of inadequate development of FINE MOTOR SKILLS.

aptitude test   A general type of test that is designed to predict a student's success in various kinds of learning, before any instruction has taken place, as opposed to an ACHIEVEMENT TEST, given after instruction. How well such tests do what they set out to achieve is a point of considerable controversy, focusing on VALIDITY. Many such tests attempt to measure academic aptitude, probably the best-known being the SCHOLASTIC APTITUDE TEST. *Mechanical aptitude tests* attempt to assess how well a student is likely to do in learning skills involving mechanical devices, normally testing reasoning in relation to mechanical things and SPATIAL RELATIONS. In the widest sense, READINESS TESTS and DEVELOPMENTAL SCREENING TESTS are kinds of aptitude tests, though they generally purport to test not general learning success but whether a child has the necessary PREREQUISITE skills and behavioral development needed to benefit fully from instruction. (For help and further information, see TESTS.)

AR   Abbreviation for AUTOSOMAL RECESSIVE, a pattern of GENETIC INHERITANCE.

arachnodactyly   Traditional name for MARFAN SYNDROME; Greek for "spider fingers."

Aran-Duchenne   A type of muscle disorder. (See MUSCULAR DYSTROPHY.)

arbitration   A procedure under which two parties submit their dispute for resolution to a neutral third party, selected by the parties or appointed by the court, often from the American Arbitration Association. The procedure is informal, though each side can present evidence and bring witnesses, and the decision is binding on both parties (unlike MEDIATION). Using arbitration, disputants can avoid the cost, delay, and hard feelings that often attend court cases, so many divorce agreements include a clause specifying that arbitration will be used in case of later disagreement. (For help and further information, see CUSTODY.)

architectural barriers   Obstacles barring people with physical HANDICAPS from free access to buildings, such as stairs, narrow doorways, and inaccessible bathrooms. Many older buildings are completely inaccessible to people with physical disabilities, but various laws are requiring that at least some be modified for free access; the EDUCATION FOR ALL HANDICAPPED CHILDREN ACT, for example, requires that school buildings be made accessible to disabled students. New construction of many kinds, especially schools and buildings supported by federal funds, must be designed for easy access.

ARMS   Abbreviation for *Adverse Reaction Monitoring System*, a reporting system for complaints about FOOD ADDITIVES.

arrearages   Back payments that have accumulated on a debt, such as unpaid, overdue CHILD SUPPORT payments; also called *arrears*. The term is sometimes also used to refer to "unpaid" visits, when VISITATION RIGHTS have been denied.

arteriogram   Alternate term for an ANGIOGRAM.

arthritis   Inflammation of the joints, often with swelling, pain, stiffness, and redness, a condition that can have a wide variety of causes and that can affect just one part of the body or many. Most forms of arthritis affect primarily older people, as the joints wear down over the years, but some forms affect children. *Juvenile rheumatoid arthritis* (JRA), also called *Still's disease*, generally attacks children, causing not only the usual pain and stiffness but sometimes muscle atrophy and deformity. If damage affects the *epiphyses*, the "growth plates" at the ends of the long bones, the child's overall growth may be impaired. JRA is thought to be a type of AUTOIMMUNE DISORDER, in which the body mistakenly attacks its own tissue. Unlike the adult form of the disease, however, JRA may pass in some children by the age of PUBERTY. Children can also have forms of arthritis as a result of injury to a joint; bacterial infection, as from GONORRHEA, TUBERCULOSIS, or LYME DISEASE; or other disorders, such as ANEMIA. A related disorder is ARTHROGRYPOSIS MULTIPLEX CONGENITA (AMC).

For help and further information

Arthritis Foundation
American Juvenile Arthritis Organization (AJAO)
1314 Spring Street, NW
Atlanta, GA 30309
404-872-7100
Clifford Clarke, President
Linda Weatherbee, Vice President for AJAO and Special Projects, Contact
Organization devoted to finding a cure for and preventing arthritis and related diseases. Provides information and referrals; offers professional training; sponsors self-help programs through local chapters; publishes many materials, including quarterly newsletter *Arthritis: Basic Facts* and *Arthritis: Diet and Nutrition*.

Arthritis Information Clearinghouse
P.O. Box 9872
Arlington, VA 22209
703-558-8250
Federally supported information clearinghouse, largely for professionals but also for public. Maintains library and bibliography of print and audiovisual material; publishes booklets.

National Institute of Arthritis and Musculoskeletal and Skin Diseases (NIAMS)
9000 Rockville Pike
Building 31, Room 9A04
Bethesda, MD 20892
301-496-3583
Federal arm, one of the U.S. National Institutes of Health, sponsoring research on arthritis, lupus, scleroderma, and related musculoskeletal and skin diseases. Provides information; publishes various materials, including *How to Cope with Arthritis*, *Arthritis: Medicine for the Layman*, and *Arthritis, Rheumatic Diseases, and Related Disorders*.

Other reference sources
Treating Arthritis: Medicine, Myth, and Magic, by Felix Fernandez-Madrid. New York: Plenum, 1989.
Arthritis: What Works, by Dava Sobel and Arthur C. Klein. New York: St. Martin's, 1989.
Rheumatoid Arthritis: Its Cause and Its Treatment, by Thomas McPherson Brown, M.D., and Henry Scammell. New York: M. Evans, 1988.
Health Care U.S.A., by Jean Carper. New York: Prentice Hall, 1987. Resource for general and specific health-care information, as for juvenile arthritis, osteoarthritis, lupus, scleroderma, brittle-bone disease, and related diseases; lists major centers for treatment or research, leading rheumatologists and immunologists, and other information.
Understanding Arthritis, by the Arthritis Foundation, edited by Irving Kusher, M.D., Ann Forer, and Ann B. McGuire. New York: Scribner, 1984.
Overcoming Arthritis: A Guide to Coping with Stiff or Aching Joints, by Dr. Frank Dudley Hart. New York: Arco, 1981.
A Manual for Arthritis Self-Management: A Joint Venture, by Dr. Frank Dudley Hart. New York: Arco, 1981.
The Arthritis Exercise Book, by Semyon Edgar and Ann Edgar. New York: Simon & Schuster/Cornerstone, 1981.
Arthritis: A Comprehensive Guide, by Dr. James R. Fries. Boston: Addison Wesley, 1979.
Arty's Arthritis Antics. Playful workbook about arthritis for children. Available from University of Alabama Multipurpose Arthritis Center, University Station, Birmingham, AL 35294.
You Have Arthritis Coloring Book. For children. Available from Dr. Gordon C. Sharp, University of Missouri Medical Center, Columbia, MO 65212.
(See also IMMUNE SYSTEM; LYME DISEASE; and HELP FOR SPECIAL CHILDREN, on page 578.)

arthrogryposis multiplex congenita (AMC)   A disorder in which the joints of the body are stiff and tend to be fixed in painful, awkward positions, partly because nerve and muscle tissue serving those joints is malformed and often replaced by fibrous tissue. The disease is *congenital* (present at birth), but its cause is unknown; it apparently is not a GENETIC DISORDER, but some suggest that AMC results from constriction of the motion of the FETUS. AMC is not PROGRESSIVE and tends to improve as an infant grows, often helped by physical therapy to enhance mobility and sometimes surgery or use of ORTHOPEDIC DEVICES to attempt to change the angle of the joint. Intelligence is not generally affected, but other abnormalities occasionally associated with arthrogryposis include CLEFT PALATE, CLUBFOOT, and undescended testicles (CRYPTORCHIDISM).

For help and further information
AVENUES (National Support Group for Arthrogryposis Multiplex Congenita)
P.O. Box 5192
Sonora, CA 95379

209-928-3688
Mary Anne Schmidt and Jim Schmidt, Executive Directors
Organization of people concerned with AMC. Gathers and disseminates information; encourages exchange of information about treatments, technical aids, and services; makes referrals; publishes newsletter *Avenues* and *What Is Arthrogryposis?*

National Institute of Arthritis and Musculoskeletal and Skin Diseases (NIAMS), 301-496-8188. (For full group information, see ARTHRITIS.)

arthroscopic surgery   Inspection and repair of the inside of a joint, using a flexible viewing tube called an *endoscope*, inserted through a small incision. The technique is most commonly used on knee joints and allows ORTHOPEDISTS to remove damaged material, repair torn tissues, and make other repairs, in a procedure that allows people (notably athletes) to resume normal activity quickly, unlike a traditional operation, in which the whole kneecap is exposed.

artificial coloring   A type of FOOD ADDITIVE that has been implicated in triggering, or at least exacerbating, HYPERACTIVITY.

artificial insemination (AI)   Introduction of SEMEN into a woman's VAGINA through a tube or other instrument, rather than by sexual intercourse, to achieve FERTILIZATION. To maximize the chances of conception, the woman normally uses various methods, such as NATURAL FAMILY PLANNING techniques, to pinpoint when OVULATION occurs. Using a HOME MEDICAL TEST (see also OVULATION METHOD), she can normally identify the time of ovulation, which is the optimum time for insemination.

There are two main kinds of artificial insemination:

• *artificial insemination–husband (AIH)*, also called *homologous insemination*, in which sperm from a woman's husband or sexual partner is used. On the appropriate day, the man provides semen, normally produced by MASTURBATION in a doctor's office and placed in a sterile container. This is then generally injected near the woman's CERVIX using a syringe or plastic tube; sometimes a small cup is used to hold the semen in place for a few hours. AIH may be used when the man has a physical disability that prevents normal intercourse, when there is a problem with the SPERM (as when there is a low sperm count, or the sperm need special treatment before being introduced), or when the fluids in the woman's vagina are hostile to the sperm (this procedure largely bypasses them). A man's semen may also sometimes be stored ahead of time if he is undergoing medical treatment, such as RADIATION or CHEMOTHERAPY, that can cause STERILITY. The procedure itself is simple, and some couples choose to perform insemination by themselves at home, though with a lower success rate. To increase the success rate, the procedure may be repeated over the several days of highest fertility.

• *artificial insemination–donor (AID)*, also called *heterologous insemination*, in which the semen used is from a donor, often anonymous. In this case, semen is obtained ahead of

time from donors who are in good general health and have been screened for known physical and mental disorders, though there is no guarantee that the man does not unknowingly carry a defective gene. Semen is frozen in liquid nitrogen and stored, often at central SPERM BANKS (also called *cryobanks*), but before use it is tested for common infections. Since AIDS and HEPATITIS can be (and have been) transmitted through donor sperm, sperm banks today are advised to use sperm only from donors who have tested negative on two widely spaced tests for these viruses. People considering AID are advised to explore such protections very carefully and especially not to use fresh sperm but only frozen sperm stored until two negative tests have been obtained. Couples may use AID when they have a history of GENETIC DISORDERS or RH INCOMPATIBILITY and in cases of INFERTILITY, as when the man has too few or defective sperm. Women without male sexual partners can also choose to have a child through AID. Physically, the procedure is much the same, with apparently no increase in BIRTH DEFECTS, but the frozen sperm has a somewhat shorter life span, so timing is even more crucial. The woman or the couple are sometimes able to choose the donor on the basis of anonymous information about the person's health and abilities, sometimes attempting to match characteristics of the donor with their own. Sperm is often ordered from a sperm bank elsewhere in the country to minimize the likelihood that a child will later unknowingly meet and marry another child with the same BIOLOGICAL FATHER.

With AIH, the legal father is also the biological father, so legal questions are at a minimum. With AID, the law generally regards the woman's husband as the legal father, regardless of who the anonymous biological father was. Legal problems and special wrinkles still remain, however. In one recent case, a woman became inseminated with what was supposed to be semen from her husband (who had since died of cancer) but was in fact someone else's semen, as genetic analysis confirmed. Women without male sexual partners who use sperm from known male friends may also be leaving open the question of the child's legal father, depending on the state laws where they live. Similar legal problems surround SURROGATE PARENTING, which often uses artificial insemination.

For help and further information

American Fertility Society (AFS), 205-933-8494. Publishes *Report of the Ad Hoc Committee on Artificial Insemination*. (For full group information, see INFERTILITY.)

National Institute of Child Health and Human Development (NICHD), 301-496-5133. (For full group information, see PREGNANCY.)

RESOLVE, Inc., 617-484-2424. Publishes fact sheet *Artificial Insemination*. (For full group information, see INFERTILITY.)

Lesbian Mothers National Defense Fund (LMNDF), 206-325-2643. Provides information on alternatives for would-be lesbian mothers, such as donor insemination. (For full group information, see HOMOSEXUALITY.)

Lesbian Rights Project (LRP), 415-621-0674. Publishes *Lesbians Choosing Motherhood: Legal Issues in Donor Insemination*. (For full group information, see HOMOSEXUALITY.)

Donor's Offspring
P.O. Box 37
Sarcoxie, MO 64862
417-548-3679
Candace Cay Turner, Executive Director
Organization for people using, considering, or conceived through donor insemination.

Other reference sources

Health Care U.S.A., by Jean Carper. New York: Prentice Hall, 1987. Resource for general and specific health-care information, including information on artificial insemination by donor (AID), in vitro fertilization, GIFT (gamete intrafallopian transfer), embryo transfer, and surrogate motherhood; lists key in vitro fertilization centers, embryo transfer centers, sperm banks, nurse-midwife centers, and other information.

Having Your Baby by Donor Insemination: A Complete Resource Guide, by Elizabeth Noble. Boston: Houghton Mifflin, 1987. Has extensive bibliography.

artificial limbs (prostheses)   A common type of ORTHOPEDIC DEVICE.

artificial respiration   Attempting to restart or maintain breathing for someone whose breathing has stopped or is inadequate to maintain functioning; also called *rescue breathing* (if done mouth-to-mouth) or *ventilation* (especially if by a machine). In CARDIOPULMONARY RESUSCITATION (CPR), *chest compressions* are also used to stimulate the heart. The Public Health Service recommmends that parents take first-aid and cardiopulmonary-resuscitation courses locally, as from the Red Cross or a nearby "Y," and review them periodically. They offer the following as general guidelines for maintaining basic life support in an infant.

asbestos   A type of ENVIRONMENTAL HAZARD.

ascorbic acid   Alternate name for VITAMIN C.

If Your Infant Is Not Breathing

Basic life support. If your baby is not breathing, no matter what the reason, or has no pulse (his or her heart has stopped beating), you must provide life support until help arrives. This means that [after calling for emergency help] you must try to stimulate the baby to start breathing again, and the heart to start pumping again, by the following steps:

Rescue breathing (ventilation)

1. Clear the mouth with your finger, quickly removing any mucus, vomit, food, or object.
2. Place the baby face up on the floor, table, or other firm surface.

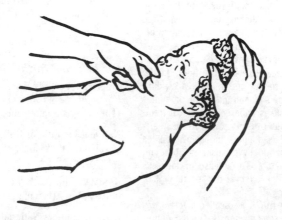

Continued on page 35.

3. If neck or spine has not been injured, tilt baby's head back slightly with chin up. Place your hand on baby's forehead to keep head in this position.

4. Cover mouth and nose with your mouth and blow gently until you see baby's chest rise.

5. Remove your mouth and let baby's lungs empty.
6. Take a quick breath yourself.
7. Repeat steps 4 and 5.

8. After breathing twice, check to be sure baby's heart is beating by feeling with your index and middle finger for pulse in the inside of baby's upper arm between the elbow and shoulder.

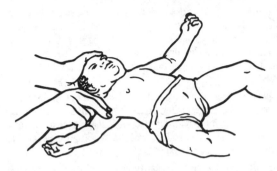

IF NO PULSE, YOU MUST TRY TO STIMULATE THE HEART BY PERFORMING CHEST COMPRESSIONS (see below).

9. If there is a pulse, continue rescue breathing at the rate of once every three seconds. Check to be sure baby's chest is rising—a sign the baby's airway is clear and air is entering freely. If air is not moving, quickly check the position of your baby's head, and try again.

10. IF STILL NO MOVEMENT, THERE IS PROBABLY SOMETHING BLOCKING THE BABY'S AIRWAY. TO CLEAR THE AIRWAY, FOLLOW STEPS UNDER CHOK-ING.

Chest compressions

1. Follow an imaginary line across the baby's chest from one nipple to the other. Place three fingers just below the middle of that imaginary line.

2. Lift the finger closest to the line, and with the two remaining fingers, press down ½ to 1 inch.

3. Keeping fingers in place, press, relax, press, relax for a total of five compressions.

4. Do one ventilation (rescue breathing).

5. Then repeat five compressions and one ventilation rapidly (the entire cycle should take less than 5 seconds to complete) 10 times.

6. Feel again for a pulse; if there is none, do 10 more cycles.

7. Repeat entire procedure until help arrives.

Source: *Infant Care* (1989). Prepared for the Public Health Service by the Health Resources and Services Administration, Bureau of Maternal and Child Health and Resources Development.

aspartame (brand name NutraSweet®) An artificial sweetener, a type of FOOD ADDITIVE.

asphyxia A severe kind of HYPOXIA (lack of oxygen). In the period just before, during, and after delivery, PERINATAL ASPHYXIA is a leading cause of infant DEATH.

aspiration The act of withdrawing fluid through a hollow needle, as in an ASPIRATION BIOPSY, or the act of breathing in or inhaling. In young children, foreign objects or substances can sometimes be inhaled directly or aspirated, such as vomit into the lungs, causing pneumonia. (See LUNG AND BREATHING DISORDERS.)

aspiration biopsy A type of BIOPSY using a hollow *aspiration needle* to obtain a sample of suspect material, such as a possible TUMOR, from the body for laboratory analysis; also, the technique of removing defective BONE MARROW from a patient, as part of a BONE MARROW TRANSPLANT.

assault In the law, a threat to cause deliberate or reckless physical injury to someone, as opposed to BATTERY, which is actual physical violence or offensive contact. *Simple assault* is a threat the person did not seriously intend to carry out or an uncompleted attempt at injury, while *aggravated assault* refers to threat with intention to do physical injury or to commit other crimes. In general usage, as in discussions of child abuse, the term is often used more loosely, as in "sexual assault," but such actions are legally considered battery. (See CHILD ABUSE AND NEGLECT.)

assessment General term for evaluation, most often used to refer to testing, as in DIAGNOSTIC ASSESSMENT TESTS. When teachers provide written evaluations of students, instead of or in addition to number or letter GRADES, it is sometimes called INFORMAL ASSESSMENT or *summative evaluation*.

assessment center In EDUCATION, an area of a school or a separate facility primarily devoted to administering various kinds of TESTS, generally to individual children, such as individually administered INTELLIGENCE TESTS, DEVELOPMENTAL SCREENING TESTS, DIAGNOSTIC ASSESSMENT TESTS, or READINESS TESTS.

assignment of support rights An agreement made by a CUSTODIAL PARENT who has not been receiving court-ordered CHILD-SUPPORT payments, specifying that such payments (including ARREARAGES) will be paid to the state, in exchange for various benefits, including a grant from AID TO FAMILIES WITH DEPENDENT CHILDREN.

associate degree The DEGREE awarded by most two-year colleges and universities to students who successfully complete their program of study, such as an Associate in Arts (A.A.), Associate in Science (A.S.), Associate in Applied Science (A.A.S.), or Associate in Occupational Studies (A.O.S.).

associative learning A type of LEARNING STYLE that focuses on relating new knowledge, skills, and concepts to prior learning.

asthma A condition involving recurrent bouts of breathlessness, wheezing, and coughing; a kind of LUNG AND BREATHING DISORDER that is closely related to ALLERGY. In an asthma attack, the bronchial tubes become constricted from muscle spasms and

swelling in the bronchial tissue, and mucus clogs the smaller tubes, so fresh oxygen-bearing air cannot enter. In severe

---

Controlling the Home Environment for the Asthmatic Child

- Avoid contact with pets and other animals.
- Avoid tobacco smoke.
- Control humidity, but beware belt-type humidifiers, which provide good growing places for fungi and bacteria.
- Install ventilator fans for stoves.
- Use air conditioners to screen particles from the air, and change filters frequently.
- Keep doors and windows closed to keep out unwanted particles, such as pollen.
- Make sure household odors are well vented.
- See that the heating system and its filters are properly maintained.
- If possible, use electric heat, rather than a forced-air heating system.
- Vacuum rooms when children are elsewhere, to avoid dust inhalation.
- Keep closet doors shut to minimize spreading of dust, and keep wool clothing in plastic garment bags.
- Use and store household chemicals carefully.
- Avoid dust-catchers like rugs, stuffed toys, cushions, pleated lampshades, venetian blinds, and cotton or wool blankets.
- Instead leave wood or tile floors bare and use plain, simple furniture; washable pillows and blankets of synthetic materials; and washable window shades.
- Air new mattresses packed in plastic until the odor is gone.
- Use nonallergenic cleaning agents, such as
  - plain ammonia for general household cleaning.
  - baking soda for general household cleaning and deodorizer (sprinkle on rugs before vacuuming).
  - oils such as beeswax, lemon oil, raw linseed oil, mineral oil and wax, and olive oil (though not on pewter) —be sure they haven't turned rancid.
  - nonchlorine bleaches for household and laundry cleaning.
  - charcoal packets as room and refrigerator deodorizers; close off rooms briefly.
  - club soda as a spot remover for clothing or rugs; pour on spot, let set, and sponge up.
  - salt as a kitchen cleaner, to loosen burned-on foods.
  - unscented, mild soaps; avoid scented deodorant soaps.
  - white or apple-cider vinegar mixed with water to remove mold, mineral deposits, crayon marks, and wallpaper.

Source: Allen & Hanbury's flyer based on "Helping Asthmatic Patients Control Their Environment," by J. C. Selner, *Journal of Respiratory Disorders*, 1986, 7:83–104.

cases, the person may turn pale or blue (CYANOSIS), especially around the lips and nails, have a rapid heartbeat (*tachycardia*), break out in a cold sweat, and indicate general distress. Though not generally fatal, asthma each year kills hundreds, with hundreds more dying from asthma-related complications. Many of these are people who develop the disease as adults, for whom the attacks are most severe, but children are also at risk and in severe cases should receive prompt medical care.

Precisely what causes asthma is not clear. Attacks can be triggered by widely varying factors at different times in different people, including respiratory infections; excitement or emotional stress; vigorous exercise; aspirin and some other anti-inflammatory drugs; weather changes and climate extremes, including sudden drafts; some kinds of foods (such as peanut butter, eggs, shellfish, chocolate, and foods containing sulfites); and a very wide range of substances carried in the air. Among these airborne substances (called *allergens*) are dust, animal hair and skin (*dander*), tobacco smoke, pollen, mold, aerosol sprays, cooking smoke, and feathers in the home and various kinds of pollutants outside and at work and school, such as automobile exhaust, industrial fumes and vapors, traces of metals and chemicals, cotton and wood dust, and the like. Asthma triggered by outside factors such as these is sometimes called *extrinsic asthma*.

In general, people are more likely to develop asthma if there is a history of allergies in the family. Except when the asthma begins before age two, the National Institute of Allergy and Infectious Diseases (NIAID) reports, the earlier the onset of asthma in a child, the less severe and long-lasting it is likely to be. Some children do "outgrow" the condition by mid-ADOLESCENCE, but what percentage is not clear. Certainly, the NIAID recommends that treatment should begin as soon as the disease is recognized, to minimize damage to the respiratory system.

The main treatment is to identify the causes of asthma attacks in a particular child and help the child avoid them whenever possible. That may take some considerable detective work and then sometimes considerable work to keep an environment free of allergens (see below for guidelines). Where the allergens are unavoidable, the child may need to undergo standard allergy treatment. For some children, a doctor may also prescribe cough medicines (*expectorants*), the drinking of water and breathing of moist air to clear air passages, *postural drainage* that uses gravity to clear mucus, drugs to relax the muscles of the air passages (*bronchodilators*), and drugs to reduce inflammation and so prevent attacks. STEROIDS have proved useful for many but are used only in severe, relatively unresponsive cases, because of their side effects. Scientific research is being done on many aspects of the disease and its causes and treatment.

For help and further information

National Heart, Lung, and Blood Institute (NHLBI), 301-496-4236. (For full group information, see BLOOD AND BLOOD DISORDERS; HEART AND HEART PROBLEMS; LUNG AND BREATHING DISORDERS.)

National Institute of Allergy and Infectious Diseases (NIAID), 301-496-5717. Publishes brochure on asthma. (For full group information, see ALLERGY.)

National Jewish Hospital/National Asthma Center
1400 Jackson Street
Denver, CO 80206
Toll-free National Jewish LUNG LINE (8–5 MT, weekdays) 800-222-LUNG [5864]

Major treatment center for lung diseases. Operates toll-free hotline staffed by specialist nurse; provides information and referrals.

American Lung Association (ALA), 212-315-8700. (For full group information, see LUNG AND BREATHING DISORDERS.)

Other reference sources

The Complete Book of Children's Allergies: A Vital Comprehensive Sourcebook for Parents, by B. Robert Feldman and David Carroll. New York: Warner, 1989.

Conquering Your Child's Allergies, by M. Eric Gershwin and Edwin L. Kingelhofer. Reading, MA: Addison-Wesley, 1989.

The Asthma Handbook: A Complete Guide for Patients and Their Families, revised edition, by Stuart H. Young with Susan A. Shulman and Martin D. Shulman. New York: Bantam, 1989.

A Parent's Guide to Asthma: How You Can Help Your Child Control Asthma at Home, School, and Play, by Nancy Sander. Garden City, NY: Doubleday, 1989.

The Asthma Self-Help Book: A Comprehensive Guide to Management of Asthma in Children and Adults, by Paul J. Hannaway. Marblehead, MA: Lighthouse, 1989.

The Essential Asthma Book: A Manual for Asthmatics of All Ages, by François Haas and Sheila S. Haas. New York: Ivy, 1988.

Asthma: A Complete Guide to Self-Management of Asthma and Allergies for Patients and Their Families, by Allan M. Weinstein. New York: Fawcett, 1988.

Breathing Easy: A Handbook for Asthmatics, by Genell J. Subak-Sharpe. Garden City, NY: Doubleday, 1988. Part of the Frontiers of Medicine Series.

Children with Asthma: A Manual for Parents, revised edition, by Thomas F. Plaut, M.D. Amherst, MA: Pedipress, 1988.

All About Asthma and How to Live with It, by Glennon H. Paul and Barbara A. Fafoglia. New York: Sterling, 1988.

The Reliable Healthcare Companions: Understanding and Managing Asthma, by John L. Decker. New York: Avon, 1988.

Asthma and Exercise, by Nancy Hogshead and Gerald S. Couzens. New York: Henry Holt, 1989.

A Portrait of Me: Featuring Christine Kontos, by Barbara Aiello and Jeffrey Shulman. Frederick, MD: 21st Century, 1989. Part of The Kids on the Block Book Series.

All About Asthma, by William Ostrow and Vivan Ostrow. Niles, IL: Albert Whitman, 1989.

The Asthma Attack by Bo B. Bear, by Charlotte L. Casterline. Dallas, PA: Info-All, 1988.

Luke Has Asthma, Too, by Alison Rogers. Burlington, VT: Waterfront, 1988. For young readers.
(See also ALLERGY.)

astigmatism   Blurring or distortion of vision from a misshapen cornea in the eye. (See EYE AND VISION PROBLEMS.)

astrocytoma   A type of BRAIN TUMOR common in children.

ataxia   Lack of coordination and balance, often resulting in a staggering, awkward, uncertain gait, with legs too far apart, lifted jerkily and abnormally high, then dropped down so the sole of the foot strikes the ground flat; jerky eye movements called NYSTAGMUS are often associated. Ataxia generally indicates some kind of damage or disorder in the SPINAL CORD or the part of the BRAIN called the *cerebellum*, as from CHILDBIRTH, infection, HEAD INJURY, BRAIN TUMOR, response to some toxin (poison), or some other disorder that causes degeneration in the CENTRAL NERVOUS SYSTEM, including MULTIPLE SCLEROSIS and GENETIC DISORDERS such as *Friedreich's ataxia* or *ataxia telangiectasia*.

Friedreich's ataxia is a very rare inherited form of ataxia, resulting from an AUTOSOMAL RECESSIVE trait, which involves muscle weakness and loss of muscle control, especially of the lower limbs but sometimes of the upper limbs as well. It generally appears between ages five and 20, most often at PUBERTY, and progresses to severe disability and premature death. Among associated symptoms are SCOLIOSIS, tremors of the head, slurred speech, and heart problems (see HEART AND HEART PROBLEMS), often the cause of death. BABINSKI'S REFLEX and ROMBERG'S SIGN may signal the presence of Friedreich's ataxia.

Another rare PROGRESSIVE genetic disease of autosomal recessive origin, ataxia telangiectasia (also called *Louis-Bar syndrome*) is associated with unusually large and numerous blood vessels (*telangiectasias*, sometimes mistakenly referred to as "broken" blood vessels) in areas of the skin, causing redness, especially around the ears and face. It appears in infancy and gradually worsens, and it is often associated with sinus and pulmonary infections and with increased risk of malignant TUMORS, especially LEUKEMIA.

For help and further information

National Ataxia Foundation (NAF)
600 Twelve Oaks Center
15500 Wayzata Boulevard
Wayzata, MN 55391
612-473-7666
Donna Gruetzmacher, Patient Services Director
Organization of people concerned with hereditary ataxia and related disorders such as Charcot-Marie-Tooth syndrome, hereditary spastic paraplegia, and ataxia telangiectasia. Provides information and referrals; publishes various materials, including quarterly newsletter *Generations*, book *Hereditary Ataxia: A Guidebook for Managing Speech and Swallowing Problems*, and brochure *Hereditary Ataxia (HA): The Facts*.

Friedreich's Ataxia Group in America (FAGA)
P.O. Box 11116
Oakland, CA 94611
415-655-0833
Raymond S. McCarthy, Executive Director
Myrna J. Lesinsky, Administrative Assistant, Contact
Organization concerned with Friedreich's ataxia. Aids patients and their families; provides information to public and health professionals; supports research; publishes newsletter.

Muscular Dystrophy Association (MDA), 212-586-0808. Runs summer camps for young people with muscular dystrophy or related neuromuscular diseases; publishes many materials, including *Learning to Live with Neuromuscular Disease: A Message for Parents of Children with a Neuromuscular Disease* and *Living with Progressive Childhood Illness: Parental Management of Neuromuscular Disease*. (For full group information, see MUSCULAR DYSTROPHY.)

National Institute of Neurological Disorders and Stroke (NINDS), 301-496-5751. (For full group information, see BRAIN AND BRAIN DISORDERS.)

Other reference sources

Health Care U.S.A., by Jean Carper. New York: Prentice Hall, 1987. Resource for general and specific health-care information, including information on neuromuscular diseases such as muscular dystrophy, amyotrophic lateral sclerosis (ALS or Lou Gehrig's disease), myasthenia gravis, and ataxia. Lists Muscular Dystrophy Association research and treatment clinics, ALS Association research and treatment centers, government research and treatment centers, and other information.
(See also HELP FOR SPECIAL CHILDREN on page 578.)

atherosclerosis   Buildup of fatty tissue in the arteries, sometimes resulting from too much CHOLESTEROL in the body.

athetosis   Slow, involuntary, writhing movements, resulting from disturbance deep within the brain, often associated with the quick, jerky movements of CHOREA, the combination called *choreoathetosis*. The condition is often found in people who have HUNTINGTON'S DISEASE, CEREBRAL PALSY, ENCEPHALITIS, or brain disorders (see BRAIN AND BRAIN DISORDERS); it can also be a side effect of certain drugs.

athletic scholarship   A type of SCHOLARSHIP offered to students with outstanding sports abilities, who are expected to make a major contribution to their school's athletic program. Many highly talented athletes are actively recruited and often offered financial and other material inducements to attend a particular school. Too often, then, the focus is only on the sport, with the COLLEGE education getting insufficient attention; as a result some athletes, who have been passed through school and college on the basis of their athletic ability, find themselves retired in their late 20s and early 30s with few other skills to fall back on, some of them actually being functionally

ILLITERATE. (For help and further information, see SPORTS under PARENT'S BOOKSHELF on page 566.)

at-home delivery   Alternate name for HOME BIRTH.

atresia   Lack or malformation of a normal body opening, often requiring surgical correction. (For help and further information, see BILIARY ATRESIA; DIGESTIVE DISORDERS.)

atrial fibrillation   Irregular rapid contractions of the heart's upper chambers (*atria*). (See HEART AND HEART PROBLEMS.)

at risk   Having increased likelihood of developing a certain disease or condition. (See RISK FACTORS.)

atrophy   The shrinking, weakening, and "wasting away" of a part of the body, as because of disease, disuse, or damage, as in MUSCULAR DYSTROPHY, SPINAL CORD INJURY, or prolonged hospitalization. In MOTOR NEURON DISEASES, for example, the muscles waste away because the nerves supplying communication with them are damaged.

attachment   Alternate term for BONDING, but applied more widely than to the primary CAREGIVER to include other people with whom a child forms a significant link, such as other family members.

attempted suicide   Alternate term for SELF-MUTILATION SYNDROME, not necessarily an attempt to commit SUICIDE, though that may result.

attendance   In EDUCATION, the presence of a student in school or in a school-sponsored activity on a day when the school is considered in session. Under COMPULSORY ATTENDANCE laws, children are required to be present when school is in session, except when having a valid excuse. An attendance or TRUANT officer is normally assigned in the school to seek out students and parents who fail to comply.

attending behavior   Ability to pay attention to a task, including alertness, focusing, vigilance, and selection from among various stimuli.

attention deficit disorder (ADD)   Alternate name for ATTENTION DEFICIT HYPERACTIVITY DISORDER (ADHD).

attention deficit hyperactivity disorder (ADHD)   A complex of behavioral problems marked especially by inattention, impulsiveness, and HYPERACTIVITY, beyond what is considered normal for the person's chronological and mental AGE; formerly called *attention deficit disorder* (ADD), *hyperactivity, hyperkinetic syndrome*, or *minimal brain dysfunction* (MBD). Definitions of and names for the disorder have varied over the years, partly because it is so hard to pin down and partly because the whole range of behaviors does not appear in all cases. Children with ADHD have difficulty finishing a task, following through a set of instructions, organizing work for completion, sometimes even watching an entire television program, often jumping into a task before instructions have been finished, interrupting others, and not waiting for their turn in school or at home. In PRESCHOOL, children with ADHD are constantly or excessively on the move, often in a disorganized or disruptive way; in older children, the disorder is more likely to show itself in squirm-

ing, fidgeting, and general restlessness, as well as in messy work and inability to complete assigned tasks. ADHD children frequently act impulsively, without reflecting on consequences, sometimes in such a way as to endanger themselves or others (as by grabbing a hot pan from a stove or riding a skateboard down a steep incline). Such behaviors interfere with learning and lead to both academic failure and low self-esteem, often accompanied by emotional instability and mood swings (LABILITY) and spurts of temper. This is sometimes complicated in young children by inability to fully control bowels and bladder and resulting wetting (ENURESIS) and soiling (ENCOPRESIS).

ADHD behaviors are not evident in all settings. They are most obvious in a setting (such as a classroom) that requires quiet, sustained listening while containing many distractions. But ADHD behaviors can be minimal in a one-to-one setting or a setting where distracting stimuli are limited. In EDUCATION, therefore, one of the common approaches to ADHD is to arrange for highly structured tutorial or small-group teaching situations. ADHD, in fact, is often not recognized until a child enters school.

Children with ADHD often have problems with MOTOR SKILLS, VISUAL SKILLS, AUDITORY SKILLS, and COMMUNICATIONS SKILLS, including difficulty in conceptualizing, using language, and remembering, as well as shortened ATTENTION SPAN, DISTRACTIBILITY, and heightened impulsiveness. For ways to help young children with ADHD, such as using modeling and BEHAVIOR MODIFICATION or breaking instructions into small steps, parents can refer to TEACHING YOUNG CHILDREN: GUIDELINES AND ACTIVITIES (page 544). The symptoms of ADHD disappear in some children during ADOLESCENCE, while in others they may continue, though perhaps masked, into adulthood, sometimes (with its related social, psychological, and educational problems) leading to JUVENILE DELINQUENCY, but other times turned to advantage in work that requires high energy level, intense bursts of activity, and considerable freedom and independence.

ADHD probably stems from a variety of causes, as yet illunderstood. It is presumed to result from damage or malfunctioning of the brain (see BRAIN AND BRAIN DISORDERS) and CENTRAL NERVOUS SYSTEM but without major brain or neurological damage; many people involved are of average or above-average intelligence. GENETIC INHERITANCE, biochemical problems, injury or damage during birth, and possibly ALLERGY to certain foods or food additives have all been implicated in causing ADHD, though how and to what extent is unknown. Boys are three to nine times more likely to have the disorder than girls. ADHD behaviors may also be triggered by an unsettled or chaotic home environment, especially one involving CHILD ABUSE AND NEGLECT, and may sometimes be linked with family history of ALCOHOL ABUSE and psychiatric problems. ADHD behaviors are often found in children with a wider set of problems, such as LEARNING DISABILITIES, TOURETTE'S SYNDROME, MENTAL RETARDATION, CEREBRAL PALSY, EPILEPSY, childhood SCHIZOPHRENIA, and other neurological or psychiatric problems.

Children whose hyperactivity interferes with their learning are often treated with a medicine such as Ritalin,® paradoxically a STIMULANT that increases brain activity and control, in the process decreasing hyperactivity and distractibility and increasing attention and muscular coordination. Among the medication's occasional side effects are INSOMNIA, diminished appetite, CONSTIPATION, and less often, stomachaches and headaches.

Another approach is prescribing a special antiallergenic diet developed by Ben Feingold. The *Feingold diet*, a type of ELIMINATION DIET, excludes any foods (or medicines) that contain:

- artificial flavorings or colorings, including those in medicines and vitamins and in many common foods, such as ice cream, soft drinks, and powdered drink mixes;
- any salicylates (a type of salt), found in aspirin and many fruits and vegetables, including blackberries, grapes, raisins, currants, peaches, strawberries, tomatoes, and cucumbers;
- the preservatives BHA (*butylated hydroxyanisole*), BHT (*butylated hydroxytoluene*), and TBHQ (*monotertiary butyhydroxylquinone*), found in such products as commercial breads and other bakery goods and cold cuts.

Though the diet has been used for some decades, proponents and critics are still sharply divided as to its usefulness for children with ADHD. The diet apparently helps at least some of those with ADHD, notably those with associated allergies, but many seem to derive little or no benefit from it. In any case, if they decide to follow the diet, parents should consult a PEDIATRICIAN to be sure that the child is getting the proper NUTRITION with such a restricted diet.

For help and further information

Center for Hyperactive Child Information (CHCI)
P.O. Box 66272
Washington, DC 20035
703-920-7495
John C. Malloy, Executive Director
Organization concerned with hyperactivity in children. Gathers and disseminates information, on diagnosis and medical and educational needs, to public and professionals; publishes CHCI brochure and distributes *Helping the Hyperactive Child*.

Co-ADD (Coalition for the Education and Support of Attention Deficit Disorder)
P.O. Box 242
Osseo, MI 55369
612-425-0423
Organization of people concerned with attention-deficit hyperactivity disorder.

National Institute of Mental Health (NIMH), 301-443-4515. (For full group information, see MENTAL DISORDERS.)

National Institute of Child Health and Human Development (NICHD), 301-496-5133. (For full group information, see PREGNANCY.)

American Association of University Affiliated Programs for Persons with Developmental Disabilities (AAUAP), 301-588-8252. Network of federally supported centers for assessment and treatment of developmental disabilities (For full group information, see HELP FOR SPECIAL CHILDREN on page 578.)

Feingold Association of the United States
Drawer AG
Holtsville, NY 11742
516-543-4658
Organization of parents and professionals interested in using the Feingold diet with hyperactive children. Sponsors local self-help groups; provides information and referrals; publishes various materials, including newsletter, food lists, and cookbook.

Other reference sources

General Works

Maybe You Know My Kid: A Parent's Guide to Identifying, Understanding and Helping Your Child with Attention Deficit Hyperactivity Disorder, by Mary Cahill Fowler. New York: Birch Lane/Carol, 1990.

Helping Your Hyperactive Child: From Effective Treatments and Developing Discipline and Self-Esteem to Helping Your Family Adjust, by John F. Taylor. Rocklin, CA: Prima, 1990.

Your Hyperactive Child, by William G. Crook. Jackson, TN: Professional Books/Future Health, 1990.

If Your Child Is Hyperactive, Inattentive, Impulsive, Distractible . . .: Helping the ADD (Attention Deficit Disorder)-Hyperactive Child, by Stephen W. Garber, Marianne Daniels, and Robyn F. Spizman. New York: Random House, 1990.

Parenting the Overactive Child: Alternatives to Drug Therapy, by Paul Lavin. Lanham, MD: Madison, 1989.

Mommy, I Can't Sit Still: Coping with Hyperactive and Aggressive Children, by Daniel O'Leary. Far Hills, NJ: New Horizon, 1989.

Your Hyperactive Child: A Parent's Guide to Dealing with Attention Deficit Disorder, by Barbara Ingersoll. Garden City, NY: Doubleday, 1988.

Attention Deficit Disorders: Hyperactivity and Associated Disorders: A Handbook for Parents and Professionals, fifth edition, by Wendy S. Coleman. Westport, CT: Calliope, 1988.

Attention Deficit Disorder: A Common but Often Overlooked Disorder of Children, by Glenn Hunsucker. Fort Worth, TX: Forresst, 1988.

The ADD Hyperactivity Workbook for Parents, Teachers and Kids, by Harvey C. Parker. Plantation, FL: Impact, 1988.

Background Works

The Attention Deficit Disorders Intervention Manual, by Stephen B. McCarney. Columbia, MO: Hawthorne Educational Service, 1990.

Ryan: A Mother's Story of Her Hyperactive-Tourette Syndrome Child, by Susan Hughes. Duarte, CA: Hope, 1990.

The Natural Way to Control Hyperactivity with Amino Acids and Nutrient Therapy, by Billie J. Sahley. San Antonio, TX: Watercress, 1988.

Allergies and the Hyperactive Child, by Doris J. Rapp. New York: Sovereign, 1979.

Why Your Child Is Hyperactive, by Benjamin Feingold, M.D. New York: Random House, 1975.

Feingold Cookbook for Hyperactive Children, by Benjamin Feingold, M.D. New York: Random House, 1979.

For Kids

Shelley, the Hyperactive Turtle, by Deborah Moss, Deborah. Kensington, MD: Woodbine House, 1989.

Otto Learns About His Medicine: A Story About Medication for Hyperactive Children, by Matthew R. Galvin. New York: Magination, 1988.

Robby Really Transforms: A Story About Grown-ups Helping Children, by Matthew R. Galvin. New York: Magination, 1988.

attention span   The amount of time someone can concentrate on a task without losing interest in or being distracted from it. Increasing attention span is one of the skills a young child develops gradually; however, children with LEARNING DISABILITIES and some other DEVELOPMENTAL DISORDERS may have heightened DISTRACTIBILITY, perhaps as part of a complex of problems known as ATTENTION DEFICIT HYPERACTIVITY DISORDER (ADHD).

atypical development   Outdated term for AUTISM.

audiologist   A health professional who specializes in screening for and diagnosing hearing problems, often in schools or clinics. Audiologists use HEARING TESTS to assess the amount of hearing loss and show just what a child can and cannot hear and also to see if a HEARING AID might help. If so, the audiologist will prescribe and fit the hearing aid and also recommend any other appropriate special devices or programs. It is wise to have children's hearing tested early and regularly, so that any hearing problems can be detected and treated before they cause communication problems. If communication disorders (see COMMUNICATION SKILLS AND DISORDERS) have resulted from hearing loss, the child is generally referred to a SPEECH-LANGUAGE PATHOLOGIST. Not physicians, audiologists refer problems treatable by drugs or surgery to medical specialists, such as OTOLARYNGOLOGISTS. (For help and further information, see EARS AND HEARING PROBLEMS.)

audiometric test   Type of HEARING TEST, often called a PURE TONE TEST.

Auditory Blending Test   Alternate name for the ROSWELL CHALL AUDITORY BLENDING TEST.

auditory brainstem response (auditory evoked response) test   A type of HEARING TEST that uses electrodes attached to the scalp to record the brain's response to sounds, a common test in assessing EAR AND HEARING PROBLEMS. It is used especially for infants and in checking for a possible ACOUSTIC NEUROMA.

auditory discrimination   A key kind of AUDITORY SKILL.

Auditory Discrimination Test (Wepman)   A widely used DIAGNOSTIC ASSESSMENT TEST focusing on AUDITORY SKILLS, used with children ages five to eight. The test presents pairs of words to the child, who is asked to tell whether they are the same or different. The results are designed to highlight possible problems with READING and communication skills. Other forms of the test are sometimes used for follow-up testing after REMEDIAL INSTRUCTION. (For help and further information, see TESTS; COMMUNICATION SKILLS AND DISORDERS.)

auditory evoked response test   See AUDITORY BRAINSTEM RESPONSE TEST.

auditory memory   A key kind of AUDITORY SKILL.

auditory nerve (eighth nerve)   The nerve that actually carries electrical signals representing sound vibrations from the inner ear to the brain. Malfunctioning of the auditory nerve leads to *sensorineural loss*, a significant EAR AND HEARING PROBLEM.

auditory skills   A set of overlapping skills that involve the ears and hearing; closely related to communication skills (see COMMUNICATION SKILLS AND DISORDERS).

Auditory discrimination is the ability to distinguish one sound from another. Children with hearing problems, LEARNING DISABILITIES, or some other DEVELOPMENTAL DISORDERS may have trouble telling the difference between words that sound similar, such as *pale* and *bale*; they also sometimes have trouble distinguishing between a familiar and an unfamiliar voice or recognizing familiar nonverbal sounds, such as an alarm clock or siren, a form of auditory AGNOSIA. Such problems can cause confusion and frustration in learning, as a child may miss the point of what is being said or be confused about who is saying it.

Auditory memory is the ability to remember for a short time what you have heard. Children with learning disabilities or some other developmental disorders often have difficulty with short-term auditory memory. No matter how hard they concentrate, they may be able to remember only three or four words in a row, often forgetting the beginning of a sentence by the end of it. They may also confuse the order of sounds heard, so *basket* might become *bakset*. Such children often ask repeatedly for things to be repeated and may repeat them out loud to themselves, trying to remember them.

Localization is the ability to identify where a sound is coming from. Some children have great difficulty with this; they may look all around the room on hearing their names called.

The CHART OF NORMAL DEVELOPMENT reproduced on page 507 indicates when between birth and age six children first *on the average* begin to develop the main communication skills. Children grow and learn at individual and varying paces, but every child can benefit from activities designed to enhance their natural development. In TEACHING YOUNG CHILDREN: GUIDELINES AND ACTIVITIES (page 544), parents will find guidance on how to develop children's skills in various areas. (For help and further information, see EAR AND HEARING PROBLEMS.)

aura   In EPILEPSY, one or more unusual sensations that sometimes precede and provide warning of a SEIZURE.

autism   A type of MENTAL DISORDER that appears in early childhood, generally before age three, marked by lack of normal social interaction with parents and others, often with resistance to physical and eye contact, and impaired development in many areas, including SOCIAL SKILLS, LANGUAGE SKILLS, communication skills (see COMMUNICATION SKILLS AND DISORDERS), and SELF-HELP SKILLS. Though the severity of the disorder differs from child to child, the child's activities and interests are often sharply restricted, with insistence on sameness in environment and routine. Repetitive movements, such as rocking, spinning, head-banging, and hand-twisting, are characteristic, as are stereotypical responses to social situations. MENTAL RETARDATION is common, and some of the most severely affected tend to develop SEIZURES. This puzzling disorder is presently classified by psychiatrists as *autistic disorder*, a type of *pervasive developmental disorder*, but it has previously gone under a variety of other names, including *atypical development, symbiotic psychosis, childhood psychosis*, and *childhood schizophrenia*. Though once assumed to have resulted from poor parental environment, recent studies have indicated nothing of the sort. The causes of the disorder are obscure, though it has been associated with various physical disorders, including maternal RUBELLA, untreated PHENYLKETONURIA, CELIAC SPRUE, ENCEPHALITIS, tuberous sclerosis, FRAGILE X SYNDROME, and lack of oxygen at CHILDBIRTH.

For help and further information
General Works

Children with Autism: A Parents' Guide, Michael Powers, ed. Kensington, MD: Woodbine House, 1989.

Background Works

Autism: A Practical Guide for Those Who Help Others, by John Gerdtz and Joel Bregman. New York: Continuum, 1990. Part of the Continuum Counseling Series.
Autism: Explaining the Enigma, by Uta Frith. Cambridge, MA: Basil Blackwell, 1989. Part of the Cognitive Development Series.
Autism: Nature, Diagnosis, and Treatment, Geraldine Dawson, ed. New York: Guilford, 1989.
Diagnosis and Treatment of Infantile Autism, C. Gillberg, ed. New York: Plenum, 1989.
Autism, by Laura Schreibman. Vol. 15 of the Developmental Clinical Psychology & Psychiatry Series. Newbury Park, CA: Sage, 1989.
Autism and Life in the Community: Successful Interventions for Behavioral Challenges, by Marcia D. Smith. Baltimore: Paul H. Brookes, 1989.

Personal Experiences

Family Pictures, by Sue Miller. New York: Harper & Row, 1990.
Without Reason: A Family Copes with Two Generations of Autism, by Charles Hart. New York: Harper & Row, 1989.
Mixed Blessings, by William Christopher and Barbara Christopher. Nashville, TN: Abingdon, 1989.

Bobby: Breakthrough of a Special Child, by Rachel Pinney and Mimi Shlachter with Anthea Courtenay. New York: St. Martin's/Marek, 1983.
(See also MENTAL DISORDERS and specific disorders listed above.)

autistic fantasy   A type of DEFENSE MECHANISM in which a child (or adult) substitutes persistent daydreaming for human contact or for dealing directly with personal problems.

autoaggression   Alternate term for SELF-MUTILATION SYNDROME.

autoimmune disorders   Disorders that result from malfunctioning of the body's IMMUNE SYSTEM, which mistakenly attacks the body's tissues or organs, regarding then as foreign invaders. Among the autoimmune disorders that are commonly found among young people are rheumatoid ARTHRITIS, DIABETES MELLITUS (Type I), systemic LUPUS ERYTHEMATOSUS, a disorder of the THYROID GLAND (*Hashimoto's thyroiditis*), a disorder of the ADRENAL GLANDS (*Addison's disease*), and pernicious ANEMIA. Problems with autoimmunity are also involved in some kinds of ALLERGY.

For help and further information

National Institute of Allergy and Infectious Diseases (NIAID), 301-496-5717. Publishes *Understanding the Immune System*. (For full group information, see ALLERGY.)

National Institute of Arthritis and Musculoskeletal and Skin Diseases (NIAMS), 301-496-8188. (For full group information, see ARTHRITIS.

(See also IMMUNE SYSTEM and specific disorders.)

autologous   In medicine, a general term referring to a type of TRANSPLANT or BLOOD TRANSFUSION that comes from the person's own body. Tissue, BONE MARROW, or blood is often taken days or weeks earlier and stored for use in a specific operation. By contrast, a transplant or transfusion from a donor whose makeup is similar to that of the patient is called ALLOGENIC.

automatic promotion   The annual passing of a student from grade to grade through a school, regardless of the student's academic performance. (See PROMOTION.)

autonomic nervous system   The part of the NERVOUS SYSTEM that controls the actions that the body makes automatically or involuntarily, such as heartbeat, breathing, production of substances by various glands, and the like.

autopagnosia   A type of AGNOSIA involving inability to recognize or localize parts of one's own body.

autosomal dominant (AD)   A pattern of GENETIC INHERITANCE in which only one copy of a particular gene needs to be present for a trait (such as brown eyes) to be expressed; though a person may carry two genes for the same dominant trait, only

Autosomal Dominant (AD) Disorders

- *Definitions:* Only one gene of a given gene pair need be abnormal to manifest the condition.
- *Characteristics:*
  An AD condition appears every generation; it usually does not skip a generation.
  On the average, one-half of the children of an affected person are affected.
  Unaffected people do not have affected children (unless the child represents a new mutation).
  Males and females are affected with equal frequency.
  Many AD human conditions are variously expressed in different affected members of the same family.
  Serious effects of the disorder are compounded if an individual receives two copies of the same AD gene.
- *Pedigree Sample* [for information on the symbols, see GENETIC COUNSELING]:

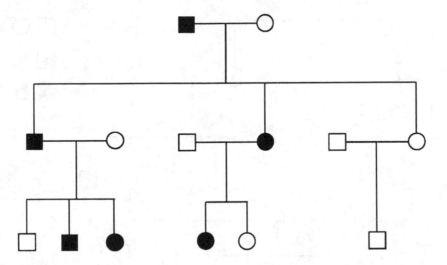

Source: *Genetic Family History: An Aid to Better Health in Adoptive Children* (1984). Published by the National Center for Education in Maternal and Child Health (NCEMCH), for the Public Health Service's Genetic Diseases Service Branch, Division of Maternal and Child Health, from materials by Catherine A. Reiser from a conference sponsored by Wisconsin Clinical Genetics Center and Waisman Center on Mental Retardation and Human Development, University of Wisconsin-Madison.

one is needed. Among the GENETIC DISORDERS that are of the autosomal dominant type are ACHONDROPLASIA, HUNTINGTON'S CHOREA, POLYDACTYLY, and NEUROFIBROMATOSIS. A disorder may affect individuals in widely varying ways; some may show mild signs of a disease, while others may have a severe form of the disorder. Even if a child is not seriously affected, it is important to diagnose a mild form of the disorder, to help prevent damage from later possible effects and also to help parents and their genetic counselors judge the likelihood that another child may be seriously affected. (For help and further information, see below; see also GENETIC COUNSELING; PEDIGREE.)

autosomal recessive (AR) A pattern of GENETIC INHERITANCE in which both copies of a particular gene pair need to carry the same trait (such as blue eyes) for a trait to be expressed. Among the GENETIC DISORDERS that are of the autosomal reces-

sive type are PHENYLKETONURIA, GALACTOSEMIA, and ALBINISM. (For help and further information, see below; see also GENETIC COUNSELING; PEDIGREE.)

autosomes The 22 pairs of genes that, with the SEX CHROMOSOMES, make up the complete set of chromosomes that form an individual's GENETIC INHERITANCE. If the paired genes are alike, the person is said to be a HOMOZYGOTE for that gene; if they differ (as with one for blue eyes and one for brown), the person is called a HETEROZYGOTE for that gene. If only one copy of a gene must be present for a trait to be expressed (regardless of what the paired gene is), it is called DOMINANT, and the pattern of inheritance is called AUTOSOMAL DOMINANT. However, if the two paired genes need to be alike for a trait to be expressed, it is called RECESSIVE and the inheritance pattern is called AUTOSOMAL RECESSIVE.

Autosomal Recessive (AR) Disorders

- *Definitions:* Both genes of a given gene pair must be abnormal to manifest the condition.
- *Characteristics:*
  The disease does not appear in every generation.
  On the average, one-fourth of the children of two carriers will be affected.
  Males and females are affected with equal frequency.
  Increased incidence of consanguinity for rare conditions is frequently noted.
  Specific AR conditions have an increased frequency in certain populations, such as Tay-Sachs disease in the Jewish population, sickle-cell anemia among Blacks, and cystic fibrosis among Caucasians.
- *Pedigree Sample* [for information on the symbols, see GENETIC COUNSELING]:

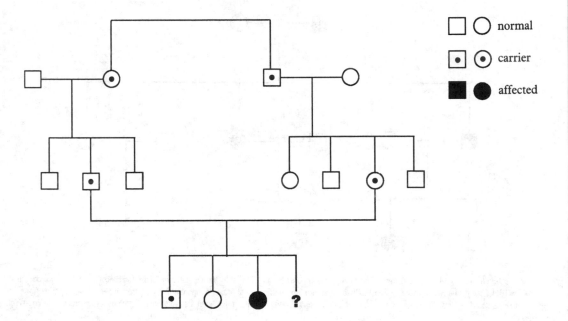

Source: *Genetic Family History: An Aid to Better Health in Adoptive Children* (1984). Published by the National Center for Education in Maternal and Child Health (NCEMCH), for the Public Health Service's Genetic Diseases Service Branch, Division of Maternal and Child Health, from materials by Catherine A. Reiser from a conference sponsored by Wisconsin Clinical Genetics Center and Waisman Center on Mental Retardation and Human Development, University of Wisconsin-Madison.

average   A number intended to give a general picture of a group of numbers, such as test scores; in statistics, called a *measure of central tendency*. The most common type of average is the *mean*, which is calculated by adding the scores and dividing by the number of scores, as in calculating a GRADE-POINT AVERAGE or CUMULATIVE AVERAGE. However, average may sometimes refer to a *median*, the score precisely in the middle when the scores are ranked in order, or to a *mode*, the score that appears most often, as when five people score 75 on a test and no more than two people have any other test score.

AV fistula   A type of surgically created artificial connection between an artery (A) and a vein (V), used in some forms of DIALYSIS.

avitaminosis   Alternate medical term for deficiency in one or more VITAMINS, a kind of DEFICIENCY DISEASE.

avoidance   A type of DEFENSE MECHANISM in which the person tries to steer clear of people, situations, or objects perceived as threatening to the self, especially if related to unconscious impulses and imagined punishment for such impulses; a common type of behavior in ANXIETY disorders.

avoidant disorder of childhood or adolescence   A type of anxiety disorder (see ANXIETY) in which children (girls more than boys) shrink excessively from contact with strangers. AVOIDANCE in children under two or two-and-a-half, popularly called *stranger anxiety*, is quite normal. However, if it appears after that, especially in the early school years, it can lead to impaired SOCIAL SKILLS, isolation, and DEPRESSION. In severe cases, the child may be so shy and anxious that he or she will be inarticulate or even MUTE. If it persists into adulthood, this condition is classified by psychiatrists as *avoidant personality disorder;* it may also be associated with some other disorders, such as SEPARATION ANXIETY DISORDER, OVERANXIOUS DISORDER, or PHOBIA. (For help and further information, see MENTAL DISORDERS.)

AV shunt   A type of SHUNT connecting an artery and a vein, used in some forms of DIALYSIS.

azoospermia   Lack of SPERM, a cause of INFERTILITY.

B

B cells   Type of white blood cells (*lymphocytes*) in the IMMUNE SYSTEM.

Babinski's reflex   Upward flexion of the big toe and fanning of the other toes, when a child's foot is firmly stroked on the outside of the sole. Babinski's reflex is normal in NEWBORNS, but its presence in children and adults can indicate brain or spinal-cord disorders (see BRAIN AND BRAIN DISORDERS and SPINAL-CORD INJURIES). The normal postnewborn response to such stroking is to curl the toes, called the *plantar response.*

baby blues   Nickname for POSTPARTUM DEPRESSION.

baby boards   Popular nickname for DEVELOPMENTAL SCREENING TESTS or DIAGNOSTIC ASSESSMENT TESTS, when used as ADMISSION TESTS; a reference to the dreaded pre-college tests offered by the College Board. (See COLLEGE ENTRANCE EXAMINATION BOARD.)

baby brokering   An illegal type of private ADOPTION in which large sums of money are paid to the intermediaries and to the birth mother.

Baby Doe Law   Legislation designed to protect the right of HANDICAPPED infants to receive medical care, whether or not the parents wish it; named after a New York case in which an anonymous baby, dubbed "Baby Jane Doe," was given lifesaving surgery for SPINA BIFIDA and other defects, despite her parents' objections. As part of the Child Abuse Amendments of 1984, Public Law 98-457, the Baby Doe Law requires that, to continue to receive federal grant money for CHILD ABUSE AND NEGLECT programs, states must institute programs to investigate suspected cases of "withholding of medically indicated treatment from disabled infants with life-threatening conditions." More specifically, the law requires that a handicapped infant must always be given appropriate nutrition, hydration (fluids), and medication, and should be given "medically indicated treatment" unless the infant is in a chronic and irreversible COMA; the treatment would merely prolong dying while not improving life-threatening conditions; or the treatment would be inhumane and futile (in terms of survival).

To be in compliance with the law, states must follow the Department of Health and Human Services (DHHS) regulations, which call for prompt notification of a state agency of cases where medical treatment is suspected of being withheld; investigation of such alleged "medical neglect," including access to medical records; and authority to initiate court proceedings to obtain medical treatment for disabled infants.

The Baby Doe regulations cover infants (defined as children under one year old) and also children who have been continuously hospitalized from birth, were extremely PREMATURE babies, or have long-term disabilities. The DHHS also made clear that the decision to give or withhold treatment should not be based on the child's anticipated "quality of life," but on "reasonable medical judgment," the decision being one "that would be made about the case and the treatment possibilities with respect to the medical conditions involved."

For help and further information

Spina Bifida Association of America (SBAA), 301-770-SBAA [7222]; toll-free number 800-621-3141. Publishes information sheet *The Baby Doe Law*. (For full group information, see SPINA BIFIDA.)

babysitter   A person, often a teenager, who provides short-term CHILD CARE.

bachelor's degree   The DEGREE awarded by most four-year colleges and universities to students who successfully complete their program of study, usually a Bachelor of Arts (B.A.) or Bachelor of Science (B.S.). Bachelor's degrees are sometimes also awarded for longer courses of study, as in architecture or pharmacy, or for some kinds of graduate study, as in theology.

back to basics   Late-20th-century phrase calling for a return to focus on teaching fundamental skills—especially the so-called three R's: reading, 'riting, and 'rithmetic—and deem-phasizing supposedly "softer" subjects, such as music, art, and social studies. (See EDUCATION.)

balanitis   Inflammation of the glans and foreskin of the PENIS, often from infections such as CANDIDIASIS, prevention of which has traditionally been one of the medical reasons advanced for CIRCUMCISION.

Band-Aid surgery   Popular name for TUBAL LIGATION, a type of STERILIZATION for a woman, employing the technique of *laparoscopy*.

banding   Alternate term for TRACKING.

baptismal certificate (church certificate)   A written form indicating the date of birth and of baptism of a child, issued by a church; such a certificate can sometimes be used as proof of age, as for entering school, when the BIRTH CERTIFICATE is unavailable.

barium X-ray examinations   Medical procedures to help diagnose DIGESTIVE DISORDERS, involving the use of barium as a contrasting medium, so that details of the digestive system will show up clearly on X-RAYS; often called a *GI (gastrointestinal) series*. For examination of the upper part of the system (an *upper GI series*) or the whole system, the patient is given a "barium milkshake" to drink and X-rays are taken at intervals as the barium passes through the system. For examination of the small intestine, a tube is fed into the system through the mouth or nose and the barium introduced directly at the site to be X-rayed. For examination of the large intestine, the patient's system is made as empty as possible, and then a tube fed through the anus introduces barium—popularly called a "barium enema"—into the body. (For help and further information, see DIGESTIVE DISORDERS.)

basal age   The age level at which a child is consistently able to correctly answer all of the items on a STANDARDIZED TEST, such as the STANFORD-BINET INTELLIGENCE TEST, the opposite being the *ceiling age*.

basal body temperature method   A technique of NATURAL FAMILY PLANNING.

basal metabolic rate (BMR)   The amount of energy needed to "run" the body at rest. (See METABOLISM.)

Basic Educational Opportunity Grant Program (BEOG)   Former name of the PELL GRANT for college FINANCIAL AID.

basic skills   Skills learned in ELEMENTARY SCHOOL that are fundamental to all other, later learning, such as READING, spelling, adding, and subtracting. Acquisition of such skills is often tested by ACHIEVEMENT TESTS, such as the IOWA TESTS OF BASIC SKILLS.

Basic Skills and Educational Proficiency Program   Federal program set up with the passage of Public Law 95-561, the Educational Amendments of 1978, its aim being to upgrade basic skills among both children and adults, especially in the areas of READING, mathematics, speaking, and writing; an expansion of the earlier RIGHT TO READ program.

battered child syndrome   A pattern of physical and other signs, including FRACTURES, BURNS, CONTUSIONS, welts, cuts, and internal damage, indicating that a child's internal and external injuries were inflicted by someone, generally a parent, other CAREGIVER, or older SIBLING, using a hand, fist, or object such as a belt, pan, or pipe; one type of child abuse, often intended as DISCIPLINE or punishment. (For help and further information, see CHILD ABUSE AND NEGLECT.)

battery   In testing, a series of two or more TESTS given to a person in roughly the same period, such as a series of ACHIEVEMENT TESTS; also a group of STANDARDIZED TESTS that have been developed and tested on the same general population, and so are considered comparable to one another. In law, battery is physical violence or contact that is offensive to and without the consent of the battered person. An adult may consent to such violence or contact, but since a MINOR child cannot legally give consent, such actions are to be considered battery, as in cases of child abuse (see CHILD ABUSE AND NEGLECT). An unintentional action causing no severe harm is called *simple battery*, while intentional violence is termed *aggravated battery*. By contrast, ASSAULT is the threat of or sometimes an uncompleted attempt at injury or violence. Battery is often (though it need not be) preceded by threats; hence, the common phrase "assault and battery."

Bayley Scales of Infant Development   An individually administered test that attempts to measure the development of mental processes and MOTOR SKILLS in infants age two to 30 months. The test administrator uses various stimulus items to evoke responses from the child, including early attempts to communicate and use of gross and fine motor skills, and describes these in the Infant Behavior Record. The Bayley Scales are often used to determine whether a child is developing normally or has DEVELOPMENTAL DELAY. (For help and further information, see TESTS.)

BBB   Abbreviation for the BLOOD-BRAIN BARRIER.

BCG vaccine   The VACCINE used for IMMUNIZATION against TUBERCULOSIS; abbreviation for *bacille Calmette-Guérin*, named after its developers.

Becker's muscular dystrophy   A relatively rare form of MUSCULAR DYSTROPHY.

bedwetting   Popular term for ENURESIS.

Beery-Buktenica Test   Alternate name for DEVELOPMENTAL TEST OF VISUAL-MOTOR INTEGRATION (VMI).

behavior disorder Alternate term for DISRUPTIVE BEHAVIOR DIS-ORDER, a classification of MENTAL DISORDER that includes ATTEN-TION DEFICIT HYPERACTIVITY DISORDER and CONDUCT DISORDER.

behavior modification A teaching and guiding technique used to mold and change behavior by rewarding desired actions and ignoring (that is, withholding reward from) unwanted actions. Such rewards are sometimes material but often are simply recognition and warm praise, and they are not offered only when a child has complete success at a task but also when the child has made honest effort or has come a step closer to success (what psychologists call *successive approximation*). The underlying principle of behavior modification is that *positive reinforcement*—rewards, including praise for effort—encourages children (and adults!) to continue to improve their skills and learn new ones, while punishment and criticism tend to discourage them from making the effort to improve and try new things. (For a fuller discussion of using behavior modifica-tion with young children, see TEACHING YOUNG CHILDREN: GUIDE-LINES AND ACTIVITIES on page 544.) Behavior modification is also widely used with teenagers and adults in programs that focus on changing behavior, such as SMOKING, regardless of its causes. (For help and further information, see DISCIPLINE.)

bell curve Alternate term for NORMAL DISTRIBUTION.

belly-button surgery Popular name for TUBAL LIGATION, a type of STERILIZATION for a woman, employing the technique of *laparoscopy*.

Bender Visual Motor Gestalt Test (Bender-Gestalt) A type of individually administered DIAGNOSTIC ASSESSMENT TEST that is used to help identify possible LEARNING DISABILITIES, brain dis-orders (see BRAIN AND BRAIN DISORDERS), MENTAL RETARDATION, MENTAL DISORDER, or general DEVELOPMENTAL DELAY in all ages. The child is given a series of designs on a card and is asked to reproduce each on blank paper. The drawings are scored by test professionals based on various aspects of form, shape, pattern, and orientation on the paper. (For help and further information, see TESTS.)

benign pseudohypertropic muscular dystrophy Alternate name for Becker's MUSCULAR DYSTROPHY.

Benton Visual Retention Test A type of individually adminis-tered DIAGNOSTIC ASSESSMENT TEST that is used to help identify possible disorders in visual memory, as in people with LEARNING DISABILITIES. Given ten designs, one by one, the child is asked to reproduce each on plain paper, with the results being profes-sionally scored. (For help and further information, see TESTS.)

BEOG Abbreviation for Basic Educational Opportunity Grant, the former name of the PELL GRANT for college FINANCIAL AID.

beriberi A DEFICIENCY DISEASE caused by lack of VITAMIN B_1.

best interests of the child In family law, a general rule guiding the court in determining such matters as CUSTODY and VISITATION RIGHTS, with the emotional and financial stability of the child being considered paramount; also called the *least det-*

rimental alternative. In cases of CHILD ABUSE AND NEGLECT, the court usually assumes that it is in the child's best interests to remain in the home, while the case is being studied or the parents undergo treatment, except where the child's life is threatened or the parents have proved unable to respond to treatment. The principle of the best interests of the child acts as a brake on overuse of institutional placement by the state but can have the unwanted result of leaving the child in danger.

beta-sitosterolemia and xanthomatosis A type of LIPID STORAGE DISEASE.

beta-thalassemia An inherited form of ANEMIA.

bifurcation In law, breaking a case or trial into two parts so that the question of divorce may often be separated from other related issues, such as CHILD SUPPORT, CUSTODY, VISITATION RIGHTS, and alimony.

Big E test Nickname for the Snellen Test. (See EYE AND VISION PROBLEMS.)

bikini cut Popular name for a kind of CESAREAN SECTION.

biliary atresia Absence or malfunctioning of the bile ducts that carry the secretion called *bile* away from the liver. Causes for the disorder are unclear, but some bile duct damage may be caused by viral infection near birth. Symptoms of biliary atresia generally appear two to six weeks after birth and include JAUNDICE and a swollen abdomen. ULTRASOUND, X-RAYS, and other radioactive scanning devices, along with BLOOD TESTS, URINALYSIS, and LIVER FUNCTION TESTS, help doctors distinguish bil-iary atresia from other disorders, including neonatal HEPATITIS. Untreated, biliary atresia will lead to CIRRHOSIS OF THE LIVER and often to death, generally in infancy. About half of the cases of biliary atresia are treatable by surgery; the *Kasai procedure*, or *hepatoportoenterostomy*, involves removing damaged bile ducts and creating artificial bypass ducts from the baby's intestine. For some children with biliary atresia, however, such as those whose damaged ducts are inside the liver, liver TRANSPLANTS at present offer the only hope for survival.

For help and further information

American Liver Foundation (ALF), 201-857-2626; toll-free number, U.S. except NJ, 800-223-0179. Sponsors network for parents of children with liver diseases, including biliary atresia, and publishes information sheet about biliary atresia. (For full group information, see LIVER PROBLEMS.)

Children's Liver Foundation, 201-761-1111. (For full group information, see LIVER PROBLEMS.)

National Institute of Diabetes and Digestive and Kidney Dis-eases (NIDDK), 301-496-3583. (For full group information, see DIGESTIVE DISORDERS.)

National Digestive Disease Information Clearinghouse (NDDIC), 301-468-6344. (For full group information, see DIGES-TIVE DISORDERS.)

Other reference sources

Your Child with Biliary Atresia. Available from Office of Educational Resources, Texas Children's Hospital, 6621 Fannin, Houston, TX 77030.

bilirubin test   A kind of BLOOD TEST, one of those considered LIVER FUNCTION TESTS.

Billings method   A technique of NATURAL FAMILY PLANNING.

biochemical tests   Alternate name for *blood chemistry*, a type of BLOOD TEST.

biological parents   The male and female whose genes actually make up the GENETIC INHERITANCE of a child and who are therefore the child's immediate ancestors and nearest BLOOD RELATIVES; also called *birth parents* or *natural parents*. The term is most widely used when a child has more than one set of parents to distinguish between the parents whose genetic inheritance the child bears and those who have legal CUSTODY of the child, such as adoptive parents (see ADOPTION), FOSTER PARENTS, or stepparents. Biological parents have PARENTS' RIGHTS and PARENTS' RESPONSIBILITIES, including the right to see the children and the duty to contribute to their support. However, some confusion has come to surround the term, because it is not always clear who are the legal parents of a child born using some of the new reproductive approaches, such as ARTIFICIAL INSEMINATION, IN VITRO FERTILIZATION, and SURROGATE PARENTING. Under the UNIFORM PARENTAGE ACT enacted in some states, for example, the father of a child born through artificial insemination is recognized as the husband of the woman who bears the child, not the donor who provided the SPERM.

biopsy   The taking of tissue or cells from the body to examine in a laboratory, often for diagnostic purposes, such as assessing whether a person has CANCER or MUSCULAR DYSTROPHY. Most biopsies involve the taking of a small piece of skin or muscle under a local ANESTHESIA. In cases of an accessible TUMOR or internal organ, a hollow *aspiration needle* is inserted into the body to suck up cells, also under local anesthetic, sometimes with the aid of ULTRASOUND or other SCAN devices. If a tumor or internal organ is not readily accessible, a biopsy may sometimes be obtained by pushing into the body an ENDOSCOPE (long viewing tube) with forceps attached, under a general anesthetic. Biopsy samples may also be obtained as part of a regular operation under general anesthesia; sometimes a whole tumor is removed and sent for analysis. (For help and further information, see MEDICAL TESTS.)

biotin   A VITAMIN, once called vitamin H but now considered one of the B vitamins, that is important in the METABOLISM of CARBOHYDRATES, PROTEINS, and FATS. Symptoms of deficiency include fatigue, DEPRESSION, nausea, INSOMNIA, and muscle pain; it is, however, rare, because bacteria produce biotin in the intestinal tract, much of which is later excreted. Biotin is abundant in eggs, milk, and meats, though raw egg white contains a factor that destroys biotin. (For help and further information, see RECOMMENDED DAILY ALLOWANCES; VITAMINS.)

bipolar disorder   A type of MOOD DISORDER involving episodes of strong DEPRESSION and mania (a state of high energy, irritability, and impulsiveness), as a person swings from "highs" to "lows," generally with intervening periods of more normal moods; a form of MENTAL DISORDER previously called *manic-depressive illness*. Bipolar disorder often goes unrecognized, unless one of the episodes is severe enough to require temporary hospitalization. Once diagnosed, it often responds to medication, such as lithium; psychotherapy and electroshock therapy may also be used. The causes of bipolar disorder are unknown, though it may be a kind of GENETIC DISORDER. In 1987, scientists found what they thought was a defective gene that caused bipolar disorder, but later studies cast doubt on that conclusion.

For help and further information

National Institute of Mental Health (NIMH), 301-443-4536 (public affairs); 301-443-4513 (publications). Publishes various materials, including brochure *Bipolar Disorder*. (For full group information, see MENTAL DISORDERS.)

bird's nest custody   A type of CUSTODY in which the children remain in the family home and the parents shuttle in and out, rather than having the children move back and forth as parents exercise VISITATION RIGHTS.

birth canal   The widened CERVIX and VAGINA through which a baby passes on its way from the UTERUS during CHILDBIRTH.

birth certificate   A formal written statement verifying a person's name and date of birth, generally based on a report by the doctor attending at the birth and filed in a government office of vital statistics. A child who has been adopted will generally be issued a new birth certificate showing the date of birth, new name, and new parents, though not usually showing the fact of adoption. A hospital form showing a child's name and date of birth may also be called a birth certificate. A birth certificate is a key personal document required for several purposes, such as to attest to the age of a child entering school, to obtain a passport, during ADOPTION procedures, and to establish information for a PEDIGREE in GENETIC COUNSELING. *Where to Write for Vital Records: Births, Deaths, Marriages, and Divorces* (published by the Public Health Service, National Center for Health Statistics) tells where to write for copies of birth certificates, if needed.

birth control   Exercise of deliberate choice over when one will conceive and bear a child, in this sense also called *family planning*. In a wider sense, birth control also refers to the social goal of limiting family size and therefore population growth by limiting CONCEPTION. In addition, birth control refers to the various methods for preventing undesired pregnancies, in this sense encompassing:

- *contraception*, which focuses on preventing conception, including methods such as the CONDOM, SPERMICIDES, SPONGE, DIAPHRAGM, CERVICAL CAP, INTRAUTERINE DEVICE (IUD), and BIRTH-CONTROL PILLS.
- STERILIZATION, including VASECTOMY and TUBAL LIGATION.
- ABORTION.
- NATURAL FAMILY PLANNING, including the calendar (rhythm) method, the basal body temperature method, the vaginal (cervical) mucus (or Billings) method, and the symptothermal method.

Parents who want to plan when and at what intervals to have their children will want to review the merits and demerits of various birth-control methods and discuss them with their doctor or clinic, deciding on which have the least risk and most effectiveness. (See BIRTH CONTROL: A GUIDE TO THE PROS AND CONS, below.) Sexually active adolescents should also be introduced to birth control, preferably by their parents. Whatever other form of birth control teenagers use for contraception, they should also use condoms for protection from various SEXUALLY TRANSMITTED DISEASES, such as GONORRHEA, HERPES, and AIDS.

For help and further information

Planned Parenthood Federation of America (PPFA)
810 Seventh Avenue
New York, NY 10019
212-541-7800
Faye Wattleton, President
Organization aimed at making available to all information about and access to the full range of birth-control methods, including contraception, abortion, and sterilization, and about infertility services. Sponsors research and disseminates knowledge about family planning, reproduction, and sexuality; attempts to influence public policy and legislation regarding these matters; operates nationwide network of centers providing services and education; maintains library; publishes various materials.

National Institute of Child Health and Human Development (NICHD), 301-496-5133. Publishes a series of "Facts About" booklets on topics such as oral contraceptives and vasectomy safety. (For full group information, see PREGNANCY.)

National Family Planning and Reproductive Health Association (NFPRHA)
122 C Street, NW, Suite 380
Washington, DC 20001
202-628-3535
Scott R. Swirling, Executive Director
Individuals and organizations concerned with family planning and reproductive health. Seeks to influence public policy and acts as advocate; publishes various materials.

Center for Population Options (CPO)
1012 14th Street, NW, Suite 1200
Washington, DC 20005
202-347-5700
Judith Senderowitz, President and Executive Director
Organization aimed at reducing the number of adolescent pregnancies through education about birth control and parenting. Attempts to influence public policy and legislation relating to teenage pregnancies; gathers research data and maintains library; publishes various materials, including fact sheets in English, Spanish, and French.

Choice
c/o Women's Way
125 South Ninth Street, Suite 603
Philadelphia, PA 19107
215-592-7644; hotline for health information 215-592-0550; hotline for day-care information 215-592-7616
Ann Ricksecker, Executive Director
Organization aiming to provide information on reproductive health care, both to teenagers and to parents wishing to educate their children. Offers seminars and workshops; maintains resource information center; provides telephone counseling and referrals; publishes various materials, including one aimed at adolescents and another for parents teaching their children about sex.

Association for Voluntary Surgical Contraception (AVSC)
122 East 42nd Street
New York, NY 10168
212-351-2500
Hugo Hoogenboom, Executive Director
Organization aiming to counter rapid population growth by encouraging voluntary sterilization internationally. Sponsors research programs and maintains library; publishes various materials, including fact sheets on both male and female sterilization.

Couple to Couple League (CCL), 513-661-7612. (For full group information, see NATURAL FAMILY PLANNING.)

Family of the Americas Foundation (FAF), 504-626-7724. (For full group information, see NATURAL FAMILY PLANNING.)

Human Life International (HLI), 301-670-7884. (For full group information, see NATURAL FAMILY PLANNING.)

Other reference sources

How Not to Get Pregnant, by Sherman J. Silber. New York: Warner, 1990.
Preventing Birth: Contemporary Methods and Related Moral Controversies, by James W. Knight and Joan C. Callahan. Salt Lake City: University of Utah, 1989.
The New Birth Control Book, by Howard Shapiro, M.D. New York: Prentice Hall, 1988.

Birth Control: A Guide to the Pros and Cons

Efficacy rates given in this chart are estimates based on a number of different studies. Methods that are more dependent on conscientious use and therefore are more subject to human error have wider ranges of efficacy than the others. For comparison, 60 to 80 percent of sexually active women using no contraception would be expected to become pregnant in a year.

Type	Estimated Effectiveness	Risks	Noncontraceptive Benefits	Convenience	Availability
Condom	64–97%	Rarely, irritation and allergic reactions	Some protection against sexually transmitted diseases, including herpes and AIDS	Applied immediately before intercourse	Nonprescription
Vaginal spermicides	70–80%	Rarely, irritation and allergic reactions	May give some protection against some sexually transmitted diseases	Applied no more than one hour before intercourse; can be "messy"	Nonprescription
Sponge	80–87%	Rarely, irritation and allergic reactions; difficulty in removal; very rarely, toxic shock syndrome	Spermicides may give some protection against some sexually transmitted diseases	Can be inserted hours before intercourse, left in place up to 24 hours; disposable	Nonprescription
Diaphragm with spermicide	80–98%	Rarely, irritation and allergic reactions; bladder infection; constipation; very rarely, toxic shock syndrome	Spermicides may give some protection against some sexually transmitted diseases	Inserted before intercourse; can be left in place 24 hours but additional spermicide must be inserted if intercourse is repeated	Rx
Cervical cap with spermicide	80–98%	Abnormal Pap test; vaginal or cervical infections; very rarely, toxic shock syndrome	Spermicides may give some protection against some sexually transmitted diseases	Can remain in place for 48 hours, not necessary to reapply spermicide upon repeated intercourse; may be difficult to insert	Rx
IUD	95–96%	Cramps, bleeding, PID (pelvic inflammatory disease), infertility; rarely, perforation of the uterus	None	After insertion, stays in place until physician removes it	Rx
Birth-control pills	97% (mini) 99% (comb.)	Blood clots, heart attacks and strokes, gallbladder disease, liver tumors, water retention, hypertension, mood changes, dizziness and nausea; not for smokers	Less menstrual bleeding and cramping; lower risk of fibrocystic breast disease, ovarian cysts, and pelvic inflammatory disease; protects against cancer of the ovaries and lining of the uterus	Pill must be taken on daily schedule, regardless of the frequency of intercourse	Rx
Periodic abstinence (NFP)	Very variable, perhaps 53–98%	None	None	Requires frequent monitoring of body functions and periods of abstinence	Instructions from physician or clinic

Continued on page 51

Type	Estimated Effectiveness	Risks	Noncontraceptive Benefits	Convenience	Availability
Vasectomy (male sterilization)	Over 99%	Pain, infection; rarely, possible psychological problems	None	One-time procedure	Minor surgery
Tubal ligation (female sterilization)	Over 99%	Surgical complications; some pain or discomfort; possibly higher risk of hysterectomy later in life	None	One-time procedure	Surgery

Source: *Comparing Contraceptives*, by Judith Levine Willis (1989). Prepared by the Food and Drug Administration for the Public Health Service. **Note:** The author of this chart meant it to be used in conjunction with discussions of each method, not alone.

What Are You Using: A Birth Control Guide for Teenagers, by Andrea Balis. Fayetteville, NC: Ed-U Press, 1981.
(See also specific types of birth control; SEX EDUCATION; ADOLESCENT PREGNANCY; ABORTION; SEXUALLY TRANSMITTED DISEASES.)

birth-control pill (oral contraceptive) The most effective form of temporary BIRTH CONTROL (as opposed to permanent STERILIZATION), though its side effects may make them not the best choice for some women. There are two main types of birth-control pills. Both act to keep SPERM from fertilizing an egg (OVUM), but do so in different ways:

- *combination pills*, made from estrogen and progestin (synthetic HORMONES similar to those produced in a woman's own body), which act on a woman's OVARIES to stop release of an egg. The Food and Drug Administration (FDA) estimates their effectiveness at about 99 percent. Among the side effects experienced are nausea, high BLOOD PRESSURE, and blood clots, which at the worst can cause severe problems, including blindness and death. The side effects may be lessened with *biphasic* or *triphasic* forms that more closely approximate a woman's normal hormonal variations, but insufficient data has so far been gathered on these.
- *mini-pills*, made only of progestin, which also suppress release of an egg, though less effectively. Less commonly used, these also act on the CERVIX and UTERUS to make them more hostile to sperm. The FDA estimates their effectiveness at about 97 percent. Among the side effects are spotting and bleeding between periods.

Women who smoke, are over 35, or have high BLOOD PRESSURE, DIABETES MELLITUS, or high CHOLESTEROL are advised by the FDA not to take birth-control pills, because of increased risk of heart attack and stroke. So are women who have previously had health problems related to these, such as heart problems, blood clots, unexplained vaginal bleeding, and CANCER of the BREASTS or UTERUS. In addition, women who are or may be pregnant should not take oral contraceptives, because they can cause BIRTH DEFECTS. Combination pills also carry increased risk of gall-bladder problems, LIVER PROBLEMS, and possibly cancer of the CERVIX but apparently not (according to recent studies) breast cancer. Some people who take combination pills also experience VOMITING, severe headaches, DEPRESSION, dizziness, EDEMA (water buildup), missed menstrual periods, and problems with contact lenses. These pills also cause adverse DRUG REACTIONS with some other common medications, including some barbiturates and antibiotics.

Oral contraceptives do, however, also carry some benefits. MENSTRUATION is usually lighter and less painful, formation of cysts in breasts and ovaries is less common, and so is PELVIC INFLAMMATORY DISEASE. ECTOPIC PREGNANCY is less likely, when pregnancy does occur, and oral contraceptives may carry some protection against cancer of the ovaries or the endometrium (lining of the uterus).

Although it must be taken every day, "the pill" is the contraceptive of choice for many sexually active teenagers. Parents may well want to explore with their daughters and doctors the best birth control to use when abstinence is not at issue. If the pill is adopted, the FDA advises: "Women prescribed birth control pills should acquaint themselves with the information in the patient package insert accompanying the prescription. [Good advice in any case.] They should also have their blood pressure checked and should have physical examinations and PAP SMEAR TESTS at least yearly. Because the risk of serious side effects in many cases decreases with a reduced hormone dose, patients should discuss with their physicians using the lowest effective dose." In 1990, the Food and Drug Administration approved a new form of birth control that is implanted under the skin in small, flexible tubes, releasing the hormone progestin over five years. Called Norplant, the method has been used in parts of Europe for several years. (For help and further information, see BIRTH CONTROL.)

birth defects Malformations, malfunctions, and other CONGENITAL disorders that appear in newborns, including GENETIC DISORDERS and CHROMOSOMAL ABNORMALITIES as well as problems resulting from other causes, such as exposure to RADIATION, drugs, disease, or injury during PREGNANCY or CHILDBIRTH. Some defects are so lethal that the FETUS fails to develop and a spontaneous abortion (MISCARRIAGE) occurs, sometimes so early in pregnancy that the woman does not even know she is pregnant. Other defects result in babies dying shortly after birth, such as those with ANENCEPHALY. Of those babies who survive, perhaps 5 to 9 percent have some sort of birth defect; the percentage may be higher because some congenital disorders (such as HUNTINGTON'S CHOREA) appear only later in life. Some birth defects can now be spotted during GENETIC SCREENING early in pregnancy, giving the parents the option of having a selective abortion; in a few special situations, repairing the defect through IN UTERO SURGERY; or preparing to raise a child with SPECIAL NEEDS. Physicians who specialize in birth defects are called TERATOLOGISTS, from the Greek word *teras*, meaning "monster."

Of the many thousands known or suspected, any single type of birth defect is rare, and their causes are generally unknown. Most birth defects seem to result from a combination of GENETIC INHERITANCE and environmental factors. Two couples with similar life-styles and home settings, exposed to the same ENVIRONMENTAL HAZARDS, may be differently affected depending on their genetic predisposition, so one couple's child may be born with a birth defect but not the other's. For unknown reasons, birth defects also appear at widely varying rates in different parts of the world. SPINA BIFIDA, for example, occurs in roughly one of every 575 births in Northern Ireland, but only once in every 20,000 births in Japan; in the U.S. the rate is about one in every 3,333 births.

In some cases, however, researchers can identify specific causes for a birth defect, such as a chromosomal abnormality, exposure to a specific disease (such as RUBELLA) or drug (such as thalidomide), or the pregnant mother's shortage of an essential VITAMIN or MINERAL. As a result, much emphasis has been placed on getting good PRENATAL CARE, avoiding known reproductive hazards (environmental hazards that have direct effects on a developing fetus), and assuring that the mother has a properly balanced diet.

Some drugs can cause birth defects at any stage during a pregnancy, including in the early weeks before a woman realizes she is pregnant, so a woman considering a pregnancy should take no medications—prescription or over-the-counter—without first consulting her GYNECOLOGIST/OBSTETRICIAN about the possible effects on a developing fetus. Fathers taking strong medications may also want to check with a physician before a planned conception. Other reproductive hazards include toxic chemicals, SMOKING, ALCOHOL ABUSE, chronic illness in either parent, SPERMICIDES used around the time of pregnancy, rubella, TOXOPLASMOSIS, viral diseases such as HEPATITIS, X-RAYS (not only in medicine or industry but also in high-altitude flying), ANESTHESIA, and STRESS.

Experts in GENETIC COUNSELING can help prospective parents review their genetic and personal histories and assess the risk of their having a child with a birth defect. Best consulted before pregnancy, genetic counselors can also advise on any life-style changes that can help parents reduce their risk of having a child with birth defects. This is important because the fetus is most vulnerable to damage during the first TRIMESTER (three months) of pregnancy. Some men and women may even wish to consider a job change to avoid some reproductive hazards, such as high-altitude radiation or toxic chemicals.

For help and further information:

National Center for Education in Child and Maternal Health (NCEMCH), 202-625-8400, and **National Maternal and Child Health Clearinghouse (NMCHC)**, 202-625-8410. Provide information to public and professionals about specific genetic diseases and general child and maternal health. Help parents locate groups of other parents with children having specific or related diseases; publish various materials, including *Genetic Screening for Inborn Errors of Metabolism* and *Learning Together: A Guide for Families with Genetic Disorders*. (For full group information, see PREGNANCY.)

March of Dimes Birth Defects Foundation
1275 Mamaroneck Avenue
White Plains, NY 10605
914-428-7100 (local chapters in telephone-directory white pages)
Charles Massey, President

Organization concerned about preventing, repairing, or treating birth defects. Provides information and referrals, as for genetic counseling; has many local chapters, some of which have certified midwives available, for normal pregnancies and for prenatal services for women with high-risk pregnancies; publishes numerous print and audiovisual materials, including booklets such as *International Directory of Genetic Services, Genetic Counseling, Birth Defects: Tragedy and Hope, Your Special Child, Drugs, Alcohol and Tobacco Abuse During Pregnancy, Will My Drinking Hurt My Baby?, Babies Don't Thrive in Smoke-Filled Wombs, Family Health Tree*, and *Family Medical Record*, and various materials (in English and Spanish) for teenagers about pregnancy, as well as information sheets on specific topics, including *Accutane, Achondroplasia, Alpha-Fetoprotein Screening, Chicken Pox During Pregnancy, Cleft Lip and Palate, Clubfoot, Cocaine Use During Pregnancy, Congenital AIDS, Congenital Heart Defects, Down Syndrome, Fetal Alcohol Syndrome, Fitness for Two, Genital Herpes, Infections During Pregnancy: Toxoplasmosis and Chlamydia, Low Birthweight, Marfan Syndrome, Neurofibromatosis, Newborn Screening Tests, PKU, Polio, Post Polio Muscle Atrophy, Pregnancy Over 35, Rh Disease, Rubella, Sickle-Cell Anemia, Spina Bifida, Stress and Pregnancy, Tay-Sachs Disease, Teen-Age Pregnancy, Thalassemia*, and *VDT Facts*.

Association of Birth Defect Children (ABDC)
3526 Emerywood Lane
Orlando, FL 32806

305-859-2821
Betty Mekdeci, Executive Director
Organization of parents, health professionals, and other individuals and organizations seeking to prevent birth defects. Gathers and disseminates information; offers support to families with birth defects; seeks to educate public and influence government policy, especially about effects of prenatal drugs; publishes quarterly newsletter *ABDC*.

National Network to Prevent Birth Defects
c/o Health and Energy Institute (HEI)
236 Massachusetts Avenue, NE, No. 506
Washington, DC 20002
202-543-1070
Kathleen M. Tucker, President
Organization of people concerned about the effects of nuclear energy and radiation on health and the environment, including reproduction. Sponsors research; seeks to educate public and influence public policy; sponsors National Network to Prevent Birth Defects; publishes various materials.

Teratology Society (TS)
9650 Rockville Pike
Bethesda, MD 20814
301-564-1493
Alexandra Ventura, Contact
Organization of health professionals and other individuals interested in birth defects and abnormal development. Publishes bimonthly *Teratology: The International Journal of Abnormal Development*.

National Foundation for Jewish Genetic Diseases, 212-753-5155. (For full group information, see GENETIC DISORDERS.)

National Organization for Rare Disorders (NORD), 203-746-6518. (For full group information, see RARE DISORDERS.)

National Genetics Federation, 212-586-5800. (For full group information, see GENETIC COUNSELING.)

DES Action, 415-826-5060. (For full group information, see DES.)

Other reference sources

The Encyclopedia of Genetic Disorders and Birth Defects, by Mark D. Ludman, M.D. and James Wyndbrandt. New York: Facts on File, 1990.
Family Diseases: Are You At Risk, by Myra Vanderpool Gormley. Baltimore: Genealogical Publishing, 1989.
Peace of Mind During Pregnancy: An A-to-Z Guide to the Substances That Could Affect Your Unborn Baby, by Christine Kelley-Buchanan. New York: Facts on File, 1988.
Health Care U.S.A., by Jean Carper. New York: Prentice Hall, 1987. Resource for general and specific health-care information; lists major genetic counseling and testing centers and other information.

New Hope for Problem Pregnancies: Helping Babies Before They're Born, by Dianne Hales and Robert K. Creasy, M.D. New York: Harper & Row, 1982.
Children Who Are Different: Meeting the Challenges of Birth Defects in Society, by Rosalyn Benjamin Darling and Jon Darling. St. Louis, C.V. Mosby, 1982.
Families Against Society: A Study of Reactions to Children with Birth Defects, by Rosalyn Benjamin Darling. Beverly Hills, CA: Sage Publications, 1979.
The Genetic Connection, by David Hendin and Joan Marks. New York: Morrow, 1978.
Know Your Genes, by Aubrey Milunsky. Boston: Houghton Mifflin, 1977.
Is My Baby All Right?, by Virginia Apgar and Joan Beck. New York: Trident, 1972.
Genes, Medicine, and You, by Alvin Silverstein and Virginia Silverstein. Hillside, NJ: Enslow, 1989. For young adult readers.
(See also GENETIC COUNSELING; GENETIC DISORDERS; PREGNANCY; specific diseases.)

birthing center   Alternate name for MATERNITY CENTER.

birthing chair   A chair designed to use gravity to ease CHILDBIRTH. Traditional in many cultures until modern times, as a simple high-backed stool with a hole in the center, the birthing chair has been revived in recent decades in modern designs that allow women to sit up or recline, with a section that can be dropped down from the chair seat during actual delivery. The chair is not used when ANESTHESIA is required. (For help and further information, see PREGNANCY; CHILDBIRTH.)

birthing room   A room in which a woman can give birth in a homelike, relaxed setting, often attached to a HOSPITAL but sometimes in a freestanding MATERNITY CENTER. Developed largely in response to the perceived coldness of traditional hospital DELIVERY ROOMS, birthing rooms often have homelike furniture, allow birth to take place without changing rooms (as from LABOR ROOM to delivery room), and sometimes allow family members (not just the BIRTH PARTNER) to attend the birth if desired. Some birthing rooms provide special birthing beds or BIRTHING CHAIRS that allow a woman to give birth from a sitting or semireclining position, often with a lower section of the chair or bed dropped down during actual delivery. Birthing rooms are used only for low-risk pregnancies, and if complications occur, the mother and child will need to be moved into regular delivery rooms; in some emergency situations this results in dangerous loss of time. (For help and further information, see PREGNANCY; CHILDBIRTH; MATERNITY CENTER; CERTIFIED NURSE-MIDWIFE.)

birthmark   Popular name for HEMANGIOMA.

birth order   The position a child occupies in a family, based on arrival and number of other children, such as only child, first-born, second-born, middle child, youngest, and so on. Traditionally, many people have believed that birth order has a strong influence on a child's development and personality. Theories abound, such as that first-born or only children are strong, self-directed, capable leaders; second-born or middle children are more relaxed, spontaneous compromisers; and third-born or youngest children are more gentle, passive, withdrawn followers. Some assert that first-born or only children tend to support the status quo, while second and later children are more likely to challenge established views. Though popular, such views are highly controversial. Some studies tend to support influence of birth order on personality, but critics charge that supposed influence of birth order often turns out, on closer analysis, to actually be due to other factors, such as the family's social and economic status, educational level, or age.

Other reference sources

On Birth Order in General

Birth Order and You: How Your Sex and Your Position in the Family Affects Your Personality and Relationships, by Ron Richardson and Lois A. Richardson. Bellingham, WA: Self-Counsel, 1990.

Birth Order Roles and Sibling Patterns in Individual and Family Therapy, by Margaret Hoopes and James Harper. Gaithersburg, MD: Aspen, 1987.

The Birth Order Book: Why You Are the Way You Are, by Kevin Leman. Old Tappan, NJ: Revell, 1985, New York: Dell, 1987.

First Child, Second Child . . . Your Birth Order Profile, by Bradford Wilson. New York: McGraw-Hill, 1981.

On Firstborn or Only Children

Parenting an Only Child: The Joys and Challenges of Raising Your One and Only, by Susan Newman. Garden City, NY: Doubleday, 1990.

Growing Up Firstborn: The Pressure and Privilege of Being Number One, by Kevin Leman. New York: Delacorte, 1989.

The Only Child: Being One, Loving One, Understanding One, Raising One, by Darrell Sifford. New York: Putnam, 1989.

birth parents   A synonym for BIOLOGICAL PARENTS.

birth partner   The person who is designated by a pregnant woman to be her "coach" during CHILDBIRTH, generally the FATHER, but sometimes a friend or relative; in any case, someone who has attended PREPARED CHILDBIRTH classes with the woman. (For help and further information, see CHILDBIRTH.)

black-market adoption   Illegal form of ADOPTION.

Blacky Pictures   A type of PROJECTIVE TEST for use with children age five and up, attempting to gain information on the child's personality. The child is given a set of 12 cartoon pictures featuring a dog named Blacky and is asked to make up a story about them, answer questions for each picture, and sort them by preference. The test is usually administered individually, but may be given to groups with the pictures on slides. (For help and further information, see TESTS.)

bleaching   A technique for restoring discolored TEETH.

Bliss Symbols

bleeding disorder   Alternative name for HEMOPHILIA, a type of blood disorder involving defects in blood clotting. (See BLOOD AND BLOOD DISORDERS; HEMOPHILIA.)

blepharitis   Inflammation of the eyelids. (See EYE AND VISION PROBLEMS.)

blindness   A severe (though not necessarily total) loss of vision. (See EYE AND VISION PROBLEMS.)

Bliss symbols   A set of standardized symbols developed for use with young children who are not able to speak clearly enough to express themselves, as when they have ORTHOPEDIC HANDICAPS that affect their speaking apparatus, and who cannot read and write. The symbols (see samples above) are moved around on CONVERSATION BOARDS to "converse" with others.

block arents   Individuals in a community, often identified by a sign in a window or on a house, who are designated as people to whom children (and adults) can go when they need help. When an urban school community is divided into "blocks" for ease of communication, the block parent—generally appointed or elected from among parents active in the school—may be the person responsible for communication between the neighborhood and the school.

blood and blood disorders   Blood disorders are problems with the vital red fluid that circulates in the body's veins and arteries. Most of the blood is made up of blood cells, all formed in the BONE MARROW, including:

* *red blood cells* (RBCs), or *erythrocytes*, which transport oxygen from the lungs, exchanging it for the waste product, carbon dioxide. *Hemoglobin* is the pigment inside the RBCs that actually carries the oxygen.

* *white blood cells* (WBCs) or *leukocytes*, larger but less numerous than RBCs, that are the blood's infection fighters

and come in various types, including *lymphocytes*, which play an important role in the IMMUNE SYSTEM.
- *platelets* or *thrombocytes*, the smallest blood cells, which control bleeding through blood clotting and speed repairs of injured blood vessels.

The balance of the blood volume is a fluid called *plasma*, in which are dissolved and transported around the body a variety of substances, including PROTEINS, MINERALS, VITAMINS, HORMONES, FATS, and sugars for use in tissues, as well as waste products such as bilirubin.

The blood is the body's barometer and often gives early indications of health problems, including blood disorders. One of the basic kinds of BLOOD TESTS, the CBC or *complete blood count*, measures the number of each kind of cell in proportion to the others. There are also blood tests that measure the amount and proportion of other substances carried in the blood.

Among the main kinds of blood disorders are:

- ANEMIA, too few healthy red blood cells. (See ANEMIA for some of the many causes.)
- *polycythemia*, too many red blood cells.
- LEUKEMIA, too many white blood cells, a form of CANCER. (See LEUKEMIA.)
- HEMOPHILIA, various bleeding disorders resulting from defective platelets and ineffective clotting.
- *thrombosis*, overactive clotting, which can cause heart problems. (See HEART AND HEART PROBLEMS.)

Some blood disorders are caused by GENETIC DISORDERS, some by poor NUTRITION. Poisons, TUMORS, RADIATION, and drugs all can have adverse effects on the proper functioning of the blood. Bacteria can enter the blood (as through injury) and multiply, producing *septicemia*; these sometimes produce toxins, or substances that act as poisons in the body, the infection then being called TOXEMIA. Both of these are commonly called *blood poisoning* and are potentially life-threatening.

Blood comes in different types, distinguished by differing ANTIGENS (PROTEIN markers). The two main kinds of markers are A and B, and the four main kinds of blood are A (with only A markers), B (with only B), AB (with A and B), and O (with neither).

Another distinguishing characteristic of some kinds of blood is the presence or absence of a complex marker called an Rh factor. Approximately 85 percent of the population has the factor (Rh positive), but 15 percent do not (Rh negative); during a PREGNANCY this can cause problems because of RH INCOMPATIBILITY, which leads to *erythroblastosis fetalis* or *hemolytic disease of the newborn*. Rh incompatibility can also lead to problems during BLOOD TRANSFUSIONS.

For help and further information

National Heart, Lung, and Blood Institute (NHLBI)
9000 Rockville Pike
Building 31, Room 4A21

Bethesda, MD 20892
301-496-4236
Federal arm, one of the U.S. National Institutes of Health, sponsoring research on heart, lung, and blood disorders and diseases. Provides information to public and health professionals; publishes various materials, including technical reports for medical specialists and more general brochures such as *Blood Cholesterol, Eating to Lower Your Blood Cholesterol, Blacks and High Blood Pressure*, and *Questions About Weight, Salt, and High Blood Pressure*.

High Blood Pressure Information Center, 301-496-1809. (For full group information, see BLOOD PRESSURE.)

(See also ANEMIA; HEMOPHILIA; LEUKEMIA; BLOOD PRESSURE; BLOOD TRANSFUSIONS.)

blood-brain barrier (BBB) A physiological protective screen surrounding the brain that keeps out or slows passage of many substances from the blood into the brain. Normally a protective mechanism, the blood-brain barrier can sometimes have negative effects, as when it keeps some kinds of drugs from reaching diseased portions of the brain. In such cases, medications may be given as intrathecal INJECTIONS, directly into the CEREBROSPINAL FLUID, or as intraarterial injections, directly into an artery feeding a BRAIN TUMOR. Some medications, given beforehand, can also temporarily allow passage of other medications through the barrier.

blood chemistry A range of BLOOD TESTS examining various substances carried in the blood.

blood gases A kind of PULMONARY FUNCTION TEST.

blood glucose monitoring A test used by people with DIABETES MELLITUS to monitor the level of the sugar GLUCOSE in their blood.

blood pressure The amount of force blood exerts on the walls of the blood vessels (arteries and veins) and the heart, as it circulates in the body. Using a device called a *sphygmomanometer*, in which an inflated rubber cuff is wrapped tightly around the upper arm, the force of the blood moving from the heart to the main artery in the arm is measured; this is the *systolic* pressure. Then, as the cuff is deflated and the blood begins to flow freely, the *diastolic pressure* is taken. The two figures are given together, so a typical reading for a young adult might be 110/75; for a mature adult, it is closer to 120/80. Blood pressure is quite variable and may rise or fall with activity, time of day, or the action of drugs, for example. But people who have blood pressure that is consistently well below normal (for example, because of illness, certain drugs, blood loss, SHOCK, heart attack, or problems with their ADRENAL GLANDS, are said to have hypotension. This can lead to reduced blood to the brain, resulting in dizziness or fainting.

Conversely, those with abnormally high blood pressure—normally above 140/90—are said to have *hypertension*. This may be in response to physical activity, stress, excess salt, certain

---

Hypertension in Pregnancy

Preeclampsia and eclampsia are hypertensive conditions induced by pregnancy. Preeclampsia is characterized by a rise in blood pressure, generalized edema that may cause sudden, large weight gain from retained water, and loss of protein in the urine. Eclampsia is the most severe form of the disorder, characterized by convulsions that may lead to coma. Both present serious health risks to mother and fetus. Pregnancy-induced hypertension occurs among younger women (especially those under 15 years); primiparas [first-time mothers], especially older primiparas; and those who are underweight or of low socioeconomic status. The cause of these conditions is uncertain. Whether dietary variables may be part of the cause cannot be determined from available data. Hypertension existing before pregnancy may also adversely affect pregnancy.

Source: *The Surgeon General's Report on Nutrition and Health.* Rocklin, CA: Prime, 1988.

---

drugs, SMOKING, and various kinds of disorders, including KIDNEY AND UROLOGICAL DISORDERS, problems with the adrenal glands, some heart problems (see HEART AND HEART PROBLEMS), and OBESITY. Hypertension can sometimes develop when a woman is taking BIRTH-CONTROL PILLS. If unchecked, it can increase the risk of stroke, heart failure, kidney damage, and EYE AND VISION PROBLEMS, notably retinopathy. Hypertension can also develop during PREGNANCY and increase the risk of serious complications, especially PREECLAMPSIA and ECLAMPSIA, if not treated promptly (see HYPERTENSION IN PREGNANCY, below). A tendency toward hypertension can run in families, but it is often controllable by lifestyle changes supplemented with drugs if necessary.

For help and further information

High Blood Pressure Information Center
120/80 National Institutes of Health
Bethesda, MD 20892
301-496-1809
Federal arm serving as information clearinghouse for public and professionals. Answers questions and makes referrals; publishes various materials, including pamphlets *High Blood Pressure and What You Can Do About It, High Blood Pressure: Facts and Fiction*, and *Blacks and High Blood Pressure*.

(See also BLOOD AND BLOOD DISORDERS.)

blood relations   People who share some close GENETIC INHERITANCE and therefore have an increased risk of passing on various traits, including GENETIC DISORDERS. Blood relatives are said to be consanguineous (see CONSANGUINITY). When someone dies intestate (without a will), the court determines the specific blood relations of KIN to decide INHERITANCE RIGHTS.

blood sugar   Alternate term for BLOOD GLUCOSE.

blood tests   A wide variety of MEDICAL TESTS done on samples of blood taken from a vein (VENIPUNCTURE), to assess the health of the body and its major systems. *Hematological tests* look at aspects of the blood itself; among such tests are *complete blood count* (CBC) and *thrombin time*, which measures blood-clotting ability. *Microbiological tests* search for infectious organisms carried in the blood and for ANTIBODIES that may have formed to counteract them; often these tests take the form of attempting to grow a CULTURE in the laboratory. *Biochemical or blood chemistry tests* examine the substances carried in the blood, such as SODIUM and other elements, VITAMINS, gases, and drugs. Using medical shorthand, doctors often refer to different groups of tests by the organ whose health is being examined (for example, KIDNEY FUNCTION TESTS) or by the information sought, such as blood gases or thyroid-stimulating hormone (T_4, T_3). (For help and further information, see MEDICAL TESTS, kidney function tests, LIVER FUNCTION TESTS, and PULMONARY FUNCTION TESTS.)

blood transfusion   The introduction of large quantities of blood or blood components (such as red blood cells) into a patient's body to replace blood lost or weakened through injury, surgery, or disease. Blood is stored in blood banks by ABO type and Rh factor (see BLOOD AND BLOOD DISORDERS) and is used only for people whose blood type is compatible. Even so, except in emergency situations, blood for transfusions is generally tested against a sample of the patient's blood to be sure no compatibility problems exist. People with blood type O, Rh factor negative are called *universal donors*, because their blood can be used in emergencies for most other people with little risk of incompatibility; otherwise solutions without blood cells might be used. If blood is incompatible, donor cells may self-destruct by bursting (*hemolysis*), leading to possibly severe reactions, such as SHOCK or kidney failure.

Blood transfusions are commonly given after severe bleeding, as from an accident, operation, hemorrhage, or bleeding ulcer. They are also often given to people with blood disorders such as ANEMIA or LEUKEMIA. When a child is born with *hemolytic disease of the newborn*, a result of RH INCOMPATIBILITY, an *exchange transfusion* may be performed, in which virtually all of the infant's blood is replaced to prevent permanent damage. Usually blood is dripped slowly into the patient's vein at the rate of about one pint over one to four hours, while the patient's condition is checked for any sign of a reaction. In an emergency, a pint of blood may be given in minutes, however.

A serious problem with blood transfusions is the possibility of being infected by disease from the donor's blood. Blood banks routinely test for infections such as AIDS, HEPATITIS B, and SYPHILIS, but some risk remains. The vulnerabilty of the blood system was demonstrated when AIDS came on the scene; numerous people, many of them children, contracted the disease before it was recognized as a major threat and before tests were developed to screen blood for it. To cut down on this risk, some hospitals have programs allowing people to donate some of their own blood over the weeks before a planned operation, called an AUTOLOGOUS blood transfusion. Others allow family and friends to donate blood designated for use by a particular patient.

For help and further information

National Heart, Lung, and Blood Institute (NHLBI), 301-496-4236. (For full group information, see BLOOD AND BLOOD DISORDERS; HEART AND HEART PROBLEMS; LUNG AND BREATHING DISORDERS.)

Safe Blood: Purifying the Nation's Blood Supply in the Age of AIDS, by Joseph Feldschuh, M.D. with Doron Weber. New York: Free Press, 1989.

bloody show In PREGNANCY, the bloody mucus that appears just before the onset of LABOR.

blue babies Babies born with congenital heart defects, causing characteristic CYANOSIS (blueness). (See HEART AND HEART PROBLEMS.)

BMR Abbreviation for basal metabolic rate. (See METABOLISM.)

BMT Abbreviation for BONE MARROW TRANSPLANT.

boards Nickname for various kinds of ADMISSION TESTS. In relation to children they often refer to DIAGNOSTIC ASSESSMENT TESTS (nicknamed *baby boards*) or the dreaded pre-college tests offered by the College Board (see COLLEGE ENTRANCE EXAMINATION BOARD).

body identity See BODY IMAGE.

body image (body identity) An awareness of one's body as being separate from the environment, of its parts and their relationship to one another and to the outside environment, and of the possibilities of body movement and action. Children must develop a sense of the body, and gradually most learn to identify the parts of their own body and recognize how they relate to objects around them so that they can avoid running into objects or can move their bodies without awkwardness. But some children, such as those with SCHIZOPHRENIA, lack a clear body image and may not, for example, be aware that their hand is attached to their body; therefore, they may lack coordination and the ability to work with objects in a predictable way. A child's sense of body is sometimes tested using PROJECTIVE TESTS such as the HOUSE-TREE-PERSON TEST or DRAW-A-PERSON TEST.

body-eye coordination Alternate name for visual-motor integration, one of the key VISUAL SKILLS.

Boehm Test of Basic Concepts-Revised (Boehm-R) A type of READINESS TEST administered individually or to small groups of children in grades K to 2, attempting to assess a child's grasp of the basic concepts used in classroom teaching. In a multiple-choice picture booklet, the child marks which one of several pictures fits the question the examiner poses orally, generally relating to quantity, space, and time. The 50-item test is then scored by a hand key, the SCORE being made part of a report to

be used in a PARENT–TEACHER CONFERENCE, if desired. A preschool version, for children ages three to five, is also sometimes used. (For help and further information, see TESTS.)

bonding The forming of special emotional ties between a baby and his or her primary CAREGIVER, often the MOTHER but sometimes the FATHER, another adult, or another child; also called *maternal–infant attachment*. After CHILDBIRTH, the newborn is often placed on the mother's abdomen to start the process of bonding between the two, considered key to the normal development of the baby. Bonding is the process of interaction by which the child develops trust and security vital for "making contact" with the world, and for learning the SOCIAL SKILLS, communication skills (see COMMUNICATION SKILLS AND DISORDERS), VISUAL SKILLS, and AUDITORY SKILLS needed to function in the world. PREMATURE or HIGH-RISK BABIES who need to stay in hospitals for some days or weeks after birth are in special need of bonding and stimulation. Indeed, children who lack such bonding often have retarded physical and mental development, leading to a variety of problem conditions, including FAILURE TO THRIVE, MATERNAL DEPRIVATION SYNDROME, and REACTIVE ATTACHMENT DISORDER OF INFANCY. And mothers who fail to bond with their children are at risk for later CHILD ABUSE AND NEGLECT. Psychologists sometimes call this early close relationship between mother and child the SYMBIOTIC STAGE.

For help and further information

The Earliest Relationship: Parents, Infants, and the Drama of Early Attachment, by T. Berry Brazelton and Bertrand Cramer. Reading, MA: Addison-Wesley, 1990.

Love Start: Pre-Birth Bonding, by Eve Marnie. Santa Monica, CA: Hay House, 1990.

Mothers and Their Adopted Children—The Bonding Process, by Dorothy W. Smith and Laurie Nehls Sherwen. New York: Tiresias, 1983.

bone disorders Problems with the skeleton that makes up the hard but resilient framework of the body, vital for the ability to move at will. In general, bone consists of three main layers. On the outside is a thin membrane (*periosteum*) containing blood vessels and nerves; below that is the dense hard shell we normally think of as bone, which gets its rigidity from large amounts of CALCIUM and phosphate; inside the shell is spongy tissue, including the BONE MARROW, where vital blood cells are produced.

An EMBRYO has no bone, only cartilage; in a process called *ossification*, this tough, resilient material begins to turn into bone in the FETUS at about the seventh to eighth week of development. But ossification proceeds very slowly and is not completed until early adulthood, which is why calcium is so important all through childhood and adolescence. (See BUILDING STRONG BONES below.) At birth, a baby's skull is soft in some places and has gaps called FONTANELLES, which later are closed with bone. In the long bones of the arms and legs, growth takes place primarily at the ends, called epiphyses. If these epiphy-

---

Building Strong Bones

As a person grows during youth, bones are metabolically active, and calcium is deposited into bone faster than it is taken out. The deposition of calcium into bone peaks at about 35 years of age in men and women. At the time of "peak bone mass," the bones are most dense and strong.

Some experts believe that the level of bone mass at this age may help determine whether a person may later lose enough bone to fracture easily. If a young woman achieves a high peak bone mass—possibly through increased calcium intake, moderate weight-bearing exercise, and other lifestyle choices—she may be less likely to develop osteoporosis later.

Source: *Osteoporosis: Causes, Prevention, Treatment* (1986). Prepared for the National Institute of Arthritis and Musculoskeletal Disorders.

---

ses ossify prematurely, for whatever reason, growth stops and short stature results.

Like all parts in the body, bone is constantly undergoing change. Cells called *osteoclasts* remove calcium from the bone, while other cells, called *osteoblasts*, deposit calcium phosphate in the bone. In a healthy body, the destruction of old, worn-out cells and the formation of new ones is well balanced, with the calcium level in the blood regulated by various HORMONES, including key hormones from the PITUITARY GLAND, ADRENAL GLANDS, and THYROID GLANDS and the sex hormones ESTROGEN and TESTOSTERONE. If the body is not healthy, however, the process will go awry, sometimes resulting in bones too hard or too soft.

Bones may be subject to several kinds of disorders:

* FRACTURE, as in direct injury or overuse;
* infection, as in OSTEOMYELITIS;
* GENETIC DISORDERS, such as OSTEOGENESIS IMPERFECTA, ACHONDROPLASIA, and OSTEOPETROSIS;
* nutritional deficiencies, such as lack of VITAMIN D and CALCIUM, which can cause RICKETS in children;
* hormone disorders, such as osteoporosis or pituitary disorders;
* TUMORS, including CANCER;
* degeneration, or wearing down, as in *osteoarthritis*, primarily in older adults;
* AUTOIMMUNE DISORDERS, such as rheumatoid ARTHRITIS;
* other diseases of unclear origin, such as CRANIOSYNOSTOSIS or PAGET'S DISEASE.

If the bone marrow is damaged or defective, a BONE MARROW TRANSPLANT may be attempted. If the bone is weakened or excessively hardened, a child may have trouble developing MOTOR SKILLS; ORTHOPEDIC DEVICES may sometimes be used as aids and to protect the bone from use after fracture or surgery.

For help and further information

National Institute of Arthritis and Musculoskeletal and Skin Diseases (NIAMS), 301-496-8188. (For full group information, see ARTHRITIS; MUSCULAR DYSTROPHY.)

American Society for Bone and Mineral Research (ASBMR)
P.O. Box 95451
Kelseyville, CA 95451
707-279-1344
Norman H. Bell, President
Organization of health professionals, including physicians, dentists, and veterinarians, interested in researching bone and mineral diseases. Has established guidelines for preventing osteoporosis; publishes newsletter and *Journal of Bone and Mineral Research*.

The Skeleton and Movement, revised edition, by Steve Parker. New York: Watts, 1989. For grades 4 to 7.
(See also MOTOR SKILLS; GROWTH AND GROWTH DISORDERS; ORTHOPEDIC DEVICES.)

bone marrow   Blood-producing tissue within the bones of the body, the factory for oxygen-carrying red blood cells, disease-fighting white blood cells, and platelets, important in blood-clotting. At birth, the most productive "red" bone marrow is present in all bones, but by ADOLESCENCE it generally becomes confined to the large central bones, including the spine, skull, chestbone (*sternum*), ribs, shoulderbone (*clavicle*), shoulder blades (*scapulae*), and hip bones. Normally well protected in its bony housing, bone marrow can be affected by infections, as in OSTEOMYELITIS, or by TUMORS; it can also malfunction, producing too few of some blood cells, as in aplastic ANEMIA, or too many, as in LEUKEMIA or polycythemia. In cases where bone marrow has been damaged, surgical removal of diseased marrow and replacement in a BONE MARROW TRANSPLANT may be necessary. (For help and further information, see BONE DISORDERS; BONE MARROW TRANSPLANT; BLOOD AND BLOOD DISORDERS.)

bone marrow transplant (BMT)   A surgical operation to replace diseased or defective BONE MARROW with healthy bone marrow, generally performed when the person faces a life-threatening disorder, such as severe aplastic ANEMIA, LEUKEMIA, CANCER, or certain serious GENETIC DISORDERS. First, the patient's defective bone marrow is destroyed by drugs or RADIATION. Then new bone marrow cells are fed into the patient intravenously, finding their way into the bone cavities, where they will—if all goes as planned—begin to produce blood.

The problem of finding compatible bone marrow is a formidable one. In an *allogenic BMT* the healthy bone marrow is provided by someone whose tissue is similar to the patient's, such as a SIBLING, but the chance of finding a match even in a close relative is only one in four and is much higher among strangers. In certain situations, bone marrow may be extracted from the patient's own body using a hollow *aspiration needle* (before the use of destructive drugs or radiation) and then frozen until ready for use; this is called an *autologous BMT*. The autologous BMT shows considerable promise in the treatment of TUMORS that might previously have been considered untreatable.

The BMT is a difficult, delicate, and dangerous procedure, and the failure rate is relatively high, but it offers hope to people who might in earlier decades have had no chance of survival. The autologous BMT, especially, holds great hope for people with cancers so severe as to have been, previously, untreatable, because the heavy doses of radiation required would kill the bone marrow.

For help and further information

National Marrow Donor Program
100 South Robert Street
St. Paul, MN 55107
800-654-1247
Jeffrey McCullough, President
Registry of unrelated potential donors for people in need of bone marrow transplant, sponsored by the American Association of Blood Banks, American Red Cross, Council of Community Blood Centers, and the National Heart, Lung, and Blood Institute. Publishes *The Chance of a Lifetime: Questions and Answers about Marrow Transplants.*

National Cancer Institute (NCI), 800-4-CANCER [422-6237]. (For full group information, see CANCER.)

Leukemia Society of America, 212-573-8484. Publishes *Bone Marrow Transplantation: Questions and Answers.* (For full group information, see LEUKEMIA.)

National Heart, Lung, and Blood Institute (NHLBI), 301-496-4236. (For full group information, see BLOOD AND BLOOD DISORDERS; HEART AND HEART PROBLEMS; LUNG AND BREATHING DISORDERS.)

National Institute of Allergy and Infectious Diseases (NIAID), 301-496-5717. (For full group information, see ALLERGY.)

(See also TRANSPLANTS.)

borderline personality disorder The adult form of the childhood IDENTITY DISORDER.

bottlefeeding Supplying an infant with nutrients in a modified MILK or milklike fluid called FORMULA, fed through a bottle with a nipple similar to that of a BREAST. Public health experts recommend BREASTFEEDING where possible, because the mother's milk provides more completely balanced NUTRITION and temporary IMMUNIZATION against various kinds of diseases. But many women find breastfeeding too inconvenient, unattractive, or difficult to arrange, especially in a world where both parents often work, and not all women who choose to breastfeed can do so. Bottlefeeding, though a second choice for doctors, is then a perfectly good alternative to breastfeeding. Mothers (and also fathers) are equally able to establish the close BOND-

ING relationship with the baby if they cuddle, rock, and talk with the child while bottlefeeding.

Some kinds of commercially available formulas come in a ready-to-use liquid form; less-expensive liquid concentrates or dry powders need water added to approximate breast milk. The preparation of the formula and the sterilization of the bottles and other equipment used are extremely important because germs can grow very quickly in warm milk, causing DIGESTIVE DISORDERS in infants, some very serious and all hindering the absorption of nutrients needed for proper growth. (See FIXING FORMULA, on page 60.) The storage of formula is equally important. The Public Health Service recommends: "Don't feed any formula that has been left at room temperature in a nursing bottle or open can for more than an hour, or in the refrigerator for more than two days."

Properly prepared formula contains all of the nutrients needed by a baby. The Food and Drug Administration monitors the nutrient content of commercially prepared formulas, under the Infant Formula Act of 1980, to be sure that it is so. Parents are advised not to give their babies additional VITAMINS or IRON unless the doctor specifically recommends it, to avoid overtaxing the baby's immature digestive system and kidneys. They should also not try to change a child's bowel movements (see DIGESTIVE DISORDERS) or spitting up (see REGURGITATION) by changing formulas; if they have concerns in this area, they should consult the doctor or clinic.

The Public Health Service's *Infant Care* provides the following guidelines for bottlefeeding:

- Hold your baby close to you in your arms, with the head a little higher than the rest of the body.
- Tilt the bottle to be sure that milk is in the nipple. Touch the nipple next to the baby's mouth and the baby will turn and grasp the nipple. Hold the bottle so that it sticks straight out at a right angle to the baby's mouth.
- The nipple's holes should be large enough so that milk drops slowly (about one drop per second) from the bottle when it is held with the nipple down.
- You should see air bubbles entering the bottle as the baby drinks (except when using plastic-lined bottles that collapse as the bottle empties). If no air bubbles appear, milk will stop flowing. Check to see that the cap is not on too tight.
- Halfway through the bottle and again when your baby is finished eating, burp your baby on your shoulder by patting him or her gently on the back until you hear a burp. (Another way is to hold your baby face down on his or her stomach in your lap over your hand or knee and pat his or her back.) Your baby will usually burp up some air and often a little of the formula.
- Don't leave a bottle containing formula—or *anything else*—with your baby to calm or help him or her sleep. Your baby's teeth are developing, and milk, formula, juices or other liquids that remain in your baby's mouth can lead to cavities. [See NURSING BOTTLE SYNDROME.] In addition, propping a bottle may result in the baby's choking or developing an ear infection.

Fixing Formula

Parents who have decided to bottlefeed their baby should consult with their doctor or clinic before the birth about the form and perhaps the brand of formula recommended. Choose a formula with iron unless there are medical reasons why you should not. Always check the expiration date, and do not buy it or use it if that date has passed.

Equipment Needed for Bottlefeeding

- *Nursing bottles with caps*. Six to eight 8-ounce bottles, or fewer if you wash them more than once a day. You may choose reusable bottles or disposable bottles with sterile plastic liners.
- *Nipples*. One for each bottle with a few spares. Those made of silicone will last longer.
- *A bottle brush and a nipple brush.*

Step-By-Step Preparation

Once you have chosen and brought home the formula, follow these easy steps to prepare it to feed your baby:

- Always wash your hands before preparing baby's formula and bottles, to prevent infection.
- Use bottles, caps, and nipples that have been washed in clean water and dishwashing soap or detergent, or in the dishwasher if you have one. (You may wash them with the family dishes). If you wash them by hand, use a bottle brush. Squeeze water through the nipple holes to be sure that they are open. Rinse well to remove all detergent, and let them stand in a rack to dry. (Check the package to see if they should be boiled before you use them the first time.)
- When you are ready to feed your baby, clean the top of the formula can (if the formula you've chosen is canned) with soap and water. Rinse.
- Open the can with a clean punch-type opener.
- Using the directions that came with the formula, pour it into the bottle. *Mix it with water if it is a concentrate or*

powder. Use only fresh water directly from the cold-water tap.
- Put on the nipple and cap.
- No warming is necessary. Babies can take cold formula, although they may prefer it warm when they are young.
- Try to feed your baby with the formula within 30 minutes of the time you make it. If it isn't used up within about an hour, throw it away and start again *with a clean bottle*.
- Keep any opened can of liquid formula covered in the refrigerator (powdered formula does not need to be kept cold until it is mixed with water).

If You Use Water from a Well

If you use water from a well instead of a community water supply, you should have it tested to make sure that it is safe before you use it for your baby. Call your local health department—they may test it or tell you how to find a company that will do it for you.

If your well water is not pure (or if you are not sure), you may choose to breastfeed or use ready-to-use formula. If you use powdered or concentrated formula, you will need to take a few extra steps to make the water safe for your baby:

- *Boil* each day's supply of water for 20 minutes.
- Pour the boiling water into a clean jar (that has been boiled or washed in a dishwasher).
- Be sure to cool the water before you use it.
- Keep the jar covered in the refrigerator for use in making formula.
- Wash the jar daily.

Note: If someone else will be feeding your baby, make sure he or she knows know exactly how to prepare the formula. Adding water when you don't need it and not adding water when you do can hurt your baby.

Source: *Infant Care* (1989). Prepared by the Bureau of Maternal and Child Health and Resources Development for the Public Health Service.

Food for Thought

The sense of taste is well developed at birth. Newborns can taste the difference between milk, water, and other liquids; and a baby's enthusiasm for various liquids can be observed by watching his or her sucking response. A baby will suck harder and longer when she or he prefers the taste.

You may be trying to decide whether to breastfeed or bottlefeed your baby. Breastfeeding has some real advantages—no formulas to fuss with, and the baby is getting a natural, nutritional food. It also gives the baby the close body contact she or he enjoys. But not all mothers can or want to breastfeed. For years babies have been flourishing on the bottle. Some mothers get their hearts set on breastfeeding and then for some reason they cannot breastfeed. Disappointment and guilt can result, which is

really too bad because it isn't necessary to breastfeed to be a good mother. Just as long as a baby is held lovingly and securely and is fed according to the doctor's directions, he or she will be well nourished—both physically and emotionally.

A baby is also sensitive to temperature, but, interestingly, it isn't necessary to heat food to make it palatable, nourishing, or digestible. Most doctors now believe that room-temperature formula is just as beneficial and acceptable as warm. It is not the warmth of the food that is important to a baby's development but rather the emotional warmth given her or him during the feeding.

Source: *Stimulating Baby Senses*, by Marilyn Sargent, in consultation with National Institute of Mental Health scientists (1978). Part of the Caring About Kids series. For more from this pamphlet, see COMMUNICATION SKILLS AND DISORDERS, MOTOR SKILLS, SENSORY MODES, and VISUAL SKILLS.

Infants are generally fed solely on formula for the first six months or so. Then some SOLID FOODS—at first not literally solids but usually cooked cerals and purées—should be added to the diet. (For help and further information, see FORMULA; MILK, including HUMAN MILK VS. FORMULA AND OTHER MILKS; BREASTFEEDING; FEEDING; NUTRITION; SOLID FOODS.)

For help and further information

National Center for Education in Maternal and Child Health (NCEMCH), 202-625-8400, and **National Maternal and Child Health Clearinghouse (NMCHC)**, 202-625-8410. (For full group information, see PREGNANCY.)

botulism   Rare but often fatal form of poisoning that results from eating food contaminated with the bacterium *Clostridium botulinium*. In adults, botulism is rare and most often results from improperly canned or preserved foods. But infants can contract botulism if the bacteria enter the body in water or some other foods (notably honey, which should not be fed to infants) or through injury that breaks the skin. The bacteria then grow in the intestinal system, producing their poison (toxin) that attacks and paralyzes the NERVOUS SYSTEM, which affects breathing. One early symptom of the infection is hypotonia, or floppy muscles. Other symptoms include difficulty swallowing or speaking, nausea, VOMITING, and double vision. Untreated, more than two out of three people will die from botulism; early treatment with an antitoxin can lower that rate, but recovery will be slow.

For help and further information

National Institute of Allergy and Infectious Diseases (NIAID), 301-496-5717. (For full group information, see ALLERGY.)

bowel problems   Alternative name for some kinds of DIGESTIVE DISORDERS, including INFLAMMATORY BOWEL DISEASE.

bowlegs   Popular term for GENU VARUM.

BPD   Abbreviation for bronchopulmonary dysplasia, a condition related to RESPIRATORY DISTRESS SYNDROME.

braces   A common type of ORTHOPEDIC DEVICE; also a type of orthodontic device used for children (see TEETH).

brachytherapy   Alternate name for interstitial radiation.

Bradley method   A popular form of natural or PREPARED CHILDBIRTH.

bradycardia   Slow heartbeat, a symptom found in various serious ailments, including PERINATAL ASPHYXIA.

Braille   A system of raised dots used to represent letters, numbers, musical symbols, and the like, used to allow blind or visually impaired people to read. (For information on where and how to find Braille materials, and to learn how to read Braille, see the various organizations under EYE AND VISION DISORDERS.)

brain and brain disorders   The brain is the command center of the body that, with the spinal cord and the network of nerves that feed information to and from every part of the body, controls every voluntary and involuntary reaction we make; it is an amazingly complex and delicate system subject to a variety of diseases and injuries.

The brain itself has three main parts:

1. The *brain stem*, which connects the spinal cord and the brain, controls key functions such as heartbeat and breathing, and is the source for the important cranial nerves that serve the eyes, ears, mouth, and other areas of the face and throat. A person in a COMA, with substantial damage to various parts of the brain, may continue to breathe if the lower part of the brain stem is still functioning. If the brain stem totally ceases to function, physicians conclude that BRAIN DEATH has occurred.

2. The *cerebrum*, the largest part of the brain, is made up of billions of nerve cells and is divided into two hemispheres, each containing a central cavity, or VENTRICLE, filled with CEREBROSPINAL FLUID (CSF). The cerebrum is where most conscious and "thoughtful" activities occur. In relation to thesenses or to motor activities, the left half of the brain generally controls the right side of the body and vice versa. For most people—right-handers and many left-handers— the so-called left brain is DOMINANT; this is the hemisphere that focuses on word comprehension, language, speech, and numbers. The right brain focuses more on spatial relationships and feelings. Some parts of the cerebrum focus on quite specific functions, such as seeing, hearing, or smelling; if these parts are damaged, the senses they serve may be dulled or lost. Other activities, such as memory, are carried on more generally and in both halves of the brain.

3. The *cerebellum*, the second-largest portion of the brain, is connected to the brain stem and lies underneath the cerebrum. The cerebellum controls many subconscious activities, especially those involving balance and coordination of movement. Among the disorders that are linked with disease or damage to the cerebellum are ATAXIA, DYSARTHRIA, and NYSTAGMUS. *Medulloblastoma*, a BRAIN TUMOR common in children, grows in the cerebellum.

Covering the brain is a membrane called the *meninges*. The brain itself is housed in a rigid bony skull or cranium, which provides protection but little room for expansion; as a result any injury or disease that causes inflammation can readily cause damage, as the brain swells and presses against its casing.

The brain can be damaged in a number of different ways, among them:

- GENETIC DISORDERS, including CHROMOSOMAL ABNORMALITIES, that affect the brain. Among the common results are MENTAL RETARDATION, as in DOWN'S SYNDROME or Tay-Sachs disease (see LIPID STORAGE DISEASES); structural defects, such as a very small head (*microcephaly*), ANENCEPHALY (absence of a brain), and HYDROCEPHALUS (water on the brain); and degeneration of brain tissue, as in HUNTINGTON'S CHOREA.

- infection and resulting inflammation, especially ENCEPHALITIS (inflammation of the brain) and MENINGITIS (inflammation of the meninges), sometimes as part of another disease, such as MEASLES or CHICKEN POX.

- lack of blood and the vital oxygen it provides to the brain cells. Many children suffer HYPOXIA (lack of oxygen) during CHILDBIRTH, drowning, SLEEP APNEA, or CHOKING; among the resulting conditions are CEREBRAL PALSY and probably LEARNING DISABILITIES.
- TUMORS, or abnormal growths in or around the brain, whether benign or malignant. (See BRAIN TUMOR.)
- degeneration of nerve or brain tissue, often for unknown causes, as in MULTIPLE SCLEROSIS and Alzheimer's disease.

Many kinds of MENTAL DISORDERS, SLEEP DISORDERS, and EATING DISORDERS are clearly linked with brain functioning, but how and why they occur is unknown. In many cases, as with DEPRESSION and SCHIZOPHRENIA, physicians believe that the underlying cause is related to disorders in the brain chemistry; such diseases are sometimes called *organic brain syndromes*. Misfunctions of the brain can also cause SEIZURES, as in EPILEPSY.

The billions of cells in the brain pass information by means of tiny electrical impulses; these can be measured by an ELECTROENCEPHALOGRAPH (EEG), which depicts electrical activity in the brain. Physical damage to or abnormalities in the brain and surrounding structures can be "seen" through various imaging techniques, such as the CT SCAN and MRI. In checking for signs of bleeding or infection, a physician may perform a LUMBAR PUNCTURE, to sample cerebrospinal fluid. (For help and further information, see specific diseases or disorders; EPILEPSY; HEAD INJURY; BRAIN TUMOR; SPINAL CORD INJURIES; MEDICAL TESTS.)

For help and further information

National Institute of Neurological Disorders and Stroke (NINDS)
9000 Rockville Pike
Building 31, Room 8A06
Bethesda, MD 20892
301-496-5751
Federal arm, one of the National Institutes of Health, focusing on the brain and related disorders. Publishes various materials for public and health professionals.

Other reference sources

The Brain: A User's Manual, by the Diagram Group. New York: Berkley, 1983.
Feeding the Brain: How Foods Affect Children, by C. Keith Conners. New York: Plenum, 1989.
The Brain and Nervous System, revised edition, by Steve Parker. New York: Watts, 1990. For young readers.
The Brain: What It Is, What It Does, by Ruth Dowling Bruun and Bertel Bruun. New York: Greenwillow, 1989. For children grades 2 to 3 but may be useful for older children as well; includes material on how drugs and alcohol affect the brain.

brain death Total cessation of all activity in the brain, generally measured by lack of electrical signals on ELECTROENCEPHALOGRAPH readings taken over a period of at least 12 to 24 hours, even though heart and lungs may still continue to function (with machine assistance). The time period is important, because some conditions, such as some kinds of poisoning or drug reactions, can suppress brain activity. Brain death (sometimes called irreversible COMA) has been variously defined and interpreted in different states and settings, but generally the patient has ceased to have reflexes, movements, and independent breathing. The definition of DEATH has become important in several areas, notably the question of whether a patient should be maintained in a VENTILATOR and whether the patient's organs might be used for transplants. Often organs for TRANSPLANTS are taken after the brain is dead but while the heart and lungs are still functioning, since blood supply to organs is important if the transplant is to have the best chance to succeed. (For help and further information, see BRAIN AND BRAIN DISORDERS; DEATH.)

brain tumor A TUMOR that occurs in or around the brain, either malignant or benign. Among children, *primary brain tumors*, which originate in the brain itself, are most common, and they are the second most common cause of CANCER death in children under 15 years old. Less common are *secondary brain tumors*, which arise from malignant cells originating elsewhere.

The causes of brain tumors are unclear, but GENETIC INHERITANCE, environmental agents, and viruses are among the many possibilities being investigated. The size and growth of tumors is affected by some events; they often increase during a PREGNANCY, for example, probably as a result of HORMONE stimulation.

Among the most common types of brain tumors affecting children are:

- *medulloblastoma*: a rapidly growing, invasive, malignant tumor of the *cerebellum*, the part of the brain governing balance and coordination of movement. Medulloblastomas tend to spread to other parts of the body, through the CEREBROSPINAL FLUID in the CENTRAL NERVOUS SYSTEM. Treatment may include surgery—complete if the tumor's location is favorable but partial otherwise—followed by radiation therapy and sometimes chemotherapy.
- *astrocytoma*: a tumor of the brain (glial) tissue, either benign or malignant. Severe tumors (Grade III—see TUMOR for grading system) are called *anaplastic astrocytomas*; even more severe forms are sometimes called *glioblastomas*. Treatment may include surgery—complete if the tumor's location is favorable but partial otherwise—followed by radiation therapy and sometimes chemotherapy.
- *glioblastoma (glioblastoma multiforme, or GBM)*: a malignant Grade IV tumor, the most common and most destructive type of brain tumor; a name given to the most serious astrocytomas. Because of their varied, invasive, and spreading nature, glioblastomas are more difficult to treat surgically

and to control through radiation and chemotherapy than many other tumors.

- *ependymoma*: a benign or malignant tumor deep inside the brain, generally in the region of the cerebellum and the small central VENTRICLE and so usually not fully treatable by surgery. Treatment may include radiation therapy, SHUNTS to relieve fluid pressure on the brain, and sometimes chemotherapy.
- *craniopharyngioma*: a benign, cystlike tumor that may appear in various parts of the brain region. It may be removed completely if it is in a favorable location; if not, radiation therapy is often used.

Symptoms of brain tumors vary widely depending on the location of the tumor, its size, and how fast it is growing; and because symptoms are so general, they may seem to be indicative of other disorders, so brain tumors are not readily diagnosed until other possibilities are eliminated. Among the most common symptoms experienced are:

- ATAXIA, or lack of coordination
- persistent VOMITING
- weakness of the facial muscles
- *dysphagia*, or difficulty in swallowing
- DYSARTHRIA, or difficulty in speaking
- EYE AND VISION PROBLEMS, such as NYSTAGMUS or STRABISMUS
- tilting of the head
- HEADACHE
- drowsiness
- EAR AND HEARING PROBLEMS
- PARALYSIS or weakness (*paresis*) on one side of the body (*hemiparesis*)
- personality changes

The nature of some symptoms, such as loss of vision in one eye or paralysis of a particular area of the body, can give physicians an early clue to the location of a possible tumor.

A wide variety of medical tests can be used to diagnose brain tumors, including MYELOGRAM, ANGIOGRAM, brain scans (such as CT SCANS, MRI IMAGING, and PET SCAN), LUMBAR PUNCTURE (spinal tap), ELECTROENCEPHALOGRAPH (EEG), and BIOPSY.

For help and further information

Association for Brain Tumor Research (AFBTR)
2910 West Montrose Avenue
Chicago, IL 60618
312-286-5571
Hal Jenkins, President
Organization dedicated to combatting brain tumors. Sponsors mutual-support self-help groups for patients with brain tumors, their families, and concerned health professionals; supports research; provides information and referrals; publishes various materials, including booklet *A Primer of Brain Tumors* (fourth edition, 1988), bibliography *Living With a Brain Tumor*, and booklets on specific topics, such as *When Your Child Is Ready to Return to School, Shunts, Coping with a Brain Tumor, About Medulloblastoma, About Meningiomas, About Glioblastoma Multiforme and Malignant Astrocytoma*, and *About Oligodendroglioma*.

Friends of Brain Tumor Research
2169 Union Street
San Francisco, CA 94123
415-563-0466
Organization that encourages formation of mutual-support self-help groups. Publishes various materials, including quarterly newsletter and *Resource Guide*.

Brain Tumor Foundation for Children
751 DeKalb Industrial Way
Decatur, GA 30033
414-292-3536
Organization that sponsors local support groups. Publishes newsletter for parents of children with brain tumors.

National Institute of Neurological Disorders and Stroke (NINDS), 301-496-5751. (For full group information, see BRAIN AND BRAIN DISORDERS.)

National Cancer Institute (NCI), 800-4-CANCER [422-6237]. (For full group information, see CANCER.)

Epilepsy Foundation of America, 301-459-3700. Publishes various materials on epilepsy, including some on seizures and medications common to children with brain tumors. (See EPILEPSY.)

Other reference sources

Health Care U.S.A., by Jean Carper. New York: Prentice Hall, 1987. Resource for general and specific health-care information, including different types of cancers; lists sources of up-to-date information on cancer treatments and major centers for treatment or research, including experimental psychological cancer therapy; provides list of children's cancer specialists and other information.

Brainstorm, by Karen Osney Brownstein. New York: Avon, 1984.

Death Be Not Proud, by John Gunther. New York: Perennial Library, 1949.

13 Is Too Young to Die, by Isaacsen-Bright. Worthington, OH: Willowisp, 1989. For ages 9 and up. Girl learns she has terminal brain tumor.

Learning About Tumors, by Joy Johnson and Marv Johnson. Omaha, NE: Centering Corporation, 1981. Address: P.O. Box 3367, Omaha, NE 68103. For children up to age 7.

(For help and further information, see TUMORS; CANCER; DEATH; also HELP FOR SPECIAL CHILDREN, including *Wishes for Terminally Ill Children*, on page 578.)

Braxton-Hicks contractions Medical name for false LABOR.

breaking of the bag of waters In PREGNANCY, the breaking of the sac holding the AMNIOTIC FLUID that protects the baby, generally just before the onset of LABOR.

breastfeeding Feeding a newborn on human MILK from a mother's BREASTS, the natural and traditional method of feeding infants. Breast milk is produced in response to a variety of HORMONES but especially prolactin, which is produced by the PITUITARY GLAND in response to the infant's SUCKING on the breast and so is maintained as long as nursing continues.

Breastfeeding has a significant number of advantages, as summarized in the Public Health Service's publication *Infant Care*:

- Mother's milk normally has just the right amount of the right nutrients to help the baby grow, with no worry about whether it is "too rich" or "too thin."
- It is easy for the baby's immature system to digest.
- Mother's milk contains ANTIBODIES that give the baby a temporary IMMUNIZATION protecting against viruses and bacteria.
- Breastfeeding lessens the likelihood that a child will later develop an ALLERGY.
- Mother's milk is clean, uncontaminated, and served at the right temperature.
- Mother's milk is ready when the baby is hungry, needing no equipment, preparation, or cleanup.
- Breastfeeding is inexpensive and costs less than BOTTLEFEEDING with FORMULA.
- Mother's milk is the only food a baby needs for the first four to six months.
- Breastfeeding uses some of the extra fat stored for this purpose in the body during PREGNANCY and so helps mothers to lose weight.
- Breastfeeding also helps the UTERUS resume its normal size more quickly.
- Breastfeeding helps with BONDING, the building of the special emotional and physical relationship between mother and child.

Given this array of advantages, it is no wonder that many doctors and clinics recommend that mothers breastfeed their children if possible.

According to the Public Health Service, over half of all babies now born in the United States are breastfed. Breastfeeding is not an automatic choice, however. In a world where many mothers return to work outside the home soon after giving birth, breastfeeding requires very special kinds of arrangements, such as special CHILD-CARE arrangements at work so that the baby can be breastfed periodically through the day or use of a BREAST PUMP to extract milk from the breast, which can then be stored and fed to the baby in a bottle later by others while the mother is gone. Parents need to explore the pros and cons of breastfeeding versus bottlefeeding as part of their preparation for the new child, to be prepared before the child arrives.

Breastfeeding, though natural, needs to be learned. Before the birth, prospective mothers will want to gather information on breastfeeding, from organizations like those below, from LACTATION SPECIALISTS, and also from friends or relatives who have recently breastfed a baby and can give practical advice on getting started. BREASTFEEDING: TIPS FOR FIRST-TIME MOTHERS should also help.

Not all women who choose to breastfeed are able to do so. Various problems can occur. Breastfeeding mothers can develop breast infections (*mastitis*), which can sometimes be treated early enough for nursing to continue. Sometimes, despite the mother's having followed dietary recommendations, the milk supply seems inadequate; this can sometimes be remedied by nursing the baby more often to stimulate the body to produce more milk. The baby may develop breastmilk JAUNDICE and need to be taken temporarily off breastfeeding. Some babies also have physical problems, such as CLEFT LIP AND PALATE, that make nursing difficult to impossible. Some mothers also find that breastfeeding conflicts with their sexual image or requires too great a time commitment in their busy schedules. These mothers may turn to bottlefeeding, either temporarily or permanently. If they wish to resume breastfeeding, they need to continue to express the milk during the days when the baby is on the bottle, to maintain milk production.

Breastfeeding: Tips for First-Time Mothers

Following these steps may help first-time new mothers to get started breastfeeding:

- It helps you and the baby learn how to breastfeed if you begin in the first few hours after birth when the baby is alert.
- Find a chair that is comfortable for you and your baby, such as a chair with arms, a footstool, and a pillow.
- Hold your baby comfortably across your lap, with his or her head in the crook of your arm, so that his or her mouth directly faces your nipple. Tuck the baby's arms out of the way so they don't get between the baby's

mouth and your nipple. Support your breast with your thumb *above* the areola (the dark part of the breast) and the rest of your fingers *below* the areola, out of the way of your baby's mouth.
- Touch your baby's cheek or lower lip with your nipple to start. The baby will open his or her mouth wider, and the tongue will move downward [see ROOTING REFLEX]. Once this happens, move your baby quickly onto your breast.
- Allow the baby to grasp the dark-colored part of the breast in his or her mouth. Your baby gets milk by pressing the areola with tongue, gums, and cheek, as well as by suction. The baby's grasp on your nipple should not

Continued on page 65

hurt if the baby is properly attached to your breast. (The baby's nose should be pressed against the breast. Even though his or her nose appears buried, your baby should be able to breathe easily. If there is a problem, press lightly on your breast to move it away from the baby's nose and make breathing easier.)

- When you want to stop nursing, break the suction by putting your finger in the corner of your baby's mouth, between the gums. This will help prevent sore nipples.
- Feed the baby at both breasts. You will probably nurse your baby for at least 10 to 20 minutes per side, about every two to three hours or *more often* during the first several weeks. If you finish feeding on the right breast, start the next feeding on the left breast. Alternate breasts in this way each time you feed your baby. It is normal for newborns to eat 8 to 12 or more times every 24 hours. This need to eat so often may taper off after several months.
- Because there is a tighter seal between the baby's mouth and your nipple than there is with a bottle, breastfed babies do not swallow as much air. That means that they do not need to burp as much after feeding. Still, you should try to burp your baby halfway through and again when your baby is finished eating by placing him or her on your shoulder and patting gently on the back until you hear a burp.
- If you have less milk than your baby seems to want, try nursing more often. This will increase your supply of milk, usually within three to four days.

Advice and practice are the best ways to learn to breastfeed. If you have questions or need help after you leave the hospital, find someone who is experienced and sympathetic to teach you. Most obstetric and nursery nurses are good helpers. Other mothers who have breastfed their babies and enjoyed it can help you and provide valuable support. "Lactation specialists" may be available in many areas, as are chapters of the La Leche League. In many communities mothers have organized La Leche League chapters or other groups especially to help new mothers with breastfeeding. Your doctor, clinic, hospital staff, or other mothers should be able to help you find such a group.

Your breasts need to be cleaned only with plain water, which may be done during your daily shower or bath. Keep yourself rested, well nourished, and relaxed, if possible. You will need to drink more liquids (8 to 12 glasses daily) and eat more protein and some extra calories when you are nursing. Be sure you eat at least three servings of lean meat, fish, poultry, eggs, dried beans or peas each day (for protein), with four glasses of milk or servings of cheese or yogurt (for calcium.) Fruits, juices, and green, leafy vegetables will give you extra vitamins and minerals. [For help and more information, see DIET FOR PREGNANT AND NURSING WOMEN and NUTRITIONAL NEEDS OF PREGNANT AND LACTATING WOMEN under NUTRITION.]

There are no special foods that will insure successful breastfeeding. Likewise, there is no basis for avoiding garlic, curry, strong-flavored vegetables, or any other nourishing food. Remember, it takes several hours for a food flavor to appear in your milk. If a particular food seems to cause you or your baby discomfort, omit that food to see if it is the cause. Do not use alcohol, drugs, or cigarettes. Ask your doctor, nurse, or pharmacist before you take any medicines.

Most women find that a good nursing bra (one with wide straps and good support that opens easily for feeding) makes breastfeeding easier and more comfortable. Many women even wear a nursing bra during their last weeks of pregnancy.

Milk may leak from your breasts between feedings. Place a small, clean absorbent pad in your bra, and change it as necessary, to keep your nipples dry and clean.

If your entire breast becomes swollen and painful, try letting your baby nurse more often. Also try warm towels or a warm shower, massaging milk from the edges of your breast toward the nipple, and expressing some milk to make yourself more comfortable.

Early signs of breast infection include a tender, red area as well as symptoms like the flu: body aches, headache, nausea, and fever. If any of these symptoms appear, contact your doctor or clinic promptly.

Sometimes it may be necessary to be away from your baby for one or more feedings. If you want to continue fully breastfeeding, you should express your milk either by hand or by using a breast pump during the time when your baby would normally feed. You can save breastmilk and have it fed to your baby while you are away—it can safely be left at room temperature for 40 minutes, in the refrigerator for 48 hours, or in your freezer for up to three months. Store it in a sterile glass or a hard plastic container (such as a bottle) or a disposable bottle. If the milk is cooled or frozen, bring it to room temperature by placing it in warm water. Don't heat breastmilk in a microwave or over boiling water.

If you are away from your baby and facilities aren't available for you to keep your expressed breastmilk, you may need to discard it. Or, if you can't express your milk, nurse your baby as soon as you get home.

Breastfeeding is recommended as the only food for baby for the first four to six months. After this time, other foods are added, while breastfeeding may continue through the first year or longer. In addition to being the most healthful way of feeding your baby, it will help mother and baby develop a special bond, or closeness. Remember, breastfeeding is *learned* by you and your baby. Don't get discouraged. Soon you and your baby will be on the way to a pleasing and successful breastfeeding experience.

Source: *Infant Care* (1989). Prepared by the Bureau of Maternal and Child Health and Resources Development for the Public Health Service.

If, for whatever reason, breastfeeding is stopped early, doctors recommend infant formula as the best substitute, and parents may want to be prepared with at least minimal provisions for BOTTLEFEEDING in case of problems. The Public Health Service suggests, however, that parents can give whole (not skim) cow's milk to babies instead, if they

- are more than six months old;
- are eating a variety of solids or spoon foods, including cereals, vegetables, and fruits; or
- are eating the equivalent of 1½ jars of baby food a day.

In any case, after about six months, the baby needs more than breastmilk or formula and should begin taking SOLID FOODS. (For help and further information, see below; see also MILK; BOTTLEFEEDING; FORMULA; SOLID FOODS.)

For help and further information

La Leche League International (LLLI)
9616 Minneapolis
P.O. Box 1209
Franklin Park, IL 60131
312-455-7730
Betty Wagner, Executive Director
International network of groups of women dedicated to breastfeeding babies. Trains group leaders and maintains libraries and resource centers; operates telephone reference service; publishes many materials, including general brochures such as *When You Breastfeed Your Baby, Does Breastfeeding Take Too Much Time?, The Breastfeeding Father, Breastfeeding after a Cesarean Birth, Nutrition and Breastfeeding, Positioning Your Baby at the Breast, Increasing Your Milk, Preparing Your Nipples, Establishing Your Milk Supply, Manual Expression of Breast-Milk—Marmet Technique, Medications for the Nursing Mother,* and *Legal Rights of Breastfeeding Mothers, USA Scene*; brochures for families in special situations, such as *Nursing My Baby with a Cleft of the Soft Palate, The Diabetic Mother and Breastfeeding, Breastfeeding the Baby with Down Syndrome, Breastfeeding Your Premature Baby, Allergies in Breastfed Babies, Nursing Your Adopted Baby, Nursing Siblings Who Are Not Twins,* and *Breastfeeding Rights Packet* for mothers whose continued breastfeeding is threatened by legal situations, such as divorce or custody; and books such as *A Practical Guide to Breastfeeding, The Womanly Art of Breastfeeding, Nighttime Parenting, Of Cradles and Careers: A Guide to Reshaping Your Job to Include a Baby in Your Life, Drugs in Pregnancy and Lactation, Breastfeeding and Drugs in Human Milk, Mothering Your Nursing Toddler, Mothering Multiples: Breastfeeding and Caring for Twins,* and *A Special Find of Parenting: Meeting the Needs of Handicapped Children,* plus various products to aid breastfeeding, such as the breast pump and breast shield.

National Center for Education in Maternal and Child Health (NCEMCH), 202-625-8400. Publishes many materials, including *Breastfeeding: Catalog of Products from Projects Supported by the Bureau of Maternal and Child Health and Resources Development. (For full group information, see* PREGNANCY.)

National Maternal and Child Health Clearinghouse (NMCHC), 202-625-8410. (For full group information, see PREGNANCY.)

Human Lactation Center (HLC)
666 Sturges Highway
Westport, CT 06880
203-259-5995
Dana Raphael, Director
Organization encouraging breastfeeding of babies. Conducts international research on lactation and consults with government and industry groups on nutrition for infants and mothers; maintains library and museum; publishes various materials.

International Association of Parents and Professionals for Safe Alternatives in Childbirth (NAPSAC), 314-238-2010. (For full group information, see CHILDBIRTH.)

Lactaid Hotline, 800-257-8650.

Other reference sources
Will It Hurt the Baby? The Safe Use of Medications During Pregnancy and Breastfeeding, by Richard S. Abrams, M.D. Reading, MA: Addison-Wesley, 1990.
Women's Experience of Breast Feeding, by Heather Maclean. Cheektowaga, NY: University of Toronto Press, 1990.
Nursing Your Baby, revised edition, by Karen Pryor, edited by Jane Chelius. New York: Harper & Row, 1990.
Breastfeeding Your Baby, by Sheila Kitzinger. New York: Knopf, 1989.
Bestfeeding, by Mary Renfrew, Chloe Fisher, and Suzanne Arms. Berkeley, CA: Celestial, 1989.
Breastfeeding Your Baby: A Practical Guide for the New Mother, 3rd edition, by Nursing Mothers' Council of the Boston Association for Childbirth Education. Garden City Park, NY: Avery, 1989.
Nursing Your Baby, by Karen Pryor. New York: Harper & Row, 1963; Pocket, 1973.

breastmilk jaundice   A yellowish discoloration of the skin, mucous membrane, and the "whites" of the eye, a symptom of HYPERBILIRUBINEMIA, which appears for unknown causes in some infants who are BREASTFEEDING. See JAUNDICE.

breast pump   A device used to draw, or *express*, milk out of the BREASTS, as when a BREASTFEEDING mother is going to be away from her baby for a few hours and wants to store some milk for the baby to have while she is away or on return. The breast pump may also be used to relieve pressure when the breasts are too full. The device is simple: a rubber suction cup is placed over the nipple and an attached rubber bulb, which is pumped (by hand or electricity) to draw out milk to go into the connected glass or plastic bottle. Women who use breast pumps should be sure that all parts are carefully sterilized before use. (For help and further information, including how and how long to store breastmilk safely, see BREASTFEEDING.)

Breast Self-Examination

The purpose of the breast self-examination is to identify any changes in the way the breasts look and feel. It is best performed at about the same time each month, preferably after a period, so that the body will be at about the same stage of the menstrual cycle and any abnormalities can be most easily detected.

The woman should first stand or sit in front of a mirror with arms down at her sides, then with each arm raised in turn, in each position looking for any changes in the shape, size, or appearance of the skin, including any kinds of moles or other marks, or edema (fluid buildup). Still standing or sitting, the woman should then feel the breast surface for any peculiarities and squeeze the nipple to test for soreness and discharge.

In the second stage of the examination, she should lie on her back with a pillow under shoulders and head. With her left arm down at her side, she should move the fingers of her flat-open right hand in a circular direction around the nipple of the left breast, working slowly outward in ever-widening circles, feeling for lumps or any other kind of abnormality. She should then raise her left arm over her head and repeat the procedure on the same breast, extending the circular feeling (in medical terms, *palpation*) up to the collarbone and into the armpit. She should then repeat this whole second stage on the other breast. Any abnormality should be reported to the doctor immediately, since if detected early enough, breast cancer can be treated effectively, before it has spread.

---

breasts (mammary glands) A pair of hemispheric structures on the chest of mature females, composed largely of fatty tissue, surrounding 15 to 20 milk-secreting glands (physiologically modified sweat glands), with milk funneled into the nipple in the middle. Children and men have undeveloped breasts. Under some conditions, as when taking female HORMONES, a child's or male's breasts can develop a condition called GYNECOMASTIA; newborns may also sometimes have enlarged breasts, in response to the mother's hormones, and may even produce breastmilk, popularly called WITCH'S MILK.

At PUBERTY, a girl's breasts begin to swell, with the nipple and the *areola* (the brownish area around the nipple) both enlarging. Breasts are key SECONDARY SEX CHARACTERISTICS that develop with the onset of sexual maturity, and their sensitivity is closely associated with sexual pleasure. The size and shape of the breasts vary widely from person to person, though the left one is slightly larger than the right. During PREGNANCY, the breasts prepare to meet their main physiological function when the hormones ESTROGEN and PROGESTERONE activate the milk-producing glands and cause the whole breast, including the nipple, to enlarge.

The main disorders affecting breasts are those of adult women. Nursing mothers sometimes may develop *mastitis*, or

inflammation of the breast. TUMORS are common, especially between ages 30 and 50; some of these are benign, but many malignant. In fact, breast cancer is the most common kind of CANCER in women and is a main cause of death for women in this age group. On rare occasions breast cancer also occurs in males, especially those with KLINEFELTER'S SYNDROME. Increased risk of cancer is associated with women who have early MENARCHE (onset of MENSTRUATION) and late MENOPAUSE (cessation of menstruation); have their first child in their late 20s or 30s; have a family history of breast cancer; have a personal history of benign tumors; are tall and heavy (as opposed to short and thin); and have a diet high in FATS. It is unclear what effect, if any, the BIRTH-CONTROL PILL has on the risk of breast cancer.

Sexually mature women of whatever age can best protect themselves by conducting regular breast self-examinations—and can best protect their female children by teaching them the procedure during their teens (see BREAST SELF-EXAMINATION, at left). *Mammography*, a type of X-RAY using minimal RADIATION and therefore posing little risk, is recommended for adult women; they should check with their doctor as to the periodicity, depending on their particular history.

For help and further information

National Institute of Child Health and Human Development (NICHD), 301-496-5133. (For full group information, see PREGNANCY.)

National Cancer Institute (NCI), 301-496-5583. Publishes *Breast Exams: What You Should Know* and *Questions and Answers About Breast Lumps*. (For full group information, see CANCER.)

Other reference sources

Your Breasts: A Complete Guide, by Jerome Levy, M.D., with Diana Odell Potter. New York: Noonday Press/Farrar, Straus & Giroux, 1990.

Dr. Susan Love's Breast Book, by Susan M. Love, M.D., with Karen Lindsey. Reading, MA: Addison-Wesley, 1990.

breathing problems Difficulties with the system that takes oxygen from the air and passes it on to the bloodstream, subject to a variety of LUNG AND BREATHING DISORDERS.

breech presentation A type of FETAL PRESENTATION in which the FETUS is buttocks or feet first.

Brigance® Diagnostic Inventory of Early Development An individually administered test that attempts to measure general development in children under age six. The test includes a variety of paper-and-pencil, oral-response, and direct-observations sections, focusing on MOTOR SKILLS, SELF-HELP SKILLS, communication skills (see COMMUNICATION SKILLS AND DISORDERS), general knowledge and comprehension, and academic skills, with the tasks arranged in the order in which such skills are generally developed. The resulting SCORES are given in terms of DEVELOPMENTAL AGE. The Brigance Inventory is widely used as a READINESS

TEST and a DEVELOPMENTAL SCREENING TEST, especially in diagnosing DEVELOPMENTAL DELAYS and developing INDIVIDUALIZED EDUCATION PROGRAMS, with the student often being tested periodically to monitor development. Other Brigance tests may also be used for screening. (For help and further information, see TESTS.)

brittle bone disease Alternate name for OSTEOGENESIS IMPERFECTA.

broken family A FAMILY that has been split, as through divorce or separation.

bronchiectasis Swelling of the bronchial tubes, a kind of LUNG AND BREATHING DISORDER.

bronchitis Inflammation of the bronchial tubes, a kind of LUNG AND BREATHING DISORDER.

bronchopulmonary dysplasia (BPD) Abnormal development of the lungs, a condition related to RESPIRATORY DISTRESS SYNDROME.

Brown v. Board of Education A landmark court case regarding SEGREGATION in the schools.

Brudzinski's sign Involuntary flexing in a patient's limbs and hips when the head is flexed; a sign that generally indicates the existence of MENINGITIS.

bruise Popular name for a HEMORRHAGE underneath the skin.

bruxism Grinding of TEETH, especially at night. A bad bite, or MALOCCLUSION, can cause children to grind their teeth; a dentist may recommend a bite plate to protect the teeth from damage at night or may refer the patient to an ORTHODONTIST to correct the problem. Bruxism can also result from tension or from worms.

Buckley Amendment The popular name for the FAMILY EDUCATIONAL RIGHTS AND PRIVACY ACT OF 1974.

buck teeth Type of MALOCCLUSION in which the jaw and upper front teeth project too far forward.

bulimia (bulimia nervosa) A type of MENTAL DISORDER, psychiatrically classified as an *eating disorder*, that involves binge eating—intake of large amounts of food in a short time—followed by induced VOMITING, use of laxatives, dieting, or fasting, to avoid gaining weight. This is commonly called the *binge–purge cycle*. Binges often take place secretly, with eating pattern quite out of control, and are halted only by abdominal pain, vomiting, sleep, or outside interruption. Sometimes associated with ANOREXIA NERVOSA, bulimia is not, by itself, generally a life-threatening disease. But it wreaks enormous havoc on the body all the same, with stomach acid causing dental decay, persistent vomiting sometimes causing tears and ruptures in the stomach and esophagus, and disturbance of the body's ELECTROLYTES and DEHYDRATION leading to severe physical problems, including heart irregularities, which can sometimes trigger death. The disorder usually occurs in adolescence or early adulthood, more among females than males, and may persist for years. As with anorexia nervosa, the causes are unknown.

For help and further information

Bulimia Nervosa, by James Mitchell. Minneapolis: University of Minnesota, 1989.

Food Addiction: The Body Knows, by Kay Sheppard. Deerfield Beach, FL: Health Communications, 1989. On food addiction as a disease.

Compulsive Eating, by Donna LeBlanc. Deerfield Beach, FL: Health Communications, 1990.

Compulsive Eaters and Relationships, by Aphrodite Matsakis. Center City, MN: Hazelden, 1990.

The Psychobiology of Bulimia, J. Hudson and H. Pope, eds. Washington, DC: American Psychiatric Association, 1987.

Bulimia: A Guide to Recovery, by Lindsey Hall and Leigh Cohn. Santa Barbara, CA: Gurze, 1986.

Bulimia: A Systems Approach to Treatment, by Maria Root, Patricia Fallon, and William Friedrich. New York: Norton, 1986.

You Can't Have Your Cake and Eat It Too: A Program for Controlling Bulimia, by Lillie Weiss, Melanie Katzman, and Sharon Wolchik. Saratoga, CA: R & E, 1986.

Bulimarexia: The Binge/Purge Cycle, by Marlene Boskind-White and William C. White, Jr. New York: Norton, 1983.

Bulimia—The Binge-Purge Compulsion, by Janice M. Cauwels. Garden City, NY: Doubleday, 1983.

New Hope for Binge Eaters: Advances in the Understanding of Bulimics, by Harrison G. Pope, Jr., and James I. Hudson. New York: Harper & Row, 1984.

(For organizations and additional references, see also ANOREXIA NERVOSA; MENTAL DISORDERS.)

buphthalmos (ox-eye) A bulging eyeball. (See EYE AND VISION PROBLEMS.)

burns Damage to skin caused by heating above 120°F, which may be caused by heat, hot water, fire, chemicals, electricity, or gases. With their tender skin, children (along with the elderly) are the most vulnerable to burns, most of which occur in the home and are preventable. Though fires are the largest and best-known cause of burns, many burns are caused by simply having the hot-water heater set too high, when children are placed in exceedingly hot water (by mistake or through CHILD ABUSE AND NEGLECT) or accidentally turn on the hot water themselves.

In the 1970s water heaters were often set at 140 to 150 degrees, which (according to the Odessa Brown Children's Clinic in Seattle) could produce third-degree burns in a child in two to five seconds. While the Consumer Product Safety Commission rejected requests to lower the settings to 120°F, many states set such guidelines, resulting in a marked decrease in tap-water burns. Parents may well want to check the temperature setting on their water heaters to be sure it is set at no more than 120°F. Antiscalding devices that turn off too-hot water right at the faucet or shower-head are also for sale.

Burns are classed by their degree of severity. *First-degree burns* are those that involve only the upper layer of the skin, the *epidermis*. For these, the Public Health Service's booklet *Infant Care* recommends:

- Rinse with cold water for 5 to 10 minutes. Don't use ointments or greases.
- Do not break blisters.
- Cover with sterile dressing or clean cloth held in place by a nonadhesive material such as aluminum foil.
- A cold pack made by putting ice cubes in a plastic bag and covering with several layers of cloth may relieve the pain of a fresh burn. Leave in place for about 15 minutes.

In many first-degree burns, such as sunburns, the damaged skin peels away in a few days.

If the burn is caused by lye, oven cleaner, pesticides, or other strong chemicals coming into contact with a baby's skin or eyes, they recommend that it be washed off with "large amounts of water immediately and for a long time"; more specifically:

- Remove any contaminated clothing.
- Place the affected area directly under a faucet, garden hose, or shower and keep rinsing for 15 minutes.
- Use a bottle, cup, or gentle faucet to wash out eyes; keep the eyelids open as much as possible and continue to flush out for at least 30 minutes.
- Call your doctor or clinic immediately.

Second-degree burns, affecting the upper and second layers of the skin, are more serious but may heal without scarring unless widespread. *Third-degree burns* involve all three layers of skin, exposing the body to infection and loss of fluids, which can quickly bring on SHOCK and possibly DEATH unless the patient is given intravenous fluids. Second-degree burns over more than 30 percent of the body or third-degree burns over more than 10 percent can be critical and life-threatening.

If a child has been burned, parents are advised (after dousing the child with water) to cover exposed burned areas with dry, clean, lint-free cloth but not to try to remove clothing stuck to wounds, and then to get medical attention as quickly as possible. Where fire is involved, heated smoke may also cause inflammation of the lungs and damage to the eyes; where electricity is involved, physicians need to check for heart damage.

In a hospital or specialized burn center, a burn victim will be given PARENTERAL NUTRITION, including antibiotics and analgesics (painkillers), and the wounds will be either covered with antibacterial dressing or left exposed in a specially controlled antiseptic setting. Skin grafts and PLASTIC SURGERY may be required, sometimes several operations.

For help and further information

National Institute of General Medical Sciences (NIGMS), 301-496-7301. (For full group information, see ANESTHESIA.)

Shriners Hospital Referral Line (for children under 18), U.S. except FL, 800-237-5055; FL, 800-282-9161.

Phoenix Society
11 Rust Hill Road
Levittown, PA 19056
215-946-4788
Network of mutual-support self-help groups of burn victims and their families. Provides information about burns and prevention of disfigurement; publishes print and audiovisual materials, including newsletter *Icarus File*.

National Burn Victim Foundation
308 Main Street
Orange, NJ 07050
201-731-3112
Organization to aid burn victims; centered in New Jersey but model for programs elsewhere. Sponsors mutual-support self-help groups and educational programs; offers professional counseling, with special programs for burned children; seeks to educate public as to needs of burn victims.

Other reference sources

Coping Strategies for Burn Survivors and Their Families, by Norman R. Bernstein, Alan Jeffry Breslau, and Jean Ann Graham, eds. Westport, CT: Praeger, 1988.
Health Care U.S.A., by Jean Carper. New York: Prentice Hall, 1987. Resource for general and specific health-care information. Lists major burn centers for treatment or research and provides other information.
The Burned Child Book, by John Davis, Jr. (7 years old). Available from North Carolina Memorial Hospital, Chapel Hill, NC 27514.
A Matter of Degree: Heat, Life, and Death, by Lucy Kavaler. New York: Harper & Row, 1981.
Manual of Burn Care, Joan Nicosia and Jane Petro, M.D., eds. New York: Raven, 1982.
See also CHILDPROOFING.

burping The audible return of air from the stomach, called *belching* in an adult. Babies swallow a good deal of air while they are feeding, more during BOTTLEFEEDING than BREASTFEEDING, because the baby's mouth generally fits more closely around the breast. Burping a baby two or three times during a feeding can help reduce the amount of REGURGITATION (spitting up) of food and fluid.

busing In EDUCATION, transporting of schoolchildren who live beyond a certain distance; but in recent decades, longer-distance transporting of children to schools beyond their neighborhood school to achieve racial balance, as part of efforts to achieve DESEGREGATION. Busing has often been mandated by federal courts, and proponents of the approach applaud the judiciary's attempt to provide equality of opportunity to students of all races when schools and other branches of government have failed to do so. Critics, however, charge that court action amounts to government by judiciary, usurping the prerogatives of the legislative and executive branches. On a personal level, some parents openly prefer a segregated school system, while many parents (regardless of their feelings about desegregation) have been concerned about the effect of the disruptive busing on young children, some of whom are transported long distances when they might otherwise have walked to their neighborhood school. As a result, many parents opted out of the PUBLIC SCHOOL system altogether, choosing instead to place their children in PRIVATE SCHOOLS or to try HOME SCHOOLING. In recent years, many school districts have tried alternative approaches to voluntary desegregation instead of involuntary busing; SCHOOLS OF CHOICE, especially MAGNET SCHOOLS, are often key features of such programs. (For help and further information, see EDUCATION; DESEGREGATION.)

C

CA Abbreviation for CHRONOLOGICAL AGE.

café au lait spots "Coffee-with-milk"-colored patches on the skin, sometimes from infancy. Some of these are quite normal and benign, but several appearing at once can be a possible early sign of NEUROFIBROMATOSIS.

calciferol Alternate name for VITAMIN D.

calcification Formation of bone through deposits of CALCIUM, which show up on X-RAYS, including the SKELETAL SURVEYS often done in cases of possible CHILD ABUSE AND NEGLECT. The amount of calcium deposited shows how well a newly broken bone is healing and also marks the location of old healed FRACTURES.

calcium A MINERAL vital to the building and maintenance of strong bones and TEETH, also important in the proper functioning of nerves and muscles, in blood clotting, and in the body's METABOLISM. Calcium is the most abundant mineral in the body and one of the most important elements overall, each adult body having over two pounds of calcium. The most important sources of calcium are milk and other dairy products, eggs, fish (especially sardines and shellfish), green leafy vegetables, dried peas and beans, and fruits (especially citrus fruits). The level of calcium in the blood is controlled by VITAMIN D in the body and by various HORMONES produced by the THYROID GLAND and parathyroid glands. Problems with these glands, kidney problems (see KIDNEY AND UROLOGICAL DISORDERS), lack of sufficient calcium in the diet, and other disorders can lead to calcium deficiency (*hypocalcemia*). In infants this can cause TETANY or RICKETS; in adults, OSTEOMALACIA. Too much calcium can cause harmful calcium deposits in tissue and DEPRESSION. (For help and further information, see MINERALS; NUTRITION; VITAMIN D; LACTATION.)

calendar method A technique of NATURAL FAMILY PLANNING.

California Achievement Tests (CAT) A series of group-administered, paper-and-pencil tests used to assess basic academic skills in children from grades K through 12. The tests are available in different forms and at overlapping levels through the 13 grades, measuring knowledge and skills appropriate to each, especially in the areas of READING, spelling, language, reference, and mathematics and sometimes STUDY SKILLS, science, social studies, and computer literacy. Tests in specific subjects are also available for end-of-course use, as in algebra or chemistry. Tests may be scored by hand or by computer, and the scores themselves may be expressed in various ways. The CAT is widely used as a READINESS TEST, to assess whether a student is ready for PROMOTION to more advanced classes and to help in class placement decisions. (For help and further information, see TESTS.)

Callier-Azusa Scale A test widely used with children with handicaps, especially those who have multiple, severe, or profound handicaps, to assess their capacity in such areas as MOTOR SKILLS, perceptual skills (including visual, auditory, and tactile skills), SELF-HELP SKILLS, communication skills (see COMMUNICATION SKILLS AND DISORDERS), cognitive skills, and SOCIAL SKILLS. The subtests focus on DEVELOPMENTAL MILESTONES in each area as they occur among children with handicaps (the CHART OF NORMAL DEVELOPMENT on page 507 shows when various skills are usually developed) and are rated according to observations from one (preferably two or more) people very familiar with the child's behavior. The results are expressed very generally in AGE EQUIVALENTS. (For help and further information, see TESTS; HANDICAPPED.)

callus New bone that forms at the point of a FRACTURE.

CAN Abbreviation for CHILD ABUSE AND NEGLECT.

Canadian crutches A common type of ORTHOPEDIC DEVICE.

cancer A general name for a wide variety of diseases that have in common unchecked growth of the cells in one or more parts of the body. The resulting abnormal growths, called TUMORS or *neoplasms*, crowd out normal cells and eventually kill the tissue or organs involved. Any part of the body can be affected, not just the major organs, such as the heart and lungs; cancer often affects the skin (see SKIN DISORDERS); the lymphatic system, as in Hodgkin's disease (see IMMUNE SYSTEM); and the BONE MARROW (see LEUKEMIA).

Not all tumors are cancerous; on the contrary, many grow so slowly that they are not considered life-threatening and are labeled *benign*. Tumors that grow rapidly enough to threaten life are termed *malignant*, or cancerous. Some otherwise benign tumors can still be life-threatening if they occur in a sensitive area, such as the brain. (For an overview of the different kinds of tumors, see TUMOR and BRAIN TUMOR.)

At the most basic level, cancer begins when *oncogenes* (genes that control cell growth and duplication) become abnormal, sometimes due to the presence of cancer-inducing substances called *carcinogens*. The growth at the original site of the cancer is termed *primary*, but cancerous growths "shed" cancer cells, which enter the bloodstream and lymphatic system. The body's immune system often tackles and kills some of these cells, but if the cancer goes undetected and untreated, the surviving cancerous cells in circulation can establish malignant tumors elsewhere in the body, called *secondary tumors* or *metastases*.

What causes cells to become cancerous in the first place is an extremely complex question with no clear and simple answers. Cancer is not directly inherited, though some people apparently inherit a susceptibility or tendency to develop cancer under certain conditions. Nor is cancer directly contagious, though some forms seem to be triggered by viruses. While the causes are unclear, a variety of RISK FACTORS have been shown to increase a person's likelihood of getting cancer. Among them are:

- SMOKING.
- ENVIRONMENTAL HAZARDS, including RADIATION, though that may also be used as a therapy (see below).
- ALCOHOL ABUSE.
- some kinds of foods, additives, and forms of cooking. For example, diets heavy in FATS are linked to higher rates of cancer (though some kinds of foods, such as those in the cabbage and broccoli family, seem to offer some protection); so are diets that include carcinogenic FOOD ADDITIVES.
- some medications, such as the AIDS drug *zidovudine* (AZT).
- sexual and reproductive history; for example, women who have children, especially while fairly young, are at less risk for some forms of cancer, while men and women who have many sexual partners are at greater risk of cancer, possibly because of viruses passed during sexual activity.

Parents will want to cut down on such risk factors, for themselves and their children, to lessen the risk of developing cancer later on.

But in many cases, the causes of the cancer are unknown, and it develops extremely rapidly. This is often the case with cancers in children, such as leukemia, brain tumors, and abdominal tumors. Many physicians recommend that parents routinely, at least once a month, lightly feel over a young child's body, especially the abdomen, and if they find any changes or abnormalities take the child to the doctor immediately. With childhood cancers, as with others, the sooner the disease is detected, the better the chance of a cure.

Cancer is identified in several ways. Sometimes, as in skin cancers or cancer of the CERVIX, doctors can visually examine the growth. In these and many other cases, they may also take a BIOPSY, a procedure that may require an operation if an internal organ is involved. Various SCANS, such as ULTRASOUND, MAGNETIC RESONANCE IMAGING, or CT SCANS, can also provide information about tumors. In addition, laboratory analysis of blood samples can sometimes provide clues to the existence of cancer.

Treatment varies with the type of cancer, the part of the body involved, and the general medical condition of the patient. Physicians will generally develop a medical treatment plan, called a *protocol*, to be followed in a particular case. Such a plan may include a variety of therapies, such as

- *surgery*: complete excision if the tumor is located so as to allow it; partial removal otherwise, at least diminishing the number of malignant cells to be treated by other therapies. In some cases, the location of the tumor may require amputation of a limb (as in the thigh) or formation of a new body opening (OSTOMY). If the tumor is located in an inaccessible position deep in the brain or in or beyond a vital structure, operation may be considered impossible.
- *radiotherapy*: use of radiation to destroy malignant cells. Often these are the "familiar" X-rays and gamma rays, the problem being to use a sufficient concentration to kill the cancer without causing other, potentially deadly health problems in the patient. Newer approaches to this problem include *interstitial radiation (brachytherapy),* in which radioactive materials are implanted directly into the tumor; *photoradiation*, in which the patient is given a light-sensitive drug and then placed under red laser light; and *hyperthermia*, which uses heat to destroy cells.

  Very promising recent work has involved BONE MARROW TRANSPLANTS, in which some of the patient's healthy bone marrow is removed and carefully cultured while the patient is subjected to massive doses of radiation, which kills the cancer (but also the remaining bone marrow). Externally "grown" healthy bone marrow is then inserted back into the body. This is a painful and dangerous procedure, so far best used on young people who are otherwise healthy, but it holds promise for previously untreatable or unresponsive life-threatening tumors.
- *chemotherapy:* use of poisonous chemicals to kill tumor cells, which are generally more vulnerable to toxins than are healthy cells. The difficulty is often to obtain sufficient concentration to destroy tumor cells without poisoning the rest of the body. If the tumor is in the brain, sometimes special techniques may be required to breach the BLOOD-BRAIN BARRIER.
- *immunotherapy*: activation or stimulation of the body's own immune system to fight tumors, a focus of considerable research though not yet used as a major standard therapy.

• *steroid therapy*: administration of various kinds of STEROIDS, as in cases of brain tumors, to hold down *edema* (fluid accumulation and resulting swelling), which can damage tissues such as the brain.

With these and other techniques, many more people have been able to beat cancer and go on to live normal lives. But the treatments themselves often have severe side effects, including loss of appetite (*anorexia*), severe weight loss and wasting of body tissues (*cachexia*), VOMITING, water retention (EDEMA), DIARRHEA, CONSTIPATION, DEHYDRATION, hair loss, mouth sores, loss or distortion of taste and smell (mouth blindness or ANOSMIA), dry mouth (XEROSTOMIA), and tooth decay. These side effects are difficult enough for adults to deal with, but much more so for young children, sometimes too young to fully understand what is occurring.

In dealing with cancer in their children, parents can turn for help to many organizations and resources (see below). For example, they should note the National Cancer Institute's *Talking with Your Child About Cancer* on when and what to tell children of different age groups and *Help Yourself: Tips for Teenagers with Cancer*, which includes such information as how to fix a fancy scarf when you have lost your hair and 35 ways to pass the time while waiting for treatment. (For information on how to deal with facing a possibly terminal illness, see DEATH; and for more on different types of hospitals and arrangements for children, see HOSPITALS.)

For help and further information

National Cancer Institute (NCI)
Office of Cancer Communications
9000 Rockville Pike
Building 31, Room 10A24
Bethesda, MD 20892
301-496-5583; Cancer Information Service (CIS) toll-free number: 800-4-CANCER [422-6237] (M–F, 9 AM–10 PM EST); in Spanish also during daytime.
Federal arm concerned with cancer research and public policy regarding cancer, one of the National Institutes of Health. Gathers and disseminates data; provides information to public and professionals; maintains computerized database (Physician Data Query, or PDQ) of experimental treatments currently being funded; publishes numerous print and audiovisual materials, including *What You Need to Know About Cancer, What You Need to Know About Hodgkin's Disease, What You Need to Know About Non-Hodgkin's Lymphoma*, and other similar pamphlets on specific types of cancers; audiocassettes and booklets *Young People with Cancer: A Handbook for Parents, Help Yourself: Tips for Teenagers with Cancer, Diet and Nutrition: A Resource for Parents of Children with Cancer, Talking with Your Child About Cancer* (for parents of young children with cancer), *Hospital Days, Treatment Ways* (coloring book for children), *When Someone in Your Family Has Cancer* (for ages 7 through early teens), *Chemotherapy and You—A Guide to Self-Help During Treatment*, and *Radiation Therapy and You—A Guide to*

Self-Help During Treatment; and research reports on specific types of cancers.

American Cancer Society (ACS)
1599 Clifton Road, NE
Atlanta, GA 30329
404-320-3333, toll-free number 800-227-2345
William Tipping, Executive Director
Organization aimed at combatting and eliminating cancer. Sponsors research, education programs, and support services to cancer patients and their families; special services include programs for people with specific types of cancers; Cancermount, matching people who have successfully dealt with cancer with current patients; I Can Cope, educating patients about living with cancer; and International Association of Laryngectomies for those whose larynx has been removed; provides information for public and professionals; publishes numerous print and audiovisual materials, including newsletter *Cancer News, When Your Brother or Sister Has Cancer* (for ages 7 through early teens), *Pain Control*, the booklets *Helping Children Understand: A Guide for a Parent with Cancer* and *What Happened to You Happened to Me* (for cancer patients ages 7 through early teens), and materials on specific types of cancer, such as *Facts on Bone Cancer* and *Facts on Leukemia*.

Candlelighters Childhood Cancer Foundation
1901 Pennsylvania Avenue, NW, Suite 1011
Washington, DC 20006
202-659-5136
Julie Sullivan, Executive Director
Network of mutual-support self-help groups for parents of children with cancer and concerned medical professionals. Provides information on childhood cancer; publishes various materials, including quarterly *Youth Newsletter*, as well as *When Your Child Has a Life-Threatening Illness, Bone Marrow Transplantation in Childhood Cancer*, and *Candlelighters Foundation Bibliography and Resource Guide*.

National Cancer Care Foundation (NCCF)
1180 Avenue of the Americas
New York, NY 10036
212-221-3300
Diane Blum, Executive Director
Organization devoted to helping patients and their families cope with cancer. Offers psychological, social, and educational services; publishes various materials.

American Institute for Cancer Research (AICR)
500 North Washington Street, Suite 100
Falls Church, VA 22046
703-237-0159
Organization devoted to cancer research. Publishes AICR Information Series of booklets and pamphlets, including *All About Fat and Cancer Risk, Dietary Fiber to Lower Cancer Risk*, and *Dietary Guidelines to Lower Cancer Risk*.

Association for Brain Tumor Research (AFBTR), 312-286-5571. (For full group information, see BRAIN TUMOR.)

DES Action, 415-826-5060. (For full group information, see DES.)

Skin Cancer Foundation
245 Fifth Avenue, Suite 2402
New York, NY 10016
212-725-5176
Organization for people concerned with skin cancer. Publishes various materials, including brochures and quarterly newsletters *The Melanoma Letter* and *Sun and Skin Use*.

Acoustic Neuroma Association, 717-249-4783. (For full group information, see ACOUSTIC NEUROMA.)

Familial Polyposis Registry
Toronto General Hospital
200 Elizabeth Street
Eaton Building 10-315
Toronto, Ontario MFG 2C4, Canada
416-595-3934
Zane Cohen, Executive Director
International network of registries for people with personal or family history of a premalignant genetic disease, familial adenomatous polyposis, juvenile polyposis, and PeutzJeghers syndrome. Provides information and makes referrals; maintains family study center; publishes various materials, including quarterly newsletter *GI Polyposis & Related Conditions*, audiovisual and print work *The Pelvic Pouch Procedure*, and print works *Familial Polyposis: A Guide for Patients and their Families* and *Ileostomy Surgery: What Does It Mean For Me?*.

G.I. Polyposis and Hereditary Colon Cancer Registry
The Moore Clinic
Johns Hopkins Hospital
600 North Wolfe Street
Baltimore, MD 21205
301-955-4040 or 955-3875
Anne Krush, Coordinator
International network of registries for people with personal or family history of G.I. polyposis and hereditary colon cancer. Seeks to identify families at risk and to educate them and health professionals working with them; provides information and makes referrals; maintains family study center; publishes various materials, including quarterly newsletter *GI Polyposis & Related Conditions*, quarterly *Ostomy*, and *Family Studies in Genetic Disorders*.

Intestinal Multiple Polyposis and Colorectal Cancer (IMPACC)
1006-1001 Brinker Drive
Hagerstown, MD 21740
301-791-7526
Dolores Boone, Administrator
Mutual-support self-help group for people with personal or family history of hereditary gastrointestinal polyposes or hereditary colon cancer. Seeks to educate public and alert affected individuals to risks; encourages research; publishes various materials, including newsletters *G.I. Polyposis & Related Conditions* and *Ostomy Quarterly*, audiovisual materials on eye and jaw lesions associated with Gardner syndrome, and print works such as *Hereditary Intestinal Polyps: A Guide for Patients & Families* and *Family Studies in Genetic Disorders*.

Corporate Angel Network
Westchester County Airport
Building 1
White Plains, NY 10604
914-328-1313
Organization that coordinates free flights to NCI-approved treatment centers for cancer patients (and one family member or attendant) on corporate airplanes, when seats are available.

Other reference sources

For Parents

A Family Doctor's Guide to Understanding and Preventing Cancer, by S.R. Kaura. Santa Fe, NM: Health, 1990. Address: P.O. Box 367, Santa Fe, NM 87501.

Cancer as a Turning Point: A Handbook for People with Cancer, Their Families, and Health Professionals, by Lawrence LeShan. New York: Dutton, 1989.

Coping Magazine, for cancer patients and families, on cancer research, services, and personal experiences. Available from Pulse Publications, P.O. Box 1677, Franklin, TN 37065, telephone 615-791-5900.

Coping with Childhood Cancer, by David Adams and Eleanor Deveau. Reston, VA: Reston, 1988.

Understanding Cancer, third revised edition, by Mark Renneker, M.D. Palo Alto, CA: Bull, 1988.

The Cancer Reference Book: Direct and Clear Answers to Everyone's Questions, revised edition, by Paul M. Levitt, Elissa S. Guralnick, Dr. A. Robert Kagan, and Dr. Harvey Gilbert. New York: Facts on File, 1983.

Health Care U.S.A., by Jean Carper. New York: Prentice Hall, 1987. Resource for general and specific health-care information, including different types of cancers. Lists sources of up-to-date information on cancer treatments and major centers for treatment or research, including experimental psychological cancer therapy; provides list of children's cancer specialists and other information.

Choices: Realistic Alternatives in Cancer Treatment, by Marion Morra and Eve Potts. New York: Avon, 1987.

Children with Cancer: A Reference Guide for Parents, by Jeanne Munn Bracken. New York: Oxford University Press, 1986.

The American Cancer Society Cancer Book. Garden City, NY: Doubleday, 1986.

Cancer: A Patient's Guide, by Chris Williams and Sue Williams. New York: Wiley, 1986.

Why Mine? A Book for Parents Whose Child Is Seriously Ill, by Joy Johnson, Marv Johnson, and Billy Williams. Omaha, NE: Centering Corporation, 1981. Address: P.O. Box 3367, Omaha, NE 68103.

Getting Well Again: A Step-by-Step, Self-Help Guide to Overcoming Cancer for Patients and Their Families, by O.C. Simonton and S. Matthews Simonton. New York: St. Martin's, 1978.

The Healing Family: The Simonton Approach for Families Facing Illness, by Stephanie Matthews Simonton. New York: Bantam, 1984.

For or by Kids

Living with Cancer, by Dr. Simon Smail. New York: Watts, 1990. For young readers.

Cancer, by Joann Rodgers. New York: Chelsea House, 1990. For young adults.

Cancer, by D.J. Herda. New York: Watts, 1989. For grades 6 to 9.

I Want to Grow Hair, I Want to Grow Up, I Want to Go to Boise, by Erma Bombeck. New York: Harper & Row, 1989.

Coping When a Parent Has Cancer, by Linda Leopold Strauss. New York: Rosen, 1988.

Cancer, by Wrynn Smith, Ph.D. New York: Facts on File, 1987.

Teenagers Face to Face with Cancer, by Karen Gravelle and Bertram A. John. New York: Messner, 1986.

Afraid to Ask: A Book About Cancer, by Judylaine Fine. New York: Lothrop, Lee & Shepard, 1986.

Home Care for the Dying: A Reassuring, Comprehensive Guide to Physical and Emotional Care, by D.W. Little. New York: Dial, 1985. Includes a chapter on pediatric care.

Miracles of Courage: How Families Meet the Challenge of a Child's Critical Illness, by M. Dickens. New York: Dodd, Mead, 1985.

Understanding Leukemia, by C.P. Margolies. New York: Scribner, 1983.

I'll Never Walk Alone, by Carol Simonides. New York: Continuum, 1983. Autobiography of a teenager with cancer.

No Dragons to Slay, by J. Greenberg. New York: Farrar, Straus & Giroux, 1983. About a 17-year-old boy with a tumor.

On with My Life, by P. Trull. New York: Putnam, 1983. Autobiography of a girl with a leg amputated to cure cancer.

RAY-DEE-A-SHUN, by Joy Johnson and Marv Johnson. Omaha, NE: Centering Corporation, 1981. Address: P.O. Box 3367, Omaha, NE 68103. For children up to age 7.

Too Old to Cry . . . Too Young to Die, Edith Pendleton, ed. Nashville, TN: Thomas Nelson, 1980. By and for terminally ill teenagers.

Waiting for Johnny Miracle, by Alice Bach. New York: Harper & Row, 1980. Novel about a teenage athlete who learns she has cancer.

You Don't Have to Die. 1988. 30-minute video from Ambrose Video, 381 Park Avenue South, New York, NY 10016. On a child who successfully fought cancer. For ages 6 to adult.

Background Works

Protect Yourself from Cancer: A Physician's Comprehensive Plan for Cancer Prevention, by Howard R. Bierman, M.D. New York: Dodd, Mead, 1988.

How to Improve Your Odds Against Cancer, by John F. Potter, M.D. Hollywood, FL: Frederick Fell, 1988.

We, the Victors: Inspiring Stories of People Who Conquered Cancer and How They Did It, by Curtis Bill Pepper. Garden City, NY: Doubleday, 1984.

You Can Fight Cancer and Win, by Jane Brody and Arthur I. Holleb, M.D. New York: Times Books, 1977.

(See also LEUKEMIA; TUMOR; BRAIN TUMOR; BONE MARROW TRANSPLANT; DEATH; HOSPITAL; OSTOMY; also HELP FOR SPECIAL CHILDREN, on page 578, including "Make-a-Wish" organizations for severely or terminally ill children.)

Candidates Reply Date Agreement An agreement among many colleges, sponsored by the COLLEGE ENTRANCE EXAMINATION BOARD, that colleges will not require students to accept or reject an offer of ADMISSION or of FINANCIAL AID before May 1. The aim is to allow the student to learn of all of the possible offers open before choosing one of them.

candidiasis Infection by the fungus *Candida albicans*. The fungus flourishes in moist parts of the body, such as the mouth, VAGINA, or under the FORESKIN of an uncircumcised male but is normally kept in check by bacteria in the body unless something upsets the body's balances. Antibiotics, in killing bacteria, can allow candidiasis to spread; drugs that suppress the IMMUNE SYSTEM can encourage candidiasis growth, as can the disease AIDS. Pregnant women, women on BIRTH-CONTROL PILLS, and people with DIABETES MELLITUS may, because of changes in the body's chemical balances, be susceptible to candidiasis. Symptoms include itchiness; a thick, white discharge from the vagina; yellowish patches in the mouth; or white, flaky patches on moist skin. Babies with diaper rash are susceptible to candidiasis, and the fungus can cause BALANITIS, inflammation of the tip of the penis. Among people weakened by other conditions, candidiasis can be not just irritating, but more serious, involving inflammation of the heart and liver and infection centering on various internal organs. Treated with antifungal medications, candidiasis is best combatted by keeping skin dry.

cap In dentistry, a popular name for a CROWN; also short for CRADLE CAP.

CAPD Abbreviation for continuous ambulatory peritoneal dialysis, a form of DIALYSIS.

carbohydrates A group of naturally occurring, organic compounds, including sugar, starch, and cellulose, that provide the main source of energy for all body functions. The National Institute of Digestive and Kidney Diseases (NIDDK) estimates that an average American adult eats about half a pound of carbohydrates each day, in such common and inexpensive foods as bread, potatoes, pastries, candy, soft drinks, rice, pasta, fruits, and vegetables. Nutritionists recommend getting carbohydrates primarily from unprocessed (unrefined) foods, such as whole-grain cereals and fresh fruits, because they have more nutrients and FIBER than refined foods, such as sugar and white flour. (For help and further information, see NUTRITION.)

carcinogens Substances that can cause or increase the risk of CANCER.

carcinoma General term for a kind of malignant TUMOR, or CANCER, that arises from the outer skin, or from skin covering or lining organs (notably the liver and kidneys) or systems (such as the digestive, respiratory, urological, and reproductive systems). (For help and further information, see TUMOR; CANCER.)

cardiac arrhythmia Disrupted rhythm of the heartbeat. (See HEART AND HEART PROBLEMS.)

cardiac monitor A type of electronic machine that monitors heartbeat, often used to alert parents or medical staff to dangerous irregularities in the heartbeat of a PREMATURE infant, such as one susceptible to SLEEP APNEA or thought at risk for SUDDEN INFANT DEATH SYNDROME. Sometimes a *cardiorespiratory monitor* is used to monitor both heartbeat and breathing. (For help and further information, see SLEEP APNEA.)

cardiomyopathy A condition in which the heart muscle has been damaged. (See HEART AND HEART PROBLEMS.)

cardiopulmonary resuscitation (CPR) A technique that uses chest compressions in addition to ARTIFICIAL RESPIRATION to maintain basic life support.

caregiver Someone responsible for a child's health and welfare, and for meeting the child's basic physical and psychological needs. Caretakers include those who have full-time legal responsibility for the child, such as parents or a GUARDIAN; others in the home, such as SIBLINGS or CO-PARENTS; and others who have shorter-term care of the child, such as BABYSITTERS or CHILD-CARE workers. More widely, the terms *caregiver* and *caretaker* refer to anyone who meets the physical, emotional, and social needs of others, especially dependent people, such as severely disabled adults.

caries The medical term for tooth decay, commonly called *cavities*. (See TEETH.)

carotene Pigment in yellow and green vegetables and fruits (especially carrots) that is used in making VITAMIN A.

carrier Someone who carries a disease or disorder, such as a malfunctioning RECESSIVE gene, and is unaffected by it but may pass it on to others; often a woman who passes on an X-LINKED GENETIC DISORDER to her sons.

CASA Abbreviation for COURT-APPOINTED SPECIAL ADVOCATE.

CAT Abbreviation for CALIFORNIA ACHIEVEMENT TESTS or CHILDREN'S APPERCEPTION TEST; also an alternate name for CT SCAN.

cataracts Loss of transparency in the lens at the back of the eye. (See EYE AND VISION PROBLEMS.)

catastrophic reaction Unrestrained actions in response to an apparently minor but, to a child, frightening, threatening, frustrating, overstimulating, or otherwise upsetting situation. The child may, for example, scream uncontrollably, bang his or her head on the floor, throw things, or cry unconsolably. Children with LEARNING DISABILITIES or MENTAL DISORDERS are especially susceptible to this kind of reaction, but many children will occasionally respond in this way to unexpected or disturbing changes in routine or to pressure to achieve more than present skills allow.

catch-up school Alternate term for REMEDIAL SCHOOL.

categorical aid Governmental financial assistance given to people who fit into a certain category, such as disabled or family with dependent children, rather than only to people who pass a MEANS TEST. Much assistance under Social Security is categorical, as under the AID TO FAMILIES WITH DEPENDENT CHILDREN program.

catheter A hollow, flexible tube that can be inserted into the body, through a blood vessel or natural body opening, to withdraw or remove fluid and sometimes to aid in diagnosis of a disorder. Using a technique called CLEAN, INTERMITTENT CATHETERIZATION, some children, such as those with SPINA BIFIDA, learn at a very early age to insert a catheter into themselves to drain urine from their bladder, to prevent kidney damage or infection.

cathexis Powerful concentration of emotion on a particular person, place, or thing, or on one's self. When such a concentration becomes painful or troubling, DISPLACEMENT may occur, in which the emotion becomes focused on another object instead.

Cattell Infant Intelligence Scale A type of INTELLIGENCE TEST used to assess the mental development of children aged three to 30 months. Various stimulus items, such as cubes, pencils, and pegboards, are used to assess the child's motor control; the test administrator takes notes on the responses and also on infant attempts to communicate. (For help and further information, see TESTS.)

cavity The popular name for tooth decay, or *caries*. (See TEETH.)

CBC Abbreviation for complete blood count, a type of BLOOD TEST. (See also BLOOD AND BLOOD DISORDERS.)

CC Medical abbreviation for *cum correction*, meaning with corrective lenses, such as glasses. (See EYE AND VISION PROBLEMS.)

CCPD Abbreviation for continuous cycling peritoneal dialysis, a form of DIALYSIS.

CdLS Abbreviation for CORNELIA DE LANGE SYNDROME.

CEEB Abbreviation for COLLEGE ENTRANCE EXAMINATION BOARD.

ceiling age The age level at which a child is unable to complete any questions correctly on a STANDARDIZED TEST, such as the STANFORD-BINET INTELLIGENCE TEST, the opposite being the BASAL AGE.

celiac disease Alternate name for *celiac sprue*.

celiac sprue (celiac disease) A type of FOOD INTOLERANCE involving a sensitivity to *gluten*, the insoluble PROTEIN that is part of wheat, rye, barley, and some other grains; also called *gluten-induced enteropathy* (literally an ailment of the intestine caused by gluten). Celiac sprue runs in families and so may be a form of GENETIC DISORDER, but its exact pattern of inheritance is not fully known. Sensitized and damaged by contact with gluten, the intestines become unable to properly absorb other kinds of nutrients, the result being MALABSORPTION and often severe MALNUTRITION. Other symptoms of celiac sprue include pale, fatty, foul-smelling feces, DIARRHEA, VOMITING, DEHYDRATION, and buildup of acids in the body, which can be severe, growth-stunting, and even life-threatening in infants. Celiac sprue is sometimes associated with LACTOSE INTOLERANCE.

The treatment is a gluten-restricted diet, avoiding all products made from wheat, rye, barley, and sometimes oats, including breads, cereals, and pasta; rice and corn are then the main grains in the diet, with the rest of the food groups all available. The symptoms generally begin to recede within a few weeks; though if the intestine has been severely damaged, recovery may be slow. Until properly diagnosed, often by a BIOPSY of the intestinal lining, celiac sprue can sometimes be mistaken for other disorders, including CYSTIC FIBROSIS or ALLERGY.

For help and further information

Celiac Sprue Association/United States of America (CSA/USA)
2313 Rocklyn Drive, Suite 1
Des Moines, IA 50322
515-270-9689
Tracey Mohns, Contact
Organization concerned with celiac sprue. Provides information and referrals to individuals with celiac sprue, their families, and health professionals; publishes various materials, including quarterly *Lifeline*, audiovisual works *Celiac Sprue in Adults and Children* and *A Basic Primer on Celiac Sprue*, and print works *Celiac Sprue* and *On the Celiac Condition*.

American Celiac Society (ACS)
45 Gifford Avenue
Jersey City, NJ 07304
201-432-1207
Anita Garrow, Executive Director
Organization concerned with gluten intolerance. Gathers and disseminates information to public and professionals, especially as to gluten-free diets; makes referrals to gluten intolerance groups; publishes various materials.

Gluten Intolerance Group of North America (GIG)
P.O. Box 23055
Seattle, WA 98102
206-325-6980
Elaine I. Hartsook, Executive Director
Organization concerned with people who have celiac sprue or dermatitis herpetiformis, and with their families and health professionals. Provides information, counseling, and referrals; publishes various print and audiovisual materials, including quarterly *GIG Newsletter*, as well as *Gluten Intolerance Group Cookbook*, *Gluten-Restricted, Gliadin-Free Diet Instruction*, and *Celiac Sprue*.

National Institute of Diabetes and Digestive and Kidney Diseases (NIDDK), 301-496-3583. (For full group information, see DIGESTIVE DISORDERS.)

central apnea Type of SLEEP APNEA that is not caused by obstruction of air passage, but possibly by a brain malfunction.

central nervous system (CNS) In anatomy, the system made up of the brain and spinal cord, which receives information from, interprets, and transmits information to the rest of the body; it is served by a network of nerves called the PERIPHERAL NERVOUS SYSTEM (PNS). The CNS is extremely sensitive to injury, and damage to it is often irreparable, causing long-term disability; by contrast, injury to nerves in the outlying peripheral nervous system is more local and responsive to surgery. (For help and further information, see BRAIN AND BRAIN DISORDERS; SPINAL CORD INJURY.)

central register In relation to CHILD ABUSE AND NEGLECT, a collection of reports held in some central agency. Arrangements vary by state, but the purpose of the central register is to provide a place for SOCIAL WORKERS and others to check, in cases of suspected child abuse, to see if any such reports have been filed previously. Critics warn that such files are not always kept fully confidential and that unverified reports are not always cleared from the register.

central visual acuity Sharpness of vision, a basic measure tested by the Snellen Test. (See EYE AND VISION PROBLEMS.)

cephalic presentation A type of FETAL PRESENTATION in which the FETUS is head first.

cephalopelvic disproportion A condition in which a baby's head is too large for its mother's pelvis, leading to difficult and sometimes impossible LABOR.

cerebral dominance A kind of DOMINANCE of one part of the brain over another.

cerebral palsy (CP) A disorder caused by damage to the brain, especially affecting ability to control movement and posture. *Palsy* is a synonym for PARALYSIS, although a more accurate description of the usual muscular symptoms might be weakness (*paresis*) and inability to make voluntary movements and to suppress involuntary ones. Depending on the location and extent of the damage, cerebral palsy can be mild, revealing itself as a kind of awkwardness, or severe, largely incapacitating a child from infancy. It is sometimes associated with other problems such as SEIZURES (EPILEPSY), MENTAL RETARDATION, EAR AND HEARING PROBLEMS, EYE AND VISION PROBLEMS, communication disorders (see COMMUNICATION SKILLS AND DISORDERS), and impairment of other senses. Some of those most severely affected may not survive infancy, but most will have a normal life span.

Cerebral palsy is not contagious. It is not progressive—it does not get worse as time passes and may instead improve somewhat with therapy (see below). It is not inherited, except in rare cases where it is associated with a GENETIC DISORDER, notably LESCH-NYHAN SYNDROME. About 10 percent of the cases are *acquired cerebral palsy*, in which the condition has been triggered by events after birth, such as HEAD INJURY, infections like MENINGITIS, and other types of brain damage, including injury from CHILD ABUSE AND NEGLECT. But most cases are caused by brain damage during PREGNANCY, CHILDBIRTH, or the neonatal period (just after birth); this is called *congenital cerebral palsy*, because it is present at or around the time of birth.

Just why cerebral palsy occurs is far from clear. In a recent study sponsored by the National Institute of Neurological Disorders and Stroke (NINDS), 58 percent of the cases of cerebral palsy occurred in children who were born at full term and full weight and in whom doctors could discern no cause of brain damage, at the present state of knowledge and technology. But studies have shown that numerous conditions are RISK FACTORS for cerebral palsy—that is, they will not necessarily lead to the disorder but increase the risk that a child will have it. Among the main risk factors are:

- infections in the mother during pregnancy, including RUBELLA (German measles); SEXUALLY TRANSMITTED DISEASES such as GONORRHEA, CHLAMYDIAL INFECTION, and SYPHILIS; and various other bacterial and viral infections, some of which attack the baby's CENTRAL NERVOUS SYSTEM.
- PREMATURE delivery.
- LOW BIRTH WEIGHT (though NINDS points out that some infants under two pounds, spending months in neonatal intensive care, are unimpaired).
- difficult or abnormal delivery, especially awkward FETAL PRESENTATION (position at birth), lengthy or too abrupt labor, or obstruction of the UMBILICAL CORD.
- HYPOXIA, or insufficient oxygen, in the brain, for a variety of reasons, such as premature separation of the PLACENTA during delivery or swelling of the brain due to illness.
- incompatability between parents' and fetus's blood types, especially RH INCOMPATIBILITY.
- JAUNDICE of the newborn, or HYPERBILIRUBINEMIA, sometimes associated with Rh incompatibility.
- medications and DRUG ABUSE.
- LEAD POISONING.
- SMOKING.
- ALCOHOL ABUSE.

With increased knowledge, developing technology (as in treating Rh incompatibility), and enhanced PRENATAL CARE, the risks of cerebral palsy can be much diminished, though not necessarily prevented. Precise figures are hard to come by because of the wide variation in forms of the disorder and lack of requirement that doctors report it, but the United Cerebral Palsy Association estimates that about 3,000 infants are born with cerebral palsy each year and about 500 other preschool-age children later acquire the condition.

Cerebral palsy is generally recognized in the early years, as DEVELOPMENTAL DELAY becomes apparent. Though various kinds of medical scans can help doctors identify some brain abnormalities, the disorder is most often seen in its symptoms.

These may include:

- retention of PRIMITIVE REFLEXES (involuntary reactions to particular stimuli that are normally found only in newborns).
- conversely, muscular weakness and "floppiness" (HYPOTONIA).
- assumption of abnormal, awkward positions, which (if uncorrected) can lead to skeletal disorders.
- favoring one side of the body over the other.
- poor muscle control and lack of coordination.
- muscle spasms or seizures.
- problems with sucking, chewing, and swallowing.
- unusual tenseness and irritability in infancy.
- inability to control bladder and bowels (INCONTINENCE).
- difficulty (DISARTHRIA) speaking.
- difficulty in concentrating, which has adverse effects on learning.
- trouble in interpreting sense perceptions, such as inability to identify objects by touch.
- other problems with the senses, especially hearing and vision.

Some children may show serious symptoms at birth; some may not show any clear signs for a long time. Most children with cerebral palsy are diagnosed by age five. It is important to diagnose the disorder early so that therapy can minimize handicaps, learning is not hindered, and the child (and parents) can adjust more readily.

Doctors classify cerebral palsy in two main ways: by the affected limbs and by the nature of the movement disturbance:

By affected limbs
- *diplegia*: limbs on opposite sides are affected, such as both legs.
- *hemiplegia* or *hemiparesis*: arm and leg on one side are affected.
- *quadriplegia* or *quadriparesis*: all four limbs are affected.

By the nature of the movement disturbance
- *spastic cerebral palsy*: muscles are tense, contracted, and resistant to movement; the most common form of cerebral palsy, especially in low-birth-weight or premature babies.
- *athetoid cerebral palsy*: the affected parts of the body perform involuntary writhing movements (CATHETOSIS), such as turning, twisting, facial grimacing, and drooling, often associated with jerky, abrupt, flailing motions (CHOREA). This form of cerebral palsy generally involves damage only to the motor centers, not to other parts of the brain, but "strange" and "unnatural" movements are often interpreted by the unknowing as signs of mental or emotional disturbance.
- *ataxic cerebral palsy*: the main characteristic is lack of balance and coordination, due to damage to the cerebellum. ATAXIA involves trouble maintaining balance and swaying when standing.
- *rigidity*: muscles are extremely tight and resistant to movement.
- *tremor*: muscles uncontrollably shake, interfering with coordination.

Sometimes several areas of the brain are involved, so the description of a particular child's condition may involve several of the above terms and symptoms.

No cure exists for cerebral palsy, but various kinds of therapies are used to help each child do as much as he or she is capable of doing. Among these are:

- *physical therapy*, the use of therapeutic exercises and activities to extend the child's range of controlled movement, generally focusing on gross MOTOR SKILLS. Some of these use the *Bobath technique*, in which exercises are directed first toward countering primitive reflexes and then on extending the range of voluntary movement, sometimes with the help of BEHAVIOR MODIFICATION, offering positive reinforcement to help children act against the body's awkward inclinations. Physical therapists also help children learn how to use ORTHOPEDIC DEVICES, such as wheelchairs and walkers.

- *biofeedback*, in which children are given information about the functioning of a particular part of the body, often by electrical machines that produce visual or auditory signals, and are taught to concentrate on changing the visual picture or sound. Through such techniques, children with cerebral palsy can gain increased control over movements and are sometimes able to do things like drink from a cup or control their bladder—things previously beyond their range of skills.

- *occupational therapy*, the use of therapeutic exercises and activities to extend the child's range of controlled movement, generally focusing on fine motor skills, many of them SELF-HELP SKILLS. For children that may mean learning how to dress themselves, comb their hair, brush their teeth, drink from a cup, or hold a pen or pencil. For young adults it includes preparation for living as self-sufficiently and independently as possible.

- *speech and language therapy*, which can help children overcome some speech and hearing impairments and also learn to use the great variety of mechanical and electronic devices that have been developed to help them, such as voice synthesizers or specially adapted computers.

- *drugs*, including muscle relaxants for spastic muscles and antiseizure drugs if epilepsy is involved. Drugs are best used sparingly, however, since the long-term side effects on the developing, already damaged nervous system are unknown.

- *surgery*, which can be helpful in dealing with certain specific problems, such as those involving eyes, ears, and gait; brain surgery may help some but is still experimental.

- *orthopedic devices*, such as wheelchairs, walkers, page-turners, specially equipped automobiles, and the like.

Many physical therapists stress that a varied and stimulating environment is in itself a powerful "treatment" for the child. Also important to both child and family are counseling, which can offer emotional support and relief of stress, advice on handling practical problems, and training to prepare for the future, as the child grows into an adult. Many public and private organizations also provide financial assistance, diagnostic and treatment centers, vocational training and guidance, RESPITE CARE for

Will My Child Ever Walk?

The diagnosis of cerebral palsy is always upsetting, and parents are inevitably anxious and concerned over the future. Will the child ever talk? Walk? Go to college? Be able to work? In mild cases the doctor can usually be reassuring. But often there are no simple answers. Every individual with cerebral palsy presents a unique set of symptoms along with a unique capacity and potential for coping. A lot may depend on rehabilitation and education programs, a lot on the cooperation and positive but realistic attitudes of all concerned. Some physicians generalize that if a child can sit up unsupported by the end of the second year, or stand by age three, the chances for independent walking are good. But there are always exceptions. Sometimes orthopedic surgery may be necessary. Almost always there will be a need for a coordinated treatment program provided by a team of skilled professionals. Still, not all children may respond.

Coordinated programs are available through the physical medicine and rehabilitation department of hospitals, state crippled children's programs, and a variety of clinics or centers for the handicapped financed by public or private agencies. Both the United Cerebral Palsy Associations, Inc., and the National Easter Seal Society, Inc., have local chapters and clinics throughout the country. In addition, special programs are available to assure that no handicapped person is denied free public education.

At the same time, it is important to maintain a stable and reassuring home environment. The presence of a handicapped child is hard on all members of the family. Parents may quarrel or feel guilty and occasionally experience such strain that the marriage is threatened. Parents are sometimes overprotective and pampering, creating serious personality and behavioral problems for the child and leading brothers and sisters to feel denied attention and love. In a few instances parents may be rejecting or show indifference to the handicapped child. Excellent advice comes from the mother of a child with cerebral palsy: "If the parents accept the child, the child will then accept himself." Many agencies and clinics providing treatment for individuals with cerebral palsy include social workers or psychologists skilled in family counseling or else can refer families to appropriate professionals to guide them through the initial adjustment and as problems arise.

The combined education and rehabilitation programs currently available will enable some children to progress to excellent control over their bodies and a nearly normal life. Those with more severe handicaps may be able to move from bed to wheelchair or from wheelchair to braces or other mechanical aids. Most authorities agree that progress in overcoming handicaps is harder if there are mental impairments.

Source: *Cerebral Palsy: Hope Through Research* (1980). Prepared by the National Institute of Neurological Disorders and Stroke for the Public Health Service.

families of children with cerebral palsy, special recreational facilities, adapted work settings, and adapted living arrangements.

For help and further information

United Cerebral Palsy Association (UCPA)
7 Penn Plaza, Suite 804
New York, NY 10010
212-268-6655, toll-free number 800-USA-5UCP (872-5827), for publications list: 717-396-7965
John D. Kemp, Executive Director
UCPA Government Activities Office
1522 K Street, NW, Suite 1112
Washington, DC 20005
202-842-1266
Organization offering wide range of services to people with cerebral palsy and related handicaps, ranging from diagnosis and treatment to counseling and job training to residences and sports activities. Provides information and referrals; acts as advocate for people with cerebral palsy, seeking to educate public and change public policy; sponsors research; sponsors National Association of Sports for Cerebral Palsy (see below); publishes many materials, including *Family Support Bulletin, Head Injury, Handling the Young C.P. Child at Home, How to Help a Baby with Developmental Delay, Programming for Adolescents with C.P., Strengthening Individual and Family Life* (including tips on mothering from wheelchair and adolescents with C.P.), *Cerebral Palsy—Facts and Figures, What Everyone Should Know About Cerebral Palsy,* various monographs, and *Augmentative Communications,* a series of books on communications devices available for people with cerebral palsy.

National Institute of Neurological Disorders and Stroke (NINDS), 301-496-5751. Publishes *Cerebral Palsy: Hope Through Research.* (For full group information, see BRAIN AND BRAIN DISORDERS.)

American Academy for Cerebral Palsy and Developmental Medicine
1910 Byrd Avenue, Suite 118, P.O. Box 11086
Richmond, VA 23230
804-282-0036
John A. Hinckley, Executive Director
Organization of medical professionals dealing with cerebral palsy and developmental disabilities. Publishes bimonthly journal and membership directory.

National Easter Seal Society, 312-726-6200 voice; 312-726-4258 TDD. (For full group information, see HELP FOR SPECIAL CHILDREN on page 578.)

American Association of University Affiliated Programs for Persons with Developmental Disabilities (AAUAP) (301-588-8252). (For full group information, see HELP FOR SPECIAL CHILDREN on page 578.)

National Association of Sports for Cerebral Palsy (NASCP)
66 East 34th Street
New York, NY 10016
212-481-6300
Arm of United Cerebral Palsy Association (see above). Arranges international sports competitions for people with various levels of disability, from minimally handicapped, ambulatory contestants to multiply handicapped people competing in wheelchairs; publishes various materials, including monthly magazine *Sportline* and manuals and guides for sports.

Other reference sources

General Works

Children with Cerebral Palsy: A Parent's Guide, by Elaine Tomlinson. Kensington, MD: Woodbine, 1990.
Health Care U.S.A., by Jean Carper. New York: Prentice Hall, 1987. Resource for general and specific health-care information; lists major cerebral palsy treatment and research centers, leading neurologists, rehabilitation centers specializing in infant and early childhood development, and other information.
Coping with Cerebral Palsy: Answers to Questions Parents Often Ask, by Jay Schleichkorn. Austin, TX: PRO-ED, 1983.
Care of the Neurologically Handicapped Child: A Book for Parents and Professionals, by A.L. Prensky and H.S. Pulkens. New York: Oxford University Press, 1982.
Handling the Young Cerebral Palsied Child at Home, by Nancie R. Finnie. New York: E.P. Dutton, 1975.
Functional Aids for the Multiple Handicapped, by Isabel P. Robinault. New York: United Cerebral Palsy Association, 1973.

For Kids

Arnie and the New Kid, by Nancy Carlson. New York: Viking, 1990. For ages 3 to 8. A boy with cerebral palsy teaches Arnie a lesson about being different.
I'm the Big Sister Now, by Gail Owens. Niles, IL: Albert Whitman, 1989. Michelle Emmert is the younger sister of Amy, who is severely handicapped with cerebral palsy.
It's Your Turn at Bat, by Barbara Aiello and Jeffrey Shulman. Frederick, MD: 21st Century, 1989. For readers age 8 to 12.
Eddie's Blue-Winged Dragon, by C.S. Adler. New York: Putnam, 1988.
Howie Helps Himself (inspirational story about cerebral palsy child's victory in wheelchair). Available from Pediatric Projects, Inc., P.O. Box 2175, Santa Monica, CA 90406.
(See also ORTHOPEDIC DEVICES; BRAIN AND BRAIN DISORDERS; head injury; and HELP FOR SPECIAL CHILDREN on page 578.)

cerebrospinal fluid (CSF)   The fluid that circulates throughout the brain and spinal cord. In some kinds of MEDICAL TESTS, such as the LUMBAR PUNCTURE or *cisternal puncture*, samples of CSF may be taken for analysis, or some removed and replaced by a dyed fluid that shows up in images, as in a MYELOGRAM. In some medical situations; such as BRAIN TUMORS, a SHUNT may be inserted in the skull to allow the cerebrospinal fluid to flow freely past an inoperable obstruction. (See BRAIN AND BRAIN DISORDERS; SPINAL DISORDERS.)

cerebrotendinous xanthomatosis (van Bogaert's disease) A type of LIPID STORAGE DISEASE.

certificate of attendance A document confirming that a student attended school during certain specified periods. Such a certificate is often given to a student who will not be obtaining either a DIPLOMA or a CERTIFICATE OF COMPLETION, such as a student with MENTAL RETARDATION who has passed beyond normal school age but has attended school regularly, taking a CURRICULUM focusing on FUNCTIONAL SKILLS.

certificate of completion A document confirming that a student has successfully completed a course of study, usually awarded for courses that do not carry credit toward GRADUATION; sometimes called *certificate of training*.

certificate of high school equivalency A document awarded to a student who has achieved passing scores on TESTS OF GENERAL EDUCATIONAL DEVELOPMENT or their recognized equivalents; also called *General Equivalency diplomas*. Such certificates, given by a state education department or other authorized agency, are accepted as the equivalent of a high school DIPLOMA for many purposes, especially in work and POST-SECONDARY SCHOOLS. High school dropouts who do not return to finish their schooling in a formal way may study on their own, as through INDEPENDENT STUDY, and obtain a high school equivalency certificate.

certificate of training Alternate term for CERTIFICATE OF COMPLETION.

certified nurse-midwife (CNM) A registered nurse with special training in advising women during normal PREGNANCY, counseling on such matters as NUTRITION, EXERCISE, and preparation for CHILDBIRTH as part of PRENATAL CARE; assisting during LABOR, DELIVERY, and PERINATAL CARE; and providing afterbirth instruction on self-care and infant care, including BREASTFEEDING or BOTTLEFEEDING. If a woman has a HIGH-RISK PREGNANCY, she is referred to a physician early in the pregnancy, usually an OBSTETRICIAN-GYNECOLOGIST or MATERNAL AND FETAL SPECIALIST; and if complications develop during the birth, a doctor may be called in or the woman and baby transported on an emergency basis to a HOSPITAL.

CNMs must meet certain training and licensing requirements, unlike *lay midwives*, who may have experience in assisting at childbirth but not necessarily formal training or certification. According to the American College of Nurse-Midwives, most CNMs (85 percent) work in hospitals or HEALTH MAINTENANCE ORGANIZATIONS (HMOs) as part of the obstetrical team delivering babies in normal or low-risk pregnancies, often in a hospital-connected birthing center. About 11 percent of CNM-attended births take place in MATERNITY CENTERS (alternative birthing centers), and about 4 percent are HOME BIRTHS.

In some states, certified nurse-midwives can practice independently, but in many states they must practice in association with a doctor. Their activities are restricted in some areas

because of the difficulty of making required associations with doctors and hospitals to provide backup medical care. That means also that the backup hospitals are not always close by, a potential danger if an emergency occurs during delivery. Parents who wish to be attended by a CNM at delivery should carefully examine the backup arrangements, should emergency medical care be needed; often parents must themselves provide emergency transportation to the hospital. Fees for CNMs (but not for lay midwives) are covered by most insurance plans, public and private.

The midwifery movement has much expanded in recent decades, partly in reaction to hospital birthing practices, which came to be seen as cold, impersonal, and invasive; in response, the hospitals themselves have changed somewhat. CNMs have been recognized for their role in providing prenatal care, especially in underserved rural and inner-city areas to "women who are at high risk of low birthweight because of social and economic factors," often being employed by public health departments for that purpose.

For help and further information

American College of Nurse Midwives (ACNM)
1522 K Street, NW, Suite 1000
Washington, DC 20005
202-289-0171
Professional organization of certified nurse midwives, many of whom work in birthing centers. Seeks to educate public and influence social policy; serves as accrediting agency for nurse-midwife education programs; provides information and referrals.

March of Dimes Birth Defects Foundation, 914-428-7100 (local chapters in telephone-directory white pages). In some localities, chapters have available certified midwives for normal pregnancies and for prenatal services for women with high-risk pregnancies. (For full group information, see BIRTH DEFECTS.)

Other reference sources

Prenatal Care: Reaching Mothers, Reaching Infants, Sarah S. Brown, ed. Washington, DC: National Academy Press, 1988. Prepared by the National Institute of Medicine. Focuses on role of CNMs.

Health Care U.S.A., by Jean Carper. New York: Prentice Hall, 1987. Resource for general and specific health-care information, as on infertility and childbirth; lists nurse-midwife centers, key in vitro fertilization centers, embryo transfer centers, sperm banks, and other information.

Nurse Practitioners, Physician's Assistants, and Certified Nurse-Midwives: A Policy Analysis, by the Office of Technology Assessment, US Congress. Washington, DC: Government Printing Office, 1986.

cervical cap A form of BIRTH CONTROL that involves a rubber cup that fits tightly over the CERVIX, used with SPERMICIDE cream or jelly. Used widely in Europe, the cervical cap has been approved for use in the United States only since 1988. The cap is harder to insert than a DIAPHRAGM, though it has roughly the same effectiveness as a contraceptive: between 90 and 98 percent, the Food and Drug Administration estimates. Women and their sex partners can have allergic reactions to the rubber or to the spermicide, and they are warned to discontinue use in case of any genital burning or irritation. (For information on other possible problems, such as BIRTH DEFECTS, see SPERMICIDE.) The cervical cap is not recommended for women who have had an abnormal PAP SMEAR TEST or who have had TOXIC SHOCK SYNDROME, since it increases the risk of the latter, as well as some other infections of the UTERUS and CERVIX. The cap should not be inserted or used during menstrual, POSTPARTUM, or postabortion periods. (For help and further information, see BIRTH CONTROL.)

cervical mucus method A type of OVULATION METHOD of BIRTH CONTROL that monitors changes in the mucus secreted by a woman's CERVIX as a guide to when OVULATION has taken place; a type of NATURAL FAMILY PLANNING employing periodic abstinence during a woman's fertile period as a means of CONTRACEPTION, or using the same techniques to identify the most likely time for CONCEPTION, in dealing with INFERTILITY. (For help and further information, see NATURAL FAMILY PLANNING.)

cervical smear test Alternate name for the PAP SMEAR TEST.

cervical sponge An over-the-counter form of BIRTH CONTROL that uses a slightly cup-shaped soft sponge, saturated with a SPERMICIDE, to form both a physical and chemical barrier to SPERM. Before intercourse, the sponge is inserted into the VAGINA and positioned to cover the CERVIX. It should be left in place for at least six hours after intercourse and up to 24 hours, during which time intercourse can be repeated if desired. Sometimes women or their sexual partners have allergic reactions to the sponges. (See SPERMICIDE for other possible problems, including BIRTH DEFECTS.) The sponge can sometimes fragment on removal, causing infection, and on rare occasions it has been linked with cases of TOXIC SHOCK SYNDROME. The effectiveness rate of the cervical sponge as a contraceptive is about 80 to 87 percent, the Food and Drug Administration estimates. (For help and further information, see BIRTH CONTROL.)

cervix The small, fibrous neck of the UTERUS. Blood passes out from the uterus during MENSTRUATION, and after sexual intercourse, SPERM pass from the VAGINA into the uterus, normally aided by a mucus secreted by the cervix, especially around the time of OVULATION. (Changes in the cervical mucus at around the time of ovulation are used in the OVULATION METHOD of birth control.) During PREGNANCY, the cervix becomes longer and more muscular, helping to hold the developing FETUS in the uterus. Then, as a woman's body prepares for LABOR and DELIVERY, the cervix shortens and widens dramatically, forming part of the BIRTH CANAL through which the baby is delivered.

The cervix is subject to a number of disorders that can affect the reproductive system, including:

• *inflammation of the cervix (cervicitis)*: This can result from a variety of infections, especially SEXUALLY TRANSMITTED DIS-

EASES such as CHLAMYDIAL INFECTIONS, GONORRHEA, HERPES SIMPLEX, and HUMAN PAPILLOMAVIRUSES. These can readily spread to infect the uterus (*endometritis*) and FALLOPIAN TUBES (*salpingitis*), causing possible INFERTILITY; some viruses also increase the risk of cancer.

• *tumors*: A variety of growths can appear in the cervix, many of them small benign growths called *polyps*, but some malignant (see CANCER, TUMORS). The PAP SMEAR TEST involves checking cells for signs of possible malignancy. Women who are sexually very active, with multiple sex partners, are at increased risk for cervical cancer, partly because of exposure to viruses.

• *injury*: The cervix can readily be torn or strained during CHILDBIRTH, especially during a long, difficult delivery or during a badly performed ABORTION. Sometimes injuries are substantial enough to cause internal bleeding and require major surgery. In most cases, the injuries heal but may leave the muscle weakened so that it does not hold the FETUS properly in place, a condition called INCOMPETENT CERVIX. If not recognized and treated, this could lead to MISCARRIAGE or PREMATURE delivery.

If a woman has cervicitis at the time of delivery, her baby can also be infected at birth, with serious consequences, including possible blindness and PNEUMONIA. Symptoms of any such condition should be discussed with the doctor before the birth and treated if possible; if not, a CESAREAN SECTION may be indicated. (For help and further information, see PREGNANCY; OVULATION.)

cesarean section (C-section) A surgical procedure to deliver a baby through an incision in a woman's abdomen, in cases where delivery through the VAGINA is impossible or dangerous to mother or child. In decades past, the incision was usually a vertical cut made high on the abdomen, the so-called *classical uterine incision*. Some doctors, for various reasons, used a vertical incision low on the abdomen (*low vertical incision*) or two incisions, one vertical, one horizontal (*inverted-T incision*). These types of incisions carry the risk of the UTERUS rupturing during future pregnancies, a risk that led to the widespread medical rule "once a cesarean, always a cesarean."

But in recent years, most physicians have instead used a horizontal incision low on the abdomen, called a *low transverse uterine incision*, or *bikini cut*. With this approach, many women have been able to deliver a later child normally through the vagina, rather than necessarily having repeat cesareans for any future children. Various organizations (see below) developed to promote this idea of *vaginal birth after cesarean section* (VBAC), which is possible because the conditions that indicated a cesarean section in one birth are often not present in a later one.

Cesarean sections are performed for a variety of reasons, generally as a matter of medical choice, for safety of mother or child, not usually from absolute necessity. Among the situations in which cesareans are often performed are:

• FETAL DISTRESS, in which the baby has insufficient oxygen during difficult LABOR.

- *problems with the* PLACENTA, the organ that nourishes the fetus.
- *active infection in the mother*, which might damage the child, as when a HERPES SIMPLEX infection in the genitals could cause blindness or other BIRTH DEFECTS.
- *abnormal* FETAL PRESENTATION, such as *breech presentation* (feet or buttocks down) or *transverse lie* (horizontal position), rather than a vertical, head-down presentation.
- *baby too large for mother's pelvis*, which may become apparent in late stages of labor.
- MULTIPLE BIRTH, which often involves some of the above difficulties as well, especially abnormal presentation and fetal distress.
- PROLAPSE of the UMBILICAL CORD, in which the cord drops down into the VAGINA, possibly endangering the baby's oxygen supply.
- DYSTOCIA, or such difficulties that labor ceases to progress, often because the mother is overtired or because of abnormalities in the shape of her internal organs.
- *previous cesarean section* with a vertical or other problem incision.

Today the C-section itself is often performed under local (epidural) ANESTHESIA, the bladder being emptied by a CATHETER, the AMNIOTIC FLUID drained off by suction, the baby delivered through the incision, and the placenta (afterbirth) removed. Though it is still major surgery, recovery is generally faster than when general anesthesia was used.

The number of cesareans has risen dramatically in the past two decades, partly because it is a safer operation, and partly because obstetricians are concerned about malpractice charges if mother or baby otherwise has problems resulting from difficult labor. Some studies have found a wide variation in the frequency of cesarean sections, depending on the area, the doctor, and to some extent the socioeconomic level of the community, with more C-sections generally being performed in affluent areas.

When choosing an obstetrician, prospective parents may want to discuss the question of C-sections and when they should and should not be used. They should be sure they are comfortable with their chosen doctor's approach—or choose another doctor. And in choosing a HOSPITAL, they should find out the hospital's policies on allowing husbands to attend a C-section delivery. Some hospitals allow fathers to be present, but others do not because of increased risk of infection, crowded operating-room quarters, and the possibility of the father fainting. Since the mother is under only a local anesthetic, the father can give her emotional support.

For births after a previous C-section, parents may want to explore the hospital's policy of allowing at least a *trial of labor*, rather than automatically assuming that the next child will also be delivered by cesarean. One advantage of the trial of labor is that it indicates when the baby is ready to be born; otherwise, when the DUE DATE is uncertain, doctors may opt for a cesarean section when the baby is in fact PREMATURE, causing medical problems that need not have existed.

For help and further information

C/SEC (Cesareans/Support, Education, and Concern)
22 Forest Road
Framingham, MA 01701
508-877-8266
Organization of individuals and medical professionals concerned with cesarean deliveries, especially with preventing unnecessary cesareans. Encourages family-centered birth and hospital care and stresses alternative of vaginal birth after cesarean; provides information and referrals; encourages formation of mutual-support groups and person-to-person contact; publishes various materials, including newsletter, pamphlets such as *Education for Vaginal Birth After Cesarean* and *Planning for Birth*, and books such as *Frankly Speaking, The Cesarean Myth, The Vaginal Birth After Cesarean (VBAC) Experience, Essential Exercises for the Childbearing Year, Having Twins*, and *Special Delivery: A Book for Kids about Cesarean and Vaginal Birth*.

Cesarean Prevention Movement (CPM)
P.O. Box 152
University Station
Syracuse, NY 13210
315-424-1942
Organization of people concerned with increased rate of cesareans. Refers women to physicians in their community who support vaginal birth after a cesarean; encourages formation of support network; publishes various materials, including quarterly newspaper and *Cesarean Facts*.

International Childbirth Education Association (ICEA), 612-854-8660. Provides information about physicians sympathetic to vaginal birth after a cesarean; organizes classes for women who have previously had a C-section. (For full group information, see CHILDBIRTH.)

La Leche League International (LLLI), 312-455-7730. Publishes *Breastfeeding after a Cesarean Birth*. (For full group information, see BREASTFEEDING.)

Other reference sources

Birth After Cesarean: The Medical Facts, by Bruce L. Flamm. New York: Prentice Hall, 1990.
The Cesarean Myth: Choosing the Best Way to Have Your Baby, by Mortimer Rosen, M.D., and Lillian Thomas. New York: Penguin, 1989.
Silent Knife: Cesarean Prevention and Vaginal Birth After a Cesarean, by Nancy Wainer Coben and Lois Estner. Available from La Leche League International.
Cesarean Childbirth: A Handbook for Parents, by Christine Coleman Wilson. New York: New American Library, 1980.

CF Abbreviation for CYSTIC FIBROSIS.

changed circumstance In family law, a substantial change in a family situation, such as a sharp drop or increase in income, a geographical move, or illness or disability of child or either parent. Such a substantial change is generally necessary before the court will consider reviewing such matters as CUSTODY, VISITATION RIGHTS, or CHILD SUPPORT.

Chapter 1 Abbreviated name for a federal program to fund educational programs for students primarily from low-income families, especially for those who have fallen below grade level in key skills such as mathematics, READING, and writing; more precisely, Chapter 1 of Title I of the Elementary and Secondary Education Act of 1965, as amended by Chapter 1 of the Education Consolidation and Improvement Act of 1981 and the Hawkins-Stafford Elementary and Secondary School Improvements Amendments of 1988. Under these laws, each year the federal government sends a grant of money to each state (to *state educational agencies*, or SEAs), which then distribute the money to school districts based on the number of low-income families they serve. Local school districts (sometimes called *local education agencies*, or LEAs) then select "target schools"—those with the most children from low-income families—and the students in those schools most in need of help (whether themselves from low-income families or not), as indicated by TEST scores, school reports, and teachers' evaluations. The LEAs then develop programs to help those students, involving parents wherever possible, setting goals and evaluating student progress along the way; these plans are reviewed and revised annually if goals are not being met. Chapter 1 funds are often used to provide smaller classes, more teachers and teaching aides, extra REMEDIAL INSTRUCTION in key skills, and more varied teaching approaches and materials.

For help and further information

National Coalition of Title I/Chapter I Parents (NCTCP)
National Parent Center
Edmonds School Building
9th & D Streets, NE, 2nd Floor
Washington, DC 20002
202-547-9286
Robert Witherspoon, Director
Organization of parents, educators, and others concerned with the education of children falling under federal Title 1 or Chapter 1 programs, primarily children educationally disadvantaged in reading or mathematics. Provides information to parents and professionals; offers training and technical help to parents and local groups; runs National Parent Center, seeking to increase parent involvement in children's education; publishes various materials, including bimonthly newsletter and handbook. (See also EDUCATION.)

Charcot-Marie-Tooth disease Alternate name for PERONEAL MUSCULAR ATROPHY.

chariot Alternate term for a type of walker. (See ORTHOPEDIC DEVICE.)

chest compressions A technique used in cardiopulmonary resuscitation (CPR). (See ARTIFICIAL RESPIRATION.)

CHF See CONGESTIVE HEART FAILURE.

chicken pox (varicella) A highly communicable disease caused by the *varicella-zoster virus* (VZV, a type of herpes virus), spread from person to person in droplets from coughing, sneezing, or just talking, or from contact with an affected person's rash. Among children, the disease takes a mild form, involving a slight fever and a rash of fluid-filled blisters, which children must be kept from scratching to avoid bacterial infection. The disease, however inconvenient, is so mild that many doctors recommend that children be exposed to chicken pox in childhood when it will do them little or no harm; most people have, in fact, had the disease by age 10 and so have lifelong IMMUNIZATION from further attacks. But among adults (or for children with lowered resistance, as with LEUKEMIA) chicken pox can be a very serious matter, sometimes involving PNEUMONIA, various breathing difficulties (partly resulting from rash blisters in the throat), and on rare occasions ENCEPHALITIS (inflammation of the brain), REYE'S SYNDROME, HEPATITIS, and *thrombocytopenia* (see BLOOD AND BLOOD DISORDERS), sometimes leading to DEATH. Like other herpes viruses, the varicella zoster virus afterward lies dormant in the body's nerve tissues and later may cause attacks of *herpes zoster* (shingles) in elderly or debilitated people.

Pregnant women are especially at risk, not only for themselves but for their child, for the disease can produce a complex of BIRTH DEFECTS called *congenital varicella syndrome*. Among these are muscle and bone defects, deformed limbs, scars, PARALYSIS, SEIZURES, and MENTAL RETARDATION. The March of Dimes reports that birth defects are most serious if the mother contracts the disease during the first TRIMESTER (three months), with few defects resulting from the disease in the second and third trimesters. The baby is also at great risk if the mother contracts chicken pox in the few days just before delivery; then up to three out of 10 newborns will contract the disease, and perhaps 30 percent of them will die from it.

Women who have never, to their knowledge, had chicken pox can have a BLOOD TEST to check their IMMUNITY. If they are shown to be susceptible to chicken pox, they should avoid exposure to the disease if at all possible. If they are exposed, they should see a doctor immediately, because an injection of IMMUNOGLOBULIN can offer temporary immunity (see PASSIVE IMMUNIZATION) to prevent or lessen chicken pox. Researchers have developed a vaccine that is in the testing stage.

For further information

National Institute of Allergy and Infectious Diseases (NIAID), 301-496-5717. (For full group information, see ALLERGY.)

National Institute of Child Health and Human Development (NICHD), 301-496-5133. (For full group information, see PREGNANCY.)

March of Dimes Birth Defects Foundation, 914-428-7100 (local chapters in telephone-directory white pages). Publishes information sheet, *Chicken Pox During Pregnancy*.

child A son or daughter of any age, though commonly a young person, especially a preteen; in law, as in the 1974 Child Abuse Prevention and Treatment Act, a MINOR, usually meaning someone under age 18.

Child Abuse Amendments of 1984, Public Law 98-457 Federal law that includes the so-called BABY DOE LAW.

child abuse and neglect (CAN) As defined in the 1974 federal Child Abuse Prevention and Treatment Act, "the physical or mental injury, sexual abuse, negligent treatment or maltreatment of a child under 18 by a person who is responsible for the child's welfare."

Child abuse refers to deliberate acts that harm or threaten to harm the child's health or welfare, including:

• *physical abuse*. Acts that result in internal and external physical injuries, most obviously FRACTURES, BURNS, BRUISES, welts, and cuts, inflicted by hand or fist or by some other object, such as a strap or pipe, often intended as DISCIPLINE or punishment. Some types of physical punishment long thought harmless, such as shaking a child, are now known to have specific and often serious physical effects. Internal and external injuries often form recognizable patterns such as the BATTERED CHILD SYNDROME or the WHIPLASH-SHAKEN INFANT SYNDROME, which Suspected Child Abuse and Neglect (SCAN) teams use as indicators of possible child abuse. Whether or to what extent any form of CORPORAL PUNISHMENT is appropriate in either the family or school settings is hotly contested.

• *sexual abuse*. Acts of a sexual nature between a child and a parent or CAREGIVER, defined by the National Center on Child Abuse and Neglect (established by the 1974 act) as "contacts or interactions between a child and an adult when the child is being used for the sexual stimulation of the perpetrator or another person. Sexual abuse may also be committed by a person under the age of 18 when that person is either significantly older than the victim or when the perpetrator is in a position of power or control over another child." Such acts involving a young child, as in a CHILD-CARE setting, or within the family, as in INCEST between father and daughter (the most common type of sexual abuse), are viewed with extreme gravity. Sexual acts of consenting adolescents, though they are legally under the AGE OF CONSENT, are viewed less seriously, though the acts may legally be considered STATUTORY RAPE.

• *psychological and emotional abuse*. Personal verbal abuse, rejection, isolation, encouragement of self-destructive behavior, or making unrealistic demands on a child that, often combined with other types of abuse, result in negative self-image and often in behavioral problems and even MENTAL DISORDERS. Long-term verbal harassment and denigration of a

child is a particularly insidious form of abuse and is in some ways more devastating than physical abuse alone.

All states have some sort of law requiring that child abuse be reported and filed in some CENTRAL REGISTER, though they have different definitions of what constitutes abuse, who must report it, and what action should then be taken. Reports of abuse are followed up, often by a specially deputed SCAN team, usually including at least a PEDIATRICIAN, a SOCIAL WORKER, and a PSYCHIATRIST or PSYCHOLOGIST; those reports that are confirmed or verified are called *founded reports*. Critics have charged that too often warnings go unheeded, until damage is irreparable; on the other hand, critics also charge that central registers fail to fully protect confidentiality and do not properly clear their files of unverified, *unfounded reports*.

By contrast, *child neglect* refers not to actions but failures to act, especially to provide for the child's basic needs. Again, state laws and definitions vary, and not all states require reporting of child neglect, but among the kinds of neglect are:

• *physical neglect*. Failure to provide the necessities of life, such as food, clothing, shelter, hygiene, and SUPERVISION. In an infant or small child, physical neglect, especially failure to provide sufficient food, can lead to FAILURE TO THRIVE. There is, however, wide disagreement about what constitutes sufficient supervision of a young child; much depends on the age of the child, the time of day during which the child is unsupervised, and the arrangements the parent has made for the child's unsupervised time. The parent of a 12-year-old LATCHKEY CHILD, who has made thorough emergency plans for unsupervised time during the day, is unlikely to be charged with physical neglect.

• *medical neglect*. Failure to provide medical or dental care for a condition that, if untreated, could cause severe damage or death to a child. Often medical neglect is part of a wider picture of neglect. But among some religious groups (such as Christian Scientists) who disavow medical treatment, charges of medical neglect sometimes bring before the courts and social agencies painful and difficult conflicts between the PARENTS' RIGHTS to make decisions about medical care and the PARENTS' RESPONSIBILITIES, as interpreted by the state, to provide essential medical care. Some cases of medical neglect, especially for infants with severe handicaps, come under the BABY DOE LAW.

• *educational neglect*. Failure to provide for a child's COGNITIVE DEVELOPMENT, and sometimes also failure to see that the child attends school regularly. Parents of chronic TRUANTS are legally liable, and in some areas government agencies are attempting to reduce or eliminate welfare payments for families whose children do not attend school regularly without a valid excuse.

• *moral neglect*. Failure to teach basic principles of right and wrong, what some call general social values. In practice, this general stricture applies to parents who knowingly allow their children to commit crimes, such as stealing or prostitution, or indeed push them into doing so.

Indicators of Child Abuse and Neglect

Category	Child's appearance	Child's behavior	Caretaker's behavior
Physical abuse	Bruises and welts (on the face, lips, or mouth; in various stages of healing; on large areas of the torso, back, buttocks, or thighs; in unusual patterns, clustered, or reflective of the instrument used to inflict them; on several different surface areas) Burns (cigar or cigarette burns; glove- or socklike burns or doughnut-shaped burns on the buttocks or genitalia indicative of immersion in hot liquid; rope burns on the arms, legs, neck, or torso; patterned burns that show the shape of the item (iron, grill, etc.) used to inflict them) Fractures (skull, jaw, or nasal fractures; spiral fractures of the long (arm and leg) bones; fractures in various states of healing; multiple fractures; any fracture in a child under the age of two) Lacerations and abrasions (to the mouth, lip, gums, or eye; to the external genitalia) Human bite marks	Wary of physical contact with adults Apprehensive when other children cry Demonstrates extremes in behavior (e.g., extreme aggressiveness or withdrawal) Seems frightened of parents Reports injury by parents	Has history of abuse as a child Uses harsh discipline inappropriate to child's age, transgression, and condition Offers illogical, unconvincing, contradictory, or no explanation of child's injury Seems unconcerned about child Significantly misperceives child (e.g., sees him as bad, evil, a monster, etc.) Psychotic or psychopathic Misuses alcohol or other drugs Attempts to conceal child's injury or to protect identity of person responsible
Neglect	Consistently dirty, unwashed, hungry, or inappropriately dressed Without supervision for extended periods of time or when engaged in dangerous activities Constantly tired or listless Has unattended physical problems or lacks routine medical care Is exploited, overworked, or kept from attending school Has been abandoned	Is engaging in delinquent acts (e.g., vandalism, drinking, prostitution, drug use, etc.) Is begging or stealing food Rarely attends school	Misuses alcohol or other drugs Maintains chaotic home life Shows evidence of apathy or futility Is mentally ill or of diminished intelligence Has long-term chronic illnesses Has history of neglect as a child
Sexual abuse	Has torn, stained, or bloody underclothing Experience pain or itching in the genital area Has bruises or bleeding in external genitalia, vagina, or anal regions Has venereal disease Has swollen or red cervix, vulva, or perineum Has semen around mouth or genitalia or on clothing Is pregnant	Appears withdrawn or engages in fantasy or infantile behavior Has poor peer relationships Is unwilling to participate in physical activities Is engaging in delinquent acts or runs away States he/she has been sexually assaulted by parent/caretaker	Extremely protective or jealous of child Encourages child to engage in prostitution or sexual acts in the presence of caretaker Has been sexually abused as a child Is experiencing marital difficulties Misuses alcohol or other drugs Is frequently absent from the home

Continued on page 86

Indicators of Child Abuse and Neglect (Continued)

Category	Child's appearance	Child's behavior	Caretaker's behavior
Emotional maltreatment	Emotional maltreatment, often less tangible than other forms of child abuse and neglect, can be indicated by behaviors of the child and the caretaker.	Appears overly compliant, passive, undemanding	Blames or belittles child
		Is extremely aggressive, demanding, or rageful	Is cold and rejecting
		Shows overly adoptive behaviors, either inappropriately adult (e.g., parents other children) or inappropriately infantile (e.g., rocks constantly, sucks thumb, is enuretic)	Withholds love
			Treats siblings unequally
			Seems unconcerned about child's problem
		Lags in physical, emotional, and intellectual development	
		Attempts suicide	

Source: *Interdisciplinary Glossary on Child Abuse and Neglect: Legal, Medical, Social Work Terms* (1980). Prepared for the National Center on Child Abuse and Neglect, Children's Bureau, Administration of Children, Youth and Families, Department of Health and Human Services by the Midwest Parent-Child Welfare Resource Center (now Region V Child Abuse and Neglect Resource Center).

• *psychological/emotional neglect*. Failure to provide support for the child's basic psychological growth and development, in essence a lack of responsiveness to the child's needs, hopes, fears, and aspirations, a quality sometimes called *nurturance*. While such neglect undoubtedly exists, it is extremely difficult to prove and few states have laws regarding it.

The procedure for handling suspected child abuse and neglect cases varies widely. In general, once a child-abuse report or a suspect hospital admission is made, the child is removed from the situation. If the charge is of parental abuse or neglect, the child is generally taken out of the home and put into protective or emergency CUSTODY, also called *detention*. Sometimes the whole family will be taken to a 24-hour residential *family shelter* for short-term diagnosis and treatment, as part of CRISIS INTERVENTION. Quickly, usually within 48 hours, a social worker, PROBATION officer, or other official files a *detention request*; this calls for a *detention hearing* to be held, usually within 24 hours of filing, to see whether the child should be kept apart from the family until a full court hearing takes place. Meanwhile, ideally in the same 72 hours, various workers evaluate the child, parent, family, and home environment, and at a multidisciplinary *dispositional conference* recommend measures needed to protect the child, long-term treatment for family members, and whether the court needs to be involved.

At a *dispositional hearing*, a JUVENILE COURT or FAMILY COURT will decide whether or not the child should be returned to the home and, if so, under what conditions, or placed in a different setting, such as with FOSTER PARENTS, in a GROUP HOME, or in a relative's home. Following the general rule of the BEST INTERESTS OF THE CHILD, the child is often kept in the home, that being seen as giving the most emotional and financial stability. Often the child and some or all family members are given *day treatment*, services that include psychological and social counseling, structured supervision, and activities designed to break the cycle of abuse and begin the process of repairing the damage. However, if the situation is regarded as sufficiently dangerous or destructive, the social workers will recommend a *dependency hearing*, in which the state takes temporary custody of the child, providing for counseling and therapy of the child and family and aiming to reunite the family. If this fails, however, the state may seek TERMINATION OF PARENTAL RIGHTS.

The National Center on Child Abuse and Neglect has recommended that people accused of child abuse or neglect—family members or other caregivers—should have their legal rights protected, including the right to

• be informed of their legal rights;
• receive written notice and information on legal rights regarding protective custody;
• have a lawyer's counsel during any trial or ADMINISTRATIVE PROCEDURE;
• appeal a decision;
• have material in a child-abuse or neglect report kept confidential.

In essence, the Center is encouraging extension of rights to DUE PROCESS into areas where they formerly seldom applied. The Center has also recommended that the government's child protective services have legal counsel and that the child's interests be represented independently, as by a court-appointed GUARDIAN *ad litem* (at law) or COURT-APPOINTED SPECIAL ADVOCATE (CASA).

Parents need to be aware of the signs that might indicate possible child abuse or neglect, because the child is in the care of many people at various times, including relatives and other people living in the household, former wives or husbands, friends, neighbors, baby-sitters, child-care workers, teachers, and others. It is only human to think that child abuse "can't happen here," but in fact it is far more common than most people recognize. Parents can best help their children by regularly taking a hardheaded look at the kinds of signs and symptoms that health, social, and other community officials look at, as outlined in INDICATORS OF CHILD ABUSE AND NEGLECT (page 85).

So much publicity has been given to child abuse in recent years that there is some danger of hysteria or overreaction, and in rightly seeking to identify cases of child abuse some people can be overzealous, catching innocent and unsuspecting parents and other caregivers in a complicated net of officialdom. Some medical conditions, such as OSTEOGENESIS IMPERFECTA or MONGOLIAN SPOT, can mistakenly be seen as indicating child abuse. Vindictive ex-spouses and others can also sometimes use charges of child abuse as part of some personal contest. Parents can therefore also protect *themselves* by looking carefully at the list, for these are the kinds of appearances and actions that make officials suspect child abuse.

Seeking to prevent child abuse and neglect, social-work professionals watch for such signals and make early intervention, trying to offer help or relieve stress before a family's problems become too severe. *Abused parents*, adults who were themselves subjected to abuse as a child, are considered at higher-than-normal risk of later inflicting child abuse. Among the factors that tag a *family at risk* for child abuse are:

- abused parents
- ALCOHOL or DRUG ABUSE
- MENTAL DISORDER of parent
- MENTAL RETARDATION of parent
- *anomie* (personal isolation and disorientation) of parent
- social isolation of family
- parental unemployment or strong stress and dissatisfaction in work
- lack of maternal–infant BONDING
- lack of resources for child care
- parental ignorance of infant care and child development
- unwanted child
- immature parents
- HANDICAPPED or HYPERACTIVE child
- baby with COLIC
- parental discord

- sudden changes in family, such as DEATH, illness, or separation

If a situation seems immediately threatening to a child's health or welfare, social workers make crisis intervention. Recognizing that family patterns can perpetuate child abuse and neglect, many organizations and self-help groups (see below) also help families try to break the cycle of child abuse and neglect, especially by getting help to deal with current problems, by linking with other families sharing similar problems, and by learning new ways of interacting within a family, including nonviolent ways of training and disciplining children.

The concept of child abuse and neglect has also been applied to the failure by state institutions, such as jails or group homes, to properly care for children, and has been used to bring legal pressure to change institutional conditions.

For help and general information
About Child Abuse (Including Sexual Abuse)

National Center on Child Abuse and Neglect
Children's Bureau/Administration for Children, Youth and Families
U.S. Department of Health and Human Services
P.O. Box 1182
Washington, DC 20013
202-245-0586

Children's Bureau Clearinghouse on Child Abuse and Neglect Information
202-245-2856

Organizations established under the federal 1974 Child Abuse Prevention and Treatment Act. Conduct, compile, and disseminate research and national statistics; act as information clearinghouse; provide technical assistance; fund pilot prevention, identification, and treatment projects, including parent self-help projects; publish various materials.

American Association for Protecting Children (AAPC)
c/o American Humane Association
63 Inverness Drive East
Englewood, CO 80112
303-792-9900; toll-free number 800-227-5242
Patricia Schene, Director

Organization of people and groups interested in preventing child abuse and neglect, a division of the American Humane Association. Promotes stronger services to protect children, offering training to community professionals and influencing legislation; operates a toll-free number for research and information; publishes various materials, including quarterly *Protecting Children* and various books and pamphlets, mostly oriented toward professionals in the medical, educational, and social services.

Childhelp U. S. A., Inc. (CUI)
6463 Independence Avenue

Woodland Hills, California 91370
818-347-7280, toll-free hotline 800-4-A-CHILD [422-4253]
Sara O' Meara, Board Chairman

Organization focusing on prevention and treatment of child abuse. Operates Village of Childhelp residential center; runs Family Evaluation Program and Aftercare Program; operates hotline; sponsors research; seeks to educate public and influence government policy; publishes various materials, including book *Assault Against Children*.

International Society for Prevention of Child Abuse and Neglect (ISPCAN)

1205 Oneida Street
Denver, CO 80220
303-321-3963
Margaret A. Lynch, M.D., President

Organization of individuals and groups concerned with preventing child neglect and abuse, especially sexual. Shares experiences through international congresses; publishes quarterly *International Journal: Child Abuse and Neglect*.

National Committee for Prevention of Child Abuse (NCPCA)

332 South Michigan Avenue, Suite 950
Chicago, IL 60604
312-663-3520
Anne Harris Cohn, Executive Director

Organization devoted to influencing public awareness of and policy regarding child abuse, sexual, physical, or emotional. Provides information and referrals; conducts child-abuse prevention programs and media campaigns; publishes various materials, including *A Future Filled with Healthy Minds and Bodies: A Call to Abolish Corporal Punishment in Schools*.

National Council on Child Abuse and Family Violence (NCCAFV)

1050 Connecticut Avenue, NW, Suite 300
Washington, DC 20036
202-429-6695, toll-free number 800-222-2000
Alan Davis, President

Organization supporting community centers for prevention and treatment of violence and abuse in families. Acts as clearinghouse for information on and funding for such centers; operates toll-free referral service; publishes newsletter and other materials.

Defense for Children International–United States of America (DCI-USA)

210 Forsyth Street
New York, NY 10002
212-353-0951
Kay Castelle, Executive Director

Part of an international organization of professionals and others interested in promoting stronger protection for the rights of children under the UN Convention on the Rights of the Child, as in cases of child labor, education, child abuse, parental kidnapping, and armed conflict. Provides information; maintains database on children's rights issues; publishes newsletter and other materials, including magazine *International Children's Rights Monitor*.

National Court Appointed Special Advocates Association, 206-328-8588. (For full group information, see COURT-APPOINTED SPECIAL ADVOCATES.)

National Legal Resource Center For Child Advocacy and Protection

American Bar Association
1800 M Street, NW, South Lobby
Washington, DC 20036
202-331-2200

Professional organization focusing on using the legal system to protect children. Gathers resources and provides information on topics such as child custody, child abuse, and missing children.

National Center for Youth Law (NCYL)

1663 Mission Street, 5th Floor
San Francisco, CA 94103
415-543-3307
John O'Toole, Director

Organization aiding legal services programs and lawyers in representing low-income young people in the United States, in areas such as child abuse and neglect, termination of parental rights, foster care, juvenile delinquency, health problems, and housing discrimination due to children. Provides consultation, training, research, drafting of legal documents, and aid in writing briefs; participates directly in litigation in certain cases; gathers and maintains library of legal and other materials relating to youth law; publishes bimonthly *Youth Law News*.

National Organization for Victim Assistance (NOVA)

717 D Street, NW
Washington, DC 20531
202-393-6682
Marlene A. Young, Executive Director

Organization of victims of crime and the whole range of professionals who work with them, medical, legal, social, and psychological. Seeks to advocate claims of victims for relief and recovery; provides direct aid and also referrals to victim assistance programs and other available services; acts as information clearinghouse; among its focuses are juvenile victimization, minority victims, sexual assault, and domestic violence; publishes various materials, including newsletter and *Victim Service Program Directory*.

National Coalition Against Domestic Violence

P.O. Box 15127
Washington, DC 20003
202-293-8860, toll-free number 800-333-SAFE [7233]
Marcia Niemann, Executive Director

Nationwide network of shelters and support services for battered women and children; operates toll-free number.

Odyssey Institute Corporation (OIC)
817 Fairfield Corporation
Bridgeport, CT 06604
203-334-3488
Judianne Densen-Gerber, M.D., President
Organization focusing on child advocacy on various issues, including child abuse and gifted children. Sponsors formation of local PACT (Protect America's Children Today) groups; publishes quarterly *Odyssey Journal*.

About Special Programs
for Abused Children, Including Sexual Abuse

Committee for Children (CFC)
172 20th Avenue
Seattle, WA 98122
206-322-5050
Alice-Ray-Keil, Executive Director
Organization that develops curriculum for children K to 12, seeking to prevent child abuse. Works to educate educators and general public as to sexual abuse; seeks to change public policy and legislation; publishes various print and video materials, including *Prevention Notes, Talking About Touching: A Personal Safety Curriculum, Talking About Touching with Preschoolers*, and videocassette *Yes, You Can Say No*.

Parents United
P.O. Box 952
San Jose, CA 95108
408-280-5055, 24-hour hotline 408-279-1957
Henry Giaretto, Executive Director
Network of professionally guided mutual-support self-help groups of individuals and families with experience of child molestation, including incest. Provides therapy for the whole family and medical, legal, and vocational counseling; active arms include Daughters and Sons United, for sexually abused children (5 to 18) and their families, and Adults Molested as Children United (AMACU), for those over 18 abused as children.

Parents Against Molesters (PAM)
P.O. Box 3357
Portsmouth, VA 23701
804-465-1582
Barbara Barker, Executive Director
Organization of children who have been sexually molested, their families, and interested others. Aims to promote public awareness of the problems faced by molestation victims and to encourage formation of self-help groups, with referral to trained counselors; publishes newsletter *Parents Against Molesters*.

People Against Rape (PAR)
P.O. Box 160
Chicago, IL 60635

312-745-1025
Marie Howard, President
Organization that aims to protect children from sexual abuse. Offers self-defense training for school-age children; publishes various materials, including booklet *Hands Off, I'm Special*.

SHARE, Inc.
P.O. Box 1342
Beverly Hills, CA 90213
213-274-5361
Judy Feder, President
Organization raising money for special programs for mentally retarded and abused children. Funds diagnostic and counseling center, infant development and preschool programs, special education for school-age children, art center, and sheltered workshops for older retarded; Citizen Advocacy Program assigns a volunteer to represent each retarded person.

Society's League Against Molestation (SLAM)
c/o Women Against Rape/Childwatch
P.O. Box 346
Collingswood, NJ 08108
609-858-7800
Joan McKenna, Director
Organization working to prevent sexual abuse and exploitation of children. Seeks to educate public and change public policy and legislation; monitors court cases and collects data; provides aid and support to child molestation victims and their families; operates telephone referral service; publishes newsletter.

End Violence Against the Next Generation (EVAN-G), 415-527-0454. Publishes *Child Abuse in Schools: A National Disgrace* and *Religious Value and Child Abuse*. (For full group information, see CORPORAL PUNISHMENT.)

National Center for the Study of Corporal Punishment and Alternatives in the Schools (NCSCPAS), 215-787-6091. (For full group information, see CORPORAL PUNISHMENT.)

Parents and Teachers Against Violence in Education (PTAVE), 415-831-1661. (For full group information, see CORPORAL PUNISHMENT.)

About Programs for Child-Abusing Parents

Parents Anonymous (PA)
6733 South Sepulveda, Suite 270
Los Angeles, CA 90045
213-410-9732, toll-free number 800-421-0353
Margot Fritz, Executive Director
Organization of child-abusing adults and interested others, on model of Alcoholics Anonymous. Mutual-support self-help groups aim at rehabilitation of child abusers; publishes newsletter and other printed materials.

Sexaholics Anonymous
P.O. Box 300
Simi Valley, CA 93062
818-704-9854
Network of mutual-support self-help programs, modeled on Alcoholics Anonymous, for people addicted to destructive or self-destructive sexual behavior, including incest. Publishes various materials, including newsletter.

Other reference sources

General Works

Recognizing Child Abuse: A Guide for the Concerned, by Douglas J. Besharov. New York: Free Press/Macmillan, 1990.

The Abusing Family, revised edition, by Blair Justice and Rita Justice. New York: Plenum, 1990.

Not My Child: A Mother Confronts Her Child's Sexual Abuse, by Patricia Crowley. Garden City, NY: Doubleday, 1990.

Children Are People Too: The Case Against Physical Punishment, by Peter Newell. London: Bedford Square, 1989.

Spare the Rod: Breaking the Cycle of Child Abuse, by Phil E. Quinn. Nashville, TN: Abingdon, 1988.

Background Books

Slaughter of the Innocents: Child Abuse Through the Ages and Today, by Sander J. Breiner, M.D. New York: Plenum, 1990.

Too Old to Cry: Abused Teens in Today's America, by Robert J. Ackerman and Lee Marvin Joiner. Summit, PA: TAB, 1990.

Sexual Assault and Child Sexual Abuse: A National Directory of Victim/Survivor Services and Prevention Programs, Linda Webster, ed. Phoenix, AZ: Oryx, 1989.

Soul Murder: The Effects of Childhood Abuse and Deprivation, by Leonard Shengold. New Haven, CT: Yale University Press, 1989.

On Trial: America's Courts and Their Treatment of Sexually Abused Children. Boston: Beacon, 1989.

The Encyclopedia of Child Abuse, by Robin E. Clark and Judith Freeman Clark. New York: Facts on File, 1989.

Family Violence, Lloyd Ohlin and Michael Tonry, eds. Chicago: University of Chicago Press, 1988.

The Violent Family: Victimization of Women, Children and Elders, Nancy Hitchings, ed. New York: Human Sciences, 1988.

Triumph over Darkness: Understanding and Healing the Trauma of Childhood Sexual Abuse, by Leslie Hatton and Wendy Wood. Hillsboro, OR: Beyond Words, 1988.

The Battle and the Backlash: The Child Sexual Abuse War, by David Hechler. Lexington, MA: Lexington, 1988.

Incest and Sexuality: A Guide to Understanding Healing, by Wendy Maltz and Beverly Holman. Lexington, MA: Lexington, 1988.

Heroes of Their Own Lives: The Politics and History of Family Violence, by Linda Gordon. New York: Viking, 1988.

Intimate Violence: The Definitive Study of the Causes and Consequences of Abuse in the American Family, by Richard J.

Gelles and Murray A. Straus. New York: Simon & Schuster, 1988.

The Politics of Child Abuse, by Paul Eberle and Shirley Eberle. Secaucus, NJ: Lyle Stuart, 1986.

Thou Shalt Not Be Aware: Society's Betrayal of the Child, by Alice Miller. New York: Farrar, Straus & Giroux, 1984.

For Your Own Good: Hidden Cruelty in Child Rearing and the Roots of Violence, by Alice Miller. New York: Farrar, Straus & Giroux, 1983.

Hope for the Children: A Personal History of Parents Anonymous, by Patte Wheat and Leonard L. Lieber. Minneapolis: Winston, 1979.

Corporal Punishment in American Education, I.A. Hyman and J.H. Wise, eds. Philadelphia: Temple University Press, 1979.

Child Abuse and Neglect: Annotated Bibliography, by Beatrice J. Kalisch. Westport, CT: Greenwood, 1978.

Wednesday's Children: A Study of Child Neglect and Abuse, by Leontine Young. New York: McGraw-Hill, 1964.

Effects of Child Abuse on Later Adults

Growing Through the Pain: The Incest Survivor's Companion, Anonymous. New York: Prentice Hall, 1990.

Soul Survivors: A New Beginning for Adults Abused as Children, by J. Patrick Gannon. New York: Prentice Hall, 1990.

The Courage to Heal Workbook: For Women and Men Survivors of Child Sexual Abuse, by Laura David. New York: Perennial Library, 1990.

Adult Children of Abusive Parents: A Healing Program for Those Who Have Been Physically, Sexually, or Emotionally Abused, by Steven Farmer. Chicago: Contemporary, 1989; New York: Ballantine, 1990.

Victims No Longer: Men Recovering from Incest and Other Childhood Sexual Abuse, by Mike Lew. New York: Harper/Perennial Library, 1990.

Reclaiming the Heart: A Handbook of Help and Hope for Survivors of Incest, by Mary Beth McLure. New York: Warner, 1990.

Abused! A Guide to Recovery for Adult Survivors of Emotional/Physical Abuse, by Dee Anna Parrish. Barrytown, NY: Station Hill, 1990.

Broken Boys/Mending Men: Recovery from Childhood Sexual Abuse, by Stephen D. Grubman-Black. Blue Ridge Summit, PA: TAB Books, 1990.

Virginia Woolf: The Impact of Childhood Sexual Abuse on Her Life and Work, by Louise DeSalvo. New York: Ballantine, 1990.

The Healing Way: Adult Recovery from Childhood Sexual Abuse, by Kristin A. Kunzman. Center City, MN: Hazelden, 1990.

Forgiveness: How to Make Peace with Your Past and Get On with Your Life, by Sidney B. Simon and Suzanne Simon. New York: Warner, 1990.

Strong at the Broken Places: Overcoming the Trauma of Childhood Abuse, by Linda T. Sanford. New York: Random House, 1990.

Reclaiming Our Lives: Adult Survivors of Incest, by Carol Poston and Karen Lison. Boston: Little, Brown, 1989.

Emotional Healing, by Karen Paine-Gernes and Terry Hunt. New York: Warner, 1989.

Secret Scars: A Guide for Survivors of Child Sexual Abuse, by Cynthia Crosson Tower. New York: Viking, 1988.

The Courage to Heal: A Guide for Women Survivors of Child Sexual Abuse, by Ellen Bass and Laura Davis. New York: Harper & Row/Perennial, 1988.

Personal Stories

What Lisa Knew: The Truths and Lies of the Steinberg Case, by Joyce Johnson. New York: Putnam, 1990.

Nap Time: The True Story of Sexual Abuse at a Suburban Day Care Center, by Lisa Manshel. New York: Morrow, 1990.

An Uncommon Hero: One Mother Who Went to Jail to Protect Her Child from Sexual Abuse, by Stephen T. Curwood. New York: Warner, 1990.

Perfect Victim: The True Story of "The Girl in the Box," by Carla Norton and Christine McGuire. New York: Morrow, 1988.

One Child, by Torey L. Hayden. New York: Putnam, 1980; Avon paperback. A therapist tells of a gifted sexually abused child, misdiagnosed as emotionally disturbed.

To a Safer Place. 1987. 58-minute film/video from AIMS Media, 6901 Woodley Avenue, Van Nuys, CA 91406. A mother explores her sexual abuse as a child. For adults.

Understanding Survivors of Abuse: Stories of Homeless and Run-away Adolescents, by Jane Levine Powers and Barbara Weiss Jaklitsch. Lexington, MA: Lexington, 1989.

Books for Professionals

Child Abuse, by E. Clay Jorgenson. New York: Cross-roads/Continuum, 1990. For caregivers helping both children and parents.

The Seduction Theory: Sexual Abuse and Psychiatric Disorders, by David Sack. Summit, NJ: PIA, 1990.

Child Sexual Abuse: An Interdisciplinary Manual for Diagnosis, Case Management, and Treatment, by Kathleen Boulborn Faller. New York: Columbia University Press, 1989.

The Sexual Abuse of Children: A Comprehensive Guide to Current Knowledge and Intervention Strategies, by Jeffrey J. Haugaard and N. Dickon Reppucci. San Francisco: Jossey-Bass, 1988.

The Dark Side of Families: Current Family Violence Research, David Finkelhor, Richard J. Gelles, Gerald T. Hotaling, and Murray Straus, eds. Beverly Hills, CA: Sage, 1983.

Child Abuse—An Interactional Event, by Alfred Kadushin and Judith A. Martin, with the assistance of James McGloin. New York: Columbia University Press, 1981.

On Children's Rights

Stolen Childhood: In Search of the Rights of the Child, by Anuradha Vittachi. Cambridge, MA: Basil Blackwell, 1990.

Up Against the Law: Your Legal Rights as a Minor, by Ross R. Olney and Patricia J. Olney. New York: Dutton, 1985.

Legal Rights of Children, Robert M. Horowitz and Howard A. Davidson, eds. Colorado Springs, CO: Shepard's/McGraw-Hill, 1984.

For Kids

Child Abuse, revised edition, by Elaine Landau. New York: Messner, 1990.

Child Abuse, by Gail Stewart. New York: Crestwood, 1990. Part of the Facts About Series.

Child Abuse, by William A. Check. New York: Chelsea House, 1989. For grades 7 to 12.

Violence and the Family, by Gilda Berger. New York: Watts, 1990. For grades 9 to 12.

My Body Is Private, by Linda Walvoord Girard. Niles, IL: Albert Whitman, 1984. For children ages 5 to 8.

Hands Off . . . I'm Special, by Dan Lema and Marie Howard. Hollywood, FL: Frederick Fell, 1988. On developing self-esteem and positive attitudes to defend oneself against assault.

(See also MISSING CHILDREN.)

childbirth   The whole process of a baby's emergence from the UTERUS into independent life, which culminates nine months of PREGNANCY in the intense activity of LABOR and DELIVERY. For most of history, a woman was attended at childbirth by a MID-WIFE. Only in the last few centuries were men even allowed in the rooms where labor and delivery took place. But with the rise of modern medicine, OBSTETRICIAN/GYNECOLOGISTS became the main health-care providers for women giving birth, and by the mid-20th century most births, especially in the United States, took place in HOSPITALS, which came to routinely use ANESTHESIA and painkillers (*analgesics*) and various kinds of medical technology and techniques, such as FETAL MONITORING, FORCEPS DELIVERY, VACUUM EXTRACTION, EPISIOTOMY, and CESAREAN SECTION. Each of these came as great advances in their day, freeing women from the great pain of childbirth and providing life- and health-saving alternatives in cases of difficult deliveries.

In recent decades, however, many people began to feel that medical technology was sometimes overused and that childbirth in the hospital was cold, impersonal, and invasive. So came the rise of the *natural childbirth* movement, often called *prepared childbirth*, *psychoprophylaxis*, or *psychophysical preparation for childbirth*, which stresses avoidance of intervention in the birth process unless absolutely necessary. Prepared childbirth emphasizes educational programs for pregnant women and their BIRTH PARTNERS, focusing on relaxation techniques for dealing with labor pains. The woman and her birth partner, usually the father but sometimes a relative or friend, normally attend a series of classes, taught by CERTIFIED NURSE-MIDWIVES or other trained childbirth educators. These often focus on a set of breathing exercises to lessen tension in the body during labor and help diminish pain or make it easier to deal with and therefore to require less in the way of anesthesia and analgesics. Designed as well to diminish fear and anxiety through knowledge, the classes educate the couple about the anatomy and physiology of pregnancy and delivery, parenting skills, PRENATAL CARE, and some of the early choices that must be made, such as BREASTFEEDING or BOTTLEFEEDING. Many also stress exercises to improve muscle tone and stamina in preparation for childbirth.

Among the best-known natural childbirth approaches are:

• *Lamaze method* or *Lamaze-Pavlov method*, the most widespread approach today, which spurred the natural childbirth movement from the 1960s in the United States. Breathing exercises stress concentrating on a focal point, to ease consciousness of pain and to keep the all-important oxygen supply flowing to the baby and the muscles of the UTERUS. The birth partner coaches the process, sometimes offering massages to encourage relaxation.

• *Read (Dick-Read) method*, an approach developed in the 1930s by the man who coined the phrase "natural childbirth," recognizing that much of the pain of labor and delivery was due to what he termed the *fear tension pain syndrome*. To counter this, he developed classes that included physical exercises, stressing the development of different breathing patterns for different stages of labor.

• *LeBoyer method*, which stresses gentle delivery in a quiet, dimly lit, relaxing room, with a minimum of interference (such as pulling on the baby's head) and avoiding overstimulation of the baby's senses. To foster maternal–infant BONDING, the newborn is placed on the mother's abdomen and massaged immediately after birth, then gently washed by the father in warm water.

• *Bradley method*, which focuses heavily on the father as coach, and so is often called *husband-coached childbirth*; it encourages continuation of normal activities during the first stage of labor.

The choice of childbirth approach is generally intertwined with the choice of health-care providers and birth sites. Along with natural childbirth, the midwife movement has revived, with practitioners now generally trained certified nurse-midwives (CNMs). At first, CNMs worked mostly in MATERNITY CENTERS or attending at HOME BIRTHS but more recently are often found in hospitals as well. Partly in response, many hospitals now offer a much wider range of alternatives, such as BIRTHING ROOMS and LABOR/DELIVERY/RECOVERY ROOMS. Not only fathers, but also in some cases other family members as well, for the first time have been able to become active participants in the childbirth process, if desired.

Women have more options in the childbirth position, too. Though lying flat on a bed has been the standard mode in recent centuries, the BIRTHING CHAIR (which goes back to at least biblical times) has been revived—a high-backed chair with a hole or semicircular cut in the seat. Other approaches have also been used, including a reclining bed with a drop-down bottom.

Parents will want to learn more about these approaches, and about the pros and cons of various birthing sites, compared with traditional hospital delivery, before deciding which approach best suits their needs and desires. Much will depend on the parents' personal inclinations, though choices are somewhat more limited in cases of HIGH-RISK PREGNANCY.

For help and further information

General Information

National Center for Education in Child and Maternal Health (NCEMCH), 202-625-8400. National Maternal and Child Health Clearinghouse (NMCHC), 202-625-8410. (For full group information, see PREGNANCY.)

National Institute of Child Health and Human Development (NICHD), 301-496-5133. (For full group information, see PREGNANCY.)

International Association of Parents and Professionals for Safe Alternatives in Childbirth (NAPSAC)
Route 1, Box 646
Marble Hill, MO 63764
314-238-2010
David Stewart, Executive Director
International organization of individuals and childbirth professionals promoting alternatives to traditional hospital-based childbirth. Areas of interest include natural childbirth, parental education about childbirth alternatives, midwifery, breastfeeding, and nutrition of pregnant women. Provides information and referrals; publishes *Directory of Alternative Birth Services and Consumer Guide*.

International Childbirth Education Association (ICEA)
P.O. Box 20048
Minneapolis, MN 55420
612-854-8660
Trudy Keller, President
Organization of individuals and groups concerned with education of parents for childbirth and breastfeeding; supports safe, low-cost alternatives and parental choice; publishes various materials.

Childbirth Education Foundation (CEF)
P.O. Box 5
Richboro, PA 18954
215-357-2792
James C. Peron, Executive Director
Organization of people concerned with reform of childbirth methods and treatment of newborns. Promotes birthing centers, certified nurse-midwives, and similar alternatives; provides training for childbirth educators, including Lamaze method, and La Leche instructors; publishes various materials.

American Academy of Husband-Coached Childbirth (AAHCC)
P.O. Box 5224
Sherman Oaks, CA 91413

818-788-6662, Pregnancy Hotline, for referrals, U.S. except CA, 800-423-2397; in CA, 800-42B-IRTH [422-4784]

James Hathaway, Executive Director

For-profit organization dedicated to spreading use of the Bradley Method® of natural childbirth. Trains instructors; provides information and referrals; operates Pregnancy Hotline; publishes various print and audiovisual materials.

American Society for Prophylaxis in Obstetrics (ASPO/Lamaze)

1840 Wilson Boulevard, Suite 204
Arlington, VA 22201
703-524-7802, toll-free number 800-368-4404

Robert H. Moran, Executive Director

Organization of medical professionals including nurse-midwives, trained instructors, parents, and others interested in the Lamaze method of natural childbirth. Operates toll-free number; trains and certifies instructors; provides information and makes referrals; publishes various materials.

Read Natural Childbirth Foundation (RNCF)

P.O. Box 956
San Rafael, CA 94915
415-456-8462

Margaret B. Farley, President

Organization of health professionals and others interested in the Grantly Dick-Read approach to natural childbirth. Publishes various materials, including *Preparation for Childbirth* and film *A Time to Be Born*.

National Association of Childbirth Education (NACE)

3940 11th Street
Riverside, CA 92501
714-686-0422

Rebecca Smith, President

Professional organization of certified childbirth educators, using the Pavlov-Lamaze method.

National Association of Childbearing Centers (NACC), 215-234-8068. (For full group information, see MATERNITY CENTER.)

American College of Nurse Midwives (ACNM), 202-289-0171. (For full group information, see CERTIFIED NURSE-MIDWIFE.)

Maternity Center Association (MCA), 212-369-7300. (For full group information, see MATERNITY CENTER.)

Informed Homebirth/Informed Birth and Parenting (IH/IBP), 313-662-6857. (For full group information, see HOME BIRTH.)

Other reference sources

Methods of Childbirth: The Completely Updated Version of a Classic Work for Today's Woman, revised edition, by Constance A. Bean. New York: Morrow, 1990.

The Midwife's Pregnancy and Childbirth Book: Having Your Baby Your Way, by Marion McCartney and Antonia Van der Meer. New York: Holt, 1990.

Preparation for Birth: The Complete Guide to the Lamaze Method, by Beverly Savage and Diana Simkin. New York: Ballantine, 1989.

The Birth Partner: Everything You Need to Know to Help a Woman Through Childbirth, by Penny Simkin. Boston: Harvard Common, 1989.

The Birth Partner's Handbook, by Carl Jones with Jan Jones. Deephaven, MN: Meadowbrook, 1989.

Labor Pains, by Kate Klimo. New York: Ivy/Ballantine, 1989. Following women from Lamaze class through birth.

Birth, by Nancy Durrell McKenna. North Pomfret, CT: David & Charles, 1989. Photographs of birth.

Your Child's First Journey: A Guide to Prepared Birth from Pregnancy to Parenthood, second edition, by Ginny Brinkley, Linda Goldberg, and Janice Kukar. Garden City Park, NY: Avery, 1988.

Fritzi Kallop's Birth Book, by Fritzi Kallop and Julie Houston. New York: Vintage, 1988.

Sense and Sensibility in Childbirth: A Guide to Negotiating Supportive Obstetrical Care, by Judith Herzfeld. New York: Norton, 1985.

Birthing: Making the Right Choices. Audiocassettes available from La Leche League International.

Natural Childbirth the Bradley Way, by Susan McCutcheon-Rosegg with Peter Rosegg. New York: E.P. Dutton, 1984.

The Whole Birth Catalog: A Source Book for Choices in Childbirth, by Janet Isaacs Ashford. Trumansburg, NY: Crossing, 1983.

Husband-Coached Childbirth, by Robert A. Bradley, M.D. New York: Harper & Row, 1981.

Assertive Childbirth, by Susan McKay. Englewood Cliffs, NJ: Prentice-Hall, 1983.

Birth Without Violence, by Frederick LeBoyer. New York: Knopf, 1975.

Background Books

Lying-In: A History of Childbirth in America, by Richard W. Wertz and Dorothy C. Wertz. New Haven, CT: Yale University Press, 1989.

Childbirth in America: Anthropological Perspectives, by Karen L. Michaelson and contributors. Granby, MA: Bergin & Garvey, 1988. On issues arising from current technology and ideology.

(See also PREGNANCY; LABOR; DELIVERY; CESAREAN SECTION; EXERCISE.)

child care Care and supervision of infants and children by people other than their parents. In past decades, when many women stayed at home with their young children, child care usually meant bringing in a baby-sitter or relative for a few hours on an evening. But today, with many more single parents and working couples, child care means a much more major commitment for many families, often for over 40 hours a week. Some employers, church and community organizations, and schools (as in the 21ST-CENTURY SCHOOL) have begun to meet this enormous need locally, but state and federal governments have so far failed to address the issue in any comprehensive way, so parents are generally on their own in arranging for child care.

The three main alternatives for temporary babysitting or longer-term child care are:

• *in the family home*—on a temporary basis a baby-sitter (often a teenager or older woman) or relative may come to care for a child; longer-term care may be provided for by a relative (such as a grandmother) or by a full-time CAREGIVER, often called a *nanny* or housekeeper.
• *in someone else's home*—child care provided in a family setting, often with five or six other children, an alternative often called *family day care*. This offers flexible hours and individual attention in a home setting and is often less expensive than a child-care center, though if the caregiver or her own family is ill, parents will need to make alternative arrangements temporarily. Some women who wish to be with their young children but also wish and/or need to keep working establish their own small family day-care centers.
• *in a separate child-care center*—providing care for larger groups of children, sometimes connected with work or community centers but often private, for-profit organizations. Parents should seek licensed child-care centers whenever possible; though no one can absolutely guarantee the safety of a center, licensing at least attempts to see that a center meets some minimum standards. Unlike family day care, child-care centers generally have backup staff but often have less flexible hours, though some are extending hours to supply coverage for parents who work evenings and nights.

Among preschool-age children in child care, over half in the mid-1980s were cared for at home (a sharp drop from over 75 percent in the mid-1960s); increasing numbers, just under a quarter of the total each, were in family day-care and child-care centers.

For many parents, just finding affordable day care is a major problem, and they need to start planning months ahead of time to be sure they have arrangements in place when they need them. Certainly they should not rely on vague "we can always take one more" promises. Friends and relatives in the neighborhood, other families with young children, local newspapers, organizations such as those listed below, and community agencies, such as local offices of the Department of Health or Social Services, can all help parents locate local child-care workers, family day care, or centers. In calculating costs, parents should take into account that some centers charge a sliding fee depending on family income, and federal and state income-tax credits are available for some child-care expenses.

In making choices about child care, parents should see that the caregiver has compatible views on such crucial matters as offering babies stimulation; developing various skills, such as LANGUAGE SKILLS and MOTOR SKILLS; using DISCIPLINE; concern for health and safety; later TOILET TRAINING; and the like. Ideally, the caregiver will have some basic training in child development

Checklist for Choosing Child Care

(For care both inside and outside of your home)

• Do you think the person who would care for your baby will really care about him or her?
• Are your suggestions for the care of your baby welcomed and listened to?
• Has the caregiver had a medical examination to show that he or she has no disease that your baby could catch and is strong and healthy enough to care for children?
• Has he or she taken first-aid and cardiopulmonary resuscitation (CPR) courses recently? Are first-aid supplies available?
• Is there a telephone which the caregiver can use to reach you or call for help in an emergency?
• Would you feel at ease leaving your baby in the person's care?
• Does the caregiver treat each baby as his or her own—talking to each while bathing or changing, holding each child while feeding, and paying attention to each child's needs?
• How does the caregiver deal with behavioral issues (such as tantrums)?

(For care outside of your home)

• Is there at least one person to care for each four or five babies at all times during the day?
• Is the home or center safe and clean, with room for play and sleep, and fresh air?
• Are there age-appropriate toys to play with?
• Do the caregivers and children seem to be happy, alert, and enjoying themselves?
• Are you welcome to visit at any time, with or without telling them in advance that you are coming?
• Will care be available for all of the hours and days (including holidays) you will need it?
• What happens if your baby becomes ill or hurt?
• Is the facility registered or licensed by the state or by another agency?
• How long has the facility been in operation, and how long have the present caregivers been on staff?
• Will they give you regular reports about how your baby is doing?
• Will they tell you about any accidents your baby may have, or any contagious disease in the group?
• Will appropriate snacks and meals be available on a regular schedule?

Before you make a final decision, ask for and *check references*. Talk with other parents whose children have been cared for by the individuals or centers you are considering. Ask whether they are satisfied or have any complaints.

Source:*Infant Care* (1989). Prepared for the Public Health Service by the Health Resources and Services Administration, Bureau of Maternal and Child Health and Resources Development.

and emergency procedures such as first aid and ARTIFICIAL RESPI-RATION; in some communities, even young baby-sitters are offered courses leading to "certification." The CHECKLIST FOR CHOOSING CHILD CARE (see page 94) can help parents in assessing whether a particular person or center is the right one for their child.

Once child-care decisions have been made, parents should periodically reassess how the arrangement is working for the child, in particular whether the child feels happy and comfortable with the caregiver and whether the caregiver is responsive to parents' needs and concerns. With increasing incidence of CHILD ABUSE AND NEGLECT, parents also should be alert to unusual or unexplained accidents or injuries, or to a child's discomfort, disquiet, fear, or upset in the caregiver's presence, apart from initial STRANGER ANXIETY and normal SEPARATION ANXIETY. (Parents will want to be familiar with INDICATORS OF CHILD ABUSE AND NEGLECT on page 85.) Infants and young children, especially, may be unable to communicate if a problem exists, but even with older children parents must be sensitive to problems with the relationship between child and caregiver and act decisively to make a change if appropriate. They should not, however, change caregivers lightly, because each such change will be a major disruption in a young child's life.

For help and further information

Children's Foundation (TCF)
725 15th Street NW, Suite #505
Washington, DC 20005
202-347-3300
Kay Hollestelle, Executive Director
Organization concerned with social and economic welfare of families with children. Provides children of low- or moderate-income families with food at child-care and family day-care centers; publishes various materials, including *National Directory of Family Day Care Associations and Support Groups, Fact Sheet on Family Day Care, A Guide for Parents Using or Seeking Home-Based Child Care,* and *Better Baby Care: A Book for Family Day Care Providers.*

Child Care Action Campaign (CCAC)
330 Seventh Ave, 18th Floor
New York, NY 10001
212-239-0138
Barbara Reisman, Executive Director
People and organizations interested in improving provision of child care and in influencing legislative action in the area. Publishes newsletter and other materials, including audiocassettes.

National Association for Family Day Care (NAFDC)
P.O. Box 71268
Murray, UT 84107
801-268-9148
Linga Geigle, Contact
For parents, caretakers, and others interested in improving provision of day care in household settings for children and in setting standards for day-care centers. Publishes newsletter

and other publications, including the brochure *What Is Family Day Care?*.

International Nanny Association
P.O. Box 26522
Austin, TX 78755
512-454-6462
Donna Lect Dixon, Contact
Organization of nannies, employment agencies, and nanny training schools. Maintains directory of placement agencies; seeks to set professional standards.

Family Service Association, 414-359-2111. Publishes *The Family Guide to Child Care: Making the Right Choices.* (For full group information, see FAMILY.)

National Association for the Education of Young Children (NAEYC), 202-232-8777, toll-free number 800-424-2460. Publishes brochures on child care. (For full group information, see PRESCHOOL.)

Choice, c/o Women's Way, 215-592-7644. Hotline for day-care information 215-592-7616. (For full group information, see BIRTH CONTROL.)

National Safety Council, 312-527-4800. Publishes *How to Find the Right Child Care Center* and *Babysitting Is Your Job* (guide for babysitters on their responsibilities). (For full group information, see LATCHKEY CHILD.)

Institute for Childhood Resources (NICR), 415-864-1169. Publishes *Choosing Child Care.* (For full group information, see PLAY GROUP.)

Other reference sources

The Parent's Guide to Daycare, by Jo Ann Miller and Susan Weissman. New York: Bantam, 1986.
The Day Care Dilemma: Critical Concerns for American Families, by Angela Browne Miller. New York: Plenum/Insight, 1990.
Child Care That Works: How Families Can Share Their Lives with Child Care and Thrive, by Ann Muscari and Wenda Wardell Morrone. Garden City, NY: Doubleday, 1989.
Day-Care: A Parent's Choice, by James Hollingsworth, Julie Hollingsworth, and Marie Bergeron. D/B Trust, 1989.
Start Your Own At Home Child Care Business, by Patricia Gallagher. Garden City, NY: Doubleday, 1989.
The Complete Guide to Affordable In-Home Childcare, by Ruth Eliott and Jim Savage. New York: Prentice Hall, 1988.
Who Cares for the Children? 1988; released 1989. Producers and directors: David Davis and Bobbie Baker for KCTS/Seattle 9. 58-minute video available from Filmmakers Library, 124 East 40th Street, New York, NY 10016. On evaluation of child-care sites. For adults.
Selecting Day Care for Your Child. 45-minute video from American Association for Vocational Instructional Materials (AAVIM), 120 Driftmier Engineering Center, Athens, GA 30602.

<u>For or by Kids</u>

Babysitting, by Frances S. Dayee. New York: Watts, 1990. For grades 6 to 8.

Max and the Babysitter, by Danielle Steele. New York: Delacorte, 1989.

Childfind   A government-sponsored program to identify young children AT RISK for having a LEARNING DISABILITY or other disability (see HANDICAPPED) that could affect learning. The purpose of these and similar programs, mandated by the EDUCATION FOR ALL HANDICAPPED CHILDREN ACT, is to identify as early as possible (preferably before kindergarten or first grade) children who need intervention or special services to be fully prepared for school.

childhood polycystic disease (CPD)   A kind of KIDNEY AND UROLOGICAL DISORDER.

childhood psychosis   Outdated term for AUTISM.

childhood schizophrenia   Outdated term for AUTISM.

Childhood Vaccine Injury Act   A federal law passed in 1986 establishing the National Vaccine Injury Compensation Program, which provides compensation for injuries or death related to IMMUNIZATION with DTP VACCINE (diphtheria-tetanus-pertussis), MEASLES-MUMPS-RUBELLA VACCINE (MMR), or polio vaccines (see ORAL POLIO VACCINE). Its aim was to help the families of affected children gain proper compensation without costly and burdensome litigation, while offering doctors and vaccine manufacturers relief from lawsuits, which had caused many companies to stop making vaccines, threatening the country's vaccine supply system.

To be eligible, someone must have incurred over $1,000 in expenses as a result of a child's vaccine-related injury or death. For injuries after October 1, 1988, claims must be filed with the U.S. Claims Court in Washington, D.C. (with two copies to the Secretary of Health and Human Services) within three years of the first symptoms and within two years of death. As described in the September 1990 *FDA Consumer*, if the court rules favorably on the claim, the person is eligible for up to $250,000 "for present and future pain and suffering. This includes past and future unreimbursed medical expenses, residential and custodial care and rehabilitation costs, and projected lost earnings from age 18. Attorney's fees may also be awarded, even if the petition is denied.... $250,000 is awarded in the event of death."

A vaccine injury table is used to establish legal links between administration of a vaccine and injury or death. As the *FDA Consumer* notes: "For example, to show that a child's seizure disorder was caused by the DTP vaccine, the child's first seizure must have occurred within three days of vaccination. To show that the MMR vaccine caused encephalitis, the injury must have occurred within 15 days of receiving the MMR vaccine. To establish that either the DTP or MMR vaccine caused a severe anaphylactic reaction or shock, the reaction must have taken place within 24 hours of immunization."

If the court's judgment is favorable, the claimant can either accept it—thereby giving up the right to take any legal action against the doctor of manufacturer—or reject it, keeping the right to bring a lawsuit.

For help and further information

National Vaccine Injury Compensation Program (NVICP)
6001 Montrose Road, Room 702
Rockville, MD 20852
Cynthia McCormick, Acting Administrator
301-443-6593

Federal arm that oversees implementation of the Childhood Vaccine Injury Act. Provides information packet.

(See also IMMUNIZATION; DTP VACCINE; MEASLES-MUMPS-RUBELLA VACCINE; ORAL POLIO VACCINE.)

child life worker   A health professional who tries to ease long HOSPITAL stays for children.

child molestation   Sexual abuse of a MINOR. (See CHILD ABUSE AND NEGLECT.)

child prodigy   A child who demonstrates unusual and superior talent at a very early age, especially in music or the arts, such as a child who begins composing music on the piano at age three. (See GIFTED CHILD.)

childproofing   Careful examination of any setting in which young children will spend any amount of time, to remove from it or place out of reach (in a closed closet or on an upper shelf, for example) anything that might prove a danger to the child, such as marbles, nuts, buttons, or removable parts (which might be swallowed), anything with sharp points or edges, or items painted with leaded or otherwise toxic paint. It also includes removing anything that might be damaged by children, such as a beautiful bowl or fine book, and covering exposed electrical outlets. Parents of infants will need to periodically analyze what their child is capable of doing and what new dangers might emerge as the child develops. When they go visiting with the child, they should also keep a watchful eye out and (if the social situation allows it) temporarily childproof the room they and the child will be in. (For an outline of what the baby can do at various stages in the first 12 months, see the SAFETY CHECKLIST: KEEPING BABY SAFE on page 504.)

For help and further information

The Childproofing Checklist, by Mary Matzger and Cynthya P. Whittaker. Garden City, NY: Doubleday, 1988.

Making Your Home Child-Safe. Menlo Park, CA: Sunset, 1988.

Curiosity Without Tears: Childproofing Your Home, revised edition. 1988; released 1989. Producer and director: Ann Biswas. 20-minute film/video from Good Health, P.O. Box 588, Dayton, OH 45405. For ages 15 to adult. Shows and explains what children can do at different ages and how to protect them.

Children's Apperception Test (CAT)   A type of individually administered PROJECTIVE TEST similar to and modeled on the THEMATIC APPERCEPTION TEST, but designed for children ages three to 10. A child is given a series of pictures, one at a time, often animals in human settings, and is asked to make up stories about them, the aim being to reveal the child's personality and maturity. (For help and further information, see TESTS.)

child support   Money that must legally be paid by parents for a MINOR child's care; part of PARENTS' RESPONSIBILITIES. The parent's duty to provide support continues at least until the child reaches legal adulthood (often beyond that if the child is disabled or incapacitated) or becomes formally emancipated (see EMANCIPATED MINOR), and otherwise ends only with the permanent TERMINATION OF PARENTAL RIGHTS, as in ADOPTION.

For most families, child support is accepted as a matter of course. Even if parents separate or divorce, they generally recognize that support must continue to be provided for the children—their main argument is over what level of support should be provided. In this they have historically had very little uniform guidance, since the amount of child support varies widely. Celebrity divorces to the contrary, a mother and children are almost invariably poorer than before a separation—and so, of course, is the father. Specialist divorce lawyers are often enlisted by each side, attempting to gain every monetary, tax, and other advantage possible for their clients, and often the court is involved in the final determination of how much should be paid in child support (and alimony).

The amount of a court's child-support order has traditionally been based on the ill-defined, open-to-wide-interpretation concepts of the two parties' ability to earn and ability to pay, though the 1984 Child Support Enforcement Act encouraged the formation of state guidelines on what is a fair amount of child support. In such situations, the lone couple trying to make an equitable child-support arrangement on their own are a rarity, and many have contacted organizations of various kinds (see below) to help them in their quest for what they believe is right.

The person who receives a court order to pay child support—generally the father, but sometimes the mother—is called the *obligated parent* or *responsible parent*. A court order for child-support payments can later be modified temporarily or permanently if the court is convinced that CHANGED CIRCUMSTANCES warrant it, such as a sharp rise or decrease in income or a change in a child's health, requiring expensive medical care.

More serious, however, is the fact that in an enormous number of cases, child support is not paid regularly, if at all. Of mothers granted CUSTODY and child support by the court, over half receive no regular child support, including families at every level of the socioeconomic scale. In 1984, the Secretary of Health and Human Services reported that 15,000,000 children lived in homes without their fathers, but that only 35 percent of them received child support; as a result nearly one-third, or 5,000,000, lived in poverty.

Some of these families are eligible for aid under the AID TO FAMILIES WITH DEPENDENT CHILDREN program; if so, they are required by law to cooperate in the state's search for the DELINQUENT parent, to obtain reimbursement for child-support payments. If the ABSENT PARENT is found, the custodial parent will be asked to sign an ASSIGNMENT OF SUPPORT RIGHTS, specifying that support payment including ARREARAGES will be paid to the state, in exchange for AFDC grants and other benefits. If the absent parent is an unwed FATHER, the state may initiate a PATERNITY SUIT to establish his legal status as father.

The problem is of such dimensions that various government agencies have been established to help obtain court-ordered back child-support payments (arrearages) and regular payment of current amounts due. The federal government in 1975 established the OFFICE OF CHILD SUPPORT ENFORCEMENT (OCSE), working through regional and state OCSE agencies and using a PARENT LOCATOR SERVICE (PLS) to first find the delinquent parent. The PLS uses computer searches, on the federal level, searching through income tax records, Social Security earnings and benefit records, and the like. Its counterparts on the state level scan voter registration, motor vehicle, driver's license, welfare, prison, worker's compensation, and similar records. While the PLS has had some success in locating missing parents, some custodial parents also use friends, relatives, colleagues, and knowledge of interests and associations to try to find the delinquent parent.

Once the absent parent has been located, the OCSE also applies increasingly effective procedures for obtaining child-support payments, including:

- withholding child-support payments automatically from paychecks;
- withholding tax refunds to pay child-support arrearages;
- requiring posting of bonds or security to guarantee payment;
- government seizure of property (*sequestration*) for sale to cover arrearages;
- reporting delinquent parents to credit agencies.

The UNIFORM RECIPROCAL ENFORCEMENT OF SUPPORT ACT (URESA) provides for enforcement of child-support payments when the obligated parent lives in a different state from the custodial parent and children. A government booklet, *Handbook on Child Support Enforcement*, provides further information about the OCSE program and addresses of state and regional OCSE agencies.

Another approach applied to the problem is WAGE ATTACHMENT, under which the obligated parent's employer is notified of any child-support order and the required amount is "attached" or taken from the paycheck and sent as child support. In some states, the wage attachment law applies automatically to everyone who has been ordered to pay child support. Sometimes the obligated parent may have wages voluntarily withheld to pay for child support.

For help and further information

Parents Without Partners (PWP), 301-588-9354, toll-free number 800-637-7974. Publishes various materials on child support. (For full group information, see CUSTODY.)

Child Support Network (CSN)
807 Colesville Road
Silver Spring, MD 20910
301-588-9354
Ginnie Nuta, Coordinator
Program for divorced women, sponsored by Parents Without Partners (see above); offers information on child support and related matters.

Association of Family and Conciliation Courts (AFCC), 503-279-5651. (For full group information, see CUSTODY.)

National Child Support Advocacy Coalition (NCSAC)
6816 Rock Creek Court
Alexandria, VA 22306
703-765-7956
Organization devoted to improving enforcement of child support. Monitors U.S. legislation and programs; provides information on enforcement techniques; seeks to educate parents and general public, and to influence public policy; makes referrals.

National Child Support Enforcement Association (NCSEA)
Hall of State
444 North Capitol, NW, #613
Washington, DC 20001
202-624-8180
Mary Nathan, Executive Director
Organization of state and local officials and agencies involved in enforcing child-support laws. Publishes various materials, including newsletter, biennial referral guide, and administrative procedures handbook.

National Committee for Fair Divorce and Alimony (NCFDAL), 212-766-4030. (For full group information, see CUSTODY.)

Academy of Family Mediators (AFM), 203-629-8049. (For full group information, see CUSTODY.)

Help Abolish Legal Tyranny (HALT), 202-347-9600. (For full group information, see CUSTODY.)

National Organization for Women's Legal Defense and Education Fund, 212-925-6635. (For full group information, see CUSTODY.)

National Center for Women and Family Law, 212-674-8200. (For full group information, see CUSTODY.)

Father's Rights of America (FRA), 818-789-4435. (For full group information, see CUSTODY.)

National Congress for Men (NCM), 202-328-4377. (For full group information, see CUSTODY.)

Other reference sources

How to Modify and Collect Child Support, third edition, by Joseph Matthews, Warren Siegel, and Mary Willis. Berkeley, CA: Nolo, 1990.

Child Support: A Complete, Up-to-Date Authoritative Guide to Collecting Child Support, by Marianne Takas. New York: Harper & Row, 1985.

Fathers' Rights: The Sourcebook for Dealing with the Child Support System, by Jon Conne. New York: Walker, 1989.

Divorced But Not Disastrous, by Susan Anderson-Khleif. Englewood Cliffs, NJ: Prentice-Hall, 1982.

(See also CUSTODY.)

CHINS   Abbreviation for children in need of SUPERVISION.

chlamydial infection   Infection by the bacterium *Chlamydia trachomatis*, the most common SEXUALLY TRANSMITTED DISEASE, infecting an estimated three to four million people each year; nicknamed the "Silent STD." Symptoms are initially mild or even absent altogether, dangerously so, because the infection can lead to serious complications, often before people are aware they have the disease. The most serious complication is PELVIC INFLAMMATORY DISEASE (PID), a major cause of INFERTILITY in women. In men, infection can cause inflammation in the urinary tract (medically called *nongonococcal urethritis* or NGU) or other parts of the reproductive system. Men and women who do have symptoms (generally starting one to three weeks after exposure) may have pain during urination, a discharge of mucus or pus from the PENIS or VAGINA, and sometimes lower abdominal pain. Chlamydia may also cause infection elsewhere in the body, such as the rectum, the lining of the eye (*conjunctivitis*), or the lymph nodes in the groin (*lymphogranuloma venerum*, or LGV).

Chlamydia is sometimes confused with, and often occurs with, GONORRHEA; both are treated with antibiotics. Chlamydia infections can be detected by any of several quick office tests, and many doctors recommend that anyone who has multiple sex partners, and especially a woman of childbearing age, should be tested annually. A child who is exposed to chlamydia during CHILDBIRTH may develop conjunctivitis or PNEUMONIA, so doctors also recommend routine testing of all pregnant women for chlamydia. (For help and further information, including how to avoid infection, see SEXUALLY TRANSMITTED DISEASES.)

chloasma (melasma)   A kind of HYPERPIGMENTATION.

chloride   A MINERAL, generally found in a compound with SODIUM as table salt, that is important in the functioning of the body's digestive juices (such as forming hydrocholoric acid in the stomach). Either too much or too little chloride can upset the chemical balance of the body. (For help and further information, see NUTRITION.)

choking Partial and complete blockage of the air passages, generally because the person has swallowed food or a foreign object that has lodged in the throat. Partial obstruction, with some air flow, can often be cleared by coughing, but total obstruction will lead to ASPHYXIA unless the airways are opened. Children are especially vulnerable to choking because their air passages are narrower and because very young children cannot recognize that they should not try to swallow small items, such as jelly beans or buttons. Danger is increased if they have physical problems involving the muscles of the mouth and neck, affecting speaking, breathing, and eating.

Prevention is best, keeping dangerous items out of the reach of young children—an important part of CHILDPROOFING. (See also SUCKING AND PACIFIERS under SUCKING.)

But if a child is choking, pounding on the back, use of the Heimlich maneuver (see page 101), and if necessary an emergency TRACHEOSTOMY may be needed to prevent suffocation, brain damage, and death. If results are not immediate, call for emergency medical help.

cholangitis Inflammation of the bile duct, the passageway carrying waste secretions away from the liver. The most common form is *acute ascending cholangitis*, which generally involves bacterial infection in the bile duct, often because of blockage, as by a gallstone, TUMOR, or worm infestation. Mild cases can be treated with antibiotics, but serious cases may require surgery, as they can lead to severe, even life-threatening LIVER PROBLEMS, KIDNEY and UROLOGICAL DISORDERS, or SEPTICEMIA. The rarer form, *sclerosing cholangitis*, involves narrowing of the bile ducts and progressive liver damage; so far no treatment has been developed for this condition except a liver TRANSPLANT. Doctors may use LIVER FUNCTION TESTS, an ULTRASOUND SCAN, or an ENDOSCOPE to help diagnose cholangitis.

For help and further information

American Liver Foundation (ALF), 201-857-2626; toll-free number, U.S. except NJ, 800-223-0179. Sponsors network for parents of children with liver diseases and information sheets about various types of liver ailments. (For full group information, see LIVER PROBLEMS.)

Children's Liver Foundation, 201-761-1111. (For full group information, see LIVER PROBLEMS.)

National Institute of Diabetes and Digestive and Kidney Diseases (NIDDK), 301-496-3583. (For full group information, see DIGESTIVE DISORDERS.)

National Digestive Disease Information Clearinghouse (NDDIC), 301-468-6344. (For full group information, see DIGESTIVE DISORDERS.)

cholesterol A fatty substance present in foods from animal sources (including meat, poultry, eggs, and dairy products) but not from plant sources. The body makes sufficient cholesterol for its own needs, which include helping in the formation of VITAMIN D and various HORMONES. But excessive amounts that are ingested in some high-fat diets are carried in the bloodstream and cause a buildup of fatty tissue in the arteries (called *atherosclerosis*) and therefore pose a risk of heart problems (see HEART AND HEART PROBLEMS). Cholesterol can also crystallize in the gall bladder to form gallstones. Not all forms of cholesterol are the same. *High-density lipoproteins* (HDLs)—the so-called good cholesterol—seem to help protect against arterial buildup, while *low-density lipoproteins* (LDLs) and *very-low-density lipoproteins* (VLDLs) tend to increase the buildup. Though the effects are normally not seen until adulthood, recent studies have shown that atherosclerosis starts in childhood, so parents would be wise to watch the cholesterol content of meals for all family members (see FATS).

For help and further information

National Heart, Lung, and Blood Institute (NHLBI), 301-496-4236. Publishes various materials, including *Blood Cholesterol* and *Eating to Lower Your Blood Cholesterol*. (For full group information, see HEART AND HEART PROBLEMS.)

Your Child and Cholesterol, by Eugene Eisman and Diane Batshaw Eisman. Hollywood, FL: Fell, 1990.

cholesteryl ester storage disease A type of LIPID STORAGE DISEASE.

chondrodysplasia A general term for abnormal skeletal development, as in GENETIC DISORDERS such as MORQUIO'S SYNDROME.

chondrodystrophy Alternate name for ACHONDROPLASIA.

chordee A CONGENITAL defect in which a male's PENIS curves downward; often associated with HYPOSPADIAS.

chorea Unpredictable, involuntary, jerky movements, especially in the face and limbs, resulting from disturbances deep within the brain; formerly called *St. Vitus's dance*. The condition is most often found in two diseases, HUNTINGTON'S CHOREA and SYDENHAM'S CHOREA. It also sometimes appears during PREGNANCY, as *chorea gravidarum*; as a side effect from some kinds of drugs, including BIRTH-CONTROL PILLS; or in CEREBRAL PALSY, often associated with the slow writhing of ATHETOSIS, the combination called *choreoathetosis*.

chorionic biopsy Alternate name for CHORIONIC VILLUS SAMPLING.

chorionic villus sampling (CVS or chorionic biopsy) A relatively new GENETIC SCREENING procedure that involves removing some cells from tiny fingerlike projections (*villi*) on the *chorion*, the outer membrane of the PLACENTA. These cells, identical to those of the FETUS, can be used to identify some GENETIC DISORDERS, such as DOWN'S SYNDROME. Usually a flexible tube,

What If an Infant Is Choking?

If your baby's airway is blocked, follow these steps:

1. *If someone is nearby, first call for help; if you are alone, try the procedures below for a minute or so before you phone for emergency help.*
2. Place the baby face down on your forearm, with his or her head lower than the body and the head and neck stable or supported. Support your forearm firmly against your body. (If your baby is large, you may lay him or her face down on your lap, with head lower than body.)
3. Slap the baby rapidly between the shoulder blades four times, with the heel of your hand.

4. Turn the baby over and thrust into the chest (just below baby's nipples—the same location as for chest compression [see ARTIFICAL RESPIRATION]) with two fingers four times rapidly.
5. If something is completely blocking the windpipe and baby still is not breathing, open mouth by grasping both tongue and lower jaw between your thumb and finger and lift. This should move the tongue away from the back of the throat, and may help open the throat. *If you can see* something blocking the windpipe, try to remove it by carefully sweeping your finger from back to front.
6. If breathing does not start again, try giving two ventilations [rescue breathing].
7. If airway is still blocked, repeat entire procedure until help arrives.

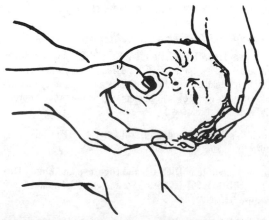

Source: *Infant Care* (1989). Prepared for the Public Health Service by the Health Resources and Services Administration, Bureau of Maternal and Child Health and Resources Development.

What If a Child Is Choking?

When food or a foreign body is sucked into the windpipe, the victim is unable to talk, turns blue, and can die within minutes. The technique described below forces air from the lungs up the windpipe, to dislodge whatever is blocking the windpipe and thereby restore breathing. *If someone is nearby, first call for help; if you are alone, try the procedures below for a minute or so before you phone for emergency help*:

1. *If the child is standing*, support his or her chest with one hand, and with the heel of the other, give the child four rapid, forceful blows between the shoulder blades. *If the child is lying down*, place your knee against his or her chest for support, and administer blows.
2. *If the obstruction is not cleared*, wrap your arms around the child, with the thumb side of your fist against his or her stomach between the navel and the rib cage. Grasp your fist with your other hand and make four quick, upward thrusts. Repeat if necessary. Watch breathing closely.

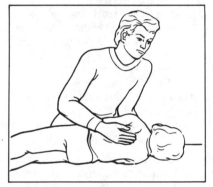

If the child is lying down, support child's chest with your knee and administer blows.

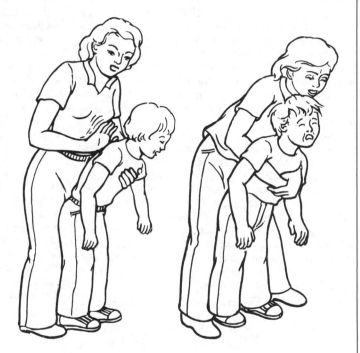

If the child is standing, support chest and give four blows between the shoulder blades.

Use the "hugging" technique if blows to the back do not dislodge the obstruction.

Source: *Mainstreaming Preschoolers: Children with Orthopedic Handicaps*, by Shari Stokes Kieran et al. (1986). Prepared for the Department of Health and Human Services by the Administration for Children, Youth and Families, Head Start Bureau.

guided by ULTRASOUND, is inserted through the pregnant woman's VAGINA, though sometimes a needle may be inserted through the abdomen. CVS can be done eight to 12 weeks into a pregnancy, much earlier than AMNIOCENTESIS, and its results are received more quickly, making an ABORTION easier, if desired. But CVS can identify fewer genetic problems and carries a higher risk of MISCARRIAGE than amniocentesis, while its long-term effects on the fetus are not yet known. (For help and further information, see GENETIC DISORDERS; GENETIC SCREENING.)

Christmas disease   Alternate name for HEMOPHILIA B.

chromosomal abnormalities   Problems resulting from mistakes in the duplication of the chromosomes that carry an individual's GENETIC INHERITANCE. Normally a baby is born with 23 pairs of chromosomes, 22 pairs called AUTOSOMES and one pair of SEX CHROMOSOMES, with XX for a female and XY for a male. But due to errors in duplication of the chromosomes, some babies will have too many chromosomes, some too few; some will be missing pieces of chromosomes, some will have extra pieces, and some will have chromosomes separated and then rejoined in the wrong places (*translocation*). Many of these errors are so serious that the FETUS cannot develop and a spontaneous ABORTION (MISCARRIAGE) occurs; or they cause the DEATH of a child just before or soon after birth.

Having one or more extra full sets of chromosomes, a condition called *polyploidy*, is lethal. So, in many cases, is having a triplet in place of a chromosome pair, a condition called TRISOMY. However, some babies with trisomy survive, including many who have a triplet for chromosome 21, their disorder being called DOWN'S SYNDROME or trisomy 21. Other, rarer trisomies include PATAU'S SYNDROME, or trisomy 13, and EDWARDS' SYNDROME, or trisomy 18. Syndromes resulting from deletion of all or part of a chromosome are rare, but include the CRI DU CHAT SYNDROME.

Problems with the sex chromosomes lead to other common chromosomal abnormalities, including TURNER'S SYNDROME, in which a girl has only one X chromosome, instead of two, and KLINEFELTER'S SYNDROME, in which a boy has extra X chromosomes. Sometimes the chromosomal abnormality has only slight effects and can go undetected, but may be passed on to the next generation. The older the prospective parents, especially after the woman is over 30, the greater the chance of having chromosomal abnormalities, so GENETIC COUNSELING and GENETIC SCREENING are often advisable. (For help and further information, see GENETIC DISORDERS.)

chronic obstructive lung disease (COLD)   A general term for a variety of chronic diseases, sometimes involving structural malformations that cause progressive blockage of air passages; also called *chronic obstructive pulmonary disease* (COPD) or *chronic obstructive respiratory disease* (CORD). (For help and further information, see LUNG AND BREATHING DISORDERS.)

chronic voice disorder   A type of communication disorder (see COMMUNICATION SKILLS AND DISORDERS).

chronological age (CA)   A child's age as measured from the birthdate, which must often be attested to by showing a BIRTH CERTIFICATE or other acceptable certificate, as on entering school. A child's age is often used in comparisons of performance, skills, or behavior with others of the same chronological age, such as EDUCATIONAL AGE or MENTAL AGE. (For help and further information, see TEST; AGE.)

Chubby Puffer syndrome   A type of SLEEP APNEA found in a child who is overweight and has large TONSILS and ADENOIDS, which can block air passages during sleep.

church certificate   Alternate name for BAPTISMAL CERTIFICATE.

church-related school   Alternate term for a PRIVATE SCHOOL with religious affiliation.

CIC   Abbreviation for CLEAN, INTERMITTENT CATHETERIZATION.

circumcision   Removal of the foreskin, a loose fold of skin that covers the head, or glans, of the PENIS; a brief operation generally performed on newborns. Long performed for religious reasons by Jews and Moslems, circumcision became widespread throughout the United States by the mid-20th century but today is somewhat less universal.

People who recommend circumcision note that:

• The circumcised penis is easier to keep clean.
• Secretions tend to be trapped under the foreskin and become infected, causing problems such as BALANITIS, an inflammation of the glans and foreskin.
• Circumcision avoids the painful possibilities of PHIMOSIS, in which the too-tight foreskin cannot be fully drawn back and impedes free urination, and PARAPHIMOSIS, in which the retracted foreskin is too tight and becomes a tourniquet.
• Cancer of the penis and of the cervix are found more often among uncircumcised men and their wives.
• The operation is less painful and traumatic when performed on a newborn than on an older child or an adult.
• Some recent studies have shown that uncircumsized men are more susceptible to SEXUALLY TRANSMITTED DISEASES.

Those against circumcision regard the operation as an unnecessary surgical intervention that creates as many problems as it is designed to prevent, carrying some risk of injury to the penis and URETHRA, as well as of infection or HEMORRHAGE. Should the child have any CONGENITAL defect of the penis, such as HYPOSPADIAS, circumcision is normally not done, since the foreskin tissue might be needed during a later surgical reconstruction. The Public Health Service's publication *Prenatal Care* comments: "Circumcision was once a routine medical procedure for male babies, thought to be necessary for cleanliness. Today, however, there is no medical indication for routine cir-

---

About Circumcision

If you want your boy circumcised, have it done while you are still in the hospital. Except for religious purposes, it is not necessary, and it should almost never be done as a special operation once you and he have left the hospital.

A circumcision should heal completely within a week to 10 days. Protect the site until it heals and keep it from sticking to diapers by putting a small amount of petroleum jelly and a strip of gauze on the penis each time you change the diaper. Do not use alcohol to clean the circumcised area.

Sources: *Infant Care* (1989). Prepared for the Public Health Service by the Bureau of Maternal and Child Health and Resources Development. *Prenatal Care* (1983). Prepared for the Public Health Service, Division of Maternal and Child Health.

cumcision of the newborn." They recommend that couples discuss the question with their doctor before the birth.

In some cultures, notably in parts of Africa, many women are circumcised, an operation that involves removing all or part of the outer GENITALS, especially the clitoris and often the labia major and minora, and sometimes constricting the opening of the VAGINA as well. Female circumcision has no medical benefits and considerable hazards, including risk of problems with urination, normal sexual relations, and childbirth.

For help and further information
General Organizations

National Center for Education in Child and Maternal Health (NCEMCH), 202-625-8400, and **National Maternal and Child Health Clearinghouse (NMCHC)**, 202-625-8410. (For full group information, see PREGNANCY.)

National Perinatal Association (NPA), 703-549-5523. (For full group information, see PERINATAL CARE.)

National Perinatal Information Center, 401-274-0650. (For full group information, see PERINATAL CARE.)

Organizations Against Circumcision

National Organization of Circumcision Information Resource Centers (NO-CIRC)
731 Sir Francis Drake Boulevard
San Anselmo, CA 94960
415-454-5669
Marilyn Fayre Milos, Executive Director
Network of groups aimed at educating the public and medical professionals about the possible dangers of circumcision, hoping to end such routine surgery. Publishes newsletter and other materials.

Newborn Rights Society (NRS)
P.O. Box 48
St. Peters PA 19470
215-323-6061
Kurt E. Bomke, Contact
Organization of people opposing routine medical procedures such as circumcision and silver nitrate in the eyes as invasive and against the rights of the newborn. Gathers and disseminates data.

Non-Circumcision Educational Foundation (NCEF)
P.O. Box 5
Richboro, PA 18954
215-357-2792
James E. Peron, Executive Director
Organization of parents, medical personnel involved in childbirth, and interested others seeking to end routine circumcision and other medical treatments regarded as invasive, such as putting silver nitrate in the newborn's eyes as a preventative. Runs seminars and workshops; publishes print and film materials.

Remain Intact Organization (RIO)
Airport Route 2, Box 86
Larchwood, IA 51241
712-477-2256
Rev. Russell Zanggner, Director
Organization of people opposing routine circumcision. Distributes printed, audio, and video materials.

Other reference sources

Circumcision: A Parents' Decision for Life, by Aaron J. Fink. Mountain View, CA: Kavanah, 1988.

Circumcision: Mothering Special Edition, revised edition, Vicki I. Stamler and Barrett Flascher Dunn, eds. Santa Fe, NM: Mothering Magazine, 1988.

Circumcision: The Painful Dilemma, by Rosemary Romberg. South Hadley, MA: Bergin and Garvey, 1985.

cirrhosis of the liver   Scarring of the liver, as fibrous tissue replaces damaged liver cells, gradually blocking blood flow within the liver and causing liver cells to die. Most people think of cirrhosis in connection with ALCOHOL or DRUG ABUSE, problems rare in young children, though found among some adolescents. But cirrhosis can also result from many other causes, including infectious diseases such as HEPATITIS, inherited METABOLIC DISORDERS such as ALPHA 1-ANTITRYPSIN DEFICIENCY and GALACTOSEMIA, and other disorders such as CYSTIC FIBROSIS and heart problems (see HEART AND HEART PROBLEMS), as well as some medications and ENVIRONMENTAL HAZARDS. If such causes are identified and treated early, the scarring process can be arrested. Early warning signs of cirrhosis include mild JAUNDICE, EDEMA (collection of fluid in body tissues), and VOMITING of blood. Routine BLOOD TESTS or LIVER FUNCTION TESTS may sometimes suggest cirrhosis, a diagnosis often confirmed by a liver BIOPSY. But if cirrhosis is not recognized early enough or if the scarring process cannot be halted, the result is a series of ever-more-serious complications, including massive hemorrhaging; damage to other organs, such as kidneys; COMA; and DEATH. Children or adults with progressive, unchecked cirrhosis may require a liver TRANSPLANT to survive. (For help and further information, see LIVER PROBLEMS.)

cisternal puncture   A type of MEDICAL TEST used as an alternative or complement to the LUMBAR PUNCTURE, in which a small amount of fluid is removed from the base of the brain.

civil proceeding   Any noncriminal legal action, such as cases in which two parties disagree over rights. Most cases in JUVENILE COURT, FAMILY COURT, or DOMESTIC RELATIONS COURT are civil proceedings and (unlike criminal court) do not involve the right to a jury trial. Rules about what kinds of evidence are admissible are also much looser than in criminal court.

Civil Rights Act for Handicapped Persons   Alternate name for REHABILITATION ACT OF 1973; Section 504 of the Act applied to schools and laid the groundwork for the EDUCATION FOR ALL HANDICAPPED CHILDREN ACT OF 1975.

classical curriculum   A type of CURRICULUM that emphasizes the traditional LIBERAL ARTS, especially on the college level.

Why Clean, Intermittent Catheterization (CIC)?

In children with spina bifida, chronic bladder infections and kidney deterioration pose the greatest potential danger after age one. The kidneys serve a vital function: they filter waste products from the blood to form urine and return salts and other important substances to the blood. Urine flows from the kidneys to the bladder for storage. Retention and elimination of urine is controlled by the sphincter, a muscle at the neck of the bladder. When the bladder is full, nerves direct the sphincter to open and the bladder to contract in a coordinate process that releases the accumulated urine through a tube called the urethra.

Children with spina bifida are usually unable to control this process. Because of nerve damage, some children may not be able to feel when their bladder is full. Some patients cannot relax their sphincters enough to let all the urine flow out, while in others the sphincter is always open so that urine dribbles from the urethra. Many children have both incomplete emptying and leakage.

In a dangerous consequence of incomplete emptying, urine accumulates in the bladder and backs up into the kidneys. Unchecked, the pressure of this reflex can cause life-threatening kidney deterioration. Or bacteria may grow in the urine that collects in the bladder, and the infection may travel to the kidneys.

In recent years, improved methods of diagnosis, treatment, and prevention of bladder problems have greatly reduced the number of infections and their severity. These same techniques have also allowed children to exert greater control over leakage problems—important for both self-esteem and acceptance by others.

Source: *Spina Bifida: Hope Through Research* (1986). Prepared for the Public Health Service by the National Institute of Neurological and Communicative Disorders and Stroke.

---

class parent   A parent, often the mother, who helps in a child's classroom, on field trips, and at other special events, generally in rotation with other parents for a specified period, though sometimes for a whole school year; also called a *room parent*.

clean hands doctrine   In family law, the general rule that a party who has acted in bad faith is judged with disfavor in future disputes. A parent who has resorted to parental kidnapping (see MISSING CHILDREN) is, for example, very unlikely to later gain CUSTODY of the child, except in very special circumstances.

clean, intermittent catheterization (CIC)   A medical technique for emptying the bladder, involving temporarily inserting a drainage tube (CATHETER) into the URETHRA, the tube through which urine passes. The tube is inserted every three to four hours, then taken out again and washed with soap and water; it has been found that, with proper care, sterilization is not necessary. Since the 1970s, CIC has generally replaced the earlier procedure of making a surgical opening into the abdomen and collecting the urine in an external bag.

Some children, such as those with SPINA BIFIDA, cannot control the nerves and muscles that normally handle emptying of the bladder, so CIC is used to handle that function. Parents or caregivers handle the catheterization until children are able to do it themselves—some learn as young as age three or four, often practicing on a special doll before performing the procedure on themselves. In school, including PRESCHOOL, a school nurse or a trained layperson must be provided to perform CIC, if a handicapped child is unable to do so, according to a 1984 Supreme Court ruling (*Irving Independent School District v. Tatro*). Commenting that "services like CIC that permit a child to remain in school during the day are no less related to the effort to educate than are services that enable a child to reach, enter, or exit the school," the Court likened CIC to transportation, as a related educational service, rather than a medical service.

cleft lip and palate   A split in the lip and the roof of the mouth (*hard palate*), sometimes extending back to the soft palate at the back of the mouth and the nostrils. Such splits are normal at an early stage of the FETUS's development but fail to close in about one of every 600 to 700 babies. The causes of cleft lip and palate are complex and unclear; genetic and environmental factors seem to be involved, as are ALCOHOL and DRUG ABUSE, some medications, and DIABETES MELLITUS in the mother. Recent studies also indicate that MALNUTRITION, especially lack of proper VITAMINS, during the first few weeks of PREGNANCY are associated with significantly higher risk of having a child with cleft lip or palate. Women AT RISK, or those with a family history including cleft lip or palate, may well want to seek GENETIC COUNSELING when considering a pregnancy. Today cleft lips and palates can be surgically repaired, generally within the first three months of life; the surgical team often includes several specialists, such as a PEDIATRICIAN, PLASTIC SURGEON, and dental specialists. Before and after surgery SPEECH-LANGUAGE PATHOLOGISTS and AUDIOLOGISTS (hearing specialists) are also often consulted. Babies with cleft lips are generally able to feed normally, but those with cleft palates must generally be bottlefed, sometimes with special help, such as an *obturator*, which covers the cleft palate during feeding. Babies with cleft palates also often have EAR AND HEARING PROBLEMS that require special attention, even after surgery, to prevent hearing loss and speech problems.

For help and further information

American Cleft Palate Association (ACPA)/Cleft Palate Foundation
1218 Grandview Avenue
University of Pittsburgh
Pittsburgh, PA 15261

412-481-1376, toll-free number 800-24-CLEFT [2-5338]
Nancy C. Smythe, Executive Director
Organization for individuals with clefts and their families. Seeks to educate public and enhance social support; maintains toll-free hotline; provides information and makes referrals; publishes various materials for parents, including *ACPA Newsletter*; sponsors organization for parents of children with cleft lip or palate, National Cleft Palate Association (contact Donnie Schlereth at above address and number).

Prescription Parents
P.O. Box 426
Quincy, MA 02269
617-479-2463
Laura I. Cohen, Executive Director
Organization of parents of children with cleft lip or palate and health professionals who work with them. Encourages formation of parent support groups; publishes various materials, including newsletter, *Caring for Your Newborn*, and *Hearing and Behavior in Children Born with Cleft Palate*.

AboutFace
99 Crowns Lane, 3rd floor
Toronto, Ontario M5R 3P4, Canada
416-944-3223
Elisabeth Bednar, Executive Director
International organization of parents and professionals concerned with cleft palate and facial disfigurement. Provides support and information; encourages formation of local groups and linking of parents with similar experiences; publishes various materials, including the brochure *AboutFace* and pamphlets on facial disfigurement and other disorders, such as craniosynostosis.

March of Dimes Birth Defects Foundation, 914-428-7100 (local chapters in telephone-directory white pages). Publishes information sheet *Cleft Lip and Palate*. (For full group information, see BIRTH DEFECTS; GENETIC DISORDERS.)

National Institute of Dental Research (NIDR), 301-496-4261. (For full group information, see TEETH.)

National Foundation of Dentistry for the Handicapped (NFDH), 303-573-0264. (For full group information, see HELP FOR SPECIAL CHILDREN on page 578.)

FACES—The National Association for the Craniofacially Handicapped, 615-266-1632. (For full group information, see PLASTIC SURGERY.)

National Foundation for Facial Reconstruction, 212-340-6656. (For full group information, see PLASTIC SURGERY.)

Other reference sources
A Parent's Guide to Cleft Lip and Palate, by Karlind T. Moller, Clark D. Starr, and Sylvia A. Johnson. Minneapolis: University of Minnesota Press, 1989.
A Practical Guide to Cleft Lip and Palate Birth Defects: Helpful, Practical Information and Answers for Parents, Physicians,

Nurses and Other Professionals, Sidney K. Wynn and Alfred L. Miller, eds. Springfield, IL: Charles C. Thomas, 1984.
Cleft Palate: The Nature and Remediation of Communication Problems, Jackie Stenglehofen, ed. Dallas, TX: Churchill, 1989.
Cleft Lip and/or Palate: Behavioral Effects from Infancy to Adulthood, by Philip Starr. Springfield, IL: Charles C. Thomas, 1983.
(See also COMMUNICATION SKILLS AND DISORDERS.)

CLEP Abbreviation for COLLEGE-LEVEL EXAMINATION PROGRAM.

clinodactyly Abnormal bending (to the side or toward the middle) of one or more fingers or toes, a BIRTH DEFECT found in some disorders, such as DE LANGE SYNDROME.

closed captions Captions on film or television that are invisible except to people with special captioning decoders, as opposed to captions superimposed on the picture for all to see. The technique, which is encouraged and partly subsidized by government funding, allows people with EAR AND HEARING PROBLEMS to have readier access to news, arts, and entertainment programs. Decoders are expensive, but current legislation aims at having computer-chip decoders available on most new television sets at the touch of a button by the mid-1990s.

closed fracture Alternate term for *simple fracture*, a kind of FRACTURE in which two bone pieces are not displaced.

closed reduction In cases of FRACTURE, repositioning the broken bones by manipulating them through the skin, without surgery.

closed scholarship A type of SCHOLARSHIP restricted to certain kinds of applicants, such as those living in a certain state.

clubfoot (talipes) A CONGENITAL deformity in which the foot or ankle is twisted and somewhat fixed into an awkward position; a common BIRTH DEFECT affecting about one in every 400 babies, boys twice as often as girls. By far the most common and most severe kind of clubfoot is *talipes equinovarus*, in which one or both feet are twisted downward and inward, or "clubbed," often with the heel cord so tight that the foot cannot be easily moved into a normal position. Less severe and more easily treatable forms of clubfoot are *talipes calcaneal valgus*, in which the foot is sharply angled upward and outward, and *talipes metatarsus varus*, in which the front part of the foot is twisted inward. The causes of clubfoot are complex and unclear but apparently involve genetic and environmental factors, including drugs, infection, or other disease, and they are sometimes associated with other birth defects, such as SPINA BIFIDA. Couples with clubfoot in their family history may wish to seek GENETIC COUNSELING when considering a pregnancy. Though once thought true of all forms of clubfoot, only the mildest cases are now thought to result from constriction in the UTERUS. Milder cases of clubfoot may respond to exercises starting shortly after birth, but more severe cases may require plaster casts or surgery to stretch or lengthen the heel cord. Mild or severe, clubfoot is best treated early.

For help and further information

March of Dimes Birth Defects Foundation, 914-428-7100 (local chapters in telephone-directory white pages). Publishes information sheet *Clubfoot*. (For full group information, see BIRTH DEFECTS.)

National Institute of Child Health and Human Development (NICHD), 301-496-5133. (For full group information, see PREGNANCY.)

National Center for Education in Child and Maternal Health (NCEMCH), 202-625-8400; **National Maternal and Child Health Clearinghouse (NMCHC)**, 202-625-8410. (For full group information, see PREGNANCY.)

(See also HELP FOR SPECIAL CHILDREN on page 578.)

CMV Abbreviation for CYTOMEGALOVIRUS.

CNM Abbreviation for CERTIFIED NURSE-MIDWIFE.

CNS Abbreviation for CENTRAL NERVOUS SYSTEM.

coach In CHILDBIRTH, popular term for BIRTH PARTNER.

coarctation of the aorta A type of CONGENITAL heart defect. (See HEART AND HEART PROBLEMS.)

cochlea A fluid-filled, snail-shaped, bony shell in the inner ear, which contains the organ of Corti, the actual organ of hearing; problems in the cochlea can lead to significant EAR AND HEARING PROBLEMS.

cochlear implant A device using a microprocessor to simulate the functions performed in the inner ear, to aid people whose EAR AND HEARING PROBLEMS are so severe that a HEARING AID is of little or no use. A tiny electrical receiver and transmitter is surgically implanted into the inner ear; there it receives electrical signals from an external microphone and speech processor and transmits them to the brain. At its present state of development, the cochlear implant does not allow for normal hearing, but used in conjunction with LIPREADING, it can allow for much greater understanding of speech. The cochlear implant is only in experimental use with children. It is most successful with POSTLINGUAL deaf people, who have some experience of spoken language.

cognitive development The process by which an infant gains knowledge and becomes a thinking being, developing the whole range of perceptual and conceptual skills needed for organizing and understanding experience of the world, including memory, discrimination, sequencing, concept formation, generalization, reasoning, and problem-solving. Psychologist Jean Piaget, pioneer in studying cognitive development, proposed that children pass through four stages of cognitive learning:

1. *sensory motor* (or *sensorimotor*). During roughly the first two years of life, a child becomes aware of sense perceptions and uses this knowledge in developing MOTOR SKILLS. Children learn OBJECT PERMANENCE and cause-and-effect, as they begin to understand and somewhat control their environment.

2. *preoperational*. Between roughly ages two and seven, a child acquires language skills, begins to use symbols (words and images), and develops reasoning ability but is as yet unable to deal with abstract concepts and deductive reasoning.

3. *concrete operations*. Between roughly ages seven and 11, a child begins to develop systematic reasoning and can apply logic to concrete, physical problems but is not yet able to deal with abstract questions. That is, children at this stage may begin to solve problems in their heads, by thinking rather than doing, but the problems still relate to concrete things.

4. *formal operations*. Between roughly ages 11 and 16, a child develops the ability to think, apply logic to, and solve problems about abstract ideas, not just concrete objects that can be readily perceived. This, for Piaget, marked the development of adult thinking, a stage at which a child begins to be able to hypothesize what might have been or what might be and to plan for the future.

Piaget's thinking on cognitive development has been enormously influential. However, many psychologists now feel that individual variations in the timing, sequence, and style of learning, especially among children who come from widely varying environments, are considerably greater than Piaget recognized. Piaget did, however, spur considerable observation and research as to just what and how children learn and when. A CHART OF NORMAL DEVELOPMENT (on page 507) indicates when between birth and age six children first *on the average* begin to develop the main cognitive skills.

Children with LEARNING DISABILITIES or other DEVELOPMENTAL DISORDERS may have malfunctions that inhibit their cognitive development. They often think in concrete terms, taking words quite literally, rather than generalizing. For example, if you tell a group of children to get into a circle, a learning-disabled child may step into a circle drawn on a carpet rather than joining hands in a ring. Such children may take much longer to learn real-life connections—for example, that grass needs rain to grow.

Children develop at individual and varying paces, but every child can benefit from activities designed to enhance their natural development. In TEACHING YOUNG CHILDREN: GUIDELINES AND ACTIVITIES (page 544), parents will find activities designed to develop children's skills in various areas, including cognitive skills. Some general suggestions are given on page 107 in HOW PARENTS CAN HELP A CHILD'S MIND TO GROW.

For help and further information

Jean Piaget Society (JPS)
College of Education
University of Delaware
Newark, DE 19716

How Parents Can Help a Child's Mind to Grow

The reactions of other people are very important to a child's development. When parents talk to and play with their baby, they stimulate her senses. The baby, in turn, becomes more confident of her abilities. Games like peek-a-boo and patty-cake increase the interaction and improve the relationship between parent and child. At the same time, they lay the groundwork for more complicated learning.

The potential for intelligent behavior does not simply unfold. Its development needs experience, encouragement, affection, and tender, loving care along with stimulation from the environment. (Enriching the environment of a culturally deprived child can bring striking improvements in intelligence test scores, especially if a child is quite young at the time of the change.)

There are many ways to stimulate the learning and thinking process. Parents can help by not using baby talk. They can also help by explaining objects and events, using more than one word, and trying to involve more than one sense. For instance, a child says, "Look!" The parent might respond, "What is it?" The child then names the object or, if she doesn't know the name, is told what it is. Other questions lead to her practicing what she already knows, or they add to her knowledge. Examples are: "What color is it?" "What is it doing?" "What does it feel like?"

Children are full of curiosity. They are full of questions that can lead to stimulation of their thought processes. When parents accept and respond to this curiosity, it grows. When they do not, it may wither—to the detriment of learning. If a parent responds receptively to each situation as it unfolds, a natural reaction takes place that helps the learning process as well as the parent–child relationship.

Therefore, when a child asks questions, be sure to give answers in such a way that she has something to think about. To encourage her to exchange information, ask her opinion about an idea, an object, or a situation. See if she can figure out more than one way to solve a problem or to find the information she needs. With increases in a child's ability to handle information, make your explanations more complex.

As a child is challenged, her learning speeds up and her world grows larger. On the other hand, if pushed so far that she can't succeed, she becomes frustrated. Also, if a parent gives too many or too complex directions, the child may give up and stop trying, or she may respond with anger and rebellion. Some adults think on such a sophisticated level that they tend to talk over a child's head. Such an adult's instructions to a young child can be like an explanation of how to fly an airplane to someone who wants only to steer a scooter.

When a child has both choice and voice in a project, she is more likely to become involved and to commit herself to goals. And when behavior is rewarded (for example, by paying attention to the child), it is more likely to be repeated.

Your child's intellectual development doesn't hang on a single act but on an attitude that encourages enthusiasm for learning and new ideas. Your child models herself after you, and a major route for learning is your child's observations of how you learn and deal with your emotions and stress.

Children also learn from watching other siblings or TV shows. However, parents should not expect educational TV programs to do all the work. Research shows that a child gains the most from television when a parent is involved and shares the experience. For example, the parent helps by explaining what the child doesn't understand and by talking about issues raised in the program.

Instead of telling children what to think or do in every situation, help them to learn how to solve their problems themselves. People who are good at problem solving are better adjusted and more able to get along with other persons than those who are not. They are less nagging, demanding, impatient, and aggressive. They also tend to be less inhibited, shy, fearful, or withdrawn. They are more concerned about others and better liked. This has been found to be true of children as young as four years of age.

When children are encouraged to choose among alternatives and judge the consequences of their actions, they learn to think about various possibilities. And they discover that, when the first idea for solving a problem does not work, there are other routes available.

In managing your child, use your imagination; put yourself in her place. Let's pretend that you are expecting guests and your child is fingerpainting. If you say, "You can't do that anymore; go ride your bike," her answer will probably be, "I don't want to." If instead you explain that you are expecting company and ask her to think of something less messy to do, she just might choose to ride her bike or may even offer to help. A child is much more likely to carry out her own idea than one suggested or imposed by an adult. Of course, there will be times when you will have to insist that a child do it your way.

Every child wants to know more. As she explores, learns, and receives encouragement and reinforcement (or rewards) from the actions and words of parents, her world of knowledge expands along with her ability to think.

Parents are a key ingredient in the development of their child's thinking abilities. When they provide interesting experiences, encouragement, affection, love, and a challenging environment, they vastly expand what a child is likely to achieve.

Source: *Learning While Growing: Cognitive Development,* by Constance Stapleton and Herbert Yahraes (1980). Prepared for the National Institute of Mental Health's Caring About Kids series.

302-451-2311
Frank B. Murray, Editor
Organization of psychologists, educators, and students interested in Piaget's ideas on cognitive development. Encourages further research on Piaget's ideas; seeks to educate public; maintains library; publishes various materials, including quarterly newsletter.

High-Scope Educational Research Foundation
600 North River Street
Ypsilanti, MI 48197
313-485-2000
David P. Weikart, President
Organization devoted to exploring alternatives to education for children from birth through adolescence and to training for teachers. Does curriculum development, including elementary curriculum incorporating Piaget's ideas of cognitive development; develops training materials, including some for home teaching of infants; maintains laboratory school; offers programs in infant education and development, for both parents and preschool education professionals; conducts research; publishes various materials, including newsletters and books.

Other reference sources

A Piaget Primer: How a Child Thinks, by Dorothy G. Singer and Travey A. Revenson. New York: Universities Press, 1978.
Alternatives to Piaget: Critical Essays on the Theory, by Linda S. Siegel and Charles J. Brainerd. New York: Academic, 1978.
Cognitive Development, by J.H. Flavell. Englewood Cliffs, NJ: Prentice-Hall, 1977.
How Children Learn, by John Holt. New York: Delta, 1969.
(See also EDUCATION.)

cognitive domain   One of three key categories of instructional content and learning objectives described by Benjamin Bloom, referring to thinking skills such as problem-solving, memory and recall, comprehension, reasoning, and judgment; the others are the AFFECTIVE DOMAIN and the PSYCHOMOTOR DOMAIN. (See DOMAIN.)

cognitive style   The type of approach that a person generally takes toward learning activities and problem-solving. One person may carefully analyze a task, break it down, and put the smaller steps in order, while another may jump impulsively into the middle of a new activity. (For help and further information, see LEARNING STYLE.)

COLD   Abbreviation for CHRONIC OBSTRUCTIVE LUNG DISEASE, a kind of LUNG AND BREATHING DISORDER.

cold sores   Popular name for mouth sores caused by the HERPES SIMPLEX virus.

colic (infantile)   A condition in which an otherwise happy, healthy, alert young baby has attacks of crying and screaming—often quite different from cries for food or attention—nearly every day, often in the evening and at about the same hour of the day. Precisely what causes the attacks is unknown, though many people think it involves severe, painful spasms in the intestines; it is often associated with gas rumbling through the intestines. The crying may last for just a few minutes or may go on for 20 minutes or more, then end suddenly, perhaps tailing off into a soft whimper, and may start up again just before sleep. Luckily, the condition generally disappears in a few weeks, with no harm except to the parents' nerves.

It is wise for parents to be sure from the baby's medical checkups that the crying does not reflect some physical prob-

---

Tips for Parents With Colicky Babies

If your baby has an attack of colic, holding him or her across your knees on the stomach often will give some comfort. Some colicky babies cry less if they are kept in motion—try rocking or pushing in a carriage.

There is little you can do except try to comfort the baby until the attack stops. Make sure your baby isn't crying for some other reason (is hungry, wet, lonely, or some clothing is uncomfortable). It is important to remember that if your baby has colic, it does not interfere with his or her general health and growth. Your baby should grow out of it by the time he or she is 12 to 16 weeks old.

"Colicky" babies do annoy and distress their mothers and fathers and anybody living in the household. Remind everyone that it is not the baby's fault, it is not your fault, and the baby will get over it. If the crying becomes too much to bear, put the baby safely in the crib and walk into another room for a few minutes of relief. If the colic becomes a real problem, it is worth a special trip to your doctor.

Source: *Infant Care* (1989). Prepared for the Public Health Service by the Bureau of Maternal and Child Health and Resources Development.

---

lem that requires attention. Beyond that, the parent's main role is to try to soothe the child—but not with feeding, for that may exacerbate the problem—and maintain their own composure. Some experts recommend against overstimulating the child or conveying any sense of anxiety, which will only make the problem worse. One option during such attacks is for parents or others in the household to take turns being with the baby, giving each other a break.

For help and further information

Parents' Book of Infant Colic, by Phyllis Schneider. New York: Ballantine, 1990.
Stopping Baby's Colic, by Ted Ayllon with Mori Freed. New York: Putnam, 1989.

colitis   Inflammation of the *colon*, the large intestine; a kind of DIGESTIVE DISORDER.

college   In general, a school offering EDUCATION beyond the HIGH SCHOOL level, but most often one that offers academic education leading to the lower-level postsecondary DEGREES. Two-year colleges (junior or community colleges) normally grant ASSOCIATE DEGREES, while four-year colleges award BACHELOR'S DEGREES. Two or more colleges, graduate schools, and professional schools grouped together make up a UNIVERSITY, which often focuses on research in addition to teaching.

Once open to relatively few people, a college education has in recent decades become available to a much wider segment of the population and has become increasingly necessary for individuals. A college degree is a prerequisite for many jobs, since the complexity of the modern technological world requires more highly skilled people. One reflection of that is the rapid spread of two-year community colleges, which provide advanced training in many occupational, technical, and cultural areas, today attended by many students who in earlier decades would have finished their schooling at the 12th grade or earlier.

Many two- and four-year public colleges and universities have been far better funded in recent decades than most private colleges and universities and therefore often have more modern and extensive libraries, laboratory equipment, and other facilities; they can often attract high-quality professors by paying better salaries. As a result, many of the highest-ranking colleges and universities in recent surveys of the professors themselves have been public universities, with some public schools (such as the University of Michigan and top branches of the University of California) sometimes edging out IVY LEAGUE schools for top honors. Parents considering both academic excellence and their own pocketbooks may well focus early on sending their children to public colleges, rather than automatically going for the far more expensive private colleges.

A college education is not necessary or even advisable for everyone, of course. Many people do not have the interest, the aptitude, or the basic skills to pursue academic education beyond the high school level. Their occupational options may be somewhat circumscribed by the lack of a college degree, but if they have other kinds of skills and interests to pursue, they may be perfectly happy to forgo college.

But for those who choose to attend college, some of the main questions are:

- identifying what they want in a college—small or large, competitive or easygoing, urban or rural, special programs offered, and so on.
- identifying which colleges will offer what they want.
- gaining ADMISSION to the schools that interest them.
- arranging to finance college costs.
- selecting which of the schools that offer them admission best fits their needs.

With all of the focus on admissions and financing, and on the prestige of this school or that, students sometimes lose sight of their own personal preferences. But it is worth analyzing very early and carefully choosing to apply to colleges that suit a student's individual needs, for those colleges are likely to make for the most successful and satisfying college career.

Among the key pre-college hurdles are STANDARDIZED TESTS such as the SCHOLASTIC APTITUDE TEST. The PRELIMINARY SCHOLASTIC APTITUDE TEST, offered in the junior year, can give the student an idea of where he or she stands relative to other students. Students and parents should use this information wisely in selecting which colleges to apply to, a process in which a school's guidance counselor can be helpful. The important point is to apply to schools that will suit the student's needs and desires but that are not so competitive that the application is likely to fail. If students (or parents) still prefer to try for riskily competitive schools, they should be sure to have one or more *safety schools*, to which admission is almost guaranteed.

Other reference sources

General Works

What Do You Mean You Don't Want to Go to College?, by Liliane Quon McCain and Larry Strauss. Chicago: Lowell House/Contemporary, 1990.

Paine Webber: How to Build a College Fund for Your Child, by Marion Buhagiar. New York: Putnam, 1990.

Financing a College Education: The Essential Guide for the 90's, by Judith B. Margolin. New York: Plenum, 1989.

The Question Is College: Guiding Your Child to the Right Choice After High School, by Herbert Kohl. New York: Times Books, 1989.

Putting Your Kids Through College, by Scott Edelstein and the editors of Consumer Reports Books. New York: Consumer Reports Books, 1989.

The Ultimate Guide to College Success, by Thomas Abdo and Penelope Pederson-Kaye. Gainesville, FL: Maupin House, 1989.

The College Guide for Parents, revised and updated edition, by Charles J. Shields. New York: College Board, 1988.

Letting Go: A Parent's Guide to the College Experience, by Karen Levin Coburn and Madge Lawrence Treeger. New York: Farrar, Straus & Giroux, 1988.

For Students

Looking Beyond the Ivy League: Finding the College That's Right for You, by Loren Pope. New York: Penguin, 1990.

The Right College 1991, compiled by College Research Group of Concord, MA. New York: Arco, 1990.

Choosing a College: The Student's Step-by-Step Decision-Making Workbook, by Gordon Porter Miller. New York: College Board, annual.

College: Getting In and Staying In, by D. Bruce Lockerbie and Donald R. Fonseca. Grand Rapids, MI: Eerdmans, 1990.

Campus Bound: How to Choose—and Get Into—the College That's Right for You, by Annette Spence. Los Angeles: Price/Stern/Sloan, 1990.

Lisa Birnbach's New and Improved College Book. New York: Prentice Hall, 1990.

Majoring in the Rest of Your Life: Career Secrets for College Students, by Carol Carter. New York: Farrar, Straus & Giroux/Noonday, 1990.

How to Prepare for College, by Margaret Gisler and Marjorie Eberts. Lincolnwood, IL: Passport Books/NTC, 1989.

Summer on Campus: College Experiences for High School Students, by Shirley Levin. New York: College Board, 1989.

Campus Health Guide: The College Students' Handbook for Healthy Living, by Carol L. Otis, M.D., and Roger Goldingay. New York: College Board, 1989.

I Wonder What College Is Like? by Meg F. Schneider. New York: Messner, 1989. For ages 12 to 16.

Coping with Stress in College, by Mark Rowh. New York: College Board, 1989.

College Bound: The Student's Handbook for Getting Ready, Moving in, and Succeeding on Campus, by Evelyn Kaye and Janet Gardner. New York: College Board, 1988.

For Information About Colleges

The College Handbook. New York: College Board, annual. Basic resource on admissions, costs, financial aid, majors, etc., for 2- and 4-year colleges.

Comparative Guide to American Colleges, by James Cass and Max Birnbaum. New York: Harper & Row, 1989.

Best Dollar Values in American Colleges, compiled by College Research Group of Concord, MA. New York: Prentice Hall/Arco, 1990.

The Almanac of Higher Education, 1989–1990, by editors of *The Chronicle of Higher Education*. Chicago: University of Chicago, 1989.

Fischgrund's Insider's Guide to the Top 25 Colleges, Tom Fischgrund, ed. Marietta, GA: Longstreet, 1989.

The Fiske Guide to Colleges, by Edward B. Fiske. New York: Times Books, 1989.

The 1990 GIS® Guide to Four-Year Colleges, by Pedro Arango and Dwight Hatcher, consultants, the editors of the Guidance Information System. Boston, MA: Houghton Mifflin, 1989.

Lovejoy's College Guide, 19th edition, by Charles T. Straughn II and Barbarasue Lovejoy Straughn. New York: Monarch, 1989.

Peterson's Guide to Four-Year Colleges 1991 and *Peterson's Guide to Two-Year Colleges 1991*. Princeton, NJ: Peterson's, 1990.

Peterson's Drug and Alcohol Programs and Policies at Four-Year Colleges, Janet Carney Schneider and Bunny Porter-Shirley, eds. Princeton, NJ: Peterson's, 1989.

Peterson's Competitive Colleges. Princeton, NJ: Peterson's, 1988.

Directory of Software Sources for Higher Education. Princeton, NJ: Peterson's, 1988.

Index of Majors. New York: College Board, annual. Lists programs at undergraduate and graduate levels, including special programs.

On College Admissions

50 College Admission Directors Speak to Parents, by Sandra F. MacGowan and Sarah M. McGinty. Orlando, FL: Harcourt Brace Jovanovich, 1990.

College Admissions: Cracking the System. New York: Villard, 1990.

College Appli-Kit: College Application System, by Eileen Cohen and Beverly Zakarian. New York: Times Books, 1989.

Peterson's Handbook for College Admissions: A Family Guide, third edition, by Thomas C. Hayden. Princeton, NJ: Peterson's, 1989.

How to Get into the Right College: Advice Straight From the Experts—Admissions Officers Themselves, by Edward B. Fiske. New York: Times Books, 1988.

A Student's Guide to College Admissions: Everything Your Guidance Counselor Has No Time to Tell You, by Harlow G. Unger. New York: Facts on File, 1990.

The Princeton Review: College Admissions: Cracking the System, by Adam Robinson and John Katzman. New York: Villard, 1988.

(For help and further information, see ADMISSIONS; FINANCIAL AID; SCHOLASTIC APTITUDE TEST.)

college boards   Popular name for pre-college tests offered by the COLLEGE ENTRANCE EXAMINATION BOARD, especially the SCHOLASTIC APTITUDE TEST.

College Entrance Examination Board (College Board or CEEB)   Nonprofit organization providing services to hundreds of colleges, universities, agencies, and other groups, primarily offering widely used tests for college-bound students, among them:

- SCHOLASTIC APTITUDE TEST (SAT), for students as an ADMISSION TEST for COLLEGE.
- PRELIMINARY SCHOLASTIC APTITUDE TEST/NATIONAL MERIT SCHOLARSHIP QUALIFYING TEST (PSAT/NMSQT), a "warm-up" for the SAT, also used for the National Merit Scholarships.
- ADVANCED PLACEMENT PROGRAM (APP), for high school students seeking college credits.
- COLLEGE LEVEL EXAMINATION PROGRAM (CLEP), for college students seeking non-course credit.

The College Board also operates the College Scholarship Service for students seeking FINANCIAL AID. Though its testing services are clearly valued by colleges and universities, critics have often complained that such tests distort the evaluation process, giving preference to those who are good at taking TESTS over those who may have other, equally valuable but less easily measurable skills and abilities.

For help and further information

The College Board
45 Columbus Avenue
New York, NY 10023
212-713-8000

The College Board and the School Curriculum, by John Valentine. Princeton, NJ: College Board, 1987.

College-Level Examination Program (CLEP)   A series of STANDARDIZED TESTS offered by the COLLEGE ENTRANCE EXAMINATION BOARD in dozens of subjects to students who are studying in EXTERNAL DEGREE PROGRAMS or who, through self-study, wish to gain college CREDIT before entering or while enrolled in a regular campus-based college program. Students would be wise to confirm that the college they are attending will accept CLEP results for credit and ADVANCED PLACEMENT.

College Work-Study (CWS)   Federally funded WORK-STUDY PROGRAM, open to undergraduate and graduate students, offering jobs on- and off-campus. Undergraduates are paid by the hour, graduates by the hour or by salary, all at least monthly, but the amount earned cannot exceed demonstrated need. (For help and further information, see FINANCIAL AID.)

colonoscope   A type of ENDOSCOPE, passed through the anus and used by doctors in visually examining the colon (large intestine). (For help and further information, see DIGESTIVE DISORDERS.)

color blindness (color vision deficiency)   Reduced ability to perceive differences in color, especially in the red and green ranges. (See EYE AND VISION PROBLEMS.)

colostomy   A type of OSTOMY performed on the *colon* (large intestine), most often because of CANCER.

colostrum   A yellowish fluid that is produced by the BREASTS in the last part of PREGNANCY and the first few days after CHILDBIRTH, before the normal LACTATION begins. The colostrum contains white blood cells, ANTIBODIES, PROTEIN, MINERALS, FATS, and sugars. Women may wish to place a small, clean pad in a bra to prevent clothes from becoming stained; they should wash the breasts with mild soap and water as necessary to avoid infection.

coma   A state of deep unconsciousness, but unlike sleep in that the person cannot be aroused and does not respond, either to external stimuli (such as shouts or pinches) or internal (such as the sensation of a full bladder). Unlike conditions of BRAIN DEATH, however, some types of brain activity remain. Even severely comatose patients can sometimes breathe on their own, move their eyes, and make other facial movements. Patients in less severe comas may even have some modest response to external stimulation, even though still unconscious. People can exist for years in a coma, if feeding, breathing, and other vital functions are maintained. Coma can result from a variety of problems, including HEAD INJURY, BRAIN TUMOR, severe cases of DIABETES MELLITUS, KIDNEY AND UROLOGICAL DISORDERS, LIVER PROBLEMS, ENCEPHALITIS, MENINGITIS, SHOCK, and HYPOXIA.

For help and further information

National Institute of Neurological Disorders and Stroke (NINDS), 301-496-5751. (For full group information, see BRAIN AND BRAIN DISORDERS.)

combination pill   A kind of BIRTH-CONTROL PILL.

comfort habits   General term for actions or things adopted by young children to enhance feelings of comfort, safety, and security. These include SUCKING a thumb, finger, or PACIFIER; adopting a TRANSITIONAL COMFORT OBJECT such as a teddy bear or old blanket; and repetitive, rhythmic activities such as rocking or hair twisting. Sucking and comfort objects generally cause no concern (unless one is accidentally lost!), but repetitive physical activities can interfere with the child's developing relationship with the world, becoming a sort of self-hypnosis. If a child seems to be withdrawing from other activities into rhythmic habits (rather than falling into them when bored or tired, as at sleeptime), and especially if the activities are potentially dangerous (such as head-banging), parents may want to consult their PEDIATRICIAN for ways to counteract or divert the habits before they become ingrained. Such habits can develop into a psychological condition called *stereotypy habit disorder*, which may require treatment. Often, however, substantial amounts of loving attention and playtime with parents can turn the child away from rhythmic habits if they have not already become well-established. (See also IMPULSE CONTROL DISORDER; MENTAL DISORDER.)

comfort object   Alternate name for TRANSITIONAL COMFORT OBJECT.

comity   A legal doctrine under which countries recognize each others' judicial decrees. In family law, CUSTODY decrees handed down in foreign countries are often recognized in those states that have enacted the UNIFORM CHILD CUSTODY JURISDICTION ACT. U.S. custody decrees are recognized in many other countries but not all.

comminuted fracture   A type of FRACTURE in which the bone is shattered into more than two pieces.

communication skills and disorders   The skills involved in using speech and language, and the problems with them, which become obvious in early childhood, when children learn to communicate with others. Speech is just one method of communicating with language, which is the ability to use symbols to represent objects and ideas. These symbols may include written characters and words used in WRITING, the gestures used in SIGN LANGUAGE, standardized BLISS SYMBOLS moved on a CONVERSATION BOARD, or the spoken sounds used in speech.

To communicate, children must learn two different kinds of language skills. The first is *receptive language*, the ability to understand or comprehend what is heard. The other is *expressive language*, the ability to express oneself verbally. Most children (like most adults) understand more than they are able to express. Many perfectly normal young children have difficulty imitating sounds and language clearly enough to be understood, but many outgrow such problems during the early grades of school. The process starts early, as described in "Your Baby Hears You Talking," on page 112.

The list of language milestones on page 113 gives a picture of the kinds of communication skills a child, *on the average*, develops in the first six years. Also, the CHART OF NORMAL DEVELOPMENT on page 507 indicates when between birth and age six children generally first develop the main communication and other skills. Parents should be forewarned that children develop at individual and widely varying paces. If they have real concerns about a child's development, they should by all means

Your Baby Hears You Talking

Although hearing is not fully developed at birth, newborns can hear moderately loud sounds, and they do distinguish between pitches. It has long been known that babies startle at loud and sudden noises, but they also react to softer sounds, usually by waving their arms and legs.

Infants seem to prefer sounds in the normal human voice range. A fascinating slow-motion film made by a researcher shows a baby moving her arms and legs rhythmically to the sounds of her mother's voice. What appears to the normal eye to be random arm and leg movements are actually muscular responses attuned to the changes in the mother's speech. Although scientists do not fully understand the connection between the baby's movements and the sound of the mother's voice, it is thought that the baby's muscular responses may somehow be part of earliest speech development.

It is well known that a baby learns, from her or his parent's reactions, to associate particular sounds with specific objects. For example, with your encouragement—your smiles, your repetition of his or her babbling with slight changing of the sounds—your baby's "d" and "m" sounds usually become "dada" and "mama." From your responses, your baby will soon learn who mama and dada are.

Talk to your baby. Don't be embarrassed about talking to an infant. She or he is probably the best audience you'll ever have. At that tender age, your baby just likes the sound of your voice. It doesn't matter whether you recite poems, talk about your day at work, or discuss the weather.

When your baby is older and beginning to talk, it is best to let her or him do most of the talking. Encourage your baby to talk, and *listen* to him or her. When babies know you care enough to listen, they will feel good about themselves and may find talking easier.

Babies also like musical sounds. Sing to your baby. She or he is not a music critic and will appreciate your songs even if off key. Singing to your baby while rocking him or her in your arms can be fun and relaxing for both of you. Music boxes and toys with firmly fastened bells are also good entertainment, not to mention the old favorite, the rattle.

As your child grows older, she or he will enjoy listening to records and stories. You may find that your toddler plays the same record over and over again, just as he or she may want to hear the same story over and over again. Children learn from the repetition and need it. Listening to the same record for three hours may not be your idea of a fun afternoon, but who knows, it could be the beginning of your child's music appreciation!

Source: *Stimulating Baby Senses*, by Marilyn Sargent, in consultation with National Institute of Mental Health scientists. Washington, DC: Government Printing Office, 1978. Part of the Caring About Kids series. For more from this pamphlet, see BOTTLEFEEDING, MOTOR SKILLS, SENSORY MODES, and VISUAL SKILLS.

have the child professionally evaluated, but many perfectly normal children did not begin to speak until *long* after the averages said they should.

Some children, however, have continuing problems. They are said to have a *language disorder* if their difficulty is in understanding language or putting words together to make sense, in which case the cause is generally some kind of malfunction of the brain. The National Institute on Deafness and Other Communicative Disorders (NIDCD) notes that such problems may show themselves in several ways:

- Children may have trouble giving names to objects and using those names to formulate ideas about how the world is organized. For example, they cannot learn that a toy they play with is called *car* or that a toy car of another color, or a real car, can also be called *car*.
- They may have trouble learning the rules of grammar. Such children might not learn, for example, how to use prepositions and other small words like *in* and *the*.
- They may not use language appropriately for the context; for example, they might respond to a teacher's question by reciting an irrelevant jingle heard on television.

Children with *speech disorders* have trouble actually producing the sounds of the language, which may stem from a malfunction in the brain or inability to properly control the muscles needed to produce the sounds. Speech is actually a highly complex activity directed by the brain, using various muscles in the tongue, lips, jaw, palate, larynx, and face to change the shape of the mouth and so shape the sound made by air being pushed from the lungs through the vocal cords in the larynx, while other consonants ("stop" sounds) are produced by the lips, teeth, and roof of the mouth. Children with certain kinds of physical problems, such as CEREBRAL PALSY or CLEFT LIP AND PALATE, have special difficulty with speech.

Speech problems are far more widespread than language problems, affecting twice as many boys as girls. The NIDCD estimates that speech disorders affect about 10 to 15 percent of preschoolers and about 6 percent of children in grades one through 12. Language disorders affect 2 to 3 percent of preschoolers and about 1 percent of older children. In either case, the child will be significantly behind other children of the same age, background, and ability in their rate of speech and language development. Professionals in the field use a wide variety of phrases to describe the kind of slowed development shown in these children, including *developmental language disorder*, *delayed speech*, *impaired language*, *motor disorder*, and *idiopathic* (of no known cause) *speech and language disorders*.

Children with communication disorders often have other kinds of problems, such as EAR AND HEARING PROBLEMS, MENTAL RETARDATION, CRI DU CHAT SYNDROME, TOURETTE'S SYNDROME, and AUTISM. These can magnify the effects of communication problems. For example, children who have trouble with AUDITORY SKILLS—auditory discrimination, auditory memory, or localization—also have trouble developing receptive language skills,

Language Milestones

Child's age	Speech behavior the child should have mastered
1 year	Says 2 to 3 words (may not be clearly pronounced) Repeats same syllable 2 to 3 times ("ma, ma, ma") Carries out simple directions when accompanied by gestures Answers simple questions with nonverbal response Imitates voice patterns of others Uses single word meaningfully to label object or person
2 years	Says 8 to 10 words by age 1½, 10 to 15 words by age 2 Puts two words together ("more cookie," "where kitty?") Points to 12 familiar objects when named Names 3 body parts on a doll, self, or another person Names 5 family members including pets and self Produces animal sound or uses sound for animal's name (cow is "moo-moo") Asks for some common food items by name when shown ("milk," "cookie," "cracker")
3 years	Produces two-word phrases combining two nouns ("ball chair"), noun and adjective ("my ball"), or noun and verb ("daddy go") Uses *no* or *not* in speech Answers *where*, *who*, and *what* questions Carries out a series of two related commands Consistently uses *ing* verb form ("running"), regular plural form ("book/books"), and some irregular past tense forms ("went," "did," "was") Uses *is* and *a* in statements ("This is a ball.") Uses possessive form of nouns ("daddy's") Uses some class names ("toy," "animals," "food")
4 years	Uses a vocabulary of 200 to 300 words Uses *is* at beginning of questions when appropriate Carries out series of two unrelated commands Expresses future occurrences with *going to, have to, want to* Changes word order appropriately to ask questions ("Can I?" "Does he?") Uses some common irregular plurals ("men," "feet") Tells two events in order of occurrence
5 years	Carries out series of three directions Demonstrates understanding of passive sentences ("Girl was hit by boy.") Uses compound and complex sentences Uses contractions *can't, don't, won't* Points out absurdities in picture Tells final word in opposite analogies Names picture that does not belong in particular class ("one that's not an animal") Tells whether two words rhyme
6 years	Points to some, many, several Tells address and telephone number Tells simple jokes Tells daily experiences Answers *why* question with an explanation Defines words

Source: *Developmental Speech and Language Disorders* (1988). Prepared for the Public Health Service by the National Institute of Neurological and Communicative Disorders and Stroke, adapted from material of the Portage Guide to Early Education, ©1976, Cooperative Educational Service Agency.

because they misunderstand or forget words. They may also have trouble learning some of the key action words (e.g., verbs such as *put, jump,* or *run*) and words showing position (e.g., prepositions such as *in, on, behind,* or *under*) and so be unable to understand simple-seeming directions, such as "Put the ball in the box."

Observational Checklist for Communication Disorders

Reception

	Often or Always	Rarely or Never
After 24 months, the child cannot point to common objects that are named.	☐	☐
After 24 months, the child cannot understand simple one-part directions, such as "Bring me the ball."	☐	☐
After 36 months, the child repeats questions rather than answering them. For example, when asked, "What did you do yesterday?" the child responds, "Do yesterday."	☐	☐
After 48 months, the child cannot follow two-part directions, such as "Put the book away and get a chair."	☐	☐
After 48 months, the child is unable to respond, even with appropriate gestures, to a slightly complex question such as "What do you do when you're thirsty?"	☐	☐
After 48 months, the child seems confused when asked a question or when the class is given instructions. The child waits to see what the other children are doing when directions are given.	☐	☐

Expression

	Often or Always	Rarely or Never
After 24 months, the child has not yet started talking.	☐	☐
After 36 months, the child cannot put words together to make simple sentences such as "Give me more juice."	☐	☐
After 48 months, the child cannot tell a recent series of events.	☐	☐
After 48 months, there are unusual word confusions or substitutions of words when the child talks. For example, the child may say "I want a crayon" for "I want a pencil," or "Give me the stove thing" for "Give me a pot."	☐	☐
After 60 months, most of the child's grammar and sentence structure seems noticeably faulty and is unlike the communication pattern used in the child's home.	☐	☐

Many of the items in this checklist were obtained from *Getting a HEAD START on Speech and Language Problems* by Susan Hansen. Copyright 1974 Meyer Children's Rehabilitation Institute, 444 South 44 Street, Omaha, Nebraska 68131.

Continued on page 115

Children with LEARNING DISABILITIES and some other DEVELOP-MENTAL DISORDERS may also have problems in learning the forms of the language, such as singular or plural or past and present tense of verbs. They may often forget the words they want to say, substitute one word for another (e.g., *table* for *chair*), or substitute sound effects for a word (e.g., *meow* for *cat*). Such children also often cannot imitate movements of the tongue or lips for actions such as blowing, and they may experience equal difficulty in body language or nonverbal communication, as in using gestures, mime, or facial expression.

But apart from these multiple problems, there are several different kinds of speech and language problems that may affect children:

- *phonological impairment*, or *misarticulation*, in which a child says the sounds wrong or omits or duplicates sounds within a word, as in *wabbit* for *rabbit*, *thnake* for *snake, dood* for *good*, and *poo* for *spoon*. The problem might be poor neuro-

logical motor skills, an error in learning, or difficulty in identifying some speech sounds. A child might also drop an unstressed syllable, as in *nana* for *banana* or *te-phone* for *telephone*. Many young children do this early in speech development, but when it persists unduly, brain dysfunction is considered the cause. Some of these misarticulations are popularly called "baby talk" or *lisping*; to make sure a child does not learn to speak improperly, experts recommend that parents avoid using "baby talk" altogether.

- *stuttering*, or *stammering*, in which speech rhythms are disrupted. A child repeatedly hesitates, stumbles, prolongs, or spasmodically pronounces certain sounds, which vary from person to person. Stuttering is common among children, especially boys, but many outgrow it or receive therapy in early childhood to help overcome it. Professionals advise parents to be patient and calm, not to make the child anxious about the stuttering and thereby exacerbate it, and to seek

Articulation

	Often or Always	Rarely or Never
After 24 months, the child uses mostly vowel sounds (oo, ah, ee) and gestures when talking.	☐	☐
After 36 months, the child leaves out the first sound in many words (says "at" for "cat" or "es" for "yes").	☐	☐
After 42 months, friends, neighbors, and teachers cannot understand most of what the child says.	☐	☐
At any age, the child seems embarrassed or disturbed about his or her speech.	☐	☐
At any age, speech sounds are more than a year late in developing.	☐	☐

Rhythm

	Often or Always	Rarely or Never
The child has noticeable difficulty and seems to struggle trying to say words or sounds.	☐	☐
The child is aware of this difficulty.	☐	☐
There is an abnormal amount of hesitation, repetition of sounds ("cuh-cuh-can") or words ("but-but-but"), and/or prolongation of sounds ("sssssomething") or words ("mmmmeeee") in the child's speech and the child seems aware of it.	☐	☐

Voice

	Often or Always	Rarely or Never
The child's voice is so soft that he or she can barely be heard.	☐	☐
The child's voice is extremely loud.	☐	☐
The child's pitch is inappropriate (too high or too low) for the child's sex and age.	☐	☐
The child's voice sounds hoarse, strained, or unusual in some way.	☐	☐
The child's speech is nasal (sounds as if he or she has a cold or sinus condition).	☐	☐
The child's speech is hypernasal (sounds seem to be spoken through the nose rather than through the mouth).	☐	☐

Source: *Mainstreaming Preschoolers: Children with Speech and Language Impairments.*

therapy early on so that the speech pattern does not become set for life. The causes of stuttering are unclear; it seems to run in families, and some feel it results from some subtle brain dysfunction, while others regard the triggers as psychological. Recent researchers have found that while, in most people, one set of vocal muscles relaxes and the other contracts during speech, in stutterers both sets of muscles contract very hard, as the NINCDS put it, "setting up a virtual tug of war for control of the cords."

- DYSPRAXIA, which is the inability to properly coordinate in sequence the movements required for speech. In this case, the vocal instruments seem to be in perfectly good working order, but there is a disruption in the instructions from the brain to the muscles involved in speech. Children with verbal dyspraxia make many of the same errors as in phonological impairment but may also speak using only vowels, making their speech virtually unintelligible.

- DYSARTHRIA, which involves problems with controlling the muscles used in speaking, often with the mouth open all the time and the tongue protruding. This is often associated with disorders affecting the CENTRAL NERVOUS SYSTEM; the child may have trouble eating as well.
- *aphasia*, the lack of language function, expressive or receptive. When resulting from HEAD INJURY that damaged the part of the brain involved in speech, after the child had begun to develop communication skills, the condition is called *acquired aphasia*.
- *chronic voice disorders*, in which the voice is unusually loud, soft, high, low, raspy, strained, hoarse, nasal, monotone, or in other ways abnormal.

The OBSERVATIONAL CHECKLIST FOR COMMUNICATION DISORDERS (see page 114) can alert parents or teachers to an undiagnosed speech or language problem in a preschooler. For each item in the five areas, parents should check either the "often or always" or the "rarely or never" column. Young children are still developing, so the age of the various questions is important. One or more checks in the "often or always" column could signal a communication problem, so parents should have the child evaluated.

Whatever the type of communication disorder, therapy is generally in the hands of a SPEECH-LANGUAGE PATHOLOGIST, also called a *speech therapist*, working with various medical specialists, including

- AUDIOLOGIST, to assess any association with hearing problems;
- OTOLARYNGOLOGIST, to examine whether there are physical conditions in the speech-making apparatus that need medical treatment, including surgery;
- NEUROLOGIST, to detect, if possible, any brain abnormalities; and
- PSYCHOLOGIST, to assess the child's mental abilities, through various TESTS.

Together these specialists will develop a program of exercises that the speech-language pathologist will use to lessen or eliminate the speech disorders. Often these are a variety of techniques, including tapes and headphones that help the child hear his or her own speech and so begin to shape the sounds more appropriately, as well as a wide variety of exercises designed to enhance COGNITIVE DEVELOPMENT. For people who stutter, various exercises are used to teach how to relax the larynx muscles and slow the rate of speech.

In school and in PRESCHOOL programs such as HEAD START, children with communication disorders are often entitled to special help under the EDUCATION FOR ALL HANDICAPPED CHILDREN ACT OF 1975. Various descriptions are used to identify who is regarded as handicapped, but Head Start's definition is as follows:

A child shall be reported as speech impaired with such identifiable disorders as receptive and/or expressive language impairment, stuttering, chronic voice disorders, and serious articulation problems affecting social, emotional and/or educational achievements; and speech and language disorders accompanying conditions of hearing loss, cleft palate, cerebral palsy, mental retardation, emotional disturbance, multiple handicapping conditions, and other sensory and health impairments. This category excludes conditions of a transitional nature consequent to the early developmental processes of the child.

More generally, children are considered handicapped if they fit under a definition like that above and, by reason of this handicap, require SPECIAL EDUCATION and related services.

For parents who want to help their children at home, TEACHING YOUNG CHILDREN: GUIDELINES AND ACTIVITIES (on page 544) includes activities designed to develop children's communication skills. Every young child can benefit from activities designed to enhance their natural development, as in imitating speech and body language.

For help and further information

National Institute on Deafness and other Communication Disorders (NIDCD)
9000 Rockville Pike
Building 31, Room 1B62
Bethesda, MD 20892
301-496-7243

Federal arm, one of the U.S. National Institutes of Health, formerly part of the National Institute of Neurological and Communicative Disorders and Stroke (NINCDS), sponsoring research on deafness and communicative disorders. Provides information to public and health professionals; publishes various materials, including research reports for professionals and brochures on topics such as aphasia, autism, cerebral palsy, developmental speech and language disorders, head injury, headache, hearing loss, stuttering, and Tourette's syndrome.

National Association for Hearing and Speech Action
10801 Rockville Pike
Rockville, MD 20852
301-897-8682 (voice and TDD, MD, AK, and HI call collect), toll-free number (U.S. except MD, AK, and HI (voice and TDD) 800-638-TALK [8255]

Organization affiliated with American Speech-Language-Hearing Association (see separate entry). Aims to provide public with information on speech, language, and hearing disorders; operates toll-free hotline; makes referrals; publishes various materials, including newsletter and brochures *Answers Questions About Child Language, How Does Your Child Hear and Talk?, Recognizing Communication Disorders, Aphasia*, and *Speech and Language Disorders and the Speech-Language Pathologist*.

American Speech-Language-Hearing Association
10801 Rockville Pike
Rockville, MD 20852
301-897-5700 (voice and TDD or TTY)

Organization of professionals concerned with speaking and hearing and their disorders. Provides information to public and professionals; makes referrals; publishes various materials.

National Easter Seal Society, 312-243-8400 (toll-free number 800-221-6827). Publishes many materials, including *Are You Listening to What Your Child May Not Be Saying, A Speech Pathologist Talks to the Parents of a Nonverbal Child, Understanding Stuttering: Information for Parents, First Aid for Aphasics, Handbook on Stuttering*, and *Same Face—New Sound: Information for Laryngectomies and Their Families*. (For full group information, see HELP FOR SPECIAL CHILDREN on page 578.)

Speech Foundation of America
P.O. Box 11749
Memphis, TN 38111
901-452-0995

Organization concerned with stuttering. Seeks to educate public and encourages research on prevention and treatment; provides information and referrals; publishes various materials, including *If Your Child Stutters: A Guide for Parents, Do You Stutter: A Guide for Teens, Stuttering: Successes and Failures in Therapy, Self-Therapy for the Stutterer*, and *To the Stutterer*.

Council for Exceptional Children, Division for Children with Communication Disorders, 703-620-3660. (For full group information, see HELP FOR SPECIAL CHILDREN on page 578.)

National Center for Stuttering (NCS)
200 East 33rd Street
New York, NY 10016
212-532-1460; toll-free hotline 800-221-2483
Lorraine Schneider, Director
Organization providing information to families of children who stutter. Provides treatment for children and adults; maintains computerized database on new approaches and theories; publishes quarterly newsletter and annual review of published literature.

National Stuttering Project (NSP)
4601 Irving Street
San Francisco, CA 94122
415-566-5324
John Ahlbach, Executive Director
Organization for children and adults who stutter, their families and friends, and speech-language pathologists. Encourages formation of local mutual-support self-help groups; provides information and referrals; seeks to educate public and assist schools and other institutions and agencies; publishes various print and audio materials, including monthly *Letting Go* and *Letting Go, Jr.*

International Foundation for Stutterers (IFS)
P.O. Box 462
Belle Mead, NJ 08502
201-359-6469
Arthur Maurice, President
Organization of people who stutter, their friends and families, speech-language therapists, and concerned others. Encourages establishment of mutual-support self-help groups to supplement and reinforce speech therapy; gathers and disseminates information on stuttering, focusing on its causes and treatments; publishes quarterly newsletter *Look Who's Talking*.

Scottish Rite Foundation
Southern Jurisdiction, U.S.A., Inc.
1733 Sixteenth Street, NW
Washington, DC 20009
202-232-3579
Masonic organization that helps children with communication disorders. Publishes pamphlet listing hospitals for special help.

Other reference sources

Helping Baby Talk: A Pressure-Free Approach to Your Child's First Words from Birth to 3 Years, by Lorraine Rocissano and Jean Grasso Fitzpatrick. New York: Avon, 1990.
The Many Voices of Paws: A Book for Young Stutterers, by Julie D. Reville. Vero Beach, FL: Speech Bin, 1989.

Literacy Begins at Birth, by Marjorie V. Fields. Tucson, AZ: Fisher, 1989.
Talk with Your Child, by Harvey S. Wiener. New York: Viking, 1988.
Fluency Criterion Program: A Stuttering Management System for Children and Adults, revised edition, by Janice P. Herring. Tucson, AZ: Communication Skill Builders, 1988.
Freedom of Fluency: The Total Program to Eliminate Stuttering in Adolescents and Adults, by David A. Daly. East Moline, IL: LinguiSystems, 1988.
Easy Does It Two: Fluency Activities for School-Aged Stutterers, by Barbara A. Heinze and Karin L. Johnson. East Moline, IL: LinguiSystems, 1987.
Mainstreaming Preschoolers: Children with Speech and Language Impairments: A Guide for Teachers, Parents, and Others Who Work with Speech and Language Impaired Preschoolers, by Jacqueline Liebergott, Aaron Favors, Jr., Caren Saaz von Hippel, and Harriet Liftman Needleman. Washington, DC: Government Printing Office, 1978. Prepared for the Head Start Bureau, Administration for Children, Youth and Families. Contains much useful information on what speech and language impairments are, how specific disorders affect learning in preschoolers, and teaching techniques and activities to help them develop their skills.
Health Care U.S.A., by Jean Carper. New York: Prentice Hall, 1987. Resource for general and specific health-care information. Lists major speech-language pathology and audiology centers and other information.
Human Communication Disorders: An Introduction, by G.H. Shames and E.H. Wiig. Columbus, OH: Merrill, 1982.
Articulation Disorders, by J.E. Berthal and N.W. Bankson. Englewood Cliffs, NJ: Prentice-Hall, 1981.
Communication Disorders: An Introduction, by R.J. Van Hattum. New York: Macmillan, 1980.
Introduction to Communication Disorders, by T.J. Hixon, L.D. Shribers, and J.H. Saxman. Englewood Cliffs, NJ: Prentice-Hall, 1980.
Before Speech: The Beginning of Interpersonal Communication, Margaret Bullowa, ed. Cambridge/New York: Cambridge University Press, 1979.
The Body Language of Children, by Suzanne Szasz. New York: Norton, 1978.
Tootsie Tanner, Why Don't You Talk?, by Patricia Reilly Giff. New York: Dell, 1990. For ages 9 to 12.
(See also HELP FOR SPECIAL CHILDREN on page 578.)

community control A decentralized approach to handling educational and related questions concerning neighborhood schools, generally found in large cities in reaction to previous highly centralized school administrations, which were seen as unresponsive to local needs. Critics charge that decentralization too often leads to lack of control and accountability, and opens the door to fraud and corruption. Programs such as SCHOOLS OF CHOICE are attempting to make schools more responsive and to involve parents in the educational process while retaining the overall centralized planning required by large cities. (For help and further information, see EDUCATION.)

compensatory education   A type of SPECIAL EDUCATION to make up lacks or deficiencies in a child's experience and skills, notably in children who are socioeconomically or culturally disadvantaged, especially members of minority groups, so that they will be on a more equal footing with other students.

competency test   The type of test used in MINIMUM COMPETENCY TESTING.

competitive admissions   A highly restrictive policy toward ADMISSION to a school.

complaint   In family law, a written document filed in court to begin a civil lawsuit, naming the person involved, the allegations or charges, and the relief or type of decision sought; sometimes called *petition* or *libel*. In a CHILD-SUPPORT complaint, for example, the desired relief would be payment of court-ordered support. A report of suspected CHILD ABUSE AND NEGLECT is also often called a complaint.

complete blood count (CBC)   Standard type of BLOOD TEST. (See also BLOOD AND BLOOD DISORDERS.)

compound fracture   Alternate term for *open fracture*, a type of FRACTURE in which pieces of bone break the skin.

compound presentation   In CHILDBIRTH, a type of FETAL PRESENTATION in which more than one part is placed first in the pelvis, such as a hand next to the head.

comprehension-level thinking   Understanding of relationships between two pieces of previously learned information or between an old and a new piece of information; from Benjamin Bloom's description of the various kinds of thinking or learning processes, the other main types being KNOWLEDGE-LEVEL, APPLICATION-LEVEL, ANALYSIS-LEVEL, SYNTHESIS-LEVEL, and EVALUATION-LEVEL thinking.

compulsory attendance   The legal requirement that all children attend school when it is in session, with the student's precise starting age (generally five or six) and the leaving age (often 16) specified by the individual states. Students who fail to attend school are considered TRUANTS, and parents who fail to send their children to school are legally liable and may be compelled to do so by the school's ATTENDANCE or truant officer.

compulsory school age   The starting and ending ages between which a child is required to attend school; the specific ages vary by state, but are usually about six and 16. (See ATTENDANCE.)

computerized axial tomography (computerized tomography)   Alternate name for CT SCAN.

conception   In relation to PREGNANCY, the act of FERTILIZATION, in which the SPERM enters the egg (OVUM) and forms a ZYGOTE. Attempts to avert conception are often called CONTRACEPTION, FAMILY PLANNING, or BIRTH CONTROL. In cases of INFERTILITY, a variety of methods are used to achieve conception. (For help and further information, see FERTILIZATION; INFERTILITY.)

conceptus   General physiological term for the result of CONCEPTION, encompassing the whole range of development from the egg (OVUM) when first fertilized by the SPERM through the complete PREGNANCY and birth, including the stages called ZYGOTE, EMBRYO, and FETUS.

concrete operations   The third stage of children's learning, according to Piaget's theory of COGNITIVE DEVELOPMENT.

condylomata acuminata   Alternate medical term for GENITAL WARTS, a SEXUALLY TRANSMITTED DISEASE.

condom   The form of BIRTH CONTROL that uses a thin, stretchable sheath over the PENIS to trap SPERM, with an effectiveness that varies from 64 to 97 percent, according to the Food and Drug Administration (FDA); also called *prophylactic*, *rubber*, or *safe*. In the age of AIDS, condoms also provide much-needed protection (although not 100 percent) against SEXUALLY TRANSMITTED DISEASES. For that purpose, the FDA notes that rubber condoms are more effective than those of natural material (lamb intestines), though the latter will be used by men who have an allergic reaction to the rubber condom. Some manufacturers have added a SPERMICIDE to the condoms to increase their effectiveness. Parents of sexually active children will want to urge them to use a condom during any sexual contact—a discussion best had by parents before a child has his or her first sexual contact. Government and schools are also attempting to spread this word through SEX EDUCATION. (For help and further information, see BIRTH CONTROL.)

conduct disorder   A type of MENTAL DISORDER, classified by psychiatrists as a DISRUPTIVE BEHAVIOR DISORDER, which commonly develops (more often among boys than girls) in late childhood or ADOLESCENCE and which involves persistent, long-term violation of the rights of others and of usual social NORMS. This often includes physical aggression and cruelty to people and animals, deliberate destruction of property (including arson), violent stealing, assault, and sometimes rape and murder, often associated with (but not necessarily caused by) DRUG ABUSE or ALCOHOL ABUSE. Children with conduct disorder often have great trouble at school, at home, and socially; they may be labeled OUT-OF-CONTROL CHILDREN or, if in legal trouble, JUVENILE DELINQUENTS, and so may find themselves placed with FOSTER PARENTS or in institutions. Among the children AT RISK for developing the disorder are those who have ATTENTION DEFICIT HYPERACTIVITY DISORDER, low self-esteem, REJECTION by or extremely rigid DISCIPLINE from parents, and lack of stable home life. If the pattern of behavior persists into adulthood, it is often called *antisocial personality disorder*. (For help and further information, see MENTAL DISORDERS.)

conductive loss   The type of EAR AND HEARING PROBLEM that involves a malfunction or disorder in the outer or middle ear, the mechanisms that gather and pass on the sound vibrations to the inner ear. Conductive losses are less severe than SENSORINEURAL LOSSES and can usually be reduced or eliminated through medical treatment. (See EAR AND HEARING PROBLEMS.)

confidentiality The practice among professionals, such as lawyers, doctors, and psychologists, of regarding conversations with their clients or patients as private and not to be revealed to other unauthorized parties. If this confidentiality is protected by law, as it commonly is with lawyers and more variably with others, the conversation is sometimes called a PRIVILEGED COMMUNICATION. Confidentiality of educational records, including those of HANDICAPPED children, have also been covered by various laws, including the FAMILY EDUCATIONAL RIGHTS AND PRIVACY ACT and the EDUCATION FOR ALL HANDICAPPED CHILDREN ACT.

congenital Something present at birth, usually a problem, including not only GENETIC DISORDERS or CHROMOSOMAL ABNORMALITIES but also problems resulting from other causes, such as exposure to RADIATION, drugs, or injury.

congenital acromicria Alternate term for DOWN'S SYNDROME.

congenital adrenal hyperplasia Alternate name for adrenogenital syndrome, a condition involving a disorder of the ADRENAL GLANDS.

congenital dislocation of the hip A congenital abnormality in which the "ball" or head of the thigh bone (*femur*) does not sit properly in its appointed socket, a cavity in the pelvis, but instead sits outside it. Why it occurs is unknown, though it is more common in girls than in boys and is especially common in cases where the child was born from a breech position (see BREECH PRESENTATION). If not discovered during routine WELL-BABY EXAMINATIONS, congenital dislocation of the hip generally becomes apparent through a limp when a baby starts WALKING. The condition is treated in infants by using splints or traction to hold the ball in the socket for a few months, usually solving the problem with no adverse effects. But if the disorder is not discovered and treated until later in childhood, surgery, hospitalization, and long-term casts are usually required, and some problems may remain.

For help and further information
National Institute of Child Health and Human Development (NICHD), 301-496-5133. (For full group information, see PREGNANCY.)

congenital lobar emphysema A type of LUNG AND BREATHING DISORDER that is found in newborns.

congenital muscular dystrophy A form of MUSCULAR DYSTROPHY present at birth.

congenital varicella syndrome A complex of BIRTH DEFECTS that may result when a baby's mother had CHICKEN POX during pregnancy.

congestive heart failure (CHF) A condition in which part or all of the heart becomes incapable of carrying out its normal functions. (See HEART AND HEART PROBLEMS.)

conjunctivitis Inflammation of the membrane that covers the eye when closed. (See EYE AND VISION PROBLEMS.)

Constipation During Pregnancy

Constipation is due to hormonal changes that tend to relax the muscles of your digestive system. Late in pregnancy, constipation may be caused by the growing uterus pressing on the lower intestine. There are several things you can do to relieve constipation. Drink six to eight glasses of liquids a day. A glass of cold water or juice before breakfast is often effective. Eat foods that provide fiber, such as whole-grain cereals and breads and raw fruits and vegetables. Get some exercise every day and make a habit of going to the bathroom every day at the same time. If you continue to be troubled after trying these things, tell your doctor. Do not take enemas, laxatives, or home remedies unless recommended by your doctor.

Source: *Prenatal Care* (1983). Prepared for the Public Health Service by the Bureau of Health Care Delivery and Assistance, Division of Maternal and Child Health.

---

consanguinity A formal term describing the relationship of BLOOD RELATIVES who share a common GENETIC INHERITANCE and as KIN have certain legal INHERITANCE RIGHTS in the absence of a will.

consent agreement In family law, a voluntary written statement from an unwed FATHER acknowledging a child as his own and recognizing his responsibility to provide CHILD SUPPORT.

conservator A kind of GUARDIAN, usually referring to a person appointed by a court to act to manage the affairs of a severely HANDICAPPED or incapacitated adult, especially one with considerable assets; in some areas, a public or private agency may be appointed to act as conservator. To avoid court involvement in appointing a conservator, parents who wish to secure the future of a handicapped child may instead prepare a durable POWER OF ATTORNEY giving a chosen person the power to act if the parents are incapacitated.

constipation Infrequent or difficult bowel movements, with hard and dry feces. Constipation can result from physical causes, such as narrowing of parts of the digestive system, painful tears (fissures) in the skin around the anus, inflammation of the intestines, or suppression or disruption of the normal bowel activity because of some disorder, such as IRRITABLE BOWEL SYNDROME. Problems in diet can also contribute, especially lack of FIBER in older children; for treating constipation in infants, see BABY'S BOWELS—WHAT'S NORMAL, WHAT'S NOT (on page 148). Sometimes constipation can result from repeatedly ignoring signals that bowels should be moved, perhaps because of misunderstandings during TOILET TRAINING. In pregnant women, constipation and associated hemorrhoids are common (see CONSTIPATION DURING PREGNANCY, above). (For help and further information, see DIGESTIVE DISORDERS.)

contact lenses Specially ground lenses placed over the cornea of the eye to correct various vision defects. (See EYE AND VISION PROBLEMS.)

contempt of court Defiance of the court's authority, either directly and disruptively challenging officials in court or indirectly, as in violating a court order. A parent who fails to provide court-ordered CHILD SUPPORT is in contempt of court, as is a parent who denies court-ordered VISITATION RIGHTS. Such contempt can call for a fine, jail, or both; but in family law situations, the court is generally reluctant to impose punishment that may harm children in the family.

content analysis A type of WORD-ATTACK SKILL necessary for effective, independent READING.

content validity In testing, a type of VALIDITY relating to how well a test measures what it sets out to measure.

continuous ambulatory peritoneal dialysis (CAPD) A form of DIALYSIS.

continuous cycling peritoneal dialysis (CCPD) A form of DIALYSIS.

contraception A form of BIRTH CONTROL that focuses on preventing CONCEPTION, including methods such as the CONDOM, SPERMICIDES, SPONGE, DIAPHRAGM, CERVICAL CAP, INTRAUTERINE DEVICE (IUD), and BIRTH-CONTROL PILLS.

contractions Powerful, spasmodic, painful, rhythmic squeezing, as of the walls of the UTERUS during LABOR.

controllable disease An illness or disorder that has no CURE but that can be treated—with medicines, physical therapy, and a wide variety of other treatments—so as to hold the disease's symptoms in check. Among common diseases that are controllable with modern technology are DIABETES MELLITUS and PHENYL-KETONURIA.

controlled choice A type of program involving SCHOOLS OF CHOICE, in which some guidelines are built in so that the schools will not become unbalanced, racially or otherwise.

controlled reading An approach to teaching READING in which the student's reading speed and the level and the content of the material are carefully paced to maximize the student's learning.

contusions Medical term for bruises, in which a blow to the body causes pain, swelling, and discoloration, though without breaking the skin; often found in cases of CHILD ABUSE AND NEGLECT, as in the BATTERED CHILD SYNDROME.

conversation board A flat surface that can be used for communication by children who are unable to speak clearly enough to communicate with others, such as children who have ORTHOPEDIC HANDICAPS affecting their speech apparatus and who are not able to write. For young children who have not yet learned to read, a set of standardized symbols called BLISS SYMBOLS have been developed; once children are able to read and spell, they can move letters and words into position on the board to "converse" with others.

converted score A test SCORE that reflects a comparison with the performance of other people who have taken the TEST.

convulsion Violent muscular contractions that accompany some kinds of SEIZURES, especially the most disruptive seizures that go under the umbrella name of EPILEPSY.

Cooley's anemia An inherited form of ANEMIA.

cooperative A type of PRESCHOOL or NURSERY SCHOOL in which parents supply much or all of the staffing and assistance, sometimes managing and financing the entire operation.

Cooperative English Tests A group-administered test of LANGUAGE SKILLS for children in grades nine through college; a paper-and-pencil test covering reading comprehension (including vocabulary level and speed of comprehension) and expression (both in conveying exact meaning and in using mechanics of grammar and punctuation). The tests are available in two levels and are often used for class placement, especially to identify those who may benefit from REMEDIAL INSTRUCTION or ACCELERATED PROGRAMS. (For help and further information, see TESTS.)

cooperative work-study program Alternate term for WORK-STUDY PROGRAM.

co-parent A person who does not have legal CUSTODY of a child and has no formal PARENTS' RIGHTS and PARENTS' RESPONSIBILITIES but who shares in the day-to-day care, support, and custody of the child, along with the CUSTODIAL PARENT. A woman sharing a household with a man and the child in his custody is called a co-parent; so is a stepfather who has not legally adopted his stepchildren. The term is commonly used among HOMOSEXUAL couples, where generally only one of them has legal responsibility for a child, through birth, custody, or ADOPTION.

COPD Abbreviation for chronic obstructive pulmonary disease, a kind of LUNG AND BREATHING DISORDER.

copper A MINERAL vital to the body, though only in trace amounts, to help form PROTEINS and enzymes that manage biochemical functions and to help form red blood cells. Copper is found in organ meats (such as liver, kidneys, and heart), shellfish, dried beans and peas, nuts, fruits (especially raisins), and mushrooms. Copper deficiency is rare, but excess can cause nausea, VOMITING, and DIARRHEA, as when people eat food cooked in unlined copper pots or drink alcohol distilled with copper tubing; if continued, this copper poisoning can lead to serious health problems, such as HEPATITIS or CIRRHOSIS OF THE LIVER. Copper can also build up in the body as a result of certain diseases, such as WILSON'S DISEASE. (For help and further information, see MINERALS; NUTRITION.)

coprolalia A rare condition in which a person involuntarily utters words seen as vulgar or obscene; literally, "fecal speech." Coprolalia often results from a brain dysfunction or MENTAL DISORDER, such as SCHIZOPHRENIA, or from a condition such as TOURETTE'S SYNDROME.

CORD Abbreviation for chronic obstructive respiratory disease, a kind of LUNG AND BREATHING DISORDER.

cordocentesus (percutaneous umbilical cord sampling or **PUBS)** A relatively new GENETIC SCREENING procedure that involves drawing a sample of blood, identical to that of the FETUS, from the UMBILICAL CORD, using a needle guided by ULTRASOUND and inserted into the abdomen of a pregnant woman. The sample can then be quickly analyzed for some serious genetic blood disorders, such as HEMOPHILIA, THALASSEMIA, or sickle-cell ANEMIA. (For organizations and reference works offering help and further information, see GENETIC DISORDERS; GENETIC SCREENING.)

core course A course that is part of a school's core CURRICULUM, which all students in the regular program must take.

core curriculum Those courses taken by all students in a particular group. (See CURRICULUM.)

Cornelia de Lange syndrome Alternate name for DE LANGE SYNDROME.

corporal punishment Physical blows or hurts to the body, defined by Parents and Teachers Against Violence in Education (PTAVE) as "hitting, paddling, spanking, grabbing, shaking, forced exercise, and any other means of inflicting pain as punishment." Once generally—and erroneously—thought almost synonymous with DISCIPLINE, corporal punishment is now under considerable attack because it can easily escalate into child abuse, especially when it results from an adult's frustration or mental disturbance (see CHILD ABUSE AND NEGLECT).

Some social workers and psychologists believe that all forms of corporal punishment are destructive and to be avoided in any situation, at home or school; some others believe that no harm is done if parents on occasion resort to a light spanking. But almost all believe that corporal punishment is unnecessary and usually represents a failure of the adult's patience and imagination in developing alternative forms of discipline.

Corporal punishment in the schools is also widely criticized as physically and psychologically harmful to the child, contribut-

ing to (not lessening) behavior problems, reducing the ability to learn, and causing SCHOOL PHOBIA. Many medical, social-work, educational, and other professionals have called for a complete ban on physical punishment in schools, and many states and cities have formally abolished the practice. In fact, though, many teachers and principals continue to administer physical punishment, and the Supreme Court has (as in *Ingraham v. Wright*, April 19, 1977) upheld the school's right to do so in some circumstances, ruling that the Eighth Amendment does not apply to children. Unfortunately, school-administered corporal punishment can cause serious injuries or medical problems—serious enough that if administered by a parent they would be considered child abuse. Some school officials are now being challenged by parents, social workers, and legal authorities. Various organizations (see below) have been fighting to protect children from violence in schools.

For help and further information

National Center for the Study of Corporal Punishment and Alternatives in the Schools (NCSCPAS)
253 Ritter Hall South
Department of School Psychology
Temple University
Philadelphia, PA 19122
215-787-6091
Irwin A. Hyman, Director
Organization of people concerned about psychological and educational effects of corporal punishment in schools. Acts as legal advocate; seeks to educate public and influence public policy; conducts research; gathers information and maintains library; operates DisciplineHelpline counseling services for parents and teachers; publishes various materials, including the journal *Discipline*, pamphlets such as *Think Twice: The Medical Effects of Physical Punishment, 1001 Alternatives to Corporal Punishment, The Bible and the Rod*, and *The Influence of School Corporal Punishment on Crime*, and numerous papers and articles.

End Violence Against the Next Generation (EVAN-G)
977 Keeler Avenue
Berkeley, CA 94708
415-527-0454
Adah Maurer, Executive Director
Organization of parents, social workers, psychologists, educators, lawyers, and others devoted to ending corporal punishment, as in schools and institutes. Seeks to educate public and influence public policy; supports and encourages research and development of alternatives to corporal punishment; acts as information exchange; provides counsel to schools; publishes various materials, including quarterly *The Last Resort*; pamphlet *Child Abuse in Schools: A National Disgrace*; and booklets *Think Twice: Medical Effects of Physical Punishment, 1001 Alternatives to Corporal Punishment* (vols. 1 and 2), *The Bible and the Rod, Corporal Punishment Handbook, Religious Value and Child Abuse*, and *The Effect of Corporal Punishment on Crime*.

On Corporal Punishment

Corporal punishment of children actually interferes with the process of learning and with their optimal development as socially responsible adults. We feel it is important for public health workers, teachers, and others concerned for the emotional and physical health of children and youth to support the adoption of alternative methods for the achievement of self-control and responsible behavior in children and adolescents.

—Dr. Daniel F. Whiteside
   Assistant Surgeon General
   Department of Health & Human Services
   (Reagan administration)

Parents and Teachers Against Violence in Education (PTAVE)
560 South Hartz Avenue, Suite 408
Danville, CA 94526
415-831-1661
Jordan Riak, President
Organization seeking to end corporal punishment, psychological torture, sexual molestation, and other child abuse in schools and institutions. Seeks to educate public as to desirability of education free from fear or violence; advises parents and educators; publishes various materials, including pamphlets *Understanding Corporal Punishment of Schoolchildren* and *The Case Against Physical Punishment of School Children* and leaflets *Facts and Quotes* and *Statement on Corporal Punishment*.

National Coalition to Abolish Corporal Punishment in Schools (NCACPS)
155 West Main Street
Columbus, OH 43215
614-891-2524
Robert Fathman, Chairman
Coalition of organizations and individuals against the use of corporal punishment in schools. Member organizations include American Bar Association, National PTA, American Medical Association, and National Center for Prevention of Child Abuse. Seeks to influence public policy and legislation; publishes various materials, including newsletters, facts sheets, and books such as *What Are My Alternatives to Corporal Punishment?*.

National Committee for Citizens in Education (NCCE), 301-997-9300; toll-free number (U.S. except MD) 800-NETWORK [638-9675]. Publishes fact sheets on special topics, including corporal punishment in schools. (For full group information, see EDUCATION.)

Other reference sources

Reading, Writing, and the Hickory Stick: The Appalling Story of Physical and Psychological Abuse in American Schools, by Irwin A. Hyman. Lexington, MA: Lexington, 1990.
Corporal Punishment in American Education: Readings in History, Practice, and Alternatives, I.A. Hyman and J.H. Wise, eds. Philadelphia: Temple University Press, 1979.
(See also CHILD ABUSE AND NEGLECT; DISCIPLINE; EDUCATION.)

cor pulmonale   Failure of the right side of the heart, generally in connection with LUNG AND BREATHING PROBLEMS, such as *emphysema*. (See HEART AND HEART PROBLEMS.)

correlation   A statistical expression of the relationship between two sets of scores, important in evaluating a test's VALIDITY.

correspondence school   Alternate term for HOME STUDY.

cosmetic surgery   A surgical operation performed primarily to change (and, in the eyes of the patient, improve) appearance, rather than to make the body better able to function; a form of PLASTIC SURGERY. Cosmetic surgery would, for example, change the way a nose looks, rather than make it easier to breathe through. Two common kinds of cosmetic surgery performed on children, especially teenagers, are RHINOPLASTY on the nose and OTOPLASTY on the ears. (For help and further information, see PLASTIC SURGERY.)

cot death   Alternate name for SUDDEN INFANT DEATH SYNDROME.

court-appointed special advocate (CASA)   A specially trained volunteer who will represent the interests of an otherwise unrepresented child in certain types of court cases, notably judicial hearings involving CHILD ABUSE AND NEGLECT.

For help and further information

National Court Appointed Special Advocates Association (National CASA Association, or NCASAA)
2722 Eastlake Avenue, East, Suite 220
Seattle, WA 98102
206-328-8588
Beth Waid, Executive Director
Organization of judicial and legal professionals and specially trained court-appointed special advocates (CASAs). Maintains network of programs; provides training seminars and other assistance to local groups; publishes various materials, including quarterlies *CASA Connection* and *Feedback*, semiannual directory, and *NCASAA Communications Manual*.

court of conciliation   An offshoot of the DOMESTIC RELATIONS COURT, staffed by professional counselors rather than legal personnel, that in some states is charged with trying to facilitate reconciliations in divorce cases.

CP   Abbreviation for CEREBRAL PALSY.

CPD   Abbreviation for childhood polycystic disease, a kind of KIDNEY AND UROLOGICAL DISORDER.

CPR   Abbreviation for CARDIOPULMONARY RESUSCITATION. (See ARTIFICIAL RESPIRATION.)

cradle cap   Harmless, waxy, yellowish scales that develop on the scalp and forehead of infants, generally in their first year, a benign kind of SKIN DISORDER that is related to the adult condition *seborrhea*. Though it does not result from poor hygiene, washing with mild soap and water may help, perhaps after putting mineral oil on the scalp; if not, or if the area is inflamed, a doctor should be consulted.

craniofacial surgery   PLASTIC SURGERY performed on the skull and face.

craniopharyngioma   A type of BRAIN TUMOR common in children.

craniosynostosis   A condition involving premature closing or absence of joints, or *sutures*, in the skull; a baby with this condition is born without FONTANELLES, or spaces between the plates of the skull to allow for growth. Causes of the disorder are unclear. Craniosynostosis is associated with some BONE DIS-

ORDERS, such as RICKETS, and with some BIRTH DEFECTS or an abnormally small brain, but it can occur in babies with no other obvious disorders. To prevent brain damage, the plates of the skull need to be separated surgically within a few months after birth.

For help and further information

Society for Children with Craniosynostosis (SCC)
P.O. Box 1522
Denver, CO 80201
303-722-9992
Marilyn Anderson, President
Organization of parents whose children have craniosynostosis. Provides support for families; offers information and referrals; supports research; seeks to educate public; publishes periodic newsletter.

AboutFace, 416-944-3223. Publishes pamphlet on craniosynostosis. (For full group information, see CLEFT LIP AND PALATE.)

National Institute of Arthritis and Musculoskeletal and Skin Diseases (NIAMS), 301-496-8188. (For full group information, see ARTHRITIS.)

National Institute of Dental Research (NIDR), 301-496-4261. (For full group information, see TEETH.)
(See also BONE DISORDERS.)

creative child A child with unusual talent in artistic areas or, more widely, a child who thinks originally and innovatively in any area. (See GIFTED CHILD; CREATIVE THINKING.)

creative thinking Mental processes that are original, flexible, and imaginative, often producing unusual and novel approaches to problems. Often thought of as the province of the arts, where creativity is essential, creative thinking is also important and valued in many other areas of work, such as science and technology. Though creative thinking is hard to define, children who have it are often deemed gifted (see GIFTED CHILD).

creativity test Test that attempts to measure CREATIVE THINKING, sometimes as a way of assessing thinking abilities of a child who comes from a disadvantaged or non-English-speaking background. Such a test might, for example, ask a child to think of new uses for a familiar object, such as a broom.

credit In EDUCATION in general, recognition for a student's successful completion of work in a course but, more specifically, a unit of value awarded by a school for such work. In HIGH SCHOOLS, each course of study is generally worth one credit unit per SEMESTER, and the student must accumulate a specified number of these credits, with appropriate numbers from various areas of study (such as English, mathematics, or science), to qualify for GRADUATION. At the COLLEGE level, varying numbers of credits are awarded to courses, generally based on the number of hours per week that a student is scheduled to spend in the class. A literature class that meets for one hour on Mon-

day, Wednesday, and Friday, for example, would generally carry three credits, sometimes called *credit-hours*. But an organic chemistry class that meets for the same three hours but also has two scheduled hours of laboratory work might carry five credits. At the end of the semester, a student's GRADE for the course and the credits carried by the course are used to calculate his or her GRADE-POINT AVERAGE.

credit by examination In EDUCATION, COLLEGE credit gained by passing a test, even though the student did not take a college course or reside on campus. Some students study in special classes while in high school that prepare them for tests in the ADVANCED PLACEMENT PROGRAM (APP); others may study independently to prepare for tests in the COLLEGE-LEVEL EXAMINATION PROGRAM (CLEP) or the PROFICIENCY EXAMINATION PROGRAM (PEP).

credit–no credit Alternate term for a PASS–FAIL grading system.

Creutzfeldt-Jakob disease A rare, fatal slow virus that attacks the brain, causing DEMENTIA, SEIZURES, and eventually DEATH, in previous years apparently sometimes transmitted to young people treated with contaminated HUMAN GROWTH HORMONE.

crib death Alternate term for SUDDEN INFANT DEATH SYNDROME (SIDS).

cri du chat syndrome (cry of the cat or 5p- syndrome) A CONGENITAL condition resulting from a CHROMOSOMAL ABNORMALITY in which part of chromosome 5 has been lost. Infants with the syndrome are marked by a kittenlike mewing cry, which disappears after the first few weeks. They suffer from physical and MENTAL RETARDATION, along with other problems, such as SYNDACTYLY and heart problems (see HEART AND HEART PROBLEMS).

For help and further information

5p- Society
11609 Oakmont
Overland Park, KS 66210
913-469-8900
Kent W. Nicholls, Executive Director
Mutual-support self-help organization for families who have a child with cri-du-chat or 5p- syndrome. Provides information to public and professionals; publishes various materials, including quarterly *5p- Newsletter* and *North American 5p- Syndrome Listing*.

criminal court The type of court that handles cases involving crimes, such as misdemeanors and (more serious) felonies, with results that can range from fines or probation to imprisonment or death. People being prosecuted in criminal court are judged innocent unless proven guilty beyond a reasonable doubt; they have the right to a jury trial, and strict rules apply about what evidence is admissible. Except in special cases, most JUVENILES charged with crimes come before a CIVIL COURT, such as a JUVENILE COURT or FAMILY COURT, and are subject to less severe penalties. If found guilty, such MINORS would—in strict legal terms—be labeled juvenile DELINQUENTS rather than criminals.

crippled Outdated term describing people with ORTHOPEDIC HANDICAPS.

crisis intervention Action taken to help relieve an immediately threatening or serious situation, the short-term aim being to remove a threat to health or welfare, the longer-term aim being to help the person or family recognize the problem and learn how to cope with it. The term may, for example, refer to emergency services provided by a social worker to relieve stress within a family or to remove a child from a possible child-abuse setting, or to a parent's confronting and providing help for a child on drugs. Similar action taken before an immediate threat exists is called *early intervention*. (For help and further information, see CHILD ABUSE AND NEGLECT; also HELP AGAINST SUBSTANCE ABUSE on page 587.)

criterion-referenced A type of TEST in which a student's performance is measured against a specific standard—such as 75 out of 100 questions correct, ability to solve a set problem, or typing 50 words a minute with no more than five errors—as opposed to a NORM-REFERENCED TEST in which performance is compared with that of a larger group. (For help and further information, see TESTS.)

Crohn's disease One of two main types of INFLAMMATORY BOWEL DISEASE (IBD).

cross-dominance Alternate term for MIXED DOMINANCE.

croup (acute laryngotracheobronchitis or LTB) A common childhood disease in which viral infection (sometimes complicated by bacteria and ALLERGIES as well) causes inflammation and narrowing of the breathing passages, with resulting hoarseness, distinctive harsh coughing, and rough breathing (STRIDOR). It often occurs in dry houses and at night and is generally helped by humidity, as from a humidifier, vaporizer, the mist from a shower or pot of boiling water, or moist night air. Soothing the child may help the muscles relax and ease breathing. But if the child has severe difficulty in breathing or begins to turn blue (CYANOSIS), hospitalization may be indicated to prevent brain damage from lack of oxygen (HYPOXIA). The alternative treatments include being placed in a tent with humidified oxygen or temporary insertion of a breathing tube, either through the mouth (using a hollow, flexible tube called an ENDOSCOPE) or through an artificial opening in the throat (in an operation called a TRACHEOSTOMY). Children generally recover in a few days, though some are subject to recurrence. Croup does not usually appear after about age four, because by then the breathing tubes are larger and firmer and so less liable to constriction.

crown An artificial "cap" to replace the natural crown of a tooth, the enamel-coated part above the gum. Crowns are used when a tooth's natural crown has been damaged beyond repair but also for cosmetic reasons, as when a tooth turns grayish after ROOT CANAL THERAPY. Crowns in the front of the mouth are normally made of porcelain or other materials that can be matched in shade to the surrounding natural teeth; crowns on the grinding teeth—bicuspids and especially molars—are made of an alloy of gold or other metal, or at least have metal on the upper surface, for strength. In recent decades, dentists have developed several alternatives for cosmetic use when the crown of the tooth is intact. (For help and further information, see TEETH.)

crowning The first glimpse of a baby's head through the VAGINA during LABOR and DELIVERY.

crutches A common type of ORTHOPEDIC DEVICE.

cryobank Alternate name for SPERM BANK.

cry of the cat syndrome Alternate name for CRI DU CHAT SYNDROME.

cryptorchidism Alternate name for UNDESCENDED TESTICLES. (See TESTES.)

C-section Abbreviation for CESAREAN SECTION.

CSF Abbreviation for CEREBROSPINAL FLUID.

CT scan (computerized tomography) A type of MEDICAL TEST that involves a high-speed X-RAY machine linked to a computer so that a series of pictures taken at different planes are combined into computer-simulated three-dimensional views; also called *computerized axial tomography* or *CAT scan*. In a CT scan, air and liquid show up as black, the densest bones as white, and tissues as various shades of gray. The CT scan gives far more precise pictures than ordinary X-ray photographs and ULTRASOUND, involves low exposure to X-rays, can be used to view any internal organ (including the brain), and is especially useful in detecting CALCIUM deposits (often signs of old healed FRACTURES), bone displacements in new fractures, accumulations of fluid, and TUMORS, sometimes giving enough detail so that physicians can judge whether the tumor is likely to be benign or malignant. Because X-rays can damage a FETUS, women who are or suspect they may be pregnant are advised not to have such a test. (For help and further information, see MEDICAL TESTS.)

cuddly Alternate name for TRANSITIONAL COMFORT OBJECT.

cued speech Enhancement of speech by making lip movements clear and using finger signs for particular sounds that are otherwise easily confused, such as "p" and "b," to ease SPEECHREADING. (For help and further information, see EAR AND HEARING PROBLEMS.)

culture In medicine, a type of TEST in which microorganisms or material taken from the body, as in BLOOD TESTS, URINALYSIS, or BIOPSY, are grown and cultivated in the laboratory. The aim is often to identify bacteria or other infectious organisms so that proper treatment can be given. Cells in laboratory cultures may also be examined as part of PRENATAL TESTING, checking for CHROMOSOMAL ABNORMALITIES or signs of possible GENETIC DISORDERS. Sometimes tissue may be grown for later use in grafts, or tissue TRANSPLANTS. (See MEDICAL TEST.)

culture-fair (culture-free) A term describing a TEST that attempts not to be biased toward children of White, comfortably middle-class, English-speaking, two-parent family backgrounds. Many tests used with children, especially INTELLIGENCE TESTS that purport to measure "pure" mental ability, have been criticized for discriminating unfairly against children of other backgrounds in the content, vocabulary, and assumptions of their questions. Many testing organizations have attempted to respond to these criticisms by rewriting their tests or by making other tests for children of differing backgrounds, but controversy still remains. Parents whose family backgrounds are in any way unusual, especially in the areas of language and culture in the home, should try to see that no tests given to their children have such built-in biases and that school officials are aware of any special circumstances in a child's background that might affect test performance.

cumulative average   The AVERAGE of a student's GRADES from entry into a school or COLLEGE to GRADUATION (or to some interim point). In HIGH SCHOOLS this generally means an average of the letter or numerical grades handed out during the period; in college it often refers to a GRADE POINT AVERAGE that takes into account the number of credits granted to each particular course.

cure   In medicine, to treat so as to achieve total disappearance of a disease's SIGNS and SYMPTOMS, restoring the patient to normal health. A temporary halt in the advance of a progressive disease or the spontaneous temporary lessening or disappearance of symptoms (*remission*) is not generally considered a cure. Many diseases are not curable, but they are CONTROLLABLE DISEASES, meaning that the symptoms can be held in check with regular treatment.

curriculum   The range of programs offered to students in a school, developed in a deliberate sequence, with the content, materials, and approaches geared to the abilities of the students and the established goals of the school. In a high school whose students have a wide range of abilities and educational aims, the curriculum might vary. For example, college-bound students would take an *academic curriculum*, such as that described under HIGH SCHOOL or in the more detailed model curriculum for secondary schools, in JAMES MADISON HIGH SCHOOL: A MODEL CURRICULUM (on page 538, along with JAMES MADISON ELEMENTARY SCHOOL: A MODEL CURRICULUM). Students seeking less demanding courses and perhaps unsure of their future direction might follow a *general curriculum*. Students who are not college-bound but want to learn skills that will help them get a job might follow a *vocational curriculum*.

However, students with severe handicaps (see HANDICAPPED) might follow a *functional curriculum*, designed to help them learn the skills basic to everyday life, the aim being to help them become as independent as possible. This kind of *adapted* or *differentiated* curriculum for students with SPECIAL NEEDS has in recent years helped to prepare some students (such as those with MENTAL RETARDATION), who would once have been fully dependent as adults, to instead take minimally demanding, carefully structured jobs in the adult world. Students with handicaps will, by law, have an INDIVIDUALIZED EDUCATION PROGRAM tailored to their individual skills and potential.

Within a particular program, the group of courses taken by all students is called the *core curriculum*; other optional courses are termed *electives*. Where the same kinds of subjects are taught, but with increasing depth and detail over the several years, the school is employing a *spiral curriculum*. Where the same material is taught to different groups of students but at different rates—for example, over five years for one group and over six for another—the result is called a *parallel curriculum*. If the school's courses heavily focus on content, rather than on the way a student learns or is taught, it is called a *subject-centered curriculum*. A *classical curriculum* is one that emphasizes the traditional liberal arts, including literature, art, music, philosophy, history, and foreign languages, normally on the college level; when the subjects of two different types of courses are taught together, such as literature and history, the result is called a *fused curriculum*.

For help and further information

The Subject Matters: Classroom Activity in Math and Social Studies, by Susan S. Stodolsky. Chicago: University of Chicago Press, 1988.

Critical Issues in Curriculum, Laurel N. Tanner, ed. Chicago: University of Chicago Press, 1988.

Cultural Literacy and the Idea of General Education, Ian Westbury and Alan C. Purves, eds. Chicago: University of Chicago Press, 1988.

Educational Wastelands: The Retreat from Learning in Our Public Schools, second edition, by Arthur Bestor. Champaign, IL: University of Illinois Press, 1988.

(See also EDUCATION.)

cursive writing   Handwriting in which letters are joined together, as opposed to the PRINTING of letters that young children first learn.

curve   Alternate term for NORMAL DISTRIBUTION.

Cushing's syndrome   A condition involving a disorder of the ADRENAL GLANDS.

custodial parent   The parent who has been awarded sole legal CUSTODY of a child, as in a divorce case without shared custody. The term sometimes applies to a nonparent who has custody, such as a friend or other relative. Where parents have shared custody, the parent with whom the child is staying at the time is considered the custodial parent.

custody   In family law, the right and duty to care for and control basic decisions regarding children who are MINORS or disabled adults; part of both PARENTS' RIGHTS and PARENTS' RESPONSIBILITIES, including provision of food, clothing, shelter, basic medical care, EDUCATION, and DISCIPLINE. *Legal custody* refers to the right to make basic decisions about a child, as regarding education and medical care; *physical custody* refers to where the child lives and who provides day-to-day care and control. Where both parents share a home with the children, custody is fully shared by both parents; where a single parent raises a child alone from the time of birth or ADOPTION, that person has sole custody.

Problems arise, however, when parents separate or divorce, and the parents must decide who shall have custody of the child. The parents may agree between themselves that one parent—the *custodial parent*—shall have full custody, with the other—the *noncustodial parent*—being granted VISITATION RIGHTS. The noncustodial parent retains the obligation to help support the child but no longer has the legal right to participate in major decisions regarding the child, though often will do so informally.

Or the parents may agree to a *shared* or *joint custody* arrangement. The terms of such arrangements vary, but generally parents share the decision-making and the child spends a substantial amount of time with each parent, perhaps spending alternate weeks, years, or months with each parent or spending most of the school year with one parent and many of the holidays with the other. (Some states award joint legal custody while awarding physical custody to one parent.) Joint custody assures the child of continuing contact with and support from both parents and so is favored by many, including some courts. But it has the disadvantage of disrupting children's lives with shuttling back and forth between parents.

One alternative form of joint custody designed to meet this problem is *bird's-nest custody* or *nesting*, in which the children stay in their home and the parents shuttle in and out periodically. Such an arrangement is expensive, since it requires that parents each maintain separate living quarters apart from the family home where the children live. And though providing a more stable base for the children, since they stay in the same surroundings and are not separated from their friends and community ties, it is more disruptive to the adult lives.

Ideally, joint custody can ease the burden otherwise felt by a single parent exercising sole custody, but it requires substantial cooperation between parents, not always a commodity in ready supply among separated couples.

A less common option, for families with more than one child, is *split custody*, in which some children go with the mother and some with the father. This choice seems "neater," in that no one shuttles back and forth, and both parents have the full experience of parenting. But the breaking apart of the family is often disruptive to the children, as children lose substantial contact with one parent and often feel rejected. Split custody can also cause sharp rivalry and resentment between the two sets of SIBLINGS over perceived advantages and disadvantages to each.

If the parents are unable to agree on custody, the court will decide for them, often a FAMILY COURT or DOMESTIC RELATIONS COURT. In the 19th century, the court decision was almost always that the father should be given custody of the children; later the equal rights of both parents were more often recognized, and custody was awarded to the "most fit" parent, the one who could best provide for the emotional and material needs of the child. Then, in the 20th century, under the popularly dubbed TENDER-YEARS DOCTRINE, courts began to award custody of children routinely to the mother, except in special circumstances, as when she was perceived to be clearly less fit than the father. In recent decades, at least since the 1960s, the court has tended to take a somewhat less dogmatic view of custody questions and in some states is even forbidden to take into account the parent's sex in awarding custody. Mothers are still often granted custody, though some experts feel that—when they choose to contest custody—fathers are sometimes favored.

Sometimes the custody fight is not between two parents but between one parent and another relative or friend. A single mother may contest custody with a grandmother who has been caring for the child for several years, for example. Or after the death of a child's mother, the court may need to decide whether to award custody to the stepfather, with whom the child has been living for years, or with the child's biological father (see BIOLOGICAL PARENTS).

The court generally assesses custody questions in light of the BEST INTERESTS OF THE CHILD and may award sole custody to one parent and visitation rights to the other, joint custody, or custody to a GUARDIAN. When sharply contested custody questions are before a court, a *guardian ad litem* (at law) is often appointed to act in the child's behalf. Among the areas the court explores in determining custody are:

- *established living pattern.* The court will tend to favor the parent or arrangement that provides the most continuity and stability for the child, especially the parent who will remain in the same family home and keep current school, community, and religious ties, as opposed to a parent who is moving away. The court also tends to keep siblings together, rather than divide them.
- *emotional ties.* The court tends to favor the parent or guardian perceived to have the strongest emotional ties with the child; this is the PSYCHOLOGICAL PARENT, the person who has been closest to the child's day-to-day hopes and fears.
- *child's age, sex, health, and physical condition.* The court tends to favor the person perceived as being best able to deal with a child's needs, including any special health needs.
- *parent's health and physical condition.* The court tends to favor the parent who is physically best equipped to care for the child, but a parent's disability is not supposed to stand in the way of a custody award.
- *parent's ability to supply basic necessities.* The court will need to be assured that the child's basic needs for food, clothing, shelter, and medical care are met but will not necessarily choose the wealthier parent, since financial arrangements can be made through CHILD SUPPORT. Failure to provide for the child can later on lead to loss of custody.
- *parent's plans for education.* The court tends to favor the parent who has formulated plans for the child's education, especially college, though the parent's own level of education or skills are not a major factor to consider.
- *parent's behavior.* The court tends to favor the parent whose behavior has been the most circumspect and traditionally "moral" and who has regular religious involvement. Adultery during the marriage can weigh heavily against custody, espe-

cially for the mother; later on, living unmarried with another sexual partner can in some states also cause a parent to lose custody. Parents who have, after the marriage relationship, openly acknowledged HOMOSEXUALITY and live with a partner of the same sex have special difficulty in custody fights. Various groups (see below) have been formed to help parents fight custody battles, especially by urging that parents' activities should be evaluated by the court only in terms of whether there is any direct harm to the child. Problems with drugs, alcohol, money handling, and the like can also tell against a parent in a custody decision.

- *parent's acrimony.* The court tends to favor a parent who wishes to ensure continuing contact between the child and the other parent and, conversely, looks with disfavor on a parent who tries to sever such contact, as by making active personal attacks on the other parent, denying visitation rights, taking the child to an undisclosed location, or outright parental kidnapping (see MISSING CHILDREN). Such actions can also lead to loss of custody later on.
- *citizenship.* For children born outside the United States, and with only one parent a U.S. citizen, and who need to live in the United States for a specified period in order to retain citizenship, the court tends to rule against awarding custody to a parent who intends to take the child out of the country, risking the loss of valuable U.S. citizenship.
- *child's preference.* The court tends to give some weight to an older child's preference for a parent or guardian but less to a younger child's views, except as they reflect on other aspects of the relationship. The judge may have a private interview with the child in camera (in chambers), with the record of the conversation sealed to anyone else.

On reviewing the child's total situation, the judge may also, in some special situations, override the parents' agreement and decide on a different custody arrangement.

A court order for custody can later be modified if the court is convinced that CHANGED CIRCUMSTANCES warrant it, as temporarily during the hospitalization of the custodial parent. But once a custody agreement or decision has been made, the court is very reluctant to alter it permanently unless some changed circumstance directly and adversely affects the child. A change in the noncustodial parent, no matter how favorable, will rarely be sufficient to change a custody decision.

Unfortunately, some parents, distressed at loss of custody or denial of visitation rights, have resorted to parental kidnapping of the child, hoping that a court in a different jurisdiction will rule in their favor. To prevent that, the federal government passed the Parental Kidnapping Prevention Act, and many states have adopted the UNIFORM CHILD CUSTODY JURISDICTION ACT (UCCJA); under these the new state will enforce the original order, rather than modify it, except in some very special circumstances. Perhaps as much to the point, the parent who has once resorted to kidnapping may irreparably damage chances to gain custody later, under the CLEAN HANDS DOCTRINE.

In cases of suspected CHILD ABUSE AND NEGLECT, when SOCIAL WORKERS or other health or public officials fear that parents are hurting children or failing to care for them properly, the state may temporarily take the child into *protective custody* or *emergency custody*, placing the child with a FOSTER PARENT, or in a GROUP HOME or other facility until a hearing has been held on the charges.

For help and general information

About Custody of Children in General

Parents Without Partners (PWP)
8807 Colesville Road
Silver Spring, MD 20910
301-588-9354, toll-free number 800-637-7974
Maurine McKinley, Executive Officer

Network of local groups of single parents, with or without custody, for whatever reason, as by choice, divorce, separation, or death of spouse. Gathers information on single parenting and maintains library, serving as information clearinghouse; operates toll-free number; provides single parents with referrals for help; publishes various materials, including the magazine *The Single Parent*; the book *My Mom and Dad Are Getting a Divorce*; brochures such as *40 Tips for Better Single Parenting, Are You a Single Parent?, Single Parenting and Education*, and *Single Parenting and Legislation*; separate bibliographies for children and teens on divorce, parents on separation and divorce, never-married parents, and widowed parents; information kit on family law, information kits for noncustodial fathers, noncustodial mothers, never-married mothers, and parents raising children alone, and information sheets on topics of concern to them, such as resource organizations, child support, visitation, and rights to examine school records.

Association of Family and Conciliation Courts (AFCC)
c/o OHSU
Department of Psychiatry
Gaines Hall, Room 149
SW Sam Jackson Park Road
Portland, OR 97201
503-279-5651

Interdisciplinary organization of professionals—in the law, the justice system, health and human services, counseling, mediation, and education—concerned with the constructive resolution of family disputes involving children. Supports research and provides assistance to professionals; publishes various materials, including quarterly newsletter, semiannual journal, and annual directory; studies on various topics, including child support, custody, and visitation, are available through its research unit at AFCC, 1720 Emerson Street, Denver, CO 80218; 303-837-1555.

Parents and Children's Equality (PACE)
2054 Loma Linda Way, South
Clearwater, FL 33575

813-461-3806
Kenneth R. Pangborn, Executive Director
For parents and professionals, such as lawyers and counselors, involved in divorce and custody questions. Seeks the child's best interests during divorce; counsels partners to divorce and aids them in gaining access to their children in cases of parental abduction or other interference with custody or visitation rights; conducts seminars and attempts to influence public policy; publishes *Directory of Divorce Reform Organizations*.

Second Wives Association of North America (SWAN)
720 Spadina Avenue, Suite 509
Toronto, Ontario, Canada M5S 2T9
416-968-1647
Glynnis Walker, President
Organization of second wives and their husbands. Aims to educate public as to special problems of second marriages; seeks to change public policy and legislation as to divorce and child custody; publishes newsletter.

About Shared or Joint Custody

Joint Custody Association (JCA)
10606 Wilkins Avenue
Los Angeles, CA 90024
213-475-5352
James A. Cook, President
For anyone involved with child custody and related issues, both parents and professionals such as psychologists, social workers, and lawyers. Offers information and support to those seeking to establish joint custody; gathers data and maintains archives.

National Council for Children's Rights (NCCR)
2001 O Street, NW
Washington, DC 20036
202-223-NCCR
David L. Levy, President
Organization for more equitable divorce, custody, and child-support arrangements, especially favoring joint custody, visitation enforcement, and mediation. Gathers research data and offers seminars; publishes various print and audio materials, including newsletter *Speak Out for Children*.

National Committee for Fair Divorce and Alimony (NCFDAL)
11 Park Place, Suite 116
New York, NY 10007
212-766-4030
Sidney Siller, General Counsel
For people who desire to reform laws regarding divorce, alimony, and child support, making them more uniform and fair, and making custody equal. Maintains archives and holds symposiums; publishes newsletter.

National Legal Resource Center for Child Advocacy and Protection, American Bar Association, 202-331-2200. (For full information, see CHILD ABUSE AND NEGLECT.)

Help Abolish Legal Tyranny (HALT)
1319 F Street, NW, Suite 300
Washington, DC 20004
202-347-9600
Organization of people interested in citizens acting as their own lawyers (termed *pro se*). Publishes various citizen's legal manuals, including one on pro se divorce.

National Congress for Men (NCM)
223 15th Street, SE
Washington, DC 20003
202-328-4377
Organization dedicated to preserving father's rights. Seeks to influence public policy and acts as advocate for fathers; publishes directory of father's rights and divorce reform groups with information on family law.

National Organization for Women's Legal Defense and Education Fund
99 Hudson Street
New York, NY 10036
212-925-6635
Organization focusing on legal problems and needs of women. Runs family law program; provides referral services.

National Center for Women and Family Law
799 Broadway, Suite 402
New York, NY 10003
212-674-8200
Organization that gathers and disseminates information on women's relationship to family law.

Father's Rights of America (FRA)
P.O. Box 7596
Van Nuys, CA 91409
818-789-4435
Woody Bren, Secretary
For divorced parents faced with questions of custody, child support, and visitation rights. Urges shared custody and alternatives to litigation; publishes newsletter.

Parents Sharing Custody (PSC)
P.O. Box 9286
Marina Del Rey, CA 90295
213-273-9042
Linda Blakeley, President
For divorced parents who have joint custody of children and others interested in such arrangements. Aims to educate others about shared custody through seminars and other programs.

About Mediation or
Arbitration of Custody Disputes

Academy of Family Mediators (AFM)
P.O. Box 4686
Greenwich, CT 06830

203-629-8049
Nancy Thode, Executive Director
Organization of attorneys and mental health professionals supporting the use of mediation in family disputes, including divorce. Provides information and makes referrals; supports mediation standards; publishes newsletter and quarterly.

Mothers Without Custody (MWOC)
P.O. Box 56762
Houston, TX 77256
713-840-1622
Angie Mease, Executive Director
Network of mutual-support self-help groups for mothers who do not live with their children for whatever reason, as by choice, by judicial or social agency intervention, by loss of custody, or by abduction of the child by an ex-husband; provides information, referrals, and legal help. Publishes newsletter *Mother-to-Mother*.

Committee for Mother and Child Rights (CMCR)
Box 481
Chappaqua, NY 10514
914-238-8672
Elizabeth Owen, President and Director
For mothers who have lost custody or have had other custody problems, and interested others. Aims to provide mutual support and to influence public opinion.

Citizen's Committee to Amend Title 18
P.O. Box 936
Newhall, CA 91321
805-259-4435
Beth Kurrus, Coordinator
Organization of parents granted custody, whose children were kidnapped by the other parent. Aims to change the law (Title 18, Section 1201A of the U.S. Code) that exempts parents from kidnapping charges regarding their children under 18.

About Custody Problems of Lesbians
and Gay Men

Lambda Legal Defense and Education Fund (LLDEF), 212-995-8585. Defends homosexuals' civil rights in child custody; publishes *Lesbians Choosing Motherhood*. (For full group information, see HOMOSEXUALITY.)

Custody Action for Lesbian Mothers (CALM)
P.O. Box 281
Narberth, PA 19072
215-667-7508
Rosalie G. Davies, Coordinator
Organization providing legal and counseling services to lesbian mothers facing child-custody battles. Offers support to individuals; seeks to influence public policy and legislation; acts as information clearinghouse for similar activities elsewhere.

Lesbian Rights Project, 415-621-0674. (For full group information, see HOMOSEXUALITY.)

Lesbian Mothers National Defense Fund (LMNDF), 206-325-2643. Offers legal, psychological, and financial support to lesbian mothers in contested child-custody situations; gathers data on gay and lesbian custody cases. (For full group information, see HOMOSEXUALITY.)

Other reference sources
General Works

How to Handle Your Child Custody Case: A Guide for Parents, Psychologists, and Attorneys, by Leonard Diamond. Buffalo, NY: Prometheus, 1989.

Child Custody, by James C. Black and Donald Cantor. Irvington, NY: Columbia University Press, 1989.

Sharing the Children: How to Resolve Custody Problems and Get On with Your Life, by Robert E. Adler. New York: Farrar, Straus & Giroux, 1988.

How to Win Custody, by Louis Kiefer. New York: Simon & Schuster, 1982.

The Complete Book of Child Custody, by Suzanne Ramos. New York: Putnam, 1979.

The Custody Handbook, by Persia Woolley. New York: Summit, 1979.

Getting Custody, by Robert Henley Woody. New York: Macmillan, 1978.

Mothers on Trial: The Battle for Children and Custody, by Phyllis Chesler. New York: McGraw-Hill, 1979. On legal biases against mothers.

Divorced but Not Disastrous, by Susan Anderson-Khleif. Englewood Cliffs, NJ: Prentice-Hall, 1982.

Before the Best Interests of the Child (1979) and *Beyond the Best Interests of the Child* (1973), by Joseph Goldstein, Anna Freud, and Albert J. Solnit. New York: Free Press. Analysis of custody practices and psychological effects on children.

Child Custody Mediation, by Florence Bienenfeld. Palo Alto, CA: Science and Behavior Books, 1983. On California's mandated mediation in disputed custody cases.

On Joint Custody

Sharing Parenthood After Divorce, by Ciji Ware. New York: Viking, 1982.

Mom's House, Dad's House: Making Shared Custody Work. New York: Macmillan, 1980.

Co-Parenting: A Source Book for the Separated or Divorced Family, by Miriam Galper. Philadelphia: Running Press, 1978.

The Disposable Parent: The Case for Joint Custody, by Mel Roman and William Haddad. New York: Holt, Rinehart & Winston, 1978.

Joint Custody: A Handbook for Judges, Lawyers and Counselors, Ann L. Milne, ed. Also useful for parents. Available (for $10) from Association of Family Conciliation Courts, 10015 Terwilliger Boulevard, SW, Portland, OR 79219.

Home Sweet Homes: Kids Talk About Joint Custody. 1982. 20-minute film/video from Filmmakers Library, 124 East 40th

Street, New York, NY 10016. For ages 8 to adult. On logistics and emotional and physical effects.

On Noncustodial Parents

Mothers Without Custody, by Geoffrey L. Greif and Mary S. Pabst. Lexington, MA: Lexington, 1988.

Who Will Take the Children?, by Susan Meyers and Joan Lakin. New York: Bobbs-Merrill, 1983. For noncustodial mothers.

Saturday Parent: A Book for Separated Families, by Peter Rowlands. New York: Continuum, 1980.

Divorced Dads—Their Kids, Ex-Wives and New Lives, by Morris A. Shepard and Gerald Goldman. Radnor, PA: Chilton, 1979.

Part-Time Father, by Edith Atkin and Estelle Rubin. New York: Vanguard, 1976.

(See also VISITATION RIGHTS; MISSING CHILDREN; CHILD ABUSE AND NEGLECT; also PARENT'S BOOKSHELF on page 566 for books on divorce and stepfamilies.)

cutoff score (cutting score) On an ADMISSION TEST, a SCORE a student must reach or risk being rejected by a school—even though test professionals always stress that no one should accept, reject, or make any other key decision on the basis of any single test score alone. If parents feel a child was unfairly rejected on the basis of a single test, they should seek a retest.

CVS Abbreviation for the GENETIC SCREENING procedure CHORIONIC VILLUS SAMPLING.

CWS Abbreviation for COLLEGE WORK-STUDY.

cyanosis A blueness, especially around the lips and nails, indicating lack of oxygen; a common symptom among infants, as in RESPIRATORY DISTRESS SYNDROME or PERSISTENT FETAL CIRCULATION, and with many other kinds of heart problems (see HEART AND HEART PROBLEMS) or LUNG AND BREATHING DISORDERS.

cystic fibrosis (CF or mucoviscidosis) A METABOLIC DISORDER in which the body's *exocrine* (externally secreting) glands, including the sweat and salivary glands, do not produce the normal clear, free-flowing fluid but a thick, sticky mucus; this mucus accumulates in various parts of the body, interfering with vital functions, such as breathing and digestion. CF is not infectious but is a GENETIC DISORDER of the AUTOSOMAL RECESSIVE type, so it can be passed on to children only if both parents carry the defective gene; the Public Health Service estimates that there are now perhaps 10,000,000 such unaffected CARRIERS in the United States. CF affects approximately one in every 6,000 newborns, most often those of Caucasian ancestry, less often Blacks, and only rarely those of Asian background. The defective gene was identified as being on chromosome 7 only in the late 1980s, and already GENETIC SCREENING tests such as CHORIONIC VILLUS SAMPLING and AMNIOCENTESIS have been used to see if a FETUS has CF. Tests for CF are in early stages, however, and lack RELIABILITY, giving a great many FALSE POSITIVES and FALSE NEGATIVES—so many that some doctors question whether they are worth giving yet. Prospective parents who have any history of CF in their families may well want to seek GENETIC COUNSEL-

ING. Knowledge of the gene should help researchers understand precisely what causes CF and how they might correct the defect. At present, however, there is no preventive or cure for CF, only treatments that may alleviate symptoms of the disease.

The symptoms of CF are easily mistaken for other disorders, so it can sometimes be difficult to diagnose accurately. The three main symptoms are:

1. *pancreatic insufficiency.* The pancreas secretes enzymes necessary for proper digestion; but in CF, mucus tends to block the passageways by which the enzymes reach the small intestine. As a result, the digestive process is seriously disrupted. Much food passes through the body undigested, so despite very large intake of food, a person with CF may show signs of MALNUTRITION. Early signs of this are fatty, foul-smelling stool and abdominal pain. Lack of digestive enzymes in the small intestines is one clue to a diagnosis of CF.

2. *respiratory problems.* Chronic LUNG AND BREATHING DISORDERS are common among people with CF because thick mucus obstructs the air passages of the lungs and bronchial tubes, causing labored breathing and chronic cough. Worse, the mucus is a prime breeding ground for bacteria, which often become resistant to treatment by antibiotics, producing chronic respiratory infections. Breathing problems lead to poor circulation and increased BLOOD PRESSURE, which in turn can cause damage to the lungs and heart, further weakening the body's ability to resist infection. It is this pattern of complications from respiratory difficulty that, the Public Health Service estimates, causes 90 percent of all deaths from CF.

3. *excessive loss of salt.* People with CF lose large amounts of SODIUM and CHLORIDE in their sweat, causing weakness and listlessness and, in summer, increased risk of DEHYDRATION or heat exhaustion. The most commonly used diagnostic test for CF is, in fact, the *sweat test*, which tests for abnormal concentrations of salt in sweat.

Other symptoms seen in severe cases of CF are short, stubby ("clubbed") fingers and bluish lips (cyanosis). For unknown reasons, not all people are affected with equal severity. Some people show serious symptoms in infancy, while others, with lesser symptoms, may be diagnosed only later in childhood. And some experience primarily breathing difficulties, without much digestive involvement, whereas others experience the reverse.

Researchers are working hard to develop more accurate diagnostic tests because it is vitally important to begin treatment early, before great damage has been done. The main treatments include:

- use of antibiotics to combat infections;
- aerosal inhalation to clear air passages;
- physical therapy, especially *postural drainage*, a technique that uses gravity and "pounding" of the chest to help dislodge and drain mucus from the lungs and bronchial tubes;
- taking pancreatic extracts to replace missing enzymes;
- consuming additional quantities of food, though well balanced and relatively low in fat; and
- using supplemental salt to replace that lost in perspiration.

Until recently, few people with CF reached school age. But treatment techniques developed in recent decades have greatly improved both the quality and length of life for CF patients, with many living into their 20s and 30s and beyond. GENE THERAPY, successful in the test tube, offers much hope for the future, though practical application in humans may be years away.

For help and further information

Cystic Fibrosis Foundation (CFF)
6931 Arlington Road
Bethesda, MD 20814
301-951-4422, toll-free number (U.S. except MD) 800-FIGHTCF [344-4823]
Robert K. Dresing, President

Organization to aid cystic fibrosis patients and their families. Funds research; helps fund cystic fibrosis medical centers; provides information and referrals; publishes various materials, including quarterly newsletter and many booklets, such as *Your Child and CF*, *Cystic Fibrosis: Questions Frequently Asked by Parents*, *Living with Cystic Fibrosis: A Guide for Adolescents*, *Cystic Fibrosis: A Summary of Symptoms, Diagnosis, and Treatment*, and *The Genetics of Cystic Fibrosis*.

National Institute of Diabetes and Digestive and Kidney Diseases (NIDDK), 301-496-3583. Publishes *Cystic Fibrosis: The Puzzle and the Promise*. (For full group information, see DIGESTIVE DISORDERS.)

Other reference sources

A Parent's Guide to Cystic Fibrosis, by Burton L. Shapiro and Ralph C. Heussner, Jr. Minneapolis: University of Minnesota Press, 1990.
Health Care U.S.A., by Jean Carper. New York: Prentice Hall, 1987. Resource for general and specific health-care information; lists major centers for cystic fibrosis treatment or research and other information.
CF in His Corner, by Gail Radley. New York: Four Winds, 1984.

Alex: The Life of a Child, by Frank Deford. New York: Viking, 1983.
(See also GENETIC COUNSELING; also HELP FOR SPECIAL CHILDREN on page 578.)

cystinosis (cystine storage disease)   A kind of KIDNEY AND UROLOGICAL DISORDER.

cystitis   Inflammation of the bladder, usually from infection. (See KIDNEY AND UROLOGICAL DISORDERS.)

cytomegalovirus infection   Infection with the cytomegalovirus (CMV), a kind of SEXUALLY TRANSMITTED DISEASE but one that is also readily spread by other forms of bodily contact, including kissing. CMV, a member of the HERPES SIMPLEX family, is a common virus, infecting most mature adults; and like its relatives, CMV often lies dormant in the body, becoming reactivated from time to time. In most healthy adults, CMV has few serious consequences, causing flulike symptoms, such as FEVER, fatigue, and swollen lymph glands, similar to INFECTIOUS MONONUCLEOSIS. But CMV can be quite dangerous to infants, whose IMMUNE SYSTEMS are not yet fully developed; to people whose immune systems are damaged or being suppressed, as during AIDS or chemotherapy; and to pregnant women, who can pass it on to the FETUS, with resulting BIRTH DEFECTS, such as MENTAL RETARDATION, EAR AND HEARING PROBLEMS, EPILEPSY, various deformities, and even DEATH. The National Institute of Allergy and Infectious Diseases estimates that CMV is the "leading cause of congenital infection," affecting 6,000 babies a year. Various diagnostic tests are not very reliable, nor are there yet any effective drugs, though some are being tested. Some doctors have cautioned pregnant women who work in CHILD CARE that they are at increased risk of catching the infection from the young children in their care, but they note that the virus is so widespread and readily transmitted that it is hard to avoid. (For help and further information, including how to avoid infection, see SEXUALLY TRANSMITTED DISEASES.)

D

DA   Abbreviation for DEVELOPMENTAL AGE.

dancing eyes   Nickname for *nystagmus*. (See EYE AND VISION PROBLEMS.)

day care   Alternate term for CHILD CARE.

day treatment   Treatment given to a child and some or all family members while they remain living in their own home. In cases of CHILD ABUSE AND NEGLECT, day treatment services may include psychological and social counseling, structured supervision, and activities designed to break the cycle of abuse and begin the process of repairing the damage.

DD Abbreviation for developmental disability and sometimes for DEVELOPMENTAL DISORDER.

deaf In general, a term referring to people with hearing so severely impaired that it cannot be used for the ordinary purposes of life, with or without a hearing aid. When hearing is impaired but can be used for the ordinary purposes of life with the use of a hearing aid, a child is generally termed *hard of hearing*. (For help and further information, see EAR AND HEARING PROBLEMS.)

dean's list A list prepared at the end of each term (traditionally by the dean's office) indicating which students at the college or university achieved a GRADE POINT AVERAGE of B or better or, if number GRADES are used, generally 90 or better; the college equivalent of a high school's HONOR ROLL.

death The cessation of life, traditionally indicated by lack of heartbeat and breathing, what some medical professionals now call *apparent death*. In recent decades, with the develop of VENTILATORS and other technology to assist in maintaining heart and lung functions, a new definition of death has emerged: BRAIN DEATH, which focuses on the lack of activity in the brain. Definitions vary from state to state, however, and the specific definition controlling in a particular area is sometimes called *legal death*.

The questions of death and the use of medical technology in cases of irreversible COMA and terminal illness have raised grave problems for the families of people lingering on the edge of death. If a terminally ill child is considered so severely ill that death is inevitable and imminent, parents may be asked to decide whether the child should be placed on a ventilator in case heart and lungs fail or be allowed to die without intervention. If the latter is decided upon, the senior physician will often write *no code* or *do not resuscitate (DNR)* on the child's medical chart. Once a child is placed on an artificial breathing machine, the decision of when (if ever) the child is later taken off is extremely difficult, because many health personnel feel that their professional standards call for doing everything possible to maintain life. In some instances parents have entered lengthy court cases to win the right to remove their child from a machine—in effect, to win the child's right to die. The legal questions in these areas have only begun to be explored. For patients who are terminally ill, a *hospice* is often a good alternative to a HOSPITAL. The hospice focuses on maintaining the quality of life for as long as it can be lived, rather than maintaining length of life regardless of all other concerns.

For many parents, the questions of death are bound up with PREGNANCY and CHILDBIRTH, as in cases of MISCARRIAGE or STILLBIRTH, when a child dies before birth, or MATERNAL MORTALITY, in which the mother dies from complications of the pregnancy.

For babies born alive, the first year—especially the first month—is the most dangerous time.

The rate of death in infants varies widely from country to country, depending on various factors, including medical care, PRENATAL CARE, and socioeconomic conditions. In the United States, the INFANT MORTALITY RATE (the number of infants per 1,000 who die in their first year) is 10 per 1,000 for White infants and 19 per 1,000 for Black infants. Of these, two-thirds die in the first month.

As shown in NEONATAL AND POSTNEONATAL MORTALITY (on page 133), in the first month babies are most at risk from RESPIRATORY DISTRESS SYNDROME, complications associated with PREMATURE birth and LOW BIRTH WEIGHT, CONGENITAL abnormalities (such as SPINA BIFIDA), and effects of maternal complications of pregnancy. In the second to twelfth months, death most often occurs because of SUDDEN INFANT DEATH SYNDROME, congenital abnormalities, and infections (bacterial or viral) such as PNEUMONIA, influenza, SEPTICEMIA, bronchitis, and MENINGITIS, followed by injuries and murder.

As CHILD MORTALITY (on page 134) outlines, among older children, ages one to 19, by far the main cause of death is injuries, followed by congenital abnormalities, CANCER (on the chart labeled *malignant neoplasms*), heart problems (see HEART AND HEART PROBLEMS), and murder. During ADOLESCENCE, SUICIDE becomes a major cause of death and murder a much more important one.

Although death may come suddenly and unexpectedly, sometimes families must together face the impending loss of a parent, grandparent, sibling, or other close relative or friend—or the possibility of their own death. Death and dying were, for centuries, almost unmentionables. Often doctors did not tell patients when they were dying, and family members pretended that nothing was wrong. The very great tragedy was that no one was fooled, but each was cut off from the possibility of support from the others.

Today there is a much greater understanding that all humans face the same questions of death and dying, that they have many of the same reactions in response to it, and that by sharing their thoughts and feelings they can all be helped to face questions of death, come to terms with it, and, with love and support from others, learn to move beyond.

This very much includes young children, because (as noted in SOMEHOW CHILDREN KNOW, on page 135) they are sensitive to changes in the home and may readily come to feel that they have caused those changes, a classic example of MAGICAL THINKING. Parents (like doctors with their patients) need to be sensitive to how much a child wants to know, to be forthcoming and responsive but not to force unwanted knowledge on a child. The main point to keep in mind is that if parents do not frankly acknowledge that something is wrong, the child is left to deal with terrible fears and felt "responsibilities" alone.

Many groups (see below), often formed by people who have been through similar experiences, now exist to help surviving family members—parents and siblings—deal with the death of

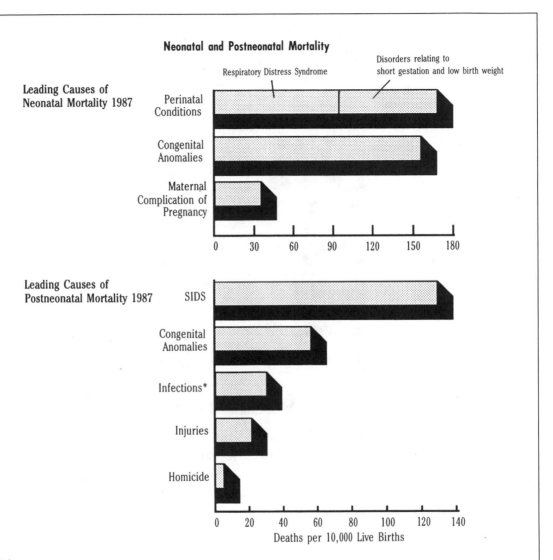

Neonatal and Postneonatal Mortality

Leading Causes of
Neonatal Mortality 1987

Respiratory Distress Syndrome

Disorders relating to
short gestation and low birth weight

Perinatal
Conditions

Congenital
Anomalies

Maternal
Complication of
Pregnancy

0   30   60   90   120   150   180

Leading Causes of
Postneonatal Mortality 1987

SIDS

Congenital
Anomalies

Infections*

Injuries

Homicide

0   20   40   60   80   100   120   140
Deaths per 10,000 Live Births

Neonatal
    In 1987, 24,627 infants under the age of 28 days died; the neonatal mortality rate was 647 deaths per 100,000 live births.
Postneonatal
    In 1987, 13,781 infants ages 28 days up to one year died; the postneonatal mortality rate was 362 per 100,000 live births.
    Of the five leading causes of postneonatal death, infections, injuries, and homicides may be prevented with appropriate inter-
vention.
    Between 1960 and 1986, the postneonatal mortality rate decreased faster for black infants than for white infants.
    *Note: The category entitled infection includes pneumonia, influenza, septicemia, meningitis, bronchitis, viral diseases.

Source: National Center for Health Statistics, as reprinted in *Child Health USA '89* (1989). Prepared for the Public Health Service by the Health Resources and
Services Administration, Bureau of Maternal and Child Health and Resources Development.

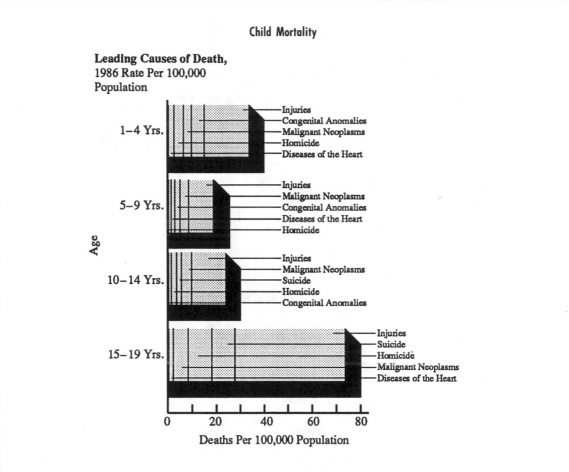

Child Mortality

Leading Causes of Death,
1986 Rate Per 100,000
Population

1–4 Yrs.
- Injuries
- Congenital Anomalies
- Malignant Neoplasms
- Homicide
- Diseases of the Heart

5–9 Yrs.
- Injuries
- Malignant Neoplasms
- Congenital Anomalies
- Diseases of the Heart
- Homicide

10–14 Yrs.
- Injuries
- Malignant Neoplasms
- Suicide
- Homicide
- Congenital Anomalies

15–19 Yrs.
- Injuries
- Suicide
- Homicide
- Malignant Neoplasms
- Diseases of the Heart

Age

0   20   40   60   80

Deaths Per 100,000 Population

Injuries are the leading cause of death among all children.
Homicide and suicide are major contributors to the causes of death in adolescents 15 through 19 years of age.
In 1986, 32,492 children of ages one through 19 died.

Source: National Center for Health Statistics, as reprinted in *Child Health USA '89*. (See previous chart.)

a child or parent. Organizations formed around specific diseases and disorders, such as cancer, can also help. Even funeral homes have begun to provide supportive services, called *bereavement counseling*, to people surviving a death in the family.

For help and further information

The Compassionate Friends (TCF)
P.O. Box 3696
Oak Brook, IL 60522

312-990-0010
Therese Goodrich, Executive Director
Nondenominational network of mutual-support self-help groups of and for parents who have lost a child. Seeks to counsel and support surviving family members, including siblings; links grieving families with "telephone friends" to talk with; publishes newsletter and other materials.

Parents of Suicides (PS)
c/o Bergen/Passaic T.C.F.
P.O. Box 373
Englewood, NJ 07631

201-894-0042
Esther Ehrenberg, Co-Chair
Network of mutual-support self-help groups of parents and siblings of suicides. Helps them deal with grief, guilt, confusion, and stigma following suicide; maintains library; publishes newsletter; affiliated with Compassionate Friends.

Parents of Murdered Children (POMC)
100 East Eighth Street, B-41
Cincinnati, OH 45202
513-721-5683
Sharon Tewksbury, Executive Director
Mutual-support self-help group of parents of a murdered child or others who have lost a family member to murder. Disseminates information about the grieving process and about dealing with the criminal justice aftermath of a homicide; publishes newsletter, *Survivors*.

SHARE (Source of Help in Airing and Resolving Experiences)
c/o St. Elizabeth's Hospital
211 South Third Street
Belleville, IL 62222
618-234-2415 or -2120, ext. 1430
Sister Jane Marie Lamb, Chairperson
Network of groups of and for families who have lost a baby through early infant death, stillbirth, or miscarriage. Aims to provide mutual support, encouraging parent-to-parent contacts; maintains library and information about resources available to surviving parents and siblings; publishes various printed and audiovisual materials, including newsletter *Share* and a children's book on grief.

Inter-National Association for Widowed People (IAWP)
P.O. Box 3564
Springfield, IL 62708
217-787-0886
Dorothy L. Doering, President
Organization for widowed people and their families. Offers referrals to self-help programs to deal with grief, loss, and loneliness; provides information on benefits available; seeks to educate the public and influence public policy and legislation regarding special needs and problems of widowed people; provides special programs in travel, living arrangements, job placement, and social contact; gathers research data and maintains library; publishes various materials, including bimonthly, *The Survivors*, and pamphlet, *Grief Curve*.

Pregnancy and Infant Loss Center (PILC)
1415 East Wayzata Boulevard, Suite 22
Wayzata, MN 55391
612-473-9372
Susan Erling, Executive Director
Organization for parents who have experienced miscarriage, stillbirth, or infant death and others concerned with these experiences. Provides information and referrals; encourages

---

Somehow Children Know

Even children sense the truth. Some parents who tried to "spare" their children from knowing [that a family member had a terminal illness] later voiced regret at not discussing the truth during the course of the disease. Children have amazing capabilities when they understand a situation. However, when their normal world is turned upside down and whispered conversations go on behind closed doors, they often imagine situations that are worse than reality. Young children dwell on "terrible" things *they* have done or said that place responsibility for the upheaval in the household on themselves. This is especially true if the child is going through a period of testing parental authority or in some other way is in disagreement with family members. Children—especially young ones—tend to view themselves as the center of the universe and see many situations only in direct relationship to themselves.

The children's ages and emotional maturity should suggest what and how much to disclose. It might help to realize that including the children among those who know comforts them by confirming their belief that something is amiss within the family. . . .

The most compelling reason for sharing the diagnosis with adults and children alike is that cancer [and other terminal illnesses] can be so terribly lonely. No one need try to bear it alone.

Source: *Taking Time: Support for People with Cancer and the People Who Care About Them* (1987). Prepared for the Public Health Service by the National Cancer Institute.

---

formation of mutual-support parent groups; maintains helpline; publishes various materials, including newsletter *Loving Arms*.

National Institute of Child Health and Human Development (NICHD), 301-496-5133. (For full group information, see PREGNANCY.)

Other reference sources

General Works

Mortal Matters: When a Loved One Dies, by Sara Engram. Kansas City, MO: Andrews & McMeel, 1990.
Death in the Family: The Importance of Mourning, by Lily Pincus. New York: Schocken, 1988.
Grieving: How to Go On Living When Someone You Love Dies, by Therese A. Rando. Lexington, MA: Lexington, 1988.
Early Winter: Learning to Live, Love and Laugh Again After a Painful Loss, by Howard Bronson. New Seabury, MA: Bestsell, 1988.
Encyclopedia of Death, Robert Kastenbaum and Beatrice Kastenbaum, eds. Phoenix, AZ: Oryx, 1989.

Living with Death and Dying, by Elisabeth Kübler-Ross. New York: Macmillan, 1981.

On Loss of a Child

Recovering from the Loss of a Child, by Katherine Fair Donnelly. New York: Dodd, Mead, 1988; Macmillan, 1982.

Beyond Endurance: When a Child Dies, by Ronald J. Knapp. New York: Schocken, 1986.

When Your Child Is Gone: Learning to Live Again, by Francine Roder. Sacramento, CA: Capital, 1986.

Surviving Pregnancy Loss, by Rochelle Friedman, M.D., and Bonnie Gradstein. Boston: Little, Brown, 1982.

Before and After My Child Died: A Collection of Parents' Experiences, by Joseph Fischhoff and Noreen O'Brien Brohl. Detroit: Emmons-Fairfield, 1981.

When Pregnancy Fails: Families Coping with Miscarriage, Stillbirth and Infant Death, by Susan Borg and Judith Lasker. Boston: Beacon, 1981.

On Loss of an Adult in the Family

When Your Spouse Dies: A Concise and Practical Source of Help and Advice, by Cathleen L. Curry. Notre Dame, IN: Ave Maria, 1990. Helping surviving adults and children deal with grief.

Learning to Say Good-Bye: When a Parent Dies, by Eda LeShan. New York: Macmillan, 1976; Avon, 1988. For children of all ages.

When Parents Die, by Edward Myers. New York: Viking, 1986.

The Kids Next Door: Sons and Daughters Who Kill Their Parents, by Gregory Morris. New York: Morrow, 1985.

On Helping Kids Deal with Death

Talking About Death: A Dialogue Between Parent and Child, revised edition, by Earl A. Grollman. Boston: Beacon, 1990.

Why Did Daddy Die? Helping Children Cope With the Loss of a Parent, by Linda Alderman. New York: Pocket, 1989.

How Do We Tell the Children? Helping Children Understand and Cope When Someone Dies, by Dan Schaefer and Christine Lyons. New York: Newmarket, 1988.

The Seasons of Grief: Helping Your Children Grow Through Loss, by Donna A. Gaffney. New York: New American Library, 1988.

Lifetimes: A Beautiful Way to Explain Death to Children, by Bryan Mellonie and Robert Ingpen. New York: Bantam, 1983.

Helping Children Cope with Death: Guidelines and Resources, Hansbore Wass and Charles A. Corr, eds. New York: Hemisphere, 1982.

Helping Children Cope with Separation and Loss, by Claudia Jewett. Cambridge, MA: Harvard Common, 1982.

Helping Children Cope: Mastering Stress Through Books and Stories, by Joan Fassler. New York: Free Press, 1978. Includes bibliographies of books related to various problems, including death, separation, hospitalization and illness, life-style changes (such as new baby, adoption, and divorce), and other stressful situations (such as financial problems, parent in prison, and natural disasters).

Explaining Death to Children, Earl Grollman, ed. Boston: Beacon, 1967.

For or by Kids

Death, by Gail Stewart. New York: Crestwood, 1990. Part of the Facts About series.

Winter Holding Spring, by Crescent Dragonwagon. New York: Macmillan, 1990. For ages 7 to 10. A girl and her father cope with a mother's death.

Sheila's Dying, by Alden R. Carter. New York: Scholastic/Point, 1989. For young adult readers.

Teenagers Face to Face with Bereavement, by Karen Gravelle and Charles Haskins. New York: Messner, 1989. Interviews with teens facing death, with advice.

Meeting Death, by Margaret Hyde and Lawrence Hyde. New York: Walker, 1989. For ages 10 and up.

Remember the Secret, by Elisabeth Kübler-Ross. Berkeley, CA: Celestial Arts, 1988. Useful for children facing life-threatening illness or the loss of a loved one.

The Kids' Book About Death and Dying: By and For Kids, by the Unit at Fayeweather Street School, E.E. Rofes, ed. Boston: Little, Brown, 1985.

Summerland: A Story About Death and Hope, by Eyvind Skeie. Elgin, IL: Brethren. For children, from a Christian point of view.

How It Feels When a Parent Dies, by Jill Krementz. New York: Knopf, 1981.

Tiger Eyes, by Judy Blume. New York: Bradbury, 1981; Dell paperback. For young adults. About a young girl dealing with her father's death.

Too Old to Cry . . . Too Young to Die, Edith Pendleton, ed. Nashville, TN: Thomas Nelson, 1980. By and for terminally ill teenagers.

On Legal and Moral Issues

Alpha and Omega: Ethics at the Frontiers of Life and Death, by Ernlé W.D. Young. Reading, MA: Addison-Wesley, 1990.

Medicine and the Law, by Neil Grauer. New York: Chelsea House, 1990. Overview of issues such as euthanasia, animal rights, abortion, genetic engineering, surrogate motherhood, and medical malpractice. For grades 7 to 10.

Euthanasia: The Moral Issues, Robert M. Baird and Stuart E. Rosenbaum, eds. Buffalo, NY: Prometheus, 1989.

By No Extraordinary Means: The Choice to Forgo Life-Sustaining Food and Water, expanded edition, Joanne Lynn, M.D., ed. Bloomington, IN: University of Indiana Press, 1989.

Born to Die?: Deciding the Fate of Critically Ill Newborns, by Earl E. Shelp. New York: Free Press, 1986.

Should the Baby Live: The Problem of the Handicapped Infants, by Helga Kihse. New York: Oxford University Press, 1985.

Euthanasia: Opposing Viewpoints, Neal Bernards, ed. San Diego, CA: Greenhaven, 1989. For grades 7 to 12.

Terminal Choices: Euthanasia, Suicide, and the Right to Die, by Robert N. Wennberg. Grand Rapids, MI: Eerdmans, 1989.

(See also MISCARRIAGE; SUICIDE; SUDDEN INFANT DEATH SYNDROME; STILLBIRTH; HOSPITALS, including hospices.)

decibels   A measure of loudness, used in HEARING TESTS.

decile   A way of ranking test scores; the same principle as a PERCENTILE but with 10 divisions.

decoding   The process of extracting meaning from symbols, such as written, spoken, or signed words or numbers. An important intellectual skill, basic to much learning, decoding poses significant problems for many people with brain dysfunction. A child with LEARNING DISABILITIES, especially DYSLEXIA, for example, may see printed words upside down, backward, or distorted in a variety of ways, and so may have trouble decoding the symbols. Similarly, a child with DYSCALCULIA may have trouble decoding and working with mathematical symbols. Such children may also have trouble with the reverse process, ENCODING. Various TESTS are used to try to identify decoding problems so that teachers and therapists can help the child learn to overcome them. (For help and further information, see LEARNING DISABILITIES.)

deductive learning   A LEARNING STYLE in which a teacher or parent presents a general rule or concept and the child learns to apply it to specific situations; also called *expository learning*.

defense mechanism   Generally involuntary patterns of thoughts, behavior, and feelings that serve to protect the self from perceived threats, including ANXIETY and guilt. Among the common defense mechanisms found among children are ACTING OUT, AUTISTIC FANTASY, DISPLACEMENT, and IDEALIZATION.

deficiency diseases   Disorders resulting from lack of some essential nutrients in the diet, such as PROTEINS, CARBOHYDRATES, MINERALS, or VITAMINS, the latter sometimes called *avitaminosis*. (See also NUTRITION.)

degree   A title conferred on a student who has successfully completed a course of study; also an alternate term for DIPLOMA. The main kinds of COLLEGE degrees are ASSOCIATE DEGREE, BACHELOR'S DEGREE, MASTER'S DEGREE, and DOCTORAL DEGREE. Degree requirements—the number of courses in various areas of study that a student must complete to be eligible for a diploma or degree—vary from school to school, but the JAMES MADISON HIGH SCHOOL MODEL CURRICULUM (on page 538) indicates what courses a typical student might have to complete in order to graduate.

Degrees of Reading Power   A TEST that measures a student's ability to comprehend READING matter of a determined level of difficulty.

Infant's Water Needs

The evaporative, fecal, and urinary water losses determine water requirements for infants. Evaporative losses in healthy, full-term normal infants range from 30 to 70 ml/kg/day. Fecal losses average one to four ml/kg/day (up to 10 ml/kg/day in breastfed infants) but can increase suddenly and vary greatly in infants with diarrhea. Because of their large surface area relative to mass, infants lose proportionately more water by skin evaporation than do adults. Infants also have less renal [kidney] concentrating capacity than do adults. Thus, infants are vulnerable to water imbalance. Nevertheless, breast milk and infant formulas provide adequate water, and healthy infants rarely require supplemental water except in very hot weather. Instead, dehydration problems are most likely to occur during episodes of vomiting, diarrhea, or fever, when dehydration can occur so suddenly as to constitute a medical emergency.

Source: *The Surgeon General's Report on Nutrition and Health*. Rocklin, CA: Prima, 1988.

---

dehydration   Dangerously low water level in the body's tissues, generally also involving loss of key substances called ELECTROLYTES that are normally dissolved in the body fluids. Where water is available and the person is conscious, powerful sensations of thirst generally prevent dehydration. But infants and small children, as well as adults who are severely ill, may be vulnerable to serious, even life-threatening damage from dehydration. (See INFANT'S WATER NEEDS, above.) DIARRHEA and persistent VOMITING can put a baby's life at risk, so medical help should be sought immediately. In addition to thirst, symptoms of dehydration include dry lips and tongue, dizziness and confusion, rapid heartbeat and breathing, and eventual COMA. Treatment involves replacing not only water but also vital substances, using *rehydration* mixtures (available in drugstores) or in hospitals PARENTERAL NUTRITION, to resupply the fluid and balance necessary for recovery.

Dejerine-Sottas disease   A type of muscle disorder. (See MUSCULAR DYSTROPHY.)

de Lange syndrome (Cornelia de Lange, CdLS, or Amsterdam syndrome)   A rare type of BIRTH DEFECT characterized by MENTAL RETARDATION and a wide variety of minor physical signs, including short stature, small head, low forehead and ears, heavy eyebrows, flattened nose with widened nostrils, small jaw, one or more limbs somewhat shortened (*micromelia*) or nearly nonexistent, with hands or feet attached almost directly to the body (PHOCOMELIA), thumb placed low on the hand, abnormal bending of some fingers or toes (*clinodactyly*), limited extension of the arm at the elbow, webbing of the second and third toes, and unusually large amounts of body hair (HIRSUTISM). Some researchers distinguish between a short-statured, large-featured form of the syndrome (called *Brachman-de Lange* or *dwarf type*) and a larger form (*Bruck-de Lange type*), characterized by a heavily muscular, wrestlerlike appearance, with broad neck and shoulders. The cause of de Lange syndrome is unknown. Prospective parents with a history of the syndrome in their family may want to seek GENETIC COUNSELING.

For help and further information

Cornelia de Lange Syndrome (CdLS) Foundation
60 Dyer Avenue
Collinsville, CT 06022
203-693-0159, toll-free number (US except CT) 800-223-8355
Julie A. Mairano, Executive Director
Organization concerned with individuals having Cornelia de Lange syndrome, especially as to early and accurate diagnosis. Provides information to public and professionals; aids families in making decisions about child's future; publishes various materials, including bimonthly *Reaching Out*, audiovisual *Unto Us This Child*, *Cornelia de Lange Syndrome: A Book for Families*, *Facts About Cornelia de Lange Syndrome*, and *CdLS Directory*.

National Institute of Child Health and Human Development (NICHD), 301-496-5133. (For full group information, see PREGNANCY.)

delayed speech Alternate name for a type of communication disorder (see COMMUNICATION SKILLS AND DISORDERS).

deliberate self-harm syndrome Alternate term for SELF-MUTILATION SYNDROME.

delinquent Term used to describe behavior or acts that lead to the conviction of a MINOR in JUVENILE COURT—often behavior that would, if performed by an adult, be labeled criminal. The term *delinquent* is also often used to refer to JUVENILES who have violated social standards or are considered UNSOCIALIZED. More loosely, the term refers to a person's failure to perform required duties or obligations, so a parent who fails to make CHILD-SUPPORT payments may be called delinquent.

delirium A confused, turbulent mental state, often including HALLUCINATIONS, DELUSIONS, LABILITY (emotional swings), and ANXIETY, generally an acute reaction in cases of ORGANIC MENTAL DISORDER, as may be caused by infection, METABOLIC DISORDERS, HEAD INJURY, or trauma. Delirium is usually reversible once the underlying condition is treated. In cases of ALCOHOL ABUSE, the state caused by withdrawal is often called *delirium tremens* (DTs)

delivery In PREGNANCY, the bringing forth of a baby from the mother's UTERUS and also the expulsion of the PLACENTA (afterbirth), which are the second and third stages of LABOR. Delivery is a general term for the ways in which a child appears or is brought out into the world—normal vaginal birth; assisted vaginal birth, such as FORCEPS DELIVERY and VACUUM EXTRACTION;

extraction through an incision in the abdomen (CESAREAN SECTION); or the various methods of natural or prepared CHILDBIRTH—as well as for birth of a child from an abnormal FETAL PRESENTATION, such as a *breech delivery*. (For help and further information, see PREGNANCY; CHILDBIRTH.)

delivery room In traditional HOSPITAL births, the room in which the child is actually born, to which a woman is normally transferred from a LABOR ROOM. In look and furniture, a delivery room is much like an operating room, which has the advantage of having medical equipment readily at hand, should they be needed if complications develop during CHILDBIRTH. But many people in recent decades have found the delivery room cold and forbidding, so (except for HIGH-RISK PREGNANCY) some have preferred to give birth in a more homey MATERNITY CENTER, a hospital-attached BIRTHING ROOM, or at home (see HOME BIRTH).

Hospitals have different rules about who will or will not be allowed in the delivery room, and prospective parents should inquire about these rules in making choices about delivery. These days the BIRTH PARTNER will be generally be allowed to remain with the woman in delivery, but some hospitals require that the birth partner have taken childbirth preparation classes and may ask the partner to leave in case of emergencies or complications, especially a CESAREAN SECTION. Some hospitals have gone to an all-in-one *labor/delivery/recovery room (LDR)*, to avoid the often-unsettling shift from labor room to delivery room. Others have gone even further, developing the *labor/delivery/recovery/postpartum room (LDRP)*, where a mother stays from arrival at the hospital, through labor and delivery, and until discharge.

delusion A false belief, firmly held though contradicted by physical reality or common sense, as when a child believes a control box has been implanted in his or her head, or a 70-pound anorexic girl insists she is obese. (For help and further information, see MENTAL DISORDERS.)

dementia Long-term or irreversible deterioration of intellectual functioning, affecting memory, personality, VISUAL SKILLS, SPATIAL RELATIONS, and general thinking ability. Dementia may result from some kinds of ORGANIC MENTAL DISORDERS, as from illness or injury, or may accompany some other kinds of mental disturbances, such as SCHIZOPHRENIA. (For help and further information, see MENTAL DISORDERS.)

demonstration school Alternate term for LABORATORY SCHOOL.

dental age A summary of the relationship between the growth of a child's teeth and the statistical average for a child of the same size and sex; if a child of six has a maturity of TEETH and jaw formation normally seen in a seven-year-old, that child's dental age is seven. (See AGE.)

dental onlay A procedure used to build up teeth in some cases of MALOCCLUSION.

dentist The dental equivalent of the family physician, the health professional who has primary care of the TEETH and gums. Modern dentists focus on prevention, not just treatment, and are oriented toward early detection and handling of dental problems before much damage has been done. Among the dental specialists to whom a patient might be referred are an ORTHODONTIST, ENDODONTIST, PERIODONTIST, and ORAL SURGEON.

dependency hearing   A hearing at which the court assesses whether or not the state should take temporary CUSTODY of a child, as in extreme cases of CHILD ABUSE AND NEGLECT.

dependent personality disorder   A type of PERSONALITY DISORDER.

depression   A type of MENTAL DISORDER in which a person is overwhelmed with feelings of worthlessness, hopelessness, dejection, apathy, fatigue, pessimism, and generally low feeling of well-being. Because its symptoms seem so general, depression can sometimes be hard to identify, but the National Institute of Mental Health suggests that clinical depression may exist if at least four of the following symptoms continue nearly every day for at least two weeks:

- change in appetite or weight
- change in sleeping patterns
- speaking and/or moving with unusual speed or slowness
- loss of interest or pleasure in usual activities
- decrease in sexual drive
- fatigue or loss of energy
- feelings of worthlessness, self-reproach, or guilt
- diminished ability to think or concentrate, slowed thinking, or indecisiveness
- thoughts of death, suicide, wishing to be dead, or suicide attempt

And, in fact, most people who attempt SUICIDE are depressed, though many who are depressed never attempt suicide.

A form of depression common among women after CHILDBIRTH is *postpartum depression*, popularly called *baby blues*. It is apparently triggered by the great hormonal changes that occur in the body after PREGNANCY, as well as broken sleep and stress at dealing with the massive life-style changes that accompany a new child. Generally a mild, short-lived condition, involving mood swings (LABILITY), irritability, confusion, and feeling miserable, postpartum depression is in some women a persistent, serious condition called *puerperal psychosis*, in which the woman may be at risk for committing suicide or harming her baby.

Long thought primarily a problem of adults, depression is now known to be common in children and adolescents as well, affecting teenage girls more than boys, with dissatisfaction often centering on BODY IMAGE. Studies indicate that as many as one in 50 school-age children show signs of clinical depression. This is often linked with other mental disorders, such as anxiety disorders (see ANXIETY) and CONDUCT DISORDERS.

In some people, depression alternates with its opposite, a manic, hyperactive state, in what used to be called *manic-depression* but is now medically known as BIPOLAR DISORDER. Recent research indicates that bipolar disorder is linked to a defective gene, making it at least partly a type of GENETIC DISORDER.

Clinical depression is often treated with drugs, counseling, and therapy, and sometimes temporary hospitalization may be required. Some women with postpartum depression, others with milder depression, or people recovering from severe depression may find relief in talking with friends, family, and perhaps mutual-support self-help groups like those below.

For help and further information

National Institute of Mental Health (NIMH), 301-443-4536. Publishes *Depressive Illnesses: Treatments Bring New Hope*, *What to Do When a Friend Is Depressed: A Guide for Teenagers*, *Helpful Facts About Depressive Disorders*, and *Bipolar Disorder: Manic-Depressive Illness*. (For full group information, see MENTAL DISORDERS.)

National Depressive and Manic-Depressive Association (NDMDA)
Merchandise Mart, Box 3395
Chicago, IL 60654
312-939-2442
Organization of and for depressive or manic-depressive patients and their families. Seeks to educate public and influence public policy and legislation; provides information.

Depression and Related Affective Disorders Association (DRADA)
The Johns Hopkins Hospital
Meyer 4-181
601 North Wolfe Street
Baltimore, MD 21205
301-987-5756, 301-955-4647, or 301-955-3246
Charles Peck, President
Organization of patients with clinical depression, including manic depression, their families, and health professionals. Fosters research and expansion of support services; publishes various materials, including quarterly newsletter *Smooth Sailing*, brochure *I Am the Greatest. I Am Depressed*, annotated bibliography, and audiovisual materials for young people.

National Foundation for Depressive Illness
P.O. Box 2257
New York, NY 10116
212-620-7637, toll-free number 800-248-4344
Organization of people concerned with depressive illness. Operates toll-free number; provides information and referrals to support groups.

Depressives Anonymous: Recovery from Depression (DARFD)
329 East 62nd Street
New York, NY 10021
212-689-2600
Dr. Helen DeRosis, Founder
Network of mutual-support self-help groups for people with depression or anxiety. Modeled on Alcoholics Anonymous; publishes newsletter and other materials.

Depression After Delivery
P.O. Box 1282
Morrisville, PA 19067
215-295-3994
Organization of and for women with postpartum depression.

Other Reference Sources

You Can Beat Depression: A Guide to Recovery, by John Preston. San Luis Obispo, CA: Impact, 1989.

The Exercise Prescription for Depression and Anxiety, by Keith W. Johnsgård. New York: Plenum, 1989.

The Good News About Depression: New Breakthrough Medical Treatments That Can Work for You, by Mark S. Gold, M.D., and Lois B. Morris. New York: Bantam, 1988.

Depression Hits Every Family, by Grace Ketterman, M.D. Nashville, TN: Thomas Nelson, 1988.

Do You Have a Depressive Illness: How to Tell, What to Do, by Donald F. Klein, M.D., and Paul H. Wender, M.D. New York: New American Library, 1988.

How to Understand and Overcome Depression, by Earnie Larsen. Available from The Johnson Institute, 7151 Metro Boulevard, Minneapolis, MN 55435.

Why Isn't Johnny Crying? Coping with Depression in Children, by Dr. Leon Cytryn, Dr. Donald H. McKnew, Jr., and Herbert Yahraes. New York: Norton, 1983.

Coping with Teenage Depression, by Dr. Richard MacKenzie. New York: New American Library, 1982.

For Kids

Beating Depression, by Dr. John Rush. New York: Facts on File, 1986.

What Can I Do When I Feel Bad? 1989. Producer: Jack Ellis for Stone Soup Productions. Director: Scott Fillingham. 30-minute film/video from Human Relations Media, 175 Tompkins Avenue, Pleasantville, NY 10570. For ages 12 to 14.

Background Works

Encyclopedia of Depression, by Roberta Roesch. New York: Facts on File, 1990.

From Cradle to Grave: The Short Lives and Strange Deaths of Marybeth Tinning's Nine Children, by Joyce Egginton. New York: Berkley/Jove, 1990. About alleged killing of children during postpartum depression.

Depression: The Mood Disease, by Francis M. Mondimore, M.D. Baltimore: Johns Hopkins, 1990.

Sex Differences in Depression, by Susan Nolen-Hoeksema. Stanford, CA: Stanford University, 1990.

Health Care U.S.A., by Jean Carper. New York: Prentice Hall, 1987. Resource for general and specific health-care information; lists centers for treatment or research, specialists in treating depression, suicide prevention centers, and other information.

Suicide and Depression Among Adolescents and Young Adults, Gerald L. Klerman, ed. Washington, DC: American Psychiatric Press, 1986.

Depression and Its Treatment, by John R. Greist, M.D., and James Jefferson, M.D. Washington, DC: American Psychiatric Press, 1984.

(See also MENTAL DISORDERS.)

depth perception (DP) Ability to perceive the distance of objects and their relative position in space. (See EYE AND VISION PROBLEMS.)

dermatomyositis A type of muscle disorder. (See MUSCULAR DYSTROPHY.)

DES (diethylstilbestrol) A drug given between 1941 and 1971 that was found to have significant adverse effects on women and their children; a synthetic form of the female HORMONE, ESTROGEN, DES was prescribed for many women with a history of MISCARRIAGE, PREMATURE delivery, slight bleeding during PREGNANCY, or DIABETES MELLITUS. Later, many women did not remember taking the drug, so they and their children were unaware of the possible long-term side effects. DES mothers have increased risk of breast CANCER. DES daughters are more likely to have a miscarriage, ECTOPIC PREGNANCY, or premature delivery; they also have some structural changes, especially in the VAGINA and CERVIX, that can make CONCEPTION more difficult (see INFERTILITY) and an increased risk of a rare cancer of the vagina or cervix (*clear-cell adenocarcinoma*). DES sons are more likely to have underdeveloped or undescended TESTES, low SPERM counts, and other genital problems.

Prospective parents who are unsure if they were exposed to DES should check with their mothers regarding medications (including some prescription vitamins) and problems during pregnancy or (since mothers may not remember) check medical records at her doctor's office, her pharmacy, or the hospital. Many DES sons and daughters have borne normal, healthy children, with no problems during pregnancy, but they are advised to have regular medical checkups to screen for possible changes in the body. Many doctors also advise that DES daughters should avoid estrogen-containing BIRTH-CONTROL PILLS, which might increase cancer risk.

For help and further information
DES Action
2845 24th Street
San Francisco, CA 94110
415-826-5060
Organization of and for women who took DES (diethylstilbestrol), their offspring, and interested others. Gathers and disseminates information about effects of DES, as in causing cancer and birth defects. Seeks to educate public and influence public policy and legislation; provides for mutual support through DES Cancer Network for DES daughters; publishes various materials, including *DES Exposure: Questions and Answers for Mothers, Daughters and Sons, Fertility and Pregnancy Guide for DES Daughters and Sons, Preventing Preterm Birth: A Parent's Guide, Every Woman's Guide to Tests During Pregnancy*, and *Natural Remedies for Pregnancy Discomforts*.

National Cancer Institute, 800-4-CANCER [422-6237]. *Questions and Answers About DES Exposure During Pregnancy and Before Birth* and *Were You or Your Daughter or Son Born After 1940?* (For full group information, see CANCER.)
(See also CANCER; BIRTH DEFECTS; GENETIC COUNSELING; INFERTILITY; PREMATURE.)

desegregation In EDUCATION, the transfer of students from some schools to others to achieve racial balance or to end other kinds of discrimination (such as separation of the HANDICAPPED), often mandated by the court in cases of SEGREGATION, whether *de jure* (deliberate and written into law) or *de facto* (in fact, often by informal social pressures). One major court-mandated approach to de facto segregation has been BUSING, but more recently some school districts have tried various voluntary methods for achieving desegregation, as through SCHOOLS OF CHOICE and MAGNET SCHOOLS.

Other reference sources
School Desegregation Research, Jeffrey Prager, Douglas Longshore, and Melvin Seeman, eds. New York: Plenum, 1986.
School Desegregation Plans That Work, by Charles V. Willie. Westport, CT: Greenwood, 1984.
(For help and further information, see EDUCATION; SCHOOLS OF CHOICE.)

designated adoption A form of ADOPTION in which an adoption agency handles arrangements for an adoption that originated privately.

detention In government social services, a synonym for protective or emergency CUSTODY; in cases of CHILD ABUSE OR NEGLECT, social workers generally file a *detention request*, calling for a *detention hearing* to be held, usually within 24 hours of filing, to see whether the child should be kept apart from the family until a full court hearing takes place. In EDUCATION, detention refers to the practice of keeping students in school outside of normal school hours, usually for misbehavior or failure to do assigned work.

developmental age (DA) In general, an alternate term for EDUCATIONAL AGE but more specifically a child's score on the GESELL PRESCHOOL TEST; sometimes called *maturational age* (MA).

developmental delay (maturation lag) A significantly longer-than-normal length of time before a child learns certain skills or begins to be able to do certain key kinds of activities, called DEVELOPMENTAL MILESTONES. (For help and further information, see DEVELOPMENTAL SCREENING TESTS; also CHART OF NORMAL DEVELOPMENT on page 507.)

developmental disorders General term used in some quite different ways, referring variously to:

• the characteristic behaviors a child shows at each stage of emotional development, such as crying, STRANGER ANXIETY, and SEPARATION ANXIETY, not in fact disorders at all;
• generally slow development and retention of infantile behavior;
• conditions that are characterized by slower-than-normal development or whose characteristics cause development to be slowed because of increased difficulty, as in MENTAL RETARDATION, AUTISM, EPILEPSY, and some speech and language disorders (see COMMUNICATION SKILLS AND DISORDERS);
• conditions appearing in childhood characterized by delay in development of specific skills or functions but not related to mental problems or inadequate teaching; sometimes called *specific developmental disorders*. Examples include communication disorders and various LEARNING DISABILITIES.
• any medical condition that becomes apparent in youth or adolescence; also called a *developmental disability* (DD).

Because the term is used is so many different ways, parents will be wise to try to get more precise descriptions from educational, psychological, or medical professionals who are evaluating their children.

developmental language disorder Alternate name for a type of communication disorder (see COMMUNICATION SKILLS AND DISORDERS).

developmental milestone The age at which a child begins to be able to do certain key kinds of activities, especially in the area of MOTOR SKILLS, COGNITIVE SKILLS, SELF-HELP SKILLS, SOCIAL SKILLS, and communication skills (see COMMUNICATION SKILLS AND DISORDERS). A CHART OF NORMAL DEVELOPMENT, reproduced on page 507, indicates when, between birth and age six, children first *on the average* begin to do certain things. Note (as the materials accompanying the chart explain) that children may vary widely from the average as to when they reach certain milestones and still be quite normal. But if a child is seriously delayed (called *developmental delay*) in one or more skills areas, parents may want to consult their PEDIATRICIAN to see if there is a problem, especially one that might benefit from early diagnosis and treatment.

developmental schedules   Tables of behavior considered appropriate to various age levels for children being tested with the GESELL PRESCHOOL TEST or the Gesell School Readiness Test—Complete Battery.

developmental screening tests   Various TESTS given to try to identify children who may have LEARNING DISABILITIES or handicaps that might affect learning. They are used to survey a child's abilities and skills in a wide range of areas, including language skills, reasoning, gross and fine MOTOR SKILLS, SOCIAL SKILLS, and general personal development, though the process itself may last no longer than 15 to 20 minutes. Among the most common developmental screening tests are the GESELL PRESCHOOL TEST, the ABC INVENTORY, BRIGANCE® DIAGNOSTIC INVENTORY OF EARLY DEVELOPMENT, EARLY SCREENING INVENTORY, JORDAN LEFT-RIGHT REVERSAL TEST, MEETING STREET SCHOOL SCREENING TEST, and SPECIFIC LANGUAGE DISABILITY TESTS. Screening sometimes includes a DRAW-A-PERSON-type test for indications as to the child's emotional development. Parents are sometimes asked to fill out a questionnaire on the child's medical and developmental background.

For the results to be most reliable, tests should be given to the child one-to-one by a psychologist, teacher, or assistant; it is important that the person be sensitive to children, that children be prepared for testing (see books below), and that the tests chosen be appropriate for the child's cultural and linguistic background. If not, or if parents disagree with the results of the test (feeling that it wrongly identified problems or failed to identify problems), they may want to try to arrange for retesting, since key decisions will made on the basis of the results. Parents should understand that testing of young children is a very uncertain affair, and many tests used for developmental screening were not originally designed for that purpose and lack RELIABILITY. Certainly, if a child was not well on the day of the testing or if the test was disrupted or disturbed in any way, retesting may well be indicated. If results are borderline, retesting after eight to 10 weeks of further development is often appropriate.

Developmental screening tests are the first step in an evaluation process mandated by the EDUCATION FOR ALL HANDICAPPED CHILDREN ACT OF 1975. Through school systems and social services, states are required to have in place programs (such as CHILDFIND) to identify children AT RISK for having such problems and arrange for developmental screening tests to be given. If these indicate a possible problem, the child would then be referred for DIAGNOSTIC ASSESSMENT TESTS, to provide more detailed information on the nature of the problem. Children with obvious handicaps would generally be referred directly for diagnosis.

For help and further information
General Works

Developmental Screening in Early Childhood: A Guide, 3rd edition, by Samuel J. Meisels. Washington, DC: National Association for the Education of Young Children, 1989.

Is Your Child Ready for School? A Parent's Guide to Preschool and Primary School Entrance Tests, by Jacqueline Robinson. New York: Arco, 1990. (Originally published as *The Baby Boards*, 1988.)

Professional Works

Preschool Screening: Identifying Young Children with Developmental and Educational Problems, by R. Richtenstein and H. Ireton. Orlando, FL: Grune & Stratton, 1984.

Preschool Screening: The Measurement and Prediction of Children At-Risk, by K. E. Barnes. Springfield, IL: Thomas, 1982.

Identifying the Developmentally Delayed Child, N. J. Anastasiow, W. K. Frankenburg, and A.W. Fandal, eds. Baltimore: University Park Press, 1982.

Screening and Evaluating the Young Child: A Handbook of Instruments to Use from Infancy to Six Years, by L.E. Southworth, R.L. Burr, and A.E. Cox. Springfield, IL: Thomas, 1981.

(See also TESTS; HANDICAPPED; and specific tests noted above.)

Developmental Test of Visual Perception   Alternate name for the FROSTIG DEVELOPMENTAL TEST OF VISUAL PERCEPTION.

Developmental Test of Visual-Motor Integration (VMI or Beery-Buktenica Test)   A test designed to identify people with problems in VISUAL SKILLS, fine MOTOR SKILLS (especially use of hands), and HAND–EYE coordination. The test offers increasingly difficult geometric figures for the child to copy; a short form is used for children ages two to eight, and a longer form is for adolescents and adults with DEVELOPMENTAL DELAY. Tests are scored according to a manual that contains NORMS by age, with results given in converted SCORES and PERCENTILES. (For help and further information, see TESTS.)

diabetes insipidus   A rare METABOLIC DISORDER, of entirely different origin from the more common DIABETES MELLITUS but with similar symptoms in the early stages, especially excessive thirst (*polydipsia*) and production of great quantities of urine (*polyuria*). Most cases of diabetes insipidus result from the PITUITARY GLAND's inadequate production of the *antidiuretic hormone* (ADH), which controls the amount of water sent out of the body as urine. Diabetes insipidus can, in fact, be a sign of a TUMOR in or damage to the pituitary. Lack of sufficient water to match the enormous output can lead to serious DEHYDRATION, ultimately resulting in COMA and possible serious damage, especially in infants and small children. This kind of diabetes insipidus can be treated with a synthetic form of ADH. A rarer form of the disorder, *nephrogenic diabetes insipidus*, can result from failure of the kidneys to respond to the ADH in the body. This can be a congenital disorder, or it may result from kidney infection (*pyelonephritis*). It cannot be treated with ADH but requires careful control of diet and water intake, with medication to suppress some thirst symptoms.

For help and further information

National Institute of Diabetes, Digestive and Kidney Diseases (NIDDK), 301-496-3583. Publishes various materials, including newsletters, such as *Diabetes Dateline*, and booklets on specific topics, such as *The Diabetes Dictionary*. (For full group information, see DIGESTIVE DISORDERS.)

diabetes mellitus (DM) A disorder in which a person's body is unable to use sugar as it should to provide for energy needs. The problem occurs when the pancreas produces too little or no *insulin*, the HORMONE that is needed to break down the sugar GLUCOSE (the body's main form of energy). As a result, the level of sugar in the blood becomes abnormally high, causing a characteristic set of symptoms, including great thirst and hunger, very frequent urination, fatigue, and weight loss.

There are two main types of diabetes mellitus:

1. *insulin-dependent (Type I)*, in which the pancreas makes very little or no insulin. This form appears quite suddenly, at any age, but usually before the age of 30 and especially in the teens, affecting about two in 1,000 under age 20. To control this form of diabetes, the person must carefully monitor the amount of glucose in the blood, eat a planned diet, get plenty of exercise, and have an injection of insulin each day. This form is also called *juvenile-onset diabetes, insulin-dependent diabetes mellitus (IDDM)*, or *ketosis-prone diabetes*.

2. *noninsulin-dependent (Type II)*, in which the pancreas makes some insulin. For some people with Type II diabetes, a careful diet and regular exercise may be sufficient to control the disease. Others may need to take insulin and other medications as well. Most people with diabetes have the noninsulin-dependent form, which also can appear at any age but usually after age 40, affecting approximately 20 people per 1,000. People with Type II diabetes tend toward OBESITY, and their bodies are thought to resist the effects of insulin. This form is also called *noninsulin-dependent diabetes mellitus (NIDDM), adult-onset diabetes, maturity-onset diabetes*, or *ketosis-resistant diabetes*.

Both main forms of diabetes seem to have some hereditary component. But not everyone who inherits a predisposition toward the disorder actually gets the disease. In Type I, the disease may result when, after a viral infection, an autoimmune reaction destroys the insulin-producing parts of the pancreas. In Type II, the triggering mechanism most often seems to be excessive weight.

If unrecognized or untreated, insulin-dependent diabetes can have serious effects. In the absence of glucose for energy, the body begins to break down its stores of fat, releasing acids (*ketones*) into the blood. The result is *diabetic ketoacidosis*, which can lead to diabetic COMA and DEATH if not reversed.

Although no cure exists, diabetes is a CONTROLLABLE DISEASE. People with insulin-dependent diabetes carefully watch their diets and generally give themselves INJECTIONS one to four times a day, with insulin of animal or synthetic (genetically engineered) origin. Alternatively, some people with hard-to-control diabetes use a device called an *insulin pump*: a needle inserted under the skin pumps a continuous low level of insulin between meals and an extra dose (when the person presses the appropriate buttons) at mealtimes. The aim is to avoid extremes in the levels of glucose in the blood. Too much glucose (*hyperglycemia*) causes symptoms of diabetes to recur. The opposite, too little glucose (*hypoglycemia* or *insulin shock*), can lead to weakness, dizziness, confusion, and sometimes unconsciousness and SEIZURES. To help keep the glucose level in the happy middle, people with Type I diabetes monitor their glucose levels carefully, generally using HOME MEDICAL TESTS.

Diabetes can have serious complications, especially if it has not been well-controlled. These include *retinopathy* (a type of EYE AND VISION PROBLEM involving damage to the retina, resulting from pressure on the blood vessels), *neuropathy* (damage to peripheral nerve fibers), ulcers (raw sores) on the feet that can turn gangrenous, KIDNEY AND UROLOGICAL DISORDERS, and periodontal problems (see TEETH). People with diabetes are also at some increased risk of later developing high BLOOD PRESSURE, CATARACTS, atherosclerosis (constriction of the arteries), and other circulatory disorders. Most people with diabetes can lead relatively normal lives, though there is a slightly reduced life expectancy. Women with diabetes can generally have a normal PREGNANCY.

During pregnancy, some women may develop a form of diabetes, called *gestational diabetes mellitus (GDM)* or *Type III diabetes*. It is important to recognize the diabetes and bring it under control early to lessen the risk of damage to the child and complications in the mother (see PREGNANCY AND DIABETES below). In most cases this form of diabetes disappears after CHILDBIRTH, though in some cases it may signal future onset of diabetes.

For help and further information

American Diabetes Association (ADA)
National Service Center
P.O. Box 25757
1660 Duke Street
Alexandria, VA 22314
703-549-1500, toll-free number (U.S. except VA) 800-232-3472
Robert S. Bolan, Executive Vice President
Organization for diabetics, their families and friends, and professionals who work with them. Provides information and services for patients and their families through programs in local

Pregnancy and Diabetes

Infants born to women with diabetes are at greatly increased risk for prematurity, congenital defects, excessively high birth weight, respiratory distress syndrome, and other conditions that increase overall mortality, especially when the mother's blood glucose levels remain high during pregnancy. Risks of maternal complications are also increased by established diabetes. These problems are reduced by maintaining strict control of blood glucose levels before and throughout pregnancy; dietary counseling is important in helping patients to achieve such control.

In some women who are not otherwise diagnosed as diabetic, pregnancy is associated with significant alterations in carbohydrate metabolism such that overnight fasting leads to lower-than-normal blood sugar and insulin levels, and carbohydrate consumption leads to higher-than-normal levels. These changes, which are most marked near the end of pregnancy, are referred to as gestational diabetes. Because current diagnostic methods cannot easily distinguish between established and gestational diabetes, it is uncertain whether gestational diabetes itself—in the absence of preexisting undiagnosed diabetes—increases risks to mothers and infants.

All authorities agree that diabetes screening is indicated for pregnant women with risk factors for overt diabetes: a previous history of gestational diabetes, a large-for-gestational-age infant, excess amniotic fluid during pregnancy, excretion of sugar in urine, increased thirst or urination, or recurrent vaginal or urinary tract infections. Because diabetes screening can identify diabetes in mothers who may not have been diagnosed previously and who might benefit from preventive services, various authorities recommend screening for all pregnant women, including administration of an oral glucose tolerance test between the 24th and 28th weeks of pregnancy, or earlier for women with risk factors. Others, however, believe that current understanding of gestational diabetes is insufficient to justify universal screening at this time.

Source: *The Surgeon General's Report on Nutrition and Health.* Rocklin, CA: Prima, 1988.

212-889-7575, toll-free number (U.S. except NY) 800-223-1138 (for local chapters only)
Gloria Pennington, Executive Director
Organization for people with juvenile diabetes or insulin-dependent diabetes. Funds research; provides information and services through local affiliates; publishes many materials, including quarterly newsletter *Tie Lines*, magazine *Countdown*, and booklets such as *Pregnancy and Diabetes*, *Your Child Has Diabetes*, *A Child with Diabetes Is in Your Care*, *What You Should Know About Diabetes*, *Information About Insulin*, and *Self Blood Glucose Monitoring*.

National Diabetes Information Clearinghouse
Box NDIC
Bethesda, MD 20892
301-468-2162

Federal information clearinghouse on diabetes as a disease. Operated by the U.S. Department of Health and Human Services. Provides information and referrals; publishes various materials, including *Facts About Insulin-Dependent Diabetes* and *Diabetic Retinopathy*.

National Institute of Diabetes, Digestive and Kidney Diseases (NIDDK), 301-496-3583. Publishes various materials, including research materials, newsletters such as *Diabetes Dateline*, and booklets on specific topics, such as *Sports and Exercise for People with Diabetes*, *Noninsulin-Dependent Diabetes*, *Periodontal Disease and Diabetes*, *A Guide for Patients*, *Dental Tips for Diabetics*, and *The Diabetes Dictionary*. (For full group information, see DIGESTIVE DISORDERS.)

Joslin Diabetes Center (JDC)
15 Joslin Place
Boston, MA 02215
617-732-2400

Private center specializing in research and treatment of diabetes. Provides information; publishes various materials, including *Joslin Magazine* and books *A Guide for Women with Diabetes Who Are Pregnant . . . or Plan to Be*, *A Guide for Parents of Children and Youth with Diabetes*, *Know Your Diabetes, Know Yourself*, and *Joslin Diabetes Manual*.

National Eye Institute (NEI), 301-496-5248. Publishes fact sheet *Early Treatment Diabetic Retinopathy Study (ETDRS)*. (For full group information, see EYE AND VISION PROBLEMS.)

La Leche League International (LLLI), 312-455-7730. Publishes *The Diabetic Mother and Breastfeeding*. (For full group information, see BREASTFEEDING.)

Other reference sources

If Your Child Has Diabetes: An Answer Book for Parents. New York: Perigee/Putnam, 1990.
The Diabetic's Book: All Your Questions Answered, revised edition, by June Biermann and Barbara Toohey. Los Angeles: Tarcher, 1990.

affiliates; publishes numerous materials, including magazines *Diabetes Forecast* and *Kid's Corner*, series of *Diabetes and You* booklets (for Children, Teens, Young Adults, and Parents), books *Children with Diabetes*, *Diabetes in the Family*, *Diabetes and Pregnancy: What to Expect*, *Gestational Diabetes: What to Expect*, and diet guidelines and cookbooks.

Juvenile Diabetes Foundation International (JDFI)
432 Park Avenue South, 16th Floor
New York, NY 10016

Living with Diabetes, by Barbara Taylor. New York: Watts, 1989.

Living with Diabetes, by Heather Maclean and Barbara Oram. Cheektowaga, NY: University of Toronto Press, 1988.

Health Care U.S.A., by Jean Carper. New York: Prentice Hall, 1987. Resource for general and specific health-care information, as for various types of diabetes and related pancreas problems; lists major centers for treatment or research, leading endocrinologists, specialists carrying out diabetes research trials, centers for pancreas transplants, manufacturers offering products for diabetics, and other information.

Diabetes: The Comprehensive Self-Mangement Handbook, by John F. Aloia. Garden City, NY: Doubleday, 1984.

The Diabetes Self-Help Method, by C.M. Peterson. New York: Simon & Schuster, 1984.

The Diabetes Fact Book, by Theodore G. Duncan. New York: Scribner, 1982.

Diabetes: A Guide to Self Management for Patients and Their Families, by Terri Kivelowitz. Englewood Cliffs, NJ: Prentice-Hall, 1981.

Diabetes, A Practical Guide to Healthy Living by Dr. James W. Anderson. New York: Arco, 1981.

The Diabetic's Total Health Book, by June Biermann and Barbara Toohey. Los Angeles: Tarcher, 1980.

A Portrait of Me, by Barbara Aiello and Jeffrey Shulman. Frederick, MD: 21st Century, 1988. Part of The Kids on the Block Book Series for readers ages 8 to 12, focusing on children with problems or disabilities.

Diabetes, Liver and Digestive Diseases, by Wrynn Smith, Ph.D. New York: Facts on File, 1987. For young readers.

diagnostic assessment test A test designed to identify specific problems and needs. In education, such tests are often given after DEVELOPMENTAL SCREENING TESTS have indicated the possible existence of LEARNING DISABILITIES or handicaps (see HANDICAPPED). Diagnostic assessment tests are then used to provide more detailed information about the problem or handicap; information from these tests are used to help plan INDIVIDUALIZED EDUCATION PROGRAMS (IEPs) for the child, under the EDUCATION FOR ALL HANDICAPPED CHILDREN ACT OF 1975. Examples of common tests used in diagnostic assessment are GESELL PRESCHOOL TEST, ILLINOIS TEST OF PSYCHOLINGUISTIC ABILITIES, KAUFMAN ASSESSMENT BATTERY FOR CHILDREN (K-ABC), McCARTHY SCALES OF CHILDREN'S ABILITIES (MSCA), STANFORD-BINET INTELLIGENCE TEST, and WECHSLER PRESCHOOL AND PRIMARY SCALE OF INTELLIGENCE (WPPSI).

Diagnostic assessment tests such as these are also often used for placement purposes, as ADMISSION TESTS (popularly dubbed "Baby Boards") for selective PRESCHOOLS, for example, or for indications of what type of class a child should be placed in.

For help and further information

Developmental Screening in Early Childhood: A Guide, third edition, by Samuel J. Meisels. Washington, DC: National Association for the Education of Young Children, 1989.

Is Your Child Ready for School? A Parent's Guide to Preschool and Primary School Entrance Tests, by Jacqueline Robinson. New York: Arco, 1990. (Originally published as *The Baby Boards*, 1988.)

(See also TESTS and specific tests noted above.)

Diagnostic Reading Scales (DMR or **Spache)** An individually administered TEST of READING skills for children, a verbal test focusing on word recognition, reading comprehension (oral and silent), PHONICS, and word analysis. The DMR is used as a DIAGNOSTIC ASSESSMENT TEST to identify a student's specific strengths and weaknesses in reading, for purposes of class placement and possible REMEDIAL INSTRUCTION. (For help and further information, see TESTS.)

dialysis Use of an artificial machine to filter waste products from the blood when a person's kidneys are unable to function, either temporarily or permanently. The two main kinds of dialysis are *hemodialysis* and *peritoneal dialysis*.

For hemodialysis, surgeons implant a connection between an artery (A) and vein (V) in a patient. In an AV SHUNT, connected tubes outside the body (covered with a sterile bandage when not in use) link an artery and vein, with blood flowing through it; during dialysis, the connector is removed, and blood flows into the dialysis machine and then (once cleansed) out of it and back into the body. In an AV *fistula*, an artificial connection is surgically created between a vein and an artery inside the body (with no part of it exposed and so no need to wear a bandage); during dialysis, the machine is connected to the fistula by needles, to do the necessary cleansing. Hemodialysis must be done two to three times a week and takes about four to six hours per visit. The patient must also follow a carefully restricted diet and take various drugs and VITAMINS.

While performing the same function as hemodialysis, peritoneal dialysis differs in that the process is continuous and takes place in the patient's abdomen (*peritoneal cavity*), using the peritoneal membrane itself as the filter. A hollow tube (CATHETER) is surgically implanted in the patient's abdomen. With *intermittent peritoneal dialysis* (IPD), a patient is hooked up to a machine several times a day in a procedure that can be performed at home. But peritoneal dialysis can also be done in ways that allow greater freedom of movement and life-style.

With *continuous ambulatory peritoneal dialysis* (CAPD), a two-liter bag of a special dialysate solution is connected to the catheter and allowed to drain by gravity into the abdomen. The still-connected empty bag is then tucked inside the patient's clothing, and while normal everyday activities continue, the blood's waste products are filtered out; then, after four to five hours, the bag is taken out, and the fluid with the filtered

---

Preventing Diaper Rash

Parents can prevent diaper rash in their infants by:

- changing diapers frequently
- rinsing the baby's diaper area with clean water at each diaper change
- rinsing cotton diapers thoroughly before washing them
- avoiding "super-absorbent" disposable diapers
- leaving off plastic pants whenever possible
- applying a layer of zinc oxide paste or diaper rash ointment to any irritated area.

If your baby gets a diaper rash in spite of this, you should:

- Leave off plastic pants (or plastic-covered disposable diapers) except when absolutely necessary. Using two or more cloth diapers together at nap time and at night will make this less messy.
- Leave the baby's diaper area completely uncovered for a few hours each day (nap time or early evening is most convenient). Be sure to place a couple of diapers under the baby to prevent soiling.
- Apply a thin layer of zinc oxide paste or diaper rash ointment to any irritated area after cleansing at each diaper change.

If the problem persists, the doctor or clinic staff may recommend another medication. Be sure to wash your hands with soap and water after diapering to avoid passing infection.

Source: *Infant Care* (1989). Prepared for the Public Health Service by the Bureau of Maternal and Child Health and Resources Development.

---

waste products drains into the bag, which is then discarded. This kind of exchange is made four to six times a day, while the person is able to go to school or to work or otherwise live a normal life. And because dialysis is continuous, diet is not restricted. It does, however, carry the risk of *peritonitis*, a dangerous infection of the lining of the peritoneal cavity, so sterility is important in carrying out this procedure. An alternative form, called *continuous cycling peritoneal dialysis* (CCPD), uses filtering during the day as in CAPD, but the actual exchange of fluids is made only at night, with a machine recycling solutions several times each night.

For help and further information

National Association of Patients on Hemodialysis and Transplantation (NAPHT)
211 East 43rd Street
New York, NY 10017
212-867-4486
Susan Kaufer, Executive Director
Organization of patients with kidney disease and their families. Provides information; encourages formation of local mutual-support groups; offers special services, such as summer camp for children on dialysis; maintains international directory of dialysis centers; publishes various materials, including magazine and pamphlets: *Living with Renal Failure*, *Renal Failure and Diabetes*, and *Na-K, Sodium-Potassium Counter* (for use in dialysis patient's special diet).
(See also KIDNEY AND UROLOGICAL DISORDERS.)

diaper rash   Localized redness and irritation of an infant's skin, from prolonged contact with urine and feces and from the ammonia produced by bacteria working on them; a benign kind of SKIN DISORDER.

diaphragm   A form of BIRTH CONTROL using a slightly cup-shaped disk of soft rubber, with a flexible rim, that fits over the CERVIX. Filled with a SPERMICIDE jelly or cream before insertion, the diaphragm forms both a physical and chemical barrier to SPERM. The spermicide or the rubber in the diaphragm can sometimes cause allergic reactions in the woman or her partner. (For other possible problems, such as birth defects, see SPERMICIDE.) Unlike the CERVICAL SPONGE, the diaphragm is a prescription device that must be fitted by a physician. It is to be inserted within an hour before intercourse and left in place for at least six hours afterward, with additions of spermicidal cream or jelly if intercourse is repeated. The diaphragm's effectiveness as a contraceptive is estimated by the Food and Drug Administration as between 80 and 98 percent. (For help and further information, see BIRTH CONTROL.) More generally, a diaphragm is a partition of muscle and tissue between the chest and abdomen.

diaphragmatic hernia   A kind of BIRTH DEFECT in which an abnormal hole in the diaphragm allows some abdominal organs, especially the intestines, to move into the space normally occupied by the lungs, a situation that can be identified by some kinds of PRENATAL TESTING, notably ULTRASOUND. Often the chest space becomes so crowded that the lungs cannot develop normally, so a baby is unable to breathe independently and often dies soon after birth. New experimental techniques allow this defect to be corrected with IN UTERO SURGERY.

diarrhea   Excessive fluids in and frequency of bowel movements, compared to what is normal in a particular person. Diarrhea often results from gastrointestinal infection but may be a symptom of a wider disorder, such as LACTOSE INTOLERANCE or IRRITABLE BOWEL SYNDROME. In children, especially infants, diarrhea can be extremely dangerous, causing a possibly fatal DEHYDRATION (loss of body fluids). (See BABY'S BOWELS—WHAT'S NORMAL, WHAT'S NOT on page 148.) Treatment often involves giving a special fluid mixture containing ELECTROLYTES, to replace what has been lost. (For help and further information, see DIGESTIVE DISORDERS.)

Dick-Read method   A popular form of natural or PREPARED CHILDBIRTH, also called the *Read method*.

diethylstilbestrol   Full name of the drug DES.

differential curriculum   Alternate term for functional curriculum (see CURRICULUM).

differentiation   The first stage of a baby's SEPARATION–INDIVIDUATION process.

diffusing capacity   A kind of PULMONARY FUNCTION TEST.

digestive disorders   Problems and diseases affecting the long, complex system by which food is broken into substances to be used in the body and waste products to be excreted. In the digestive system, food enters the mouth, where is it chewed and softened with saliva and then swallowed in the throat and the long tube called the *esophagus*, where muscle contractions (*peristalsis*) propel the food into the stomach. The stomach produces hydrochloric acid and various digestive enzymes, mixing these with the food by muscle action for two to four hours.

From the stomach, the food, by now semiliquid, is moved on to the *duodenum*, the first part of the small intestine, where more digestive enzymes (from the liver, gall bladder, and pancreas) are added to further break down the food, and then on through the small intestine, which produces more enzymes to complete the digestive process. Nutrients from the digested food are absorbed from the lining of the small intestine into the blood and lymph vessels. The undigested material is moved on from the last part of the small intestine (*ileum*) into the large intestine (*colon*), where most remaining fluid is absorbed by the lining. The balance is then moved into the last part of the large intestine, the *rectum*, to be excreted through the *anus* as *feces*, or *stool*.

The body produces various HORMONES that direct the digestive operation, triggering different organs to produce enzymes and to move the food with muscular contractions. Between various sections of the digestive system are ringlike muscles called *sphincters* that control the movement of food; the one between the stomach and the esophagus is the *lower esophageal sphincter* (LES), that between the stomach and the small intestine is the *pyloric sphincter*, and that at the anus, which controls bowel movements, is the *anal sphincter*.

The digestive process can be disrupted in a number of ways. Among those that commonly affect children are:

1. *congenital abnormalities*, malformations of the digestive system present at birth.

   • CLEFT LIP AND PALATE, making feeding difficult.
   • *atresia* (abnormal closure), requiring immediate surgical correction. In *esophageal atresia*, the esophagus reaches a dead end; atresia may also affect the intestines. In BILIARY ATRESIA, openings for the liver's bile ducts are absent or malformed.
   • *stenosis* (abnormal narrowing), often requiring surgical correction. In *pyloric stenosis*, the stomach outlet (pyloric sphincter) is narrowed so that food cannot freely pass into the small intestine. Stenosis can also affect the intestines; in *anal stenosis*, the passage is too small to allow for excreting stool.

   • *Meckel's diverticulum*, a small hollow sac near the end of the small intestine; a common disorder, which can be symptomless but can cause infection, obstruction, or sometimes severe bleeding, so surgery and BLOOD TRANSFUSIONS may be required. Symptoms of an inflamed diverticulum are similar to those of APPENDICITIS.
   • *imperforate anus*, in which the anus is closed off and needs to be surgically opened immediately after birth.

2. *infection and inflammation*:

   • The esophagus can become inflamed and sometimes even torn or ruptured if there is frequent VOMITING (as in BULIMIA or some KIDNEY AND UROLOGICAL DISORDERS), if a foreign body is swallowed, or if corrosive chemicals are swallowed. This can cause narrowing the esophagus, making swallowing difficult.
   • The stomach, though normally protected by stomach acids, is prey to various gastrointestinal infections, going under the umbrella term *gastroenteritis*. Infections of the ileum and colon are called *ileitis* and *colitis*. These may be caused by bacteria, viruses, worms, or parasites, such as the protozoa *giardiasis* and *amebiasis*. Some of these come under the rough heading of "food poisoning," and some can be quite serious, including cholera, typhoid fever, and BOTULISM. It is important to treat such infections with whatever medical means are available, because continuing inflammation and infection can seriously weaken the body.
   • infections in localized areas, such as APPENDICITIS (inflammation of the APPENDIX, a tiny projection off the small intestine).
   • INFLAMMATORY BOWEL DISEASE (*Crohn's disease* and *ulcerative colitis*), affecting the digestive tract, especially the small intestine.

3. *other disorders*, including rarer problems.

   • *achalasia*, in which the muscle that controls the passage between the esophagus and the stomach fails to relax, sometimes causing vomiting and swallowing difficulty.
   • *peptic ulcer*, a raw sore in the gastrointestinal tract, generally in the stomach, esophagus, or duodenum. Generally a disorder affecting adults, it can sometimes occur in children, especially if peptic ulcers "run in the family." They are exacerbated by alcohol, coffee, tea, aspirin, large meals, and general stress but often respond to some medication and change of eating patterns. When serious, considerable bleeding may result and surgery may be required.
   • telescoping (*intussusception*, or *prolapse*) or twisting (*volvulus*) of the small intestine, sometimes linked with Meckel's diverticulum, a small polyp, or volvulus of the stomach. These disorders are most often found in young children, leading to COLIC-like reactions, vomiting, and blood in the stool. Often diagnosed by BARIUM X-RAY EXAMINATION, surgery may be required to clear the obstruction.

Baby's Bowels—What's Normal, What's Not

Babies' first bowel movements, usually in the hospital, are sticky and greenish-black. After a week or two, they will become lighter, gradually turn yellow, be less sticky, and remain that way for the next year. A baby may have anywhere from four to 10 movements a day to one movement every three or four days. After the first month, the number of bowel movements will usually be less—three or four times a day or as few as once a week. As long as the bowel movements are soft, your baby is not constipated.

Movements may be as firm as those of a normal adult or as soft as loose scrambled eggs and may be yellow, green, or brown. The color, consistency, and odor will be different with breast milk or different kinds of formulas.

For a breastfed infant, the bowel movements usually look yellow or yellow-green and are soft to runny. Generally, your baby should have at least two to three bowel movements a day for the first few weeks. This is a sign that your baby is getting enough milk.

Your baby may turn red in the face and cry with each bowel movement or may seem totally unaware of them. Both of these are normal.

Soiled diapers should be changed soon after a bowel movement to keep the baby as clean and comfortable as possible.

Constipation

Constipation is when the bowel movements are hard, dry, and difficult to pass, no matter how frequent or infrequent they may be. Constipation should not be a problem if you breastfeed. If you bottlefeed, one tablespoon of light corn syrup in a four-ounce bottle of water (for infants younger than three months) or one tablespoon of prune juice added to one of the baby's bottles (for older babies) may soften the bowel movements. If not, ask your doctor or clinic staff what to do. Do *not* use mineral oil, castor oil, adult laxatives, or enemas without medical advice.

Diarrhea

Sometimes your baby will have frequent loose or watery bowel movements. Watery bowel movements can cause a baby to lose more fluid than he or she is drinking. This "dehydration" (loss of liquid) can be a true medical emergency. Even a single, huge, explosive, watery bowel movement can be an emergency in an infant one to two months old, especially if he or she has a poor appetite or is vomiting. *Call or visit your doctor or clinic right away when there is one or more large watery bowel movements*.

Blood in bowel movement

Slight blood streaking on the outside of a bowel movement is usually caused by a small sore or tear ("fissure") in the anus and is not a cause for alarm. The tear and the bleeding can often be cured by keeping the stools soft with light corn syrup or prune juice or a remedy from your doctor.

Do not delay calling or going to your doctor or clinic right away if there is bloody diarrhea or if fresh blood or blood clots are passed with the bowel movements.

Source: *Infant Care* (1989). Prepared for the Public Health Service by the Bureau of Maternal and Child Health and Resources Development.

- *familial polyposis*, a rare inherited disease in which many polyps grow in the colon; associated with later high risk of colon CANCER.
- *malabsorption*, impaired ability to digest food, especially to absorb nutrients from it, as in cases of METABOLIC DISORDERS or other types of digestive problems.
- IRRITABLE BOWEL SYNDROME, also called *spastic colon*.

Many seemingly more minor ailments can be serious in young children, including vomiting, DIARRHEA, and CONSTIPATION (see BABY'S BOWELS—WHAT'S NORMAL, WHAT'S NOT, above). Inability to control bowel movements, as because of neurological impairment, is called INCONTINENCE; if it seems without physical cause, it may be called *soiling* or ENCOPRESIS.

Many other kinds of disorders are closely related to digestive disorders, including pernicious ANEMIA, DIABETES MELLITUS, CELIAC SPRUE (gluten intolerance), CYSTIC FIBROSIS, hematochromatosis, kidney problems, LACTOSE INTOLERANCE, LIVER PROBLEMS, and various metabolic disorders, such as ALPHA-1 ANTITRYPSIN DEFICIENCY and GLYCOGEN STORAGE DISEASE.

Among the specialists who work with the digestive system are the GASTROENTEROLOGIST and PROCTOLOGIST. Various kinds of MEDICAL TESTS, devices, and procedures may be used in relation to digestive disorders, including COLONOSCOPE, GASTROSCOPE, PROCTOSCOPE, SIGMOIDOSCOPE, OSTOMY (including *colostomy* and *ileostomy*), and barium X-ray examinations.

For help and further information

American Digestive Disease Society (ADDS)
7720 Wisconsin Avenue, NW
Bethesda, MD 20814
301-223-0179, Gutline 301-652-9293 (business hours and Tues. 7–9 PM EST)
Organization for people with digestive diseases. Provides information and referral; offers counseling; operates hotline; publishes various materials, including magazine *Living Healthy*, diet books such as *The Irritable Bowel Diet*, *The Inflammatory Bowel Diet*, *The Lactose Intolerance Diet*, and *The Ulcer Diet*, and booklets such as *Living Healthy: Food and Why It Hurts*.

National Institute of Diabetes and Digestive and Kidney Diseases (NIDDK)
9000 Rockville Pike
Building 31, Room 9A04
Bethesda, MD 20892
301-496-3583
Federal arm, one of the U.S. National Institutes of Health, sponsoring research on diabetes, digestive diseases, kidney diseases, and related ailments. Provides information; publishes various materials, including *Digestive Health and Disease: A Glossary*, *Facts and Fallacies About Digestive Diseases*, *Your Digestive System and How It Works*, *Smoking and Your Digestive System*, *About Stomach Ulcers*, and *Diagnostic Tests for Digestive Diseases: X-rays and Ultrasound*.

National Digestive Disease Information Clearinghouse
Box NDDIC
Bethesda, MD 20892
301-468-6344
Federally funded clearinghouse for information on digestive diseases, a service of the National Institute of Diabetes and Digestive and Kidney Diseases (NIDDK). Provides information to public and health professionals; makes referrals; publishes various materials, including brochures *Facts and Fallacies About Digestive Diseases* and *Digestive Health and Disease: A Glossary* and fact sheets: *Irritable Bowel Syndrome*, *About Stomach Ulcers*, *Inflammatory Bowel Disease*, *IBD and IBS: Two Very Different Problems*, *Diarrhea: Infectious and Other Causes*, *What Is Constipation?*, *What Is Hiatal Hernia?*, *Lactose Intolerance*, *Resources on Dietary Fiber*, *Your Digestive System and How It Works*, and *Diagnostic Tests for Digestive Diseases: X-Rays and Ultrasound*.

National Foundation for Ileitis and Colitis (NFIC), 212-685-3440. (For full group information, see INFLAMMATORY BOWEL DISEASE.)

Familial Polyposis Registry, Toronto General Hospital, 416-595-3934. International network of registries. Publishes various materials, including quarterly newsletter *GI Polyposis and Related Conditions* and *Familial Polyposis: A Guide for Patients and their Families*. (For full group information, see CANCER.)

G.I. Polyposis and Hereditary Colon Cancer Registry, The Moore Clinic, Johns Hopkins Hospital, 301-955-4040 or 955-3875. International network of registries. Publishes various materials, including quarterly newsletter *GI Polyposis and Related Conditions*, quarterly *Ostomy*, and *Family Studies in Genetic Disorders*. (For full group information, see CANCER.)

Intestinal Multiple Polyposis and Colorectal Cancer (IMPACC), 301-791-7526. Publishes various materials, including newsletters *G.I. Polyposis and Related Conditions* and *Ostomy Quarterly*, *Hereditary Intestinal Polyps: A Guide for Patients and Families*, and *Family Studies in Genetic Disorders*. (For full group information, see CANCER.)

United Ostomy Association (UOA), 213-413-5510. (For full group information, see OSTOMY.)

Other reference sources

Gut Reactions: Understanding Symptoms of the Digestive Tract, by W. Grant Thompson. New York: Plenum, 1989. Includes material on irritable bowel syndrome.
Health Care U.S.A., by Jean Carper. New York: Prentice Hall, 1987. Resource for general and specific health-care information, as for various digestive diseases, including bowel diseases, ulcers, liver transplants and donations, and liver problems such as hepatitis, biliary atresia, hemochromatosis, alpha-1 antitrypsin deficiency, and Wilson's disease; lists centers for treatment or research in gastroenterology and digestive diseases, centers and specialists performing liver transplants, manufacturers offering products for diabetics, and other information.
The Great American Stomach Book, by Maureen Mylander. New York: Ticknor and Fields, 1982.
Food and Digestion, revised edition, by Steve Parker. New York: Watts, 1990. For young readers.
(See also CONSTIPATION; DIARRHEA; DIABETES; INFLAMMATORY BOWEL DISEASE; IRRITABLE BOWEL SYNDROME; KIDNEY AND UROLOGICAL DISORDERS; LIVER PROBLEMS; METABOLIC DISORDERS; OSTOMY.)

dilation During LABOR, the widening of the CERVIX, generally to about four inches, in preparation for the actual DELIVERY of a baby.

diphtheria A bacterial illness that was once a major childhood killer but is now extremely rare in those areas in which most people have received IMMUNIZATION—usually from a combination DTP VACCINE, which also immunizes against TETANUS (lockjaw) and PERTUSSIS (whooping cough). Passed through droplets in the air, as from coughing or sneezing, from infected people or unaffected CARRIERS, the diphtheria bacteria cause a membrane to form in the throat; this may obstruct swallowing and breathing and sometimes requires a TRACHEOSTOMY to maintain breathing. Although generally responsive to antibiotics such as penicillin in the early stages, if diphtheria takes hold, it produces a powerful, life-threatening toxin (poison). This can sometimes be treated with ANTITOXINS but causes PARALYSIS, heart failure, and bronchial PNEUMONIA in many, causing death in one out of 10 patients. The diphtheria vaccine does not provide lifelong protection, and a booster is recommended every 10 years, generally combined with tetanus in the TD VACCINE.

For help and further information

National Institute of Allergy and Infectious Diseases (NIAID), 301-496-5717. (For full group information, see ALLERGY.)

National Institute of Child Health and Human Development (NICHD), 301-496-5133. (For full group information, see PREGNANCY.)

diplegia PARALYSIS of like parts on both sides of the body, such as both legs or both sides of the face.

Comparison of Discipline and Punishment

Discipline	Punishment
Can be given before, during, or after an event	Is usually given after an event
Focuses on developing internal controls to affect future behavior	Focuses on external control, which may or may not affect behavior
Stresses generalizing learning	May focus only on past event
Has a rational, educational purpose	May result from frustration or anger and irrationally inflict pain
Recognizes individual worth and capabilities	Is often dehumanizing and denigrating of abilities
Can forge stronger interpersonal bonds	Usually causes deterioration of relationships
Uses authority figure as role model	Stresses submission to authority figure

---

diploma A formal document certifying that a student has successfully completed a course of study, generally offered at GRADUATION from a HIGH SCHOOL, COLLEGE, or GRADUATE SCHOOL; sometimes called a *degree, parchment,* or *sheepskin,* especially at the college level. Colleges that give degrees too easily or even fraudulently, for no work at all, are sometimes called *diploma mills* or *degree mills.*

diplopia Double vision, as may result from a BRAIN TUMOR or HEAD INJURY. (See EYE AND VISION PROBLEMS.)

disabilities A general term used alternatively with handicaps (see HANDICAPPED). DEVELOPMENTAL DISORDERS or disabilities is a widely used umbrella term, often referring to those handicaps that emerge during the course of a child's growth and development.

discipline Within the family, guidance and training to help someone—usually a child or someone less experienced—to develop self-control and conduct appropriate to given situations. As regards children, discipline is both a PARENTS' RIGHT and a PARENTS' RESPONSIBILITY, the primary training of a child being a parental prerogative and the state requiring that the parent exercise SUPERVISION and control in the process of teaching the child self-control.

Discipline was long considered almost synonymous with punishment, especially CORPORAL PUNISHMENT, but the line between acceptable corporal punishment and child abuse is in considerable flux (see CHILD ABUSE AND NEGLECT), with social norms changing and state laws having various definitions of what constitutes child abuse. More important, some crucial distinctions are now made between discipline and punishment, with discipline seen as a positive, corrective approach and punishment as a negative, often destructive one.

One key underlying idea in the modern view of discipline is *positive reinforcement,* an idea taken from psychology. In essence, it holds that you should focus on rewarding children for doing things you want them to keep on doing or for making attempts in the right direction, the rewards often being smiles, hugs, and attention, though sometimes more tangible treats. The corollary is to withhold reinforcement (rather than negatively punish) for behavior that you do not wish to see. Reserve sharp no's or punishment, if necessary, for dangerous situations, where you must protect the child first, before guiding behavior for future situations.

Among the many alternatives to punishment, perhaps the most important, if the child's behavior is unruly, is a brief time-out, a cooling-off period with the child separated from general activity but without humiliation or great fuss. Parents sometimes need a time-out, too. Punishment given in frustration or anger can escalate to child abuse; wise parents will not act in anger but will cool off in another room, after first seeing that a young child is in a safe setting, such as a crib or playpen.

Beyond that, experts agree, it is important to set basic rules for behavior, make sure the child is clear as to what they are, and be consistent about application of the rules. No matter what the child's age, but especially with very young children, you should try to make very clear precisely what behavior you are focusing on and be consistent in your approach. Effective discipline also benefits from some foresightedness—such as forestalling problems before they begin by distracting the child or by planning a situation to avoid the problem in the first place—and creativity in coming up with alternatives.

Ideally, parents should involve children in discussing and developing alternatives to problem behavior (incidentally, also improving the child's problem-solving skills), helping them to see the longer-term consequences of their behavior, which will aid in their SOCIAL SKILLS and COGNITIVE DEVELOPMENT. Parents are role models for their children, who will tend to copy parental behavior, so the parent's most important role is to guide the child in developing rules of action.

For help and further information

National Association for the Education of Young Children (NAEYC), 202-232-8777; 800-424-2460. Publishes pamphlet *A Guide to Discipline* and flyers *Helping Children Learn Self-Control: A Guide to Discipline* and *Love and Learn: Discipline for Young Children.* (For full group information, see PRESCHOOL.)

National Parents and Teachers Association (National PTA—National Congress of Parents and Teachers), 312-787-0977. Publishes materials on specific topics, including discipline.

National Center for the Study of Corporal Punishment and Alternatives in the Schools (NCSCPAS), 215-787-6091. Publishes journal *Discipline*. (For full group information, see CORPORAL PUNISHMENT.)

National Center to Abolish Corporal Punishment in Schools (NCACPS), 614-221-8829. Publishes newsletter, fact sheets, and book *What Are My Alternatives to Corporal Punishment?*. (For full group information, see CORPORAL PUNISHMENT.)

Toughlove
P.O. Box 1069
Doylestown, PA 18901
215-348-7090
Teresa Quinn, Executive Director
Network of mutual-support groups of and for parents of problem adolescents, including those involved with drug and alcohol abuse. Encourages setting of basic behavior standards and withdrawal of privileges for breaking rules; in extreme cases advises barring children from home, with members providing shelter until rules are agreed to; runs Toughlove for Kids program, designed to encourage teenagers to stay in school; publishes various materials, including *Toughlove, A Self-Help Manual for Kids in Trouble* and *Toughlove, A Self-Help Manual for Parents Troubled by Teenage Behavior*.

Other reference sources

Teach Your Child to Behave: Disciplining with Love from Two to Eight Years, by Dr. Charles E. Schaefer and Theresa Foy DiGeronimo. New York: New American Library, 1990.
Good Kids, Bad Behavior: Helping Children Learn Self-Discipline, by Peter A. Williamson. New York: Simon & Schuster, 1990.
Teaching Children Self-Discipline . . . at Home and at School, by Thomas Gordon. New York: Times Books, 1989.
Disciplining Your Preschooler: And Feeling Good About It, by Mitch Golant and Susan Golant. Chicago: Contemporary, 1989.
The Time-Out Solution: A Parent's Guide for Handling Everyday Behavior Problems, by Lynn Clark. Chicago: Contemporary, 1989.
Don't Take It Out on Your Kids! A Parent's and Teacher's Guide to Positive Discipline, by Katharine C. Kersey. Washington, DC: Acropolis, 1989.
Loving Your Child Is Not Enough: Positive Discipline That Works, by Nancy Samalin with Martha Moraghan Jablow. New York: Penguin, 1988. Available from La Leche League International.
Discipline: Kids Are Worth It!, by Barbara Coloroso. Audiocassette available from La Leche League International.
Saying No and Meaning It: A Guide for Parents. New York: National Urban League, 1986.
How to Talk So Kids Will Listen, by Adele Faber and Elaine Mazlish. Book and/or audiocassette available from La Leche League International.

Making Children Mind Without Losing Yours, by Kevin Leman. Old Tappan, NJ: Revell, 1984.
For Your Own Good: Hidden Cruelty in Child Rearing and the Roots of Violence, by Alice Miller. New York: Farrar, Straus & Giroux, 1983.
Lee Canter's Assertive Discipline for Parents, by Lee Canter, with Marlene Canter. Santa Monica, CA: Canter & Assoc., 1982.
Toughlove. 1985; released 1989. Producer: Ervin Zavada. Director: Glenn Jordan. 95-minute video from Fries Home Video, 6922 Hollywood Boulevard, Los Angeles, CA 90028. For ages 11 to adult.
(See also CORPORAL PUNISHMENT; CHILD ABUSE AND NEGLECT; also PARENT'S BOOKSHELF on page 566.)

disclosing tablets In dental care, tablets that harmlessly tint areas of the TEETH that have not been brushed thoroughly. Such tablets are especially useful for young children, up to perhaps age eight, as they are learning to brush their own teeth.

discovery learning A LEARNING STYLE in which a child is given information or materials about a variety of specific situations and learns to draw a general conclusion or rule from them; also called *inductive learning*.

disinhibition Pattern of responding to situations without constraint, often found in children with LEARNING DISABILITIES or MENTAL DISORDERS who are unable to stop themselves from responding to the variety of distracting stimuli in their environment.

displaced child syndrome A group of responses sometimes seen in a child after the birth of a SIBLING, including jealousy, feelings of rejection by others, irritability, and easy discouragement; related to SEPARATION ANXIETY.

displacement A type of DEFENSE MECHANISM in which a child (or adult) transfers emotional focus (CATHEXIS) away from a troubling thought or feeling to a less frightening or painful one.

dispositional conference A multidisciplinary meeting, often involving a SOCIAL WORKER, PEDIATRICIAN, and PSYCHOLOGIST or PSYCHIATRIST, at which decisions are made about short-term CUSTODY of a child in cases of possible CHILD ABUSE AND NEGLECT. At a later *dispositional hearing*, a court or administrative official decides longer-term questions about the child's custody.

disruptive behavior disorder A classification of MENTAL DISORDERS that includes ATTENTION-DEFICIT HYPERACTIVITY DISORDER and CONDUCT DISORDER.

dissociative disorders A class of MENTAL DISORDERS in which the key feature is disturbance and sometimes fracturing (dissociation) of consciousness, memory, and identity; also called *hysterical neuroses, dissociative type*. Among those commonly affecting children is MULTIPLE PERSONALITY DISORDER. (For help and further information, see MENTAL DISORDERS.)

distal muscular dystrophy A form of MUSCULAR DYSTROPHY.

distractibility Inability to focus for very long on any single task, tending to shift attention to new sights, sounds, or activities in the environment; a common problem among children with LEARNING DISABILITIES, especially ATTENTION DEFICIT HYPERACTIVITY DISORDER.

diverticulum An abnormal pouch off the intestines; a form of DIGESTIVE DISORDER.

dizygotic Medical term referring to *nonidentical* or *fraternal twins*, who grew from two separate fertilized eggs, or ZYGOTES; literally, "two eggs." (For further information, see MULTIPLE BIRTHS.)

DM Abbreviation for DIABETES MELLITUS.

Dmitri's disease Alternate name for STURGE-WEBER SYNDROME.

DMR Abbreviation for DIAGNOSTIC READING SCALES.

DNA Complex molecules that make up genes and carry the basic information about a person's GENETIC INHERITANCE.

DNR Medical abbreviation for *do not resuscitate*, sometimes indicated on a patient's medical chart as *no code*. (See DEATH.)

doctoral degree (doctor's degree or **doctorate)** The highest degree offered for GRADUATE studies, beyond the MASTER'S DEGREE. A doctorate, often a *Ph.D.* (doctorate of philosophy), is generally awarded to a student who has successfully completed a specified program, normally taking at least three or four years of study beyond the BACHELOR'S DEGREE.

domains In EDUCATION, a general term for areas of learning and behavior, introduced in the 1950s by Benjamin Bloom and referring to three key categories of instructional content and learning objectives: *affective domain, cognitive domain*, and *psychomotor domain*. The affective domain refers to feelings, emotions, values, and attitudes (AFFECT being a psychological word for shown feelings). The cognitive domain covers thinking skills such as problem-solving, memory and recall, comprehension, reasoning, and judgment. The psychomotor domain refers to a child's physical and muscular functioning. These domains are often referred to by educators planning a CURRICULUM, as in an INDIVIDUALIZED EDUCATION PLAN for a HANDICAPPED child, with specific learning objectives planned for each area. The term *domain* has also been used to refer to other categories of learning.

domestic relations court The type of civil court that handles divorces and CUSTODY cases resulting from divorce or separation. In some states, the role of the domestic relations court is taken over by the FAMILY COURT. Some domestic relations courts also have an affiliated COURT OF CONCILIATION, staffed by professional counselors, rather than legal personnel, to facilitate reconciliations.

dominance The tendency of a person to rely most heavily on and to be most easy and proficient at using one eye, ear, hand, or foot over the other; sometimes called *sidedness*. In relation to preference for the right or left hand, dominance is often called HANDEDNESS. Dominance in hands, eyes, and feet is

believed to reflect *cerebral dominance* of one hemisphere of the brain over the other, the right side of the brain corresponding to the left side of the body, and vice versa. Generally, the preferred eye, hand, and foot are all on the same side of the body, left or right. But in some people, including many with LEARNING DISABILITIES, they are not. So a child might, for example, be right-footed and right-eyed but left-handed. Such a condition is called *cross dominance* or *mixed dominance*. In some young learning-disabled children, dominance (including handedness) is not fully established, and they often confuse left with right. A condition in which neither eye dominates is called *ambieyedness*, as equal use of hands is called AMBIDEXTROUS.

dominant In GENETIC INHERITANCE, a gene that produces its effect regardless of the information coded on its paired gene. If a father contributes a dominant gene for curly hair, for example, his child will have curly hair, no matter what gene the mother contributed to the pair. With normal genes, this causes no problem, but if the dominant gene is defective, then the child will inherit a GENETIC DISORDER. The expression of a gene may be modified by other genes, by a person's unique environment, and sometimes even by which parent contributed the gene. In the case of a defective gene, this means that symptoms can range from severe to unnoticeable. Because of this, parents who have a family history of any genetic disorder may want to seek GENETIC COUNSELING to see if they are unknowingly carrying a dominant gene for a genetic disorder. Among the common disorders carried by dominant genes are HUNTINGTON'S CHOREA, ACHONDROPLASIA, POLYDACTYLY, MARFAN'S SYNDROME, NEUROFIBROMATOSIS, OSTEOGENESIS IMPERFECTA (brittle bone disease), and hypercholesterolemia (high blood CHOLESTEROL). If a parent carries a gene for a dominant disorder, he or she has a 50-percent chance of passing that gene on to a child (for more information, see AUTOSOMAL DOMINANT), so GENETIC SCREENING of the FETUS may be advisable. (For help and further information, see GENETIC DISORDERS.)

donor insemination Alternate term for ARTIFICIAL INSEMINATION–DONOR.

Down's syndrome A CONGENITAL condition resulting from a CHROMOSOMAL ABNORMALITY, usually the existence of three copies (TRISOMY) of chromosome 21, instead of the normal two; also called *Down syndrome, trisomy 21*, or *congenital acromicria*. Down's syndrome is the most common cause of MENTAL RETARDATION, affecting one in approximately 600 to 650 births. Children with Down's syndrome characteristically have eyes that slope upward at the outer corners and are partly covered by *epicanthal folds*, folds of skin on the inner corners, giving them a supposedly "Asian" appearance (hence, the earlier name, *mongolism*). They also tend to have small facial features, a large tongue, a skull flattened in the back, and hands with a single horizontal palm crease. Down's syndrome children are unusually likely to have heart problems (see HEART AND HEART PROBLEMS), ATRESIA (narrowing) in the intestinal system, EAR AND HEARING PROBLEMS, LEUKEMIA, and ATHEROSCLEROSIS (narrowing of the arteries)—so much so that, until recent medical advances, relatively few reached full adulthood. No treatment is known to alter the course of Down's syndrome.

Children with Down's syndrome are generally warm, affectionate, and even-tempered, and they benefit markedly from a stimulating home environment. They do, however, require special care throughout their lifetimes, the amount depending on the severity of their mental retardation. This can place an enormous strain on a family, especially when both parents work. As a result, in the past parents were often advised to place a Down's syndrome child in a LONG-TERM CARE facility soon after birth, or later if the child's needs became more than the family could handle. Today, however, such placement is rare. With the wide range of services available, especially under the EDUCATION FOR ALL HANDICAPPED CHILDREN ACT OF 1975, such a child more often attends a series of stimulating educational programs from infancy through the normal school years (see MENTAL RETARDATION). The development of GROUP HOMES, as an alternative to large institutions, has provided comfortable living settings for many adolescents and adults with Down's syndrome. As adults, many are able to work and live independently, though often in supervised settings.

Women who are over 35 or have Down's syndrome in their family history are at special risk of having a child with the syndrome and may want to seek GENETIC COUNSELING before PREGNANCY or consider GENETIC SCREENING during pregnancy, as with AMNIOCENTESIS and CHORIONIC VILLUS SAMPLING, to see if the FETUS has Down's syndrome, leaving open the options of selective ABORTION or of preparing for a child with SPECIAL NEEDS.

For help and further information

National Down Syndrome Congress (NDSC)
1800 Dempster Street
Park Ridge, IL 60068
312-823-7550, toll-free number (U.S. except IL) 800-232-NDSC [6372]
Diane M. Crutcher, Executive Director
Organization for parents of children with Down's syndrome, teachers and medical professionals who work with them, and interested others. Seeks to enhance the dignity and personal horizons of people with Down's syndrome; advises parents and parent groups; maintains library and services as information clearinghouse; operates toll-free number; publishes various materials, including *Down Syndrome News, Facts About Down Syndrome*, pamphlet *Down Syndrome* (in English and Spanish), and bibliography of materials on Down's syndrome.

National Down Syndrome Society (NDSS)
141 Fifth Avenue, Suite 7S
New York, NY 10010
212-460-9330, toll-free number (U.S. except New York) 800-221-4602
Donna M. Rosenthal, Executive Director
Organization supporting research on Down's syndrome, its causes and treatment. Operates toll-free number; publishes various materials, including biannual newsletter; audiovisual,

Gifts of Love; booklet for new parents of Down's syndrome children, *This Baby Needs You Even More*; bibliography of works on Down's syndrome, and directory (maintained on computer) of support groups for parents and early intervention programs for Down's syndrome children; as well as *Fact Sheet: Down Syndrome, Questions and Answers About Down Syndrome*, and *The Connection Between Down Syndrome and Alzheimer's Disease*.

Association for Children with Down Syndrome (ACDS)
2616 Martin Avenue
Bellmore, Long Island, NY 11710
516-221-4700
Fredda Stimell, Executive Director
Organization seeking to ease children with Down's syndrome into the mainstream, from preschool through youth, supporting special social, recreational, and educational programs to that end. Encourages parental advocacy; seeks to educate public and influence public policy; conducts research; publishes various print and audiovisual materials, including bimonthly newsletter *Spot Lite*.

National Association for Down's Syndrome (NADS)
P.O. Box 4542
Oakbrook, IL 60521
312-325-9112
Sheila Hebein, Executive Director
Organization seeking to enhance lives of people with Down's syndrome. Offers support to families; fosters formation of mutual-support self-help parent groups; seeks to educate public; provides information to public and professionals; encourages research; publishes various materials, including bimonthly *NADS Newsletter*, audiovisual works *Down's Syndrome: New Expectations* and *You Don't Outgrow Down's Syndrome: Counseling Parents*, and brochures *Parent Support Program* and *NADS*.

Down's Syndrome International (DSI)
11 North 73rd Terrace, Room K
Kansas City, KS 66111
913-299-0815
Jessie M. Bennett, Administrator
For parents of children with Down's syndrome. Promotes support and counseling among parents; funds research and provides referral service.

National Institute of Child Health and Human Development (NICHD), 301-496-5133. Publishes various materials, including *Facts About Down Syndrome* and *Facts About Down Syndrome for Women over 35*. (For full group information, see PREGNANCY.)

March of Dimes Birth Defects Foundation, 914-428-7100; local chapters in telephone-directory white pages. (For full group information, see BIRTH DEFECTS; GENETIC DISORDERS.)

National Down's Syndrome Adoption Exchange, 914-428-1236. (For full group information, see ADOPTION.)

La Leche League International (LLLI), 312-455-7730. Publishes *Breastfeeding the Baby with Down Syndrome*. (For full group information, see BREASTFEEDING.)

Other reference sources

Teaching the Infant with Down Syndrome: A Guide for Parents and Professionals, by Marci J. Hanson. Austin, TX: Pro-Ed, 1987.

The Young Child with Down's Syndrome, by S.M. Pueschel. New York: Human Sciences, 1983.

Down's Syndrome: An Introduction for Parents, by C. Cunningham. London: Souvenir Press, 1982; distributed in U.S. by Brookline Books, 460 Broadway, Cambridge, MA 02238.

Secret Places of the Stairs, by Susan Sallis. New York: Harper & Row, 1984.

Angel Unaware, by Dale Evans Rogers. Old Tappan, NJ: Revell, 1984.

Our Special Child, by Bette M. Ross. New York: Walker, 1981.

A Little Time, by Anne Norris Baldwin. New York: Viking, 1978.

(See also GENETIC DISORDERS; GENETIC COUNSELING; MENTAL RETARDATION; also HELP FOR SPECIAL CHILDREN on page 578.)

DP   Abbreviation for DEPTH PERCEPTION.

DPT vaccine   Alternate name for DTP VACCINE, against DIPHTHERIA, TETANUS (lockjaw), and PERTUSSIS (whooping cough).

Draw-a-Person Test   A type of PROJECTIVE TEST in which psychologists attempt to discern a child's personality characteristics from drawings of the self and others; also a general term for a draw-a-person task in various other tests, such as the GOODENOUGH-HARRIS DRAWING TEST or the ABC INVENTORY, where it may be used to measure nonverbal intelligence.

dropout   A student who has stopped attending school before graduating or completing a given course of study, whether under COMPULSORY SCHOOL AGE or over. Considerable attention, effort, and analysis have gone into understanding why students drop out and how to keep them from doing so. Some schools have special programs to try to maintain students identified as potential dropouts or to bring back to school some who have already left. Dropouts who later wish to continue their schooling can study, on their own or in groups, to take a series of TESTS OF GENERAL EDUCATIONAL DEVELOPMENT; if they pass, they are awarded a certificate of high school equivalency, commonly called a GENERAL EQUIVALENCY DIPLOMA (GED).

For help and further information

When I Was Young I Loved School: Dropping Out and Hanging In, by Children's Express; edited by Anne Sheffield and Bruce Frankel. Westport, CT: Meckler, 1989. About teenage dropouts, near-dropouts, and returnees.

drug abuse   Physical and psychological dependence on chemical substances, including over-the-counter drugs, prescribed medications, or illicit substances, used primarily for the physical and emotional effects they produce rather than for therapeutic reasons. While some drug abuse results when a person becomes dependent on a drug initially used for therapeutic reasons, such as tranquilizers, among young people drug abuse more often results from experimentation with so-called recreational drugs, especially during the vulnerable and uncertain period of ADOLESCENCE. With regular or heavy use, various physical changes occur as the body becomes dependent on the drug so that, if use ends, severe physical and mental distress called *withdrawal symptoms* result. Once drug abuse is established, a person often needs to enter a special treatment program to undergo withdrawal. Drug abuse is certainly one of the major social problems in the world today and one of the major challenges facing parents of young children, not only for itself but also for the possibly life-threatening infections that are often linked with drug use, notably AIDS and HEPATITIS. Many parents are working actively on prevention programs aimed at young children, hoping to head off drug use before it begins. (For an overview of the effects and signs of drug and other substance abuse, plus organizations, reference works, and recommendations for parents, see HELP AGAINST SUBSTANCE ABUSE on page 587.)

drug reactions and interactions   Undesired effects from medications in a particular person or from mixing two or more noncomplementary drugs. Reactions or effects from interactions can range from a mild rash to life-threatening shock, as in cases of penicillin ALLERGY.

For parents, the most important rule regarding drugs may be for pregnant women and children to take *no* drugs without a doctor's supervision. During PREGNANCY, a fetus is enormously vulnerable to BIRTH DEFECTS, especially during the early months, so drugs should be avoided if possible. If medication is required, doctors will prescribe only those believed to have no adverse effects on the pregnancy.

Children, too, are enormously vulnerable to damage from drugs. Parents should not assume that children are just "small adults" and give them small doses of adult medicines. In fact, the vital organs, such as the liver, kidneys, and intestinal tract of infants and young children, mature only over some years; during that development, a child's body cannot break down, use, and eliminate drugs the way an adult's can, so the drug can build up to toxic levels.

More generally, parents should be aware of the known side effects of any medicines prescribed, asking their doctors to explain them and checking books on drugs; be sure the doctor knows what other medications are being taken at the same time; monitor children for any possible side effects; and consult a doctor quickly if they occur. (For books describing drugs, their side effects, interactions, and recommended use, see General Works on Drugs and Medicines in PARENT'S BOOKSHELF on page 566.)

For help and further information

Food and Drug Administration
U.S. Department of Health and Human Services
Office of Consumer and Professional Affairs
5600 Fishers Lane
Rockville, MD 20857
301-295-8012
Federal department charged with answering public queries about drug safety and proper drug use.

National Health Information Clearinghouse, 800-336-4797.

dry mouth   Popular name for XEROSTOMIA.

DTP vaccine   Type of VACCINE given to provide IMMUNIZATION against three life-threatening childhood diseases: DIPHTHERIA, TETANUS (lockjaw), and PERTUSSIS (whooping cough); also called *DPT vaccine*. Administration of the pertussis portion of this vaccine has been somewhat controversial, since some serious reactions can occur in response to the vaccine (see below). But recent large-scale studies have indicated that the risk of SEIZURES and CONVULSIONS is no greater among children receiving the pertussis vaccine than among those who do not. And the risks of not receiving the vaccine are considerable; in England, where many parents chose not to give their children the pertussis vaccine, over 500 children died of whooping cough between 1977 and 1983, and many others suffered brain damage. On balance, then, the Public Health Service and the Centers for Disease Control continue to recommend that the full DTP vaccine be administered, including the pertussis portion, with certain cautions (see below). The vaccine is generally given as a series of five injections between the ages of two months and six

---

Possible Side Effects and Adverse Reactions to DTP Immunization

With DTP vaccine, most children will have a slight fever and will be irritable for up to two days after getting the shot. One-half of children develop some soreness and swelling in the area where the shot was given. More serious side effects can occur. A temperature of 105°F or greater may follow one in every 330 DTP shots. Continuous crying lasting three or more hours may occur after one in every 100 shots, and unusual, hours may occur after one in every 100 shots, and unusual, high-pitched crying may occur after one in every 900 shots. Convulsions or episodes of limpness and paleness may each occur after one in every 1,750 shots. Children who have previously had a convulsion may be more likely to have another one after pertussis shots. Rarely, after about one in every 110,000 shots, other more severe problems of the brain may occur, and permanent brain damage may occur after about one in every 310,000 shots. Side effects from DT (diphtheria–tetanus) or Td (tetanus–diphtheria booster) are not common and usually consist only of soreness and slight fever. As with any drug or vaccine, there is a rare possibility that allergic or more serious reactions or even death could occur. Although some people have questioned whether DTP shots might cause Sudden Infant Death Syndrome (SIDS), the majority of evidence indicates that DTP shots do not cause SIDS.

If your child meets any of the following conditions, you should check with your child's doctor before any of the diphtheria, tetanus, and pertussis vaccines are given:

1. Anyone who is sick at the time with something more serious than a cold.
2. Anyone who has had a convulsion or is suspected to have a problem of the nervous system.

3. Anyone who has had a serious reaction to DTP, DT, or Td shots before, such as an allergic reaction to any vaccine component; a temperature of 105°F or greater; an episode of limpness and paleness; prolonged continuous crying; an unusual, high-pitched cry; or a convulsion or other more severe problem of the brain.
4. Anyone taking a drug or undergoing a treatment that lowers the body's resistance to infection, such as cortisone, prednisone, certain anticancer drugs, or irradiation, as the degree of protection provided by DTP may be decreased.

Who Should Not Receive the DTP Vaccine

Some children who are less than seven years of age and have had certain reactions, such as a convulsion, following receipt of a previous DTP shot should not receive the pertussis vaccine. Children who have a history of a convulsion prior to receipt of any DTP vaccine or who have other neurologic disorders should check with their doctor before receiving DTP vaccine. A diphtheria and tetanus vaccine preparation called DT is available for children who should not receive pertussis vaccine. Children who have a family history of convulsions in parents or siblings have a very small increase in risk for a convulsion following a DTP shot. However, because of the overall risk of whooping cough, such children should be immunized with DTP. In the event of a convulsion at any time, including following the receipt of DTP, the child should be seen by a doctor as soon as possible.

You should report any reactions to your health-care provider. He or she can then determine whether your child should continue to receive DTP or receive DT instead.

Source: *Parents' Guide to Childhood Immunization* (1988). Prepared for the Public Health Service and the Centers for Disease Control.

years. All 50 U.S. states require children to be immunized against diphtheria before entering school; almost all require tetanus immunization, and about two-thirds of the states require pertussis immunization. Parents who feel their child has been injured or has died because of a DTP vaccination can bring a claim under the CHILDHOOD VACCINE INJURY ACT.

For help and further information

Dissatisfied Parents Together (DPT)
128 Branch Road
Vienna, VA 22180
703-938-3783
Kathi Williams, Director
Organization of parents whose children have had adverse reactions to or damage from vaccines, especially the DPT vaccine. Seeks to reform vaccine system and develop safer vaccines; provides information and makes referrals; publishes various materials, including *DPT News* and *Parent Information Packet*. (See also IMMUNIZATION, which includes a recommended schedule for immunization.)

DTs   Abbreviation for *delerium tremens*, a form of DELIRIUM resulting from withdrawal after ALCOHOL ABUSE.

DT vaccine   Alternative to the DTP VACCINE, with the PERTUSSIS (whooping cough) portion omitted.

dual grading system   In EDUCATION, an evaluative approach that gives two marks, one for achievement as compared to others in the class (the usual GRADE) and one for achievement relative to one's ability, sometimes popularly called "for effort."

Duchenne muscular dystrophy   The most common form of MUSCULAR DYSTROPHY.

duck walk   Alternate name for METATARSUS VALGUS, or toeing out.

due date   The date on which a baby's birth is expected, traditionally calculated by doctors as 280 days (40 weeks) from the beginning of the woman's last MENSTRUATION, even though FERTILIZATION probably did not take place until two weeks later, at the time of OVULATION; also called *expected date of confinement (EDC)* by doctors. To calculate a due date, start with the day on which the last period began (say July 15), add nine months (making it April 15), and add seven days (making the due date April 22). By contrast the average period of GESTATION is 266 days (38 weeks), figured from the date of fertilization. If the fertilization date is known, subtracting two weeks from the due date gives a more accurate expected delivery date. Because the 40-week due date calculation is imprecise, obstetricians may give a more accurate date toward the end of the PREGNANCY, guided by a variety of tests and examinations, including when the first heartbeat is heard.

due process   A person's right to be treated with fairness in any legal proceeding, one of the most basic rights of a U.S. citizen; from the phrase in the Constitution "no person shall be deprived of life, liberty, or property without due process of law." Due process often includes the rights to receive adequate notice of hearings, to receive notice of allegations or charges, to have a lawyer's counsel, to confront and cross-examine witnesses, to refuse to give self-incriminating testimony, to be presumed innocent, and to receive a jury trial. However, the precise details of what constitutes fairness in what settings, for what types of cases, and for what people is a complex matter that changes somewhat as courts rule on specific cases. Family law and many types of matters dealt with in ADMINISTRATIVE PROCEDURES have in the past often not been accorded the basic legal protection of due process. A series of cases over the years have resulted in due-process safeguards gradually being extended into some of these areas, as in relation to separation and divorce, schools, and social services, including CUSTODY and TERMINATION OF PARENTS' RIGHTS. Even so, in some circumstances, parents or students may be adversely affected by a hearing—or even a decision without a hearing—at which they have had no opportunity to be heard and may be obliged to prove that they have been denied due process to get a new, fair hearing. Due-process hearings are common in connection with the EDUCATION FOR ALL HANDICAPPED CHILDREN ACT OF 1975, when parents disagree with the INDIVIDUALIZED EDUCATION PROGRAM the school prepares for their child. (For an outline of parents' rights in such cases, see EDUCATION FOR ALL HANDICAPPED CHILDREN ACT OF 1975; for an overview of Supreme Court rulings regarding student suspensions or expulsions from school, see SUSPENSION.)

Durrell Analysis of Reading Difficulty   An individually administered test of READING skills for children in grades one through six, including oral reading, silent reading, listening comprehension, listening vocabulary, word recognition/word analysis, spelling, auditory analysis of words and word elements, pronunciation of word elements, visual memory of words, and prereading PHONICS abilities. The Durrell test is often used as a DIAGNOSTIC ASSESSMENT TEST, for the planning of REMEDIAL INSTRUCTION, as well as to attempt to predict a child's future reading skills. (For help and further information, see TESTS.)

dwarfism   Abnormally short stature and general underdevelopment of the body, which may result from a wide variety of causes, among them:

- GENETIC DISORDERS, such as MUCOPOLYSACCHARIDOSES or ACHONDROPLASIA;
- malfunctioning of some part of the ENDOCRINE SYSTEM, especially the PITUITARY or THYROID GLAND;
- chronic illnesses that sap strength and slow growth;
- persistent MALNUTRITION, as in nutritional disorders such as RICKETS;
- kidney failure (see KIDNEY AND UROLOGICAL DISORDERS);
- defects in the digestive and absorptive systems (see DIGESTIVE DISORDERS);
- psychosocial stress, as in MATERNAL DEPRIVATION SYNDROME.

Dwarfism is often associated with other problems or defects, such as MENTAL RETARDATION. (For help and further information, see GROWTH AND GROWTH DISORDERS.)

dysarthria   Difficult, often unclear speech, resulting from malfunctioning of the muscles used in pronouncing words, often because of damage to the nerves serving the area. Dysarthria may result from a BRAIN TUMOR. Total inability to speak is called *anarthria*. (For help and further information, see COMMUNICATION SKILLS AND DISORDERS.)

dyscalculia   Difficulty in working with mathematical symbols and functions, presumably because of some brain dysfunction; one of the kinds of LEARNING DISABILITIES. Total inability to work with numbers is called *acalculia*.

dysgraphia   Difficulty in writing, especially in producing handwriting legible to others, generally because of problems with *visual-motor integration*, one of the key VISUAL SKILLS. Total inability to write is called *agraphia*, a type of APHASIA.

dyslexia   Difficulty in READING or partial word blindness, despite unimpaired vision and intelligence; a type of learning disability relating to specific reading problems. A dyslexic child may see printed words upside down, backward, or otherwise distorted. Total inability to read—that is, to interpret written symbols—is called *alexia* or *word blindness*. (For help and further information, see LEARNING DISABILITIES.)

dysmenorrhea   A disorder association with MENSTRUATION.

dysphagia   Difficulty in swallowing, or inability to swallow, a symptom of a variety of disorders, including BRAIN TUMOR.

dysphasia   A kind of communication disorder, involving inability to speak the words in one's mind or to find the correct words to speak, as well as the inability to understand spoken or written words (see COMMUNICATION SKILLS AND DISORDERS); a condition that may result from certain kinds of damage to the brain, such as a BRAIN TUMOR or HEAD INJURY.

dyspraxia   A type of communication disorder (see COMMUNICATION SKILLS AND DISORDERS).

dystocia   Medical term for difficult (sometimes impossible) LABOR, when labor fails to progress. It may occur when a mother is overtired or her internal organs are shaped abnormally and is often an indication for assistance, including FORCEPS DELIVERY, VACUUM EXTRACTION, or CESAREAN SECTION.

dystolic pressure   The lower figure in a measurement of BLOOD PRESSURE.

EA   Abbreviation for EDUCATIONAL AGE.

ear and hearing problems   Difficulties or impairment in the twin structures involved in receiving and registering sounds and transmitting information about them to the brain for interpretation. The *outer ear* (the visible part) acts as a funnel for sound and transmits it to the *eardrum*, a membrane that vibrates like a drum when sound strikes it.

This vibration is passed on to the *ossicles* (the *malleus*, the *incus*, and the *stapes*), a set of tiny bones in the *middle ear* that amplify the sound. The middle ear is connected to the throat by a narrow canal called the *eustachian tube*, which helps protect the delicate eardrum and ossicles from too-rapid, potentially dangerous changes in pressure, as in an airplane, or from loud noises.

The amplified vibrations are then passed on to the *cochlea*, a fluid-filled, snail-shaped, bony shell in the *inner ear*. Within the cochlea is the actual organ of hearing, the *organ of Corti*, a minute duct filled with microscopic hair cells that take the incoming sound vibrations and transform them into electrical signals. These are picked up by nearby nerve cells, which trans-

mit the signals to the brain by way of the *auditory nerve*, also called the *eighth nerve*.

How the brain then takes these signals and interprets them is little known but is the subject of much research. Scientists do know that different parts of the brain are primarily associated with various activities, such as interpreting speech and music, thinking, memory, and learning. But researchers do not yet know how we can focus on one sound in a noisy setting, "tuning out" other unwanted sounds, or how we identify the source of a sound from some distance away.

Clearly, such a delicate set of mechanisms is easily disrupted, and hearing impaired. Many hearing defects are associated with problems in the outer and middle ear involving the gathering and passing on of the sound vibrations; this type of hearing impairment is called *conductive loss*. By contrast, *sensorineural* loss occurs when there is a problem in the inner ear, especially with the delicate hair cells or with the nerves that carry sound to the brain. Both types of loss may occur either before or after birth. Hearing loss that is present at birth—the child having no experience of sound or spoken language—is called PRELINGUAL; hearing loss after a person has had some experience of sound and language is called POSTLINGUAL.

Conductive losses are less severe than sensorineural losses and can usually be reduced or eliminated through medical treatment. Sensorineural losses are permanent and more severe. At present, they cannot be cured or even reduced by doctor's treatment. But most children with such losses can be helped greatly by a HEARING AID. It is important that children with sensorineural loss see a doctor regularly to make sure infections or other problems do not further impair their hearing or present a medical problem that may otherwise be physically damaging. Sometimes a child may have *mixed hearing loss*, involving problems in all parts of the ear.

Conductive losses may be caused by:

- infections that fill the ear with fluid, the most common being the middle ear infection called *otitis media*. Researchers estimate that two out of three children have at least one episode of otitis media before reaching school age. Often, during colds or other respiratory illnesses, mucus and pus drain into the middle ear, causing swelling, inflammation, pain, and temporary or sometimes permanent hearing impairment. The infection also may spread to the nearby mastoid bone, causing inflammation, or *mastoiditis*. With modern antibiotics, many infections can be cleared up with no lasting damage. But some children have chronic otitis media, with five or six bouts a year, creating the risk of some permanent hearing loss. Then an OTOLOGIST or OTOLARYNGOLOGIST may make a tiny incision in the eardrum to drain built-up fluid; if fluid continues to build up, the surgeon may insert a minute drainage tube in the eardrum, in a procedure called a *tympanostomy*. Such an operation can ease the problem but can have the side effect of thickening or scarring the eardrum. If children (or parents) have middle-ear infections, they should not fly on airplanes because the changes in pressure can cause ear damage.
- ruptured eardrum, which can result from an injury, a too-sudden, too-drastic pressure drop, or damage caused by a foreign object, such as a pencil, stick, or hairpin. Using the modern techniques of MICROSURGERY, ear specialists can now repair or rebuild an eardrum in many such cases. Using a technique called MYRINGOPLASTY, surgeons can close a hole in the eardrum using a tissue graft from elsewhere in the body.
- external blockage, such as a buildup of ear wax in the ear or a foreign object, such as a bead or a bug. Such blocks should be removed only by a medical specialist, such as an otologist or otolaryngologist, because the eardrum can be damaged in the process. Buildup of wax and other debris from the air can serve as a medium for growth of agents such as bacteria, yeasts, fungi, or viruses, especially if the ear is often underwater. The result is the common ear ailment called *otitis externa*, or *swimmer's ear*, which is infection or inflammation in the outer ear; often associated with this is MYRINGITIS, inflammation of the eardrum. The debris needs to be professionally cleaned out and the area medicinally disinfected. Showers rather than baths are less conducive to otitis externa, and a child vulnerable to ear infections may need to limit swimming.

- deformity in the ear structures, such as the hereditary hearing problem called *otosclerosis*, in which one or more of the bones in the middle ear has excess bone and therefore cannot transmit sound vibrations effectively. Modern surgery can remove excess bone and, if necessary, replace part of the bone with an artificial part.
- missing or occluded (obstructed) ear canal, a rare condition.
- ALLERGIES.

In rare cases, a child may have a hearing loss that comes and goes. Such a child has normal hearing but may occasionally suffer a significant hearing loss because of allergies and chronic colds. This kind of hearing loss can be very hard to detect and treat. One week you may notice inconsistent responses, like those of a hearing-impaired child who doesn't know he or she is being spoken to. The next week and for some time thereafter, the child will respond as though he or she has normal hearing. You should bring this kind of problem to the attention of a doctor.

Sensorineural losses may be caused by many different things:

- diseases during pregnancy. German measles (RUBELLA) and common MEASLES (rubeola) once caused numerous cases of hearing impairment at birth. Luckily, vaccines now exist for both of these diseases; any woman considering pregnancy should be sure to be vaccinated well before becoming pregnant. Other common infections that can cause hearing loss, and for which no vaccines currently exist, are CYTOMEGALOVIRUS INFECTION and HERPES SIMPLEX type 2 virus, which causes genital infection.
- heredity. Of the 4,000 babies born deaf in the United States each year, perhaps half have lost their hearing because of GENETIC DISORDERS; many more have substantial hearing impairment, which may appear only later. If prospective parents have hereditary deafness in their personal or family history, they may want to seek GENETIC COUNSELING to assess the risk that their child might have hearing impairment.
- difficult LABOR and DELIVERY. If the baby's oxygen supply is temporarily cut off during labor, for example, hearing damage may result.
- drugs taken by a pregnant woman during pregnancy or by a child. Aspirin, some antibiotics (such as streptomycin or neomycin), and some diuretics (water-reducing medications) can on occasion damage hair cells or other parts of the inner ear; so can some anti-CANCER drugs. Anyone taking such drugs and experiencing change in hearing, dizziness, balance problems, or TINNITUS (ringing in the ears) should check promptly with a physician. Parents should be alert to such symptoms in their children.

- childhood diseases, such as MUMPS, measles, or CHICKEN POX.
- viral infections, such as MENINGITIS and ENCEPHALITIS.
- prolonged high FEVER.
- TUMORS. Most common are ACOUSTIC NEUROMAS, also called *eighth nerve tumors*; associated symptoms are hearing loss in one or both ears, HEADACHES, dizziness, tinnitus, and numbness in the face. If detected early, the tumor can be removed without hearing damage; but if diagnosed late, acoustic neuromas can be life-threatening or surgical removal can at least involve hearing loss, disturbance of the sense of balance (related to the inner ear), and loss of feeling or paralysis in the face.
- physical damage to head or ear. A severe blow to the head, an accident, brain HEMORRHAGE, or similar trauma may damage hearing ability.
- excessive or intense noise. Brief exposure to extremely loud, intense, explosive sound can cause temporary but possibly reversible hearing loss. Continued exposure can cause permanent damage to the vital hair cells of the inner ear, causing irreversible hearing loss—a serious problem in a society that is surrounded by noise, not least in personal earphones.

Sometimes hearing impairment is associated with other diseases or disorders, among them HUNTER'S SYNDROME, ALBERS-SCHÖNBERG DISEASE, and THYROID GLAND problems.

Sensorineural loss affects sound at some frequencies more than others, so even with a hearing aid, a person with sensorineural loss often hears distorted sounds, making the use of an aid impossible. A COCHLEAR IMPLANT, which uses a microprocessor to simulate the functions performed by the cochlea, may help such people.

It is extremely important that any hearing impairment be identified early so that a child can get treatment, aid, and training to minimize damage and loss. Deafness itself does not affect intellectual capacity, but the language and sounds children hear from birth provide vital experience, and many aspects of learning depend on a child's communication skills (see COMMUNICATION SKILLS AND DISORDERS). As a result, undiagnosed hearing-impaired children may quickly fall behind in developing skills. Some kinds of hearing loss can be identified in newborns, but many cases of hearing impairment go undiagnosed for years, with children being mistakenly thought to have MENTAL RETARDATION. Government agencies now have programs to try to identify hearing and other such problems in infancy, but parents can often spot hearing loss best. The U.S. Surgeon General's office published the following guidelines for parents.

Sometimes hearing impairment, especially if it is mild, is not diagnosed until the child enters nursery school. The Observation Checklist on page 160 was designed to help Head Start teachers tell if children in their preschool classes might have an undiagnosed hearing problem, but parents can use the checklist to assess whether their young child needs to be referred to an AUDIOLOGIST for HEARING TESTS. If a child is found

Parents Are the First to Know If Their Infants Cannot Hear

When you check your baby's hearing, he or she should be happy and the room quiet.

Does Your Baby Sometimes

From birth to age three months

- Startle or jump when there is a sudden loud sound?
- Stir or wake up and cry when someone talks or makes a noise?
- Recognize and be quieted and sometimes pacified by the sound of your voice?

By age three to six months

- Turn his or her eyes to look for an interesting sound?
- Respond to mother's or father's voice?
- Turn his or her eyes toward you when you call his or her name?

By age six to 12 months

- Turn toward interesting sound and toward you when his or her name is called from behind? (Sounds need *not* be loud.)
- Understand "no" and "bye-bye" and similar common words?
- Search or look around when hearing new sounds?

If your baby cannot do these things, check with your doctor. Parents must persist until their concerns are answered! If you need any help regarding your infant's hearing, call the Surgeon General's Hotline 800-922-9234.

Source: U.S. Surgeon General's Office.

to have a significant hearing loss, he or she will be entitled to special educational and other services under the EDUCATION FOR ALL HANDICAPPED CHILDREN ACT OF 1975.

Hearing loss is defined in different ways by different people for various purposes. Government agencies use specific *categorical definitions* for administrative reporting purposes; these set out the kinds of categories and test results that would make a child eligible for certain government services, as under the Education of All Handicapped Children Act. Mild impairments that can be readily corrected are not considered handicaps unless they fall within specified governmental definitions and, because of the handicap, require SPECIAL EDUCATION and related services.

More important for parents and teachers is the *functional definition* of a child's impairment; this describes how an indi-

Observation Checklist for Possible Hearing Impairment

Using an Observation Checklist

The checklist of behaviors that follows can alert you to undiagnosed hearing loss in a child and help you know when to refer that child for professional evaluation. There are certain aspects of the child's medical history that are important to note on your checklist, in addition to observable behaviors. Look through the child's records or ask the child's doctor to help you answer the ''medical history'' questions. Then continue to fill in your checklist from your observations.

If a child displays one or two of the behaviors listed, watch him or her more closely and in a variety of situations. Look carefully for other listed behaviors. You may also want to ask teachers or child-care staff if they have observed any of the behaviors on the checklist. If you can't decide whether something is wrong, request that a specialist, such as a teacher in a special program for the hearing-impaired, observe the child, too.

Medical History

	Yes	No
Is there a history of earaches or ear infections in the child's records?	☐	☐
Does the child complain of earaches, ringing, or buzzing in the ears?	☐	☐
Does the child have allergies or what appear to be chronic colds?	☐	☐
Has the child had a disease (mumps, measles) accompanied by a high fever?	☐	☐
Do parents say that they have wondered if the child has a hearing loss?	☐	☐

Hearing

	Yes	No
Does the child fail to respond to loud, unusual, or unexpected sounds?	☐	☐
Does the child fail to respond to communication that excites the other children? (For example, "Who wants ice cream?")	☐	☐
Does the child frequently fail to understand or respond to instructions or greetings when he or she doesn't see the speaker?	☐	☐
Does the child seem to watch other children rather than listen to the teacher in order to learn what to do next?	☐	☐
Does the child have difficulty finding the source of a sound?	☐	☐
Does the child constantly turn the television, radio, or record player up louder?	☐	☐
Does the child's attention wander or does the child look around the room while the teacher is talking or reading a story?	☐	☐

Speech

	Yes	No
Does the child frequently say "Huh?" or "What?" or show other signs of not understanding what has been said?	☐	☐
Does the child use very little speech?	☐	☐

	Yes	No
Does the child have difficulty controlling how loudly or softly he or she speaks?	☐	☐
Does the child have trouble putting words together in the right order?	☐	☐
Does the child's voice seem too high-pitched, too low-pitched, or too nasal?	☐	☐
Is the child's speech full of words and sentences that cannot be understood or recognized?	☐	☐
Does the child have poor articulation?	☐	☐

Other Behavior

	Yes	No
Does the child have a short attention span?	☐	☐
Does the child seem frequently restless?	☐	☐
Does the child breathe with his or her mouth open?	☐	☐
Is the child seldom the first one to do what the teacher has asked the group to do?	☐	☐
Is the child easily frustrated or distracted in a group?	☐	☐
Does the child tend to play in the quietest group?	☐	☐
Does the child tend to play alone more than the other children do?	☐	☐
Does the child seem unaware of social conventions? For example, does the child:	☐	☐
• never say automatically "thank you," "excuse me," or "sorry"?	☐	☐
• generally tap or grab another person instead of calling his or her name?	☐	☐
• not become quiet in quiet areas or activities (church, story corner, naptime)?	☐	☐
• not ask permission to leave the room, go to the bathroom, get a drink?	☐	☐
• appear unaware of disturbing others with noises?	☐	☐

Source: *Mainstreaming Preschoolers: Children with Hearing Impairment* (See General Works on page 165).

vidual child can and cannot use hearing for the ordinary purposes of life.

Few people have total loss of hearing. Most children commonly termed *deaf* have some level of hearing that is demonstrable on a hearing test. This is called *residual hearing*. It is the extent to which this remaining hearing is useful for functioning in life that determines whether a person is considered deaf or hard of hearing. Being able to use hearing for the "ordinary purposes of life" means being able to understand speech through hearing alone or hearing combined with SPEECH-READING (lipreading) and being able to hear enough of ordinary sounds—such as telephones, traffic, and voices—to be able to make sense out of them. A child who functions this way is termed *hard of hearing*; a child who cannot use his or her hearing to function this way is termed *deaf*.

A second type of functional definition is based on the degree of hearing loss and is determined by hearing tests, normally performed by an audiologist. In this definition, all children, whether they are categorized as deaf or hard of hearing, are referred to as *hearing-impaired*. The government publication *Mainstreaming Preschoolers: Children with Hearing Impairment* explains it this way:

Hearing impairment covers the entire range of degree of hearing loss and is broken down into four categories: *mild*, *moderate*, *severe*, and *profound*. [For a fuller discussion, see HEARING TESTS.] Children who have the same degree of hearing loss may function quite differently from one another, however. One child with a severe hearing impairment may be functionally hard of hearing, while another child with a severe hearing impairment may be functionally deaf.

While audiometric testing tells how loud a sound must be to be heard by a hearing-impaired child (without a hearing aid), it does not tell how distorted sounds may be for that particular child. Two children with the same measurable degree of hearing loss may hear sounds with differing degrees of clarity, which greatly affect what each is able to understand. Categories of loss also do not tell what a child's potential for hearing or listening may be. And they do not tell how a child will function on a daily basis.

For these reasons, the measured degree of hearing loss in a child (mild, moderate, severe, or profound) cannot be used to predict behaviors or functioning of that child. Many hearing-impaired children can learn to use the hearing they have to understand and to speak, although these skills will vary from child to child.

Hearing-impaired children have two different problems in receiving sound. First, sounds are not as loud as they are for children without hearing impairment. Sounds may be slightly softer than normal, very soft, or even impossible for hearing-impaired children to hear. Through testing, a professional can determine how loud a sound has to be for a child to be able to hear it.

Second, for children with more severe hearing loss, sounds may be distorted, as well as soft. When sounds are distorted, they can be mistaken for other sounds or be impossible to understand. The amount of distortion cannot be measured by a test, but it greatly affects how children function. It is necessary to be aware of these two problems—loudness and distortion—to understand fully the effects of hearing loss.

The results of audiological tests and of observations in the classroom and in the home allow teachers, in consultation with parents, to develop INDIVIDUALIZED EDUCATION PROGRAMS for children with hearing impairment.

A hearing-impaired child's central problem is learning to communicate. In order to communicate, children need to send and receive messages. Hearing-impaired children have a harder time than other children in learning to talk and to understand the conversation of others. This is because hearing-impaired children may not hear a message clearly, may hear it at a reduced intensity, or may not hear it at all. Therefore, the ability to communicate through spoken language is developed more slowly in hearing-impaired children than in other children. A CHART OF NORMAL DEVELOPMENT (on page 507) indicates when between birth and age six unimpaired children first *on the average* begin to develop the main communication and other basic skills. TEACHING YOUNG CHILDREN: GUIDELINES AND ACTIVITIES (on page 544) describes activities designed to develop children's skills in various areas.

Children with prelingual hearing loss—those who were deaf at birth and so had no experience of sound and spoken language or those who lost their hearing before age three, before they learned how to speak—have the most difficulty. Such children—95 percent of the hearing-impaired children—need much more special training to develop fluent communication skills and special skills such as speechreading, SIGN LANGUAGE (such as American Sign Language), and FINGERSPELLING.

Considerable dispute exists among people who work with the deaf, between those who believe deaf people should avoid any form of MANUAL COMMUNICATION and focus totally on oral speech and those who believe that they should use any and all means of communication open to them, an approach called TOTAL COMMUNICATION. SPEECH-LANGUAGE PATHOLOGISTS use a variety of approaches to teach speech to deaf children, including having the child learn to mimic the "voiceprint" that shows up on a computer screen and feeling the vibrations in the jaw, throat, and neck muscles (as Helen Keller learned from her teacher).

Various kinds of technical aids have also been developed to aid hearing-impaired people. Among these are:

- TELECOMMUNICATION DEVICES FOR THE DEAF (TDDs or TTYs);
- alerting systems that use flashing lights or vibrations to signal particular sounds, such as the ringing of a phone, the crying of a baby, or the beep of a smoke detector;
- electronic mail, using typed messages on computers as a main avenue of communication, such as DeafNet (operated by the Deaf Communications Institute) and Disabilities Forum (operated by CompuServe);

- interactive instruction, using computers or videodiscs, especially for speech and language development;
- computers for word processing, making writing and corrections much easier;
- computers for speech recognition, in which words spoken in a classroom are translated by a computer into print on a screen;
- SPEECH SYNTHESIS, computer programs that allow a deaf person to type into a computer and have the computer "speak" the words;
- systems that funnel sound directly into a hearing aid and so deliver sound to the ear more efficiently, using various technologies, including electromagnetic fields, radiowaves, and infrared systems;
- CLOSED CAPTIONS for visual materials.

Such devices and others surely to come are gradually increasing the independence of people who are deaf or hearing-impaired. Among other special arrangements possible are use of specially trained dogs to act as "alerting systems," generally only for adolescents or adults who are old enough to care for the dog, or provision of an interpreter or translator in some test situations, as for the SCHOLASTIC APTITUDE TEST (see below).

For help and further information

About Deafness and Hearing Impairment

American Society for Deaf Children (ASDC)
814 Thayer Avenue
Silver Spring, MD 20910
301-585-5400 (voice/TDD)
Roberta Thomas, Executive Director
Organization for families with deaf children and professionals who work with them. Encourages parent-to-parent mutual support and formation of local self-help groups; offers Two Years of Love, special program for new parents of deaf children; maintains library and disseminates information relating to families with deaf children; publishes various materials, including bimonthly newsletter *The Endeavor* and summer camp directory.

National Association for Hearing and Speech Action (NAHSA)
10801 Rockville Pike
Rockville, MD 20852
301-897-8682, voice and TDD, MD, AK, and HI call collect; toll-free number, U.S. except MD, AK, and HI, voice and TDD, 800-638-TALK [8255]
Judith Shannon, President
Consumer affiliate of the American Speech-Language-Hearing Association. Answers questions on any hearing and speech problems, provides information, and makes referrals; operates toll-free line; publishes various materials, including *How Does Your Child Hear and Talk?* and *NAHSA Answers Questions About:*

Noise and Hearing Loss, Otitis Media and Language Development, Recognizing Communication Disorders, and *Tinnitus.*

National Information Center on Deafness (NICD)
Gallaudet University
800 Florida Avenue, NE
Washington, DC 20002
202-651-5051 (voice)
202-651-5052 (TDD)
Loraine DiPietro, Executive Director
Information clearinghouse run by university for the deaf. Answers questions and provides information to public and to professionals on all aspects of deafness and hearing impairment, including deafness in children, technical aids, methods of communication with the deaf and hearing-impaired, and careers working with the deaf; publishes *American Annals of the Deaf*, a directory of programs and services available to deaf people in the United States.

National Institute on Deafness and Other Communication Disorders (NINDS)
9000 Rockville Pike
Building 31, Room 1B62
Bethesda, MD 20892
301-496-7243
Federal arm, one of the U.S. National Institutes of Health, sponsoring research on deafness and communication disorders. Provides information; publishes various materials, including *Hearing Loss: Hope Through Research* and *Dizziness,* booklet encompassing Ménière's disease.

National Association of the Deaf (NAD)
814 Thayer Avenue
Silver Spring, MD
301-587-1788 (voice and TTY)
Gary Olsen, Executive Director
Nationwide organization with state affiliates acting as advocates for the deaf. Seeks to educate public and influence public policy and legislation; acts as information clearinghouse; publishes many books and other print and audiovisual materials, including magazine *Deaf American*, newsletter *Broadcaster*, and books *Deaf Heritage, They Grow in Silence: The Deaf Child and His Family, For Parents of Deaf Children*, and *A Basic Course in Manual Communication* (primer on sign language).

Alexander Graham Bell Association for the Deaf (AGBAD)
3417 Volta Place, NW
Washington, DC 20007
202-337-5220 (voice and TDD)
Donna McCord Dickman, Executive Director
Organization concerned with deafness and other hearing problems. Acts as information clearinghouse for public and professionals, on any hearing problems such as tinnitus, medical treatments such as cochlear implants, training, lipreading, deaf children's rights, and technical aids such as home signaling devices; includes special sections for deaf adults and the Inter-

national Parent Organization for parents; publishes various materials, including monthly newsletter *Newsounds*, quarterly *Our Kids Magazine, Deafness and Adolescence*, and *A Parent Kit.*

American Speech-Language-Hearing Association (ASHA)
10801 Rockville Pike
Rockville, MD 20852
301-897-5700 (voice/TDD)
Frederick T. Spahr, Executive Director
Organization of professionals concerned with speaking and hearing and their disorders. Provides information to public and professionals; makes referrals; publishes various materials.

Better Hearing Institute (BHI)
Box 1840
Washington, DC 20013
703-642-0580, toll-free Hearing Helpline, 800-EAR-WELL [327-9355]
Organization of professionals and others concerned with hearing impairments. Provides information to public and professionals; operates toll-free line; publishes various print and audiovisual materials, including *Sounds or Silence?, Tinnitus or Head Noises*, and *Nerve Deafness and You.*

Deafpride
1350 Potomac Avenue, SE
Washington, DC 20003
202-675-6700
Ann Champ-Wilson, Executive Director
Organization of people concerned about the rights and problems of the deaf. Seeks to educate public and influence public policy; supports bilingual approach to education, with English and American Sign Language taught to all; focuses on services to families and community organizations; publishes various materials, including newsletter *Deafpride Advocate Quarterly.*

Helen Keller National Center for Deaf-Blind Youths and Adults
111 Middle Neck Road
Sands Point, NY 11050
516-944-8900
Steve Barrett, Director
Organization to serve people with substantial hearing and vision loss, established by Congress; operated by The Industrial Home for the Blind.

American Association of the Deaf-Blind (AADB)
814 Thayer Avenue
Silver Spring, MD 20910
301-588-6545
Rod Macdonald, President
Organization of deaf-blind people and their families. Provides information and makes referrals; encourages independent living for the deaf-blind; publishes quarterly *Deaf-Blind American* in large print and braille.

Self-Help for Hard of Hearing People (SHHH)
7800 Wisconsin Avenue
Bethesda, MD 20814
301-657-2248 (voice), 301-657-2249 (TTY)
Howard E., Stone, Sr., Executive Director
Organization for hard-of-hearing individuals, their families, and concerned professionals. Publishes bimonthly *SHHH Journal* and monthly *SHHH Newsletter.*

National Center for Law and the Deaf
Gallaudet University
800 Florida Avenue, NE
Washington, DC 20002
202-651-5373 (voice/TDD)
Jack Gannon, Executive Director
Public service of Gallaudet University. Provides help for hearing-impaired people with legal problems in many areas, including social security, insurance, welfare, TDDs, and hearing ear dogs; publishes various materials.

House Ear Institute
256 South Lake Street
Los Angeles, CA 90057
213-483-4431; (TDD) 213-484-2642
John W. House, M.D., President
Organization that researches and develops new approaches to ear and hearing disorders. Operates Center for Deaf Children; runs support groups for parents of deaf children; trains and updates medical professionals; maintains professional library; publishes various materials, including quarterlies *House Cochlear Implant Associates Newsletter* and *OTO Review*, series of *A Discussion of* booklets on specific topics (such as acoustic neuromas, chronic ear infection, and cochlear implant) for general public, and many professional materials.

National Cued Speech Association (NCSA)
P.O. Box 31345
Raleigh, NC 27622
919-828-1218
Mary Elsie Daisy, Executive Director
Organization of people with hearing impairment, their families and friends, and interested professionals. Provides information on use of cued speech; publishes various materials, including quarterly newsletter *On Cue*, professional journal *Cued Speech Annual*, and annual directory.

Children of Deaf Adults (CODA)
Box 30715
Santa Barbara, CA 93130
805-682-0997
Millie Brother, Founder
Organization of hearing children of deaf parents. Encourages sharing of experiences; seeks to act as advocate; publishes quarterly newsletter and bibliography, *Hearing Children/Deaf Parents.*

American Tinnitus Institute, 503-248-9985. (For full group information, see TINNITUS.)

National Crisis Center for the Deaf, TDD only. 800-446-9876, U.S. except Virginia; 800-552-3723, Virginia.

Tripod Grapevine Hearing Impairment Hotline, US except CA, 800-352-8888; CA, 800-346-8888.

On Special Programs and Aids for the Deaf and Hearing-Impaired

National Hearing Aid Society, 313-478-2610, Hearing Aid Hotline (U.S. except MI) 800-521-5247. Distributes Better Business Brochure pamphlet *Facts About Hearing Aids*. (For full group information, see HEARING AID.)

Registry of Interpreters for the Deaf, Inc. (RID)
51 Monroe Street
Rockville, MD 20850
301-279-0555
Don D. Roose, Executive Director
Organization of professional interpreters, translators, and transliterators. Maintains register of people trained in use of American Sign Language and other signing systems; provides information on interpreting for the deaf; trains and certifies interpreters for the deaf; publishes various materials, including texts on interpretation, transliteration, and translation.

Telecommunications for the Deaf, Inc. (TDI)
814 Thayer Avenue
Silver Spring, MD 20910
301-589-3006
Thomas M. Mentkowski, Executive Director
Organization of hearing-impaired people and others who use telecommunications devices (TDDs). Publishes international telephone directory of people and organizations who use TDDs for personal or commercial purposes; seeks to extend placement of TDDs in public places; promotes closed captioning and provides necessary decoders; publishes various materials, including annual *International Telephone Directory of TDD Users* and quarterly *GA-SK Newsletter*.

Hearing Dog Programs

Dogs for the Deaf (DD)
10175 Wheeler Road
Central Point, OR 97502
503-826-9220
Robin Dickson, Director
Organization that trains and provides listening dogs for the deaf. Publishes quarterly newsletter *Canine Listener*.

International Hearing Dog, Inc. (IHDI)
5901 East 89th Avenue
Henderson, CO 80640

303-287-EARS [3277] (voice and TTY)
Martha Foss, President
Organization that trains and supplies hearing dogs cost-free in the United States and Canada, normally for hearing-impaired individuals living in homes without hearing people. Publishes newsletter *Paws for Silence*.

New England Assistance Dog Service (NEADS)
P.O. Box 213
West Boylston, MA 01583
508-835-3304
Sheila O'Brien, Executive Director
Organization that trains guide dogs for individuals with hearing impairment and service dogs for those with physical handicaps. Publishes quarterly newsletter.

About Special College Programs for the Deaf

College and Career Programs
Center for Assessment and Demographic Studies
Gallaudet University
800 Florida Avenue, NE
Washington, DC 20002
202-651-5000
Distributes *College and Career Programs for Deaf Students*, describing over 100 community college and technical school programs in the United States for deaf students.

Scholastic Aptitude Test (SAT), Admissions Testing Program for Handicapped Students, 609-734-5068. Offers special testing arrangements for students documented to have hearing disabilities, including untimed tests or additional time, interpreter, and rest breaks. (For full group information, see HELP FOR SPECIAL CHILDREN on page 578.)

Other reference sources
General Works

How to Survive Hearing Loss, by Charlotte Himber. Washington, DC: Gallaudet University Press, 1989.
At Home Among Strangers, by Jerome D. Schein. Washington, DC: Gallaudet University Press, 1989.
Living with Deafness, by Barbara Taylor. New York: Watts, 1989.
Seeing Voices: A Journey into the World of the Deaf, by Oliver Sacks. Berkeley: University of California, 1989.
Health Care U.S.A., by Jean Carper. New York: Prentice Hall, 1987. Resource for general and specific health-care information, as for various types of hearing-loss and related disorders such as tinnitus and Ménière's disease; lists key otolaryngologists, ear donation centers and ear banks, and other information, such as about hearing aids, audiologists, and hearing dogs.
The Silent Garden: Understanding the Hearing Impaired Child, by Paul Ogden and Suzanne Lipsett. New York: St. Martin's, 1982.
Can't Your Child Hear? A Guide for Those Who Care About Deaf Children, by Roger Freeman, Clifton Carbin, and Robert Boese. Baltimore: University Park Press, 1981.

A Difference in the Family, by Helen Featherstone. New York: Viking-Penguin, 1981.

Mainstreaming Preschoolers: Children with Hearing Impairment: A Guide for Teachers, Parents, and Others Who Work with Hearing Impaired Preschoolers, by Rita Ann LaPorta et al. (1978). Prepared for the Head Start Bureau, Administration for Children, Youth and Families. Contains much useful information on what hearing impairments are and how they affect learning in preschoolers, various types of communications systems, and teaching techniques and activities to help develop skills.

The Deaf Child in the Public Schools: A Handbook for Parents of Deaf Children, second edition, by L. Katz, S. Mathis, and E. C. Merrill, Jr. Danville, IL: Interstate Printers and Publishers, 1978.

On Sign Language

Gallaudet Survival Guide to Signing, expanded edition, by Leonard G. Lane. Washington, DC: Gallaudet University Press, 1990.

Signs for Me: Basic Sign Vocabulary for Children, Parents and Teachers, by Benjamin Bahan and Joe Dannis. Berkeley, CA: Dawn Sign, 1990. Distributed by Publishers Group West.

From Mime to Sign, by Gilbert C. Eastman et al. Silver Spring, MD: T. J. Publishers, 1989. Address: 817 Silver Spring Avenue, 206, Silver Spring, MD 20910.

Signing Exact English. Producers: Gary Noe and Larry Noe. 1989. 116-minute video available from Hearing-Impaired Products Co., P.O. Box 12217, Fort Wayne, IN 46863. For ages 12 to adult.

American Sign Language: A Comprehensive Dictionary, by Martin Sternberg. New York: Harper and Row, 1981.

A Show of Hands: Say It in Sign Language, by Mary Beth Sullivan and Linda Bourke. Boston: Addison-Wesley, 1980.

Sesame Street Sign Language Fun, with Linda Bove. New York: Random House/Children's Television Workshop, 1980. For children.

Background Works

Manual Communication: Implications for Education, Harry Bornstein, ed. Washington, DC: Gallaudet University Press, 1990.

Educational Developmental Aspects of Deafness, Donald F. Moores and Kathryn P. Meadows-Orlans, eds. Washington, DC: Gallaudet University Press, 1990.

Dancing Without Music: Deafness in America, reprint, by Beryl Lieff Benderly. Washington, DC: Gallaudet University Press, 1990.

The Quiet Ear: Deafness in Literature, compiled by Brian Grant. Winchester, MA: Faber and Faber, 1988.

Gallaudet Encyclopedia of Deaf People and Deafness, 3 volumes, John V. Van Cleve, ed. New York: McGraw-Hill, 1987.

When the Mind Hears: A History of the Deaf, by Harlan Lane. New York: Random House, 1984.

Legal Rights of Hearing Impaired People, by National Center for Law and the Deaf. Washington, DC: Gallaudet University Press, 1982.

Professional Works

Educating the Deaf: Psychology, Principles, and Practices, third edition. Boston: Houghton Mifflin, 1987.

Hearing and Deafness, fourth edition, by H. Davis and R.S. Silverman. New York: Holt, Rinehart & Winston, 1978.

Sound and Sign: Childhood Deafness and Mental Health, by H. Schlesinger and K. Meadow. Berkeley: University of California, 1974.

For and by Kids

The Other Side of Silence, by Arden Neisser. Washington, DC: Gallaudet University Press, 1990.

Finding a Common Language: Children Living with Deafness, by Thomas Bergman. Milwaukee, WI: Gareth Stevens, 1990. For grades 3 to 5.

Annie's World, by Nancy Smiler Levinson. Washington, DC: Gallaudet University Press, 1990.

Ears Are for Hearing, by Paul Showers. New York: Crowell/Harper, 1990. For ages 4 to 8.

The Ear and Hearing, revised edition, by Steve Parker. New York: Watts, 1989. For grades 4 to 7.

Children of Silence: The Story of My Daughter's Triumph over Deafness, by Kathy Robinson. New York: Dutton, 1988.

Just Like Everybody Else, by Lillian Rosen. New York: Harcourt Brace Jovanovich, 1981.

Silent Dancer, by Bruce Hlibok. New York: Simon & Schuster, 1981.

Deaf Like Me, by T.S. Spradley and J.P. Spradley. Washington, DC: Gallaudet University Press, 1978.

(See COMMUNICATION SKILLS AND DISORDERS; also HELP FOR SPECIAL CHILDREN on page 578.)

Early and Periodic Screening, Diagnosis, and Treatment (EPSDT) A federal program established in 1967 under Medicaid, as part of Title 19 of the Social Security Act, that works through local social services to foster early detection of potentially disabling conditions in poor children, seeking through early health care to diminish the consequences of physical or mental problems and to lessen the later need for remedial services, enhancing in the long run the child's ability to live an independent life. Although too poorly funded to carry out its mission properly, EPSDT has helped diagnose and obtain treatment for many otherwise undetected, potentially debilitating conditions.

Early Screening Inventory (ESI) A DEVELOPMENTAL SCREENING TEST, administered individually or by group to children ages four to six, that attempts to assess ability to acquire new skills. Among the test's four sections are tasks calling for free-drawing and copying figures, language comprehension and expression, reasoning and counting, and balancing and motor coordination. Parents are asked to fill out a questionnaire on the child's family background, including medical history. Scoring is done according to a manual, and results may be used to indicate that a child needs further evaluation, as with a DIAGNOSTIC ASSESSMENT TEST. (For help and further information, see TESTS.)

early admission   In EDUCATION, formal acceptance of a student into COLLEGE before completion of high school studies, a form of ACCELERATION. (For help and further information, see ADMISSION.)

early childhood education   A general term with varying meanings, sometimes referring to PRESCHOOL education, including NURSERY SCHOOL, HEAD START, or any other programs before KINDERGARTEN level; sometimes referring to any school-based EDUCATION from PREPRIMARY level through PRIMARY SCHOOL.

early decision plan   In education, a program involving early student applications, usually in autumn of the senior year, and early response by a COLLEGE, usually in December. (For help and further information, see ADMISSION.)

eating disorders   A group of MENTAL DISORDERS, a psychiatric classification including ANOREXIA NERVOSA, BULIMIA, PICA, and RUMINATION DISORDER OF INFANCY.

Eaton-Lambert syndrome   A type of muscle disorder. (See MUSCULAR DYSTROPHY.)

EB   Abbreviation for EPIDERMOLYSIS BULLOSA.

ecchymosis   A large bruise or HEMORRHAGE under the skin.

ECG   Abbreviation for ELECTROENCEPHALOGRAPH.

echocardiography   A medical procedure for examining heart problems using ULTRASOUND (see HEART AND HEART PROBLEMS).

echolalia   Repetition of someone else's words or phrases, in a parrotlike, meaningless way; behavior found among some people with brain dysfunctions or MENTAL DISORDERS, such as SCHIZOPHRENIA, or with conditions such as TOURETTE'S SYNDROME.

eclampsia   A rare but extremely serious condition affecting women late in PREGNANCY, during LABOR, and shortly after DELIVERY. It generally occurs following unchecked PREECLAMPSIA. (Preeclampsia and eclampsia are sometimes considered mild and severe forms of a condition called *toxemia of pregnancy*.) Many symptoms of preeclampsia—such as hypertension (high BLOOD PRESSURE), edema (fluid buildup), and PROTEIN in the urine (*proteinuria*)—become more severe and are often accompanied by SEIZURES that threaten both mother and baby, sometimes resulting in COMA or DEATH. Emergency delivery is often performed, by CESAREAN SECTION if necessary, because the condition generally clears soon after CHILDBIRTH, though severe damage may already have been done to many body systems. With proper PRENATAL CARE, preeclampsia need not progress to eclampsia, but once severe symptoms of eclampsia develop, perhaps one out of four babies and one out of 10 mothers will die. The cause is unknown, though some have suggested that preeclampsia and eclampsia are triggered by a toxin (poison) produced by the PLACENTA, the fetus-nourishing organ in the UTERUS. (For help and further information, see PREGNANCY.)

ecological inventory   A survey performed by a SPECIAL EDUCATION teacher to identify skills that a HANDICAPPED child needs to develop in order to function successfully as an adult in work and in everyday living situations, such as those of stores, restaurants, parks, and buses.

ectopic pregnancy   Any PREGNANCY that is implanted and develops outside the UTERUS, generally in the FALLOPIAN TUBES (called a *tubal pregnancy*) but sometimes in one of the OVARIES, or on rare occasions in the CERVIX or elsewhere in the abdominal cavity. A woman who has previously had an operation on or infection in the fallopian tubes is at increased risk for having an ectopic pregnancy; use of an IUD, CONGENITAL abnormalities, use of some kinds of BIRTH-CONTROL PILLS, and earlier attempted STERILIZATION may also increase risk.

Ectopic pregnancy is a common condition, affecting perhaps one or two out of 100 pregnancies. In some cases, the fertilized egg (CONCEPTUS) is not VIABLE and simply dies, being reabsorbed into body tissues at a very early stage. Early signs of ectopic pregnancy often include missed menstrual periods, severe abdominal pain, and spotting (light bleeding) from the VAGINA.

If the ectopic pregnancy is undiscovered and the tube ruptures, HEMORRHAGE can lead to SHOCK and in some cases to DEATH. As well as through PREGNANCY TESTS, diagnosis is often made through ULTRASOUND and LAPAROSCOPY. If confirmed, an emergency operation (*laparotomy*) is performed to remove the developing EMBRYO and any associated tissues and to repair (or remove) the tube. Often BLOOD TRANSFUSIONS are needed if the tube has ruptured. Chances of normal conception are reduced after an ectopic pregnancy, but IN VITRO FERTILIZATION can bypass the tubes by implanting an embryo directly into the uterus. (For help and further information, see PREGNANCY.)

ectopic testicles   TESTES that have descended but not into their proper place in the SCROTUM.

EDC   Abbreviation for *expected date of confinement*, a medical term for DUE DATE.

edema   Abnormal accumulation of fluid in the body's tissues, causing swelling; a sign of imbalances and disruptions of the body's chemistry that can result from a wide variety of diseases and disorders, such as KIDNEY AND UROLOGICAL DISORDERS or ECLAMPSIA. Drugs called *diuretics* are often prescribed, and salt is restricted in the diet to lessen fluid retention.

education   The process by which a child (and later an adult) acquires new knowledge and skills, especially those necessary for independent living, whether by informal exposure to new data, ideas, and experiences, by the semiformal teaching of a parent, or by formal, organized instruction in a school.

Parents are a child's first teachers, the ones through whom the child begins to learn that the world is an interesting place and worth communicating with. They have the important task of establishing from birth regular contact between the baby and the world, encouraging the baby's efforts to interact with the

Baby's Growth and Development: The First Year

Here are some of the things you can usually expect your baby to do in the first year of life.

By about six weeks

- Holds head off of bed for a few moments while lying on stomach
- Follows an object with eyes for a short distance
- Pays attention to sounds
- Makes a few vocal sounds other than crying
- Looks at your face
- Smiles when you smile or play with him or her
- Moves arms and legs in an energetic manner

By about five months

- Holds head upright while lying on stomach
- Holds head steady when held in a sitting position
- Laughs, squeals, and babbles
- Turns to your voice
- Rolls over
- Follows with eyes from side to side
- Recognizes parents
- Bring hands together in front of the body
- Reaches for and holds objects
- Passes object from one hand to the other
- Begins to chew
- Stretches out arms to be picked up
- Smiles by him or herself

By about eight months

- Sits without support when placed in sitting position
- Takes part of weight on own legs when held steady
- Creeps (pulls body with arm and leg kicks)
- Starts to make recognizable sounds (''baa'' or ''daa'')
- Responds to ''no'' and his or her name
- Grasps object off of flat surface
- Feeds crackers to self
- Looks around for the source of new sounds

By about 10 months

- Gets into sitting position on his or her own
- Stands, holding on
- Crawls
- Picks up a small object with thumb and fingers
- Tries to get an object that is out of reach
- Pulls back when you pull a toy in his or her hand
- Drinks from a cup when it is held
- Plays peek-a-boo
- Uses voice to get attention

By about 12 months

- Brings together two toys held in hand
- Imitates your speech
- Uses ''Dada'' or ''Mama'' to mean a specific person
- Plays pat-a-cake
- Can walk holding onto something
- Finds one object under another
- Waves bye-bye
- Understands simple words and phrases (''come here'')

Soon after baby's first birthday

- Stands alone, then walks alone
- Scribbles with a pencil or crayon
- Drinks from a cup by self
- Uses a spoon (spills a little!)
- Plays with a ball on the floor
- Can say two or three words (may not be clear)

Don't worry if your baby is different—each baby develops in his or her own way. However, if you notice large variations from what you might expect, or if you have other concerns, ask your doctor or clinic staff. (**Note**: If your baby arrived early—was premature—he or she may develop a little later in some things and not in others.)

Source: *Infant Care*. Washington, DC: Government Printing Office, 1989. Prepared for the Public Health Service, Bureau of Maternal and Child Health and Resources Development.

people and things in his or her environment. Some suggestions for STIMULATING BABY'S SENSES are given on page 418, under SENSORY MODES. Working parents need to be sure that, if others are caring for their baby, these CAREGIVERS give the infant the necessary attention and stimulation. Babies who do not get the required physical contact and sensory stimulation can lapse into a kind of apathy or DEPRESSION, ceasing attempts to make contact with the world, and as a result can become retarded in development, a condition known medically as MARASMUS, or FAILURE TO THRIVE. Much teaching, of course, goes on under the heading of play. Many everyday household items such as pots

and pans can be used fruitfully as toys for babies. (See CHILDPROOFING for cautions about safety.)

BABY'S GROWTH AND DEVELOPMENT, above, gives some sense of what babies, *on the average*, learn to do within their first year. This chart will help parents adjust to their baby's development, rather than frustrating themselves or making their baby uncomfortable by trying to teach the baby something most babies don't learn until they are older. Knowledge of how a baby grows and develops can also help parents plan ahead to keep an environment safe. The SAFETY CHECKLIST: KEEPING BABY SAFE on page 504 is a guide to how to keep a baby's environment safe in the early years, depending on what the baby can do at each stage of development.

Parents should not be concerned if their baby reaches a DEVELOPMENTAL MILESTONE later (or earlier!) than on the chart, but they should examine why this might be. Babies are individuals, and variations in the timing of development of skills does not mean that they have problems. If a child develops late in just one or two areas, and average or fast in others, this may be a mark of the child's individual learning pattern. But if the baby is late in developing most skills, parents should ask themselves the following:

• Have they been giving the child an opportunity to learn?
• Have they been praising and encouraging the child's efforts?
• Is the child a premature baby or physically ill?

If they do not see a reason for the late development, and the child does not improve, they should have a doctor or clinic staff check the child. If such professionals say the baby will "grow out of it" but the child still does not seem to be developing, parents should seek another opinion. If there is a health problem or some lack of opportunity to learn and develop, the sooner the problem is recognized and either corrected or dealt with, the better for the child's long-term development.

In families where the parent or parents work outside the home, an infant is likely to be in the care of others from a very early age, such as a nanny in the home, family day care in someone else's home, or CHILD CARE in a variety of other settings. During the day, in the parent's absence, these caregivers are responsible for teaching the baby. From about age two or three, many babies are part of PLAY GROUPS, which begin to develop their social skills. From about ages three to five, many children join somewhat more formal, organized groups and classes, in various PRESCHOOL programs, including NURSERY SCHOOLS, HEAD START programs, PREKINDERGARTEN, and MONTESSORI METHOD schools.

During these years, children develop a wide range of skills. The CHART OF NORMAL DEVELOPMENT, on page 507, indicates when between birth and age six children first *on the average* begin to develop the key skills: MOTOR SKILLS (gross and fine), COGNITIVE SKILLS, SELF-HELP SKILLS, SOCIAL SKILLS, and communication skills (understanding and speaking language, see COMMUNICATION SKILLS AND DISORDERS). Children develop at individual and varying paces, but all children can benefit from activities designed to enhance their natural development. In TEACHING YOUNG CHILDREN: GUIDELINES AND ACTIVITIES, on page 544, parents will find activities designed to develop children's skills in various areas, as well as general guidelines for teaching that apply to children of any age. (For information on evaluating early childhood programs, see PRESCHOOLS.)

At about age five many children enter the formal school system in KINDERGARTEN; where no kindergarten exists, some enter ELEMENTARY or PRIMARY SCHOOL at about age six, in first grade. By law, children are required to be in COMPULSORY ATTENDANCE at a school between specified ages, usually about six to 16. At the age of six, therefore, legal requirements, rights, and responsibilities begin to impinge on the parent's educational choices.

Some parents at this stage choose to educate their children themselves, through HOME SCHOOLING; if they do, they need to meet whatever requirements have been set for children's education in their state of residence. Some parents educate their children at home in the early years, later sending them to formal schools; but others follow home schooling through their children's ADOLESCENCE, often using correspondence materials for INDEPENDENT STUDY. This very demanding course is taken by relatively few families, however.

Considerably more children—about one in eight—are at this point entered into PRIVATE SCHOOLS, for a variety of reasons, including differing views on DISCIPLINE (stricter or freer), more varied educational methods, desire for religious schooling, attempts to avoid DESEGREGATION, prestige (as with elite boarding schools), and smaller classes. Parents who send their children to private schools are not exempt from taxes for PUBLIC SCHOOLS, a situation some wish to change with a VOUCHER SYSTEM, under which tax funds could be used for either public or private schools. Critics stress that this would undermine the public school system and run counter to separation of church and state, since many private schools are religiously oriented or affiliated. Many parents keep their children in private schools only until it is time to enter JUNIOR HIGH SCHOOL or HIGH SCHOOL, where public institutions are better funded and therefore likely to have the kinds of laboratory and other educational materials needed for high school classes, especially in the sciences.

Most students, however, enter the public schools at age five or six and stay in them from elementary school through MIDDLE SCHOOL, or junior high school, and on to high school (secondary school). These schools vary widely around the country in terms of CURRICULUM and resources. Partly, that is because Americans have long resisted any standardization of education. Recognition of the flaws and shortcomings of the current educational system, however, have led many to be more receptive to model curricula, like that for secondary schools in JAMES MADISON HIGH SCHOOL: A MODEL CURRICULUM, on page 538, and the corresponding one for elementary schools on page 530.

The distribution of resources also varies widely. Rural schools, especially in poor, sparsely populated areas, and inner-city schools with limited resources may have trouble attracting high-quality teachers, for example, and may not have the kind of equipment needed for a full science or technical program. On the other hand, some rural schools have the advantage of smaller classes and more personal education. Suburban schools may have resources both for physical plant and for attracting good teachers but may sometimes be impersonal and focus too heavily on achievement, rather than on developing the individual. Inner-city schools have the considerable cultural resources of the city itself to draw on, but many individual schools have been starved of funds, are filled with violence, and cannot attract and hold top teachers.

Under the circumstances, parents concerned with their children's education must look very carefully at the schools in their area. If they are moving into an area, they are well advised to learn as much as they can about the strengths and weaknesses of the various schools available and to make the school part of the decision about where to live. The importance of schooling and the desire to provide more varied programs for many students have led to the popularity of SCHOOLS OF CHOICE, in which schools are deliberately varied to provide educational experiences among which parents and children can choose. Portions of the U.S. Department of Education's pamphlet *Choosing a School for Your Child*, including a checklist for evaluating schools (including PRIVATE SCHOOLS), are reproduced on page 516.

Wherever they live, parents are advised to become actively involved in school life and help improve the quality of education in the area. Virtually every study of education indicates that schools are improved and children's learning benefits with strong parental involvement. Numerous laws and policy changes have, in fact, brought parents much more into the public education system than in the past.

The federal EDUCATION FOR ALL HANDICAPPED CHILDREN ACT of 1975 requires states and local school districts to actively seek out, from infancy and then throughout the school years, any child with a handicap (see HANDICAPPED) that affects learning. Children who may have learning problems undergo DEVELOPMENTAL SCREENING and DIAGNOSTIC ASSESSMENT TESTS, depending on what kind of problem is suspected. If a problem is diagnosed, the child is entitled to special educational services, and school officials must draw up an INDIVIDUALIZED EDUCATION PROGRAM designed to overcome, eliminate, or ameliorate the problem—but none of this can take place without the parent's knowledge and consent. Parents are involved at every stage, asking questions, getting answers, acting as advocate for their child (sometimes with other advocates to help), monitoring the child's progress, and helping modify the program if necessary. If school and parents disagree on what is appropriate, a whole sequence of appeals and hearings, many of them based on considerations of DUE PROCESS, have been developed that may eventually extend to the court system.

CHAPTER 1 (of Title I of the Elementary and Secondary Education Act of 1965) is also a federal program, one providing funds to students of low-income families who are performing below GRADE level. Parents in these programs are equally involved in the processes of selecting the schools, and the students within those schools, to be eligible for funds.

Another federal law that affects all parents of school-age children is the FAMILY EDUCATIONAL RIGHTS AND PRIVACY ACT OF 1974 (FERPA), which gives parents (and students after age 18) access to school records and control over who gets to see them outside of the school system, except for court-mandated disclosures. On page 202 is a summary of parents' rights and schools' responsibilities under FERPA and guidelines on what to look for and how to act when reviewing and attempting to revise or correct school records. Under this law, too, a whole appeal system operates.

As parents have increasingly become active advocates of their children's educational rights and participants in the school system that teaches them, the once-informal PARENT–TEACHER CONFERENCES have often been turned into multidisciplinary team discussions of test results and educational programs. Numerous organizations (see below) have developed to help parents prepare themselves for these new responsibilities, not least to explain to them the nature and significance of the many and varied TESTS given to young children (many of which are described by name in separate entries in this book). The National Committee on Citizens in Education has prepared a summary of PARENTS' RIGHTS TO INVOLVEMENT IN PUBLIC SCHOOLS and notes on their recommended ANNUAL EDUCATION CHECKUP (pages 170–72).

For help and further information

General Organizations

National Committee for Citizens in Education (NCCE)
10840 Little Patuxent Parkway, Suite 301
Columbia, MD 21044
301-997-9300, toll-free number 800-NETWORK [638-9675]
William Rioux, Executive Director

Organization of parents and interested others devoted to increasing parent and community participation in education. Conducts research; acts as information clearinghouse, including foundation-funded ACCESS computerized information; operates toll-free number for information and advice about public school education; offers special programs for single parents and their children; publishes various print and audiovisual materials, including newspaper *NETWORK for Public Schools*; "Information for Parents" pamphlets on educational issues, such as school records, parent–teacher conferences, and parent involvement in schools; fact sheets on special topics, such as *School Records, Corporal Punishment, Gifted Education, Parent Involvement, School Evaluation, Parent's Rights* regarding handicapped education, *Individualized Education Programs, When You Disagree* (about handicapped programs), *Home Schooling, Single-Parent Families, Parents Organizing, Suspension and Due Process*, and *How to Appeal*; and books (some also in Spanish) such as *Parents Can Understand Testing, The Middle School Years: A Parent's Handbook, Beyond the Open Door: A Citizen's Guide to Increasing Public Access to Local School Boards, Parents, Schools and the Law, Parents Organizing to Improve Schools, The Evidence Continues to Grow: Parent Involvement Improves Student Achievement: An Annotated Bibliography, You Can Improve Your Child's School: Practical Answers to Questions Parents Ask Most About Their Public Schools, Your School: How Well Is It Working?*, and *A Citizen's Guide to School Evaluation, School Closings and Declining Enrollment: A Guide to Effective Parent/Citizen Involvement*, as well as handy pocket-size cards such as Parent's Rights Card, Annual Education Checkup Card, and Special Education Checkup Card.

Parents' Rights to Involvement in Public Schools

The National Committee for Citizens in Education (NCCE) believes parents should have a number of "rights" to become involved in the public schools their children attend. Most of those rights listed might better be classified as "expectations" parents have for their relationship with their child's school and specific tasks or activities parents can do to become active participants in the educational process. A few are based on the Constitution, federal or state laws, or Supreme Court rulings. Others have been identified by many research studies which show that any and all types of parent involvement have a positive effect on a child's success in school.

Many school districts afford these basic "rights" automatically to the parents and citizens in the community. Others do not yet feel comfortable with encouraging parents to become equal partners in the educational process. We urge parents to assert their right to participate in and be consulted about their children's education.

Why Parents Have Rights

It is the belief of NCCE that parents of children in the public schools have fundamental rights to become involved based on the following:

- Children do better in school when their parents are involved.
- Public schools are supported by tax dollars.
- Teachers, principals, and other school personnel are public officials accountable to the school board, which in turn is accountable to the public.
- The public school system was organized to serve the citizens of the community, especially the children and their parents. As such, it should have an open atmosphere and be responsive to their needs.

Parents Have a Right to Information About:

- Teachers and principals—their background and experience;
- School policies, rules, and regulations in areas of:
    Health and medical regulations, such as
        required examinations and inoculations,
        procedures if a child is sick at school;
    Attendance regulations:
        How many days may a student be absent or late without a penalty?
        What should you do if your child is sick and cannot attend school?
        Will the school inform you if your child is absent?
    Disciplinary policy, behavior standards, and grounds for suspension and exclusion, including procedures to
        be followed;
    Schedule for the school year, such as
        dates of parent/teacher conferences
        holidays
        parent meetings
        report cards;
    Sources of all rules and policies, whether state law, local district policy, or policy of the school principal;
- Grievance procedures—how you can appeal rules and regulations with which you disagree;
- Academic requirements, criteria for student evaluation, homework regulations, standards for promotion, and problems your child may have with schoolwork or behavior;
- Curriculum—what is being taught, how the curriculum is organized, how students are grouped for instruction, and what methods are being employed in the classes.

Parents Have Rights of Access to:

- Review all records kept by the school about your child and to challenge inaccurate information or material which you believe is an invasion of privacy.
- Visit the school and your child's classroom after making arrangements with the school office and the classroom teacher.
- See your child's teacher and the school principal without "red tape" and delay.
- Have individual teacher conferences several times a year, in privacy, with a translator if needed, at a time convenient to both parent and teacher, and at home if that is the only feasible way for the meeting to be held.

Continued on page 171

Parents Have Rights to Participate and Be Consulted:

- Before a change in placement, retention in grade, or assignment to a special classroom;
- To get help for a child who is not doing well;
- To appeal school decisions affecting your child;
- To organize and participate in parent organizations;
- To attend and speak at school board meetings.

What Research Reveals About Parent Involvement

The forty-nine studies annotated in the report *The Evidence Continues to Grow* document and corroborate that "when parents are involved, children do better in school, and they go to better schools."

Programs designed with strong parent involvement produce students who perform better than otherwise identical programs without parent involvement. Children whose parents help them at home and stay in touch with the school score higher than children of similar aptitude and family background whose parents are *not involved*. Schools where children are failing improve dramatically when parents are called in to help.

Some of the major benefits of parent involvement are:

- High grades and test scores;
- Long-term academic achievement;
- Positive attitudes and behavior;
- More successful programs;
- More effective schools.

How Schools Benefit from Parent Involvement

When parents can expect the "rights" to information, access, and consultation to be honored by school personnel, an atmosphere of trust and collaboration will develop between school and home, children will perform at a higher level, and the educational system will benefit.

Source: National Committee for Citizens in Education.

Home and School Institute (HSI)
Special Projects Office
1201 16th Street, NW
Washington, DC 20036
202-466-3633
Dorothy Rich, President

Organization stressing the importance of home and community in education, as by use of household items and activities to teach basic educational and coping skills. Develops methods and materials to assist parents in helping children learn at home, including some for bilingual, handicapped, and disadvantaged children; operates MegaSkills® Education Center and Workshops; publishes various materials, including pamphlets, books on home and school curriculum, and other works, such as *Survival Guide for Busy Parents, The Forgotten Factor in School Success—Parents, Careers and Caring, Special Solutions, Get Smart: Advice for Teens with Babies,* and *Families Learning Together*.

National Education Association (NEA)
1201 16th Street, NW
Washington, DC 20036
202-822-7200

Don Cameron, Executive Director
Mary H. Futrell, President
Professional organization of educators at all levels. Affiliated with National Coalition for Parent Involvement in Education (NCPIE). Publishes various materials, including *NEA Today*, annual reviews, and NCPIE's "Guidelines for Schools and School Districts."

United States Department of Education
Office of Educational Research and Improvement
555 New Jersey Avenue, NW
Washington, DC 20208
202-401-3032
Federal arm researching education and aiming to improve it.

ACCESS/ERIC
Aspen Systems Corporation
1600 Research Boulevard
Rockville, MD 20850
800-USE-ERIC [873-3792]
Federally funded clearinghouse for information on education.

On Parental Involvement in Schools

National Congress of Parents and Teachers (National PTA)
700 North Rush Street
Chicago, IL 60611

Annual Education Checkup

Most parents are convinced of the importance of an annual medical checkup for their children, but what about an Annual Education Checkup? The National Committee for Citizens in Education (NCCE) suggests that a good way to help assure a child's progress in school is for every parent of a school-age child to conduct an Annual Educational Checkup. This checklist tells you how.

Basic steps include reviewing home and school files kept on your child and interviewing your child's teacher and possibly other members of the school staff. If your child is having special problems in school, you may need to consult some of the school system's specialists.

If, after talking to your child's teacher or counselor and reviewing and correcting the school record, any aspect of your child's schooling remains unsatisfactory to you, there are some steps you can take toward resolving the situation. You can appeal to the principal, superintendent, or school board if you disagree with disciplinary action or school policies and practices. Keep in mind that when you request a hearing, it is your right to bring your own expert, a doctor, lawyer, interpreter, or parent advocate.

Working together with the school is the best way to help your child in school. It is NCCE's hope that this review will help discover school problems early and give parents and teachers a chance to work out a plan for each child to guarantee school success.

Review of Material at Home

Check on school-related materials sent home during the last year. It's a good idea to keep a separate file for each child. As you review the file, ask your child for his or her comments on school. You might ask, "What do you like best? What least?" and "What would you like to change?" The checklist below lists other questions to consider.

Checklist for Review of Material at Home

	Yes	No	Need More Info		Yes	No	Need More Info
Do I have all previously issued report cards?				If our school does not have a handbook, do I know to whom to go for answers to questions?			
Does any correspondence with teachers and principal remain unanswered?				Are my child's immunizations against contagious diseases up to date, and have I made an appointment for my child's annual school medical checkup for next fall?			
If our school produces a handbook, do I have a copy? Does it clearly answer any questions I may have about school policies on such subjects as suspension, promotion, graduating procedures, attendance, and due process rights?				Have I made a list of questions I want to ask my child's teacher, and have I set aside materials from my home file that I plan to take with me?			

To complete the checkup, you should also review the TIPS FOR PARENT–TEACHER CONFERENCES on page 362 under PARENT–TEACHER CONFERENCE and the CHECKLIST FOR REVIEW OF SCHOOL RECORDS on page 204 under FAMILY EDUCATIONAL RIGHTS AND PRIVACY ACT OF 1974.

Source: National Committee for Citizens in Education

312-787-0977
Manya Ungar, President
Jeanne Koepsell, Contact

Organization of parents, teachers, school administrators, students, and others dedicated to improving education, health, and safety of children. Acts as advocate for children's interests; seeks to educate public and influence public policy and legislation; publishes various materials, including *PTA Today*, quarterly *National PTA Directory*, newsletter *What's Happening in Washington*, *PTA Handbook*, *Looking In on Your School: A Workbook for Improving Public Education*, and other materials on topics such as parent–school relations, single parents, latchkey children, education to prevent alcohol and drug abuse, absenteeism, teenage sexuality, discipline, seatbelts, improving education quality, and parent education.

Institute for Responsive Education (IRE)
605 Commonwealth Avenue
Boston, MA 02215
617-353-3309
Don Davies, President
Organization advocating increased citizen participation in schools and educational decision-making. Gathers and disseminates information; seeks to educate public and influence policy; operates National Partnership for Parent Choice in the Public Schools; publishes various materials, including magazine *Equity and Choice.*

National Association of Hebrew Day School PTA's
160 Broadway
New York, NY 10038
212-406-4190
Mrs. Samuel Brand, Executive Director
Organization of PTA associations of Hebrew elementary and secondary schools. Counsels individual groups on programs and fund-raising; publishes various materials, including *National PTA Bulletin.*

National Forum of Catholic Parent Organizations (NFCPO)
c/o National Catholic Educational Association
1077 30th Street, NW, #100
Washington, DC 20007
202-293-5954
Mary Lynch Barnds, Executive Director
Organization of Catholic parent groups, schools, and other interested individuals and groups; arm of National Catholic Educational Association. Advises parents on at-home religious training and parents' rights in education; acts as advocate for government support of nonpublic schools; publishes *The Catholic Parent* quarterly.

National Lutheran Parent-Teacher League (NLPTL)
123 West Clinton Place, Room 102
St. Louis, MO 63122
314-821-5135
Betty Brusius, Executive Director
Organization of parent–teacher groups linked with the Lutheran Church–Missouri Synod. Advises parents on religious training of their children; publishes newsletter *Training Wheels.*

Parents for Quality Education (PQE)
P.O. Box 50025
Pasadena, CA 91105
213-684-1881
Forrest L. Turpen, Executive Director
Organization of parents, teachers, school administrators, and pastors seeking to enhance children's Christian education. Publishes bimonthly magazine *Visions*, arm of Christian Educators Association International.

Parents Rights Organization (PRO)
12571 Northwinds Drive
St. Louis, MO 63146

314-434-4171
Mae Duggan, President
Organization of parents, teachers, educators, churches, and students seeking freedom of choice in education. Aims to gain legal recognition for parents' rights to control their children's education; seeks to educate public and influence public policy; publishes various materials, including *Parents Rights Newsletter.*

About Preschool and Elementary Education and
Child Development

National Association for the Education of Young Children (NAEYC), 202-232-8777; toll-free number 800-424-2460. (For full group information, see PRESCHOOL.)

Association for Childhood Education International (ACEI), 301-942-2443. (For full group information, see PRESCHOOL.)

National Head Start Association (NHSA), 703-739-0875. (For full group information, see HEAD START.)

American Montessori Society (AMS), 212-924-3209. (For full group information, see MONTESSORI METHOD.)

Parent Cooperative Pre-Schools International (PCPI), 317-849-0992. (For full group information, see PRESCHOOL.)

National Coalition of Title I/Chapter I Parents (NCTCP), National Parent Center, 202-547-9286. (For full group information, see CHAPTER 1.)

Institute for Childhood Resources (INICR), 415-864-1169. (For full group information, see PLAY GROUP.)

Society for Research in Child Development (SRCD), 312-962-7470. (For full group information, see PRESCHOOL.)

World Organization for Early Childhood Education, U.S. National Committee, 209-224-0924. (For full group information, see PRESCHOOL.)

American Institute for Character Education (AICE)
Box 12617
342 West Woodlawn Avenue
San Antonio, TX 78212
512-734-5091
Ray S. Erlandson, Chairman, Board of Governors
Organization aiming to help teachers teach grade-school children basic values. Trains and advises teachers; maintains library; publishes various materials, including quarterly *Character Education Today* and kits and manuals for teachers.

National Black Child Development Institute (NBCDI)
1463 Rhode Island Avenue, NW
Washington, DC 20005
202-387-1281
Evelyn K. Moore, Executive Director
Organization acting as advocate for Black children. Encourages development of full potential; seeks to educate public and

influence government policy; provides services and programs on curriculum, play schools, and materials and equipment for all Black children, including handicapped; publishes various materials for parents and teachers.

About Discipline in Schools

End Violence Against the Next Generation (EVAN-G), 415-527-0454. (For full group information, see CORPORAL PUNISHMENT.)

National Center for the Study of Corporal Punishment and Alternatives in the Schools (NCSCPAS), 215-787-6091. (For full group information, see CORPORAL PUNISHMENT.)

Parents and Teachers Against Violence in Education (PTAVE), 415-831-1661. (For full group information, see CORPORAL PUNISHMENT.)

On Private and Alternative Elementary and Secondary Schools

Council for American Private Education (CAPE), 202-659-0016. (For full group information, see PRIVATE SCHOOL.)

National Association of Independent Schools (NAIS), 617-723-6900. (For full group information, see PRIVATE SCHOOL.)

National Association of Private, Nontraditional Schools and Colleges (NAPNSC), 303-243-5441. (For full group information, see PRIVATE SCHOOL.)

National Home Study Council (NHSC), 202-234-5100. (For full group information, see HOME STUDY.)

National Coalition of Alternative Community Schools (NCACS), 615-964-3670. (For full group information, see ALTERNATIVE SCHOOL.)

Education Voucher Institute (EVI), 313-881-2337. (For full group information, see VOUCHER SYSTEM.)

Citizens for Educational Freedom (CEF)
Rosslyn Plaza
1611 North Kent Street, Suite 805
Arlington, VA 22209
703-524-1991
Sr. Renee Oliver, Executive Director
Nonsectarian organization of parents and others interested in establishing free choice among educational alternatives. Supports voucher system for school tuition and tax deductions or credits for educational expenses; encourages increased public participation in education; publishes various materials, including bimonthly *Freedom in Education* and semiannual *Educational Freedom*.

High-Scope Educational Research Foundation, 313-485-2000. (For full group information, see COGNITIVE DEVELOPMENT.)

National Council for Better Education (NCBE)
1800 Diagonal Road, Suite 635

Alexandria, VA 22314
703-684-4404
Sally D. Reed, Chairman
Organization of parents, teachers, and others who believe that the National Education Association (page 171) is "radical left" tool to control U.S. education. Supports parents' rights in education and teaching of values; publishes various materials, including books *NEA: Propaganda Front of the Radical Left* and *A Parent's Survival Guide to the Public Schools*.

On Equal Treatment in Schools

NAACP Legal Defense and Educational Fund (LDF)
99 Hudson Street, 16th Floor
New York, NY 10013
212-219-1900
Julius LeVonne, Director-Counsel
Arm of the National Association for the Advancement of Colored People using the law to fight discrimination in many areas, including education. Finances court actions; seeks to influence public policy; publishes various materials, including newsletter and watchdog reports.

National Urban League (NUL)
500 East 62nd Street
New York, NY 10021
212-310-9000
John E. Jacob, President
Organization seeking to end segregation and discrimination in many areas, including education. Seeks to influence public policy; publishes various materials.

A Better Chance (ABC)
419 Boylston Street
Boston, MA 02116
617-536-5270
Organization of private and some public secondary schools to provide educational opportunity for talented minority students. Finds and selects students for placement in special secondary school programs, preparatory for selective colleges and universities; provides financial and technical aid as needed; conducts research; operates affiliated Women's Committee for a Better Chance; publishes various materials.

Project on Equal Education Rights (PEER)
1413 K Street, NW, 9th Floor
Washington, DC 20005
202-332-7337
Leslie R. Wolfe, Director
Arm of National Organization of Women (NOW), seeking to eliminate sex discrimination in schools, especially by enforcement of Title IX. Gathers and disseminates information on treatment of girls and women in education; sponsors special programs about problems for minority and disabled girls and women, especially in computer and other technical and vocational training; publishes various materials, including newsletter *Equal Education Alert* and policy papers, such as *Sex Bias at*

the Computer Terminal—How Schools Program Girls, Learning Her Place—Sex Bias in the Elementary Classroom, and Black Women in a High Tech World.

Sex Equity in Education Program (SEEP)
370 Lexington Avenue, Room 603
New York, NY 10017
212-532-8330
Jo Sanders, Director
Arm of Women's Action Alliance, aiming to foster nonsexist educational environment for children. Gathers and disseminates information; generates and makes available nonsexist educational materials; operates Computer Equity and Training Project to give female students full access to computer skills; publishes various materials, including biennial journal *Equal Play* and *The Neuter Computer*.

Council on Interracial Books for Children (CIBC), 212-757-5339. Operates Racism and Sexism Resource Center for Educators. (For full group information, see READING.)

On Other Special Approaches or Areas of Concern

Council for Basic Education (CBE)
725 15th Street, NW
Washington, DC 20005
202-347-4171
A. Graham Down, Executive Director
Organization of parents, educators, and others interested in liberal arts education, including English, science, mathematics, history, geography, government, the arts, and foreign languages. Reviews educational research; advises schools; supports Writing to Learn workshops; publishes various materials, including quarterly *Basic Education: Issues, Answers, and Facts*.

Association for Experiential Education (AEE)
Box 249-CU
Boulder, CO 80309
303-492-1547
Mitchell Sakofs, Executive Director
Organization of schools, groups, and individuals interested in fostering experience-based education, not only in regular classrooms but also for special situations and populations, such as mentally retarded or mentally ill, handicapped, and juvenile delinquents. Acts as information clearinghouse; publishes various materials, including *Journal of Experiential Education*.

Quest National Center
6655 Sharon Woods Boulevard
Columbus, OH 43229
614-882-6400
Rick R. Little, President
Organization to support parents and teachers in helping school-age children to learn basic life skills, such as problem-solving and interpersonal communication. Seeks to prevent alcohol and drug abuse; provides training and children's services; conducts research; publishes various materials, including *Skills for Living Curriculum* and *Skills for Adolescence Curriculum*.

People United for Rural Education (PURE)
R.R. Box 35
Kamrar, IA 50132
515-325-6059
Claudia Jones, President
Organization of parents, educators, government officials, and others interested in rural education. Seeks to influence public policy, especially toward maintaining values of rural schools and ensuring equal educational opportunities for all; supports local control of schools; opposes centralization; publishes various materials, including newsletter and occasional *Legislative Alerts*.

National Rural Education Association (NREA)
c/o Joseph T. Newlin, Executive Director
Office for Rural Education
300 Education Building
Colorado State University
Fort Collins, CO 80523
303-491-7022
Organization of educators, school administrators, parents, community leaders, and others interested in education in rural and small schools. Seeks to educate public and influence policy as to the special needs of rural schools and the importance of providing equal educational opportunities for all; encourages development of materials and programs for rural schoolchildren; publishes various materials, including quarterly *National Rural Education News* and journal *The Rural Educator*.

Association for Individually Guided Education (AIGE)
c/o Shirley Hutcherson, Executive Officer
Hutchinson United School District #308
P.O. Box 1908
Hutchinson, KS 67504
316-662-4461
Organization of educators and other interested in education tailored to "the individual needs of all educable children and adults." Seeks to educate public and professionals about individually guided education (IGE); provides information, materials, and suggestions for teachers and schools, including focus on slow learners and mainstreaming programs; maintains library; publishes various materials, including quarterly newsletter.

National Association for Core Curriculum (NACC), 216-672-2792. (For full group information, see CURRICULUM.)

National Association for Year-Round Education (NAYRE), 619-292-3679. SCHOOL.)

On Legal Problems Relating to Education

National Organization on Legal Problems of Education (NOLPE)
3601 SW 29th Street, Suite 223

Topeka, KS 66614
913-273-3550

Organization serving as a clearinghouse for information on law in the schools. Publishes various materials, including newsletters and books on education law.

Center for Law and Education (CLE)
Larsen Hall, 6th Floor
14 Appian Way
Cambridge, MA 02138
617-495-4666
Paul Newman, Executive Director

Organization of legal professionals focusing on legal questions related to education, including students' rights, special education, competency testing, discrimination (by sex or race), and bilingual education. Provides information and referrals to individuals and professionals; engages in some litigation directly, especially on behalf of low-income families; publishes various materials; funded by the Legal Services Corporation.

National Association for Legal Support of Alternative Schools (NALSAS), 505-471-6928. (For full group information, see ALTERNATIVE SCHOOL.)

Home School Legal Defense Association (HSDLA), 703-882-3838. (For full group information, see HOME SCHOOLING.)

Community Dispute Services (CDS)
140 West 51st Street
New York, NY 10020
212-484-4000
Robert Coulson, President

Organization aiming to encourage use of mediation, arbitration, and fact-finding in community disputes, including those involving welfare agencies, schools, and landlords; an arm of the American Arbitration Association. Offers training programs for community members; provides neutral third parties from Community Disputes Settlement Panel, on request.

Children's Rights Project
American Civil Liberties Union (ACLU)
132 West 43rd Street
New York, NY 10036
212-944-9800
Ira Glasser, Executive Director
Marcia R. Lowry, Project Director

Organization that acts as advocate for "the rights of people set forth in the Declaration of Independence and the Constitution: freedom of inquiry and expression (speech, press, assembly, and religion); due process of law and fair trial for everybody; equality before the law for everybody regardless of race, color, national origin, and political opinion or religious belief." Publishes wide variety of materials; focuses on issues concerning children and families.

Other reference sources

On General Education and Success in School

The National PTA Talks to Parents: How to Get the Best Education for Your Child, by Melitta J. Cutright. New York: Delacorte, 1989.

Learning All the Time, by John Holt. Reading, MA: Addison-Wesley, 1989.

Hassle-Free Homework: A Six-Week Plan for Parents and Children to Take the Pain Out of Homework, by Faith Clark and Cecil Clark. New York: Delacorte, 1989.

Help Your Child Make the Most of School, by Terri Fields. Tucson, AZ: Fisher, 1989.

You Are Your Child's First Teacher, by Rahima Baldwin. Berkeley, CA: Celestial Arts, 1989.

The School-Smart Parent: A Guide to Knowing What Your Child Should Know—from Infancy Through the End of Elementary School, by Gene I. Maeroff. New York: Times Books, 1989.

Parents' Guide to Raising Kids Who Love to Learn: Infant to Grade School, by the Children's Television Workshop. New York: Prentice Hall, 1989.

Smart Kids with School Problems: Things to Know and Ways to Help, by Priscilla L. Vail. New York: New American Library, 1989.

Your Child's Growing Mind: A Guide to Learning and Brain Development from Birth to Adolescence, by Jane M. Healy. Garden City, NY: Doubleday, 1988.

Helping Your Child Get A's in School, by Alan M. Solomon and Penelope B. Grenoble. Chicago: Contemporary, 1988.

The Learning Child, by Dorothy Cohen. New York: Schocken, 1988.

Megalearning: A Course in Enhancing Learning Skills and Applying Knowledge, by Ron Gross. Los Angeles: Tarcher, 1988.

Your Child in School, by Thomas Sobol and Harriett Sobol. New York: Arbor House, 1986–87.

Ending the Homework Hassle: How to Help Your Child Succeed Independently in School, by John Rosemond. Kansas City, MO: Andrews and McMeel, 1990.

Growing Up Writing: Teaching Our Children to Write, Think, and Learn, by Arlene Silberman. New York: Random House, 1989.

Countdown to College: A Student's Guide to Getting the Most Out of High School, by Zola Dincin Schneider and Phyllis B. Kalb. New York: College Board, 1989.

MegaSkills: How Families Can Help Children Succeed in School and Beyond, by Dorothy Rich. Boston: Houghton Mifflin, 1988.

Coping with Kids and School: A Guide for Parents, by Linda Albert. New York: Dutton, 1984.

Your Child's Education: A School Guide for Parents, by Mark Wolraich, Landis Rick, and Nicholas Karagan. Springfield, IL: Charles C. Thomas, 1984.

Bringing Learning Home: How Parents Can Play a More Active and Effective Role in Their Children's Education, by Mary Susan Miller. New York: Lippincott & Crowell, 1981.

On Dealing with Problems at School

Improving Schools from Within: Teachers, Parents, and Principals Can Make a Difference, by Roland S. Barth. San Francisco: Jossey-Bass, 1990.

When Your Child Isn't Doing Well in School, by Ann Thiel, Richard Thiel, and Penelope B. Grenoble. Chicago: Contemporary, 1988.

Smart Kids with School Problems: Things to Know and Ways to Help, by Priscilla L. Vail. New York: Dutton, 1987. Focuses on elementary grades.

Is Your Child in the Wrong Grade?, revised edition, by Louise Bates Ames. Rosemont, NJ: Programs for Education, 1987.

Stop School Failure, revised edition, by Louise Bates Ames et al. Rosemont, NJ: Programs for Education, 1987.

What Do They Mean I'm Difficult, by Louise Bates Ames. Rosemont, NJ: Programs for Education, 1986.

What Am I Doing in This Grade? A Book for Parents about School Readiness, by Louise Bates Ames. Rosemont, NJ: Programs for Education, 1985.

The Special Education Handbook: A Comprehensive Guide for Parents and Educators, by Kenneth Shore. New York: Teachers College Press, 1986.

The Powerful Parent: A Child Advocacy Handbook, by David M. Gotesman. Norwalk, CT: Appleton-Century-Crofts, 1982.

Background Books

Eager to Learn: Helping Children Become Motivated and Love Learning, by Raymond J. Wlodkowski and Judith H. Jaynes. San Francisco: Jossey-Bass, 1990.

Endangered Brains: Why Our Children Can't Think, by Jane Healy. New York: Simon & Schuster, 1990.

Teachers at Work: Achieving Success in Our School, by Susan Moore Johnson. New York: Basic, 1990.

Schooling, by Sylvia Farnham-Diggory. Cambridge, MA: Harvard University Press, 1990.

Small Victories: The Real World of a Teacher: Her Students and Their High School, by Samuel G. Freedman. New York: Harper & Row, 1990.

Volunteers in Public Schools. Washington, DC: National Academy Press, 1990.

Privatization and Educational Choice, by Myron Lieberman. New York: St. Martin's, 1989.

Our Children and Our Country: Improving America's Schools and Affirming the Common Culture, by William J. Bennett. New York: Touchstone, 1989.

Innumeracy: Mathematical Illiteracy and Its Consequences, by John Allen Paulos. New York: Vintage, 1989.

The Facts on File Dictionary of Education, by Jay M. Shafritz, Richard P. Koeppe, and Elizabeth Soper. New York: Facts on File, 1988.

Public and Private High Schools: The Impact of Communities, by James S. Coleman and Thomas B. Hoffer. New York: Basic, 1987.

Places Where Children Succeed: A Profile of Outstanding Elementary Schools, by Bruce L. Wilson and Thomas B. Corcoran. Washington, DC: Government Printing Office, 1987.

What Works: Research About Teaching and Learning, by the U.S. Department of Education. Washington, DC: Government Printing Office, 1986.

A Nation At Risk: The Imperative for Educational Reform, by the National Commission on Excellence in Education. Washington, DC: Government Printing Office, 1983.

All Our Children Learning, by Benjamin Bloom. New York: McGraw-Hill, 1981.

How Children Learn, by John Holt. New York: Delta, 1969.

How Children Fail, by John Holt. New York: Delta, 1964.

On Education and the Law

Your Child's School Records: Questions and Answers About a Set of Rights for Parents and Students. Washington, DC: Children's Defense Fund, 1986.

Inequality in Education. Cambridge, MA: Center for Law and Education, July 1977 (special issue). Address: Larsen Hall, 6th Floor, 14 Appian Way, Cambridge, MA 02138; 617-495-4666.

Home Schooling Laws: All Fifty States. Steve Deckard, 11144 Riaza, Apt. #5, St. Louis, MO 63138; 1989; $18.

School Law News. Newsletter published by Capitol Publications, 1300 North 17th Street, Arlington, VA 22209.

School Law Bulletin. Quarterly published by the Institute of Government, University of North Carolina at Chapel Hill, Chapel Hill, NC 27599.

The Schools and the Courts. Briefs of selected court cases related to elementary or secondary schools. Quarterly published by College Administration Publications, P.O. Box 8492, Asheville, NC 28814.

The Journal of Law and Education. Quarterly published by Jefferson Law Company, P.O. Box 1936, Cincinnati, OH 45201.

West's Education Law Reporter. Reprints of cases and articles related to education law. Published by West Publishing Company, 50 West Kellogg Boulevard, P.O. Box 64526, St. Paul, MN 55164.

For or by Kids

Smarten Up! How to Increase Your Brain Power, by Roger Yepsen. Boston: Little, Brown, 1990. For ages 10 and up.

Make the Grade! Tests: How to Study For, Take and Ace Any Test!, by E. Richard Churchill. Los Angeles: Price Stern Sloan, 1989.

Make the Grade! Essays and Reports: What It Takes to Research, Write and Present an A+ Paper! by E. Richard Churchill. Los Angeles: Price Stern Sloan, 1989.

Scholastic's A+ Junior Guide to Book Reports, by Louise Colligan. New York: Scholastic, 1989. For grades 5 to 6.

Scholastic's A+ Junior Guide to Giving a Speech, by Louise Colligan. New York: Scholastic, 1989. For grades 5 to 6.

Student's Guide to Good Writing: Building Writing Skills for Success in College, by Rick Dalton and Marianne Dalton. New York: College Board, 1990.

Everything You Needed to Learn About Writing in High School, But . . ., by Beth Means and Lindy Lindner. Englewood, CO: Libraries Unlimited, 1989.

Improve Your Grades: Effective Study and Test-Taking Techniques Not Taught in School, by Veltisezar B. Bautista. East Detroit, MI: Bookhaus, 1989.

You Can Do It Guide to School Success, by Rebecca Allen. Worthington, OH: Willowisp, 1989.

Martha's New School, by Danielle Steel. New York: Delacorte, 1989. For ages 4 to 7.

Starting School, by Allan Ahlberg. New York: Viking Kestrel, 1988.

Can You Find It? 50 Scavenger Hunts to Sharpen Your Research Skills, by Randall McCutcheon. Minneapolis: Free Spirit, 1988.

The Student's Memory Book: Easy-to-Master Techniques That Will Revolutionize Your Study Habits, by Bill Adler, Jr. Garden City, NY: Doubleday, 1988.

(See also specific types or levels of schools, such as PRE-SCHOOL, KINDERGARTEN, HIGH SCHOOL, COLLEGE, PRIVATE SCHOOL, ALTERNATIVE SCHOOL, HOME SCHOOLING, and SPECIAL EDUCATION; also specific topics, such as DROPOUT; GIFTED CHILD; HANDI-CAPPED; READING; COGNITIVE DEVELOPMENT; LEARNING STYLE; and MASTERY LEARNING.)

educational age (EA) A summary reflecting how a child's SCORE relates to a wide range of other scores on the same ACHIEVEMENT TEST; also called *achievement age*. If an eight-year-old child's score on an achievement test is the score normally achieved by children half a year older, that child's educational age will be eight years, six months. (For help and further information, see TEST; NORM-REFERENCED TEST; AGE.)

Educational Amendments of 1978 (Public Law 95-561) The federal statute that included the GIFTED AND TALENTED CHIL-DREN'S ACT OF 1978 and the BASIC SKILLS AND EDUCATIONAL PROFI-CIENCY PROGRAM.

educational approach Alternate term for some kinds of LEARNING STYLES.

Educational Testing Service (ETS) A company that prepares and administers many tests for organizations, the best-known being the SCHOLASTIC APTITUDE TEST, written by the ETS for the COLLEGE ENTRANCE EXAMINATION BOARD.

Education for All Handicapped Children Act of 1975 (EHC, or Public Law 94-142) The federal law that established the rights of children with handicaps to a free and appropriate EDU-CATION, where previously many of them had received little or no benefit from the PUBLIC SCHOOL system. An earlier, closely related statute was the *Civil Rights Act for Handicapped Persons*, specifically *Section 504 of the Rehabilitation Act of 1973*, which barred any organization or institution receiving federal funds from discriminating in any way against qualified people with disabilities.

As applied to public education, this meant that schools must provide an appropriate education to children (up to age 21) with disabilities and must ensure children access to educational services, or the schools risk losing all federal funds. (Private and parochial schools, which receive no federal funds, are not covered by the law.) The EHC was amended in 1986 (*Public Law 99-457*) to cover disabled children from ages three to five; states were required to provide appropriate preschool programs for disabled children by school year 1990–91 and to have early intervention programs in place by school year 1991–92, available to disabled children from birth to age two.

These laws produced a revolution on paper, but many parents found that they had to do an enormous amount of work to arrange for that "appropriate education" and access to educational services for their disabled children. As a result many parents formed *advocacy groups* to share experiences and information on how best to get local public school systems to comply. Throughout this book, under entries on many kinds of physical and mental disabilities and ailments, you will find such groups listed. Under HELP FOR SPECIAL CHILDREN on page 578 you will find many other more general groups geared to helping parents and advocacy groups work with local school districts.

Among the HANDICAPPED children covered by the above laws are those with:

- hearing impairment or deafness.
- speech impairment.
- visual impairment or blindness.
- emotional disturbance.
- AUTISM.
- MENTAL RETARDATION.
- LEARNING DISABILITIES.
- physical impairments.
- chronic illness or long-term health problems.
- other conditions, including any not specified, that require children to receive SPECIAL EDUCATION.

Children below the state's COMPULSORY SCHOOL AGE are covered, as well as other children who are eligible for special educational services under the law if they are receiving educational services in federal programs, such as HEAD START, or if state law or court order specifies their eligibility. These laws cover children regardless of where they are living—with their parents, with FOSTER PARENTS, in an institution, in a GROUP HOME, or anywhere else.

By "appropriate education" the law has been interpreted to mean not the best or the most expensive programs possible but specialized programs designed to suit each child's individual needs and to allow each to make meaningful progress, the overriding goal being to provide the disabled child with the basic skills necessary to be self-sufficient: SELF-HELP SKILLS, READING skills, and writing, speaking, and arithmetic skills. The interpretation of what is required to do this is a main area of contention between parents and school districts and one reason for the emergence of so many advocacy groups.

Among the services that may be provided under the EHC are speech and language therapy, medical services for diagnostic or evaluation purposes, physical therapy, occupational therapy, school health services, psychological services, vocational education, educational programs extending year-round or beyond the normal school year, counseling (for student and parent), training for parents, specially trained teachers and teacher's aides, special materials and equipment, special transportation to school and to activities within school, college placement services, and the like.

The laws cover extracurricular activities as well, giving disabled children the same rights as their peers to participate in programs and activities such as clubs and other special-interest activities (including music, arts, crafts, homemaking, and industrial arts), meals, recess periods, physical education (with a specially designed *adaptive physical education* program, if necessary), school athletic programs, before- and after-school CHILD-CARE programs, health services, career and educational counseling, employment services, and referrals to agencies providing special aid to people with disabilities.

All school and extracurricular activities are to be provided on a fully integrated basis, or similar opportunities provided, because the underlying approach is MAINSTREAMING, bringing children with disabilities into regular and thoroughgoing contact from early childhood with their peers, as preparation for living as adults with the greatest possible independence. In connection with this, the law emphasizes that at the school the child should be in the LEAST RESTRICTIVE ENVIRONMENT, meaning the most natural, most integrated setting possible. The school is barred from shunting children with disabilities into separate buildings and trailers because of ARCHITECTURAL BARRIERS but is obliged to make the regular building accessible, as through building ramps and relocating classes. Any new buildings (from preschool to college and postsecondary vocational schools) must be fully accessible.

Only if evaluation and experience indicate that the child's disabilities are so great that the school is unable to provide appropriate education—and even then only if the parents approve—is a child referred to a separate program, as in a PRIVATE SCHOOL, day program, or residential program. However, the program must meet federal and state standards, and all costs (including educational expenses, room, board, transportation, and nonmedical care) must be paid for by the school district; the law also requires that such a residential program be as near to the child's home as possible. If parents on their own place the child in a residential program, the school district does not have to pay, but the child is still eligible for the school district's special education services.

The EHC law places parents at the center of decisions regarding the child. Parents are encouraged to attend any discussions affecting their child, and they have the right to bring with them anyone they choose, such as a lawyer, friend, or other advocate. The school must keep parents fully informed in writing of alternatives discussed and decisions made, with reasons spelled out; school districts need parental approval before they can conduct an evaluation of the child's abilities and educational needs, determine what special educational services may be necessary, or move the child from regular classes into a special education program. Another federal law, the FAMILY EDUCATIONAL RIGHTS AND PRIVACY ACT OF 1974, gives parents the right to inspect the child's STUDENT RECORD. If parents disagree with the child's identification, evaluation, and placement—for example, if they feel that a child has been incorrectly classed as mentally retarded because she has limited English-speaking skills—they may call for a DUE PROCESS hearing to review the decision.

An evaluation is recommended whenever someone has reason to suspect that a child has some problem interfering with learning—if the child has trouble understanding, for example, or difficulty speaking. Under the law, state and local school districts are required to have special programs for identifying children who may need special attention. Approaches vary by state, but among the people who may refer a child for evaluation are parents, teachers, social workers, doctors, agencies, and community services. Except for obvious physical or mental problems likely to be spotted soon after birth by a physician, parents and teachers are the people most likely to sense a possible problem and call for an evaluation. If there is any question about whether a child has any impairment or disability, parents should have the child evaluated by a physician or other appropriate specialist immediately. In most cases, the earlier the condition is identified the sooner special services can be started to minimize the handicap. Below is one advocacy group's PARENT'S GUIDELINES TO THE EVALUATION PROCESS.

Checklists on what kinds of behavior and other signs might indicate problems in young children are provided in several areas in this book, notably under these headings: EAR AND HEARING PROBLEMS, EYE AND VISION PROBLEMS, LEARNING DISABILITIES, MENTAL RETARDATION, MENTAL DISORDERS, PHYSICAL DISABILITIES, and COMMUNICATION SKILLS AND DISORDERS. Checklists and other descriptions can help parents assess whether or not to send their child for SCREENING TESTS. The entries listed above also will provide descriptions of some kinds of tests that might be given to a child to screen for different kinds of problems.

If a child has been evaluated and some sort of disability identified, information from the DEVELOPMENTAL SCREENING TESTS and DIAGNOSTIC ASSESSMENT TESTS, along with observations by parents and educational staff, will be used to develop an INDIVIDUALIZED EDUCATION PROGRAM (IEP). This will be modified as the child progresses, but IEPs will form a significant part of the child's education throughout the school years. (For help and further information, see EDUCATION; SPECIAL EDUCATION.)

Edwards' syndrome (trisomy 18) A congenital condition stemming from a CHROMOSOMAL ABNORMALITY that results from the existence of three copies (*trisomy*) of chromosome 18. Infants with Edwards' syndrome have severe MENTAL RETARDATION and often numerous defects, such as CLEFT LIP AND PALATE, SYNDACTYLY, CLUB FOOT, and malformation of internal organs. Most die within a few months.

Parent's Guidelines to the Evaluation Process

Why do school officials recommend that children be tested?

There are many reasons, most of which concern the suitability of the child's placement or program. School officials may recommend testing if a child has difficulty learning or accepting school rules when usual methods of dealing with such problems have not been effective. They hope that educational or psychological tests will provide them with information about the way in which the child learns, the child's strengths and weaknesses, the nature of his/her problems, and the kind of special help he/she may need.

Should I agree to have my child tested?

Public Law 94-142, the Education for All Handicapped Children Act of 1975, states that children attending public school can be given educational and psychological tests only with the approval of their parents or guardians. Your child's teacher, counselor, principal, or other staff member should explain to you the reasons for the request to test, discuss the tests that will be given, and tell you what school people hope to learn from the tests. Based on this you can decide whether to give permission or not.

May I request testing for my child if school officials do not?

Yes, Public Law 94-142 gives you the right to a free series of tests to determine whether a handicapping condition exists and the right to have an Individual Educational Program designed for your child if tests confirm the presence of such a condition.

If I agree to have my child tested what should I do before testing takes place?

There are several important steps you can take to ensure that the testing will be useful and that your child will profit from it:

a. Be sure you know what tests will be used, why these particular tests were selected, and what information these tests may provide that can help in planning a more suitable program for your child. Be sure to ask for definitions and explanations of any terms that are not clear to you and ask school officials to be specific regarding the skills, aptitudes, and/or behaviors they will be testing.

b. Discuss and agree upon the child's preparation for the evaluation. Usually the child should be told about the testing and the reasons for it in advance, although there are instances where this may not be the best procedure. If the child is to be informed in advance, you should determine whether he/she will respond better to being told by you or by some member of the school staff. Tests results can be influenced by the child's attitude toward the testing process; thus, the person who discusses it with him/her should guard against words and actions which may make the child anxious or heighten feelings of inadequacy.

c. Be sure that the examiner or the person who schedules the testing is aware of anything which might adversely affect your child's performance. If your son is pitching his first Little League game on Wednesday, he may have more than usual trouble concentrating on that day.

d. Find out what the physical setting for the testing will be. Individual tests should be given in a quiet, comfortable room. Some evaluations include observations of the child as he/she participates in a variety of daily activities.

What are my rights and responsibilities after my child has been tested?

P. L. 94-142 clearly guarantees certain important rights, including these:

a. The right to receive a copy of the results of all testing and evaluation and to have these results explained.

b. The right to be present at all meetings of the team which plans your child's program. Your child's teacher, the testers and evaluators, the learning specialist and others responsible for your child's education are members of this team. They are responsible for studying the results and the interpretations of all the testing and evaluation your child has had and for preparing an Individual Educational Program (IEP) for your child.

c. The right to be accompanied by a friend, lawyer, or child advocate at all meetings at which test results are discussed and plans for the child's program and placement are considered.

d. The right to request retesting in areas where test results disagree with your assessment of your child's abilities, achievements, or behavior patterns.

e. The right to obtain an outside evaluation if you question the accuracy or fairness of the evaluation completed by school staff. You must be prepared to pay for outside evaluations.

f. The right to accept or reject the IEP and to request modifications in the IEP after it has been accepted.

For detailed information about your rights under P.L. 94-142, refer to *The Rights of Parents and the Responsibilities of Schools*, compiled by James G. Meade, Ph.D., and published in paperback by Educators Publishing Services, Inc., 75 Moulton Street, Cambridge, MA 02138.

What kinds of programs might the IEP include?

Based on the results of evaluations and the meetings of the team, the IEP may provide for special help in any of several settings. The overriding goal of P.L. 94-142 is to provide the help each child needs in the least restrictive setting. Depending on the extent of your child's needs, the IEP may call for:

a. a modified program in the regular classroom,

Continued on page 181

b. regular class placement with supplemental tutoring, remedial instruction, counseling, or therapy,

c. special class placement, or

d. special school placement.

In addition to the rights guaranteed you by law, you have several important responsibilities to fulfill if your child is to have the best chance to overcome or compensate for his/her handicap. These include:

a. Understanding the results of testing and evaluation. Psychological and educational language can be confusing. Never hesitate to ask for clarification of anything you do not understand.

b. Being sure that the goals in the IEP are those agreed upon by the team of which you are a member and being sure that these goals are specific and realistic for your child.

c. Working to establish and maintain a cooperative rather than an adversarial relationship with members of the team who are responsible for carrying out the IEP.

d. Sharing with school personnel information about your child and his/her life outside of school which may affect school performance or behavior.

Source: Orton Dyslexia Society, 724 York Road, Baltimore, MD 21204 (301-296-0232). Reprinted by permission.

For help and further information

Support Organization for Trisomy 18/13 and Other Related Disorders (SOFT 18/13)
5030 Cole
Pocatello, ID 93202
208-237-8782
Pat Farmer, President
Organization for families of children with trisomy 18 or 13 or related disorders. Provides support for families; publishes various materials, including bimonthly newsletter *S.O.F.T. Touch* and *Trisomy 18: A Book for Families*.
(See also GENETIC DISORDERS.)

EEG   Abbreviation for ELECTROENCEPHALOGRAPH.

effacement   In PREGNANCY, the softening and flattening of the CERVIX during LABOR and its merging with the UTERUS wall in preparation for the actual DELIVERY of a baby.

EFM   Abbreviation for electronic FETAL MONITORING.

egg   In relation to PREGNANCY, the OVUM that unites with a SPERM at the point of CONCEPTION, or FERTILIZATION.

EHC   Abbreviation for EDUCATION FOR ALL HANDICAPPED CHILDREN ACT OF 1975.

eighth nerve   Alternate name for AUDITORY NERVE.

eighth nerve tumor   Alternate name for ACOUSTIC NEUROMA.

Eisenmenger complex   A complication connected with *ventricular septal defect*, a type of CONGENITAL heart defect. (See HEART AND HEART PROBLEMS.)

ejaculation   The emission of SEMEN from a male's PENIS at the point of ORGASM. In response to rhythmic pressure on the penis, muscles in the area move SPERM from the EPIDIDYMIS through the VAS DEFERENS, fluids from the PROSTATE GLAND, and secretions from the SEMINAL VESICLES into the URETHRA, to be released from the body. (A valve normally closes off the bladder so that urine does not leak into the semen.) Ejaculation can sometimes occur too quickly, a condition called *premature ejaculation*, common in ADOLESCENCE but also occurring in adult-

hood, frequently from overstimulation or anxiety. On the other hand, it sometimes fails to occur at all, in *inhibited ejaculation*, sometimes as a result of drugs, disorders such as DIABETES MELLITUS, or psychological problems. If medical problems have been ruled out, sex therapy can sometimes help. Occasionally, especially in cases of neurological damage or pelvic surgery, the valve to the bladder fails to operate properly, and semen is released into the bladder instead of into the penis. Adolescents often have ejaculations during sleep, called *nocturnal emissions* or *wet dreams*; these are quite normal, though they may cause anxiety or embarrassment to teenagers.

ejaculatory duct   A short tube in which SPERM from the EPIDIDYMIS (by way of the VAS DEFERENS) mixes with fluids from the PROSTATE GLAND and secretions from the SEMINAL VESICLES; the resulting mixture is SEMEN, which is released into the URETHRA during EJACULATION at the point of ORGASM.

EKG   Abbreviation for ELECTROENCEPHALOGRAPH.

elective   An optional course that a student may take, as opposed to the courses in a school's core CURRICULUM, which all students must take.

electroencephalograph (ECG or EKG)   A MEDICAL TEST that records the electrical activity of the heart, used in seeking to diagnose heart disorders (see HEART AND HEART PROBLEMS). Electrodes are attached painlessly to the chest, wrists, and ankles; these transmit information about the electrical changes in the heart as it undergoes each rest–contraction cycle, generally recorded as a graph on a sheet of paper (sometimes also on a screen), which physicians analyze for information about normalities and abnormalities in the heart's functioning. An ECG can be done in a doctor's office, clinic, or hospital; in some cases, as in an INTENSIVE CARE UNIT, the ECG machine may remain attached for hours or days, until the need for such monitoring has passed. (For help and further information, see MEDICAL TESTS; HEART AND HEART PROBLEMS.)

electroencephalograph (EEG)   A MEDICAL TEST that records the electrical activity of the brain, as an aid in the diagnosis of such disorders as EPILEPSY, BRAIN TUMORS, MENTAL RETARDATION, and MENTAL DISORDERS. Electrodes are painlessly attached to the patient's scalp and, as an extremely weak current is passed between them, the electroencephalograph records the brain's electrical activity during a variety of activities, including responses to bright lights, drugs, visual exercises, or sleep. (For help and further information, see BRAIN AND BRAIN DISORDERS; MEDICAL TESTS.)

electrolytes Substances that break up into electrically charged particles when dissolved or melted in fluids, such as the blood, and are vital to the normal functioning of the body. Some kinds of disorders, such as METABOLIC DISORDERS, more general disorders, such as DEHYDRATION resulting from DIARRHEA, and sometimes DRUG or ALCOHOL ABUSE can cause loss of electrolytes or imbalance between them (acid–base imbalance), disrupting the body and sometimes even threatening life. Among the key electrolytes are SODIUM (important in maintaining fluid balance), CALCIUM (needed for the relaxation of skeletal muscle and contraction of heart muscle), POTASSIUM (needed for contraction of skeletal muscle and relaxation of heart muscle), CHLORIDE, hydrogen, MAGNESIUM, bicarbonate, PROTEINS, PHOSPHATE, and sulfate.

electromyogram (EMG) A MEDICAL TEST in which the electrical activity in a set of muscles is recorded and analyzed, a harmless test in which small electrodes are placed on or in the skin and the patterns of electrical activity projected on a screen or over a loudspeaker. An EMG is used to test for muscle disorders, such as MUSCULAR DYSTROPHY.

electronic fetal monitoring (EFM) Alternate term for FETAL MONITORING.

elementary school An institution providing EDUCATION to grades one through five, and sometimes also KINDERGARTEN and grades six through eight if these are housed in the same set of buildings; also called a PRIMARY SCHOOL, *grade school*, or *grammar school*. From elementary school, children move either into MIDDLE SCHOOL or directly into HIGH SCHOOL. While kindergarten is largely preparatory, in the first grade children begin to learn the THREE R'S—reading, 'riting, and 'rithmetic—and are gradually introduced to material in science, geography, and history, simplified at first, but increasingly sophisticated as the grades progress. The U.S. Department of Education has also recommended that children have some exposure to foreign languages, computers, music, and art in elementary school.

Americans have in the past resisted attempts at formulating a national CURRICULUM for elementary and HIGH SCHOOLS, but in recent decades concern over the decline of some basic educational skills among students has inclined many to view more favorably the idea of specific matter to be covered by each grade. Though no national agreement yet exists, the Department of Education has formulated the JAMES MADISON ELEMENTARY SCHOOL: A MODEL CURRICULUM, reproduced on page 530.

In general, children in elementary school spend most of their time in a single classroom with one teacher, going to other locations only for special activities, such as art or gym. The Department of Education has also recommended that par-

ents exercise choice in finding the right school for their child; see CHOOSING A SCHOOL FOR YOUR CHILD on page 514, which provides a checklist for evaluating schools.

For help and further information

National Committee for Citizens in Education (NCCE), 301-997-9300; toll-free number, U.S. except Maryland, 800-NETWORK (638-9675). (For full group information, see EDUCATION.)

Association for Childhood Education International (ACEI), 301-942-2443. (For full group information, see EDUCATION.)

National Education Association (NEA), 202-822-7200. (For full group information, see EDUCATION.)

Other reference sources

The Elementary School Handbook: Making the Most of Your Child's Education, by Joanne Oppenheim. New York: Pantheon, 1989.

We've All Got Scars: What Boys and Girls Learn in Elementary School, by Raphaela Best. Bloomington: University of Indiana Press, 1989.

(See also EDUCATION.)

Elephant Man disease Alternate name for NEUROFIBROMATOSIS.

elimination diet Alternate term for the FEINGOLD DIET, used in the treatment of ATTENTION DEFICIT HYPERACTIVITY DISORDER; also used more widely to refer to a restrictive diet that eliminates all foods or additives thought to trigger or worsen the problem in question, such as ALLERGIES or DIGESTIVE DISORDERS.

elimination disorder Psychiatric classification for ENCOPRESIS, or soiling, and ENURESIS, or bedwetting.

emancipated minor A child of an age to be classed as a MINOR (generally under 18) but who has become free of parental control and CUSTODY. Minors who leave home, join the military, or otherwise assume legal responsibility for themselves and show their full independence from parental support may legally be declared emancipated by a court; those who marry or who have a court-supervised legal agreement with their parents may be emancipated without court order, though in some states they will require a court order or their parents' consent to the marriage. Once emancipated, minors have all the legal rights and responsibilities of an adult, including the ability to sign a contract or make a will. In some circumstances, however, parents may still have CHILD-SUPPORT responsibilities unless these are formally canceled by the court.

embryo Medical designation for the growing being during a PREGNANCY, from the time of IMPLANTATION, when the fertilized egg attaches itself to the lining of the UTERUS, through the first eight weeks of GESTATION. After that point, the being is generally known as a FETUS. Soon after implantation, some of the egg's cells begin to develop the nourishing PLACENTA. Also a sac filled with AMNIOTIC FLUID begins to form, cushioning the developing embryo. (It is this fluid that is sampled in the GENETIC SCREENING test called AMNIOCENTESIS.) These early weeks of embryonic development are crucial to the new being; it is during this period that all of the major organs begin to develop (by the fifth week). And it is during this period, often before a woman even realizes that she is pregnant, that great damage can be done by ingestion of alcohol and drugs and exposure to RADIATION and other hazards that can lead to BIRTH DEFECTS. (For help and further information, see PREGNANCY; BIRTH DEFECTS.)

embryo transfer   Treatment for INFERTILITY that involves a female egg (OVUM) donor, who volunteers to be inseminated with a man's sperm; after the fertilized egg has been implanted in her UTERUS for a few days, the developing EMBRYO is flushed out and implanted into the uterus of the man's wife or female sex partner. For the procedure to work, the two women's MENSTRUAL CYCLES must be in unison. No surgery is involved, but the donor faces two potential problems: the embryo may resist flushing, leaving her pregnant, or it may be flushed up into the fallopian tubes, causing a life-threatening ECTOPIC PREGNANCY and necessitating emergency surgery. Various legal questions need to be resolved, not the least of which is: which woman is the legal mother? Though this technique has long been used with animals, it is still so new among humans that its success rate—and problem rate—are not yet clear. (For help and further information, see INFERTILITY; CHILDBIRTH.)

EMG   Abbreviation for ELECTROMYOGRAM.

emphysema   A kind of LUNG AND BREATHING DISORDER, one type of which—*congenital lobar emphysema*—affects newborns.

encephalitis   Infection and inflammation of the brain itself, most commonly by a virus but sometimes by bacteria, often in connection with MENINGITIS or other infections, such as AIDS, MEASLES, MUMPS, or CHICKEN POX. The virus most often responsible is a form of HERPES SIMPLEX that causes cold sores. In *St. Louis encephalitis*, the virus is introduced to the body by a mosquito bite. Symptoms include FEVER, headache, confusion, disturbed perception and behavior, PARALYSIS and weakness, and SEIZURES; it sometimes leads to loss of consciousness, COMA, and DEATH. Physicians may use a variety of methods to diagnose the disease, such as CT SCAN, LUMBAR PUNCTURE, ELECTROENCEPHALOGRAPH, BLOOD TESTS, and even BIOPSY. Little can be done to treat most forms of the disease, though an antiviral drug can be used against the herpes simplex virus. Recovery depends on the patient's age and condition; those who do recover often have some kinds of brain damage. (For help and further information, see BRAIN AND BRAIN DISORDERS; MENINGITIS.)

encephalocele   A BIRTH DEFECT related to SPINA BIFIDA.

encephalotrigeminal angiomatosis   Alternate name for STURGE-WEBER SYNDROME.

encopresis (soiling)   Inability to fully control bowel movements, deliberate holding in of feces, or defecation somewhere other than in a toilet. Encopresis generally refers to otherwise physically normal children who have passed the usual age by which bowel control is normally achieved (not those with physi-

cal handicaps causing INCONTINENCE). Since bowel movements are generally easier for young children to control than urination, encopresis is much rarer than ENURESIS, or bedwetting. An occasional "accident," especially when a child has DIARRHEA, may occur in a child who normally has bowel control, and many young children go through a brief period of resisting use of the toilet for defecation; but encopresis refers to persistent problems involving defecation in diapers, underpants, in "private places" such as corners—in short, at times and places other than adults wish.

Unlike enuresis, which many children outgrow, encopresis often seems to stem from emotional problems and parent–child battles that center around TOILET TRAINING and may require deliberate changing of parental tactics and parent–child dynamics, often with the help of health professionals, if the child is not to develop a distorted self-image and become socially isolated. Parents need to be supportive and to try to defuse any parent–child conflict—anger and scorn are counterproductive here, but help and therapy are important. Chronic "holding-in" of feces can also cause CONSTIPATION and other physical problems. Soiling can sometimes occur in older children who have previously shown bowel control and may signal DIGESTIVE DISORDERS or emotional disturbance. Psychiatrists class enuresis and encopresis as *elimination disorders*.

For help and further information

Clouds and Clocks: A Story for Children Who Soil, by Matthew Galvin. New York: Brunner/Mazel/Magination, 1990. For ages 4 to 7.
(See also TOILET TRAINING; INCONTINENCE; DIGESTIVE DISORDERS; MENTAL DISORDERS.)

encoding   The process of converting spoken or signed words or numbers into written symbols. An important intellectual skill, basic to much learning, encoding poses significant problems for many people with brain dysfunction. A child with LEARNING DISABILITIES, especially DYSLEXIA, for example, may see printed words upside down, backward, or distorted in a variety of ways and so may have trouble encoding the symbols. Similarly, a child with DYSCALCULIA may have trouble encoding and working with mathematical symbols. Such children may also have trouble with the reverse process, DECODING. (For help and further information, see LEARNING DISABILITIES.)

endocarditis   Inflammation of the lining of the heart, generally from infection. (See HEART AND HEART PROBLEMS.)

endocrine system   The set of glands that produce many of the key HORMONES needed to regulate the body's functioning, including the HYPOTHALAMUS, PITUITARY GLAND, THYROID GLAND, parathyroid glands, THYMUS, ADRENAL GLANDS, and the sex organs called GONADS (TESTES in the male and OVARIES in the female).

endodontist   A DENTIST who specializes in treating the living pulp of TEETH, especially in doing ROOT-CANAL THERAPY.

endometrial biopsy   A common type of BIOPSY performed in evaluating INFERTILITY problems.

endometriosis   Abnormal growth in the body of tissue (*endometrium*) that normally lines the UTERUS, sometimes forming cysts in other reproductive organs or elsewhere in the body. Often painful, though sometimes without symptoms, the condition becomes increasingly common as a woman grows older and is a leading cause of INFERTILITY. Normally confirmed by a LAPAROSCOPY (visual examination of the abdomen through a small incision), the condition does not necessarily require treatment unless it is painful or if the woman wants to have children. If a woman does become pregnant, the symptoms of endometriosis (which vary with the MENSTRUAL CYCLE) decline sharply.

For help and further information

Endometriosis Association (EA)
P.O. Box 92187
Milwaukee, WI 53202
414-962-8972, toll-free number 800-992-ENDO [3636]
Mary Lou Ballweg, Executive Director
North American organization of individuals and professionals concerned about endometriosis, including its role in infertility. Provides information and referrals; operates toll-free number; publishes various materials, including newsletter, pamphlets, and information sheets.

RESOLVE, Inc., 617-643-2424. Publishes fact sheet *Endometriosis*. (For full group information, see INFERTILITY.)

Other reference sources

The Endometriosis Answer Book: New Hope, New Help, by Neils H. Lauersen, M.D., and Constance deSwaan. New York: Rawson, 1988; Fawcett, 1989.
Coping with Endometriosis, by Lyle Breitkopf and Marion Gordon Bakoulis. New York: Prentice Hall, 1988.
(See also INFERTILITY; UTERUS.)

endometritis   Inflammation of the UTERUS, which can cause INFERTILITY.

endometrium   The lining of the UTERUS, which grows and later is shed in MENSTRUATION if no fertilized egg is implanted in it.

endophthalmitis   Inflammation of the inner eye. (See EYE AND VISION PROBLEMS.)

endoscope   A hollow, generally flexible viewing tube, often fitted with a light, used by physicians to look at the body's internal organs directly, rather than indirectly as with a SCAN. The endoscope may be inserted through one of the body's natural openings, such as the mouth, nose, anus, or VAGINA, or through a surgical incision in the chest or abdomen or near a joint. An endoscope can also be used for a variety of other purposes, such as to assist in obtaining a BIOPSY, to aid in delicate operations such as FETAL SURGERY or ARTHROSCOPY, or to inflate internal cavities with air for better examination. *Endo-scope* is a general term; often the tube is given a more specific name indicating the purpose for which it is being used, such as a *bronchoscope* for viewing the bronchial tubes or a *gastroscope* for looking at the stomach.

end-stage renal disease (ESRD)   Medical term for the permanent and irreversible loss of kidney function. (See KIDNEY AND UROLOGICAL DISORDERS.)

engagement   In PREGNANCY, the beginning of the baby's movement into the BIRTH CANAL in preparation for DELIVERY. This engaging, "falling," or "dropping" of the baby is often quite noticeable, since the mother can suddenly breathe much more easily. In the most typical FETAL PRESENTATION, it will be the head of the FETUS that settles first into the pelvis; this may occur two or three weeks before the DUE DATE or not until the beginning of LABOR. Abnormal presentation can prevent proper engagement and cause difficult delivery. (For help and further information, see LABOR; PREGNANCY; CHILDBIRTH.)

enrichment   In EDUCATION, use of special kinds of subject matter and experiences, often going beyond the basic content of the CURRICULUM, to expand and deepen the knowledge and understanding of students. Enrichment is often used with college-bound students, especially those who are gifted, to enhance their education and keep their interest, when the ordinary curriculum might not be sufficiently challenging and stimulating (see GIFTED CHILD). In PRESCHOOL programs and in COMPENSATORY EDUCATION, enrichment might be used to help students gain experience and skills they might not have obtained from their home environment, as through field trips, audiovisual presentations, and visiting experts.

enuresis (bedwetting)   Inability to exercise full control of urination, especially during the night but also sometimes during the day; a term generally referring to otherwise normal children of school age, younger children being seen as still developing control. (By contrast, children who have physical disorders, such as SPINA BIFIDA or PARALYSIS, that prevent them from exercising control are said to have INCONTINENCE.)
   Primary enuresis is when a child has never developed the ability to stay dry reliably through the night; *secondary enuresis* is when a child who has been dry for months or years begins again to wet the bed. Secondary enuresis can result from diseases, disorders, or upset in a child's life, such as hospitalization or the birth of a SIBLING. Certainly, the child should be examined by a physician for possible physical problems.
   The causes of primary enuresis are less clear, but it often seems to run in families. Smaller bladders, delay in development of the nerves and muscles involved, insufficiency of ANTIDIURETIC HORMONE, and other such subtle factors may be part of an enuretic child's GENETIC INHERITANCE, while unsatisfactory TOILET TRAINING from one generation to the next may exacerbate the problem. If a child is still wetting the bed by school age (or before, if the child is anxious about or socially restricted by the bedwetting), parents may want to seek help from among the network of health professionals in their community.

One of the most commonly used approaches is a buzzer-alarm, triggered by the first few drops of urine, which is used to help children gradually train themselves to wake up during the night to urinate. This is effective for many children, though it may be counterproductive for some children already feeling anxiety and stress. Medications also can sometimes help, though some are dangerously toxic. One promising new approach is a nasal spray (*desmopressin acetate*) that stimulates the antidiuretic hormone. If emotional disturbance is involved, psychological therapy may be recommended; for psychiatrists, enuresis is an *elimination disorder*, a kind of MENTAL DISORDER. Whatever approach is taken, children with enuresis require considerable understanding and support from their families.

For help and further reference

Dry All Night: The Picture Book Technique That Stops Bedwetting, by Alison Mack. Boston: Little, Brown, 1989.

Toilet Training and Bed Wetting: A Practical Guide for Today's Parents, by Heather Welford. New York: Harper and Row, 1988.

Waking Up Dry: How to End Bedwetting Forever, by Martin Scharf. Cincinnati: Writer's Digest, 1986.

Bedwetting: A Guide for Parents and Children, by Arthur C. Houts and Robert M. Liebert. Springfield, IL: Charles C. Thomas, 1984.

A Parent's Guide to Bedwetting Control: A Step by Step Method, by Nathan H. Azrin and Victoria A. Besalel. New York: Pocket, 1981.

Nocturnal Enuresis: Psychological Perspectives, by R.J. Butler. Stoneham, MA: Butterworth, 1987.

Sammy the Elephant and Mr. Camel: A Story to Help Children Overcome Enuresis While Discovering Self-Appreciation, by Joyce C. Mills and Richard J. Crowley. New York: Magination, 1988.

(See also TOILET TRAINING; INCONTINENCE; KIDNEY AND UROLOGICAL DISORDERS; MENTAL DISORDERS.)

environmental hazards Substances in home, work, or community that can have adverse effects on health; when they affect the health of a FETUS during PREGNANCY, they are often called *reproductive hazards*. Some of these occur naturally, such as RADIATION from the sun; many others result from human activities, often involving chemicals and human-induced radiation. The catalog of possible environmental hazards is enormous, but parents should be alert to some that pose particular hazards to children's growth and development. Among these are:

• *radiation*, which can seriously affect both the fetus and the growing child. Prospective parents in high-radiation activities (such as flying) may want to change work temporarily before conceiving a child. They also will want to be alert to news about possible sources of radiation in daily life; much atten-

tion has, for example, focused recently on the radiation from computers, televisions, and other appliances, as well as from electrical power lines. CANCER and other types of health problems can result from excess exposure to radiation.

• *pesticides*, chemicals used on growing plants, especially food. Recent studies have shown that pesticides are especially dangerous to children under age eight, whose developing bodies are less able to ward off harmful effects.

• *radon*, a radioactive gas that occurs naturally in the earth, often building up to dangerous levels in homes built in high-radon areas or using radon-producing building materials. Parents will want to check radon levels in the home, employing an environmental engineer or using home kits designed for the purpose.

• *asbestos*, a fiber linked with increased risk of LUNG AND BREATHING DISORDERS and cancer. Apart from industrial use, asbestos was (before its dangers were fully known) widely used in homes and schools for insulation. Since the 1970s much of that asbestos has been removed. Some recent studies indicate that, unless it is exposed and breaking apart, asbestos may be better sealed from the air but otherwise left alone, since removal causes the fibers to be widely dispersed in the air, making them more dangerous.

• *lead*, which builds up in the body and can permanently harm the brain, NERVOUS SYSTEM, and other parts of the body, often causing MENTAL RETARDATION, and can even be fatal if large amounts enter the body in a short time. Once common in paints and gasoline, lead is now far more controlled. It can still, however, be found in many places, including some cans used for foods; since it is not possible to detect by eye, lead-testing kits are available for parents. Food intended for young children, however, is generally packed in lead-free containers, such as glass jars of baby food. Old paint is also a significant hazard.

Beyond these, parents will want to be especially aware of the potential dangers of ordinary household substances. Some of these are clearly marked "Poison," but many others are often not recognized as dangerous, including those used as art supplies for children or adults (see Art Hazards Information Center, below).

Certainly, parents should have clearly posted for themselves and their children the phone numbers of the local poison control center. For more general information, they can contact groups like those below.

For help and further information

National Pesticide Telecommunications Network, 800-858-7378 (24 hours, 365 days).

National Safety Council, 312-527-4800. Publishes quarterly *Family Safety and Health*, community program kit for poison prevention, and booklets on specific topics, such as *Preventing Accidental Poisonings* and *Radon . . . What You Need to Know*. (For full group information, see EXERCISE.)

Art Hazards Information Center
Center for Safety in the Arts (CSA, formerly **Center for Occupational Hazards**)
Five Beekman Street
New York, NY 10038
212-227-6220
Chris Proctor, Director
Organization exploring and disseminating information on hazardous chemicals used in arts and crafts. Provides information, suggests precautions and alternatives, and makes referrals; maintains library; publishes various materials including newsletter *Art Hazards News*, reprints of articles and lists of acceptable arts and craft materials, and data sheets on specific types of art hazards and precautions.

Other reference sources

Packages of fact sheets on the 100 most commonly used pesticides, funded by the Environmental Protection Agency. Available as a set from Cornell University, Distribution Center, Building 8, Ithaca, NY 14853; 607-255-7660.
Dumb Cane and Daffodils: Poisonous Plants in the House and Garden, by Carol Lerner. New York: Morrow Junior Books, 1990. For all ages.
Deadly Deceit: Low-Level Radiation, High-Level Cover-up, by Jay M. Gould and Benjamin A. Goldman. New York: Four Walls Eight Windows, 1990.
The Indoor Radon Problem, by Douglas G. Brookins. New York: Columbia University Press, 1990.
Peace of Mind During Pregnancy: An A-to-Z Guide to the Substances That Could Affect Your Unborn Baby, by Christine Kelley-Buchanan. New York: Facts on File, 1989.
For Our Kids' Sake: How to Protect Your Child Against Pesticides in Food, by Natural Resources Defense Council. San Francisco: Sierra Club, 1989.
Currents of Death: Power Lines, Computer Terminals, and the Attempt to Cover up Their Threat to Your Health, by Paul Brodeur. New York: Simon & Schuster, 1989.
Risk Assessment of Neurotoxic Chemicals. Washington, DC: National Academy Press, 1989.
Living with Radiation: The Risk, the Promise, by Henry N. Wagner, Jr., M.D., and Linda E. Ketchum. Baltimore: Johns Hopkins University Press, 1989.
Pesticide Alert: A Guide to Pesticides in Fruits and Vegetables, by Lawrie Mott and Karen Snyder. San Francisco: Sierra Club Books and Natural Resources Defense Council, 1988.
Pregnant and Working: What Are Your Rights? (1986). Available from New York Committee on Occupational Safety and Health (NYCOSH), 275 Seventh Avenue, New York, NY 10001.
Double Exposure: Women's Health Hazards on the Job and at Home, by Wendy Chavkin. New York: Monthly Review Press, 1984.
Women's Work, Women's Health: Myth and Realities, by Jeanne Stellman. New York: Pantheon, 1977.
Reproductive Hazards of Industrial Chemicals, by Susan M. Barlow and Frank M. Sullivan. New York: Academic, 1973.

Environment and Birth Defects, by James G. Wilson. New York: Academic, 1973.
(See also the general numbers at the beginning of HOTLINES, HELPLINES, AND HELPING ORGANIZATIONS, on page 601.)

enzyme replacement therapy   An experimental type of treatment being explored for LIPID STORAGE DISEASES.

ependymoma   A type of BRAIN TUMOR common in children.

epidemic parotitis   Alternate name for MUMPS.

epidermolysis bullosa (EB)   A rare condition in which skin and mucous membranes blister from injury or friction and, in severe cases, simply from normal activities, as internally in the digestive system. Though one form can be acquired during ADOLESCENCE or later, most forms of epidermolysis bullosa are GENETIC DISORDERS; some are of the AUTOSOMAL DOMINANT type, others are AUTOSOMAL RECESSIVE, and some are apparent at birth. Blisters resemble serious BURNS and must be treated as carefully to avoid infection; some blisters form permanent scars, which can cause immobility and deformity. In severe forms, some infants can die during the first year of life, from infections and loss of fluid, though sometimes the symptoms lessen in children who survive. EB can be detected during PREGNANCY using FETOSCOPY and by BLOOD TESTS and BIOPSY. Prospective parents with EB in their personal or family history may want to seek GENETIC COUNSELING.

For help and further information

Dystrophic Epidermolysis Bullosa Research Association of America (DEBRA)
Kings County Hospital Center
Building E, 6th Floor, Room E6101
4512 Clarkson Avenue
Brooklyn, NY 11203
718-774-8700
Arlene Pessar, Executive Director
Organization of and for EB victims, their families, and interested others. Supports research; offers support; provides information to public and professionals; publishes newsletter *EB Current*.

National Institute of Arthritis and Musculoskeletal and Skin Diseases (NIAMS), 301-496-8188. Publishes *Living with Epidermolysis Bullosa*. (For full group information, see ARTHRITIS.)

National Center for Education in Child and Maternal Health (NCEMCH), 202-625-8400. (For full group information, see PREGNANCY.)

(See also GENETIC COUNSELING; SKIN DISORDERS.)

epididymis   The area behind the TESTES, including a long coiled tube where a man's SPERM mature.

epididymo-orchitis Inflammation of one or both TESTES and the EPIDIDYMIS, the SPERM storage area behind the testes, by a variety of organisms; often associated with CHLAMYDIAL INFECTIONS and GONORRHEA. Cold packs to reduce swelling, painkillers (*analgesics*), support for the SCROTUM, and antibiotics are often used to treat the condition. By contrast, ORCHITIS—inflammation of the testes alone—is generally caused by the MUMPS virus.

epilepsy Not a single disease but a general term for a wide range of symptoms, most notable of which is the tendency to have recurring SEIZURES (convulsions)—sudden periods of involuntary, uncontrolled electrical activity in the brain—often accompanied by violent muscular contractions. Instead of the normal generation of about 80 impulses a second, some of the brain's nerve cells may "fire" 500 times a second during an epileptic seizure, disrupting normal brain activities with electrical overload.

The various types of epileptic seizures are classed under two main headings: *generalized seizures*, which affect the whole brain, and *partial seizures* (*focal seizures*), which are localized in one part of the brain. Within these two categories, the main kinds of epileptic seizures are these.

1. Generalized Seizures

   • *Tonic-clonic seizure* (*grand mal*). The best-known type of seizure, though not the most common, involving involuntary, uncontrolled electrical activity in the brain, often (but not necessarily) accompanied by violent muscular contractions called CONVULSIONS. People having a tonic-clonic seizure may cry out hoarsely, then fall to the ground unconscious, their body stiffening and jerking. The person may lose control of the bladder and bowels, have a froth of saliva at the mouth, and turn somewhat bluish as oxygen intake is slowed. Then, after a minute or two, the brain restores normal activity, the jerking movements end, and the seizure is over, leaving the person confused and drowsy; after a period of sleep, the person can usually resume normal activity. A tonic-clonic seizure is sometimes presaged by an *aura*, a variable complex of unusual sensations such as an odd smell or taste, light, slight sick feeling, or warmth; if recognized, it can give the person time to move away from any hazards nearby.

   • *Absence* (*petit mal seizure*): A seizure that lasts only a few seconds, involving brief loss of consciousness, often seeming like daydreaming or blank staring, sometimes with rhythmic twitching of the eyelids or facial muscles but generally without any aura. A child may stumble and fall, then get up and continue running, with no one—including himself—realizing that he has had a seizure.

2. Partial Seizures

   • *Simple partial seizure* (*Jacksonian seizure*). A seizure involving disturbances in movement only, in which the person retains consciousness but cannot control his or her movements, generally trembling or jerking an arm or leg, sometimes starting with just a finger. Another form of simple partial seizure involves seeing strange, illusory people or sounds, or having a strong, disconcerting feeling of déjà vu—that the events being experienced have happened before.

   • *Complex partial seizure* (*psychomotor* or *temporal lobe seizure*). A trancelike seizure in which the person moves through a set of motions (often much the same in each attack) as in a daze; not totally out of contact, the person can often respond to simple directions given calmly by a familiar voice, as of a friend or family member. The person returns to awareness in a minute or two with no recollection of what happened but perhaps with some confusion and irritability.

   • *Secondarily generalized seizure*. A seizure that was initially partial but spreads to become generalized.

Epilepsy can begin at any time of life but generally appears first in childhood, normally between ages two and 20. In at least half of the cases, the cause is completely unknown. In the rest, though the precise mechanism remains obscure, some of the disorder's many and various triggering factors can be identified, including HEAD INJURY; BRAIN TUMOR; CONGENITAL damage or disorders of the brain (such as MENTAL RETARDATION or CEREBRAL PALSY, sometimes as a result of difficult CHILDBIRTH); GENETIC DISORDERS; lead poisoning (see ENVIRONMENTAL HAZARDS); severe infections, such as MENINGITIS, ENCEPHALITIS, TUBERCULOSIS, malaria, and MEASLES; and poor NUTRITION. To the extent that these and like causes can be reduced or eliminated—as by PRENATAL CARE, SAFETY, and IMMUNIZATION against infections—many kinds of epilepsy are preventable.

Epilepsy is generally diagnosed by a PEDIATRICIAN, family PHYSICIAN, or NEUROLOGIST on the basis of a parent's descriptions of a child's seizures and a review of his or her medical history. Doctors may also use an ELECTROENCEPHALOGRAPH (EEG) to record the electrical activity of the brain. By comparing the record with normal brain waves, they may be able to diagnose epilepsy, but not all types of epilepsy show up on an EEG. Doctors may also use various kinds of SCANS to look for physical abnormalities, such as tumors or signs of head injuries, that might be causing seizures.

When epilepsy has a precise, treatable cause, the problem may be eliminated, as by surgery, a change in medications for other illnesses, or a special diet. But in many cases, epilepsy is best controlled by drugs, the precise medication used depending on the type of seizure and the response of the person. These drugs generally need to be taken regularly to keep a steady level in the body; if that is done, the Epilepsy Foundation of America estimates that seizures can be controlled in four out of five patients. More promising, there are some indications that, if children on medication have been seizure-free for some years, some might be very slowly withdrawn from the medication and remain free of symptoms. In any case, with some forms of epilepsy, especially absence seizures, many children tend to "grow out of it."

Other approaches tried in some situations include a special high-FAT diet, called a *ketogenic diet*; supplemental VITAMINS;

What Should You Do If Someone Has a Seizure?

Convulsive Seizure

First aid for epilepsy is basically very simple. It keeps the person safe until the seizure stops naturally by itself. These are the key things to remember about a convulsive seizure:

- Keep calm and reassure other people who may be nearby.
- Clear the area around the person of anything hard or sharp.
- Loosen ties or anything around the neck that may make breathing difficult.
- Put something flat and soft, like a folded jacket, under the head.
- Turn the person gently onto one side. This will help keep the airway clear. Do *not* try to force the mouth open with any hard implement or with fingers. It is not true that a person having a seizure can swallow the tongue. Efforts to hold the tongue down can injure teeth or jaw.
- Don't hold the person down or try to stop movement.
- Don't attempt artificial respiration except in the unlikely event that a person does not start breathing again after the seizure has stopped.
- Stay with the person until the seizure ends naturally.
- Be friendly and reassuring as consciousness returns.
- Offer to call a taxi, friend, or relative to help the person get home if he or she seems confused or unable to get home alone.

If you know the person has epilepsy, it is usually not necessary to call an ambulance unless the seizure lasts longer than a few minutes, unless another seizure begins soon after the first, or unless the person cannot be awakened after the jerking movements have stopped.

Other Kinds of Seizures:

You don't have to do anything if a person has brief periods of staring or shaking of the limbs. If someone has the kind of seizure that involves a dazed state and automatic behavior, the best thing to do is:

- Watch the person carefully and explain to others what is happening. Often people who don't recognize this kind of behavior as a seizure will think that the dazed person is drunk or on drugs.
- Speak quietly and calmly in a friendly way.
- Guide the person gently away from any danger, such as a steep flight of steps, a busy highway, or a hot stove. Don't grab hold, however, unless some immediate danger threatens. People having this kind of seizure are on "automatic pilot" as far as their movements are concerned, and instinct may make them struggle or lash out at the person who is trying to hold them.
- Stay with the person until full consciousness returns, and offer help in returning home.

Source: *Questions and Answers About Epilepsy.* Epilepsy Foundation of America.

and *biofeedback* (see FEEDBACK). But these are best tried, if appropriate, only under a doctor's direction.

Beyond that, people with epilepsy can often live quite normal lives. They have the normal range of intelligence and need only exercise caution in sports, work, and other activities that involve potential hazards, such as alcoholic drinks (which can bring on seizures in some), water (as in swimming and boating), exposed heights, automobiles, and other dangerous machinery. If they are shown to have been seizure-free for a certain time (depending on the state), they can usually get a driver's license. They may have difficulty getting insurance; where it is available, they may be subject to high rates and be placed in special risk "pools." Antidiscrimination laws protecting the HANDICAPPED apply to people with epilepsy, though they often may have to fight discrimination in employment and social situations. Various organizations (see below) can help in such areas.

Women with epilepsy would be wise to consult a doctor and perhaps receive GENETIC COUNSELING before becoming pregnant. Because PREGNANCY changes the balance of HORMONES in the body, it also changes the response of the body to medication, so in some women it can increase the number of seizures; in others, the reverse can occur. More important, the Epilepsy Foundation of America estimates that women taking epilepsy medications have a two to three times greater risk of having a baby with a BIRTH DEFECT. It is unclear what proportion of the defects are caused by the epilepsy itself and what by the medication, but because most such birth defects occur in the first three months of pregnancy, planning ahead seems indicated. Certain medications seem to be associated with certain kinds of birth defects, including CLEFT LIP AND PALATE, heart problems (see HEART AND HEART PROBLEMS), FETAL HYDANTOIN SYNDROME, and SPINA BIFIDA. Women taking epilepsy medications may want to seek PRENATAL TESTING. If they are planning on BREASTFEEDING, they should also discuss medications with their doctors beforehand, since some amount of the drugs in their system will be passed on in the milk.

For help and further information

Epilepsy Foundation of America (EFA)
4351 Garden City Drive, Suite 406
Landover, MD 20785
301-459-3700
William McLin, Executive Director

Organization concerned with preventing and controlling epilepsy and improving lives of people affected. Seeks to educate public and influence social policy, as advocate; provides information and referrals; maintains National Library and Resource Center on Epilepsy; publishes various materials, including newsletter *National Spokesman*, book *Epilepsy: You and Your Child: A Guide for Parents*, pamphlets *Epilepsy and the Family*, *Questions and Answers About Epilepsy* and *Epilepsy: Medical Aspects*, and information sheet *Epilepsy in Pregnancy*.

National Easter Seal Society, 312-726-6200 voice; 312-726-4258 TDD. (For full group information, see HELP FOR SPECIAL CHILDREN on page 578.)

National Institute of Neurological Disorders and Stroke (NINDS), 301-496-5751. Publishes many materials, including *Epilepsy: Hope Through Research.* (For full group information, SEE BRAIN AND BRAIN DISORDERS.)

Other reference sources

General Works

Health Care U.S.A., by Jean Carper. New York: Prentice Hall, 1987. Resource for general and specific health-care information; lists major epilepsy treatment and research centers and other information.

Children with Epilepsy: A Parents Guide, E. McElroy, ed. Kensington, MD: Woodbine House, 1988.

Epilepsy and the Family, by Richard Lechtenberg. Cambridge, MA: Harvard University Press, 1984.

Does Your Child Have Epilepsy?, by J.E. Jan, R.G. Ziegler, and G. Erba. Austin, TX: PRO-ED, 1983.

Epilepsy: A Handbook for Patients, Parents, Families, Teachers, Health and Social Workers, by A. Middleton, A. Attwell, and G. O. Walsh. Boston: Little, Brown, 1981.

The Epilepsy Handbook, by Robert J. Gumnit. New York: Raven, 1983.

Epilepsy: A Handbook, by Allen H. Middleton, Arthur A. Attwell, and Gregory Walsh. Boston: Little, Brown, 1982.

For or by Kids

Epilepsy, by Tom McGowen. New York: Watts, 1989. For grades 6 to 9.

Halsey's Pride, by Lynn Hall. New York: Scribner, 1990. For ages 12 and up. About a girl with epilepsy.

Trick or Treat or Trouble, by Barbara Aiello and Jeffrey Shulman; illustrated by Loel Barr. On epilepsy; part of The Kids on the Block Book Series for readers age 8 to 12, focusing on children with problems or disabilities.

Epilepsy, by Alvin Silverstein and Virginia B. Silverstein. Philadelphia: Lippincott, 1975. For young people.

A Handful of Stars, by Barbara Girion. New York: Scribner, 1981. A novel for young people.

What Difference Does It Make, Danny?, by Helen Young. London: Andre Deutsch, 1980. For young people. Available from British Epilepsy Association, Anstey House, 40 Hanover Square, Leeds LS3 1BE, West Yorkshire, United Kingdom.

Dreams Come True, by Elizabeth J. Kornfield. For young people. Available from Rocky Mountain Press, 1520 Shaw Mountain Road, Boise, Idaho 93812. $5.95 plus $1.00 shipping; profits go to EFA.

(See also HELP FOR SPECIAL CHILDREN, on page 578.)

epiphyses The ends of the long bones in the limbs, where growth takes place in children. (See GROWTH AND GROWTH DISORDERS.)

episiotomy A controversial medical procedure in which a surgical incision is made in the tissue between a woman's VAGINA and anus during CHILDBIRTH to ease DELIVERY of the baby.

It is generally done when the tissue is under pressure by the baby's head and seems likely to tear, almost always in cases of FORCEPS DELIVERY or breech FETAL PRESENTATION, where a larger opening is needed, and often when there are signs of FETAL DISTRESS. Advocates note that an episiotomy causes less pressure on the head of a PREMATURE baby and enlarges the vaginal opening neatly, preventing the tears in tissue that can otherwise occur, which are harder to repair afterward and can lead to complications. Critics say that episiotomies have been overused, with some obstetricians performing episiotomies almost routinely, and that it sometimes causes discomfort long after the birth. In exploring childbirth alternatives, parents will want to explore a doctor's or hospital's policies on episiotomies. (For help and further information, see CHILDBIRTH.)

epispadias A congenital defect similar to HYPOSPADIAS, in which a male's URETHRA opens on the upper side of his PENIS, rather than at its head.

EPSDT Abbreviation for EARLY AND PERIODIC SCREENING, DIAGNOSIS, AND TREATMENT.

erythema infectiosum An infectious viral disease that causes a striking red rash on the cheeks, giving it an alternate name, *slapped cheeks disease*. It is also called *the fifth disease*, because it is the least well known of the common childhood diseases, the other main ones being MEASLES, MUMPS, CHICKEN POX, and RUBELLA (German measles). Erythema infectiosum causes only mild symptoms in children, but it is presently being examined closely, because some medical researchers suspect that it can cause BIRTH DEFECTS, especially a dangerous form of ANEMIA, in the babies of pregnant women who contract the disease.

For help and further information

March of Dimes Birth Defects Foundation, 914-428-7100; local chapters in telephone-directory white pages. Publishes information sheet *Chicken Pox During Pregnancy*, with comments on erythema infectiosum.

National Institute of Allergy and Infectious Diseases (NIAID), 301-496-5717. (For full group information, see ALLERGY.)

National Institute of Child Health and Human Development (NICHD), 301-496-5133. (For full group information, see PREGNANCY.)

erythroblastosis fetalis A serious disorder that affects a fetus in cases of RH INCOMPATABILITY between the baby and its mother.

erythrocytes Alternate name for red blood cells. (See BLOOD AND BLOOD DISORDERS.)

ESI Abbreviation for EARLY SCREENING INVENTORY.

esotropia A type of STRABISMUS in which the crossed eye is turned toward the nose. (See EYE AND VISION PROBLEMS.)

ESRD   Abbreviation for *end-stage renal disease*, the medical term for permanent and irreversible loss of kidney function. (See KIDNEY AND UROLOGICAL DISORDERS.)

estrogen   A key female HORMONE produced in the OVARIES, which triggers the physical changes that take place in a girl during PUBERTY and which helps to regulate the MENSTRUAL CYCLE that is the key to the functioning of the reproductive system. Estrogen is also produced in the PLACENTA during PREGNANCY and in small amounts in males.

etiology   The study of the causes of a disease, in both general and specific cases, including investigation of a patient's susceptibility, the specific agent causing the disease, and the way in which the agent was introduced into the body. In cases of severe communicable diseases, such as AIDS, examination of the means of transmission are key to preventing its spread to others.

ETS   Abbreviation for EDUCATIONAL TESTING SERVICE.

eustachian tube   A narrow canal connecting the middle ear with the throat, helping to protect the delicate eardrum and ossicles (tiny middle-ear bones) from potentially dangerous changes in pressure or explosive noises; if the tube is blocked, significant EAR AND HEARING PROBLEMS can result.

evaluation-level thinking   Making judgments on the basis of established criteria; from Benjamin Bloom's description of the various kinds of thinking or learning processes, the other main types being KNOWLEDGE-LEVEL THINKING, COMPREHENSION-LEVEL THINKING, APPLICATION-LEVEL THINKING, ANALYSIS-LEVEL THINKING, and SYNTHESIS-LEVEL THINKING.

exceptional child   Alternate term for a child with SPECIAL NEEDS.

exchange transfusion   A BLOOD TRANSFUSION that is virtually a total replacement of a baby's blood, as in cases of RH INCOMPATIBILITY, to avoid permanent damage.

exercise   Physical activity to improve the health and functioning of the body, as by increasing blood circulation and muscle strength. In response to concerns about being "unfit," many parents and children have turned to exercise, often establishing regular exercise programs. Both pregnant women and children should use some caution, however.

Ideally, women should have been exercising before becoming pregnant; that way they would start off relatively fit and be familiar with their body's response to exercise. In any case, women are advised to have a thorough medical examination before embarking on an exercise program during pregnancy. Doctors may suggest restrictions or recommend against exercise, as when a woman has heart problems, will have a MULTIPLE BIRTH, or shows signs indicating possibility of MISCARRIAGE or PREMATURE DELIVERY.

Most women will want to do some basic exercises to prepare them for CHILDBIRTH and delivery, like those in BASIC EXERCISES FOR DURING AND AFTER PREGNANCY on page 488. These can serve as warm-up exercises for a more extensive exercise program, if desired. The American College of Obstetrics and Gynecology suggests, however, that pregnant women should avoid the following:

- strenuous activities calling for twisting, turning, deep flexion, extension, or bouncy, jerky motion;
- competitive sports calling for stamina and endurance;
- activities depending on balance, which might lead to a fall;
- activities that raise body temperature too high (including sauna and whirlpool);
- exercises done lying flat on the back, which can cut normal blood flow through the vena cava to the fetus (see HEART AND HEART PROBLEMS);
- high-risk activities such as diving or skiing.

They also recommend exercising no more than three times a week, with sessions of 15 minutes tops (not counting warm-up and cool-down) and with maximum heartbeat of 140 beats per minute, halting exercise with any sign of strain, fatigue, dizziness, bleeding, contractions, nausea, chest pain, or the like.

Some cautions are recommended for children, too. In their *Pediatric Athlete*, the American Academy of Orthopaedic Surgeons (see below) notes that children are not miniature adults; rather, their bodies are still developing and have different needs and requirements from those of adults. They use more calories and tire faster, build up more body heat (and risk of heat-related illnesses), and breathe faster (making them more susceptible to pollution), for example. The AAOS warns against using adult training programs for children, suggesting instead that sports and activities should be chosen with the child's DEVELOPMENTAL AGE in mind, noting that before PUBERTY boys and girls have generally equivalent athletic potential.

For help and further information

National Safety Council
444 North Michigan Avenue
Chicago, IL 60611
312-527-4800
T.C. Gilchrest, President
Nationwide organization promoting safety in all areas of life. Seeks to educate public on accident prevention, offering training courses to that end; maintains library; publishes materials in many areas, including quarterly *Family Safety and Health*, newsletter *Recreational Safety, Preschool Pedestrian Safety Program* (for presentation to ages 3 to 5), *Bicycle Safety Program* (for presentation in schools), *Overexertion: What You Don't Know Can Hurt You* (slide show for groups), and booklets on specific topics, such as *Playing It Safe, a Pocket Guide to Fitness, The Millers Beat the Heat! The National Safety Council's Summer Activities Guide, Cruisin' Rules* (on bicycle safety rules for ages 8 to 14), *Bicycling for Fitness, Bicycling Skills*, and *Bicycle Safety Maintenance Manual*.

American College of Obstetricians and Gynecologists (ACOG)
600 Maryland Avenue, SW, Suite 300
Washington, DC 20024

202-638-5577
Warren H. Pearse, M.D., Executive Director
Professional organization of obstetricians and gynecologists.
Establishes guidelines for exercises during pregnancy.

American Academy of Orthopaedic Surgeons (AAOS)
222 South Prospect Avenue
Park Ridge, IL 60068
708-823-7186
Thomas C. Nelson, Executive Director
Professional organization of orthopaedic surgeons. Publishes
The Pediatric Athlete.

Positive Pregnancy and Parenting Fitness, 203-822-8573; toll-
free number 800-433-5523. (For full group information, see
PREGNANCY.)

C/SEC (Cesareans/Support, Education, and Concern), 508-
877-8266. Publishes book *Essential Exercises for the Childbearing Years.*

March of Dimes Birth Defects Foundation, 914-428-7100; local
chapters in telephone-directory white pages. Publishes information sheet *Fitness for Two.* (See BIRTH DEFECTS.)

Other reference sources

Jane Fonda's New Pregnancy Workout and Total Birth Program,
  by Femmy DeLyse. New York: Simon & Schuster, 1989.
Pregnancy and Sports Fitness, by Lynne Pirie and Lindsay Curtis,
  Tucson, AZ: Fisher, 1989.
The Postnatal Exercise Book, by Barbara Whiteford and Margie
  Polden. Available from La Leche League International.
The Exercise Prescription for Depression and Anxiety, by Keith
  W. Johnsgård. New York: Plenum, 1989.
*The Complete Prenatal Water Workout Book: A Safe, Low-Impact
  Exercise Alternative for Expectant Women*, by Helga Hughes.
  Garden City Park, NY: Avery, 1989.
(See also Sports and Leisure Activities in the PARENT'S BOOK-
  SHELF on page 566.)

exotropia   A kind of STRABISMUS in which the crossed eye is
turned away from the nose. (See EYE AND VISION PROBLEMS.)

expected date of confinement (EDC)   Medical term for DUE
DATE.

experiential learning   Alternate term for a LEARNING STYLE
focusing on student discovery of rules and conclusions from
given materials.

experimental school   Alternate term for LABORATORY SCHOOL.

expository learning   A LEARNING STYLE in which a teacher
presents a general rule or concept and the student learns to
apply it to specific situations; also called *deductive learning*.

expressive language   The ability to express oneself in
words, as opposed to RECEPTIVE LANGUAGE, which is passively
understood. (See COMMUNICATION SKILLS AND DISORDERS.)

expulsion   In EDUCATION, an order for a student to leave a
school, generally only after repeated serious misbehavior,
though sometimes for grossly inadequate performance at
schoolwork. Unlike SUSPENSION, which is temporary, expulsion is
long-term, either for the balance of the school year or permanently at that school, though the student may be enrolled elsewhere. Some states require that an expelled student be provided with alternative education if he or she is under
COMPULSORY SCHOOL AGE. Various Supreme Court rulings have
affected the legal rights of students and schools in cases of
suspension and expulsion. (See PROCEDURAL GUIDELINES FOR SUS-
PENSION AND EXPULSION, under SUSPENSION.)

expunged records   Records that have been destroyed as if
they had never existed. Documents of JUVENILE COURT proceedings are often restricted or even SEALED; then, after a specified
number of years, the JUVENILE, parent, or GUARDIAN may apply for
the records to be expunged, generally on showing that the
problem behavior has been improved. An unverified report of
possible CHILD ABUSE AND NEGLECT may also be—though sometimes is not—removed from a CENTRAL REGISTER.

extended family   A type of FAMILY that goes beyond the
nucleus of parents and children to include other generations or
more distant relatives.

external cephalic version   A medical procedure performed
when there are problems with FETAL PRESENTATION, in which a
doctor tries to turn the baby into the normal head-downward
position for delivery.

external degree programs   In EDUCATION, especially at the
COLLEGE level, programs that allow students to learn material
and fulfill course requirements (such as tests, papers, and laboratory work) largely on their own, with little or no attendance
at scheduled classes on a college campus. Some external
degree students use INDEPENDENT STUDY via correspondence;
others, a form of *open university* combining correspondence
study with learning via radio and television broadcasts. Such
students generally earn CREDIT for their courses by taking examinations, either tests offered by the individual school or STAN-
DARDIZED TESTS such as those in the COLLEGE-LEVEL EXAMINATION
PROGRAM. External degree programs are especially attractive to
people who prefer to study on their own or those who have
time commitments that preclude their attending regular
classes, such as parents with children at home or adults whose
jobs involve travel and irregular hours.

extrinsic asthma   A type of ASTHMA.

eye and vision problems   The organs of sight and the widely
varied disorders that affect them. A number of vision disorders
can affect children, some of which can permanently damage the
child's vision if they are not diagnosed and treated in early
childhood. Though newborns can see, their vision develops
substantially in their early years, especially in the first few
months, with development normally complete by about age
nine. For the eyes to develop normally, they must both be used
equally, or the sight in the weaker eye may be impaired or
totally lost.

Observational Checklist for Possible Vision Problems

The checklist that follows can help you identify if a child has a vision problem. Check any behavior that applies. If a child shows *any* of these symptoms, there *may* be eye trouble, and the child should be referred for evaluation.

Behavior	YES	NO
Rubs eyes excessively.	☐	☐
Shuts or covers one eye, tilts head, or thrusts head forward.	☐	☐
Has difficulty in work that requires close use of the eyes (such as putting puzzle parts together or matching identical shapes).	☐	☐
Blinks more than usual or is irritable when doing close work.	☐	☐
Holds objects close to eyes.	☐	☐
Is unable to see distant things clearly.	☐	☐
Squints eyelids together or frowns.	☐	☐

Appearance		
Has crossed eyes.	☐	☐
Eyelids are red-rimmed, crusty, or swollen.	☐	☐
Eyes are inflamed or watery.	☐	☐
Has recurring styes (small inflamed swellings on the rim of the eyelid).	☐	☐

Complaints		
Eyes itch, burn, or feel scratchy.		
Cannot see well.	☐	☐
Has dizziness, headaches, or nausea following close eye work.	☐	☐
Has blurred or double vision.	☐	☐

Source: *Mainstreaming Preschoolers: Children with Visual Handicaps* (see General Works on page 000). Adapted from "Signs of Possible Eye Trouble in Children," by the National Society for the Prevention of Blindness.

The Observational Checklist above can help parents spot signs of possible vision problems. If glasses or other corrective measures, such as contact lenses or eye patches, are prescribed, it is extremely important for the child's future sight that they be worn regularly.

Parents will also want to protect their children from eye injuries by educating them from a very young age about the dangers of injuries, as from:

- sharp, pointed objects, such as pencils, knives, and pieces of glass, metal, or wood, as well as less hard but still dangerous items such as cards and straws;
- projectile toys such as BB guns, bows and arrows, darts, and slingshots;
- fireworks;
- unsupervised work in shop or laboratory, at home or in school, where goggles should always be worn; and
- sports accidents.

The National Society to Prevent Blindness estimates that sports injuries alone affect approximately 11,000 children a year, with nearly 25 percent of the injuries to children age five to 14 resulting from baseball accidents. They recommend that children protect their eyes by wearing safety eyeguards or industrial-quality safety glasses, with either plain (*plano*) or corrective lenses, and where appropriate (as in hockey), helmets as well.

The eyes themselves are a pair of round structures set deep into a bony eye socket on either side of the nose; each is protected largely by the whitish *sclera*. In the center of the sclera is the transparent *cornea*, which controls focusing for the eye. Behind the cornea is a depression filled with fluid (*aqueous humor*), in which is set the *iris* (the colored part). In the center of iris is the *pupil*, which widens (dilates) or contracts in response to dark or light, controlling the amount of light entering. Behind the iris is the *lens*, set in a ring of delicate muscles called the *ciliary body*, which changes the shape of the lens to help the eye focus. Behind the lens is a jelly-like substance called the *vitreous humor*.

Deep in the back of the eye is the *retina*, which receives the image as gathered and focused by the cornea and lens. The retina's light-sensing structures, called *rods* and *cones*, convert the light impulses into electrical impulses that they transmit along the *optic nerve* to the brain. The rods, situated mostly around the edges of the retina, are light sensors; cones, the color sensors, are generally grouped more in the center of the retina. The retina itself is kept supplied with necessary oxygen and sugar by a network of blood vessels called the *choroid plexus*.

For rest and protection, the whole mechanism can be sealed off from the outside by closing the eyelids, to each of which is attached a thin, flexible membrane called the *conjunctiva*. This and the eyelid itself contain glands that secrete tears and mucus that continually coat the eye and keep it moist, a process helped by blinking.

For the brain to interpret the information transmitted along the optic nerve, and especially to blend the two separate images into a single image and be able to judge distances, the two eyes must work together in a coordinated way. This so-called *stereoscopic vision* or *binocular vision* is managed by a set of small muscles, which align the eyes according to signals received, in turn, from the brain. If the action of the eyes is abnormal in some way, the brain cannot properly coordinate images from the two eyes, causing a wide variety of problems.

Few of these problems involve total loss of sight, though many can result in legal blindness if undiagnosed and untreated. Many involve vision impairment of various kinds and severity, some of which can be partly corrected, as through glasses (external lenses ground to correct vision defects), contact lenses (specially ground lenses placed directly over the cornea), drugs, or surgery, especially LASER SURGERY or MICROSURGERY.

Many eye disorders appear only with age, but many others affect young people, and some are present at birth. The most common of these involve the muscular coordination and structure of the eyes, including the following:

- *strabismus*, or crossed eyes, in which one eye turns or squints because of a muscle or neurological problem. Often the squinting eye has impaired vision. If that eye is turned toward the nose, the condition is called *esotropia*; if turned outward, it is *exotropia*. Children with this problem may use the eyes alternately, but if (as often happens) they use one eye continuously, they risk losing sight in the other eye, a condition called *amblyopia* (see below). Ophthalmologists may try to prevent this by using an eye patch over the stronger eye. Glasses and surgery may also be required to treat the problem.
- *amblyopia*, permanently impaired vision, though the eye shows no structural abnormality when examined by an ophthalmologist; the problem therefore apparently lies in the nerves connecting the retina with the brain. Amblyopia can result from nutritional deficiency or toxic levels of alcohol, tobacco, or other poisons. But in children, amblyopia often results from use of a single eye in strabismus, sometimes called *suppression amblyopia*, *amblyopia ex anopsia*, or *lazy eye blindness*. Cataracts and astigmatism (see below) can also cause amblyopia. An eye patch over the stronger eye, glasses, and surgery may be used to treat the problem.
- *ametropia*, or errors in focusing the eye, which can occur in various forms, including:
  – *myopia*, or *nearsightedness*, in which near vision (within eight to 20 inches) is strong, but far vision is blurred. Children with uncorrected myopia often tire easily and are restless or inattentive when doing work requiring distance vision. The problem is easily corrected with glasses.
  – *hyperopia*, or *farsightedness*, in which vision is blurred for near vision (and sometimes far vision as well), easily corrected with glasses. Children with uncorrected hyperopia may be fussy and irritable and may tire easily when doing work requiring near vision.
  – *astigmatism*, in which the cornea is slightly misshapen, causing blurring and distortion of vision. In mild cases, the distortion can be offset by specially ground lenses in glasses, but in severe cases, *contact lenses* are needed to provide a smooth, undistorted focusing surface.
  – *anisometropia* or *aniseikonia*, in which the two eyes vary markedly in what they see, because of unequal focusing power of the eyes or differences in the size and shape of the eyes. As a result, one eye sees an object of one size and shape, while the other sees the same object as a different size and shape, as when one eye is myopic and the other hyperopic. Glasses are not fully effective in treating this problem, though contact lenses are somewhat better.
- *size defects*, including eyes smaller than normal (*microcornea*), larger than normal (*megalocornea*), or bulging (*buphthalmos*, or "ox-eye"), which can lead to infantile *glaucoma* (see below).

In additional to structural problems, disorders may affect various parts of the eye, one of the most sensitive parts being the retina. Among the retinal disorders found in young people (as well as adults) are:

- *damage to or detachment of the retina*, when the light-sensitive membrane of the retina is torn or pulled apart from the layer behind it, allowing vitreous humor to leak in between. This can occur after a major injury but sometimes occurs spontaneously, especially in people with severe myopia, the first sign usually being flashes of light at the edge of the *field of vision* (the area the eye can see looking straight ahead without shifting position). This is an emergency, requiring immediate surgical repair; otherwise, if the central part of the retina (the *macula*) becomes detached, central vision may be lost, even though some *peripheral vision* may remain from the edges of the field of vision.
- *retinopathy*, a general disease or disorder of the retina, usually referring to damage to the retina from long-term high BLOOD PRESSURE or DIABETES MELLITUS, which can lead to blindness. It can also occur in PREMATURE babies.
- *retinitis pigmentosa* (RP), a progressive disease in which the rods of the retina degenerate and become pigmented, sometimes starting in early childhood as poor night vision but sometimes not recognized until later, gradually reducing vision. Cones are less slowly affected, so central vision remains longer, but RP sometimes leads to total blindness. RP is a GENETIC DISORDER, but though often AUTOSOMAL RECESSIVE, its inheritance pattern is not entirely clear. Some children also have an inherited disposition for the center of the

retina to degenerate, a condition called *macular degeneration*. Retinal degeneration may also accompany some other genetic disorders, such as LAURENCE-MOON-BIEDL SYNDROME and TAY-SACHS DISEASE (see LIPID STORAGE DISEASES).

- *retinoblastoma*, a malignant TUMOR that commonly occurs in very young children, for which a susceptibility may be inherited. Often seen first in a whitened pupil, retinoblastoma may cause blindness in the eye, sometimes accompanied by strabismus, and can spread along the optic nerve to the brain. RADIATION therapy is the main treatment, with the eye being removed if necessary. Any eye abnormality in an infant should be brought to the doctor's attention immediately. Tumors may also form elsewhere in the eye, some of them benign, some secondary tumors from elsewhere in the body.
- *retrolental fibroplasia*, in which a mass of scar tissue forms in back of the lens, usually affecting both eyes. Severe cases can lead to complete loss of sight.
- *color blindness*, more accurately called *color vision deficiency*, because it involves reduced ability to perceive differences in color, especially in the red and green ranges. Absolute color blindness is very rare and would involve seeing everything in shades of black and white. Color vision deficiency is a common GENETIC DISORDER of the sex-linked type (see X-LINKED), so it affects mostly men, though women are CARRIERS. Lessened color discrimination is not a serious problem unless the child is in a situation where inability to distinguish colors can be dangerous.

The eye's other focusing part, the cornea, is also subject to various disorders, including:

- *corneal abrasion*, or scratching, which can then become infected and ulcerated, with the resulting scar leading to some loss of vision.
- *injury by corrosive substances*, where the eye is splashed by substances such as acids or alkalis; the eye must be washed with large amounts of water to attempt to save sight.
- *xerophthalmia* (dry eye), involving severe dryness of the cornea and conjunctiva, resulting from severe VITAMIN A deficiency; if uncorrected, it can result in *keratomalacia*, a softening of the cornea, often leading to perforation, a condition that can cause blindness.
- *keratoconjunctivitis sicca* (dry eye and conjunctiva), in which the film of tears coating the eye is inadequate to protect the eye, as in some disorders, such as SJÖGREN-LAHRSSON'S SYNDROME.
- *uveitis*, inflammation of the iris, choroid, or ciliary body (called *uveal tissues*), often from infection but sometimes in connection with an AUTOIMMUNE DISORDER.

If the cornea has become damaged beyond repair, a cornea TRANSPLANT may restore sight, using a donor's cornea stored in an *eye bank*. Cornea transplants are far easier and more likely to be successful than other kinds of transplants because the cornea is relatively insulated from the body's IMMUNE SYSTEM, so rejection is less likely.

In addition, the eye is subject to other disorders, among them:

- *infections*, as by bacteria, viruses, and parasites, especially in people with weakened immune systems. Among the most common infections is *conjunctivitis* ("pink eye"), the inflammation of the membrane that covers the eye when closed, which can also result from ALLERGIES. Newborns often pick up conjunctival infections called *ophthalmia* from the mother during birth, whether bacterial or related to various SEXUALLY TRANSMITTED DISEASES, such as GONORRHEA or HERPES SIMPLEX, which can spread and damage vision. A severe form of conjunctivitis, called *trachoma*, is caused by CHLAMYDIAL INFECTION; if not effectively treated with antibiotics, it can scar the cornea and reduce vision to light only. PERINATAL CARE, notably use of silver nitrate and antibiotic ointments, has made such infections rare in developed countries. Inflammation and infection of the internal eye, called *endophthalmitis*, can also be extremely serious. Inflammation of the eyelids, *blepharitis*, often involves itchiness and pus or mucus on the lids and lashes.
- *glaucoma*, a condition involving abnormally high pressure on the aqueous fluid of the eye, which can damage the optic nerve and result in severe loss of sight or sometimes in *tunnel vision*, in which the child has only central vision, with no peripheral vision. In children, glaucoma is sometimes associated with buphthalmos (bulging eye); it can also result from injury, disease, or other disorders, such as PIERRE ROBIN SYNDROME. If diagnosed in time, the condition can be controlled with drugs before damage occurs.
- *cataracts*, loss of transparency in the lens at the back of the eye, gradually decreasing transmission of light to the retina. Most cases of cataracts occur in elderly people, but one form occurs in infants at birth. These congenital cataracts may result from the mother's infection with RUBELLA or ingestion of certain drugs during PREGNANCY; it is also associated with some GENETIC DISORDERS, such as DOWN'S SYNDROME. A child with GALACTOSEMIA is at risk for developing cataracts unless kept on a restricted diet. In most cases, surgery can be performed to remove the clouded lens and restore sight, replacing the lens with special glasses or lens implants.
- *nystagmus*, sometimes called *dancing eyes*, in which the eyes make involuntary, rapid, jerky movements from side to side, often in combination with some other kind of visual handicap or health disorder. Young children with nystagmus may be able to focus more clearly if they are taught to put a finger on what they want to see and use a marker for close work.
- *optic atrophy*, in which the optic nerve has been damaged, as by some causes noted above, impairing both central visual acuity and color vision. Children with optic atrophy have a much easier time perceiving black print on white paper, for example, than on colored paper. Hand-held magnifiers can also help.
- *hyphema*, HEMORRHAGE in the front of the eye, often looking like a bloodshot eye, which can be caused by violent shaking or a blow to the head; it is one sign of possible child abuse

(see CHILD ABUSE AND NEGLECT and WHIPLASH-SHAKEN INFANT SYN-DROME).

• *papilledema (choked disk)*, a swelling of the optic nerve, as may result from a BRAIN TUMOR increasing the fluid pressure inside the skull.

• *diplopia*, or double vision, which may result from a variety of causes, including a brain tumor.

Various parts of the eye can also be damaged by poisons, by MALNUTRITION, by heavy SMOKING and ALCOHOL ABUSE, by metals such as lead, and by some kinds of drugs.

In checking a child's eyes, ophthalmologists generally first examine the physical appearance of the eyes and the surrounding skin, the movement of the eyes (checking for strabismus, for example), visual acuity (sharpness of vision), field of vision, and color vision. In the process they use a variety of techniques.

Best known is the *Snellen Test*, the wall chart of letters, numbers, or symbols, often starting with a "Big E" on the top, each row below it smaller and each labeled with the distance at which it can be read by people with normal vision. For preschoolers, the big E alone is used, placed in different positions. This tests *central visual acuity*, or sharpness of vision in the direct line of sight. It is generally used for testing vision at a distance of 20 feet, using one eye at a time. A child who, from 20 feet away, can read a line that people of normal vision can read from 20 feet away is said to have 20/20 vision. If a child has 20/30 vision, that means that the child can read at 20 feet what most normal people can read at 30 feet. A Snellen rating of 20/30 or less is one of the common descriptions of people with "reduced vision." A similarly graded test for near vision is called the *Jaeger Test*. Where appropriate, *visual field tests* will be used to check peripheral vision.

In examining the inner part of the eye (possible because the main parts are transparent), the ophthalmologist will generally use a *slit-lamp microscope* and *ophthalmoscope* to provide magnification to check for possible abnormalities or damage, sometimes after the pupil has been widened with eye drops. If infection is suspected, a sample of cells will be scraped off and a CULTURE made in the laboratory. If abrasions or ulcers are suspected, a dye may be put into the eye to show up any damage. To check for possible glaucoma, pressure within the eye is measured by a test called *applanation tonometry*. Where appropriate, the doctor may also check *depth perception* (DP), the ability to perceive the distance of objects and their relative position in space, and *light perception* (LP), the ability to distinguish light from dark.

Finally, a variety of *refraction tests* will help the ophthalmologist decide whether corrective lenses—glasses or contact lenses—are needed. Glasses are sufficient for many mild eye problems, such as myopia. Many people, however, prefer contact lenses of various kinds, which also have some advantages in correcting certain conditions (as noted above). They have some disadvantages, however, in that wearing them for too long a period (even when supposedly designed for long-term use) can cause eye damage, and infections can easily occur if they are not properly sterilized. In addition, some people's eyes are sensitive and irritated by contact lenses. If children are using contact lenses, parents should note for how long a period the lenses are worn and should be very careful about sterilization; at any sign of a problem—sensitivity, redness, mucus, discomfort—contact lenses should be removed and the child taken to the doctor.

In cases where serious vision problems exist, the ophthalmologist's report will be made available to the school and often to the preschool, where appropriate. Reports are sometimes rather technical; in medical reports, for example, ophthalmologists will often use the abbreviations *OD* (*oculus dexter*) to refer to the right eye, *OS* (*oculus sinister*) for the left eye, *OU* (*oculus uterque*) if a condition affects both eyes, and *CC* (*cum correction*) to indicate corrective lenses, such as glasses. These reports are used in determining whether the child is HANDICAPPED and therefore eligible for SPECIAL EDUCATION assistance and, if so, of what kind.

In the HEAD START program, for example, various categories of visual impairment are described. In these, a child is considered *blind* when any *one* of the following exist:

(A) The child is sightless or has such limited vision that he/she must rely on hearing and touch as his/her chief means of learning; (B) a determination of legal blindness in the state of residence has been made; (C) central [visual] acuity does not exceed 20/200 in the better eye, with correcting lenses, or visual acuity is greater than 20/200 but is accompanied by a limitation in the field of vision such that the widest diameter of visual field subtends an angle of no greater than 20 degrees [this is a physical description of tunnel vision].

As implied above, few children are totally sightless; most have some remaining sight, sometimes described as *low vision*.

The much wider category in Head Start is *visually impaired*, described as follows:

A child shall be reported as visually impaired if central [visual] acuity, with corrective lenses, does not exceed 20/70 in either eye, but who is not blind; or whose visual acuity is greater than 20/70, but is accompanied by a limitation in the field of vision such that the widest diameter of visual field subtends an angle of no greater than 140 degrees, or who suffers any other loss of visual function that will restrict learning processes, e.g., faulty muscular action. *Not to be included in this category are persons whose vision with eyeglasses is normal, or nearly so.*

It is important for both parents and teachers, however, to focus not on the technical categories that are used for reporting purposes but on how well a child can use remaining vision for everyday purposes. Some are able to use their residual vision far more effectively than others, and some kinds of visual problems cause more difficulties than others in everyday life. A child's vision may also be affected by other outside factors, such as illness, fatigue, or stress; so something they can do one week they might not be able to do the next—if a mother has been hospitalized and the child is worried, for example. It is important, also, to talk much more to the child than normal—when going in or out of the room, for example, or when something unusual is happening—to maximize the child's development by providing satisfying contact with the outside world. This should start immediately after birth if blindness is recognized then (see the American Foundation for the Blind's booklet *Touch the Baby* and the Blind Children's Center's *Talk to Me*).

In any case, children should be encouraged to use whatever vision capabilities they have, regardless of how slight they may be. The Head Start program recommends: "The eyes, especially in early childhood, benefit from use. You should encourage a child to look both far and near and to examine objects close up. If necessary, encourage a child to hold objects close to the face, even if only part of the object is seen in this manner." In some programs, such as Head Start, special assistants called *orientation and mobility instructors* or *peripatologists* are available to help visually handicapped children learn the concepts and skills they need to understand where they are and to move about safely and easily. With special assistance such as this, and somewhat ADAPTED EDUCATION, many students with impaired vision are able to attend local schools, either in regular classrooms or special ones or both; some others may instead go to residential schools for the blind or the multiply handicapped.

In TEACHING YOUNG CHILDREN: GUIDELINES AND ACTIVITIES, on page 544, parents will find some suggestions for activities at home that are especially useful for children with visual impairments. Various kinds of programs are available to help visually impaired children. Materials printed in BRAILLE, large-print books, video aids for children with low vision, and audio recordings of books on records and tape, including textbooks, are available at little or no cost. In addition, many colleges and testing programs have special arrangements to accommodate blind or visually impaired students who attend regular colleges (no separate colleges for the blind exist). Guide dogs are often used to give people mobility where sight is extremely low. Government assistance and tax credits are also often available, as through Social Security. Parents seeking help and assistance for their visually impaired child should see below.

For help and further information

Organizations Focusing on Children

National Association for Parents of the Visually Impaired, Inc. (NAPVI)
P.O. Box 562
Camden, NY 13316
315-245-3442, toll-free number 800-562-6265
Keitha Robinson, Acting Director
Organization of and for parents of visually impaired children, organizations and agencies serving them, and interested others. Seeks to educate public, influence public policy and legislation, and strengthen services to blind and visually impaired children; provides information and support; offers training and operates workshops; operates toll-free number; publishes various print and taped materials, including books and booklets *Take Charge! A Guide to Resources for Parents of the Visually Impaired, Parents to the Rescue, Your Child's Information Journal, Preschool Learning Activities for the Visually Impaired Child—A Guide for Parents;* tapes from national conferences, such as *Equipment and Toys, Family Dynamics, Words of Wisdom from Parents of Older Blind Children;* and reprints on specific topics, such as *Choosing Toys for the VI Child, Parents Should Plan for IEP Meetings, Too!, Parent to Parent: Letting Him Try, A Practical Letter to Parents About Reaching Independence, Back to School: A Tough Parental Task, If Your Child Is Going Away to School,* and *Parent and Child: Defusing Anger.*

International Institute for Visually Impaired, 0-7 (IIVI, 0-7)
1975 Rutgers Circle
East Lansing, MI 48823
517-332-2666
Organization for parents and teachers of vision-impaired children from birth to age seven. Operates information center for parents and teachers of visually impaired preschoolers; consults and offers workshops; publishes quarterly newsletter and pamphlets.

Division for the Visually Handicapped, c/o Council for Exceptional Children, 703-620-3660. (For full group information see HELP FOR SPECIAL CHILDREN on page 578.)

Blind Children's Center
4120 Marathon Street
P.O. Box 29159
Los Angeles, CA 90029
213-664-2153; toll-free number (U.S. except CA) 800-222-3566; toll-free number (CA) 800-222-3567
Organization for parents of vision-impaired children. Publishes various materials, including *Heart to Heart* (English and Spanish), for parents of children without sight, and *Talk to Me,* language guide for parents of blind children.

Helen Keller National Center for Deaf-Blind Youths and Adults, 516-944-8900. (For full group information, see EAR AND HEARING PROBLEMS.)

Blind Children's Fund
230 Central Street
Auburndale, MA 02166
617-332-4014
Sherry Raynor, President
Organization for parents and professionals working with visually impaired infants, toddlers, and preschoolers. Publishes wide range of materials for teaching and stimulating children at different stages and levels of impairment, including works such as *Get A Wiggle On* and *Move It.*

Parents and Cataract Kids (PACK)
P.O. Box 73
Southeastern, PA 19399

215-352-0719
Geraldine Miller, President
Organization of parents whose children have cataracts. Encourages formation of local groups; maintains telephone networking service for parents facing similar situations; publishes quarterly newsletter *In-Sight*.

General Organizations

American Foundation for the Blind (AFB)
15 West 16th Street
New York, NY 10011
212-620-2000
(TTY) 212-620-2158, toll-free number 800-AFBLIND
William F. Gallagher, Executive Director
Organization for people who are blind or visually impaired, their families, and professionals who work with them. Provides information and referrals; helps blind people and their families develop self-help programs; makes for sale technical aids for visually impaired people; maintains library and National Consultant on Early Childhood; publishes extensive list of general materials in large type, recording, and braille, as well as basic guide to services for the blind from birth on, *Directory of Services for Blind and Visually Impaired Persons in the United States* (23rd edition, 1988), and other informative materials about blindness, including books *Blindness and Early Childhood Development* and *Understanding Low Vision* and pamphlets such as *Touch the Baby: Blind and Visually Impaired Children as Patients: Helping Them Respond to Care, Parenting Preschoolers: A Guide to Raising Young Blind and Visually Impaired Children, Getting Help for a Disabled Child—Advice from Parents, How to Thrive, Not Just Survive: A Guide to Developing Independent Life Skills for Blind and Visually Impaired Children and Youth, Reach Out and Teach* (teaching materials for parents), *Show Me How* (for parents teaching young children), *Blindness and Diabetes, Facts About Blindness and Visual Impairment,* and *Environmental Modifications for the Visually Impaired.*

National Society to Prevent Blindness (NSPB)
500 East Remington Road
Schaumburg, IL 60173
312-843-2020, toll-free number 800-221-3004
Michael Weamer, Executive Director
Organization for professionals and others concerned about blindness and preserving sight. Provides information to public about proper eye care, eye diseases, and treatments; supports research and operates screening programs; publishes various materials, including pamphlets and flyers such as *Children's Eye Problems, Sports Eye Injuries, Eye Injuries Among Schoolchildren, Home Eye Injuries, Hereditary/Congenital Conditions, Diabetic Retinopathy, Cataract, Glaucoma: Sneak Thief of Sight,* and multimedia eye safety education programs for school use: *The Eyes Have It* (for primary grades), *The Magic of Sight,* and *An Option to See* (for students in laboratory and shop classes).

American Council of the Blind (ACB)
1010 Vermont Avenue, NW, Suite 1100
Washington, DC 20005
202-393-3666, toll-free number (U.S. except DC) 800-424-8666; Legislative Information Hotline 202-393-3664
Oral O. Miller, National Representative
Organization for people who are blind or visually impaired, their friends and families, and interested others. Provides information and makes referrals; seeks to educate public and influence public policy and legislation, often in coalition with other national disability groups; operates toll-free numbers for general information and for legislative information; records talking books and maintains library about vision problems; evaluates and consults on consumer products; publishes various materials in large type, recording, and braille, including *The Braille Forum* (monthly), *Journal of Visual Impairment and Blindness, Directory of Agencies Serving the Visually Handicapped in the U.S.,* catalog *Products for People with Vision Problems,* brochures on specific topics, and radio program *ACB Reports*; has numerous special-interest affiliates, such as ACB Parents, Council of Citizens with Low Vision, Guide Dog Users, Friends-In-Art, Library Users of America, and National Association of Blind Students.

National Association for Visually Handicapped (NAVH)
22 West 21st Street
New York, NY 10010
212-889-3141
Lorraine H. Marchi, Executive Director
Organization acting as information clearinghouse and providing services for the visually impaired. Offers counseling to parents of partially seeing children, as well as adults; maintains lending library of large-print materials; publishes various materials, including large-print newsletter for children *In Focus*, newsletter for adults *Seeing Clearly*, and catalog of large-type publications.

National Eye Institute (NEI)
Building 31, Room 6A32
Bethesda, MD 20892
301-496-5248
Federal arm, one of the U.S. National Institutes of Health, sponsoring research on eyes and vision disorders. Provides information; publishes various materials, for professionals and public, on eye disorders.

RP (Retinitis Pigmentosa) Foundation Fighting Blindness
1401 Mt. Royal Avenue
Baltimore, MD 21217
(voice) 301-225-9400, (TDD) 301-225-9409, toll-free number 800-638-2300, Eye Donation Hotline, 24 hours a day, toll-free, 800-638-1818
Robert Gray, Executive Director
Organization of people concerned about retinitis pigmentosa and related inherited degenerative diseases of the retina, such as Usher syndrome and macular degeneration. Gathers and disseminates information; sponsors research and runs screening

centers; operates toll-free numbers, including eye donation hotlines; encourages formation of mutual-support self-help groups through local affiliates; publishes various print and audiovisual materials.

Association for Macular Diseases
210 East 64th Street
New York, NY 10021
212-605-3719
Nicholai Stevenson, President
Organization for people concerned with macular diseases.

Council of Citizens with Low Vision (CCLV)
1400 North Drake Road, #218
Kalamazoo, MI 49007
616-381-9566
Elizabeth Lennon, President
Organization for people with partial sight or low vision, their families, and the professionals who work with them. Encourages such people to use technical aids and services to enhance residual vision; seeks to educate public and bring people of low vision into the mainstream; publishes newsletter in large print.

National Federation of the Blind (NFB)
1800 Johnson Street
Baltimore, MD 21230
301-659-9314, toll-free Job Opportunity number 800-638-7518
Organization of groups representing blind people. Seeks to educate public about importance of equality and integration and to influence government policy; maintains toll-free number; operates National Blindness Information Center; publishes various materials.

Other reference sources
General Works

20/20 Is Not Enough: The New World of Vision, by Arthur S. Seiderman and Steven E. Marcus, with David Hapgood. New York: Knopf, 1990.

Encyclopedia of Blindness and Sight Impairments, by Jill Sardegna. New York: Facts on File, 1990.

Living with Blindness, by Steve Parker. New York: Watts, 1989.

Health Care U.S.A., by Jean Carper. New York: Prentice Hall, 1987. Resource for general and specific health-care information, including eye and vision problems such as retinitis pigmentosa, diabetic retinopathy, cataracts, and glaucoma; lists major eye disease treatment and research centers, leading ophthalmologists, diabetic retinopathy research centers, screening centers for Night Vision Aid for people with retinitis pigmentosa, sources of recorded and large-print materials, and other information.

Can't Your Child See?, by E. Scott, J. Jan, and R. Freeman. Baltimore: University Park Press, 1977; Austin, TX: Pro-Ed, 1985.

Mainstreaming Preschoolers: Children with Visual Handicaps: A Guide for Teachers, Parents, and Others Who Work with Visually Handicapped Preschoolers, by Lou Alonso et al. Washington, DC: Government Printing Office, 1984. Prepared for the Head Start Bureau, Administration for Children, Youth and Families. Contains much useful information on what visual handicaps are and how they affect learning in preschoolers, and teaching techniques and activities to help them develop their visual skills.

Practical Guidance for Parents of the Visually Handicapped Preschooler, by Patricia L. Maloney. Springfield, IL: Charles C. Thomas, 1981.

Raising the Young Blind Child: A Guide for Parents and Educators, by S. Kaastein, I. Spaulding, and B. Scharf. New York: Human Sciences, 1980.

Touch Toys and How to Make Them. Available from Touch Toys, P.O. Box 2224, Rockville, MD 20852.

Insight into Eyesight: The Patient's Guide to Visual Disorders, by Paul E. Michelson, M.D. Chicago: Nelson-Hall, 1980.

For or by Kids

Why Do I Have to Wear Glasses? by Sandra Lee Stuart. New York: Carol Communications/Lyle Stuart, 1989.

Seeing in Special Ways, by Thomas Bergman. Milwaukee, WI: Gareth Stevens, 1990. For grades 3 to 5.

Business Is Looking Up, by Barbara Aiello and Jeffrey Shulman. Frederick, MD: 21st Century, 1988. On vision impairment; part of The Kids on the Block Book Series for readers age 8 to 12, focusing on children with problems or disabilities.

The Eye and Seeing, revised edition, by Steve Parker. New York: Watts, 1990. For grades 4 to 7.

One Step at a Time, by Deborah Kent. New York: Scholastic, 1989. For ages 10 to 14. About a girl dealing with eye disease.

Lifeprints, quarterly magazine for blind or visually impaired youth (junior–senior high school). Available from Blindskills, Inc., P.O. Box 5181, Salem, OR 97304.

(See also VISUAL SKILLS; also HELP FOR SPECIAL CHILDREN on page 578.)

Fabry's disease   A type of LIPID STORAGE DISEASE.

FAE   Abbreviation for fetal alcohol effects, a mild form of FETAL ALCOHOL SYNDROME.

fail   In EDUCATION, to have a level of performance too low to be acceptable as evidence of learning, whether on a single TEST or piece of work or for a whole course; in the latter case a teacher would not allow a student CREDIT for taking a course. Sometimes the failing level is a preset GRADE, such as below a D average or a numerical average below 65 or 70; but sometimes the "fail" label simply distinguishes those who did not receive credit from those who did, in a PASS–FAIL system.

failure to thrive   Abnormally slow growth and development of a child, compared to the usual pattern for children of their weight at birth. Failure to grow normally can result from a wide variety of causes, including:

1. MALNUTRITION, which itself can result from a variety of causes, such as
   • poverty in the family;
   • lack of knowledge by the mother and father about how and what to feed the child;
   • CHILD ABUSE AND NEGLECT;
   • severe MATERNAL DEPRIVATION SYNDROME, as from outright rejection of the child by the mother and father or allowing an infant to be left in a hospital without stimulation, warmth, or human contact;
2. CHROMOSOMAL ABNORMALITIES, including TURNER'S SYNDROME, DOWN'S SYNDROME, and other forms of TRISOMY;
3. acute illness, such as an infection;
4. chronic illness or general health problems, such as heart problems (see HEART AND HEART PROBLEMS) or kidney problems (see KIDNEY AND UROLOGICAL DISORDERS), which are sapping the child's ability to grow and develop;
5. METABOLIC DISORDERS or MALABSORPTION, which keep the child from getting the proper NUTRITION, even though the diet is sufficient.

If unrecognized and unreversed, failure to thrive can lead to permanent retardation of physical, mental, and social development. Extreme failure to thrive leads to a severe condition called MARASMUS. That is a main reason for WELL-BABY EXAMINATIONS, including careful monitoring of height and weight; and if the parent–child relationship seems deficient, social services attempt INTERVENTION. (For help and further information, see GROWTH AND GROWTH DISORDERS.)

fallopian tubes   A pair of narrow tubes that arc around the lower abdomen from the two OVARIES to the UTERUS. The ends of the fallopian tubes, which lie above the ovaries, appear as upside-down, flowerlike funnels. When a mature egg (OVUM) is released by an ovary, the petal-like ends (*fimbriae*) of the fallopian tube open to receive it, drawing it inside by the action of millions of hairlike cells (*cilia*), which move, wavelike, to draw the powerless egg into the tube. In the fallopian tube, the egg undergoes division (*meiosis*) once more; its 23 chromosomes, each made of double strands of DNA, reduce themselves to 23 single strands of DNA, ready for FERTILIZATION, with the duplicate strand passing out of the picture. The egg is capable of being fertilized if a SPERM arrives in the fallopian tube during the next 12 to 24 hours and penetrates the double-layer coating of the egg. If it does, the fertilized egg will gradually move out of the fallopian tube to implant itself in the *endometrium* (lining of the uterus), becoming an EMBRYO. If not, the egg will gradually pass out of the fallopian tube and into the uterus, later to be expelled in the next MENSTRUATION.

Several things can occur to hinder this delicate process taking place in the fallopian tube, including the following:

• The egg may not make it across the space between the follicle where it matured and the fimbriae that will sweep it into the fallopian tube.
• The fallopian tubes may be inflamed, a condition called *salpingitis*, often as a result of infection. This is a very common cause of INFERTILITY.
• The fertilized egg may not be moved on into the uterus, often because the tube is naturally too narrow or has been damaged, as from infection, previous operation, or use of an IUD. Instead, the fertilized egg may implant itself in the fallopian tube, resulting in an ECTOPIC (or tubal) PREGNANCY. The tube will rupture as the embryo grows, causing possibly life-threatening hemorrhaging and possibly diminishing future chances for conception, though the other tube (if undamaged) is still open for use.

Women whose fallopian tubes are damaged or otherwise unsuitable for natural conception may turn to techniques such as IN VITRO FERTILIZATION or GAMETE INTRA FALLOPIAN TUBE TRANSFER (GIFT) to become pregnant. (For help and further information, see PREGNANCY; INFERTILITY.)

false labor   Popular name for *Braxton-Hicks contractions*, often confused with true LABOR contractions.

false negative   A TEST result that wrongly indicates that a person does not have the characteristics being tested for. If a child is given a SCREENING TEST for hearing problems and the test fails to identify an existing hearing impairment, the result is a false negative.

false positive   A TEST result that wrongly indicates a person has the characteristics being tested for. If a child is given a SCREENING TEST that indicates he has AIDS, when in fact he does not, the result is called a false positive.

familial polyposis   A rare inherited DIGESTIVE DISORDER.

Families Anonymous   An umbrella name for self-help groups for parents attempting to break the cycle of CHILD ABUSE AND NEGLECT and also for self-help groups of families of people involved in DRUG ABUSE.

family   Two or more people living together, sharing common responsibilities and obligations, among them physical, emotional, social, and economic care, and related to each other by blood, ADOPTION, marriage, or mutual agreement; also all of one's relatives, regardless of where they live. The most basic form is the *nuclear family*, consisting of two generations in one household. The classic type of nuclear family is made up of FATHER, MOTHER, and children, but single-parent families are also nuclear, as is a HOMOSEXUAL couple raising a child. The head of the family is the person who primarily supports one or more others in the family; for income tax purposes, the head of the household is the person who contributes more than half of the necessary support of a family member other than a spouse.

A family that has never been through a divorce or separation is sometimes called an *intact family*; conversely, a family that has been split is often termed a *broken family*, though many single parents object to the term because it indicates that the family needs to be "fixed." Many broken families re-form themselves into nuclear *stepfamilies*, often made up of a previously married mother and father and the children from their respective marriages, plus any new children they may have together.

Such families can have rather complicated living relationships, with ex-spouses having VISITATION RIGHTS or with other children from a previous marriage shuttling in and out of the house according to various CUSTODY arrangements. Relationships between step-siblings and half-SIBLINGS, and between step-parents and stepchildren, also often take some delicate handling.

Legal relationships in such families vary widely. Often a stepfather, despite having practical day-to-day authority in the house, will in fact have no formal legally recognized custody relationship with a stepchild. Such a father is sometimes called a *co-parent*. Some step-parents clarify the legal relationship by formal adoption of their stepchildren, if the biological father consents or has abandoned the child.

Many modern families involve co-parents. In a household where a man and woman live unmarried with the woman's son from a previous marriage, the man is co-parent to the woman's son but has no formal legal relationship to him. Similarly, in a household where a lesbian couple has adopted a child, only one woman can legally be the adoptive parent; the other is the co-parent.

With far more freedom in choosing marriage partners, many families today are formed by couples from different religious, cultural, or racial backgrounds. *Interfaith* or *interracial* marriages sometimes pose special strains, most of all regarding how the children should be brought up; such problems are extremely painful and difficult in cases of separation and divorce, when the court often has to decide questions parents are unable to resolve. In one case, for example, the court ruled that the child be raised by one parent but educated in the religion of the other parent.

An *extended family* is one that includes more than parents and their children. The term generally refers to those relatives beyond parents and children who are living in the FAMILY HOME, such as grandparents, aunts, and cousins, but sometimes to the whole network of relatives with whom the family is in regular contact. Extended families used to be far more common and still are in many parts of the world; in the United States today, nuclear families predominate, though the trend may be slowing somewhat for economic and health reasons. Whatever the disadvantages to the individual in terms of conservatism and traditionalism, the extended family has the advantages of providing a strong personal context for family members, ideally with older people receiving respect and younger ones learning from them; they also provide a support system now lacking in more separated households. In truth, some of the social movements of recent decades may have their roots in the desire to re-create such a support system.

Multiparent families are one approach. Common among some polygamous societies and groups, multiparent families are also found on some kinds of collective households or communes, such as kibbutzes, where adults share the rearing of the children.

Another approach is to choose a *surrogate family*, a family-like network based on chosen friends and often shared work, culture, interests, or neighborhoods. The now-common mutual-support self-help groups may partly represent an attempt by some people to replace the support individuals once had from extended families. Many organizations have formalized these attempts to create a nonbiological family, such as Big Brothers/Big Sisters of America (see below) and others.

Most families function more or less on their own, with occasional help from the government's social support system. But some families find themselves unable to cope with the problems they face, and in particular are unable to care for the children; such families are labeled *dysfunctional*. Health and social-work professionals have studied the family intensively in the past decades, analyzing the dynamics of family relationships and trying to identify signals that a family is dysfunctional and at high risk for problems such as CHILD ABUSE AND NEGLECT. Their aim is to try to detect signs of impending trouble and to prevent full-blown problems by means of CRISIS INTERVENTION.

For help and further information

About Families and Family Welfare

United Families of America (UFA)
220 I Street, NE, Suite 150
Washington, DC 20002
202-546-1600
Gordon S. Jones, Executive Director
Organization of people concerned about families in society. Aims to shape public policy and legislation so that it will not interfere with the strength of the family; conducts educational seminars and training sessions about lobbying; publishes *National Family Reporter*.

Family Service Association of America (FSA)
(formerly Family Welfare Association of America)
11700 West Lake Park Drive
Milwaukee, WI 53224
414-359-2111
Geneva B. Johnson, President and CEO
Network of community-based agencies aimed at educating families, enhancing their social and mental health, and working on their behalf in the community. Maintains library and publishes various materials, including *The Family Guide to Child Care: Making the Right Choices*.

Family Resource Coalition (FRC)
200 South Michigan Avenue, Suite 1520
Chicago, IL 60604
312-341-0900
Judy Langford Carter, Executive Director
Network of local family-support organizations seeking to strengthen families, give them greater access to community services, and enhance the quality of child development. Acts as information clearinghouse for family resource programs; attempts to influence public policy and legislation related to families and child development; publishes materials including *Program to Strengthen Families: A Resource Guide*.

Interracial Family Alliance (IFA)
P.O. Box 16248
Houston, TX 77222
713-454-5018
Organization for families that are interracial through marriage or adoption. Aims to strengthen interracial families, giving special support to their biracial children; encourages public acceptance of interracial families; maintains library and computerized network of interracial family organizations; publishes various materials.

National Council on Family Relations
1910 West County Road B, Suite 147
St. Paul, MN 55113
612-633-6933
Mary Jo Czaplewski, Executive Director
Organization of professionals who work with families. Provides information and referrals; maintains research data bank; publishes various materials for professionals.

Big Brothers and Big Sisters of America (BB/BSA)
230 North 13th Street
Philadelphia, PA 19107
215-567-7880
Thomas M. McKenna, Executive Director
Network of local, volunteer-run agencies to provide an adult friend for children from single-parent homes. Publishes various materials, including newsletter.

About Organizations For Stepfamily Members

Stepfamily Association of America (SAA)
602 East Joppa Road
Baltimore, MD 21204
301-823-7570
Barbara Muller, Executive Director
Network of mutual-support groups for stepfamilies and interested others. Helps stepfamily members enhance their relationships, through various programs and meetings, including some especially directed at children; works as advocate for stepfamily rights; offers referral services; publishes various materials, including *Learning to Step Together*.

Step Family Foundation (SFF)
333 West End Avenue
New York, NY 10023
212-877-3244
Jeannette Lofas, Executive Director
For stepfamily members and professionals who work with them. Gathers and disseminates information on stepfamily relationships; offers counseling and training groups; publishes various materials.

Second Wives Association of North America (SWAN), 416-968-1647. (For full group information, see CUSTODY.)

(See also CUSTODY; CHILD SUPPORT; GRANDPARENTS' RIGHTS; MOTHER; FATHER; also PARENT'S BOOKSHELF on page 566, for range of books on various kinds of families and parenting.)

family abduction   Alternate term for parental kidnapping. (See MISSING CHILDREN.)

family-at-risk   A family that, in the opinion of social workers, is more than usually likely to be dysfunctional, as in cases of child abuse. (See CHILD ABUSE AND NEGLECT for list of risk factors.)

family car doctrine   A legal rule in some states that the registered owner of a family car is responsible for any damage caused by a family member using the car with the owner's knowledge and consent.

Summary of the Family Educational Rights and Privacy Act of 1974 (FERPA)

Parent's Rights

Under the Family Educational Rights and Privacy Act of 1974 (FERPA), you as parents (or students who have reached the age of 18) have the right to:

• inspect all recorded information about your child maintained anywhere and in any form by the school system;
• challenge information in the records which you consider inappropriate, inaccurate, misleading, or which violates the privacy or other rights of you and your child, and to request amendment or deletion;
• provide or withhold written consent prior to disclosure of the records to any individual, agency, or organization outside the school system;
• receive a list of those who have been permitted to see your child's records;
• request that your child's name, address, and phone number not be released as part of a list to anyone outside the school system.

When reviewing their child's record, parents may want to use the Checklist for Review of School Records on page 204.

School's Responsibilities

FERPA requires schools receiving federal funds to assist parents in the following ways:

• inform you at least once a year of your right to examine and challenge your child's school record;
• provide a list of the types and locations of all records kept by the school in any and all media (handwritten, print, tapes, microfiche, computers, etc.);
• respond within 45 days (some schools have shorter time limits) to your written or oral request to inspect records;
• not remove or destroy material in the record after you have made a request to see it;
• provide copies of the record to you only if you are not able to review them at the school (schools may charge a reasonable fee for this service);
• hold an impartial hearing to consider your request to amend the records if the initial request is denied;
• place a statement in the record of your objection to specific material and/or information.

Continued on page 203

---

family court The type of civil court that in some states combines the functions of DOMESTIC RELATIONS COURT, JUVENILE COURT, and PROBATE COURT. On occasion, criminal cases involving families, such as CHILD ABUSE AND NEGLECT cases, also are handled in the family court.

family day care A type of CHILD CARE in a home or homelike setting.

Family Educational Rights and Privacy Act of 1974 (FERPA) A law, popularly called the *Buckley Amendment*, under which schools risk loss of federal funds if they fail to give parents access to the STUDENT RECORDS of their children under 18. Under the law, the school can release information from the student record to people outside the school only with the parent's authorization; over age 18 the student has control over access to the record and must authorize any access, including that by parents.

The school is obliged to respond to parents' reasonable requests for interpretations or explanations and may charge a nominal fee to cover time and expenses. The law also provides that parents can request corrections in the file and provides for

an appeals procedure if the request is denied. NONCUSTODIAL PARENTS retain the right to examine the student's record; the school may inform the CUSTODIAL PARENT of such a request but cannot ask permission.

For help and further information
FERPA Office
Department of Education
Washington, DC 20202
202-732-2057
Patricia Ballinger, Contact
Federal office monitoring compliance with the FERPA law. Offers information on FERPA laws and regulations; in case of problems, will on written request describing the problem contact the school.

National Committee for Citizens in Education (NCCE), 301-997-9300, toll-free number (U.S. except MD) 800-NETWORK [638-9675]. Publishes various materials, including "Information for Parents" pamphlets and fact sheets on educational issues,

Other Provisions

- *disclosure of school records*: Prior consent of parents is not required for disclosure of records to officials within the school system, to officials of a school to which the child is transferring, to authorized state and federal officials, or to comply with a court order.
- *divorced parents*: In the case of divorced parents, either or both natural parents, custodial and noncustodial, must be provided access to the child's records, unless there is a legally binding document to the contrary.
- *enforcement*: The FERPA law applies to all educational agencies or institutions that receive funds administered by the U.S. Commissioner of Education. Federal funds may be withheld from schools that do not comply.
- *private schools*: Private, parochial, and independent schools are not required to comply with FERPA. Some do so voluntarily.

Correcting the Records

If you think information in your child's school record is inaccurate, misleading, false, inappropriate, outdated, an invasion of family privacy, or otherwise harmful to your child:

1. Meet with the principal and request that the document be removed or revised.
2. If the principal does not agree to do so, request a hearing, as provided for in the federal law.
3. Present your case to the impartial hearing officer.
4. If the outcome of the hearing is not in your favor, prepare a written statement for the record explaining your reasons for disagreeing with the record.

Filing a Complaint with the Federal Government

If the school denies access to your child's records or releases student information without proper consent, a complaint may be sent (in writing) to:

Leroy Rooker, Director
Family Policy and Regulations Office
RM 3021, 400 Maryland Avenue, SW
Washington, DC 20202
202-732-2058

Names of students, school principal, dates, and specific description of what has occurred should be included, with copies of any correspondence. The FERPA Office will investigate the complaint and will inform you and the school of their findings and whether any action is required.

Source: National Committee for Citizens in Education

such as school records, parent–teacher conferences, parent involvement in schools, suspension and due process, and how to appeal. (For full group information, see EDUCATION.)

Other reference sources

Your Child's School Records: Questions and Answers About a Set of Rights for Parents and Students. Washington, DC: Children's Defense Fund, 1986. 122 C Street NW, Washington, DC 20001; 202-628-8787.

Inequality in Education. Cambridge, MA: Center for Law and Education, July 1977 (special issue). Larsen Hall, 6th Floor, 14 Appian Way, Cambridge, MA 02138; 617-495-4666.

family home In family law, the owned home in which a family lived before a divorce or separation. In many states, the court will not allow the house to be sold, or award the NONCUSTODIAL PARENT with half of its estimated value, as long as there are MINOR children living there, but will do so only after the children leave home or the CUSTODIAL PARENT moves or remarries.

In cases of threatened child abuse (see CHILD ABUSE AND NEGLECT) or parental kidnapping (see MISSING CHILDREN), the offending parent may sometimes be barred from the family home by a TEMPORARY RESTRAINING ORDER.

family-life education Courses that educate people about aspects of family living, such as parenting, child development, and communication skills. Such courses are increasingly taught in schools to prepare adolescents for adulthood and marriage, though these often focus primarily on SEX EDUCATION. Family-life education has been recommended for parents who have been, or are at risk of, committing CHILD ABUSE AND NEGLECT, as part of the 21ST-CENTURY SCHOOL, for example.

family planning Alternate term for BIRTH CONTROL.

family practice physician Alternate term for *general practitioner*, a type of PHYSICIAN who provides medical care to people of any age and either sex.

family practitioner (FP) A physician who specializes in providing general health care to the whole family, including children and women during PREGNANCY, though any family member

---

Checklist for Review of School Records

Have I received satisfactory answers to questions about the location and content of my child's school records?

	Yes	No	Need More Info
Has my child's entire school record been gathered in the school office?	☐	☐	☐
If not, where are the other parts of the record? Are parts of the record on tape, in a computer data bank, or on microfilm or microfiche?	☐	☐	☐
In looking through the record, are there any unexplained labels used to describe my child, like hyperactive, learning disabled, or antisocial?	☐	☐	☐
Have I seen the following parts of the record and had them explained to me? (Do not expect to see all of the following. Some entries may not apply to your child.)	☐	☐	☐
Grades, year by year	☐	☐	☐
Health records	☐	☐	☐
Attendance records	☐	☐	☐
Test scores	☐	☐	☐
Psychologist's and school social worker's reports to school staff or recommendations. (Psychologist's and school social worker's notes as part of treatment may be held confidential.)	☐	☐	☐
Reports from welfare and social service agencies	☐	☐	☐
Transcripts from other schools	☐	☐	☐
Guidance counselor's career or college recommendations	☐	☐	☐
Disciplinary actions	☐	☐	☐
Honors, awards	☐	☐	☐

This checklist is recommended as part of the ANNUAL EDUCATION CHECKUP described on page 172 under EDUCATION.

Source: National Committee for Citizens in Education.

---

having special problems will be referred to a specialist, such as an OBSTETRICIAN-GYNECOLOGIST.

family shelter   A residence to which many or all members of a family might go or be taken, as in cases of possible CHILD ABUSE AND NEGLECT. Often 24-hour counseling, along with short-term diagnosis and treatment, is available as part of CRISIS INTERVENTION.

Fanconi's anemia   An inherited form of ANEMIA.

Fanconi's syndrome   A kind of KIDNEY AND UROLOGICAL DISORDER.

Farber's disease   A type of LIPID STORAGE DISEASE.

FAS   Abbreviation for FETAL ALCOHOL SYNDROME.

father   The male who has PARENTS' RIGHTS and PARENTS' RESPONSIBILITIES toward a child, especially a MINOR. The male whose GENETIC INHERITANCE contributed directly to the child and who is one of the child's nearest BLOOD RELATIVES is the child's biological father (see BIOLOGICAL PARENT), also called the *natural father* or *birth father*. If the biological father gives up his rights and allows his child to be placed for ADOPTION, a male who adopts the child is called the *adoptive father*.

If a child's parents are unmarried, and the father has not acknowledged the child as his, the presumed biological father is known legally as the *putative father*, or sometimes the *unwed father*. Before the child is actually born, the unwed father generally has no legal right to be involved in the unwed mother's decision on a possible ABORTION; but after the birth, an unwed father has at least the right to visit the child and the obligation to contribute to the child's support. And if the unwed mother decides to place the child for adoption, the unwed father can protest TERMINATION OF PARENTS' RIGHTS. Whether or not he succeeds will depend on highly variable state laws, some of which may grant him CUSTODY, if he desires, while others may allow the adoption, especially if the child is a newborn.

If an unwed mother is receiving benefits under the AID TO FAMILIES WITH DEPENDENT CHILDREN and some other programs, the state will attempt to locate the father to have him reimburse the state for money paid for CHILD SUPPORT. The putative father, once located, may voluntarily sign a CONSENT AGREEMENT acknowledging the child and his responsibility for support; otherwise the state may institute a PATERNITY SUIT to establish that he is the *legal father* or *acknowledged father*. Under the

UNIFORM PARENTAGE ACT, enacted in some states, a man is presumed to be a child's father if:

- he has acknowledged the child as his own, as by raising the child in his own home as his child;
- he and the mother were married at the child's birth, or the child was born within 300 days of the marriage's end; or
- he and the mother married, or tried to do so, after the child's birth, and he either acknowledged in writing that the child was his, allowed his name to appear on the birth certificate, or has voluntarily or by court order assumed child-support obligations.

Under this Act, the legally recognized father of a child born through ARTIFICIAL INSEMINATION is the mother's husband, not the man who provided the SPERM. However, a stepfather is not regarded as a child's legal father unless he adopts the child.

Until recently, the husband of a child's mother was automatically considered to be the child's legal father, whatever evidence there may have been to the contrary. But with the advent of BLOOD TESTS that can exclude paternity with high accuracy, even if they cannot always say with equal accuracy who the father was, courts have sometimes allowed the paternity of a legal father to be questioned.

In recent decades, as the FAMILY has been in considerable turmoil and massive social changes have been taking place, many fathers are playing a more active role in bringing up their children, even while (through divorce and separation) many are obliged to see their children only when CUSTODY and VISITATION RIGHTS allow.

For help and further information

Fatherhood Project (FP)
c/o Families and Work Institute
330 Seventh Avenue
New York, NY 10001
James A. Levine, Director
212-268-4846; main number 212-465-2044
Organization to promote fathers' participation in raising children. Explores innovative programs in work, law, education, health, and social services that foster fatherly participation; provides information and referrals; conducts research and maintains library.

Parents Without Partners (PWP), 301-588-9354; toll-free number 800-637-7974. (For full group information, see CUSTODY.)

(See also FAMILY; CUSTODY; CHILD SUPPORT; VISITATION RIGHTS; and also PARENT'S BOOKSHELF, on page 566, for works on fathering and families.)

fats   A key source of energy for the body, as well as the carrier of the fat-soluble VITAMINS A, D, E, and K and part of the structure of the body's cells; often called *lipids*. Nutritionists recommend that fats should compose only 30 percent of daily caloric intake; but since most foods contain fats, people in Western countries generally consume far too much fat. The major component of fats are fatty acids, which come in various types, including:

1. *saturated fatty acids*, which are solid or nearly so at room temperature, found most abundantly in food from animal sources. These are especially undesirable in the diet because they tend to increase the amount of CHOLESTEROL in the blood.
2. *unsaturated fatty acids*, which are liquid at room temperature. These often come from plant sources and tend to decrease the amount of cholesterol in the blood. The two types of unsaturated fatty acids are:
   - *monounsaturated fatty acids*, such as olive oil and peanut oil;
   - *polyunsaturated fatty acids*, such as safflower, sunflower, corn, soybean, and cottonseed oils, which tend to reduce cholesterol most effectively.

Nutritionists and others researching the relationship between diet and heart disease have reached wide agreement in recommending that the diet for adults should lean heavily toward polyunsaturated types of fats in the diet. This means not only in cooking—the so-called *visible fats*—but also in the choice of foods, since meat, fish, poultry, and dairy products all contain so-called *invisible fats*. More recently, some key pediatric health organizations have called for restricting saturated fats to just 10 percent of the diet, though the American Academy of Pediatricians (AAP) cautions that fats should not be restricted before age two, when they are needed for proper growth.

Among the problems associated with fats are some METABOLIC DISORDERS in which abnormal amounts of fats are stored in the body. These disorders are sometimes called LIPID STORAGE DISEASES or *lipidoses*, and include *Gaucher's disease, Krabbe's disease, Niemann-Pick disease,* and *Tay-Sachs disease.* EATING DISORDERS such as OBESITY are generally linked to overconsumption of fat. (For help and further information, see CHOLESTEROL; LIPID STORAGE DISEASES; OBESITY.)

favism   A variant form of G6PD DEFICIENCY.

fear tension pain syndrome   A complex of feelings and reactions that are believed to be the source of much of the pain of labor and delivery, recognition of which by Dr. Grantly Dick-Read led to the development of natural CHILDBIRTH, now often called PREPARED CHILDBIRTH.

Federal Parent Locator Service   The federal branch of the nationwide PARENT LOCATOR SERVICE.

feedback   Information about the results of previous actions, which can then be used as a guide to future action. In relation to one's body, for example, feedback may be the sense of motion or pain that comes from moving your arm, information that can then be used to decide whether or not to move the arm further or pull it back. Children with an inadequate BODY IMAGE get inadequate feedback or do not know how to interpret

---

Feeding Baby: How Often? How Much?

How Often to Feed

Feed your baby when he or she seems hungry. Most babies will fall into a pattern of six to eight feedings about three to five hours apart. It is easier and better to get a regular schedule by working from the baby's own timing than by just deciding to feed at certain times whether the baby is hungry or not. You will soon be able to tell from your baby's crying and fussing what his or her needs are.

After a few weeks, most babies will begin to sleep through one of the feedings. Most parents prefer to skip the night feeding rather than a daytime feeding. If your baby sleeps through a daytime feeding, wake and feed at the usual time in the hope that the baby will give up one of the nighttime feedings.

How Much to Feed

Don't worry about how much is taken at a single feeding; most babies will have times when they just aren't hungry and other times when they take more than you expect. If your baby is growing at a satisfactory rate, he or she is probably getting the right amount.

If you are breastfeeding, you don't have to concern youself about how much to feed—your baby decides. Most mothers who are breastfeeding worry at some time about whether they have enough milk. Actually, too little milk is unusual and *more frequent feeding naturally increases the supply*. The best reassurance is your baby's normal activity and growth.

If you are bottlefeeding, most babies, after the first few days, take two to three ounces of milk each day for each pound of their body weight. Most bottlefed babies want six or seven feedings each day. For a seven-pound baby, this would mean 14 to 21 ounces of formula a day ($2\frac{1}{2}$ to $3\frac{1}{2}$ ounces in each six or seven feedings).

You might begin by offering three ounces in each bottle. When your baby begins to empty the bottle completely at two or three feedings a day, add an additional one ounce to the bottle. Stay a little ahead of the baby and let the baby decide how much to take. If your baby takes much more or less than two or three ounces per pound per day, talk with your doctor or clinic staff.

Source: *Infant Care* (1989). Prepared by the Bureau of Maternal and Child Health and Resources Development for the Public Health Service.

---

it, so they often cannot judge the effect of their actions, nor can they learn for the future the likely result of an action. People with EATING DISORDERS sometimes get faulty feedback about their actions, which causes them to act in ways harmful to themselves. More generally, feedback refers to the response of others to ourselves and our actions, which helps shape our view of how we feel about ourselves and how we will act in the future; in this sense, feedback can be used positively to shape behavior, as in BEHAVIOR MODIFICATION, or negatively to inhibit behavior.

feeding   The supplying of nutrients to someone who is unable to eat independently or in the normal way. The term often applies to infants, who receive their nutrition either through BREASTFEEDING or BOTTLEFEEDING using FORMULA. But in a hospital setting, the term *feeding* generally refers to the provision of nutrients other than by eating, as by a tube inserted into the stomach or intestines (often through the mouth or nose) or by nutritional fluids fed directly into the bloodstream intravenously (called PARENTERAL NUTRITION or *intravenous feeding*). Such artificial feeding is often used for PREMATURE babies, whose SUCKING or ROOTING REFLEX is insufficiently developed for normal feeding, as well as for children (and adults) who have various DIGESTIVE DISORDERS, MALABSORPTION, KIDNEY AND UROLOGICAL DISORDERS, brain disorders (see BRAIN AND BRAIN DISORDERS), high FEVER, or severe BURNS. (For help and further information, see BREASTFEEDING; BOTTLEFEEDING; SOLID FOODS, which includes material on eating patterns, on page 432.)

For help and further information

Poor Eaters: Helping Children Who Refuse to Eat, by Joel Macht. New York: Plenum, 1990.
Solving Your Child's Eating Problems, by Jane Hirschmann and Lela Zaphiropoulos. New York: Fawcett/Columbine. Formerly titled *Are You Hungry?*.

Feingold diet   A special diet developed by Dr. Ben Feingold that eliminates items such as food colorings that he believed to cause or worsen HYPERACTIVITY in children; a type of ELIMINATION DIET. (For help and further information, see ATTENTION DEFICIT HYPERACTIVITY DISORDER.)

Fernald method   A type of VAKT approach to teaching READING.

FERPA   Abbreviation for the FAMILY EDUCATIONAL RIGHTS AND PRIVACY ACT OF 1974.

fertility drugs   Medications given to treat some problems associated with INFERTILITY, associated with an increased risk of MULTIPLE BIRTHS in the pregnancies that occur.

fertility enhancement techniques   Alternate term for INFERTILITY treatments.

fertility specialist   An OBSTETRICIAN/GYNECOLOGIST or UROLOGIST who specializes in the particular problems of INFERTILITY and ways to overcome them, a fairly new medical specialty on the cutting edge of that branch of medical technology, often part of a team of specialists, including physicians and counselors.

fertility workup   A major medical and sexual evaluation done in cases of INFERTILITY.

fertilization (conception)   The union of an egg (OVUM) and a SPERM, which normally takes place in a woman's FALLOPIAN TUBE, the sperm (one of millions released in an EJACULATION) having traveled from the VAGINA through the CERVIX and UTERUS to the site. A single sperm burrows through the two outer layers of the egg, at which point the egg's membrane immediately bars the way to other sperm. The resulting fertilized egg is called a ZYGOTE. If two sperm enter, the egg will not be VIABLE, having lethal duplication of DNA, and a spontaneous ABORTION will occur, so early that the tissue will probably simply be reabsorbed by the body or flushed out in MENSTRUATION. (The same is true of many other fertilized eggs that have defects so severe that they are clearly, at a very early stage, incompatible with life.) If two eggs are fertilized by two different sperm, the result will be *dizygotic, nonidentical*, or *fraternal* twins (see MULTIPLE BIRTH); if a zygote separates into two separate EMBRYOS, the result is *monozygotic* or *identical* twins.

The egg, formed by an earlier cell division (*meiosis*), undergoes another cell division on penetration by the sperm, producing 23 single strands of DNA in the main egg and leaving the rest (called a *polar body*) to wither away. The sperm's DNA and the egg's DNA now begin to pair up, to form 23 double strands of DNA, which then duplicate themselves to form the 46 chromosomes needed for a new human being. It is in cell divisions and in this pairing-up process that some CHROMOSOMAL ABNORMALITIES can occur, as genetic material breaks apart and does not always recombine perfectly.

With the joining of egg and sperm, a unique being has been created, and his or her sex is determined. The egg (except in case of chromosomal abnormality) carries an X SEX CHROMOSOME; if the sperm's sex chromosome is also an X, the baby will be a girl; if a Y, a boy.

The zygote quickly starts dividing to form new duplicate cells, as it travels slowly down the fallopian tube. (Medically, the ball of cells, which soon develops a hollow center, is called a *blastocyte*.) On reaching the uterus (roughly a week after fertilization), the egg becomes implanted in the uterus wall and there begins to develop as an embryo.

In some cases, for a variety of reasons, fertilization cannot take place in the way described. Various alternatives have been developed for circumventing and treating this resulting INFERTILITY, including IN VITRO FERTILIZATION, EMBRYO TRANSFER, GAMETE INTRAFALLOPIAN TUBE TRANSFER (GIFT), and ARTIFICIAL INSEMINATION, sometimes with sperm from a donor. (For help and further information, see specific topics noted above; see also PREGNANCY; GENETIC DISORDERS; BIRTH CONTROL; INFERTILITY, for methods of achieving fertilization.)

fetal alcohol syndrome (FAS)   A combination of physical and mental BIRTH DEFECTS resulting from alcohol consumed by a mother during PREGNANCY. Only recognized in the early 1970s, FAS is now known to be one of the most common causes of MENTAL RETARDATION. Among the common characteristics of an FAS baby are an abnormally small head and brain; small, wide-spaced eyes; short, upturned nose; flat cheeks; various irregularities or malformations of face, joints, and limbs; and malformations of internal organs, especially the heart (see HEART AND HEART PROBLEMS). Babies with FAS are also shorter and weigh less than normal when born, and they fail to "catch up" even when special POSTNATAL CARE is provided. They often continue to

have poor coordination, HYPERACTIVITY, short ATTENTION SPAN, extreme nervousness, and behavioral problems.

In the United States, FAS affects perhaps one out of every 750 newborns (about 5,000 babies a year). And, as the Public Health Service's booklet *My Baby . . . Strong and Healthy* points out:

> . . . for every infant born with fetal alcohol syndrome, there are several more born with only some of the features of the syndrome. When only some of the characteristics are present, they are called "alcohol-related birth defects [or fetal alcohol effects]."

Pregnant women who drink during pregnancy are also at increased risk of having a STILLBIRTH or MISCARRIAGE; in the fourth to sixth months of pregnancy, a heavy drinker's risk of miscarriage is two to four times normal. And women who drink during pregnancy are two to three times more likely to lose their baby from the 28th week of GESTATION through the first week after birth.

Precisely how the alcohol does all this damage is not yet entirely clear. What is known is that the alcohol goes into the mother's bloodstream and quickly passes across the PLACENTA to the FETUS; but because a baby's organs are still developing, they cannot break down the alcohol as quickly as those of an adult can, so the alcohol is much more concentrated in the fetal bloodstream.

How much is too much? No one knows. In some women, the alcohol contained in six mixed drinks or cans of beer daily can produce the full fetal alcohol syndrome; in many women, the equivalent of two to five drinks daily also produces damage. The individual woman's system also apparently plays a significant role; some can drink heavily to no apparent effect on the fetus, while others can drink very little and still have babies with *fetal alcohol effects* (FAE). For this reason, women are best advised to stop drinking totally from the time when they are planning or anticipating possible CONCEPTION (or from the time they suspect they may be pregnant) through birth, and through BREASTFEEDING as well, for alcohol can continue to cause damage then.

Nor should women assume, because they have abstained for most of the time, that drinking heavily at a single party or celebration will be safe. In fact, some evidence suggests that sudden heavy drinking may be the most harmful of all. The main point to keep in mind is that fetal alcohol syndrome, unlike many other possible birth defects, is entirely preventable.

For help and further information

March of Dimes Birth Defects Foundation, 914-428-7100; local chapters in telephone-directory white pages. Publishes information sheets on specific topics, including *Fetal Alcohol Syndrome*. (For full group information, see BIRTH DEFECTS.)

National Institute of Child Health and Human Development (NICHD), 301-496-5133.

On Drinking During Pregnancy

The safest choice is not to drink at all during pregnancy or if you are planning or anticipating pregnancy. In addition, women who breastfeed should continue abstaining from alcohol until their babies are weaned.

—U.S. Surgeon General

National Center for Education in Child and Maternal Health (NCEMCH), 202-625-8400. (For full group information, see PREGNANCY.)

fetal and maternal specialist   Alternate name for MATERNAL AND FETAL SPECIALIST.

fetal distress   General term for problems experienced by a FETUS, especially with getting enough oxygen during the period of LABOR and DELIVERY. FETAL MONITORING seeks to identify early signs of fetal distress so that death and damage can be avoided. If a sample of blood from the baby's scalp shows high acidity, that may also indicate insufficient oxygen (HYPOXIA). So can the presence of MECONIUM (fetal stool) in the AMNIOTIC FLUID. In cases of fetal distress, prompt delivery is indicated, either by FORCEPS DELIVERY, VACUUM EXTRACTION, or CESAREAN SECTION. (For help and further information, see LABOR; CHILDBIRTH.)

fetal hydantoin syndrome (FHS)   A group of BIRTH DEFECTS found in women with EPILEPSY who have taken antiseizure medication derived from the chemical hydantoin. Among the symptoms are a small head (*microcephaly*), growth deficiency (see GROWTH AND GROWTH DISORDERS), abnormalities of the nails and fingers, and sometimes MENTAL RETARDATION.

fetal–maternal exchange   Exchange of nutrients and oxygen from the mother's blood for waste products from the baby's blood, accomplished through the PLACENTA.

fetal monitoring (electronic fetal monitoring or EFM)   Use of an electronic device that allows medical staff to track a FETUS's heart rate and the contractions of the mother's UTERUS. Monitoring can be done externally by using ULTRASOUND to detect the fetal heartbeat and by using a sensor placed on a woman's abdomen to register contractions. In late 1990, the Food and Drug Administration gave approval to the first external monitor for home use, for pregnant women AT RISK of having a PREMATURE birth, to be used under a doctor's direction and by prescription only. Internal monitoring involves the implantation of an electrode on the baby's scalp, by way of a CATHETER fed in through the VAGINA; a catheter also allows for internal detection of the uterine contractions. Physicians often use internal fetal monitoring when there are indications of possible problems, especially if the mother is two weeks past her DUE DATE, the aim being to detect problems—generically called FETAL DISTRESS—in time to save the baby's life and possibly to prevent damage.

In the past many doctors have thought such internal monitoring to be risk-free, though some parents have regarded it as needlessly invasive. More recently, however, research has indicated that use of internal fetal monitoring is associated with a higher risk of neurological problems, such as CEREBRAL PALSY, and that signs of fetal distress are equally well detected by using external means, including the stethoscope.

For help and further information

National Institute of Child Health and Human Development (NICHD), 301-496-5133. (For full group information, see PREGNANCY.)

Food and Drug Administration, 301-443-3170.

fetal presentation   The orientation of a FETUS in the mother's pelvic cavity in preparation for CHILDBIRTH. The main types of presentation include:

1. *cephalic presentation*, the usual head-first presentation. Often the fetus has been oriented head upward during the pregnancy, but in most cases (about 96 percent) the baby turns around with head downward in the pelvic cavity in the last weeks before delivery. A cephalic presentation can be described more precisely by the part of the head that first appears in the pelvis, such as:
   - *vertex presentation*, with the top of the head (crown) first, the easiest and safest position for delivery;
   - *brow presentation*, with forehead first, which can cause difficulty in delivery; or
   - *chin presentation*, with chin first, which can also complicate delivery.
2. *breech presentation*, with buttocks, or sometimes feet or knees, first at the opening of the pelvis. A common position earlier in pregnancy, breech presentation occurs only in about 3 percent of babies at the time of delivery, most commonly in cases of MULTIPLE BIRTH. If the baby is in a breech position at about the 38th week, the doctor may try to maneuver the fetus around, working from the outside (*external cephalic version*), a delicate procedure because it risks premature separation of the PLACENTA. Sometimes this maneuver does not work, or the baby returns to the breech position, perhaps because of a too-small pelvis or abnormally shaped UTERUS. Breech birth makes for a considerably more difficult delivery, often requiring some assistance, such as FORCEPS DELIVERY, EPISIOTOMY, or VACUUM EXTRACTION. FETAL MONITORING is frequently used to check for signs of FETAL DISTRESS. Sometimes a CESAREAN SECTION may be indicated, especially if a woman has not previously borne a child. Breech presentations can be more precisely described, such as:
   - *complete breech*, in which the legs are folded on the thighs, which are tucked up on the abdomen;

- *frank breech*, in which the legs are straight and bent upward so that feet are near the shoulder, a position these newborns may retain for a few days after birth; or
- *footling breech*, in which one or both feet are tucked backward under the buttocks at the pelvic opening, with one foot being called *single footling* and both feet called *double footling*.
3. *compound presentation*, in which more than one part is placed first in the pelvis, such as a hand next to the head.

Cephalic and breech presentations are both described as *longitudinal lies*, since the axis of the fetus is in the same direction as that of the mother, generally up-and-down. But in about one in every 500 presentations, a baby will lie crosswise, or horizontally, in the uterus, with a shoulder toward the pelvis. This is termed a *transverse lie*. If the baby cannot be turned, a transverse lie generally requires a cesarean section. In general, any types of presentation other than cephalic are termed *malpresentation* or *abnormal presentation*. (For help and further information, see CHILDBIRTH; DELIVERY.)

fetal rickets   Alternate name for ACHONDROPLASIA.

fetal surgery   Alternate term for IN UTERO SURGERY.

feticide   The killing of a living FETUS in the UTERUS, as through ABORTION. Recently, some antiabortion activists have taken to using the term *infanticide* instead, for rhetorical purposes.

fetoscopy   A prenatal diagnostic procedure in which a flexible tube containing a periscopelike device called a *laparoscope* is inserted through a small incision in a pregnant woman's abdomen and the UTERUS wall. Using this special form of LAPAROSCOPY, physicians can then visually examine the fetus for signs of abnormal development and, in certain cases, repair defects through IN UTERO SURGERY. Samples of blood, fluid, and fetus cells can also be taken for testing, though other GENETIC SCREENING procedures are often used for this. (For help and further information, see GENETIC DISORDERS; PREGNANCY.)

fetus   The being developing in the mother's UTERUS, from the eighth week through birth (earlier known as an EMBRYO); literally "offspring" or "little one." The fetus floats in protective AMNIOTIC FLUID and is nourished by the PLACENTA, to which it is connected by the UMBILICAL CORD. In the eighth week, on the average, the fetus is only about 1 to 1½ inches long and weighs about two-thirds of an ounce, but by the 40th week, at FULL-TERM, the baby that is born more likely measures 20 inches and weighs on the average about 7½ pounds. (See PREGNANCY for a description of month-by-month development.)

fever (pyrexia)   An abnormally high body temperature, above the normal 98.6°F (37°C), generally due to infections caused by bacteria or viruses but sometimes stemming from other types of problems within the body, including reaction to medications. Fever is a natural part of the body's reaction to invasion by disease organisms, but it can have serious effects, especially in young children. Most serious, very high fever can cause CONVULSIONS, COMA, and even DEATH in some situations. Other common accompanying symptoms are confusion; DELIR-

Fever and Babies

Temperatures will vary during the day. However, if your baby feels particularly warm, take the baby's temperature. If your baby's temperature taken rectally is above 100°F, you should call your doctor or clinic.

Fever is the body's natural response to many infections. If your baby has a fever, there is something wrong. If your baby is less than two months old, call your doctor or clinic immediately. If an infant with a high fever (above 102°F) is playful and cheerful, the sickness is not likely to be serious, but you should call your doctor to be sure. An older baby with only a slight fever or no fever who appears to be sick and weak also needs medical attention. Fever should warn you to watch carefully, but it doesn't tell you how sick your child may be.

Many babies will have a fever with every cold. Many have a fever for a day or two with no other signs of illness except tiredness and fussiness.

Give plenty to drink and take off any extra sweaters or blankets. A "sponge bath" with a cloth dampened with lukewarm water may help if your baby's temperature is high. You may also try a bath in lukewarm water. If your baby seems uncomfortable or particularly jittery, call your doctor or clinic.

It will be helpful to take your baby's temperature before you call the doctor or clinic so that you can report the number to them.

Source: *Infant Care* (1989). Prepared by the Bureau of Maternal and Child Health and Resources Development, Public Health Service.

IUM; shivering; headache; thirst; flushed, hot skin; rapid breathing; and alternating shivering and sweating.

Apart from treating the underlying cause, if possible, the main aim is to bring down the body temperature, as by giving a sponge bath with lukewarm water or giving acetaminophen (not aspirin to children, because of its link to REYE'S SYNDROME). Parents should in any case consult a physician about any fever, especially in a very young child, so that the causative condition can be treated. Some serious diseases, such as MENINGITIS, can progress extremely rapidly, so prompt attention is important.

fever blisters   Popular name for mouth sores caused by the HERPES SIMPLEX virus.

FHS   Abbreviation for FETAL HYDANTOIN SYNDROME.

fiber   In the diet, that portion of plants that is indigestible by humans. It helps avoid CONSTIPATION and maintain normal bowel movements, because it soaks up water and so eases passage of feces through the intestines. Dietary fiber, found in whole-grain products, fruits, and root vegetables, can also help ease problems associated with IRRITABLE BOWEL SYNDROME and cut the risk of developing CANCER. (For help and further information, see NUTRITION.)

fifth disease   Alternate name for ERYTHEMA INFECTIOSUM.

figure–ground discrimination   Ability to distinguish between important and unimportant information in an environment, such as a child's ability to focus on a teacher's voice and ignore the singing in the next room. Children with a high degree of DISTRACTIBILITY are often unable to select and attend to one aspect of the environment and "tune out" others. Some psychological tests ask people to look at pictures and identify which is the "figure" and which the "background"; people with brain dysfunction, including LEARNING DISABILITIES, often are uncertain about doing so.

financial aid   For students, a variety of programs providing help in handling the costs of attending a COLLEGE or PRIVATE SCHOOL, some applying only to TUITION costs but others covering additional expenses, such as room and board, books, and other supplies. Financial aid comes in many forms, including SCHOLARSHIPS, GRANTS, SUBSIDIZED LOANS, WORK-STUDY PROGRAMS, and (generally in graduate school) fellowships and assistantships. A school's financial aid administrator works with a student to put together a financial aid "package," consisting of several types of aid, to meet the student's needs. Many types of federally subsidized financial aid will be suspended or terminated if a student is convicted of possessing or distributing drugs.

For help and further information

Federal Student Aid Information Center, 800-333-INFO [4636]. Offers students information about federal student financial aid programs.

Citizens' Scholarship Foundation of America (CSFA)
Box 297
St. Peter, MN 56082
507-931-1682
Marlys C. Johnson, Vice President
Organization that originated the Dollars for Scholars program, under which local communities raise money (emphasizing small contributions from many people) for college and technical training for local students. Aims to help average as well as top students and to fund technical as well as college education; helps local communities organize scholarship programs; publishes various materials, including monthly newsletter.

United Student Air Funds (USA FUNDS)
200 East 42nd Street
New York, NY 10017
212-661-0900, toll-free number 800-428-9250
J. Wilmer Mirandon, Chairman
Organization providing low-cost loans to college students needing financial aid. Funded by corporations and foundations; operates toll-free number and WHIZ-KID on-line computer processing; publishes various materials, including quarterly newsletter and pamphlets.

National Scholarship Service and Fund for Negro Students (NSSFNS)
965 Martin Luther King, Jr. Drive

Atlanta, GA 30314
404-577-3990
Samuel Johnson, Executive Director
Organization providing college scholarships for low-income minority students. Provides advice and referral to interested students, especially those in Talent Search and Upward Bound projects; arranges student–college interview sessions; advises guidance and admissions counselors; publishes brochure and annual report.

Other reference sources

Financing a College Education: The Essential Guide for the 90s, by Judith B. Margolin. New York: Plenum, 1989; paper, 1990.

The Tuition Dilemma: Assessing New Ways to Pay for College, by Arthur M. Hauptman. Washington, DC: Brookings Books, 1990.

The College Cost Book. New York: College Board, annual. Includes costs and financial aid available at two- and four-year colleges.

The Scholarship Book, third edition, by Daniel Cassidy. New York: Prentice Hall, 1990.

College Financial Aid Annual, compiled by College Research Group of Concord, MA. New York: Arco, annual.

Lovejoy's Guide to Financial Aid, third edition, by Anna Leider. New York: Monarch, 1989.

Peterson's College Money Handbook 1990. Princeton, NJ: Peterson's, 1989.

Don't Miss Out: The Ambitious Student's Guide to Financial Aid, 1990–1991, 14th edition, by Anna Leider and Robert Leider. Chicago: Longman, 1989.

College Check Mate: Innovative Tuition Plans That Make You a Winner, 1990–1991, third edition, by Octameron Staff. Chicago: Longman, 1989.

The Student Entrepreneur's Guide: How to Start and Run Your Own Business, revised edition, by Brett Kingstone. New York: McGraw-Hill, 1990.

fine motor skills   The types of MOTOR SKILLS that use the small muscles of the fingers, toes, wrists, lips, and tongue to perform precision tasks such as writing or tying shoes.

fingerspelling   Use of hand shapes to stand for letters of the alphabet, to spell out words. Fingerspelling is often used by people with EAR AND HEARING PROBLEMS when they are being taught using a TOTAL COMMUNICATIONS approach, but it is avoided by those teachers of the deaf who believe that no form of MANUAL COMMUNICATION should be used.

fish-skin disease   Popular alternate name for ICHTHYOSIS.

5p- syndrome   Alternate name for CRI DU CHAT SYNDROME.

floppy infant syndrome   A general term for a condition in which some babies, especially PREMATURE infants, have unusually limp, slack, or flaccid muscles (HYPOTONIA). This generally disappears as they mature, but in some children it remains and is associated with a variety of conditions, including CEREBRAL PALSY,

MOTOR NEURON DISEASES, DOWN'S SYNDROME, heart problems (see HEART AND HEART PROBLEMS), THYROID GLAND problems, and MALNUTRITION. *Floppy infant syndrome* is sometimes used specifically to refer to SPINAL MUSCULAR ATROPHIES. (For help and further information, see MUSCULAR DYSTROPHY.)

fluoridation   In dentistry, treatment of TEETH with the chemical FLUORINE, which helps strengthen the tooth's protective enamel and also reduces the cavity-causing acid formed by bacteria in the mouth. In the last few decades, fluoridation in the public water supply has helped cut tooth decay by 50 percent or more. The process is not without controversy; some people have always criticized fluoridation as introducing risks of unknown magnitude into people's lives, and they cite some animal studies suggesting that large amounts of fluorine can increase the risk of CANCER. The main scientific community, however, has found no convincing data of such a risk to humans and continues to strongly recommend fluoridation.

If the family water supply does not contain adequate fluoride, parents are advised to see that their children get daily fluoride supplements from infancy, because it is most effective when teeth are forming. Fluoride may be administered in the form of drops (for infants) or tablets (once children can swallow pills), or it may be applied directly to the teeth in a solution or gel, in toothpaste or mouthwashes; it should be continued at least through age 14. Fluoride administration should be done under the direction of a dentist or physician, however, since too much fluoride can cause discoloration of teeth. To avoid this, dentists recommend using only a pea-sized portion of fluoride toothpaste for preschoolers. They also suggest that mouth rinses not be used until age six, since younger children tend to swallow rather than rinse. Some schools conduct weekly fluoride mouth-rinsing programs for school-age children or provide tablets for students. (For help and further information, see TEETH.)

fluorine   A MINERAL vital to the body, though only in small amounts, for proper formation and maintenance of bone, especially in children. It is fluorine that is widely used in FLUORIDATION programs, to help prevent tooth decay. Some have suggested that additional amounts of fluorine used in fluoridation also *cause* health problems, such as increased risk of CANCER, but public health experts generally feel that the scientific data so far does not support that view. In large amounts (for example, if fluorine-containing pesticides are ingested), it can cause poisoning and even DEATH. (For help and further information, see FLUORIDATION; MINERALS; NUTRITION; TEETH.)

fluoroscopy   A type of RADIOGRAPHY in which X-RAYS are used to give not still pictures, but moving ones. Fluoroscopy is especially useful as a guide to the physician in certain delicate procedures, such as when giving a BLOOD TRANSFUSION to a FETUS still in the UTERUS.

FNP   Abbreviation for FAMILY NURSE PRACTITIONER.

folacin   Alternate name for FOLIC ACID.

folic acid (folacin)   A VITAMIN important in the manufacturing of red blood cells and in energy METABOLISM. Symptoms of deficiency are DIARRHEA and a form of ANEMIA, while overconsumption can obscure the presence of pernicious anemia. Recent studies have also suggested that deficiency of folic acid—from improper diet or from drugs that decrease the body's supply of folic acid—can contribute to neural tube defects, such as SPINA BIFIDA. Folic acid is abundant in liver, beans, and green leafy vegetables and is also found in nuts, fresh oranges, and whole-wheat products. (For help and further information, see RECOMMENDED DAILY ALLOWANCES; VITAMINS.)

follicles   Egg-producing structures in the OVARIES, the one producing the "lead" egg being called the *graafian follicle*; also a general name for the sites from which teeth or strands of hair emerge.

fontanelles   Two soft spots in a baby's skull, covered only by membranes at birth, where the bones of the skull fuse and harden later; the rear one fuses in about two months and the top front one in about 18 months. It is the softness of a baby's skull that allows the head to pass through the BIRTH CANAL during CHILDBIRTH. Some babies, especially those with DOWN'S SYNDROME, have more than two fontanelles. Abnormalities of the fontanelles are associated with some brain disorders. They may temporarily bulge when a baby cries, but persistent tension in the membrane can indicate physical problems, such as HYDROCEPHALUS. (For help and further information, see BRAIN AND BRAIN DISORDERS.)

food additives   Any substance added to food during processing. In the United States and many other countries, such additives are regulated and tested for safety, though problems can still occur. Additives are used for a variety of reasons, including the following:

- *to preserve storage quality.* Preservatives retard growth of bacteria, molds, and yeasts that can spoil food and otherwise cause FOOD POISONING; some ANTIOXIDANTS prevent other kinds of food changes, such as discoloration or growing rancid, during normal storage life. One common group of preservative used in meats is NITRITES.
- *to improve texture.* Some additives, including stabilizers, emulsifiers (to prevent separation), thickeners, and gelling agents, help make the food's texture more attractive.
- *to improve taste and color.* Colors and flavorings are added to enhance the food's original taste and color, to make up for qualities lost during processing, or to make foods appropriate for use by people with specific health problems, as artificial sweeteners are used in products for people with DIABETES MELLITUS.
- *to enhance the food's performance.* A variety of additives are used to make the food respond in an enhanced or more standardized way during cooking, such as flour to be used for baking bread.

The Food and Drug Administration (FDA) has, since 1958, been charged with ensuring the safety of food additives (1960 for colorings). For its regulatory purposes, the FDA divides food additives into different groups:

- *generally recognized as safe (GRAS) substances.* These are things like sugar and salt, two of the most widespread food additives, and also many spices, herbs, and vitamins, that are considered "safe based either on a history of safe use before 1958 or on published scientific evidence." Though these may be safe, many parents will want to select foods not overloaded with sugar and salt, which can cause tooth decay and high BLOOD PRESSURE, even if they are not implicated in the more serious problems tested for (see WHAT IS SAFE?, on page 213).

- *prior-sanctioned substances.* These are substances that had been sanctioned before the 1958 amendment for use in a specific food, by either the FDA or the U.S. Department of Agriculture. Nitrites, for example, are prior-sanctioned substances as common preservatives in meats (though not in vegetables).

- *food additives.* This is the FDA's category for additives that have no proven track record. The artificial sweetener ASPARTAME (brand name NutraSweet®), for example, was simply unknown at the time it was proposed for use, so it had to undergo substantial testing before approval. Substances used in food packaging can also end up in food and so require testing by the FDA.

- *color additives.* These are dyes used in foods, drugs, cosmetics, and other medical products, which are subjected to testing similar to that for food additives. Those being used in 1960 were given provisional approval at the time; some were later dropped because testing showed them unsafe or because manufacturers were no longer interested in using them. Food dyes have been suspected of triggering or exacerbating HYPERACTIVITY, but no real consensus on the question has developed in the scientific community.

Neither GRAS, prior-sanctioned substances, nor provisionally approved color additives remain on the FDA's approved list unreviewed. If later data indicates that a substance is unsafe, it will be removed. Both saccharin and cyclamates were once on the GRAS list, for example, but evidence showed that they might cause cancer in animals. As a result, cyclamates were banned altogether and saccharin was kept only by special exemption from Congress because of need by people with diabetes. Since then aspartame has become the most widely used artificial sweetener.

Nitrites have come under some fire because, in the intestines, they are converted into chemical compounds called *nitrosamines*, which have been shown to cause cancer in animals. Though nitrites have not been barred from use, partly because the scientific evidence is indirect and partly because no good substitute is readily available, many parents may wish to control carefully their family's consumption of nitrite-containing meats, such as hot dogs.

Approved additives are safe for most people but can cause severe and sometimes life-threatening allergic reactions in some. Through its *Adverse Reaction Monitoring System* (ARMS), the FDA has, since 1985, collected information on complaints received directly by them or indirectly from the manufacturer, classifying the complaints by the severity of the symptoms reported and the directness of the relationship between the product and the symptom. Among the additives about which such complaints are most often received are aspartame, sulfites, monosodium glutamate (MSG, a flavor-enhancer), nitrites, polysorbate (an emulsifier), and some color dyes. Some reactions are extremely severe; according to the ARMS records, more than two dozen people may have died from allergic reaction to sulfites before they were banned from use in salad bars in 1986. On the other hand, sometimes reactions are so widely diverse, general, or vague that thay cannot be substantiated. For example, while early studies indicated that some people have an allergic-type reaction to aspartame, at least one study showed reactions to aspartame were less than to a neutral placebo.

The FDA suggests that if you or anyone in your family has an allergic reaction to a food additive, you should first contact your local physician for treatment. Then you or the doctor should contact the nearest FDA field office (in the blue pages of the telephone book) to report information about the reaction. (For help and further information, see NUTRITION; ALLERGY; FEINGOLD DIET.)

For help and further information

Food and Drug Administration (FDA), 301-443-3170. Publishes *A Primer on Food Additives*. (For full group information, see NUTRITION; DRUG REACTIONS AND INTERACTIONS.)

Other reference sources

A Consumer's Dictionary of Food Additives, third edition, by Ruth Winter. New York: Crown, 1989.
Aspartame (Nutrasweet): Is It Safe?, by H.J. Roberts. Philadelphia: Charles, 1990. P.O. Box 15715, Philadelphia, PA 19103. (See also POISONS.)

food intolerance A general term for a regular adverse reaction to a food or FOOD ADDITIVE, not stemming from FOOD POISONING or a psychological reaction. It can refer to a wide range of responses, from a mild upset stomach after eating fried foods to ALLERGIES involving possibly life-threatening ANAPHYLACTIC SHOCK, as to monosodium glutamate (MSG). Many forms of food intolerance are related to a biochemical deficiency, either inherited or environmentally triggered, that makes the body unable to digest certain foods; among these are LACTOSE INTOLERANCE, CELIAC SPRUE (gluten intolerance), and even DIABETES MELLITUS (a sort of glucose intolerance). In a wider sense, some kinds of METABOLIC DISORDERS, involving the body's inability to break down essential nutrients and use them for energy, might also be considered examples of food intolerance. When first starting a baby on SOLID FOODS, public health experts recommend that parents try one simple food at a time, and only for a few days each, to identify any adverse reactions to foods.

What Is Safe?

The Food and Drug Administration is charged with ensuring the safety of food additives, but what is "safe"?

"Congress has defined safety as a reasonable certainty that no harm will result from use of an additive," says Gerad McCowin, director of the FDA's division of food and color additives. "In our evaluation we examine to see whether the additive has any toxic effects, whether it may cause birth defects. Does it interfere with nutrition? Does it affect individuals with allergies?"

When an additive is tested, it is usually fed in large doses over an extended period to at least two kinds of animals. These feeding studies, usually done by or for a food company that wants to use or sell the additive, are designed to determine whether the substance causes cancer, birth defects, or other injury to the animals.

Cancer is of particular concern. A special provision of the 1958 and 1960 additive amendments, the so-called Delaney clause, states that if an additive is found to cause cancer in humans or animals it may not be added to food.

The company submits the results of all these tests to the FDA for review. If the FDA review finds that the additive is safe, the agency establishes regulations for how it can be used in food. This commonly includes a 100-fold margin of safety. This means that the substance may be used in food at a level that is no more than one-100th of the highest level at which it was fed to test animals and did not produce any harmful effects.

Source: *A Primer on Food Additives* (1989). Prepared for the Public Health Service by the Food and Drug Administration.

(For help and further information, see NUTRITION, and specific topics noted above.)

food labels Information that the Food and Drug Administration requires to be on all food products from manufacturers, including information on the ingredients; the net contents or net weight (including liquid); the name and business address of the manufacturer, packer, or distributor; and (where appropriate) the date by which it should be sold. More specifically, labels should include:

- a full list of the ingredients (including FOOD ADDITIVES), in descending order by weight, using their common or usual names. Color and flavor additives do not normally need to be listed specifically by name, except for color Yellow No. 5, which can cause allergic reactions in some people.
- nutrition information, actually required only when a manufacturer adds nutrients to a product (such as to make a food more nutritious or to replace nutrients lost in processing) or makes a claim like "now contains fewer calories"; but most manufacturers include nutrition information to meet consumer demand, listing some of the key nutrients and to what

extent the product meets the RECOMMENDED DAILY ALLOWANCE of each.
- grades, where appropriate, such as for meat, poultry, fish, or milk.
- product dating, required by the FDA on only a very few products (such as an expiration date for infant FORMULA) but widely used nevertheless, usually as "pull dates" (indicating when to take from the store shelf) or "use-by dates" (meaning not to use after that date).
- code dating, required by the FDA for most canned foods and used also on other products with a long shelf life, giving information about the manufacturer and the place of packaging, should a recall be required.

The FDA has established basic standards for ingredients if certain names (such as ketchup or mayonnaise) are to be used. Minimum standards for these so-called *standardized foods* are aimed at helping consumers avoid being cheated by cheap substitutes and fraudulent packaging. If a product does not meet the minimum standard, it cannot be called by that name; a peanut-butter-like product that does not contain 90 percent peanuts cannot, for example, legally be called peanut butter. Also, a less nutritious product resembling a standardized food must be called an imitation; even if it is equally nutritious, it still needs to be given a different name. The basic ingredients required to meet the standard need not be listed on the food label, but any other ingredients added by a specific manufacturer must be shown.

Various FDA requirements also govern labeling of incomplete products. For example, only products that contain 100 percent juice can be called juices; if they are diluted, they must be called drinks or beverages. Similarly "helper" products must clearly indicate what needs to be added to make the dish a complete dinner—such as a chicken to a chicken-casserole dinner package.

For help and further information

Food and Drug Administration (FDA), 301-443-3170. Publishes *A Consumer's Guide to Food Labels*. (For full group information, see NUTRITION; DRUG REACTIONS AND INTERACTIONS.)

footling breech A type of FETAL PRESENTATION in which one or both feet are tucked backward under the buttocks at the pelvic opening, with one foot being called *single footling* and both feet called *double footling*.

foramen ovale A hole in the septum, the wall that divides the right and left sides of the heart, which normally closes at birth. (See HEART AND HEART PROBLEMS.)

forceps delivery Use of a hinged device with two curved arms that are inserted into a woman's VAGINA during CHILDBIRTH and fit around a child's head, being then used to aid DELIVERY. Forceps are generally removed as soon as the head is delivered, allowing the rest of the delivery to proceed normally, but they can leave some temporary marks on the head and face.

They are used sometimes in cases of FETAL DISTRESS, especially early in the delivery or when the mother is unable to push out the baby on her own. Forceps have been used somewhat less often in recent years, as VACUUM EXTRACTIONS and CESAREAN SECTIONS have become more common. (For help and further information, see CHILDBIRTH.)

foreskin (prepuce)   The loose fold of skin over the head, or *glans*, of the PENIS, which is often removed shortly after birth for medical or religious reasons in an operation called CIRCUMCISION.

formal operations   The fourth stage of children's learning, according to Piaget's theory of COGNITIVE DEVELOPMENT.

form constancy   The ability to recognize an object or shape, regardless of what position or angle it is viewed from or with slight changes in color or size; an important element in SPATIAL ORIENTATION and in VISUAL SKILLS that often gives difficulty to children with LEARNING DISABILITIES or other DEVELOPMENTAL DISORDERS.

formula   A fluid preparation designed to simulate BREASTMILK in its balance and amount of nutrients (though it cannot give the natural IMMUNIZATION provided by mother to child). Commercially sold formulas can come in various forms:

- *ready-to-use*, the most expensive form, to which no water is added;
- *liquid concentrate*, to which some water is added; and
- *dry powder*, the cheapest form, to which water is added.

Packages of formula are required to carry expiration dates as part of their FOOD LABELS; parents should always carefully check the expiration date, and if it is past, they should throw the formula away unused. Parents who have decided to bottlefeed their baby should consult with their doctor or clinic before the birth about the form and perhaps the brand of formula recommended, generally one with added iron unless there are medical reasons otherwise.

Cow's milk, the basis of most formulas, is incomplete nutritionally, difficult for a newborn to digest, and has too-high concentrations of some FATS and MINERALS. But in formula some milk fats are replaced by vegetable oils, minerals are diluted, VITAMINS and some minerals are added, and the resulting mixture is heated to make the PROTEIN more digestible. If a child proves to have LACTOSE INTOLERANCE (inability to properly digest milk) or sensitivity to something in cow's milk, other formulas are available as substitutes, including one based on soy.

To ensure that infants get proper nutrition, the Food and Drug Administration (under the Infant Formula Act of 1980) has set standards for the nutrient composition of commercially available infant formulas. It is vitally important, however, that formula be used or prepared precisely according to directions (see FIXING FORMULA, under BOTTLEFEEDING). Too diluted a formula can lead to MALNUTRITION and serious imbalances in body chemistry, while too concentrated a formula can overtax the infant's immature system, causing other kinds of imbalances and sometimes severe KIDNEY AND UROLOGICAL DISORDERS. (For help and further information, see also HUMAN MILK VS. FORMULA AND OTHER MILKS, under MILK.)

forty-five/fifteen plan   An experimental educational schedule under which students alternate 45 days of schooling with 15 days of vacation throughout the year. (For help and further information, see EDUCATION.)

foster/adoption   A form of ADOPTION that is provisional, pending completion of formal requirements.

foster parents   Adults appointed by the court to care for a MINOR in their home temporarily, until the child can return home or reaches the legal age of adulthood; such adults often receive payments to help in supporting the child. In cases of TERMINATION OF PARENTAL RIGHTS, the child may later become available for ADOPTION; in such cases, foster parents are often able to adopt the child if they wish. LONG-TERM CARE—residential care in a homelike setting—may also be provided for minors and some adults judged to be INCOMPETENT, such as those who have severe handicaps (see HANDICAPPED), MENTAL DISORDERS, or MENTAL RETARDATION; facilities for such care are generally called GROUP HOMES. Some communities sponsor foster grandparents programs, in which retired older people (paid or as volunteers) develop a supplementary relationship with a child who has special needs, as because of disabilities or family problems at home.

For help and further information

Where Is Home: Living Through Foster Care, by E.P. Jones. New York: Four Walls, Eight Windows, 1990.

Foster Child. 1987. 43-minute film/video from National Film Board of Canada, 1251 Avenue of the Americas, New York, NY 10020. Documentary of adult director's search for his natural parents.

FP   Abbreviation for FAMILY PRACTITIONER.

FPLS   Abbreviation for Federal PARENT LOCATOR SERVICE.

fractures   Breaks in bones, as from a fall or a blow, but sometimes during normal use, as in certain disorders such as OSTEOPOROSIS. Fractures may be classified by the nature of the break. *Simple fractures*, also called *closed fractures*, are those in which the two bone pieces are not displaced and so do not break the skin or damage surrounding tissue. Breaks in which the pieces of the bone break the skin and damage surrounding tissue are called *open*, or *compound, fractures*. Some other special types of fractures include the *comminuted fracture*, when bone is shattered into more than two pieces, as in an automobile accident; a *transverse fracture*, in which the two pieces of bone are dislocated sideways by a sharp blow or from stress after excessive use; and *greenstick fracture*, common in young children, in which the bone bends and breaks only partway through (as in a young growing twig, rather than an old dry stick). Breaks resulting from overuse, as in overexercising as part of a sports program, are called *stress fractures*. X-RAYS or other SCANS are often used to give physicians a picture of the exact nature of the break.

The most serious kind of fracture is one that involves possible SPINAL CORD INJURY; people with such injuries should be treated only by trained health professionals and moved only in extreme emergency. Otherwise, the fractured bone should be immobilized as much as possible but without attempts to force the bone back into position, and medical care should be sought immediately.

If the pieces of the bone have been displaced, they must be *reduced*, or put back into their original position, so that the bone can heal properly. Often the bones can be manipulated through the skin, in a *closed reduction*, but sometimes surgery is necessary to expose the pieces for repositioning, in what is called an *open reduction*. Once replaced, the bones are immobilized so that they can heal, growing new bone, called *callus*, at the point of the break. A plaster cast may be used to immobilize the bones, but in some cases pins are temporarily inserted surgically and sometimes affixed to external metal rods, depending on the type of fracture.

In general, fractures in children mend much more quickly than in adults, and fractures in non-weight-bearing bones, such as arms or collarbones (*clavicles*), heal more quickly than do weight-bearing bones, such as legs. In some cases the fracture fails to heal properly, and surgery may be necessary. PHYSICAL THERAPISTS may provide guidance in restoring full strength and mobility to the affected part, and ORTHOPEDIC DEVICES may be needed to provide mobility while protecting the healing bone.

Multiple fractures, as revealed in a SKELETAL SURVEY, may be taken as signs of CHILD ABUSE AND NEGLECT. If a child's bones fracture more readily than seems typical, parents should have the child checked for a possible BONE DISORDER, such as OSTEOGENESIS IMPERFECTA.

For help and further information

National Institute of Arthritis and Musculoskeletal and Skin Diseases (NIAMS), 301-496-8188. (For full group information, see ARTHRITIS; MUSCULAR DYSTROPHY.)

(See also BONE DISORDERS.)

fragile X syndrome (X-linked mental retardation)   A CONGENITAL condition resulting from a CHROMOSOMAL ABNORMALITY in which a male's X SEX CHROMOSOME is malformed (termed fragile because it often breaks during chromosome analysis). Many children with fragile X syndrome are mentally retarded, as often are their mothers, CARRIERS of the defective chromosome; but many people with the syndrome have normal mental capacity. In mature males, the syndrome is characterized by large TESTICLES, protruding ears, and pronounced chin and forehead. The fragile X syndrome affects one in every 2,000 to 3,000 births; a child of a mother who carries the fragile X chromosome has a one in two chance of inheriting the disorder. Some evidence suggests that fragile X syndrome is associated with LEARNING DISABILITIES; it may also be linked with AUTISM, though some recent research indicates otherwise.

For help and further information

Fragile X Foundation
P.O. Box 30023
Denver, CO 80203
Toll-free number 800-835-2246, ext. 58
Tad Jackson, Executive Director
Organization concerned with fragile X syndrome and other forms of X-linked mental retardation. Seeks to educate public; provides information to public and professionals about diagnosis and treatment; encourages research; publishes various materials, including quarterly newsletter and brochure, *Fragile X Foundation*.

Fragile X Support
1380 Huntington Drive
Mundelein, IL 60060
312-680-3317
David Franklin, Executive Director
Organization concerned with fragile X syndrome. Aids families in enhancing lives of children with fragile X syndrome; seeks to educate public; provides information; publishes brochure, *Fragile X Syndrome*.

(See also GENETIC DISORDERS.)

frank breech   A type of FETAL PRESENTATION in which the legs are straight and bent upward so that the feet are near the shoulder.

Friedreich's ataxia   A rare GENETIC DISORDER that is a hereditary form of ATAXIA.

Frostig Developmental Test of Visual Perception   A widely used type of DIAGNOSTIC ASSESSMENT TEST, administered individually or to groups, that is used to help identify possible LEARNING DISABILITIES or neurological handicaps in children in prekindergarten through grade 3. Focusing on VISUAL SKILLS, the Frostig test covers five main areas: HAND–EYE COORDINATION, FIGURE–GROUND DISCRIMINATION, FORM CONSTANCY, SPATIAL RELATIONS, and SPATIAL ORIENTATION. Test results are compared to NORMS that are correlated with likely READING skills in first-grade classes. (For help and further information, see TESTS.)

fruitarian   A VEGETARIAN whose diet includes only plant products that fall off naturally so that the plant is not destroyed during harvesting; these include nuts, beans, peas, corn, cucumbers, tomatoes, berries, and fruits such as apples, pears, and peaches.

fucosidosis   A type of LIPID STORAGE DISEASE.

full-term   In relation to birth, a child who is born at the completion of GESTATION and so has had the normal amount of time to develop in the UTERUS, as opposed to a PREMATURE child, who is born without having the full nine months (medically, 40 weeks) to develop.

functional curriculum   A type of CURRICULUM that focuses on teaching SELF-HELP SKILLS for everyday life, aiming to increase the independence of students with severe handicaps (see HAND-ICAPPED); also called an *adapted* or *differential curriculum*.

functional skills   Skills necessary to everyday life, a term especially used in SPECIAL EDUCATION to identify skills that a child with handicaps (see HANDICAPPED) must learn or forever be dependent on others to perform, such as brushing teeth or writing a check; sometimes called *survival skills*. A school program that focuses on such skills may be called a functional CURRICULUM. In EDUCATION in general, functional skills are those that can be immediately applied in daily life, such as typing or auto mechanics. Functional reading skills means reading ability sufficient for the purposes of daily life—reading signs, train schedules, application forms, and the like. People (including nonhandicapped adults) who are unable to read such materials are called functionally illiterate (see ILLITERACY).

fused curriculum   A type of CURRICULUM in which some courses are taught jointly, such as literature and history.

GAL   Abbreviation for *guardian ad litem*. (See GUARDIAN.)

galactosemia   A rare GENETIC DISORDER of the AUTOSOMAL RECESSIVE type, a kind of METABOLIC DISORDER that results from the lack of a key liver enzyme (*galactose-1-phosphate uridyl transferase*), making the body unable to break down galactose, part of the milk sugar LACTOSE. If not quickly recognized and treated, galactosemia soon causes FAILURE TO THRIVE and a variety of specific consequences, including CIRRHOSIS OF THE LIVER, JAUNDICE, CATARACTS, and MENTAL RETARDATION. Various MEDICAL TESTS for galactosemia can be performed, from the child's first week of life, using blood and urine specimens. Treatment simply involves lifelong avoidance of normal MILK, substituting lactose-free milk when available. If the condition is diagnosed late, however, some damage may be irreversible.

For help and information

American Liver Foundation (ALF), 201-857-2626; toll-free number, U.S. except NJ, 800-223-0179. Sponsors network for parents of children with liver diseases; publishes information sheet *Galactosemia* (For full group information, see LIVER PROBLEMS.)

Children's Liver Foundation, 201-761-1111. (For full group information, see LIVER PROBLEMS.)

Parents of Galactosemic Children
20981 Solano Way
Boca Raton, FL 33433
407-852-0266
Linda Manis, Contact

Mutual-support group for families of children with galactosemia. Publishes newsletter and videotape of conferences.

National Institute of Diabetes and Digestive and Kidney Diseases (NIDDK), 301-496-3583. (For full group information, see DIGESTIVE DISORDERS.)

National Institute of Child Health and Human Development (NICHD), 301-496-5133. (For full group information, see PREGNANCY.)

National Institute of Neurological Disorders and Stroke (NINDS), 301-496-5751. (For full group information, see BRAIN AND BRAIN DISORDERS.)

(See also METABOLIC DISORDERS; LIVER PROBLEMS; DIGESTIVE DISORDERS; LACTOSE INTOLERANCE.)

gambling, pathological   A kind of IMPULSE CONTROL DISORDER.

gamete intrafallopian tube transfer (GIFT)   A treatment for INFERTILITY that involves removing eggs (see OVUM) from a woman's OVARIES and inserting eggs and a man's SPERM in her FALLOPIAN TUBE, allowing FERTILIZATION to take place in the normal environment, though with some scientific assistance. The procedure for maturing and removing eggs is similar to that in IN VITRO FERTILIZATION, but the eggs are immediately mixed with the ready sperm and (while the woman is still on the operating table) inserted into the fallopian tubes by a CATHETER. If all goes well, fertilization takes place, and the fertilized egg moves down the fallopian tube into the UTERUS, where the crucial IMPLANTATION takes place. It is vital to see that this has occurred, for if a fertilized egg implants itself in the fallopian tubes (or anywhere other than the uterus), the result is a life-threatening ECTOPIC PREGNANCY, which will require emergency surgery to remove. GIFT is still a fairly new technique, so its long-term success rate is not yet known. (For help and further information, see INFERTILITY; PREGNANCY.)

gargoylism   A combination of defects often found in (and an outdated term for) HURLER'S SYNDROME but found in some other GENETIC DISORDERS as well. Among the characteristics of gargoylism are DWARFISM; MENTAL RETARDATION; large head with protruding tongue and prominent brows; thick arms, legs, hands, and ribs, along with various other skeletal deformities; enlarged liver and spleen; and some eye defects, such as clouded cornea (see EYE AND VISION PROBLEMS).

gastroenteritis   Inflammation of the stomach and intestines, often because of infection. (For help and further information, see DIGESTIVE DISORDERS.)

gastroenterologist   A medical PHYSICIAN who specializes in treating disorders of the digestive system, especially the stomach and intestines.

gastroscope   A type of lighted ENDOSCOPE, swallowed by the patient and used by doctors in visually examining the stomach. (For help and further information, see DIGESTIVE DISORDERS.)

Gates-MacGinitie Reading Test (GMRT)   A group-administered TEST of READING skills for children in grades 1 to 12, a paper-and-pencil test focusing on reading comprehension and vocabulary development, and sometimes also on letter recognition and letter sounds, at various grade levels. The GMRT is often used as a DIAGNOSTIC ASSESSMENT TEST to identify students who need REMEDIAL INSTRUCTION or, conversely, ACCELERATED PROGRAMS, as well as to evaluate school instructional programs. (For help and further information, see TESTS.)

Gates-McKillop-Horowitz Reading Diagnostic Tests   An individually administered TEST of READING skills for children in grades 1 to 6, evaluating oral reading, recognition of isolated words, knowledge of word parts, recognition and ability to blend common word parts, reading words, giving letter sounds, naming letters, writing, and AUDITORY SKILLS such as identifying vowel sounds, auditory blending, and discrimination. The test is generally given for class placement purposes, and not all parts will be used with all students. (For help and further information, see TESTS.)

Gaucher's disease (glucosyl cerebroside lipidosis)   The most common of the LIPID STORAGE DISEASES.

GBM   Abbreviation for GLIOBLASTOMA.

GDM   Abbreviation for *gestational diabetes mellitus,* a generally temporary form of DIABETES MELLITUS that first appears in a woman during PREGNANCY.

gender-identity disorders   The psychiatric term for MENTAL DISORDERS in which a person's inner sense of gender is different from the gender assigned by the outside world. Psychiatrists note that such disorders are rare and are not to be confused with nonconformity to sex roles, normally labeled as "tomboyish" or "sissyish"; with a feeling of inadequacy in meeting social expectations of one's gender role; or with the desire to have the social advantages accorded to the opposite sex. Instead, people with gender-identity disorders feel that they *are* a sex other than that perceived by the rest of the world and have intense distress about their gender "assignment." Such feelings generally appear in childhood and are often accompanied by a mild to total repudiation of not just clothing and activities but their sexual anatomy, with young children often asserting that they will grow up to be of the "opposite"—to them the true—sex. Children with gender-identity disorders can have significant social problems, often leading to or associated with DEPRESSION, SEPARATION ANXIETY, or general withdrawal. After PUBERTY, many develop a homosexual orientation, sometimes cross-dressing and in some cases having surgery to change their sex.

For help and further information

National Institute of Mental Health, 301-443-4536 (public affairs); 301-443-4513 (publications). (For full group information, see MENTAL DISORDERS.)

(See also HOMOSEXUALITY; MENTAL DISORDERS.)

genealogy   Alternate term for PEDIGREE.

general curriculum   A type of CURRICULUM that is less rigorous than an academic curriculum aimed at college-bound students.

General Equivalency Diploma (GED)   A certificate of high school equivalency given to a school DROPOUT who later took and passed a series of TESTS OF GENERAL EDUCATIONAL DEVELOPMENT. (For help and further information, see EDUCATION.)

generalized (G$_{M2}$) gangliosidosis   Alternate name for *Tay-Sachs disease,* a type of LIPID STORAGE DISEASE.

generally recognized as safe substances (GRAS)   Types of FOOD ADDITIVES such as sugar, salt, herbs, and spices that are considered safe and not subject to testing by the Food and Drug Administration.

general practitioner (GP)   A type of PHYSICIAN who provides medical care to people of any age and either sex, today more commonly called *family physician.* A general practitioner treats a wide variety of health problems, sometimes (especially in rural areas) including health needs of children and women during PREGNANCY, though someone having special problems will be referred to a specialist such as an OBSTETRICIAN-GYNECOLOGIST.

gene therapy   A new, still largely experimental approach to treating GENETIC DISORDERS, which involves inserting into the body (by various means) cells containing healthy genes to replace the defective ones, and perhaps in the future also actually manipulating the body's genes to correct defects. It is still in its infancy but holds great promise for potentially all genetic disorders. Already, as of this writing, gene therapy seems likely to yield positive results for several disorders, such as CYSTIC FIBROSIS (which show promising test-tube results), MUSCULAR DYSTROPHY (for which the earliest human experiment was promising), and *severe combined immunodeficiency* (a disorder in which the therapy was first tried in humans, with early indications of success; see IMMUNE SYSTEM). As experience accretes, new approaches and applications for gene therapy seem to be introduced almost every day. Concerned families will want to keep in touch with breaking events, not only through newspapers and government health information lines, but also by joining one or more of the organizations relating to the particular genetic disorder affecting them.

genetic counseling A guidance service, often offered by a physician with special training in medical genetics, that helps prospective parents assess their risk of having a child with a GENETIC DISORDER or the likelihood that a disorder that might affect one child will appear in other, later children. Counselors explain the pattern of GENETIC INHERITANCE that leads to such disorders and give parents the background information necessary for deciding whether or not to try to have a child.

People with a family or ethnic history of genetic abnormalities, couples who are near BLOOD RELATIONS, and older couples are all prime candidates for genetic counseling, since they all have a higher-than-normal risk of bearing a child with a genetic disorder. So are couples who have had a previous MISCARRIAGE or infant DEATH, those who have a previous child with a genetic disorder, and those whose work exposes them to ENVIRONMENTAL HAZARDS that might put a PREGNANCY at risk.

Generally, genetic counseling starts with the preparation of a PEDIGREE, a medical family tree that shows the inheritance patterns of traits and disorders in both families. If a couple had a previous child born with genetic problems, counselors might arrange for analysis of the chromosomes of the parents and child, trying to identify abnormalities that might affect a future birth. Here they would draw on the information gradually being built up by scientific researchers as to the location and makeup of the tens of thousands of genes in the human body. They would also explore environmental influences that might have contributed to the abnormality, such as exposure to RADIATION, drugs, malnutrition, or injury.

Genetic counselors also advise on the various methods of GENETIC SCREENING by which a FETUS can be tested to see if it has inherited some major genetic disorders. If so, the counselors can explain the outlook for a child with that abnormality and what special treatment might be necessary so that the couple can decide whether to prepare for a SPECIAL CHILD or have a selective ABORTION. In some cases counselors might also explore with the couple other alternatives, such as ADOPTION, ARTIFICIAL INSEMINATION using a donor's sperm, or even surrogate motherhood (see SURROGATE PARENTING).

For help and further information

National Society of Genetic Counselors (NSGC)
Division of Medical Genetics
Michael Reese Hospital and Medical Center
31st Street and Lakeshore Drive
Chicago, IL 60616
312-791-4436
Beth A. Fine, President
Organization of trained genetic counselors and other interested health professionals. Provides training; seeks to educate public; publishes various materials, including quarterly *Perspectives in Genetic Counseling* and biennial *NSGC Membership Directory*.

National Genetics Federation (NGF)
555 West 57th Street
New York, NY 10019
212-586-5800
Ruth Y. Bernini, Executive Director
Organization dedicated to the advancement of medical genetics. Sponsors genetic counseling network and clearinghouse; provides information and referrals, including computerized analyses; publishes various materials, including brochures *How Genetic Disease Can Affect You and Your Family* and *Can Genetic Counseling Help You?*.

Other reference sources

Backdoor to Eugenics, by Troy Duster. New York: Routledge, 1990.

Before Birth: Prenatal Testing for Genetic Disease, by Elena O. Nightingale and Melissa Goodman. Cambridge, MA: Harvard University Press, 1990.

The Ethics of Genetic Control: Ending Reproductive Roulette, by Joseph Fletcher. Buffalo, NY: Prometheus, 1988. Addresses questions about nontraditional baby-making.

The Tentative Pregnancy: Prenatal Diagnosis and the Future of Motherhood, by Barbara Katz Rothman. New York: Viking, 1986.

Playing God in the Nursery, by Jeff Lyon. New York: Norton, 1985.

(See also GENETIC DISORDERS; GENETIC SCREENING; CHROMOSOMAL ABNORMALITIES.)

genetic disorder An abnormal trait or disease that results from mistakes in an individual's "genetic blueprint," such as a problem in the DNA coding of the genes or errors in duplication of the chromosomes. The defective gene may have been received from one or both parents, as part of the individual's GENETIC INHERITANCE, or it may stem from a MUTATION in the genetic material in the SPERM or egg (OVUM) that joined at CONCEPTION to form the new individual.

Disorders that result from just a single gene or gene pair are known as *unifactorial disorders*. If the problem is on the pair of SEX CHROMOSOMES, that almost always means that it is on the X chromosome. Such disorders are called X-LINKED, sex-linked, or sex-limited, because they usually affect only male children, being passed on by mothers who are CARRIERS. Among such X-linked diseases are HEMOPHILIA, color blindness (see EYE AND VISIONS PROBLEMS), MUSCULAR DYSTROPHY (Duchenne type), G6PD DEFICIENCY, FRAGILE X SYNDROME, and spinal ATAXIA. Single-gene disorders that appear on any of the other 22 pairs of chromosomes (AUTOSOMES) are called AUTOSOMAL DISORDERS.

Some single-gene disorders are DOMINANT, meaning that they need only be passed on by one parent to affect the child. Among these AUTOSOMAL DOMINANT disorders are HUNTINGTON'S CHOREA, MARFAN'S SYNDROME, NEUROFIBROMATOSIS, ACHONDROPLASIA,

OSTEOGENESIS IMPERFECTA, and POLYCYSTIC KIDNEY DISEASE. A parent who carries the gene for an autosomal dominant disorder has a 50-percent chance of passing it on to a child.

Other single-gene disorders are RECESSIVE, meaning that a child must receive the defective gene from both parents to get the disorder. Among these AUTOSOMAL RECESSIVE disorders are CYSTIC FIBROSIS, PHENYLKETONURIA, sickle-cell ANEMIA, some LIPID STORAGE DISEASES such as Gaucher's disease and Tay-Sachs disease, GALACTOSEMIA, FRIEDREICH'S ATAXIA, and HURLER'S SYNDROME. If both parents carry the gene for an autosomal recessive disorder, they have a 25-percent chance of having an affected child, with a 50-percent chance that their child will be a carrier of the recessive gene.

A great many genetic disorders, however, are not caused by a single gene but by a mixture of various genes affected by environmental influences. Among these *multifactorial disorders* are CLEFT LIP AND PALATE, CLUBFOOT, *neural tube defects* such as SPINA BIFIDA, EPILEPSY, DIABETES MELLITUS, ARTHRITIS, and CONGENITAL DISLOCATION OF THE HIP. Sorting out the relative importance of genetic and environmental factors in such diseases is extremely difficult, but genetic researchers are making ever more accurate estimates of the heritability of these diseases—that is, the likelihood that they will appear in the next generation, apart from environmental effects. Such information is of great value in GENETIC COUNSELING. Serious genetic disorders can also result from CHROMOSOMAL ABNORMALITIES.

In the past, most treatments have (of necessity) focused on the symptoms of genetic disorders, but experimental GENE THERAPY now holds the hope of correcting or replacing the defective genes themselves.

For help and further information

National Center for Education in Child and Maternal Health (NCEMCH), 202-625-8400, and **National Maternal and Child Health Clearinghouse**, 202-625-8410. Provide information to public and professionals about specific genetic diseases and general child and maternal health; help parents locate groups of other parents with children having specific or related diseases; publish various materials, including *Genetic Screening for Inborn Errors of Metabolism, A Guide to Selected National Genetic Voluntary Organizations, Genetic Family History: An Aid to Better Health in Adoptive Children,* and *Learning Together: A Guide for Families with Genetic Disorders.* (For full group information, see PREGNANCY.)

National Genetics Federation, 212-586-5800. Publishes *How Genetic Disease Can Affect You and Your Family.* (For full group information, see GENETIC COUNSELING.)

March of Dimes Birth Defects Foundation (MDBDF)
1275 Mamaroneck Avenue
White Plains, NY 10605

914-428-7100 (local chapters in telephone-directory white pages)
Charles Massey, President

Organization concerned about preventing, repairing, or treating birth defects. Provides information and referrals, as for genetic counseling; has many local chapters, some of which have available certified midwives for normal pregnancies and for prenatal services for women with high-risk pregnancies; publishes numerous print and audiovisual materials, including booklets such as *International Directory of Genetic Services, Genetic Counseling, Birth Defects: Tragedy and Hope, Your Special Child, Drugs, Alcohol and Tobacco Abuse During Pregnancy, Will My Drinking Hurt My Baby?, Babies Don't Thrive in Smoke-Filled Wombs, Family Health Tree,* and *Family Medical Record,* and various materials (in English and Spanish) for teenagers about pregnancy, as well as information sheets on specific topics, including *Accutane, Achondroplasia, Alpha-Fetoprotein Screening, Chicken Pox During Pregnancy, Cleft Lip and Palate, Clubfoot, Cocaine Use During Pregnancy, Congenital AIDS, Congenital Heart Defects, Down Syndrome, Fetal Alcohol Syndrome, Fitness for Two, Genital Herpes, Infections During Pregnancy: Toxoplasmosis and Chlamydia, Low Birthweight, Marfan Syndrome, Neurofibromatosis, Newborn Screening Tests, PKU, Polio, Post Polio Muscle Atrophy, Pregnancy Over 35, Rh Disease, Rubella, Sickle-Cell Anemia, Spina Bifida, Stress and Pregnancy, Tay-Sachs Disease, Teen-Age Pregnancy, Thalassemia,* and *VDT Facts.*

National Organization for Rare Disorders (NORD)
P.O. Box 8923
New Fairfield, CT 06812
203-746-6518
Abbey S. Meyers, Executive Director

Organization of health professionals and other individuals and organizations interested in rare disorders. Gathers and disseminates information; makes referrals to organizations regarding specific disorders; monitors availability of medicines for rare disorders under the Orphan Drug Act; publishes quarterly *Orphan Disease Update* and occasional legislative newsletter *NORD On-Line.*

National Foundation for Jewish Genetic Diseases (NFJGD)
250 Park Avenue, Suite 1000
New York, NY 10017
212-682-5550
Joan Samsen, Executive Director

Organization of and for people concerned with genetic diseases that particularly affect Jews. Seeks to educate public; provides information; publishes fact sheet *You Have a Right to Know . . . About Jewish Genetic Diseases.*

Hereditary Disease Foundation (HDF), 213-458-4183. (For full group information, see HUNTINGTON'S CHOREA.)

Other reference sources

The Encyclopedia of Genetic Disorders and Birth Defects, by Mark D. Ludman, M.D., and James Wyndbrandt. New York: Facts on File, 1990.

The Family Genetic Sourcebook, by Benjamin A. Pierce. New York: Wiley, 1990.

Genetic Engineering: Opposing Viewpoints, William Dudley, ed. San Diego, CA: Greenhaven, 1990.

Genome, by Jerry E. Bishiop and Michael Waldholz. New York: Simon & Schuster, 1990.

Genetics: The Clash Between the New Genetics and Human Values, by David Suzuki and Peter Knudtson. Cambridge, MA: Harvard University Press, 1989.

Family Diseases: Are You At Risk, by Myra Vanderpool Gormley. Baltimore: Genealogical Publishing, 1989.

New Hope for Problem Pregnancies: Helping Babies Before They're Born, by Dianne Hales and Robert K. Creasy, M.D. New York: Harper & Row, 1982.

Mapping Our Genes: The Genome Project and the Future of Medicine, by Lois Wingerson. New York: Dutton, 1989.

Genes, Medicine, and You, by Alvin Silverstein and Virginia Silverstein. Hillside, NJ: Enslow, 1989. For young adult readers.

Health Care U.S.A., by Jean Carper. New York: Prentice Hall, 1987. Resource for general and specific health-care information; lists major genetic counseling and testing centers and other information.

The Genetic Connection, by David Henden and Joan Marks. New York: Morrow, 1978.

Know Your Genes, by Aubrey Milunsky. Boston: Houghton Mifflin, 1977.

(See also GENETIC COUNSELING; CHROMOSOMAL ABNORMALITIES; BIRTH DEFECTS; PREGNANCY; PEDIGREE; specific diseases.)

genetic inheritance   The pattern by which information is passed from parents to child, creating a unique individual. The basic units of inheritance are genes, molecules of DNA in a cell's nucleus that are organized in linear sequence on 23 threadlike pairs of structures called chromosomes. One pair, the SEX CHROMOSOMES, determines the new being's gender. A normal female has two X chromosomes; a normal male has an X and a Y. The other 22 chromosome pairs, called AUTOSOMES, carry the majority of the being's genetic inheritance.

The complete set of genes, or *genome,* for an individual is set at the point of CONCEPTION, when the father's SPERM and the mother's egg (OVUM) each contribute half of the paired genetic material for the new being. As each parent forms sperm and eggs, the chromosomes in the nucleus are first duplicated, then divided, creating four "daughter cells." This cell-dividing process, called *meiosis,* results in each daughter cell having half of the chromosomes needed by a new being and each having a different selection of the genetic material. These differing selections are then incorporated into each parent's sperm and eggs.

Later, when a sperm and egg join, the half-selection of chromosomes from each parent join to make a unique new being. The fertilized egg then created receives 50 percent of its genes from its mother and 50 percent from its father; and because the parents' genetic inheritance was formed in the same way, 25 percent of the egg's genes come from each of its four grandparents.

The pattern of genes in that fertilized egg will be duplicated over and over, being part of the nucleus of every cell in the new being. Given the tens of thousands of genes involved, it is not surprising that errors sometimes occur that are passed on to the new being. Errors in the cell-division process of meiosis give rise to CHROMOSOMAL ABNORMALITIES; inherited mistakes in the coding of the genes themselves lead to GENETIC DISORDERS; some abnormalities arise from a spontaneous change in the genes of sperm or egg, called a *mutation.*

Most genetic information, however, is passed on normally. How the new pattern of genes will be expressed in the new being depends on the nature of each gene and its relation to other genes. Genes operate in pairs, the paired genes for each site being called *alleles.* If a pair is identical, the person is called a *homozygote* for that gene; if the paired genes differ, the person is a *heterozygote.* If one gene is DOMINANT, it will affect the individual no matter what the other gene is. If either of the paired genes for eye color is brown, for example, the baby will have brown eyes, since brown eyes are dominant. If a gene is RECESSIVE, it will affect the individual only if its paired gene is identical. For a baby to have blue eyes, a recessive trait, both parents must give it a gene for blue eyes.

The exception to that is the genes that appear on the sex chromosomes. The Y chromosome is small and carries little genetic information apart from male sexual development; but the X chromosome carries a full complement of genetic information. So if a recessive gene is on a male's X chromosome, it will affect him, because no paired dominant gene is present; the same gene on a female's X chromosome would not affect her if the paired gene were dominant, only if both were recessive. That partly explains why many men, but few women, are partially bald; the gene relating to baldness is recessive and resides on the X chromosome. Traits and disorders that affect mostly males because they appear on the X chromosome are often called X-LINKED, sex-linked, or sex-limited. Traits and disorders that are controlled by a single gene are called *unifactorial;* those that are affected by many genes, as well as by the individual's environment, are called *multifactorial.*

Each gene occupies a specific site on a particular chromosome, and considerable scientific research is focused on mapping the position of genes, especially noting the site of malfunctioning genes that cause common genetic disorders. Such sites, or *genetic markers,* can then be used to identify CARRIERS, people who, though healthy themselves, carry defective genes and could pass them on to their children. Researchers are exploring ways to correct such defects, using the techniques of genetic engineering. Physicians use genetic markers in GENETIC SCREENING, attempting to identify whether or not a FETUS has inherited a defective gene. All this new information has given rise, in recent decades, to GENETIC COUNSELING, a service that attempts to advise prospective parents on genetic risks.

Other reference sources

Nature's Thumbprint: The New Genetics of Personality, by Peter B. Neubauer, M.D., and Alexander Neubauer. Reading, MA: Addison-Wesley, 1990. About impact of heredity on personality.

Grandfather's Nose: Why We Look Alike or Different, by Dorothy Hinshaw. New York: Watts, 1989. For young readers.

(See also GENETIC DISORDERS; AUTOSOMAL DOMINANT; AUTOSOMAL RECESSIVE; X-LINKED; MULTIFACTORIAL DISORDER.)

genetic screening   A range of PRENATAL MEDICAL TESTS aimed at identifying possible BIRTH DEFECTS. Some, such as AMNIOCENTESIS, CHORIONIC VILLUS SAMPLING, CORDOCENTESUS, or ALPHA FETOPROTEIN testing, involve taking samples of material shed by the FETUS and analyzing the genetic content for clues as to possible abnormalities. Others, such as FETOSCOPY or ULTRASOUND scanning, look directly or indirectly at the fetus for visual signs of defects. If abnormalities are identified, parents may choose to terminate the pregnancy with an ABORTION, attempt correction of the defect through IN UTERO SURGERY, or prepare for a SPECIAL CHILD. Differing medical conditions and family histories call for the use of different tests, each with its own strengths and weaknesses, but no test, nor all the known tests combined, can identify all possible birth defects.

For help and further information

National Center for Education in Child and Maternal Health (NCEMCH), 202-625-8400 or 625-8410.

National Institute of Child Health and Human Development (NICHD), 301-496-5133. (For full group information, see PREGNANCY.)

Genetics Society of America (GSA)
American Society of Human Genetics (ASHG)
9650 Rockville Pike
Bethesda, MD 20814
301-571-1825
Gerry Gurvitch, Executive Director
Organization of professionals and other individuals and organizations interested in genetics.

Committee for Responsible Genetics (CRG)
186-A South Street
Boston, MA 02111
617-423-0650
Nachama Wilker, Executive Director
Organization of people interested in social implications of biotechnology and new reproductive technology.

(See also GENETIC COUNSELING; GENETIC DISORDERS; MEDICAL TESTS.)

genital warts   Groups of growths in the genital area caused by infection with one or more of the HUMAN PAPILLOMAVIRUSES (HPVs); a kind of SEXUALLY TRANSMITTED DISEASE that needs to be dealt with quickly because its presence can increase the risk of some kinds of CANCERS, especially in the CERVIX but also sometimes in the PENIS. Genital warts (also called *condylomata acuminata* or *venereal warts*) also often grow during PREGNANCY, making urination and, later, DELIVERY difficult. In addition, a child can be infected during the CHILDBIRTH process, developing warts in the throat (*laryngeal papillomatosis*), a possibly life-threatening condition sometimes requiring corrective surgery.

Within three weeks to three months of contact with an infected person, small, hard, visible spots develop in many infected people; however, the National Institute of Allergy and Infectious Diseases found in one study that almost half of the infected women had no symptoms. Genital warts are generally diagnosed by visual examination, sometimes including a *colposcopy* by means of a lighted magnifying instrument; sometimes a BIOPSY of cervical tissue may be taken and analyzed, along with other laboratory tests.

Once diagnosed, genital warts are treated with a chemical solution (except during pregnancy, since the medication can cause BIRTH DEFECTS) or sometimes removed by freezing, burning, and, if necessary, surgery, including LASER SURGERY. Other promising drugs, including interferon, are being tried experimentally. (For help and further information, including how to avoid infection, see SEXUALLY TRANSMITTED DISEASES.)

genitals   General name for the reproductive organs, especially the external sex organs. In the male these include the PENIS and the pouch called a SCROTUM containing two TESTES. In the female these are generally called the VULVA or *pudendum* and include the *clitoris*, a small bit of tissue responsive to sexual stimulation, and the opening of the VAGINA, partly blocked by tissue called the HYMEN and enclosed by two sets of "lips," the *labia majora* and the *labia minora*. The labia are sometimes joined in newborns, but generally separate without outside intervention. The condition of having underdeveloped genitals is called HYPOGENITALISM.

genius   A person of extremely high intellectual ability, who has made or is considered likely to make a significant contribution in one or more fields; often considered to be someone with an IQ of 140 or over, despite the lack of reliability of INTELLIGENCE TESTS. A child whose IQ is in the "genius" range is usually considered a GIFTED CHILD.

genu valgum   An abnormality in which the legs bend inward, with the knees close together; medical parlance for "knock-knees." (See WALKING.)

genu varum   An abnormality in which the legs bend outward at the knees; medical parlance for "bowlegs." (See WALKING.)

germ cells   General name for the special cells that give rise to an egg (OVUM) in females and SPERM in males.

Gesell Preschool Test   A widely used, individually administered DEVELOPMENTAL SCREENING TEST for assessing the emotional, physical, and behavioral development of children 2½ to 6 years old. The test includes various tasks (subtests), among them:

- building increasingly more complex structures with cubes (sometimes following a demonstration), testing fine MOTOR SKILLS, HAND–EYE COORDINATION, ATTENTION SPAN, and other skills;
- an interview that tests accuracy of personal and family knowledge as well as LANGUAGE SKILLS;
- a pencil-and-paper test, in which a child is to write his or her name, testing DOMINANCE, NEUROMUSCULAR DEVELOPMENT, fine motor skills, and TASK-APPROPRIATE behavior, followed by tasks involving copying various geometric designs, writing numbers, and completing a picture of a partially drawn person;
- naming animals and talking about their favorite activities, indicating level of attention and interests;
- discriminating among prepositions, such as *on* and *in*, testing both language skills and understanding of SPATIAL RELATIONS; and
- repeating numbers, testing various memory and attention skills.

Other tasks include a picture vocabulary test, a "color forms" test to assess recognition of shapes, a formboard test, and other motor tests.

For children 4½ to 9 who are being considered for entry into kindergarten through third grades, several other tests are added, the result being called the *Gesell School Readiness Test—Complete Battery*. Additional tasks include copying more complex forms, a labeling and naming exercise focusing on right or left orientation, and two visual tests, one involving matching cards and the other drawing designs from memory after being shown cards.

In the course of the test, the specially trained examiners make various notes about the child's behavior, including behavior not directly related to the task (called OVERFLOW BEHAVIOR). They then compare these with a variety of *developmental schedules* that outline what is considered the age level for behavior in each of the areas listed, based on NORMS observed in children's behavior. These are summarized to give an overall DEVELOPMENTAL AGE (DA).

Many questions have been raised about the RELIABILITY and predictive VALIDITY of the Gesell tests. Children develop in highly individual and variable ways, and many children assigned low DAs turn out to have visual or other undiagnosed perceptual problems (as in much childhood testing). In addition, as Samuel Meisels commented in his *Developmental Screening in Early Childhood*, published under the auspices of the National Association for the Education of Young Children: "Classification data concerning predictive validity of these tests [including Gesell] is inadequate. As a result, they . . . cannot be recommended for use in a developmental screening program." Many others disagree, and in fact the Gesell materials are widely used. But parents whose child runs into difficulty in school placement because of a too-low DA should certainly explore, protest, retest, and do whatever is appropriate to right a situation if it seems wrong to them.

For help and further information

Developmental Screening in Early Childhood: A Guide, third edition, by Samuel J. Meisels. Washington, DC: National Association for the Education of Young Children, 1989.

Is Your Child Ready for School? A Parent's Guide to Preschool and Primary School Entrance Tests, by Jacqueline Robinson. New York: Arco, 1990. (Originally published as *The Baby Boards*, 1988.) Gives a full description of the Gesell tests and advice on how to "prepare" a child for one.

(See also TESTS; INTELLIGENCE TESTS.)

Gesell School Readiness Test—Complete Battery Fuller form of the GESELL PRESCHOOL TEST, used for somewhat older children.

gestation The period during which a FETUS is developing in the UTERUS, from CONCEPTION to CHILDBIRTH. If a baby is PREMATURE, its stage of development is indicated by its GESTATIONAL AGE, the number of weeks from the beginning of the mother's last MENSTRUATION. The average length of gestation is 266 days (38 weeks) from the date of FERTILIZATION. But since the date of fertilization may be unknown or uncertain, doctors traditionally calculate the DUE DATE as being 280 days (40 weeks) from the beginning of the mother's last menstruation.

gestational age The age of a FETUS still in the UTERUS or of a PREMATURE newborn, indicating the number of weeks of development, usually measured by physicians as the number of weeks from the beginning date of the mother's last MENSTRUATION. Gestational age is important because premature infants are less fully developed; and the younger they are, the more vulnerable they are to certain kinds of disorders. SLEEP APNEA, for example, occurs in about 35 to 50 percent of premature infants, but it occurs among nearly 90 percent of those who are less than 29 weeks in gestational age (as opposed to the normal 40 weeks).

gestational diabetes mellitus (GDM) A generally temporary form of DIABETES MELLITUS that appears in a woman during PREGNANCY.

GIFT Abbreviation for GAMETE INTRAFALLOPIAN TUBE TRANSFER.

Gifted and Talented Children's Act of 1978 (Public Law 95-561) A federal law intended to provide for the special educational needs of unusually talented and gifted children (see GIFTED CHILD), unevenly implemented because of widely differing definitions of "gifted."

gifted child A child who has very superior abilities, especially in academic areas, but also sometimes in artistic or athletic fields. It is widely agreed that such children have SPECIAL NEEDS and benefit most from ADAPTED EDUCATION programs. However, the definition of "gifted" varies widely. The classic early description (see book by Barbe and Renzulli, on page 224) focused on a gifted child's special combination of high COGNITIVE DEVELOPMENT, intellectual superiority, creativity, and motivation, such that they are set off from their peers and have the potential of making significant contributions to society. The GIFTED AND TALENTED CHILDREN'S ACT OF 1978 had a wider and more controversial definition of gifted and talented youngsters as:

> . . . children and, whenever applicable, youth, who are identified at the preschool, elementary, or secondary level as possessing demonstrated or potential abilities that give evidence of high performance capabilities in areas such as intellectual, creative, specific academic, or leadership ability, or in the performing and visual arts, and who by reason thereof, require services or activities not ordinarily provided by the school.

Though differing definitions and inadequate funding have meant that federal programs have not been made widely available, still parents who believe that their child truly is gifted in one or more areas may well want to contact local school officials to get help in planning the child's PRESCHOOL program. They may also want to contact one of the organizations below or the child-study unit of some nearby university.

Children develop at widely differing rates, however, and parents should beware of putting pressure on a child they proudly think is "gifted"; conversely, parents should not fear that their child is too precocious or "learning too fast." Both pushing a child and holding a child back can be harmful, and parents would be wise to let a child's talents develop naturally, providing all of the stimulation and experiences that a child seems ready and eager for, without being overwhelming.

For help and further information

Gifted Child Society (GCS)
190 Rock Road
Glen Rock, NJ 07452
201-444-6530
Gina Ginsberg Riggs, Executive Director

Organization of gifted children, their parents, and educators working with them. Acts as advocate for special needs of gifted children; sponsors Saturday Workshop Program for enrichment classes, special preschool programs, and Whiz Kids programs for multiethnic gifted children; provides clinical support services, as for testing, counseling, and special treatment for gifted children, including learning-disabled; encourages formation of parent discussion groups; publishes various materials, including semiannual newsletter, semiannual catalog of Saturday Workshop Activities, periodic directory, and advocacy packets *How to Help Your Gifted Child* and *Private Sector: New Answers to Old Budget Questions*.

National Association for Gifted Children (NAGC)
4175 Lovell Road, Suite 140
Circle Pines, MN 55014
612-784-3475
Joyce Juntune, Executive Director

Organization of parents and educators concerned with gifted children. Provides information to parents and professionals; counsels on development of curriculum and special programming; publishes various materials, including *Gifted Child Quarterly*.

The Association for the Gifted (TAG)
c/o James Delisle
401 White Hall
Kent State University
Kent, OH 44242
216-672-2477

Organization of educators and parents interested in gifted children; division of the Council for Exceptional Children. Develops educational programs; publishes various materials, including *Update* and quarterly *Journal for the Education of the Gifted*.

American Association for Gifted Children (AAGC)
P.O. Box 2745
140 East Monument Avenue
Dayton, OH 45401
513-461-1687
James T. Webb, President

Organization to aid gifted children in developing their talents, especially for social good. Seeks to educate public; offers scholarships; publishes various materials for family members and other working with gifted children.

National Business Consortium for the Gifted and Talented (NBCGT)
1751 N Street, NW, Suite 402
Washington, DC 20036
202-293-6894
Jacqueline A. Meers, Executive Director

Organization of business leaders seeking to expand educational opportunities of school-age gifted and talented children. Seeks to increase involvement of government agencies, schools, businesses and community; publishes bimonthly newsletter.

National/State Leadership Training Institute on Gifted and Talented
One Wilshire Boulevard
624 South Grand Avenue, Suite 1007
Los Angeles, CA 90017
213-489-7470
Irving S. Sato, Director

Organization of school- and college-level educators, government agencies, legislators, and parents, seeking to coordinate planning for and information about gifted and talented children. Provides information about special resources; runs Project GREAT (Gifted Resources Education Action Team) to aid agencies and educators in planning programs; publishes various materials, including quarterly bulletin and books.

World Council for Gifted and Talented Children (WCGTC)
HMS Room 414
University of South Florida
Tampa, FL 33620

813-974-3638
Dorothy Sisk, Executive Secretary
Organization of educators, schools, and parents of gifted children. Encourages international exchange of information; seeks to educate public about special needs; publishes various materials, including newsletter *World Gifted*.

National Association for Creative Children and Adults (NACCA)
8080 Springvalley Drive
Cincinnati, OH 45236
513-631-1777
Ann F. Isaacs, Executive Director
Organization seeking to encourage creativity among gifted children and adults. Sponsors research; encourages artistic development; acts as clearinghouse on creativity research and endeavors; publishes various materials, including quarterly *Creative Child and Adult*.

Other reference sources

Child Prodigies and Exceptional Early Achievement, by John Radford. New York: Free Press/Macmillan, 1990.
Your Gifted Child: How to Recognize and Develop the Special Talents in Your Child from Birth to Age Seven, by Joan Franklin Smutny, Kathleen Veenker, and Stephen Veenker. New York: Facts on File, 1989.
Developing Talent in Young People, Benjamin S. Bloom, ed. New York: Ballantine, 1988.
Conceptions of Giftedness, by Robert J. Sternberg and Janet E. Davidson. New York: Cambridge University Press, 1986.
Parents' Guide to Raising a Gifted Child, by James Alvino and the editors of *Gifted Children Monthly*. Boston: Little, Brown, 1985.
Parenting the Gifted, by Sheila Perino and Joseph Perino. New York: Bowker, 1981.
Educating the Gifted: Acceleration and Enrichment, by William C. George et al. Baltimore: Johns Hopkins University Press, 1979.
Psychology and Education of the Gifted, by W.B. Barbe and J.S. Renzulli. New York: Irvington, 1975.

gigantism   A condition involving abnormal growth, in height and weight. (See GROWTH AND GROWTH DISORDERS.)

Gilles de la Tourette syndrome   Alternate name for TOURETTE'S SYNDROME.

Gillingham method   A type of VAKT approach to teaching READING.

gingivitis   Mild inflammation of the gums (*gingiva*), in which the gums become reddish, swollen, tender, and prone to bleed, especially during brushing. Gingivitis normally results from infection due to PLAQUE that has collected on teeth because of inadequate cleaning. Local irritation from too much brushing or flossing or from MALOCCLUSION can also lead to gingivitis, as can some nutritional diseases, such as scurvy, and some types of medications that cut saliva flow, such as antihistamines. Because of hormonal changes in the body, pregnant women and women taking BIRTH-CONTROL PILLS are susceptible to gingivitis. So are people with diabetes, including perhaps 20 percent of teenagers who developed insulin-dependent DIABETES MELLITUS (IDDM) as children. Treatment of gingivitis involves regular, careful cleaning of the teeth by the dentist at least once a year. If gingivitis is untreated, the gums loosen their hold on the teeth and form pockets where plaque collects. Eventually, infection attacks both the bone and tissues surrounding the teeth, resulting in an advanced stage of gingivitis called *periodontitis*, in which teeth are loosened and may be lost. Dentists or specialist PERIODONTISTS may still be able to save some teeth by cutting away diseased gum tissue, a procedure called *gingivectomy*, to see if healthy gum tissue will grow back around the tooth. If that fails, periodontists may attempt to rebuild the tooth support through a combination of bonelike laboratory materials and grafts of healthy gum tissue from elsewhere. Though often associated with adults, gingivitis also affects adolescents and causes serious damage and premature loss of teeth. (For help and further information, see TEETH.)

GI series   Abbreviation for gastrointestinal series, an alternate name for BARIUM X-RAY EXAMINATIONS.

glaucoma   A condition involving abnormally high pressure on the aqueous fluid of the eye. (See EYE AND VISION PROBLEMS.)

glioblastoma (glioblastoma multiform or **GBM)**   A type of BRAIN TUMOR common in children.

glioma   General term for a TUMOR arising from within the brain, generally malignant (see BRAIN AND BRAIN DISORDERS; BRAIN TUMOR).

globoid leukodystrophy   Alternate name for Krabbe's disease, a type of LIPID STORAGE DISEASE.

glomerulonephritis   A kind of KIDNEY AND UROLOGICAL DISORDER.

glucose   A type of sugar that forms the body's main form of energy (also called *dextrose*). People with DIABETES MELLITUS lack the HORMONE INSULIN needed to convert the sugar to usable form; as a result, glucose builds up in the blood, leading to *hyperglycemia* and perhaps diabetic COMA. People under insulin treatment can sometimes have too little glucose in the blood, a condition called *hypoglycemia* or *insulin shock*. To prevent either of these extremes, many people with diabetes carefully monitor the levels of glucose in their blood, often using a HOME MEDICAL TEST. (For help and further information, see DIABETES MELLITUS.)

glucose-6-phosphate dehydrogenase   The full name of the abnormal enzyme in G6PD DEFICIENCY.

glucosyl cerebroside lipidosis   Alternate name for Gaucher's disease, the most common of the LIPID STORAGE DISEASES.

gluten   The insoluble PROTEIN that is part of wheat, rye, barley, and some other grains, such as oats. Sensitivity to gluten is a type of FOOD INTOLERANCE called CELIAC SPRUE or *gluten-induced enteropathy*.

glycogen storage diseases A group of GENETIC DISORDERS involving storage of excess glycogen—the CARBOHYDRATE storage form of the sugar GLUCOSE—in the liver. Symptoms vary, but they often involve enlarged liver or CIRRHOSIS OF THE LIVER and damage to various types of muscle, including the heart. At least a dozen of these metabolic liver diseases have been identified. Two forms of glycogen storage disease are fatal; some others can be treated with special diet or a liver TRANSPLANT. These disorders often lead to retarded growth and CONVULSIONS, resulting from insufficient sugar in the blood.

For help and further information

Association for Glycogen Storage Disease
Box 896
Durant, IO 52747
319-785-6038
Hollie Arp, President
Organization seeking to aid people affected by glycogen storage disease. Acts as advocate, encouraging expansion of facilities and services for treatment; gathers and disseminates information; publishes various materials, including quarterly newsletter.

American Liver Foundation (ALF), 201-857-2626; toll-free number, U.S. except NJ, 800-223-0179. Sponsors network for parents of children with liver diseases. (For full group information, see LIVER PROBLEMS.)

Children's Liver Foundation, 201-761-1111. (For full group information, see LIVER PROBLEMS.)

National Institute of Diabetes and Digestive and Kidney Diseases (NIDDK), 301-496-3583; **National Digestive Disease Information Clearinghouse**, 301-468-6344. (For full group information, see DIGESTIVE DISORDERS.)

National Institute of Child Health and Human Development (NICHD), 301-496-5133. (For full group information, see PREGNANCY.)

(See also METABOLIC DISORDERS; GROWTH AND GROWTH DISORDERS.)

G$_{M2}$ gangliosidosis Alternate name for *Tay-Sachs disease*, a type of LIPID STORAGE DISEASE.

GMRT Abbreviation for GATES-MACGINITIE READING TEST.

goiter A disorder involving enlargement of the THYROID GLAND.

Goldman-Fristoe Test of Articulation An individually administered test designed to assess the speaking skills of children age 2 to 16, focusing on articulation of the major speech sounds in various positions, of sounds in ordinary speech, and of sounds difficult for the child to pronounce. The nonverbal test uses a picture format and so can be used with many children, including mentally retarded or distractible children, as a guide to planning REMEDIAL INSTRUCTION. (For help and further information, see TESTS.)

gonads The sex glands, the parts of the reproductive system that produce the cells that can join together to form a fertilized egg at CONCEPTION. The male gonads, the TESTES, produce the SPERM; the female gonads, the OVARIES, produce the OVUM (egg).

gonorrhea Infection by the bacterium *gonococcus*, a common SEXUALLY TRANSMITTED DISEASE and one of the traditional *venereal diseases*, infecting at least one million people each year, with an estimated one million more unreported, generally teenagers and young adults. Initial symptoms are mild, sometimes absent altogether, so gonorrhea can readily be spread unknowingly. Infection often takes hold in moist, warm parts of the body, such as the VAGINA, CERVIX, urinary tract, mouth, and rectum. Probably the most common serious complication is infection of the OVARIES and FALLOPIAN TUBES, resulting in PELVIC INFLAMMATORY DISEASE (PID), a major cause of INFERTILITY; other complications include infection in joints, heart, and brain.

Symptoms (if any) generally occur two to 10 days after contact with an infected partner and include painful or burning urination or bowel movements; discharge from the vagina or PENIS; and in women, more seriously, abdominal pain, nonmenstrual vaginal bleeding, vomiting, and FEVER. Doctors often use two laboratory tests to make a positive diagnosis of gonorrhea; the first, a quick office procedure. Gonorrhea is sometimes confused with and often occurs with CHLAMYDIAL INFECTION; both are treated with antibiotics, though some strains of gonorrhea have developed resistance to some antibiotics. Pregnant women who have gonorrhea can pass the infection on to their children, possibly causing BLINDNESS; to prevent that, many doctors recommend that women be tested for gonorrhea at least once during pregnancy, and many states require that silver nitrate or other medication be put into the eyes of newborns to prevent vision-impairing infection. The presence of gonorrhea in young children is often taken as an indication of possible child abuse. A VACCINE to produce IMMUNIZATION against gonorrhea is currently under experimental testing. (For help and further information, including how to avoid infection, see SEXUALLY TRANSMITTED DISEASES.)

Goodenough-Harris Drawing Test A type of INTELLIGENCE TEST used with children age 3 to 15, including a Draw-a-Man Test, a Draw-a-Woman Test, and sometimes an optional, experimental Self-Drawing Test, administered either to groups or to individuals. Drawings are scored for a variety of characteristics, with separate NORMS for males and females, the result being an attempt to measure intelligence without reliance on verbal skills. A different DRAW-A-PERSON TEST is used as a PROJECTIVE TEST. (For help and further information, see TESTS; INTELLIGENCE TESTS.)

GORT-R Abbreviation for GRAY ORAL READING TESTS–REVISED.

GP Abbreviation for GENERAL PRACTITIONER.

GPA Abbreviation for GRADE-POINT AVERAGE.

graafian follicle Of the egg-producing structures in the OVARIES, the one that produces the lead egg (OVUM) ready for fertilization.

grades In EDUCATION, levels of instruction corresponding roughly to age levels (such as KINDERGARTEN, age five; grade 1, age six; grade 2, age seven), with an established CURRICULUM to be covered during a particular school year; also a mark (such as a number or letter) given by a teacher to indicate the student's level of performance on a piece of work or in the course as a whole. If number grades are used (as is common in HIGH SCHOOLS), the PASSING grades usually range from 100 to 70 or 65, with lower numbers indicating FAILING work. If letter grades are used, the range is usually:

A—excellent, roughly equivalent to 90–100 or 95–100

B—above average, 80–90 or 85–94

C—average, 70–80 or 75–84

D—below average, 65–70 or 65–74

F—failure, below 65

In COLLEGE, letter grades are often converted into GRADE-POINT AVERAGES to indicate relative academic rank. Some schools have a *dual grading system*, in which a teacher gives a student two separate grades: one for achievement compared to others in the class (the usual grade) and one for achievement relative to one's ability, sometimes popularly called "for effort." (For help and further information, see EDUCATION; GRADE-POINT AVERAGE.)

grade-equivalent (grade-level) A score indicating how a student's performance on a TEST ranks in terms of the average performance of students of various grades on the same or a similar test. For example, if the NORM for students in the fifth month of seventh grade is a score of 85 on a particular test, and your sixth-grader gets an 85 on the test, her grade-equivalent score is seventh grade, fifth month, and she may be described as "above grade level" in the subject area of the test. (For help and further information, see TESTS.)

grade-level Alternate term for GRADE-EQUIVALENT.

grade-point average (GPA) Conversion of letter GRADES into numerical figures to indicate relative academic rank, usually at the college level; often A = 4.0, B = 3.0, C = 2.0, and D = 1.0. Because courses differ in length and difficulty and are given varying numbers of CREDITS (an organic chemistry course with heavy laboratory work might be five credits, for example, while a course on literature might be three credits), the grade for each course is multiplied by the number of credits the college awards to the course. The resulting grade-point values for all of the courses taken are then totaled, and the sum is divided by the total number of credits (also called *hours of study*) to give the student's grade-point average for the period examined—a semester, a year, or a whole college career. If a student received a B (3.0) in the five-credit organic chemistry course and an A (4.0) in a three-credit art course, then the calculation would work like this:

$$(3 \times 5) + (4 \times 3) / 8 = (15 + 12) / 8 = 27/8 = 3.375 \text{ GPA}$$

Colleges and universities vary somewhat in the points and credits assigned to letter grades and courses, but most use variations of this approach. Students who receive a grade-point average of B or better (in this case, 3.0 or above) are honored by being placed on the school's DEAN'S LIST. An average from a student's entry into a school or college to graduation (or to an interim point) is called a CUMULATIVE AVERAGE.

grade school Alternate term for ELEMENTARY SCHOOL.

grading on the curve An educational policy in which a teacher gives GRADES according to a student's relative performance in a class, rather than on the basis of how well each student met a preestablished standard of skill or knowledge; more specifically, the policy of assigning grades so that the distribution (if graphed) would roughly resemble the bell-shaped NORMAL DISTRIBUTION curve. With a hard test, grading on the curve has the advantage of sorting out the actual distinctions of knowledge levels among students without unduly discouraging them. With an easy test, it keeps everyone from getting A's and B's, which would obscure the real differences in skill levels among them.

For example, the grades given out might read this way: three A's, five B's, nine C's, five D's, three F's. But in fact, if the TEST were very easy, most people would have done well—well enough to have received an A or B if measured against a preset standard. Conversely, if the test were very hard, perhaps only one or two would have passed, according to a preset standard. Because of the widespread use of statistics, grading on the curve has been common in many schools for decades. However, the practice tends to keep students in the same relative position on tests and so can tend to discourage learning. An alternative is to focus on some form of PASS–FAIL system or MASTERY LEARNING, in which the main effort is to bring all students up to a particular level of skill and knowledge. (For help and further information, see EDUCATION; GRADES; TESTS.)

graduate One who has successfully completed the course of study offered at a school, often receiving a CERTIFICATE or DIPLOMA; the term also describes educational programs beyond the BACHELOR'S DEGREE level.

graduation In EDUCATION in general, moving on from one level of learning to another, such as from addition to subtraction, or PROMOTION from one GRADE to another; more specifically completion of a set course of study, for which a student receives formal recognition. Graduation ceremonies, or exercises, are often held to honor students who have completed study at a school and are ready to move on to another section of the school system (as from ELEMENTARY SCHOOL to MIDDLE SCHOOL), to another school (as from HIGH SCHOOL to COLLEGE), or out of the school system (as from HIGH SCHOOL to work). When students are ranked academically, the highest-ranked student at a graduation is called the VALEDICTORIAN and often gives the ceremony's closing speech; the second-ranked student, the SALUTATORIAN, generally gives the opening speech.

grammar school Alternate term for ELEMENTARY SCHOOL.

grand mal seizure   The most striking kind of SEIZURE that goes under the umbrella name of EPILEPSY; also called a *tonic-clonic seizure*.

grandparents' rights   The legally supported ability of grandparents to visit their grandchildren even if the parents have separated or divorced. In practice, many parents wish to continue relationships between grandparent and grandchild, but some do not, and their attempt to bar such contact has led to a great deal of lobbying for legal protection of grandparents' VISITATION RIGHTS. Most states now have laws supporting grandparents' rights. One state, Illinois, has even passed a landmark law guaranteeing grandparents' visitation rights while the parents remain together, regardless of the parents' wishes in the matter. However, in cases of ADOPTION, which involves TERMINATION OF PARENTAL RIGHTS, grandparents often lose their visitation rights, although some states formally protect them when the adoption is by a stepparent.

For help and further information

Grandparents Association of America (GAA)
P.O. Box 2410
Peachtree, GA 30269
404-455-1616
Mike Goldgar, Executive Director
Organization seeking to strengthen bonds between grandparents and grandchildren. Urges establishment of Grandparents' Days; publishes *Grand Times*.

Grandparents'/Children's Rights (GCR)
5728 Bayonne Avenue
Haslett, MI 48840
517-339-8663
Lee and Lucille Sumpter, Study Directors
For grandparents and others concerned with protecting the rights of children and grandparents to have access to each other. Works to protect grandparents' visitation rights and other rights affecting children's emotional, mental, and physical health, especially regarding child abuse; seeks to influence public policy and legislation, and serves as information clearinghouse.

(See also "Grandparenting" in the PARENT'S BOOKSHELF.)

grant   In EDUCATION, a type of FINANCIAL AID, money that can be applied to the costs of attending COLLEGE or PRIVATE SCHOOLS, such as a SCHOLARSHIP, or for carrying out a specified academic project, but that does not have to be repaid. Many grants are offered on the basis of special need, including several federal programs, such as the PELL GRANT and the SUPPLEMENTAL EDUCATIONAL OPPORTUNITY GRANT. (For help and further information, see FINANCIAL AID.)

GRAS   Abbreviation for generally recognized as safe substances, a type of FOOD ADDITIVE.

grasping reflex   The automatic response of a baby to clutch any object placed in his or her palm; a type of PRIMITIVE REFLEX found only in babies and normally disappearing in the first few months of life.

gravida   Medical term for a pregnant woman, often used with a prefix indicating the number of pregnancies, such as *primigravida* for a first pregnancy or *multigravida* for multiple pregnancies.

gray market adoptions   Legal but nontraditional ADOPTIONS.

Gray Oral Reading Tests-Revised (GORT-R)   An individually administered TEST of READING skills for children age 7 to 17, used to evaluate the development of oral reading and as a DIAGNOSTIC ASSESSMENT TEST to identify reading difficulties. A child reads aloud a series of increasingly difficult passages and orally answers several comprehension questions on each. The results are given in converted SCORES and PERCENTILES. (For help and further information, see TESTS.)

greenstick fracture   A type of FRACTURE common in young children, in which a bone breaks only partway through.

grip age   A summary of the relationship between a child's growth and the statistical average for a child of the same size and sex; if a child of six has gripping power normally seen in a seven-year-old, that child's grip age is seven. (See AGE.)

gross motor skills   A type of MOTOR SKILL that involves the large muscles of the arms, legs, torso, and feet and is used in activities requiring strength and balance, such as walking, running, and jumping.

group home   A residential facility providing LONG-TERM CARE in a homelike setting for MINORS or adults who require substantial help or supervision, such as those who have serious handicaps (see HANDICAPPED), MENTAL DISORDERS, or MENTAL RETARDATION, or those classed as JUVENILE DELINQUENTS or INCORRIGIBLE children, the aim being to place them in the LEAST RESTRICTIVE ENVIRONMENT. Normally staffed 24 hours a day, group homes serve generally fewer than 50 people and provide the kind of supervision a family on its own might not be able to provide. Children in group homes generally attend local public schools, often in special programs. Children who have no parents or GUARDIANS and who once would have been placed in large orphanages are now more likely to be placed in group homes, pending placement with FOSTER PARENTS or for ADOPTION.

growing pains   General aches and pains in the muscles and joints of children's limbs, appearing for unknown causes, often at night. Public health experts note that these are no cause for medical concern unless they are severe or are linked with other symptoms, which may require diagnosis and treatment. "Growing pains" is also a popular phrase referring to the emotional and social trials and tribulations of ADOLESCENCE.

growth and growth disorders   Increase in a child's height and weight, and associated changes in body parts and their relative proportions, processes that form the physical basis for a child's development and can be adversely affected in a variety of ways. Apart from the enormous growth of the EMBRYO and

Baby's First Year: Height and Weight Changes

The charts below show the average lengths and weights of large, small, and average-size babies, and indicate about how much they will gain from month to month during the first year of life. If you think your baby is behind in growth, you should talk with your doctor or clinic staff.

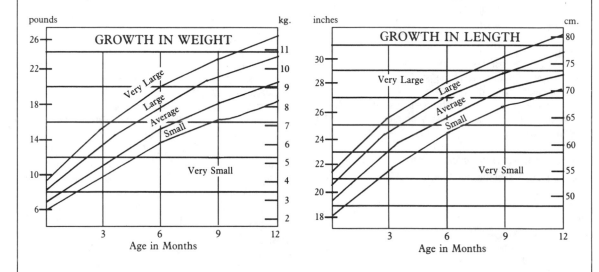

Source: *Infant Care* (1989). Prepared for the Public Health Service by the Health Resources and Services Administration, Bureau of Maternal and Child Health and Resources Development.

FETUS (see PREGNANCY for a month-by-month description of fetal development), a child experiences two major growth spurts.

The first is during the first year of life. Infants average about 7½ pounds at birth, though some may weigh a good deal more and some much less. (Those under 5½ pounds are termed LOW BIRTH WEIGHT and have increased risk of various medical problems.) But within a year most infants have tripled their weight and added about 50 percent to their height (see BABY'S FIRST YEAR: HEIGHT AND WEIGHT CHANGES, above). The head grows markedly in this first year, starting out at about one-quarter of the body's length and ending the year at almost full adult size. By about 18 months, the FONTANELLES (soft spots) disappear, as the skull hardens and fuses; the brain it encases will grow more slowly, approaching adult size only after age five.

In newborns, the legs account for only about three-eighths of the body's length. In the months and years of early childhood, much of the increase in length takes place in the limbs—more precisely at the ends of the long bones, called *epiphyses* (or more popularly, *growth plates* or *growth centers*). (In this period, also, enormous development occurs in skills, outlined in the CHART OF NORMAL DEVELOPMENT on page 507.)

The immediate concern in childhood is that the growth be steady. In general, children from age two to puberty grow at a relatively steady rate of two to three inches a year. If growth suddenly slows down or if the child's growth lags far behind the average, that may indicate a physical disorder that should be diagnosed and treated before long-term damage is done. Another main concern in early childhood is that the epiphyses not be damaged in cases of FRACTURES, sometimes even in what appear to be sprained ankles.

The second great growth spurt occurs during PUBERTY. Since puberty normally starts earlier in girls, they sometimes grow temporarily taller than boys, but boys overall tend to be taller in the long run. In this period, the trunk grows faster than before, while the limbs also continue to grow, reaching their limit of growth only in the late teens, when the growth plates turn completely to bone, forming the adult skeleton. By that time, the legs will account for about one-half of the body's height, and the head for only about one-eighth. (For an overview of growth, see NORMAL GROWTH AND DEVELOPMENT on page 229.)

The rate, timing, and overall height of a child depend on many factors. GENETIC INHERITANCE is important among these, but it is very much affected by environmental factors, including

Normal Growth and Development

In humans, intrauterine growth and development require about 40 weeks of gestation. From the third month until term, fetal weight increases nearly 500-fold, from about 6 g (0.2 oz) to 3,000 to 3,500 g (6.5 to 7.6 lb) at birth.

Infants

Immediately after birth, weight is lost, but birth weight is usually regained by the 10th day. After this time, weight increases at a rapid but decelerating rate. Most infants double their birth weight by the age of four months and triple it within one year. Length increases by 50 percent during the first year. These changes are accompanied by changes in body composition. Fat accumulates rapidly; by six months, it makes up about 25 percent of the total body weight. During the second six months, the relative increase in lean body mass is much greater than the increase in fat.

Children and Adolescents

The very rapid rate of growth in infancy is followed by slower growth during the preschool and early school-age years. Weight gain approximates 2.5 kilograms a year until nine to 10 years of age. Length increases by an average of 11 to 12 centimeters in the second year, about 7 centimeters during each of the next three. Children become leaner between six months and six years, after which a gradual increase of fat thickness occurs in both males and females until puberty; females have a relatively greater body fat content than males at all stages of development. The brain reaches 50 percent of its adult size by age two, 75 percent by age four, and 100 percent by age six to 10. Body growth is measured by increases in length and weight; skin-fold measurements may be used to evaluate body fat. The heights and weights for representative samples of boys and girls have been used to establish growth reference curves developed by the National Center for Health Statistics (NCHS). As a general rule, growth patterns follow percentile lines on these growth charts.

When growth performance for a given child is measured at regular intervals and plotted on such charts, unusual changes in weight and height percentile can identify children who are at nutritional risk from either under- or overnutrition. Growth patterns are highly individual, however, and average growth rates do not always apply to individual children. This observation is especially applicable in adolescence.

The velocity of physical growth in adolescence is second only to that of infancy. The most rapid period of growth in adolescence is known as the growth spurt. It precedes menarche in females and spermatogenesis in males. In males, the age at which peak growth occurs is later and the growth spurt more intense than in females. There are also differences in its timing and length. The growth spurt usually begins between ages eight and 12 in females and between ages 10 and 16 in males. Linear growth stops toward the end of adolescence, usually between the ages of 14 and 16 in females and between 16 and 18 in males. The magnitude and duration of growth vary widely in adolescents, making chronologic age an unsatisfactory index of nutritional needs. Instead, individual body size, stage of sexual maturation, and current rate of growth must be considered.

Source: *The Surgeon General's Report on Nutrition and Health.* Rocklin, CA: Prima, 1988.

NUTRITION and general physical and mental health. Long-term MALNUTRITION, FAILURE TO THRIVE, or chronic illness (such as ASTHMA or TUBERCULOSIS) can slow growth significantly. Among the many other disorders that can retard growth are ACHONDRO-PLASIA (in which the epiphyses turn to bone prematurely), CYSTIC FIBROSIS, CELIAC SPRUE (gluten intolerance), disorders of the THYROID GLAND, CHROMOSOMAL ABNORMALITIES such as DOWN'S SYNDROME and TURNER'S SYNDROME, and METABOLIC DISORDERS such as PHENYLKETONURIA. Children treated with chemotherapy and some other drugs can also have slowed growth. ADOLESCENT PREGNANCY, too, often causes short stature because teenage girls have not completed their own growth when the fetus is calling on needed nutritional resources.

The growth process itself is triggered and regulated largely by several HORMONES, including HUMAN GROWTH HORMONE (hGH), thyroid hormone, and the sex hormones that bring on puberty and regulate sexual development. Deficiency or excess of any of these hormones can cause a child to be abnormally short or tall.

In particular, too much human growth hormone, as from a tumor of the PITUITARY GLAND, can cause excessive height and weight, a condition called *gigantism* (in adults, *acromegaly*). Great height is also associated with some other disorders, such as MARFAN'S SYNDROME.

On the other hand, too little human growth hormone leads to markedly short stature, in the past often called DWARFISM. The range of "normal" height is a very wide one. But if any other physical disorders have been treated and the child's growth is still extremely slowed, doctors may administer some human growth hormone to bring the child's growth to normal level.

For help and further information

Human Growth Foundation (HGF)
Montgomery Building
4720 Montgomery Lane
Bethesda, MD 20814

301-656-7540
Denise Orenstein, Executive Director
Organization of and for families of children with growth problems and interested others. Gathers and disseminates information to public and professionals; supports research; publishes various materials, including monthly *Fourth Friday*, quarterlies *Growth Chart* and *HGF Ink*, and *Growth Series* brochures.

National Institute of Diabetes and Digestive and Kidney Diseases (NIDDK), 301-496-3583. Publishes fact sheet *Human Growth Hormone and Creutzfeldt-Jakob Disease*. (For full group information, see DIGESTIVE DISORDERS.)

National Hormone and Pituitary Program (NHPP), 301-837-2552. (For full group information, see PITUITARY GLAND.)

Little People of America
P.O. Box 633
San Bruno, CA 94066
415-589-0695
Harriet Stickney or Al Stickney, Contacts
Organization for people with dwarf-type growth disorders, generally under four feet ten inches, and normal-sized adults who have dwarf children. Aims to provide mutual support and understanding, exchanging information on all aspects of life; works through agencies to arrange for adoption of dwarf children by similar parents; encourages and cooperates in medical research; publishes newsletter *LPA Today* and booklet *My Child Is a Dwarf*.

Tall Clubs International (TCI)
911 South Oakwood Drive
Tempe, AZ 85282
602-969-8933, toll-free number 800-521-2512
Marlene Klatt, Executive Vice President
Network of clubs of and for tall people (women 5'10" or more, men 6'2" or more). Provides forum for exchanging experiences and ideas for how to deal with special problems of tall people, as in getting suitable clothing and accommodations; seeks to educate public as to needs of tall people; operates toll-free number; publishes various materials, including *Tall Topix*.

Other reference source

Growth, by James M. Tanner. Alexandria, VA: Time-Life Books, 1981.

growth spurt A child's most rapid period of growth after infancy, normally starting shortly before the onset of PUBERTY, specifically before MENARCHE in females and production of SPERM in males. (For help and further information, see GROWTH AND GROWTH DISORDERS.)

G6PD deficiency A GENETIC DISORDER, more specifically a type of METABOLIC DISORDER, in which the body's red blood cells produce abnormal molecules of a key enzyme called *glucose-6-phosphate dehydrogenase* (G6PD). This makes the blood cells vulnerable to damage, disease, and destruction and often results in severe ANEMIA. An X-LINKED recessive disease, G6PD deficiency is carried and passed on by women CARRIERS but affects mostly males, being especially common among Black males. Some Whites of Mediterranean ancestry have a related disorder called *favism*, so named for their adverse reaction to fava beans. Some types of drugs, such as antibiotics, can trigger destruction of red blood cells among people with G6PD deficiency and favism. The G6PD deficiency can be detected by a BLOOD TEST; although the condition cannot be cured, its effects can be moderated.

For help and further information

National Heart, Lung, and Blood Institute, 301-496-4236. (For full group information, see BLOOD AND BLOOD DISORDERS; HEART AND HEART PROBLEMS; LUNG AND BREATHING DISORDERS.)

GSL Abbreviation for Guaranteed Student Loans, former name of STAFFORD LOANS.

Guaranteed Student Loans (GSL) Former name of STAFFORD LOANS.

guardian An adult who has been given long-term or temporary legal responsibility for a MINOR (called a WARD), acting in place of the BIOLOGICAL PARENTS, though not necessarily having day-to-day CUSTODY and care of the child. FOSTER PARENTS are often appointed guardians to the children in their care. In some circumstances, as in legal proceedings about CHILD ABUSE AND NEGLECT or CUSTODY, the court may appoint a *guardian ad litem (GAL)* to represent the child's interests during the case. A guardian may also be appointed for adults who have been judged legally INCOMPETENT or HANDICAPPED adults unable to care for themselves; in such cases, the guardian is sometimes called a CONSERVATOR.

Parents of young children, especially those with disabilities that will require care into adulthood, should designate a guardian in their will; otherwise, in case of their death, the court will appoint one. A good choice is a close friend or relative, one who is willing and able to serve as guardian—young enough, strong enough, and with a life-style compatible with children. Discussing the idea, getting the prospective guardian's agreement, and informing other relatives about the choice can avoid possible unhappiness and even court battles over custody in case of the parents' death.

For help and further information

Guardian Association (GA)
P.O. Box 1826
Pinellas Park, FL 33565
813-381-5129
Donna H. Hicks, Executive Officer
For legal guardians and interested others. Offers education to prospective guardians and others in the court system, aimed at improving the quality of guardianship; publishes newsletter.

Mental Retardation Association of America (MRAA), 801-328-1575. (See MENTAL RETARDATION.)

Guthrie test   A MEDICAL TEST used in screening for PHENYLKE-TONURIA, routinely given (often by law) to most newborns.

gynecologist   A physician who specializes in providing medical and surgical care relating to women's reproductive system, often working as an OBSTETRICIAN-GYNECOLOGIST.

gynecomastia   Abnormal enlargement of the BREASTS of a male, generally resulting from too much of the female sex hormone ESTROGEN. Temporary swelling of a male's breasts can occur in newborns (from HORMONES from his mother) and at PUBERTY, when the body is going through many hormonal changes. Gynecomastia is also common in males who have KLINEFELTER'S SYNDROME, and it can be a sign of disease in a male, especially a grown man, such as CIRRHOSIS OF THE LIVER or a TUMOR in the TESTES or breast. It can be treated with hormones or surgery.

For help and further information

National Institute of Child Health and Human Development (NICHD), 301-496-5133. (For full group information, see PREGNANCY.)

habits   Alternate term for COMFORT HABITS.

Haemophilus influenzae type b conjugate vaccine (Hib vaccine)   A type of VACCINE normally given by injection to children at age 15 to 18 months, though it can be given as late as 60 months, to provide IMMUNIZATION against HAEMOPHILUS INFLUENZAE TYPE B DISEASE. Newer forms of the Hib vaccine may be available for younger children in the near future. The vaccine provides protection for at least 1½ to 3 years, the most dangerous period for this disease in children.

Haemophilus influenzae type b disease (Hib)   A very serious disease caused by a parasitic bacterium (unlike influenza, which is caused by a virus), especially threatening to children under five years old. In the United States, Hib disease strikes about one in every 200 children under age five, with 70 percent of the cases—generally the most serious ones—occurring under the age of 18 months. Hib disease can cause PNEUMONIA and infections of the blood, joints, bones, soft tissues, throat, and, worst of all, the covering of the heart and brain. About 12,000 cases of MENINGITIS (inflammation of the membranes covering the brain) occur in the United States each year, causing death in one of every 20 affected children and permanent brain damage in one of four. Fortunately a VACCINE now exists to protect children from this potentially devastating illness. (For help and further information, see HAEMOPHILUS INFLUENZAE TYPE B VACCINE.)

half-brother and **half-sister**   SIBLINGS who share one, rather than two, parents. With modern complicated patterns of divorce and remarriage, many more children are living in families with half-brothers and half-sisters. (See FAMILY.)

halitosis   The medical term for bad breath. It often results from poor dental care, as in a teenager who fails to keep up regular toothbrushing, but it can also be a symptom of illness, such as mouth infection or sinusitis.

Possible Side Effects and Adverse Reactions to Hib Immunization

This vaccine is among the safest of all vaccine products. The vaccine cannot cause meningitis. About one in every eight children who receive the current Hib vaccine will have some slight redness or swelling or tenderness in the area where the shot was given. About one in every 140 children will develop a fever higher than 102.2°F. These reactions begin within 24 hours after the shot, but usually go away quickly.

Source: *Parents Guide to Childhood Immunization* (1988). Prepared for the Public Health Service and the Centers for Disease Control.

hallucination Apparent perception of something that is not, in fact, present (as opposed to an ILLUSION, which is a misinterpretation of something that *is* present); a common symptom of PSYCHOSIS. Hallucinations may be labeled by the main sense involved, such as *auditory* (as in hearing voices), *visual* (as in seeing objects), *haptic* or *tactile* (as in touching or feeling objects), *olfactory* (smelling), and *gustatory* (tasting), as well as *somatic* (perception within the body, such as feeling a current of electricity). Drugs or chemicals that induce hallucinations are called *hallucinogens*. (For help and further information, see MENTAL DISORDERS; DRUG ABUSE.)

handedness The tendency of a person to rely more heavily on and to be more easy and proficient at using one hand than the other; also called *chirality*. The preference for one hand over the other is believed to reflect the DOMINANCE of one side of the brain over the other, but why this occurs is unknown. About two-thirds of the population—with males and females in equal proportions—are right-handed for fine MOTOR SKILLS, with as many as 90 percent writing right-handed. Some people are *ambidextrous*, or able to use both hands equally well. Though few parents and teachers any longer force left-handed children to use their right hands for writing and other fine motor activities, social pressure is still great to use the right hand. The equipment in this technological world is generally geared to right-handed people, so many left-handed people come to use their right hand a good deal. No special artistic or intellectual abilities are clearly linked with left-handedness. Lefthanders do have a higher proportion of accidents—due, many people feel, to the right-handed orientation of the things around them. Parents of left-handed children may well want to select left-handed versions of various tools and equipment, commonly available in special catalogs.

For help and further information

Lefthanders International (LHI)
P.O. Box 8249
Topeka, KS 66608
913-234-2177
Dean R. Campbell, President

Organization publishing *Lefthander Magazine* and *Lefthander's Catalog*, focusing on products, research, and success stories of special interest to lefthanders.

Southpaws International (SI)
P.O. Box 31170
Birmingham, AL 35222
205-324-2596
Herman Moore, President

Organization of and for lefthanders. Seeks to gain greater public recognition for southpaws and their achievements; publishes newsletter *Lefties Unite.*

Other reference source

Left-handed Kids, by James T. de Kay. New York: M. Evans, 1989.

hand–eye coordination Alternate name for visual-motor integration, one of the key VISUAL SKILLS.

handicapped An umbrella term referring to a wide range of people with minor or major physical or mental disabilities who have some degree of difficulty in certain activities such as walking, seeing, hearing, speaking, and learning. In children, that generally means that they have significant delay in reaching key DEVELOPMENTAL MILESTONES.

Often used loosely in the past, the term "handicapped" came to be given rather a more precise definition regarding children with the passage of the EDUCATION FOR ALL HANDICAPPED CHILDREN ACT OF 1975. This federal law defines handicapped children as those who are "mentally retarded, hard of hearing, deaf, speech impaired, visually handicapped, seriously emotionally disturbed, orthopedically impaired, other health impaired, blind, multihandicapped, or having specific learning disabilities" and who require special educational services because of such disabilities. The various arms of government have set up a variety of programs (such as CHILDFIND) to try to identify such children as early as possible, so as to provide treatment and other special services quickly and minimize the impact of disabilities. Any child in a public school or program who has such a handicap is provided with an INDIVIDUALIZED EDUCATION PROGRAM, outlining what the school will be teaching the child, how they will go about it, how they will evaluate progress and measure success, and what special educational services will be provided.

Given this very wide definition, many children are seen to have some kind of minor handicap, and given modern medical technology, many children are surviving with severe handicaps. Partly as a result, many organizations have been formed to support, educate, and act as advocates for handicapped children and their parents, especially in ensuring that they get their rights, and many books have been written to help them maximize their independence. Some of these organizations and works are listed in this book under specific disabilities, notably under such headings as EAR AND HEARING PROBLEMS, EYE AND VISION PROBLEMS, LEARNING DISABILITIES, MENTAL RETARDATION, MENTAL DISORDERS, and COMMUNICATION SKILLS AND DISORDERS. Many other organizations and written works deal with overarching general needs of all kinds of handicapped people—so many that we have listed them separately under HELP FOR SPECIAL CHILDREN, on page 578.

haptic A general term for a physical, hands-on approach to learning, one of the main MODALITIES for receiving and processing information. (See LEARNING STYLE.)

hard of hearing A general term referring to people with EAR AND HEARING PROBLEMS whose hearing is impaired but can be used for the ordinary purposes of life with a hearing aid.

hard signs Clear differences in the way a child's CENTRAL NERVOUS SYSTEM functions and responds, compared to that of the average child. NEUROLOGISTS sometimes use the term when referring to inappropriate responses or the absence of appropriate responses in a child with LEARNING DISABILITIES or other DEVELOPMENTAL DISORDERS. Less clear-cut observations are called *soft signs*, the term SIGNS indicating an objective finding by a physician, rather than a subjective SYMPTOM described by the patient.

hard-to-place children   Children who are available for ADOPTION, but for whom it is hard to find adoptive parents. Many unplaced children are less attractive to would-be adoptors because they are older, have SIBLINGS who wish to stay together, are of minority background, or have SPECIAL NEEDS, such as those who have physical handicaps (see HANDICAPPED) or MENTAL RETARDATION or are victims of CHILD ABUSE AND NEGLECT. To encourage adoption of hard-to-place children, the government has developed *adoption subsidies* or *adoption assistance plans* to cover some of the costs incurred by parents. (For help and further information, see ADOPTION.)

hay fever   A common type of ALLERGY.

hCG   Abbreviation for human chorionic gonadotropin, a key HORMONE used in tests for PREGNANCY.

HDLs   Abbreviation for high-density lipoproteins, the so-called good form of CHOLESTEROL.

head injury   Damage to the head as a result of a fall or other accident, assault, or wound, the main concern being whether the brain is affected. The brain is protected by a bony skull, and sometimes even if the skull itself is fractured, damage may still be superficial. However, the brain can be damaged by certain types of head injuries that leave little or no external sign, as in some kinds of child abuse in which a child is violently shaken (see CHILD ABUSE AND NEGLECT). Even mild head injuries commonly produce headaches and may involve unconsciousness, COMA, or amnesia. Associated symptoms may include PARALYSIS, sometimes with muscle weakness and loss of feeling, continual VOMITING, loss or deterioration in clarity and consciousness, and EYE AND VISION PROBLEMS, such as double vision or pupils of unequal size. Any head injury should be referred to a physician; if a child loses consciousness, even briefly, the doctor may want to take X-RAYS of the skull to check for skull fracture or a CT SCAN to check for HEMORRHAGE or clots in the brain and may well suggest that the child be hospitalized for observation.

For help and further information

National Head Injury Foundation
333 Turnpike Road
Southboro, MA 01772
617-485-9950
Marilyn Price Spivack, Executive Director
Organization of people concerned with head injuries. Encourages formation of support groups; acts as information clearinghouse and makes referrals.

National Institute of Neurological Disorders and Stroke (NINDS), 301-496-5751. (For full group information, see BRAIN AND BRAIN DISORDERS.)

Head Start   A federally funded, locally operated program that provides PRE-KINDERGARTEN educational opportunities, as well as health, social, psychological, and nutritional services, for disadvantaged three- to five-year-olds from low-income families, including many HANDICAPPED children, who are given special individualized help. Started in 1965, it is presently run by the ADMINISTRATION FOR CHILDREN, YOUTH, AND FAMILIES (ACYF), surviving the many social cuts of the 1980s because its value was so widely recognized.

The Head Start program produced a valuable series of books, *Mainstreaming Preschoolers*, about how to recognize young children with handicaps, how their handicaps affect their learning and behavior, and how to help them. Selections from some of these (modified for wider use by parents) are reproduced in this book:

- under specific topics, such as LEARNING DISABILITIES, EAR AND HEARING PROBLEMS, EYE AND VISION PROBLEMS, MENTAL RETARDATION, CHOKING, ARTIFICIAL RESPIRATION, and ORTHOPEDIC DEVICES, including some Observational Checklists for spotting problems;
- in TEACHING YOUNG CHILDREN: GUIDELINES AND ACTIVITIES (on page 544).

Parents should find these materials useful in assessing whether or not their young children have problems of any sort, since early diagnosis and treatment will minimize the effects of any problems and maximize the child's chance to develop normally.

For help and further information

National Head Start Association (NHSA)
1309 King Street, Suite 200
Alexandria, VA 22344
703-739-0875
Jim Matlock, Executive Director
Organization of parents, Head Start staff, and others concerned with the Head Start program. Seeks to expand and enhance Head Start services; publishes various materials, including quarterly *NHSA Newsletter* and *Tell the Head Start Story*.

The Impact of Head Start on Children, Families and Communities, by Ruth H. McKey et al. Washington, DC: Government Printing Office, 1985.
(See also PRESCHOOL and EDUCATION.)

health maintenance organization (HMO)   A type of medical practice that provides general health care, including hospitalization and surgery, to individuals and families who pay a flat monthly or yearly fee, regardless of the amount or kind of medical services needed. Some HMOs cover dental, mental, and eye care, and prescription drugs as well, for a supplemental fee. HMOs (such as Kaiser-Permanente) attempt to keep medical costs down, reduce unnecessary hospitalization, and eliminate the need for health insurance, while still maintaining quality health care. Some HMOs operate under federal regulations and others under state laws with various requirements. Some own their own hospitals, while others have contract arrangements with hospitals. In some HMO plans, doctors work on salaries; in others, they are private doctors who bill the HMO. One disadvantage of HMOs, especially for families considering maternity care and perhaps special care for a child with chronic illness, is the patient's limited choice of doctor, hospital, or both.

hearing aid   An electronic aid used by people with certain kinds of hearing impairment to make sounds louder. The effect of a hearing aid depends on the seriousness and type of the hearing loss. As explained in *Mainstreaming Preschoolers: Children with Hearing Impairment*:

> For some children a hearing aid makes spoken words understandable. For others, it only helps them to hear speech partially. And for still others, it may only help them know that sounds are being made. One problem with a hearing aid is that it makes all sounds louder, not just speech. This means that sounds such as radiators, outside traffic, the crashing of blocks, people walking, and so on will be made louder and will interfere with the child's listening.

Improvements in digital signal processing are lessening those problems somewhat.

Most hearing aids today are small devices worn at ear level, consisting of five basic parts:

1. a microphone to pick up the sound;
2. batteries to provide power to make the sound louder, in a case behind the ear, attached to eyeglasses, or in an earpiece (ear mold);
3. a receiver that adapts the sound so that the ear can use it;
4. an ear mold that holds the receiver and carries the sound into the ear;
5. wires to connect the system.

Such small devices have largely replaced the larger devices on a chest harness worn until recently. In rare cases in which a child is unable to use a standard ear mold and receiver (due to a missing ear or ear canal), a small vibrator may be worn on a headband near the ear to act as a receiver. For some profoundly deaf children, *tactile devices* can transmit speech signals in the form of vibrations or codes that are felt, rather than heard.

Hearing aids are often prescribed by an AUDIOLOGIST or OTOLOGIST after HEARING TESTS have indicated hearing impairment. The sooner a hearing-impaired child is properly diagnosed and fitted with a hearing aid, the less the negative impact on the child's development in communication skills (see COMMUNICATION SKILLS AND DISORDERS) and therefore in many other areas, such as COGNITIVE DEVELOPMENT. Infants and young children need to be taught how to use and listen with hearing aids and other such devices.

For help and further information

National Hearing Aid Society (NHAS)
20361 Middlebelt
Livonia, MI 48152
313-478-2610, Hearing Aid Hotline (U.S. except MI) 800-521-5247
Trade association of certified hearing-aid dealers. Aims to assure that members meet professional standards; provides information to public on hearing aids and possible sources of financial aid; makes referrals to local hearing-aid specialists; operates toll-free line; distributes Better Business Brochure pamphlet *Facts About Hearing Aids*.

(See also EAR AND HEARING PROBLEMS.)

hearing loss   Inability or impaired ability to hear and interpret sounds, the two general types of EAR AND HEARING PROBLEMS being *conductive losses* and *sensorineural losses*.

hearing tests   A series of MEDICAL TESTS, normally performed by an AUDIOLOGIST, OTOLOGIST, or OTOLARYNGOLOGIST, designed to screen for possible hearing loss, to assess the amount of hearing loss, and to identify the location of the problem causing the loss.

Basic hearing loss is assessed by a *Pure Tone Test (audiometric test* or *sweep-check test)*, which measures two things: the *frequency* (high or low pitch) and the *loudness* of tones the child is able to hear. For the Pure Tone Test the audiologist places earphones on a child and, using a machine called an *audiometer*, sends tones of different pitch and loudness through the earphones (testing one ear at a time). The audiologist asks the child to do something—such as raise a hand or put a toy in a bucket—when he or she hears the tone. The results—what pitches the child can hear and how loud sounds must be for the child to hear them—are recorded on a chart called an audiogram.

The audiometric test measures hearing in a range of zero to 110 *decibels* (a measure of loudness). People with unimpaired hearing begin to hear sounds at approximately zero to 10 decibels. People with hearing loss do not begin to hear sounds until higher decibel levels are reached. If, for example, a child cannot begin to hear sounds until they are at least 50 decibels loud, then the child is said to have a 50-decibel hearing loss.

These decibel levels serve as the basis for the categories of hearing impairment:

- *mildly hearing impaired*: loss between 20 and 40 decibels;
- *moderately hearing impaired*: loss between 40 and 70 decibels;
- *severely hearing impaired*: loss between 70 and 92 decibels;
- *profoundly hearing impaired*: loss greater than 92 decibels.

In everyday terms, a faint whisper three feet away would be about 10 decibels; average conversation, about 60 decibels; an auto horn about 100 decibels; and a propellor airplane revving up 15 feet away, about 120 decibels.

Tips for Parents of Children with Hearing Aids

For the hearing aid to help, it must be turned on and working well. You should check a child's aid several times every day. Make sure it is turned on. Take the ear mold out of the child's ear and listen through it to make sure the aid is working. The ear mold can be removed and reinserted by a gentle pushing and twisting motion. If the ear mold is not in the ear properly, or if it falls out, you will hear a whistling sound. This is simply feedback noise, which can be eliminated by inserting the ear mold into the ear snugly. If the squeal is constant, the child may need a new ear mold. You might ask an audiologist or a teacher of the deaf to give you guidance in how to put in the ear mold, check the hearing aid, and take care of it. Below is a short checklist to assist you.

Daily Hearing Aid Check

1. Is the equipment in good condition?
   * Look at the aid and ear mold. They should be free of dirt and wax.
   * Look at the cord. It should be free of breaks or cuts.
2. Is the hearing aid turned on?
   * The switch should be on "M" for microphone.
3. Is it loud enough?
   * Ask the audiologist what the volume should be and check to make sure it is correct. If it isn't correct, adjust the volume to the proper setting.
4. Is it working well?
   * Listen through the ear mold. The sound should be clear—not fuzzy, intermittent, or static. The sound should be strong, not weak. If you discover a problem (for example, the hearing aid sounds weak, there is no sound at all, there is static sound, or the sound cuts on and off), you should check the aid immediately. Perhaps the aid only needs a new battery. Or perhaps it needs to be repaired.

   Often the problem will be a weak or dead battery. The average life span of a battery is five to seven days. Since you may have to change a hearing aid's battery quite often, it is important to keep some spare batteries on hand. Wires wear out and break and children grow out of ear molds quickly. Your daily hearing aid checks will help to spot any problem with either the wire or the ear mold. The hearing aid must be kept dry and clean.

   Parents are often reluctant to allow their children to wear hearing aids all day at school or even at home. While it is wise to be cautious, the aid can only help a child if he or she is wearing it. Parents may not know that the hearing aid dealer can help them obtain insurance for the aid to cover loss and damage.

Source: *Mainstreaming Preschoolers: Children with Hearing Impairment: A Guide for Teachers, Parents, and Others Who Work with Hearing Impaired Preschoolers*, by Rita Ann LaPorta et al. (1978). Prepared for the Head Start Bureau of the Administration for Children, Youth, and Families.

If your child has an audiometric test, the results will be recorded on an audiogram like the one on page 236. In that audiogram, the results for the right ear are marked with a circle and those for the left ear with an X. As often happens, this child has better hearing in the lower frequencies than in the higher ones, so high-pitched sounds must be louder for the child to hear them. Because the lines are in the regions marked "moderate" and "severe" loss, this child is said to have "moderate to severe hearing loss."

In the *auditory brainstem response* (or *auditory evoked response*) test, the audiologist attaches electrodes to the child's scalp to record how the brain responds to sounds. This test is commonly used with infants, mentally retarded children, and others who are unable to respond appropriately in the Pure Tone Test, and also to check for possible *acoustic neuroma*.

Tuning fork tests are generally used to determine the type of hearing loss: conductive (in the ear) or sensorineural (in the transmission to the brain). In the *Rinne test*, the tuning fork is held at the opening of the outer ear (with sound traveling through air) and against the mastoid bone behind the ear (with sound traveling through bone). The person is asked to say which sounds louder. If there is conductive hearing loss, bone conduction will be greater or equal to air conduction; air conduction is greater in normal hearing and with sensorineural loss. In *Weber's test*, the tuning fork is held to the center of the child's forehead, and he or she is asked to tell whether the sound appears louder in one ear than the other. With conductive hearing loss, the sound will appear louder in the ear that is more impaired.

An *impedance audiometry test* may be used in cases of conductive hearing loss to assess the kind of middle-ear problem involved. A probe is tightly fitted into the ear canal and emits a steady sound; air is pumped through the probe and the miniature microphone in the probe records the changes in the sound as it bounces off the eardrum. The results, recorded on a chart called a *tympanogram*, indicate the elasticity of the eardrum, the pressure in the middle ear, and the flexibility of the middle-ear bones.

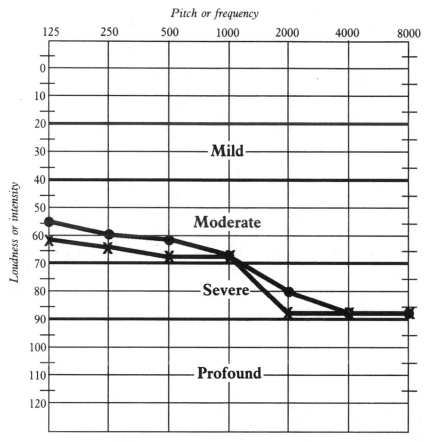

Audiogram: Hearing Loss in a Particular Child

Hearing tests that require responses from children can be inaccurate and the degree of hearing loss hard to diagnose, for a variety of reasons, as explained in *Mainstreaming Preschoolers: Children with Hearing Impairment*:

Taking Tests Is a Learned Skill

Up to ages three and four, the child may not understand what to do during the test. For example, when Jan was 2½ years old, she was diagnosed as having an average loss of 80 decibels. Later tests showed that Jan had an average loss of 72 decibels. Jan's hearing had not improved, however. She had simply learned how to take the test.

Tests May Be Inadequately Administered

Hearing screening tests are often conducted under adverse circumstances. The room may be noisy or the testing may be rushed, so a child may not do as well as he or she might. In other cases, the screening diagnosis may indicate "normal" hearing, even though the teacher or parent suspects a hearing loss.

As a teacher or parent, you should definitely request a more thorough hearing test if you have any suspicion of hearing loss in a child.

Hearing Impairment May Be Misdiagnosed

One of the most common problems is that a hearing impairment can be diagnosed as another problem. For example, Timothy is a four-year-old with an undiagnosed moderate hearing loss. Because his hearing loss had gone untreated, he had missed out on learning a lot of the words that other four-year-olds know. When he didn't understand questions asked of him on a psychological test, he either guessed or didn't respond. His test score was very low, and he was misdiagnosed as mentally retarded.

This kind of mistake doesn't happen often. But it can occur. If your observation of a child tells you something different from the information on diagnostic reports, or from what others tell you, follow it up.

Parents can use an Observation Checklist (see EAR AND HEARING PROBLEMS) to help them assess whether their child might have an undiagnosed hearing problem and need to be referred to an audiologist for hearing tests. From the child's point of view, referral is better than nonreferral. If you find out that the child does not have a handicap, no harm has been done.

heart and heart problems   Disorders affecting the fist-shaped muscular organ that continuously pumps blood throughout the body. The bulk of the heart is made up of muscle called *myocardium*, which in a healthy, well-nourished body contracts regularly, normally about 70 times a minute, providing the heart's pumping action.

Inside the heart are four chambers. The heart is divided by a vertical wall called the *septum* and each half has an upper chamber (*atrium*) and a lower one (*ventricle*). The pumping action in the four chambers is timed so as to move the blood along smoothly in the desired direction. One-way "doors" called *valves* are situated at each of the entrances and exits to the chambers to prevent blood from flowing backward.

From the lungs, blood newly freshened with oxygen pours into the heart's left atrium, by way of the *pulmonary veins*; when the valve between the two left-side chambers opens, this blood moves into the left ventricle. From there the blood, bright red and carrying its fresh oxygen, is pumped on through the body's main artery, the *aorta*, and then on into the artery network into the rest of the body. On its return from the body's tissues—having "dropped off" oxygen and picked up the waste product carbon dioxide, in the process becoming increasingly darker—the blood gathers into two large veins (the *vena cava*), which empty into the right atrium. After being transferred into the right ventricle, this blood is then pumped through the *pulmonary artery* into the lungs to receive fresh oxygen, and the process starts all over again.

In the unborn FETUS, the blood circulates differently, since lungs are not the source of oxygen. Blood carrying oxygen is received not from the lungs, but from the mother through the PLACENTA and UMBILICAL CORD to the liver and then into the lower (*inferior*) vena cava and right atrium. It is then forced through a hole in the septum into the left atrium and then into the left ventricle, from which it is pumped to the upper part of the body. (This hole in the septum, the *foramen ovale*, normally closes at birth, when the baby begins to use its lungs, but can remain open for a time in some PREMATURE babies.) On its return to the heart, blood flows into the right atrium through the upper (*superior*) vena cava and then on into the right ventricle. From there it is pumped through the pulmonary artery and into the *ductus arteriosus* (a connection that normally exists only in the fetus) and then into the lower branch of the aorta to supply the lower part of the body. Having completed its circuit, the blood (now carrying carbon dioxide and other waste products) exits through the umbilical cord to the placenta. The key role of the vena cava in circulating blood during PREGNANCY is the reason pregnant women are advised not to sleep or EXERCISE lying on their backs, since the weight of the fetus can press on the vena cava and cut off blood flow.

As such a central organ, the heart is subject to a variety of disorders. Many of them apply to adults, reflecting the wear and strain of years, but some affect young children. In particular, children often have structural or functional abnormalities in the heart at birth. Taken together, these CONGENITAL heart defects are the most common kind of BIRTH DEFECT, occurring in at least one out of every 100 live births and, by some estimates, a good many more. The causes of most heart defects are unknown, though RUBELLA is one known cause (now preventable by vaccination), and some defects accompany other birth defects and GENETIC DISORDERS, such as DOWN'S SYNDROME. Congenital heart defects are not themselves passed as part of GENETIC INHERITANCE.

Some of these congenital heart defects may disappear on their own, as the infant's body completes its development. On the other hand, some can be so severe that infants die within the first year, especially the first month. Most are not immediately life-threatening but can severely impair the child's development, since the body is receiving insufficient oxygen, and can leave the child susceptible to infection—especially *endocarditis*, infection of the heart's lining. But with modern medical advances, many more heart defects are correctible by surgical or other techniques, and the life expectancy of many such children is near normal.

Immediate symptoms of congenital heart problems are CYANOSIS ("blueness" from lack of oxygen) and breathlessness. In fact, newborns with congenital heart defects are often called *blue babies* for their characteristic cyanosis and often require emergency aid, sometimes including surgery, to correct the defect. Some defects may not be immediately apparent but may develop as the child gets older; undetected, they may cause slowed growth, thickening (*clubbing*) of fingers and toes, poorly developed muscles, and fatigue from even small amounts of exercise.

Among the main kinds of congenital heart defects are:

- *ventricular septal defect* (VSD), a hole in the septum, popularly called a "hole in the heart" (see above), the most common congenital heart defect. If this fails to close on its own, it may need to be repaired surgically, preferably in early childhood. If not detected and corrected, this could later in life lead to the *Eisenmenger complex*, in which the blood vessels of the lungs are damaged and increasingly resist blood flow, eventually reversing the blood flow back across the hole in the septum. When such damage has occurred, life expectancy is shortened to the 30s or 40s, though a heart-lung TRANSPLANT offers some hope.

- *transposition of the great vessels*, in which the pulmonary artery exits from the left (instead of the right) ventricle and the aorta from the right (instead of the left) ventricle. Unless a hole remains in the septum, by which oxygen-rich blood can be exchanged for oxygen-poor blood, a child cannot live with this malformation uncorrected. Where possible, however, surgery is delayed for a few months, to give the baby a better chance of survival.

- *coarctation of the aorta*, in which the aorta is narrowed and so cuts down the flow of blood to the the body, normally to the lower part. Surgery is generally performed to prevent complications, such as high BLOOD PRESSURE and congestive heart failure (see below).
- *patent ductus arteriosus* (PDA), in which the ductus arteriosus (see fetal heart circulation, above) fails to close at birth, a defect common in premature babies. Sometimes the artery closes off on its own as the baby develops, but if not, surgery will need to be performed.
- *pulmonary* STENOSIS, in which the pulmonary valve or sometimes the upper right ventricle is abnormally narrow, cutting blood flow to the lungs, a problem that can also occur after birth in connection with other disorders. Surgery may be required in infancy and sometimes also later in childhood.
- *tetralogy of Fallot*, a common combination of four heart defects, including a hole in the septum, misplaced aorta, pulmonary stenosis, and thickening of the right ventricle. Newborns with this combination of problems often need urgent medical help after birth, but where possible surgery is postponed until the child is somewhat older.

Once immediate, life-threatening conditions are dealt with, the doctor's main concern is to assure sufficient blood circulation to supply the brain and so prevent MENTAL RETARDATION and allow for normal growth. Various techniques are used to help the infant's body repair defects, including drugs and sometimes insertion of small inflatable balloons through CATHETERS, which can be used to widen narrow passages.

But sometimes *open-heart surgery* may need to be performed in cases of congenital heart defects, though doctors will often, if possible, delay such an operation until after the child is six months old or perhaps even three to four years old. In open-heart surgery, a machine is used to maintain blood flow in the child's body; the heart itself is drained of blood and kept very cool to avoid tissue damage while surgeons make appropriate repairs, including implantation of artificial valves where necessary.

Young people sometimes, though more rarely, experience other kinds of heart problems, including:

- *cardiomyopathy*, in which the heart muscle itself is damaged, reducing pumping ability and causing *atrial fibrillation* (irregular rapid contractions of the heart's upper chambers). In some cases this may be an inherited condition, but more often it is caused by viral infection, VITAMIN deficiency, ALCOHOL ABUSE, or an AUTOIMMUNE DISORDER. It can be somewhat controlled by drugs but gradually deteriorates, in severe cases sometimes requiring a heart transplant. (It was cardiomyopathy that, in early 1990, felled college basketball star Hank Gathers in midgame.)
- *myocarditis*, inflammation of the heart muscle, generally as a result of bacterial or viral infection, such as RHEUMATIC FEVER, but sometimes from drugs, radiation, or even parasites. Doctors recommend that exercise be limited until the inflammation subsides.

- *endocarditis*, inflammation of the heart valves from infection, a common side effect of rheumatic fever and increasingly likely with some kinds of congenital heart defects.
- *valvular heart disease*, in which the valves narrow and restrict blood flow or malfunction and allow backflow. This can occur as a congenital heart defect or as a result of some other disorder, such as rheumatic fever. The characteristic abnormal sound of the valve action is called a *heart murmur* or *cardiac murmur*.
- *cardiac arrhythmia*, disrupted rhythm of the heartbeat.
- *heart block*, uncoordinated heartbeat of the heart's chambers.
- *cor pulmonale*, failure of the right side of the heart, generally in connection with LUNG AND BREATHING PROBLEMS, such as *emphysema*.

If repairs cannot be made, if the heart is damaged before the defect is detected, or if the heart is damaged by some other disorders, *congestive heart failure* (CHF) may develop. This simply means that part of the heart becomes incapable of carrying out its normal functions. If the other parts of the heart are still functioning, life may continue, though on a carefully monitored basis with restricted diet and activity. In the long run, however, congestive heart failure places great strain on the heart and circulatory system, often with enlargement of the heart; the result is generally a somewhat shortened life span.

Pregnant women who have heart problems, either from congenital defects or later damage, need to exercise special care, since theirs will be a HIGH-RISK PREGNANCY. They may well want to consult with their doctors before considering PREGNANCY, to assess the possible risks to mother and child and, if the decision is to go ahead, to allow time to get in the best possible physical condition before CONCEPTION.

NUTRITION is vital to the health of the heart. Lack of proper nutrients can cause the heart to work less effectively, leaving the whole body functioning at a sub-par level. It is also important to avoid harmful substances, such as FATS and especially CHOLESTEROL, which can build up in the body's arteries and lead to heart disease later in life. Recent research has shown that even young children begin to show signs of narrowed arteries from cholesterol build-up, so parents will do their children a favor by avoiding fatty and cholesterol-rich foods in the family's diet.

Among the medical tests used in diagnosing heart disorders are the ELECTROENCEPHALOGRAPH and *electrocardiography* (see ULTRASOUND).

For help and further information

American Heart Association (AHA)
7320 Greenville Avenue
Dallas, TX 75231
214-750-5300 (see telephone-directory white pages for local number)
Organization of health professionals, affected individuals and families, and others interested in heart disease. Provides information and educates public; offers services to heart patients

and their families; encourages mutual-support groups; publishes many print and audiovisual materials, including *E Is for Exercise* and *High Blood Pressure*.

Council on Cardiovascular Disease in the Young
American Heart Association National Center
7320 Greenville Avenue
Dallas, TX 75231
214-373-6300
Dudley Hafner, Executive Director
Organization concerned with cardiovascular disease in children. Seeks to educate public and encourages research; publishes various materials, including *Safeguarding Your Health During Pregnancy, Feeding Infants with Congenital Heart Disease, If Your Child Has a Congenital Heart Defect, Abnormalities of Heart Rhythm—A Guide for Parents, Your Child and Rheumatic Fever*, and *Innocent Heart Murmurs*.

Mended Hearts (MH)
c/o American Heart Association
7320 Greenville Avenue
Dallas, TX 75231
214-750-5442
Mutual-support organization for people with heart problems. Provides information and referrals; publishes quarterly *Heartbeat*.

National Heart, Lung, and Blood Institute
National Institutes of Health
9000 Rockville Pike
Building 31, Room 4A21
Bethesda, MD 20892
301-496-4236
Federal arm, one of National Institutes of Health, dedicated to research and dissemination of information about cardiovascular disease, including heart problems, blood vessel disease, and hypertension or high blood pressure. Publishes many materials, including *Exercise and Your Heart, A Handbook of Heart Terms, Heart Attacks: Medicine for the Layman*, and fact sheets on specific topics, such as *Arteriosclerosis, Diabetes and Cardiovascular Disease*, and *Venous Thrombosis and Pulmonary Embolism*.

March of Dimes Birth Defects Foundation, 914-428-7100; local chapters in telephone-directory white pages. Publishes fact sheet *Congenital Heart Defects*. (For full group information, see BIRTH DEFECTS; GENETIC DISORDERS.)

Other reference sources
A Parent's Guide to Heart Disorders, by James H. Moller, M.D., William A. Neal, M.D., and William Hoffman. Minneapolis: University of Minnesota Press, 1988.
Living with Heart Disease, by Steve Parker. New York: Watts, 1989.
Taking Heart, by A.C. Greene. New York: Simon & Schuster, 1990. On undergoing a heart transplant operation.

Take Care of Your Heart: The Complete Book of Heart Facts, by Ezra A. Amsterdam, M.D., and Ann M. Holmes. New York: Facts on File, 1984.
Cardiovascular Disease, by Wrynn Smith, Ph.D. New York: Facts on File, 1987.
Health Care U.S.A., by Jean Carper. New York: Prentice Hall, 1987. Resource for general and specific health-care information, as for various kinds of heart problems and related cardiovascular ailments, such as high blood pressure and stroke; lists key cardiologists, major heart transplant centers, cardiovascular research and treatment centers, cerebrovascular research and treatment centers, and other information.
Heart Care, by American Medical Association. New York: Random House, 1982.
The Heartbook, by American Heart Association. New York: Dutton, 1980.
Boston University Medical Center's Heart Risk Book: A Practical Guide to Preventing Heart Disease, by Aram V. Chobanian, M.D. New York: Bantam, 1982.
Cardiac Rehabilitation for the Patient and Family, by Judy A. David. Reston, VA: Reston, 1980.
The Heart and the Blood, revised edition, by Steve Parker. New York: Watts, 1989. For grades 4 to 7.

heat rash (prickly heat) A type of RASH associated with local irritation from perspiration; in babies it is often found in the diaper area and folds of the skin, and generally responds to loose clothing and exposure to air. (See DIAPER RASH.)

Hegge-Kirk-Kirk method An approach to teaching READING that stresses use of PHONICS, with extensive drill and practice.

Heimlich maneuver (hug) A procedure to use in cases of CHOKING, when a person's air passages are obstructed by food or a foreign object. Standing behind the choking person, the rescuer makes a fist, with thumb side up but thumb tucked in; wraps the other hand around it, placing the fist in the choking person's abdomen, just above the navel and below the rib cage; and makes a quick thrust upward and inward, attempting to use air from below to push the obstruction out of the throat. If the maneuver fails after several tries, an emergency TRACHEOSTOMY may be required to restore breathing before the person suffocates. (See CHOKING for an illustration of the Heimlich maneuver with young children.)

helpline A telephone number that can be called for information, counseling, or referrals, often staffed by trained counselors. Unlike HOTLINES, which are designed more for real emergency situations and are often staffed 24 hours a day, helplines generally have more limited hours, such as standard business hours. Many helplines do, however, have toll-free (800) numbers that people can use to call long distance. (For those in this book, see HOTLINES, HELPLINES, AND HELPING ORGANIZATIONS, on page 601, or look under specific topics.)

hemangioma   General name for a variety of discolorations on the skin of newly born infants, sometimes called *birthmarks*. These are a form of NEVUS (skin blemish) caused by an abnormal mass of blood vessels, sometimes called a *vascular nevus*. The most common hemangiomas are:

* *stork bites*, small, flat marks on the back of the neck and sometimes elsewhere as well in newborns. These marks generally disappear harmlessly in early childhood; they are a localized form of TELANGIECTASIA.
* *strawberry marks*, raised, bright red marks (but sometimes blue if fed by a vein) that are essentially benign blood-filled TUMORS, sometimes called *capillary hemangiomas*. They grow quickly in the first few months of life and often disappear on their own by the time the child is of school age. They normally require attention only in cases of trauma and bleeding.
* *port-wine stains*, large, flat, purplish-red marks, though sometimes pale red, often on the back of the head but also elsewhere on the body, that are present at birth and permanent; also called *nevus flammeus*. No technique has yet been successful in removing such "stains," but some hold future promise. In rare instances, the port-wine stain on the face is associated with STURGE-WEBER SYNDROME, which involves brain abnormalities, including MENTAL RETARDATION.

Though birthmarks are not generally dangerous, for safety parents should closely examine and take notes on the size, location, and color of any markings on the skin of a young child and then check them periodically. Any changes or problems, such as darkening, growing, bleeding, or appearance of new marks, should be noted and reported to the doctor immediately, to be sure no CANCER is developing.

For help and further information

National Congenital Port Wine Stain Foundation
125 East 63rd Street
New York, NY 10021
212-755-3820
Martha Woodhouse, Executive Director
Organization for people concerned with port-wine stains. Provides information. (See also SKIN DISORDERS.)

hematemesis   VOMITING of blood from the stomach, a sign of serious DIGESTIVE DISORDERS or of possible child abuse, resulting from internal injuries (see CHILD ABUSE AND NEGLECT).

hematological test   A type of BLOOD TEST.

hematoma   A swelling resulting from blood collecting in a restricted space, such as under the skull or skin; often found among victims of child abuse (see CHILD ABUSE AND NEGLECT). A *subdural hematoma* is blood collected between the brain's covering membrane and the spinal cord, as may be caused by accidental injury or by some types of child abuse, including violent shaking or a blow to the head. In some locations, especially in the head, the clot that forms can cause severe brain damage or

be fatal. It can, however, sometimes be located by a CT or MRI SCAN and removed.

hemiplegia   PARALYSIS affecting one half of the body, as from a BRAIN TUMOR or CEREBRAL PALSY.

hemodialysis   A form of DIALYSIS using an artificial machine to replace the kidney's functions.

hemoglobin   Oxygen-carrying pigment in red blood cells. (See ANEMIA; BLOOD AND BLOOD DISORDERS.)

hemolysis   Medical term for the bursting or self-destruction of red blood cells, as in some cases of RH INCOMPATIBILITY. (See also BLOOD AND BLOOD DISORDERS.)

hemolytic disease of the newborn   A serious type of ANEMIA that results in a newborn in cases of RH INCOMPATIBILITY between the baby and its mother.

hemophilia   A group of disorders in which the blood fails to clot properly, usually because of deficiency or total lack of one or more enzymes, called *coagulation factors*, needed for proper clotting. These are called *bleeding disorders*, because the dominant characteristic is that blood fails to clot and so keeps on flowing, from external cuts as well as internally, with blood often gathering painfully in the knee and elbow joints. The disorders are identified as a result of various BLOOD TESTS, such as *prothrombin time*.

Some types of hemophilia are inherited and are identified by the missing coagulation factor. Classic hemophilia, called *hemophilia A*, is caused by a deficiency in factor VIII, or *antihemophiliac globulin* (AHG); whereas *hemophilia B* (also called *Christmas disease*) is due to a shortage of factor IX, or *plasma thromboplastin component*; and *hemophilia C*, or *Rosenthal's syndrome*, results from lack of factor XI, or *plasma thromboplastin antecedent*. These forms are GENETIC DISORDERS of the X-LINKED type, meaning that they generally affect males. By contrast, *von Willebrand's disease*, also missing factor VIII, is a genetic disorder that affects males and females equally. Prospective parents, women as well as men, with a family history of hemophilia may want to seek GENETIC COUNSELING to assess the risk of having a child with the disorder.

Some other types of hemophilia may result from other causes, including:

* DIGESTIVE DISORDERS, especially those that affect absorption of VITAMIN K, important in clotting;
* effects of various medications;
* *thrombocytopenia*, a deficiency in *platelets* (*thrombocytes*), blood cells important in clotting, which can result from LEUKEMIA;
* conditions that affect the blood vessels, such as SCURVY (vitamin C deficiency).

The underlying cause of hemophilia is treated where possible. Beyond that, the main treatment is to supply the patient with the missing factor or platelets, though this carries the risk of infection, as with other BLOOD TRANSFUSIONS.

For help and further information

National Hemophilia Foundation (NHF)
Soho Building
110 Greene Street, Suite 406
New York, NY 10012
212-219-8180
Alan P. Brownstein, Executive Director
Organization concerned with individuals who have hemophilia and related bleeding disorders. Provides support for patient and families; serves as information clearinghouse on hemophilia for public and professionals; acts as advocate for increased social services; supports research; publishes various materials, including quarterly *Hemophilia Newsnotes*, directories of treatment centers and summer camps for hemophiliacs, and pamphlets such as *What You Should Know About Hemophilia, Comprehensive Care for the Person with Hemophilia*, and *Control of Pain in Hemophilia*.

World Federation of Hemophilia
Suite 902
1155 Dorchester Boulevard, West
Montreal, Quebec H3B 2L3, Canada
514-933-7944
International organization that provides information, including special advice to hemophiliac travelers. Publishes *Passport*, guide to world's hemophilia treatment centers.

National Heart, Lung, and Blood Institute (NHLBI), 301-496-4236. For full group information, see BLOOD AND BLOOD DISORDERS.

(See also BLOOD TRANSFUSIONS.)

Other reference sources

Health Care U.S.A., by Jean Carper. New York: Prentice Hall, 1987. Resource for general and specific health-care information; lists major hemophilia treatment and research centers and other information.
Journey, by Robert Massie and Suzanne Massie. New York: Warner, 1976.
Living with Hemophilia, by Peter Jones. Philadelphia: David Co., 1974.
Go Toward the Light, by Chris Oyler, with Laurie Becklund and Beth Polson. New York: Harper & Row, 1988. On children with hemophilia who contracted AIDS.

hemoptysis   Coughing or spitting of blood from the lungs or respiratory tract; often found among victims of child abuse, as a result of internal injuries (see CHILD ABUSE AND NEGLECT).

hemorrhage   Bleeding from the blood vessels, often as the result of an accident or disease, such as HEMOPHILIA, but also an indicator of possible CHILD ABUSE AND NEGLECT. Bleeding under the skin is called a BRUISE or *intradermal hemorrhage*; very small bruises are called *petechiae*, small ones or groups of petechiae are *purpura*, and a larger bruise (over one centimeter) is an

ecchymosis. Severe hemorrhage is one of the main hazards facing women after a HIGH-RISK PREGNANCY and a difficult CHILDBIRTH. Treatment focuses primarily on stopping the bleeding, whether by repairing a wound or operating to stop internal bleeding, and on replacing lost blood.

hepatitis   Inflammation of the liver, often signaled by JAUNDICE; it can be either acute—short and limited, though perhaps severe—or chronic, sometimes leading to CIRRHOSIS OF THE LIVER, liver failure, and DEATH. Acute hepatitis is often caused by one of several viruses, for some of which vaccines now exist. *Type A viral hepatitis (infectious* or *epidemic hepatitis)* is relatively mild and primarily preventable by good hygiene, being passed largely through direct contact with infected people or contaminated food and water. Young people who contract type A hepatitis generally recover fully and are thereafter immune. *Type B viral hepatitis (serum hepatitis)* is more serious, often becoming chronic and involving increased risk of liver CANCER; sometimes the symptoms initially are not severe, and the disease is not recognized until liver damage has occurred. The type B hepatitis virus is spread by contact with infected blood, saliva, semen, and other body fluids, as through blood transfusions, shared intravenous drug or ear-piercing needles, and sex. Not everyone exposed to the virus contracts hepatitis; many people carry the type B hepatitis virus without even knowing it. Babies are at risk of catching type B hepatitis if their mothers are CARRIERS; while mostly protected in the UTERUS, babies are exposed to the virus during birth and through later contact, especially BREASTFEEDING. Many such cases of *neonatal hepatitis* can be prevented by administration of hepatitis B immune globulin and hepatitis B vaccine quickly after birth. Pregnant women at high risk for exposure to the virus, such as health-care workers, are advised to have screening for the type B virus. Less is known about other types of hepatitis, once called *non-A, non-B hepatitis*, now labeled *Type C viral hepatitis*. Hepatitis—acute or chronic—can also result from damage to the liver by some drugs, chemicals, or poisons, from certain GENETIC DISORDERS such as WILSON'S DISEASE, or from disorder in the body's IMMUNE SYSTEM. (For help and further information, see LIVER PROBLEMS.)

hepatologist   A medical PHYSICIAN who specializes in treating LIVER PROBLEMS.

hepatoportoenterostomy (Kasai procedure)   A surgical procedure for correcting malfunctioning of the liver's bile ducts in some cases of BILIARY ATRESIA.

herpes simplex   Infections caused by one of the two forms of *herpes simplex virus (HSV)*, producing sores generally on the mouth or genital area, the latter being a form of SEXUALLY TRANSMITTED DISEASE.

HSV type 1 often causes *oral herpes*, resulting in "fever blisters" or "cold sores" around the mouth. But HSV type 1, as well as HSV type 2, can also affect the genital area and other parts of the body that might come into contact with the genitals or mouth of an infected person. The National Institute of Allergy and Infectious Diseases (NIAID) says: "It is unlikely that the virus can be spread by contact with an object such as a toilet seat."

Within two to 10 days of contact with an infected person, small, red bumps often appear around the nose, mouth, and GENITALS, over several days developing into blisters or open sores (*lesions*), which then crust over and heal. This *primary* episode lasts about two to three weeks and is sometimes accompanied by flulike symptoms, such as FEVER, headache, muscle aches, painful urination, and swollen glands. After the infection, the virus lies dormant in the body, and is thought not to be contagious in this state. But occasionally the virus is reactivated (precisely when and why is unclear), affecting the same area as the original sores, but generally in a milder form; such recurrences are sometimes signaled by tingling in the genitals or pain in the buttocks or legs (medically termed *prodromal symptoms*). During these recurrences, the activated virus can be spread to others.

If genital herpes is active in a woman giving birth, the child can be infected, with extremely severe results, including BLIND-NESS, brain damage, or even DEATH. Many doctors recommend that pregnant women carrying the virus be tested each week in the latter stages of PREGNANCY and that if any question exists as to whether the virus might be active, a CESAREAN SECTION should be used to protect the baby. In addition, a woman who is infected during pregnancy faces increased risk of MISCARRIAGE, PREMATURE delivery, and infection of the FETUS, possibly with resulting BIRTH DEFECTS. Herpes simplex can also have serious effects in some people with weakened IMMUNE SYSTEMS, such as those with AIDS or LEUKEMIA.

To keep from spreading an active infection, the NIAID recommends:

- Keep the infected area clean and dry to prevent the development of secondary infections.
- Try to avoid touching the sores directly, and if unavoidable, wash hands afterward.
- Avoid sexual contact from the first recognized symptoms until the sores are completely healed.

Herpes simplex sores are visible, but doctors need a variety of laboratory tests to tell if they are caused by an HSV or something else. No cure yet exists, but the drug acyclovir has been used in ointment form to treat initial outbreaks and experimentally to "speed healing and limit the severity of a herpes outbreak" in an oral form. (For information on how to avoid infection, see SEXUALLY TRANSMITTED DISEASES.)

A different virus, *varicella-zoster virus* (VZV), causes CHICKEN POX and (sometimes later in life) shingles, medically termed *herpes zoster*. Also in the herpes family is the cytomegalovirus (see CYTOMEGALOVIRUS INFECTION).

For help and further information
Herpes Resource Center (HRC)
Box 100

Palo Alto, CA 94302
415-328-7710
Alice Robinson, Associate Director
Organization of and for people with genital herpes. Provides support and encourages formation of local chapters; affiliated with American Social Health Association (see below).

National Institute of Allergy and Infectious Diseases (NIAID), 301-496-5717. Publishes brochures *Genital Herpes* and *Sexually Transmitted Diseases*. (For full group information, see ALLERGY.)

American Social Health Association (ASHA), 415-321-5134; toll-free VD national hotline, U.S. except CA 800-227-8922; CA 800-982-5883. (For full group information, see SEXUALLY TRANSMITTED DISEASES.)

Other reference source
Herpes, by Alan E. Nourse. New York: Watts, 1985.

heterogeneous grouping   A class that includes students of a wide range of achievement and ability, as opposed to the *homogeneous groups* found in a TRACKING system.

heterologous insemination   Alternate name for ARTIFICIAL INSEMINATION using SEMEN from a donor.

heterozygote   In GENETIC INHERITANCE, a person carrying two different forms of a particular gene in a chromosome pair.

heuristic learning   Alternate term for a LEARNING STYLE focusing on student discovery of rules and conclusions from given materials, with emphasis on independent problem-solving.

Hib   Abbreviation for HAEMOPHILUS INFLUENZAE TYPE B DISEASE.

Hib vaccine   Abbreviation for HAEMOPHILUS INFLUENZAE TYPE B CONJUGATE VACCINE.

high blood pressure   See BLOOD PRESSURE.

higher education   Programs offering academic education beyond the HIGH SCHOOL level, normally referring to programs at two- or four-year COLLEGES or universities, graduate schools, and professional schools, that are designed to lead to a further degree, such as an ASSOCIATE, BACHELOR'S, MASTER'S, or DOCTORAL DEGREE. The phrase *higher education* does not usually apply to PROPRIETARY SCHOOLS focusing on occupational and technical fields and not offering advanced degrees.

high-risk babies   Infants who have an increased risk of dying or developing diseases or disorders, especially during the *neonatal period*, the first month of life; also called *special babies*. Among these are babies of LOW BIRTH WEIGHT or low GESTATIONAL AGE because of PREMATURE delivery and those considered high-risk because of signs observed by the medical staff or information from POSTNATAL TESTS. If medical problems are recognized before mother and child go home, the baby may need to remain

---

Special Care for Special Babies

Each new baby is unique. All newborns need love, attention, and care. Some will need medical attention as well.

If your baby is premature (early), very small, or has another medical problem, your baby may need special medical care and you may not be able to bring him or her home from the hospital as soon as you expected. You and your family may be faced with disappointment and worry at a time usually reserved for great joy. It is normal to be upset and confused. Sharing your feelings with your partner, family, or friends may help deal with your and your partner's pain and problems.

The hospital may have a separate nursery for babies who need special care. This nursery may be called a "Neonatal Intensive Care Unit" (NICU) or a "High Risk Nursery." These nurseries have a specially trained health-care team to help your baby. They are there to help you and your family through this hard time as well. These tips may help you:

- Ask if there is a social worker to help you and your family with your questions and concerns. This person can be your "contact point" each time you have a question.
- If you don't understand something that is happening, or are confused about what you have been told, *ask* your doctor, social worker, nurse, or someone else on the health-care team. It might help if you keep a small notebook with you and write down questions when you think of them. When you are at the hospital, you can write down the answers and read them again later.
- Most nurseries will let you visit 24 hours a day. You and your partner should be there often to touch and hold your baby. This contact will help your baby and you become a famliy.
- You may still be able to provide your breastmilk for your baby. Be sure to discuss this with your doctor as early as possible.
- There may be meetings of parents like you ("support groups") where you can discuss your problems and feelings. There may be other sources of help in your community as well. Ask the hospital social worker about resources that may be helpful for you and your partner.
- When you take your baby home, he or she may need special kinds of care. Be sure to get clear written instructions from the hospital staff before you leave. You and your partner or another family member, if possible, should be there, so that you both know what you should do. If you think that you may need help at home caring for your baby, ask the hospital social worker about sources of assistance.

What to ask your doctor or nurses

Don't be afraid to ask about anything you want to know. Your baby's doctor and the nursing staff are there to help you, and if you don't ask about caring for your baby, they may think you already know. If you forget something they said, or don't understand, *ask again*. Keep asking questions until you understand. The kind of advice you get will depend upon how much you tell them you want to understand and learn. Remember:

- Think about all the questions you have about your baby and those things you want to learn.
- Make a list of questions if you want. You may want to write down the answers, too.
- Ask your doctor or nurse to explain anything you don't understand.
- Ask them to explain any medical terms you don't know.
- If they give you advice that sounds hard to follow, keep asking questions to find out what they really mean, to help you follow their advice.

Source: *Infant Care* (1989). Prepared for the Public Health Service by the Health and Resources Administration, Bureau of Maternal and Child Health and Resources Development.

---

in the hospital, often in a NEONATAL INTENSIVE CARE UNIT (NICU), also called a *high-risk nursery*, equipped with the special equipment and trained staff necessary for proper medical care. Then parents will need to make special arrangements to stay close to their baby, for BONDING in a child's early life is important (see SPECIAL CARE FOR SPECIAL BABIES, above).

For help and further information

National Institute of Child Health and Human Development (NICHD), 301-496-5133. (For full group information, see PREGNANCY.)

(See also MORBIDITY; INFANT MORTALITY; DEATH.)

high-risk nursery   Alternate term for NEONATAL INTENSIVE CARE UNIT.

high-risk pregnancy   A PREGNANCY in which there is an increased likelihood of complications developing because of the presence of various RISK FACTORS in the woman or her life situation. Most women with high-risk pregnancies will, with proper PRENATAL CARE, go on to bear healthy, FULL-TERM babies without difficulties; the label simply means that they are somewhat more likely than normal to have problems during pregnancy or CHILDBIRTH and so should exercise due caution. A woman with a high-risk pregnancy will be well advised, for example, to have her child in a well-equipped HOSPITAL (Level II or III), rather than considering a community hospital, MATERNITY CENTER, or

HOME BIRTH. Among the factors that increase risk during a pregnancy are:

- ADOLESCENT PREGNANCY, in which a girl is bearing a child before her own body has fully matured. (See separate entry on ADOLESCENT PREGNANCY.)
- *age over 35 years*, which carries a greater risk of BIRTH DEFECTS, especially CHROMOSOMAL ABNORMALITIES, such as DOWN'S SYNDROME, and for complications such as high blood pressure (*hypertension*), DIABETES MELLITUS, and AUTOIMMUNE DISORDERS. Older women also have an increased chance of having twins or triplets, themselves a risk factor.
- *too little time between pregnancies*, especially CONCEPTION within three months of a previous delivery, before the woman's body has fully recovered. If the woman is still BREASTFEEDING a previous child, she is generally advised to wean the infant as soon as possible, to see that the FETUS gets all necessary NUTRITION.
- *use of* CONTRACEPTION *at the time of* CONCEPTION, some forms of which may cause BIRTH DEFECTS, including INTRAUTERINE DEVICES and possibly SPERMICIDES and BIRTH-CONTROL PILLS, though scientific studies are so far unclear.
- MULTIPLE BIRTHS, both because of highly increased NUTRITION needs and the strain on the mother's body. (See separate entry on MULTIPLE BIRTHS.)
- *maternal–fetal blood-group incompatibility*, especially problems with RH INCOMPATIBILITY, which can cause severe BLOOD DISORDERS in newborns.
- *DES daughters*, women whose mothers took the medication *diethylstilbestrol* between 1946 and 1970 during their own pregnancies. (See separate entry on DES.)
- *previous delivery of a* PREMATURE *baby*, though prenatal care can focus on lowering the risk of premature delivery by stressing proper nutrition, avoidance of alcohol, smoking, and drugs, and change of work patterns and by teaching women to recognize and stop premature CONTRACTIONS if they occur.

Numerous diseases and conditions in the mother can also increase risk in a pregnancy, affecting fetal development or putting the woman herself in poorer medical condition. Among these are hypertension, EPILEPSY, ASTHMA, LUPUS, thrombocytopenia (see BLOOD AND BLOOD DISORDERS), diabetes mellitus, MULTIPLE SCLEROSIS, heart problems, HERPES SIMPLEX, and HEPATITIS. (For help and further information, see specific topics noted above; see also PREGNANCY; CHILDBIRTH.)

Other reference sources

Intensive Caring: New Hope for High-Risk Pregnancy, by Dianne Hales and Timothy R.B. Johnson, M.D. New York: Brown, 1990.

How to Prevent Miscarriages and Other Crises of Pregnancy, by Stefan Semchyshyn, M.D. New York: Macmillan, 1989.

New Hope for Problem Pregnancies: Helping Babies Before They're Born, by Dianne Hales and Robert K. Creasy, M.D. New York: Harper & Row, 1982.

Safe Delivery: Protecting Your Baby During High-Risk Pregnancy, by Roger K. Freeman and Susan C. Pescar. New York: Facts on File, 1982.

high school (secondary school) An institution providing EDUCATION to students after MIDDLE SCHOOL or directly after ELEMENTARY SCHOOL; sometimes used to refer only to grades 9 to 12, with grades 7 and 8 considered *junior high school* or *early secondary school*. In high school, students generally have a homeroom to which they report at the beginning and ending of each day for ATTENDANCE checking and school announcements. But, unlike elementary school, they then generally change classrooms and teachers with every subject. During the high school years, most students pass the age of COMPULSORY ATTENDANCE, so the schools have a major challenge in preventing student DROPOUTS.

Americans have traditionally resisted any attempts at formulating a national CURRICULUM for elementary and secondary schools, but in recent decades concern over the decline of some basic educational skills among students has led many to view the idea more favorably. Though no national agreement yet exists on what specific matter should be covered in the various grades, the U.S. Department of Education, in its 1983 report, *A Nation at Risk*, recommended this basic high school curriculum:

- *four years of English*, emphasizing literary heritage and requiring students to understand, discuss, and write effectively about what they have read.
- *three years of mathematics* courses that include an understanding of algebra, geometry, probability, and statistics, and that teach students to apply math to everyday problems.
- *three years of science* that cover the major concepts and methods of the physical and biological sciences along with their applications to everyday life.
- *three years of social studies* that explain world economic and political systems, the differences between free and repressive societies, and "the broad sweep of ancient and contemporary ideas that have shaped our world."
- *one-half year of computer science*.
- *two years of foreign-language study* for all college-bound students.

The Department of Education also formulated a more detailed model curriculum for secondary schools, in JAMES MADISON HIGH SCHOOL: A MODEL CURRICULUM (on page 538). Most students, of course, take a far less demanding set of courses in high school, especially those who are not college-bound.

High schools vary widely, depending on their location—inner city, suburban, or rural, for example—and on their purpose. While most students have traditionally simply attended their neighborhood or district high school, some areas, especially those with heavy populations, are increasingly offering choices to parents and students, including MAGNET SCHOOLS, VOCATIONAL SCHOOLS, or ALTERNATIVE SCHOOLS. The Department of Education urges parents and students to exercise choice in education, not simply by selecting the area in which to live. For their advice to parents on finding the right school for their child, see CHOOSING A SCHOOL FOR YOUR CHILD, which includes a checklist for evaluating schools, on page 514. Specially oriented public schools—any school beyond the neighborhood public school—are called SCHOOLS OF CHOICE. Many parents choose to educate their children outside the public school system altogether, as in a PRIVATE SCHOOL or through HOME SCHOOLING. (For help and further information, see EDUCATION.)

Other reference sources

Ending the Homework Hassle: How to Help Your Child Succeed Independently in School, by John Rosemond. Kansas City, MO: Andrews and McMeel, 1990.

Countdown to College: A Student's Guide to Getting the Most Out of High School, by Zola Dincin Schneider and Phyllis B. Kalb. New York: College Board, 1989.

MegaSkills: How Families Can Help Children Succeed in School and Beyond, by Dorothy Rich. Boston: Houghton Mifflin, 1988.

Small Victories: The Real World of a Teacher, Her Students and Their High School, by Samuel G. Freedman. New York: Harper & Row, 1990.

Public and Private High Schools: The Impact of Communities, by James S. Coleman and Thomas S. Hoffer. New York: Basic, 1987.

The College Board Guide to High Schools. New York: College Board, 1990. Directory of over 25,000 public and private high schools.

high school equivalency Popular name for the GENERAL EQUIVALENCY DIPLOMA (GED).

hip The ball-and-socket joint between the pelvis and the thigh bone (*femur*), abnormally formed in newborns who have CONGENITAL DISLOCATION OF THE HIP.

hirsutism A condition of having excessive amounts of coarse body hair growing in a masculine pattern, especially in a woman; also called *hypertrichosis*. Hirsutism can occur as a result of levels of male HORMONES, medication, disease or disorder (such as *porphyria, adrenal hyperplasia*, or *polycystic ovary syndrome*), or BIRTH DEFECTS such as those giving rise to DE LANGE SYNDROME. Hair can be removed in a variety of ways, such as electrolysis or rubbing with pumice, or can be bleached.

For help and further information

National Institute of Arthritis and Musculoskeletal and Skin Diseases (NIAMS), 301-496-8188. (For full group information, see ARTHRITIS; MUSCULAR DYSTROPHY.)

histocompatibility testing The medical technique used in attempting to match organs and tissue for use in TRANSPLANTS; also called *tissue typing*. (For help and further information, see IMMUNE SYSTEM.)

histrionic personality disorder A type of PERSONALITY DISORDER.

HMD Abbreviation for hyaline membrane disease, an alternate term for RESPIRATORY DISTRESS SYNDROME.

HMO Abbreviation for HEALTH MAINTENANCE ORGANIZATION.

hold back Informal alternate term for RETENTION, in which a student is required to remain in a GRADE for another year, rather than being promoted to the next.

home birth DELIVERY of a baby in the home, under the care of a midwife, rather than in a HOSPITAL. Partly in reaction to traditional hospital deliveries, seen as cold, invasive, and impersonal, some people have chosen to deliver their babies at home, often with a CERTIFIED NURSE-MIDWIFE in attendance. The main hazards here are loss of time in getting to a hospital if complications arise and the possibility of infection, since the setting cannot be made as antiseptic as a hospital's DELIVERY ROOM or a MATERNITY CENTER'S BIRTHING ROOM would be. People considering home birth should be even more careful than usual about PRENATAL CARE and checkups, since any complication could be disastrous. They should also make very careful arrangements for obtaining backup medical care, should emergencies arise. (For help and further information, see PREGNANCY; CHILDBIRTH; CERTIFIED NURSE-MIDWIFE.)

homebound student A school-age child who is confined to home and so must be taught by a VISITING TEACHER, or *itinerant teacher*, sometimes linked with a classroom by means of telephone or television; often a severely HANDICAPPED child or one with severe MENTAL RETARDATION.

home medical tests Simple, generally inexpensive MEDICAL TESTS designed for people to perform themselves at home. While most medical tests and procedures require special equipment and training, an increasing number of tests are being developed for home use. In the Food and Drug Administration's *Do-It-Yourself Medical Testing*, Dixie Farley noted that the three main categories of self-testing products are:

1. tests that help diagnose a specific condition or disease in people with symptoms, such as PREGNANCY TEST kits to be used after a menstrual period is missed;

2. SCREENING tests that identify indications of disease in people without symptoms;

3. doctor-recommended monitoring devices that provide ongoing checkups on an existing disease or condition—BLOOD GLUCOSE MONITORING by diabetics, for instance. Many of these tests analyze urine, blood, or other fluid or tissue samples taken from the body.

Self-tests allow people to get a much more detailed picture of their body's functioning. Using a self-test, for example, a

Cautions in Using Home Medical Tests

To promote self-testing safety and effectiveness, here are some general precautions (all precautions do not necessarily apply to all tests):

- For test kits that contain chemicals, note the expiration date. Beyond that date, chemicals may lose potency and affect results. Don't buy or use a test kit if the date is past.
- Consider whether the product needs protection from heat or cold. If so, don't leave it in the car trunk or by a sunny window on the trip home. At home, follow storage directions.
- Study the package insert. First read it through to get a general idea of what the test is about. Then go back and study the instructions and pictures until you fully understand each step.
- If something isn't clear, don't guess. Consult a pharmacist or other health professional. Or check the insert for a toll-free ''800'' number to call.
- Learn what the test is *intended* to do and what its limitations are. Remember: The tests are not 100-percent accurate.
- If color is part of the test and you're color blind, be sure someone who *can* discern color interprets the results.
- Note special precautions, such as avoiding physical activity or certain foods and drugs before testing.
- Follow instructions exactly, including the specimen collection process if that is a part of the test. Sequence is important. Don't skip a step. If a step to validate the test or calibrate an instrument is included, do it.
- When collecting a urine specimen—unless you use a container from a kit—wash the container thoroughly and rinse out all soap traces, preferably with distilled water, which is generally purer than tap or other bottled water.
- When a step is timed, be precise. Use a stopwatch or at least a watch with a second hand.
- Note what you should do if the results are positive, negative, or unclear. Keep accurate records of results.
- As with medications, keep test kits that contain chemicals out of the reach of children. Promptly discard used test materials as directed.

Any malfunction of a self-test should be reported to the manufacturer or to the FDA through the agency's reporting system at the U.S. Pharmacopeia. To report a problem to the pharmacopeia, write to: USP, Problem Reporting Program, 12601 Twinbrook Parkway, Rockville, MD 20852, Attn: Dr. Joseph G. Valentino. Another reporting option, especially in an emergency, is to call the nearest FDA district office listed in the telephone directory. Describe the product completely, stating the product name, type, and—as appropriate—serial and lot numbers, dosage strength, and expiration date. Explain all details of the problem, including the date it occurred.

Source: *Do-It-Yourself Medical Testing*, by Dixie Farley (1989). Prepared for the Public Health Service, Food and Drug Administration.

---

woman can pinpoint her time of OVULATION, important information if she is being treated for INFERTILITY. And monitoring of blood glucose has allowed people with DIABETES MELLITUS to live much healthier, more normal lives.

It is important, however, to note what self-tests can and cannot do. No self-test can tell you definitively that you have a disease or that you are free from the disease. No test is 100-percent accurate and reliable. But more to the point, self-test does not mean *self-diagnosis*. As Farley points out:

... considering the results of one test to be a diagnosis is risky. ... The fact is, a diagnosis by a physician involves an evaluation of the patient's medical history, a physical examination, most likely other tests, and sometimes consultation with other medical experts. And even a carefully gathered patient profile is subject to error.

With self-tests, error may be compounded precisely because the test is being performed by people untrained in either testing or interpretation and in conditions not specifically designed for scientific testing. As Farley continues: "The inexperienced, untrained user may misinterpret results, a mistake that can be compounded by the fact that no test is 100 percent accurate

even under the best conditions and that results can differ from brand to brand." This is especially true of tests that were originally designed for use only by medical professionals but that individuals have purchased from medical supply firms. Such tests may indeed be useful but generally only when used under a doctor's guidance.

An additional concern about self-tests is that individuals may not seek medical advice when they should—that is, when there are symptoms. For example, if a menstrual period is overdue, a home pregnancy test is not the only step that should be taken. The missed period may be due to a TUMOR or other condition that should be diagnosed and treated quickly, not ignored if the pregnancy test is negative. The greatest value of a pregnancy self-test in that situation is that a woman may go to her doctor early in the first TRIMESTER, and so she and her baby may get the maximum benefit of PRENATAL CARE.

Home medical tests hold great promise for the future, allowing individuals to have better information and therefore more meaningful control of their own health and that of their children. In the meantime, while self-tests are still relatively new, people using them should keep in mind the cautions below. Among the home medical tests discussed in this book are blood glucose monitoring, OVULATION monitoring, and pregnancy. (For help and further information, see MEDICAL TESTS.)

home monitor   General term for electronic devices used in the home to check the breathing and/or heartbeat of a child susceptible to SLEEP APNEA or considered to be AT-RISK for SUDDEN INFANT DEATH SYNDROME (SIDS); most commonly some type of CARDIAC MONITOR or *cardiorespiratory monitor*. In late 1990, the Food and Drug Administration gave approval to the first FETAL MONITORING device intended for home use. The aim of cardiac or cardiorespiratory monitors is to alert parents or CAREGIVERS to problems so that they can attempt to relieve the problems before the brain and other organs are damaged. While home monitors are clearly useful in some situations, as among infants who have already experienced an APPARENT LIFE-THREATENING EVENT (ALTE), evidence is less clear or simply unavailable about their usefulness among other infants.

Home monitors are not wholly reliable, sometimes giving a FALSE POSITIVE (indicating a problem where none exists) or a FALSE NEGATIVE (failing to signal that a problem does exist). The Public Health Service's report on *Infantile Apnea and Home Monitoring* (1986) defines these as the essential features of an infant cardiorespiratory monitor:

> Primary among these [essential criteria] is the ability to recognize central, obstructive, or mixed apneas and/or bradycardia as they occur. Alarms that accurately reflect the predisposing condition must consistently be alert and be understandable to the caregiver. In other words, the monitor must be efficacious in recognizing apnea and triggering its alarm for prolonged apnea. In addition, the monitor must be capable of monitoring its own internal essential functions to assure proper operation. It must be noninvasive and easy to use and understand.

Because of the life-and-death importance of meeting such criteria, they recommend that monitoring devices should not be sold "over the counter" to consumers, but supplied only with professional recommendation, training, supervision, and support. Parents need, for example, to have been taught techniques to use in cases of emergency, such as ARTIFICIAL RESPIRATION. For information about any particular home monitor, you can call the Food and Drug Administration at 301-443-3170. (For help and further information, see SUDDEN INFANT DEATH SYNDROME; FETAL MONITORING.)

home school district   The school district serving the area of a student's legal place of residence. In cases where a student is found to have SPECIAL NEEDS that the home school district cannot meet, the student is assigned an OUT-OF-DISTRICT PLACEMENT to a school with appropriate services, at the expense of the home school district. If, however, parents voluntarily place the child in a school outside the home district, they are responsible for most if not all costs. (For help and further information, see EDUCATION FOR ALL HANDICAPPED CHILDREN ACT OF 1975.)

home schooling   EDUCATION of children at home, under parental supervision, rather than in a public or PRIVATE SCHOOL, in some cases using materials prepared by the parents, in many using materials prepared by organizations specializing in home-school education. For children in the United States, COMPULSORY ATTENDANCE at school is required between ages set by various state laws, often six to 16. States have different rules about what parents must do to meet compulsory schooling requirements. Some require parents to register as home schoolers, to submit a formal CURRICULUM plan, or to obtain a state teaching certificate. Parents considering home schooling should carefully explore the laws in their state, contacting their state department of education or the organization listed below. They should also read about and talk with others who have been involved in home schooling, to get a full appreciation of the substantial commitment required. Home schooling has been successful in some families, with children achieving educational levels comparable to (and sometimes even higher than) those children attending HIGH SCHOOL, even when the parents in the family were not themselves highly educated in formal terms. Critics cite, in addition to the enormous commitment involved, the loss in "intangible" education from socializing with other students in a school setting. Perhaps 100,000 to 250,000 students are presently being educated at home. For adults or former DROPOUTS enrolled in a correspondence school course and studying at home, the term more commonly used is HOME STUDY.

For help and further information

Home School Legal Defense Association (HSLDA)
Paeonian Springs, VA 22129
703-882-3838
Michael Farris, President
Organization to provide low-cost legal assistance for member parents operating HSLDA-accepted home schools. Provides legal defense for "families who choose to exercise their God-given and constitutional right to teach their children at home"; seeks to educate public and influence public policy; publishes quarterly *Home School Court Report*.

Other reference sources

"An Overview of Home Instruction," by Patricia M. Lines. *Phi Delta Kappan*, March 1987, pp. 510–17.

Survivor's Guide to Home Schooling, by Luanne Shackleford and Susan White. Westchester, IL: Crossways, 1988.

Home School: Taking the First Step: Program Planning Handbook, by Borg Hendrickson. Available from Mountain Meadow Press, P.O. Box 447, Kooskia, ID 83539.

Famous Home Schoolers. Booklet available from Unschoolers Network, 2 Smith Street, Farmingdale, NJ 07727.

home study   1. Analysis of the family situation of parents wishing to adopt, required by law to be prepared by a licensed social worker, often from an ADOPTION agency, whether the planned adoption is from within the United States or from abroad. Would-be adoptors meet with the social worker in the home or agency setting over a period of several weeks or months. Some agencies use a group approach, in which parents are evaluated during a parenting preparation course. The social worker who writes the home-study report is attempting to screen out parents who might be unsuitable as adoptive parents, as because of financial or psychological instability. Would-be parents also often contribute autobiographies or other personal statements that help social workers understand what they have to offer children. As part of the evaluation process, parents often have to supply many other materials, including personal references and numerous certificates (see ADOPTION). The final home-study report is to be sent every time parents make an application for a child. Papers submitted abroad for an international adoption often need to be notarized and authenticated.

2. Enrollment in a school that has, instead of classes, sequenced materials for a student to study at home, which are then evaluated and graded by school staff; also called *correspondence courses*. These may be courses as part of degree programs (as for a HIGH SCHOOL or COLLEGE degree), courses combined with on-the-job training, or stand-alone courses to gain certain skills or enhance interests. Some can be completed in a few weeks; others require several years of intensive study. Home study courses are generally taken by adults, many of them former DROPOUTS. Children studying at home under their parent's supervision are generally said to be in HOME SCHOOLING.

For help and further information

National Home Study Council (NHSC)
1601 18th Street, NW
Washington, DC 20009
202-234-5100
William A. Fowler, Executive Director
Organization acting as information clearinghouse on home study or correspondence schools. Establishes standards and supplies accreditation; maintains library; publishes various materials, including semiannual *News*, annual *Directory of Accredited Home Study Schools*, brochure *Facts About NHSC*, and books such as *We Succeeded Through Home Study*, *The Effectiveness and Acceptance of Home Study*, *Home Study Course Development Handbook*, *Home Study Student Services Handbook*, and *Bibliography on Home Study Education*.

Other reference source

Peterson's The Independent Study Catalog, fourth edition. Princeton, NJ: Peterson's, 1989.

homogeneous group   A grouping of students with similar achievement and ability, as in a TRACKING system, in contrast to a *heterogeneous group*.

homologous insemination   Alternate name for ARTIFICIAL INSEMINATION using semen from the woman's husband or sexual partner.

homosexuality   Sexual attraction to people of the same sex, a pattern of sexual preference that exists in substantial segments of the population. Though reliable and current data is lacking, perhaps 5 percent of the population is estimated to be fully homosexual by preference (women homosexuals often being called *lesbians*), while another 15 to 35 percent may be *bisexual*, having both homosexual and heterosexual relationships at various points during their lives.

For much of history, those with same-sex preferences have been shunned and harassed and so have kept silent about their sexual orientation, an approach that led to enormous emotional stress and isolation among homosexuals. But in recent years, many of them have elected to "come out of the closet," openly showing their sexual preferences. This change affected the parent–child relationship in a variety of ways.

Some men and women who had been bisexual, often attempting to conform to the heterosexual life-style, had been married and had children. On later becoming openly homosexual, many of them risked losing CUSTODY of and sometimes even access to their children. At the very least, they faced the delicate task of explaining their stance to the children.

Some homosexual couples, desiring to form their own families, arranged for ADOPTION of a child, sometimes one born to a surrogate mother (see SURROGATE PARENTING), or (in the case of lesbians) for birth by one of the women following ARTIFICIAL INSEMINATION. Such arrangements carry their own hazards. The nontraditional family arrangement can be confusing to young children and can lead to some taunts and discrimination from others, so the parents need to prepare the children very carefully to understand the special family situation. If such couples break up, they have all of the usual battles over custody, VISITATION RIGHTS, and CHILD SUPPORT, but these are made more difficult because they do not come under the usual protection of marital laws.

The new openness has also changed the situation for parents of children who are—or think they may be—gay. In the past, such young people were generally isolated and alone, especially during the difficult period of ADOLESCENCE, often feeling (and often rightly) that they could not talk to their parents and lacking other sources of help. That is still the case for many, but in at least some areas, various groups now openly offer assistance, and even some school systems provide counseling for children uncertain about their sexual orientation. More such young people also feel that they can tell their parents about their feelings, when in the past they might have spent decades painfully hiding the truth. The situation has been complicated by the advent of AIDS, which is readily transmitted by some forms of homosexual intercourse.

In the not-so-distant past, homosexuality was considered a form of MENTAL DISORDER. Though that is no longer true, some related disorders may be treated by psychologists or psychiatrists, including GENDER IDENTITY DISORDER, in which people's inner sense of gender (male or female) does not match their external SECONDARY SEX CHARACTERISTICS. This may lead to *transsexualism*, in which the person desires to live like one of the opposite sex and sometimes also seeks surgical and hormonal treatment to perform a sex change.

Various organizations (see below) have been formed to help homosexual parents and children deal with their special problems and concerns.

For help and further information

Federation of Parents and Friends of Lesbians and Gays (ParentsFLAG)
P.O. Box 27605
Washington, DC 20038
202-638-4200
Paulette Goodman, President
Network of mutual-support self-help groups of parents of homosexuals. Seeks to maintain and strengthen parent–child communication; aims to educate public and influence legislation; publishes audiovisual and print materials, including *About Our Children* and *Coming Out to Your Parents*.

Gay and Lesbian Parents Coalition International (GLPCI)
Box 50360
Washington, DC 20004
703-548-3238
E. Jeremy Hutton, Secretary
Network of mutual-support self-help groups of organizations for homosexual parents. Seeks to influence public policy and legislation for rights of homosexual parents; publishes newsletter, directory of affiliates, and other materials.

National Federation of Parents and Friends of Gays (NF/PFOG)
8020 Eastern Avenue, NW
Washington, DC 20012
202-726-3223
Eugene M. Baker, Executive Secretary
Network of peer-counseling groups aimed at helping families and friends of homosexuals understand the problems faced by gay men and lesbians. Seeks to educate public and professionals and to change public policy and legislation; publishes various materials, including recommended reading list.

Lambda Legal Defense and Education Fund (LLDEF)
666 Broadway
New York, NY 10012
212-995-8585
Thomas B. Stoddard, Executive Director
Organization to defend homosexuals' civil rights in many areas, including housing, child custody, and AIDS. Acts as information resource and referral service to gay men and lesbians; assists individual homosexuals and their attorneys, and also litigates test cases; seeks to educate public and change public policy and legislation; maintains library of cases affecting homosexual rights; publishes various materials, including *Lesbians Choosing Motherhood*.

Lesbian Mothers National Defense Fund (LMNDF)
P.O. Box 21567

Seattle, WA 98111
206-325-2643
Nancy Rickerson, Executive Officer
Organization to aid lesbians who are or would like to be mothers. Offers legal, psychological, and financial support to lesbian mothers in contested child-custody situations; provides information on alternatives for would-be lesbian mothers, such as donor insemination and adoption; gathers data on gay and lesbian custody cases and acts as information resource; offers referrals to lawyers; publishes quarterly *Mom's Apple Pie*.

Lesbian Rights Project (LRP)
1370 Mission Street, 3rd Floor
San Francisco, CA 94103
415-621-0674
Roberta Achtenberg, Directing Attorney
Public-interest law firm aimed at protecting rights of homosexuals, especially lesbians, in many areas, including child custody, parenting, and housing. Publishes various materials, including *Lesbians Choosing Motherhood: Legal Issues in Donor Insemination, Lesbian Mothers and Their Children*, and *Reorganizing Lesbian and Gay Families: Strategies for Extending Employment Benefits*.

Custody Action for Lesbian Mothers (CALM), 215-667-7508. (For full group information, see CUSTODY.)

Other reference sources

For Parents

Different Daughters: A Book by Mothers of Lesbians, Louise Rafkin, ed. Garden City, NY: Doubleday, 1989.

There's Something I've Been Meaning to Tell You, Loralee Macpike, ed. Tallahassee, FL: Naiad, 1989. About gay and lesbian parents telling children of their homosexuality; includes review of legal implications.

Mother, I Have Something to Tell You, by Joe Brans. Garden City, NY: Doubleday, 1987.

The Complete Guide to Gay Parenting, by Joy Schulenburg. Garden City, NY: Doubleday, 1985.

Parents of the Homosexual, by David K. Switzer and Shirley Switzer. Philadelphia: Westminster, 1980.

For or By Kids

Heather Has Two Mommies, by Lesléa Newman. Northampton, MA: In Other Words, 1990. For ages 3 to 5. Address: 351 Pleasant Street, Suite 233, Northampton, MA 01060.

Coping with Your Sexual Orientation, by Deborah A. Miller and Alex Waigandt. New York: Rosen, 1990. For adolescents. On exploring sexual identity.

Jack, by A.M. Holmes. New York: Macmillan, 1989. For young adult readers. About a teenage boy adjusting to his father's homosexuality.

How Will I Tell My Mother?, by Jerry Arterburn with his brother Steve. Nashville, TN: Thomas Nelson, 1988.

Counter Play, by Anne Snyder. New York: New American Library, 1981. Novel about a teenage boy confronting his homosexuality.

Background Works

Encyclopedia of Homosexuality, Wayne R. Dynes et al, eds. New York: Garland, 1990.

Male Homosexuality: A Contemporary Psychoanalytic Perspective, by Richard C. Friedman. New Haven, CT: Yale University Press, 1990.

The Psychoanalytic Theory of Male Homosexuality, by Kenneth Lewes. New York: New American Library, 1989.

Coping with Your Sexual Orientation, by Deborah A. Miller and Alex Waigandt. New York: Rosen, 1990. For adolescents. On exploring sexual identity.

(See also SEX EDUCATION; also NONTRADITIONAL FAMILIES in the PARENT'S BOOKSHELF on page 566.)

homozygote In GENETIC INHERITANCE, a person carrying identical forms of a particular gene in a chromosome pair.

honor roll A list prepared by a school at the end of each marking period indicating which students achieved an AVERAGE of B or better or, if number GRADES are used, generally 90 or better; the high school equivalent of a college or university's DEAN'S LIST.

horizontal lie A type of FETAL PRESENTATION in which the axis of the fetus is crossways, or horizontal, in the UTERUS, rather than the normal up-and-down position.

hormones A wide variety of chemicals produced by organs to help control various body functions, including METABOLISM, growth (see GROWTH AND GROWTH DISORDERS, development of SECONDARY SEX CHARACTERISTICS, a woman's MENSTRUAL CYCLE, a man's SPERM production, the changes involved in PREGNANCY and LACTATION, and the general circulatory system. Some hormones are produced by body organs such as the kidneys or intestines (and during pregnancy, the PLACENTA), but most are produced by the ENDOCRINE SYSTEM, among them the HYPOTHALAMUS, PITUITARY GLAND, THYROID GLAND, parathyroid glands, thymus, ADRENAL GLANDS, and the sex organs called GONADS (TESTES in the male and OVARIES in the female).

For help and further information

National Institute of Child Health and Human Development (NICHD), 301-496-5133. (For full group information, see PREGNANCY.)

National Institute of Diabetes and Digestive and Kidney Diseases (NIDDK), 301-496-3583. (For full group information, see DIGESTIVE DISORDERS.)

Other reference source

Hormones: The Woman's Answerbook, by Lois Jovanovic, M.D., and Genell J. Subak-Sharpe. New York: Fawcett/Columbine, 1988.

hospitals Institutions providing medical care of a type or level that cannot generally be offered at home. Many hospitals are government institutions, run by federal, state, county, community, or city governments, sometimes at least partly funded by local contributions; many others are owned and operated by religious groups; some are linked with university research and teaching programs; and some are run on a for-profit basis by medical-care corporations. Hospitals are often classed by the level and kind of care they are equipped to provide, such as:

- *the primary-care level (Level I)*, including many community hospitals, where the care is basic and generally directed toward handling routine medical emergencies. In relation to PREGNANCY, these Level I hospitals are generally geared to handle normal or low-risk pregnancies. HIGH-RISK PREGNANCIES are better handled by more sophisticated facilities; and if complications develop during LABOR or DELIVERY, the medical staff may stabilize the mother and/or infant and transport them to a higher-level facility. Some Level I hospitals offer homelike BIRTHING ROOMS that may include such things as a bed, stereo, and rocking chair. These have the advantage of providing a relaxed atmosphere and more natural setting (though it cannot be made as antiseptic), close to emergency hospital facilities, as necessary.

- *the secondary-care level (Level II)*, an intermediate level of care, serving a larger area and population than a Level I hospital and having more sophisticated medical equipment and laboratory facilities, sometimes including a NEONATAL INTENSIVE CARE UNIT (ICU). In relation to pregnancy, a Level II hospital would handle normal or moderate-risk pregnancies, referring pregnancies with high risk or complications to a Level III facility.

- *the tertiary-care level (Level III)*, which provides far more sophisticated facilities for diagnosis and treatment, including highly specialized staff and extensive support systems. Level III hospitals are often associated with university research and training facilities, in which case they are sometimes called UNIVERSITY-AFFILIATED FACILITIES (UAFs). A woman with a high-risk pregnancy will be wise to arrange to have her child in a tertiary-care facility or UAF, if possible, where the specialist staff will be best trained and equipped to deal with any complications that may occur.

If a woman decides to give birth in a hospital, she and her partner will want to assess (with the doctor's help) any risk factors in the pregnancy and also the policies of the hospital regarding such questions as the administration of enemas, FETAL MONITORING, EPISIOTOMIES, intravenous supplements, and BIRTH PARTNERS, including who will or will not be allowed to attend the birth and what training (if any) is required of birth

---

Before Delivery: What to Pack for the Hospital

Approximately two weeks before your delivery date, pack a bag with the personal things you will want to take with you. You will probably want to include:

- bathrobe
- two nightgowns (opening in front if you plan to breastfeed)
- slippers
- two bras (nursing bras if you plan to breastfeed)
- underpants
- sanitary-pad belt (or bring your own self-adhesive sanitary pads)
- toothbrush and toothpaste
- comb, brush, and curlers, if desired
- cosmetics
- books or magazines
- something to wear home (remember to choose something a little loose fitting; you won't quite have your figure back!)

You should also take any prenatal reports or hospitalization papers. Pack the clothes you will want to take the baby home in and tell the person who will be coming to take you home where they are. Depending on the weather, the baby will need a blanket, sweater, or cap. If it is warm weather, all you need are diapers, safety pins, shirt, and receiving blanket.

Plan on how you will get to the hospital, both during the day and at night. You should have telephone numbers in an obvious and handy place so that you can call your husband, friend, mother, or a taxicab when you are ready to go.

It is usually an exciting time and it is easy to forget phone numbers. Have the doctor's phone number on your list so that you can call to either find out if it is time to go to the hospital or to report that you are going.

Source: *Prenatal Care* (1983). Prepared for the Public Health Service by the Bureau of Health Care Delivery and Assistance, Division of Maternal and Child Health.

---

partners. The couple can then assess what level of hospital and which particular facility will be most appropriate. Before delivery, they should also plan ahead, packing a bag of items ready to take to the hospital (see above).

Parents whose children have severe diseases or disorders are also often referred to tertiary-care facilities or UAFs for diagnosis and extensive or sophisticated treatment, such as BONE MARROW TRANSPLANT or open-heart surgery. In such situations, both parents and children will need special preparation and support. They should make use of the support facilities often provided. Some such facilities, including special children's hospitals or large hospitals with children's sections, have made special arrangements for children who spend long periods hospitalized. *Recreational* therapists, sometimes called

child life workers, attempt to develop recreational programs in homelike quarters, in some cases even having social rooms where adolescents can entertain their friends. Parents may also find assistance from the various self-help groups that have been formed by other parents dealing with severe health problems, often linked with hospital facilities. (See entries under the particular type of health problem faced, such as CANCER, LIVER PROBLEMS, or CYSTIC FIBROSIS.)

Other reference sources

In the Blink of an Eye: Inside a Children's Trauma Center, by Alan Doelp. New York: Prentice Hall, 1989.

In the Hospital. (1989) 67-minute cassette and book, performed by Peter Alsop and Bill Harley, available from Moose School Records, P.O. Box 960, Topanga, CA 90290. For ages 6 to 12.

Max's Daddy Goes to the Hospital, by Danielle Steel. New York: Delacorte, 1989. For ages 4 to 7.

Going to the Hospital, by Fred Rogers. Photographs by Jim Judkis. New York: Putnam, 1988. For preschoolers.

The Hospital Book, by J. Howe. New York: Crown, 1981. Orientation guide, with photos, for school-age children.

Hospital Roadmap: A Book to Help Explain the Hospital Experience to Young Children, by I.G. Elliott (1981). Available from: Resources for Children in Hospitals, P.O. Box 10, Belmont, MA 02178, 617–6220.

hospital hold Hospitalization of a child when medical or social-work staff suspect possible CHILD ABUSE AND NEGLECT, often against the wishes of the parent or caretaker who has brought the child to an emergency room for treatment. Usually, SOCIAL WORKERS are quickly called in, as the state takes temporary CUSTODY of the child.

hotline A telephone number that can be called in times of emergency, often staffed 24 hours a day by trained counselors. Classic hotlines are special-purpose numbers, as for runaways, drug addicts, people considering SUICIDE, or people reporting CHILD ABUSE AND NEGLECT. Some hotlines are local; many others are toll-free (800) numbers that can be called long distance. Many organizations operate general information lines on a toll-free basis, sometimes for limited hours but occasionally around the clock; these are more properly called HELPLINES. (For those in this book, see HOTLINES, HELPLINES, AND HELPING ORGANIZATIONS on page 601, or look under specific topics.)

House-Tree-Person (H-T-P) Projective Technique A type of individually administered PROJECTIVE TEST for people from ages three to adult, used to assess personality and especially to highlight any emotional disturbance. The child is asked to make separate drawings of a house, a tree, and a person and then to interpret each of the drawings, responses to which the administrator then gives SCORES according to the test manual. (For help and further information, see TESTS.)

HPV Abbreviation for human papillomaviruses, viruses that cause GENITAL WARTS.

HSV Abbreviation for herpes simplex virus, the cause of HERPES SIMPLEX infections.

HTP Abbreviation for HOUSE-TREE-PERSON (H-T-P) PROJECTIVE TECHNIQUE.

human chorionic gonadotropin (hCG) A HORMONE produced by the PLACENTA during PREGNANCY, which triggers the formation of the additional ESTROGEN and PROGESTERONE needed during pregnancy. Excreted in urine, hCG is used in testing to see whether PREGNANCY has occurred. In cases of INFERTILITY, hCG is also sometimes given to stimulate OVULATION in a woman or SPERM production in a man. It may also be administered as a preventive for MISCARRIAGE and as a treatment for some forms of undescended TESTES. (For a description of a HOME MEDICAL TEST using hCG, see PREGNANCY TESTS.)

human growth hormone (hGH) The key HORMONE in regulating growth, produced by the PITUITARY GLAND, sometimes administered when a child's growth has been extremely slow. From 1963, this hGH extract was made from human pituitary glands, but in 1985 it was discovered that a few people had died of a rare slow brain virus (see CREUTZFELDT-JAKOB DISEASE), apparently from contaminated pituitary tissue in the extract. Since that time a synthetic form of hGH has been used that does not carry that risk of contamination but seems to work as well to bring a child's growth into the normal range. (For help and further information, see below; see also GROWTH AND GROWTH DISORDERS.)

For help and further information

Food and Drug Administration, 301-295-8012. (For full grup information, see DRUG REACTIONS AND INTERACTIONS.)

National Hormone and Pituitary Program (NHPP), 301-837-2552. (See PITUITARY GLAND.)

(See also GROWTH AND GROWTH DISORDERS.)

human papillomaviruses (HPVs) Viruses that cause GENITAL WARTS, a SEXUALLY TRANSMITTED DISEASE.

humpback Outdated popular name for KYPHOSIS.

Hunter's syndrome (MPS II) A GENETIC DISORDER of the X-LINKED recessive type, affecting only males, and resulting from a defect in a specific enzyme; one of a group of disorders called MUCOPOLYSACCHARIDOSES (MPS). Children affected with MPS II generally have MENTAL RETARDATION, skeletal deformity (especially of the face), retarded growth often resulting in DWARFISM, and a shortened life expectancy, often dying in childhood or ADOLESCENCE, though some with a mild form of the disorder may live a relatively normal life. In addition, the specific characteristics of Hunter's syndrome include KYPHOSIS (excessive curvature of the spine), EAR AND HEARING PROBLEMS, and a combination of defects commonly known as GARGOYLISM. Parents with a family history of MPS II may well want to seek GENETIC COUNSELING before a pregnancy. The defective gene, carried by females and with one chance in two of being passed on to a male child, can

be detected by GENETIC SCREENING TESTS before PREGNANCY. Hunter's syndrome can be detected during pregnancy with PRE-NATAL TESTING, as through AMNIOCENTESIS, or after birth through URINE TESTS and X-RAY analysis of skeletal development. (For help and further information, see MUCOPOLYSACCHARIDOSES.)

Huntington's chorea (HD or Huntington's disease) A GENETIC DISORDER that causes the brain to deteriorate, resulting in the quick, jerky movements called CHOREA and gradual mental degeneration. Passed on by a single, defective, DOMINANT gene and appearing equally in both sexes, Huntington's chorea often does not appear until middle age, so people may have children and pass on the disease before realizing that they have it themselves. Prospective parents with Huntington's chorea in their family history may well want to seek GENETIC COUNSELING for advice on the likelihood of passing it on to possible children. As genetic researchers continue to study the defective gene, they hope to refine a test to tell whether or not someone carries the abnormal gene and possibly to learn how to correct it through genetic engineering. Recent medications have eased the effects of Huntington's chorea, but no cure is known.

For help and further information

Huntington's Disease Society of America (HDSA)
140 West 22nd Street
New York, NY 10011
212-242-1968
Gary Wallach, Executive Director
Organization concerned with families affected by Huntington's disease. Provides information and makes referrals; supports research; operates Brain Donor program, under which families donate tissue vital for research; publishes various materials, including newsletter, *The Marker*, and brochures *Huntington's Disease, Caring for the HD Patient at Home*, and *Experiences of a Huntington's Disease Patient*.

Hereditary Disease Foundation (HDF)
606 Wilshire Boulevard, Suite 504
Beverly Hills, CA 90401
213-458-4183
Nancy S. Wexler, President
Organization supporting research into causes, prevention, diagnosis, and treatment of genetic disorders, especially Huntington's disease. Gathers and disseminates information; maintains tissue banks for research purposes.

National Institute of Neurological Disorders and Stroke (NINDS), 301-496-5751. Publishes booklet *Huntington's Disease: Hope Through Research* and brochure *A Neurologist Speaks with Huntington's Disease Families*. (For full group information, see BRAIN AND BRAIN DISORDERS.)

Other reference sources

Health Care U.S.A., by Jean Carper. New York: Prentice Hall, 1987. Resource for general and specific health-care information. Lists major Huntington's disease treatment and research centers, key neurologists, and other information, as on brain tissue banks and confidential national research roster for Huntington's disease patients and their families.

Living with Huntington's Disease: A Book for Patients and Families, by Dennis Phillips. Milwaukee: University of Wisconsin Press, 1982.

Heirloom, by Dorothy Snyder. Boulder, CO: Stonehenge, 1981. 381 Ponderosa Drive, Boulder, CO 80303.

The 36-Hour Day, by Nancy Mace and Peter Rabins, M.D. Baltimore: Johns Hopkins University Press, 1981.

Hurler's syndrome (MPS I)   A GENETIC DISORDER of the AUTOSOMAL RECESSIVE type, resulting from a defect in a specific enzyme; one of a group of disorders called MUCOPOLYSACCHARIDOSES (MPS). Children affected with MPS I generally have MENTAL RETARDATION, skeletal deformity (especially of the face), retarded growth often resulting in DWARFISM, and a shortened life expectancy, often dying in childhood or adolescence, though some with a mild form of the disorder may live a relatively normal life. Also among the common characteristics are a group of defects called GARGOYLISM (a now-outdated popular name for Hurler's syndrome). Children with MPS I often also have HYDROCEPHALUS, heart problems (see HEART AND HEART PROBLEMS), and LUNG AND BREATHING DISORDERS, which generally lead to DEATH in childhood. Characteristics of Hurler's syndrome become identifiable at about six to 12 months of age. Parents with a family history of MPS I may well want to seek GENETIC COUNSELING; MPS I defects can be detected before birth with PRENATAL TESTING, as through AMNIOCENTESIS. (For help and further information, see MUCOPOLYSACCHARIDOSES.)

husband-coached childbirth   Alternate name for the *Bradley method*, a popular form of natural or PREPARED CHILDBIRTH.

hyaline membrane disease (HMD)   Alternate term for RESPIRATORY DISTRESS SYNDROME.

hydramnios (polyhydramnios)   A condition of having too much AMNIOTIC FLUID during a PREGNANCY.

hydrocele   An accumulation of fluid, literally a "water sac," in the area around the TESTES and within the SCROTUM, sometimes resulting from inflammation or injury and generally painless. Though often found in middle-aged men, hydroceles sometimes occur in male babies shortly after birth. In their booklet *Infant Care*, the Public Health Service notes:

One or both of a [newborn] boy's testicles may seem particularly large, and may be surrounded by a water sac or "hydrocele." Seek medical care for any swelling in the groin, and go to the doctor or clinic immediately if there is a red or painful swelling in the groin or testicles. Hydroceles are painless, cause no harm and go away without treatment, usually within a few months.

hydrocephalus   A condition involving excessive amounts of CEREBROSPINAL FLUID circulating in the BRAIN and SPINAL CORD and sometimes blockage of the normal circulation; popularly called "water on the brain." Hydrocephalus may be present at birth,

as the result of a GENETIC DISORDER such as SPINA BIFIDA, or it may result from other causes, such as HEAD INJURY, a BRAIN TUMOR, or infections such as MENINGITIS or ENCEPHALITIS.

With hydrocephalus, the fluid in the brain is generally under increased pressure, expanding the fluid-filled cavities (VENTRICLES) in the center of the brain, and in the process compressing and damaging brain tissue. In infants, whose skulls are still soft and expandable, the skull becomes abnormally large, while in older children and adults, the pressure soon becomes dangerously high.

If unchecked, hydrocephalus can lead to EPILEPSY, severe brain damage, SEIZURES, and sometimes DEATH. The condition can be diagnosed using a variety of MEDICAL TESTS, notably the CT SCAN or MRI. Treatment generally involves draining away excess fluid, as through a SHUNT, and (where possible) dealing with the underlying cause.

For help and further information

National Hydrocephalus Foundation (NHF)
Route One, River Road
Box 210A
Joliet, IL 60436
815-467-6548
James A. Mazzetti, Executive Director
Organization seeking to aid individuals and families affected by hydrocephalus. Provides information and makes referrals; maintains library; publishes various print and audiovisual materials, including quarterly newsletter.

National Institute of Neurological Disorders and Stroke (NINDS), 301-496-5751. (For full group information, see BRAIN AND BRAIN DISORDERS.)

National Institute of Child Health and Human Development (NICHD), 301-496-5133. (For full group information, see PREGNANCY.)

hymen   A thin piece of membrane that mostly covers the opening of the VAGINA, generally with a small opening in the center, which is stretched or torn during the first penetration of the area, as in sexual intercourse, use of tampons during MENSTRUATION, or a medical examination. In some rare cases, a girl's hymen will have no opening—a condition called *imperforate hymen*—often discovered at MENARCHE, since menstrual blood cannot be released; it may need to be opened surgically.

hyperactivity (hyperkinetic syndrome)   A behavior pattern in which a person is constantly or excessively moving about and making rapid motions, often in a disorganized or disruptive way, or if seated is fidgeting or squirming. Hyperactivity is a general term, used loosely to refer to a wide range of behaviors; in psychiatric parlance, it is no longer considered a separate disorder but part of a wider complex of behaviors called ATTENTION-DEFICIT HYPERACTIVITY DISORDER (ADHD). (For help and further information, see ATTENTION-DEFICIT HYPERACTIVITY DISORDER.)

hyperbilirubinemia   An excess amount of *bilirubin* (a yellow-ish substance formed by the breakdown of "retired" red blood cells) in the blood, which causes JAUNDICE, a yellowish discolor-ation of the skin, mucous membranes, and the "whites" of the eyes. Often associated with liver malfunction or obstruction of ducts in the liver, or with hemolytic ANEMIA, hyperbilirubinemia can result from a variety of causes. Many infants have a slight touch of jaundice at birth, but some have *hyperbilirubinemia of the newborn*, involving larger amounts of bilirubin. Sometimes infants being breastfed will develop *breast-milk jaundice* for unknown reasons and may need to be switched to FORMULA for one or two days and given PHOTOTHERAPY (light therapy).

In a condition called *kernicterus*, however, greatly excessive amounts can accumulate causing widespread damage to the brain and other parts of the body, including MENTAL RETARDATION, CHOREA, ATHETOSIS, CEREBRAL PALSY, EAR AND HEARING PROBLEMS, some EYE AND VISION PROBLEMS, and sometimes DEATH. Hyperbili-rubinemia is generally treated with phototherapy and fluids; treatment must also involve attempting to identify the cause of the buildup of bilirubin, such as some kind of LIVER PROBLEM, ANEMIA, ALPHA 1-ANTITRYPSIN DEFICIENCY, or CYSTIC FIBROSIS.

For help and further information

National Institute of Child Health and Human Development (NICHD), 301-496-5133. (For full group information, see PREG-NANCY.)

National Institute of Diabetes and Digestive and Kidney Dis-eases (NIDDK), 301-496-3583. (For full group information, see DIGESTIVE DISORDERS.)

(See also LIVER PROBLEMS.)

hyperdactyly   Alternate term for POLYDACTYLY.

hyperglycemia   Abnormally high levels of GLUCOSE (a sugar used in the body for energy) in the blood, a common result of DIABETES MELLITUS.

hyperkinesis   Alternate term for *hyperactivity*, now generally called ATTENTION DEFICIT HYPERACTIVITY DISORDER (ADHD).

hyperkinetic syndrome (hyperkinesis)   Alternate term for *hyperactivity*, now generally called ATTENTION DEFICIT HYPERACTIV-ITY DISORDER (ADHD).

hyperlipidemias   A group of METABOLIC DISORDERS that involves abnormally high levels of CHOLESTEROL (especially *low-density lipoproteins*, or LDLs) in the bloodstream, increasing the risk of buildup of fatty tissue in the arteries (*atherosclerosis*) and resulting in heart problems (see HEART AND HEART PROBLEMS). Some kinds of hyperlipidemias are evidently GENETIC DISORDERS, so people with a family history of heart disease before age 50 should have their own and their children's blood levels checked. The buildup often starts in childhood and can cause heart problems in early adulthood if not recognized and treated, usually by drugs and low-fat diets to bring down the cholesterol level.

For help and further information

National Heart, Lung, and Blood Institute (NHLBI), 301-496-4236. (For full group information, see HEART AND HEART PROB-LEMS.)

hyperlordosis   Alternate term for LORDOSIS.

hyperopia   Farsightedness. (See EYE AND VISION PROBLEMS.)

hyperpigmentation (melasma or chloasma)   A SKIN DISORDER involving excess amounts of the dark pigment *melanin* in the skin, making dark brown patches, especially on the forehead, temples, and cheeks, which are accentuated by exposure to sun. Generally resulting from hormonal imbalance, hyperpig-mentation is associated with ADDISON'S DISEASE and also some-times occurs when a woman is using BIRTH-CONTROL PILLS or with PREGNANCY, then often called *melasma gravidarum* (mask of pregnancy). The condition is benign and usually clears up when balance is restored.

hypertension   Medical term for abnormally high BLOOD PRES-SURE.

hyperthermia   General term for excessively high body tem-perature, as in MALIGNANT HYPERTHERMIA.

hyperthyroidism   A disorder involving too much production from the THYROID GLAND.

hypervitaminosis A   A condition resulting from excessive consumption of VITAMIN A.

hyphema   HEMORRHAGE in the front of the eye, often looking like a bloodshot eye. Hyphema can be caused by violent shaking or a blow to the head and is one sign of possible child abuse (see CHILD ABUSE AND NEGLECT).

hypoactive   Listless, lethargic, or considerably less active than is normal for a particular age group, seeming almost to move in slow motion, a characteristic found among some chil-dren with LEARNING DISABILITIES, MENTAL RETARDATION, or MENTAL DISORDERS; the opposite of hyperactive.

hypogammaglobulinemia   An inherited deficiency in the IMMUNE SYSTEM.

hypogenitalism   Underdevelopment of the reproductive organs, or GENITALS, as through disorders of the sex glands (GONADS) or wider disorders such as LAURENCE-MOON-BIEDL SYN-DROME.

hypoglycemia   Abnormally low levels of GLUCOSE (a sugar used in the body for energy) in the blood, common among peo-ple with diabetes mellitus who are treating themselves with INSULIN; also called *insulin shock*. (For more information, see DIABETES MELLITUS.)

hypogonadism   Underactivity of the sex glands (GONADS), the TESTES in the male and the OVARIES in the female. The condition can result from a problem with the PITUITARY GLAND, which trig-gers production of male and female HORMONES, and by disorders in the gonads themselves, sometimes as a result of wider prob-lems, such as LAURENCE-MOON-BIEDL SYNDROME.

hypopigmentation   Alternate term for ALBINISM.

hypospadias   A CONGENITAL defect in which the URETHRA, the tube by which urine and SEMEN pass through the PENIS, is misplaced. In males, the opening is found on the underside of the penis, rather than in its head, and may be associated with a downward curving of the penis, called *chordee*. Sometimes the urethra's opening is found on the upper surface, a condition called EPISPADIAS, often associated with an upward curving of the penis. Such conditions can be corrected during infancy, with surgical reconstruction of the urethra and penis so that the adult male will be able to direct his urine stream and have normal sexual relations. In rare cases, females may have a urethra opening into the VAGINA.

hypotension   Medical term for abnormally low BLOOD PRESSURE.

hypothalamus   A cherry-sized portion of the brain behind the eyes (and under the brain section called the *thalamus*, as its name implies), which manages a wide range of functions in the body:

• It controls the *sympathetic nervous system* (part of the AUTONOMIC NERVOUS SYSTEM), which prepares our bodies to meet alarm or excitement—it increases the heart and breathing rates, increases blood flow to the muscles, and widens the pupils of the eyes.
• It controls responses to heat and cold, triggering sweating or shivering, as appropriate.
• It responds to information from elsewhere in the body regarding thirst and hunger.
• It coordinates the NERVOUS SYSTEM and ENDOCRINE SYSTEM, which produce the HORMONES that run many other body systems and therefore much influence the important PITUITARY GLAND, the sex glands (GONADS), the THYROID GLAND, and the brain (especially the adrenal cortex).

Because of its many functions, problems with the hypothalamus, such as a brain HEMORRHAGE or a TUMOR (as in the pituitary), can have wide-ranging consequences. LAURENCE-MOON-BIEDL SYNDROME is believed to be associated with a malfunction of the hypothalamus.

For help and further information
National Institute of Child Health and Human Development (NICHD), 301-496-5133. (For full group information, see PREGNANCY.)

National Institute of Diabetes and Digestive and Kidney Diseases (NIDDK), 301-496-3583. (For full group information, see digestive disorders.)

hypothyroidism (myxedema)   A disorder involving too little production from the THYROID GLAND.

hypotonia   Abnormal limpness of the muscles, when the muscles do not have the "tension" they normally have even in relaxation. Some babies with hypotonia have what is called the FLOPPY INFANT SYNDROME, which is especially common among PREMATURE infants, who develop normal muscle tension as they mature. But hypotonia is also associated with several other kinds of health disorders, such as heart problems (see HEART AND HEART PROBLEMS); MALNUTRITION or nutritional deficiencies and related diseases such as RICKETS and SCURVY; MOTOR NEURON DISEASES; MUSCULAR DYSTROPHY and related juvenile spinal *muscular atrophies*, including *Werdnig-Hoffmann disease* and *Wohlfart-Kugelberg-Welander disease*; and a variety of other disorders such as severe SLEEP APNEA, CEREBRAL PALSY, and DOWN'S SYNDROME.

For help and further information
National Institute of Neurological Disorders and Stroke (NINDS), 301-496-5751. (For full group information, see BRAIN AND BRAIN DISORDERS.)

hypoxia   Lack of oxygen vital to the cells of the brain (see BRAIN AND BRAIN DISORDERS), a condition resulting when blood or flow of the precious oxygen it carries are cut off, as during CHILDBIRTH, drowning, or CHOKING. Hypoxia during the birth process is regarded as a main cause of CEREBRAL PALSY and a possible cause of LEARNING DISABILITIES.

hysterectomy   A surgical operation to remove the UTERUS.

hysterosalpingogram   An X-RAY of a woman's reproductive organs, a picture enhanced by dyes pumped in through the VAGINA, often during a search for causes of INFERTILITY. Most reliably performed at the early part of a woman's MENSTRUAL CYCLE, the test is aimed at identifying structural problems that might be interfering with CONCEPTION, such as fibroid TUMORS or blockage of the FALLOPIAN TUBES. On occasion the pumping of the dye into the region even clears partially blocked fallopian tubes.

hysteroscopy   A medical procedure in which an *endoscope*, a flexible tube containing a periscope-like viewing device, is introduced into the UTERUS through the VAGINA and CERVIX; often performed during a search for causes of INFERTILITY. Most reliably performed at the early part of a woman's menstrual cycle, the hysteroscopy can help physicians detect fibroid TUMORS, polyps, or other abnormalities that might interfere with CONCEPTION.

IBD   Abbreviation for INFLAMMATORY BOWEL DISEASE.

IBS   Abbreviation for IRRITABLE BOWEL SYNDROME.

ichthyosis   The condition of having dry, thickened, darkened, scaly, "fishlike" skin (the literal implication of the name), due to a problem with production of *keratin,* an important protein in skin; sometimes popularly called the *fish-skin disease.* Ichthyosis is inherited, often as part of disorder such as SJÖGREN-LAHR-SSON SYNDROME, appearing soon after birth, especially on the arms, thighs, and backs of the hands. Soap and dry air make the condition worse, and the skin easily blisters and sheds, but lubricants, oils, and humid air ease the condition, which moderates through childhood.

For help and further information

Foundation for Ichthyosis and Related Skin Types (FIRST)
3640 Grand Avenue, Suite Two
Oakland, CA 94610
415-763-9839
Charles Eichhorn, Executive Director
Organization of people with ichthyosis and related skin disorders, health professionals, and interested others. Encourages formation of self-help mutual-support groups; gathers and disseminates information; publishes bimonthly newsletter *Ichthyosis Focus.*

National Institute of Arthritis and Musculoskeletal and Skin Diseases (NIAMS), 301-496-8188. (For full group information, see ARTHRITIS; MUSCULAR DYSTROPHY.)

National Cancer Institute (NCI), 301-496-5583. (For full group information, see CANCER.)

(See also SKIN DISORDERS.)

ICU   Abbreviation for INTENSIVE CARE UNIT.

IDDM   Abbreviation for *insulin-dependent diabetes mellitus,* a form of DIABETES MELLITUS.

idealization   A type of DEFENSE MECHANISM, in which a child (or adult) grossly exaggerates the positive qualities of someone or something.

identified adoption   A form of ADOPTION in which an adoption agency handles arrangements for an adoption that originated privately.

identity disorder   A type of MENTAL DISORDER that affects young people, in which the child is unable to mesh the various aspects of self into a coherent and acceptable identity (called *borderline personality disorder* if it persists into adulthood). Though many people have uncertainties about such questions as long-term goals, sexual orientation, religious and moral beliefs, and social relations with friends and groups, adolescents with identity disorder are so uncertain that they experience ANXIETY and DEPRESSION. Some become almost immobilized as a result, often with harm to their everyday functioning at home and school, while others experiment impulsively.

For help and further information

I Hate You—Don't Leave Me! Understanding Borderline Personality Disorders, by Jerold Kreisman and Hal Straus. Los Angeles: Price Stern Sloan, 1989.
On the Edge: The Love/Hate World of the Borderline Personality, by Neil D. Price. Summit, NJ: PIA, 1989.
Borderline Personality Disorder, by J.G. Gunderson. Washington, DC: American Psychiatric Press, 1984.
(See also MENTAL DISORDER; ADOLESCENCE.)

idiopathic   Medical term meaning "of no known cause," or a disorder of the individual.

idiot savant   Former name for what is now more commonly called SAVANT SYNDROME.

IEP   Abbreviation for INDIVIDUALIZED EDUCATION PROGRAM.

ileitis   Inflammation of the *ileum,* the last and largest part of the small intestine; a kind of DIGESTIVE DISORDER.

ileostomy   A type of OSTOMY performed on the *ileum* (small intestine), often because of INFLAMMATORY BOWEL DISEASE (ulcerative colitis and Crohn's disease).

illegitimate   Now-seldom-used term for a child whose parents have not been legally married. In some states, illegitimate children have no INHERITANCE RIGHTS from their FATHERS; and in some states, if the child dies a WRONGFUL DEATH, an UNWED FATHER cannot file a suit against the party responsible (though all mothers and married fathers can do so). But in most states, if the father acknowledges the child as his own, or a PATERNITY SUIT successfully identifies him as the father, an illegitimate child has much the same rights as one born to parents who were married at the time of birth or later.

Illinois Test of Psycholinguistic Abilities (ITPA)
A widely used, individually administered DIAGNOSTIC ASSESSMENT TEST used to measure the communication skills of children ages two to 10, especially to identify any specific problems, as in children with possible LEARNING DISABILITIES. Test examiners use a variety of materials, including booklets, picture books, and other objects, in assessing VISUAL SKILLS and AUDITORY SKILLS in reception, expression, association, and sequential memory, and other skills. (For help and further information, see TESTS; COMMUNICATION SKILLS AND DISORDERS.)

illiteracy Inability to read and write, but more specifically the inability to read and write so as to operate effectively in our information-packed society—reading signs, filling out forms, calculating figures, and dealing with words and numbers in all of their many aspects. Adults who cannot read, write, or calculate beyond eighth-grade level are often considered *functionally illiterate* and are the focus of many adult-education or continuing-education classes, sometimes attended by parents wishing to gain the skills they need to work with their own children in school. Many functional illiterates received automatic PROMOTION while in school, but failed to learn the basic skills, sometimes because they had undiagnosed handicaps, such as LEARNING DISABILITIES or EAR AND HEARING PROBLEMS, that hindered learning.

For help and further information
CETA Services
Contact Literacy Center
P.O. Box 81826
Lincoln, NE 68501
Literacy Hotline, 800-228-8813
Referral service for people wishing to learn how to read, in English or Spanish. Operates toll-free hotline for mainland U.S., Hawaii, Alaska, Guam, and Puerto Rico.

Other reference sources
Coping with an Illiterate Parent, by Nancy N. Rue. New York: Rosen, 1990. Counseling teenagers about how to deal with their parents' reading problems.
Education's Castaways: Literacy Problems of Learning Disabled Adults, by Helen Ginandes Weiss and Martin S. Weiss (1990). Available from Treehouse Associates, Box 1992, Avon, CO 81620.
Illiterate America, by Jonathan Kozol. Garden City, NY: Anchor/Doubleday, 1985.
(See also READING; LEARNING DISABILITIES.)

illusion A faulty perception or misinterpretation of something perceived, such as hearing a train whistle as a woman's scream; a common symptom of PSYCHOSIS. By contrast, HALLUCI-

NATION is a perception of something that is not present. (For help and further information, see MENTAL DISORDERS.)

immersion course A course in which students focus entirely and intensively on one subject area for a certain period of time, as in a weeklong course where students speak only a foreign language.

immune system A complex network of specialized cells and organs that work to defend the body against attack from what are perceived as "foreign" invaders. Often these invaders, including bacteria, viruses, fungi, and parasites, are indeed foreign and dangerous, and the immune system routinely saves the body from threatening and potentially lethal attack.

The key to the immune system's operation is the distinction between "self" and "not-self." Normally, the body's own cells carry markers that identify them as part of the self. Anything without those markers is perceived as not-self and attacked accordingly; any substance that is capable of triggering this immune response is called an *antigen*. (It is such antigens that distinguish the different types of blood, such as A, B, or O; see BLOOD AND BLOOD DISORDERS.)

Physically, the heart of the immune system is a network of vessels called the *lymphatic system*. These carry a milky fluid, called *lymph,* containing *lymphocytes* (a type of white blood cell), PROTEINS, and FATS, from near the blood vessels through various filtering mechanisms, including *lymph nodes* in the groin and underarm areas and in other organs, such as the *spleen* in the lower left side of the chest, the TONSILS and ADENOIDS in the neck, and even the APPENDIX, a projection off the intestines. There foreign substances, such as bacteria, are trapped and neutralized or destroyed. In cases of illness or infection, when much matter is being trapped in these filtering tissues, the area can become swollen, as when someone has "swollen glands." The body can function without some of these organs, such as the tonsils, adenoids, spleen, and appendix, if necessary, but their filtering is an important part of the body's protective defenses, and a ruptured spleen is a life-threatening emergency.

Lymphocytes form the body's defensive army. There are two main types of lymphocytes, B cells and T cells, both originally formed in the BONE MARROW. B cells, which also mature in the bone marrow, work by triggering the creation of substances called ANTIBODIES, which connect with and destroy antigens.

If a person has previously been exposed to a disease or had a VACCINATION against it, antibodies will be present in the body; then the person is said to have IMMUNITY against that particular disease. Babies are often born with temporary natural immunity from their mothers, which is enhanced during BREASTFEEDING. Antibodies belong to a wider class of immune-system molecules called *immunoglobulins*. In some situations, immunoglobulins may be injected into the body to provide temporary immunity, as when a pregnant woman has been exposed to RUBELLA. It is *immunoglobulin E* (IgE) that is mainly responsible for the reactions in ALLERGY and ASTHMA.

T cells, which mature in a chest gland called the THYMUS, directly attack cells that have been taken over by foreign organisms, such as viruses, or become abnormal, as in CANCER. They do this in a variety of ways. Some kinds (*suppressor cells*) turn

---

Immunology and Transplants

Since organ transplantation was introduced over a quarter of a century ago, it has become a widespread remedy for life-threatening disease. Several thousand kidney transplants are performed each year in the United States alone. In addition, physicians have succeeded in transplanting the heart, lungs, liver, and pancreas.

The success of a transplant—whether it is accepted or rejected— depends on the stubbornness of the immune system. For a transplant to "take," the body of the recipient must be made to suppress its natural tendency to get rid of foreign tissue.

Scientists have tackled this problem in two ways. The first is to make sure that the tissue of the donor and the recipient are as similar as possible. Tissue typing, or histocompatibility testing, involves matching the markers of self on body tissues; because the typing is usually done on white blood cells, or leukocytes, the markers are referred to as human leukocyte antigens (HLA). Each cell has a double set of six major antigens, designated as HLA-A, B, C, and three types of HLA-D—DR, DP, and DQ.

Each of the HLA antigens exists—in different individuals—in as many as 20 varieties, so the number of possible HLA types reaches about 10,000. Histocompatibility testing relies on antibodies to determine if a potential organ donor and recipient share two or more HLA antigens and thus are likely to make a good "match." The best matches are identical twins; next best are close relatives, especially brothers and sisters.

The second approach to taming rejection is to lull the recipient's immune system. This can be achieved through a variety of powerful immunosuppressive drugs. Steroids suppress lymphocyte function; the drug cyclosporine holds down the production of the lymphokine interleukin-2, which is necessary for T-cell growth. When such measures fail, the graft may yet be saved with a new treatment: OKT3 is a monoclonal antibody that seeks out the T3 marker on all mature T cells. By either destroying T cells or incapacitating them, OKT3 can bring an acute rejection crisis to a halt.

Not surprisingly, any such all-out assault on the immune system leaves a transplant recipient susceptible to both opportunitistic infections and lymphomas. Although such patients need careful medical follow-up, many of them are able to lead active and essentially normal lives.

Source: *Understanding the Immune System,* by Lydia Woods Schindler (1988). Prepared for the Public Health Service by the National Institute of Allergy and Infectious Diseases and the National Cancer Institute.

---

off or suppress problem cells, while others trigger growth of beneficial cells, destroy problem cells, and encourage *phagocytes* (cell-eaters). Though a key part of the body's defenses, these T-cell activities cause problems in TRANSPLANTS, because tissue from other people (except identical twins) is rejected. To counter this reaction, transplant patients are given *immunosuppressive drugs*. (For more, see IMMUNOLOGY AND TRANSPLANTS, above.)

The immune system can also fail to function properly in defending against disease. This *immunodeficiency* can result from a variety of factors:

• inherited immunodeficiency, in which children are born with flawed immune systems, conditions sometimes called *agammaglobulinemia* or *hypogammaglobulinemia*, in which they are highly susceptible to infections. Sometimes these can be treated with injections of immunoglobulin or transplants of thymus tissue. Rarely, babies are born totally or mostly lacking immune defenses, resulting in *severe combined immunodeficiency disease* (SCID); such children must be kept in totally germ-free settings, or "bubbles." A few SCID patients have been sucessfully treated with BONE MARROW TRANSPLANTS, and early results of experimental GENE THERAPY have shown promise.

• *acquired immunodeficiency*, which can occur temporarily and partially with some viral infections, such as MEASLES, MONONUCLEOSIS, and influenza, or under other conditions, such as BLOOD TRANSFUSIONS, surgery, MALNUTRITION, or stress. It can also occur in a permanent, devastating way in the disease called *acquired immunodeficiency syndrome*, or AIDS, in which a virus destroys helper T cells and is harbored by other immune cells, leaving the body defenseless against infections and cancers.

• *side effects of anticancer therapy*, such as RADIATION or *chemotherapy*.

The immune system itself is sometimes affected by *cancer*, such as LEUKEMIA (abnormal proliferation of the white blood cells), *multiple myeloma* (abnormal growth of the cells that produce antibodies), and *lymphomas*, cancers of the lymph organs, including *Hodgkin's disease*.

Sometimes the immune system malfunctions and mistakenly attacks part of the body itself, as if it were foreign. The result is an AUTOIMMUNE DISORDER, such as rheumatoid ARTHRITIS or LUPUS ERYTHEMATOSUS. In allergies, the body responds in excessive and harmful ways to foreign substances; in this case the antigens are generally termed *allergens*.

For help and further information

National Institute of Allergy and Infectious Diseases (NIAID), 301-496-5717. Publishes *Understanding the Immune System*. (For full group information, see ALLERGY.)

National Cancer Institute (NCI), 301-496-5583. (For full group information, see CANCER.)

Immune Deficiency Foundation (IDF)
P.O. Box 586
Columbia, MD 21045
301-461-3127
Marcia Boyle, President
Organization concerned with immune-deficiency diseases. Gathers and disseminates information to public and professionals; encourages formation of local chapters; supports research into cause, prevention, treatment, and cure; publishes various materials, including annual *IDF Newsletter*, audiovisual *Moment to Moment: The Story of Immune Deficiency*, and works such as *Immune Deficiency Diseases: An Overview, Patient and Family Handbook* and *List of Suggested Readings in Immunology*.

Other reference sources

Health Care U.S.A., by Jean Carper. New York: Prentice Hall, 1987. Resource for general and specific health-care information, as for asthma, allergies, and related immunological diseases; lists major centers for treatment or research and specialists in "alternative" approach of clinical ecology, and other information.
Defending the Body: Unraveling the Mysteries of Immunology, by Joel Davis. New York: Atheneum, 1990.
The Body at War: The Miracle of the Immune System, by John M. Dwyer, M.D. New York: New American Library, 1989.
Immunity and Survival: Keys to Immune System Health, by Sylvia S. Greenberg. New York: Plenum, 1989.
Your Immune System, revised edition, by Alan E. Nourse. New York: Watts, 1989. For grades 6 to 8.
The Immune System, by Edward Edelson. New York: Chelsea House, 1990.
(See also specific disorders mentioned in article.)

immunity In medicine, the state of being unaffected by or unsusceptible to a disease because the body's IMMUNE SYSTEM is operating effectively— specifically because ANTIBODIES are present to fight off the disease organisms. Babies are born with *natural immunity* from antibodies they have received from their mother's bloodstream, reinforced during BREASTFEEDING, which wears off during the first year of life. In centuries past, this meant that a child one year old lacked internal defenses against some of the most serious diseases, so INFANT MORTALITY was high. But in this century, VACCINES have been developed to give children an *acquired* or *induced* immunity that allows them to survive attack by various disease organisms. (For help and further information, see IMMUNIZATION.)

immunization The process of inducing IMMUNITY, or internal resistance to disease, in a person of any age but especially in children, who are very vulnerable to diseases after the first year as the natural immunity they received from their mothers wears off. Immunization can be induced in two main ways. The first, and most familiar, is *active immunization*, in which a VACCINE is introduced into a person's system, either by injection or by mouth, triggering the formation of ANTIBODIES and the development of immunity for a limited time or a lifetime, depending on the vaccine. In the less common *passive immunization*, antibodies are directly injected into a person's body, supplying a short-term immunity. This approach is sometimes used during PREGNANCY when a woman has been exposed to a dangerous disease or has RH INCOMPATIBILITY.

Among children, some of the most important diseases to guard against are DIPHTHERIA, TETANUS (lockjaw), PERTUSSIS (whooping cough), POLIO, MEASLES, RUBELLA (German measles), MUMPS, and HAEMOPHILUS INFLUENZAE TYPE B. The Public Health Service and the Centers for Disease Control have recommended a schedule (see page 260) on which children should receive various vaccines. (Different schedules are used for children whose immunization was not started at the recommended time.) They recommend that parents keep a record of their children's immunizations, the specific vaccines given, and the dates. That will act as a reminder of visits coming up for remaining immunization and booster doses. It also acts as a record that the child is protected. Most doctors or clinics will provide an immunization record form for parents, often an official state record. The doctor should date and sign the record each time an immunization is given, to keep the record current and correct. The signed document should be kept in a safe, accessible place. In many places state law requires that children who have not yet been properly immunized against specific diseases (with some exceptions) will not be allowed to enter or attend school until started on a course of immunization.

In general, vaccines are safe and effective, protecting against life-threatening diseases, but they can cause side effects. These are usually mild and temporary, such as a slight fever, a sore arm, or a rash, but can sometimes be more serious. The Public Health Service and the Centers for Disease Control recommend that if a child gets sick and visits a doctor, hospital, or clinic during the four weeks after an immunization, parents should report this to the doctor's office or clinic where the vaccine was given. (For more information on the side effects of the various vaccines, see DTP VACCINE, ORAL POLIO VACCINE, MEASLES-MUMPS-RUBELLA VACCINE, and HAEMOPHILUS INFLUENZAE TYPE B CONJUGATE VACCINE. For information on recourse in case of problems, see CHILDHOOD VACCINE INJURY ACT.)

For help and further information

National Institute of Allergy and Infectious Diseases (NIAID), 301-496-5717. (For full group information, see ALLERGY.)

National Institute of Child Health and Human Development (NICHD), 301-496-5133. (For full group information, see PREGNANCY.)

Centers for Disease Control (CDC)
Department of Health and Human Services
Public Inquiries, Building 1, Room B63

Immunization Schedules

Vaccines work best when they are given at the recommended time and on a regular schedule. Measles vaccine, for example, is not usually given to infants before they reach the age of 15 months. When it is given earlier than that, it may not be as effective. Oral polio and DTP (diphtheria-tetanus-pertussis, also called DPT) vaccines must be given over a period of time, in a series of properly spaced doses and shots.

Recommended Immunization Schedule for Infants and Children

The following immunization schedule is recommended for infants and children who are being immunized for the first time. This schedule shows all of the immunizations that a child should receive, beginning at the age of two months.

Recommended Age	Vaccines
2 months	DTP-1 (1st diphtheria-tetanus-pertussis); OPV-1(1st oral polio vaccine)
4 months	DTP-2, OPV-2
6 months	DTP-3
15 months	DTP-4; OPV-3; MMR (measles-mumps-rubella)
18 months	Hib (Haemophilus influenzae type b) [often now given at 15 months]
4–6 years	DTP-5; OPV-4
14–16 years, and every 10 years thereafter	Td (tetanus-diphtheria booster)

Source: *Parents Guide to Childhood Immunization* (1988). Prepared for the Public Health Service and the Centers for Disease Control.

1600 Clifton Road, NE
Atlanta, GA 30333
404-329-3534
Federal agency charged with investigating, identifying, controlling the spread of, preventing, and if possible eradicating diseases.

Other references sources

The Immunization Decision: A Guide for Parents, by Randall Neustaedter. Berkeley, CA: North Atlantic, 1990.
Immunization: Miracle or Myth?: The Story Behind Immunizations and Their Long Term Effects, by Walene James. Granby, MA: Bergin & Garvey, 1988.

immunoglobulin A class of substances produced by the IMMUNE SYSTEM, including ANTIBODIES. One type, *immunoglobulin E* (IgE), is mainly responsible for the reactions in ALLERGY and ASTHMA. (For help and further information, see IMMUNE SYSTEM.)

immunotherapy Treatment for some malfunctions or overreaction of the IMMUNE SYSTEM. (See ALLERGY.)

impacted tooth A tooth blocked from appearing in the mouth because the jaw is already overcrowded with TEETH. An impacted tooth can become infected and painful, requiring extraction; it can also damage other teeth or cause the opposite tooth to grow abnormally long.

impaired language Alternate name for a type of communication disorder. (See COMMUNICATION SKILLS AND DISORDERS.)

impedance audiometry A type of HEARING TEST sometimes used to assess the kind of middle-ear damage involved in hearing loss.

imperforate anus The lack of an outer opening for the anus, a BIRTH DEFECT that requires immediate surgical correction. (For help and further information, see DIGESTIVE DISORDERS.)

imperforate hymen A rare condition in which a girl's HYMEN has no central opening.

implantation The point at which the fertilized egg, having traveled down the FALLOPIAN TUBE, attaches itself to the lining of the UTERUS (*endometrium*), there receiving nourishment to grow. The egg, after implantation called an EMBRYO, then begins to grow, while some of its cells begin to develop the nourishing PLACENTA. If implantation takes place outside the uterus, such as in the fallopian tubes, the result is a potentially life-threatening ECTOPIC PREGNANCY. (For help and further information, see PREGNANCY; UTERUS.)

impulse control disorder A type of MENTAL DISORDER that involves a person failing to resist a drive or temptation to do something harmful. People with the disorder may or may not consciously plan to do harm and may not be conscious of resisting the impulse, but they characteristically feel a sense of tension or arousal beforehand and a sense of release, pleasure, or gratification afterward, often followed by self-reproach, guilt, or regret.

Among the main kinds of impulse control disorders are:

- *intermittent explosive disorder*, in which a person has episodes—generally self-described as "spells" or "attacks"—during which he or she loses control of aggressive impulses and assaults others or destroys property, often soon expressing regret over the damage done and inability to maintain control. Between episodes, aggressive impulses are not particularly noticeable. The disorder can appear at any age, but most often in the teens and 20s, and especially in males.
- *kleptomania*, in which a person is unable to resist impulses to steal items, not for their value or use and not because money is lacking to buy them. Often the items are thrown or given away, returned, or hidden and not used. Kleptomania can begin at any age, including childhood.
- *pyromania*, in which a person has irresistible impulses to start fires, deliberately and often with considerable planning, rather than accidentally. Pyromania often begins in childhood, but psychiatrists consider it most destructive during ADOLESCENCE and adulthood.
- *trichotillomania*, in which a person fails to resist the impulse to pull out his or her own hair, but not because of any skin problem or delusion; a condition often beginning in childhood and somewhat more common among children with MENTAL RETARDATION. Mostly hair from the scalp is involved, but the person may also pull eyebrows, eyelashes, and less frequently other body hair.
- *pathological gambling*, in which a person is unable to resist impulses to gamble, regardless of the disruption caused in his or her life, a pattern that often begins in adolescence in males, though somewhat later in females.

Such behaviors may also be associated with other kinds of mental disorders. They may also appear in people without particular disorders, such as children who pull their hair absentmindedly (see COMFORT HABITS) but apparently without the feeling of tension or gratification and release associated with impulse control disorders. (For help and further information, see MENTAL DISORDERS.)

inactivated polio vaccine (IPV or Salk vaccine) A vaccine made from killed polio viruses, given as a series of injections between ages two months and six years. ORAL POLIO VACCINE made from "live" viruses is used for most polio immunizations, but because the viruses can spread, IPV is preferred when the child or a family member has low resistance to serious infections. IPV is not known to produce any side effects other than minor local pain and redness.

inborn errors of metabolism A medical phrase referring to the genetic deficiencies behind a group of METABOLIC DISORDERS that cause disruption of the chemical and physical processes by which food is broken down for use in the body.

incest Sexual relations between close relatives, generally those who are too close to be permitted by law to marry, including at least parents, children, SIBLINGS, grandparents, great-grandparents, grandchildren, great-grandchildren, uncles, aunts, nieces, and nephews, and in some states also first cousins, stepchildren, stepparents, parents-in-law, children-in-law, and spouse's grandchildren or grandparents. Laws vary, and some states consider sexual relations to be incest, and therefore criminal, only if the parties are BLOOD RELATIVES; if a MINOR child is involved, however, sexual relations constitute child abuse. The most common kind of incest is between fathers and daughters, though same-sex incest also occurs. (For help and further information, see CHILD ABUSE AND NEGLECT.)

incompetent In the law, unable, unqualified, or inadequate to act or fulfill responsibilities. MINORS and some severely HANDICAPPED people may be considered legally incompetent, and in some cases the state may act on their behalf under the doctrine of PARENS PATRIAE.

incompetent cervix A condition of PREGNANCY in which the muscles of a woman's CERVIX are too weak to hold the FETUS within the UTERUS for the full term of GESTATION. Normally, the cervix widens only just before birth, in preparation for LABOR and DELIVERY, but in some women, the cervix begins to widen gradually months earlier, as can be detected with ULTRASOUND scanning. A woman who has had previous MISCARRIAGES or who is diagnosed as having an incompetent cervix may have a stitch placed across the end of the cervix to hold it together, generally under an *epidural anesthetic* (see ANESTHESIA) in the hospital at about the 14th week of pregnancy. She is also advised to limit activity for the rest of the pregnancy, when (once the suture is taken out) she should be able to deliver normally. (For help and further information, see PREGNANCY.)

incontinence Inability to control the release of urine from the bladder and of feces from the bowels, including inability to sense fullness, to empty thoroughly, and to close completely. Incontinence can have a variety of causes. Among toilet-trained children (as well as adults), short-term bouts of incontinence can occur as a result of local inflammation in the anus or urethra, temporary damage to the muscles in the area (as after CHILDBIRTH or surgery), infection (such as that which causes DIARRHEA), or physical stress, as in heavy athletic activity. In children, long-term or permanent incontinence most often occurs as a result of damage to the NERVOUS SYSTEM or to muscles in the area, as in cases of SPINA BIFIDA or PARAPLEGIA. The procedure of CLEAN, INTERMITTENT CATHETERIZATION helps such children handle bladder-emptying functions. By contrast, bedwetting (ENURESIS) and soiling (ENCOPRESIS) are not the result of physical damage alone, though some physical factors may be involved.

incorrigible In family law, a term for JUVENILES who refuse to obey their parents, such as juvenile DELINQUENTS, runaways (see MISSING CHILDREN), or chronic TRUANTS. Where parents are unable to exercise parental control, the police, social-work system, school, or the parents themselves may bring the child to court. If found incorrigible, the child is then made a WARD of the court and may either be returned home under the SUPERVISION of a PROBATION officer or placed elsewhere, as with FOSTER PARENTS or in an institution. Incorrigible children are often STA-

TUS OFFENDERS, who would not be brought before the court except that they are MINORS.

incubator   A special device providing control of the environment, including heat, light, oxygen, and humidity. In NEONATAL INTENSIVE CARE UNITS (NICUs), incubators are often used for PRE-MATURE or LOW-BIRTH-WEIGHT infants, or newborns with health problems. Sometimes these incubators may include tubes that assist in breathing (see VENTILATOR) and feeding (see PARENTERAL NUTRITION). Incubators may have portholes in the sides so that parents and nursing staff can handle the baby, for BONDING and stimulation of the senses.

independent study   A self-directed course of learning in which a student works outside a regular classroom but under the guidance of a teacher, who also evaluates the completed work, often for academic credit (depending on the school setting); sometimes also called HOME STUDY. Independent study is used in many ALTERNATIVE SCHOOLS and in some honors classes for "fast-track" students in a TRACKING system. (For help and further information, see HOME STUDY; EDUCATION.)

index case   Alternate term for PROBAND in constructing a family PEDIGREE during GENETIC COUNSELING.

individualized education program (IEP)   A written plan outlining the SPECIAL EDUCATION and other services to be provided for a HANDICAPPED child, as specified under the EDUCATION FOR ALL HANDICAPPED CHILDREN ACT OF 1975. This act specifies that the plan shall outline:

- the child's present levels of educational performance. This would vary depending on the nature of the child's handicap but might include the child's level of ability in a variety of areas, including communication skills (see COMMUNICATION SKILLS AND DISORDERS), SOCIAL SKILLS, SELF-HELP SKILLS, MOTOR SKILLS, academic achievement, and the like;
- annual goals;
- short-term instructional objectives, the individual steps by which the annual goal is to be reached;
- the special educational and other specific services to be provided to the child and who will provide them;
- the extent to which such a child will be able to participate in regular educational programs;
- the projected date for initiation and anticipated duration of special educational and other services;
- appropriate objective criteria and evaluation procedures and schedules for determining, on at least an annual basis, whether instructional objectives are being achieved.

An IEP is prepared for every child who has been evaluated and found to have some sort of handicap that would hinder learning. It is developed at a meeting involving one or both of the child's parents, the child's teacher (if he or she has more than one, the state may specify which should be involved), sometimes the child, another representative of the school or public agency (such as the special education teacher, LEARNING DISABILITIES specialist, or school principal), and perhaps other people brought by the parents or a state agency.

To prepare for such a meeting, parents may well want to visit the child's classes, talk with the child about school, perhaps talk with the teacher, and think realistically about the child's strengths and weaknesses and what he or she should reasonably be expected to accomplish in a year. No decisions can be made without parental permission, and parents should be as well informed as possible before the IEP meeting, being sure to convey to the others their special view of the child.

If everyone at the meeting agrees on a reasonable IEP for the child, all well and good. Then parents will want to keep in touch with the school and monitor how well the child is progressing with the program; if progress is not being made, the program may need to be revised.

But if, at the IEP meeting, parents and others are not able to agree on a reasonable program for the child (or if the program is found not to work and the school fails to modify it appropriately), parents have the right to appeal the program suggested by the school, by calling in writing for a DUE PROCESS hearing before an impartial hearing officer appointed by a public agency. For such a hearing, the parents may:

- have full access to all records;
- require full explanations of all records;
- request clarification, explanation, or removal of false or misleading information in the records;
- have with them people of their choice, including legal counsel, an advocacy group representative, an impartial educator, or an independent evaluator;
- call and question officials and call other witnesses;
- obtain an independent educational evaluation (at their own expense);
- prevent introduction of any document not made available to them at least five days earlier (school officials have the same right);
- have the child attend, if appropriate;
- have the hearing closed to the public, if desired.

The hearing officer may accept or reject the school's proposed IEP or may require that the school provide other services not mentioned in the original IEP.

If parents fail to obtain satisfaction at the due process hearing, they can appeal to the state department of education (unless the hearing was handled by that department) and ultimately to civil court if necessary, though it is, of course, preferable to settle matters informally where possible. Since 1986, a new provision of the Education for All Handicapped Children Act provides that parents who win at a hearing, appeal, or court proceeding may be awarded reimbursement from the school for legal and evaluative fees, and the U.S. Supreme Court has ruled that in some cases such parents may be able to collect from the school the costs of private schooling for a child if the court agrees with the parents that the school's original program for the child was incorrect.

One area of substantial disagreement has been the initial evaluation of a child. Because many TESTS are geared toward middle-class students speaking standard English, children who speak nonstandard English or another language, or who come from a disadvantaged or non-middle-class background, have sometimes been wrongly diagnosed as mentally retarded or having communications disorders. As a result, the law now specifies that children cannot be placed in special education programs on the basis of only one test, that the tests must be given in the child's language, and that the evaluation must include observation of the child. Schools are also obliged to communicate with the parents using their primary language.

Parents who believe their child has been wrongly diagnosed may call for a due process hearing. Conversely, many parents have found that their children had undiagnosed LEARNING DISABILITIES and have had to use the due process hearing to obtain proper educational services for their children. While such questions are in dispute, the child generally stays in whatever program he or she was placed in. (See PARENT'S GUIDELINES TO THE EVALUATION PROCESS under EDUCATION FOR ALL HANDICAPPED CHILDREN ACT OF 1975.)

For help and further information

Children's Defense Fund (CDF)
122 C Street, NW, Suite 400
Washington, DC 20001
202-628-8787
Marian Wright Edelman, President
Organization acting as advocate for children and their rights. Carries on research, assists local community groups, and helps shape public policy and legislation, especially in such areas as child health and welfare, preventing adolescent pregnancy, child care, child development, and family services; publishes newsletter and other materials, including *94-142 and 504: Numbers That Add Up to Educational Rights for Handicapped Children, How to Help Handicapped Children Get an Education: A Success Story, It's Time to Stand Up for Your Children—A Parent's Guide to Child Advocacy,* and *Where Do You Look? An Information Resource for Child Advocates.*

Other reference sources

The Rights of Parents and the Responsibilities of Schools, by James G. Meade. Available from Educators Publishing Service, 75 Moulton Street, Cambridge, MA 02138.
How to Write an I.E.P., by John Arena. 1978. Available from Academic Therapy Publications, 20 Commercial Boulevard, Novato, CA 94947. Reviews rights of handicapped children and their parents.
How to Get Services by Being Assertive, by Charlotte Des Jardins. 1980. Available from Coordinating Council for Handicapped Children, 407 South Dearborn, Room 680, Chicago, IL 60605. Includes advice on IEP (Individualized Education Plan) meetings, due process hearings, and gaining access to school records.
(See also EDUCATION; SPECIAL EDUCATION; entries under specific types of handicaps, which include information on specific advocacy groups; HELP FOR SPECIAL CHILDREN on page 578, which includes information on general children's or parents' advocacy groups.)

inductive learning A LEARNING STYLE in which a child is given information or materials about a variety of specific situations and learns to draw a general conclusion or rule from them; also called *discovery learning.*

infant A very young child, usually one not yet able to walk. In law, the term generally refers to a MINOR, usually meaning a person under age 18, but the BABY DOE LAW defines *infant* as a child under one year.

infanticide The killing of a baby. Historically, and still in a few cultures, many unwanted babies—especially girls, infants of unacknowledged paternity, or babies with BIRTH DEFECTS—were simply abandoned, if not directly killed. Such ABANDONMENT is rare and rejected in most cultures today, but the term *infanticide* has more recently been applied with rhetorical emphasis to the killing of a FETUS (more properly called *feticide*).

infant mortality The DEATH of an infant during the first year of life, normally expressed as a rate of the number of deaths per specified number of pregnancies. Two thirds die during the first month (called *neonatal mortality*). Infant mortality has declined in recent years, because of a variety of factors, including better PRENATAL CARE, improved NUTRITION, availability of NEONATAL INTENSIVE CARE UNITS (NICUs), and a wide variety of advancements in medical technology. However, the improvement has not been felt uniformly. In the United States, the infant mortality rate among Blacks is almost twice as high as that for Whites. And in the world, the United States ranked 22nd in 1985, with an overall rate of 10.6 per 1,000 live births, while in some parts of the world the rate is almost 10 times that high. (For help and further information, including charts of the main causes of infant mortality, see DEATH.)

For help and further information
National Institute of Child Health and Human Development (NICHD), 301-496-5133. (For full group information, see PREGNANCY.)

Death Before Life: The Tragedy of Infant Mortality, by the National Commission to Prevent Infant Mortality. Washington, DC: Government Printing Office, 1988.

infection and antibody tests A common set of tests performed on SEMEN in evaluating INFERTILITY problems.

infectious mononucleosis Alternate term for MONONUCLEOSIS.

infectious parotitis Alternate name for MUMPS.

infertility Inability to conceive a baby, also often encompassing the related inability to carry a child, once conceived, to FULL TERM in a healthy birth. In practice, infertility is often not permanent and absolute (a condition called *sterility*) but temporary or a matter of decreased odds, more properly called *subfertility*. Among specialists in the field, infertility is often defined as the inability to conceive after two years of trying, without medical intervention. Sometimes the problem is simply the result of not timing sexual intercourse with OVULATION in such a way as to maximize the chances of CONCEPTION. But a wide variety of problems can lead to temporary or permanent infertility, including:

- *poor general physical condition,* such as being overweight, being underweight, or having ANEMIA.
- *abuses of the body,* such as ALCOHOL ABUSE, SMOKING, or DRUG ABUSE, which can lower the SPERM count.
- *hostile conditions in the woman's reproductive system,* such as acidic or impenetrable mucus in the VAGINA or CERVIX, but also sometimes a woman's ALLERGY to her partner's sperm, and perhaps in both partners the formation of ANTIBODIES that cause sperm to clump together.
- GENETIC DISORDERS, such as TURNER'S SYNDROME (for women), KLINEFELTER'S SYNDROME (for men), and CYSTIC FIBROSIS (for men).
- *problems with* HORMONES *and glands,* such as the PITUITARY, THYROID, or ADRENAL GLANDS.
- *problems with the* OVARIES, as in not producing eggs, a condition called *anovulation,* or irregularity of ovulation.
- *problems with the sperm,* such as a low sperm count, insufficiently active sperm, or too short a life span. Lack of sperm is called *azoospermia,* while too few sperm is termed *oligospermia.*
- *physical malformations,* such as deformed UTERUS, undescended testicles, undeveloped ovaries or TESTES (as in HYPOGONADISM), lack of essential organs (such as the uterus or FALLOPIAN TUBES), or blocked tubes or ducts through which the sperm and egg must pass (sometimes because of infection or injury, as noted below). An INCOMPETENT CERVIX may make it impossible for a child to be held in the uterus for the full term.
- *problems in getting the sperm into the vagina,* including impotence and problems with EJACULATION.
- *problems with development of the sperm,* sometimes apparently caused by the testicles being too hot, as in cases of VARICOCELE (a swollen vein in a testicle, easily treated surgically).
- *current infection or damage from previous infection,* affecting various reproductive organs. SEXUALLY TRANSMITTED DISEASES are common culprits, especially in women, including PELVIC INFLAMMATORY DISEASE, CHLAMYDIAL INFECTIONS, and GONORRHEA.
- *other abnormalities,* such as ENDOMETRIOSIS, scarring or adhesions in the fallopian tubes, cervical polyps, or fibroid TUMORS in women and HYDROCELE in men; scars and damage from previous injuries, as from an INTRAUTERINE DEVICE; or operations, such as for ECTOPIC PREGNANCY.
- *the effects of earlier diseases that might affect fertility,* such as MUMPS, MEASLES, WHOOPING COUGH, DIPHTHERIA, RUBELLA, DIABETES MELLITUS, TUBERCULOSIS, and EPILEPSY.

Among the changes that have led to wider infertility are the rise in sexually transmitted diseases in recent decades, partly linked to multiple sexual partners, use of intrauterine devices, delay of childbearing until later (since a woman's fertility decreases with age), and exposure to various ENVIRONMENTAL HAZARDS, the effects of which are often unknown. Women are more likely to have infertility problems than are men, but in many cases where a couple cannot conceive, both partners have problems that decrease their chances of achieving a pregnancy (such as low sperm count and irregular ovulation). In some cases, perhaps one in 10, it proves impossible to identify the cause of the infertility. And in many cases, couples conceive children while they are consulting about infertility but without any treatment being given.

If a couple decides to seek help with an infertility problem, they should probably start with their INTERNIST or FAMILY PRACTICE PHYSICIAN, since general health problems (rather than problems with the reproductive system itself) may be causing the difficulty. The next step would be the GYNECOLOGIST or UROLOGIST. Only if no solution is offered should the couple then consult a FERTILITY SPECIALIST, preferably part of a team, who will do a *fertility workup.* This is a major medical evaluation, including several office sessions, sometimes a brief hospital stay, and numerous tests over a period of months that may cost one to several thousand dollars in sum. It includes a detailed medical and sexual history and a series of tests.

Some of the main tests included in a fertility workup are noted below, the first three being performed in most cases. Which other tests are given and in what sequence depends on the particulars of the couple's background.

- *semen analysis,* in which semen produced by masturbation (usually after two days of sexual abstinence) is analyzed in the laboratory. The number of sperm per volume are noted, as are the shape and "swimming power" of the sperm. If a low sperm count is found, further tests might explore the cause.
- *postcoital test,* in which samples of mucus are taken from a woman's cervix a few hours after intercourse, to see whether sperm are present and active, dead, or sluggish.
- *endometrial biopsy,* in which a sample (BIOPSY) is taken of the endometrium (lining of the uterus) late in the MENSTRUAL CYCLE as a possible indication of whether ovulation has in fact occurred. Sometimes this shows that ovulation *has* occurred, but a hormonal imbalance prevents the endometrium from being properly developed to receive a fertilized egg.
- *infection and antibody tests,* in which semen is examined for bacteria and also antibodies that might cause death or clumping of the sperm.
- *ovulation tests,* to see whether ovulation has occurred.
- *basal temperature record,* a temperature chart using a specially calibrated thermometer, to see if and when ovulation occurs. (See NATURAL FAMILY PLANNING for a fuller description.)
- BLOOD TESTS, various laboratory analyses, some of them quite esoteric and expensive, to monitor the rise and fall of hormones, especially when a woman has no or irregular menstruation and other tests have proved uninformative.
- ULTRASOUND SCAN, in some special situations, to detect evidence of ovulation.
- HYSTEROSALPINGOGRAM, an X-RAY using a contrast dye to see whether the fallopian tubes are open.

- HYSTEROSCOPY, visual examination of the uterus through a lighted flexible tube (ENDOSCOPE) passed in through the vagina and cervix and sometimes equipped to take a biopsy as well.
- LAPAROSCOPY, visual examination of the reproductive organs through a device inserted through a small abdominal incision to look for evidence of ovulation or scarring, especially to see whether the fallopian tubes are blocked and to assess whether an operation could correct the condition.

Treatment of infertility varies according to the results of the tests. Sometimes it is simply a matter of the couple not being well enough attuned to the changes in their bodies to maximize their chances of conception. If ovulation does indeed take place, and other obstructions do not exist, use of natural family-planning techniques to identify the woman's most fertile time can lead to successful conception. And sometimes an underlying physical problem needs to be treated, such as a tumor in a PITUITARY GLAND or a thyroid disorder. But often other kinds of treatments are indicated, including:

- *fertility drugs,* which can be used in men to improve a low sperm count and in women can help correct problems with ovulation by acting on the glands that produce key hormones. In women, fertility drugs are associated with a significantly higher risk of MULTIPLE BIRTHS than normal, since sometimes more than one egg is produced in response to the drug and becomes fertilized.
- *surgery,* as to correct a VARICOCELE or to unblock ducts or tubes, where that is technically feasible, or to remove a section of an ovary containing cysts and thickened tissue (a procedure called an *ovarian wedge resection*), in an effort to restart ovulation, though the scar itself can cause problems.
- *lowering the heat of the man's* SCROTUM, sometimes by spending less time in a sauna or hot tub, wearing looser briefs and pants (which allow the testicles to lie further away from the body and therefore be cooler), and perhaps temporarily changing work that involves long exposure to heat.
- *modifying the semen* (where it hinders movement of the sperm), then using the modified semen in ARTIFICIAL INSEMINATION, a fairly new approach.

Beyond these are several other techniques, some of them relatively new, that have been breaking the bounds of reproductive technology and raising a great many social and ethical questions—which go much discussed but unresolved, as medical technology proceeds apace. Some of these techniques are still experimental and very expensive and have a high failure rate, yet for couples seeking a child, they offer a promise not available to previous generations. Among these techniques, dealt with in separate entries, are EMBRYO TRANSFER, GAMETE INTRAFALLOPIAN TUBE TRANSFER (GIFT), IN VITRO FERTILIZATION (IVF), and SURROGATE PARENTING.

For help and further information

American Fertility Society
2140 11th Avenue South, Suite 200
Birmingham, AL 35205
205-933-8494
Nancy C. Hayley, Administrative Director

Organization of medical professionals, acting as information clearinghouse on fertility and infertility. Provides information and referrals to physicians specializing in areas such as fertility workups, artificial insemination, reversing vasectomies, and in vitro fertilization; publishes various materials, including monthly *Fertility and Sterility Journal* and *How to Organize a Basic Study of the Infertile Couple* (written for medical professionals), *Report of the Ad Hoc Committee on Artificial Insemination,* and *Vasectomy: Facts About Male Sterilization*.

RESOLVE, Inc.
5 Water Street
Arlington, MA 02174
617-643-2424
Beverly Freeman, Executive Director
Karen Berkeley, Contact

Network of mutual-support self-help groups of couples dealing with infertility, counseled by trained professionals. Provides information and referrals in infertility-related areas, including infertility treatment, artificial insemination, in vitro fertilization, and adoption services; publishes various materials, including newsletter and fact sheets on specific topics, such as *Adoption, Artificial Insemination, Choosing a Specialist, Endometriosis, In Vitro Fertilization, Laparoscopy: What to Expect, Medical Evaluation of the Couple, Medical Management of Male Infertility, Miscarriage: Medical Facts, Semen Analysis, Surgical Techniques for Tubal Repair, Varicocele: Surgical and Medical Treatment.*

de Miranda Institute for Infertility and Modern Parenting Issues
3535 East Coast Highway, Box 95
Corona del Mar, CA 92625
714-833-9898

Organization that provides pamphlets and news updates on in vitro fertilization and related issues.

National Institute of Child Health and Human Development (NICHD), 301-496-5133. (For full group information, see PREGNANCY.)

Center for Surrogate Parenting (CSP), 213-655-1974. (For full group information, see SURROGATE PARENTING.)

Endometriosis Association (EA), 414-962-8972; toll-free number 800-992-ENDO [3636]. (For full group information, see ENDOMETRIOSIS.)

Other reference sources

General Works

New Options for Fertility: A Guide to In Vitro Fertilization and Other Assisted Reproduction Methods, by Arthur L. Wisot, M.D., and David R. Meldrum, M.D. New York: Pharos, 1990.

In Pursuit of Fertility: A Consultation with a Specialist, by Robert R. Franklin and Dorothy Kay Brockman. New York: Holt, 1990.

The Couple's Guide to Fertility: How New Medical Advances Can Help You Have a Baby, by Gary S. Berger, M.D., and Mark Fuerst. Garden City, NY: Doubleday, 1989.

A Stairstep Approach to Fertility, Margot Edwards, ed. Freedom, CA: Crossing, 1989.

Infertility: A Guide for the Childless Couple, revised reprint, by Barbara Eck Manning. New York: Prentice Hall, 1988.

The New Fertility and Conception: Today's Essential Guide to Childless Couples, by John J. Stangel, M.D. New York: New American Library, 1988.

The Infertility Maze: Finding Your Way to the Right Help and the Right Answers, by Kassie Schwan. Chicago: Contemporary, 1988.

Health Care U.S.A., by Jean Carper. New York: Prentice Hall, 1987. Resource for general and specific health-care information, as on infertility and childbirth, including treatments such as artificial insemination by donor (AID), in vitro fertilization, GIFT (gamete intrafallopian transfer), embryo transfer, and surrogate motherhood; lists key in vitro fertilization centers, embryo transfer centers, sperm banks, sexual dysfunction clinics, nurse-midwife centers, and other information.

In Pursuit of Pregnancy: How Couples Discover, Cope With, and Resolve Their Fertility Problems, by Joan Liebmann-Smith. New York: Newmarket, 1987.

Give Us a Child: Coping with the Personal Crisis of Infertility, by Lynda Rutledge Stephenson. San Francisco: Harper & Row, 1987.

You Can Have a Baby: Everything You Need to Know About Fertility, by Joseph H. Bellina and Josleen Wilson. New York: Bantam, 1986; Crown, 1985.

Infertility: How Couples Can Cope, by Linda P. Salzer. Boston: G.K. Hall, 1986.

Miracle Babies and Other Happy Endings for Couples with Fertility Problems, by Mark Perloe and Linda Gail Christie. New York: Rawson, 1986.

New Conceptions: A Consumer's Guide to the Newest Infertility Treatments, Including In Vitro Fertilization, Artificial Insemination, and Surrogate Motherhood, by Lori B. Andrews, J.D. New York: St. Martin's, 1984.

Conquering Infertility, by Dr. Stephen L. Corson. Norwalk, CT: Appleton-Century-Crofts, 1983.

Coping with Infertility, by Judith A. Stigger. Minneapolis: Augsburg, 1983.

Understanding: A Guide to Impaired Fertility for Family and Friends, by Pat Johnston. Fort Wayne, IN: Perspectives, 1983.

Getting Pregnant in the 1980s, by Robert H. Glass and Ronald J. Ericsson. Berkeley: University of California Press, 1982.

Your Search for Fertility, by Graham H. Barker. New York: Morrow, 1981.

The Fertility Handbook, by Aaron S. Lifchez, M.D., and Judith A. Fenton. New York: Clarkson N. Potter, 1980.

How to Get Pregnant, by Sherman J. Silber. New York: Scribner, 1980; Warner, 1981.

Infertility: A Guide for the Childless Couple, by Barbara Eck Menning (founder of RESOLVE, Inc.). Englewood Cliffs, NJ: Prentice-Hall, 1977.

Background Works

Making Babies: The New Science and Ethics of Conception, by Peter Singer and Deane Wells. New York: Scribner, 1985.

The Mother Machine: Reproductive Technologies from Artificial Insemination to Artificial Wombs, by Gena Corea. New York: Harper & Row, 1985.

Birth Trap: The Legal Low-Down on High-Tech Obstetrics, by Y. Brackhill, J. Rice, and D. Young. St. Louis: Mosby, 1984.

Test-Tube Babies: A Guide to Moral Questions, Present Techniques and Future Possibilities, by William Walters and Peter Singer. Oxford: Oxford University Press, 1982.

A Matter of Life: The Story of a Medical Breakthrough, by Robert Edwards and Patrick Steptoe (the first physician to perform successful in vitro fertilization). New York: William Morrow, 1980.

Trying Times: Crisis in Fertility. 1980. 33-minute film/video from Fanlight Productions, 47 Halifax Street, Boston, MA 02130. For adults. Strong on the emotional effects of infertility.

Personal Stories

Waiting for Baby: One Couple's Journey Through Infertility to Adoption, by Mary Earle Chase. New York: McGraw-Hill, 1989.

Sweet Grapes: How to Stop Being Infertile and Start Living Again, by Jean W. Carter and Michael Carter. Indianapolis: Perspectives, 1989. P.O. Box 90318, Indianapolis, IN 46290. On accepting infertility and childlessness and resuming control of lives and marriage.

Searching for the Stork: One Couple's Struggle to Start a Family, by Marion Lee Wasserman. New York: New American Library, 1988.

(See also PREGNANCY.)

inflammatory bowel disease (IBD) An umbrella name for a group of chronic DIGESTIVE DISORDERS affecting the small and large intestines. These disorders go by many names, some of them indicating simply inflammation of the affected part, such as *ileitis* (ileum, part of the small intestine), *enteritis* (small intestine), *colitis* (colon, or large intestine), *ileocolitis* (ileum and colon), *enterocolitis* (small and large intestines), or *procti-*

tis (rectum and anus). More often doctors divide IBD into two groups:

- *ulcerative colitis,* which involves ulcers (raw sores) and inflammation of the lining (*mucosa*) of the colon;
- *Crohn's disease,* which involves inflammation in the deeper layers of the intestinal wall and may also affect not only the colon but the whole digestive tract, including the mouth, esophagus, stomach, *duodenum* (upper part of the small intestine), and even the *appendix,* the tiny but troublesome projection off the intestines.

Symptoms of IBD include DIARRHEA, chronic pain in the abdomen, occasional FEVER, and sometimes bleeding from the rectum (especially from ulcerative colitis), which can lead to ANEMIA and weight loss. In children, persistent symptoms can stunt growth (see GROWTH AND GROWTH DISORDERS), especially affecting the joints, cause DEVELOPMENTAL DELAY, and slow sexual maturation. Ulcerative colitis is relatively easy to diagnose through visual examinations using a PROCTOSCOPE or SIGMOIDOSCOPE or BARIUM X-RAY EXAMINATIONS. The same examinations are not so helpful with Crohn's disease, because the affected areas are not always so accessible.

No cure is yet available for IBD. Drugs can help suppress cramps and diarrhea. Many people are helped by avoiding foods that trigger symptoms; these vary from person to person but often include MILK, alcohol, hot spices, and FIBER. The National Institute of Diabetes and Digestive and Kidney Diseases (NIDDK) notes that "maintaining good general nutrition and adequate intake is far more important than emphasizing or avoiding any particular food. Also, large doses of vitamins are useless and may even produce harmful side effects." Doctors sometimes recommend nutritional supplements, often high-calorie liquid formulas, to growing children. In severe cases, when patients need extra NUTRITION, their bowels need complete rest, or their bowels are too inflamed to absorb sufficient nourishment from food, doctors may place patients on PARENTERAL NUTRITION, supplied intravenously.

Among the complications of IBD are the formation of holes (*perforations*) and abnormal openings (*fistulas*), which may spread infection and inflammation to the abdominal cavity, including the potentially dangerous *peritonitis* (inflammation of the *peritoneum,* the abdomen's lining). Ulcerative colitis carries an increased risk of colon or rectal CANCER. And with Crohn's disease, obstructions or blockages may form and need surgical correction. IBD can also have wider effects on the body, being associated with some forms of ARTHRITIS, SKIN DISORDERS, inflammation of the eyes and mouth, kidney stones, gallstones, and some LIVER PROBLEMS.

Both main forms of IBD may go into REMISSION for long periods, sometimes years, for unknown reasons and then recur equally unexpectedly, though sometimes with obvious triggers. In the long run, the NIDDK estimates, perhaps one-third of the people with ulcerative colitis may need to have part or all of the colon removed, sometimes making an artificial opening called an OSTOMY in the abdomen for emptying of the bowels. Likewise, the NIDDK estimates that about two out of three patients with Crohn's disease will require intestinal surgery at some time during their lives. Unfortunately, removing sections of the intestine does not solve the problem, because the inflammation tends to reappear in the sections near those removed (as it does not in ulcerative colitis).

The NIDDK estimates that one to two million people suffer from IBD, men and women equally and people of all backgrounds. The disorder appears to be especially common among Jews and in general more common among Whites than Blacks, Hispanics, Native Americans, and people of Asian ancestry. In about one case in four, a person with IBD has a blood relative, often a SIBLING, who also has the disorder, but researchers are not sure to what extent that connection is genetic and to what extent environmental. The disorder seems to be on the rise around the world, but for unknown reasons.

Women with active Crohn's disease may have slightly increased difficulty in conceiving, perhaps because of associated symptoms, such as fever and anemia. They also have a higher-than-normal risk of having a STILLBIRTH, MISCARRIAGE, or PREMATURE delivery. Because IBD can worsen during pregnancy, women should try to bring the disorder under control before attempting conception. They will also wish to consult with their doctor about the effect that any medication may have on the developing FETUS or on the baby if BREASTFEEDING is chosen.

For help and further information

National Foundation for Ileitis and Colitis (NFIC)
444 Park Avenue, 11th Floor
New York, NY 10016
212-685-3440
George Theobald, Jr., Executive Director
Organization devoted to exploring problems from and cure for ileitis and colitis. Sponsors research; supports formation of local mutual-support groups for patients and their families; provides information and referrals; publishes many materials, including quarterly newsletters *IBD News* and *National Newsletter,* books such as *The Crohn's Disease and Ulcerative Colitis Fact Book* and *People . . . Not Patients: A Source Book for Living with Inflammatory Bowel Disease,* and booklets such as *Crohn's Disease, Ulcerative Colitis and Your Child, Coping With Crohn's Disease and Ulcerative Colitis* (for young people), *Living with IBD* (for young people), and *Questions and Answers About Pregnancy in Ileitis and Colitis.*

National Institute of Diabetes, Digestive and Kidney Diseases (NIDDK), 301-496-3583. Publishes various materials, including *Inflammatory Bowel Disease, IBD and IBS: Two Very Different Problems,* and *Bleeding in the Digestive Tract. (For full group information, see* DIGESTIVE DISORDERS.)

Other reference sources

Eating Right for a Bad Gut: The Complete Nutritional Guide to Ileitis, Crohn's Disease and Inflammatory Bowel Syndrome, by James Scala. New York: New American Library, 1990.

Treating IBD: A Patient's Guide to the Medical and Surgical Management of Inflammatory Bowel Disease, Lawrence J. Brandt and Penny Steiner-Grossman, eds. New York: Raven, 1989. Produced by the National Foundation for Ileitis and Colitis.

Inflammatory Bowel Disease: A Guide for Patients and Their Families, by Stephen B. Hanauer and Joseph B. Kirsner. New York: Raven, 1985.

The Crohn's Disease and Ulcerative Colitis Fact Book, by National Foundation for Ileitis and Colitis. New York: Scribner, 1983.

The Bowel Book: A Practical Guide to Good Health, by David Ehrlich and George Wolf. New York: Schocken, 1981.

Inflammatory Bowel Disease, third edition, J.B. Kirsner and R. G. Shorter, eds. Philadelphia: Lea & Febiger, 1988. Medical textbook.

(See also DIGESTIVE DISORDERS.)

informal assessment   A method of evaluating student performance by writing evaluations rather than assigning numerical or letter GRADES; sometimes called *summative evaluation.* Informal assessments are used in some ALTERNATIVE SCHOOLS or other types of experimental institutions and are common in PRE-SCHOOL and early PRIMARY SCHOOLS. While providing more information about a student, such written evaluations do not readily allow for comparison of students, as for applications to COL-LEGE.

informed consent   Formal written permission to be obtained from a patient by medical personnel before invasive and possibly risky MEDICAL TESTS or other medical procedures, such as operations, are performed. By law, the doctor is required to tell patients, in language they can understand, the risks as well as the benefits of the test or procedure to be performed and to give patients information about possible alternative tests to find the same or similar information. Before certain types of procedures, the patient may be asked to sign a document outlining that information in language understandable to nonprofessionals, often before a witness and generally a specified number of hours or days ahead of time. Because children, as MINORS, are usually not legally able to sign such documents, parents must obtain and analyze the information and give consent for them. (For help and further information, see MEDICAL TESTS.)

inheritance rights   Legal rights to inherit a share of the estate of someone who has died. If the person died with a valid will, these rights are spelled out in that document, which must be affirmed as valid by a PROBATE COURT. But if the person died *intestate* (without a will), the *intestate succession* laws of the particular state will determine precisely who is entitled to what share of the estate, if any. Among those who usually have inheritance rights by state law are BLOOD RELATIVES or KIN, adopted children, ADOPTIVE PARENTS, and a surviving spouse. Someone who would normally have inheritance rights but who was deliberately or inadvertently (such as an AFTER-BORN child)

left out of the will is termed *disinherited,* or more formally a *pretermitted heir.*

injection   In medicine, the technique of forcing a liquid into the body by means of a *syringe,* a hollow-barreled cylinder with a plunger (though sometimes a rubber bulb) affixed to a needle. Health professionals name injections for the different parts of the body into which the fluid is being introduced, common forms being:

• *intra-arterial:* directly into an artery, such as one that supplies a TUMOR;
• *intradermal:* directly into the skin, specifically the *dermis*;
• *intramuscular:* directly into the muscle;
• *intravenous:* directly into a vein, as after an operation;
• *intrathecal:* directly through the membrane enclosing the spinal cord and into the CEREBROSPINAL FLUID (CSF);
• *subcutaneous:* directly into the tissue beneath the skin, such as the upper arm or thigh, like most common "shots."

Sometimes nutrients and medications may be introduced into the body by any of various types of injections, bypassing the digestive system; such injections are termed parenteral (see PARENTERAL NUTRITION).

Where carefully sterile conditions are maintained, such injections pose little risk, and we have come to accept them as everyday occurrences. But where proper caution is not exercised, injections can introduce infections, since they are INVASIVE procedures, a matter of special concern in the AIDS era.

inkblot test   Popular name for a test such as the RORSCHACH PSYCHODIAGNOSTIC TEST.

in loco parentis   The legal term for the duties and rights of an organization or GUARDIAN acting as temporary parent to a child, as in a boarding school or camp; from the Latin for "in place of a parent."

insomnia   A type of SLEEPING DISORDER.

insulin   A HORMONE produced by the pancreas, lack of which produces the disease DIABETES MELLITUS. Too much insulin, as during treatment, can cause HYPOGLYCEMIA or *insulin shock.*

intact family   A FAMILY that has never been split, as through divorce or separation.

integration   Ability to use all of the available MODALITIES or senses to gain new learning. (See LEARNING STYLE.)

intelligence quotient (IQ)   The final score on an INTELLIGENCE TEST, relating a child's score on the test, notably the STANFORD-BINET INTELLIGENCE TEST, with NORMS determined for other children of the same age, by means of a formula; a somewhat outdated concept.

intelligence tests   TESTS intended to measure general mental abilities, dubbed "intelligence"; the VALIDITY of such tests has been greatly attacked in recent years, as it is unclear what intelligence tests actually measure (a question of *content validity*) and how well the tests estimate future intellectual performance (*predictive validity*). Old-style, strongly verbal intelligence tests, such as the STANFORD-BINET INTELLIGENCE TEST, have been accused of unfairly discriminating against children who are not from White, comfortably middle-class, two-parent families; the charge is that—far from measuring innate abilities—they are measuring experience of certain kinds, leaving children without those experiences at a distinct disadvantage. Some testers have attempted to get around the thorny cultural problem by trying to devise tests that are independent of (or at least even-handed regarding) cultural experience, tests called CULTURE-FAIR or *culture-free*. Others have developed kinds of tests that do not depend on either verbal ability or cultural background and, as a result, also measure different aspects of "intelligence." Examples include the GOODENOUGH-HARRIS DRAWING TEST, KOHS BLOCK DESIGN TEST, MERRILL-PALMER SCALES OF MENTAL DEVELOPMENT, and STANDARD PROGRESSIVE MATRICES. In addition, some intelligence tests have been developed for very young, even preverbal children, such as the CATTELL INFANT INTELLIGENCE SCALE. Other intelligence tests in wide use for children today include the WECHSLER INTELLIGENCE SCALE FOR CHILDREN—REVISED (probably the most widely used) and the KAUFMAN ASSESSMENT BATTERY FOR CHILDREN.

For help and further information

Perspectives on Bias in Mental Testing, C. Reynolds, ed. New York: Plenum, 1984.
The Science and Politics of IQ, by L. Kamin. New York: Wiley, 1974.
(See also STANFORD-BINET INTELLIGENCE TEST, including the standard IQ categories; TESTS.)

intensive care unit (ICU)   A division of a HOSPITAL designed to provide continuous monitoring and medical care for people with acute, life-threatening conditions, such as severe BURNS, multiple injuries, and certain heart problems (see HEART AND HEART PROBLEMS). ICUs have far more sophisticated monitoring and treatment equipment than do ordinary hospital wards and have specially trained staff. LOW-BIRTH-WEIGHT, PREMATURE, or seriously ill infants are often placed in an ICU; some large, sophisticated hospitals (Level III or tertiary care) have separate NEONATAL INTENSIVE CARE UNITS (NICUs).

interfaith   Description of a FAMILY in which partners and perhaps children are of different religions.

intermediate school   Alternate term for MIDDLE SCHOOL; the term *intermediate* is sometimes used to refer to the upper elementary grades, 4 to 6.

intermittent explosive disorder   A kind of IMPULSE CONTROL DISORDER.

intermittent peritoneal dialysis (IPD)   A form of DIALYSIS.

internist   A physician who specializes in treating diseases affecting the internal organs of adults and in providing primary health care for adults.

interracial   Description of a FAMILY in which partners or children are of different racial backgrounds.

intervention   Action to relieve a stressful situation or series of problems threatening someone's health or welfare; generally called CRISIS INTERVENTION.

intra-arterial   A type of INJECTION made directly into an artery, such as one that supplies a TUMOR.

intradermal   A type of INJECTION made directly into the skin, specifically the *dermis*.

intramuscular   A type of INJECTION made directly into a muscle.

intrapartal care   Medical care for a pregnant woman throughout the whole of LABOR, from the onset of CONTRACTIONS through the DELIVERY of the baby and expulsion of the PLACENTA (afterbirth); a part of the MATERNITY CYCLE. Care for the baby in the same period is called *newborn intrapartal care*. (For help and further information, see POSTNATAL CARE.)

intrathecal   A type of injection made directly through the membrane enclosing the SPINAL CORD and into the CEREBROSPINAL FLUID (CSF).

intrauterine device (IUD)   A form of BIRTH CONTROL that involves the insertion of a metal or plastic device into a woman's UTERUS, to prevent IMPLANTATION of a fertilized egg. Some IUDs are biochemically neutral, but others contain HORMONES that also aid in CONTRACEPTION; a string hangs down to allow women to check that the IUD is still in place. IUDs were popular for some years because the neutral (inert) types could remain in place for up to five years, and they had a high effectiveness rate as contraceptives of 95 to 96 percent. However, some types of IUDs, especially the Dalkon Shield, were linked with increased risk of many serious problems, including infection in the reproductive system, septic ABORTION (with severe infection), perforation of the uterus, PELVIC INFLAMMATORY DISEASE, ECTOPIC PREGNANCY, and other causes of INFERTILITY. Other less serious side effects occurred shortly after insertion, including cramping, dizziness, backache, bleeding, and heavy MENSTRUATION. The Dalkon Shield was removed from the market in 1974; later the manufacturer agreed to pay medical costs of women injured by their IUDs. Because of these medical and legal problems, many manufacturers have ceased making IUDs in the United States. Some are still available and being used, however. (For help and further information, see BIRTH CONTROL.)

intrauterine growth retardation   Slow growth of the FETUS during a PREGNANCY, often resulting in a child labeled SMALL FOR GESTATIONAL AGE. Growth can be slowed when the mother has certain medical conditions, such as PREECLAMPSIA, high blood pressure (HYPERTENSION), or chronic KIDNEY AND UROLOGICAL DISORDERS, as well as improper NUTRITION, SMOKING, or ALCOHOL ABUSE. Slow growth can also result from failure of the PLACENTA to provide appropriate nutrients, from viral infection caught from the mother, such as RUBELLA (German measles), or from conditions resulting from CHROMOSOMAL ABNORMALITIES, such as DOWN'S SYNDROME. (For help and further information, see LOW BIRTH WEIGHT; GESTATIONAL AGE; PREGNANCY.)

intravenous   Describing a type of INJECTION made directly into a vein, as during or after an operation.

intraventricular hemorrhage (IVH)   Severe bleeding into the VENTRICLES of the brain, a problem often associated with PREMATURE babies. (For help and further information, see PREMATURE.)

intussusception   Telescoping of the small intestine, a painful DIGESTIVE DISORDER common in young children, causing COLIC-like symptoms and often requiring surgical correction; also known by the more general term PROLAPSE.

in utero surgery   A medical procedure in which a physician, using FETOSCOPY, operates on the FETUS in the UTERUS to correct abnormalities; also called *fetal surgery*. One common type of fetal surgery is the insertion of a catheter to bypass a fetus's blocked urinary tract, to prevent kidney damage. For a fetus suffering from RH INCOMPATIBILITY in the blood an EXCHANGE TRANSFUSION can also be carried out. In utero surgery holds enormous promise for correction of BIRTH DEFECTS, and numerous life-saving or life-enhancing operations have been performed or are planned on an experimental basis.

invasive   General descriptive term for something that tends to spread or intrude into its surroundings, such as CANCER or a TUMOR. In relation to MEDICAL TESTS, the term *invasive* describes a procedure that involves "breaching the body's defenses." It is generally used to refer to tests in which foreign substances are introduced by a potentially risky procedure, as when a dyed fluid is injected into the body by way of a LUMBAR PUNCTURE in a MYELOGRAM. A simple procedure such as inserting a needle into a child's arm to take a blood sample can also be regarded as invasive. In most medical establishments in the United States, where standards of hygiene are high and needles are either new and sterile or carefully sterilized, there is little risk from the taking of a blood sample. But where needles are reused without being carefully sterilized, even the seemingly simple puncture of a needle can lead to serious infection—deadly in the case of AIDS. By contrast, an ULTRASOUND scan would be regarded medically as noninvasive, because nothing is injected or ingested into the body. (For help and more information, see MEDICAL TESTS.)

in vitro fertilization (IVF)   Treatment for INFERTILITY in which the SPERM and egg (OVUM) are brought together for FERTILIZATION, not in a woman's FALLOPIAN TUBES but in a glass laboratory dish (*in vitro* means literally "in glass"); also called *test-tube fertilization*. The technique is especially useful if the woman's fallopian tubes are so damaged or clogged that they cannot be used as a site for fertilization but the rest of her reproductive organs are functioning.

In the actual procedure, the woman is given fertility drugs during the first week of her MENSTRUAL CYCLE to stimulate the maturation of eggs, which is monitored using ULTRASOUND SCANS and BLOOD TESTS during the next few days. At about the 14th day of the cycle, just before OVULATION, which is sometimes pushed along by injections of HORMONES, doctors remove as many ripe eggs as possible, using a technique such as LAPAROSCOPY or ASPI-

RATION. Then, after a few hours, the eggs are mixed with the man's sperm in a glass dish and placed in an incubator. Fertilization, if it occurs, will take place within 12 hours, and the fertilized eggs will begin to divide.

At that point, several fertilized eggs are drawn into a CATHETER, which is then inserted through the woman's CERVIX, and the eggs deposited into the UTERUS, after which the woman is assigned bed rest while the embryos—it is hoped—implant.

Several eggs are used because the failure rate is so high, with many eggs failing to implant or spontaneously aborting in the weeks that follow, some because of CHROMOSOMAL ABNORMALITIES. On the other hand, the insertion of multiple fertilized eggs has often led to MULTIPLE BIRTHS. Questions also abound about the legal status of the fertilized eggs, some of which may be frozen for future use. Some states have even barred the procedure because of ethical questions regarding the test-tube-created EMBRYOS.

In vitro fertilization, though dramatic, still has a very low success rate. The procedures are enormously expensive, with costs not covered by many insurance policies, as well as being emotionally and physically very taxing, involving travel to the clinic, loss of work time, and cost of accommodations for at least two weeks each time the procedure is tried. Fertility experts recommend that IVF should not be entered into lightly and should be the last resort, chosen only after full fertility workups and thorough exploration of other options. IVF clinics also vary widely in their success rates, some having nearly zero. A couple exploring IVF should certainly question clinics carefully about the actual number of live births that have resulted from their clinic's work.

For help and further information

In Vitro Fertilization: Building Policy from Laboratories to Legislatures, by Andrea Bonnicksen. Irvington, NY: Columbia University Press, 1989.
(See also INFERTILITY; IMPLANTATION; PREGNANCY.)

iodine   A MINERAL needed in the body, though only in trace amounts, for the normal functioning of the THYROID GLAND, which through HORMONES controls the body's METABOLISM, growth, and development. The best natural source of iodine is seafood, but to ensure that they get enough iodine, many people use iodized salt—table salt with iodine added. Iodine deficiency can lead to various thyroid problems, including a thyroid-related kind of physical and MENTAL RETARDATION sometimes called *cretinism*. Radioactive forms of iodine are sometimes used to treat thyroid problems and as part of some kinds of RADIOISOTOPE SCANS. Iodine is also sometimes used as an antiseptic. (For help and further information, see MINERALS; NUTRITION.)

Iowa Tests of Basic Skills (ITBS)   A set of group-administered paper-and-pencil tests that attempt to measure basic academic skills, available in various forms for children in grades K to 9. The tests cover vocabulary, READING, language, spelling,

Do Pregnant Women Need Extra Iron?

The need for iron is increased during pregnancy, with about 500 mg needed to increase the number of maternal red blood cells, about 600 mg needed for the fetus and placenta, about 200 mg needed to replace normal maternal losses, and another 200 mg needed to replace the red blood cells lost during delivery. Because menstruation ceases for nine months, about 300 mg of iron are saved, and the total additional iron needed for a pregnancy with a normal delivery is about 1,200 mg, or about 4 mg/day. As discussed under anemia, iron deficiency occurs infrequently in the general population. Nevertheless, the National Research Council [Food and Nutrition Board, National Academy of Sciences, which advises the Food and Drug Administration] recommends an iron supplement of 30 to 60 mg/day to prevent depletion of iron stores during pregnancy and lactation. Even when women are not anemic, they may complete pregnancy with low iron reserves. Clinical studies indicate that iron absorption increases progressively throughout pregnancy. Although as much as 90 percent may be absorbed under these defined experimental conditions, the true efficiency of dietary iron absorption under normal situations of food intake is unknown. For these reasons, pregnant women should be evaluated periodically to determine their level of iron stores and should receive supplements when stores are low.

Source: *The Surgeon General's Report on Nutrition and Health.* Rocklin, CA: Prima, 1988.

capitalization, punctuation, usage, work and STUDY SKILLS, visual materials, reference materials, concepts in mathematics, problem solving, and computation, and sometimes also listening, word analysis, science, and social studies. For older students, in grades 9 to 12, schools may use the *Iowa Tests of Educational Development (ITED),* which focus on more sophisticated material and skills, such as critical analysis, understanding scientific material, distinguishing between different literary approaches, and using common information tools. Any of these tests may be hand- or computer-scored, and student SCORES are compared with national NORMS. The "Iowas" are used to identify strengths and weaknesses in a student's basic skills, to evaluate the effectiveness of classroom instruction, and to monitor a student's progress year by year. (For help and further information, see TESTS.)

IPD Abbreviation for intermittent peritoneal dialysis, a form of DIALYSIS.

IPV Abbreviation for INACTIVATED POLIO VACCINE.

IQ Abbreviation for INTELLIGENCE QUOTIENT.

iron A MINERAL required by the body, though in trace amounts, to work with PROTEIN to make HEMOGLOBIN, the vital blood substance that transports oxygen from the lungs to the

cells, and *myoglobin,* which stores oxygen in muscles. Iron is found in many foods, including meat (especially liver), egg yolks, shellfish, green leafy vegetables, dried fruits such as prunes and raisins, apricots, whole-grain and enriched breads and cereals, and beans. Deficiency is uncommon with a balanced diet, but public health officials advise women to take iron supplements during PREGNANCY or extremely heavy MENSTRUATION. Lack of sufficient iron can lead to iron-deficiency ANEMIA. Excess iron should also be avoided, however, since it can build up in the internal organs, causing problems such as CIRRHOSIS OF THE LIVER. (For help and further information, see MINERALS; NUTRITION.)

irritable bowel syndrome (IBS) A chronic DIGESTIVE DISORDER of the colon (large intestine) of unknown cause. The disorder has also been called *mucous colitis, spastic colon, colitis, spastic bowel,* and *functional bowel disease.* The National Institute of Diabetes and Digestive and Kidney Diseases (NIDDK) points out that at least some of these terms are inaccurate, since they wrongly imply the presence of inflammation, as in the quite different disorder INFLAMMATORY BOWEL DISEASE (IBD). Symptoms of IBS include abdominal pain, gas, bloating, CONSTIPATION, DIARRHEA, or alternating constipation and diarrhea; it apparently stems partly from abnormalities in the movement of the large intestine, which sometimes leads to muscle spasms and resulting cramps. Because it is hard to identify precisely, physicians need to eliminate other more serious diseases before IBS is diagnosed. Symptoms can be lessened by careful management of diet, especially eating smaller meals and restricting the amount of fats in a meal, and by minimizing stress. Dietary FIBER can help, as can reduction of some kinds of dairy products, but people with IBS must be sure that the rest of their diet gives them sufficient CALCIUM. Antispasmodic drugs, laxatives, and tranquilizers are sometimes used, but doctors tend to prescribe them in moderation, to avoid potential DRUG ABUSE. Recent studies suggest that some cases of IBS may be caused by undiagnosed chronic giardiasis, which is infection by various protozoa.

For help and further information

The Wellness Book of I. B. S.: A Guide to Lifelong Relief from Symptoms of One of America's Most Common and Least-Talked-About Ailments: Irritable Bowel Syndrome, by Deralee Scanlon and Barbara Cottman Becnel. New York: St. Martin's, 1990.

(See also DIGESTIVE DISORDERS.)

issue The legal term for a person's biological descendants—children, grandchildren, and so on—commonly used in reference to wills and INHERITANCE RIGHTS; before an ADOPTION, parents should make sure to change their insurance policies and wills to include not only issue but also adopted children. An issue is also the main point being contested in a case, a *material issue* being one that must be settled before another can be resolved, as a question of paternity must be settled before the court can address CHILD SUPPORT.

ITBS Abbreviation for IOWA TESTS OF BASIC SKILLS.

ITED Abbreviation for Iowa Tests of Educational Development. (See IOWA TESTS OF BASIC SKILLS.)

ITPA Abbreviation for ILLINOIS TEST OF PSYCHOLINGUISTIC ABILITIES.

IUD Abbreviation for INTRAUTERINE DEVICE.

IVF Abbreviation for IN VITRO FERTILIZATION.

IVH Abbreviation for INTRAVENTRICULAR HEMORRHAGE.

Ivy League A group of COLLEGES and universities that include seven of the oldest such institutions in the United States, the eight members being Brown, Columbia, Cornell, Dartmouth, Harvard, Princeton, Pennsylvania (University of), and Yale. Their counterparts among formerly all-female colleges are the Seven Sisters: Barnard, Bryn Mawr, Mt. Holyoke, Radcliffe, Smith, Vassar, and Wellesley. Such private institutions and others on their level—such as Stanford and the Massachusetts Institute of Technology—have traditionally high prestige and often maintain high academic standards. However, in recent decades some public colleges and universities have attained equal or even greater academic excellence, partly because public funding has often allowed for better plants and equipment, salaries, and materials. In recent ratings by American professors themselves, for example, the top schools in several subject areas have been public universities, notably the University of California (Berkeley or Los Angeles) and University of Michigan. Parents looking ahead to college for their children may want to explore public colleges, not automatically look to private ones; the difference in cost is enormous. (For help and further information, see COLLEGE.)

Jaeger test A widely used test for near vision. (See EYE AND VISION PROBLEMS.)

jaundice Yellowish discoloration of the skin, mucous membrane, and whites of the eyes, due to a buildup in the blood of *bilirubin*, a pigment in bile, a fluid secreted by the liver; a symptom of HYPERBILIRUBINEMIA, a condition of excess bilirubin. Jaundice is a common sign of liver disease or problems with associated bile ducts, often suggesting the advisability of various diagnostic tests. In *hemolytic jaundice*, the liver is unable to handle the amount of bilirubin; newborns often have this kind of jaundice, which gradually clears up as the body matures. In *hepatocellular jaundice*, buildup of bilirubin results from inflammation or failure of the liver, as in severe cases of HEPATITIS or CIRRHOSIS OF THE LIVER. In *obstructive jaundice*, bile is unable to exit from the liver because of blockage or absence of bile ducts; the latter condition, a GENETIC DISORDER, is called BILIARY ATRESIA. Jaundice also occurs temporarily in some infants during BREASTFEEDING, in a condition called *breastmilk jaundice*. (For help and further information, see LIVER PROBLEMS; BILIARY ATRESIA; BREASTFEEDING.)

JINS Abbreviation for juveniles in need of SUPERVISION.

JLRRT Abbreviation for JORDAN LEFT-RIGHT REVERSAL TEST.

Jordan Left-Right Reversal Test (JLRRT) A paper-and-pencil TEST used with children ages five to 12 to measure the frequency of TRANSPOSITIONS, that is, reversals of letters, numbers, and words. The test asks students to pick out errors (reversed or upside down) among groups of letters and numbers and to identify which words have similar errors; children with perceptual problems often miss the real transpositions while perceiving others. The JLRRT may be administered to individuals or groups; the tests are scored by hand, and the SCORES are converted into a DEVELOPMENTAL AGE. Sometimes used as a kind of DEVELOPMENTAL SCREENING TEST, it may also be used as a DIAGNOSTIC ASSESSMENT TEST, especially for children thought to have possible LEARNING DISABILITIES. (For help and further information, see TESTS.)

JRA Abbreviation for juvenile rheumatoid ARTHRITIS.

junior high school Alternate term for MIDDLE SCHOOL.

junior primary Alternate term for KINDERGARTEN.

juvenile court The type of court that handles most cases involving MINORS. JUVENILES involved in criminal cases generally appear in juvenile court rather than CRIMINAL COURT, as do children considered INCORRIGIBLE. In cases of CHILD ABUSE AND NEGLECT or TERMINATION OF PARENTAL RIGHTS, parents may sometimes be called before a juvenile court, with the minor's interest often represented by a court-appointed GUARDIAN *ad litem* (at law) or a COURT-APPOINTED SPECIAL ADVOCATE (CASA). In some states, the role of the juvenile court is taken over by the FAMILY

COURT. Judges sometimes appoint referees or commissioners to handle actual hearings in juvenile court.

juveniles Young persons who are not old enough to be treated as adults under criminal law. (By contrast, the term MINOR refers to a young person's legal ability to act as an adult.) The age limit varies, but the Juvenile Justice and Delinquency Prevention Act of 1974 defined a juvenile as someone under the age of 18; cases involving juveniles are generally tried in JUVENILE COURT. If found to have committed a crime, a minor

is—in strict legal terms—labeled a juvenile DELINQUENT, a term often applied more loosely and widely to adolescents who are disruptive or troublesome, or UNSOCIALIZED. Juveniles are often STATUS OFFENDERS, and so may be made WARDS of the court and committed to an institution for acts that, if committed by an adult, would not be considered criminal.

juvenile rheumatoid arthritis (JRA) A form of ARTHRITIS affecting children, sometimes called *Still's disease*.

K-ABC Abbreviation for KAUFMAN ASSESSMENT BATTERY FOR CHILDREN.

Kasai procedure (hepatoportoenterostomy) A surgical procedure for correcting malfunctioning bile ducts in some cases of BILIARY ATRESIA.

Kaufman Assessment Battery for Children (K-ABC or ABC) An individually administered test designed to act as both INTELLIGENCE TEST and ACHIEVEMENT TEST, used with children from ages 2½ to 12½. Its various subtests focus on mental processing (both sequential and simultaneous), which are scored separately and then together, as well as acquired knowledge, READING, and arithmetic, which yields a SCORE for achievement. The K-ABC is often used as a DIAGNOSTIC ASSESSMENT TEST for preschoolers and older children, attempting to learn more about the strengths and weaknesses of children who may have learning problems, such as those with LEARNING DISABILITIES and MENTAL RETARDATION, or those who are exceptional in other ways, such as GIFTED CHILDREN and those from minority backgrounds. The test may be given in the child's native language, if not English, or using gestures for those with EAR AND HEARING PROBLEMS. Test scores may be converted to comparative rankings, such as national PERCENTILES, AGE-EQUIVALENTS, or GRADE-EQUIVALENTS. (For help and further information, see TESTS.)

keratomalacia A softening of the cornea of the eye. (See EYE AND VISION PROBLEMS.)

Kernig's sign Pain and resistance at flexing the thigh at the hip and extending the leg at the knee; a SIGN that generally indicates the existence of MENINGITIS.

ketoacidosis A result of unchecked DIABETES MELLITUS, in which the body begins to break down its stores of fat, releasing acids (*ketones*) into the blood. The resulting ketoacidosis can lead to diabetic COMA and DEATH if not reversed.

ketogenic diet A special high-fat diet, used in some cases of EPILEPSY.

key words The words most commonly taught to children in the early grades and generally found in materials written for them; lists of these words, such as the *Dolch Word List*, are used by authors and publishers in preparing new materials for children of various age and grade levels. (See READING.)

kidney and urological disorders Problems with the system that filters unwanted substances from the blood and excretes waste products and fluids, maintaining the proper balance of ELECTROLYTES in the body. The two kidneys are on either side of the spinal column, toward the back and above the waistline, with the left one slightly higher than the right. About one-quarter of the blood being pumped from the heart goes directly to the kidneys, where it is pushed through a delicate *mesangial membrane* into tiny structures called *nephrons*, about one million of them in each kidney. Blood passes through a cluster of tiny blood vessels called the *glomerulus*, which filters out larger particles such as blood cells and proteins and sends the smaller particles and fluid through another filtering structure called a *tubule*. Depending on the body's blood chemistry at the time, the tubule will select out certain chemicals and some amounts of water to be returned to the system. The rest will then be sent out of the kidney as urine, pouring down thin tubes called *ureters* that empty into the *bladder*. There it is stored until the bladder is full, at which point signals of "fullness" are sent to the brain. The person then decides, at an appropriate time and place, to release the urine through the URETHRA, which in women is an opening above the VAGINA and in men is a thin tube that exits through the PENIS.

The kidneys' filtering structures maintain a delicate balance (called the *acid–base balance*) in the body's chemistry by:

- regulating how much water stays in the blood and how much is removed from the body in urine;
- regulating the concentration of key substances in the body, such as SODIUM, POTASSIUM, CHLORIDE, bicarbonate, CALCIUM, and PHOSPHORUS, ensuring that the body retains the nutrients it needs for normal functioning, such as building bone, but does not have too much of harmful substances;
- removing potentially harmful waste products from the blood, primarily urea (also called *blood urea nitrogen*, or BUN), creatinine, and uric acid.

The kidneys also regulate BLOOD PRESSURE, partly by regulating blood volume and partly by producing HORMONES that cause blood vessels to expand or contract, and produce a hormone, *erythropoietin*, that stimulates the BONE MARROW to make red blood cells. That such a complex system works so well so much of the time is actually quite remarkable. But because of its many and complex functions, the kidneys and urological system are subject to a wide variety of problems in children and pregnant women, some of them easily treatable, some life-threatening.

To recognize the abnormal, we first need to know what is normal. The American Kidney Foundation offers these guidelines for parents of young children:

- Urine is normally clear to medium yellow, though it may be dark yellow in the morning when a child has had nothing to drink overnight and the urine has become concentrated, and it may change color temporarily after a child has eaten certain foods, such as beets. But bloody or tea-colored urine is *never* normal, and a doctor should be consulted if an infant's diapers have red or brown stains.
- Urine has a mild odor when passed, becoming strong only after some exposure to air, except after eating foods such as asparagus that impart a strong smell. Foul-smelling odor in fresh urine can be a sign of infection.
- It is hard to judge what is normal or abnormal frequency of urination, since it depends on the amount of fluid consumed. As a rough guide, parents might expect infants to have 12 to 20 wet diapers in 24 hours, toddlers to urinate six to 10 times, and preschoolers to school-age children, four to seven times. Children will sometimes seem to have more frequent urination but really have only a dribble rather than a full urination each time. It is important, however, to see a doctor if the frequency or amount of urination changes from a previously normal pattern, as that may signal some sort of problem.
- The stream of urine should be strong and steady, without interruption, fanning, or excessive dribbling, especially for boys; if it is not, check with your doctor to see if there is any abnormality or problem.
- Urination should be painless, so if your baby cries when wetting a diaper or your older child has pain on urinating,

it may be a sign of infection, and a visit to the doctor is in order.

Because the kidneys play such an important role in the body, any infection, injury, or disorder affecting them can have widespread affects. Among the warning signs of kidney disease, in addition to those noted above, are poor FEEDING, VOMITING, or chronic DIARRHEA; slow growth or slow weight gain (see GROWTH AND GROWTH DISORDERS); persistent abdominal pain; lack of energy; pale, washed-out appearance; frequent severe headaches; lower back pain; unexplained low-grade FEVER; bedwetting (ENURESIS) in children over four to five years old, especially if they have previously been dry through the night; and EDEMA (collection of fluid in the tissues, especially swelling or puffiness about the eyes and ankles, especially in the morning, and distension of the belly later in the day). Lack of bladder control (INCONTINENCE) can be a problem for young children and also for pregnant women, since the developing FETUS presses on the bladder.

The main kinds of kidney problems affecting children are:

- *urinary tract infection (UTI)*. Bacteria readily infect the urethra, bladder, ureters, and kidneys. In infants, such infections are hard to recognize, but failure to gain weight, vomiting, persistent loose stool, and fussiness when diapers are wet may be clues that a problem exists. In a newborn the problem is sometimes discovered to be an obstruction somewhere in the system, blocking the normal flow of urine. Young girls should be taught to wipe their stool backward, rather than forward, which can spread bacteria to the urethral opening. For sexually active girls and women, some doctors recommend urination just after sexual intercourse to cut down the risk of bacterial infection. This especially true of pregnant women, since changes in the body and pressure on the urinary tract increase the risk of infections that inflame the bladder (*cystitis*) and kidneys (*pyelonephritis*). If untreated these can lead to serious illness, possibly involving SEPTICEMIA (blood poisoning), scarring of the kidneys, and even kidney failure.

  Urinary tract infection is normally diagnosed by URINALYSIS. Once a laboratory CULTURE has shown the type of bacteria involved, the appropriate antibiotic is normally prescribed. Drinking additional quantities of fluids is also important in helping "flush" the infection from the body. In severe cases, hospitalization may be needed, to provide fluids and medicines intravenously. In cases of recurring infection, urinalysis may be repeated several times to be sure the infection has been cleared up.

- *nephrosis (nephrotic syndrome)*. This is an umbrella term for a group of kidney disorders in which the glomerular filter in the nephrons has been damaged; as a result, large protein molecules that normally remain in the blood leak into urine, starving the body of necessary proteins and upsetting the body's chemistry. The result is often edema, paleness, waxy skin, rapid increase in body weight (from fluid retention), poor appetite, stomachache, CONSTIPATION, and susceptibility to infections and skin injuries. The American Kidney Fund notes that nephrotic syndrome is the most common serious kidney disease in children but that it is usually very responsive and seldom leads to total kidney failure. Treatment often includes medication (commonly prednisone), restriction of salt in the diet, diuretics (drugs to control edema), and on occasion hospitalization. Children may sometimes have relapses periodically until they have reached full adulthood.

- *glomerulonephritis*. This is a general term for a result—inflammation of the glomerulus in the nephrons—that can have a variety of causes, most often from infection with the bacterium called *streptococcus*, best known for causing STREP THROAT. Urination will often be abundant and more frequent and may contain blood; children will often have edema, headaches, blurred vision, and general aches and pains. The American Kidney Foundation notes that with careful control of high BLOOD PRESSURE and excess body fluids, often requiring hospitalization to manage fluid and food intake, 90 percent of the children affected with streptococcus glomerulonephritis will recover completely. Glomerulonephritis from other causes is rare but more serious; while some forms may respond, damage may remain, and in many the illness becomes progressive, culminating in total kidney failure.
- *hypertension (high blood pressure)*. Some children have very seriously high blood pressure because of abnormalities in the kidneys or in the network of blood vessels linked with the kidneys or associated with other diseases or disorders. Because high blood pressure can damage the body's delicate internal organs, it is important to spot it quickly and begin the search for a cause and treatment. This is one of the areas normally checked today in a WELL-BABY EXAMINATION. This childhood hypertension stems from different causes than the high blood pressure common in adults, though some teenagers may be subject to the adult form of high blood pressure.

In searching for the cause of various kinds of kidney disorders, UROLOGISTS—physicians specializing in kidney and urological disorders—use a range of KIDNEY FUNCTION TESTS, which attempt to determine how well the kidneys are operating and what problems they may have.

Some rarer kidney and urological disorders that affect children are:

- *congenital abnormalities*: kidney and urological abnormalities present at birth, most commonly that the two kidneys are joined (called a *horseshoe kidney*), but sometimes absence of a kidney, both kidneys on one side, double ureters in a kidney, or improper development from birth of the kidneys, bladder, and their related structures. Some of these are not serious or are correctible. Sometimes an artificial opening must be created for release of urine from the bladder, a surgical procedure called *urostomy* or *urinary ostomy* (see OSTOMY).
- *polycystic kidney disease (PKD)*: a disease in which many cysts (fluid-filled sacs) grow in the kidneys, gradually increasing so as to destroy most of the normal kidney tissue; often diagnosed by a SCAN such as ULTRASOUND. *Childhood polycystic disease (CPD)* is a GENETIC DISORDER, of the AUTOSOMAL DOMINANT type, which affects both the kidneys and liver in young children. Most infants born with the disease die in the first few months; with forms that initially involve less of the kidney, and generally are recognized later in childhood, some children may survive into adolescence.
- *cystinosis (cystine storage disease)*, *Fanconi's syndrome*, and *renal tubular acidosis*: rare congenital disorders involving loss into the urine of key nutrients and chemicals, such as AMINO ACIDS, CALCIUM, and PHOSPHATE important to growth, sometimes because of inability to respond to HORMONES designed to balance these substances in the body. The causes are unclear; some are apparently GENETIC DISORDERS, while others result from poisons ingested or created within the body.
- *Wilm's tumor (nephroblastoma)*: a malignant tumor that often affects children, mostly under age five, accounting for 20 percent of the CANCERS in children and affecting boys more than girls. The tumor spreads rapidly and is generally diagnosed by hypertension, a hard mass in the abdomen, pain, and blood in the urine. If caught and treated early, by surgery and RADIATION therapy, many children can survive, but sometimes the cancer spreads too quickly to other parts of the body. (For help and further information, see CANCER; TUMOR.)

In cases where kidney problems are undiagnosed, untreated, untreatable, or unresponsive to treatment, one or both kidneys can become so diseased or damaged that they can no longer function properly. The result is kidney (renal) failure. Sometimes this is acute kidney failure, resulting from a severe, temporary situation, such as surgery, severe infection, BURNS, ALLERGIES to medicines, poisons, or severe DIARRHEA or vomiting. Hospitalization, with careful control of food and fluids, is indicated, and sometimes an artifical machine will be used to take over the kidney's functions temporarily, in a procedure called DIALYSIS. Children suffering acute kidney failure almost always regain normal kidney function, with little permanent damage, though that may take as long as a year or more.

More serious is *chronic kidney (renal) failure*, in which kidney function is gradually, irreversibly, and permanently lost. This is called *end-stage renal disease* (ESRD), and the life-threatening condition that develops from ESRD is *uremia* (literally, urine in the blood). As the kidneys fail, every aspect of a child's life will be affected, from growth to ATTENTION SPAN. In addition to control of diet and medication, dialysis treatments will be required on a regular basis. Children suffering from chronic kidney failure are, depending on the health of the body otherwise, often prime candidates for kidney TRANSPLANTS.

For help and further information

American Kidney Fund (AKF)
6110 Executive Boulevard, Suite 1010
Rockville, MD 20852
301-881-3052, toll-free number (U.S. except MD) 800-638-8299; (MD) 800-492-8361
Francis J. Soldovere, Executive Director

Organization concerned with kidney problems. Provides information; supplies financial aid to qualified needy patients with kidney problems; publishes various materials including pamphlets such as *Children and Kidney Disease, The Kid* (for children), *Dialysis Patient, Facts About Kidney Diseases and Their Treatment*, and *Give A Kidney*.

National Kidney Foundation (NKF)
2 Park Avenue, Suite 908
New York, NY 10016
212-889-2210
John Davis, Executive Director

Organization of patients with kidney disease, their families, medical professionals working with them, and interested others. Provides information and makes referrals; offers patient services through local groups; operates an organ donor program; publishes various materials including quarterly newsletter, medical journal, and pamphlets such as *Questions Parents Ask About Nephrosis, Transplantation, Dialysis, What Everyone Should Know About Kidneys, How Can Urinary Tract Obstructions Affect You?*, and *If You Needed a Kidney or Other Vital Organ to Live, Would You Be Able to Get One?*

National Institute of Diabetes and Digestive and Kidney Diseases (NIDDK), 301-496-3583. Publishes *Understanding Urinary Tract Infections*. (For full group information, see DIGESTIVE DISORDERS.)

National Kidney and Urologic Disease Information Clearinghouse
Box NKUDIC
Bethesda, MD 20892
301-468-6345

Organization sponsored by federal government to provide information on kidney and urological problems. Publishes various materials for medical professionals and general public, including *When Your Kidneys Fail . . . A Handbook for Patients and Their Families*, second edition.

Polycystic Kidney Research Foundation (PKR)
922 Walnut Street
Kansas City, MO 64106

816-421-1869
Jean G. Bacon, Executive Director

Organization supporting research into cause and cure of polycystic kidney disease. Publishes various materials, including newsletter *PKR Progress, Polycystic Kidney Disease?, Problems in Diagnosis and Management of Polycystic Kidney Disease*, and *Your Diet and Polycystic Kidney Disease*.

Cystinosis Foundation (CF)
477 15th Street, Suite 1500
Oakland, CA 94612
415-834-7897
Jean Hotz, President

Organization providing support for families whose children have cystinosis. Provides support; seeks to educate public and health professionals; supports research; publishes various materials, including quarterly newsletter *Help Us Grow*, pamphlet *Facts about Cystinosis*, and information sheets.

National Association of Patients on Hemodialysis and Transplantation (NAPHT), 212-867-4486. Publishes pamphlet *Living with Renal Failure*. (For full group information, see DIALYSIS; TRANSPLANT.)

Other reference sources

Overcoming Bladder Disorders: Compassionate, Authoritative Medical and Self-help Solutions for Incontinence, Cystitis, Interstitial Cystitis, Prostrate Problems, and Bladder Cancer, by Rebecca Chalker and Kristene E. Whitmore. New York: Harper, 1990.

Health Care U.S.A., by Jean Carper. New York: Prentice Hall, 1987. Resource for general and specific health-care information, as on kidney and urinary tract diseases of all kinds; lists key kidney transplant specialists and centers, specialists in lithotripsy (shock-wave therapy), kidney-stone research centers, and other information, as on CAPD (continuous ambulatory peritoneal dialysis).

When Your Kidneys Fail: A Handbook for Patients and Their Families, by Mickie Hall Faris. Los Angeles: National Kidney Foundation of Southern California, 1982. Address: 6820 La Tijero Boulevard, Suite, 111, Los Angeles, CA 90045; second edition in both English and Spanish also available from National Kidney and Urologic Diseases Clearinghouse, Box NKUDIC, Bethesda, MD 20892, 301-468-6345.

A Patient's Guide to Dialysis and Transplantation, by Roger Gabriel, M.D. Hingham, MA: Kluwer Boston, 1983. Address: 190 Old Derby Street, Hingham, MA 02043.

Understanding Your New Life with Dialysis: A Patient's Guide for Physical and Psychological Adjustment, by Edith T. Oberley and Terry D. Oberley. Springfield, IL: Charles C. Thomas, 1983.

Gary Coleman: Medical Miracle, by the Coleman Family and Bill Davidson. New York: Coward, McCann & Geoghegan, 1983.

(See also TRANSPLANTS; DIALYSIS; ENURESIS; DIABETES INSIPIDUS.)

kidney function tests A series of tests seeking to assess, from analyzing the chemistry of the body, how well the kidney is carrying out its tasks of filtering unwanted substances out of the blood and excreting waste products and fluid as urine. The simplest kind of kidney function test is URINALYSIS, which involves testing the urine for the presence of various substances. BLOOD TESTS may also be used to assess kidney function; if substances such as urea (blood urea nitrogen, or BUN) and creatinine are found concentrated in the blood, it may indicate kidney disease. The kidneys can also be examined by various imaging techniques, including SCANS or a *pyelography*, in which contrasting material is injected into a vein so that the kidney and ureters (and possible kidney stones) will show up well with RADIOGRAPHY. (For help and further information, see KIDNEY AND UROLOGICAL DISORDERS; MEDICAL TESTS.)

kin Alternate term for BLOOD RELATIVES. When someone dies *intestate* (without a will) the PROBATE COURT uses the specific relationships of kin to determine INHERITANCE RIGHTS.

kindergarten Full-day or half-day classes for children of about age five, offered in the year before the first grade, either in the same building as the ELEMENTARY SCHOOL or in a separate structure; sometimes called *preprimary, junior primary*, or *primary*. Kindergarten classes traditionally focused on play activities and SOCIAL SKILLS, as some PRESCHOOLS and nursery schools still do. Today, in addition, kindergarten educators stress educational skills, especially those that prepare children for READING and writing, and many schools give students tests to assess their READINESS for school and to identify any learning problems that might require SPECIAL EDUCATION. The U.S. Department of Education also recommends that parents exercise choice in finding the right school for their child; see CHOOSING A SCHOOL FOR YOUR CHILD on page 514, which provides a checklist for evaluating schools.

For help and further information

A Place Called Kindergarten, by L. Katz, J. Raths, and R. Torres. Urbana, IL: ERIC Clearinghouse on Elementary and Early Childhood Education, no date.

(See also EDUCATION; DEVELOPMENTAL SCREENING TESTS.)

kinesthetic Referring to the sense of body motion, often employed in MULTISENSORY approaches to learning, such as VAKT, for children with LEARNING DISABILITIES.

kissing disease Popular nickname for MONONUCLEOSIS.

kleptomania A type of IMPULSE CONTROL DISORDER.

Klinefelter's syndrome A CONGENITAL condition resulting from a CHROMOSOMAL ABNORMALITY, in which a male has not just the usual two SEX CHROMOSOMES (XY), but one or more additional X chromosomes. Males with one extra X chromosome (labeled 47,XXY) are often tall and lean, with some tendency to

LEARNING DISABILITIES in the verbal area; in many, the syndrome is recognized only during a search for causes of INFERTILITY, since most lack SPERM. Even for those with two or more additional X chromosomes, Klinefelter's syndrome generally shows itself only at PUBERTY, when such males tend to develop enlarged breasts (GYNECOMASTIA) and other SECONDARY SEX CHARACTERISTICS that tend toward the female, though these can sometimes be modified surgically or through hormone treatment. The TESTES, however, remain small, giving the syndrome an alternate name, *primary micro-orchidism*. People with Klinefelter's syndrome are somewhat more likely than most to have some MENTAL RETARDATION and difficulty in social adaptation.

For help and further information

National Institute of Child Health and Human Development (NICHD), 301-496-5133. (For full group information, see PREGNANCY.)

(See also CHROMOSOMAL ABNORMALITIES.)

knock-knees Popular term for GENU VALGUM.

knowledge-level thinking Simple recall of previously learned information; from Benjamin Bloom's description of the various kinds of thinking or learning processes, the other main types being COMPREHENSION-LEVEL THINKING, APPLICATION-LEVEL THINKING, ANALYSIS-LEVEL THINKING, SYNTHESIS-LEVEL THINKING, and EVALUATION-LEVEL THINKING.

Kohs Block Design Test A type of INTELLIGENCE TEST for children or adults with a MENTAL AGE of three to 19 years, especially HANDICAPPED people with defects of language or hearing, as well as disadvantaged children or those from non-English-speaking backgrounds. The child is given a variety of colored blocks with which to copy designs shown on a series of cards. The test administrator, often working one to one, evaluates not only success in copying the design but also attention to the task, ADAPTIVE BEHAVIOR, and self-criticism. The Kohs Block Design Test is sometimes included in other tests, such as the MERRILL-PALMER SCALES OF MENTAL DEVELOPMENT. (For help and further information, see TESTS.)

Krabbe's disease (globoid leukodystrophy) A type of LIPID STORAGE DISEASE.

kyphosis Excessive curving of the spine, producing a rounded or "humped" upper back, a type of SPINAL DISORDER often associated with SCOLIOSIS or LORDOSIS; once popularly called *humpback*. In adults, it is often related to OSTEOPOROSIS (bone weakening from CALCIUM loss); in children, kyphosis more often results from injury, a TUMOR on the spine, or a GENETIC DISORDER, such as HUNTER'S SYNDROME. (For help and further information, see SCOLIOSIS.)

L

labeling Tagging a child as good or bad, bright or dull, pretty or plain, and the like; a destructive habit, because such labels can damage a child's SELF-ESTEEM and (because children often live up to adults' expectations for them) may become SELF-FULFILLING PROPHECIES. Child-development experts recommend that parents and teachers avoid labels such as a "problem child" or "slow learner" (sometimes on the basis of a single unreliable TEST) and focus instead on what children can and cannot do, helping them to grow in areas where their skills are weak.

lability Emotional instability or mood swings, found in mild form in some children with LEARNING DISABILITIES and in more severe form in some MENTAL DISORDERS such as BIPOLAR DISORDERS and some kinds of SCHIZOPHRENIA.

labor In PREGNANCY, the events and actions involved in bringing forth a baby, from the beginning of the dilation (widening) of the CERVIX to the expulsion of the PLACENTA (afterbirth); also the period in which these activities occur.

Several changes often take place in the previous weeks and days before actual labor starts, including:

- the settling of the baby into its final FETAL PRESENTATION in the mother's pelvis, an action called ENGAGEMENT, "dropping," or "falling," which may not happen until later.
- a burst of energy in the days before labor.
- a dull ache in the lower back or pelvis, somewhat like menstrual cramps.
- appearance of a bloody mucus discharge from the VAGINA, called *show* or *bloody show*, with the expulsion of a mucus plug from the cervix before labor.
- appearance of small or large amounts of watery fluid (AMNIOTIC FLUID) from the vagina; this is the "rupture of the membranes" or "breaking of the bag of waters" that results when the amniotic sac protecting the FETUS breaks, often within about 12 hours of the start of labor. The time of the first fluid release should be reported immediately to the doctor or midwife; since the baby is no longer protected by the amniotic fluid, some health professionals wish to bring the mother into the hospital or birthing center at this time.

Any or all of these signs can (but will not necessarily) indicate that labor will start in a matter of days or hours.

Labor itself generally has three stages:

1. *first stage*, which begins with regular, intense contractions and ends when the cervix has become fully dilated, to about four inches. In a first pregnancy this stage often takes 13 hours or longer but is generally significantly shorter in subsequent pregnancies. It starts with mild, brief, often irregular stop-and-start *contractions*, which are powerful, spasmodic, painful, rhythmic squeezings of the walls of the UTERUS. These settle into a regular pattern, gradually coming closer together, lasting longer, and intensifying, while the cervix *effaces*—that is, shortens, flattens, and merges with the uterus walls—and opens. During the early part of this first stage, the mother should be making her way to where the child will be delivered; in a HOSPITAL she will go into a LABOR ROOM or sometimes a combination LABOR/DELIVERY/RECOVERY (LDR) ROOM. There the extent of the cervix's dilation will be measured periodically. If it has not occurred earlier, engagement generally takes place at this time. In HIGH-RISK PREGNANCIES, and sometimes routinely, FETAL MONITORING may be used to detect early signs of FETAL DISTRESS.

2. *second stage*, the actual delivery, which starts when the baby's head reaches the pelvic floor muscles, with contractions and an accompanying urge to push the baby on through the BIRTH CANAL, which can be much helped by preparation in PREPARED CHILDBIRTH classes. How long this stage of labor takes depends on many factors, including the position of the baby and its size in relation to the mother's pelvis. As the baby's head begins to appear in the VAGINA, an event called *crowning*, the tissue (*perineum*) between the vagina and anus is stretched very thin. If a woman is in a hospital's labor room, she will at this point (if not before) be moved to a DELIVERY ROOM. If it appears that the perineum will tear, and sometimes routinely, a doctor may perform an EPISIOTOMY, making a surgical incision to provide more room for the baby. Once the head emerges, the doctor or midwife will check to be sure the UMBILICAL CORD is not wrapped around the baby's neck and may use a suction bulb to clear out the nose and mouth so that the baby can begin to breathe freely. The baby then normally rotates the head and with it the body somewhat, a process the doctor or midwife will assist; this allows shoulders, angled sideways, to come

out more easily—one first, then the other. After that, the rest of the baby comes out relatively easily, along with the remaining amniotic fluid. The baby may then be placed on the mother's abdomen and lightly massaged. Immediately or within a few minutes, the umbilical cord is clamped and cut. At this point, in many states, silver nitrate or erythromycin ointment is placed in the baby's eyes to prevent damage from possible infection, as from GONORRHEA; the baby may also be given an injection of VITAMIN K, to aid in blood clotting. In a hospital, identification bands will be placed on mother and infant, and the baby's footprint may be taken; the baby may also be briefly placed in a warmer before being returned to the mother. At one minute and again at five minutes after the birth, an APGAR SCORE will be taken, to identify any urgent health needs.

3. *third stage*, which is the period between the baby's actual delivery and the delivery of the placenta, literally the *afterbirth*. Contractions starting a few minutes after the birth expel the tissue, though some medical assistance may be necessary if not all of the tissue is delivered. Some drugs may be given to help with the expulsion and then to help control the bleeding that often follows. Then, while the mother holds the baby, the doctor generally cleans the mother's genital area and stitches up any tears or cuts.

In most births, labor roughly follows this pattern, with the child born normally. But sometimes, for various reasons, labor is difficult and does not proceed normally, as when the cervix fails to dilate enough, the baby's head is too large for the mother's pelvis (CEPHALOPELVIC DISPROPORTION), the baby has an abnormal fetal presentation, the mother is hemorrhaging, the mother has ECLAMPSIA, or the mother is having a MULTIPLE BIRTH. Then other forms of delivery may be used, including FORCEPS DELIVERY, VACUUM EXTRACTION, or CESAREAN SECTION.

In certain cases, physicians may decide that labor must be *induced*, that is, brought on by artificial means, as in cases of POSTMATURE babies, Rh INCOMPATIBILITY between mother and baby, or PREECLAMPSIA or eclampsia in the mother. If the amniotic fluid has not already been released, the physician may release it by breaking open the amniotic sac, which may in itself bring on labor. Otherwise, various HORMONES can be given, either as vaginal suppositories or intravenous INJECTIONS, to stimulate labor. If they fail to do so, cesarean section may be necessary. However, it is important not to induce labor before the DUE DATE, unless serious medical conditions warrant it, since the baby will then be PREMATURE and so subject to a variety of other health problems.

Sometimes, for a variety of reasons, many of them unknown, labor starts well before the due date, the result being premature delivery, though some drugs can halt the process. Sometimes a woman experiences *false labor*, medically called *Braxton-Hicks contractions*, in which contractions occur for an hour or two, not coming more often or intensifying, then stop, often going away when the woman relaxes, unlike true labor contractions.

For help and further information

Mind over Labor, by Carl Jones. New York: Viking, 1987. (See also CHILDBIRTH; PREGNANCY.)

laboratory school   An ELEMENTARY or HIGH SCHOOL linked with a teacher's college or university and staffed largely by student teachers under their professors' direction; also called a *model*, *demonstration*, or *experimental school*.

labor companion   Alternate term for BIRTH PARTNER.

labor/delivery/recovery room (LDR)   A room in which the mother stays from arrival in some hospitals until shortly after CHILDBIRTH, at which point she moves to a POSTPARTUM ROOM, generally a regular room in a maternity ward. The aim is to avoid the often-unsettling shift from LABOR ROOM to DELIVERY ROOM. On the model of the BIRTHING ROOM, some hospitals have gone even further, developing the *labor/delivery/ recovery/ postpartum room (LDRP)*, where a mother stays from arrival at the hospital, through labor and delivery, and until discharge.

labor room   In traditional HOSPITAL births, the room where the woman waits during LABOR until delivery is imminent, at which point she is moved into the DELIVERY ROOM.

lactase deficiency   Alternate term for LACTOSE INTOLERANCE.

lactation   The production of milk by a new mother. (See BREASTFEEDING.)

lactation specialists   People who offer advice on BREASTFEEDING, generally with experience and some training, though not necessarily any formal certification, and often associated with local groups formed especially to advise new mothers.

lacto-ovo-vegetarian   A type of VEGETARIAN diet that eliminates meat, poultry, and fish but allows eggs, milk, and other dairy products, such as cheese. A *lactovegetarian* diet permits dairy products but not eggs. (For help and further information, see VEGETARIAN; NUTRITION.)

lactose intolerance   A type of DIGESTIVE DISORDER involving inability to break down milk sugar (*lactose*) into forms that can be used by the body, generally because of shortage of the enzyme LACTASE; also called *lactase deficiency*. Sometimes lack of lactase results from disorders or injuries affecting the intestinal tract, but in many cases, especially after age two, children's bodies begin to produce less lactase. Common symptoms of indigestion of lactose are nausea, cramps, bloating, gas, and DIARRHEA, about 30 to 120 minutes after eating foods containing lactose. The problem is especially common among people of Black African, Asian, or Jewish ancestry, and less common among those of Caucasian background from northern Europe. Lactose intolerance is in itself not a danger, but because CALCIUM is so important to growth and repair of bones, especially in the growing years, it is necessary to be sure that children (and adults) get anough calcium from other sources, such as those in CALCIUM AND LACTOSE IN COMMON FOODS, on page 280. (For help and further information, see TREATMENT OF

Calcium and Lactose in Common Foods

	Calcium Content*	Lactose Content**
Vegetables		
Broccoli (pieces cooked), 1 cup	94–177 mg	0
Chinese cabbage (bok choy, cooked), 1 cup	158 mg	0
Collard greens (cooked), 1 cup	148–357 mg	0
Kale (cooked), 1 cup	94–179 mg	0
Turnip greens (cooked), 1 cup	197–249 mg	0
Dairy Products		
Ice cream/ice milk, 8 oz	176 mg	6–7 g
Milk (whole, low-fat, skim, buttermilk), 8 oz	291–316 mg	12–13 g
Processed cheese, 1 oz	159–219 mg	2–3 g
Sour cream, 4 oz	134 mg	4–5 g
Yogurt (plain), 8 oz	274–415 mg	12–13 g
Fish/Seafood		
Oysters (raw), 1 cup	226 mg	0
Salmon with bones (canned), 3 oz	167 mg	0
Sardines, 3 oz	371 mg	0
Shrimp (canned), 3 oz	98 mg	0
Other		
Molasses, 2 tbsp	274 mg	0
Tofu (processed with calcium salts), 3 oz	225 mg	0

*Nutritive value of foods. Values vary with methods of processing and preparation.

**Derived from *Lactose Intolerance: A Resource Including Recipes*, Food Sensitivity Series, American Dietetic Association, 1985.

Source: *Lactose Intolerance* (1987). Prepared by the National Institute of Diabetes and Digestive and Kidney Diseases (NIDDK).

LACTOSE INTOLERANCE = CONTROL OF SYMPTOMS, on page 281; see also DIGESTIVE DISORDERS.)

Lamaze method   A popular form of natural or PREPARED CHILD-BIRTH.

laminate veneer   A technique used for restoring discolored or damaged TEETH.

Landau's reflex   The automatic response of an infant three to 12 months old, when laid face downward, to raise the head and arch the back; absence of this REFLEX can suggest possible problems that affect MOTOR SKILLS, such as CEREBRAL PALSY or MENTAL RETARDATION.

language disorder   Difficulty in understanding language or putting words together to make sense, often resulting from some kind of malfunction of the brain. (For help and further information, see COMMUNICATION SKILLS AND DISORDERS.)

language skills   Alternate phrase for communication skill. (See COMMUNICATION SKILLS AND DISORDERS).

lanugo   Downy hair found on newborns, especially those who are PREMATURE; it may also be found among some people with ANOREXIA NERVOSA.

laparoscopy   A surgical procedure in which a physician passes a flexible tube through an incision in the patient's abdomen and then uses a small periscope-like device, called a *laparoscope* or *peritoneoscope*, to view the internal organs. Because of the small size and placement of the incision, the procedure is sometimes called popularly nicknamed *Band-Aid surgery* or *belly-button surgery*. Used in a wide range of medical situations, laparoscopy is an important tool in identifying causes of INFERTILITY in women, such as TUBAL BLOCKAGE, PELVIC INFLAMMATORY DISEASE, or ENDOMETRIOSIS, or other reproductive problems, such as ECTOPIC PREGNANCY. Laparoscopy is also employed in some treatments of infertility, such as IN VITRO FERTILIZATION and GIFT; in some female STERILIZATION methods, notably TUBAL LIGATION; and in examining a fetus in the womb, a procedure called FETOSCOPY.

laparotomy   A form of operation used in TUBAL LIGATION.

laser surgery   Use of a narrow, highly concentrated beam of light, focused through a microscope, to do extremely precise, delicate surgery; a kind of MICROSURGERY. In eye surgery, for example, lasers can be used in treating tears in the retina, retinopathy, macular degeneration, glaucoma, and removal of cataracts. Laser beams may also be used in a wide variety of

Treatment of Lactose Intolerance = Control of Symptoms

Small children born with lactase deficiency should not be fed any foods containing lactose. Most older children and adults need not avoid lactose completely, but they differ in the amounts of lactose they can handle. For example, one person may suffer symptoms after drinking just a small glass of milk, while another can drink one glass but not two. Others with lactase deficiency may be able to manage ice cream and aged cheeses, such as Cheddar and Swiss, but not other dairy products. Dietary control of the problem depends on each person's knowing, through trial and error, *how much* milk sugar and *what forms* of it his or her body can handle.

For those who react to very small amounts of lactose or have trouble limiting their intake of foods that contain lactose, lactase additives are available from drug stores without a prescription. One form is a liquid for use with milk. A few drops are added to a quart of milk, and after 24 hours in the refrigerator, the lactose content is reduced by 70 percent. The process works faster if the milk is heated first, and adding a double amount of lactase liquid produces milk that is 90 percent lactose free. A more recent development is a lactase tablet that helps people digest solid foods that contain lactose. One to three tablets are taken just before a meal or snack.

At somewhat higher cost, shoppers can buy lactose-reduced milk at most supermarkets. It contains all of the other nutrients found in milk and remains fresh for about the same time. Some stores also have cottage cheese and ice cream with decreased lactose content.

Source: *Lactose Intolerance* (1987). Prepared by the National Institute of Diabetes and Digestive and Kidney Diseases (NIDDK).

other ways, including some kinds of STERILIZATION, removal of small birthmarks or scar tissue, and destruction of abnormal or CANCER cells. (For help and further information, see EYE AND VISION PROBLEMS.)

latchkey child A child who returns from school or play to an empty home, so called because the child must carry a key to enter the house or apartment. With the rise in single parents and working couples, increasing numbers of children fall into this category, often because of the inadequacy, unavailability, or expense of CHILD CARE. If parents are obliged to leave their children unattended, though certainly not before age seven or eight, they should take great care to prepare the children to meet potential emergencies.

Among the most important areas in which a child needs protection are:

- *key safety*—the key should be hidden on a chain or pinned inside clothing so that no one is alerted that the child is

alone. A spare should be available in a safe place (such as a neighbor's house) in case the child's is lost, and the child should understand that it is to be given to no one.
- *dealing with potentially dangerous people*—young children need help in recognizing strangers and dangerous people or situations. Role-playing may help the child recognize trouble and learn how to deal with it. (See MISSING CHILDREN for more suggestions.)
- *handling traffic*—apart from teaching children how to cross roads safely at intersections (not between), parents should map out with the children safe routes and alternative plans if a child misses a bus or car pool.
- *handling the telephone*—children need to know how to reach key numbers, such as those of parents, police, fire department, poison-control center, ambulance, and neighbors, as well as to dial 911 for emergencies. Parents should be sure the children have memorized and know how to give their address and phone number and explain the nature of the emergency. Children also need to know how to respond to telephone calls received, including prank calls, and to beware telling anyone they are at home alone. (The same holds for answering the door.)
- *handling fire*—children should know how to handle matches and gas appliances safely, if necessary, what to do if their clothes are on fire, how to put out a small fire, and, most important, how to escape. Parents should stress escape first (not hiding, as from fear of being blamed for the fire), then calling the fire department from a neighbor's house.
- *other household or weather emergencies*—children need to know how to respond in case of power failure, household breakdowns such as plumbing problems, or a storm that prevents parents from reaching home. Parents may want to prepare a survival kit for children for such emergencies, including flashlight, transistor radio, extra batteries, and the like, and also give their child some basic first-aid training and supply a first-aid kit, with bandages, gauze, iodine, and so on. Firearms should be unloaded and locked up, and any other dangerous appliances the child should not be using should be unplugged or otherwise disabled.
- *recreation*—children alone should be clear on what kinds of activities are safe and allowed and which are dangerous and not allowed. Parents should try to arrange for the child to join community or after-school recreation programs, such as at a local YMCA or YWCA. The main danger occurs around unsupervised activities such as swimming, bicycling, or playing in dangerous areas.

Whatever the area of concern, the child should have places to turn and alternative plans to follow in case of emergency. (For more suggestions, see the books below; see also MISSING CHILDREN.) Most important, parents need to help children accept and deal with their natural fears about being alone, including seemingly small things like having the child listen to and identify household noises so that they will not seem strange when the child is home alone.

For help and further information

National Safety Council, 312-527-4800. Publishes *Child Alone* for latchkey children. (For full group information; see EXERCISE.)

National Congress of Parents and Teachers (National PTA), 312-787-0977. Publishes materials on latchkey children. (For full group information, see EDUCATION.)

Other reference sources

For Parents

Home-Alone Kids: A Parent's Guide to Providing the Best Care for Your Child, by Bryan E. Robinson, Bobbie H. Rowland, and Mick Coleman. Lexington, MA: Lexington, 1989.

Safe and Sound: A Parent's Guide to the Care of Children Home Alone, by Trudy K. Dana. New York: McGraw-Hill, 1988.

Alone After School: A Self-Care Guide for Latchkey Children and Their Parents, by Helen L. Swan and Victoria Houston. New York: Prentice Hall, 1987.

The Latchkey Children, by Eric Allen. New York: Oxford University Press, 1987.

For Kids

Latchkey Children, by Judy Monroe. New York: Crestwood, 1990. Part of the Facts About series.

Playing It Smart: What to Do When You're on Your Own, by Tova Navarra. Hauppauge, NY: Barron's, 1989. For ages 7 to 13. On how to deal with problems such as fire, accidents, answering phone, and fear of dark.

What Would You Do If . . .? A Safety Game for You and Your Child, by Jeanne Ebert. Boston: Houghton Mifflin, 1985. For young children.

School's Out, Now What, by Joan Bergstrom. Berkeley, CA: Ten Speed, 1984. For older children.

In Charge: A Complete Handbook for Kids with Working Parents, by Kathy S. Kyte. New York: Knopf, 1983. For older children.

By Yourself, by Sara Gilbert. New York: Lothrop, Lee & Shepard, 1983. For young children.

late bloomer   Informal term for a student thought to be an UNDERACHIEVER who, somewhat later than other students, begins to fulfill the expected potential indicated by previous performance on STANDARDIZED TESTS of ability; sometimes called *latent achiever*.

For help and further information

Leo the Late Bloomer, by Robert Kraus. New York: Windmill, 1971.
(See also EDUCATION.)

late fetal death   Alternate term for STILLBIRTH.

latent achiever   Alternate term for LATE BLOOMER or UNDERACHIEVER.

laterality   An awareness of the two sides of one's body and which is left and which is right. Some children with RIGHT–LEFT DISORIENTATION have a poor sense of laterality and often confuse left and right; these are often children who lack DOMINANCE of one eye, ear, hand, and foot for most proficient use.

Laurence-Moon-Biedl syndrome (Laurence-Moon-Bardet-Biedl syndrome or retinodiencephalic degeneration)   A rare GENETIC DISORDER of the AUTOSOMAL RECESSIVE type that is characterized by INCREASING OBESITY, RETINITIS PIGMENTOSA, which often leads to blindness, mild-to-severe MENTAL RETARDATION, underactive TESTES or OVARIES (HYPOGONADISM), underdeveloped genitals (HYPOGENITALISM), and extra fingers or toes (POLYDACTYLY). Although the complex of symptoms seems to be caused by a problem with the HYPOTHALAMUS, which controls HORMONE balance, the precise cause of the syndrome is unknown and no treatment currently exists. Prospective parents with a history of the syndrome in their family may want to seek GENETIC COUNSELING.

For help and further information

National Institute of Neurological Disorders and Stroke (NINDS), 301-496-5751. (For full group information, see BRAIN AND BRAIN DISORDERS.)

lay midwife   A MIDWIFE with no formal training or certification, though generally with wide practical experience, allowed to practice in only a few states. Most states require formally trained, licensed practitioners called CERTIFIED NURSE-MIDWIVES. (For help and further information, see CERTIFIED NURSE-MIDWIFE.)

lazy eye blindness   Alternate term for suppression amblyopia, a serious eye condition that may involve loss of sight in one eye. (See EYE AND VISION PROBLEMS.)

LBW   Abbreviation for LOW BIRTH WEIGHT, meaning under 5.5 pounds (2,500 g).

LD   Abbreviation for LEARNING DISABILITIES.

LDLs   Abbreviation for low-density lipoproteins, a so-called bad form of CHOLESTEROL.

LDR and **LDRP**   Abbreviations for LABOR/DELIVERY/RECOVERY ROOM and LABOR/DELIVERY/RECOVERY/POSTPARTUM ROOM.

LEA   Abbreviation for local educational agency, which receives and distributes federal moneys under CHAPTER 1.

lead poisoning   A type of ENVIRONMENTAL HAZARD.

learning block   A general term for anything that might hinder a student's gaining of new knowledge and skills, including handicaps (see HANDICAPPED) of various kinds and lack of the necessary skills, such as READING.

learning disabilities (LD)   An umbrella term for a wide range of educational problems that involve continuing difficulties in speaking, listening, READING, writing, interpreting, understanding, and remembering but are not due to any other kind of handicap (such as MENTAL RETARDATION), unfamiliarity with the culture and its language, or failure of instructional methods, though they may involve uneven development or DEVELOPMENTAL DELAY in certain areas. The kinds of problems and the ways in which they show themselves vary widely from person to person, but in general learning disabilities involve difficulties in four major areas:

- *input*: the process of receiving and registering information in the brain. People with LD often have trouble seeing and hearing accurately, though their ears and eyes function normally; they have problems DECODING, or extracting meaning from symbols, such as written, spoken, or signed words or numbers. They often confuse letters or words, as because of REVERSALS (transpositions), and so may misunderstand directions and be easily distracted. Input problems also affect HAND–EYE coordination and other VISUAL SKILLS and MOTOR SKILLS.
- *integration*: the process of putting information together in a meaningful sequence and understanding it. Partly because of input problems, people with LD often have difficulty in putting letters, words, gestures, and ideas in correct order. They may have trouble recalling the order of events in a story or steps in a group of instructions.
- *memory*: the process of storing information in the brain and retrieving it as desired. People with LD may have trouble with short-term memory, as in being unable to remember instructions long enough to carry them out. Part of the problem may be that input and integration problems cause information to be "scrambled" in storage. They may also have trouble with long-term memory, or "permanent" storage, as in remembering their address and phone number.
- *output*: the process of carrying out commands given by the brain, such as communicating (writing, signing, or speaking) or doing physical things that require muscular coordination, in gross motor skills (such as jumping) or fine motor skills (as in the physical act of writing). People with LD have problems with ENCODING, or converting spoken or signed words or numbers into written symbols, and often grope for or misuse words.

Children with LD often have associated problems, including a short ATTENTION SPAN and HYPERACTIVITY (as in ATTENTION DEFICIT HYPERACTIVITY DISORDER); DISTRACTIBILITY; problems with socializing, partly due to lack of communication skills (see COMMUNICATION SKILLS AND DISORDERS); and general frustration at having trouble with learning tasks that seem easy to most, which can in turn lead to behavioral problems.

Many other people have learning problems, too, but if these are people with physical handicaps (see HANDICAPPED), mental retardation, MENTAL DISORDERS, or socioeconomic disadvantages, they are not considered to be learning-disabled. By contrast, people with LD have average or above-average intelligence, but some malfunction bars them from being able to learn as effectively as their mental ability would seem to indicate. They are

also not simply UNDERACHIEVERS, though some so-called underachievers may have undiagnosed learning disabilities.

The causes of learning disabilities are so far obscure. At the heart of the problem seems to be some disorder in the brain and NERVOUS SYSTEM. Among the causes that may be linked with such neurological problems are:

- injuries at or during birth or in early childhood;
- PREMATURE birth;
- serious illness in infancy or early childhood;
- GENETIC INHERITANCE, since learning disabilities tend to run in families;
- gender, since boys are five times more likely than girls to have LD. Their problems are compounded because they tend to mature more slowly as well.

The erratic spelling and form of the English language, and modern society's increasing dependence on floods of words and numbers, on paper and on screens, exacerbate these problems.

Because learning disabilities are various and often subtle, they can be hard to diagnose, especially in young children. Although learning problems may be recognized early, some experts do not feel it possible to diagnose these as learning disabilities in PRESCHOOL children because the problems may have other causes, such as unfamiliarity with structured learning, cultural differences, language differences (as when a language other than English is spoken in the home), or simply widely different rates of development. But the important thing is for learning problems to be identified as soon as possible and special training or services be provided if necessary.

In brief, the Association for Children with Learning Disabilities outlines several warning signs for learning disabilities:

- *in spoken language*: delays, disorders, and deviations in listening and speaking;
- *in written language*: difficulties with reading, writing, and spelling;
- *in arithmetic*: difficulties in performing mathematical operations or in understanding basic mathematical concepts;
- *in reasoning*: difficulties in organizing and integrating thoughts;
- *in memory*: difficulties in remembering information and instructions.

Parents can use the OBSERVATION CHECKLIST FOR POSSIBLE LEARNING DISABILITIES on page 286 to help them assess (with the help of the child's preschool teacher or CHILD-CARE provider, if appropriate) whether or not their child needs professional evaluation. TEACHING YOUNG CHILDREN: GUIDELINES AND ACTIVITIES (on page 544) gives some general advice on how parents can help children overcome learning disabilities.

Learning disabilities are increasingly being recognized as a common problem—but how common is still not known, because experts believe that many people with LD have not been diagnosed (including both children and adults). Some experts believe that learning disabilities are behind many behavioral problems in schools, and that many people who are

UNDERACHIEVERS, DROPOUTS, or DELINQUENTS have undiagnosed (and therefore untreated) learning disabilities. Government and educational organizations have been making increasingly stronger efforts to identify people who suffer from LD and to get them the special educational and other services they need, focusing especially on preschool- and ELEMENTARY-SCHOOL-age children.

One problem with identification of learning disabilities is that people define them in different ways for different purposes, often using different names and terms. The set of problems known as learning disabilities has in the past been given dozens of names, including PERCEPTUAL HANDICAPS, *minimal brain dysfunction (MBD)*, *perceptual disturbances*, *minimal cerebral dysfunction*, or *minimal neurological dysfunction*, and some professionals still use these names. And the term *learning disabilities*, as it is used today, often includes a number of specific kinds of disabilities, such as:

- *dyslexia*—difficulty with reading and understanding written words;
- *dyscalculia*—difficulty with numbers and mathematical calculations;
- *dysgraphia*—difficulty in producing readable handwriting;
- *dysarthria*—difficulty in producing readily understandable speech.

The result is a thicket of definitions and descriptions that many parents must be prepared to cut through if their child may have learning disabilities. As the people of the HEAD START program point out in their booklet series, *Mainstreaming Preschoolers*:

It is usually more helpful to describe what children with learning problems are like rather than to classify them. This is partly because different diagnosticians use different definitions of learning disabilities and follow different theories in labeling problems. This means that three children for whom you have the same diagnostic information could be classified or categorized in three different ways, depending on the diagnostician or diagnostic team. On the other hand, just because two children are both diagnosed as learning-disabled doesn't mean that they will behave in the same way. The only way to understand a child's problem is to consider what he or she currently can and cannot do.

Classifying can, however, serve several purposes. Current special education laws require that a diagnostic category be assigned to each handicapped child, in order to provide that child with special education services and to receive necessary state and federal reimbursement. So, for that purpose, categories are required. Also, when there is a need for common understanding, categories can be a useful shortcut. You will want to be familiar with certain terms and categories that may appear in medical reports. They may guide you in asking further questions about a child's strengths and weaknesses.

Various definitions may determine whether or not a child is eligible for certain kinds of aid and special services, so parents whose children may have learning disabilities will need to "decode" them as preparation for helping their children. The federal EDUCATION FOR ALL HANDICAPPED CHILDREN ACT OF 1975 (Public Law 94-142) defines learning disabilities this way:

Specific learning disability means a disorder in one or more of the basic psychological processes involved in understanding or in using language, spoken or written, which may manifest itself in an imperfect inability to listen, think, speak, read, write, spell, or to do mathematical calculations. The term includes such conditions as perceptual handicaps, brain injury, minimal brain dysfunction, dyslexia, and developmental aphasia. The term does not include children who have learning problems that are primarily the result of visual, hearing, or motor handicaps, of mental retardation, of emotional disturbance, or of environmental, cultural, or economic disadvantage.

Because PUBLIC SCHOOLS must comply with Public Law 94-142 to continue to receive federal funds, the above definition is widely used.

But state laws vary, as do interpretations. As a result there are wide variations in the number of people diagnosed as being learning disabled. The Association for Children with Learning Disabilities (ACLD) reports, for example, that (as of 1980) 5.7 percent of students in Maryland were diagnosed as having learning disabilities; while in Massachusetts, the figure was only 1.5 percent. Overall, the U.S. Department of Education estimates that about 4.4 percent (about 1,750,000) of American schoolchildren are classed as learning-disabled.

As the prevalence of learning disabilities has become recognized, numerous organizations (see below) have emerged to explore and coordinate research into the causes of LD and the best ways to help children overcome learning problems. Many of these have emphasized the lifelong nature of learning disabilities and the need to make long-term plans for children with LD. For example, the ACLD defines LD this way:

Specific Learning Disabilities is a chronic condition of presumed neurological origin which selectively interferes with the development, integration, and/or demonstration of verbal and/or nonverbal abilities.

Specific Learning Disabilities exists as a distinct handicapping condition in the presence of average to superior intelligence, adequate sensory and motor systems, and adequate learning opportunities. The condition varies in its manifestations and in degree of severity.

Throughout life the condition can affect self-esteem, education, vocation, socialization, and/or daily living activities.

Organizations such as ACLD help parents obtain proper diagnoses for their children's learning disabilities and then arrange for special educational services.

Many children can be helped by a variety of special programs, often using more than one SENSORY MODE to reinforce learning. Among approaches that have had some success are:

- using recorded material to supplement printed matter, such as textbooks;
- using a typewriter or tape recorder, instead of writing by hand;
- having students make outlines and run through drills before testing;
- supplying outlines of classroom presentations;
- focusing on PHONICS in reading, or on highly structured multisensory reading approaches (such as VAKT), rather than on learning whole words.

(See LEARNING STYLES for suggestions on how to use different sensory modes in learning.)

Where learning disabilities are severe, or parents are unable to obtain proper services for their child (despite the guarantee of the Education for All Handicapped Children Act), special schools are available (see organizations and other reference sources below). Increasing numbers of camps and college programs are tailored to the needs of learning-disabled students, and special arrangements can be made for LD students in some testing situations, as with the SCHOLASTIC APTITUDE TEST. Some vocational training programs and employment situations are also now being modified to help learning disabled people, including people who only learn as adults that their educational difficulties were caused by learning disabilities.

For help and further information

Orton Dyslexia Society (ODS)
724 York Road
Baltimore, MD 21204
301-296-0232, toll-free number 800-ABCD-123 (222-3123)
Anne L. O'Flanagan, Executive Director
Organization of parents, educators, health professionals, and other people concerned with the study, treatment, and prevention of dyslexia, named for dyslexia pioneer Dr. Samuel Orton. Provides information to public and professionals; publishes various print and audio materials, including quarterly *Perspectives on Dyslexia* and journal *Annals of Dyslexia*, books such as *The Many Faces of Dyslexia, Language and the Developing Child*, and *Sex Differences in Dyslexia*, booklets and pamphlets such as *The Dyslexic Child, Guidelines for Seeking Help for Dyslexic Students, Parents' Guidelines to the Evaluation Process, The Problem of Dyslexia, What Is Dyslexia?*, and *Checklist* (for schools, camps, and colleges), and reprints, including some in packets such as *Readings for Parents*.

Association for Children and Adults with Learning Disabilities (ACLD)
4156 Library Road
Pittsburgh, PA 15234
412-341-1515
Jean Petersen, Executive Director
Organization of and for adults and children with learning disabilities, their families, and professionals in the field. Aims to educate parents and the public in general; helps state and local groups of similar membership, especially providing information on special programs in schools and camps; offers referral services; publishes various materials, including *ACLD Newsbriefs*.

National Center for Learning Disabilities (NCLD)
99 Park Avenue, 6th Floor
New York, NY 10016
212-687-7211
Arlyn Gardner, Executive Director

Organization aimed at educating the public about learning disabilities and raising funds to provide programs for those affected. Publishes *Their World* and *NCLD Learning Disabilities Resource Guide*, indispensable guide to state-by-state programs, schools, services, and organizations for learning-disabled children and adults, including overview, such as warning signals, rights of LD children, moving into adulthood and work, bibliography, and glossary of terms.

Council for Exceptional Children (CEC), ERIC Clearinghouse on Handicapped and Gifted Children, CEC Information Center, 703-620-3660. Organization of educators working with children with special needs; has 17 special education divisions, including Division for Learning Disabilities (DLD). (For full group information, see HELP FOR SPECIAL CHILDREN on page 578.)

AVKO Educational Research Foundation (AVKOERF)
3084 West Willard Road
Birch Run, MI 48415
313-686-9283
Don McCabe, Research Director

Organization of educators and others interested in audio, visual, kinetic, and oral (AVKO) techniques for teaching reading and spelling, especially for people with dyslexia or other learning disabilities. Conducts research; gathers and disseminates information; operates reading and spelling center; provides training for adult tutors; maintains library; publishes various materials, including quarterly newsletter and dictionary of phonograms *Word Families Plus*.

Council for Learning Disabilities (CLD)
9013 West Brooke Drive
Overland Park, KS 66212
913-492-3840
Kirsten McBride, Executive Secretary

Organization for professionals in the field of learning disabilities and interested others, including parents. Publishes professional newsletter and journal.

National Institute of Child Health and Human Development (NICHD), 301-496-5133. Publishes various materials, including the brochures *Developmental Dyslexia and Related Reading Disorders* and *Learning Disabilities: A Report to Congress*. (For full group information, see PREGNANCY.)

Observational Checklist for Learning Disabilities in Preschoolers

Note: This checklist is from materials prepared for teachers and parents of Head Start preschoolers, to help them decide whether or not screening is advisable for possible learning disabilities.

Children with learning problems generally exhibit certain behaviors that can be observed by the child's teachers and parents. [**Note**: At preschool age, they may be hard to diagnose as learning disabilities.] The checklist of behaviors that follows can alert you to undiagnosed learning problems, and help you know when to refer a child for professional evaluation. This checklist is intended to help you carry out systematic observations, which you can then share with others who might, if necessary, diagnose your child.

Using the Checklist

The "red flag." The checklist is only one of several observational devices that you can use to learn more about your child. Its main purpose is to help you to identify needs that have not been identified before. It should be considered only the first step in an overall program of systematic observation and assessment of a child's performance over time. It acts as a red flag because it can call your attention to behaviors that require much more careful observation and ongoing assessment. It can send you a signal that something may be wrong.

Knowing when to refer a child. Some behaviors may require urgent attention, while others can wait while you observe them more carefully over time. For instance, if a child complains of an earache (question 30) he or she requires immediate medical attention. It is important to find out whether the earache is a symptom of an infection, because untreated ear infections may result in hearing loss. Similarly, in case of dizziness, feverish forehead, and other possible signs of illness, the child should be taken to a doctor or clinic right away.

But other behaviors need to be watched carefully over time. For example, if your initial observations tell you that Jack really does have two tantrums a day (question 21), then that is the red flag that alerts you to continue, in a systematic way, to observe and assess these tantrums. You need to have time to examine these behaviors to find whether something happening in the home or classroom is causing them—something that can be changed to reduce or stop the tantrums. If, after all of your efforts to modify and adjust your home or classroom situation and teaching techniques [see TEACHING YOUNG CHILDREN: GUIDELINES AND TECH-

NIQUES on page 544], you find that Jack's tantrums continue and are highly disruptive to the family or other children, it is time to seek additional services.

If Tina is not using at least two- and three-word phrases to ask for what she wants (question 1), you need time to find out why. Is Tina not using phrases because she really cannot do so, or because she has simply never needed to use them or been expected to do so? Perhaps she has always gotten what she wanted just by pointing to the object or by saying only one word. She may need some prompting from you, the teachers in her class, and her friends and classmates to get her to use words to ask for what she wants. However, if you try for some time and have no success, Tina should be referred to an appropriate professional or team of professionals for help.

Parents and teachers are the best judges of when they have watched long enough to decide whether diagnostic services outside the classroom are necessary.

How often should this checklist be used? This observational checklist is a part of the first step in identifying problems and seeking help for them. But observation, like assessment or evaluation, should be a continuous process. This is because behavior is always changing, and some behavior changes may signal a problem. In addition, some children have secondary or associated problems that are very slow to develop and hard to detect—but that need to be identified and helped. It is not possible to give a surefire rule or formula for how often to use this observation form. But once you become familiar with the behaviors listed and the questions asked, you will probably find that these questions occur to you naturally as you watch your child and other children. The checklist form should help you to organize the information that you collect.

Using Checklist Results

It is important to remember that any child may exhibit one of the behaviors described under a particular skill area. This does not mean that the child is learning-disabled. Learning-disabled children will exhibit several of the behaviors described in one or several of the skill areas. There are many different combinations of behaviors that learning-disabled children display.

If your answers fall in the gray boxes on a number of observational questions in one or more skill areas, this may indicate potential problems and the need for extra help in those areas.

If you observe the same behaviors frequently in a child, you should concentrate on helping the child acquire skills in the areas you have checked. If your efforts are unsuccessful, and if the specific problems interfere with the child's general success in learning, you may need to refer the child for an evaluation.

Communicative Skills	Yes	No	Sometimes
1. Does the child use at least two- and three-word phrases to ask for what he or she wants? (For example, "more juice" or "more juice please."	☐	☐	☐

Continued on page 287

	Yes	No	Sometimes
2. Does the child use complete sentences to tell you what has happened? (For example, "My doggie ran away" versus "doggie gone.")	☐	☐	☐
*3. When the child is asked to describe something, does he or she use at least two sentences to talk about it?	☐	☐	☐
4. Does the child ask questions? (For example, "Where is Juan?")	☐	☐	☐
5. Does the child seem to have difficulty following directions?	☐	☐	☐
6. Does the child respond to questions with an appropriate answer?	☐	☐	☐
7. Does the child seem to talk too softly or too loudly?	☐	☐	☐
8. Are you able to understand the child?	☐	☐	☐
9. Does the child have difficulty paying attention to group activities for more than five minutes at a time?	☐	☐	☐

Question applies if child is four years or older.

Motor Skills	Yes	No	Sometimes
10. Does the child stumble often, or appear awkward when he or she moves?	☐	☐	☐
11. Does the child seem afraid of or unable to use stairs, climbing equipment, or tricycles?	☐	☐	☐
12. When the child walks or runs, does one side of his or her body seem to move differently than the other side? For instance, does the child seem to have better control of the leg and arm on one side than on the other?	☐	☐	☐
13. Can the child hop on one foot?	☐	☐	☐
*14. Is the child capable of dressing him- or herself except for tying shoes?	☐	☐	☐
15. Does the child hold a pencil or a crayon appropriately with the thumb, index, and middle fingers?	☐	☐	☐
16. Does the child continually switch a crayon from one hand to the other when coloring?	☐	☐	☐
17. Do the child's hands appear clumsy or shaky when he or she is using them?	☐	☐	☐
18. When the child is coloring with a crayon, does the hand that he or she is *not* using appear tense? (For example, clenched into a fist.)	☐	☐	☐
19. Can the child color inside a circumscribed area with any accuracy?	☐	☐	☐
20. Can the child cut with a pair of scissors?	☐	☐	☐

Question applies if child is four years or older.

Social Skills	Yes	No	Sometimes
21. Does the child engage in at least two disruptive behaviors a day? (For example, tantrums, fighting, screaming.)	☐	☐	☐
22. Does the child appear withdrawn from the outside world? (For example, fiddling with pieces of string, staring into space, rocking his or her body, banging his or her head, talking to him- or herself.)	☐	☐	☐
23. Does the child appear extremely shy in group activities? (For example, does the child avoid volunteering answers or answering direct questions, even when you think he or she knows the answers?)	☐	☐	☐
24. Does the child play alone and seldom talk to the other children?	☐	☐	☐
25. Does the child spend most of the time trying to get attention from the adults?	☐	☐	☐
26. Does the child have toileting problems (wet or soiled) at least once a week?	☐	☐	☐

Vision or Hearing Skills	Yes	No	Sometimes
27. Do the child's eye movements appear jerky or uncoordinated?	☐	☐	☐

Continued on page 288

28. Does the child seem to have difficulty seeing objects?	□	□	□
. . . tilt his or her head to look at things?	□	□	□
. . . hold objects close to his or her eyes?	□	□	□
. . . squint?	□	□	□
. . . show sensitivity to bright lights?	□	□	□
. . . have uncontrolled eye-rolling?	□	□	□
. . . complain that his or her eyes hurt?	□	□	□
. . . bump into things constantly?	□	□	□
29. Does the child appear awkward in tasks requiring eye-hand coordination? (For example, pegs, puzzles, coloring.)	□	□	□
30. Does the child seem to have difficulty hearing?	□	□	□
. . . consistently favor one ear by turning the same side of his or her head in the direction of the sound?	□	□	□
. . . ignore, confuse, or not follow directions?	□	□	□
. . . rub or pull on his or her ear frequently, or complain of earache?	□	□	□
. . . complain of head noises or dizziness?	□	□	□
. . . have a high, low, or monotonous tone of voice?	□	□	□
. . . respond to your voice when he or she is not looking at you?	□	□	□
. . . ask "what?" excessively?	□	□	□
. . . have speech that is very difficult for you to understand?	□	□	□

General Health	Yes	No	Sometimes
31. Does the child seem to have an excessive number of colds?	□	□	□
32. Does the child have frequent absences because of illness?	□	□	□
33. Do the child's eyes water?	□	□	□
34. Does the child have a discharge from his or her eyes?	□	□	□
. . . his or her ears?	□	□	□
35. Does the child have periods of unusual movements (such as rapid eye blinking) or "blank spells" that seem to appear and disappear without relationship to the social situation?	□	□	□
36. Does the child have hives or rashes?	□	□	□
Does the child wheeze?	□	□	□
37. Does the child have a persistent cough?	□	□	□
38. Is the child excessively thirsty?	□	□	□
. . . ravenously hungry?	□	□	□
39. Have you noticed any of the following conditions?			
. . . constant fatigue	□	□	□
. . . irritability	□	□	□
. . . restlessness	□	□	□
. . . tenseness	□	□	□
. . . feverish cheeks or forehead.	□	□	□
40. Is the child overweight?	□	□	□
41. Is the child physically or mentally sluggish?	□	□	□
42. Has the child lost weight without being on a diet?	□	□	□

Source: *Mainstreaming Preschoolers: Children with Learning Disabilities: A Guide for Teachers, Parents, and Others Who Work with Learning Disabled Preschoolers,* by Alice H. Hayden et al. [see page 290]. The checklist was adapted from materials prepared by the OCD/BEH Collaborative Project with Head Start, Model Preschool Center for Handicapped Children, Experimental Education Unit, Child Development and Mental Retardation Center, University of Washington.

National Institute of Neurological Disorders and Stroke (NINDS), 301-496-5751. Publishes *Learning Disabilities due to Minimal Brain Dysfunction: Hope Through Research*. (For full group information, see BRAIN AND BRAIN DISORDERS.)

National Institute of Mental Health (NIMH), 301-443-4515. (For full group information, see MENTAL DISORDERS.)

National Easter Seal Society, 312-243-8400; toll-free number 800-221-6827. Network of societies to aid people with disabilities of any kind, including problems stemming from learning disabilities. (For full group information, see HELP FOR SPECIAL CHILDREN on page 578.)

American Association of University Affiliated Programs for Persons with Developmental Disabilities (AAUAP), 202-737-1511. (For full group information, see HELP FOR SPECIAL CHILDREN on page 578.)

Co-ADD (Coalition for the Education and Support of Attention Deficit Disorder), 612-425-0423. (For full group information, see ATTENTION DEFICIT HYPERACTIVITY DISORDER.)

HEATH Resource Center, National Clearinghouse on Postsecondary Education for Handicapped Individuals, 202-833-4707. (For full group information, see HELP FOR SPECIAL CHILDREN on page 578.)

National Association of Private Schools for Exceptional Children (NAPSEC), 202-296-1800. (For full group information, see HELP FOR SPECIAL CHILDREN on page 578.)

Scholastic Aptitude Test (SAT) Admissions Testing Program for Handicapped Students, 609-734-5068. Offers special testing arrangements for students documented to have learning disabilities, visual or hearing disabilties, or dyslexia, including untimed tests or additional time, tests in large type or braille, tests on tape cassette or read to student, scribe, interpreter, and rest breaks. (For full group information, see EAR AND HEARING PROBLEMS; HELP FOR SPECIAL CHILDREN on page 578.)

ACT Special Testing, ACT Test Administration, 319-337-1332. (For full group information, see HELP FOR SPECIAL CHILDREN on page 578.)

Other reference sources

Guides For Parents

Help Me to Help My Child: A Sourcebook for Parents of Learning Disabled Children, by Jill Bloom. Boston: Little, Brown, 1990.

Smart Kids with School Problems: Things to Know and Ways to Help, by Priscilla L. Vail. New York: Dutton, 1987. Focuses on elementary grades.

Unlocking Potential: College and Other Choices for Learning Disabled People—A Step-by-Step Guide, by Barbara Scheiber and Jeanne Talpers. Bethesda, MD: Adler and Adler, 1987.

Your Child in School, by Thomas Sobol and Harriett Sobol. New York: Arbor House, 1986–87. Focuses on elementary grades, with sections on learning disabilities.

The Misunderstood Child: A Guide for Parents of Learning Disabled Children, by Larry B. Silver. New York: McGraw-Hill, 1984.

Helping Children with Specific Learning Disabilities: A Practical Guide for Parents and Teachers, by Donald H. Painting. Englewood Cliffs, NJ: Prentice-Hall, 1983.

Your Child Can Win, by Joan Noyes and Norma Macneill. New York: Morrow, 1983. Describes many games, home and commercial, to improve skills.

Life After High School, by Helen Ginandes Weiss and Martin S. Weiss (1990). Available from Treehouse Associates, Box 1992, Avon, CO 81620. For parents and educators.

A Survival Manual: Case Studies and Suggestions for the Learning Disabled Teenager, by Helen Ginandes Weiss and Martin S. Weiss (1976). Available from Treehouse Associates, Box 1992, Avon, CO 81620.

Caring for Little People: A Handbook of Diagnostic and Remedial Materials, by Helen Ginandes Weiss and Martin S. Weiss (1985). Available from Treehouse Associates, Box 1992, Avon, CO 81620. For preschool educators, child-care workers, and parents of children 3 months to 5 years. Includes readiness evaluation chart, learning-style observational checklist, neurosensory developmental screening, glossary, and remedial suggestions.

A Home-School Cookbook: Parents and Teachers Guide to Learning Disabilities, by Helen Ginandes Weiss and Martin S. Weiss (1983). Available from Treehouse Associates, Box 1992, Avon, CO 81620. Hands-on collection of simple games and activities for LD children grades K to 6.

Basic Language Kit: A Teaching-Tutoring Aid for Adolescents and Young Adults, by Helen Ginandes Weiss and Martin S. Weiss (1979). Available from Treehouse Associates, Box 1992, Avon, CO 81620. Materials and approaches for language skills.

Home Is a Learning Place: A Parents Guide to Learning Disabilities, by Helen Ginandes Weiss and Martin S. Weiss. Boston: Little, Brown, 1976. Available from Treehouse Associates, Box 1992, Avon, CO 81620.

The Learning Disabled Child: Ways That Parents Can Help, by Suzanne H. Stevens. Winston-Salem, NC: John F. Blair, 1980. 1406 Plaza Drive, SW, Winston-Salem, NC 27103.

Mainstreaming Preschoolers: Children with Learning Disabilities: A Guide for Teachers, Parents, and Others Who Work with Learning Disabled Preschoolers, by Alice H. Hayden et al. Prepared for the Head Start Bureau, Administration for Children, Youth, and Families. Washington, DC: Government Printing Office, 1978.

On Parent Advocacy and Student's Rights

Your Child's Education: A School Guide for Parents, by Mark Wolraich, Landis Rick, and Nicholas Karagan. Springfield, IL: Charles C. Thomas, 1984. Aims to make parents effective advocates for their children in school; includes section on learning disabilities.

The Powerful Parent: A Child Advocacy Handbook, by David M. Gottesman. Norwalk, CT: Appleton-Century-Crofts, 1982.

Due Process in Special Education, by James A. Shrybman. Gaithersburg, MD: Aspen Systems Corporation, 1982. P.O. Box 6018, Gaithersburg, MD 20877.

How to Get Services by Being Assertive, by Charlotte Des Jardins. 1980. Includes advice on IEP (Individualized Education Plan) meetings, due process hearings, and gaining access to school records. Available from Coordinating Council for Handicapped Children, 407 South Dearborn, Room 680, Chicago, IL 60605.

Legal Rights Primer for the Handicapped: In and Out of the Classroom, by Joseph Roberts and Bonnie Hawk. Novato, CA: Academic Therapy Publications, 1980. 20 Commercial Boulevard, Novato, CA 94947. Includes text of Education for All Handicapped Children Act.

How to Write an I.E.P., by John Arena. 1978. Available from Academic Therapy Publications, 20 Commercial Boulevard, Novato, CA 94947. Includes chapter on learning disabilities; reviews rights of handicapped children and their parents.

Background Books

Learning Disabilities, by Jean McBee Knox. New York: Chelsea House, 1989.

Reading, Writing and Rage, by Dorothy Ungerleider. Rolling Hills, CA: Jalmar, 1985.

Overcoming Dyslexia, by Beve Hornsby. New York: Arco, 1984.

An Uncommon Gift, by James S. Evans. Philadelphia: Westminster, 1983.

Learning Disabilities Explained, by Stanley S. Lamm and Martin L. Fisch. Garden City, NY: Doubleday, 1982.

No One to Play With: The Social Side of Learning Disabilities, by Betty B. Osman, in association with Henriette Blinder. New York: Random House, 1982. Spanish translation also available.

No Easy Answers—The Learning Disabled Child, by Sally L. Smith. New York: Bantam, 1980.

How to Raise Your Child to Be a Winner, by Gene R. Hawes, Helen Ginandes Weiss, and Martin S. Weiss. New York: Rawson, Wade, 1980. Includes section on learning disabilities.

Available from Treehouse Associates, Box 1992, Avon, CO 81620.

The Hidden Handicap, by Dr. Judith Ehre Kranes. New York: Simon & Schuster, 1980.

Learning Disabilities: The Struggle from Adolescence Toward Adulthood, by William M. Cruickshank, William C. Morse, and Jeannie S. Johns. Syracuse: Syracuse University Press, 1980.

Learning Disabilities: A Family Affair, by Betty B. Osman. New York: Random House, 1979.

Something's Wrong with My Child, by Milton Brutten, Sylvia O. Richardson, and Charles Mangel. San Diego/New York: Harcourt Brace Jovanovich, 1979.

Dyslexia and Your Child, by Rudolph F. Wagner. New York: Harper & Row, 1979.

Square Pegs Round Holes—The Learning Disabled Child in the Classroom and at Home, by Harold B. Levy, M.D. Boston: Little, Brown, 1973. Focuses on elementary grades.

Directories and Guides

For Learning-disabled Children

The School Search Guide to Private Schools for Students with Learning Disabilities, by Midge Lipkin. Belmont, MA: Schoolsearch, 1989. 127 Marsh Street, Belmont, MA 02178.

Campus Access for Learning Disabled Students: A Handbook for a Successful Postsecondary Education, by Barbara Scheiber and Jeanne Talpers. 1985. Available from Closer Look/Parents' Campaign for Handicapped Children and Youth.

Directory for Exceptional Children. Available from Porter Sargent Publishers, 11 Beacon Street, Boston, MA 02108.

Directory of College Facilities and Services for the Handicapped, Charles S. McGeough, Barbara Jungjohan, and James L. Thomas, eds. 1983. Available from Oryx Press, 2214 North Central at Encanto, Phoenix, AZ 85004.

Directory of Facilities and Services for the Learning Disabled. Available from Academic Therapy Publications, 20 Commercial Boulevard, Novato, CA, 94947.

Directory of Summer Camps for Children with Learning Disabilities. Available from Association for Children and Adults with Learning Disabilities (ACLD).

Guide to College Programs for Learning Disabled Students. Available from National Association of College Admissions Counselors.

Peterson's Guide to Colleges with Programs for Learning Disabled Students. Princeton, NJ: Peterson's, 1988.

Books For or By Kids

Survival Guide for Kids with LD (Learning Differences), by Gary Fisher and Rhoda Cummings. Minneapolis: Free Spirit, 1990. Book and cassette about learning disabilities, for ages 8 and up. Available from Free Spirit, 123 N. Third Street, Suite 716, Minneapolis, MN 55401.

Dyslexia, by Christopher A. Raccioppi. Photo-essay by a learning-disabled teenager. Available from RMR Educational Consultation, 124 Washington Street, Tappan, NY 10983.

Josh—A Boy with Dyslexia, by Caroline Janover. Burlington, VT: Waterfront, 1988. For grades 3 to 7.

Secrets Aren't (Always) for Keeps, by Barbara Aiello and Jeffrey Shulman. Frederick, MD: 21st Century, 1988. On learning disabilities; part of The Kids on the Block Book Series for readers age 8 to 12, focusing on children with problems or disabilities.

M.E. and Morton, by Sylvia Cassedy. New York: Crowell, 1987.

Wrongway Applebaum, by Marjorie Lewis. New York: Coward, 1985. For early elementary grades.

Will the Real Gertrude Hollings Please Stand Up?, by Sheila Greenwald. Boston: Atlantic/Little, Brown, 1983. For grades 4 to 8.

Do Bananas Chew Gum?, by Jamie Gilson. New York: Lothrop, 1980. For grades 4 to 8.

He's My Brother, by Joe Lasker. Niles, IL: Albert Whitman, 1974. For beginning readers.

Other Useful Reference Works

Reading Disability, 4th edition, by Florence G. Roswell and Gladys Natchez. New York: Basic, 1989.

Assessment of Developmental Learning Disorders: A Neuropsychological Approach, by Rita G. Rudel with Jane M. Holmes and Joan Rudel Pardes. New York: Basic, 1988.

Health Care U.S.A., by Jean Carper. New York: Prentice Hall, 1987. Resource for general and specific health-care information, including sections on mental retardation, developmental disabilities, and learning disabilities; lists key rehabilitation centers specializing in infant and early childhood development, government-supported university-affiliated facilities (UAFs) for learning disabilities and UAF-associated specialists, mental retardation research centers, special schools for dyslexic children, and other information.

Journal of Learning Disabilities, Austin, TX: PRO-ED.

Developmental Variation and Learning Disorders, by Melvin D. Levine, M.D. Cambridge, MA: Educators Publishing Services, 1987.

Learning Disabilities: Theories, Diagnosis, and Teaching Strategies, by J. Lerner. Boston: Houghton Mifflin, 1985.

The Complete Handbook of Children's Reading Disorders, by Hilde L. Mosse. New York: Human Sciences, 1982.

(See also BRAIN AND BRAIN DISORDERS; COMMUNICATION SKILLS AND DISORDERS; ATTENTION DEFICIT HYPERACTIVITY DISORDER; READING.)

learning readiness skill   Alternate term for PREREQUISITE, in the sense of a simpler skill that is regarded as fundamental to the mastering of a more complex, higher-level skill. Such skills are sometimes measured on various READINESS TESTS.

learning style   The way a child most readily receives and processes new information, a general term used in many different ways, depending on how educators and psychologists themselves approach the question; also called *cognitive style*.

Sometimes a child might be classified as an *analytic learner*, one who tends to first grasp a concept and then focus on the parts or supporting details; at the opposite pole would be a *synthetic learner*, who learns best when presented with various aspects or parts of a skill or concept, then moving on to the general.

Sometimes discussions of learning style will focus on the SENSORY MODES or MODALITIES a child uses to receive and process information most efficiently and easily. An acronym often used for these modes is VAKT, for visual, auditory, kinesthetic, and tactile; but sometimes the term *haptic* is used to refer to physical, hands-on learning, in a sense combining kinesthetic and tactile. Children (and adults) can use these various modes for learning, a process often called *integration*. But some kinds of learning focus on some modes more than on others, and children with handicaps (see HANDICAPPED), including LEARNING DISABILITIES, may not be able to use some modes as well as others. The chart of children's LEARNING STYLES on page 292 describes some of the main characteristics of these styles of learning and offers some tips for helping children learn more easily. The MONTESSORI METHOD uses materials designed to increase the child's use of all the sensory modes, in what is called *sensory education*.

Sometimes learning styles refer to the way in which material is taught or presented, as a synonym for *educational approach*. If a parent or teacher lectures while a child sits and listens, what results is *passive learning*. By contrast, when a child is doing something, such as building a model or conducting an experiment, in the process using a variety of sensory modes, the result is *active learning*. If the parent or teacher presents a general rule and then has students learn to recognize or work with that rule in specific situations, the result is *expository learning* or *deductive learning*. Conversely, if the child is given information or materials on a number of specific situations and is asked to draw general conclusions, the result is *discovery learning, inductive learning*, sometimes *experiential learning*, or (if the emphasis is on independent problem solving) *heuristic learning*. When the student primarily memorizes material, without necessarily understanding it in context, it is called *rote learning*; when the focus is on relating new information to prior knowledge, the result is *associative learning*; and when the information is carefully structured with ever-more-difficult tasks building on earlier material, it is called *sequential learning*.

Concepts and skills acquired in daily life without specific instruction result from what is called *trial-and-error learning* or (if the focus is on learning from the experience of others) *vicarious learning*. Conscious use of these skills, expecting that a child will imitate a teacher or parent, is sometimes called *modeling*.

Learning Styles

CLUES	LEARNING TIPS
VISUAL • Needs to see it to know it. • Strong sense of color. • May have artistic ability. • Difficulty with spoken directions. • Overreaction to sounds. • Trouble following lectures. • Misinterpretation of words.	• Use of graphics to reinforce learning—films, slides, illustrations, diagrams, doodles. • Color coding to organize notes and possessions. • Written directions. • Use of flow charts and diagrams for notetaking. • Visualizing spelling of words or facts to be memorized.
AUDITORY • Prefers to get information by listening—needs to hear it to know it. • Difficulty following written directions. • Difficulty with reading. • Problems with writing.	• Inability to read body language and facial expressions. • Use of tapes for reading and for class and lecture notes. • Learning by interviewing or by participating in discussions. • Having test questions or directions read aloud or put on tape.
HAPTIC • Prefers hands-on learning. • Can assemble parts without reading directions. • Difficulty sitting still. • Learns better when physical activity is involved. • May be very well coordinated and has athletic ability.	• Experiential learning (making models, doing lab work, and role playing). • Frequent breaks in study periods. • Tracing letters and words to learn spelling and remember facts. • Use of computer to reinforce learning through sense of touch. • Memorizing or drilling while walking or exercising. • Expressing abilities through dance, drama, or gymnastics.

Reprinted by permission from *Unlocking Potential*, by Barbara Scheiber and Jeanne Talpers, © 1987. (Available for $12.95 + $2.50 shipping & handling per copy, from Adler & Adler Woodbine House, 5614 Fishers Land, Rockville MD 20852, toll-free number 800-843-7323, in MD 301-468-8800.)

For help and further information

In Their Own Way: Discovering and Encouraging Your Child's Personal Learning Style, by Thomas Armstrong. Los Angeles: Tarcher, 1987.

(See also EDUCATION; also TEACHING YOUNG CHILDREN: GUIDELINES AND ACTIVITIES on page 544.)

least detrimental alternative   Alternate phrase for BEST INTERESTS OF THE CHILD, as in CUSTODY or CHILD ABUSE AND NEGLECT cases.

least restrictive environment (LRE)   Specification in the EDUCATION FOR ALL HANDICAPPED CHILDREN ACT OF 1975 emphasizing that at school HANDICAPPED children should be in the most natural, most integrated, least inhibiting setting possible and that they should be educated in the same settings with non-handicapped children to the extent possible. LRE is a key concept in mainstreaming, designed to maximize the social and cultural contacts of children with handicaps and maximize their growth and independence.

LeBoyer method   A popular form of natural or PREPARED CHILD-BIRTH.

left-handed   A type of HANDEDNESS in which a person relies more heavily on and is more proficient at using the left hand than the right.

legal risk adoption   A form of ADOPTION that is provisional, pending completion of formal requirements.

Lesch-Nyhan syndrome   A rare GENETIC DISORDER of the X-LINKED, RECESSIVE type, only recognized in the early 1960s, involving a deficiency of HGPRT enzyme (*hypoxanthine-guanine-phosphoribosyltransferase*). Lacking this enzyme, the body is unable to break down and use a group of compounds called PURINES, some of which are produced naturally in the body, while others result as a by-product of the digestion of PROTEINS. In a mild form this might produce gout. But in its most severe form, the syndrome is characterized by MENTAL RETARDATION, impaired kidney function (see KIDNEY AND UROLOGICAL DISORDERS), abnormal physical development, CHOREA (jerky, fidgeting movements), ATHETOSIS (slow writhing movements), spasticity (increasing rigidity of the muscles), and most strikingly SELF-MUTILATION, in which the child compulsively bites away lips and fingers. No treatment is yet known, and most children with the syndrome die before PUBERTY.

For help and further information

National Institute of Arthritis and Musculoskeletal and Skin Diseases (NIAMS), 301-496-8188. (For full group information, see ARTHRITIS; MUSCULAR DYSTROPHY.)

National Institute of Neurological Disorders and Stroke (NINDS), 301-496-5751. (For full group information, see BRAIN AND BRAIN DISORDERS.)

National Institute of Mental Health (NIMH), 301-443-4515. (For full group information, see MENTAL DISORDERS.)

(See also GENETIC DISORDERS; X-LINKED; RECESSIVE.)

lesion A general term for an abnormality anywhere in or on the body, due to injury or disease, including a wound, an injury, a tumor, a change in body tissue, a sore, or a rash.

leukemia A form of CANCER that involves unchecked production of white blood cells in the BONE MARROW. These gradually crowd out the red blood cells and platelets required for health, leading to severe ANEMIA and HEMORRHAGES (see BLOOD AND BLOOD DISORDERS). In children, leukemia often develops rapidly and, if untreated, can cause death within weeks or months. But a variety of drugs are used to try to halt the process, producing REMISSIONS and sometimes full cures. (For more on chemotherapy, and on dealing with possibly terminal illness in children, see CANCER.) If relapses occur, physicians may consider a BONE MARROW TRANSPLANT, though the operation is risky, and finding a donor with matching bone marrow is difficult. As with cancer in general, the causes of leukemia are obscure, though some forms seem to be triggered by a virus or by ENVIRONMENTAL HAZARDS such as RADIATION or individual cancer-causing chemicals (*carcinogens*). People with some GENETIC DISORDERS or CHROMOSOMAL ABNORMALITIES, such as DOWN'S SYNDROME, are at increased risk for leukemia.

For help and further information

Leukemia Society of America
733 Third Avenue
New York, NY 10017
212-573-8484
Peter N. Cakridas, Executive Director
Organization devoted to helping patients and their families cope with leukemia, lymphomas, and multiple myelomas. Provides direct financial aid, transportation, and other services; seeks to educate public; provides information to public and professionals; publishes various materials, including the bimonthly *Society News* and *What It Is That I Have, Don't Want, Didn't Ask For, Can't Give Back, and How I Feel About It* (book to help teens handle feelings, not specific to leukemia).

National Leukemia Association
585 Stewart Avenue, Suite 536

Garden City, NY 11530
516-222-1944
Allan D. Weinberg, Executive Director
Organization dedicated to combatting leukemia. Funds research; supplies financial aid to qualified needy leukemia patients, upon application.

National Cancer Institute (NCI), 800-4-CANCER [422-6237]. (For full group information, see CANCER.)

Other references sources

For Parents

Understanding Leukemia, by C.P. Margolies. New York: Scribner, 1983.
A Child's Fight Against Leukemia, by Jonathan B. Tucker. New York: Holt, Rinehart & Winston, 1982.
Eric, by Doris Lund. New York: Dell, 1976. A mother's story of her son with leukemia.

For Kids

One Day at a Time: Children Living with Leukemia, by Thomas Bergman. Milwaukee, WI. Gareth Stevens, 1990. For grades 3 to 5.
Patty Gets Well, by P.D. Frevert. Mankato, MN: Creative Education, 1983.
Friends till the End, by Todd Strasser. New York: Delacorte, 1981.
You and Leukemia: A Day at a Time, revised edition, by Lyn S. Baker. Philadelphia: Saunders, 1978. For ages 9 and up.
(See also CANCER; BLOOD AND BLOOD DISORDERS; BONE MARROW; BONE MARROW TRANSPLANT; DEATH; HOSPITAL; also HELP FOR SPECIAL CHILDREN, on page 578, including "Make-a-Wish" organizations for severely or terminally ill children.)

leukocytes Alternate name for white blood cells. (See BLOOD AND BLOOD DISORDERS.)

Levels I, II, and III Designations sometimes used for HOSPITALS of various categories, based on the kind and sophistication of the medical care they offer, the highest being Level III, including many UNIVERSITY-AFFILIATED FACILITIES (UAFs).

LH Abbreviation for luteinizing hormone, a HORMONE used in a HOME MEDICAL TEST. (See OVULATION.)

liberal arts Traditionally, the courses that made up the classical CURRICULUM, such as literature, art, philosophy, history, music, and foreign languages, usually referring to COLLEGE-level education. Today the term is more widely used to refer to a broad, general, "liberal" education, including study of the humanities, the social sciences, and the sciences, as opposed to a narrowly specialized, vocationally oriented education.

lie In PREGNANCY, a general term for whether the FETUS is *longitudinal* (up-and-down) or *transverse* (horizontal) in the UTERUS. (See FETAL PRESENTATION.)

lien A legal claim on someone's property, to prevent sale or transfer until a debt is satisfied; in certain cases, as to satisfy unpaid CHILD SUPPORT, the property may be sold to pay the debt.

life-support machine Alternate name for a VENTILATOR.

light perception (LP) The ability to distinguish light from dark. (See EYE AND VISION PROBLEMS.)

limb-girdle muscular dystrophy A form of MUSCULAR DYSTROPHY.

Lincoln-Oseretsky Motor Development Scale A type of individually administered TEST to assess the development of MOTOR SKILLS in children and adolescents, more specifically fine and gross motor skills, finger dexterity and speed, and hand–eye coordination (see VISUAL SKILLS). The 36 tasks include such activities as walking backward, catching a ball, winding a thread, tapping with feet and fingers, and balancing on tiptoe while opening and closing hands. NORMS for test results are given for both sexes for ages six to 14, with PERCENTILES. (For help and further information, see TESTS.)

linea nigra A dark streak that sometimes develops between a woman's NAVEL and pubic area during PREGNANCY, later fading away.

lipids Alternate term for FATS.

lipid storage diseases (lipidoses) A group of METABOLIC DISORDERS in which abnormal amounts of FATS, or *lipids*, are stored in the body. Fats are found in almost all of the body's cells; when these cells are ready to be routinely replaced, certain substances called *enzymes* normally help break down the worn-out cells, with each enzyme acting on a different part of the lipid molecule. But in some people, an inherited defect keeps the body from producing any or enough of a particular enzyme, so lipids that are normally broken down instead accumulate in various tissues of the body, causing progressive damage, sometimes including MENTAL RETARDATION, enlarged spleen and liver (see LIVER PROBLEMS), bone degeneration, and even DEATH.

The abnormal fat accumulation is often named for the missing or deficient enzyme; in *Gaucher's disease*, for example, the defective enzyme is *glucocerebrosidase*, and the fat that accumulates is called *glucocerebroside*. Some forms of lipid storage disease show themselves in infancy, but others do not appear until later childhood or adulthood.

Lipid storage diseases are generally rare, but among the more common ones so far identified are:

- *Gaucher's disease (glucosyl cerebroside lipidosis)*, the most common of the lipid storage diseases, the adult form of which affects perhaps 20,000 people in the United States. The main symptoms are enlarged spleen and liver, eroded bones, and mental retardation or MENTAL DISORDERS, as fats are stored in the brain. The most severe form (Type II or the *acute infantile neuronopathic form*) strikes in infancy, producing major neurological damage and an enlarged spleen, and usually brings death within one to two years. Type III, the *juvenile form*, generally strikes later in childhood, progresses more slowly, and involves less neurological damage.

Children with Gaucher's disease who survive to adolescence may live for many years. The most common and least severe form of Gaucher's disease is Type I, the *adult chronic non-neuronopathic form*, which produces enlarged spleen and liver and eroded bones but does not involve neurological damage.

- *Fabry's disease (angiokeratoma corporis diffusum universale* or *alpha-galactosidase deficiency)*, which affects about 2,000 people in the United States, mostly males. Symptoms include skin abnormalities (*angiokeratomas*), opacity of the cornea (see EYE AND VISION DISORDERS), episodes of FEVER, and burning pain in the extremities.

- *Tay-Sachs disease (G_{M2} gangliosidosis)*, which strikes infants, usually around the age of six months, bringing physical and mental retardation, PARALYSIS, BLINDNESS, DEMENTIA, and generally death by age three or four, as fats (*gangliosides*) accumulate in the brain. Because of public education and PRENATAL TESTS, Tay-Sachs disease has become quite rare. A related variant is *Sandhoff's disease*.

- *generalized (G_{M2}) gangliosidosis*, in which the gangliosides accumulate in the NERVOUS SYSTEM, often bringing death by age two.

- *Niemann-Pick disease (sphingomyelin lipidosis)*, in which sphingomyelin accumulates in the BONE MARROW, spleen, and lymph nodes. The disorder may appear at different ages and with varying severity, involving an enlarged spleen and liver and some mental retardation, but often brings death within a few years.

- *Krabbe's disease (globoid leukodystrophy)*, involving a deficiency of *galactocerebroside beta-galactosidase*, which leads to progressive physical and mental retardation, paralysis, blindness, deafness (see EAR AND HEARING PROBLEMS), and death in infancy.

- *metachromatic leukodystrophy (sulfatide lipidosis)*, in which a deficiency of the enzyme *cerebroside sulfatase* causes accumulation of fats in the CENTRAL NERVOUS SYSTEM, kidneys (see KIDNEY AND UROLOGICAL DISORDERS), and spleen. Apparent by about age two, it generally brings progressive paralysis and dementia until death by about age 10.

Among other rare lipid storage diseases are *fucosidosis, Farber's disease, Wolman's disease (acid cholesteryl ester hydrolase deficiency), cholesteryl ester storage disease, cerebrotendinous xanthomatosis (van Bogaert's disease), beta-sitosterolemia and xanthomatosis*, and *Refsum's syndrome (phytanic acid storage disease)*.

Lipid storage diseases are GENETIC DISORDERS, almost all of them so far identified being of the AUTOSOMAL RECESSIVE type, in which a child inherits a defective gene from both parents, who may be unaffected CARRIERS. Of the known lipid storage diseases, Fabry's disease is the exception, being an X-LINKED DISORDER, passed on to a son by a carrier mother.

Most lipid storage diseases first appear in infancy and show themselves in retarded physical and mental skills. Diagnosis is often confirmed by a BLOOD TEST that measures the enzymes active in the white blood cells and by a CULTURE of the skin cells, in which the enzyme activity can be measured. These techniques can also be used as GENETIC SCREENING tests to detect carriers. Parents with any family history of lipid storage diseases should seek GENETIC COUNSELING, especially those whose ancestry is Ashkenazi Jewish, from Central and Eastern Europe, since several of the lipid storage diseases are found predominantly among people of this background. The same people may also want to consider PRENATAL TESTS, such as AMNIOCENTESIS or CHORIONIC VILLUS SAMPLING, to see if a FETUS has a lipid storage defect. Tests and screening have sharply reduced the number of children born with lipid storage diseases, especially Tay-Sachs disease.

For the children and adults already living with lipid storage diseases, often no therapy exists other than attempting to minimize pain and other symptoms. Several promising approaches are being explored, however. One is *enzyme replacement therapy*, in which healthy enzymes taken from the PLACENTA of newborns is injected into the bloodstream to replace or supplement the person's defective enzymes. But problems exist with obtaining enough purified enzymes and directing them to the places where they are needed. Another approach is BONE MARROW TRANSPLANT, a risky, expensive form of treatment. Genetic-engineering researchers are also attempting to find ways to create and insert healthy replacement genes, to create the missing enzymes, but considerable work remains to be done on this experimental GENE THERAPY. (For help and further information, see GENETIC DISORDERS; GENETIC COUNSELING.)

For help and further information

National Institute of Neurological Disorders and Stroke (NINDS), 301-496-5751. Publishes *Lipid Storage Disease*. (See BRAIN AND BRAIN DISORDERS.)

National Tay-Sachs & Allied Diseases Association (NTSAD)
385 Elliot Street
Newton, MA 02164
617-964-5508
Dale I. Carre, Executive Director
Organization of families with children suffering from Tay-Sachs or related diseases, including Gaucher disease, Krabbe disease, Niemann-Pick disease, and Sandhoff disease. Encourages formation of local mutual-support self-help groups, especially with experienced parents supporting new ones; provides information and makes referrals; maintains directory of test centers and laboratories; publishes various materials, including newsletter *Breakthrough*, *What Every Family Should Know About Tay Sachs and Allied Diseases*, *Prevent a Tragedy*, *Services to Families*, and *One Day at a Time*.

National Gaucher Foundation (NGF)
1424 K Street, NW
Washington, DC 20005
202-393-2777
Karen Cohen, Executive Director
Organization promoting medical research and clinical programs directed toward finding treatment and cure for Gaucher's dis-

ease. Encourages formation of self-help groups for affected individuals and their families; provides information and seeks to educate public; publishes various materials, including bimonthly newsletter *Gaucher's Disease Registry Newsletter*, audiovisual *Gaucher's Disease: Coping, Caring and Searching for a Cure*, and pamphlets and other material on genetic background.

National Institute of Diabetes and Digestive and Kidney Diseases (NIDDK), 301-496-3583. (For full group information, see DIGESTIVE DISORDERS.)

National Center for Education in Child and Maternal Health (NCEMCH), 202-625-8400. (For full group information, see PREGNANCY.)

National Foundation for Jewish Genetic Diseases (NFJGD), 212-682-5550. (For full group information, see GENETIC DISORDERS.)

National Genetics Federation, 212-586-5800. (For full group information, see GENETIC DISORDERS.)

March of Dimes Birth Defects Foundation (MDBDF), 914-428-7100; local chapters in telephone-directory white pages. Publishes booklets such as *International Directory of Genetic Services*, *Family Health Tree*, and *Genetic Counseling*, and information sheet *Tay-Sachs*. (For full group information, see BIRTH DEFECTS; GENETIC DISORDERS.)

Other reference sources

Health Care U.S.A., by Jean Carper. New York: Prentice Hall, 1987. Resource for general and specific health-care information, as on Tay-Sachs disease, Gaucher's disease, Niemann-Pick disease, and Sandhoff's disease; lists genetic counseling centers, research and treatment centers, and other information.

lipreading   Alternate term for SPEECHREADING.

lisp   Alternate name for a type of communication disorder (see COMMUNICATION SKILLS AND DISORDERS).

literacy   The ability to read and write but, more specifically, the ability to read, write, and calculate at above an eighth-grade level, which is considered the minimum for an adult to operate effectively in modern society. Someone who is unable to do so is termed *functionally illiterate*. In recent years the term has been extended to new fields; people who can readily work with computers are called *computer literate*—a term that applies to many young children, although sometimes their parents are *computer illiterates*. (For help and further information, see ILLITERACY; READING.)

liver function tests   A series of BLOOD TESTS seeking to learn, from analyzing the chemistry of the body, how well the liver is carrying out its various tasks, including METABOLISM (breaking down substances from food for use in the body), storage, filtering out unwanted substances, and excreting them from the body. Among the common liver function tests are:

- *alkaline phosphatase test*: checking the level of the enzyme *alkaline phosphatase* in the blood; high levels are found in some kinds of LIVER PROBLEMS, such as HEPATITIS and blockage of the flow of bile, and also in some disorders of the bones and gall bladder.
- *prothrombin time (PT)*: checking the time it takes for blood to clot, a slow clotting time being an indication of various liver disorders, as well as deficiency in VITAMIN K. The test is often used to check how well anticoagulant medicine (designed to slow clotting in heart disease) is working.
- *bilirubin test*: checking the amount of *bilirubin*, a yellowish substance formed by the breakdown of "retired" red blood cells; high levels of bilirubin in the blood can indicate liver malfunction or obstruction of ducts in the liver.
- *aminotransferases (transaminases) test*: checking the amount of the enzyme *aminotransferase (transaminase)* in the blood; it is normally present in heart and liver tissues, so high amounts in the blood could signal damage to those organs.

(For help and further information, see LIVER PROBLEMS; MEDICAL TESTS.)

liver problems   Disorders in the complex internal organ in the upper right abdomen, which has hundreds of functions, mainly to produce key PROTEINS and other chemicals, to regulate the chemistry of the blood, to store the sugar GLUCOSE as glycogen until needed, and to clear drugs, poisons, and other unwanted substances from the blood, excreting these waste products in bile. Children may experience various kinds of problems with the liver. Inherited abnormalities may cause the liver to malfunction, as in ALPHA 1-ANTITRYPSIN DEFICIENCY, GALACTOSEMIA, GLYCOGEN STORAGE DISEASES, and WILSON'S DISEASE. Infections, structural problems, or other disorders may cause HEPATITIS, inflammation of the liver, or CHOLANGITIS, inflammation of the bile duct. Ailments of even more complicated or obscure origin may also affect the liver, including BILIARY ATRESIA and REYE'S SYNDROME.

For help and further information

American Liver Foundation (ALF)
998 Compton Avenue
Cedar Grove, NJ 07009
201-857-2626, toll-free number (U.S. except NJ) 800-223-0179
Thelma King Thiel, President
Organization for people with liver diseases and interested others. Encourages formation of local mutual-support self-help groups; provides information and referrals; operates Gift of Life Organ Donor Program; sponsors network for parents of children with liver diseases, including biliary atresia, congenital hepatic fibrosis, alpha 1-antitrypsin deficiency, sclerosing cholangitis, and choledochal cyst; publishes many materials, including newsletter for parents of children with liver diseases *Sharing Cares and Hopes*, leaflets such as *Liver Disease: A Problem*

for the Child?, and information sheets about various types of liver ailments, such as *Neonatal Hepatitis, Hemochromatosis, Alpha-Antitrypsin Deficiency, Biliary Atresia, Type 1 Glycogen Storage Disease, Viral Hepatitis: Everybody's Problem*, and *Galactosemia*.

Children's Liver Foundation
76 South Orange Avenue, Suite 202
South Orange, NJ 07079
201-761-1111
Maxine Turon, President
Organization concerned with liver disease in children. Provides support for children and their families; seeks to educate public and acts as advocate for children with liver disease; fosters research; publishes quarterly newsletter *CLF Lifeline*, and various materials such as *Your Child Has Been Diagnosed as Having a Liver Disorder: How Do You Cope?, What Common Liver Deficiency Spares Some Children, Dooms Many Others? Alpha-1 Antitrypsin (a_1AT), What Kills Children at Higher Rate Than Childhood Leukemia?*, and *What Liver-Destroying Illness in Children May Respond Well to Bold Drug Therapy?*.

National Institute of Diabetes and Digestive and Kidney Diseases (NIDDK), 301-496-3583; **National Digestive Disease Information Clearinghouse**, 301-468-6344. (For full group information, see DIGESTIVE DISORDERS.)

loan   In FINANCIAL AID for COLLEGE costs, generally a SUBSIDIZED LOAN.

localization   The ability to identify where a sound is coming from; a kind of AUDITORY SKILL.

locational skills   A set of READING skills necessary for a child to be able to find information in printed sources; these are PREREQUISITE skills such as understanding how to find an item in an alphabetized dictionary or index, how to find material using the page numbers in a table of contents, or how to find a book in the library.

lockjaw   Alternate name for TETANUS.

longitudinal lie   A type of FETAL PRESENTATION in which the axis of the fetus is generally up-and-down, like that of the mother.

long-term care   Medical, social, and personal care for people with chronic illness or MENTAL DISORDERS, often in a large institution but increasingly (where appropriate) in a GROUP HOME or private home. Such care often includes treatment of symptoms, maintenance of physical and mental stability, and rehabilitation.

lordosis (hyperlordosis)   Excessive curving of the lower spine, a type of SPINAL DISORDER often associated with SCOLIOSIS or KYPHOSIS; popularly called *swayback*. In adults it is often related to OSTEOPOROSIS (bone weakening from CALCIUM loss); in children, kyphosis more often results from injury, a TUMOR on the spine, or a GENETIC DISORDER. It can be exaggerated by poor posture. (For help and further information, see SCOLIOSIS.)

Surgeon General's Report on Low Birth Weight

In the United States, the most important factor contributing to the infant mortality rate is a low birth rate—less than 2,500 g, or 5.5 pounds. Low birth weight occurs as a result of birth prior to 37 weeks' gestation, intrauterine growth retardation, or both. Infant deaths and illnesses increase sharply as birth weight declines within the normal weight ranges and even more sharply below 2,500 g. They are highest among infants of very low birth weight (VLBW), below 1,500 g. LBW infants are at increased risk for developmental handicaps, birth defects, respiratory and other infectious diseases, behavior problems, and complications of medical interventions. These conditions greatly increase the emotional and financial burden to the infant's family and to the nation.

Although overall rates of infant mortality have decreased greatly, the prevalence of LBW has declined more slowly. In 1971, babies with weights below 2,500 g accounted for 7.6 percent of all live births; in 1985, they accounted for 6.8 percent. Infants of moderately low birth weight (1,500 to 2,500 g) accounted for over 5.5 percent of all live births in 1985 and those of VLBW for over 1.2 percent. Together, the 6.8 percent of infants born at weights less than 2,500 g are responsible for 67 percent of infant deaths during the first month of life and approximately 60 percent of all infant deaths.

Risk Factors for Low Birth Weight

Medical, social, behavioral, and dietary factors before and during pregnancy contribute to the risk for LBW. Medical risk factors include a previous reproductive history that includes many pregnancies, anemia, hypertensive disorders of pregnancy, inadequate weight gain, or delivery of a LBW infant; low prepregnancy weight; chronic illnesses such as diabetes or hypertension; and poor weight gain during pregnancy. Social, demographic, and behavioral risk factors have been identified as low socioeconomic status, low educational level, minority race, single marital status, adolescence, inadequate prenatal care, and use of drugs, alcohol, and cigarettes.

Dietary risk factors include an inadequate intake of calories or essential nutrients such as protein, vitamins, and minerals. Evidence indicates that the more of these risk factors present, the greater the risk to mother and child. Because these risk factors interact and affect one another, it is difficult to determine the role of nutrition separate from other risk factors.

Source: *The Surgeon General's Report on Nutrition and Health.* Rocklin, CA: Prima, 1988.

Lou Gehrig's disease A type of MOTOR NEURON DISEASE.

Louis-Bar syndrome Alternate name for ataxia telangiectasia, a rare GENETIC DISORDER that is a hereditary form of ATAXIA.

low birth weight (LBW) Term referring to a baby who is under 5.5 pounds (2,500 g) when born, while those who are under 3.3 pounds (1,500 g) are called *very low-birth-weight* (VLBW) infants. Infants of low birth weight are considered to be AT RISK because LBW is associated with higher rates of illness (MORBIDITY) and DEATH (INFANT MORTALITY) than are infants who weigh above 5.5 pounds. This does not mean that every LBW or even VLBW infant has medical problems. Many have quite normal development, outgrowing any temporary problems. Some PREMATURE BABIES have LBW because they have not sufficiently developed and may (when they have reached the full 40 weeks that would have completed their GESTATION) develop normally.

Low birth weight can have many causes, but it is found especially often in ADOLESCENT PREGNANCIES, when mothers have poor NUTRITION, when problems with the PLACENTA prevent the FETUS from receiving sufficient nutrients, and in cases of DRUG ABUSE by the mothers during PREGNANCY. LBW babies frequently experience FETAL DISTRESS during LABOR, especially from lack of oxygen (HYPOXIA). They often experience retarded growth in childhood.

For help and further information

National Institute of Child Health and Human Development (NICHD), 301-496-5133. (For full group information, see PREGNANCY.)

Preventing Low Birthweight: Summary, by the National Institute of Medicine. Washington, DC: National Academy Press, 1985.

low blood sugar Alternate phrase for HYPOGLYCEMIA.

low vision Visual impairment with some residual sight remaining. (See EYE AND VISION PROBLEMS.)

LP Abbreviation for light perception. (See EYE AND VISION PROBLEMS.)

LTB Abbreviation for acute laryngotracheobronchitis, medical term for CROUP.

lumbar puncture (spinal tap) Medical procedure involving insertion of a hollow needle (*aspiration needle*) into the base of the spine, to withdraw CEREBROSPINAL FLUID for analysis, generally to test for such conditions as infections, brain HEMORRHAGE, or TUMORS. Though often done under local ANESTHESIA, the procedure is uncomfortable, but serious side effects are relatively rare—including possible introduction of infection and the risk of tearing the *arachnoid membrane* that surrounds the spinal cord. Lumbar puncture is also used as part of some other medical procedures, such as a MYELOGRAM. An alternative or complement to the lumbar puncture is the *cisternal puncture*, in which a small amount of fluid is removed from the base of the brain. (For help and further information, see MEDICAL TESTS.)

lung and breathing disorders   Disorders involving the *respiratory system*, including the lungs and the network of air passages that take in air, remove oxygen from it, pass the oxygen on to the bloodstream, and then expel unwanted carbon dioxide. From the mouth, air passes through the windpipe (*trachea*) and the large bronchial tubes (*bronchi*) and narrower *bronchioles* into the lungs, more precisely into the tiny air sacs called *alveoli* that line the lungs. From the alveoli, oxygen from the air is passed into the blood, while waste carbon dioxide from elsewhere in the body is sent to the lungs to be expelled from the body in exhaled breath.

The respiratory system can be threatened in a number of ways, leading to lung and breathing disorders:

• *infection*: bacteria, viruses, and fungi can all infect the air passages, involving sometimes life-threatening inflammation, including *tracheitis* (inflammation of the trachea), *bronchitis* (inflammation of the bronchial tubes), *bronchiolitis* (inflammation of the bronchioles), *bronchiectasis* (swelling of the bronchi), and *pneumonia* (inflammation of one or both lungs). Such infections are often associated with other diseases, such as TUBERCULOSIS, WHOOPING COUGH, or MEASLES, and some can become chronic (recurrent). Many forms (though not all) can be treated with antibiotics.

• ALLERGY: reactions to foreign irritants in the body, including ASTHMA and allergic *alveolitis* (inflammation of the alveoli).

• TUMORS: abnormal growths, sometimes CANCERS, often associated with SMOKING.

• *injury*: Penetration of the respiratory area, as in an accident, can cause collapse of the lung.

• *toxic substances*: Inhalation of poisonous gases or dusts can injure the delicate lungs and can sometimes (as in the case of inhalation of silica or asbestos) cause the lungs to become scarred and fibrous, impairing ability to breathe.

• *foreign substances*: Through inhalation (*aspiration*), children can sometimes draw foreign objects into their lungs directly, or indirectly from vomit, causing pneumonia. During childbirth babies sometimes inhale MECONIUM (intestinal waste), being then vulnerable to pneumonia.

• *blockage of air passages*: Bodily substances can sometimes be produced in abnormal amounts, hindering breathing, as in CYSTIC FIBROSIS. If CONGENITAL, chronic, or progressive conditions tend increasingly to block air passages and decrease breathing capacity, the condition is often called *chronic obstructive lung disease* (COLD), *chronic obstructive pulmonary disease* (COPD), or *chronic obstructive respiratory disease* (CORD).

• *impaired blood and oxygen supply*: These can result from a variety of causes. A blood clot may block an artery feeding the lungs. Heart problems (see HEART AND HEART PROBLEMS) may cause EDEMA (collection of fluid) in the lungs. In *emphysema*, which is often associated with chronic bronchitis and asthma, the walls of the alveoli are impaired, cutting down their ability to exchange oxygen; some infants are born with *congenital lobar emphysema*. In newborns, RESPIRATORY DIS-TRESS SYNDROME (*hyaline membrane disease*) can cut down on the vital oxygen supply, as can PERSISTENT FETAL CIRCULATION (PFC).

Young children are especially vulnerable to lung and breathing diseases. In PREMATURE babies, the lungs are not yet as fully developed as they should be at birth. Even full-term babies have no more than one-tenth of the alveoli they will have as adults, and the lungs do not reach full maturity until ADOLESCENCE, so damage in this period (especially before age eight) can have compound effects. Children's air passages are also much narrower and more readily blocked than are those of adults. The American Lung Association estimates that of all the infants who die in their first year, about one-third die of respiratory disorders (see DEATH). Breathing problems are also involved in SLEEP APNEA and implicated in SUDDEN INFANT DEATH SYNDROME.

It is important to the overall health of a baby that a steady flow of oxygen be provided to the lungs. If breathing is difficult, or for some reason is not supplying sufficient oxygen to the body, the child may be placed in a VENTILATOR to assist breathing, often with electronic monitoring of pulse, respiration, and heartbeat.

Lung and breathing disorders are diagnosed using a variety of MEDICAL TESTS, including X-RAYS of the chest, PULMONARY FUNCTION TESTS, SPUTUM ANALYSIS, BLOOD TESTS, and BIOPSY.

For help and further information

American Lung Association (ALA)
National Headquarters
1740 Broadway
New York, NY 10019
212-315-8700
James A. Swomley, Executive Director
Organization of people concerned about lung diseases and related conditions, such as asthma. Seeks to educate public and patients; provides information directly and through local affiliates; publishes various print and audiovisual materials, such as *Lung Diseases of Children: An Introduction, About Lungs and Lung Diseases, As You Live . . . You Breathe, Histo Facts, Health Hazards in the Arts, In Defense of the Lung*, and *Tuberculosis Facts*.

National Heart, Lung, and Blood Institute (NHLBI)
National Institutes of Health
9000 Rockville Pike
Building 31, 4A21
Bethesda, MD 20892
301-496-4236
One of the federally supported divisions of the National Institutes of Health, focusing on lung diseases. Sponsors research and helps shape public policy; seeks to educate public; provides information and referrals; publishes many materials, including booklets such as *The Lungs: Medicine for the Layman* and *Chronic Obstructive Pulmonary Disease*.

National Institute of Allergy and Infectious Diseases (NIAID), 301-496-5717. (For full group information, see ALLERGY.)

National Cancer Institute (NCI), 301-496-5583. (For full group information, see CANCER.)

National Institute of Environmental Health Sciences (NIEHS), 919-541-3345. (For full group information, see ENVIRONMENTAL HAZARDS.)

National Jewish Hospital/National Asthma Center, National Jewish LUNG LINE, 8–5 Mountain Time, M–F, 800-222-LUNG (5864). (For full group information, see ASTHMA.)

Other reference sources

The Chronic Bronchitis and Emphysema Handbook, by François Haas and Sheila Sperber Haas. New York: Wiley, 1990.

The Breath Connection: How to Reduce Psychosomatic and Stress-Related Disorders with Easy-to-Do Breathing Exercises, by Robert Fried. New York: Plenum, 1990.

Health Care U.S.A., by Jean Carper. New York: Prentice Hall, 1987. Resource for general and specific health-care information, as for various lung diseses, including bronchitis, chronic obstructive pulmonary disease (COPD) or chronic obstructive lung disease (COLD), emphysema, asthma, allergies, and cancer; lists key lung-disease specialists and treatment and research centers, some of which specialize in pediatric problems, leading pulmonary specialists, and other information.

Enjoying Life with Emphysema, by Dr. Thomas L. Petty. Philadelphia: Lea & Febiger, 1984.

Respiratory and Infectious Disease, by Wrynn Smith, Ph.D. New York: Facts on File, 1987.

The Lungs and Breathing, revised edition, by Steve Parker. New York: Watts, 1989. For grades 4 to 7.

(See also ASTHMA; ALLERGY; TUBERCULOSIS.)

lupus erythematosus An AUTOIMMUNE DISORDER in which the body mistakenly attacks the connective tissue in the body, often called *systemic lupus erythematosus* (SLE). It is far more common in women than in men, especially from late childhood through early childbearing age, and occurs more often in some ethnic groups, especially Blacks. The causes of lupus are unclear, though some susceptibility may be inherited; it may be triggered by a virus or sometimes by a drug. The disease ranges in severity from mild to life-threatening, depending on what parts of the body, such as the kidneys, heart, or CENTRAL NERVOUS SYSTEM, are affected. SLE may start suddenly with a high FEVER or may develop slowly, and intermittently, over months or even years, with only occasional mild bouts of fever and fatigue. Among the common symptoms are a reddish butterfly-shaped patch on the cheeks and nose, ARTHRITIS, ANEMIA, and *pleurisy* (inflammation of the lining of the lungs). SLE is difficult to diagnose in its early stages, often being confused

with other disorders, such as rheumatoid arthritis; generally, doctors use BLOOD TESTS and BIOPSY in diagnosis to check for characteristic ANTIBODIES. Drugs are used to try to control inflammation, and often patients are advised to avoid the sun, which can worsen the condition. In addition, treatment of related conditions, such as KIDNEY AND UROLOGICAL DISORDERS, means that, with early diagnosis and close monitoring, the MORTALITY RATE for severe cases of lupus has been sharply cut. A mild form of lupus, called *discoid lupus erythematosus* (DLE), primarily affects the skin and is found mostly among women in their 30s.

A woman who has lupus may decide to have children if her heart and kidneys are not badly affected; hers would, in any case, be a HIGH-RISK PREGNANCY, with increased likelihood of MISCARRIAGE and flareups of the disease after DELIVERY. Indeed, in some studies, miscarriages that occurred for unknown reasons have occasionally been linked to undiagnosed lupus in the mother.

For help and further information

Lupus Foundation of America (LFA)
1717 Massachusetts Avenue, NW, Suite 203
Washington, DC 20036
202-328-4550, toll-free number 800-558-0121 for printed material
Margaret Gibelman, Executive Director
Organization of lupus patients, their families, and health professionals. Aims to support lupus patients, encouraging patient-to-patient contact; gathers and disseminates information; supports research and facilitates exchange of medical data; seeks to educate public about problems associated with lupus; publishes various materials, including *Lupus News* and *Lupus Erythematosus: A Handbook for Physicians, Patients and their Families*.

American Lupus Society
23751 Madison Street
Torrance, CA 90505
213-373-1335
Milton H. Abram II, President
Network of mutual-support self-help groups for people with lupus and their families. Provides information and referrals; publishes various materials including newsletter, *Lupus Erythematosus* (in English and Spanish), and *The Butterfly Mask* (writing by lupus patients).

National Institute of Arthritis and Musculoskeletal and Skin Diseases (NIAMS), 301-496-8188. Publishes *Update: Lupus Erythematosus Research* and *Arthritis, Rheumatic Diseases, and Related Disorders*. (For full group information, see ARTHRITIS.)

Arthritis Foundation, 402-872-7100. Publishes *Systemic Lupus Erythematosus*. (For full group information, see ARTHRITIS.)

National Institute of Neurological Disorders and Stroke (NINDS), 301-496-5751. (For full group information, see BRAIN AND BRAIN DISORDERS.)

Other reference sources

Lupus: My Search for a Diagnosis, by Eileen Radziunas. Claremont, CA: Hunter House, 1990.

Embracing the Wolf: A Lupus Victim and Her Family Learn to Live with Chronic Disease, by Joanna Baumer Permut. Marietta, GA: Cherokee, 1989.

Health Care U.S.A., by Jean Carper. New York: Prentice Hall, 1987. Resource for general and specific health-care information, as for juvenile arthritis, osteoarthritis, lupus, scleroderma, brittle bone disease, and related diseases; lists major centers for treatment or research and other information.

Coping with Lupus, by Robert H. Phillips. Garden City Park, NJ: Avery, 1984.

Lupus: The Body Against Itself, by Dr. Sheldon Paul and Dodi Schultz. New York: Doubleday, 1977.

The Sun Is My Enemy, by Henrietta Aldjem. Boston: Beacon, 1976. By a lupus patient.

luteinizing hormone (LH)   A kind of HORMONE produced by the PITUITARY gland that stimulates the production of other hormones from the OVARIES and the TESTES, among them *follicle-stimulating hormone* (FSH) (see FOLLICLES), ESTROGEN, and PROGESTERONE. High levels of LH, triggered in turn by estrogen, stimulate OVULATION, so levels of LH are used in some self-tests to indicate ovulation. (For a description of a HOME MEDICAL TEST using LH, see OVULATION.)

Lyme disease   A bacterial disease that can cause serious ARTHRITIS, neurological disorders, and heart problems if not recognized and treated quickly. The bacteria, *Borrelia burgdorferi*, is spread by poppy-seed-sized ticks (*Ixodes dammini*) carried by several woodland animals, including deer and mice. Within a few days of a bite by an infected tick, various symptoms appear, including, most characteristically, a red "bull's-eye" rash at the site; swollen, aching joints and muscles; FEVER, fatigue, weakness, and dizziness; and other generalized symptoms.

But sometimes the symptoms are absent—the rash is found only about 75 percent of the time—or indistinct, often being mistaken for influenza, especially since people may be unaware that they were bitten. In that case, the infection goes unrecognized and untreated and so is able to remain in the body and damage the joints, heart, and NERVOUS SYSTEM, while the early symptoms gradually decline, sometimes flaring up in cycles. Even when suspected by doctors, Lyme disease is often hard to diagnose; MEDICAL TESTS exist, but they are of varying reliability, and in many cases the bacteria's presence is effectively masked.

When recognized and treated quickly, Lyme disease responds to antibiotics in most cases. If unresponsive or recognized only weeks, months, or years after the initial infection, intravenous antibiotic treatments, along with anti-inflammatory drugs and other treatments, are often needed to combat the infection. Long-term experience is limited, however, since the bacteria responsible was discovered only in 1982, so it is unclear whether or how much permanent damage may remain.

Originally discovered in Connecticut, after a mother noticed an unusual incidence of arthritis in young people in her heavily wooded Old Lyme neighborhood (hence the early name *Lyme arthritis*), and at first concentrated on the East Coast, Lyme disease is spreading rapidly across North America. (In Europe, its effects have been known from the 19th century, although it was not recognized as a distinct disease.) Parents can best protect themselves and their children by dressing in long clothing, with pants tucked into socks, in wooded or grassy areas; by checking themselves for ticks after an outdoor excursion; by checking pets as well, since they both carry and can be infected by the ticks; and by being alert to possible symptoms and seeing a doctor promptly.

For help and further information

National Institute of Arthritis and Musculoskeletal and Skin Diseases (NIAMS), 301-496-3583. Publishes *Arthritis, Rheumatic Diseases, and Related Disorders* (including Lyme disease). (For full group information, see ARTHRITIS; MUSCULAR DYSTROPHY.)

National Institute of Allergy and Infectious Diseases (NIAID), 301-496-5717. (For full group information, see ALLERGY.)

Other reference sources

Ticks and What You Can Do About Them, by Roger Drummond. Berkeley, CA: Wilderness, 1990.

Lyme Disease, by Elaine Landau. New York: Watts, 1990. For grades 4 to 7.

Lyme Disease: The Great Imitator, by Alvin Silverstein, et al. Lebanon, NJ: Avstar, 1990. For grades 6 to 10.

lymphatic system   The network of vessels and organs through which the body's IMMUNE SYSTEM operates.

lymphocytes   A type of white blood cell. (See BLOOD AND BLOOD DISORDERS; IMMUNE SYSTEM.)

MA   Abbreviation for MENTAL AGE, relating to INTELLIGENCE TESTS, or maturational age; an alternate term for DEVELOPMENTAL AGE.

macronutrient   General term for any element or compound, notably VITAMINS or MINERALS, that is necessary for proper health and functioning of the body, in relatively large amounts (as opposed to MICRONUTRIENTS). Examples include oxygen, carbon, hydrogen, nitrogen, CALCIUM, PHOSPHORUS, MAGNESIUM, POTASSIUM, SULFUR, SODIUM, and CHLORIDE.

macular degeneration   Breakdown of the center of the retina of the eye. (See EYE AND VISION PROBLEMS.)

magical thinking   The idea or belief that one's thoughts or feelings influence people or the environment around them and trigger events. Such thinking is common in children under age five and may also occur among some uneducated adults or among people with some kinds of MENTAL DISORDERS.

magnesium   A MINERAL vital to the formation of bones and TEETH, the proper functioning of nerves and muscles, and the work of enzymes (substances promoting biochemical reactions in the body). It is abundant in green leafy vegetables, nuts, whole-grain products, and soy beans; it is also found in various antacids and laxatives. Lack of magnesium can lead to muscle weakness; severe deficiency is sometimes associated with DIARRHEA, DIABETES MELLITUS, ALCOHOL ABUSE, and KIDNEY AND UROLOGICAL DISORDERS and is sometimes found in infants fed on cow's milk or FORMULA containing insufficient magnesium. Too much magnesium, as in overuse of antacids and laxatives, can cause nausea, disruption of normal heart function, and confusion. (For help and further information, see MINERALS; NUTRITION.)

magnetic resonance imaging   Full name for the SCAN commonly called MRI.

magnet school   A school that attracts students from many different neighborhoods or backgrounds because of special interests, needs, or approaches, usually found in a heavily populated area; a type of ALTERNATIVE SCHOOL or SCHOOL OF CHOICE. A HIGH SCHOOL that focuses on music and art, science, or foreign languages, for example, might be considered a magnet school, as might a school with an intensive college-oriented program, a vocationally oriented school, a nontraditional educational approach, or a "second chance" program for former

DROPOUTS. Some magnet schools have been developed as part of voluntary DESEGREGATION plans, which attempt to attract a mix of students rather than rely on involuntary BUSING. The term *magnet school* is also sometimes used to apply to a school district's centralized special services for children with handicaps (see HANDICAPPED). CHOOSING A SCHOOL FOR YOUR CHILD, on page 514, contains a useful checklist for evaluating schools.

For help and further information

Different by Design: The Context and Character of Three Magnet Schools, by Mary Haywood Metz. New York: Routledge & Kegan Paul, 1986.

Dare to Choose: Parental Choice at Independent Neighborhood Schools, by Joan Davis Ratteray and Mwalima Shujaa. Washington, DC: Institute for Independent Education, 1987.

(See also EDUCATION; ALTERNATIVE SCHOOLS.)

mainstreaming   An approach to EDUCATION that involves integrating children with handicaps (see HANDICAPPED) as much as possible into a school or organization's main classes and activities, the aim being to help the child to develop to the fullest extent possible, as opposed to the previous pattern of segregating children with mental or physical disabilities from other children, and so markedly limiting their opportunities and possibilities. The EDUCATION FOR ALL HANDICAPPED CHILDREN ACT OF 1975 has been extremely important in making mainstreaming a widespread approach, requiring that public schools provide a "free, appropriate education" in the LEAST RESTRICTIVE SETTING to children ages 3 to 21. It has helped to make mainstreaming work by providing programs for identifying disabilities in early childhood—in the PRESCHOOL years or even in infancy—and services to help children overcome these disabilities to the greatest extent possible before the school years.

For help and further information

Center on Human Policy (CHP), 315-423-3851. Publishes many materials, focusing on the fullest possible integration of people with severe disabilities, including mental retardation, into community life. (For full group information, see HELP FOR SPECIAL CHILDREN on page 578.)

Other reference sources

Program Models for Mainstreaming: Integrating Students with Moderate to Severe Disabilities. Rockville, MD: Aspen, 1987. (See also EDUCATION FOR ALL HANDICAPPED CHILDREN ACT OF 1975; HANDICAPPED; EDUCATION; SEGREGATION; also TEACHING YOUNG CHILDREN: GUIDELINES AND ACTIVITIES on page 544.)

majority   In family law, adulthood. The age of majority is the age at which a child is no longer considered a MINOR and can legally act and be treated as an adult, set by state law but usually around 18.

malabsorption   Impaired ability to digest food, especially to absorb nutrients from it. (For help and further information, see METABOLIC DISORDERS; DIGESTIVE DISORDERS.)

maladie des tics   Alternate name for TOURETTE'S SYNDROME.

Malcomesius Test   Alternate name for SPECIFIC LANGUAGE DISABILITY TESTS.

malignant   In medicine, a general term for a progessive condition, especially a TUMOR, that is expected to worsen and may cause DEATH. By contrast, a benign condition is a mild one, not expected to be life-threatening.

malignant hyperthermia (MH)   A GENETIC DISORDER of the AUTOSOMAL DOMINANT type in which a person has an often-fatal reaction to ANESTHESIA. In those affected, the temperature rises dangerously (sometimes to 110°F or higher), METABOLISM is speeded up, and the muscles become rigid. Treatment involves attempting to bring down body temperature and right resulting imbalances. Parents with MH in their family must inform their doctor and any medical workers who may be treating their children.

For help and further information

Malignant Hyperthermia Association of the United States (MHAUS)
P.O. Box 3231
Darien, CT 06820
203-655-3007, MH/Medic Alert Hotline, 209-634-4917
Suellen Gallamore, Executive Director
Organization of people who are susceptible to MH and interested health professionals, including anesthesiologists and dentists. Gathers and disseminates information; seeks to educate public and professionals; operates hotline; supports research; publishes various materials, including quarterly *The Communicator* and emergency booklet *Understanding Malignant Hyperthermia.*

malnutrition   A condition of having an improper amount and balance of nutrients to maintain proper body functioning. Malnutrition is most often thought of as referring to deficiencies in the diet, such as insufficient PROTEIN, VITAMINS, and MINERALS, which can lead to DEFICIENCY DISEASES. But malnutrition also can stem from excessive amounts of food or vitamin and mineral supplements and from a wide variety of disorders that hinder the body from properly absorbing and using the nutrients found in foods. In Western countries, various government programs are available to help combat nutrient deficiency; apart from poor and homeless families not reached by such programs, general nutrient deficiency is most often associated with ALCOHOL ABUSE, DRUG ABUSE, or EATING DISORDERS such as ANOREXIA NERVOSA and BULIMIA. (For help and further information, see NUTRITION; MINERALS; VITAMINS.)

malocclusion   The dental term for a bad bite, in which the TEETH meet unevenly. Ideally, the upper front teeth should be slightly forward of the lower front teeth, and the rear teeth should meet evenly, but most people have some slight malocclusion. If the jaw and upper front teeth project too far forward, the result is *overbite* or *buck teeth*, which dentists call *retrognathism;* this can be caused or exaggerated by continual sucking on a thumb or pacifier for long periods beyond infancy. The reverse, with the lower jaw and front teeth in front of the upper ones, is called *underbite* or *prognathism.* Even when the two jaws meet each other properly, malocclusion can result when teeth are badly spaced or twisted out of normal position. Too many teeth or teeth too large for the size of the jaw can lead to *overcrowding.* Malocclusion can lead to pain in the joint of the jaw from an awkward bite, BRUXISM (teeth-grinding), and tooth decay and loss, especially where teeth do not meet and so are not used in chewing.

Dentists can often deal with slight malocclusion by smoothing off uneven surfaces of teeth or building up teeth with a *dental onlay.* More serious cases may require treatment by an ORTHODONTIST, generally *orthodontic braces* to gradually bring teeth into proper position. The braces may be fixed in place for a year or more, then replaced by a removable retainer plate, or the braces may be removable from the start. The fixed braces require more careful fitting and so are more expensive but interfere less with speaking, though they can tend to trap plaque. The removable braces are more cumbersome and sometimes interfere with speech so much that children stop wearing them. Sometimes one or more teeth must be extracted to make room for the straightening of the remaining teeth. In severe cases, the jaw may need to be reshaped or repositioned; this requires a procedure called *orthognathic surgery,* normally performed by an ORAL SURGEON in a hospital. Work to correct malocclusion is best carried out during childhood and ADOLESCENCE, when the young bones are still growing, but it can be done later if necessary. (For help and further information, see TEETH.)

malpresentation   General term for FETAL PRESENTATION other than the usual head-downward.

mammary glands   Scientific name for BREASTS.

manic-depression   Alternate term for BIPOLAR DISORDERS.

manual communication   Use of expressive gestures of hands, face, and body to communicate with others, whether as part of a "private language," FINGERSPELLING, or a widely taught and used SIGN LANGUAGE. Some people believe that children with EAR AND HEARING PROBLEMS should not be allowed to use any form of manual communication but should instead be trained to use and understand oral speech, especially through SPEECHREADING. Others stress a TOTAL COMMUNICATION approach, which holds that deaf children should be taught to use any communication skills at their disposal.

manuscript writing   Alternate term for PRINTING.

marasmus   Extreme MALNUTRITION and resulting emaciation, resulting from insufficient calories and PROTEIN for growth. Most often found in regions where starvation or semistarvation are common, marasmus can also result when children have been fed solely on breast MILK for too long, or when they were weaned onto a nutritionally inadequate diet (see WEANING). Marasmus can also be found in children who exhibit FAILURE TO THRIVE, for physical, social, or emotional reasons. (For help and further information, see NUTRITION; GROWTH.)

marble bones   Alternate name for OSTEOPETROSIS.

Marfan syndrome (arachnodactyly)   A rare GENETIC DISORDER of the body's connective tissue, affecting the heart and circulatory system, lungs, eyes, and skeletal system. Common symptoms include long fingers (the traditional name, *arachnodactyly,* means "spider fingers"); long, thin skeleton; SCOLIOSIS (sidewise curvature of the spine); dislocated lens in the eye; and outsize valves and aorta in the heart (see HEART AND HEART PROBLEMS). Though the disorder is sometimes recognizable nearly from birth, people occasionally grow to adulthood not knowing they have the syndrome until their lungs collapse or heart suddenly fails. Women with Marfan syndrome are especially prone to heart problems during PREGNANCY. Because it is passed on by a single AUTOSOMAL DOMINANT gene, people with a family history of Marfan syndrome may want to seek GENETIC COUNSELING when considering pregnancy.

For help and further information

National Marfan Foundation (NMF)
382 Main Street
Port Washington, NY 11050
516-883-8712
Priscilla Ciccariello, Executive Director
Organization seeking to provide information and support to people with Marfan syndrome, their families, and the professionals who work with them. Encourages sharing of family experiences; encourages research; publishes various materials, including quarterly newsletter *Connective Issues,* book, *The Marfan Syndrome,* children's picture book *How John Was Unique,* article reprints, and audiovisual works, including *Do You Know Marfan?*

National Institute of Arthritis and Musculoskeletal and Skin Diseases (NIAMS), 301-496-8188. (For full group information, see ARTHRITIS.)

National Heart, Lung, and Blood Institute (NHLBI), 301-496-4236. (For full group information, see HEART AND HEART PROBLEMS.)

March of Dimes Birth Defects Foundation, 914-428-7100; local chapters in telephone-directory white pages. Publishes information sheet *Marfan Syndrome.* (For full group information, see BIRTH DEFECTS.)

marrow transplant   Alternate term for BONE MARROW TRANSPLANT.

mask of pregnancy (melasma gravidarum)   Alternate name for HYPERPIGMENTATION during PREGNANCY.

master's degree   A DEGREE awarded to a student who has successfully completed a course of study beyond the BACHELOR'S DEGREE level, normally after a one- or two-year course of full-time enrollment; the first degree awarded for most GRADUATE work, sometimes later followed by a DOCTORAL DEGREE.

mastery learning   An educational approach that emphasizes teaching every student to meet preset instructional objectives, such as learning skills, acquiring knowledge, or solving certain types of problems, the idea being to have all students meet at least a minimum standard level. In mastery learning, students are allowed varying amounts of time—as much time as each needs—to meet the objectives, as opposed to the traditional approach of giving passing (see PASS) grades to those who can learn material within a limited time and failing (see FAIL) the rest.

For help and further information

Implementing Mastery Learning, by Thomas R. Guskey. Belmont, CA: Wadsworth, 1985.
Mastery Learning in Classroom Instruction, by James H. Block and Lorin W. Anderson. New York: Macmillan, 1975.
Schools, Society and Mastery Learning, James H. Block, ed. New York: Holt, Rinehart & Winston, 1974.
Mastery Learning: Theory and Practice, by Benjamin Bloom. New York: Holt, Rinehart & Winston, 1971.
(See also EDUCATION.)

mastoiditis   Inflammation of the mastoid bone, often because of *otitis media,* infection in the middle ear, a common EAR AND HEARING PROBLEM.

masturbation   Stimulation of one's GENITALS, in young children often general stimulation but in adolescents and adults usually massaging of the PENIS or clitoris to orgasm. Though for centuries believed to cause physical or psychological damage, masturbation is now thought to cause no harm, though parents can sometimes mistake orgasmic convulsions in their children for SEIZURES.

maternal and child health (MCH) services   General name for facilities and programs that focus on medical and social care for mothers and children, especially PRENATAL CARE, POSTNATAL CARE, BIRTH-CONTROL advice, and infant care.

maternal and fetal specialists OBSTETRICIAN-GYNECOLOGISTS who specialize in the care of mother and FETUS in HIGH-RISK PREGNANCIES.

maternal deprivation syndrome A pattern of retarded growth and development, or FAILURE TO THRIVE, that occurs mainly in infants who have experienced physical and emotional deprivation. Sometimes the normal BONDING failed to take place between parent and child, as in cases when the MOTHER has a MENTAL DISORDER, insecurity or lack of knowledge about caring for a baby, or disappointment in the child (based on unrealistic expectations or because of health problems in the child). Sometimes family poverty makes the parents unable to provide for the child's physical or emotional needs. An infant kept in a HOSPITAL without sufficient stimulation, warmth, and human contact, especially from a parent, may also experience maternal deprivation syndrome. Among the symptoms are slow growth, low weight (for the child's age), MALNUTRITION, withdrawal, irritability, unusual stiffness in posture and movements, and slow reactions to others. If the syndrome is not recognized and the situation changed—as by educating the parents or helping them better understand the child or by having volunteers visit babies in hospital—permanent physical, social, and emotional damage may result. However, physical causes should be explored, since not all cases of failure to thrive result from maternal deprivation. (For help and further information, see FAILURE TO THRIVE.)

maternal mortality The DEATH of a MOTHER that is immediately related to or significantly contributed to by a PREGNANCY, as during CHILDBIRTH, MISCARRIAGE, or ABORTION. Maternal mortality, normally expressed as a rate of the number of deaths per specified number of pregnancies, has much declined in recent years, to about eight per 100,000 in 1983. Among the factors involved in this reduction are better PRENATAL CARE, better NUTRITION, antibiotics, ready access to BLOOD TRANSFUSIONS, and availability of CONTRACEPTION, which allows women to space and limit the number of pregnancies. Women who are relatively poor, are not well-educated, and lack proper prenatal care have higher-than-average risk of mortality; so do women under 20 and over 30 and those having their first pregnancy or their fifth or more. Among the conditions that can cause maternal death are hypertension (see BLOOD PRESSURE), eclampsia, abortion, miscarriage, CESAREAN SECTION, ECTOPIC PREGNANCY, and HEMORRHAGING before or after birth (*antepartum* or *postpartum*). Other conditions that increase a woman's risk of mortality are heart problems, ANEMIA, THYROID GLAND problems, DIABETES MELLITUS, and CANCER.

maternal serum alpha-fetoprotein (MSAFP) The full name of the GENETIC SCREENING test that monitors levels of ALPHA-FETOPROTEIN (AFP) produced by a FETUS, as an indication of possible abnormalities.

maternity center A free-standing institution—one not directly attached to a HOSPITAL—where women come to give birth, often attended by CERTIFIED NURSE-MIDWIVES; also called *alternative birthing centers* or simply *birthing centers*. Maternity centers have been developed with the resurgent midwife movement, partly in response to what was seen as the cold, invasive, impersonal nature of what had become traditional hospital delivery. Maternity centers encourage a more relaxed, personal approach to CHILDBIRTH, with birth taking place in a relatively homelike atmosphere and with BIRTH PARTNERS and sometimes also other family members in attendance.

Maternity centers are only for women with low-risk, normal pregnancies. Others are generally referred to doctors and hospitals that can give them the more sophisticated medical care they may need. And if complications develop during delivery, the mother and infant are stabilized and transferred to a hospital for emergency care. Therein lies the main hazard, the loss of time in what may be an emergency situation, along with the slightly increased risk of infection, since birthing rooms cannot necessarily be made as antiseptic a setting for the birth. Parents considering alternative birthing centers should carefully investigate the emergency medical arrangements, including how transport is arranged.

For help and further information

National Association of Childbearing Centers (NACC)
Road 1, Box 1
Perkiomenville, PA 18074
215-234-8068
Eunice K.M. (Kitty) Ernst, Director
Organization of birth centers and interested individuals and organizations. Acts as information clearinghouse for public and professionals; makes referrals; helps set standards; publishes various materials, including quarterly newsletter.

Maternity Center Association (MCA)
48 East 92nd Street
New York, NY 10128
212-369-7300
Ruth Watson Lubic, Director
Organization of health professionals and others interested in maternity centers. Provides information and education; seeks to improve maternity care; sponsors research; publishes various materials, including quarterly newsletter *Special Delivery*, pamphlets, and books such as *Preparation for Childbearing* and *Newborn Needs*.

American College of Nurse Midwives (ACNM), 202-289-0171. (For full group information, see CERTIFIED NURSE-MIDWIFE.)

(See also PREGNANCY; CHILDBIRTH)

maternity cycle The period from CONCEPTION to about six weeks after CHILDBIRTH. In terms of medical care, the cycle is divided into three periods: PRENATAL, or *antepartal* (before the birth); INTRAPARTAL (during LABOR); and POSTNATAL, or POSTPARTAL (after the birth), with care offered in the 28 days after the birth also being termed PERINATAL.

maternity leave Unpaid time off for a mother before and after CHILDBIRTH, ideally without prejudice to the mother's returning to her job on the same level and promotion track. In many large corporations, maternity leave (often of about three months) and related fringe benefits are routinely provided to pregnant women. But in many others, especially smaller firms, such leave and benefits are not guaranteed, and indeed the announcement of PREGNANCY can lead to summary firing (see PREGNANCY DISCRIMINATION ACT OF 1978). Even in those firms where maternity leave and benefits are offered, many women who return to work after leave find that they have been shunted onto a slower promotion track, the so-called *mommy track*. Recognizing the need for a national policy regarding maternity leave, the wider PARENTAL AND MEDICAL LEAVE, and related ADOPTION LEAVE, numerous federal legislators have attempted to pass a Parental and Medical Leave Act allowing both parents time off with their newborn or adopted babies or in cases of serious illness in the family. As of mid-1990, however, no compromise has been reached on such a law.

For help and further information

Women's Legal Defense Fund
2000 P Street NW, Suite 400
Washington, DC 20036
202-887-0364

Organization of people concerned with issues involving women, such as family and medical leaves, reproductive health, sex discrimination in the workplace, and custody disputes. Acts as advocate for women's rights; publishes various materials, including *State Leave Laws Chart* (regarding family and medical leave), *Sex Discrimination in the Workplace: A Legal Handbook*, and *Custody Handbook*.

Catalyst
250 Park Avenue South
New York, NY 10003
212-777-8900
Felice Schwartz, President

Organization that sponsors research and advises corporations on issues involving women in the work force. Operates Information Center; publishes various materials, including monthly *Perspective on Current Corporate Issues*.

Other reference sources

General Works

Your Maternity Leave: How to Leave Work, Have a Baby and Go Back to Work Without Getting Lost, Trapped or Sandbagged Along the Way, by Jean Marzollo. New York: Poseidon/Simon & Schuster, 1989.
Managing Your Maternity Leave, by Marcie Schorr Hirsch. Boston: Houghton Mifflin, 1983.

Background Works

Costs to Americans of Lack of Family Leave, by Roberta M. Spalter-Roth and Heidi Hartmann. Washington, DC: Institute for Women's Policy Research, 1989.
Unneccessary Losses: The Costs to Workers in the States of the Lack of Family and Medical Leave, by Roberta M. Spalter-Roth, Heidi Hartmann, and Sheila Gibbs. Washington, DC: Institute for Women's Policy Research, 1989.
The Parental Leave Crisis: Toward a National Policy, Edward F. Zigler and Maryl Frank, eds. New Haven, CT: Yale University Press, 1988.
Parental Leave: Judicial and Legislative Trends: Current Practices in the Workplace, by Mary E. Radford. Brookfield, WI: International Foundation of Employee Benefit Plans, 1988.
Costs to Women and Their Families of Childbirth and the Lack of Parental Leave, by Roberta M. Spalter-Roth and Heidi Hartmann. Washington, DC: Institute for Women's Policy Research, 1987.
Pregnancy and Employment. Washington, DC: Bureau of National Affairs, 1987.
The Corporate Guide to Parental Leaves. New York: Catalyst, 1986.
(See also PREGNANCY DISCRIMINATION ACT.)

maturation lag Alternate term for DEVELOPMENTAL DELAY.

maturity A general term referring to a child's relative stage of development, in areas such as growth (see GROWTH AND GROWTH DISORDERS), SOCIAL SKILLS, and communication skills (see COMMUNICATION SKILL AND DISORDERS), compared to the development of other children of the same AGE. Various TESTS (such as the GESELL PRESCHOOL TEST) may be used to help estimate a child's maturity, with the results sometimes being converted to AGE-EQUIVALENT scores, indicating whether a child's development stands at, above, or below the AVERAGE for children of his or her age.

maxillofacial surgery PLASTIC SURGERY performed on the upper jaw, nose, and cheek.

MBD Abbreviation for minimum brain dysfunction, an alternate term for LEARNING DISABILITIES or ATTENTION DEFICIT HYPERACTIVITY DISORDER.

McCarthy Scales of Children's Abilities An individually administered TEST designed to assess the MOTOR SKILLS and COGNITIVE DEVELOPMENT of children ages 2½ to 8½. Using a wide variety of puzzles, toylike materials, and gamelike tasks, the test focuses on five areas: verbal ability, numerical ability, and perceptual performance (which are combined to give a General Cognitive Index), plus short-term memory and motor coordination. One-third of the lower-level tasks are sometimes used as a DEVELOPMENTAL SCREENING TEST for the early grades, called the *McCarthy Screening Test*. (For help and further information, see TESTS.)

Possible Side Effects and Adverse Reactions to Measles, Mumps, and Rubella Immunization

Measles—About one in every five children will develop a rash or slight to moderate fever beginning one to two weeks after receiving measles vaccine and lasting for a few days. These common reactions usually do not harm the child in any way.

Mumps—In very rare instances, mumps vaccine produces a mild brief fever. This fever may occur one to two weeks after receiving the mumps vaccine. Occasionally, there is some swelling of the salivary glands. Serious reactions are extremely rare.

Rubella—About one in every seven children will develop a rash or some swelling in the lymph glands within a week or two after receiving rubella vaccine. These side effects usually last only a day or two. About one in every 20 children and as many as 40 percent of adults who receive the vaccine will have some pain and stiffness in the joints. This condition may appear from one to three weeks after the immunization. It is usually mild and lasts for only two or three days. Other temporary side effects, such as pain, numbness, or tingling in the hands and feet, have also occurred but are uncommon. It is safe to have a child immunized even if there is a pregnant person in the household. The rubella vaccine virus is not spread from one person to another.

Although experts are not sure, it seems that on rare occasions, children who receive these vaccines (i.e., measles, mumps, and rubella) may have a more serious reaction, such as inflammation of the brain (encephalitis). Parents should be aware of this possibility. Medical authorities agree that the benefits of immunization far outweigh the risks.

Source: *Parents Guide to Childhood Immunization* (1988). Prepared for the Public Health Service and the Centers for Disease Control.

McCarthy Screening Test A DEVELOPMENTAL SCREENING TEST for the early grades, using some tasks from the McCARTHY SCALES OF CHILDREN'S ABILITIES.

MCH Abbreviation for MATERNAL AND CHILD HEALTH SERVICES.

MD Abbreviation for MUSCULAR DYSTROPHY; also for doctor of medicine.

mean The most common kind of AVERAGE, as in a GRADE-POINT AVERAGE or CUMULATIVE AVERAGE.

means test Evaluation of a person's financial resources to judge eligibility for a benefit. Assistance programs such as Medicaid, food stamps, and AID TO FAMILIES WITH DEPENDENT CHILDREN (AFDC), for example, are available only to those who do not have the means to pay for them otherwise. The same is true of some kinds of SCHOLARSHIPS. Some other programs, such as Social Security and ADOPTION assistance to people who adopt children with special needs, apply no means test.

measles (rubeola) A serious, highly contagious disease caused by a virus passed from affected people to others in droplets from coughs, sneezes, or even just talking. Measles commonly causes a widespread rash, high FEVER, cough, runny nose, and watery eyes, and runs its course in one to two weeks. But sometimes it can be far more severe. One out of every 10 children with measles develops an ear infection or pneumonia, and about one in every 1,000 develops ENCEPHALITIS (inflammation of the brain), which can lead to CONVULSIONS, EAR AND HEARING PROBLEMS, and MENTAL RETARDATION. Measles causes death in about two children in every 10,000.

Before the development of a measles vaccine, almost every child caught measles before age 15, and more than 400 died from it each year. Measles can also cause death in adults, and among pregnant women it can cause MISCARRIAGE or PREMATURE birth. Today measles is largely preventable, though some epidemics occur because of laxness in IMMUNIZATION. The measles vaccine is normally given in a combination injection of the MEASLES-MUMPS-RUBELLA (MMR) VACCINE at about age 15 months. Earlier forms of the vaccine were not as effective as immunization, so some adults (such as couples considering PREGNANCY) who have not had measles but who were immunized before 1967 may need to be reimmunized. A pregnant woman who has never had measles, was immunized before 1967, and is exposed to someone with measles is advised to get an injection of IMMUNOGLOBULIN within five days, to provide so-called PASSIVE IMMUNIZATION. Parents should keep careful records of either immunization or evidence of their child's having measles, since states require one or the other before admitting a child into school.

For further information

National Institute of Allergy and Infectious Diseases (NIAID), 301-496-5717. (For full group information, see ALLERGY.)

National Institute of Child Health and Human Development (NICHD), 301-496-5133. (For full group information, see PREGNANCY.)

National Institute of Neurological Disorders and Stroke (NINDS), 301-496-5751. (For full group information, see BRAIN AND BRAIN DISORDERS.)

National Institute on Deafness and Other Communication Disorders (NIDCD), 301-496-7243. (For full group information, see EAR AND HEARING PROBLEMS.)

Centers for Disease Control (CDC), 404-329-3534. (For full group information, see IMMUNIZATION.)

March of Dimes Birth Defects Foundation, 914-428-7000; local chapters in telephone-directory white pages. Publishes information sheet *Rubella*. (For full group information, see BIRTH DEFECTS.)

(See also MEASLES-MUMPS-RUBELLA VACCINE.)

measles-mumps-rubella vaccine (MMR) A combination VACCINE normally given to children at about age 15 months, to provide IMMUNIZATION against several serious childhood diseases: MEASLES (rubeola), MUMPS, and RUBELLA (German measles). Sometimes the child may be given the measles vaccine alone or just measles and rubella (MR) vaccine.

One injection of the current measles vaccine provides lifelong immunization in most people, but some adults (such as couples considering PREGNANCY) who have not had measles but who were immunized before 1967 may need to be reimmunized, since the earlier type of vaccine was less effective. All 50 U.S. states require that a child must either show immunization to measles or evidence (such as a doctor's statement) of having had the disease before being allowed to enter and attend school.

As with measles, one injection of the current mumps vaccine provides lifelong immunization in most people, but some adults who have not had mumps but who were immunized before 1967 may need to be reimmunized, since the earlier type of vaccine was less effective. About two-thirds of the states require that a child must either show immunization to mumps or evidence (such as a doctor's statement) of having had the disease before being allowed to enter and attend school. The mumps vaccine alone can be given by age 12 months but is normally given at 15 months as part of the MMR vaccine.

The current rubella vaccine, in use since 1969, also gives lifelong protection to most people and can be given from age 15 months. Though the disease is not serious among children, rubella can cause devastating BIRTH DEFECTS in the FETUS in a pregnant women. So any adult who has not previously had rubella itself or immunization to the disease is recommended to take the vaccine; a woman should take the vaccine at least three months before beginning a pregnancy. If desired, a BLOOD TEST can tell if someone is already immune, but reimmunization is safe if any doubt exists. (For help and further information, including a recommended immunization schedule, see IMMUNIZATION. For information on recourse in case of problems, see CHILDHOOD VACCINE INJURY ACT.)

Meckel's diverticulum A type of DIGESTIVE DISORDER.

meconium Dark, thick, sticky material that collects in the intestines of a FETUS and makes up the first bowel movement of the newborn. Sometimes the meconium is released into the AMNIOTIC FLUID, generally a sign of FETAL DISTRESS. The material can then be inhaled and taken into the lungs (a process called *meconium aspiration*), causing pneumonia. (For help and further information, see LUNG AND BREATHING DISORDERS.)

median A type of AVERAGE.

mediation A procedure under which two parties submit their dispute for resolution to a neutral third party. Like ARBITRATION, mediation is a way to avoid the cost, delay, and hard feelings that often attend court cases. However, unlike arbitration, in mediation the neutral party has no power to impose a solution, instead attempting to help the disputants reach a solution themselves. In some states, such as California, mediation is mandatory in cases of disputes over CUSTODY and VISITATION RIGHTS, and counseling services often act as court-associated mediators in divorce and other family law situations. (For help and further information, see CUSTODY.)

medical neglect A form of CHILD ABUSE AND NEGLECT specified as part of the BABY DOE LAW.

medical tests A variety of procedures that help doctors diagnose ailments and disorders. Some medical tests are entirely benign, uninvasive, and risk-free, such as—at the simplest level—the placing of a stethoscope on a child's chest or collecting a urine sample for testing. By contrast, some tests are INVASIVE—that is, they involve intruding into the body, as with an INJECTION of dyed fluid—and involve pain or risk; they should not be used unless the information to be gained is of sufficient importance to warrant their use.

Before subjecting children (or themselves) to any test, parents should be sure they understand what the procedure entails and what risks it may carry. By law, medical personnel are required to give patients the information they require about tests and procedures—about the risks, as well as the benefits—and to obtain INFORMED CONSENT before the test or procedure is carried out. Since a child is not legally able to make such decisions, parents must obtain and weigh medical information and give informed consent on their child's behalf.

Also to be considered is the test's RELIABILITY. No test is 100-percent accurate. One major area of unreliability is in giving false readings—either FALSE POSITIVES, indicating that you have a disorder when in fact you do not, or FALSE NEGATIVES, indicating that you are free from a disorder when in fact you have it. If a test is considered 80-percent accurate, that means that one out of every five times it gives a false reading. That would seem far too much for a test carrying any risk, but in fact, many tests are far less accurate than that. Ideally, for a diagnostic test (as opposed to a SCREENING TEST) to be useful, it would be reliable enough that, in most cases, another test will not be necessary to confirm the results of the first test.

But even when they are relatively reliable, medical tests rarely give definitive answers. Some tests are "disease-specific," so a positive (abnormal) result is strongly suggestive of the disease; but in most tests, positive results could suggest the presence of a range of disorders. In cases where serious questions hang on the results of a test, it may well be appropriate to have a second test, of the same or different type, to confirm the results. For example, if a test showed that your child had a BRAIN TUMOR and the doctor suggested an operation, you should certainly seek a second opinion and possibly a second test or kind of test, to confirm that the operation is necessary.

Similarly, you would not want to embark on a major course of treatment, as for DIABETES MELLITUS, on the basis of a single test result. Tests can give inaccurate results for many reasons. A sample may be kept at the wrong temperature or confused with someone else's; a machine may be set improperly; a tech-

What to Ask About a Medical Test

- *What is the test designed to show*? For example, is the test to rule out possible diseases, to narrow down the field for diagnosis? Is the test to confirm a diagnosis already tentatively made? Is it to screen for possible signs of a disorder?
- *How accurate is the test*? What is the probability that the test will give a false negative or false positive, for example?
- *How definitive is the test*? Will the test give an answer reliable enough to act on if necessary? Or is it a preliminary test that will probably need to be followed by more sophisticated tests if a positive result is obtained?
- *Where will it be done*? For example, will the test be performed in the doctor's office, in the hospital on an outpatient basis, or in a hospital as an inpatient? And if there are alternatives, what is the balance between safety and cost among them?
- *How much will it cost*? For example, are there separate charges for the attending physician, anesthetist (if necessary), nurse, laboratory work, and hospital quarters, or are all charges included in one fee?
- *Is the test covered by insurance*? Depending on the kind of health insurance you carry, you may need to obtain rather precise information about some tests and even sometimes obtain prior permission for it to be covered; or it may need to be performed in a specified place.
- *What kind of side effects are there, and how long might they last*? Side effects may range from a pin prick to active discomfort to severe pain to disability for some hours or longer, depending on the test, including the kind of anesthesia, if any, and the initial physical condition of the patient. You need as much information as possible to prepare yourself and your child to deal with possible side effects.
- *What are the risks of taking the test*? If few or none, excellent. But if there are substantial risks, you need to know them. Is there, for example, risk of infection, injury to internal organs, allergic reaction to foreign substances introduced into the body, paralysis, or even death from the test itself? Do not confuse serious risks with side effects which are simply temporary discomforts.
- *Does the test pose any special risks for pregnant women or children*? Tests that might be reasonably safe for others can prove unacceptably risky if a woman is or suspects she may be pregnant. And children, whose bodies are still growing and developing, may respond differently to a test than would a fully mature adult.
- *What are the risks of* not *taking the test*? Nothing in life is risk-free, and sometimes inaction can be more dangerous than action. If a physician suggests that your child may have a brain tumor, for example, taking a test would allow such a tumor to be diagnosed and possibly treated, while not taking the test would mean a tumor could be growing without being diagnosed and treated. Many situations are not so clear-cut, but you need to weigh the risks, side effects, and cost against the danger of leaving a disorder undiagnosed and untreated.
- *What is necessary to prepare for the test*? You or the child may, for example, need to stop taking all medication some days or hours before the test, and may need to avoid certain kinds of foods. Many tests require that the patient not eat or drink for a specified number of hours beforehand; some may also require an enema. Because tests may be highly sensitive to changes in the body, the patient may need to get a good rest before the test, in order not to throw off the results.
- *What does the test result mean*? After a test has been taken, what does the result actually indicate—that a disorder exists, that is does not exist, that it may exist? If the result is a numerical value, what is the "normal" value and how does your result compare to it? Are the results clear-cut or ambiguous? Do they indicate action now, retesting, or a "wait-and-see" attitude?

nician may misread a test; or a test may be thrown off by something special in the patient's blood or chemical makeup, especially if the patient is taking other medications or lacks rest. Especially unreliable are many results from health fairs. In their *Patient's Guide to Medical Tests*, Cathey Pinckney and Edward Pinckney put it bluntly:

Never, under any circumstances, rely upon the good or bad results of a single medical test. Any medical test report that could change your life must be repeated at least twice—and in different settings, such as another laboratory or another doctor's office—before it can be considered a valid part of your medical record.

The advice above very much applies to tests that can be performed in the home. (For a list of special precautions regarding medical self-tests, see HOME MEDICAL TESTING.)

In addition to giving informed consent *before* a test or procedure, patients have the right to expect full, understandable explanations of test results. In some states this "consumer" right has been given legal force, with laws that allow patients to review their medical records and obtain copies of them on request (though sometimes with a court order). In such states, if you fail to get the information you require from your doctor, you can go to court to obtain access to the documents. If your doctor is not giving you the information you require, however, a new doctor would seem to be in order, with your old records being transferred to the new doctor.

Various books (see below) discuss medical tests, what they entail, the risks they involve, and their reliability. Many medical books for home or professional use (see PARENT'S BOOKSHELF on page 566) provide further information on such tests in the context of the various diseases and disorders they are designed to identify. Among the general types of medical tests briefly described in this book are:

- *specimen tests,* such as BIOPSY, BLOOD TESTS, and URINE TESTS;

- *radiography,* such as FLUOROSCOPY and X-RAYS;
- *scans,* such as CT SCAN, ULTRASOUND, and MRI, including NUCLEAR SCANS, such as PET SCAN;
- *prenatal tests,* such as AMNIOCENTESIS, CHORIONIC VILLUS SAMPLING, AND ALPHA-FETOPROTEIN;
- medical tests that can be performed at home, such as BLOOD GLUCOSE MONITORING, OVULATION monitoring, and PREGNANCY tests;
- other types of tests, such as ECHOCARDIOGRAPHY, ELECTROMYOGRAM (EMG), MYELOGRAM, LUMBAR PUNCTURE (spinal tap), CISTERNAL PUNCTURE, ELECTROENCEPHALOGRAPH (EEG), and ANGIOGRAM (arteriogram).

For help and further information

Food and Drug Administration (FDA), 301-443-3170. (See DRUG REACTIONS AND INTERACTIONS.)

Other reference sources

Medical Tests and Diagnostic Procedure: A Patient's Guide, by Philip Shtasel. New York: Harper & Row, 1989.

Do-It-Yourself Medical Testing: More Than 170 Tests You Can Do at Home, third edition, by Cathey Pinckney and Edward R. Pinckney, M.D. New York: Facts on File, 1989.

Medical Tests, by H. Winter Griffith, M.D. Tucson, AZ: Fisher, 1988.

The Patient's Guide to Medical Tests, third edition, by Cathey Pinckney and Edward R. Pinckney, M.D. New York: Facts on File, 1986.

medulloblastoma   A type of BRAIN TUMOR common in children.

Meeting Street School Screening Test   A type of individually administered DEVELOPMENTAL SCREENING TEST that is used to help identify possible LEARNING DISABILITIES in kindergarteners and first-graders, ages 5 to 7½. Subtests focus on three main areas, MOTOR SKILLS (including SPATIAL RELATIONS), VISUAL SKILLS, and LANGUAGE SKILLS. Tests are scored from a behavior rating scale and book of NORMS at half-year intervals (based on 1966 testing). (For help and further information, see TESTS.)

megadoses   Amounts of VITAMINS or MINERALS that are greatly in excess of the RECOMMENDED DAILY ALLOWANCE of vitamins, which can sometimes lead to serious health problems.

megalocornea   Eyes larger than normal. (See EYE AND VISION PROBLEMS.)

meiosis   Process by which the SPERM and egg (OVUM) divide to obtain the genetic material each will contribute to a new being if the egg is fertilized. (See GENETIC INHERITANCE.)

melasma gravidarum (mask of pregnancy)   Alternate name for HYPERPIGMENTATION during pregnancy.

menarche   The onset of the first MENSTRUATION, which marks the beginning of the regular MENSTRUAL CYCLES that signal a woman's sexual maturity and FERTILITY; also called *pubarche.*

meningitis   Infection and inflammation of the *meninges,* the membranes that cover the brain and spinal cord. Although meningitis can occur at any age, it is especially a disease of children under five. The most common types of meningitis are caused by viruses; these are generally relatively mild, clearing up in a short period with little or no damage, though some rare forms can be more serious. Some yeasts can also cause meningitis, but these are rare.

The most dangerous type of meningitis is caused by bacteria, which often reach the brain from infection elsewhere in the body, though sometimes may be introduced through a HEAD INJURY. In the days before antibiotics, bacterial meningitis caused DEATH in nearly all afflicted with it. Even today, unless the disease is diagnosed and treated promptly and responds quickly, it still can cause DEATH or serious brain damage in many children. The Public Health Service estimates that "in about 8 percent of the patients (particularly those with *meningococcal meningitis*) the disease progresses so rapidly that death occurs during the first 48 hours, despite early treatment with antibiotics."

The most common forms of bacterial meningitis follow:

- *neonatal meningitis,* which affects as many as 40 to 50 of every 100,000 newborns, is particularly dangerous. The Public Health Service estimates that if the disease occurs during the first week of life, as many as half will die, and half of the survivors will have some neurological damage. Babies often get the infection during DELIVERY, as from their mothers or birthing staff or equipment. PREMATURE or LOW-BIRTH-WEIGHT infants are especially at risk, because their IMMUNE SYSTEMS are as yet insufficiently developed to protect them from infection. The main culprits are *Streptococcus group B* and *Escherichia coli.*
- *Haemophilus meningitis* has traditionally been the most common type of meningitis in children up to age 10. In recent years, however, the HIB VACCINE has been developed that protects children from HAEMOPHILUS INFLUENZAE TYPE B DISEASE. Parents should be sure to include this vaccine on their IMMUNIZATION schedule.
- *Meningococcal meningitis,* caused by *Neisseria meningitidis,* is more common in older children and young adults. It is slightly less severe but still causes a significant proportion of deaths (about 13 percent, the Public Health Service estimated in the mid-1980s) but somewhat less lasting damage. A vaccine is available against some forms of this bacteria and is used sometimes in epidemic situations.
- *Pneumococcal meningitis,* caused by *Streptococcus pneumoniae,* is less common but perhaps the most dangerous, with a death rate estimated at over 30 percent and with much lasting damage. Found in infants as well as older children and adults, it usually follows a respiratory infection or head injury.

The key to preventing death and damage from meningitis is to get help quickly. Suspicious symptoms (see SIGNS OF BACTERIAL

Signs of Bacterial Meningitis

Meningococcal and pneumococcal meningitis usually begin suddenly, with high fever, lack of energy, headache, and vomiting. There may also be stiffness of the neck, shoulders, and other joints. In about half of the meningococcal cases there is a rash—consisting of small red spots or irregular bruise-like lesions—scattered over the whole body. Young children are likely to be irritable and restless during the early stages of the disease.

Within 24 to 48 hours, the patient usually becomes drowsy and mentally confused and may slip into a coma. There may also be convulsions.

The symptoms of haemophilus meningitis are similar, but the onset of the disease may be more gradual, with fever and lack of energy lasting for several days before the other symptoms appear.

With neonatal meningitis, the picture is very different because the infant may show no signs of disease or infection other than general irritability, poor feeding, and unstable temperature. Since such symptoms are common to a number of disorders, any unexplained fever or other sign of infection should be regarded with extreme suspicion, particularly in infants who may be at special risk for meningitis.

Source: *Bacterial Meningitis* (1984). Public Health Service.

MENINGITIS, above) should be reported as quickly as possible. Often diagnosis will involve a LUMBAR PUNCTURE to remove some of the CEREBROSPINAL FLUID for analysis; this is important because doctors must identify which bacteria are involved in order to tell which antibiotics to prescribe.

Among the most common kinds of problems resulting from meningitis are MENTAL RETARDATION, EAR AND HEARING PROBLEMS, EPILEPSY, HYDROCEPHALUS, various LEARNING DISABILITIES, and sometimes problems with movement or coordination. Because damage is not always apparent until later, children who have had meningitis, especially neonatal meningitis, should be checked by a NEUROLOGIST over the next two years to identify any damage quickly and undertake therapy as necessary.

For help and further information

National Institute of Allergy and Infectious Diseases (NIAID), 301-496-5717. Publishes brochure *Bacterial Meningitis*. (For full group information, see ALLERGY.)

National Institute of Neurological Disorders and Stroke (NINDS), 301-496-5751. (For full group information, see BRAIN AND BRAIN DISORDERS.)

meningocele A form of SPINA BIFIDA.

Menke's syndrome A CONGENITAL disorder related to WILSON'S DISEASE.

menopause Cessation of the regular cycle of MENSTRUATION, either gradually or suddenly, marking the end of a woman's ability to bear children naturally, generally occurring between ages 45 and 55. During menopause, the eggs (see OVUM) stop being produced and the body makes less of the HORMONE called ESTROGEN, sometimes causing physical problems. Women approaching menopause generally do not conceive as readily as they would earlier in their lives for a variety of reasons, not the least of which is that fewer follicles (egg-forming cells) are available or suitable for possible FERTILIZATION. Some surgical procedures, such as hysterectomy (removal of the UTERUS), or

physiological problems can bring on *premature menopause*, ending early a woman's ability to reproduce. EMBRYO TRANSFER techniques have been applied experimentally to allow some women in menopause to bear children.

menorrhagia A disorder associated with MENSTRUATION.

menstrual cycle (reproductive cycle) The regular growth of the *endometrium* (lining of the UTERUS) to prepare for a possible fertilized egg and, if no PREGNANCY occurs, the expulsion of the unused lining in a bloody fluid at the end of the cycle, in the process called MENSTRUATION. The cycle itself is managed by several of the body's HORMONES and goes through various phases:

- *proliferative or follicular phase*: In response to ESTROGEN hormones, the endometrium begins to thicken in the uterus; if the woman becomes pregnant during the cycle, this endometrium will continue to grow and supply nourishment for the fertilized egg.
- *secretory or luteal phase*: OVULATION (release of an egg, or OVUM) occurs roughly midway through the cycle (measured from the beginning of the previous menstrual period). At the same time the body begins to produce the hormone PROGESTERONE, which causes swelling and thickening of the endometrium, to further prepare the uterus to accept a fertilized egg. It is during this period that a woman is able to become pregnant.
- *menstruation*: If no pregnancy occurs, the production of estrogen and progesterone declines and the unfertilized egg and unused lining are gradually expelled by contractions of the uterus, after which the process begins again.

The cycle will normally repeat, though sometimes with breaks and irregularities, from its onset (MENARCHE) during PUBERTY to its final cessation (MENOPAUSE). (For help and further information, see MENSTRUATION; CONCEPTION.)

menstrual extraction A type of ABORTION performed early in a PREGNANCY, using a procedure called VACUUM EXTRACTION.

menstruation   The periodic drainage of a bloody fluid through the VAGINA of a woman who is not pregnant; the fluid contains the unused *endometrium* (lining of the UTERUS) and the unfertilized egg (OVUM). On the average, menstruation occurs approximately once every four weeks, generally every 24 to 35 days, and lasts four to five days, though sometimes it is as short as one day and as long as eight days. For most girls, MENARCHE, the onset of the first menstruation, occurs as part of PUBERTY between ages 10 and 16. It can occur much earlier, as part of what is termed *precocious puberty*, or somewhat later; but if a girl has not begun menstruating by age 16, parents should probably consult a doctor to see if there is some underlying physical problem (see below). Girls who are overweight tend to begin their periods earlier, while those who are very thin, involved in strenuous physical activity (such as ballet and some sports), or have chronic illness may begin to menstruate later. In recent decades, partly because of improved NUTRITION, menstruation has tended to start ever earlier.

The establishment of a regular MENSTRUAL CYCLE is a sign of sexual maturity and fertility, and its cessation (either gradually or all at once) later in life (MENOPAUSE) marks the end of a woman's fertile life. Although many schools have SEX EDUCATION courses, parents who do not wish to leave such matters in the hands of others should be alert to the signs of puberty in a girl and prepare her for the coming of menstrual periods before they occur.

In the complicated and delicate process of menstruation, various kinds of disorders can occur, including:

*   *dysmenorrhea*, painful menstruation, often resulting from contractions of the UTERUS and slight dilation of the CERVIX and often accompanied by nausea, VOMITING, and intestinal cramps. Why dysmenorrhea occurs is not entirely clear, but perhaps one woman in 10 has menstrual periods so painful that they cause partial or complete disability for a few hours to a few days. BIRTH-CONTROL PILLS can provide some relief, as can some painkillers (*analgesics*). Dysmenorrhea can also accompany other kinds of disorders, such as abnormalities of the pelvis, ENDOMETRIOSIS, fibroid TUMORS, or PELVIC INFLAMMATORY DISEASE (PID). Where possible, the cause is treated, as by surgery.
*   *amenorrhea*, absence of menstruation. When a girl has failed to begin menstruating by age 16, it is called *primary amenorrhea*, which can result from a variety of reasons, including hormonal disorder, TURNER'S SYNDROME, CONGENITAL absence of reproductive organs, or lack of perforation in the HYMEN to allow blood to escape. By contrast, *secondary amenorrhea* is the halting of the menstrual cycle after establishment of regular periods, as during periods of stress or starvation (as in ANOREXIA NERVOSA) or in cases of hormonal imbalance. This can be caused by a TUMOR in the reproductive system, by hormonal disorders, or by surgical removal of the uterus. The most common causes of secondary amenorrhea are, of course, PREGNANCY and menopause.
*   *polymenorrhea*, periods that come in a cycle of less than 22 days.

*   *oligomenorrhea*, periods that occur infrequently or with very small loss of blood.
*   *menorrhagia*, excessive bleeding during periods, which can also result from hormonal imbalance, from fibroid tumors or polyps, or from an INTRAUTERINE DEVICE (IUD).
*   *metrorrhagia*, bleeding at extremely irregular intervals, often not menstrual periods at all but bleeding associated with abnormalities such as CANCER.
*   *premenstrual syndrome* (PMS), a series of physical and emotional symptoms that occur in the week or two between OVULATION and the onset of menstruation, presumably triggered by cyclical hormonal changes. Symptoms of PMS include breast soreness, EDEMA (fluid buildup), headache, aches in the back and lower abdomen, DEPRESSION, fatigue, tension, and irritability, in some cases mild, in others severe enough to disrupt personal life. Among the treatments tried, though with varied success, are diuretic drugs to counter fluid buildup, hormonal supplements or birth-control pills to smooth out hormonal swings, and elimination of foods that can cause fluid retention or headaches, such as salt, caffeine, and chocolate.

Many of these menstrual disorders can make conception more difficult, if not impossible, and so would need careful exploration and treatment to maximize the chance of becoming pregnant.

For help and further information

PMS Access, 800-222-4767. (M-F, 9 A.M.–5 P.M., CST).
Getting Your Period: A Book About Menstruation, by Jean Marzollo. New York: Dial, 1990. For ages 9 and up.
Premenstrual Syndrome Self-Help Book, by Susan M. Lark, M.D. Berkeley, CA: Celestial Arts, 1989.
(See also INFERTILITY.)

mental age (MA)   A numerical summary reflecting a child's comparative performance on a mental ability or INTELLIGENCE TEST, such as the STANFORD-BINET INTELLIGENCE TEST, relating a child's score to NORMS for others of the same age. (See also AGE.)

mental disorder   A pattern or SYNDROME of behavior that causes distress, disability, increased risk of pain or death, or grossly impaired functioning in a person to such an extent that it becomes a clinical problem. Individuals may have conflicts with society, and they may have personal behavior that is nonstandard, in areas relating to political, religious, or sexual NORMS. Many such conflicts and behavior were once regarded as signs of "mental illness." But under the American Psychiatric Association's widely accepted current classification of mental disorders (see *Diagnostic and Statistical Manual of Mental Disorders*, below), they would not be considered mental disorders unless they involved severe personal dysfunction.

Many mental disorders primarily affect adults, but some appear first during childhood or have their roots in childhood trauma. Some symptoms of mental disorders appear in early childhood, and under the EDUCATION FOR ALL HANDICAPPED CHIL-

DREN ACT OF 1975, states are charged with identifying children with *emotional disturbances* as early as possible, through such programs as CHILDFIND, so that they can receive treatment. The aim of such programs is to put children in the best possible position to benefit from public EDUCATION, with special services provided where a child needs it. For reporting purposes under the Act, programs such as HEAD START use the following definition:

A child shall be considered seriously emotionally disturbed who is identified by professionally qualified personnel (psychologist or psychiatrist) as requiring special services. This definition would include but not be limited to the following conditions: dangerously aggressive towards others, self-destructive, severely withdrawn and non-communicative, hyperactive to the extent that it affects adaptive behavior, severely anxious, depressed or phobic, psychotic or autistic.

A child thought to have possible emotional disturbance will be referred for screening (as with a DEVELOPMENTAL SCREENING TEST) and possibly then evaluation (often using a DIAGNOSTIC ASSESSMENT TEST) by a PSYCHOLOGIST or PSYCHIATRIST. The evaluation generally outlines the child's development—both strengths and weaknesses—and explains what special services the child should receive in the schools. Sometimes, however, evaluations say only that the child is emotionally disturbed or give the name of a particular disturbance. Though useful as shorthand, since a single word can convey a whole range of related behaviors, such labels can sometimes get in the way of seeing the child as an individual, as noted in Head Start's *Mainstreaming Preschoolers: Children with Emotional Disturbance*:

Classifying a child usually limits rather than extends our understanding, and often produces negative and inaccurate expectations for that child. The use of these names doesn't allow us to think of the range of skills and behaviors a child may demonstrate. It doesn't describe the severity of the child's problem with a particular skill or set of skills. For example, the term "disturbed" cannot possibly tell you whether a child has problems with sharing. One disturbed child may have problems sharing a certain toy with certain people, while another disturbed child may have trouble sharing anything with anyone. Still another disturbed child may have no special difficulty sharing. A word or phrase cannot possibly describe all of the possibilities to [teachers and parents]. Describing children in terms of strengths and weaknesses is much more valuable to [them] than being able to fit them into a category.

Another real disadvantage of classifying is that the terms tend to stick with a child for a long time, regardless of whether the handicapping condition is still present. This can lead to social isolation and incorrect assumptions about a child's ability. Young children change and grow so rapidly that some children with handicaps may overcome their disabilities before entering public school. Names acquired in preschool are likely to follow children into public schools, and may be used as a basis for excluding them from the regular school program. It is hard to outlive or live down how you have been classified.

Parents should try their best to see that teachers get to know the whole child and do not focus on simply a label. They also need to be sure that the diagnosis is a correct one; they should be sure that all possible physical causes of emotional problems are thoroughly checked so that a child is not misdiagnosed and severely disadvantaged. For example, a child who has an undiagnosed problem with hearing or vision may be thoroughly frustrated in his or her attempts to communicate with others, which can show itself in severe aggression, withdrawal, or other problem ways.

Similarly, parents need to be sure that cultural or language differences at home do not make the child seem emotionally disturbed in the new and alien setting of a classroom; when any evaluation is being done, it is important that the evaluator be fully aware of the child's home background. As the Head Start program comments:

Some children are "street wise" at an early age: they know how to fight for their rights and take care of themselves. This behavior might include using physical force and yelling to settle problems, rather than talking things out. These children may be very assertive in this way because it is how they have learned to respond and, perhaps, because this way is acceptable to other people around them. They may in fact not be disturbed at all.

All that being said, however, parents may need to know something about the kinds of mental disorders that can affect children. Among those that normally appear during infancy, childhood, or adolescence are:

- MENTAL RETARDATION.
- AUTISM, classified by psychiatrists as a *pervasive developmental disorder*.
- LEARNING DISABILITIES and communication disorders (see COMMUNICATION SKILLS AND DISORDERS), classified by psychiatrists as *specific developmental disorders*.
- ATTENTION-DEFICIT HYPERACTIVITY DISORDER (ADHD) and CONDUCT DISORDER, classified by psychiatrists as *disruptive behavior disorders*.
- *anxiety disorders* (see ANXIETY), including PANIC DISORDERS, phobic disorders (see PHOBIA), SEPARATION ANXIETY DISORDER, AVOIDANT DISORDER, and OVERANXIOUS DISORDER.
- ANOREXIA NERVOSA, BULIMIA NERVOSA, PICA, and RUMINATION DISORDER OF INFANCY, classified by psychiatrists as *eating disorders*.
- GENDER IDENTITY DISORDERS.
- TOURETTE'S SYNDROME, classified by psychiatrists as a *tic disorder*.
- ENCOPRESIS (soiling), classified by psychiatrists as an *elimination disorder*, as are some cases of ENURESIS (bedwetting).

- IDENTITY DISORDER.
- REACTIVE ATTACHMENT DISORDER.
- *stereotypy/habit disorder* (see COMFORT HABITS).

In addition, some other disorders may appear at any age and affect children and adults in many of the same ways, including:

- ORGANIC MENTAL DISORDERS, resulting from physical problems in the brain.
- MOOD DISORDERS, including DEPRESSION and BIPOLAR DISORDERS (manic-depression).
- other anxiety disorders, including OBSESSIVE COMPULSIVE DISORDER.
- DISSOCIATIVE DISORDERS, including MULTIPLE PERSONALITY DISORDER.
- IMPULSE CONTROL DISORDERS, including *intermittent explosive disorder, pyromania, kleptomania, trichotillomania,* and *pathological gambling.*
- ADJUSTMENT DISORDERS.
- PERSONALITY DISORDERS, including *dependent personality disorder, paranoid personality disorder, passive agressive personality disorder, schizoid personality disorder, schizotypal personality disorder, histrionic personality disorder,* and *narcissistic personality disorder.*

For help and further information

General Organizations

Council for Exceptional Children (CEC), 703-620-3660
Has separate division for Children with Behavioral Disorders. Operates information center; provides list of agencies serving exceptional children and their families; publishes various materials, including *Not All Little Wagons Are Red: The Exceptional Child's Early Years.* (For full group information, see HELP FOR SPECIAL CHILDREN on page 578.)

National Institute of Mental Health (NIMH)
Alcohol, Drug Abuse, and Mental Health Administration
Parklawn Building, 15C-05
5600 Fishers Lane
Rockville, MD 20857
301-443-4536 (public affairs), 301-443-4513 (publications)
Federal arm, part of the National Institutes of Health, overseeing and providing public information on mental health and illness. Sponsors research and provides information to public and professionals; publishes various materials, including *A Consumer's Guide to Mental Health Services, Schizophrenia: Questions and Answers,* and series of "Useful Information On" booklets on topics such as obsessive-compulsive disorder, anorexia nervosa and bulimia, paranoia, phobias and panic, sleep disorders, and medications for mental illness.

American Mental Health Fund (AMHF)
2735 Hartland Road, Suite 335
Falls Church, VA 22043

703-573-2200, toll-free number 800-433-5959 (for ordering brochure below)
David George, President
Organization concerned with mental illness. Seeks to educate public about warning signals and problems and need for understanding and help; supports research; publishes various materials, including *Understanding Mental Illnesses.*

National Mental Health Association (NMHA)
1021 Prince Street
Alexandria, VA 22314
703-684-7722
Preston J. Garrison, Executive Director
Organization acting as advocate for mentally ill. Seeks to improve care and prevention; supports community centers; seeks to educate public and influence government policy; publishes various print and audiovisual materials.

American Academy of Child and Adolescent Psychiatry (AACAP)
3615 Wisconsin Avenue, NW
Washington, DC 20016
202-966-7300
Professional organization of physicians in child and adolescent psychiatry. Fosters research on causes and treatment of psychiatric problems in children; provides information and some special services for children; publishes various materials, including journal, newsletters, and books.

American Association of Psychiatric Services for Children (AAPSC)
1133 15th Street, NW, Suite 1000
Washington, DC 20005
202-429-9440
John H. Gance, Executive Director
Organization concerned about psychiatric and related services for children. Encourages coordinated efforts between psychiatrists, psychologists, and social workers; provides information and referrals; publishes newsletters.

Division of Child and Youth Services
c/o American Psychological Association (APA)
1200 17th Street, NW
Washington, DC 20036
202-955-7600
Leonard S. Goodstein, Executive Officer
Division of American Psychological Association of professionals devoted to studying, preventing, and treating emotional disturbances in children. Fosters development of services for troubled children; provides information; publishes various materials.

Anxiety Disorders Association of America (ADAA)
6000 Executive Boulevard

Rockville, MD 20852 301-231-9350

Jerilyn Ross, President

Organization for people with anxiety disorders, their families and friends, and professionals involved in their treatment. Encourages formation of local mutual-support self-help groups; aims to educate public about anxiety disorders and resources available; acts as information clearinghouse; publishes various print and audio materials, including *Breaking the Panic Cycle* and *Phobia: A Comprehensive Summary of Modern Treatments*.

American Association of University Affiliated Programs for Persons with Developmental Disabilities (AAUAP), 202-737-1511. (For full group information, see HELP FOR SPECIAL CHILDREN on page 578.)

National Association for the Dually Diagnosed (NADD), 914-331-4336. (For full group information, see MENTAL RETARDATION.)

American Psychiatric Association (APA)

1400 K Street, NW

Washington, DC 20005

202-682-6000

Melvin Sabshin, M.D., Medical Director

Professional organization of psychiatrists, including special council on children, adolescents, and their families.

American Society for Adolescent Psychiatry (ASAP)

24 Green Valley Road

Wallingford, PA 19086

215-566-1054

Mary Staples, Executive Secretary

Professional organization of psychiatrists who work with adolescents.

National Association of Psychiatric Treatment Centers for Children (NAPTCC)

440 First Street, NW, Suite 310

Washington, DC 20001

202-638-1991

Claudia Waller, Executive Secretary

Organization of accredited residential centers treating emotionally disturbed children.

Mental Disability Legal Resource Center (MDLRC)

c/o American Bar Association

1800 M Street, NW

Washington, DC 20036

202-331-2240

John Parry, Director

Arm of the American Bar Association formed to monitor court decisions, legislation, and administrative rulings relating to people with mental or physical disabilities, including civil commitment, rights of the disabled, education of handicapped children, discrimination against the handicapped, and environmental barriers. Publishes various materials, including bimonthly *Mental and Physical Disability Law Reporter, Mental Disability Law Primer*, and *Right to Refuse Antipsychotic Medication*.

National Alliance for the Mentally Ill (NAMI)

1901 North Fort Myer Drive, Suite 500

Arlington, VA 22209

703-524-7600

Laurie M. Flynn, Executive Director

Network of mutual-support self-help groups of and for families and friends of people with serious mental illnesses. Seeks to educate public and influence government policy; provides information; publishes various materials, including bimonthly newsletter, *Anti-Stigma Handbook, Consumer's Guide to Mental Health Services*, and brochures on mental illnesses.

Self-help Groups For the Mentally Ill

Emotional Health Anonymous (EHA)

2420 San Gabriel Boulevard

Rosemead, CA 91770

818-573-5482

Mary Thomas, Office Manager

Network of mutual-support self-help groups for people who are recovering from emotional illness. Inspired by Alcoholics Anonymous; publishes various materials, including bimonthly *Hang-Up*.

Emotions Anonymous (EA)

P.O. Box 4245

St. Paul, MN 55104

612-647-9712

Network of mutual-support self-help groups for people who are recovering from emotional illness. Modeled on Alcoholics Anonymous; publishes various materials, including *Emotions Anonymous World Directory*.

Neurotics Anonymous International Liaison (NAIL)

P.O. Box 4866, Cleveland Park Station

Washington, D.C. 20008

202-232-0414

Grover Boydston, Chairman

Network of mutual-support self-help groups for people who are recovering from emotional illness. Modeled on Alcoholics Anonymous; publishes various materials, including *Journal of Mental Health*.

Other reference sources

General Works

Healthier Children, by Barbara Kahan. New Canaan, CT: Keats, 1989. On nutritional and environmental changes relating to mental disorders.

Children and Adolescents with Mental Illness: A Parents' Guide, by E. McElroy. Kensington, MD: Woodbine House, 1988.

Hidden Victims: An Eight-Stage Healing Process for Families and Friends of the Mentally Ill, by Julie Tallard Johnson. Garden City, NY: Doubleday, 1988.

Health Care U.S.A., by Jean Carper. New York: Prentice Hall, 1987. Resource for general and specific health-care information; lists centers for treatment or research, specialists in treating depression, suicide prevention centers, and other information.

Emotional Illness in Your Family: Helping Your Relative, Helping Yourself, by Harvey R. Greenberg, M.D. New York: Macmillan, 1989.

The Anxiety Disease, by David V. Sheehan, M.D. New York, Scribner, 1984.

Panic Disorder: The Great Pretender, by Michael Zal, D.O. New York: Plenum, 1990.

Helping the Fearful Child: A Parent's Guide to Everyday and Problem Anxieties, by Jonathan Kellerman. New York: Norton, 1981.

A Parents' Guide to Child Therapy, by Richard Bush. New York: Delacorte, 1980.

Troubled Children/Troubled Parents: The Way Out, by Stanley Goldstein. New York: Atheneum, 1979.

Help for Your Child, by Sharon Brehm. New York: Prentice-Hall, 1978.

A Circle of Children, by Mary MacCracken. New York: New American Library, 1973.

Background Works

The Untouched Key: Tracing Childhood Trauma in Creativity and Destructiveness, by Alice Miller. Translated by Hildegarde and Hunter Hannum. Garden City, NY: Doubleday, 1990.

Insanity: The Idea and Its Consequences, by Thomas Szasz. New York: Wiley, 1990.

The New Harvard Guide to Psychiatry, Armand M. Nicholi, Jr., M.D., ed. Cambridge, MA: Belknap/Harvard, 1988.

Relationship Disturbances in Early Childhood: A Developmental Approach, Arnold J. Sameroff and Robert N. Emde, eds. New York: Basic, 1989.

The Family Mental Health Encyclopedia, by Frank J. Bruno. New York: Wiley, 1989.

Child Psychopathology: A Social Work Perspective, Francis J. Turner, ed. New York: Free Press, 1989.

Psychiatric Skeletons: Tracing the Legacy of Mental Illness in the Family, by Steven D. Targum. Summit, NJ: PIA, 1989.

The Science of Mind, by Kenneth Klivington. Cambridge, MA: MIT Press, 1989.

Psychiatric Disorders in America, Lee Robins and Darrel A. Regier, eds. New York: Free Press, 1989.

The Encyclopedia of Phobias, Fears, and Anxieties, by Ronald M. Doctor and Ada P. Kahn. New York: Facts on File, 1989.

The Uses of Enchantment: The Meaning and Importance of Fairy Tales, by Bruno Bettelheim. New York: Vintage, 1977.

The Child in His Family: Children at Psychiatric Risk, by J. Anthony and C. Koupernik. New York: Wiley, 1974.

Personal Stories of Patients and Therapies

Rickie, by Frederick F. Flach. New York: Ballantine/Fawcett/Columbine, 1990. A psychiatrist's account of his adolescent daughter's 10 years of mental illness.

My Angry Son: Sometimes Love Is Not Enough, by Barbara Bartocci. New York: D.I. Fine, 1985.

Dibs: In Search of Self, by Virginia Axline. New York: Ballantine, 1976.

Lovey, by Mary MacCracken. New York: Lippincott, 1976.

I Never Promised You a Rose Garden, by Hannah Green. New York: New American Library, 1964.

Professional Works

Diagnostic and Statistical Manual of Mental Disorders, third edition revised (DSM-III-R). Washington, DC: American Psychiatric Association, 1987. Descriptions of currently recognized mental disorders, in understandable language.

Anxiety and the Anxiety Disorders, A.H. Tuma and J. Maser, eds. Hillsdale, NJ: Erlbaum, 1985.

Anxiety Disorders and Phobias—A Cognitive Perspective, by A.T. Beck, G. Emery, and R.L. Greenberg. New York: Basic, 1985.

Teaching Disturbed and Disturbing Students: An Integrated Approach, by P. Zionts. Austin, TX: PRO-ED, 1985.

Diagnosis and Treatment of Anxiety Disorders, R. Pasnau, ed. Washington, DC: American Psychiatric Press, 1984.

Genetics of Neurological and Psychiatric Disorders, by S.S. Kety, L.P. Rowland, R.L. Sidman, and S.W. Matthysse. New York: Raven, 1983.

Teaching the Emotionally Handicapped Child, by C.G. Collins. Danville, IL: Interstate Printers and Publishers, 1983.

Comprehensive Handbook of Psychotherapy, H. Adams and P. Sutker, eds. New York: Plenum, 1983.

Cure and Care of Neuroses, by I.M. Marks. New York: Wiley, 1981.

Anxiety: New Research and Changing Concepts, D.F. Klein and J.G. Rabkin, eds. New York: Raven, 1981.

Adolescent Psychiatry, S. Feinstein, P. Giovacchini, J. Looney, A. Schwartzberg, and A. Sorosky, eds. Chicago: University of Chicago Press, 1980.

Adolescence: The Psychoanalytic Study of the Child, by Anna Freud. New York: International Universities Press, 1958.

On Legal Matters

Child Psychiatry and the Law, D.H. Schetky and E.P. Benedek, eds. New York: Brunner/Mazel, 1980.

The Mentally Disabled and the Law, by S.J. Brakel, J. Parry, and B.A. Weiner. Chicago: American Bar Association, 1986.

Law, Psychiatry, and Morality, by A.A. Stone. Washington, DC: American Psychiatric Press, 1984.

Law and Psychiatry: Rethinking the Relationship, by M. Moore. Cambridge: Cambridge University Press, 1984.

Observational Checklist for Possible Mental Retardation

Information Coming from the Environment	Often or Always	Rarely or Never
The child doesn't understand directions, reacts slowly to them, or waits to see what the other children are doing first.	☐	☐
The child seems confused and doesn't do what other children are doing along with them.	☐	☐
The child doesn't know what to do with materials and toys, or uses them for the wrong purposes.	☐	☐
Loud sounds disturb the child.	☐	☐
A lot of unorganized moving around in the classroom confuses the child.	☐	☐
The child has trouble noticing fine details.	☐	☐
The child doesn't answer to his or her name.	☐	☐
The child can't carry out a one-step direction.	☐	☐
The child can't concentrate on one thing for very long, and is easily distracted.	☐	☐
The child doesn't show interest in classroom surroundings.	☐	☐

Processing the Information	Often or Always	Rarely or Never
The child has trouble remembering what he or she has seen or heard, or what has happened.	☐	☐
The child can't match colors and shapes.	☐	☐
The child can't sort colors and shapes.	☐	☐
The child can't answer simple questions (such as "What's your name?") or gives answers that make no sense.	☐	☐
The child doesn't know things that other children in the class know.	☐	☐
The child does things in the wrong order (such as drying the pan before it has been washed).	☐	☐
The child can't preduct dangerous consequences of actions before he or she does them.	☐	☐
The child can't hear small differences in words (such as boy/toy, Fred/red).	☐	☐
The child can't retell a simple story.	☐	☐
The child has trouble following two or more directions in the right order.	☐	☐
The child doesn't understand common environmental sounds (for example, can't tell you "a car" upon hearing the beep of a car horn).	☐	☐
The child doesn't remember the classroom routine.	☐	☐
The child forgets what he she is doing in the middle of it.	☐	☐
The child has trouble inventing stories and and actions in pretend play.	☐	☐
The child doesn't understand basic concepts such as relationships, time, space, and quantity as well as other children do.	☐	☐

Continued on page 317

For or By Kids

Diagnosing and Treating Mental Illness, by Alan Lundy. New York: Chelsea House, 1990. For young adults.

Emotional Illness in Your Family: Helping Your Relative, Helping Yourself, by Harvey R. Greenberg. New York: Macmillan/Collier, 1989. For young adults.

Mental Illness and Substance Abuse, by Wrynn Smith, Ph.D. New York: Facts on File, 1988.

Stress and Mental Health, by Annette Spence; Mario Orlandi and Donald Prue, series eds. New York: Facts on File, 1988.

Notes for Another Life, by Sue Ellen Bridgers. New York: Knopf, 1981; Bantam paperback. For young adults. A brother and sister cope with their father's mental illness and mother's absence.

The Keeper, by Phyllis Reynolds Naylor. New York: Atheneum, 1986; Bantam paperback. For young adults. About a boy trying to understand his mentally ill father.

(See also SUICIDE; various specific disorders listed above; also HELP FOR SPECIAL CHILDREN on page 578.)

mental retardation   Significantly lower-than-normal capacity for learning and COGNITIVE DEVELOPMENT. As the name implies, the condition shows itself by clear delays in reaching DEVELOPMENTAL MILESTONES (see CHART OF NORMAL DEVELOPMENT on page 507). But where children of normal mental capacity can overcome initial DEVELOPMENTAL DELAY from other causes, mentally retarded children develop only to a certain plateau. Traditionally, they have been classed by their mental ability, as measured by standard INTELLIGENCE TESTS, the usual classifications being:

mild—IQ 50–55 to 70, formerly termed *educable*
moderate—IQ 35–40 to 50–55, formerly *trainable*
severe—IQ 20–25 to 35–40

Using the Information	Often or Always	Rarely or Never
Verbal Responses: Talking		
The child doesn't talk at all.	☐	☐
You can't understand the child's speech.	☐	☐
The child can't communicate using words and gestures, either alone or together.	☐	☐
The child can't name or describe familiar objects.	☐	☐
Motor Responses: Moving the Body		
The child trembles or shakes.	☐	☐
The child falls down or bumps into things a lot.	☐	☐
The child walks unevenly, or limps.	☐	☐
The child has poor eye–hand coordination (for example, knocks things over a lot).	☐	☐
The child can't pull simple clothing on or off.	☐	☐
The child has trouble using toys such as blocks and puzzles.	☐	☐
The child can't copy simple forms, such as a line, circle, square.	☐	☐
The Child's Behavior in the Classroom	Often or Always	Rarely or Never
The child resists change and variety in activities by crying, throwing tantrums, or refusing to participate.	☐	☐
The child cannot make choices about what to do or select activities independently.	☐	☐
The child imitates the games of other children rather than inventing his or her own games.	☐	☐
The child withdraws from participating in most or all of the activities.	☐	☐
The child is constantly disrupting the class.	☐	☐

Source: *Mainstreaming Preschoolers: Children with Mental Retardation: A Guide for Teachers, Parents, and Others Who Work with Mentally Retarded Preschoolers*, by Eleanor Whiteside Lynch et al. (1978). Prepared for the Head Start Bureau of the U.S. Administration for Children, Youth, and Families.

profound—IQ under 20–25

In psychology and education, these categories are now somewhat outmoded, but they are still widely used, if only because they are written into many laws relating to mental retardation. For parents and educators, however, it is much more important to focus on what the individual child can and cannot do, especially on ADAPTIVE BEHAVIOR, and to focus on enhancing skills and independence as much as possible.

Though its precise causes are unknown, mental retardation is associated with a variety of other problems, including GENETIC DISORDERS, CHROMOSOMAL ABNORMALITIES, and difficulties relating to PREGNANCY and CHILDBIRTH. By definition it appears in children during development, though similar retardation can result from later problems, such as HEAD INJURY, severe FEVER and illness, or MALNUTRITION. Where associated with a specific disorder, such as DOWN'S SYNDROME, FETAL ALCOHOL SYNDROME, or PHENYLKETONURIA, mental retardation often appears with other characteristics. If not, it is sometimes hard to diagnose properly, especially in young children, since they develop at varying rates and may have other problems.

Parents who are concerned that their preschooler might be mentally retarded may want to use the above OBSERVATIONAL CHECKLIST FOR POSSIBLE MENTAL RETARDATION. The checklist should be used only as a guideline in judging when to refer a child for evaluation. It is important for parents to realize that slow mental development is not necessarily mental retardation.

Medical and educational files abound with cases of children misdiagnosed as mentally retarded. Many of these children had normal intelligence but had other problems that interfered with learning and led to apparent retardation, including EAR AND HEARING PROBLEMS, EYE AND VISION PROBLEMS, LEARNING DISABILITIES, communication problems (see COMMUNICATION SKILLS AND DISORDERS), and sometimes lack of stimulation and learning opportunities at home, different cultural background, and inability to use English fluently from lack of experience. Parents who suspect possible mental retardation should have their child evaluated promptly but should be sure that other areas are also checked so that *any* problems are properly diagnosed and treated.

In the past, the outlook for many children with mental retardation was grim, as they were often shunted aside or institutionalized in notoriously unresponsive and often abusive settings. But since the EDUCATION FOR ALL HANDICAPPED ACT OF 1975, much more concerted attention has been paid toward reaching each child's highest potential. Special PRESCHOOL and school programs are available and, for adults, often supervised work programs.

Children with mental retardation learn basic skills more slowly, but those with mild retardation (about 85 percent of the mental retarded) can learn skills up to about the sixth-grade level. They do best if skills or tasks are simple and presented in small, concrete steps. (TEACHING YOUNG CHILDREN: GUIDELINES

AND ACTIVITIES, on page 544, gives some useful guidelines for doing this and for enhancing skills development.) Those with moderate retardation (about 10 percent) can learn skills up to about the second-grade level.

As adults, some of those with mild and moderate retardation can support themselves and live independently in the community, with some supportive services. Others can perform some kinds of unskilled or semiskilled work under close supervision but need more support and guidance, often living in supervised apartments or GROUP HOMES.

Children with severe mental retardation (3 to 4 percent) have poor MOTOR SKILLS, and communication skills are limited in early childhood, though during the usual school-age period they may respond to TOILET TRAINING and learn to talk and may be able to learn some "survival" words like *stop* or *men* and *women.* Those with profound retardation (1 to 2 percent) have extremely limited capacity for skill development and require continuous supervision and help in a carefully structured environment. As adults, many of these would formerly have been institutionalized but now are more often living in group homes or remaining at home with their families.

Parents with mentally retarded children will need to make long-term plans for their welfare and care. Many parents choose to keep such children in the home environment as long as possible, moving them into group homes only later. With severe or profound retardation, however, some parents find the enormous amount of care and supervision required to be beyond their capacities. Many social and educational services are available, but parents often need to fight to get such services for their children. Parents also need to make special arrangements for the care of a mentally retarded child or adult, often appointing a GUARDIAN to look out for the child's interests, should something happen to them. Organizations and reference works, such as those below and in HELP FOR SPECIAL CHILDREN on page 578, can help by providing experience from those who have faced similar problems and are keeping up to date on new approaches.

Other reference sources

Mainstreaming Preschoolers: Children with Mental Retardation: A Guide for Teachers, Parents, and Others Who Work with Mentally Retarded Preschoolers, by Eleanor Whiteside Lynch et al. (1978). Prepared for the Department of Health and Human Services by the Administration for Children, Youth, and Families, Head Start Bureau. Discusses how mental retardation affects 3-to-5-year-olds and their learning, with suggestions for teaching activities to enhance their skills.

We Have Been There: Families Share the Joy and Struggles of Living with Mental Retardation, by T. Cougan and L. Isbell. Nashville, TN: Abingdon, 1983.

Hope for the Families: New Directions for Parents of Persons With Retardation or Other Disabilities, by R. Perske. Nashville, TN: Abingdon, 1981.

Teaching Children with Developmental Problems—A Family Care Approach, by Kathryn E. Barnard and Marcene L. Erickson. St Louis: Mosby, 1976.

A Step-by-Step Learning Guide for Retarded Infants and Children, by Vicki M. Johnson and Roberta A. Werner. Syracuse, NY: Syracuse University Press, 1975.

For or By Kids

We Laugh, We Love, We Cry: Children Living with Mental Retardation, by Thomas Bergman. Milwaukee, WI: Gareth Stevens, 1990. For grades 3 to 5.

More Time to Grow: Explaining Mental Retardation to Children: A Story, by Sharon Hya Grollmen and Robert Perske. Boston: Beacon, 1977. A story about a young girl with a retarded brother, to help young children understand about mental retardation; also includes a guide for parents and teachers about working with retarded children.

Background Works

Dictionary of Mental Handicaps, by Mary P. Lindsey. New York: Routledge, 1989.

Transitions to Adult Life for People with Mental Retardation—Principles and Practices, by B. Ludlow, A. Turnbull, and R. Lukasson. Baltimore: Paul H. Brookes, 1988.

Health Care U.S.A., by Jean Carper. New York: Prentice Hall, 1987. Resource for general and specific health-care information, including mental retardation, developmental disabilities, and learning disabilities; lists key rehabilitation centers specializing in infant and early childhood development, government-supported, university-affiliated facilities (UAFs) for learning disabilities and UAF-associated specialists, mental retardation research centers, special schools for dyslexic children, and other information.

The Mentally Disabled and the Law, by S.J. Brakel, J. Parry, and B.A. Weiner. Chicago: American Bar Association, 1986.

Increasing Behaviors of Severely Retarded and Autistic Persons, by R.M. Foxx. Champaign, IL: Research Press, 1982.

Developmental Programming for Infants and Young Children: Volume 3, Stimulation Activities, by Sara L. Brown and Carol M. Donovan. Ann Arbor: University of Michigan Press, 1977.

Brothers and Sisters of Retarded Children: An Exploratory Study, by F.K. Grossman. Syracuse, NY: Syracuse University Press, 1972.

(See also HELP FOR SPECIAL CHILDREN on page 578.)

For help and further information

Association for Retarded Citizens (ARC)
P.O. Box 6109
2501 Avenue J
Arlington, TX 76005

817-640-0204
Alan Abeson, Executive Director

Organization for parents of the mentally retarded, professionals who work with them, and interested others. Seeks to increase services for mentally retarded; works to educate public and change public policy and legislation; maintains library; publishes various materials, including booklets and brochures such as *How to Provide for Their Future, An Overview of Down Syndrome, Toilet Training for Children with Mental Retardation, Mental Retardation: The Search for Cures, Have You Heard . . . About Alcohol and Pregnancy?* (for teenagers, about preventing fetal alcohol syndrome), *Opportunities After High School for Persons Who Are Severely Handicapped, Values and Principles Guiding Establishment of Corporate Guardianship Programs, Directory of Self-Advocacy Programs, The Truth About Mental Retardation*, and *To Our Future . . . And Theirs*, flyers such as *If You Are the Parent of a Child Who Is Mentally Retarded . . ., Developmental Checklist, Test Your School's IQ: Integration Quotient, Guidelines for Quality Individual Plans*, and *Take Care of Yourself* (for and about pregnant women), and fact sheets on general topics such as *Introduction to Mental Retardation, Public Law 99-457 Amendments to the Education of the Handicapped Act, Employment of People with Mental Retardation, Family Support, Mental Illness in Persons with Mental Retardation*, and *Community Living* and on specific diseases such as *Facts About Hepatitis B, Down Syndrome, Fragile X Syndrome, Facts About Hib Disease*, and *Facts About Alcohol and Other Drug Use During Pregnancy*.

Council for Exceptional Children (CEC), 703-620-3660. Has a separate Division on Mental Retardation. Focuses on mental retardation in young people; operates information center; provides list of agencies serving exceptional children and their families; publishes various materials, including *Not All Little Wagons Are Red: The Exceptional Child's Early Years*. (For full group information, see HELP FOR SPECIAL CHILDREN on page 578.)

Mental Retardation Association of America (MRAA)
211 East 300 South Street, Suite 212
Salt Lake City, UT 84111
801-571-8011
Ernest H. Dean, President

Association of family, friends, and professional counselors of the mentally retarded. Aims to improve quality of life for the mentally retarded, especially through fostering group homes, educating public, and influencing public policy and legislation; supports research; aids parents and legal guardians as to rights of and services available to mentally retarded.

National Association for the Dually Diagnosed (NADD)
110 Prince Street

Kingston, NY 12401
914-331-4336
Robert J. Fletcher, Executive Director

Organization concerned with people who have been diagnosed as having both mental illness and mental retardation.

American Association on Mental Retardation (AAMR)
1719 Kalorama Road, NW
Washington, DC 20009
202-387-1968, toll-free number 800-424-3688
M. Doreen Croser, Executive Director

Organization of professionals working with people with mental retardation. Seeks to strengthen rights and public image of mentally retarded; sponsors research, training, and program development for mentally retarded people; sets standards for services for mentally retarded; seeks to educate public and influence public policy and legislation; publishes many materials, mostly for professionals.

SHARE, Inc., 213-274-5361. Raises money for special programs for mentally retarded children; funds diagnostic and counseling center, infant-development and preschool programs, special education for school-age children, art center, and sheltered workshops for retarded adults; Citizen Advocacy Program assigns a volunteer to represent each retarded person. (For full group information, see CHILD ABUSE AND NEGLECT.)

People First International (PFI), 503-362-0336. (For full group information, see HELP FOR SPECIAL CHILDREN on page 578.)

National Institute of Child Health and Development (NICHD), 301-496-5133. (For full group information, see PREGNANCY.)

National Institute of Neurological Disorders and Stroke (NINCDS), 301-496-5751. (For full group information, see BRAIN AND BRAIN DISORDERS.)

mental status examination   An organized attempt by a PHYSICIAN or PSYCHOLOGIST to assess a person's orientation to time and place and general level of functioning, intellectually, emotionally, and socially, as when a person has been through a trauma. The examiner observes general appearance, attitudes, and behavior and attempts to assess orientation by asking questions such as "What is your name?" or "What day is today?" and tests mental grasp by asking the person to complete some basic mental tasks, such as interpreting a common saying or counting backward and forward.

Merrill-Palmer Scales of Mental Development   A type of INTELLIGENCE TEST used with young children, ages 18 months to four years. A variety of items, such as pegboards, formboards, cubes, KOHS DESIGN BLOCKS, buttons, scissors, sticks, strings, and the like are used in 19 subtests, designed to indicate development in LANGUAGE SKILLS, MOTOR SKILLS, manual dexterity, and matching. The test administrator evaluates the child's performance by reference to a manual, and the child's final SCORE is converted into various forms, including a MENTAL AGE and PERCENTILE. (For help and further information, see TESTS.)

metabolic disorders   A group of GENETIC DISORDERS that cause disruption of the chemical and physical processes by which food is broken down for use in the body. Dozens of such disorders are known, many of them extremely rare, but each of them caused by a defect in the production of a single enzyme or protein. Many of them are classed as STORAGE DISORDERS, because the deficiency leads to abnormal and damaging accumulation of certain compounds in the body tissues, often especially affecting the brain. Among the diseases regarded as metabolic disorders are PHENYLKETONURIA, GALACTOSEMIA, various types of MUCOPOLYSACCHARIDOSES (including HURLER'S SYNDROME, HUNTER'S SYNDROME, and MORQUIO'S SYNDROME), MUCOLIPIDOSES, LIPID STORAGE DISEASES (including *Tay-Sachs disease* and *Gaucher's disease)*, LESCH-NYHAN SYNDROME, and GLYCOGEN STORAGE DISEASES. Diagnoses of such disorders are often made on the basis of the signs and symptoms linked with that particular disorder, often followed by LIVER FUNCTION TESTS and KIDNEY FUNCTION TESTS. Some metabolic disorders can now be detected by using various kinds of GENETIC SCREENING tests, such as AMNIOCENTESIS or CHORIONIC VILLUS SAMPLING. Sometimes treatment involves avoidance of particular types of foods or other things to which the body is sensitive; taking enzymes orally or by INJECTION can, in some metabolic disorders, help make up the deficiency. Researchers have also shown some early, experimental success in GENE THERAPY, transplanting healthy cells to replace deficient ones in some disorders, though therapy by manipulation of genes is still some distance in the future.

For help and further information

National Institute of Neurological Disorders and Stroke (NINDS), 301-496-5751. (For full group information, see BRAIN AND BRAIN DISORDERS.)

National Institute of Diabetes and Digestive and Kidney Diseases (NIDDK), 301-496-3583. (For full group information, see DIGESTIVE DISORDERS.)

National Tay-Sachs & Allied Diseases Association (NTSAD), 617-964-5508. (For full group information, see LIPID STORAGE DISEASES.)

(See also specific types of disorders, such as MUCOPOLYSACCHARIDOSES.)

metabolism   General term for all of the biochemical processes that take place in the body, including two main types of processes: conversion of foods to energy (*catabolism*), in which complex substances are broken down to simpler ones, in the process often releasing energy for the body's use, such as breaking down GLUCOSE (a sugar); and building complex substances out of simpler ones (*anabolism*), usually using energy, as in making PROTEINS out of AMINO ACIDS. Any activities, such as EXERCISE, fighting infection, or intellectual effort, increase the *metabolic rate*, which is the amount of calories needed to supply necessary energy. The amount needed when the body is healthy and completely at rest is called the *basal metabolic rate* (BMR). Abnormalities in or absence of various kinds of *enzymes*, substances that trigger metabolic activities, can lead to a wide variety of serious medical disorders, called METABOLIC DISORDERS or *inborn errors of metabolism*, such as PHENYLKETONURIA (PKU). Many VITAMINS are necessary for the basic metabolic processes to occur, and MALNUTRITION can also cause metabolic problems. (For help and further information, see METABOLIC DISORDERS; NUTRITION.)

metachromatic leukodystrophy (sulfatide lipidosis)   A type of LIPID STORAGE DISEASE.

metastasis   The medical term for a condition in which a TUMOR or CANCER is spreading beyond its original site.

metatarsus valgus (duck walk or **toeing out)**   A common abnormality in which the foot and toes point somewhat outward because of rotation of the leg or foot; generally left to correct itself but in severe cases corrected surgically. (See WALKING.)

metatarsus varus (pigeon toes or **toeing in)**   A common abnormality in which the foot and toes point somewhat inward because of rotation of the leg or foot; generally left to correct itself but in severe cases corrected surgically. (See WALKING.)

Metropolitan Achievement Tests   A series of group-administered ACHIEVEMENT TESTS for grades K to 12, paper-and-pencil tests geared to measure acquisition of general language and arithmetic skills and READING comprehension at various graded levels. Additional material is covered in a fuller series of tests (BATTERY). The results are often recorded as GRADE-EQUIVALENTS. (For help and further information, see TESTS.)

Metropolitan Readiness Tests   READINESS TESTS widely used in schools for children from prekindergarten to first grade, assessing development of skills necessary for early learning. The two levels, one for early KINDERGARTEN AND the other for first grade, partly overlap, and each may be given either individually or in a group. They are paper-and-pencil tests that can be computer scored. The result is shown as a raw SCORE, a national performance rating, and a PERCENTILE (and STANINE) ranking. Among the areas in the subtests (called *composites*) of Level I are Letter Recognition, Visual Matching, School Language and Listening, Quantitative Language, Auditory Memory, and Rhyming. Level II also includes Visual Matching and School Language and Listening and then adds Beginning Consonants, Sound-Letter Correspondences, Finding Patterns, Quantitative Concepts, and Quantitative Operations, some parts of which are optional. The Metropolitan Readiness Tests are not generally used as ADMISSIONS TESTS, but rather as aids to class placement according to levels of skills in READING, language, and mathematics, and also sometimes to aid in making a decision about PROMOTION to first or second grade. (For help and further information, see TESTS.)

metrorrhagia   A disorder association with MENSTRUATION.

microbiological test   A type of BLOOD TEST.

microcephaly   An abnormally small head, a common BIRTH DEFECT, as from exposure to ACCUTANE.

microcornea   Eyes smaller than normal. (See EYE AND VISION PROBLEMS.)

micromelia   A BIRTH DEFECT in which someone has abnormally short arms or limbs, as in some disorders such as DE LANGE SYNDROME.

micronutrient   General term for any element or compound, notably VITAMINS or MINERALS, that is necessary for proper health and functioning of the body, though only in small amounts (as opposed to MACRONUTRIENTS). Examples include *trace elements* such as IRON, COPPER, IODINE, ZINC, and FLUORIDE.

microsurgery   A highly complex, precise, and delicate type of surgery, in which the surgeon works through a special operating microscope, often employing LASER SURGERY. Microsurgery is used in a wide variety of areas, including eye surgery (as for cataracts or a cornea TRANSPLANT), ear surgery, unblocking a woman's FALLOPIAN TUBES, attempted reversal of a VASECTOMY, or reconnecting a severed body part.

middle school   An institution providing education to students between ELEMENTARY SCHOOL and HIGH SCHOOL, if the middle grades—for example, grades 5 to 8, 6 to 8, or 7 to 8—are taught in a separate set of buildings; sometimes called *junior high school* or *intermediate school*. Some school districts have only elementary and SECONDARY SCHOOLS, with no distinct middle school. School districts vary widely in their handling of middle schools. In some, students continue to spend much of their time with a single teacher in a single classroom, as in elementary school; in others, students follow the high school model, going to a different teacher and classroom for most subjects; some middle schools try a different approach, organizing students and teachers into smaller units, or teams. Though no national agreement yet exists on what subjects should be covered in the various grades, the U.S. Department of Education has formulated a model curriculum, outlined on pages 530 and 538 as JAMES MADISON ELEMENTARY SCHOOL: A MODEL CURRICULUM and JAMES MADISON HIGH SCHOOL: A MODEL CURRICULUM. The Department of Education also increasingly recommends that parents exercise choice in finding the right school for their child; see CHOOSING A SCHOOL FOR YOUR CHILD on page 514, which provides a checklist for evaluating schools. (For help and further information, see EDUCATION.)

midwife   A person, usually a woman, who assists a woman during PREGNANCY and CHILDBIRTH. Most often today, the term refers to a CERTIFIED NURSE-MIDWIFE (CNM), who meets training and licensing requirements set by various states. Midwives without formal training or certification, though they may have extensive practical experience, are called *lay midwives* and are allowed to practice in only a few states. (For help and further information, see CERTIFIED NURSE-MIDWIFE.)

milk   The nutritious fluid secreted by the mammary glands of mammals, BREASTS in humans and udders in many other mammals, such as cows or goats. Milk is made up of various nutrients, including PROTEIN, FATS, CARBOHYDRATES (primarily LACTOSE), and various VITAMINS and MINERALS. The proportion and kind of these nutrients varies somewhat between human milk and milk from other mammals (see HUMAN MILK VS. FORMULA AND OTHER MILKS and the accompanying table on page 322). Human milk itself varies from person to person and even in the same person at different times of the day and stages of nursing or with varied diets. Human milk also has important antibodies to provide early IMMUNIZATION to infants during BREASTFEEDING. In addition, it is quite digestible by most newborns, even those who a few months later will show signs of LACTOSE INTOLERANCE, or inability to digest and absorb milk's nutrients.

For infants in the first few months of life, a mother's milk generally provides all of the nutrition necessary. However, that assumes that the mother's diet is such that the milk contains the proper proportion of nutrients. Mothers with special health problems that might hinder their own ability to absorb nutrients from food, or those who are on some kinds of VEGETARIAN diets, must consult closely with their doctors or clinics to be sure that the infant is experiencing no nutritional deficiency, especially in IRON, FOLIC ACID, and VITAMINS B_{12}, D, and K.

Milks other than mother's milk often lack the right amount and balance of nutrients the newborn needs; in addition, they put a strain on the infant's immature gastrointestinal system and kidneys, sometimes causing intestinal bleeding, kidney problems (see KIDNEY AND UROLOGICAL DISORDERS), MALNUTRITION, and other health problems. It is to overcome just such problems that infant FORMULAS were developed, for feeding infants whose mothers choose not to or are unable to breastfeed. The most common formulas are based on cow's milk, made more easily digestible and more properly balanced for newborns' systems to handle, assuming it is properly prepared. If a child proves unable to digest this properly, soy-based or other formulas are also available to simulate human milk. The actual composition of commercially prepared formulas is set by the Food and Drug Administration, to ensure that they include the proper amount and balance of nutrients (though they cannot, of

Human Milk vs. Formula and Other Milks

Human milk is the food of choice for infants. It provides appropriate amounts of energy and nutrients, it contains factors that provide protection against infections, and it rarely causes allergic responses.

Breastfeeding of the newborn in the hospital increased from 24.7 percent in 1971 to 62.5 percent in 1984, but only 27.5 percent of infants are still breastfed by six months of age. Rates of breastfeeding are highest among mothers who live in the western part of the United States, have had at least some college education, are from upper income families, and are white. Numerous investigations and reports have discussed the unique values of human milk, trends in rates of breastfeeding in the United States, and methods for promoting breastfeeding.

The table below compares the average content of selected nutrients in human milk, infant formulas, and other kinds of milk used to feed full-term infants. The nutrient content of human milk reflects the maternal diet, the time of day the milk is expressed, and the length of time the mother has been breastfeeding. Protein concentrations, for example, decrease from the first week through the sixth to ninth month, and the concentrations of iron, copper, and zinc also decrease during that period.

Content of Selected Nutrients in Human Milk, Commercial Formulas, and Other Milks Used for Feeding Normal Full-Term Infants

Nutrient	Per Liter	Mature Human Milk[a] (21.6 ± 1.5 kcal/oz)	Milk-based Formulas[b] (20 kcal/oz)	Soy Protein-based Formulas (20 kcal/oz)	Whole Cow Milk (20 kcal/oz)	Skimmed Milk (11 kcal/oz)	Goat Milk (21 kcal/oz)
Protein	g	10.5 ± 0.2	15	18–21	34	35	37
Fat	g	39.0 ± 0.4	36–38	36–39	37	2	43
Carbohydrate	g	72.0 ± 0.25	69–72.3	66–69	48	50	46
Calcium	mg	280 ± 26	400–510	630–700	1,219	1,270	1,380
Phosphorus	mg	140 ± 22	300–390	420–500	959	1,050	1,140
Sodium	mEq	7.8 ± 1.7	7–10	9–15	22	23	23
Potassium	mEq	13.4 ± 0.9	14–21	19–24	38	44	54
Chloride	mEq	11.8 ± 1.7	11–14	11–15	27	31	44
Iron	mg	0.3 ± 0.1	1.1–1.5 (12–12.7)[c]	12–12.7	0.4	0.4	0.5
Estimated renal solute load	mOsm	73	92–105	122–138	226	240	269

[a]Average values with standard deviations for comparison.
[b]Values listed are subject to change. Refer to product label or packaging for current information. Milk-based formulas contain lactose, and soy protein-based formulas do not.
[c]Iron content of iron-fortified formulas.

Source: Table adapted from the American Academy of Pediatrics Committee on Nutrition, 1985.

Fat provides about 50 percent of the calories in human milk, most in the form of triglyceride, with the fatty acid pattern reflecting the maternal diet. Linoleic acid provides an average of four percent of the calories in human milk. The cholesterol content averages 20 mg/100 ml but varies considerably, and values up to 47 mg/100 ml have been reported. Lactose is the major carbohydrate. Human milk has a lower content of the amino acids tyrosine and phenylalanine and a higher content of taurine and cystine than cow milk.

The concentrations of water-soluble vitamins in human milk generally reflect the maternal dietary intake and nutritional status. Providing folate supplementation to a woman deficient in this vitamin increases milk folate levels. Vitamin B_{12} deficiency has been reported in breastfed infants whose mothers are strict vegetarians. Breastfed infants require supplemental vitamin K at birth and may require vitamin D supplementation if exposure to the sun is inadequate.

In addition to nutrients, human milk contains antibodies and other anti-infective factors that are thought to protect infants against gastrointestinal infections. For example, lactoferrin may slow bacterial growth by depriving infective organisms of necessary iron. Lysozymes may destroy bacterial cell membranes after they have been inactivated by peroxidases and ascorbic acid present in human milk. Secretory immunoglobulins in milk protect against organisms that infect the gastrointestinal tract. Perhaps most important, breast milk fosters colonization of the infant digestive tract with protective *Lactobacilli*. In addition, a number of other cellular and soluble factors may provide specific and nonspecific defenses against infectious agents.

Continued on page 323

Infant Formulas

The Food and Drug Administration specifies the nutrient composition of commercial infant formulas (CFR, Title 21, Section 107.100—Nutrient Specifications). As suggested by the table above, infant formulas are designed to simulate human milk. Manufacturers modify cow milk by replacing its fat with vegetable oils that are well absorbed, diluting it to a more appropriate concentration of minerals and other solutes, heating it to improve protein digestibility, and adding vitamins and minerals. Soy–based substitutes are available for infants who develop allergic or other sensitivities to substances in cow milk–based formulas. Soy formulas contain isolated soy protein, methionine, corn syrup or sucrose, vegetable oils, vitamins, minerals, carnitine, taurine, and stabilizers. Other products are available for infants who cannot tolerate either soy or cow milk. When properly prepared, commercial formulas support normal growth and development. Errors in preparation, however, have resulted in medical problems. Inadequately diluted formula increases the concentrations of calories, protein, and solutes circulated to the kidney for excretion and can increase levels of sodium and other substances in blood, resulting in disturbances of acid-base balance and toxic symptoms. Overdiluting the formula reduces the level of sodium and other salts in the blood, thereby causing adverse reactions, and it does not provide adequate energy and nutrients for growth.

Imitation Milks

Substitute or imitation milks inadequate in calories and nutrients are not suitable for feeding to infants. Malnutrition has been observed in infants fed a formula made of barley water, corn syrup, and whole milk, and in those fed nondairy creamer.

Cow Milk

Unmodified whole cow milk is inappropriate to feed to young infants because it causes occult bleeding from the gastrointestinal tract in some infants, leading to anemia and, occasionally, to allergies. Its lipids are less digestible than the lipids of human milk or most vegetable oils, and its concentrations of minerals and other solutes nearly exceed the excretory capacity of the immature kidney. Intestinal blood loss has been noted in younger infants and those who have consumed large volumes of milk, although this usually presents no problem after the age of six months or so. As indicated in the table above, cow milk has a higher renal solute load than either human milk or infant formulas. By six months of age, the kidneys of most normal infants have matured and can excrete excess solutes sufficiently. If infants receive at least one-third of their calories from foods and consume no more than one liter of milk per day, there is little disadvantage to the use of whole cow milk after six months of age. Sometimes, however, infants consuming whole cow milk may not receive adequate dietary iron to meet their nutritional requirements.

For infants, 2-percent and nonfat milks are deficient in energy, essential fatty acids, and certain vitamins, and they contain excessive protein and minerals per calorie provided. They are not recommended during the first year of life. When supplemented with vitamin C and iron, evaporated milk formula (3 ounces of evaporated milk, 4.5 ounces of water, 2 teaspoons of corn syrup) is an acceptable, low-cost substitute for infants less than six months of age.

Goat Milk

Goat milk should be used carefully during infancy because it is low in iron, folate, and vitamins B, C, and D. It requires supplementation with these nutrients. As shown in the table above, solute concentration is even higher than in cow milk.

Source: *The Surgeon General's Report on Nutrition and Health.* Rocklin, CA: Prima, 1988.

---

course, reproduce the immunization that a mother's milk gives).

After the baby is about six months old, the body has matured, and SOLID FOODS generally begin to be introduced into the diet. Then cow's milk becomes an extremely important part of a child's diet, a major source of CALCIUM; public health experts recommend that young children be fed whole milk, not skimmed milk, which provides insufficient nutrition. (For help and further information, see BREASTFEEDING; VITAMINS; MINERALS.)

minerals Elements that must be in the diet for the proper health and functioning of the body. At least 13 of them have been identified as necessary. Those needed in relatively large amounts are called MACRONUTRIENTS or *macrominerals*, including CALCIUM, POTASSIUM, MAGNESIUM, SODIUM, CHLORIDE, PHOSPHORUS, and SULFUR. Those needed in relatively small amounts are called *microminerals* or MICRONUTRIENTS, including IRON, COPPER, IODINE, ZINC, and FLUORIDE.

While these elements are vital to the body, excess amounts can cause severe health problems, even death, for some of these minerals are dangerous poisons in concentration and others can cause disruption or failure of vital body organs, such as the heart, kidneys, and liver. Public health officials advise parents not to give their children any mineral supplements without first consulting their doctor or clinic. The Food and Drug Administration has established RECOMMENDED DAILY ALLOWANCES (RDAs) for key minerals, which include increased amounts for women during PREGNANCY, especially of IRON, and for infants and young children (see MINERALS FOR GROWING BODIES, on page 324). For tables showing the suggested amounts, see RECOMMENDED DAILY ALLOWANCES.

Minerals for Growing Bodies

Minerals and the Fetus

Mineral requirements of the fetus, estimated from studies on fetal body composition, seem to be higher during the last few weeks of pregnancy than at any other time during prenatal or postnatal development. Little is known, however, about the specific needs for individual minerals. In experimental animals, prenatal calcium deficiency causes rickets in the infant. In animals and humans, iron is stored in fetal red blood cells, and term infants are born with ample reserves. Because premature infants have a smaller red cell mass, they are at increased risk for iron deficiency at birth.

Minerals and Infants

Although infant requirements for micronutrients are not as well defined as those for energy and protein, RDAs have been established for many vitamins and minerals. The bioavailability of minerals generally is greater from human milk than it is from formulas. The RDA for calcium is designed to meet the need of formula-fed infants, who retain 25 to 30 percent of the calcium in cow milk–based formula. Breastfed infants retain about 65 percent of the calcium consumed. Studies suggest that the bioavailability of zinc from human milk is 41 percent, compared with 28 percent from cow milk, 31 percent from cow milk formulas, and 14 percent from soy formula.

Iron deficiency is the most common nutrient deficiency in infancy [see ANEMIA]. Rapidly growing infants absorb 49 percent of the iron in human milk, 10 percent of the iron in cow milk, and 3 percent of the iron in iron-fortified formulas. For this reason, some authorities believe that breastfed infants do not need additional iron until the age of about six months. Current recommendations are that infants begin consuming iron-fortified cereals at four to six months of age to prevent anemia. Because human milk is low in fluoride and because enamel development in permanent teeth is significant during the first year of life, a fluoride supplement may be desirable for children who do not have access to adequately fluoridated drinking water. Requirements for other minerals have been reviewed.

Minerals and Children

Inadequate intakes of vitamins and minerals will be reflected in slow growth rates, inadequate mineralization of bones, and very low body reserves of micronutrients. The most common mineral deficiency, iron, appears to be declining, although children from low-income families are at greater risk. With the relatively low prevalence of clinical signs of vitamin and mineral deficiency in the general population of children, there is no evidence that supplementation is necessary for this group. Although vitamin and mineral supplements increase the quantity of these nutrients in the diet, they have not been shown to improve biochemical indices of nutrient status in children who are already well nourished. For this reason, recommendations on vitamin and mineral supplementation for children target those at high risk, those from socioeconomically deprived families, and those who have poor appetites or eating habits.

Source: *The Surgeon General's Report on Nutrition and Health*. Rocklin, CA: Prima, 1988.

For help and further information

Food and Drug Administration (FDA), 301-443-3170. (For full group information, see NUTRITION; DRUG REACTIONS AND INTERACTIONS.)

(See also VITAMINS.)

minicourse   A short course, as opposed to one lasting a full school TERM, such as a one-to-three-week course in the period between two college SEMESTERS.

minilaparotomy   A type of medical procedure for female STERILIZATION akin to TUBAL LIGATION.

minimal (or minimum) brain dysfunction (MBD)   A minor delay or disorder in the development of MOTOR SKILLS and ability to use the senses appropriately; a general term that has often been used (though mostly in the past) to describe disorders now called LEARNING DISABILITIES and ATTENTION DEFICIT HYPERACTIVITY DISORDER (ADHD).

minimum (or minimal) competency testing   The use of a testing program to ensure that no students will be promoted from one grade to the next, or graduated from HIGH SCHOOL, without demonstrating that they have acquired certain minimum skills and knowledge. The aim is to ensure that students will not receive automatic PROMOTION and graduate functionally illiterate (see ILLITERACY). But use of ACHIEVEMENT TESTS for minimum competency testing has been criticized because it may cause general educational standards to be lowered, as teachers focus on preparation for the minimum test. Even so, as part of a BACK-TO-BASICS move, many states have adopted some form of the program, often locally optional; most test every second or third year, not each year. A similar approach designed to assure that teachers meet basic standards is called *teacher competency testing*.

For help and further information

Minimum Competency Achievement Testing, R.M. Jaeger and C.K. Tittle, eds. Berkeley, CA: McCutchan, 1980.

Minimal Competency Testing, by Peter W. Airasian et al. Englewood Cliffs, NJ: Educational Technology Publications, 1979.

mini-pill   A kind of BIRTH-CONTROL PILL.

Minnesota Multiphasic Personality Inventory (MMPI)   A test widely used to gather information on personality, mental condition, and attitudes in people age 16 or older. Existing in various forms for administration to groups or individuals, the test consists of hundreds of true–false items designed to highlight aspects of personality, including those that may be related to MENTAL DISORDERS. The results are graphed on a personality profile sheet. (For help and further information, see TESTS.)

minor   A person under the legally defined age of adulthood (MAJORITY) and therefore normally required to be in the CUSTODY of parent, FOSTER PARENT, GUARDIAN, or other legally responsible SUPERVISION; in legal terms, a CHILD or INFANT unable to act as an adult in many respects, as in signing a contract. The age defining a minor varies by state, but in the federal 1974 Child Abuse Prevention and Treatment Act, "child" is specified as someone under 18. In some states, a HANDICAPPED adult may be legally classed as a minor. Minors who have been freed from parental control and care, as by marriage or military service, are called EMANCIPATED MINORS. The term *minor* refers to legal ability to act as an adult; by contrast a JUVENILE is someone who is not yet old enough to be treated as an adult under criminal law.

MINS   Abbreviation for minors in need of SUPERVISION.

mirror sign   Standing in front of a mirror or other shining surface for an unusually long time; a SIGN that is generally associated with MENTAL DISORDERS such as SCHIZOPHRENIA.

misarticulation   Alternate name for a type of communication disorder (see COMMUNICATION SKILLS AND DISORDERS).

miscarriage   The loss of a FETUS before the 28th week of GESTATION; an involuntary termination of a PREGNANCY, often medically called a spontaneous abortion. (Death of a fetus at a later stage is called a STILLBIRTH.) Miscarriage is extremely common, affecting at least 10 percent of all pregnancies, and perhaps as many as 30 percent, since many of these spontaneous abortions occur in the first 10 weeks, often without the woman even being aware that she is pregnant.

Most miscarriages result from CHROMOSOMAL ABNORMALITIES and GENETIC DISORDERS so severe that they are incompatible with life, though exposure to ENVIRONMENTAL HAZARDS, such as poisons and RADIATION, severe illness of the MOTHER, and AUTOIMMUNE DISORDERS in the mother may also trigger loss of the fetus. Later in the pregnancy, miscarriage can also be caused by an INCOMPETENT CERVIX, fibroid TUMORS in the UTERUS, and structural abnormalities, but public health experts say it is very rarely caused by injury or overactivity.

Warning signs of miscarriage are bleeding, cramping, and dizziness. Sometimes bed rest can save the pregnancy. But often the spontaneous abortion, once started, cannot be stopped. Bleeding becomes heavier, the CERVIX dilates, the AMNIOTIC FLUID spills out, and the fetus and its associated tissues, such as the PLACENTA and amniotic sac, are expelled. This would be termed a *complete abortion*. Sometimes the fetus dies but is not expelled, though the associated tissues die, the uterus returns to its normal size, and the symptoms of pregnancy cease. This is called a *missed abortion*, and the dead fetus and tissue must be removed in order to avoid infection and other disorders in the mother. In most cases of miscarriage, doctors will perform an operation called a *dilation and curettage (D & C)*, in which they remove the dead tissue. Before attempting another conception, doctors advise couples to let themselves recover physically and emotionally for a few months after a miscarriage while they go through the grieving process. Though one miscarriage may not necessarily signal trouble in later pregnancies, they would medically be treated as HIGH-RISK PREGNANCIES for the safety of mother and baby.

For help and further information

SHARE (Source of Help in Airing and Resolving Experiences), 618-234-2415 or -2120, ext. 1430. (For full group information, see DEATH.)

Pregnancy and Infant Loss Center (PILC), 612-473-9372. (For full group information, see DEATH.)

Resolve Through Sharing, 608-785-0530, ext. 3675. (For full group information, see DEATH.)

RESOLVE, Inc., 617-484-2424. Publishes fact sheet, *Miscarriage: Medical Facts*. (For full group information, see INFERTILITY.)

Other reference sources

Tender Miscarriage: An Epiphany, by Paula Saffire. Tucson, AZ: Harbinger House, 1989.
Nothing to Cry About, by Barbara J. Berg. New York: Bantam, 1983.
Surviving Pregnancy Loss, by Rochelle Friedman, M.D., and Bonnie Gradstein. Boston: Little, Brown, 1982.
When Pregnancy Fails: Families Coping with Miscarriage, Stillbirth and Infant Death, by Susan Borg and Judith Lasker. Boston: Beacon, 1981.
(See also DEATH; INFERTILITY; ABORTION; PREGNANCY.)

miscue   An error that a person makes in READING, such as dropping a word, adding a word, or substituting one word for another.

missing children   Children who have disappeared from the home of the parent or parents who legally have CUSTODY of them. Because disappearance of children, temporary or permanent, causes enormous anguish, a great deal of furor has surrounded the issue in recent years. More heat than light was often shed, however, until 1990 when a three-year study on missing children, under the auspices of the Congress and Justice Department, clarified the nature of the problem.

The results were surprising. Although many parents' greatest fear is that a child will be kidnapped by a stranger, such abductions in fact accounted for only a very small proportion of missing children, about 200 to 300 a year, while another 3,200 to

4,600 children a year were temporarily abducted by someone outside the family, often for purposes of sexual assault.

These figures were dwarfed by the more than 350,000 kidnappings by parents or other family members, often in dissatisfaction over custody arrangements. Many of these children were taken to undisclosed locations, often out of state, though in most family abductions the children were returned within a week.

Beyond even that are the 450,000 children who run away from home each year, many of them with no secure place to stay, and the 125,000 children who are thrown out of the home by their parents, with no other arrangements made for their care. Many of these so-called runaways and throwaways, some of whom later return home, are victims of CHILD ABUSE AND NEGLECT. In addition, over 430,000 children at some point during each year become lost (generally for less than a day), injured and unable to return home, or otherwise missing.

These numbers are truly staggering and reflect enormous disruption and dislocation in the lives of the children involved. They also suggest that social emphasis has been somewhat misplaced. Certainly, parents and children's organizations are right to be concerned about possible kidnapping or abuse by strangers or others outside the family and to prepare children to deal with such eventualities. (For help on that, see organizations below; also LATCHKEY CHILD; CHILD ABUSE AND NEGLECT.)

But for prevention, as the figures make clear, it is perhaps more important for divorced or separated parents to work out any differences between them, putting the best interests of the children ahead of any custody or related parental dispute they may have; to keep lines of communication open with their children during the difficult period of ADOLESCENCE, rather than allowing conflict to result in teenagers leaving home; and to be alert to possible child abuse within the home or local situation that might cause a child to run away.

Parents considering kidnapping their children over a custody dispute should realize that, under both the UNIFORM CHILD CUSTODY JURISDICTION ACT and the more general CLEAN HANDS DOCTRINE, they may be risking any possibility of later gaining more favorable custody arrangements. Under a federal law labeled Title 18, Section 1201A, parents are, however, exempt from kidnapping charges regarding their children under 18, a state of affairs many custodial parents who have lost their children are trying to change.

For families with missing children, the focus is very different—on finding, identifying, making contact with, helping, and obtaining the return of their children. In this, many of the organizations below can help. Some are geared to help families find children who are lost or kidnapped. Because young children change so much as they develop, some parents prepare fingerprints, footprints, identification bracelets or buttons, and even stored samples of DNA so that if missing children are found years later, they can be identified with certainty. Other organizations provide a contact point between runaways and their families, serving to reopen a dialogue while shielding the runaway's location, if desired, and to provide needed services, as for health care or DRUG ABUSE treatment.

For help and further information

On Missing Children in General

National Center for Missing and Exploited Children (NCMEC)
2101 Wilson Boulevard, Suite 550
Arlington, VA 22201
703-235-3900, toll-free number (voice; U.S. and Canada) 800-843-5678; toll-free number (for hearing impaired; U.S. and Canada) 800-826-7653
Ernest Allen, President

Organization that acts as clearinghouse for parents and agencies searching for missing children. Seeks to influence legislation and public policy; helps individuals arrange for return of the children, once found; publishes various print and video materials, including handbook on parental kidnappings and material on searching techniques.

Missing Children . . . Help Center (MCHC)
410 Ware Boulevard, Suite 400
Tampa, Florida 33619
813-623-5437, toll-free hotline 800-USA-KIDS [872-5437]
Ivana DiNova, Executive Director

Organization seeking to serve as contact point for missing children, their parents, private and public agencies, and other interested parties. Collects data on missing children and on child-search agencies nationwide; seeks to educate public and influence legislation and government policy.

Missing Children of America (MCA)
P.O. Box 10-193B
Anchorage, AK 99510
907-248-7300
Dolly Whaley, Executive Director

Organization to help locate missing children. Advises parents on preparation of identification packages and obtaining of media coverage; maintains computer files and seeks to educate public and children about problem; publishes various materials.

Child Find of America (CFA)
P.O. Box 277
New Paltz, NY 12561
914-255-1848, toll-free number 800-I-AM-LOST [426-5678]
Carolyn Zogg, Executive Director

Network of individuals, many of them parents of missing children, and groups. Aims to provide a contact point for separated children and parents, working with other concerned organizations around the country to pool information in a registry of missing children; publishes newsletter and annual directory with physical descriptions and photographs.

Search Reports, Inc./Central Registry of the Missing
345 Boulevard
Hasbrouck Heights, NJ 07604

201-288-4445
Charles A. Sutherland, President

Organization aiming to locate missing people. Collates flyers on missing persons and data on unidentified corpses; resulting *National Missing Persons Report* is sent to various public and private agencies and institutions, including hospitals, runaway shelters, and counseling services.

Hug-A-Tree and Survive (HAT)
6465 Lance Way
San Diego, CA 92120
619-286-7536
Jacqueline Heet, Executive Officer

Program for training young children on what to do if they are lost—that is, hug a tree until they are rescued. Produces slide show for training chldren.

For Runaway Children

National Runaway Switchboard (NRS)
3080 North Lincoln
Chicago, IL 60657
Toll-free number 800-621-4000
Laura Thomas, Executive Director

Confidential switchboard service for runaways and their families. Can convey messages from runaways to parents without revealing location, or set up conferences between them; provides referrals to social services nationwide, including shelters, drug treatment centers, and other hotlines; partly funded by the U.S. Health and Human Services Office of Youth Development.

Runaway Hotline (RH)
Governor's Office
P.O. Box 12428
Austin, TX 78711
Toll-free number (U.S. except TX) 800-231-6946; toll-free number (TX only) 800-392-3352

Confidential switchboard service for runaways, allowing them to pass messages to their families without revealing their location. Operates 24-hour, seven-day-a-week hotline; provides referral to social services, including medical and legal help, transportation, and shelter.

National Network of Runaway and Youth Services (NNRYS)
1400 I Street NW, Suite 330
Washington, DC 20005
202-682-4114
Della M. Hughes, Executive Director

Organization of agencies, programs, and other groups dealing with runaways and troubled adolescents. Gathers and disseminates information; seeks to educate public and influence public policy and legislation, especially to strengthen services to families of troubled youths; publishes various materials, including bimonthly *Network News* and *To Whom Do They Belong? A Profile of America's Runaway and Homeless Youth*.

Mothers Without Custody (MWOC), 713-840-1622. (For full group information, see CUSTODY.)

Defense for Children International—United States of America (DCI-USA), 212-353-0951. Promotes stronger protection for the rights of children under the UN Convention on the Rights of the Child, as in parental kidnapping. (For full group information, see CHILD ABUSE AND NEGLECT.)

Other reference sources

For Parents

Understanding Survivors of Abuse: Stories of Homeless and Runaway Adolescents, by Jane Levine Powers and Barbara Weiss Jaklitsch. Lexington, MA: Lexington, 1989.

A Cry of Absence: The True Story of a Father's Search for His Kidnapped Children, by Andrew Ward. New York: Viking, 1988.

How to Deal with a Parental Kidnapping, by Margaret Strickland. Moore Haven, FL: Rainbow, 1983.

Children in the Crossfire: The Tragedy of Parental Kidnapping, by Sally Abrahms. New York: Atheneum, 1983.

Have You Seen My Son?, by Jack Olsen. New York: Atheneum, 1982. Novel about parental kidnapping.

Stolen Children, by John Gill. New York: Seaview, 1981.

Somewhere Child, by Bonnie Lee Black. New York: Viking, 1981.

Legal Kidnapping, by Anna Demeter. Boston: Beacon, 1977.

For or By Kids

Missing Children, by JoAnn Bren Guernsey. New York: Crestwood/Macmillan, 1990. For "reluctant" young readers.

Runaways: In Their Own Words Kids Talking About Living on the Streets, by Jeffrey Artenstein. New York: Tor, 1990.

Mittelschmerz The slight abdominal pain some women feel at the time of OVULATION.

mixed dominance (cross-dominance) A condition in which DOMINANCE in hands, feet, and eyes is not clearly established on one side of the body or the other.

ML Abbreviation for MUCOLIPIDOSES.

MMPI Abbreviation for MINNESOTA MULTIPHASIC PERSONALITY INVENTORY.

MMR vaccine Abbreviation for MEASLES-MUMPS-RUBELLA VACCINE.

modalities General term referring to the senses by which a child takes in information for learning, the *preferred modality* being the sense that a child uses most easily and efficiently. These modalities are sometimes described as VAKT (for visual, auditory, kinesthetic, and tactile); but sometimes the term HAPTIC is used to refer to physical, hands-on learning, in a sense combining kinesthetic and tactile. (See LEARNING STYLE; SENSORY MODES.)

mode   A type of AVERAGE; also an alternate term for MODALITIES or SENSORY MODES.

modeling   A type of LEARNING STYLE that involves teaching by example, expecting that children will imitate the teacher. (For examples, see TEACHING YOUNG CHILDREN: GUIDELINES AND ACTIVITIES, on page 544.)

model school   Alternate term for LABORATORY SCHOOL.

mole   Popular name for the skin blemish called a NEVUS.

mommy track   A slower promotion track to which some women are shunted on their return to work after MATERNITY LEAVE.

Mongolian spot   A large area of skin colored pale blue, found in some relatively dark-skinned infants, generally on the buttocks or lower spine; a benign kind of SKIN DISORDER that usually disappears or becomes less obvious as the child grows older. Parents must be sure that others do not mistake the area for a large bruise and a sign of possible child abuse (see CHILD ABUSE AND NEGLECT).

moniliasis   Alternate name for the fungal infection CANDIDIASIS.

mononucleosis (infectious mononucleosis or "mono")   An acute infection generally caused by the *Epstein-Barr virus* (EBV), which is related to the HERPES SIMPLEX virus and (like herpes) remains in the body for life. The virus reproduces in the salivary glands and is probably spread through saliva, as during kissing (hence, its nickname, the "kissing disease") or sharing drinks, but it is not highly contagious. Much is unknown about mononucleosis, including how long a person remains infectious and why infections are often extremely mild or even symptomless in young children but are severe and long-lasting in people between 15 and 30, where perhaps 70 to 80 percent of the cases are found. Symptoms start slowly, characteristically including FEVER, sore throat, and "swollen glands" (actually lymphatic tissue acting as filters in the IMMUNE SYSTEM) in the neck, but also under the arms and in the groin. Often the spleen is enlarged, and sometimes the liver (see LIVER PROBLEMS) as well, and secondary bacterial infections may also result, especially since immune-system activity is somewhat depressed. In itself, mononucleosis is not generally a severe disease, but the Public Health Service reports:

> There are rare cases of death from the [mononucleosis] infection, following airway obstruction, rupture of the spleen, inflammation of the heart or tissues surrounding the heart, or central nervous system involvement. Steroid drugs are used to treat these complications. If the spleen should rupture, surgery to remove it, and transfusions and other therapy for shock, must be initiated immediately.

Mononucleosis is difficult to diagnose at first because its symptoms are vague and resemble those of other ailments. The main concern is often to distinguish mononucleosis from the generally more serious HEPATITIS, which can be done through a BLOOD TEST to detect antibodies to the EB virus. Mononucleosis cannot be treated, only its symptoms, though associated infections may respond to antibiotics. In years past, the standard treatment was bed rest for four to six weeks and limited activity for three months after symptoms disappeared. Today, however, doctors in general recommend that activity levels be limited on the basis of the individual's symptoms, with the proviso that strenuous exercise should be avoided, because it can damage an enlarged spleen.

For help and further information

National Institute of Allergy and Infectious Diseases (NIAID), 301-496-5717. Publishes brochure *Infectious Mononucleosis*. (For full group information, see ALLERGY.)

monounsaturated fatty acids   A type of FAT derived mostly from plant sources.

monozygotic   A medical term referring to identical twins who grew from one fertilized egg, or ZYGOTE; literally, "one egg." (For further information, see MULTIPLE BIRTH.)

Montessori method   An approach to the EDUCATION of PRESCHOOL-age children developed by Italian physician-educator Maria Montessori, featuring special materials for teaching numbers, letters, and abstract ideas. Materials are designed to foster independent thinking and creativity and to enhance a child's use of the various SENSORY MODES or MODALITIES for learning, in what is called *sensory education*. From Italy the Montessori approach spread worldwide, with small Montessori schools springing up locally in many countries; many follow Montessori's original methods, while those in the United States were somewhat modified. In recent years, Montessori approaches have been widely used in public schools, as well.

For help and further information

American Montessori Society (AMS)
150 Fifth Avenue
New York, NY 10011
212-924-3209
Bretta Weiss, Executive Director

Organization of educators, parents, schools, and other interested individuals and groups interested in Montessori's methods of teaching young children. Sets standards and offers accreditation; advises operating schools and aids new schools in getting started; maintains library; publishes various materials, including quarterly magazine *Constructive Triangle* and annual *School Directory*.

Other reference sources

Modern Montessori at Home: A Creative Teaching Guide for Parents of Children Six Through Nine Years of Age. Rossmoor, CA: American Montessori Consulting, 1989.

(See also PRESCHOOL; EDUCATION.)

mood disorders A general classification of MENTAL DISORDERS that involve prolonged disturbance of mood, coloring the person's outlook, such as DEPRESSION and BIPOLAR DISORDERS (popularly called *manic-depression*); formerly called *affective disorders*. Mood disorders sometimes occur in connection with other mental or physical disorders. (For help and further information, see MENTAL DISORDERS.)

morbidity The condition of having a disease or disorder. In medicine, the morbidity ratio is the number of people with a particular disease or disorder (such as CEREBRAL PALSY, DOWN'S SYNDROME, or MEASLES) compared to the total number of people in a group (such as all babies, only LOW-BIRTH-WEIGHT babies, or all female babies).

morning sickness Nausea and VOMITING that often accompany the early months of PREGNANCY. (For help and further information, see VOMITING.)

Moro's reflex (startle reflex) The automatic response of a baby—on hearing a loud noise or when the head is left momentarily unsupported—to swing arms outward and then together, as if embracing something, to flex the legs, and often to cry. A type of PRIMITIVE REFLEX found only in babies, it normally disappears in three to four months.

Morquio's syndrome (MPS IV) A GENETIC DISORDER resulting from a defect in a specific enzyme; one of a group of disorders called MUCOPOLYSACCHARIDOSES (MPS). Characteristics of Morquio's syndrome are retarded growth often resulting in DWARFISM and abnormal muscular and skeletal development (*chondrodysplasia*) leading to KYPHOSIS (excessive curvature of the spine), enlarged breastbone (*sternum*), fused or missing vertebrae, and knock-knees. The syndrome is often first diagnosed, when the child is learning to walk, by the unusual waddling gait. (For help and further information, see MUCOPOLYSACCHARIDOSES.)

mortality rate The number of people who die, on the average, in a specified group of a certain number, such as one per 1,000 newborns. (See INFANT MORTALITY; MATERNAL MORTALITY; DEATH.)

mother The woman who has PARENTS' RIGHTS and PARENTS' RESPONSIBILITIES toward a child, especially a MINOR. The woman whose GENETIC INHERITANCE contributed directly to the child and who is one of the child's nearest BLOOD RELATIVES is the child's biological mother (see BIOLOGICAL PARENTS), also called *natural mother* or *birth mother*. With some new reproductive techniques, the question of who the biological mother is can be clouded, as when an EMBRYO from one woman's body is transferred to another woman's UTERUS to grow and develop (see EMBRYO TRANSFER). If the biological mother gives up her rights and allows her child to be placed for ADOPTION, a female who adopts the child is called the *adoptive mother*.

If a pregnant woman is unmarried, as an *unwed mother* she has the option of having an ABORTION without getting the father's consent, though in some states a pregnant adolescent under the AGE OF CONSENT may need to notify or obtain the consent of her parents or the court before having an abortion. As laws and legal precedents change, women are increasingly becoming responsible and accountable for the health of the FETUS; some women have even been charged in criminal court for failing to heed medical advice that could harm or kill the fetus, though the issue has just in recent years begun to be addressed in the courts and is far from resolution.

Immediately after the birth, in most cases, the mother and newborn begin to form a specially close attachment called BONDING. In some cases where this does not occur, for whatever reason, lack of a warm and stimulating relationship between mother and child (or another older person and the child) can lead to MATERNAL DEPRIVATION SYNDROME, a complex of symptoms including general physical and MENTAL RETARDATION, a condition sometimes called FAILURE TO THRIVE.

Traditionally, motherhood has, along with the flag and apple pie, been almost a sacred status in the eyes of many, and it was long assumed that the rightful place of a mother was at home caring for her child. But social conditions have changed. While some women still stay at home during the early years of their children, many others choose to return to work soon after a child's birth. And many other mothers, including some who might wish to stay home, find themselves forced by economics to go to work, either because a marriage breaks up and they find themselves relatively impoverished *single parents* or because the family economy requires two incomes to stay afloat.

In any case, the role of the mother and the relationship between child and mother is in a considerable state of flux. The mother still tends to be the PSYCHOLOGICAL PARENT, the one closest to the child's aspirations and fears, but much of the child's waking, growing, and learning hours are spent in the care of others, whether babysitters, nannies, or other CHILD-CARE workers. Both mothers and FATHERS, then, have to carefully think through what kind of approach they want others to take toward the child and what kind of stimulation the child should have so that the child is presented with a relatively consistent, and consistently loving and stimulating, view of the world.

For help and further information

Mothers at Home
P.O. Box 2208
Merrifield, VA 22116
703-352-2292

Organization of and for mothers who choose to stay at home and raise their children. Aims to raise morale and image of mothers at home; gathers and disseminates information; publishes monthly *Welcome Home*.

Parents Without Partners (PWP), 301-588-9354; toll-free number 800-637-7974. (For full group information, see CUSTODY.)

(See also PREGNANCY; CHILDBIRTH; CUSTODY; CHILD SUPPORT; FAMILY; also the PARENT'S BOOKSHELF on page 566 for books on motherhood.)

motor disorder   Alternate name for a type of communication disorder (see COMMUNICATION SKILLS AND DISORDERS).

motor neuron diseases   General term for a group of diseases involving damage to the nerves that supply communication between muscles and nerves and resulting in weakness and wasting (*atrophy*) of the muscles. The group includes *amyotrophic lateral sclerosis (ALS or Lou Gehrig's disease)*, which appears during middle age, and *spinal muscular atrophies*, which mostly affect children.

The most common of the spinal muscular atrophies is labeled "Type 1," also called *infantile spinal muscular atrophy*, or *Werdnig-Hoffmann disease*. This condition involves HYPOTONIA (floppiness), PARALYSIS, and deformities appearing in the first few months of life, often apparent at birth. Infants have difficulty SUCKING, swallowing (DYSPHAGIA), and breathing, and they generally die in early childhood, often from respiratory illnesses, though some survive with severe disabilities into their teens. Infantile spinal muscular atrophy is a GENETIC DISORDER of an AUTOSOMAL RECESSIVE type.

Other forms that appear less often or somewhat later are *Type 2, or intermediate spinal muscular atrophy; Type 3, juvenile spinal muscular atrophy, or Wohlfart-Kugelberg-Welander disease;* and *benign congenital hypotonia (Aran-Duchenne type)*.

For help and further information

Amyotrophic Lateral Sclerosis Association (ALSA)
21021 Ventura Boulevard, Suite 321
Woodland Hills, CA 91364
818-340-7500
Rodney L. Houts, President
Organization of people concerned with ALS. Raises funds and supports research; provides information and makes referrals; publishes various materials, including newsletter, book *Managing ALS: Managing Muscular Weakness*, and brochures *What Is ALS? Some Questions and Answers, Managing ALS: Finding Help,* and *Home Care for the Patient with Amyotrophic Lateral Sclerosis.*

Families of S. M. A.
P.O. Box 1465
Highland Park, IL 60035
312-432-5551
Audrey N. Lewis, Executive Director
Organization of people concerned with spinal muscular atrophy, including adult progressive S.M.A. (Aran-Duchenne type), juvenile S.M.A. (Kugelberg-Welander disease), benign congenital hypotonia, and Werdnig-Hoffmann disease. Provides support for affected individuals and families; raises money for research; seeks to educate public; publishes various materials, including newsletter, audiovisuals *Living with S.M.S.* and slide presentation, and booklet on Werdnig-Hoffmann disease.

National Institute of Neurological Disorders and Stroke (NINDS), 301-496-5751. Publishes *ALS: Lou Gehrig's Disease:*

Hope Through Research. (For full group information, see BRAIN AND BRAIN DISORDERS.)

Muscular Dystrophy Association, 212-586-0808. Publishes brochures *Learning to Live with Neuromuscular Disease: A Message for Parents of Children with a Neuromuscular Disease, Living with Progressive Childhood Illness: Parental Management of Neuromuscular Disease*, and *ALS: Amytophic Lateral Sclerosis*. (For full group information, see MUSCULAR DYSTROPHY.)

Other reference sources
Health Care U.S.A., by Jean Carper. New York: Prentice Hall, 1987. Resource for general and specific health-care information, including neuromuscular diseases such as muscular dystrophy, amyotrophic lateral sclerosis (ALS or Lou Gehrig's disease), myasthenia gravis, and ataxia; lists Muscular Dystrophy Association research and treatment clinics, ALS Association research and treatment centers, government research and treatment centers, and other information. (See also MUSCULAR DYSTROPHY.)

motor skills   Skills relating to motion, involving both the muscles that carry out the motion and the brain and nervous system that direct the activity (see BRAIN AND BRAIN DISORDERS).

Gross motor skills involve the large muscles of the arms, legs, torso, and feet. For a growing child, many of the major DEVELOPMENTAL MILESTONES, such as crawling, sitting up, and WALKING, are gross motor skills. So are the even more complex skills of body control and rhythm, as in jumping, hopping, skipping, moving rhythmically to music, throwing, kicking, pushing, pulling, and lifting things; *bilateral movement*, or using both arms and hands at the same time; *cross-lateral movement*, or using opposite arms and legs at the same time; *crossing the midline*, as in using a right hand to pick up a toy placed at the left side; and balance. The CHART OF NORMAL DEVELOPMENT (on page 507) lists the age at which each major milestone is reached, *on the average*, in each of various skill areas.

Closely related to the gross motor skills are SPATIAL ORIENTATION and SPATIAL RELATIONS. Children who have LEARNING DISABILITIES and some other DEVELOPMENTAL DISORDERS may show problems in gross motor skills by reaching developmental milestones later than most, by jerky or uncoordinated movements, and by clumsiness, as with tripping, bumping into things, or dropping things. Some may also need ORTHOPEDIC DEVICES to help provide the strength and balance to move about.

Fine motor skills are those that use the small muscles of the fingers, toes, wrists, lips, and tongue. Among the developmental milestones involving fine motor skills are grasping an object and putting it in the mouth, picking up an object with thumb and one finger, transferring an object from one hand to another, building a tower, putting rings on sticks or pegs into peg boards, scribbling, turning knobs, throwing a small ball, and painting with sweeping strokes. Children who have learning disabilities and some other developmental disorders may have trouble handling small objects, such as buttons and snaps, tying

---

It's Rock Time

Babies love to be rocked. For years parents have rocked their babies in cradles, carriages, and in their arms. Rocking chairs, an old standby, are fun for both baby and parents.

Another way of "rocking" babies has been rediscovered by many modern parents—the papoose carrier. The new and varied versions of the carrier are handy for giving babies both the sense of motion and the close body contact they seem to need. Now you often see infants snuggled happily in canvas slings carried on the backs or chests of mothers and fathers as they go about their errands or enjoy recreational activities.

Babies also enjoy wind-up canvas swings, some of which have built-in music boxes. In this way, a baby can swing and sway even when it's inconvenient for someone to hold her or him.

As babies grow older, they often enjoy bouncing up and down under their own steam in canvas "jumpers," and when they graduate to the toddler stage, rocking horses can be a real joy.

Source: *Stimulating Baby Senses*, by Marilyn Sargent, in consultation with National Institute of Mental Health scientists. Washington, DC: Government Printing Office, 1978. Part of the Caring About Kids series. For more from this pamphlet, see BOTTLEFEEDING, COMMUNICATION SKILLS AND DISORDERS, MOTOR SKILLS, and VISUAL SKILLS.

---

and untying ties, using scissors smoothly, holding pencils and crayons securely, gripping or picking up small things between thumb and index finger, copying vertical or horizontal lines or circles, using rhythm instruments, or stringing beads. They may also lack the fine motor coordination between lips and tongue needed for clear speech and so may sometimes be reluctant to talk. The inability to produce in sequence the movements necessary to draw shapes and figures or to copy words and letters is called *apraxia*.

Closely related to the fine motor skills are the VISUAL SKILLS, especially those sometimes called the *perceptual motor skills*, involving hand–eye, body–eye, or visual-motor coordination. Among the other kinds of skills crucial in the development of the child are AUDITORY SKILLS, COGNITIVE SKILLS, SELF-HELP SKILLS, SOCIAL SKILLS, and communication skills (see COMMUNICATION SKILLS AND DISORDERS). Children develop at individual and varying paces, but can benefit from activities designed to enhance their natural development. In TEACHING YOUNG CHILDREN: GUIDELINES AND ACTIVITIES (on page 544), parents will find activities designed to develop children's skills in various areas. (See also EXERCISE.)

MPS Abbreviation for MUCOPOLYSACCHARIDOSES, a group of GENETIC DISORDERS involving defective enzymes; among the best-known of these disorders are HURLER'S SYNDROME (MPS I), HUNTER'S SYNDROME (MPS II), and MORQUIO'S SYNDROME (MPS IV).

MR Abbreviation for measles-rubella vaccine; see MEASLES-MUMPS-RUBELLA VACCINE.

MRI (magnetic resonance imaging) A type of MEDICAL TEST similar to a CT SCAN in its use of computers to give physicians three-dimensional pictures of the inside of the body, but different in using measurement of the natural magnetism in the atoms within the body; formerly called *nuclear magnetic resonance (NMR)*. It is not an INVASIVE procedure and has no known adverse effects, but for safety, women who are pregnant are advised not to have MRI. Since the patient must lie in a narrow tunnel-like tube, people with claustrophobia sometimes are unable to complete the test or do so only under sedation.

MS Abbreviation for MULTIPLE SCLEROSIS.

MSAFP Abbreviation for the maternal serum alpha-fetoprotein test, a GENETIC SCREENING test using ALPHA-FETOPROTEIN.

mucolipidoses (ML) A type of STORAGE DISORDER in which the body tissues accumulate abnormal and damaging amounts of certain compounds, called *mucolipids*, due to lack of enzymes needed to break them down. (For help and further information, see MUCOPOLYSACCHARIDOSES.)

mucopolysaccharidoses (MPS) A group of GENETIC DISORDERS that involve defects in certain enzymes, resulting in abnormal and damaging accumulations of substances called *mucopolysaccharides* in the tissues, medically classed as METABOLIC DISORDERS or STORAGE DISORDERS. Each of the various MPS disorders has an MPS number and a name, the best-known being HURLER'S SYNDROME (MPS I), HUNTER'S SYNDROME (MPS II), and MORQUIO'S SYNDROME (MPS IV). Children affected with MPS generally have MENTAL RETARDATION, skeletal deformity (especially of the face), retarded growth often resulting in DWARFISM, and a shortened life expectancy, often dying in childhood or adolescence, though some with a mild form of the disorder may live a relatively normal life. Other characteristics are specific to the individual types. There is as yet no specific treatment. The disorders can be detected before birth with PRENATAL TESTING, as through AMNIOCENTESIS, or after birth through URINALYSIS and X-RAY analysis of skeletal development. Parents with a family history of MPS may well want to seek GENETIC COUNSELING before or early in pregnancy. Related storage disorders, each also with several variant forms, are *mucolipidoses* (ML), in which compounds called *mucolipids* accumulate, and LIPID STORAGE DISEASES (*lipidoses*).

For help and further information

National MPS Society
17 Kraemer Street
Hicksville, NY 11801
516-931-6338
Marie Capobianco, President
Organization concerned with people who have mucopolysaccharidoses or mucolipidoses. Offers support to parents; provides information and referrals; supports research; publishes newsletter *Courage* and *What Is MPS?*.

Zain Hansen M. P. S. Foundation
1200 Fernwood Drive
P.O. Box 4768
Arcata, CA 95521
707-822-5421
Carl Zichella, President

Organization aiding children and families with muco-polysaccharidoses and related disorders. Offers some financial and other aid; supports research; acts as information clearing-house for public and professionals; operates medical equip-ment exchange bank; publishes various materials, including quarterly newsletter, brochure on MPS, *Directory of Medical Professionals Experienced in MPS*, and *Directory of MPS Research Programs*.

March of Dimes National Registry for MPS/ML Disorders (MPS/ML Registry)
c/o Program Department
53 West Jackson Boulevard, Suite 1550
Chicago, IL 60604
312-341-1370

Organization maintaining register of families with muco-polysaccharidoses (MPS) or mucolipidoses (ML). Gathers and disseminates information to members, public, and profession-als; makes referrals; publishes booklet *Parent to Parent*.

ML (Mucolipidosis) IV Foundation
Six Concord Drive
Monsey, NY 10952
914-425-0639
Lynn Goldblatt, Executive Director

Organization seeking to support families of children with mucolipidosis. Provides information; supports research; pub-lishes brochure *ML4*.

National Tay-Sachs & Allied Diseases Association (NTSAD), 617-964-5508. (For full group information, see LIPID STORAGE DIS-EASES.)

National Institute of Neurological Disorders and Stroke (NINDS), 301-496-5751. (For full group information, see BRAIN AND BRAIN DISORDERS.)

National Institute of Diabetes and Digestive and Kidney Dis-eases (NIDDK), 301-496-3583. (For full group information, see DIGESTIVE DISORDERS.)

(See also GENETIC DISORDERS; METABOLIC DISORDERS.)

mucoviscidosis   Alternate name for CYSTIC FIBROSIS, generally used in Europe.

multifactorial disorder   A pattern of GENETIC INHERITANCE that involves several factors—some genetic, some environmental—for the disorder to be expressed. Among the characteristics of multifactorial disorders are the following:

• They occur in a given family with no discernible pattern (unlike AUTOSOMAL DOMINANT, AUTOSOMAL RECESSIVE, or X-LINKED disorders).
• Conditions often vary in severity.
• Frequency may vary with race and sex.
• The risk of a particular disorder occurring in a particular per-son is assessed on the basis of statistical data.

Examples of multifactorial disorders are CLEFT LIP AND PALATE, CLUBFOOT, ASTHMA, SPINA BIFIDA, EPILEPSY, DIABETES MELLITUS, ARTHRITIS, certain heart problems (see HEART AND HEART PROB-LEMS), CONGENITAL DISLOCATION OF THE HIP, and some forms of CANCER.

multigravida   Medical designation for a woman who has been pregnant more than once.

multipara   Medical designation for a woman who has given birth to more than one live baby.

multiparent family   A type of FAMILY in which adults living in a collective household or commune share the rearing of children in the house.

multiple birth   Two or more babies developing during a sin-gle PREGNANCY. Approximately one out of three multiple births develop from a single ZYGOTE (fertilized egg), which divides after conception; these twins (or other multiples) are called *monozygotic, monovular,* or *identical.* Because they have the same genetic material, they are always of the same sex and look alike, though one is generally larger than the other at birth. Identical twins also share the same PLACENTA and chorion in the UTERUS, though with individual UMBILICAL CORDS and gener-ally separate sacs of AMNIOTIC FLUID. About one out of four pairs of identical twins are *mirror twins,* meaning that they have the same features but on opposite sides, sometimes even including internal organs, such as the heart. If division of the single egg is not fully complete, the two may be joined in some part of the body, often the chest, and need to be separated surgically after birth, where possible; these so-called *Siamese twins* occur about once in very 50,000 births.

But two out of three cases of multiple births involve fertiliza-tion of separate eggs (see OVUM) by separate SPERM and so are called *dizygotic, binovular, fraternal,* or *nonidentical.* They are genetically distinct beings, may look quite different, and may be of the same or different sexes. Each has its own placenta, but because these may be placed near each other in the uterus, laboratory tests are sometimes needed to determine whether twins are identical or fraternal. Fraternal twins are more likely to occur in women who are older or have borne several chil-dren previously and those who have a personal or family history of multiple births. Blacks have a somewhat higher-than-normal likelihood of having fraternal twins than Whites, while people of Asian background have a lower rate.

With pregnancies of three or more babies, all may be identi-cal or all fraternal, or they may be a mixture of the two forms.

Births of such *supertwins* are rare, accounting for only less than 3 percent of all multiple births.

Use of fertility drugs has made multiple births more common, as have various techniques to counter INFERTILITY, some of which (such as IN VITRO FERTILIZATION) deliberately implant multiple eggs to increase the chances of achieving pregnancy. BIRTH-CONTROL PILLS are also associated with somewhat higher rate of twinning. By the late 1980s multiple births were about 2.25 percent of all births and still rising.

Because of such increased likelihood, doctors are more alerted to the possibility of twins than in the past, when perhaps half of the cases of multiple births were not recognized until the seventh month and a quarter not until the actual DELIVERY. Multiple pregnancy is generally identified by a larger-than-usual abdomen for the woman's time of GESTATION and by the doctor's hearing more than one fetal heartbeat. An ULTRASOUND SCAN is often used to confirm the diagnosis of multiple pregnancy.

Multiple births are, almost by definition, HIGH-RISK PREGNANCIES. Two or more beings are competing for space and nourishment normally meant for a *singleton*, and one fetus is normally larger and better nourished than the other (or others), though all may have relatively LOW BIRTH WEIGHT (on the average, a little over five pounds). LABOR often starts two to four weeks early, resulting in PREMATURE DELIVERY, with its attendant risks and problems. Later-born multiple babies are likely to suffer some mild-to-severe ANOXIA during the birth of the first baby and so may have some DEVELOPMENTAL DELAY or other problems in later growth (see GROWTH AND GROWTH DISORDERS). To lessen FETAL DISTRESS, especially since MALPRESENTATION is common, doctors perform more CESAREAN SECTIONS with multiple than with single pregnancies. Even so, there is an increased risk of losing one or more babies. For mothers, multiple pregnancy is also associated with increased risk of high BLOOD PRESSURE (*hypertension*), excess amniotic fluid (HYDRAMNIOS), and POSTPARTUM HEMORRHAGE.

Twins and other multiples are generally extremely close from birth, with their own special BONDING. One of the major decisions parents must make during twins' development is when and how much to separate them. While in the past it was the fashion to dress twins alike, many parents and child-development experts today believe it more important to dress twins differently and emphasize their individuality, often sending them to different schools (either at the start or at some point during grade school) and directing them toward different kinds of activities, especially since one is often somewhat better coordinated and quicker than the other, presumably because of influences in the womb. Various organizations and studies (see below) can help parents make such decisions about raising their multiples.

For help and further information

Twins Foundation
P.O. Box 9487
Providence, RI 02940

401-274-TWIN [8946]
Kay Cassill, President
Organization of and for people of multiple birth. Seeks to enhance the welfare of twins in general.

National Organization of Mothers of Twins Clubs (NOMOTC)
12404 Princess Jeanne, NE
Albuquerque, NM 87112
505-275-0955
Lois Gallmeyer, Executive Secretary
Network of clubs of and for parents of twins and other multiple births, seeking to share special aspects of raising twins from experienced parents, teachers, and medical professionals. Aims to educate public about individuality of twins; maintains library and aids in research on twins; publishes *MOTC's Notebook*.

Twin Services
P.O. Box 10066
Berkeley, CA 94709
415-524-0863
Patricia M. Malmstrom, Executive Director
Organization of people interested in multiple births, a partly state-funded family service agency. Offers Twinline phone counseling service; provides information and referrals; publishes various materials, packaged by age group.

Triplet Connection (TC)
2618 Lucile Avenue
Stockton, CA 95209
209-474-0885
Janet Bleyl, President
Mutual-support group for parents or parents-to-be of triplets. Help parents prepare for high-risk birth; shares information and experiences of mutual interest; operates Tender Hearts program for mothers who lost one or more children in a multiple birth; publishes newsletter.

C/SEC (Cesareans/Support, Education, and Concern), 508-877-8266. Publishes *Having Twins*. (For full group information, see CESAREAN SECTION.)

La Leche League International (LLLI), 312-455-7730. Publishes brochure *Nursing Two, Is It for You?* and book *Mothering Multiples: Breastfeeding and Caring for Twins*. (For full group information, see BREASTFEEDING.)

Other reference sources

General Works

Having Twins: A Parent's Guide to Pregnancy, Birth, and Early Childhood, second edition, by Elizabeth Noble. Boston: Houghton Mifflin, 1990.

The Parents Guide to Raising Twins, second edition, by Elizabeth Griedrich and Cherry Rowland. New York: St. Martin's, 1990.

Twins, by Roxanne Pulitzer. New York: Villard, 1990.

The Joy of Twins: Having, Raising, and Loving Babies Who Arrive in Groups, by Pamela Patrick Novotny. New York: Crown, 1988.

Twins: From Conception to Five Years, by Averil Clegg and Anne Woolett. New York: Van Nostrand, 1983; Ballantine, 1988.

Make Room for Twins: A Complete Guide to Pregnancy, Delivery, and the Childhood Years, by Terry Pink Alexander. New York: Bantam, 1987.

Being a Twin, Having a Twin, by Maxine B. Rosenberg. New York: Lothrop, 1985. For grades 1 to 4.

Twins: The Parent's Survival Guide, by Carole Zentner. North Pomfret, VT: David & Charles, 1975; New York: State Mutual, 1983.

Twins: Nature's Amazing Mystery, by Kay Cassill. New York: Atheneum, 1982.

Background Works

Psychology of Twinship, by Ricardo C. Ainslie. Lincoln: University of Nebraska Press, 1985.

Identity and Intimacy in Twins, by Barbara Schave and Janet Ciriello. New York: Praeger, 1983.

Heredity, Environment and Personality: A Study of 80 Sets of Twins. Austin: University of Texas Press, 1976.

The Biology of Twinning in Man, by M.G. Buklmer. Oxford: Clarendon, 1970.

multiple handicaps   The presence of more than one kind of handicap in a child, such as DEAFNESS and BLINDNESS, or MENTAL RETARDATION and ORTHOPEDIC HANDICAPS. (For help and further information, see HANDICAPPED.)

multiple personality disorder (MPD)   A type of DISSOCIATIVE DISORDER in which a person has two or more distinct personalities in the same body, often opposites (like Dr. Jekyll and Mr. Hyde). Though sometimes not diagnosed until adulthood, MPD often begins during childhood, almost always as a result of severe CHILD ABUSE AND NEGLECT, especially sexual abuse, or other emotional trauma. The term *split personality* is sometimes popularly applied to both MPD and SCHIZOPHRENIA, but the type of split is quite different; in schizophrenia it is not between personalities but between thought and feeling.

For help and further reference

A Mind of My Own: The Woman Who Was Known as "Eve" Tells the Story of Her Triumph over Multiple Personality Disorder, by Chris Costner Sizemore. New York: Morrow, 1989.

Katherine, It's Time: An Incredible Journey into the World of Multiple Personality, by Kit Castle and Stefan Bechtel. New York: Harper & Row, 1989.

Through a Mind Divided: A Doctor's Story of Multiple Personality Patients, by Dr. Robert S. Mayer. Garden City, NY: Doubleday, 1988.

Childhood Antecedents of Multiple Personality, R. Kluft, ed. Washington, D.C.: American Psychiatric Press, 1985.

(See also MENTAL DISORDERS.)

multiple sclerosis (MS)   A disorder in which *myelin*, the fatty substance protecting nerve cells in the brain and spinal cord, is damaged or partly destroyed and replaced by scar tissue (*sclerosis*). This process gradually disrupts communications in the NERVOUS SYSTEM. Symptoms vary widely, depending on what parts of the body are most affected and how severely, but they can include tingling sensations, numbness, muscle weakness (PARESIS), muscle cramps, lack of coordination, PARALYSIS, blurred or double vision, abnormal fatigue, confusion, forgetfulness, INCONTINENCE (difficulty in controlling bladder and bowels), and impaired sexual function. The disorder is also highly variable. Some people may have a single attack, with no recurrence afterward. Some other people have periods when the disease is active, called *exacerbations*, and times when they are free of symptoms, called REMISSIONS. In still others, the disease is chronic and progressive, becoming increasingly severe.

The cause of the disease is unknown. It is not a GENETIC DISORDER, nor is it thought to be contagious, though it is possible that some families may be more susceptible to it, either because of hereditary predisposition or sharing the same environment. It most often strikes in young adulthood, affecting women somewhat more than men, and Whites more often than Blacks or Asians. It is also more common in the world's temperate zones than in tropical climates, and the area in which a child spends the first 15 years of life affects future risk of contracting MS. It is unclear why all this is so, but speculation is that a virus picked up early in life triggers an AUTOIMMUNE DISORDER in which the body mistakenly attacks its own tissue.

Recent animal studies indicate that some kinds of antibodies in the IMMUNE SYSTEM can help repair myelin, and this may help both to explain the disease's unusual REMISSION cycles and to offer promise of a treatment or even a cure in the future if these antibodies can be boosted in the body. At present, however, no cure exists, though some drugs and therapy can help alleviate syptoms.

Because the symptoms of the disease are so variable and are similar to those of many other disorders, MS is often hard to diagnose. Doctors may need to perform a variety of MEDICAL TESTS, including LUMBAR PUNCTURE, CT SCANS, and MRI SCANS. Multiple sclerosis does not affect life expectancy and most people with MS can live relatively normal lives. Though in the past it was thought that PREGNANCY could cause the disease to worsen, more recent studies, according to the National Multiple Sclerosis Society, have "not shown there to be any effects of pregnancy on the long-term course of multiple sclerosis. In general pregnancy is no longer held to be necessarily detrimental." They caution, however, that a woman with MS may not have the physical stamina to care for a baby and active child and needs to consider whether she will have the resources to help her do so.

For help and further information

National Multiple Sclerosis Society (NMSS)
205 East 42nd Street
New York, NY 10017
212-986-3240
Thor Hanson, President
Organization of people with multiple sclerosis, their families, and interested others. Provides information and referrals; offers community services, including counseling, training programs for caregivers, swimming programs, vocational rehabilitation, and medical equipment on loan; publishes various materials, including quarterly magazine, *Plain Talk: A Book about Multiple Sclerosis for Families*, and brochures *Someone You Know Has Multiple Sclerosis: A Book for Families, What Everyone Should Know About Multiple Sclerosis, Emotional Aspects of MS*, and *Living with MS: A Practical Guide*.

National Institute of Neurological Disorders and Stroke (NINDS), 301-496-5751. Publishes brochure *Multiple Sclerosis: Hope Through Research*. (For full group information, see BRAIN AND BRAIN DISORDERS.)

Other reference sources

Multiple Sclerosis: A Self-Help Guide to Its Management, revised edition, by Judy Graham. Rochester, VT: Inner Traditions, 1989.
All of a Piece: A Life with Multiple Sclerosis, by Barbara D. Webster. Baltimore: Johns Hopkins University Press, 1989. A personal account.
Health Care U.S.A., by Jean Carper. New York: Prentice Hall, 1987. Resource for general and specific health-care information; lists major multiple sclerosis treatment and research centers, and other information.
Multiple Sclerosis: A Guide for Patients and Families, by Labe C. Scheinberg, M.D. New York: Raven, 1983.
Therapeutic Claims in Multiple Sclerosis, by The International Federation of Multiple Sclerosis Societies. Available from DEMOS Publications, 156 Fifth Avenue, Suite 1018, New York, NY 10010.
Research on Multiple Sclerosis, by B.H. Waksman, M.D., and W.E. Reynolds, M.D., National Multiple Sclerosis Society. Available from DEMOS Publications, 156 Fifth Avenue, Suite 1018, New York, NY 10010.
Multiple Sclerosis: The Facts, by Walter Bryan Matthews. London: Oxford University Press, 1980.
Multiple Sclerosis: A Personal View, by Cynthia Birrer. New York: Thomas, 1979.
The Pursuit of Hope, by Miriam Ottenberg. New York: Rawson, Wade, 1978.
(See also HELP FOR SPECIAL CHILDREN on page 578.)

multisensory Employing all or most of the senses, including *auditory* (hearing), *visual* (seeing), *tactile* (touch), *olfactory* (smell), *gustatory* (taste), and *kinesthetic* (body motion). Some approaches for teaching children with LEARNING DISABILITIES or others kinds of learning difficulties employ various of the senses to enhance success at learning, as in the VAKT approach to teaching READING.

mumps A highly contagious disease caused by a virus that is passed from person to person in droplets from coughing, sneezing, or just talking; also called *epidemic parotitis* or *infectious parotitis*. Common symptoms of the disease are FEVER, headache, and inflammation of the salivary glands, causing the cheeks to swell. In some cases, however, mumps can cause more severe complications. About one affected child in 10 has MENINGITIS (inflammation of the membranes covering the brain and SPINAL CORD) or the even more serious ENCEPHALITIS (inflammation of the brain itself: see BRAIN AND BRAIN DISORDERS). This sometimes disappears without damage, but mumps can cause DEAFNESS. In addition, mumps poses a threat to adolescent or adult males; one in four affected males experience painful inflammation and swelling of one or occasionally both of the TESTES, a condition called *orchitis*, in some instances causing STERILITY. Fortunately, since 1967 a mumps VACCINE has existed, often given to children at about 15 months of age as part of a combination MEASLES-MUMPS-RUBELLA (MMR) VACCINE. Older adults who have never had mumps and have not been immunized can also take the vaccine. Parents should keep careful records of either immunization or evidence of their child's having had the disease, since many U.S. states require one or the other before admitting a child into school.

For help and further information

National Institute of Allergy and Infectious Diseases (NIAID), 301-496-5717. (For full group information, see ALLERGY.)

National Institute of Child Health and Human Development (NICHD), 301-496-5133. (For full group information, see PREGNANCY.)

(See also MEASLES-MUMPS-RUBELLA VACCINE.)

mumps vaccine A type of VACCINE that is normally given in a combination as MEASLES-MUMPS-RUBELLA VACCINE.

muscular dystrophy (MD) Not a single disease but a group of relatively rare diseases, mostly appearing during childhood and adolescence, that result from muscle destruction or degeneration, with fatty tissue often replacing the wasted (*atrophied*) muscle. MD is a group of GENETIC DISORDERS apparently resulting from abnormality in production of key proteins. It can be diagnosed by medical TESTS for certain substances released from damaged muscle cells; by an ELECTROMYOGRAM, which detects electrical activity in muscles; or by a BIOPSY (tissue sample). The forms of MD vary in their inheritance pattern, AGE of onset, muscles initially affected, and rate of progression.

The main types of muscular dystrophy affecting young people are:

- *Duchenne muscular dystrophy* or *pseudohypertrophic MD*: the most common form of MD, affecting one to two in 10,000 boys and accounting for 50 percent of MD cases. Duchenne normally appears between ages two and five, often first affecting the muscles of the pelvic girdle, then progressing rapidly to nearby muscles. Affected children are slow to sit up and walk, have trouble climbing stairs, and often have LORDOSIS (swayback). By age 12 most children with Duchenne MD are confined to a wheelchair and are experiencing progressively worsening heart and lung problems as those muscles are attacked. This generally brings death by the late teens, often from sudden heart failure. Duchenne may arise spontaneously, but usually is an X-LINKED RECESSIVE trait passed on to male children by unaffected mothers who are CARRIERS.

- *Becker's muscular dystrophy* or *benign pseudohypertropic muscular dystrophy*: a less common form of MD, appearing in males between age two and 20 and progressing more slowly and with less life-threatening results; affected people often reach age 50. Like Duchenne MD, it has an X-linked recessive hereditary pattern.

- *myotonic dystrophy*: a form of MD that affects both sexes and can appear at any age, though generally between ages 20 and 40, involving weakness or floppiness (HYPOTONIA) and MYOTONIA, the inability to readily relax muscles after use. Myotonic dystrophy often affects hands, feet, face, and neck first and may be associated with abnormalities in the heart, ENDOCRINE SYSTEM, and CENTRAL NERVOUS SYSTEM, sometimes including MENTAL RETARDATION. It has an AUTOSOMAL DOMINANT inheritance pattern and can be passed on by either mother or father.

- *limb-girdle muscular dystrophy*: a form of MD that may actually be several disorders, appearing in either sex from late childhood to early adulthood, differing greatly in severity and rate of progression, and characteristically affecting the shoulder or pelvic area. Limb-girdle MD is an AUTOSOMAL RECESSIVE trait, which both parents must pass on.

- *facioscapulohumeral muscular dystrophy,* or *Landouzy-Dejerine muscular dystrophy*: a form of MD that primarily affects the face and shoulder regions and sometimes also the pelvic region, appearing between infancy and early adulthood but most often in adolescence. Like myotonic dystrophy, it affects both sexes and is passed as an autosomal dominant trait, but its progression is slow and does not generally cause severe disability.

- *congenital muscular dystrophy*: a form of MD present at birth and not usually progressive, causing weakness in muscles of the limbs, trunk, and face, as well as overall limpness. Its inheritance progression is not fully clear, but it affects both sexes and is probably autosomal recessive, like limb-girdle dystrophy.

- *distal muscular dystrophy*: a form of MD that may actually be several disorders, which appears at various ages and first affects the muscles of the hands and feet, perhaps progressing to hips and shoulders. Its inheritance pattern is unclear, but it affects both sexes and some forms seem to be autosomal dominant, like myotonic dystrophy.

Other, rarer muscular dystrophies also exist.

No successful treatment currently exists. In the past, treatment of MD has of necessity focused on slowing the progress and severity of symptoms, but experimental GENE THERAPY has given hope that the defective genes can be corrected or replaced. Meanwhile, the main options are supportive measures. PHYSICAL THERAPISTS help MD patients keep the unaffected muscles in working condition for as long as possible, and ORTHOPEDIC DEVICES can help prevent deformity. But researchers are following various lines, including some drugs that may slow the progression of muscle-wasting.

Prospective parents with a personal or family history of muscular dystrophy may well want to seek GENETIC COUNSELING. Prepregnancy tests can detect whether or not a parent carries a defective gene. During PREGNANCY, some kinds of MD can be detected through GENETIC SCREENING tests such as CHORIONIC VILLUS SAMPLING and AMNIOCENTESIS.

Research and helping organizations (see below), both public and private, that focus on muscular dystrophy generally also encompass several other kinds of muscular diseases, including:

- MOTOR NEURON DISEASES, a group of diseases involving damage to the nerves that supply communication between muscles and nerves and resulting in weakness and wasting of the muscles. The group includes *amytrophic lateral sclerosis* (*ALS* or *Lou Gehrig's disease*) and *spinal muscular atrophies*, including *Type 1, infantile*, or *Werdnig-Hoffmann disease; Type 2, intermediate; Type 3, juvenile*, or *Kugelberg-Welander disease*; and *Aran-Duchenne type*.

- *myotonias*, inherited disorders in which the muscles do not readily relax after use but remain bulging and stiff, as in MYOTONIA CONGENITA (*Thomsen's disease*) and *paramyotonia congenita*.

- *diseases of neuromuscular junction*, in which voluntary muscles cannot contract normally, leaving the person very weak, such as MYASTHENIA GRAVIS and *Eaton-Lambert syndrome*.

- *diseases of the peripheral nerve*, such as PERONEAL MUSCULAR ATROPHY (*Charcot-Marie-Tooth disease*), Friedreich's ATAXIA, and *Dejerine-Sottas disease*.

- *inflammatory myopathies*, such as *polymyositis, dermatomyositis*, and *myositis ossificans*, in which the muscles become inflamed and weak.

- METABOLIC DISORDERS that affect muscles, such as GLYCOGEN STORAGE DISEASE and *periodic* PARALYSIS.

- *myopathies due to endocrine abnormalities*, such as *hyperthyroid myopathy* and *hypothyroid myopathy*, which result from THYROID GLAND problems.

Other even rarer muscle disorders, or *myopathies*, also exist. The organizations below can be useful for families facing any of them.

For help and further information

Muscular Dystrophy Association (MDA)
810 Seventh Avenue, 27th Floor
New York, NY 10019
212-586-0808
Robert Ross, Executive Director
Organization concerned with muscular dystrophy and related neuromuscular diseases. Operates nationwide network of diagnostic, research, and treatment clinics, offering free care to families not covered by health insurance; provides social service and genetic counseling to patients and families and special services such as assistance for transportation costs and repair of orthopedic aids; sponsors research; runs summer camps for young people with muscular dystrophy or related neuromuscular diseases; seeks to educate public and influence public policy and legislation regarding the handicapped; publishes many materials, including quarterly news magazine, *Learning to Live with Neuromuscular Disease: A Message for Parents of Children with a Neuromuscular Disease, Living with Progressive Childhood Illness: Parental Management of Neuromuscular Disease, Everybody's Different, Nobody's Perfect, Hey! I'm Here, Too!* (for siblings of MD children), *What Everyone Should Know About Muscular Dystrophy, Muscular Dystrophy Fact Sheet, 101 Questions About Muscular Dystrophy, Duchenne Muscular Dystrophy, Myotonic Dystrophy, Spinal Muscular Atrophy, Who Is At Risk? The Genetics of Duchenne Muscular Dystrophy, The CPK Test for Detection of Female Carriers of Duchenne Muscular Dystrophy, Charcot-Marie-Tooth Disease, ALS: Amytophic Lateral Sclerosis, Myasthenia Gravis, Plasmapheresis,* and *Polymyositis/Dermatomyositis*.

National Institute of Neurological Disorders and Stroke (NINDS), 301-496-5751. (For full group information, see BRAIN AND BRAIN DISORDERS.)

National Institute of Arthritis and Musculoskeletal and Skin Diseases (NIAMS), 301-496-8188. (For full group information, see ARTHRITIS.)

Other reference sources

Health Care U.S.A., by Jean Carper. New York: Prentice Hall, 1987. Resource for general and specific health-care information, including neuromuscular diseases such as muscular dystrophy, amyotrophic lateral sclerosis (ALS, or Lou Gehrig's disease), myasthenia gravis, and ataxia; lists Muscular Dystrophy Association research and treatment clinics, ALS Association research and treatment centers, government research and treatment centers, and other information.
Under the Shadow, by Anne Knowles. New York: Harper & Row, 1983.
(See also ATAXIA; MOTOR NEURON DISEASES; MYASTHENIA GRAVIS; also HELP FOR SPECIAL CHILDREN on page 578.)

mutation A change in the coding for the DNA in the genes and chromosomes that form a being's GENETIC INHERITANCE. Some-

times mutations can be beneficial, or at least neutral. But most mutations are dangerous and possibly life-threatening, giving rise to GENETIC DISORDERS and CHROMOSOMAL ABNORMALITIES. Some mutations occur spontaneously, as mistakes in the duplication of DNA in the cells that are then duplicated in the normal process of reproduction. If the mutation occurs in the "sex cells" from which the SPERM and egg (OVUM) are formed, it may be passed on to any children. But if the mutation occurs in other parts of the body, it will not be heritable, though its effects may be deadly, such as a cancerous TUMOR. Some mutations are at least partly triggered by environmental influences, such as RADIATION or *carcinogens* (cancer-causing substances). (For help and further information, see GENETIC DISORDERS; ENVIRONMENTAL HAZARDS.)

mute The state of silence, or being without speech, for whatever reason. Some children are *aphasic* and unable to speak, because of damage to the speech apparatus or the connections to the brain. Some are almost totally unresponsive, except perhaps for a whispered "yes" or "no," for physical reasons such as BRAIN TUMORS or HYDROCEPHALUS; this is called *akinetic mutism*. But some children, who are physically able both to speak and to understand language, choose not to speak, communicating instead mostly by gestures or nods. This *elective mutism* is often found in young children, usually under age five, and is sometimes associated with shyness or SEPARATION ANXIETY, though the possibility of MENTAL RETARDATION or speech problems should always be explored. In somewhat older children, elective mutism may be linked with SCHOOL PHOBIA, and may respond to a change of school. Mutism also may be a symptom of some kinds of MENTAL DISORDER. (For help and further information, see COMMUNICATION SKILLS AND DISORDERS and other specific topics.)

myasthenia gravis A rare AUTOIMMUNE DISORDER affecting the conjunction of nerves and muscles, in which voluntary muscles cannot contract normally, leaving the person very weak. Eye movements, facial expression, chewing, swallowing, and breathing are often first affected, and later arm and leg muscles. This rare disorder can appear at any age but most commonly in young women and older men.

For help and further information

Myasthenia Gravis Foundation (MG)
7-11 South Broadway
White Plains, NY 10601
914-328-1717
Valerie M. Tennent, Executive Administrator
Organization of patients with myasthenia gravis, their families, medical professionals who work with them, and interested others. Sponsors research and treatment centers; provides information and referrals; operates discount "drug banks"; publishes various materials, including *Facts About MG for Patients and Families and Myasthenia Gravis—The Disease: A Case History*. (See also MUSCULAR DYSTROPHY.)

myelogram X-RAY examination of the spinal cord and brain to see if there is evidence of TUMORS, SPINAL CORD INJURY, or dislocated disks, such as might show up in narrowing or obstruction of the spaces where the CEREBROSPINALFLUID flows (see BRAIN AND BRAIN DISORDERS). In a procedure called a LUMBAR PUNCTURE (spinal tap), a small amount of cerebrospinal fluid is removed and replaced with a fluid that will show up with contrast on the X-ray. The patient is tilted on a table while a series of X-rays are taken at different angles, and then most or all of the contrast fluid is removed. The procedure is uncomfortable; common side effects include nausea, VOMITING, flushing, pressure, headaches, and some pain, especially as fluid is removed. Serious side effects are relatively rare, but involve possible introduction of infection and ALLERGY to the contrasting fluid. (For help and further information, see MEDICAL TESTS.)

myelomeningocele A severe and common form of SPINA BIFIDA.

myocarditis Inflammation of the main muscle of the heart, often from infection. (See HEART AND HEART PROBLEMS.)

myopia Nearsightedness. (See EYE AND VISION PROBLEMS.)

myositis ossificans A type of muscle disorder. (See MUSCULAR DYSTROPHY.)

myotonia Inability of a muscle to relax readily after use, a symptom seen in diseases such as *myotonic dystrophy*, a form of MUSCULAR DYSTROPHY, and MYOTONIA CONGENITA.

myotonia congenita (Thomsen's disease) A rare inherited disorder in which muscles do not readily relax after use but remain bulging and stiff, especially when the person is tired and has been inactive; a mild, nonprogressive muscular disorder. A related disorder brought on by exposure to cold is *paramyotonia congenita*. (For help and further information, see MUSCULAR DYSTROPHY.)

myotonic dystrophy A form of MUSCULAR DYSTROPHY.

myringitis Inflammation of the eardrum, a common type of EAR AND HEARING PROBLEM, often related to *otitis externa*, inflammation or infection of the outer ear.

myringoplasty A technique by which surgeons are able to repair a hole in an eardrum, using a tissue graft from elsewhere in the body; this technique, which uses MICROSURGERY, helps relieve a significant EAR AND HEARING PROBLEM.

myxedema Alternate name for *hypothyroidism*, a disorder involving too little production from the THYROID GLAND.

narcissistic personality disorder A kind of PERSONALITY DISORDER.

narcolepsy A type of SLEEPING DISORDER.

National Direct Student Loan Program (NDSL) Former name of PERKINS LOANS.

National Merit Scholarship Qualifying Test (NMSQT) Alternate name for PRELIMINARY SCHOLASTIC APTITUDE TEST/NATIONAL MERIT SCHOLARSHIP QUALIFYING TEST.

National Vaccine Injury Compensation Program (NVICP) A federal program established under the CHILDHOOD VACCINE INJURY ACT.

natural childbirth General term for an approach to LABOR and DELIVERY that attempts to minimize medical intervention during CHILDBIRTH; in effect, often an alternative term for PREPARED CHILDBIRTH. (For help and further information, see CHILDBIRTH; PREGNANCY.)

natural family planning (NFP) A method of BIRTH CONTROL that attempts to avoid CONCEPTION by abstaining from sexual activity around the time of a woman's OVULATION, when an egg is available to be fertilized; in this sense also called *periodic abstinence*. The same methods used in NFP can also be used in reverse fashion by couples concerned about INFERTILITY to pinpoint the time when the chances of conception are greatest, whether during normal sexual intercourse, using ARTIFICIAL INSEMINATION, or extracting an egg (*oocyte*) for use in such techniques as IN VITRO FERTILIZATION.

There are three main NFP approaches:

• *calendar (rhythm) method*: This is the traditional approach, which involves keeping track of the woman's regular MENSTRUAL CYCLE and calculating when ovulation is likely to occur, generally based on the assumption that (whatever the length of the menstrual cycle) ovulation takes place about 14 days before the beginning of the next MENSTRUATION. The effectiveness of the calendar method alone for contraception is highly variable; the Public Health Service comments: "It is now generally agreed that this method is effective only when used in conjunction with one or both of the other methods."

- *basal body temperature method*: In this approach, a woman takes her temperature every morning at about the same time, before arising, using a special basal thermometer calibrated to measure very small temperature changes. When the basal body temperature (temperature of the body at rest) rises one-half to one degree and stays elevated for three days, this signals that ovulation is taking place.
- *cervical (vaginal) mucus method (Billings method)*: This approach involves observing and charting the changes in the consistency of mucus in the VAGINA, because mucus secreted by the CERVIX changes at around the time of ovulation, allowing easier passage for SPERM. For contraception, couples are advised to avoid intercourse from the time the mucus changes until at least three days afterward and also during menstruation, since the mucus cannot then be tested. Where conception is desired, these changes indicate the most fertile period. Women must learn from doctors or specially trained groups (see below) precisely what to look for.

When the latter two (or all three) methods are used together, it is called the *symptothermal method*; the effectiveness rate in preventing conception "can approach 76 to 98 percent," according to the Public Health Service. In a related approach, the OVULATION METHOD can be used to pinpoint ovulation, using release of hormones to do so. (See OVULATION METHOD for a description of an ovulation monitoring home medical test.)

For help and further information

Couple to Couple League (CCL)
P.O. Box 111184
Cincinnati, OH 45211
513-661-7612
R. Patrick Homan, Executive Director
For couples interested in using natural birth control, following the woman's fertility cycle, rather than artificial means. Helps train CCL teaching couples who teach techniques through local groups; supports premarital chastity; publishes newsletter and *The Art of Natural Family Planning*.

Family of the Americas Foundation (FAF)
P.O. Box 219, 1150 Lovers Lane
Mandeville, LA 70488
504-626-7724
Mercedes Wilson, Executive Director
Organization fostering the Billings Ovulation Method, in which a couple uses the woman's cycle to determine the period of fertility, either for birth control or to conceive. Trains teachers who conduct workshops in the method, offer sex education to teenagers, and help parents teach their children about sex; provides referral services; maintains library; publishes various materials, including films on the method and charting kits in English, Spanish, French, Portuguese, Chinese, and Arabic.

Human Life International (HLI)
7845 East Airpark Road

Gaithersburg, MD 20879
301-670-7884
Paul Marx, President
Organization opposing medical or mechanical intervention into the reproductive and life processes, including abortion and euthanasia. Fosters natural family planning and Christian sexuality; maintains library; publishes various materials, including *The Best of Natural Family Planning, Deceiving Birth Controllers*, and *Death Without Dignity*.

Food and Drug Administration, 301-472-4750. Publishes *Comparing Contraceptives*, including natural family planning. (For full group information, see NUTRITION; DRUG REACTIONS AND INTERACTIONS.)

Other reference source

The Billings Method, by Dr. Evelyn Billings and Ann Westmore. New York: Ballantine, 1989.

natural parents A synonym for BIOLOGICAL PARENTS.

navel (umbilicus) The scar left on the outside of the abdomen after the cut end of the UMBILICAL CORD falls off, some days after birth. During the first week after birth, while the scar is

---

Care of the Baby's Navel

The end of the umbilical cord, attached to the baby's navel cut at birth, usually falls off within days. You can keep the umbilical cord clean and dry until it falls off by dabbing it with rubbing alcohol on a cotton ball. Then, the navel may slightly bleed or ooze for a few days. If it does, clean it once or twice a day with alcohol. If it looks red and irritated or continues to bleed or ooze for more than two or three days after the cord falls off, you should call your doctor or clinic.

About one fourth of all babies develop a bulging at the navel. This gets larger for several months, then grows gradually with the baby for several months, then gets smaller and disappears. Large bulges (or "umbilical hernias") may not go away until the child is four to six years old. The bulge often gets tight or tense when the baby cries or coughs.

Since these bulgings almost always go away if they are left alone for long enough, there is usually no reason to have them repaired by surgery. They almost never cause any kind of trouble or pain. Occasionally a four- to six-year-old may be embarrassed by a particularly large hernia, and it can be repaired at that time. By waiting, you will probably save your baby an unpleasant and unnecessary operation. If you have concerns, discuss them with your doctor or clinic staff.

Source: *Infant Care* (1989). Prepared for the Public Health Service by the Bureau of Maternal and Child Health and Resources Development.

healing, public health experts recommend that the baby not be immersed in water but rather washed with a cloth and warm water. Often the abdominal wall will be pushed out somewhat because of weakness near the navel (in boys somewhat more often than girls), a condition called an *umbilical hernia*; that should be no cause for concern (see CARE OF THE BABY'S NAVEL, on page 339). Umbilical hernias can also sometimes occur in women after CHILDBIRTH.

NDSL Abbreviation for National Direct Student Loan Program, the former name of PERKINS LOANS.

near-miss SIDS Alternate term for APPARENT LIFE-THREATENING EVENT (ALTE).

neck righting reflex A type of REFLEX normally found in newborns in which, if the head is turned toward one side while the INFANT is lying face upward, the baby will turn the shoulders and trunk in the same direction. If this reflex is absent in newborns, or if it persists beyond infancy, physicians may suspect and test for damage to the CENTRAL NERVOUS SYSTEM.

neglect Maltreatment stemming largely from acts of omission, often linked with active mistreatment, as in CHILD ABUSE AND NEGLECT.

neonatal Referring to the first four weeks after birth, during which the newborn, or *neonate*, is often cared for by a NEONATOLOGIST, especially if a HIGH-RISK or PREMATURE baby.

neonatal intensive care unit (NICU) A type of INTENSIVE CARE UNIT that specializes in the care of LOW-BIRTH-WEIGHT, PREMATURE, or seriously ill newborns; sometimes called a *high-risk nursery*.

neonatal mortality INFANT MORTALITY in the first month of life. (For a chart of most common causes, see DEATH.)

neonatal screening tests Tests routinely given to many newborns, often involving analysis of blood samples taken from the baby's heel a few days after delivery. Though the precise tests vary from region to region, the aim of all is to identify possible BIRTH DEFECTS and medical problems, especially META-BOLIC DISORDERS that can cause MENTAL RETARDATION and sometimes DEATH unless detected and treated in the first few months of life. Among the disorders commonly screened for are PHENYL-KETONURIA, GALACTOSEMIA, and certain THYROID GLAND problems. Couples who have their baby outside a HOSPITAL should be careful to have such tests done soon after the birth, to prevent unnecessary damage to the baby's development. (For help and further information, see MEDICAL TESTS; METABOLIC DISORDERS.)

neonatologist A medical specialist who cares for newborns, generally for the first four weeks of life but sometimes longer, as when an infant is PREMATURE or is a LOW-BIRTH-WEIGHT baby. The neonatologist is often the doctor who gives the first major SCREENING TESTS for BIRTH DEFECTS, including GENETIC DISORDERS, and manages early treatment of infant health problems. After 28 days, a PEDIATRICIAN normally takes over an infant's care, with other medical specialists called in, as necessary.

neoplasm Alternate name for TUMOR.

nephroblastoma Alternate name for WILM'S TUMOR, a childhood CANCER of the kidney. (See CANCER; KIDNEY AND UROLOGICAL DISORDERS.)

nephrosis (nephrotic syndrome) A kind of KIDNEY AND URO-LOGICAL DISORDER.

nervous system The network of connections that receives and registers information from within and outside the body, interprets it, and transmits information that causes the body to take actions. In terms of the body's anatomy, the "command center" is the CENTRAL NERVOUS SYSTEM (CNS), made up of the brain and spinal cord. Transmitting information between the CNS and the outlying parts of the body is a network of nerves called the PERIPHERAL NERVOUS SYSTEM (PNS). In terms of the body's functioning, the nervous system is divided differently. The *autonomic nervous system* controls the actions that the body makes "automatically" or "involuntarily," such as heartbeat, breathing, production of substances by various glands, and the like. The autonomic nervous system is itself made up of two complementary systems: The *sympathetic nervous system* (controlled by the HYPOTHALAMUS) responds to situations such as danger or EXERCISE by speeding up heartbeat and breathing and raising BLOOD PRESSURE, while the *parasympathetic nervous system* slows heartbeat and breathing, causing a general relaxation, as when danger has passed or during sleep. Parallel with the autonomic nervous system is the *somatic nervous system*, which responds to and provides the brain with information about voluntary movements of the body, as in walking or moving an arm. (See BRAIN AND BRAIN DISORDERS, SPINE AND SPINE DISORDERS.)

nesting Alternate term for BIRD'S NEST CUSTODY.

neural tube defects Alternate medical name for a group of CONGENITAL abnormalities more popularly referred to as SPINA BIFIDA.

neurinoma Alternate name for ACOUSTIC NEUROMA.

neurofibromatosis (NF) A rare GENETIC DISORDER of the AUTO-SOMAL DOMINANT type that involves the growth of many TUMORS of nerve cells under the skin (or deeper); also called *Von Recklinghausen's disease* or *Elephant Man disease*. Though benign (not cancerous), these tumors can be disfiguring (as in the case of the so-called Elephant Man) and may grow in sensitive areas, such as the nerves serving the eyes or ears, and so can cause DEAFNESS and BLINDNESS. In most cases, however, the number and size of the tumors is less severe, and the person can lead a relatively normal life. Early signs of neurofibromatosis, often present at birth, are large tan spots called *café au lait* spots (French for "coffee with milk"), which darken and become more numerous over the years, especially during PUBERTY, PREGNANCY, and other times when the body's HORMONES are imbalanced. Neurofibromatosis is often associated with SCOLIOSIS and LEARNING DISABILITIES. If tumors are painful or very disfiguring or if they are near eye or ear nerves, they can be removed by surgery, but the hazard is that they will grow back in greater numbers. The 1990 discovery of the gene that causes NF holds the promise of earlier diagnosis, more effective treatment, and possible detection by PRENATAL TESTING. Prospective parents with NF in their family history may want to seek GENETIC COUNSELING.

For help and further information

National Neurofibromatosis Foundation (NNF)
141 Fifth Avenue, Suite 7-S
New York, NY 10010
212-460-8980, toll-free number 800-323-7938 (U.S. except NY)
Peter R. W. Bellerman, Executive Director
Organization of people with neurofibromatosis and interested others. Offers support; provides information to public and professionals; makes referrals; operates toll-free number; publishes various materials, including quarterlies *National Neurofibromatosis Foundation Newsletter* and *Research Newsletter*, and *Neurofibromatosis: A Handbook for Parents, Neurofibromatosis: Information for Kids*, and *Neurofibromatosis: Information for Patients and Families*.

National Institute of Neurological Disorders and Stroke (NINDS), 301-496-5751. Publishes fact sheet *Neurofibromatosis*. (For full group information, see BRAIN AND BRAIN DISORDERS.)

March of Dimes Birth Defects Foundation (MDBDF), 914-428-7100; local chapters in telephone-directory white pages. (For full group information, see BIRTH DEFECTS.)

Other reference sources

Health Care U.S.A., by Jean Carper. New York: Prentice Hall, 1987. Resource for general and specific health-care information; lists neurofibromatosis specialists and clinics for research and treatment, and other information.
Neurofibromatosis, by Vincent M. Riccardi and John J. Mulvihill, eds. New York: Raven, 1981.
(See also GENETIC COUNSELING; GENETIC DISORDERS.)

neurologist A physician who specializes in diagnosing and treating disorders of the brain (see BRAIN AND BRAIN DISORDERS) and NERVOUS SYSTEM and also performs surgery in those areas. If a child has abnormal behavior, a neurologist will seek to find whether that is caused by a brain or nervous system problem. The neurologist performs a variety of physical examinations and MEDICAL TESTS—such as an ELECTROENCEPHALOGRAPH (EEG) or LUMBAR PUNCTURE—aimed at seeing how the body gains information from the sense organs and how it uses the muscles to perform MOTOR SKILLS.

neuromuscular development The growth of a child's control over fine and gross MOTOR SKILLS, especially in the early childhood and preschool years; a term often used by child PSYCHOLOGISTS.

neuro-otologist A medical physician who focuses on the subspecialty of EAR AND HEARING PROBLEMS involving the acoustic nerve.

neurosurgeon A medical physician who specializes in performing surgery of the NERVOUS SYSTEM.

nevus (plural: nevi) General name for a variety of blemishes on the skin, popularly called *moles*. Nevi formed by abnormal collections of blood vessels, popularly called *birthmarks*, are medically termed *vascular nevi* or HEMANGIOMAS. The other main kind of nevus is caused by abnormal production of skin cells producing the pigment *melanin*. Among the most common of these *pigmented nevi* are freckles and *café au lait* spots (the color of coffee with milk). However, some nevi, such as the large, multicolored, often hairy mole called the *giant hairy nevus*, can be or become MALIGNANT. Though most nevi are not dangerous, for safety parents should closely examine and take notes on the size, location, and color of any markings on the skin of a young child and then check them periodically. Any changes or problems, such as darkening, growing, bleeding, or appearance of new marks, should be noted and reported to the doctor immediately, to be sure no CANCER is developing. (For help and further information, see SKIN DISORDERS.)

newborn intrapartal care Medical care for the baby through the whole of LABOR, from the onset of CONTRACTIONS through the actual DELIVERY of the baby and expulsion of the PLACENTA (afterbirth); care of the mother in the same period is called INTRAPARTAL CARE.

next friend (prochein ami) In the law, a person who acts on behalf of a MINOR or someone who is legally INCOMPETENT when that party's parent or legal GUARDIAN is not available. Someone appointed to act for a minor only in a specific lawsuit is called a *guardian ad litem* (at law).

next of kin A person's closest BLOOD RELATIVES; more precisely, in its legal origin, those people who have INHERITANCE RIGHTS and would receive a share of the estate of a person who died intestate, or without a will.

NF Abbreviation for NEUROFIBROMATOSIS.

NFP Abbreviation for NATURAL FAMILY PLANNING.

niacin (nicotinamide or nicotinic acid) A VITAMIN that is important to the health of tissue and nerve cells and to normal appetite and digestion, including the use of CARBOHYDRATES. Niacin is found in poultry, fish, and meat, especially liver, as well as whole-grain or fortified grain products, peas, and beans. Severe deficiency of niacin causes *pellagra*, once a common DEFICIENCY DISEASE that involves mouth sores, rough skin, DIARRHEA, and MENTAL DISORDERS. Less severe symptoms of deficiency include weakness and dizziness, changes in skin and intestinal lining, loss of appetite, and irritability. Overconsumption of some forms of niacin can lead to headache, cramps, and nausea. (For help and further information, see RECOMMENDED DAILY ALLOWANCES; VITAMINS.)

nicotinamide (nicotinic acid) Alternate names for NIACIN.

NICU Abbreviation for NEONATAL INTENSIVE CARE UNIT.

NIDDM Abbreviation for noninsulin-dependent diabetes mellitus, a form of DIABETES.

Niemann-Pick disease (sphingomyelin lipidosis) A type of LIPID STORAGE DISEASE.

nightmares A type of SLEEPING DISORDER.

night terrors (pavor nocturnus) A type of SLEEPING DISORDER.

nitrites A kind of FOOD ADDITIVE, a common and controversial preservative in meats.

NMR Abbreviation for nuclear magnetic resonance, former name for MRI (magnetic resonance imaging).

NMSQT Abbreviation for National Merit Scholarship Qualifying Test. (See PRELIMINARY SCHOLASTIC APTITUDE TEST/NATIONAL MERIT SCHOLARSHIP QUALIFYING TEST.)

no code Medical notation on a patient's chart meaning *do not resuscitate*. (See DEATH.)

nocturnal emission An EJACULATION that occurs during sleep, often among adolescent males; also called a *wet dream*.

noncustodial parent A parent whose ex-partner has been awarded sole legal CUSTODY of a child, as in a divorce case without shared custody. Noncustodial parents normally retain VISITATION RIGHTS.

nondextrous Unskilled in both hands, as opposed to AMBIDEXTROUS, or skilled with both hands; often occurring in young children where HANDEDNESS or lateral DOMINANCE is not yet established.

nongraded class Alternate term for UNGRADED CLASS.

nonrapid eye movement (NREM) One of the two main stages of sleep (see SLEEPING DISORDERS).

nonresident student A student whose legal place of residence is not in the district served by a school and who therefore is not necessarily eligible for services or TUITION breaks, as opposed to a RESIDENT STUDENT; at the ELEMENTARY SCHOOL or SECONDARY SCHOOL level, often called an *out-of-district student*.

Noonan's syndrome A CONGENITAL condition with characteristics similar to TURNER'S SYNDROME.

normal distribution A bell-shaped curve that graphically represents statistical data called NORMS, such as test scores; an ideal form that tends to result when large numbers of data are depicted on a graph. This form, like an upturned tulip-shaped bowl, with most scores falling in the middle and many fewer scores at the top and bottom ranges, is also used by teachers in GRADING ON THE CURVE. A curve that does not have the standard shape but instead has scores clustered at either the high or low end of the graph is called a *skewed distribution*.

norm-referenced test A type of TEST in which a student's performance is measured not against a set standard (such as 75 out of 100 right) but against the performance of a large group, as in the case of STANDARDIZED TESTS. The range of scores on the test are often published in tables, with the average scores for a particular group (such as all fifth-graders) being called the NORM for that group. The particular student's behavior may then be compared with the norm, giving an ACHIEVEMENT AGE or a DEVELOPMENTAL AGE. (For help and further information, see TESTS.)

norms In testing, usually the average scores of groups of people who have taken a particular STANDARDIZED TEST, used as a basis of comparison for those taking the test later. A child's test score is compared with the norm, and the comparison is sometimes expressed as a GRADE-EQUIVALENT score or AGE-EQUIVALENT score. Most widely used, numerically scored tests are developed and standardized on large populations, and the scores tend to be distributed evenly along a NORMAL DISTRIBUTION or *bell curve*, like an upturned tulip-shaped bowl, with most scores falling in the middle and many fewer scores at the top and bottom ranges. *Norms* may also, more generally, refer to social expectations about behavior and to the "average" behavior seen in a group. Some kinds of tests, such as the GESELL PRESCHOOL TEST, use the term *norm* more in this sense, as a behavior observed in more than half of the children of a particular age group. Confusion results when many who use the test wrongly treat the Gesell norms as if they were standardized norms with a strong statistical basis. (For help and further reference, see TESTS.)

Norplant A kind of BIRTH-CONTROL PILL implanted under the skin.

NREM Abbreviation for nonrapid eye movement, one of the two main stages of sleep.

nuclear family A type of FAMILY that includes basically two generations, parents and children.

nuclear magnetic resonance (NMR) The former name for MRI (magnetic resonance imaging).

nuclear medicine A medical specialty that involves the use of radioactive materials in diagnosis and therapy, in techniques such as NUCLEAR SCANS.

nuclear scan A type of MEDICAL TEST similar to a CT SCAN but involving the use of slightly and temporarily radioactive materials to more clearly show up certain aspects of the body's organs; also called *radioisotope scanning* or *radionuclide imaging*. These are INVASIVE procedures, in which the radioactive materials are introduced into the body, as by INJECTION or inhalation. The principle behind nuclear scanning is that various kinds of substances tend to be absorbed or concentrated in specific body organs; the material introduced will depend on which organ is to be studied, and its concentration in that organ can indicate if there is any abnormality, such as a LIVER PROBLEM or a TUMOR. In the PET SCAN, for example, radioactive glucose helps indicate the functioning of the circulatory system. (For help and further information, see MEDICAL TESTS.)

nullipara The medical designation for a woman who has never given birth to a live baby, often noted on a hospital medical chart as "para 0."

number facts Basic information about how the digits 1 to 10 are added, subtracted, multiplied, and divided, often referred to separately as *addition facts, subtraction facts*, and so on.

The number facts are basic to later number work and so are considered important PREREQUISITE skills.

nurse practitioner A nurse with special training (often including a MASTER'S DEGREE) and experience in a particular area of nursing. WELL-BABY EXAMINATIONS are sometimes given by a *pediatric nurse practitioner* (PNP), working alone or as part of a doctor/nurse team. A *family nurse practitioner* (FNP) often works in collaboration with PRIMARY HEALTH CARE PROVIDERS to help families who have continuing long-term medical needs, such as a child with SPINA BIFIDA.

nursery school A separate school for children of pre-KINDER-GARTEN age, from ages two or three to five; a type of PRESCHOOL educational program. Many nursery schools are cooperative, local groups, in which parents donate some of their time to serve as teachers' aides, in such areas as dressing or undressing children (and teaching them to do both themselves) and serving as an extra adult on a field trip. Because of parents' help, *cooperative nursery schools* generally have lower fees. Some are staffed, managed, and financed entirely by parents. Nursery schools follow various approaches to teaching and play for children, such as the MONTESSORI METHOD. (For help and further information see PRESCHOOL; EDUCATION.)

nursing bottle syndrome The rapid decay of a baby's TEETH when the infant is allowed to go to sleep with a bottle containing anything other than water. During sleep, little saliva is available to wash away sugars from liquids such as MILK, juice, or FORMULA, so bacteria quickly attack the tooth enamel, especially on the front teeth. The same is true if the baby falls asleep during BREASTFEEDING. Many dentists recommend that parents clean the infant's teeth with gauze or a damp washcloth after feeding, to prevent nursing bottle syndrome.

nurturance Support for a child's basic psychological growth and development and responsiveness to the child's needs, hopes, fears, and aspirations. For the child to develop nor-mally, at least one person in his or her life—often, but not necessarily, a parent—must supply that nurturance, a process that usually starts with BONDING. Failure to supply that support constitutes a real, though rarely provable, form of CHILD ABUSE AND NEGLECT, and can lead to MATERNAL DEPRIVATION SYNDROME or FAILURE TO THRIVE.

nutrition The provision of food substances in sufficient amounts and variety so that the body functions in a normal, healthy way; also the study of how the body uses foods and the proper amounts for daily consumption. Quantity alone is insufficient without quality and balance. The diet must contain several necessary elements every day: PROTEINS, CARBOHYDRATES, FAT, FIBER, VITAMINS, MINERALS, and water.

To get these vital elements, the diet should contain five main food groups:

- fruits and vegetables;
- milk and milk products;
- meat, fish, poultry, eggs, dried beans and peas, seeds, nuts, and peanut butter;
- whole-grain or enriched breads, cereals, and cereal products; and
- fats and sweets.

DIET DURING PREGNANCY (below) gives the Public Health Service's recommended diet for a woman during PREGNANCY, designed to give the right amount and balance of nutrients. The Food and Nutrition Board of the National Academy of Sciences is charged with making recommendations about how much of various kinds of nutrients each person should ideally have every day. These are the RECOMMENDED DAILY ALLOWANCES (RDAs), which are updated every five to 10 years on the basis of new research. (For more information and a table of RDAs, see RECOMMENDED DAILY ALLOWANCES.)

Diet During Pregnancy

1. *fruits and vegetables*: four or more servings of one-half cup of fruit or vegetable or one-half cup of juice daily. Fruits and vegetables contain vitamins, minerals, and fiber, a natural laxative. The dark green, leafy vegetables and deep yellow vegetables are rich in VITAMIN A. The dark green, leafy vegetables are also valuable for iron, VITAMIN C, MAGNESIUM, folic acid, and VITAMIN B$_2$ (riboflavin). Recommendations:

   - *at least one serving of a good source of vitamin A every other day*, such as apricots; broccoli; cantaloupe; carrots; dark green, leafy vegetables (beet greens, chard, collards, kale, mustard greens, spinach, turnip greens); pumpkin; sweet potatoes; winter squash.
   - *at least one serving of a good source of vitamin C every day*, such as broccoli; brussels sprouts; cantaloupe; cauliflower; green or sweet red pepper; grapefruit or grapefruit juice; orange or orange juice; tomatoes; dark green, leafy vegetables (beet greens, chard, collards, kale, mustard greens, spinach, turnip greens); cabbage; strawberries; watermelon.
   - *two servings of other vegetables and fruits every day*, such as beets, corn, eggplant, green and wax beans, lettuce, peas, potatoes, squash, apples, bananas, cherries, grapes, pears, pineapple, plums.

Continued on page 344

Diet During Pregnancy (continued)

2. *milk and milk products*: two to four eight-ounce glasses of milk or milk products daily (four for pregnant women). These have the calcium and other nutrients needed for strong bones and teeth, including the baby's. Choose milks that have vitamin D added. You may select whole milk, buttermilk, low-fat milk, or dry or fluid skim milk. Low-fat and skim milk have fewer calories than whole milk. Milk or cheese used in making soup, pudding, sauces, and other foods counts toward the total amount of milk you use.

   • *These amounts equal the calcium in one eight-ounce glass of milk*:
   one cup liquid skim milk, low-fat milk. or buttermilk
   one-half cup evaporated milk (undiluted)
   two one-inch cubes or two slices of cheese
   one-third cup instant powdered milk
   one cup plain yogurt, custard, or milk pudding
   • *These amounts equal the calcium in one-third cup of milk*:
   two-thirds cup cottage cheese
   one-half cup ice cream

   Note: If your child cannot drink milk, discuss this problem with your doctor or someone at the clinic. [See also LACTOSE INTOLERANCE.]

3. *meat, fish, poultry, eggs, dried beans and peas, nuts*: three or more servings daily. Meat, fish, poultry, eggs, dried beans and peas, seeds, nuts, and peanut butter supply protein as well as vitamins and minerals. Protein is needed to help build new tissues for you and your baby and to maintain the health of body cells. Three servings of these foods daily will supply you with enough protein during pregnancy. When you use dried beans or dried peas or cereals as main dishes, combine them with a small amount of cheese, milk, or meat to increase the protein value of the meal. Some examples include chile con carne, blackeyed peas and ham, chicken and rice, pizza, macaroni and cheese, and spaghetti and meatballs. Also, by combining grains with beans and peas, you will increase the amounts of protein your body can use. Some examples would be beans and rice or peanut butter on whole-wheat bread.

   • *Count as one serving*:
   two or three ounces of lean meat (remove the extra fat when possible). Some examples: one hamburger; two thin slices of beef, pork, lamb, or veal; one lean pork chop; two slices of luncheon meat; two hot dogs.
   two or three ounces of fish. Some examples: one whole small fish, one small fish fillet, one-third of a 6½-ounce can of tuna fish or salmon.
   two or three ounces of chicken, turkey, or other poultry. Some examples: two slices of light- or dark-meat turkey, one chicken leg, one-half chicken breast.
   • *Count as one-half serving*:
   one-half to three-fourths cup of cooked dried beans,
   peas, lentils, or garbanzos (chickpeas)
   two to three tablespoons of peanut butter
   one or two slices of cheese
   one egg
   one cup of tofu
   four to six tablespoons of nuts or seeds

4. *whole grain or enriched breads, cereals, and cereal products*: four or five servings daily. Breads and cereal foods provide minerals and vitamins, particularly the B vitamins and iron, as well as protein. Whole-grain breads and cereals provide essential trace elements, such as zinc, and also fiber, a natural laxative. Check the labels on breads and cereals to make sure that they are made with whole wheat or whole-grain flour or are enriched with minerals and vitamins.

   • *Count as one serving*:
   one slice of bread
   one muffin
   one roll or biscuit
   one tortilla or taco shell
   one-half to three-fourths cup of cooked or ready-to-eat cereal, such as oatmeal, farina, grits, raisin bran,
   or shredded wheat
   one cup of popcorn (1½ tablespoons unpopped)
   one-half to three-fourths cup of noodles, spaghetti, rice, bulgar, or macaroni

Continued on page 345

- two small pancakes
  one section of waffle
  two graham crackers or four to six small crackers
- *Count as two servings*:
  one hamburger bun or hot-dog roll
  one English muffin

5. *fats and sweets*: variable, according to calories needed. This group of foods includes margarine, butter, candy, jellies, sugars, syrups, desserts, soft drinks, snack foods, salad dressings, vegetable oils, and other fats used in cooking. Most of these foods are high in fat, sugar, or salt. Use them to meet additional caloric needs after basic nutritional needs have been met. Eating too much fat and too many sweets may crowd out other necessary nutrients.

Source: *Prenatal Care* (1989). Prepared for the Public Health Service by the Bureau of Health Care Delivery and Assistance, Division of Maternal and Child Health.

"Diet During Pregnancy" translates these RDAs into the specific types of foods and serving amounts needed to meet a pregnant woman's basic nutritional needs in each of these food groups. Parents can use these serving amounts, along with the RDAs, as basic guidelines in planning equally well-balanced nutrition for a growing family. Infants and young children have special nutrition needs, dealt with under the entries on BREASTFEEDING, BOTTLEFEEDING, MILK, and FEEDING, which includes a special feature on eating patterns. (See also NUTRITIONAL NEEDS OF PREGNANT AND NURSING WOMEN on page 346.)

Many people take vitamin and mineral supplements to be sure they meet the RDAs for vital nutrients. Nutrition experts say it is best to get vitamins and minerals from the foods you eat. When you select an adequate diet, you usually will not need other vitamin and mineral supplements. For pregnant women, IRON and FOLIC ACID are exceptions. Because of increased needs during pregnancy, it is difficult to obtain adequate amounts of those nutrients from food alone, so some doctors prescribe iron and folic acid supplements. Such pills do not, however, supply all of the other essential nutrients, such as protein, carbohydrate, fat, and some vitamins and minerals, so eating balanced meals is still important. The same holds for supplying nutrition to growing children, though some doctors suggest that vitamin and mineral supplements may be useful for those days when parents know their child has not eaten well-balanced meals.

In addition, our bodies need water and other fluids. For pregnant women, the recommendation is six to eight glasses of water or other liquids each day. Fruit and vegetable juices and milk, as well as water, count as fluids, though some doctors recommend that pregnant women should only sparingly drink (or eat) foods containing caffeine. Fluids are especially important for infants (see DEHYDRATION).

The diet described above is in the traditional mainstream of nutrition. But for a variety of reasons, some people choose to have more restricted diets, such as the VEGETARIAN or the even more restricted VEGAN diet. If such a diet eliminates meat and fish but retains milk and eggs, the nutritional balance is thought to be adequate, even during pregnancy. But because protein from animal sources is easier for the body to use than that from plant sources, people on a diet that also eliminates milk and eggs will probably get properly balanced nutrition only with very careful planning and vitamin and mineral supplements. They should check with a doctor and nutritionist, especially when planning a pregnancy or providing a diet for growing children.

Many other people are on restricted diets for medical reasons, such as ALLERGY to or intolerance of certain kinds of foods (such as milk; see LACTOSE INTOLERANCE). They too will need careful counseling to be sure they and their children are getting all of the nutrients necessary. Various eating disorders can also disrupt nutrition (see separate entries on ANOREXIA NERVOSA, BULIMIA, OBESITY, and PICA).

For people with any kind of DIGESTIVE DISORDER and for pregnant women, the Public Health Service recommends eating smaller meals, saving some food to snack on a couple of hours later. They also recommend raw vegetables and fruits, juices, milk, breads, and cereals for between-meal snacks; these are especially good to have available for children and adolescents, as alternatives to "junk food" of little or no nutritional value and with excess fat, and may in fact help build up habits of good nutrition from the early years.

Some people have inadequate nutrition because of poverty. For these, various federal, state, and local programs exist, including WIC (Supplemental Food Program for Women, Infants and Children), which provides selected foods for pregnant or breastfeeding mothers and preschool children. These groups reflect the widespread recognition that inadequate nutrition leads to a variety of health problems, such as LOW BIRTH WEIGHT and many associated disorders. The Food Stamp program can also help stretch food budgets. People in need should contact their local clinic or health department for help.

In selecting food for themselves and their families, parents also need to be concerned about FOOD ADDITIVES, some of which can have harmful effects on health; naturally occurring contaminants such as AFLATOXIN or salmonella; and other kinds of contaminants that can affect food (see ENVIRONMENTAL HAZARDS). They may well want to subscribe to some periodicals that give frequent updates on new information about hazards to food and nutrition; one available from the U.S. government is the Food and Drug Administration's *FDA Consumer* (see page 347).

Nutritional Needs of Pregnant and Nursing Women

Extra energy and nutrients are needed to support the growth of maternal tissues, such as the uterus and breast, and the increased metabolic demands of pregnancy, as well as the growth of the fetus and placenta. During lactation, the energy and nutrients provided in the milk, and those required for its production, must be replaced.

Weight Gain

Research has demonstrated that both maternal prepregnancy weight and weight gained during pregnancy are important determinants of infant birth weight. Inadequate weight gain during pregnancy combined with low prepregnancy weight are associated with lower-than-average infant birth weights and greater risks for fetal or neonatal death and neonatal disease; these problems decline as weight gain increases.

Such associations do not necessarily prove causality, however; healthy infants of average birth weight have been born to women whose weight change during pregnancy ranged from loss to high gain. For this reason, and because genetic and behavioral factors other than weight gain also influence infant birth weight, it has been difficult to define the optimal weight gain during pregnancy for women or varying prepregnancy weights. Most studies that have correlated average weight gain with birth outcome in normal-weight adult women with normal pregnancies have found the optimal weight gain to fall within the range of 22 to 27 pounds, yet one-fifth of white adult women and one-fourth of black adult women did not gain this much during normal pregnancies of 40 or more weeks' duration in 1980. When all pregnancies in this study, regardless of length of gestation, were considered, one-third of black mothers gained no more than 20 pounds, and black mothers were nearly twice as likely as white mothers to gain less than 16 pounds (20 percent as compared with 11 percent). Nevertheless, most of these women gave birth to healthy babies.

The influence of prepregnancy weight on birth outcome also makes it difficult to define an optimal weight gain; a low weight gain by women with a low prepregnancy weight is associated with the highest incidence of LBW [low birth weight], but higher weight gains during pregnancy reduce the risk. The relationship may not hold for adolescents, however. Although the mean weight gain of adolescent women during normal pregnancy has been shown in several studies to average about 35 pounds, their risk of having an LBW infant was still higher than that for adult women.

The effect on infant birth weight of differing levels of weight gain by obese women during pregnancy is also uncertain. Obesity during pregnancy is linked to an increased risk of maternal complications such as hypertensive disorders, gestational diabetes, infections, and surgical deliveries. These risks are reduced when obese women do not gain more than 24 pounds during pregnancy, but the lower limit of weight gain that can produce optimal birth outcome has not been defined. This issue is important because caloric restriction and diet-induced weight loss in pregnancy by obese women has been associated with reduced infant birth weight, suggesting that obese women should gain at least some weight during pregnancy.

Energy

The recommended intake of energy during pregnancy includes an increment of 300 kcal/day over the energy allowances for nonpregnant women. This amount was obtained by calculating the total energy cost of synthesizing maternal and fetal tissues and dividing this figure by the number of days of pregnancy. Although the 300 kcal/day increment has been widely accepted, actual measurements of the energy balances of pregnant women in several international populations have demonstrated that they may consume as few as 50 kcal/day over prepregnancy energy intake levels yet gain weight normally and produce infants of normal birth weight. Although the reason for this discrepancy is not yet known, preliminary observations suggest that the metabolic needs of pregnant women do not increase significantly. Nevertheless, caloric supplementation of pregnant women in a poor community where the average caloric intake was 1,500 kcal/day increased the average birth weight and reduced the incidence of LBW infants.

Recent investigations show that lactating also requires fewer calories than the 500 kcal/day calculated as needed above prepregnant energy levels. Present knowledge thus does not permit the precise definition of caloric requirements during pregnancy and lactation.

[For further information, see VITAMINS, MINERALS, IRON, and PROTEIN; for nutritional needs of the fetus, see PLACENTA.]

Source: *The Surgeon General's Report on Nutrition and Health.* Rocklin, CA: Prima, 1988.

The government publication *Nutritive Value of Foods* (see page 348) provides useful information on the amounts of various kinds of nutrients to be found in common foods. Parents can also get important information from FOOD LABELS on processed products, not only about nutrition but also about substances they may want to avoid, especially in the case of allergies. Other good sources of nutrition information (in addition to those listed below) are local branches of the Public Health Service and County Extension departments.

For help and further information

Human Nutrition Information Service
Room 325A

Federal Building
Hyattsville, MD 20782
301-436-7725
Federal arm of the U.S. Department of Agriculture (USDA). Sponsors research; publishes various materials, including (jointly with the Department of Health and Human Services) *Dietary Guidelines for Americans*.

Food and Drug Administration
HFI-40
5600 Fishers Lane
Rockville, MD 20857
301-472-4750
Federal arm of the U.S. Department of Health and Human Services. Publishes *FDA Consumer* 10 times a year.

Center for Science in the Public Interest (CSPI)
1501 16th Street, NW
Washington, DC 20036
202-332-9110
Michael Jacobsen, Executive Director
Organization of health professionals and others of many backgrounds concerned about the adverse effects of science and technology, especially on food safety and nutrition. Seeks to educate public and influence government policy, especially in testing, labeling, and advertising; publishes various materials, including *Nutrition Action Healthletter*.

American Home Economics Association (AHEA)
2010 Massachusetts Avenue, NW
Washington, DC 20036
202-862-8300
Joan R. McFadden, Executive Director
Professional organization of home economists. Seeks to educate public and influence public policy; operates Center for the Family; publishes various materials.

American Public Health Association (APHA)
1015 15th Street, NW
Washington, DC 20005
202-789-5600
William H. McBeath, M.D., Executive Director
Organization of public health professionals and interested others. Seeks to raise the level of health in the population, including physical, mental, and environmental; publishes wide variety of materials, including journal, newspaper, and many books and pamphlets.

Society for Nutrition Education (SNE)
1700 Broadway, Suite 300
Oakland, CA 94612
415-444-7133
J. Michael McKenchnie, Executive Director
Professional organization of nutritional educators. Seeks to educate and raise nutritional level of the public; publishes various materials.

International Association of Parents and Professionals for Safe Alternatives in Childbirth (NAPSAC), 314-238-2010. (For full group information, see CHILDBIRTH.)

Other reference sources

General Works

The Tufts University Guide to Total Nutrition, by Stanley Gershoff with Catherine Whitney. New York: Harper & Row, 1990.

What's In My Food? A Book of Nutrients, by Xandria Williams. Garden City Park, NY: Avery, 1990.

Jean Mayer's Diet and Nutrition Guide, by Jean Mayer and Jeanne P. Goldberg. New York: Pharos, 1990.

Everywoman's Guide to Nutrition, by Judith E. Brown. Minneapolis: University of Minnesota Press, 1990.

Nutrition Smarts: A Cookbook and Guide from Toddler to Teen, by Carolyn Moore, Mimi Kerr, and Robert Shulman, M.D. Hauppauge, NY: Barron's, 1990.

Kidfood, by Lisa Tracy. New York: Dell, 1989.

Superimmunity for Kids: The First Truly Scientific Guide to Health Through Nutrition for Children from Infancy through Adolescence, by Leo Galland, M.D., with Dian Buchman. New York: Dutton, 1988; Delacorte/Delta, 1989.

No-Nonsense Nutrition for Your Baby's First Year, second edition, by Annette Natow and Jo-Ann Heslin. New York: Prentice Hall, 1988.

Taming the C.A.N.D.Y. Monster: A Cookbook to Get Kids to Eat Less Junk Food, revised edition, by Vicky Lansky. Deephaven, MN: Book Peddlers, 1988.

Special Diets and Kids: How to Keep Your Child on Any Prescribed Diet, by John F. Taylor and R. Sharon Latta. New York: Dodd, Mead, 1988.

How To Be Your Own Nutritionist, by Stuart M. Berger, M.D. New York: Morrow, 1987.

The Complete Guide to Health and Nutrition, by Gary Null. New York: Delacorte, 1984.

The Natural Baby Food Cookbook, by Margaret Kenda and Phyllis Williams. New York: Avon, 1982.

Healthy Snacks for Kids, by Penny Warner. San Leandro, CA: Bristol, 1989.

Adolescent Nutrition, Myron Winick, ed. New York: Wiley, 1982.

Growing Up Healthy: A Parent's Guide to Good Nutrition, by Myron Winick. New York: Morrow, 1980.

Background Works

The Nutrition Desk Reference, revised edition, by Robert H. Garrison, Jr., and Elizabeth Somer. New Canaan, CT: Keats, 1990.

Nutrition During Pregnancy, Part 1: Weight Gain; Part 2: Nutrient Supplements. Washington, DC: National Academy Press, 1990.

Prescription for Nutritional Healing: A Practical A–Z Reference to Drug-Free Remedies, by James Balch, M.D., and Phyllis Balch. Garden City Park, NY: Avery, 1990.

The Complete Book of Food, by Carol Rinzler. New York: Pharos, 1989.

The Columbia Encyclopedia of Women's Nutrition, by Carlton Fredericks. New York: Putnam, 1989.

Nutritional Influences on Illness: A Sourcebook of Clinical Research, by Melvyn R. Werbach, M.D. New Canaan, CT: Keats, 1989.

Nutritive Value of Foods, by Susan E. Gebhardt and Ruth H. Matthews. Washington, DC: United States Department of Agriculture, Human Nutrition Information Service, Home and Garden Bulletin Number 72, 1988. Provides key tables indicating what the edible part of a wide range of foods, in various forms (raw or processed), contain in the way of nutrients, including food energy, protein, fat, fatty acids (saturated, monounsaturated, and polyunsaturated), cholesterol, carbohydrates, calcium, phosphorus, iron, potassium, sodium, vitamin A, thiamin, riboflavin, niacin, and ascorbic acid (vitamin C).

For Kids

New Theories on Diet and Nutrition, by Sally Lee. New York: Watts, 1990. For grades 7 to 12.

Nutrition, by Mario Orlandi, Donald Prue and Annette Spence. New York: Facts on File, 1988. For young adults.

(See also VITAMINS; MINERALS.)

nutritional supplements   General term for VITAMINS and MINERALS taken in addition to those gained from the regular diet.

nutritionist   A health professional who specializes in the study and application of principles of NUTRITION. Nutritionists evaluate the healthfulness of eating habits and advise on changes in diet, for normal diets or therapeutic diets for people with special health problems. They may also advise HANDICAPPED people on mechanical aids and techniques that will allow them to feed themselves independently.

nystagmus   Jerky oscillation of the eyeballs, a kind of EYE AND VISION PROBLEM that usually indicates some other disorder affecting the brain, such as a BRAIN TUMOR or hereditary forms of ATAXIA.

obesity   Condition of being 20 percent or more over the maximum weight considered ideal for a person's height and age. The American diet—plentiful food, rich in FATS—plus a more sedentary, TV-dominated life has led to an epidemic of obesity. By the late 1980s, some studies estimate, nearly one out of four children were so overweight as to be considered obese.

Though some obese people eat far more than normal, many obese people eat no more than their leaner counterparts. Recent studies have confirmed what many researchers have long suspected: that obesity has genetic and biochemical components. In particular, they find that obese people have a tendency to store extra calories as fat, where leaner people tend to burn up extra calories or convert them to muscle, and that when dieting, the bodies of obese people produce an enzyme that tends to make weight *gain* easier.

These results point up the difficulty of losing weight. But the excess weight came originally from excess fat in the diet, and it is there that parents can best help themselves and their children: by feeding them a balanced diet with fats controlled after age two (see NUTRITION and FATS). Beyond that, if parents or

children are obese, EXERCISE may be employed in the difficult process of taking the weight down. In past decades, doctors sometimes advised obese women not to gain any weight during PREGNANCY, but medical opinion now is that they should gain weight as do other pregnant women, though in a controlled way (see NUTRITIONAL NEEDS OF PREGNANT AND NURSING WOMEN on page 346).

Some obese children later develop EATING DISORDERS that require clinical treatment. Surprisingly, however, many adolescents with ANOREXIA NERVOSA and BULIMIA, which involve obsessions with food coupled with compulsions to diet and purge, are not obese but more often only slightly overweight.

For help and further information

National Institute of Diabetes, Digestive and Kidney Diseases (NIDDK), 301-496-3583. Publishes *Obesity and Energy Metabolism*. (For full group information, see DIGESTIVE DISORDERS.)

Other reference sources

Big Kids: A Parent's Guide to Weight Control for Children, by Gregory Archer. Oakland, CA: New Harbinger, 1989.

Taking It Off and Keeping It Off: Based on the Successful Methods of Overeaters Anonymous, by Helene R. Chicago: Contemporary, 1989.

Fat-Proofing Your Children . . . So That They Never Become Diet-Addicted Adults, by Vicki Lansky. New York: Bantam, 1988.

How to Get Your Kids to Eat . . . But Not Too Much, by Ellyn Satter. Palo Alto, CA: Bull, 1987.

Fat is a Family Affair, by Judi Hollis. Minneapolis, MN: Hazelden, 1985.

Obesity and the Family, by David Kallen and Marvin Sussman. New York: Haworth, 1984.

One Fat Summer, by Robert Lipsyte. New York: Harper, 1977; Bantam paperback. For young adults. About the changing self-image of an overweight teenage boy.

Eating Disorders, Obesity, Anorexia Nervosa and the Person Within, by Hilde Bruch. New York: Basic, 1973.

OB-GYN   Short form for OBSTETRICIAN-GYNECOLOGIST.

objective test   A type of TEST that is designed to be presented equally to all, regardless of who administers the test. The administrator follows a "script" in introducing the test and presenting the specific questions. Scoring does not depend on the administrator's discretion and may even be done by machine, often requiring only counting up the number of correct "boxes" checked or checking answers against a key. Examples of objective tests include the WECHSLER PRESCHOOL AND PRIMARY SCALE OF INTELLIGENCE (WPPSI), the WECHSLER INTELLIGENCE SCALE FOR CHILDREN, REVISED (WISC-R), METROPOLITAN ACHIEVEMENT TESTS, and SCHOLASTIC APTITUDE TESTS, as well as classroom tests that have clear right and wrong answers and unambiguous answer keys, as opposed to SUBJECTIVE TESTS.

object permanence   The understanding that an object continues to exist even though one does not have immediate knowledge of it through the senses, such as touch, sight, or smell; a key concept children develop in the sensory motor stage of COGNITIVE DEVELOPMENT, according to Jean Piaget.

obligated parent   The parent who has been ordered by a court to pay CHILD SUPPORT, such as a NONCUSTODIAL PARENT pays to help support the child in the CUSTODY of the CUSTODIAL PARENT; also called the *responsible parent*.

obsessive-compulsive disorder (OCD)   A type of MENTAL DISORDER, classed by psychiatrists as an *anxiety disorder*, in which a person focuses persistently on certain thoughts and behaviors, enough so that the person's normal working and living routine is affected, significant amounts of time are consumed, social activities or relationships are hindered, or the person feels intense distress. Common obsessions—thoughts, ideas, impulses, or images—center around violence, contamination (such as fear of being infected from shaking someone's hand), and doubt about whether something has been done (such as a light turned off) or has happened (such as an accident). Common compulsions—repeated, deliberate behaviors, often performed in a stereotyped way and related to obsessive thoughts—involve hand-washing, counting, touching, and checking, as to see that something has been done or has happened. People with OCD often build up great tension in trying to resist their obsessions and compulsions, with release of tension on yielding to them. Obsessive-compulsive disorder often begins in ADOLESCENCE or early adulthood but can appear in childhood, and it is often associated with or complicated by ANXIETY, DEPRESSION, TOURETTE'S SYNDROME, and DRUG and ALCOHOL ABUSE.

For help and further information

OCD Foundation
P.O. Box 9573
New Haven, CT 06535
203-772-0565; 772-0575
Organization of and for people with obsessive-compulsive disorder and their families.

National Institute of Mental Health, 301-443-4536 (public affairs); 301-443-4513 (publications). Publishes booklet *Useful Information On Obsessive-Compulsive Disorder*. (For full group information, see MENTAL DISORDERS.)

Other reference sources

The Boy Who Couldn't Stop Washing: The Experience and Treatment of Obsessive-Compulsive Disorder, by Judith L. Rappaport, M.D. New York: New American Library/Plume, 1990.

obstetrician-gynecologist (OB-GYN)   A physician who specializes in providing medical and surgical care related to the female reproductive system, throughout their adult lives, including during PREGNANCY. Some obstetricians specialize only in care of women during pregnancy, and some gynecologists specialize only in care of the female reproductive system apart from pregnancy, but most carry out both activities. Obstetricians who specialize in caring for women having HIGH-RISK PREGNANCIES are called *maternal and fetal specialists* or PERINATOLOGISTS.

obturator   A device that covers a child's cleft palate during feeding. (See CLEFT LIP AND PALATE.)

occupational therapist   A health professional who evaluates, treats, and counsels people whose physical activity has been limited by illness, injury, DEVELOPMENTAL DISORDERS, LEARNING DISABILITIES, or other causes and whose aim is to help such people maximize independence and maintain health. For example, occupational therapists may help people learn or relearn the physical control and coordination necessary to perform independently such everyday tasks as dressing, eating, washing, and going to the toilet and to be able eventually to work at some form of meaningful employment. Working with children, they may also focus on developing PERCEPTUAL-MOTOR SKILLS and the ability to play or carry out school-related activities, such as sitting, walking, handling physical objects, drawing and other paper-and-pencil activities, cutting, pasting, and general hand–eye and body–eye coordination (see VISUAL SKILLS; MOTOR SKILLS). Occupational therapists often work at hospitals and outpatient clinics but may also work in the person's home.

OCSE Abbreviation for OFFICE OF CHILD SUPPORT ENFORCEMENT, a federal agency for helping CUSTODIAL PARENTS obtain court-ordered CHILD SUPPORT payments.

OD Medical abbreviation for oculus dexter, the right eye; also for overdose. (See EYE AND VISION PROBLEMS; DRUG ABUSE.)

Office of Child Support Enforcement (OCSE) A federal agency, an arm of the U.S. Department of Health and Human Services, that helps CUSTODIAL PARENTS obtain court-ordered CHILD SUPPORT payments, as through its PARENT LOCATOR SERVICE.

offset In relation to CHILD SUPPORT, the amount of money taken from the income tax refund of an OBLIGATED PARENT to pay off a court-ordered child support debt.

OI Abbreviation for OSTEOGENESIS IMPERFECTA.

oligohydramnios A condition of having too little AMNIOTIC FLUID during a PREGNANCY.

oligomenorrhea A disorder associated with MENSTRUATION.

oligospermia A condition of low SPERM count, an INFERTILITY problem.

oncologist A medical professional who specializes in the treatment of TUMORS and CANCER.

only child A child with no SIBLINGS. (See BIRTH ORDER.)

oophoritis Inflammation of the OVARIES, which can cause INFERTILITY.

open admissions A largely unrestricted policy toward ADMISSION to a school.

open adoption A form of ADOPTION in which birth and adoptive parents have some full or direct contact with each other.

open-book test A TEST in which a student can consult any materials desired, sometimes meaning simply that a child can look up information in a textbook during a classroom exam but often (especially in college) meaning that the student can take the examination questions home overnight and look into any sources available for information. Open-book tests are designed to focus not on the student's ability to memorize information but on the ability to use reference sources relating to the particular topic in an intelligent, knowledgeable way.

open fracture A type of FRACTURE in which pieces of bone break the skin.

open-heart surgery A complex kind of surgery performed in cases of heart defects. (See HEART AND HEART PROBLEMS.)

open reduction In cases of FRACTURE, use of surgery to expose the broken bones so that they can be repositioned.

open scholarship A type of SCHOLARSHIP for which anyone may apply, without restrictions.

Open University A type of EXTERNAL DEGREE PROGRAM that allows people to gain college CREDIT with little or no attendance at regular courses on a college campus, often offering a combination of CORRESPONDENCE SCHOOL study and learning via radio and television broadcasts.

ophthalmia A severe eye infection in newborns. (See EYE AND VISION PROBLEMS.)

ophthalmologist A physician who specializes in diagnosing and treating disorders of the eyes, as from disease, injury, or birth defects, including performing surgery on the eyes. Ophthalmologists often work with other physicians because eye problems frequently result from other medical problems, such as DIABETES MELLITUS, BRAIN TUMOR, or various BIRTH DEFECTS. With children, they may use lights, simple pictures, or special instruments to examine the eyes to see if vision needs correction, as with glasses (though these may be prescribed by an OPTOMETRIST), or if an eye condition needs medication. In some cases, an ophthalmologist may recommend that special materials or seating arrangements be used for the child in school. (For help and further information, see EYE AND VISION PROBLEMS.)

ophthalmoscope The basic equipment used to explore the interior of the eye in an eye examination. (See EYE AND VISION PROBLEMS.)

optic atrophy A condition in which the eye's optic nerve has been damaged. (See EYE AND VISION PROBLEMS.)

optician A health professional who specializes in grinding and fitting eyeglasses or contact lenses, according to prescriptions given by an OPTOMETRIST or OPHTHALMOLOGIST.

optometrist A health professional who specializes in screening for and diagnosing vision problems and may prescribe glasses or contact lenses as needed. The lenses themselves are generally ground and fit by an OPTICIAN. Not physicians, optometrists refer to OPHTHALMOLOGISTS any eye problems that may need to be treated with drugs or surgery.

OPV Abbreviation for ORAL POLIO VACCINE.

oral contraceptive More formal name for BIRTH-CONTROL PILL.

oral herpes A type of HERPES SIMPLEX infection affecting the mouth area.

oral polio vaccine (OPV or Sabin vaccine) A vaccine made from "live" POLIOMYELITIS viruses, generally given by mouth in several doses between ages two months and six years. OPV is recommended for the IMMUNIZATION of most people under age 18 because it is easier to administer than the INACTIVATED POLIO VACCINE (IPV), is more effective in the intestinal tract (where infection first occurs), and is more effective in preventing the spread of the polio virus. Over 90 percent of those receiving the OPV vaccine have immunity for life. Some viruses can spread from the immunized person to others with whom they come into contact; that may provide immunization to those

<hr>

Possible Side Effects and Adverse Reactions to Polio Immunization

Very rarely (with about one in every 7.8 million doses distributed), oral polio vaccine (OPV) causes paralytic polio in the person who is immunized. The risk is higher following receipt of the first dose of OPV and in persons with abnormally low resistance to infection and may be higher in adults being immunized. Also, on rare occasions (about once in every 5.5 million doses of OPV distributed), paralytic polio may develop in a close contact of a person recently immunized with OPV. This risk also is somewhat higher to contacts of persons receiving their first dose of OPV. These risks are very low, but they should be recognized and balanced against the risk of disease. Inactivated polio vaccine (IPV) is not known to produce any side effects other than minor local pain and redness.

Source: *Parents Guide to Childhood Immunization* (1988). Prepared for the Public Health Service and the Centers for Disease Control.

<hr>

others as well, but in very rare cases it can produce polio itself. In special cases, such as when the child or a family member has low resistance to serious infections, IPV, made from killed polio viruses, may be given instead. Polio immunization is required by all 50 U.S. states for children entering or attending school. (For help and further information, see POLIO-MYELITIS; for a recommended immunization schedule, see IMMUNIZATION. For information on recourse in case of problems, see CHILDHOOD VACCINE INJURY ACT.)

oral surgeon   A dental-medical professional who specializes in performing surgery on the mouth, face, TEETH, or jaw. An oral surgeon must be a trained dentist with an additional specialty in oral and maxillofacial (upper face) surgery and is often trained as a physician as well. Oral surgeons perform ORTHOGNATHIC SURGERY in severe cases of MALOCCLUSION, fix broken jaws, remove some benign TUMORS from the mouth, repair CLEFT LIP AND PALATE, and do some other forms of craniofacial surgery (see PLASTIC SURGERY).

orchioectomy   An operation to remove one or both TESTES. In adults such an operation is often performed in cases of CANCER of the testicles; but in infants or young boys, orchioectomy may be done to remove a testicle that has failed to develop normally or in cases of irreparable damage due to TORSION OF THE TESTIS. Removal of one testicle does not affect the other one or the male's ability later to have children and have a normal sex life.

orchiopexy   An operation to bring one or both undescended TESTES down into the SCROTUM when they have failed to descend on their own before or after birth. Normally performed in a HOSPITAL under general ANESTHESIA when the boy is between ages one and five, orchiopexy involves making a small incision in the

groin and, through that, maneuvering the testicles into proper position and sometimes fixing them there with sutures.

orchitis   Inflammation of one or both TESTES, often with the MUMPS virus but sometimes with a bacterial infection, as in EPIDIDYMO-ORCHITIS. Cold packs to reduce swelling, painkillers (*analgesics*), support for the SCROTUM, and antibiotics are often used to treat the condition. Orchitis is sometimes followed by shrinking of the testes but rarely results in INFERTILITY.

order   In law, a formal, written directive from a judge, administrative officer, or other judicial officer, as in a case involving CHILD SUPPORT or CUSTODY.

order to show cause hearing (OCS)   An order issued by a judge for a person to tell in court why a judge should not take a specified action. In a case of threatened child abuse (see CHILD ABUSE AND NEGLECT), for example, the judge may issue a TEMPORARY RESTRAINING ORDER against the abusive parent and then call for an OCS hearing to hear the accused parent's side of the story. Someone who does not appear in court in response to an OCS is in CONTEMPT OF COURT.

organic brain syndrome   General medical term for MENTAL DISORDERS that have no precisely known physical cause but are presumed to result from disorders in the chemistry of the brain (see BRAIN AND BRAIN DISORDERS).

organic mental disorder   MENTAL DISORDERS that result from physical causes in or affecting the brain, such as infection, HEAD INJURY, BRAIN TUMOR, DRUG ABUSE, ALCOHOL ABUSE, or METABOLIC DISORDERS; when the cause is known, sometimes called *organic mental syndrome*. A wide variety of disorders can result, including DEMENTIA, DELIRIUM, HALLUCINATIONS, DELUSIONS, and MOOD DISORDERS. (For help and further information, see MENTAL DISORDERS.)

organismic age   A summary of a whole range of AGE comparisons—including educational, mental, dental, carpal (wrist), height, weight, and social—as compared to established norms. (See AGE.)

organ of Corti   The organ of hearing in the inner ear, a minute duct filled with microscopic hair cells that take incoming sound vibrations and transform them into electrical signals, which are then transmitted to the brain. Damage to the organ of Corti causes significant EAR AND HEARING PROBLEMS.

orgasm   Powerful, climactic sensations involving involuntary muscular contractions in the genital area following rhythmic sexual excitement. While orgasm brings intense pleasure to both men and women, it plays a role in reproduction only in men, by triggering the EJACULATION of the SEMEN that carries the SPERM.

orientation and mobility instructors (peripetologists)   Specialists who help visually handicapped children learn the concepts and skills they need to understand where they are and to move about safely and easily. (See EYE AND VISION PROBLEMS.)

orphan   A child who has no parents and often no guardian. Such a child would once have routinely been placed in a large institutional orphanage but is now more likely to be placed in a

GROUP HOME and then with FOSTER PARENTS until arrangements can be made for the child's ADOPTION. Under immigration law, for purposes of adoption, an orphan is defined as a child under age 16 at the date on which a visa application is filed and whose parents are dead, have disappeared, or have abandoned the child or whose surviving parent is unable to provide proper care and has formally consented to the emigration and adoption.

orphan drug A medication that pharmaceutical companies generally do not produce because it is used to treat a rare condition affecting relatively few people. This is so especially if the patent has run out on the drug and competitors might enter the field at any time they wish. In 1983, the federal government passed the Orphan Drug Act, which offers financial inducements to encourage the development, testing (including testing of drugs developed in other countries), and distribution of such drugs to the people who need them, such as medication for TOURETTE'S SYNDROME.

For help and further information

Food and Drug Administration (FDA), 301-443-3170; main number, 301-472-4750. (For full group information, see ALLERGY.)

National Organization for Rare Disorders (NORD), 203-746-6518. Monitors availability of medicines for rare disorders under the Orphan Drug Act; publishes the quarterly *Orphan Disease Update*, (203-746-6518). (For full group information, see RARE DISORDERS.)

Other reference source

Orphan Drugs, by Kenneth Anderson and Lois Anderson. Los Angeles: Body Press, 1988.
(See also specific rare disorders.)

orthodontic braces Devices used by dentists to correct some types of MALOCCLUSION, in which teeth are not in proper positions.

orthodontist A dentist who specializes in treating MALOCCLUSION, or problems with the bite, when TEETH meet unevenly.

orthognathic surgery An operation to reshape or reposition the jaws, as to correct severe cases of MALOCCLUSION, in which the TEETH do not meet evenly. Such surgery is normally performed by an ORAL SURGEON in a hospital.

orthopedic devices A variety of mechanical aids and equipment developed to help people with ORTHOPEDIC HANDICAPS, especially in the areas of sitting, standing, walking, and using their hands, as well as maintaining balance and protecting the body from harm. These are basic necessities if the child is to develop other skills to the fullest. Among the most common kinds of orthopedic devices are:

- *wheelchairs*, which for children should always be equipped with seat belts, used whenever the child is in the chair. Some techniques for maneuvering a wheelchair and for help-

ing a child into and out of one are given on page 353 in HELPING CHILDREN WITH WHEELCHAIRS.
- *walkers*, which help children move about independently. Of the several types available, some have four wheels and are quite easy for children to push. Some have two parallel railings and an enclosed front, offering support on three sides, sometimes called *chariots*.
- *carts* or *boards*, low-to-the-ground, hand-propelled devices with four wheels that allow a child to lie on his or her stomach and push around the room using hands and arms. (If not available locally, contact the National Easter Seal Society; see HELP FOR SPECIAL CHILDREN on page 578.)
- *canes* and *crutches*, traditional items, built child-size. Some canes are tripods, with three feet on the floor, offering more support than a single-pronged cane. In addition to the crutches that fit under the armpits, children may use shorter *Canadian crutches* (or *elbow crutches*), which have bands around the arm, above or below the elbow, and handles at waist height. Some children put their crutches ahead of them, then swing their bodies behind, while others use a four-point "crutch-foot-crutch-foot" type of walking pattern. Parents should check with the doctor or physical therapist to learn the best way for the child's particular condition.
- *braces*, mechanical devices of metal bars and bands designed to provide support, to hold part of the body in place, to protect it from further injury, or to prevent deformities. Ankle braces fit into the sole of the child's shoe and limit movement. Some children have braces that run the length of the leg, sometimes extending to the pelvis, with locks at the knees and joints. These lock joints have sliding catches that the child releases to bend at the knees and hips and then relocks for walking. These tasks become routine for children, though they (and parents) may need help at first.
- *helmets*, lightweight protective gear (like bicycling helmets) to protect children from HEAD INJURY, especially those with poor balance or those who have had surgery, as for a BRAIN TUMOR.
- *artificial limbs*, or *prostheses*, which replace a lost limb or a limb absent at birth. The limb helps the child maintain balance and normal development, allows for easier activity, and in all makes for a more normal life. Artificial legs often take more activity because they are used in walking. Children who have had amputations will need special training in walking, at first often using canes or crutches. An artificial hand may simply be two hooks that open and close together but can allow a child to develop many important MOTOR SKILLS. Children will need training in using it and occasionally some adjustment. Physical therapists stress that it is important that the child wear the artificial limb all day (unless medical advice is otherwise) so that it becomes accepted as part of the body.

In making a home setting convenient for children with orthopedic handicaps, parents might also use bolsters, rolls, and slanting wedges to allow children to be supported while they play on the floor. Sometimes an old chair, with high back and arms but with the legs cut off, may be placed on the floor for sitting,

Helping Children with Wheelchairs

If you are pushing a wheelchair, always go at walking speed, to keep firm control. When a curb or step appears, tilt the chair back by stepping on the extension at the base of the chair and ease the front wheels onto the higher surface. Going down a curb is sometimes more difficult, particularly since some children are afraid of falling out of the chair. Discuss with the child (if appropriate) suggestions on how to do it. If you turn the chair around as you go down a step or curb, hold on to the handles, and go to the lower level before the chair does, the child will probably have less fear of falling. Some children feel more comfortable when two people are present: one in back of the chair and one in front of the chair guiding the chair as it is lowered. This is a great help when going down more than one step. If you can arrange access to an adult-size wheelchair, you and the school or therapy staff can practice these procedures on each other. This practice will help you identify and solve problem situations in advance.

The main technique for assisting a child from a wheelchair to another seat is called *forward transfer* [illustrated on page 354]. When the child is moving from a wheelchair to a regular chair at a table, be sure that the chair the child is moving to is steady. You might have to hold it or brace it against a wall. Steadiness is particularly important if the child is moving to a seat or toilet directly in front of him or

her. To transfer to a chair, the wheelchair must be positioned so that it faces the seat, with the footrests up and the brakes locked securely. The child should then place his or her feet to one side of the chair and slide forward onto the chair. After the wheelchair has been pulled out of the way, the child can scoot his or her feet around to the chair front.

If a child is going to a toilet seat, the front wheels can be right up against the toilet. Put the footrests up and lock the brakes. Then have the child slide right onto the toilet facing the back of the toilet. After toileting, the child can then slide back toward the wheelchair, grab hold of both armrests, and lift him- or herself back into the wheelchair.

If the child cannot lift or slide him- or herself to the chair or toilet, you will have to assist. Place the wheelchair at right angles to the seat, lock the brakes, and raise the footrests. Next, bend your knees (keeping your back straight), and put your hands under the child's armpits. Stand up and turn your body so that you are facing toward the seat to which the child is going. With this pivot movement, you can place the child with his or her back to the receiving seat, and lower the child to that seat as you again bend your knees. By all means, ask the physical or occupational therapist to demonstrate the most appropriate way to assist the child.

Source: Mainstreaming Preschoolers: Children with Orthopedic Handicaps, by Shari Stokes Kieran et al. (1986). Prepared for the Department of Health and Human Services by the Administration for Children, Youth and Families, Head Start Bureau.

with seat belts, pillow, or sandbags for added support. If tables are too low for the wheelchair's arms, blocks can be used to raise the table, or trays can be placed over the wheelchair's arms for playing, working, and eating. Frames can be added to tricycles to give vertical support to the body, and doll carriages can be weighted to help provide balance.

The main objective should be to allow the child the maximum scope for exploration and development while providing for the child's safety and comfort. In school settings, this is called the LEAST RESTRICTIVE ENVIRONMENT. (For help and further information, see HELP FOR SPECIAL CHILDREN on page 578; see also organizations related to the child's particular physical problems.)

orthopedic handicap   In education, a general term for a physical condition that adversely affects a child's mobility and development of normal MOTOR SKILLS; also called *physical handicap*. In the HEAD START PRESCHOOL programs, for example, the definition reads:

A child shall be reported as crippled or with an orthopedic handicap who has a condition which prohibits or impedes normal development of gross or fine motor abilities. Such functioning is impaired as a result of conditions associated with congenital anomalies, accidents, or diseases; these conditions include, for example, spina bifida, loss of or

deformed limbs, burns which cause contractures, and cerebral palsy.

If children meet the definitions that apply in their school and state, they will be entitled to SPECIAL EDUCATION services under the EDUCATION FOR ALL HANDICAPPED CHILDREN ACT OF 1975. (For help and further information, see EDUCATION FOR ALL HANDICAPPED CHILDREN ACT OF 1975, and specific types of physical disabilities; also HELP FOR SPECIAL CHILDREN on page 578.)

orthopedist   A physician who specializes in diagnosing and treating diseases and injuries of bones and joints and associated muscles, tendons, cartilage, and ligaments. Orthopedists set and put casts on FRACTURES as needed; perform surgery, as to repair BIRTH DEFECTS or remove TUMORS, including ARTHROSCOPIC SURGERY; and may also replace joints, as in a knee, hip, or finger. Sports injuries are often treated by orthopedists, some of whom specialize in sports medicine.

Orton-Gillingham method   A type of VAKT approach to teaching READING.

OS   The medical abbreviation for oculus sinister, the left eye. (See EYE AND VISION PROBLEMS.)

ossicles   A set of tiny bones—the *malleus*, the *incus*, and the *stapes*—in the middle ear that amplify sound; malformations of

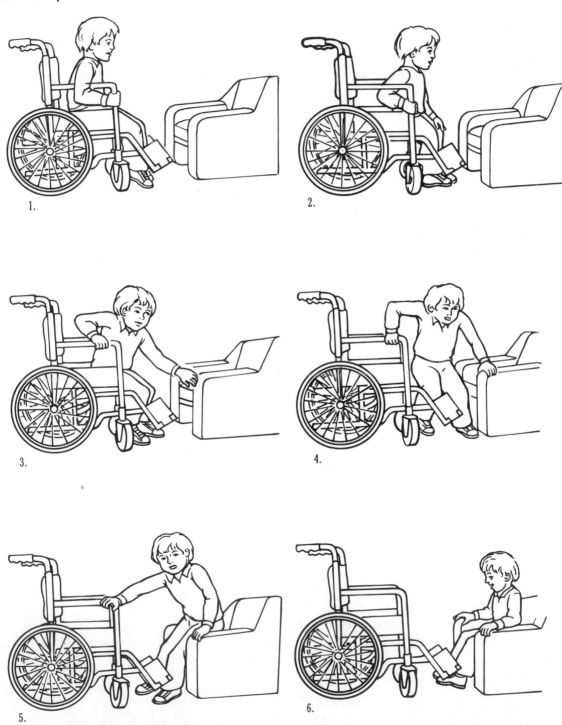

This forward transfer is the most common technique used by preschool children. (See previous page.)

the bone, as in the hereditary hearing problem *otosclerosis*, cause significant EAR AND HEARING PROBLEMS.

osteogenesis imperfecta (OI or **brittle bone disease)** A type of GENETIC DISORDER involving defective development of the normally hard bones of the body, resulting in abnormally brittle, fragile bones. Some cases are so severe that infants are born with multiple fractures, a soft skull, and often deformities; most of these die shortly after birth or survive with growth retardation (see GROWTH AND GROWTH DISORDERS). Milder cases may not be so obvious and may not be detected until ADOLESCENCE or later. These children have multiple fractures from minimal traumas and are sometimes mistaken as victims of CHILD ABUSE AND NEGLECT. Many have related EAR AND HEARING PROBLEMS, especially because of OTOSCLEROSIS, or deformities of the bones in the middle ear. They are especially susceptible to skull fractures, which may readily cause brain damage (see BRAIN AND BRAIN DISORDERS) or DEATH. Among other signs of this BONE DISORDER are blue sclera (the normally white part of the eye), loose joints, poor TEETH, and excessive sweating. Research continues on the precise defect that causes OI, but no cure presently exists.

For help and further information
Osteogenesis Imperfecta Foundation (OIF)
P.O. Box 245
Eastport, NY 11941
516-325-8992
Rosalind James, President
Organization of people with osteogenesis imperfecta, their families, and concerned health professionals. Seeks to educate public; gathers and disseminates information, supports research; publishes various materials, including quarterly newsletter *Breakthrough*, annual *Osteogenesis Imperfecta Update*, *Directory for Osteogenesis Imperfecta Care*, and *Directory of Physicians and Clinics Treating OI*.

National Institute of Arthritis and Musculoskeletal and Skin Diseases (NIAMS), 301-496-8188. (For full group information, see ARTHRITIS.)

(See also BONE DISORDERS.)

osteomalacia The adult form of RICKETS, the DEFICIENCY DISEASE affecting children.

osteomyelitis Infection of the bone and BONE MARROW, often by bacteria, as in some cases of compound FRACTURES or TUBERCULOSIS; in children, the infection generally involves the long bones of the arms and legs and the vertebrae of the spine. If promptly diagnosed, as by a bone SCAN, culture of the infectious organism, or X-RAY, the disease can often be successfully treated with antibiotics; if not, an operation may be needed to clean out infected tissue and bone. In neglected or unresponsive cases, pain, deformity, and stunted growth can occur as osteomyelitis becomes chronic; sometimes whole sections of the bone may need to be removed and replaced with bone grafts from elsewhere in the body. Among populations with good NUTRITION, high resistance, and accessible medical care, osteomyelitis is seen less often than it once was, but it is still a risk for a child who has a compound fracture, which allows infectious organisms to come into contact with bone.

For help and further information
National Institute of Allergy and Infectious Diseases (NIAID), 301-496-5717. (For full group information, see ALLERGY.)

National Institute of Arthritis and Musculoskeletal and Skin Diseases (NIAMS), 301-496-8188. (For full group information, see ARTHRITIS.)

(See also BONE DISORDERS.)

osteopathic physician A health professional with the degree of doctor of osteopathy, or D.O., who has trained in and is licensed to perform general medicine and surgery, including use of drugs, but who works within the system of osteopathic medicine, which sees the body's nerve-muscle-skeletal network as key to health functioning and uses various manipulative techniques as part of therapy to restore what are seen as imbalances in the system.

osteopetrosis A GENETIC DISORDER in which the bones become abnormally hard and dense (*petros* is Greek for "stone"), causing excess bone creation because of disruption in the normal breaking down and rebuilding of the bone; also called *Albers-Schönberg disease, marble bones*, or *osteosclerosis fragilis*. People with severe osteopetrosis often have a high susceptibility to FRACTURES, severe ANEMIA as bone fills in cavities in the blood-making BONE MARROW, and growth deformities, especially in the skull. Resulting pressure on nerves often leads to EAR AND HEARING PROBLEMS, EYE AND VISION PROBLEMS, PARALYSIS of the face, and early DEATH. The severe form of osteopetrosis is passed on from parents to child as an AUTOSOMAL RECESSIVE trait. A milder form, passed on as an AUTOSOMAL DOMINANT trait, generally involves short stature, easily fractured bones, and a tendency toward OSTEOMYELITIS, or infection in the bone.

For help and further information
National Institute of Arthritis and Musculoskeletal and Skin Diseases (NIAMS), 301-496-8188. (For full group information, see ARTHRITIS.)
(See also BONE DISORDERS; GROWTH AND GROWTH DISORDERS.)

osteoporosis Weakening and fracturing of the bone due to decrease in the density of bone, resulting in pain, injury, and sometimes deformities; literally "porous bone." This condition is generally seen in older people, especially women after MENOPAUSE or hysterectomy (since CALCIUM loss from the bones speeds up with decline in the production of ESTROGEN). However, it is a condition that young couples should keep in mind for themselves and their children, because bone mass is built primarily in youth; later on it cannot easily be replaced, only the loss of bone slowed. Osteoporosis is also associated with some HORMONE disorders, such as CUSHING'S SYNDROME; with some LUNG AND BREATHING DISORDERS, such as BRONCHITIS and EMPHYSEMA; with lack of EXERCISE; with SMOKING and ALCOHOL ABUSE; with use of steroids; and with some ethnic backgrounds and body types, particularly tall, thin northern Europeans. Young women who exercise at such an extreme level that they stop MENSTRUATION are also at risk for bone loss. Pregnant and nursing women should be sure to take extra calcium, especially if they are under age 20.

For help and further information

National Osteoporosis Foundation (NOF)
1625 Eye Street, NW, Suite 1011
Washington, DC 20006
202-223-2226
Sandra C. Raymond, Executive Director
Organization of people concerned about osteoporosis. Seeks to educate public and professionals and to influence social policy; provides information and referrals; supports research; publishes various materials, including quarterly newsletter, *Osteoporosis: A Woman's Guide*, and booklets.

American Society for Bone and Mineral Research (ASBMR), 707-279-1344. Has established guidelines for preventing osteoporosis. (For full group information, see BONE DISORDERS.)

National Institute of Arthritis and Musculoskeletal and Skin Diseases (NIAMS), 301-496-8188. Publishes *Osteoporosis: Causes, Prevention, Treatment*. (For full group information, see ARTHRITIS.)

(See also BONE DISORDERS, including BUILDING STRONG BONES.)

osteosclerosis fragilis   Alternate name for OSTEOPETROSIS.

ostomy   A surgical procedure in which an artificial opening is created on the body's surface, generally referring to an opening in the abdomen for the release of stool or urine. An *ileostomy* is one performed on the *ileum* (small intestine), often because of INFLAMMATORY BOWEL DISEASE (ulcerative colitis and Crohn's disease). A *colostomy* is performed on the *colon* (large intestine), most often because of CANCER. A *urinary ostomy* provides a new outlet for the bladder. Among the other causes for ostomies are BIRTH DEFECTS, obstructions, inflammations, injury, and nerve damage. If the air passages in the throat are blocked, an emergency TRACHEOSTOMY, or hole in the trachea, may be performed. (For help and further information, see CHOKING; DIGESTIVE DISORDERS; KIDNEY AND UROLOGICAL DISORDERS.)

For help and further information

United Ostomy Association (UOA)
2001 West Beverly Boulevard

Can People With Ostomies Become Parents?

Men who have colostomies can vary anywhere from full potency (the ability to have an erection and orgasm) to complete impotence (the inability to have an erection). It is estimated that about 10 to 20 percent of men with ileostomies suffer impairment of sexual function and potency, although, fortunately, this is only temporary in many cases. Males who have urinary ostomies early in life can usually perform sexually but may be sterile. Most males who have their urinary surgery for cancer of the bladder as adults are impotent.

Having an ostomy does not lessen a woman's sexual or reproductive capabilities. In a few cases, the condition that necessitates ostomy surgery (or an unrelated condition) may also necessitate additional surgery, such as hysterectomy. Hysterectomies make it impossible to conceive but have no effect on sexual desire or the ability to have sexual relations.

Source: *Facts and Fallacies About Digestive Diseases.* Prepared by the National Digestive Diseases Information Clearinghouse.

Los Angeles, CA 90057
213-413-5510
Organization of and for people who have had colostomy, ileostomy, or urostomy and for their families. Encourages patient-to-patient contact for mutual support; provides information and referrals; publishes various materials, including *Ostomy Quarterly*, booklets such as *My Child Has an Ostomy*, *Chris Has an Ostomy* (coloring book for children), *Anatomy of Ostomy*, *Colostomies: A Guide*, and *Ileostomy: A Guide*.

National Institute of Diabetes and Digestive and Kidney Diseases (NIDDK), 301-496-3583; **National Digestive Disease Information Clearinghouse (NDDIC)**, 301-468-6344. (For full group information, see DIGESTIVE DISORDERS.)

National Foundation for Ileitis and Colitis (NFIC), 212-685-3440. (For full group information, see INFLAMMATORY BOWEL DISEASE.)

Other reference sources

These Special Children: The Ostomy Book for Parents of Children with Colostomies, Ileostomies and Urostomies, by Katherine F. Jeter. Los Angeles: Bull, 1982. Also available from United Ostomy Association.

Managing Your Ileostomy, 18-page booklet, and *Managing Your Colostomy*, 22-page booklet. Available free from Hollister, Inc., Customer Service, 2000 Hollister Drive, Libertyville, IL 60048.

(See also DIGESTIVE DISORDERS.)

otitis externa Inflammation or infection of the outer ear, a common type of EAR AND HEARING PROBLEM; popularly called *swimmer's ear.*

otitis media A common infection of the middle ear, which can lead to EAR AND HEARING PROBLEMS.

otolaryngologist (otorhinolaryngologist, ear-nose-throat doctor, or **ENT)** A physician who specializes in identifying and treating ear, nose, and throat disorders, including performing surgery in these areas. A doctor who specializes exclusively in ear disorders is called an *otologist.*

otologist A medical professional who specializes in the diagnosis and treatment of EAR AND HEARING PROBLEMS; a subspecialist who focuses on treatment of disorders involving the acoustic nerve is called a *neuro-otologist.* Those who specialize in treating ear, nose, and throat together are called OTOLARYNGOLOGISTS.

otoplasty The surgical procedure performed to reconstruct or repair an ear that is damaged or missing, a kind of PLASTIC SURGERY, or to flatten protruding ears, as a kind of COSMETIC SURGERY.

otosclerosis A type of EAR AND HEARING PROBLEM in which one or more bones of the middle ear have excess bone and cannot therefore transmit sound vibrations effectively.

OU Medical abbreviation for oculus uterque, meaning both eyes. (See EYE AND VISION PROBLEMS.)

out-of-control children Children who refuse to obey their parents and are therefore labeled INCORRIGIBLE and can be made WARDS of the court.

out-of-district placement Assignment of a student to a school outside his or her HOME SCHOOL DISTRICT, the one serving the area of the student's legal residence. Such a NONRESIDENT STUDENT may be assigned by a court order or be placed in a school providing special services under the EDUCATION FOR ALL HANDICAPPED CHILDREN ACT OF 1975, in which case the home school district must bear the cost. Parents may also choose to place their child in an out-of-district school, but they (not the home school) would bear most if not all of the cost of such voluntary placement.

ovarian wedge resection A surgical procedure sometimes performed in treating INFERTILITY problems.

ovaries A pair of small, oval-shaped sex glands (GONADS) in a woman, which produce the key female sex HORMONES, ESTROGEN and PROGESTERONE, as well as the eggs (*ova;* singular, OVUM). The ovaries are on either side of the UTERUS in the lower abdomen, lying under the FALLOPIAN TUBES. At birth, a baby girl's ovaries each contain about one million FOLLICLES, egg-producing structures that remain immature until PUBERTY.

When a girl becomes sexually mature, *follicle-stimulating hormone* (FSH), produced by the PITUITARY GLAND, begins periodically to signal the ovaries to ripen some of these immature eggs. At the beginning of the MENSTRUAL CYCLE, on the first day of bleeding, FSH signals the ovaries to mature a group of eggs, which also produce the hormone estrogen. At this point each

egg cell, which carries 46 chromosomes in 23 pairs, subdivides into two identical cells, each with 23 chromosomes, to prepare for CONCEPTION. (Unlike other cells in the body, the SPERM also undergoes this division process, called *meiosis.*) The duplicate cell, called a *polar body,* shrivels up and disappears. Gradually, one of the group of surviving egg cells becomes dominant, while the others also pass out of the picture. This dominant egg cell, called the *graafian follicle,* develops a four-layered protective coating and prepares to burst out of its growth site in the ovaries.

At about 14 days into the menstrual cycle, the pituitary gland sends out a surge of LUTEINIZING HORMONE (LH), which breaks down the outer wall of the graafian follicle, releasing the single mature egg, still enclosed in two outer layers. This is OVULATION. The third and fourth layers shed by the egg, called the *corpus luteum,* remain behind in the ovary; there they trigger release of progesterone, which causes the *endometrium* (the lining of the uterus) to thicken, in preparation for a fertilized egg. (This is the *proliferative phase* of the menstrual cycle.) Meanwhile, the egg released from the uterus must make its way into the fallopian tube suspended above the ovary, where fertilization, if it occurs, will take place.

This same process takes place month after month from sexual maturity until MENOPAUSE but each time with a diminishing number of potential eggs, one reason why a woman's chances of conception decline as she grows older. Of the approximately two million potential eggs in the two ovaries, only a few hundred will ever mature and be available for possible fertilization.

A number of problems can interfere with the workings of this complicated, delicate egg-developing system in the ovaries, including:

- *oophoritis,* inflammation of the ovaries, sometimes as a result of infections such as MUMPS, GONORRHEA, or PELVIC INFLAMMATORY DISEASE.

- *ovarian cysts,* fluid-filled or semisolid sacs that form in the ovaries, mostly benign, sometimes so many as to be called *polycystic syndrome.* Aside from hindering the normal workings of the ovaries themselves, these cysts can trigger production of male sex hormones, which can lead to *amenorrhea* (lack of MENSTRUATION) and INFERTILITY.

- *ovarian cancer,* a form of CANCER generally found in women over 50.

- *ovarian failure,* in which, for unknown reasons, menopause comes abnormally early and the ovaries cease to function.

- *abnormality in or absence of ovaries,* a rare defect associated with some CHROMOSOMAL ABNORMALITIES, such as TURNER'S SYNDROME.

- *anovulation,* failure of the ovaries to produce, ripen, and release eggs. This happens during PREGNANCY and LACTATION (which acts as a natural form of CONTRACEPTION). It also may occur during puberty and approaching menopause and sometimes because of hormonal imbalance, illness, stress, or drugs. BIRTH-CONTROL PILLS using hormones act by suppressing ovulation.

Any of these and more can cause problems in conception, some of them being susceptible to treatment, but many not. (For help and further information, see INFERTILITY; PREGNANCY.)

overachiever   A student whose academic performance is well above educators' estimate of his or her potential, especially a student whose scores on STANDARDIZED TESTS of ability are consistently lower than those on ACHIEVEMENT TESTS. Outperforming expectations may result when a student has strong motivation to succeed and the ability to focus effort, sometimes with a specific long-term goal in mind.

overanxious disorder   A type of ANXIETY disorder in which children worry excessively and needlessly about future events, past behavior, and personal characteristics and competence; they are often self-conscious and require constant reassurance, as about social or academic achievement, though the child is often seen as at least average and often superior. Persistent anxiety and associated tension bring with them physical complaints. The disorder affects boys and girls equally, seems to be found often among elder or only children in affluent families concerned about academic and social achievement, and in severe cases can be incapacitating. (For help and further information, see MENTAL DISORDERS.)

overbite   A type of MALOCCLUSION in which the jaw and upper front teeth project too far forward.

overflow behavior   In individual testing, such as DEVELOPMENTAL SCREENING TESTS, any of a child's actions or interplay that are not directly related to the test items, including innocuous small talk and attempts to distract the examiner from continuing with a test item that seems difficult.

overplacement   A GRADE placement for which a child is of the right chronological AGE but too low a DEVELOPMENTAL AGE. Some experts in child development believe that overplacement is a major cause of failure at school, and as a result some parents have held their children back to have them be the oldest, and presumably, therefore, the most developed, in the class. This can boomerang, however, as the child grows older, especially during ADOLESCENCE, and is more mature than the rest of the class, perhaps becoming bored in class as well as restless and socially isolated.

ovulation   Release of a mature egg (OVUM) from a woman's OVARIES into the FALLOPIAN TUBES, where fertilization may take place. Ovulation generally occurs monthly, as a key part of the MENSTRUAL CYCLE, but regular menstruation does not necessarily mean a woman is ovulating. Especially during PUBERTY and approaching MENOPAUSE, a woman may have *anovulatory* (without ovulation) periods. If a couple and their doctor are exploring possible INFERTILITY, one of the earliest questions to determine is whether or not ovulation is actually taking place. At about the time of ovulation, the body's temperature rises slightly, the nature of the mucus at the CERVIX changes, and the woman sometimes experiences slight abdominal pain (called *Mittelschmerz*). These signs are used in some types of BIRTH CONTROL in which couples avoid intercourse between ovulation

---

Ovulation Monitoring Home Medical Test

Function

Measures the amount of luteinizing hormone (LH) in urine. A woman's body produces LH throughout the menstrual cycle, but at midcycle that production suddenly increases. Called the LH surge, the sudden hormone increase triggers ovulation, or the release of an egg from the ovary. Usually, ovulation occurs 24 to 36 hours after the LH surge begins. This test is *not* intended for use in contraception.

How It Works

Once a day for about a week in the middle of the menstrual cycle, a chemically treated strip is dipped in a urine specimen. Comparing the strip with a color should indicate when an LH surge begins. In diluted urine the test may not detect the hormone, so keep liquid intake fairly constant, urinate every three hours or so, and avoid excess liquid intake just before collecting the urine.

Time for Results

20 minutes to one hour

Comments

If an LH surge of more than four days in a row is indicated, consult a physician promptly. This could be caused by such conditions as pregnancy, ovarian failure, early menopause, endometriosis, or response to a medication.

Source: *Do-It-Yourself Medical Testing*, by Dixie Farley (1989). Prepared for the Public Health Service by the Food and Drug Administration.

---

and menstruation. Conversely, they are used by prospective parents to identify when the chances of CONCEPTION are the greatest. (For help and further information, see OVULATION METHOD.)

ovulation method   A method of BIRTH CONTROL that involves monitoring various changes in the body, to identify when OVULATION has occurred; a kind of NATURAL FAMILY PLANNING. Couples who do not wish to have a child can then avoid sexual intercourse at that time, while those attempting to conceive can time their intercourse or ARTIFICIAL INSEMINATION to maximize their chances.

ovum (plural, ova)   The egg cell produced by a female, one of over a million in each of the two OVARIES at birth. Normally, only one ovum is fully matured and released each month, in the process called OVULATION. If a SPERM (male sex cell) unites with the ovum, FERTILIZATION or CONCEPTION results. Then, if all goes normally, the fertilized egg travels to the UTERUS, to develop into an EMBRYO.

ox-eye   Nickname for *buphthalmos*, a bulging eyeball. (See EYE AND VISION PROBLEMS.)

P

pacifier A device for babies to suck on, given to prevent them from sucking on thumbs and fingers. Though widely used, pacifiers can cause severe problems, such as CHOKING, and can be a source of infection if they fall on the floor and are put back into the mouth without being cleaned. (For help and further information, see SUCKING.)

Paget's disease (osteitis deformans) A BONE DISORDER involving disruption of the normal processes that break down old and rebuild new bone tissue; as a result, bones weaken, thicken, become deformed, and fracture easily. Paget's disease generally affects people of middle or old age and men more often than women; its causes are unknown, though some suggest an infection, possibly from a virus. The disease sometimes runs in families, but evidence is unclear as to whether it is a GENETIC DISORDER.

For help and further information

Paget's Disease Foundation (PDF)
165 Cadman Plaza East
Brooklyn, NY 11201
718-596-1043
Charlene Waldman, Executive Director
Organization of people with Paget's disease and the medical professionals who treat them. Serves as information clearinghouse for public and professionals; encourages research into causes, prevention, and treatment; answers questions and makes referrals; offers discount drug services; publishes various materials, including newsletter and brochures such as *Paget's Disease in Families, New Direction . . . New Hope*, and *Understanding Paget's Disease*.

National Institute of Arthritis and Musculoskeletal and Skin Diseases (NIAMS), 301-496-8188. Publishes various materials, including *Understanding Paget's Disease*. (For full group information, see ARTHRITIS.)

Other reference sources

Health Care U.S.A., by Jean Carper. New York: Prentice Hall, 1987. Resource for general and specific health-care information; lists key Paget's disease specialists and other information.

palilalia A rare condition in which a person repeats a phrase over and over with increasing rapidity; it often results from a brain dysfunction or disease, such as ENCEPHALITIS, or from a condition such as TOURETTE'S SYNDROME.

Palmer method The traditional technique for teaching young children legible WRITING.

panic attack A brief abrupt period of intense apprehension, fear, or terror, often with accompanying physical symptoms such as difficult breathing, heart palpitations, chest pain, sensations of CHOKING, trembling or shaking, nausea, and fear of losing control, going crazy, or dying; a key characteristic of PANIC DISORDERS but also found in other MENTAL DISORDERS, such as SCHIZOPHRENIA or DEPRESSION.

panic disorders A group of MENTAL DISORDERS, classed as ANXIETY disorders, in which a person experiences sudden, unexpected PANIC ATTACKS, often without obvious triggers; sometimes associated with PROLAPSE of the mitral valve (see HEART AND HEART PROBLEMS). (For help and further information, see MENTAL DISORDERS; PHOBIA; and specific disorders.)

pantothenic acid A VITAMIN that is important in the body's growth, maintenance, and energy METABOLISM. Symptoms of deficiency include headache, fatigue, poor muscle coordination, nausea, and cramps. Deficiencies are rare, however, because pantothenic acid is found in many foods, including meats (especially liver and kidneys), MILK, egg yolks, whole grains (especially wheat), peanuts, peas, white and sweet potatoes, and most other vegetables. (For help and further information, see RECOMMENDED DAILY ALLOWANCES; VITAMINS.)

Pap smear (cervical smear) test A test to detect abnormal cells (*cervical dysplasias*) in the CERVIX, these being warning signs of possible CANCER formation; named after its developer, George Papanicolaou. In this simple test, some cells and mucus are painlessly scraped off the end of the cervix and analyzed in the laboratory for possible abnormalities; if found, the usual follow-up would be a BIOPSY of tissue, and then treatment as indicated, possibly delayed if the woman is pregnant. Women (including sexually active teenagers) are advised to have cervical smears regularly, starting a few months after beginning sexual activity and thereafter once a year if they have many sex partners, perhaps every two to three years if they do not, as their doctor or family-planning clinic recommends. (For help and further information, see CERVIX; CANCER.)

papilledema (choked disk)   Swelling of the optic nerve. (See EYE AND VISION PROBLEMS.)

parallel curriculum   A type of CURRICULUM in which two groups of students cover the same amount of material but at different speeds.

paralysis   Complete or partial loss of the ability to move one or more muscles at will in a controlled way, often accompanied by loss of feeling as well; sometimes called *palsy*. Paralysis does not necessarily imply total immobility, as is sometimes assumed. Muscles can be rigid, a condition termed *spastic*, but they may also be weak and "floppy," lacking the tension that muscles normally have even at rest. Weakness alone is sometimes called *paresis*.

Paralysis can be permanent (at least at the present stage of medical technology), as when a spinal cord is severed, or temporary, as in response to something pressing on a nerve. It may affect only one small muscle, such as a muscle in the face, or a major network of muscles, as in severe SPINAL CORD INJURY.

Paralysis affecting all four limbs and the trunk, as from a neck injury, is termed *quadriplegia*. Paralysis affecting the legs and part of the trunk, as with an injury to the lower back, is called *paraplegia*. Paralysis affecting one half of the body, as from a BRAIN TUMOR or sometimes CEREBRAL PALSY, is called *hemiplegia*. Paralysis of like parts on both sides of the body, such as both legs or both sides of the face, is called *diplegia*. Some young people suffer from PERIODIC PARALYSIS, a rare GENETIC DISORDER characterized by brief periods of paralysis, lasting from a few minutes to two days and recurring every few weeks.

For help and further information

American Paralysis Association (APA), 201-379-2690; toll-free number (U.S. except NJ) 800-225-0292. (For full group information, see SPINAL CORD INJURY.)

National Institute of Neurological Disorders and Stroke (NINDS), 301-496-5751. Publishes *Spinal Cord Injury: Hope Through Research*. (For full group information, see BRAIN AND BRAIN DISORDERS.)

paralytic polio   A severe form of POLIOMYELITIS.

paramyotonia congenita   A type of muscle disorder. (See MUSCULAR DYSTROPHY.)

Paranoid personality disorder   A type of PERSONALITY DISORDER.

para 1   The medical designation for a woman who has given birth to one live baby, standing for PRIMIPARA. A woman who has never borne a live infant is designated NULLIPARA, or *para 0*.

paraphimosis   A condition in which a retracted foreskin is too tight and acts like a tourniquet on a PENIS, an extremely painful condition, especially during an erection. Its avoidance is one of the medical reasons traditionally advanced for CIRCUMCISION, since it may need to be treated surgically.

paraplegia   PARALYSIS or weakness affecting the legs and part of the trunk, as in a person who has suffered a SPINAL-CORD INJURY below the neck.

parens patriae   The legal doctrine of the state's power to act for those who are INCOMPETENT to act for themselves, including MINORS and people with some handicaps (see HANDICAPPED).

parentage action   Alternate term for PATERNITY SUIT.

parental access   Alternate term for VISITATION RIGHTS.

parental and medical leave   Provision of time off for *both* parents around the time of a child's birth, ADOPTION, or serious illness; a policy that exists in some countries, notably in Scandinavia, and is offered by some firms in the United States but is very far from widely accepted. In practice, while many women are provided MATERNITY LEAVE—though many are not—men who wish to be with their children at these crucial times generally do so with a combination of vacation time, sick days, and personal days. (For help and further information, see MATERNITY LEAVE.)

parental liability   A parent's obligation for damage caused by a MINOR child, whether through criminal acts, intention, or negligence. State laws vary as to the extent and nature of parental liability. Most states hold parents responsible for willful or malicious property damage caused by their children; more than half hold parents liable for willful or malicious personal injuries caused by children. Most states do, however, limit the dollar amount of parental liability and do not hold parents liable for actions of children under age eight or so, except in cases where the parent was grossly negligent, as in giving a loaded gun to a young child. Under the FAMILY CAR DOCTRINE, the parent also may be liable for actions caused by a child driving a car owned by the parent.

parenteral nutrition   Nutrients and medications introduced to a patient's body by various forms of INJECTION, bypassing the digestive system. Parenteral nutrition is often administered to PREMATURE newborns in NEONATAL INTENSIVE CARE UNITS and to patients generally after surgery or in other special situations, as in cases of SHOCK, COMA, MALNUTRITION, or failure of the kidneys or liver (see KIDNEY AND UROLOGICAL DISORDERS, LIVER PROBLEMS). Often among the nutrients contained in parenteral fluids are saline (salt) solution, GLUCOSE, AMINO ACIDS, VITAMINS, and ELECTROLYTES, the aim being not to supply full nutrition but to stabilize the electrolyte balance in the patient's system.

Parent Locator Service (PLS)   A service of the OFFICE OF CHILD SUPPORT ENFORCEMENT, an arm of the U.S. Department of Health and Human Services, designed to help locate ABSENT PARENTS, generally to obtain CHILD SUPPORT payments but also in cases of parental kidnapping (see MISSING CHILDREN). The Federal PLS (FPLS) uses computer searches through income tax records, Social Security earnings and benefit records, and the like, while state PLSs scan voter registration, motor vehicle registration, driver's license, welfare, prison, worker's compensation, and similar records.

parents' night   An evening or a weekend day when parents are invited to visit their child's school, meet the teachers, and see work of the students, such as art displays or plays. Most schools hold parents' nights at least once a year, some more often. They are not, however, an effective substitute for a PARENT–TEACHER CONFERENCE.

parents' responsibilities   The legal duty of parents to take care of their MINOR children, a duty running alongside their PARENTS' RIGHTS; part of a wider (though in the law less clear) concept of people's responsibilities to take care of family members, including HANDICAPPED adults. Parents are responsible for providing the basic necessities of life—food, clothing, shelter, and medical treatment—as well as EDUCATION and DISCIPLINE. If a parent fails to provide proper care, SUPERVISION, and control (or attempts at control), charges of CHILD ABUSE AND NEGLECT may be brought; these can, in some cases, lead to temporary or permanent TERMINATION OF PARENTAL RIGHTS. If parents are unable to exercise control of their JUVENILE children, as in cases of juvenile DELINQUENTS, chronic TRUANTS, or runaways, the children may be legally labeled INCORRIGIBLE, put under court supervision, and placed with FOSTER PARENTS or in a GROUP HOME or institution.

parents' rights   The legal rights of parents, in the United States protected under the Constitution, to have CUSTODY and SUPERVISION of their own MINOR children, including making decisions about their medical care. Running alongside these rights are PARENTS' RESPONSIBILITIES, legal duties to care for minors and some HANDICAPPED adult children. Parents can lose these rights under certain circumstances, as in certain cases of ABANDONMENT and CHILD ABUSE AND NEGLECT. Legal proceedings to negate parents' claims on their child are called TERMINATION OF PARENTAL RIGHTS (TPR). In some cases, as when a child is judged INCORRIGIBLE, the parents may voluntarily transfer their rights to the state. In cases of divorce or separation, a NONCUSTODIAL PARENT may lose some parental rights when custody of a child is awarded to the other parent, but they generally retain VISITATION RIGHTS.

parent–teacher conference   A meeting between a child's teacher and parent or parents to discuss the child's educational progress. Here parents and teacher can get to know each other, ask questions and exchange experiences clarifying the child's situation, and discuss ways that each might enhance the child's performance. At such conferences, parents also have a chance to ask questions about classroom approaches, DISCIPLINE policies, teaching styles, CURRICULUM, GRADES, and other policies that may affect the child. (See TIPS FOR PARENT–TEACHER CONFERENCES, on page 362.)

Many schools schedule regular parent–teacher conferences in October or November, after the child has settled into the school year but soon enough so that any problems that have emerged can be dealt with expeditiously. Some schools hold conferences several times a year, after report cards are issued. If the school does not initiate such conferences, parents can do so. They should certainly do so at any time if the child seems unhappy or anxious about school, or if they have any concerns about the child's academic progress or social and emotional development. If the child has special needs or problems, or if anything in the child's health or family situation has changed or presents problems that may affect the child's performance at school—for example, if there has been a DEATH, serious illness, or divorce in the family—the parent may want to schedule a conference for the beginning of the school year to inform the teacher.

If the child lives with both parents, it is best if both parents meet with the teacher to avoid or minimize confusion or misinterpretation later on, as in the recollection or retelling. If that is not possible, or if the child has a single parent, a friend or relative might go along to take notes on important points raised in the conference, for later reference if necessary. If parents cannot meet at school during the day because of a job or family situation, many teachers will make arrangements to meet early in the morning or in the evening; and if parents do not speak English, they can request that an interpreter for their language be present at the conference.

Where possible, parents should try to give the conference a cooperative tone, stressing both parents' and teacher's desires to help a child do well. If appropriate, parents should take the time to note the positive things occurring with the child and to express thanks for the teacher's part in them, rather than focusing solely on complaints or problems.

Parents who expect a difficult, confrontational meeting, however, should try to have an impartial third party join in, possibly along with another school official (such as principal, assistant principal, or guidance counselor) and an advocate to act as advisor. But even where problems are serious, it is important to emphasize the need to work together to solve them, rather than blaming anyone for them. If parents think the teacher is incorrect about something, they should explain carefully why they think so and ask for specific examples of the teacher's position. The key point is not to let the discussion become personally critical and argumentative but to keep the focus on joint efforts to improve the child's situation.

For help and further information

National Committee for Citizens in Education (NCCE), 301-997-9300, toll-free number (U.S. except MD) 800-NETWORK [638-9675]. Publishes *Information for Parents* pamphlets on parent–teacher conferences and parent involvement in schools. (For full group information, see EDUCATION.)

paresis   Alternate term for a type of PARALYSIS in which the muscles are not rigid but rather weak and floppy.

parochial school   A church-related PRIVATE SCHOOL, generally a school affiliated with the Roman Catholic church but also sometimes referring to schools of other religious denominations, such as Baptist, Quaker, Methodist, or Jewish schools.

Tips for Parent–Teacher Conferences

Your preparation for the parent–teacher conference should include a review of the materials you file at home—including report cards, progress reports, and any papers brought home from school—*and* the child's school records. If the school provides a parent handbook, curriculum materials, or other information, review them beforehand. Talk with your child about his or her experiences, especially about which subjects he or she likes and which he or she dislikes. Explore how your child feels about all classes and teachers, and encourage discussion of any problems at school. Make a list of questions or topics you wish to raise during the conference, and be sure to cover those in the checklist below. But remember that time is limited, so focus on those areas of special concern to your child's educational progress.

Checklist for Parent–Teacher Conference

Have I received satisfactory answers to the following questions?	Yes	No	Need More Info
Is my child performing at, above, or below grade level in basic skills, such as math and reading?			
Has my child taken achievement, intelligence, or aptitude tests in the past year? What do the scores mean?			
Does my child have strengths and weaknesses in major subject areas?			
Can we go over some examples of my child's classwork together?			
Does my child need special help in any academic subject?			
If so, what help and special services are available?			
Does my child need special help in social adjustment?			
Would you recommend referral to other school specialists?			
Has my child regularly completed homework you assigned?			

Have I received satisfactory answers to the following questions?	Yes	No	Need More Info
Has my child attended class regularly?			
Does my child participate in class?			
How are my child's work habits and attitude?			
Does my child get along well with classmates?			
Have you observed any changes in learning progress during the year? Has learning improved or declined dramatically?			
Have you noticed any changes in behavior, such as squinting, extreme fatigue, or irritability, which may be signals of medical problems?			
How do teachers keep parents informed about their children's progress or problems?			
Are there specific ways I can help my child at home?			

[**Note**: This checklist is recommended for use as part of the "Annual Education Checkup" described on page 172 under EDUCATION. If your child has been identified as learning-disabled or has other physical or mental handicaps (see HANDICAPPED), Public Law 94-142 requires that you be involved in the annual development and review of an INDIVIDUALIZED EDUCATION PROGRAM (IEP) for your child. Ask about your school's plan for compliance with this federal law. On page 178, under the EDUCATION FOR ALL HANDICAPPED CHILDREN ACT OF 1975, you will find an overview of the education process.]

Conference Follow-up

If issues or problem areas arise during a parent–teacher conference, be sure that—before the meeting ends—everyone is clear about what the next step will be, who will do what, and what the timetable is for each action. Carefully think through your part of the plan to help your child. Afterward, talk to your child about what happened at the conference, discussing the positive aspects and the areas where improvement is needed.

Continued on page 363

Keep in touch with the teacher, by phone, by written notes, or through additional conferences. In any case, it would be wise to schedule an end-of-the-year conference to review your child's progress. At this meeting you might ask if the teacher has suggestions for summer activities such as summer school, remedial help, or home learning activities. The child's class, grade, and teacher assignment for next year may also be discussed at this time.

If your conference results in strong disagreements between you and the teacher, set up another meeting, including the school principal, to try to resolve them. If you are still dissatisfied, you can appeal to the superintendent, possibly the school board, and sometimes a state or federal agency. But appeal procedures are long, difficult, and often unsatisfactory and are best avoided if at all possible.

Source: National Committee for Citizens in Education.

---

parotitis Alternate name for MUMPS, usually prefaced by the term *epidemic* or *infectious*.

parturition Medical term for the process of CHILDBIRTH.

pass In EDUCATION, to have a level of performance that is considered evidence of satisfactory learning, whether for a specific test or piece of work or for a whole course; in the latter case a teacher will award the student CREDIT (formal or informal) for the course. Sometimes the passing level is a preset GRADE, such as a D average or a numerical average above 65 or 70; sometimes no grade or ranking is assigned, and the "pass" label only distinguishes those who received credit for the course from those who failed (see FAIL) and so received no credit, in a PASS–FAIL system.

pass–fail A grading system in which students receive no letter or numerical GRADES and therefore nothing that indicates differences in their level of performance or their relative ranking. They are given only one of two evaluations: PASS, for which credit is granted, or FAIL, with no credit allowed. This grading system is sometimes called *credit–no credit*.

passive abuser Someone who, while not actively abusive, fails to intervene to stop CHILD ABUSE AND NEGLECT by another person, in the home or other institution.

passive-aggressive personality disorder A type of PERSONALITY DISORDER.

passive immunization A type of IMMUNIZATION in which antibodies are directly injected into a person's body, supplying a short-term immunity; as opposed to the more common ACTIVE IMMUNIZATION.

passive learning A LEARNING STYLE in which the child sits and listens while others lecture.

passive vocabulary Words that a person can recognize or understand in context in hearing or READING matter, as opposed to the ACTIVE VOCABULARY that can be used independently in speaking or writing. Because children, like adults, always understand much more than they can express, their passive vocabulary is much larger than their active one. (See also RECEPTIVE LANGUAGE.)

Patau's syndrome (trisomy 13) A CONGENITAL condition resulting from a CHROMOSOMAL ABNORMALITY in which a child has three copies (*trisomy*) of chromosome 13. Infants with Patau's syndrome have severe MENTAL RETARDATION and often numerous defects, such as MYELOMENINGOCELE and CLEFT LIP AND PALATE, and brain deformities, such as failure of the brain to divide properly. Less than one in five survive the first year.

For help and further information

Support Organization for Trisomy 18/13 and Other Related Disorders (SOFT 18/13)
5030 Cole
Pocatello, ID 93202
208-237-8782
Pat Farmer, President
Organization for families of children with trisomy 18 or 13 or related disorders. Provides support for families; publishes various materials, including bimonthly newsletter S.O.F.T. TOUCH and TRISOMY 18: A BOOK FOR FAMILIES.

(See also GENETIC DISORDERS.)

patch test A kind of MEDICAL TEST used in indentifying which substances might be causing allergic reactions. (See ALLERGY.)

patent ductus arteriosus (PDA) A type of CONGENITAL heart defect. (See HEART AND HEART PROBLEMS.)

paternity suit A legal action to identify the FATHER of a child, especially one born outside marriage; also called a *parentage action*. Often brought in order to require the father to provide CHILD SUPPORT, many paternity suits are filed under the AID TO FAMILIES WITH DEPENDENT CHILDREN (AFDC) program, by mothers who otherwise risk losing welfare money. A successful paternity action also generally involves granting VISITATION RIGHTS to the father if he desires them. MEDICAL TESTS can show (or rule out) paternity with great accuracy, using analysis of DNA showing the child's GENETIC INHERITANCE compared to that of the presumed father.

pathologic apnea Abnormally long pauses in breathing, as can occur during SLEEP APNEA.

pathologist A physician who specializes in studying the nature, cause, development, and effects of disease, both in general and in specific cases, often working in a laboratory, hospital, medical school, or research institute. Apart from their own research, pathologists are often consultants to other

---

Selecting a Doctor or Clinic

Before your baby is born is a good time to select your baby's doctor (such as a pediatrician or family physician). You may also choose a doctor/nurse practitioner team or a pediatric nurse practitioner to take care of your baby. It is better to make this decision while you have the time to carefully choose who will advise you about your baby's health over the years. You may ask your own doctor or a nurse at the clinic for a recommendation; your friends or family members who have children of their own are good sources, too. If you have other children, you will probably find it easier to use the same care provider for all of your children. Once you have located a potential care provider, make an appointment to meet him or her if you can. Think about these questions as you decide whether this person is the one for you:

• What has been the experience of friends (or family) with this care provider?
• Do you feel comfortable with and trust him or her?
• Do you feel that he or she will take the time to answer your questions or help you deal with new situations?
• How does he or she feel about issues of importance to you (such as breastfeeding or toilet training)?
• Is the office in a convenient location, so that you and your baby can get there easily?
• Will he or she be available by telephone if you need advice?
• What are the office hours, telephone hours, and fees?
• How can he or she be reached in an emergency?
• What hospital does the doctor work at?
• Does this care provider have any special training?

Remember, your doctor, nurse, or clinic staff will be your partner in looking after your baby's health and development. You can get a head start on developing that partnership by choosing a care provider before your baby is born.

Source: *Infant Care* (1989). Prepared for the Public Health Service by the Bureau of Maternal and Child Health and Resources Development.

---

physicians, using their expert knowledge of how disease changes the tissues and fluids of the body to help in diagnosing disorders, as in analyzing material from SPECIMEN TESTS. Some specialize in doing autopsies, attempting to learn for the future from detailed analysis of the effects of a disease in someone who has died.

pavor nocturnus Alternate name for *night terrors*, a type of SLEEPING DISORDER.

PDA Abbreviation for *patent ductus arteriosus*, a type of CONGENITAL heart defect. (See HEART AND HEART PROBLEMS.)

Peabody Picture Vocabulary Test (PPVT) An individually administered DIAGNOSTIC ASSESSMENT TEST used to measure LAN-GUAGE SKILLS—and by extension, academic aptitude—from early childhood through adulthood. The examiner says a word, and the child is asked to point to the one of four pictures that depicts the word; the words and four-picture sets become increasingly complex, but the test is continued only to the limit of the child's ability. Because the test focuses on RECEPTIVE LANGUAGE—that is, the ability to understand language, as opposed to speaking or reading it—it is widely used with children for whom English is a second language and with those who may be mentally retarded, as well as with GIFTED CHILDREN. The PPVT is a NORM-REFERENCED TEST, and the result of the test is a PERCENTILE (and STANINE) and AGE EQUIVALENT (EDUCATIONAL AGE). (For help and further information, see TESTS.)

peak flow meter A device used in a kind of PULMONARY FUNCTION TEST.

pediatrician A physician who specializes in treating children and their disorders from birth through ADOLESCENCE. (If a newborn has special medical problems, such as being PREMATURE or of LOW BIRTH WEIGHT, a specialist called a NEONATOLOGIST may care for the baby during the first month of life, as in a NEONATAL INTENSIVE CARE UNIT.) Pediatricians advise on infant care, conduct WELL-BABY EXAMINATIONS, give vaccinations, treat childhood disorders and diseases, and screen for any possible health problems, among them EAR AND HEARING PROBLEMS, EYE AND VISION PROBLEMS, DEVELOPMENTAL DISORDERS, and NUTRITION problems. If specific health problems are found, the pediatrician will either treat them directly or refer the child to a specialist. If the child has long-term impairment, the pediatrician will assess the kind of activity the child is capable of handling and will recommend, for example, whether or not a child should spend a full day in the classroom.

pedigree A carefully constructed family tree showing the pattern of GENETIC INHERITANCE of traits and disorders, for purposes of research and often for GENETIC COUNSELING for prospective parents, especially those who are concerned about passing on GENETIC DISORDERS to their children; sometimes more generally called a *genealogy*. Such information is not always easy to come by, given the prevalence of immigration, divorce, separation, and ADOPTION, but various government departments can help in gathering genealogical data for reconstruction of meaningful family ancestry information. *Where to Write for Vital Records: Births, Deaths, Marriages, and Divorces*, published by the Public Health Service, National Center for Health Statistics, can help you locate and get copies of key records.

In a pedigree, males are represented by squares, females by circles, and members of each generation appear on the same line. SIBLINGS are attached to the line by "branch bars" in order of birth, where possible; information about deceased siblings, STILLBIRTHS, MISCARRIAGES, and spontaneous ABORTIONS is vitally important. (See PHYSICAL TRAITS, CHARACTERISTICS, AND MEDICAL PROBLEMS NOTED IN CONSTRUCTION OF A PEDIGREE, on page 366.) Symbols and rules for charting are not universally standard, but the most common ones are given in COMMON PEDIGREE SYMBOLS AND SAMPLE OF A PEDIGREE, on page 365.

Common Pedigree Symbols and Sample of a Pedigree

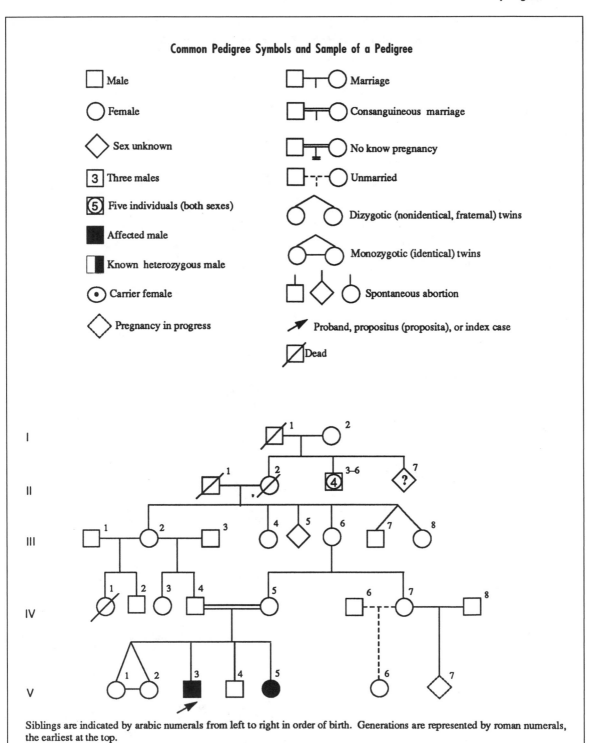

Siblings are indicated by arabic numerals from left to right in order of birth. Generations are represented by roman numerals, the earliest at the top.

Physical Traits, Characteristics, and Medical Problems Noted in Construction of a Pedigree

Sensory Organs
  Eyes
    Blindness
    farsighted/nearsighted
    cataracts
    glaucoma
    retinal detachment/retinal problems
    thick glasses/eye surgery/eye patch
    color blindness/night blindness
    different-colored eyes (e.g., one blue, one brown)

  Ears
    unusual shape
    hearing loss—deafness/hard of hearing
    hearing aids
  Absent sense of smell
  Numbness

Hair/Skin/Teeth
  psoriasis/eczema
  birthmarks—pink, brown, white
  moles
  skin tags
  premature balding or graying
  white patch of hair
  extra/missing/misshapen teeth

Nerve/Muscle/Bone
  slow learners
  learning disabilities
  mental retardation
  seizures/convulsions/epilepsy/fits
  fainting spells/dizziness
  mental illness—depression/schizophrenia
  speech difficulties
  migraine headaches
  shaking/twitching
  weakness
  dystrophy
  back problems
  bone brittleness
  club feet
  dislocated hips at birth
  tall/short stature
  pilonidal cysts

loose joints
double jointed
arthritis

Respiration
  allergies/asthma/sinus/emphysema
  cystic fibrosis

Digestion/Metabolism
  ulcers/colitis
  high cholesterol
  gall bladder problems
  restricted diet
  thyroid/goiter
  diabetes

Reproduction/Excretion
  bladder/kidney infections
  variation in size/number of kidneys
  prostate problems
  undescended testes
  infertility
  unusual reproductive organs (internal and external)
  hemorrhoids

Circulation
  heart murmurs
  varicose veins
  clotting
  bleeding disorders/hemophilia
  anemias
  high blood pressure/hypertension

Other
  cysts/lumps/growths/tumors
  extra fingers/toes
  webbing—fingers/toes
  hole in heart/congenital heart defects
  open spine/spina bifida
  hydrocephalus/waterhead
  surgeries
  serious illnesses
  cancer/leukemia
  alcoholism/drug abuse
  hernia

Source: *Genetic Family History: An Aid to Better Health in Adoptive Children* (1984). Published by the National Center for Education in Maternal and Child Health (NCEMCH) for the Public Health Service's Genetic Diseases Service Branch, Division of Maternal and Child Health, from materials from a conference sponsored by Wisconsin Clinical Genetics Center and Waisman Center on Mental Retardation and Human Development, University of Wisconsin–Madison.

For help and further information

Unpuzzling Your Past: A Basic Guide to Genealogy, second edition, by Emily Anne Croom. Crozet, VA: Betterway, 1989.

The Great Ancestor Hunt: The Fun of Finding Out Who You Are, by Lila Perl. New York: Clarion, 1989. For ages 9 and up.

My Family, Our Family, by Ira Wolfman. New York: Workman, 1989. "A kids' book of genealogy."

Roots for Kids: A Genealogy Guide for Young People, by Susan Provost Beller. Crozet, VA: Betterway, 1989.

What Makes You What You Are, by Sandy Bernstein. New York: Messner, 1989. For young readers.

(See also GENETIC COUNSELING; GENETIC DISORDERS; GENETIC INHERITANCE.)

peer tutoring (student tutoring)

The use of students to help teach skills to other students, especially those who need extra help, often in HETEROGENEOUS GROUPING of students of varying abilities but sometimes as part of a formal program in which older students tutor students in lower grades. With peer tutoring, students get extra help when they need it, the peer tutors have their own skills reinforced during the teaching, and both learn valuable SOCIAL SKILLS. Because children vary in their skills, peer tutoring is not always one-way. A student might coach another in math and herself be coached by a peer in hitting a softball. Many people also encourage peer tutoring among SIBLINGS.

For help and further information

Peer Teaching, by Lilya Wagner. Westport, CT: Greenwood, 1982.

A Guide for Student Tutors, by Patricia S. Koskinen and Tobert M. Wilson. New York: Teachers College Press, 1982.

(See also EDUCATION.)

pellagra A DEFICIENCY DISEASE caused by lack of the VITAMIN NIACIN.

Pell Grant A type of GRANT in FINANCIAL AID that helps undergraduate students meet the expenses of attending COLLEGE. The amounts of grants depend on the program funding, but they ranged up to $2,200 in 1988–89, the money being paid either directly to the student or credited to the school account. Pell Grant recipients have priority in receiving SUPPLEMENTAL EDUCATIONAL OPPORTUNITY GRANTS. As one of the conditions of receiving a Pell Grant, a student must sign a statement certifying that he or she will not make, distribute, dispense, possess, or use drugs during the period covered by the grant, and the grant may be suspended or terminated by a court if the student is convicted of possessing or distributing drugs. (For help and further information, see FINANCIAL AID.)

pelvic inflammatory disease (PID) Infection of the upper genital tract in woman, including the UTERUS, OVARIES, FALLOPIAN TUBES, and other parts of the reproductive system; a SEXUALLY TRANSMITTED DISEASE that is a major cause of INFERTILITY and ECTOPIC (tubal) PREGNANCY, with other dangerous complications. The National Institute of Allergy and Infectious Diseases (NIAID) estimates that PID affects one million women annually, nearly 200,000 of them teenagers; of these, one in 10 becomes infertile, and tens of thousands experience possible life-threatening ectopic pregnancies.

Pelvic inflammatory disease can be caused by many kinds of organisms, including some normally present in the VAGINA and CERVIX, but most often results from GONORRHEA or CHLAMYDIAL INFECTIONS; women seem to be most vulnerable to infection during MENSTRUATION. The disease-causing organisms apparently travel up into the fallopian tubes, possibly by attaching themselves to SPERM; there they penetrate and destroy the lining of the tubes, producing pus, which spreads the infection elsewhere, and leaving scarred tissue behind. This blocks the normal passage of the egg (OVUM) to the uterus and so can cause the fertilized egg to plant itself and start to grow in the tubes, which threatens the life of both mother and FETUS. Women who have had PID (even if they had no recognizable symptoms) are six to 10 times more likely to have an ectopic pregnancy. The risk rises with the age of the woman, the severity of the infection, and the number of episodes of PID.

PID may produce only mild symptoms in the early stages, so serious damage can sometimes be done before the disease is recognized. Symptoms include pain in the lower abdomen, discharge from the VAGINA, and FEVER. But diagnosis is generally made by laboratory tests and confirmed by a LAPAROSCOPY, visual examination of the region through a slit in the abdomen. Once the condition and causative organisms have been identified, it is generally treated with some form of antibiotic. Serious acute cases, as where ectopic pregnancy or APPENDICITIS have resulted, may require emergency surgery. Less severe, chronic cases can cause long-term chronic pelvic pain. (For help and further information, including how to avoid infection, see SEXUALLY TRANSMITTED DISEASES.)

penis The male organ of sexual reproduction, made up largely of spongy tissue, which on stimulation fills with blood and becomes erect. Running through the penis is the URETHRA, the passageway for both urine and SEMEN, exiting through an opening at the head of the penis, called the *glans*. A loose fold of skin over the glans is called the *foreskin* or *prepuce*, which is often removed in an operation called CIRCUMCISION. Though small through childhood, the penis grows significantly larger with PUBERTY as part of the development of SECONDARY SEXUAL CHARACTERISTICS. Among the disorders that may affect a child's penis are BALANITIS, CHORDEE, EPISPADIAS, HYPOSPADIAS, PARAPHIMOSIS, and PHIMOSIS.

PEP Abbreviation for PROFICIENCY EXAMINATION PROGRAM.

Cleaning a Baby Boy's Penis

A newborn boy's penis and scrotum are usually rather large at birth. They get slightly smaller over the next few weeks. If your son was not circumcised, ask your pediatrician to advise you on how to clean the foreskin. Don't try to pull the skin back over the tip of the penis; it will hurt and irritate. As the child grows, the skin will gradually loosen until it will pull back with ease (this could take as long as three or four years).

Source: *Infant Care* (1989). Prepared for the Public Health Service by the Bureau of Maternal and Child Health and Resources Development.

percentile One of 100 divisions into which a group of SCORES is ranked, such as children's scores from a STANDARDIZED TEST; the particular division into which the child's score falls is often the reported score for the test. The percentile indicates the percentage of people doing less well on the test, rather than the actual number or percentage of questions answered correctly. If a child scores in the 79th percentile, for example, that means that he or she did better than 79 percent of all the students who took the test during its development and standardizing. The *decile* operates on the same principle but has divisions from 1 to 10, while a *stanine* runs from 1 to 9 and a *quartile* from 1 to 4 (often simply called *quarters*). Among the many children's tests that commonly use percentiles are the WECHSLER PRESCHOOL AND PRIMARY SCALE OF INTELLIGENCE (WPPSI), the WECHSLER INTELLIGENCE SCALE FOR CHILDREN, REVISED (WISC-R), and METROPOLITAN ACHIEVEMENT TESTS.

perceptual handicap The inability to interpret stimuli received through the senses, though the sense organs themselves—eyes, ears, and so on—are in normal functioning order; a disorder of the sensory skills, including VISUAL SKILLS and AUDITORY SKILLS.

perceptual-motor skills A type of VISUAL SKILLS requiring hand–eye and body–eye coordination; closely related to MOTOR SKILLS.

percutaneous umbilical cord sampling (PUBS) Alternate name for the GENETIC SCREENING procedure CORDOCENTESUS.

perinatal General term for the period around the time of birth.

perinatal asphyxia A severe kind of HYPOXIA (lack of oxygen) affecting a baby in the period just before, during, and after DELIVERY. For physiological reasons not fully understood, babies can generally survive temporary loss of oxygen better than an older child or adult can; that allows them to survive the usually brief period between the time the PLACENTA separates from the UTERUS wall and the time the newly born infant begins to breathe independently. Even so, perinatal asphyxia is a leading cause of DEATH both in the FETUS and in newborns. Babies may be at risk for perinatal asphyxia when LABOR is long and difficult, when FETAL PRESENTATION (position at birth) is abnormal, when the placenta separates prematurely, with RH INCOMPATIBILITY of the mother and fetus's blood types, with long-standing high BLOOD PRESSURE in the mother, and in MULTIPLE BIRTHS. Obstetricians often check fetal position and heartbeat, as with FETAL MONITORS, looking for early warning signs of FETAL DISTRESS, including perinatal asphyxia. Infants with this oxygen starvation often gasp for breath or do not breathe at all (*apnea*) and have slow heartbeat (*bradycardia*), limited activity, low body temperature, pale color or blueness (CYANOSIS), and abnormally high levels of hydrogen in the body (*acidosis*). An asphyxiated infant receives immediate RESUSCITATION, often including pure oxygen poured into the air passages through a tube; cardiac massage; and various medications, depending on the analysis of blood samples from the infant. One of the main reasons for women with HIGH-RISK PREGNANCIES to give birth at high-level HOS-

PITALS, such as regional medical centers, is that these hospitals are best equipped to deal with asphyxia. Even with the best treatment, however, many babies who survive may have serious complications affecting one or more of the main systems of the body. (For help and further information, see DELIVERY; LUNG AND BREATHING DISORDERS.)

perinatal care Medical care offered in the first 28 days after CHILDBIRTH, especially immediately afterward. Often suction is used to clear mucus from the infant's air passages and silver nitrate or other ointment is put in the child's eyes to prevent blinding infections. An APGAR SCORE is performed in the minutes after DELIVERY to assess quickly whether any special medical intervention is needed to aid the child. In the days just after childbirth, if the parents choose it and the child has no special medical problems, CIRCUMCISION may also be performed. Some of these procedures have sparked considerable controversy: Some groups support actions seen as ensuring continuing good health in a baby, while others criticize those actions as INVASIVE. Perinatal care overlaps with POSTNATAL CARE, which extends through the first six weeks after delivery.

For help and further information

National Perinatal Association (NPA)
101½ South Union Street
Alexandria, VA 22314
703-549-5523
Sandra Butler Whyte, Executive Director
Organization of individuals and groups interested in perinatal health care. Publishes a newsletter.

National Perinatal Information Center
One Blackstone Place
668 Eddy Street
Providence, RI 02903
401-274-0650
David Gagnon, Executive Director
Organization that provides public and professionals with information on perinatal care.

National Organization of Circumcision Information Resource Centers (NOCIRC), 415-454-5669. (For full group information, see CIRCUMCISION.)

Newborn Rights Society (NRS), 215-323-6061. (For full group information, see CIRCUMCISION.)

Non-Circumcision Educational Foundation (NCEF), 215-357-2792. (For full group information, see CIRCUMCISION.)

Remain Intact Organization (RIO), 712-477-2256. (For full group information, see CIRCUMCISION.)

(See POSTNATAL CARE; DELIVERY; PREGNANCY.)

perinatologist An OBSTETRICIAN-GYNECOLOGIST who specializes in caring for women with HIGH-RISK PREGNANCIES, including those involving ADOLESCENT PREGNANCY; women over age 35; those with medical problems, such as DIABETES MELLITUS, HYPERTENSION, and SEXUALLY TRANSMITTED DISEASES; women with a personal or immediate family history of GENETIC DISORDERS; and women who have previously had problems during pregnancy.

periodic abstinence   Alternate term for NATURAL FAMILY PLANNING.

periodic paralysis   A rare GENETIC DISORDER affecting young people and characterized by brief periods of PARALYSIS, lasting from a few minutes to two days, and recurring every few weeks. The cause of the paralysis is unclear but seems to be associated with a drop in POTASSIUM (a MINERAL vital for muscle functioning) as a result of excessive consumption of CARBOHYDRATES. Restriction of carbohydrates, taking potassium supplements, and modest exercise at onset moderate the effects of the condition, which generally disappears by about age 30. (For help and further information, see MUSCULAR DYSTROPHY.)

periodontist   A dental specialist who treats advanced cases of GINGIVITIS, or gum inflammation.

peripatologists   Alternate name for ORIENTATION AND MOBILITY INSTRUCTORS.

peripheral nervous system (PNS)   The network of nerves that transmits information to and from the CENTRAL NERVOUS SYSTEM (CNS). Damage to the PNS tends to be local and can sometimes be repaired surgically, unlike damage to the CNS, which tends to affect wide areas of the body long-term. (See NERVOUS SYSTEM.)

peripheral vision   Vision at the sides, rather than straight ahead, lost in some kinds of visual impairment. (See EYE AND VISION PROBLEMS.)

peritoneal dialysis   A form of DIALYSIS using the lining of the abdomen, the PERITONEAL MEMBRANE, to filter out waste products from the blood when the kidneys have failed to function properly.

Perkins Loans   A federally SUBSIDIZED LOAN program under which the school lends money to undergraduate and graduate COLLEGE students; formerly called the *National Direct Student Loan Program*. The amounts available are (as of 1990) a maximum of $4,500 for vocational programs or the first two years of a college program leading to a BACHELOR'S DEGREE; up to $9,000 after two years in a bachelor's program; and up to $18,000 for graduate or professional study (this would include amounts borrowed under the program for undergraduate study). The student signs a promissory note, and money is either paid to the student directly or credited to the school account. Interest charged is only 5 percent, and the repayment period is up to 10 years. Repayments of at least $30 a month do not begin until nine months after the student either leaves school or drops below half-time, though payments may be further delayed under certain circumstances. (For help and further information, see SUBSIDIZED LOAN.)

permanent teeth   The full set of 32 TEETH found in adults, which start appearing and replacing PRIMARY TEETH when a child is about six to seven years old.

pernicious anemia   An inherited form of ANEMIA.

peroneal muscular atrophy (Charcot-Marie-Tooth disease)   A rare GENETIC DISORDER that involves weakness and wasting (ATROPHY) of the muscles in the lower limbs and sometimes the upper limbs as well, as a result of damage to the PERIPHERAL NERVOUS SYSTEM. The disorder generally appears in late childhood or ADOLESCENCE, more often in boys than girls, and progresses slowly, sometimes stopping altogether. Life expectancy is not generally affected, but people with the disorder may need ORTHOPEDIC DEVICES.

For help and further information

CMT International
34-B Bayview Drive
St. Catharines, ON, Canada L2N 4Y6
416-937-3851
Linda Crabtree, President
Organization of people concerned with Charcot-Marie-Tooth disease. Gathers and disseminates information; makes referrals; provides psychological and genetic support; maintains registry for research purposes; encourages formation of local chapters and mutual-support self-help groups; publishes bimonthly *CMT Newsletter* and pamphlets.

(See also MUSCULAR DYSTROPHY.)

perseveration   The tendency to repeat tasks, motions, or spoken words over and over, often long after the occasion for them has passed, a pattern of activity found in some children with LEARNING DISABILITIES, MENTAL RETARDATION, or MENTAL DISORDERS.

persistent fetal circulation (PFC)   A condition in which a newborn has not made the appropriate transition from a fluid-filled environment (as in the UTERUS) to an air-dependent one. Blood flow temporarily fails to effectively exchange carbon dioxide for the needed oxygen, resulting in insufficient oxygen in the blood. In these cases the baby may turn blue (CYANOSIS), breathe rapidly (*tachypnea*), and seem to have RESPIRATORY DISTRESS SYNDROME. (For help and further information, see CHILDBIRTH; LUNG AND BREATHING DISORDERS; HEART AND HEART PROBLEMS.)

personality disorder   A type of MENTAL DISORDER in which affected people have a view of themselves and their social and personal environment that is so rigid and ill-suited as to cause them distress and to significantly impair their ability to function in society. Among the various personality disorders found among children and adolescents (and treated in this book in separate entries) are CONDUCT DISORDER (in adults called *antisocial personality disorder*), AVOIDANT DISORDER OF CHILDHOOD OR ADOLESCENCE (in adults called *avoidant personality disorder*), IDENTITY DISORDER (in adults called *borderline personality disorder*), and OBSESSIVE-COMPULSIVE PERSONALITY DISORDER.

In addition to those noted above, personality disorders include:

- *paranoid personality disorder*, in which a person has a characteristic tendency, from at least early adulthood, to see others as threatening or hateful and accordingly to be suspicious and excessively vigilant of personal rights, being extremely sensitive to perceived insults or attacks.
- *schizoid personality disorder*, in which a person feels perpetually divided (the literal meaning of *schizoid*) from other people, being indifferent to most or all social relationships and having an extremely limited range of emotions, as both felt and expressed.
- *schizotypal personality disorder*, in which a person has disturbances in thought, self-perception, and behavior that are not so severe as to be classified as schizophrenic.
- *histrionic personality disorder*, in which a person is excessively emotional and dramatic in continually drawing attention to him- or herself, exaggerating personal roles, such as that of "victim."
- *narcissistic personality disorder*, in which a person has a grandiose sense of his or her abilities, self and "specialness," and unreasonably expects attention, admiration, and favorable treatment.
- *dependent personality disorder*, in which a person relies excessively on others for advice and reassurance, being unable to make everyday decisions without massive support.
- *passive-aggressive personality disorder*, in which a person characteristically resists personal and social demands indirectly, as by procrastinating, working slowly or ineffectively, protesting "unreasonable demands," or claiming to have forgotten them.

Many of the characteristics of personality disorders overlap with those of other kinds of mental disorders, including DEPRESSION and SCHIZOPHRENIA. (For help and further information, see MENTAL DISORDERS.)

personality tests   A general term for psychological tests focusing on a person's self, emotions, and behavior; also alternate term for PROJECTIVE TESTS.

pertussis (whooping cough)   A serious, highly contagious disease caused by bacteria spread in droplets from coughs and sneezes of people infected with it, which causes violent, uncontrollable spells of coughing (with a characteristic "whooping" sound) that can interfere with eating, drinking, and breathing. Pertussis hits hardest at young children; one-half of the cases are in children under the age of one year, and two-thirds are in children under five. The disease can last for weeks, and perhaps 50 percent of the children need to be hospitalized. Common complications include pneumonia (see LUNG AND BREATHING DISORDERS), CONVULSIONS, and ENCEPHALITIS (inflammation of the brain). Once a leading killer of young children, pertussis is now largely preventable through IMMUNIZATION, generally in a series of five injections of the combination DTP VACCINE between ages two months and six years. As a result, a disease that once killed thousands of children every year now

kills only a handful. Some controversy exists about the pertussis vaccine, but public health authorities recommend vaccination, feeling that it is far safer than the threat of disease. (For help and further information, see DTP VACCINE.)

pertussis vaccine   A type of VACCINE that is normally given in a combination DTP VACCINE, covering DIPHTHERIA, TETANUS (lockjaw), and PERTUSSIS (whooping cough). (For help and further information, see DTP VACCINE.)

pervasive developmental disorder   The psychiatric classification for AUTISM.

pesticide   A type of ENVIRONMENTAL HAZARD.

petechiae   Very small bruises or HEMORRHAGES under the skin.

petition   In family law, a synonym for COMPLAINT.

petit mal seizure   In EPILEPSY, a kind of SEIZURE that involves brief periods of staring unconsciousness; also called *absence seizure.*

PET scan (positron emission transaxial tomography, or **PETT)**   A type of NUCLEAR SCAN similar to a CT SCAN but using slightly radioactive glucose introduced into the body, as by inhaling or INJECTION. The PET scan is especially useful in examining the activity of internal organs, including the brain, the heart, and the circulatory system in general, and in diagnosing and studying CANCER. (For help and further information, see MEDICAL TESTS.)

PFC   Abbreviation for PERSISTENT FETAL CIRCULATION.

phagocytes   A type of "cell-eating" cell in the IMMUNE SYSTEM.

Ph.D.   Abbreviation for *doctor of philosophy*, the most common kind of DOCTORAL DEGREE.

phenylketonuria (PKU)   A GENETIC DISORDER in which children have a defect in the liver enzyme that normally converts the PROTEIN *phenylalanine* into a useful form. In children with PKU, the phenylalanine (sometimes abbreviated as "phe") builds up in the bloodstream, blocking normal development of the brain. The defect affects at least one baby in every 16,000, most commonly those of northern European background, less often those of Jewish, Asian, or African descent. Undetected, PKU can cause MENTAL RETARDATION by the time a child is one year old; if detected but not properly treated or responsive to treatment, it can lead to behavioral disturbances and LEARNING DISABILITIES. To prevent this, the *Guthrie (PKU) test* is routinely given (often by law) to newborns; a few drops of blood taken from the baby's heel will show if there is excess phenylalanine in the blood. Treatment involves a diet low on foods with phenylalanine, such as cow's MILK, meat, regular FORMULA, and other protein-rich foods, with regular monitoring of the blood's phenylalanine level. Infants may be given a special formula containing no phenylalanine; later the child is well-advised to follow a low-protein, largely VEGETARIAN diet. Most cases of PKU respond to such a diet, but how long the diet should be maintained is controversial. In practice, many children go off the special diet on reaching their teens. Women who have PKU must be extremely careful to maintain a low-protein diet during pregnancy—or when there is a possibility that they may become pregnant—because the buildup of phenylalanine can cause irreparable brain damage to the FETUS in the UTERUS. This is a special problem because some women were never told that they had PKU and may not remember being on a special diet when young.

For help and further information

March of Dimes Birth Defects Foundation, 914-428-7100; local chapters in telephone-directory white pages. Publishes information sheet *PKU*. (For full group information, see BIRTH DEFECTS.)

National Institute of Child Health and Human Development (NICHD), 301-496-5133. (For full group information, see PREGNANCY.)

PKU Parents (PKU-P)
8 Myrtle Lane
San Anselmo, CA 94960
415-457-4632
Dale Hillard, President
Organization of parents and professionals involved with children who have PKU. Provides support for parents; offers information and exchange of experiences; publishes quarterly newsletter.

National Center for Education in Child and Maternal Health (NCEMCH), 202-625-8400; **National Maternal and Child Health Clearinghouse (NMCHC)**, 202-625-8410. (For full group information, see PREGNANCY.)

(See also LIVER PROBLEMS.)

phimosis A condition in which a too-tight foreskin cannot be fully drawn back over the head, or glans, of the PENIS, and so impedes free urination. Avoidance of phimosis is one of the medical reasons traditionally advanced for CIRCUMCISION, since it may need to be treated surgically.

phlegm Alternate term for *sputum*, often tested in SPUTUM ANALYSIS.

phobia A powerful, persistent fear of an object or situation, where in fact no danger or threat exists; sometimes thought to be a kind of DEFENSE MECHANISM called DISPLACEMENT, in which unconscious fears are attached to an external object. Phobia is a key characteristic of *phobic disorders* (see below) but is also a symptom of other MENTAL DISORDERS, such as PANIC DISORDERS and other ANXIETY disorders. A much milder problem, SCHOOL PHOBIA, is more often a form of SEPARATION ANXIETY or reflects other kinds of social or academic problems.

Phobic disorders are a type of anxiety disorder characterized by phobia, an irrational fear of an object or setting, a fear so strong it brings on anxiety and a PANIC ATTACK if the sufferer is confronted with it and so leads to AVOIDANCE behavior; it is also called *phobic neurosis*. The most common kind of phobia, especially among children, is *simple phobia*, involving fear of a spe-

cific thing. Phobias about dogs, cats, snakes, mice, or bugs often begin in childhood, but other phobias, such as of blood, cuts, closed spaces (*claustrophobia*), heights (*acrophobia*), and air travel, more often begin in ADOLESCENCE or early adulthood. *Social phobia*, or fear of social situations, often begins during adolescence, when children fear they will be humiliated or embarrassed and so may drastically curtail their activities. Perhaps most severe is *agoraphobia*, or fear of open, exposed places, in which the person's fear of the situation may trigger incapacitating symptoms such as a panic attack and also temporary loss of identity, VOMITING, or INCONTINENCE. To avoid such possible symptoms (or their recurrence), many people with agoraphobia stay at home, venturing out only with a trusted companion. Such a restricted life often leads them to seek professional help, with therapy often involving BEHAVIOR MODIFICATION and desensitization.

For help and further information

Anxiety Disorders Association of America (ADAA), 301-231-9350. Publishes *Phobia: A Comprehensive Summary of Modern Treatments*. (For full group information, see MENTAL DISORDERS.)

National Institute of Mental Health (NIMH), 301-443-4515. Publishes *A Consumer's Guide to Mental Health Services* and booklets on Phobias and Panic. (For full group information, see MENTAL DISORDERS.)

Terrap Programs (Territorial Apprehensiveness)
1010 Doyle Street
Menlo Park, CA 94025
415-329-1233
Mara Woloshin, Executive Officer
For-profit organization of locally franchised programs for sufferers of anxieties and phobias, especially agoraphobia. Operates centers offering TERRAP method of treatment; supplies self-help information and counseling; maintains library and conducts research; offers correspondence program for those who cannot attend clinics; publishes various print and audio materials, including newsletter *Terrap Times*.

CALL (Concerned Agoraphobics Learning to Live)
380 Tolosa Way
San Luis Obispo, CA 93401
805-543-3764
Daryl Woods, Contact
Mutual-support self-help group of and for agoraphobics. Maintains telephone and mail contacts nationwide with housebound sufferers.

Other reference sources

The Anxiety and Phobia Workbook, by Ed Bourne. Oakland, CA: New Harbinger, 1990.
No More Fears, by Douglas Hunt, M.D. New York: Warner, 1988.
Phobia Free: A Medical Breakthrough Linking 90% of All Phobias and Panic Attacks to a Hidden Physical Problem, by Harold N. Levinson, M.D., with Steven Carter. New York: M. Evans, 1988.

Health Care U.S.A., by Jean Carper. New York: Prentice Hall, 1987. Resource for general and specific health-care information; lists major phobia treatment and research centers and other information.

Panic: Facing Fears, Phobias and Anxiety, by Stewart Agras, M.D. New York: Basic, 1985.

Your Phobia: Understanding Your Fears Through Contextual Therapy, by Manual Zane, M.D., and Harry Milt. Washington, DC: American Psychiatric Press, 1984.

Fears and Phobias, by Tony Whitehead. New York: Arco, 1983.

Helping the Fearful Child: A Parent's Guide to Everyday and Problem Anxieties, by Jonathan Kellerman. New York: Norton, 1981.

Everything You Wanted to Know About Phobias But Were Afraid to Ask, by Neal Olshan. New York: Beaufort, 1981.

Our Useless Fears, by Joseph Wolpe, M.D., and David Wolpe. Boston: Houghton Mifflin, 1981.

Agoraphobia, by Dr. Claire Weekes. New York: Hawthorn, 1977.

I Never Stayed in the Dark Long Enough, by Dr. Manual Zane. Available from Phobia Materials, P.O. Box 807, White Plains, NY 10601.

Background Works

The Encyclopedia of Phobias, Fears and Anxieties, by Ronald M. Doctor and Ada P. Kahn. New York: Facts on File, 1989.

Phobics and Other Panic Victims: A Practical Guide for Those Who Help Others, by Janice N. McLean and Sheila Knight. New York: Crossroad/Continuum, 1989.

Phobia: A Comprehensive Summary of Modern Treatments, R. L. DuPont, ed. New York: Brunner/Mazel, 1982.

Agoraphobia: Symptoms, Causes, Treatment, by Arthur B. Hardy. Available from TSC Management Corporation, 1010 Doyle Street, Menlo Park, CA 94025.

For Kids

Fears and Phobias, by Renardo Barden. New York: Crestwood, 1990. For young readers.

(See also MENTAL DISORDERS.)

phobic disorders   A group of MENTAL DISORDERS. (See PHOBIA.)

phocomelia   A BIRTH DEFECT in which a person has nearly nonexistent limbs, with hands or feet attached almost directly to the body; also called *seal limbs*. Phocomelia is associated with some disorders such as DE LANGE SYNDROME and with certain drugs, such as thalidomide, but occasionally occurs with no known triggering event.

phonics method   The traditional method of teaching READING by having the child sound out the letters and learn how they fit together to form words, one of the key WORD-ATTACK SKILLS; also called the *phonetics, alphabet,* or *ABC method*. Some children, such as those with LEARNING DISABILITIES, may need extra help in effectively learning the connections between sounds and written letters, especially if they are being taught by the WHOLE WORD METHOD; for them, phonics methods may be needed, such

as the highly structured *Hegge-Kirk-Kirk* method or VAKT, which takes a MULTISENSORY approach, having students write letters while sounding them out and reading them.

For help and further information

Up with Phonics: Short and Long Vowel Sounds, by Leah Jane Sadden and Peggy Burychka. Videocassette available from Up Video, 16720 Stuebner-Airline Drive, Suite 178, Spring, TX 77379, 713-376-8404.

(See also READING.)

phonological impairment   Alternate name for a type of communication disorder (see COMMUNICATION SKILLS AND DISORDERS).

phosphorus   A MINERAL that works with CALCIUM to build strong bones and TEETH and helps in the body's METABOLISM. Some significant sources of phosphorus are MILK, cheese, meats, egg yolks, fish, poultry, whole-grain products, beans, and nuts. Lack of sufficient phosphorus can cause weakness, bone pain, and abnormal growth. Too much phosphorus can hinder the body's use of calcium. More than that, phosphorus as an element used in pesticides and industrial materials can be a dangerous poison, with chronic exposure causing ANEMIA, CIRRHOSIS OF THE LIVER, and KIDNEY AND UROLOGICAL DISORDERS. Acute phosphorus poisoning can cause VOMITING, bloody DIARRHEA, failure of the heart, kidneys, or liver, DELIRIUM, SEIZURES, and DEATH. (For help and further information, see MINERALS; NUTRITION; poisons.)

phototherapy   The medical treatment of diseases with light, in any of a variety of forms, including sunlight, ultraviolet light, visible blue light (as in fluorescent bulbs), and LASERS. Newborns who are affected with JAUNDICE or HYPERBILIRUBINEMIA are often exposed nude to fluorescent lights, the blue range of which speeds decomposition of the BILIRUBIN that gives a yellowish cast to the skin. Some SKIN DISORDERS, such as VITILIGO and severe forms of PSORIASIS, may be treated with light plus drugs, a type of phototherapy called PUVA (for the drug *psoralen* plus *ultraviolet A*).

For help and further information

The Light Book: How Natural and Artificial Light Affect Our Health, Mood and Behavior, by Jane Wegscheider Hyman. Los Angeles: Tarcher, 1990.

physical handicaps   Alternate term for ORTHOPEDIC HANDICAPS.

physical therapist (physiotherapist)   A health professional who uses various physical techniques and agents to help a patient gain or regain mobility, strength, and control over joints and muscles damaged by disease, disorder, or injury and to reduce pain, inflammation, and muscle spasms. Physical therapists may give a child various muscle tests to assess strength and mobility and decide what methods or agents of treatment to use, including EXERCISE, massage, heat treatment, ULTRASOUND treatment, ice packs, hydrotherapy, and PHOTOTHERAPY. Physical therapists help people learn to use ORTHOPEDIC DEVICES, such as wheelchairs, braces, and crutches, as necessary, the aim being to help the patient to be self-sufficient in the gross MOTOR SKILLS such as WALKING, shifting, and shifting position and beyond that to hopping, skipping, and going up and down stairs. Physical therapists may prescribe exercises to be done at home. (See ORTHOPEDIC DEVICES for help and further information on mechanical aids.)

physician   A health professional who has the degree of doctor of medicine, or M.D. The term may also be used to refer to an OSTEOPATHIC PHYSICIAN, a health professional who has the degree of doctor of osteopathy, or D.O. Many physicians are *general practitioners* (GPs), today more often called *family-practice physicians*, who provide medical care to people of any age and of either sex, treating all aspects of a patient's care; they are PRIMARY HEALTH CARE PROVIDERS who act as a patient's "first port of call." If the condition warrants it, a patient will be referred to a *specialist*, a physician with advanced training and experience in certain areas of medical care, such as a PEDIATRICIAN, who specializes in treating children, or a NEONATOLOGIST, who specializes in treating newborns.

phytanic acid storage disease   Alternate name for Refsum's syndrome, a type of LIPID STORAGE DISEASE.

pica   A craving or compulsive desire to eat substances that are not food, such as dirt, clay, paint, laundry starch, chalk, wood, glue, hair, or ice; a kind of EATING DISORDER that often stems from a nutritional deficiency, especially of IRON. It also sometimes occurs during PREGNANCY and may be associated with some forms of MENTAL DISORDERS.

PID   Abbreviation for PELVIC INFLAMMATORY DISEASE.

Pierre Robin syndrome (Robin triad)   A CONGENITAL disorder, presumably of genetic origin, which involves various craniofacial abnormalities, such as CLEFT LIP AND PALATE, small lower jaw (*hypoplasia of the mandible*), and malformation of the tongue; defects of the eyes and ears, such as *glaucoma* (damage caused by too-high fluid pressure in the eye); and sometimes MENTAL RETARDATION. PLASTIC SURGEONS, SPEECH-LANGUAGE PATHOLOGISTS, ORTHODONTISTS, and other medical specialists often must work together to treat resulting communication and respiratory disorders. Because the tongue is often too large for the mouth in newborns, it sometimes falls back into the throat, blocking air passages and making feeding difficult; in severe cases, a physician will suture the tongue to the lower lip for a few months, to allow the jaw to grow.

For help and further information

National Institute of Dental Research (NIDR), 301-496-4261. (For full group information, see TEETH AND DENTAL PROBLEMS.)

National Foundation of Dentistry for the Handicapped (NFDH), 303-573-0264. (For full group information, see HELP FOR SPECIAL CHILDREN on page 578.)

National Institute of Child Health and Human Development (NICHD), 301-496-5133. (For full group information, see PREGNANCY.)

(See also COMMUNICATION SKILLS AND DISORDERS; LUNG AND BREATHING DISORDERS.)

pigeon toes   Alternate name for METATARSUS VARUS.

pill, the   Popular name for BIRTH-CONTROL PILL.

pink eye   Popular term for conjunctivitis. (See EYE AND VISION PROBLEMS.)

PINS   Abbreviation for persons in need of SUPERVISION.

pituitary gland   One of the key organs that produce HORMONES, a tiny gland attached to the HYPOTHALAMUS in the brain; sometimes called the master gland, because it regulates the activities of so many other glands and organs in the body. The pituitary secretes a number of key hormones:

- HUMAN GROWTH HORMONE (hGH), which stimulates the growth of the body;
- *thyroid-stimulating hormone* (TSH), which stimulates the THYROID GLAND;
- *prolactin*, which stimulates the development of a woman's BREASTS and LACTATION during BREASTFEEDING;
- LUTEINIZING HORMONE (LH);
- *follicle-stimulating hormone* (FSH) (see FOLLICLES);
- *melanocyte-stimulating hormone* (MSH), which regulates the pigmentation of the skin;
- *adrenocorticotropic hormone* (ACTH), which stimulates the ADRENAL GLANDS;
- *antidiuretic hormone* (ADH), which stimulates the kidneys to decrease the amount of water sent to form urine;
- *oxytocin*, which stimulates contractions of the UTERUS during CHILDBIRTH and also affects MILK released from the breasts.

Because of its wide range of functions, any abnormality in the pituitary gland that causes excess or deficiency in production of these hormones can seriously affect the rest of the body.

Among the pituitary disorders that can affect children are:

- *growth disorders*, resulting from GENETIC DISORDERS, other CONGENITAL disorders (such as from injury during childbirth), or later HEAD INJURY that affected the pituitary. (See GROWTH AND GROWTH DISORDERS.)
- TUMORS, usually benign in themselves, but possibly causing substantial problems because of a malfunctioning pituitary. (See BRAIN TUMORS.)
- *loss of blood supply*, as from a tumor or HEMORRHAGE; in a woman with massive hemorrhaging during childbirth, this can lead to SHEEHAN'S SYNDROME.
- *underactivity of the pituitary* as a result of RADIATION or radiation therapy.

Disorders of the pituitary are investigated using a variety of MEDICAL TESTS, including X-RAYS, CT SCANS, MRI SCANS, and ANGIOGRAMS.

For help and further information

National Hormone and Pituitary Program (NHPP)
210 West Fayette Street, Suite 501-9
Baltimore MD 21201
301-837-2552
Mildred O. Jones, Executive Secretary
Organization of health professionals concerned with hormones of the pituitary gland. Collects glands and makes extracts for research purposes; seeks to increase number of pituitary donations.

National Institute of Neurological Disorders and Stroke (NINDS), 301-496-5751. (For full group information, see BRAIN AND BRAIN DISORDERS.)

National Institute of Diabetes and Digestive and Kidney Diseases (NIDDK), 301-496-3583. (For full group information, see DIGESTIVE DISORDERS.)

Human Growth Foundation (HGF), 301-656-7540. (See GROWTH AND GROWTH DISORDERS.)

PKD Abbreviation for polycystic kidney disease, a kind of KIDNEY AND UROLOGICAL PROBLEM.

PKU Abbreviation for PHENYLKETONURIA.

placenta An organ that develops in the UTERUS, the site of the exchange of nutrients and oxygen from the mother's blood for waste products from the baby's blood. The placenta grows from the outer layer of the fertilized egg (OVUM) implanted in the lining of the uterus and is connected to the baby by the UMBILICAL CORD. It also produces HORMONES—ESTROGEN, PROGESTERONE, and HUMAN CHORIONIC GONADOTROPIN (hCG)—which are detectable in a woman's urine and are the basis of PREGNANCY TESTS. The placenta normally remains in place until after the child has been delivered, when it is expelled as the *afterbirth*.

In some cases, it begins to separate from the uterus wall prematurely, a condition called *abruptio placentae*, sometimes signaled by bleeding from the VAGINA during PREGNANCY. The separation may be only partial, as indicated on an ULTRASOUND scan and by only small amounts of bleeding. Then the pregnancy may continue, if the mother has bed rest for the balance of the pregnancy. But if the separation is severe and heavy bleeding ensues, the baby may need to be delivered immediately, either by induced LABOR, if possible, or CESAREAN SECTION. Increased risk of abruptio placentae occurs with PREECLAMPSIA, hypertension (high BLOOD PRESSURE), ANEMIA, SMOKING, and sometimes TRAUMA, such as an automobile accident.

The placenta may sometimes be placed abnormally low in the uterus so that it covers the opening of the CERVIX, a condition called *placenta previa*. Bleeding often results, with possible risk of severe HEMORRHAGE, which can cause life-threatening

SHOCK. The woman will often be hospitalized and confined to complete bed rest for as long as possible; the baby is often delivered by cesarean section, especially when the cervix is completely covered. (For help and further information, see PREGNANCY; CHILDBIRTH.)

placenta previa A disorder in which the PLACENTA that provides nourishment to a FETUS is placed abnormally low, over the CERVIX. (See PLACENTA.)

plaintiff In law, the person who makes a COMPLAINT in a civil lawsuit.

plantar response In children and adults, a normal REFLEX of curling the toes when the foot is firmly stroked on the outside of the sole. In newborns, the normal response is a flexing upward of the big toe and fanning of the other toes, called BABINSKI'S REFLEX; if this occurs in children and adults, it can indicate brain or spinal-cord disorders (see BRAIN AND BRAIN DISORDERS, SPINE AND SPINE DISORDERS).

plaque A mixture of bacteria, saliva, and leftover food that forms a deposit on TEETH and eats into the enamel, causing tooth decay, or *caries*. If plaque is not cleaned off routinely, it hardens into a mineral deposit called *calculus* or *tartar*, which the dentist must remove by scaling.

plasma Fluid that makes up much of the volume of blood, which carries the various blood cells. (See BLOOD AND BLOOD DISORDERS.)

plastic surgeon A PHYSICIAN who specializes in reconstructive or COSMETIC SURGERY to correct damage and defects or to alter appearance, through the techniques of PLASTIC SURGERY.

plastic surgery Surgical operations performed to reconstruct, repair, or alter skin and associated tissue, especially when it has been damaged by injury or disease, such as BURNS or CANCER, or is deformed because of CONGENITAL disorders, such as CLEFT LIP AND PALATE or HYPOSPADIAS; in adults, it often is performed to reverse the effects of the aging process. In attempting to correct serious damage, plastic surgeons may use a variety of skin grafts, sometimes drawn from elsewhere on the patient's own body, and sometimes must also deal with the bony structures underneath, as when a child has substantial skull deformities and requires *craniofacial* (skull and face) or *maxillofacial* (upper jaw, nose, and cheek) reconstructive surgery. The aim in general is to give the person as natural and normal a look as possible. Plastic surgery performed for appearance's sake alone, such as RHINOPLASTY (to alter the nose) or OTOPLASTY (to flatten the ears), is generally termed COSMETIC SURGERY.

For help and further information

The Teen Face Book: A Question and Answer Guide to Skin Care, Cosmetics, and Facial Plastic Surgery, by American Academy of Facial Plastic and Reconstructive Surgery. Washington, DC: Acropolis, 1989.

Plastic Surgery: The Kindest Cut, by John Camp. New York: Henry Holt, 1989.

The Complete Book of Cosmetic Surgery: A Candid Guide for Men, Women & Teens, by Elizabeth Morgan, M.D. New York: Warner, 1988.

platelets (thrombocytes)   Blood cells important in clotting. (See BLOOD AND BLOOD DISORDERS.)

play group   A circle of PRESCHOOL-age children who are gathered together (by their parents or CAREGIVERS) on a fairly regular basis at the home of one child or another, often in rotation, the idea being to help children learn to develop SOCIAL SKILLS by playing with others and to give them the stimulation of new people and activities. Such experience is especially important for children who are otherwise relatively isolated from other children of their age, whether far out in the country, in a suburban home, or in a high-rise apartment, including an only child or one with much older brothers and sisters. Children who have no experience of either play group or preschool programs (or the rough-and-tumble of brothers and sisters) before they enter KINDERGARTEN may be at a distinct disadvantage in learning how to be with others and to cooperate in activities. Such children have to deal with normal SEPARATION ANXIETY on entering school, where the shocking transition may interfere with learning, rather than at a play group or preschool. But children who have SIBLINGS at home and others their age nearby may not need any regularly established play group. Parents are well advised not to push their children into a group if they are made unhappy by it but to wait for some time to pass and more development to occur; what is "too much too soon" for a child of two might be just right for a three-year-old. TEACHING YOUNG CHILDREN: GUIDELINES AND ACTIVITIES, on page 544, gives many tips for organizing play activities for preschoolers.

For help and further information

Institute for Childhood Resources (INICR)
210 Columbus Avenue, #611
San Francisco, CA 94133
415-864-1169
Stevanne Auerbach, Director

Organization of parents, educators, and others interested in growth, development, and education of children; consults with individuals and groups involved with services to children; provides education to parents, as on parenting, childhood education, child care, and toys and games; maintains library; publishes various materials, including *The Whole Child: A Sourcebook, Choosing Child Care*, and *The Toy Chest*.

Kids and Play, prepared by the Bank Street College of Education, Joanne F. Oppenheim. New York: Ballantine, 1984.
(See also EDUCATION; SPORTS AND ACTIVITIES in the PARENT'S BOOK-SHELF on page 566.)

P.L. 94-142   Abbreviation for Public Law 94-142, the formal legal name for the EDUCATION FOR ALL HANDICAPPED CHILDREN ACT OF 1975.

PLS   Abbreviation for PARENT LOCATOR SERVICE.

PLUS Loans/Supplemental Loans for Students (SLS)   Federally SUBSIDIZED LOAN program under which banks, credit unions, or other financial institutions lend to parents or students money for educational expenses, in addition to other loans, such as STAFFORD LOANS. PLUS Loans are taken out and are to be repaid by parents; SLS loans are taken out and paid by students. Borrowers sign promissory notes. PLUS loan amounts are paid directly to parents; SLS loans are paid either directly to the student or to both student and school, sometimes in installments. Amounts available are up to $4,000 a year, to a total of $20,000, in addition to Stafford Loans, though in no case can this be more than the actual cost of the education, minus any other FINANCIAL AID the student receives. Interest varies yearly, and an insurance premium of up to three percent may be charged. Payments begin within 60 days after the last installment of the loan was received, but principal payments may be deferred in certain circumstances. (For further information, see SUBSIDIZED LOAN.)

PMS   Abbreviation for premenstrual syndrome, a disorder associated with MENSTRUATION.

pneumonia   Inflammation of one or both lungs, a kind of LUNG AND BREATHING DISORDER.

pneumothorax or **pneumomediastinum**   Leakage of air into the chest area around the lungs. While small air leaks are common and not of great concern, severe air leaks can be life-threatening, exposing the lungs to infection. Such leaks are often associated with treatment for RESPIRATORY DISTRESS SYNDROME.

PNP   Abbreviation for pediatric NURSE PRACTITIONER.

PNS   Abbreviation for PERIPHERAL NERVOUS SYSTEM, the network of nerves that transmits information to and from the CENTRAL NERVOUS SYSTEM.

poisons   Various types of ENVIRONMENTAL HAZARDS.

poliomyelitis   A severe, highly contagious disease caused by a virus that inhabits the nose, throat, and intestinal tract and is spread from person to person, by affected people or by unaffected CARRIERS. In mild cases, which might last only a few days, people with polio have fever, sore throat, nausea, headache, stomachache, and often pain and stiffness in the neck, back, and legs. More severe cases, called *paralytic polio*, start the same way but often involve severe muscle pain and PARALYSIS as soon as the first week. About half of the people with paralytic polio recover with only mild disabilities, sometimes none, but the rest may suffer permanent paralysis and occasionally even DEATH. Adults who remember the days before the 1954 discovery of the first polio VACCINE by Jonas Salk recall the fear among parents of young children, as epidemics of polio swept many regions, leaving many children disabled and dependent on ORTHOPEDIC DEVICES for mobility and often on VENTILATORS ("iron lungs") for breathing. Fortunately, use of the ORAL POLIO VACCINE (Sabin vaccine) and (less often today) the INACTIVATED POLIO VACCINE (Salk vaccine) have made cases of polio extremely rare in those parts of the world, such as the United States, where immunization is widespread.

For help and further information

National Institute of Allergy and Infectious Diseases (NIAID), 301-496-5717. (For full group information, see ALLERGY.)

National Institute of Child Health and Human Development (NICHD), 301-496-5133. (For full group information, see PREGNANCY.)

March of Dimes Birth Defects Foundation, 914-428-7100; local chapters in telephone-directory white pages. Publishes information sheets on specific topics, including *Polio* and *Post Polio Muscle Atrophy*. (For full group information, see BIRTH DEFECTS.)

Gazette International Networking Institute (GINI), 314-361-0475. Publishes *Polio Network News* and *Rehabilitation Gazette*. (For full group information, see HELP FOR SPECIAL CHILDREN on page 578.)

(See also ORAL POLIO VACCINE.)

polycystic kidney disease (PKD)   A kind of KIDNEY AND UROLOGICAL DISORDER.

polycythemia   A disorder of too many red blood cells. (See BLOOD AND BLOOD DISORDERS.)

polydactyly (polydactylism, polydactylia, or **hyperdactly)** A BIRTH DEFECT in which a baby is born with extra fingers or toes, either fully formed digits or small stumps. The condition, which in the United States affects approximately one baby in every 2,000 births, is often corrected by surgery soon after birth. Polydactyly is often a GENETIC DISORDER, of the AUTOSOMAL DOMINANT type, but it is sometimes associated with LAURENCE-MOON-BIEDL SYNDROME.

For help and further information

National Institute of Child Health and Human Development (NICHD), 301-496-5133. (For full group information, see PREGNANCY.)

polyhydramnios (hydramnios)   A condition of having too much AMNIOTIC FLUID during a PREGNANCY.

polymenorrhea   A disorder association with MENSTRUATION.

polymyositis   A type of muscle disorder. (See MUSCULAR DYSTROPHY.)

polyploidy   A lethal kind of CHROMOSOMAL ABNORMALITY in which a child has one or more extra full sets of chromosomes.

polyunsaturated fatty acids   A type of FAT mostly from plant sources.

positron emission transaxial tomograph   Full formal name of the MEDICAL TEST known as the PET SCAN.

postcoital test   A common test performed in evaluating INFERTILITY problems.

postlingual   Term referring to people with EAR AND HEARING PROBLEMS who developed deafness after some experience of sound and spoken language, especially after age three—about 5 percent of hearing-impaired people.

postmature   Term referring to an infant born at 42 weeks or more—that is, two or more weeks after the DUE DATE, normally calculated as 40 weeks from the beginning of the woman's last MENSTRUATION. Postmaturity is a problem because the PLACENTA, which nourishes the developing FETUS, no longer does its job as efficiently late in the PREGNANCY, after about the 30th week. The child may be larger-boned than average and have less moldable bones because of the longer development. Indeed, largeness itself is sometimes a cause of postmaturity if the baby's head is too big to descend properly. All of these factors make for difficult DELIVERY and attendant damage, with the risk of STILLBIRTH much increased by the 43rd and 44th weeks of pregnancy. To avoid this, doctors often act by the 42nd week to either induce LABOR (if appropriate) or to perform a CESAREAN SECTION. The baby itself will often look gaunt, since fat has been lost from the body, and will have wrinkled, peeling skin and long fingernails. There is often considerable imbalance in the key MINERALS in the blood, notably CALCIUM and POTASSIUM, which needs correction to prevent SEIZURES and possible neurological damage. (For help and further information, see PREGNANCY.)

postnatal care (postpartal care)   The medical care of mother and newborn in the first few days to six weeks after birth. In a normal birth, this is the period in which BONDING takes place between infant and mother (and father), starting immediately after the birth. After one or more days, the baby usually is able to go home with the parents. But if the baby was PREMATURE, was of LOW BIRTH WEIGHT, or had special medical problems, he or she may have to be placed in a NEONATAL INTENSIVE CARE UNIT (NICU). Then parents may need to make special arrangements to go to the HOSPITAL to be with the child for BONDING. For the mother, the main medical hazards in the postpartal period are possible infection or HEMORRHAGE, along with possible postpartum DEPRESSION. The baby's health and development are monitored by a series of WELL-BABY EXAMINATIONS. Care offered in the first 28 days after the birth may also be called PERINATAL CARE. (For help and further information, see PERINATAL CARE; PREMATURE BABIES.)

For help and further information

National Institute of Child Health and Human Development (NICHD), 301-496-5133. (For full group information, see PREGNANCY.)

National Center for Clinical Infant Programs (NCCIP)
733 15th Street, Suite 912
Washington, DC 20005
202-347-0308
Eleanor S. Szanton, Executive Director
Organization of health professionals and others interested in improving care of infants and young children and their families. Supports development of clinics focusing on early intervention and prevention; publishes various materials, including *Zero to Three* and *Clinical Infant Reports*.

postneonatal mortality   INFANT MORTALITY in the second through 12th months of life. (See DEATH for chart of postneonatal mortality.)

postpartum   General medical term for the period after CHILDBIRTH.

postpartum depression   A form of DEPRESSION common among women after CHILDBIRTH, popularly called the *baby blues*.

postpartum room   The room in a HOSPITAL to which a woman is moved after CHILDBIRTH, often from the RECOVERY ROOM but sometimes from the LABOR/DELIVERY/RECOVERY (LDR) ROOM.

postsecondary education   Any formal education beyond HIGH SCHOOL (secondary school). The term usually refers to undergraduate and postgraduate COLLEGE programs but sometimes also includes a wide range of nondegree programs for continuing education for adults, including special programs for people with handicaps.

post-traumatic stress disorder (PTSD)   A pattern of ANXIETY-related symptoms found in people who have undergone frightening or stressful experiences, such as rape, child abuse, military combat, incarceration in concentration camps, or living through earthquakes or other mass disasters. Symptoms commonly include reliving the experiences in daydreams or nightmares, other SLEEPING DISORDERS, a sense of separation and lack of responsiveness to others, DEPRESSION, disorders in memory and concentration, and exaggerated startle responses. If many or most others involved in the experience died, the disorder is often called *survivor syndrome* and involves strong guilt at having survived. Children (and adults) who have survived a car crash, fire, or airplane accident in which many or most others died are often given special counseling to help them deal with the questions of DEATH and their own survival. If PTSD stems from military situations, it is sometimes called *battle fatigue* or *shell shock*. With emotional support and counseling, many people are able to recover their "sense of balance," but in some people the experience can last for months, years, or a lifetime, sometimes being retriggered by reminders of the event.

For help and further information
National Institute of Mental Health (NIMH), 301-443-4515. (For full group information, see MENTAL DISORDERS.)

Other reference sources
Too Scared to Cry: Psychic Trauma in Childhood, by Lenore Terr, M.D. New York: Harper & Row, 1990.
Aftershock: Overcoming Post-traumatic Stress in Your Everyday Life, by Andrew E. Slaby, M.D. New York: Villard, 1989.

postural drainage   A physical-therapy technique used for patients with CYSTIC FIBROSIS and other kinds of disorders that obstruct the air passages. The patient's chest is "pounded" to dislodge mucus, and the body is positioned so that gravity will help the mucus drain from the body.

potassium   A MINERAL that is vital to maintaining the body's normal heart rhythm, water balance, and functioning of nerves and muscles, often working in combination with SODIUM and CALCIUM. Potassium is found in many foods, but especially good sources are orange juice, bananas, dried fruits, peanut butter, and potatoes. Too little potassium (*hypokalemia*) can cause muscle weakness and irregular heartbeat; it is associated with loss of body fluids through VOMITING and DIARRHEA and is especially common in children with DIABETES MELLITUS and CUSHING'S SYNDROME. Too much potassium (*hyperkalemia*), as from taking excess potassium supplements or as a result of KIDNEY AND UROLOGICAL DISORDERS, can also cause heart irregularities and even cardiac arrest. (For help and further information, see MINERALS; NUTRITION.)

power of attorney   A formal written document in which one person (the *principal*) gives another (the *attorney in fact*) the power to act in place of the principal in certain specified situations, as in financial transactions or medical decisions; a *durable* power of attorney continues in effect even after the principal has become incapacitated. Parents of children who are no longer MINORS but are unable to care for themselves (such as in MENTAL RETARDATION or with severely HANDICAPPED adults) may wish to draw up a durable power of attorney, giving the person of their choice power to act in case the parents become incapacitated, as through illness. Without such a power of attorney, the court would appoint a CONSERVATOR to act.

PPO   Abbreviation for PREFERRED PROVIDER ORGANIZATION.

PPVT   Abbreviation for PEABODY PICTURE VOCABULARY TEST.

practicing   The second stage of a baby's SEPARATION-INDIVIDUATION process.

precocious puberty   The onset of the physical changes of PUBERTY abnormally early, in girls before age nine and in boys before age 10. (For help and further information, see PUBERTY.)

precollege program   A program that specifically prepares a student for COLLEGE, often a student with handicaps or educational deficiencies that require some special training to reach college-entry level; sometimes a general term referring to any formal education below college level.

precursor skill   Alternate term for PREREQUISITE, in the sense of a skill that is regarded as fundamental to the mastering of a more complex, higher-level skill.

predictive validity   In testing, a type of VALIDITY relating to how successfully a test predicts future performance, such as student success in PRESCHOOL or COLLEGE.

preeclampsia   A condition affecting women late in PREGNANCY, generally after the 20th week; it occurs in about 5 to 7 percent of all pregnancies. Symptoms include *hypertension* (high BLOOD PRESSURE), EDEMA (fluid buildup), and PROTEIN in the urine (*proteinuria*), as well as more general symptoms such as headache, nausea, VOMITING, abdominal pain, and blurred vision. If unchecked, preeclampsia can cause severe disorders in both mother and child, especially separation of the PLACENTA (*abruptio placentae*), which cuts off nourishment to the fetus, and ECLAMPSIA, which can threaten the life of both. (Preeclampsia and eclampsia are sometimes considered a mild and more severe form of a disorder called *toxemia of pregnancy*.) Preeclampsia is most common in first pregnancies, in women under 20 and over 40, and in those with a personal or family history of related disorders, including DIABETES MELLITUS or KIDNEY AND UROLOGICAL DISORDERS. Good NUTRITION, rest, and regular EXERCISE lessen risk of the disorder. PRENATAL CARE includes regular screening for signs of preeclampsia, which is normally treated with bed rest and drugs to bring down blood pressure. In severe cases, hospitalization and intravenous blood pressure medication may be advised; and once the mother's condition has been stabilized, emergency delivery may be necessary, as through induction of LABOR or CESAREAN SECTION. Causes of preeclampsia are unknown; its effects diminish after the pregnancy ends, though some damage may have been done. (For help and further information, see PREGNANCY.)

preferred modality   The SENSORY MODE (one of the senses) the child uses most easily or efficiently for gaining knowledge and information. (See MODALITIES; LEARNING STYLE; SENSORY MODES.)

preferred provider organization (PPO)   An organization of independent physicians, HOSPITALS, and pharmacists who work under contract with an employer or insurance company to provide health care to subscribing patients for set fees, usually lower than elsewhere. Like HEALTH MAINTENANCE ORGANIZATIONS, PPOs have the advantage of holding down medical costs and seeming to eliminate the need for health insurance, but they can limit the patient's choice of medical care in special situations, such as maternity care and severe chronic illness in a child.

pregnancy   The process of a mother growing a baby in her body, from the fertilized egg (OVUM) no bigger than the dot on this letter "i" to a child perhaps 20 inches long and typically seven to eight pounds. FERTILIZATION—the joining of the egg and SPERM—normally takes place in the woman's FALLOPIAN TUBES, with the resulting ZYGOTE then traveling into the UTERUS (womb) for IMPLANTATION and growth. Usually, the sperm and egg are brought together as a result of sexual intercourse; but when a couple has INFERTILITY problems, a variety of other methods might be used to achieve conception, including ARTIFICIAL INSEMINATION, IN VITRO FERTILIZATION, GAMETE INTRAFALLOPIAN

TRANSFER (GIFT), and EMBRYO TRANSFER, as well as SURROGATE PARENTING.

The new being—at first called an EMBRYO and then (after about eight weeks) called a FETUS—develops for an average of 266 days (38 weeks) from the date of fertilization, a period called GESTATION. However, doctors generally calculate the DUE DATE and length of pregnancy as 280 days (40 weeks) from the beginning date of the last MENSTRUATION. Changes take place in the baby and in the mother's body every day, but in general the 9⅓ months of pregnancy are divided into three periods, each three months long, called *trimesters*. For an overview of the changes over these periods, see THE BABY'S GROWTH AND DEVELOPMENT and CHANGES IN THE BODY DURING PREGNANCY AND LACTATION on pages 380 and 381.

There are several early signs of possible pregnancy. Best known is the missed menstrual period, though MENSTRUATION can temporarily cease for other reasons, and some menstrual bleeding can occur early in pregnancy. Sore or tender BREASTS, nausea, VOMITING, heartburn, reflux of stomach acids, frequent urination, fatigue, weight gain, swelling of the abdomen, and EDEMA (fluid buildup) are also common signs in early pregnancy. A woman who is using the *basal body temperature method* as part of NATURAL FAMILY PLANNING will notice that her temperature remains high if she is pregnant.

The most reliable signs of pregnancy, however, are the presence of certain hormones in the blood or urine; these are used as the basis of PREGNANCY TESTS, done either in a medical laboratory (through a doctor or clinic) or with a HOME MEDICAL TEST. (See PREGNANCY TESTS for a description of a home pregnancy test.) In their publication *Prenatal Care*, the Public Health Service recommends: "It is important to have a pregnancy test as soon as possible after you miss your first period or as soon as you think you might be pregnant. Some tests can be done as early as a few days after a single missed period." They also recommend that, if you use a do-it-yourself test, you see your doctor *whatever* the result, as long as the missed period does not arrive.

Early detection is stressed because of the importance of PRENATAL CARE. The first two to three months of the baby's development are crucial, and the sooner a woman realizes she is pregnant, the sooner she can organize her life to maximize her chances of bearing a healthy baby. Among other things, she needs to:

- stop any activities that could damage the fetus, such as SMOKING, drinking alcohol, taking drugs (medical or "recreational") that might cause BIRTH DEFECTS, exposure to RADIATION or poisons, and potentially dangerous EXERCISES or sports activities such as ski jumping.
- modify her diet so that she provides sufficient nutrition for herself and her baby. (See NUTRITION for a recommended diet during pregnancy.)
- identify and take steps to treat any health problems that might affect the pregnancy, such as high BLOOD PRESSURE; DIABETES MELLITUS; SEXUALLY TRANSMITTED DISEASES such as GONORRHEA, SYPHILIS, or HERPES SIMPLEX; blood disorders such as ANE-

MIA or RH INCOMPATIBILITY with the baby (see BLOOD AND BLOOD DISORDERS); and lack of IMMUNITY to RUBELLA.

As part of prenatal care, physicians will also check the woman's general health and advise on how to prepare for the pregnancy. (See PRENATAL CARE for more information.)

Because many of these questions are so important, couples who are planning a pregnancy in advance are well advised to take many of the above steps some weeks ahead of the planned time of conception so that both mother and father are in top physical condition and the baby is not exposed to dangers before a woman even realizes she is pregnant. A woman may want to start getting physically fit before conceiving, for example, because doctors recommend against starting any new exercise regimen once pregnancy has been confirmed. (See EXERCISE for general advice during pregnancy; see also BASIC EXERCISES FOR DURING AND AFTER PREGNANCY on page 488.) Similarly, if the prospective mother or father are normally exposed to radiation (as pilots or flight attendants, for example) or chemicals, they may want to move to different work temporarily before conceiving.

Another area that couples will want to explore, either as soon as pregnancy is confirmed or suspected or, even better, beforehand, is whether they or anyone in their families has any history of GENETIC DISORDERS, CHROMOSOMAL ABNORMALITIES, or difficulties with pregnancy, such as MISCARRIAGES or STILLBIRTHS. If so, they may want to seek GENETIC COUNSELING (see separate entry) to assess the risk of their having similar problems in a pregnancy.

Once a pregnancy is confirmed, couples may want to consider various kinds of PRENATAL TESTS or GENETIC SCREENING tests to see if the fetus has any identifiable health problems. Among these tests are AMNIOCENTESIS, ALPHA FETOPROTEIN, CHORIONIC VILLUS SAMPLING, and ULTRASOUND scans. Some kinds of problems can now be corrected in the womb, as through IN UTERO SURGERY. With other kinds of problems, couples may be faced with difficult choices if a child is diagnosed as having a serious genetic disorder. Some will decide to bear the child, in which case the test will have given them time to prepare for the child's SPECIAL NEEDS; others will choose to have an elective ABORTION. If abortion is being considered, the sooner such testing is done the better.

Not all pregnancies are planned or even wanted, of course. In some cases the couple, or the mother alone, decides not to keep the baby and then faces the difficult choice of having an abortion or placing the child for ADOPTION, both of which can be traumatic in their way.

But if the mother is going to bear the child, a number of decisions have to be made. First, and most basic, is who the basic health-care provider will be during the pregnancy, such as an OBSTETRICIAN-GYNECOLOGIST, FAMILY PRACTICE PHYSICIAN, CERTIFIED NURSE-MIDWIFE, or a clinic. Who is chosen depends partly on personal attitudes and partly on medical concerns. If the mother is under 20 or above 35, if she or the fetus has any medical problems, if too little time has elapsed since a previ-

ous pregnancy, or if the mother is having a MULTIPLE BIRTH, hers would be considered a HIGH-RISK PREGNANCY. In that case, she is generally advised to be under the care of a MATERNAL AND FETAL SPECIALIST, who specializes in handling high-risk births, and to plan to deliver in a relatively sophisticated (Level II or III) HOSPITAL.

Women who do not fall into the high-risk group have other options. They may choose to have their child in a community hospital, at a MATERNITY CENTER, or even in a HOME BIRTH. Closely connected with these choices is the kind of delivery the parents envision, which may range from a high-tech birth in a hospital, using all of the painkillers (*analgesics*), ANESTHESIA, and sophisticated equipment available, to a PREPARED CHILDBIRTH that tries to avoid medical intervention unless absolutely necessary in favor of a more natural approach.

When investigating possible health-care providers and hospitals, parents will want to find those who agree on issues they feel strongly about, such as prepared childbirth, BREASTFEEDING or BOTTLEFEEDING, CIRCUMCISION, the father's presence or participation in the DELIVERY ROOM, ROOMING-IN, and prenatal classes. Among the questions the Public Health Service recommends couples consider in choosing health-care providers are:

- their reputation with other patients and physicians.
- their office hours and location of the office and the hospital.
- their fees.
- the couple's feelings of well-being during the first few visits.

The couple will want to explore their options carefully and make their decisions early so that they will have consistent follow-through from whichever health-care provider they choose and can, if desired, plan to take prepared childbirth classes, especially if the man is going to be the BIRTH PARTNER.

Both proper prenatal care and careful choice of health-care provider are important, because pregnancy is not a no-risk activity. Indeed, though better NUTRITION, better health care, availability of BLOOD TRANSFUSIONS, and use of CONTRACEPTION to limit the number of pregnancies have all combined to bring down the rate of MATERNAL MORTALITY, still, in the mid-1980s, approximately eight out of every 100,000 women in the United States died because of problems related to or made worse by pregnancy. In addition to the high-risk factors noted above, women most at risk are those having their first pregnancy or their fifth or more and those who are relatively poor, not well educated, and lacking proper prenatal care. Among the specific conditions that can cause maternal death are hypertension (high BLOOD PRESSURE), eclampsia, ABORTION, miscarriage, CESAREAN SECTION, ECTOPIC PREGNANCY, and hemorrhaging before or after birth (*antepartum* or *postpartum*). Other conditions that increase maternal mortality are heart problems (see HEART AND HEART PROBLEMS), anemia, THYROID GLAND problems, DIABETES MELLITUS, and CANCER. Most pregnancies, however, proceed normally through LABOR, DELIVERY, and the whole process of CHILDBIRTH.

The Baby's Growth and Development

Your baby starts out as a fertilized egg, no bigger than the period at the end of this sentence. The baby will change and grow almost every single day, and your body will change and grow too. It will take 280 days or 40 weeks before the baby is fully developed and is ready to live outside your uterus (womb). This is about 9⅓ calendar months. Pregnancy is often divided into three periods called trimesters. Each is about three months long.

The First Trimester

During the first trimester, you may find it difficult to believe you are pregnant. You may experience few signs of pregnancy and gain only three to four pounds. Yet, the first three months of pregnancy are critical to your baby's health. During this time the baby will grow to three inches long and will have developed all of the major organs. Untreated illness or disease, radiation, or the use of tobacco, drugs, or alcohol during this time may harm your baby for life. Make sure you eat well, rest, and don't take any medication that has not been prescribed by your doctor. Tell any doctor, nurse, or dentist you visit that you are pregnant. Prenatal care, good nutrition, and adequate rest should be started immediately.

Your First Month. For the first six weeks, the baby is called an embryo. The heart, lungs, and brain are beginning to develop and the tiny heart will beat by the 25th day. The embryo is enclosed in a sac of fluid to protect it from bumps and pressure. The baby will grow in this sac until birth.

Your baby's umbilical cord is also developing. The cord is made up of blood vessels which carry nourishment from your body to feed the baby and carry away the baby's wastes.

During this time you may not notice a weight gain, but your breasts may be larger and may feel tender. You may also have some "morning sickness" or nausea.

Consumption of alcohol and smoking of cigarettes should be stopped as soon as you think you might be pregnant. Take only those drugs prescribed by a physician who knows you are pregnant.

You should schedule your first prenatal exam.

Your Second Month. During this month the embryo becomes a fetus, which means "young one." Arms with tiny hands and fingers and legs with the beginnings of knees, ankles, and toes are starting to form. Organs such as the stomach and liver have also begun to develop. The head now seems very large compared to the rest of the body because the brain is growing so fast. Tiny ears and the beginnings of hair are forming on the head. You still may not have a weight gain but may tire more easily and need to urinate more frequently. Also, you still may be experiencing some nausea.

It is very important to eat the right foods, because you and your baby are changing and growing every day, and you both need proper nourishment.

Your Third Month. Your baby is now about three inches long, weighs about one ounce, and signs of the baby's sex are beginning to appear. Finger and toe nails are developing. The mouth opens and closes, and the baby is now starting to move the hands, legs, and head. At this point, though, you will not feel this movement.

You may have gained about three to four pounds, and your clothes will begin to feel a little tight. You may also feel warmer than usual.

The Second Trimester

The second trimester begins with your fifteenth week of pregnancy. Many of the minor discomforts of the first trimester will disappear, and you will begin to feel especially good. You can feel the baby move, and you will start to look pregnant. Your baby starts to gain weight and is clearly a boy or a girl. Good nutrition will help you and your baby gain at the right rate. Your doctor will now begin listening to your abdomen for your baby's heartbeat with a special instrument called a fetoscope.

Your Fourth Month. Your baby, now weighing about six ounces, is growing very fast and is about eight to 10 inches long by the end of this month. The umbilical cord continues to grow and thicken in order to carry enough blood and nourishment.

During the fourth month you will gain three to four pounds and start to "show." Maternity clothes and a maternity bra may now be more comfortable. You may start to feel a slight sensation of movement in your lower abdomen. This feeling is like "bubbles" or fluttering. When you first feel this movement, called "quickening," write down the date. This date will help the doctor determine when your baby is due.

Your Fifth Month. By the end of the month, your baby will weigh about one pound and be about 12 inches long. The doctor will now be able to hear the baby's heartbeat, and you will begin to feel more definite movements.

This month you may gain three to four pounds and begin to breathe deeper and more frequently. The area around your nipples may look darker and wider as your breasts prepare to make milk.

Your Sixth Month. You are now carrying a fully formed miniature baby except that the skin is wrinkled and red and there is practically no fat under the skin. The baby still needs to grow, being now only about 14 inches long and weighing only about 1½ pounds. The baby cries and sucks on the thumb and you regularly feel the baby's movement.

You may gain three or four more pounds. You may experience some backache, but wearing low-heeled shoes will give you a better sense of balance and comfort.

The Third Trimester

You have now completed 24 weeks of pregnancy. During these last three months, your baby will continue to grow and gain weight. As the baby grows larger, you may experience some discomfort from the pressure on your stomach

Continued on page 381

or bladder. You will feel the baby's stronger and more frequent movements. Now is the time to start preparing yourself and your home for the baby's arrival.

Your Seventh Month. Your baby is now about 15 inches long and weighs about two to 2½ pounds. The baby exercises by kicking and stretching and changing position from side to side. You might even be able to see the movement when one of the tiny heels pokes you.

You may gain another three or four pounds this month and may also notice some slight swelling in your ankles. A slight amount of swelling is normal. You may feel better if you lie down or prop your feet up during the day.

Your Eighth Month. Your baby has grown to about 16 inches long and weighs about four pounds. The eyes are open and the baby changes position in the uterus. This position is maintained until the baby is born. During this month, you may gain three to five pounds. Continue your daily activities, with rest periods, but stop doing any heavy lifting or work that causes strain.

Your Ninth Month. At 36 weeks your baby is about 19 inches long and weighs about six pounds. The baby's weight gain is about ½ pound per week. At 40 weeks, the baby is ''full-term'' and weighs from six to nine pounds. Your baby settles further down into your pelvis, and people will say that your baby has ''dropped.'' You may feel more comfortable, and your breathing will be easier, although you may need to urinate more frequently. You will be visiting your doctor every week until your baby is born.

Source: *Prenatal Care* (1989). Prepared for the Public Health Service by the Health Resources and Services Administration, Bureau of Health Care Delivery and Assistance, Division of Maternal and Child Health.

Changes in the Body During Pregnancy and Lactation

Normal pregnancy is accompanied by anatomical and physiologic changes that are necessary to promote fetal growth and development and prepare the mother for labor, birth, and lactation. Many of these changes are apparent in the early weeks of pregnancy.

Physiological Changes

During both pregnancy and lactation, hormonal changes affect retention, utilization, and excretion of nutrients. These changes lead to physiologic adjustments that result in expansion of blood volume and accumulation of fluid. They include an increase in cardiac output, heart rate, and basal metabolic rate. Preparation of the mammary glands for lactation begins during pregnancy, when the duct system enlarges and the alveolar cells proliferate. Lactation is initiated and maintained by hormonal changes that occur in response to the infant's sucking stimulus. Milk proteins, lipids, and lactose are synthesized by the alveolar cells. Stored fats are secreted into the milk, as are a variety of nutrients and other compounds. Although recent evidence suggests that lactation is associated with physiologic changes that conserve energy and reduce the need for increased energy intake, additional studies are needed to evaluate this matter.

Biochemical

During pregnancy, decreases in plasma concentrations of albumin, most minerals, and most water-soluble vitamins occur as a result of the dilution effect of the expanded plasma volume. Because expansion in red cell mass is not as great as the expansion in plasma volume, the hematocrit, which is the percentage of red blood cells in a sample of centrifuged blood, typically drops during pregnancy. Other nutrients, however, increase in plasma concentration, perhaps as a result of improved intestinal absorption.

Physical

During pregnancy, body weight, lean body tissue, and fat increase. Increases in tissue fluid levels are most significant in the third trimester, but women vary substantially in the timing and degree of fluid accumulation. After childbirth, blood volume and extracellular fluids return to prepregnant levels. The uterus also returns to normal size, but breast size remains enlarged throughout lactation. Loss of the body-fat stores accumulated during pregnancy occurs gradually and is usually complete by the time the nursing infant is about six months old.

Source: *The Surgeon General's Report on Nutrition and Health*. Rocklin, CA: Prima, 1988.

For help and further information

About Pregnancy and Childbirth in General

Pregnancy Helpline, 800-228-0332.

National Center for Education in Maternal and Child Health **(NCEMCH)** and **National Maternal and Child Health Clearinghouse (NMCHC)**
38th and R Streets, NW
Washington, DC 20057
202-625-8400 or 625-8410
Robert C. Baumiller, Director

Federally funded organization supplying education and information to public and professionals on matters relating to maternal and child health, including human genetics. Makes referrals to appropriate hotlines; publishes many materials, including newsletters, directories, bibliographies, resource guides, and brochures.

National Institute of Child Health and Human Development (NICHD)
9000 Rockville Pike
Building 31, Room 2A32
Bethesda, MD 20892
301-496-5133
Federal arm, one of the U.S. National Institutes of Health, sponsoring research on child health and human development. Provides information to public and health professionals; publishes various materials, including technical reports for medical specialists, more general brochures, such as *Diagnostic Ultrasound Imaging in Pregnancy* and *Pregnancy Basics (What You Need to Know and Do to Have a Good Healthy Baby)*, and a series of "Facts About" booklets on topics such as *Cesarean Childbirth* and *Premature Birth*.

Healthy Mother, Healthy Babies National Coalition (HMHB)
409 12th Street
Washington, DC 20024
202-638-5577
Lori Cooper, Executive Director
Network of national and local organizations concerned with maternal and child health. Acts as information clearinghouse; publishes various materials, including quarterly newsletter.

International Childbirth Education Association (ICEA), 612-854-8660. (For full group information, see CHILDBIRTH.)

National Association of Childbirth Education (NACE), 714-686-0422. (For full group information, see CHILDBIRTH.)

Childbirth Education Foundation (CEF), 215-357-2792. (For full group information, see CHILDBIRTH.)

Positive Pregnancy and Parenting Fitness
51 Saltrock Road
Baltic, CT 06330
203-822-8573, toll-free number 800-433-5523
Sylvia Klein Olkin, Executive Director
Organization concerned with training and supporting pregnant women and new mothers. Trains people to teach pregnancy and parenting fitness classes; includes exercises with the baby; provides mail-order catalogs; publishes newsletter.

National Organization of Adolescent Pregnancy and Parenting (NOAPP), 703-435-3948. (For full group information, see ADOLESCENT PREGNANCY.)

DES Action, 415-826-5060. Publishes *Fertility and Pregnancy Guide for DES Daughters and Sons, Preventing Preterm Birth: A Parents' Guide, Every Woman's Guide to Tests During Pregnancy,* and *Natural Remedies for Pregnancy Discomforts.* (For full group information, see DES.)

Other reference sources

General Works

A Wise Birth: Bringing Together the Best of Natural Birth with Modern Medicine, by Penny Armstrong and Sheryl Feldman. New York: Morrow, 1990.

The Complete Book of Pregnancy and Childbirth, revised edition, by Sheila Kitzinger. New York: Schocken, 1989.

Dr. Miriam Stoppard's Pregnancy and Birth Book, by Dr. Miriam Stoppard. New York: Ballantine, 1989.

The Columbia University College of Physicians and Surgeons Complete Guide to Pregnancy, Donald F. Tapley, M.D., and W. Duane Todd, M.D., eds. New York: Crown, 1988.

What Every Pregnant Woman Should Know, by Gail Brewer and Tom Brewer, M.D. New York: Penguin, 1985.

What to Expect When You're Expecting, by Arlene Eisenberg, Heidi E. Murkoff, and Sandee E. Hathaway. New York: Workman, 1984.

A Good Birth, A Safe Birth, by Diana Korte and Roberta Scaer. New York: Bantam, 1984.

Childbirth With Love: A Complete Guide to Fertility, Pregnancy, and Childbirth for Caring Couples, by Niels H. Lauersen. New York: Putnam, 1983.

Pregnancy and Childbirth, third edition, by Tracy Hotchner. New York: Avon, 1990.

On Planning for Pregnancy

Getting Pregnant: How Couples Can Protect Their Reproductive Powers Throughout Their Childbearing Years, by Niels H. Lauersen, M.D., and Colette Bouchez. New York: Rawson, 1990.

Before You Conceive: The Complete Prepregnancy Guide, by John R. Sussman, M.D., and B. Blake Levitt. New York: Bantam, 1989.

Preconceptions: Preparation for Pregnancy, by John T. Queenan, M.D., and Kimberly K. Leslie, M.D. Boston: Little, Brown, 1989.

Pre-Conceptions: What You Can Do Before Pregnancy to Help You Have a Healthy Baby, by Norra Tannenhaus. Chicago: Contemporary, 1988.

How to Get Pregnant, by Sherman J. Silber. New York: Warner, 1988.

The Baby Makers, by Diana Frank and Marta Vogel. New York: Carroll & Graf, 1988.

The Baby Decision: How to Make the Most Important Choice of Your Life, by Merle Bombardieri. New York: Rawson Wade, 1981.

Fetal Development

A Child Is Born, new edition, photographs by Lennart Nilsson, text by Lars Hamberger, M.D. New York: Delacorte, 1990. Color photos of life before birth, from conception.

How Your Baby Grows in Pregnancy, by Glade B. Curtis, M.D. Tucson, AZ: Fisher, 1989.

Fetal Development: A Nine-Month Journey. Producer: Milner-Fenwick Productions. 1988; released 1989. Video or film, available from AIMS Media, 6901 Woodley Ave., Van Nuys, CA 91406.

Being Born, by Sheila Kitzinger. New York: Putnam/Grosset, 1986. For ages 5 to 10. Intrauterine photographs of fetus development.

The Miracle of Life, 1982. 57-minute video from Random House Home Video, 400 Hahn Road, Westminster, MD 21157. For ages 12 to adult. *Nova* film of developments inside male and female reproductive organs, showing conception and fetal development.

On New Reproductive Technology

Science and the Unborn: Choosing Human Futures, by Clifford Grobstein. New York: Basic, 1990.

Science and Babies: Private Decisions, Public Dilemmas. Washington, DC: National Academy Press, 1990.

Reproductive Technologies: Gender, Motherhood, and Medicine, Michelle Stanworth, ed. Minneapolis: University of Minnesota Press, 1988.

On Special Considerations

Making Love During Pregnancy, by Elisabeth Bing and Libby Colman. New York: Farrar, Straus & Giroux, 1989.

Having a Baby After 30, by Elisabeth Bing and Libby Colman. New York: Farrar, Straus & Giroux, 1989.

Pregnancy and Dreams: How to Have a Peaceful Pregnancy by Understanding Your Dreams, Fantasies, Daydreams, and Nightmares, by Patricia Maybruck. Los Angeles: Tarcher, 1989.

Pregnant and Chic, by Lynn Sutherland with Audrey Brooks. New York: Workman, 1989.

Pregnant and Working: What Are Your Rights? (1986). Available from New York Committee on Occupational Safety and Health (NYCOSH), 275 Seventh Avenue, New York, NY 10001.

Enriching Heredity: The Impact of the Environment on the Anatomy of the Brain, by Marian Diamond. New York: Free Press, 1988.

How to Choose the Sex of Your Baby: The Newly Revised Edition of the Method Best Supported by the Scientific Evidence, by Landrum B. Shettles, M.D., and David Rorvick. Garden City, NY: Doubleday, 1988.

Background Works

The Woman in the Body: A Cultural Analysis of Reproduction, by Emily Martin. Boston: Beacon, 1989.

Beyond Conception: The New Politics of Reproduction, by Patricia Spallone. Granby, MA: Bergin & Garvey, 1989.

Cradle and All: Women Writers on Pregnancy and Birth, Laura Chester, ed. Winchester, MA: Faber and Faber, 1989.

Pregnancy, Childbirth and the Newborn, by Penny Simkin. Deephaven, MN: Meadowbrook, 1984.

The Illustrated Dictionary of Pregnancy and Childbirth, by Carl Jones. Deephaven, MN: Meadowbrook, 1989.

The Secret Life of the Unborn Child, by Thomas Verny, M.D., and John Kelly. New York: Delta, 1988.

Obstetrics and Gynecology, by Wrynn Smith. New York: Facts on File, 1986.

(See also HIGH-RISK PREGNANCY; CHILDBIRTH; LABOR; DELIVERY; EXERCISE; PRENATAL CARE; PERINATAL CARE; POSTNATAL CARE; ADOLESCENT PREGNANCY; MISCARRIAGE; STILLBIRTH; DEATH; BIRTH CONTROL; DES; PREGNANCY DISCRIMINATION ACT OF 1978; and other specific topics noted in article.)

Pregnancy Discrimination Act (PDA) of 1978   Federal law specifying that discrimination based on PREGNANCY, CHILDBIRTH, or related medical conditions is unlawful; an addition to the Civil Rights Act of 1964, which extends civil rights protection for disabled people to women working in firms with more than 15 employees. Such firms are barred from refusing to hire, firing, demoting, or penalizing a woman, including denying her promotion, because she is pregnant. In addition, they may not refuse pregnant women health insurance, disability leave, and fringes such as vacation, seniority, and raises if such benefits are available to other disabled employees. Contrary to popular opinion, the law does not provide for any particular kind of benefits or policies for pregnant women (though some state laws do), only that firms not discriminate against them.

Unfortunately, in practice (as in other civil rights arenas), discrimination cases are hard to bring and win in court. As a result, some firms still discriminate with relative impunity, routinely firing or harassing women who announce their pregnancy, immediately or sometimes when they are out on MATERNITY LEAVE. While various organizations (see some below) are fighting for stronger protection for pregnant women in the workplace, working women who become pregnant have some delicate decisions to make about how and when to announce the fact. They would be wise to review the laws operating in their state and, before making any announcements, think through their own personal and family plans, as regards such questions as maternity leave, BREASTFEEDING, and desire to return to work, change to part-time, at-home work, or stay at home.

For help and further information

9 to 5, National Association of Working Women
614 Superior Avenue, NW, Room 852
Cleveland, OH 44113
216-566-5420, 9 to 5 Office Survival Hotline 800-245-9865 (10 AM–4 PM EST, M–F)
Karen Nussbaum, Executive Director

Organization of people concerned with the rights of working women. Operates hotline on legal questions regarding hiring, promotions, and firings, including pregnancy discrimination.

Women's Rights Project, American Civil Liberties Union (ACLU), 212-944-9800. (For full group information, see EDUCATION.)

Women's Legal Defense Fund, 202-887-0364. Publishes *Sex Discrimination in the Workplace: A Legal Handbook.* (For full group information, see MATERNITY LEAVE.)

National Organization for Women (NOW)
1000 16th Street, NW, Suite 700
Washington, DC 20036
202-331-0066
Molly Yard, President
Organization active in support of women's rights in many areas. Seeks to educate public and influence legislation.

pregnancy tests   MEDICAL TESTS designed to tell if a woman is pregnant or not, generally by measuring the level of HUMAN CHORIONIC GONADOTROPIN (hCG), produced by the PLACENTA during PREGNANCY) in the blood or urine. Urine tests are most common (see PREGNANCY HOME MEDICAL TEST, at right), and some can detect a pregnancy within a few days after a missed menstrual period. They can readily be redone, so if the first result is negative but a period still does not arrive, the tests can be performed again. The level of hCG produced by a woman or detected by a test may vary. A period can also be missed for other reasons, so if a test remains negative, a woman should explore other causes with her doctor.

prekindergarten   Organized school-affiliated class for children in the year (or two) before KINDERGARTEN, taught by a professional educator and physically held either in an ELEMENTARY SCHOOL as a separate GRADE or in a NURSERY SCHOOL housed elsewhere.

Preliminary Scholastic Aptitude Test/ National Merit Scholarship Qualifying Test (PSAT/NMSQT)   A test similar to the SCHOLASTIC APTITUDE TEST but offered to high school juniors for test experience and also used as a qualifying test for National Merit SCHOLARSHIPS. (For help and further information, see SCHOLASTIC APTITUDE TEST.)

prelingual   A term referring to people with EAR AND HEARING PROBLEMS who were deaf at birth and so had no experience of sound and spoken language; the term is also used to refer to children who lost their hearing before age three, before they learned how to speak. Such people—95 percent of people who are hearing-impaired—need much more special training to develop fluent communication skills (see COMMUNICATION SKILLS AND DISORDERS).

premature   In PREGNANCY, referring to an infant born well before the DUE DATE, especially before the 37th week of GESTATION, either because labor began prematurely or because a physician induced LABOR, as when the mother's or infant's health was endangered or when the infant was mistakenly thought to

---

Pregnancy Home Medical Test

Function

Detects human chorionic gonadotropin (hCG) hormone in urine. The hCG hormone is produced by a developing placenta.

How It Works

In a small test tube, chemicals are mixed with a urine specimen. A positive result is signaled (this varies from brand to brand) by the presence or absence of a ring formation, seen by the user looking down into the tube, or by a color change in the solution or on a dipstick. Because all pregnant women don't produce the hormone at the same rate, a positive result is more likely if testing is delayed until at least seven to nine days after the missed period should have occurred.

Time for Results

20 minutes to 2 hours.

Comments

If the test results are positive, consult a physician promptly. If the results are negative, you still could be pregnant, so test again in a week. If a second negative result occurs but you're not yet menstruating, consult a physician promptly. When there's a pregnancy outside the uterus—in a fallopian tube, for instance—the hCG hormone level remains low and may not trigger the test's signal. Meanwhile, without medical treatment, you may be at risk of hemorrhaging. False results may be caused by such factors as infection, an ovarian cyst, excess urinary protein, or certain medications. Placing the test on a vibrating surface, such as a refrigerator, or allowing it to incubate or reach its end point in sunlight could also produce a false result.

Source: *Do-It-Yourself Medical Testing,* by Dixie Farley (1989). Prepared by the Food and Drug Administration for the Public Health Service.

---

be POSTMATURE. Various medical conditions can trigger premature labor and DELIVERY, including PREECLAMPSIA, hypertension (high BLOOD PRESSURE), KIDNEY AND UROLOGICAL DISORDERS, DIABETES MELLITUS, heart problems (see HEART AND HEART PROBLEMS), HEMORRHAGE as a result of problems with the PLACENTA, excess AMNIOTIC FLUID, and MULTIPLE BIRTHS. Premature infants are often common among ADOLESCENT PREGNANCIES; women with poor NUTRITION; women who smoke, drink alcohol, or use drugs during pregnancy; and those who have a previous history of childbearing problems. But in many cases, it is unclear why labor started prematurely. Sometimes a doctor may administer a drug to try to halt premature, or *preterm*, labor.

Premature babies—perhaps one in 10 of all babies born in the United States—are small, and their organs are not fully developed, so at birth many of them are not yet capable of fully independent life. Often, for example, they are unable to suck effectively, to maintain body temperature, and to fight off infection. As a result, many premature babies must be placed in an INCUBATOR and carefully monitored for some days or weeks, often until they reach five pounds. (For advice to parents on how to handle this difficult period, see SPECIAL CARE FOR SPECIAL BABIES under HIGH-RISK BABIES.) Premature babies are generally of LOW BIRTH WEIGHT and so are subject to all of the problems associated with LBW. They are at special risk for RESPIRATORY DISTRESS SYNDROME, LIVER PROBLEMS, hemorrhage in the VENTRICLES of the brain (*intraventricular hemorrhage*, or IVH), JAUNDICE, and HYPOGLYCEMIA.

In the past, the INFANT MORTALITY associated with premature infants was extremely high, but advances in medical technology have allowed many more to survive. Even some born weighing under two pounds or with a GESTATION AGE (dating from FERTILIZATION) of under 23 weeks have survived, though that is rare. Of those born at 28 weeks gestation age, approximately four of five survive today, and that ratio is rising.

For help and further information

National Institute of Child Health and Human Development (NICHD), 301-496-5153. Publishes "Facts About" booklets on topics such as *Premature Birth*. (For full group information, see PREGNANCY.)

Parent Care (PC)
1010 1/2 South Union Street
Alexandria, VA 22314
703-836-4678
Nan Streeter, Administrative Liaison
Organization of parents of premature or high-risk babies and the professionals who work with them. Fosters formation of local support groups of parents and professionals; maintains library and seeks to educate the public as to these infants' special problems; publishes a newletter and *Parents of Prematures Resource Directory*.

National Center for Clinical Infant Programs (NCCIP), 202-347-0308. (For full group information, see POSTNATAL CARE.)

La Leche League International (LLLI), 312-455-7730. Publishes *Breastfeeding Your Premature Baby*. (For full group information, see BREASTFEEDING.)

Other reference sources

Parenting Your Premature Baby: A Complete Guide to Birth, Postpartum Care, and Early Childhood, by Janine Jason, M.D., and Antonia van der Meer. New York: Henry Holt, 1989; Delacorte, 1990.
The Premature Baby Book: A Parent's Guide to Coping and Caring in the First Years, by Helen Harrison and Ann Kositsky. New York: St. Martin's, 1978.
Born to Die?: Deciding the Fate of Critically Ill Newborns, by Earl E. Shelp. New York: Free Press, 1986.

(See also PREGNANCY; HIGH-RISK PREGNANCY.)

premenstrual syndrome (PMS)   A disorder associated with MENSTRUATION.

prenatal care (antepartal care)   Medical care of a pregnant woman and the FETUS she is carrying during the whole period of PREGNANCY, the aim being to ensure the health and ease of both. In medical terms, prenatal care is the long early part of the MATERNITY CYCLE. With much heavier stress on prenatal care in recent decades, it has become clear that the earlier a woman begins prenatal care, the better for both herself and her baby in the long run. A woman is advised to see her doctor or clinic as soon as she suspects she might be pregnant. The doctor or clinic staff will perform PREGNANCY TESTS to confirm the pregnancy, will explore the woman's and her family's medical history to be alerted to any likely problems, and will give a variety of tests to identify any medical problems that might threaten the health or continuance of the pregnancy. At this time also, the doctor or clinic staff will advise the mother on what she should and should not do during the pregnancy, in such areas as NUTRITION, EXERCISE, and avoiding SMOKING, alcohol, and drugs (unless the doctor confirms that specific medications are known not to harm a FETUS).

The first prenatal visit will be lengthy and extensive, as described on page 386 in PRENATAL VISITS: WHAT TO EXPECT. The medical and social history and the various tests will allow health-care providers to assess whether the pregnancy should be classed as a HIGH-RISK PREGNANCY or whether it is expected to be normal. This classification will affect a couple's CHILDBIRTH options, since alternatives such as HOME BIRTH, birth at a MATERNITY CENTER, or even delivery in a community HOSPITAL will generally be open only to those with no RISK FACTORS. Women with high-risk pregnancies are advised to plan on delivery in a relatively sophisticated hospital (see HOSPITAL for levels of care). Similarly, a woman with a high-risk pregnancy may be wise to be under the care of a MATERNAL AND FETAL SPECIALIST, while other women may choose to have prenatal care and delivery in the hands of an OBSTETRICIAN/GYNECOLOGIST, FAMILY PRACTICE PHYSICIAN, or CERTIFIED NURSE-MIDWIFE.

Later prenatal visits will be briefer, generally monthly for the first six months, then every two weeks through the eighth month, and then weekly, though visits may be spaced more closely if problems exist. During these later visits, once the results of earlier tests are known, other tests may be performed, among them GENETIC SCREENING TESTS, such as AMNIOCENTESIS, ALPHA FETOPROTEIN (AEP), CHORIONIC VILLUS SAMPLING, FETOSCOPY, and ULTRASOUND scanning, as well as follow-up tests to see that the woman is not developing any health problems as a result of the pregnancy, such as DIABETES MELLITUS or PREECLAMPSIA. In high-risk pregnancies, hospitalization may be required for diagnosis or treatment at some period during the pregnancy.

For help and information

Pregnancy Helpline, 800-228-0332.

National Center for Education in Child and Maternal Health (NCEMCH), 202-625-8400; **National Maternal and Child**

Prenatal Visits: What to Expect

Your First Visit

Your first visit will probably take more time than later appointments. In addition to a physical examination, you will need to give information about yourself and your pregnancy.

First there will be questions about:

- your previous pregnancies, miscarriages, or abortions.
- your periods—when they started and what they are like.
- your medical history—illnesses you have had, illnesses the father has had, illnesses in members of either family.
- your diet and life-style.

Then there will be a physical examination. This will include:

- the measurement of your height, weight, and blood pressure.
- an examination of your eyes, ears, nose, throat, and teeth.
- an examination of your heart, lungs, breasts, and abdomen.
- an internal examination (pelvic examination) of the growth of your uterus and the amount of room in your pelvis for the baby.

In addition, several laboratory tests will be performed:

- A Pap smear to detect any signs of cervical cancer.
- A pregnancy test (even if you have done a test with a home urine kit)
- A culture of the cervix to check for gonorrhea
- Blood tests
    to see if you are anemic
    to learn your blood type and Rh factor
    to check for syphilis
    to check whether you have had rubella (German measles)

- Urine tests
    for diabetes
    for kidney function and toxemia
    to check for the possibility of infection

It is very important that you ask the doctor or nurse any questions you have about your pregnancy, your general health, or your examination and tests. If you don't ask, they may assume you understand. Remember, there is no such thing as a foolish question.

Tell your doctor if you have any physical problems, if you are under stress, or if you have any other special concerns. It is important for your doctor to understand how your pregnancy is affecting you and your family. In some instances the doctor or nurse may refer you to someone else for help with certain problems.

Later Visits

Usually you will return about once a month during the first six months of pregnancy. During the seventh and eighth months, you will make visits every two weeks and after that, every week until delivery. During these visits, your weight, blood pressure, and urine will be checked. Your abdomen may be measured to see how the baby is growing. These examinations help ensure that your pregnancy is progressing normally. Internal (pelvic) examinations and blood tests are not performed on every routine visit. If you have questions or concerns between visits, write them down and bring them to your next appointment.

Remember, it's important for your doctor to know about any medical problems you or your family may have had, particularly such chronic conditions as diabetes, kidney disorders, thyroid problems, heart conditions, and respiratory illnesses. Once the doctor knows about them, the necessary steps can be taken to reduce any risk to you or to the baby.

Source: *Prenatal Care* (1989). Prepared for the Public Health Service by the Health Resources and Services Administration, Bureau of Health Care Delivery and Assistance, Division of Maternal and Child Health.

Health Clearinghouse (NMCHC), 202-625-8410. (For full group information, see PREGNANCY.)

National Institute of Child Health and Human Development (NICHD), 301-496-5133. (For full group information, see PREGNANCY.)

March of Dimes Birth Defects Foundation (MDBDF), 914-428-7100; local chapters in telephone directory white pages. Some local chapters have certified midwives available for normal pregnancies and prenatal services for women with high-risk pregnancies. Publishes numerous useful materials. (For full group information, including many publications, see BIRTH DEFECTS.)

Other reference sources

Prenatal Care: Reaching Mothers, Reaching Infants, Sarah S. Brown, ed. Washington, DC: National Academy Press, 1988. Prepared by the National Institute of Medicine.

(See also PREGNANCY; CHILDBIRTH; and specific topics noted in article.)

prenatal test A type of MEDICAL TEST performed on a woman during PREGNANCY but before CHILDBIRTH, generally focusing on the health and condition of the FETUS. Many such tests are given to identify GENETIC DISORDERS before birth, often at a stage when ABORTION or FETAL SURGERY IN UTERO can be performed if appropriate. Among the common prenatal tests are AMNIOCENTESIS, ALPHA FETOPROTEIN (AFP), and CHORIONIC VILLUS SAMPLING (CVS) FETOSCOPY, and ULTRASOUND SCAN.

For help and further information

Prenatal Tests: What They Are, Their Benefits and Risks, and How to Decide Whether to Have Them or Not, by Robin J.R. Blatt. New York: Vintage, 1988.

The Tentative Pregnancy: Prenatal Diagnosis and the Future of Motherhood, by Barbara K. Rothman. New York: Penguin, 1986.

Background Books

Catalog of Prenatally Diagnosed Conditions, by David D. Weaver. Baltimore: Johns Hopkins, 1989.

Prenatal Screening, Policies and Values: The Example of Neural Tube Defects, Elena O. Nightingale and Susan B. Meister, eds. Cambridge, MA: Harvard University Press, 1987.

Prenatal Diagnosis. New York: Wiley, 1987.

(See also MEDICAL TESTS; GENETIC DISORDERS; GENETIC SCREENING; GENETIC COUNSELING.)

preoperational   The second stage of children's learning, according to Piaget's theory of COGNITIVE DEVELOPMENT.

preparatory (prep) school   A type of PRIVATE SCHOOL, generally a boarding school, geared to providing intensive secondary education aimed at putting the students on a "fast track" to prestigious COLLEGES and universities, such as the IVY LEAGUE schools.

prepared childbirth   An approach to CHILDBIRTH that emphasizes educational programs for pregnant women and their BIRTH PARTNERS, focusing on relaxation techniques for dealing with LABOR pains, with the aim of minimizing medical intervention in the childbirth process; in general, a synonym for *natural childbirth*, also called *psychoprophylaxis* or *psychophysical preparation for childbirth*. (For help and further information, see CHILDBIRTH; PREGNANCY.)

preprimary   Alternate term for KINDERGARTEN.

prerequisites   Learning that must be accomplished successfully before more advanced learning can be started. More specifically, a prerequisite is often a course that a student is required to take before taking another (algebra before calculus, for example). A prerequisite is also a skill that is felt necessary before a high-level skill can be learned, in this sense also called a PRECURSOR SKILL or learning READINESS skill. For example, a young child must learn to distinguish between an apple and a pear before beginning to learn their names, so telling the two fruits apart is a prerequisite or precursor skill. WORD-ATTACK SKILLS are regarded as prerequisites for effective, independent READING, and reading is itself a prerequisite for most other academic learning.

preschool   General term for a range of programs for pre-KINDERGARTEN children, generally from ages two or three to five; sometimes used synonymously with EARLY CHILDHOOD EDUCATION. Although the term does not cover informal PLAY GROUPS, *preschool* refers to any group or class organized for educational experience for children before they enter ELEMENTARY SCHOOL (either in kindergarten or first grade). That includes NURSERY SCHOOLS, schools following the MONTESSORI METHOD, HEAD START programs, and similar schools that are not established as part of a graded system in a school.

Preschool programs vary widely in their approach and in their relative emphasis on play and education. But it is widely accepted that preschool programs give students a literal head start on learning, helping them develop the PREREQUISITE skills basic to more advanced skills—in essence, developing learning READINESS. Children need not attend preschool programs to do well in school, of course, but if they do not, they do need to have available to them in the home the kind of stimulation and range of experiences that a preschool provides.

The preschool years are extremely important in the child's overall development. The CHART OF NORMAL DEVELOPMENT, on page 507, indicates when between birth and age six children first, *on the average,* begin to develop the key skills: MOTOR SKILLS (gross and fine), communication skills (see COMMUNICATION SKILLS AND DISORDERS), cognitive skills (see COGNITIVE DEVELOPMENT), self-help skills, and SOCIAL SKILLS. If the home is stimulating and active, with people, other children, and new experiences, and if the child gets sufficient attention and teaching, the child may develop these skills in the normal course of everyday life. But many parents feel that approach to be too haphazard and prefer to place their child in some kind of preschool program that is especially designed to help the child develop these skills.

Preschool programs have special value for children who may have handicaps (see HANDICAPPED). There the children are under the eyes of trained observers, who may recognize early warning signs of problems that the parents are not tuned to recognize—or that they have seen but do not want to acknowledge. Observational checklists for spotting signs of learning problems or handicaps in preschool-age children are given in this book under these headings: LEARNING DISABILITIES, EAR AND HEARING PROBLEMS, EYE AND VISION PROBLEMS, COMMUNICATION SKILLS AND DISORDERS, and MENTAL RETARDATION. Parents may want to use these checklists if they wonder whether their child has a problem that might interfere with learning; if they have any serious question about it, they should have the child professionally evaluated at once.

The earlier children's learning problems are diagnosed, the sooner special services can be provided, under the EDUCATION FOR ALL HANDICAPPED CHILDREN ACT OF 1975, and the less trouble the children are likely to have later on when they actually start school. Studies have generally shown that when high-risk or AT-RISK children have preschool programs, including diagnosis and treatment of any special problems, they are more likely to graduate from HIGH SCHOOL, less likely to have to REPEAT A GRADE, less likely to need special services later on in school, more likely to be able to get and hold a job after high school, and less likely to become DELINQUENTS. Families benefit from such early intervention, too, generally feeling less stress and isolation because services are being provided.

Most children do not have learning problems of any significance. But children develop at individual and varying paces, and all children can benefit from activities designed to enhance their natural development. In TEACHING YOUNG CHILDREN: GUIDELINES AND ACTIVITIES, on page 544, parents will find activities designed to develop various kinds of skills for children ages three to five, as well as general guidelines for teaching that apply to children of any age. These may be useful at home, shared with CHILD-CARE workers, or used in preschool situations, especially if the program is parent-run or parent-assisted.

Because preschool programs vary widely in approach, parents will want to visit those available locally to see the schools in action and assess which program seems most appropriate for their child. Since preschools are generally local and privately run, the question of evaluation is even more important than with many other schools. The National Association for the Education of Young Children (NAEYC) suggests that parents ask the following questions in evaluating preschools:

- Are the children in the program generally comfortable, relaxed, and happy and involved in play and other activities?
- Are there sufficient numbers of adults with specialized training in early childhood development and education?
- Do adult expectations vary appropriately for children of differing ages and interests?
- Are all areas of a child's development stressed equally, with time and attention being devoted to cognitive, social and emotional, and physical development?
- Does the staff meet regularly to plan and evaluate the program?
- Are parents welcome to observe, discuss policies, make suggestions, and participate in the work of the program?
- Is the staff alert to the health and safety of young children and of themselves?

Questions like these are part of NAEYC's ACCREDITATION criteria for early-childhood programs; if possible, parents should seek a preschool program that has been accredited as meeting basic professional standards. The U.S. Department of Education's *Choosing a School for Your Child* (excerpted on page 514), while intended for evaluating ELEMENTARY and SECONDARY SCHOOLS, may also be usefully applied to preschools.

In some highly selective preschools, the shoe is somewhat on the other foot, with children being given various kinds of DEVELOPMENTAL SCREENING TESTS as ADMISSIONS TESTS for preschool, even when the tests were not originally developed for that purpose. Parents should be wary of pushing their children into too-competitive situations and of the possible negative effects of LABELING if a student does poorly on a particular test. They should be sure that they and the school are aware that children vary widely in their rates of development.

For help and further information

National Association for the Education of Young Children (NAEYC)
1834 Connecticut Avenue, NW
Washington, DC 20009
202-232-8777, toll-free number 800-424-2460
Organization of teachers and directors of preschool groups, kindergartens, child care centers, cooperatives, play groups, religious schools, and other programs for young children, as well as early childhood educators, parents, and others concerned with high-quality education for young children (to age eight). Has network of 390 affiliate groups; provides accreditation for early childhood programs through National Academy of Early Childhood Programs; encourages professional development among early childhood educators; seeks to educate public and influence public policy; provides information and referrals; operates toll-free number; publishes various print and video materials, including bimonthly magazine *Young Children*, quarterly *Early Childhood Research*, resource guides on topics such as child care and computers for young children, policy reports on topics such as child care and early childhood teacher certification, books such as *Young Children and Picture Books: Literature From Infancy to Six, Play in the Lives of Children, Speaking Out: Early Childhood Advocacy,* and *Opening Your Door to Children: How to Start a Family Day Care Program*, video training tapes on such topics as discipline and appropriate curriculum for young children, and brochures on child care and early education (some also in Spanish), such as *Beginner's Bibliography—1989, Finding the Best Care for Your Infant and Toddler, Helping Children Learn Self-Control, How to Choose a Good Early Childhood Program, Love and Learn: Discipline for Young Children, Off to a Sound Start: Your Baby's First Year, Play Is FUNdamental, Teaching Young Children to Resist Bias: What Parents Can Do,* and *So Many Goodbyes: Ways to Ease the Transition Between Home and Groups for Young Children.*

Association for Childhood Education International (ACEI)
1141 Georgia Avenue, Suite 200
Wheaton, MD 20902
301-942-2443
A. Gilson Brown, Executive Director
Organization of teachers, parents, and others seeking to promote sound education for children from birth through adolescence. Seeks to advance children's rights and well-being and to see that programs are designed with them in mind; encourages continuing professional growth for educators; works closely with schools, government agencies, and designers and manufacturers of materials for children; publishes various materials, including monthly *ACEI Exchange* and *Bibliography of Books for Children.*

Parent Cooperative Pre-Schools International (PCPI)
P.O. Box 90410
Indianapolis, IN 46290

317-849-0992
Kathy Mensel, Executive Secretary
Organization of parents and other individuals and groups concerned with parent-run cooperative nursery schools for preschool children. Provides information and counsel to cooperatives; acts as information clearinghouse; sets standards for cooperative programs; publishes various materials, including *Cooperatively Speaking*, annual *PCPI Directory, Health and Safety in the Pre-school*, and *How to Start a Co-op*.

Society for Research in Child Development (SRCD)
University of Chicago Press
5801 Ellis Avenue
Chicago, IL 60637
312-962-7470
Dorothy H. Eichorn, Executive Officer
Interdisciplinary organization of scholars and clinical professionals interested in child development, including educators, pediatricians, psychologists, psychiatrists, dentists, nutritionists, anthropologists, and sociologists. Encourages research; publishes various materials, including bimonthly *Child Development*.

World Organization for Early Childhood Education
U.S. National Committee
P.O. Box 931
Fresno, CA 93714
209-224-0924
Joyce Higgins, President
Professional organization of educators, psychologists, social workers, and others working in early childhood education and development. Seeks to foster preschool education; supports research; consults with UNESCO; publishes various materials, including semiannual *International Journal of Early Childhood*.

National Head Start Association (NHSA), 703-739-0875. (For full group information, see HEAD START.)

American Montessori Society (AMS), 212-924-3209. (For full group information, see MONTESSORI METHOD.)

Institute for Childhood Resources (NICR), 415-864-1169. (For full group information, see PLAY GROUP.)

Play Schools Association (PSA)
19 West 44th Street, Suite 615
New York, NY 10036
212-921-2940
Joseph Corrado, Executive Director
Service organization that consults with and trains teachers and parents in organizing play activities. Helps develop curriculum and evaluate materials and teaching approaches; shapes special programs for children who have emotional or physical handicaps, brain injuries, or long-term illness; publishes printed materials and training films.

U.S.A. Toy Library Association (USATLA)
104 Wilmot Avenue, Suite 201

Deerfield, IL 60015
312-940-8800
Judith Q. Iacuzzi, Executive Director
Organization for parents, professionals, and others interested in the use of toys with young children. Urges the development of toy libraries, as in schools, libraries, hospitals, and play schools, and promotes understanding of their use in child development and in therapy for troubled or disabled children.

Other reference sources

Books For Parents

The Preschool Handbook: Making the Most of Your Child's Education, by Barbara Brenner. New York: Pantheon, 1990.
Prepping Your Preschooler: A Sourcebook for Helping Your Child Succeed in School, by Patsy Lord and Margaret Sebern. New York: McGraw-Hill, 1990.
Kindergarten Ain't What It Used to Be: Getting Your Child Ready for the Positive Experience of Education, by Susan Golant and Mitch Golant. Chicago: Lowell House/Contemporary, 1990.
Teach Your Baby Math, revised and updated, by Glenn Doman. New York: M. Evans, 1990.
Help Me Learn: A Handbook for Teaching Children from Birth to Third Grade, by Mary Forman Rice and Charles H. Flatter. Englewood Cliffs, NJ: Prentice Hall, 1989.
The Preschool Letters and Notes to Parents Book, Kathy Charner, ed. Mt. Rainer, MD: Gryphon House, 1989.
The Elementary School Handbook: Making the Most of Your Child's Education, by Joanne Oppenheim. New York: Pantheon, 1989.
Modern Montessori at Home: A Creative Teaching Guide for Parents of Children Six through Nine Years of Age, by Heidi A. Speitz. Rossmoor, CA: American Montessori Consulting, 1989.
Literacy Begins at Birth, by Marjorie V. Fields. Tucson, AZ: Fisher, 1989.
Don't Push Your Preschooler, revised edition, by Louise Bates Ames and Joan A. Chase. New York: Harper & Row, 1981.

Background Books

Early Schooling: The National Debate, Sharon L. Kagan and Edward F. Zigler, eds. New Haven, CT: Yale University Press, 1988.
Pre-School Play, by Edwina Conner. New York: Pantheon, 1988.
Developmentally Appropriate Practice in Early Childhood Programs Servicing Children form Birth Through Age 8, expanded edition, S. Bredekamp, ed. Washington, DC: National Association for the Education of Young Children, 1987.
First Lessons: A Report on Elementary Education in America, by the U.S. Department of Education. Washington, DC: Government Printing Office, 1986.
Effectiveness of Early Education, by Brian McNulty, David Smith, and Elizabeth Soper. Denver: Colorado Department of Education, 1983.

Changed Lives: The Effects of the Perry Preschool Program on Youths Through Age 19, by H.R. Berrcuta-Clement et al. Ypsilanti, MI: High Scope, 1984.

The Gesell Institute's Child from One to Six: Evaluating the Behavior of the Pre-School Child, by Louise Bates Ames et al. New York: Harper & Row, 1979.

Early Childhood Education, by Marjorie L. Hipple. Pacific Palisades, CA: Goodyear, 1975.

(See EDUCATION; TESTS.)

presentation   Short for FETAL PRESENTATION, referring to the way a FETUS is oriented in the UTERUS near the time of CHILDBIRTH.

preservatives   A type of FOOD ADDITIVE.

preterm   Alternate term for PREMATURE.

prickly heat   Alternate name for HEAT RASH.

primary amenorrhea   A disorder associated with MENSTRUATION.

primary-care-level hospital (Level I)   A medical facility such as a community HOSPITAL primarily directed toward handling routine medical emergencies.

primary health care provider   A health professional who is a patient's first "port of call" in dealing with disease or disorder and who refers the patient to the appropriate medical specialist as necessary. Primary health care providers may be PHYSICIANS, specially trained NURSE PRACTITIONERS, or CLINICS. They often also provide advice on general health and disease prevention.

primary micro-orchidism   Alternate term for KLINEFELTER'S SYNDROME.

primary school   Alternate term for ELEMENTARY SCHOOL; the term *primary* is also used to refer to the lower elementary grades, 1 to 3, sometimes including KINDERGARTEN.

primary teeth (baby, milk, or **deciduous teeth)**   The set of 20 TEETH that push through the gums in an infant's mouth in the first 25 to 33 months of life.

primary tumor   A kind of TUMOR that originated at the site where found, as opposed to a *secondary tumor* started by malignant cells originating elsewhere in the body.

primigravida   The medical designation for a woman who is pregnant for the first time.

primipara   The medical designation for a woman who has given birth to one live infant, often noted on the hospital medical chart as "para one."

primitive reflexes   A group of REFLEXES—involuntary, automatic movements in reaction to particular stimuli or events—that are normally found only in newborns and that disappear in the first few months. Among them are the GRASP REFLEX, TONIC NECK REFLEX, MORO'S REFLEX (STARTLE REFLEX), WALKING (or stepping) REFLEX, and ROOTING REFLEX. In at least some children with CEREBRAL PALSY, such SENSORIMOTOR reactions are retained and can interfere with the ability to learn voluntary control of movement.

primogeniture   A system of laws under which the family property is passed intact to the first-born son, with none going to other children, male or female. Once common in Europe and elsewhere, such laws do not apply in the modern United States.

printing (manuscript writing)   The first form of writing that children learn in ELEMENTARY SCHOOL, in which each letter is formed separately and looks approximately like its counterpart in printed books, as opposed to CURSIVE WRITING, in which letters are joined together.

private school   A school that is under the control of a person, board, or agency not responsible to the public and that is not primarily supported by federal funds; sometimes a SCHOOL OF CHOICE; an alternative to a PUBLIC SCHOOL. Parents send their children to private schools for a wide variety of reasons. Many want their children to be taught in a religious context, as in a Catholic *parochial school*, a Protestant Christian-oriented school, or a school for Jews, Moslems, Buddhists, or other groups. Some wish to have the child taught in a more tightly disciplined, structured setting, while others, conversely, want the child to be freer to develop with individualized or independent learning, as might be provided in an ALTERNATIVE SCHOOL. Some parents are simply dissatisfied with the quality of the education offered in their local schools and so opt for private schools; others are unhappy with BUSING and DESEGREGATION plans. Some parents choose a private school primarily for the prestige or intensive academic programs, as in PREPARATORY SCHOOLS, and some are attempting to meet special needs of students, such as those with severe LEARNING DISABILITIES.

In recent years, since passage of the EDUCATION FOR ALL HANDICAPPED CHILDREN ACT OF 1975, many parents have had some legal support in pushing public schools to provide the kind of instruction needed for their children, especially those with handicaps. But they should be aware that private schools are not a cure-all for public school deficiencies. Some private schools are poorly funded, equipped, and staffed, and lack any kind of ACCREDITATION. Parents must carefully evaluate any private school before entering their children. The U.S. Department of Education's *Choosing a School for Your Child*, excerpted on page 514, includes a checklist for evaluating schools.

Clearly, private schools continue to meet felt needs in the community. In 1985 approximately one out of every eight school-age children was being educated in a private school.

For help and further information

Council for American Private Education (CAPE)
1625 I Street NW
Washington, DC 20006
202-659-0016

Organizations concerned with private-school education, K to 12. Seek to educate the public and influence government policy; encourage good relationships with public schools and government; publish monthly newsletter and *Directory of Private Schools of the United States*.

National Association of Independent Schools (NAIS)
18 Tremont Street
Boston, MA 02108
617-723-6900
John C. Esty, Jr., President
Organization of independent elementary and secondary schools and associated organizations. Provides help on curriculum and administrative questions; offers education; publishes various materials, including *Independent School*.

Committee on Boarding Schools (CBS)
18 Tremont Street
Boston, MA 02108
617-723-3629
Richard H. Cowan, Director
Organization of boarding and day schools, affiliated with National Association of Independent Schools (NAIS). Publishes annual *Boarding Schools Directory* and *Directory of Schools With Special Programs*.

National Association of Private, Nontraditional Schools and Colleges (NAPNSC)
182 Thompson Road
Grand Junction, CO 81503
303-243-5441
H. Earl Heusser, Executive Director
Organization of institutions that provide education through alternative methods, including highly flexible learning approaches, often using sophisticated and elaborate development of educational objectives and assessment, sometimes with little or no classroom instruction. Develops standards for, evaluates, and accredits nontraditional educational institutions; aids formation of new alternative or experimental schools; conducts research and maintains library; publishes various materials, including annual *Accreditation Fact Sheet and Newsletter* and *Handbook for Accreditation: Guidelines for Accreditation by Contract*.

National Coalition of Alternate Community Schools (NCACS), 615-964-3670. (For full group information, see ALTERNATIVE SCHOOLS.)

Other reference sources
Privatization and Educational Choice, by Myron Lieberman. New York: St. Martin's, 1989.
Keeping Them Out of the Hands of Satan: Evangelical Schooling in America, by Susan D. Rose. New York: Routledge, 1990.
The Boarding School Guide, by Kiliaen V. R. Townsend. Athens, GA: Agee, 1989. P.O. Box 526, Athens, GA 30603.
The School Search Guide to Private Schools for Students with Learning Disabilities, by Midge Lipkin. Belmont, MA: Schoolsearch, 1989. 127 Marsh Street, Belmont, MA 02178.
Dare to Choose: Parental Choice at Independent Neighborhood Schools, by Joan Davis Ratteray and Mwalima Shujaa. Wash-

ington, DC: Institute for Independent Education, 1987. 1313 North Capitol Street, NW, Washington, DC 20002.
Preparing for Power: America's Elite Boarding Schools, by Peter W. Cookson, Jr. and Caroline H. Persell. New York: Basic, 1985.
Religious Schooling in America, James C. Carper and Thomas C. Hunt, eds. Birmingham, AL: Religious Education, 1984.
Handbook of Private Schools. Boston: Porter Sargent, annual.
The College Board Guide to High Schools. New York: College Board, 1990. Directory of over 25,000 public and private high schools.
Peterson's Independent Secondary Schools 1989–1990. Princeton, NJ: Peterson's, 1989.
(See also ALTERNATIVE SCHOOLS; EDUCATION.)

privileged communication Conversations that are legally regarded as confidential and cannot be disclosed in court if the persons involved object. In general, a person's conversations with a lawyer or a priest are seen as privileged communications. Doctors and psychologists generally consider conversations with their patients as private under their professional code of CONFIDENTIALITY, but whether or not they are legally considered privileged communications depends on the law. If the state law allows it, these and other professionals, such as social workers, may be required to testify in court in certain circumstances, as in cases involving CHILD ABUSE OR NEGLECT.

proband The person about whom medical and genetic information is being gathered for the construction of a family PEDIGREE during GENETIC COUNSELING; also called *propositus* (female: *proposita*) or *index case*.

probate court The type of court that handles questions regarding the estates of people who have died, either affirming the validity of an existing will or handling distribution of assets if the person died intestate (without a will), under the state's laws of INHERITANCE RIGHTS. Probate court may also handle some questions relating to ADOPTION and GUARDIANS. In some states, the role of the probate court has been partly taken over by the FAMILY COURT.

probation In the law, suspending a sentence imposed by a court, on certain conditions, often including good behavior, some kind of treatment, and supervision by a court-appointed professional probate officer. JUVENILES convicted of a crime, especially a first offense, are often made WARDS of the court and put on probation; so are parents convicted of CHILD ABUSE AND NEGLECT. Violation of set conditions may cause the probation to be withdrawn and the sentence to take effect; in the case of abusive parents, that may mean TERMINATION OF PARENTS' RIGHTS.

probationary promotion Passing a student to a higher grade even when academic performance has not been fully satisfactory, on the understanding that the PROMOTION will become permanent only if the student shows ability to handle the more advanced work.

problem child A child who exhibits disruptive behavior, often one who has some kind of MENTAL DISORDER or undiagnosed or untreated handicaps that interfere with learning and so lead to frustration and emotional disturbance (see HANDICAPPED).

prochein ami Original French phrase for NEXT FRIEND.

proctologist Medical PHYSICIAN who specializes in treating disorders of the anus and rectum, the final parts of the digestive system (see DIGESTIVE DISORDERS).

proctoscope A type of ENDOSCOPE used by doctors in visually examining the anus and rectum, the last parts of the digestive system. (For help and further information, see DIGESTIVE DISORDERS.)

prodigy An unusually talented individual, a term generally used in referring to a CHILD PRODIGY (see GIFTED CHILD).

Proficiency Examination Program (PEP) A program run by the American College Testing Program (ACT) in which students are able to earn college CREDIT if they take and pass a set examination, having studied on their own, in a special course, or through INDEPENDENT STUDY.

progesterone A key female HORMONE produced in the OVARIES that works with the hormone ESTROGEN to regulate the MENSTRUAL CYCLE and is important to the development of the PLACENTA and the FETUS during PREGNANCY. A drop in the level of progesterone in the body helps bring on LABOR.

prognathism A type of MALOCCLUSION in which the lower jaw and front teeth jut out in front of the upper ones.

projective test A TEST designed so that the responses given will stem from the person's underlying mental condition, personality, and mood, rather than from the test material itself. The best-known example is the RORSCHACH PSYCHODIAGNOSTIC TEST, in which the person is asked to interpret a series of inkblots. Other projective tests commonly used with children include the HOUSE-TREE-PERSON PROJECTIVE TECHNIQUE, DRAW-A-PERSON TEST, BLACKY PICTURES, THEMATIC APPERCEPTION TEST, and CHILDREN'S APPERCEPTION TEST.

prolapse A condition in which an organ has fallen out of its normal position, as sometimes happens to the UTERUS after CHILDBIRTH, to a long UMBILICAL CORD during LABOR, or in children with INTUSSUSCEPTION (telescoping of the bowel).

promotion In EDUCATION, the advancement of a student from one GRADE to another or, in an UNGRADED CLASS, from one instructional level to another. Promotion implies that the student has developed the skills, learned the material, and met the academic standards of the grade and is therefore academically ready to move on to the next grade; as a corollary, any student who has not fulfilled those requirements will be retained in the class until he or she does so. But no one—parents, students, or school officials—is happy about RETENTION, so in practice, many students have been given *automatic promotion*, being passed on from grade to grade, regardless of performance. This is sometimes called *social promotion*, as based on social, rather than educational, reasons. As a result, some students have been graduated from HIGH SCHOOL even

though they remained functionally illiterate (see ILLITERACY), creating significant social problems because such students lack the basic skills needed to operate within society. Public recognition of that fact, not least from the highly publicized cases of sports figures who have later returned to ELEMENTARY SCHOOL to learn to read or adults who have sued the school system for failing to teach them to read, has led schools to focus more on the development of basic skills as a basis for promotion. Sometimes a student may be given *probationary promotion*; if he or she is able to satisfactorily handle the work in the higher grade, the promotion will be considered permanent. Since students have variable levels of skills, some may REPEAT course material in one subject area while being promoted to the next level in other areas. More to the point should be an examination of why and how the student failed and especially whether the student has any undiagnosed handicaps (see HANDICAPPED), such as LEARNING DISABILITIES or EAR AND HEARING PROBLEMS, that prevented learning. (For help and further information, see EDUCATION.)

pro per Alternate form for PRO SE.

prophylactic Alternate name for a CONDOM.

propositus Alternate term for PROBAND in constructing a family PEDIGREE during GENETIC COUNSELING; the female form is *proposita*.

proprietary school A nonpublic or PRIVATE SCHOOL providing education primarily as a business for profit. The term most often refers to POSTSECONDARY SCHOOLS teaching noncollege subjects, such as cosmetology or secretarial skills, or providing coaching for college-related examinations, such as the SCHOLASTIC APTITUDE TEST.

pro se A legal term for a person acting in court without representation by a lawyer; literally, Latin for "for himself," sometimes called *pro per*. Some people feel that family issues are best not dealt with by lawyers, who are by definition advocates, accustomed to adversarial stances, and so may exaggerate divisions within a family, rather than conciliators, who might more readily attempt to resolve them reasonably. However, if one party in a family dispute has retained a lawyer, other members may be in a weakened position if they adopt a *pro se* approach.

For help and further information

Help Abolish Legal Tyranny, 202-347-9600. Publishes various citizen's legal manuals, including one on pro se divorce. (For full group information, see CHILD SUPPORT; CUSTODY.)

prostate gland An oval organ in males that secretes fluid that mixes with SPERM to form SEMEN. The prostate gland sits just under the bladder, and the URETHRA passes through it. Tiny at birth, the prostate begins to grow at PUBERTY, triggered by male sex HORMONES, reaching adult size by the end of the teens. In older men the prostate becomes further enlarged, which can cause painful urination, and sometimes becomes cancerous. In younger men, the main prostate problem is bacterial infection, often from SEXUALLY TRANSMITTED DISEASES.

Protein Needs

For Women During Pregnancy and Lactation

The RDA for protein during pregnancy includes an additional 30 grams per day beyond the 44 grams recommended for nonpregnant women. Protein is abundant in the American diet, and inadequate intake during pregnancy is reported infrequently. However, studies that have associated diets containing 20 percent of total calories from protein (as compared with the 13 to 14 percent usually recommended) with a higher risk of premature deliveries and neonatal mortality suggest that protein intakes significantly higher than those recommended may be harmful.

For the Fetus During Pregnancy

A fetus near term requires about 6 to 8 grams of protein per day. Most of this comes as small amounts of essential and nonessential amino acids received continuously from the placental circulation. The free amino-acid concentrations in the umbilical artery and vein are higher than those in the mother's blood, indicating that amino-acid transport across the placenta is an active metabolic process. Presumably, active transport of amino acids protects the fetus against inadequate maternal protein intake. Another source of protein occurs in amniotic fluid the fetus swallows. This could amount to as much as 750 milligrams per day.

Animal studies indicate that glucose and amino acids can be taken up from amniotic fluid more rapidly than can be accounted for by swallowing alone. Administration of nutrients directly into the fetal stomach can normalize the birth weight and length of fetuses born to nutritionally deprived dams [mothers].

For Infants

Protein requirements are proportionately greater in infants than in adults. Dietary protein must be sufficient to support increases in body protein that range on average from 3.7 grams per day for the first month in males and 3.3 in females down to 1.8 and 1.7 grams per day, respectively, for months 9 to 12. These needs generally can be met by protein intakes of about 1.8 grams (100 kilocalories) for infants during the first month of life, decreasing to 1.2 grams (100 kilocalories) for infants four to six months of age. The Infant Formula Act of 1980 established a minimum standard for the protein content of infant formulas, 1.8 grams (100 kilocalories), which is based on a protein equivalent in nutritive quality to casein. The RDA of 2.2 grams per kilogram for the first six months and 2.0 grams per kilogram for months 7 to 12 also considers protein quality.

Source: *The Surgeon General's Report on Nutrition and Health.* Rocklin, CA: Prima, 1988.

---

prostheses The medical name for artificial limbs, a common type of ORTHOPEDIC DEVICE.

proteins Complex chemical compounds, made up of AMINO ACIDS, that are vital to the body's functioning, not only forming the structure of many parts of the body but also promoting many of the most basic biochemical reactions in the body. Common sources of protein are meat, poultry, fish, eggs, MILK, and cheese, called *complete proteins* because they contain all of the essential amino acids. Other sources of proteins that contain some, but not all, essential amino acids are nuts, beans, and peas.

In the digestive system, proteins are broken down into usable components, which are then re-formed to make up basic body tissues, HORMONES, and vital parts of the blood; the basic building blocks of life, DNA, are codes for proteins. Protein deficiency in children leads to MARASMUS, or FAILURE TO THRIVE, and more seriously (as in Ethiopia's starving children) to the life-threatening stunting and malfunctioning called *kwashiorkor*. In adults, lack of protein leads to weakness, DEPRESSION, lack of resistance, and slow recovery from illness or injury. (For help and further information, see NUTRITION.)

prothrombin time (PT) A kind of BLOOD TEST, often considered one of the LIVER FUNCTION TESTS, which can also indicate VITAMIN K deficiency and help physicians monitor use of anticoagulant (anti-blood-clotting) medicine.

PSAT Abbreviation for PRELIMINARY SCHOLASTIC APTITUDE TEST.

pseudohypertrophic muscular dystrophy Alternate name for Duchenne muscular dystrophy, the most common form of MUSCULAR DYSTROPHY.

psoriasis A common SKIN DISORDER that involves thickened, reddened skin, often covered by silvery scales, as a result of excessive formation of skin cells; the parts of the body affected vary, especially with different forms of the disease. A chronic condition, psoriasis may go into REMISSION and then erupt again, as in response to illness, stress, or injury to the skin. Mild forms are sometimes treated with light (see PHOTOTHERAPY) and steroid creams. More severe forms, sometimes linked with ARTHRITIS, require more varied measures. Though the cause of the disease is unknown, it is apparently a GENETIC DISORDER, affecting both sexes and appearing at any age, sometimes in infancy but generally in the teens or 20s. (For help and further information, see SKIN DISORDERS.)

For help and further information

National Psoriasis Foundation
Suite 210

6443 Southwest Beaverton Highway
Portland, OR 97221
503-297-1545

Organization of people who have or are concerned with psoriasis. Encourages formation of self-help groups and person-to-person contact, as through Pen Pal Club for children; acts as clearinghouse for information; provides referrals; offers mail-order discount arrangement for drugs; publishes various materials, including *My Child Has Psoriasis, A Guide to Understanding Psoriasis, Update on Psoriasis Research* (including experimental treatments), and *Climatotherapy at the Dead Sea.*

Other reference sources

Health Care U.S.A., by Jean Carper. New York: Prentice Hall, 1987. Resource for general and specific health-care information. Lists leading psoriasis specialists and centers for treatment and research, including day-care centers and climatotherapy clinic, and other information.

Psoriasis: A Guide to One of the Commonest Skin Diseases, by Dr. Ronald A. Marks. New York: Arco, 1981.

psychiatrist   A PHYSICIAN who specializes in diagnosing, preventing, and treating people with MENTAL DISORDERS and other psychological, emotional, behavioral, and developmental problems. All psychiatrists are able to prescribe medications, but they vary widely in their orientation: some focus on genetic and biochemical causes of mental problems; others (such as PSYCHOANALYSTS) focus on environmental and personal experience. Some psychiatrists specialize in treating children or adolescents with behavioral or developmental problems. A psychiatrist does not generally do formal testing (normally done by a PSYCHOLOGIST) but talks with, plays with, and observes the child, both alone and with others, looking for underlying physical problems that may produce mental problems.

psychoanalyst   A health professional who treats mental, emotional, and behavioral problems using a therapeutic technique based on Freudian theory or related approaches; a kind of PSYCHOTHERAPIST. Often medically trained as PSYCHIATRISTS, psychoanalysts offer deep exploratory therapy, sometimes over a period of years, especially probing the patient's unconscious and early childhood experiences. Some psychoanalysts, such as followers of Melanie Klein, specialize in psychoanalysis of children and adolescents.

psychological parent   The person who has the strongest emotional ties with the child and is closest to the child's day-to-day activities, hopes, and fears, usually one of the child's legal parents or GUARDIANS but sometimes a neighbor or other relative with no legal responsibility for the child, such as a stepparent or aunt. If it appears that breaking such a relationship would be harmful to the child, some courts will grant such psychological parents VISITATION RIGHTS.

psychologist   A health professional who specializes in diagnosing and treating people with social, emotional, psychological, behavioral, and developmental problems. *Clinical psychologists*—who treat patients, rather than focusing on the general study of human behavior—often offer testing and counseling services, among them psychotherapy (see PSYCHOTHERAPIST). Not trained as PHYSICIANS, most psychologists are unable to prescribe medications (though in some areas that is changing). Children who may have problems, such as possible LEARNING DISABILITIES, will often be referred either to a *child psychologist* or a *school psychologist* for assessment. The psychologist will meet and talk with the child and often with the parents and will observe the child at play and with the parents; depending on the potential problem, the psychologist may also administer INTELLIGENCE TESTS, PROJECTIVE TESTS (personality tests), DEVELOPMENTAL SCREENING TESTS, and DIAGNOSTIC ASSESSMENT TESTS. The psychologist will then suggest a course of therapy, perhaps including recommendations about educational programs and activities best suited to enhancing the child's skills.

psychomotor domain   One of three key categories of instructional content and learning objectives described by Benjamin Bloom, referring to the physical and muscular functioning of an individual; the others are the AFFECTIVE DOMAIN and the COGNITIVE DOMAIN. (See DOMAIN.)

psychoprophylaxis   General medical term referring to relaxation methods used in PREPARED CHILDBIRTH. (See CHILDBIRTH.)

psychosis   A general mental condition in which the person has gross misperceptions of reality, including creation of a "new" reality, as in DELUSIONS or HALLUCINATIONS; also, used loosely, a synonym for MENTAL DISORDERS. Psychosis may be part of various other mental disturbances, such as DEPRESSION and SCHIZOPHRENIA. (For help and further information, see MENTAL DISORDERS.)

psychotherapist   A health professional who treats mental, emotional, and behavioral problems, using an approach in which a patient talks about problems in a regular therapeutic relationship. The aim is for patients to learn more about themselves, both their deep personal thoughts and feelings and their relationships with others, and to change some aspects of their behavior. Psychotherapists vary widely in their orientation and background. Some are PSYCHOLOGISTS with advanced, though not medical, training, who offer relatively short-term counseling services; others, especially PSYCHOANALYSTS, may have medical training as PSYCHIATRISTS and offer deeply exploratory therapy that can last for years. Psychiatric SOCIAL WORKERS and others with special training may also work as psychotherapists. Some psychotherapists specialize in treating children and adolescents.

PT   Abbreviation for PROTHROMBIN TIME, a type of MEDICAL TEST.

PTSD   Abbreviation for POST-TRAUMATIC STRESS DISORDER.

pubarche   Alternate term for MENARCHE, the onset of the first MENSTRUATION.

puberty   The series of physical changes that occur during the development of sexual maturity, usually starting in girls between ages 10 and 12 and in boys between ages 12 and 13. Puberty results from a series of hormonal changes. The brain begins to secrete a HORMONE called *luteinizing hormone-*

Dealing with Precocious Puberty

Mental development is normal in children with precocious puberty, and developmental milestones such as sitting, standing, and walking generally occur at the same ages as in normal children. Behavior, however, may change to that typical of adolescence.

Some girls who start puberty prematurely go through periods of moodiness and irritability, much like teenage girls. Some boys become more aggressive than their peers and develop a sex drive. Many school-age children with precocious puberty become self-conscious about their bodies, often to the point where they will no longer undress in front of other people, including their parents.

Premature puberty can have adverse psychological effects on the child and the family. While this is true of many chronic disorders, it may be especially true when an issue as sensitive as sexuality is involved. Perhaps the hardest thing a child with precocious puberty has to endure is teasing from other children about his or her sexual development. Such teasing is especially common for girls who develop breasts.

Social workers at the National Institute of Child Health and Human Development (NICHD) who work with parents of children with precocious puberty suggest the parents keep alert for signs that their child is troubled by teasing and discuss it with the child. Parents can help, they say, by acknowledging that teasing is very upsetting and by helping the child find a way to deal with it.

Children with precocious puberty may feel isolated and rejected socially. Some children who mature early, particularly boys, become more aggressive and hyperactive than their peers. This behavior can cause problems in getting along with other children their age and may make it difficult to pay attention in school. Because of their physical appearance, children who start puberty early may feel more comfortable around older children than with their peers. In general, however, they are not mature enough emotionally to be accepted by the older children.

It is easy for people to forget that the child who started puberty prematurely is not as old as he or she looks. As a result, teachers, relatives, and neighbors often expect the child to act older than his or her age, and the child may become frustrated at not being able to live up to expectations. Parents of children with precocious puberty are sometimes criticized by other adults for "babying" their child, when in fact they are treating the child in a manner appropriate for his or her age.

How the parents cope with the changes in their child will determine largely how the child copes. Parents are naturally uncomfortable about sexual development in their young children, but their main concern is how to prevent the child from developing a poor self-image as a result of early puberty.

NICHD social workers recommend that parents give their child a simple, frank explanation of what is happening to him or her. They should explain that what is occurring is a normal process but that it is happening sooner than is good for the child. Parents should maintain open communication with the child and help the child to gain perspective on his or her condition. The goal is for the child and family to accept the child's sexual development without dwelling on it.

Source: *Precocious Puberty*, a pamphlet in the "Facts About" series. Prepared by the National Institute of Child Health and Human Development for the Public Health Service.

releasing hormone (LHRH) in periodic bursts; this triggers the PITUITARY GLAND to produce hormones called *gonadotropins*, which in turn stimulate the GONADS (OVARIES in girls and TESTES in boys) to make sex HORMONES, primarily ESTROGEN for girls and TESTOSTERONE for boys.

These hormones begin to produce the outward physical changes—the SECONDARY SEX CHARACTERISTICS—by which young people signal that they are approaching sexual maturity. In girls, BREASTS and *labia* (lips of the VULVA) develop, hair grows in the underarm and pubic area, the hips widen, fat is deposited in the adult female distribution, the UTERUS enlarges, and MENSTRUATION and OVULATION begin. In boys, the PENIS and testes develop; hair appears on the face, underarms, and pubic area; shoulders widen; the voice deepens; SPERM are produced; and spontaneous erections begin to occur. The hormones also trigger a GROWTH SPURT, of perhaps four to six inches a year, until full height is reached in the late teens. Then the ends of the skeletal bones, where the growth takes place, close off, and growth ends.

The changes of puberty are the physical part of the massive changes that take place in ADOLESCENCE. These changes are made more difficult for children—perhaps one out of 10,000, more girls than boys—who experience puberty abnormally early. *Precocious puberty* generally refers to puberty that begins in girls before age nine and in boys before age 10. What triggers precocious puberty is unclear, though in some cases it seems to be a benign TUMOR in the part of the brain that releases LHRH. Other causes include BRAIN TUMORS, disorders of the CENTRAL NERVOUS SYSTEM such as NEUROFIBROMATOSIS, disorders of the ADRENAL GLANDS, and rare syndromes such as *McCune-Albright syndrome*. Some forms of precocious puberty are apparently inherited, especially in males (sometimes by way of unaffected female CARRIERS). Though in precocious puberty sex hormones speed up growth initially, growth stops sooner than usual, so these children often end up shorter than normal, with many females under five feet and many males under five feet two inches.

Early therapies to halt or slow precocious puberty had little success. But therapy that involves desensitizing the pituitary gland to the effects of LHRH has not only stopped maturation but reversed it in some cases. Long-term effects of this therapy are unknown, however.

DEALING WITH PRECOCIOUS PUBERTY (on page 395) offers suggestions for helping a child deal with precocious puberty, but much of the advice can also help parents of a young child experiencing puberty within the normal range, though earlier than his or her friends.

For help and further information

National Institute of Child Health and Human Development (NICHD), 301-496-5133. Publishes "Facts About" booklet on *Precocious Puberty*. (For full group information, see PREGNANCY.)

public assistance   A synonym for welfare, generally preferred by social-work agencies.

Public Law (P.L.) 94-142   The formal legal name for the EDUCATION FOR ALL HANDICAPPED CHILDREN ACT OF 1975.

Public Law (P.L.) 95-561   The official designation for the federal statute that included the Educational Amendments of 1978, encompassing the GIFTED AND TALENTED CHILDREN'S ACT OF 1978 and the BASIC SKILLS AND EDUCATIONAL PROFICIENCY PROGRAM.

Public Law (P.L.) 98-457, Child Abuse Amendments of 1984   The federal law that includes the so-called BABY DOE LAW.

public school   A school funded and controlled mainly by community and government, under the direction of a school board or publicly elected or appointed officials, as opposed to a PRIVATE SCHOOL, which is controlled and funded mostly by individuals not responsible to the public. (For help and further information, see EDUCATION.)

PUBS   Abbreviation for percutaneous umbilical cord sampling, alternate name for the GENETIC SCREENING procedure CORDOCENTESUS.

pudendum   Alternate name for a woman's VULVA, a region sometimes anesthetized during CHILDBIRTH using a *pudendal block*. (See ANESTHESIA.)

puerperal psychosis   The medical name for a severe form of postpartum DEPRESSION.

puerperal sepsis   Infection of the UTERUS following CHILDBIRTH, sometimes a cause of MATERNAL MORTALITY.

puerperium   The medical term for the six weeks or so after a woman gives birth, during which the body begins to normalize after its massive anatomical and physiological changes and the woman begins to adjust to the changed family life involving the new infant. (See POSTNATAL CARE.)

pulmonary embolism   A blood clot in the lungs, sometimes a cause of MATERNAL MORTALITY.

pulmonary function tests   A group of MEDICAL TESTS to assess how well a person's lungs are operating; sometimes to help in diagnosing a LUNG AND BREATHING DISORDER, sometimes to evaluate a person's condition before an operation. Among the assessments performed are:

- *spirometry*, in which the patient exhales air through a tube into a machine that measures the volume exhaled and the speed of the exhalation. Children with ASTHMA cannot exhale as fast as normal.
- *peak flow meter*, a device that measures how fast air can be expelled from the lungs as a person exhales into the meter's mouthpiece. In children with asthma, the rate is slower than normal because the air passages are constricted; this test is sometimes used to assess a child's response to various treatments and is sometimes used as a daily monitor.
- *blood gases*, a test that measures the acidity or alkalinity of the blood, using just a few drops; an emergency procedure to assess the acidity or alkalinity of the blood (to spot possible acidosis) and to read the amount of oxygen, carbon dioxide, and hydrogen in the blood, as in monitoring cases of possible respiratory failure.
- *diffusing capacity*, a test that indicates how efficient the lungs are in transferring oxygen into the blood.

(For help and further information, see LUNG AND BREATHING DISORDERS; MEDICAL TESTS.)

pulmonary stenosis   A type of CONGENITAL heart defect. (See HEART AND HEART PROBLEMS.)

punishment   A negative approach to DISCIPLINE, often referring to CORPORAL PUNISHMENT.

Pure Tone Test (audiometric test)   A type of HEARING TEST that measures the frequency and loudness of sounds that a person is able to hear, a common test in assessing EAR AND HEARING PROBLEMS.

purpura   A small bruise or HEMORRHAGE under the skin.

putative father   The legal term for the presumed biological FATHER if a child's parents are not married and paternity has not been acknowledged or established; sometimes called *unwed father*, against whom a PATERNITY SUIT may be brought in some situations.

PUVA   Abbreviation for a type of PHOTOTHERAPY, for the drug *psoralen* plus *ultraviolet A*.

pyelography   A kind of KIDNEY FUNCTION TEST using a form of RADIOGRAPHY.

pyelonephritis   Inflammation of one or both kidneys, usually from infection. (See KIDNEY AND UROLOGICAL DISORDERS.)

Pygmalion effect   Alternate name for the result of a SELF-FULFILLING PROPHECY.

pyrexia   The medical term for FEVER.

pyridoxine, pyridoxal, or **pyridoxamine**   Alternate names for VITAMIN B$_6$.

pyromania   A type of IMPULSE CONTROL DISORDER.

quadriplegia PARALYSIS or weakness affecting all four limbs and the trunk, as in a person who has suffered a SPINAL-CORD INJURY in the neck.

quarter A fourth. In EDUCATION, the school year is sometimes divided into four equal periods, instead of two SEMESTERS or three TRIMESTERS; also an alternative term for *quartile*, a way of ranking test scores, on the same principle as a PERCENTILE, but from 1 to 4.

quartile A way of ranking test scores, on the same principle as a PERCENTILE, but with four divisions.

quickening The baby's first movements in the UTERUS, generally felt by mothers during the 18th to 20th weeks of the PREGNANCY, sometimes as early as the 16th week, especially in second and subsequent pregnancies. It often starts as a flutter, but later the woman should be able to feel—and sometimes even see on her abdomen—distinct kicks.

quinmester Educational schedule that divides the school year into five 45-day units, plus one 30-day vacation unit. Students are expected to attend at least four or, if they wish, all five of the units. (See EDUCATION.)

quinsy Infection of one or both TONSILS.

rabies A life-threatening disease caused by a virus, transmitted from the saliva of an infected animal through a bite or other break in the skin. The virus travels through the NERVOUS SYSTEM to the brain, where it incubates, causing at first generalized symptoms, such as FEVER and restlessness, then inflammation (ENCEPHALITIS), intense thirst but inability to drink due to violent muscle spasms in the throat (source of the alternate name for rabies, *hydrophobia*), sometimes PARALYSIS of the face and eye muscles, and COMA. Once symptoms have appeared (usually four to eight weeks after infection but sometimes after only nine days and sometimes after months), rabies is almost always fatal, though some people have survived with special treatment in INTENSIVE CARE UNITS. The main focus, however, is on preventing the spread of the disease among wild or domestic animals and, if a child or adult is bitten, to clean the wound or break thoroughly and seek medical treatment immediately.

If rabies is at all at question, the physician will normally begin a course of injections of *immunoglobulin*, ANTIBODIES that provide passive IMMUNIZATION against the virus during the period of hazard. While these injections have some side effects, they are no longer the painful injections in the stomach of earlier decades, and if started promptly (within two days of the exposure) almost always prevent development of the disease. If possible, the biting animal is captured, killed, and examined for signs of rabies; if none are found, the injection series may be ended. Because of prevention measures, especially vaccinating dogs, rabies is no longer common, but parents who live in areas where rabies is known to exist should be alert to the possibility if a child is bitten or has contact with a questionable animal.

For help and further information

National Institute of Allergy and Infectious Diseases (NIAID), 301-496-5717. Publishes brochure *Rabies*. (For full group information, see ALLERGY.)

radiation Electromagnetic rays produced either naturally, as from the sun, or artificially, as from computers. Radiation has been linked with increased risk of CANCER and acts as an ENVIRONMENTAL HAZARD in causing other kinds of health problems, including possible BIRTH DEFECTS. It can also, however, be harnessed for useful purposes, as in X-RAYS, RADIOGRAPHY, or treatment for some kinds of cancers. (For help and further information, see ENVIRONMENTAL HAZARDS.)

radiography General medical term for the use of RADIATION or X-RAYS, either in still pictures, as in a chest X-ray, or in moving images, as in FLUOROSCOPY, to give a picture of the internal workings of the body. Some kinds of radiography are regarded as INVASIVE procedures, meaning that they involve INJECTION or ingestion of foreign substances into the body, such as the dyed fluid in a MYELOGRAM. Most X-rays are considered noninvasive, but because they can damage a FETUS, women who are or suspect they may be pregnant are advised not to have such a test. (For help and further information, see MEDICAL TESTS.)

radioisotope scanning Alternate term for a type of MEDICAL TEST called NUCLEAR SCANNING.

radionuclide imaging Alternate term for a type of MEDICAL TEST called NUCLEAR SCANNING.

radon A type of ENVIRONMENTAL HAZARD.

rank Relative standing in a group, in EDUCATION generally referring to the numerical order in which students rank by their GRADE POINT AVERAGES. In a graduating class, the highest-ranking student is the VALEDICTORIAN and the second-highest is the SALUTATORIAN, with other students listed in numerical order (third, fourth, fifth, etc.). In addition to GRADE average, class rank is one of the key criteria considered by COLLEGES in evaluating students for possible ADMISSION. However, a student who was 20th in the graduating class of a highly competitive science-oriented school may be considered more favorably than someone who was 10th in graduating from a small central school; though in practice, college admissions teams would look at a variety of measures in assessing a student.

rape In human sexuality, intercourse or other sexual acts done without a person's consent and under force, threats, or intimidation, often between parties known to one another, such as relatives or neighbors. In relation to children, see CHILD ABUSE AND NEGLECT, STATUTORY RAPE, and POST-TRAUMATIC STRESS DISORDER.

rapid eye movement (REM) One of the two main stages of sleep, associated with dreaming (see SLEEPING DISORDERS).

rapprochement The third stage of a baby's SEPARATION-INDIVIDUATION process.

rare disorders Disorders that appear in relatively few people, including GENETIC DISORDERS, CHROMOSOMAL ABNORMALITIES, unusual infectious diseases, and other health problems of unknown origin. For information on the many rare disorders not covered in this book, parents may want to contact the orga-

nizations listed below, as well as checking with any local self-help clearinghouses to see if self-help groups exist.

For help and further information

National Institutes of Health, 301-496-4000. For referral to the government organization dealing with specific health questions.

National Health Information Clearinghouse, 800-336-4797. For referrals to other hotlines or helplines.

National Organization for Rare Disorders (NORD)
P.O. Box 8923
New Fairfield, CT 06812
203-746-6518
Abbey S. Meyers, Executive Director
Organization of health professionals and other individuals and organizations interested in rare disorders. Gathers and disseminates information; makes referrals to organizations regarding specific disorders; monitors availability of medicines for rare disorders under the Orphan Drug Act; publishes quarterly *Orphan Disease Update* and occasional legislative newsletter *NORD On-Line*.

(See also medical books in PARENT'S BOOKSHELF on page 566.)

rash A general term for reddish spots or reddish, inflamed skin, often associated with itching or FEVER and with local irritation, as in DIAPER RASH or HEAT RASH. They are also associated with numerous disorders common in children, such as CHICKEN POX and SCARLET FEVER, as well as some less common diseases such as ROCKY MOUNTAIN SPOTTED FEVER, some AUTOIMMUNE DISORDERS such as LUPUS ERYTHEMATOSUS, and some kinds of VITAMIN deficiency. Treatment depends on the cause and the type of spots distinguished by a physician.

Raven's Coloured Progressive Matrices Alternate name for STANDARD PROGRESSIVE MATRICES.

RDAs Abbreviation for RECOMMENDED DAILY ALLOWANCES.

reactive attachment disorder A type of MENTAL DISORDER affecting infants and children under five, in which they have disturbances in their social interactions. Infants, for example, often have poor VISUAL SKILLS and communication skills (see COMMUNICATION SKILLS AND DISORDERS), and lack the reciprocal visual contact and playfulness to develop such skills. Slightly older children are often apathetic and incurious and lack social interest, or they may be indiscriminately sociable, as with strangers. Some of the symptoms mentioned are similar to those in AUTISM, but this disorder is termed *reactive* because it is generally a response to lack of BONDING between child and CAREGIVER, to CHILD ABUSE AND NEGLECT, and to absence of stable family attachments, as when a child has been moved from one set of FOSTER PARENTS to another. It often is the psychosocial accompaniment to FAILURE TO THRIVE or MATERNAL DEPRIVATION SYNDROME. (For help and further information, see MENTAL DISORDERS.)

readability   A measure of the difficulty of a passage of READING matter.

readiness   Possession of the skills and MATURITY necessary to learn new skills; sometimes used in the general sense of being ready for EDUCATION of any sort but often used in relation to young children and READING. A child's readiness for reading is important, because if the child is not ready, he or she will quickly fall behind the rest of the class academically, since so much other learning depends on the ability to read. As a result, educators use various READING READINESS TESTS to help them assess whether or not a child is ready to learn to read, in addition to other READINESS TESTS relating to other kinds of skills.

readiness class   A school class for children who are AGE-ELIGIBLE—that is, measured by CHRONOLOGICAL AGE they are eligible and perhaps even required to enter school—but whose DEVELOPMENTAL AGE is considered too low for entry into regular classes, based on various READINESS TESTS or DEVELOPMENTAL SCREENING TESTS.

readiness tests   TESTS that are intended to discover whether a child has the necessary skills and development to benefit fully from instruction, as in READING READINESS TESTS. Sometimes mistakenly confused with DEVELOPMENTAL SCREENING TESTS, which focus on a child's ability to learn, readiness tests instead focus on whether the child has acquired skills needed for more advanced learning. Doing poorly on a readiness test may mean that a child has not had experience or teaching at home, not necessarily that the child has a learning problem (of the type developmental screening tests are supposed to identify). Examples of widely used readiness tests are CALIFORNIA ACHIEVEMENT TEST, METROPOLITAN READINESS TEST, BOEHM TEST OF BASIC CONCEPTS, and BRIGANCE® INVENTORY OF EARLY DEVELOPMENT. Such tests are widely used for class placement and CURRICULUM planning for children, even though current research indicates that tests for young children are notorious for having very poor RELIABILITY and VALIDITY because children change so fast and grow at such individual and varying rates.

For help and further information

Developmental Screening in Early Childhood: A Guide, third edition, by Samuel J. Meisels. Washington, DC: National Association for the Education of Young Children, 1989.
(See also TESTS.)

reading   The process of perceiving and recognizing written symbols and translating them into words that individually and together convey meaning. Though many of us take reading for granted, it is, in fact, a highly complex process, and many people have difficulty with one or another stage of the process.

Most notably, some people with DYSLEXIA, sometimes called *word blindness*, or other kinds of LEARNING DISABILITIES have difficulty transmitting an accurate picture of letters and words to the brain; these are often scrambled, with REVERSALS such as *saw* for *was*, or *word test* for *test word*. Some people have problems with their short-term memory; they cannot remember letters and words they have read long enough to be able to put them together in a meaningful way. The general term for an error that a person makes in reading (such as dropping a word, adding a word, or substituting one word for another) is a *miscue*. The difficulty of reading has been pointed out with some poignancy in recent years by the public acknowledgment of many adults that, although they are graduates of high school and sometimes even of COLLEGE, they are functionally illiterate (see ILLITERACY).

Such problems point up some of the complexities that young children face in learning how to read. Because reading is such an important skill (sometimes called a PREREQUISITE or PRECURSOR SKILL), much attention is placed on evaluating whether or not a child has the skills and maturity—what educators call READINESS—to learn how to read effectively. To assess these, educators employ various READING READINESS TESTS.

Traditionally, reading was taught primarily through the PHONICS METHOD, by which the child learned to associate letters with sounds and "sounded out" words, later applying that method to new words. But in recent decades, many educators have preferred some variation of the WHOLE-WORD APPROACH (also called the *word-recognition* or *sight method*), in which children learn words as whole units, only later breaking them down into parts and learning how to put them together in new words. The whole-word approach has the advantage of focusing on meaning and context, but children who have PERCEPTUAL HANDICAPS that cause reading difficulty often seem to fare better with heavy use of the phonics approach, usually highly structured, as in the ORTON-GILLINGHAM METHOD, VAKT, the FERNALD METHOD, and the SPALDING (unified phonics) METHOD.

Beginning readers often practice *oral reading*, in which they speak the words out loud; later they move to *silent reading* but sometimes with *subvocalization*, in which the words are formed by the lips or even whispered while reading. Subvocalization can significantly slow reading speed but may be useful for students with reading difficulties, such as dyslexia.

Because reading is a skill basic to many other kinds of learning, much attention is paid to evaluating how well a student has progressed. Among the aspects of reading that educators assess are:

* *reading comprehension*, or the ability to understand and recall data from material just read;
* *speed*, or rate of reading;
* *scanning*, or running the eye down a page to find information, as in an index or catalog (a kind of LOCATIONAL SKILL);
* *skimming*, a type of speeded-up reading in which a person gets a general idea of a selection's content, without reading word for word;
* WORD-ATTACK SKILLS, the skills a child needs to deal with new or unfamiliar words;
* *passive vocabulary*, words that a child can recognize or understand in context but cannot use independently;

- *active vocabulary*, words that a child can use independently in his or her own speaking or writing, always more limited than the passive vocabulary because children (like adults) understand more than they can actively express;
- *sight vocabulary*, words that a student can read and understand without looking them up, as in a dictionary;
- *sight words*, words that a student recognizes and understands in a reading selection without needing to sound them out.

Often a student's scores on STANDARDIZED TESTS of various aspects of reading ability are compared with the average test scores of students on such tests, the result being expressed as a reading AGE or GRADE-EQUIVALENT.

Reading researchers have also developed numerous ways to measure the difficulty of reading passages. Various kinds of formulas (named for their developers, such as Lorge, Dale-Chall, Flesch, Washburne-Vogel, or Yoakam) measure *readability*, taking into account the number of syllables per word and the average number of words per sentence. The numerical results are related to the typical level of reading matter for certain age or grade levels and are used to judge whether reading matter is appropriate for given students or grades. The ability of a student to comprehend reading matter of a certain level of difficulty is sometimes expressed as *reading power* and is measured by a test called *Degrees of Reading Power*.

Reading experts have also formulated lists of *key words* (such as the Dolch Word List), those targeted for teaching in the early grades, partly because they are most common in material written for children. In preparing textbooks for young readers, educators often take into account both the readability of the work and the specific vocabulary included in it.

Parents are often the key to the child's reading ability. In *Becoming a Nation of Readers*, the U.S. Department of Education's Commission on Reading concluded that "a parent is a child's first tutor in unraveling the fascinating puzzle of written language. A parent is a child's one enduring source of faith that somehow, sooner or later, he or she will become a good reader." The commission made a number of suggestions for how parents can help their children not only learn to read but want to read, recognizing it as an opening to the whole world and time; most important are the following:

- *Parents should read to preschool children and informally teach them about reading and writing*. Reading to children, discussing stories and experiences with them, and—with a light touch—helping them learn letters and words are practices that are consistently associated with eventual success in reading.
- *Parents should support school-aged children's continued growth as readers*. Parents of children who become successful readers monitor their children's progress in school, become involved in school programs, support homework, buy their children books or take them to libraries, encourage reading as a free-time activity, and place reasonable limits on such activities as TV viewing.

Some more practical suggestions for parents on how to help their children become good readers are given under HELP YOUR CHILD BECOME A GOOD READER, on page 520.

In the SPECIAL HELP SECTION parents will find a list of the main reference books available to parents and librarians for selecting books on specific topics. (See GUIDES TO CHILDREN'S READING, on page 561, and also MEDAL-WINNING CHILDREN'S BOOKS, on page 563. Also, throughout the A-to-Z portion of this book, parents will find books for children under specific problem topics, such as AIDS or ASTHMA; some books on family situations, such as single-parent or divorced families, are listed in the PARENT'S BOOKSHELF on page 566.

For help and further information

On Reading in General

Reading Is Fundamental (RIF)
600 Maryland Avenue, SW, Suite 500
Washington, DC 20560
202-287-3220
Ruth P. Graves, President
Address for ordering brochures: Publications Department, Smithsonian Institution, 600 Maryland Avenue, SW, Suite 500, Washington, DC 20024
Organization of educators, librarians, parents, community leaders, and others forming network of local reading motivation programs, supported by corporate, foundation, private, and government funding. Aims to excite interest in reading in children from preschool through high school; offers services to parents to encourage home reading; stresses child's personal choice and ownership of books; publishes various materials, including quarterly *RIF Newsletter* and parent guides.

AVKO Educational Research Foundation (AVKOERF)
3084 West Willard Road
Birch Run, MI 48415
313-686-9283
Don McCabe, Research Director
Organization of educators and others interested in audio, visual, kinetic, and oral (AVKO) techniques for teaching reading and spelling, especially for people with dyslexia or other learning disabilities. Conducts research; gathers and disseminates information; operates reading and spelling center; provides training for adult tutors; maintains library; publishes various materials, including quarterly newsletter and dictionary of phonograms *Word Families Plus*.

Reading Reform Foundation (RRF)
7054 East Indian School Road
Scottsdale, AZ 85251
602-946-3567
Mrs. Paul B. Hinds, President
Organization devoted to restoration of phonetics in reading instruction. Gathers and disseminates information on phonetics in reading; provides referrals to trained phonetic teachers; maintains library; publishes various materials, including quarterly *The Reading Informer*.

What Is Reading?

Many people believe that reading is just the process of turning printed words into their spoken equivalents. However, this view of reading represents only part of the picture. Years of research have shown reading to be far more than just knowing how sounds correspond to letters and words.

Skilled readers do much more than just turn printed words into spoken ones. They use their knowledge of the world, of how information is organized on a page, and their awareness of whether something makes sense to guide their efforts to construct meaning. For example, children faced with the sentence "Mommy and Daddy gave the waiter a tip" might be able to say the words in the sentence. But if those children had eaten only at a fast-food restaurant and had never seen a waiter or observed their parents leaving money on the table, they might completely fail to understand the meaning of the sentence.

Consequently, for all readers, beginning or skilled, the capacity to understand a written message or text depends as much on experience with the world (including books) outside of school as on the formal education provided by the school. Hence the fundamental importance of home-based experiences.

To reflect this expanded idea of what reading is, the Commission on Reading defines reading as "the process of constructing meaning from written texts. It is a complex skill requiring the coordination of a number of interrelated sources of information."

Becoming a Nation of Readers goes on to describe skilled reading in five ways:

- Reading is a *constructive process*. According to the report, "Good readers skillfully integrate information in the text with what they already know." Since no piece of text can possibly tell readers everything they need to know, readers must "fill in the blanks" from their experience.
- Reading must be *fluent*. "Readers must be able to recognize words quickly and accurately so that this process can coordinate fluidly with the process of constructing the meaning of the text."
- Reading must be *strategic*. "Skilled readers are flexible. How they read depends upon the complexity of the text, their familiarity with the topic, and their purpose for reading." They will read difficult things slowly and with care; they might skim an advertisement; and they will probably fly through an exciting story.
- Reading requires *motivation*, "one of the keys to learning to read." This motivation develops from the recognition that reading can be interesting and informative.
- Skilled reading is a *lifelong pursuit*. "Reading, like playing a musical instrument, is not something that is mastered once and for all at a certain age. Rather, it is a skill that continues to improve through practice."

Because reading is a complex skill that develops over a lifetime, teachers alone are not enough. Learning to read begins when you talk with and listen to your children, especially when you read with them and let them see you reading for your own enjoyment. In doing just those few things, you teach your children the most important lessons about reading.

Source: *Becoming a Nation of Readers: What Parents Can Do*, prepared by Marilyn R. Binkley et al. Published by D. C. Heath and Company in cooperation with the Office of Educational Research and Improvement of the U.S Department of Education, 1988.

Laubach Literacy Action (LLA)
Box 131, 1320 Jamesville Avenue
Syracuse, NY 13210
315-422-9121
Peter Waite, Executive Director
Organization serving other volunteer literacy programs for adolescents or adults, including those for whom English is a second language. Provides training for tutors, trainers, and program leaders; acts as information exchange; sets standards and certifies literacy volunteers; counsels on development of literacy materials, depending on group being served; publishes various materials, including quarterly *Literacy Advance* and annual directory; arm of Laubach Literacy International (LLI), which runs New Readers Press, with books for adolescent or adult beginning readers.

International Reading Association
P.O. Box 8139
800 Barksdale Road
Newark, DE 19714
302-731-1600
Organization of teachers, other professionals, and parents concerned with reading. Gathers and disseminates information; encourages research; publishes various materials, including directory and journals on research and theory.

On Selecting Books and Stories

Children's Literature Association (ChLA)
c/o Jill P. May, Publications Manager
210 Education
Purdue University
West Lafayette, IN 47907
317-494-2355
Organization of college-level teachers, librarians, authors, publishers, parents, and others interested in children's literature. Fosters research and scholarship in field; gathers and disseminates information about children's literature; publishes various

materials, including quarterly journal, annual *Children's Literature: An International Journal*, and annual directory.

National Story League (NSL)

c/o E. Gertrude Stirnamen, President
3508 Russell, #6
St. Louis, MO 63104
314-773-5555

Organization of teachers, librarians, parents, and others interested in storytelling, especially to children. Publishes various materials, including quarterly *Story Art Magazine* and annual *Story Art Magazine Yearbook*.

Young Adult Services Division (YASD)

c/o American Library Association
50 East Huron Street
Chicago, IL 60611
312-944-6780
Evelyn Shaevel, Executive Director

Division of American Library Association devoted to evaluating, selecting, and circulating books and other library materials to young adult readers. Provides training for librarians; publishes various materials, including *Best Books for Young Adults, Sex Education for Adolescents*, and *Outstanding Books for the College Bound*.

Parents Choice Foundation

P.O. Box 185
Waban, MA 02168
617-965-5913
Diana H. Green, President

Organization that provides information to parents and educators about books, movies, television, toys, games, records, videos, and computer software that children might encounter. Publishes quarterly *Parents' Choice*.

Council on Interracial Books for Children (CIBC)

1841 Broadway, Room 500
New York, NY 10023
212-757-5339
Anne Johnson, Interim Administrator

Organization devoted to encouraging development and use of books and other learning materials that are free from discrimination, as related to race, sex, physical or mental disability, or age. Reviews new books and screens programs; provides teachers with guidelines for detecting and combatting such bias; operates Racism and Sexism Resource Center for Educators, which promotes nondiscriminatory materials; publishes various materials, including *Interracial Books for Children Bulletin*.

Great Books Foundation (GBF)

40 East Huron
Chicago, IL 60611
312-332-5870, toll-free number 800-222-5870
Richard P. Dennis, President

Organization encouraging reading of classic books among children and adults. Offers programs and reading aids for discussion groups; trains teachers and volunteer discussion leaders; operates toll-free number; publishes various materials, including paperback versions of Great Books and Junior Great Books.

Other reference sources

General Works

How to Teach Your Baby to Read, revised and updated, by Glenn Doman. New York: M. Evans, 1990.

Early Literacy, by Joan Brooks McLane and Gillian Dowley McNamee. Cambridge, MA: Harvard University Press, 1990.

Rx for Reading, by Barbara Fox. New York: Penguin, 1989.

First Teachers. Washington, DC: Barbara Bush Foundation for Family Literacy, 1989.

For Love of Reading: A Parent's Guide to Encouraging Young Readers and Writers from Infancy through Age 5, by Masha K. Rudman et al. New York: Consumer Reports Books, 1988.

Getting Ready to Read, by Betty D. Boegehold and The Bank Street College of Education. New York: Ballantine, 1988.

Learning to Read in a Multicultural Society, by Catherine Wallace. New York: Pergamon Institute of English, 1986.

Ready to Read: A Parents' Guide, by Mary Ann Dzama and Robert Gilstrap. New York: Wiley, 1983.

Background Works

The Reading Crisis: Why Poor Children Fall Behind, by Jeanne S. Chall, Vicki A. Jacobs, and Luke E. Baldwin. Cambridge, MA: Harvard University Press, 1990.

The Open Door: When Writers First Learned to Read, by Steven Gilbar. Boston: Godine, 1989.

Reading Comprehension: New Directions for Classroom Practice, by John D. McNeil. Glenview, IL: Scott, Foresman, 1987.

Reading: What Can Be Measured?, by R. Farr and R. Carey. Newark, DE: International Reading Association, 1986.

What's Whole in Whole Language, by Ken Goodman. Portsmouth, NH: Heinemann, 1986.

A Nation of Readers: The Report of the Commission on Reading, by R. C. Anderson et al. Urbana, IL: University of Illinois Center for the Study of Reading, 1985.

Whole Language: Theory in Use, Judith M. Newman, ed. Portsmouth, NH: Heinemann, 1986.

Improving Classroom Reading Instruction: A Decision-Making Approach, by Gerald G. Duffy and Laura R. Roehler. New York: Random House, 1986.

Teaching Reading to Slow and Disabled Learners, by Samuel A. Kirk et al. Boston: Houghton Mifflin, 1978.

The Writing Road to Reading, by Ronalda B. Spalding and Walter T. Spalding. New York: Morrow, 1969.

(See also LEARNING DISABILITIES; ILLITERACY; EDUCATION; READING READINESS TESTS.)

reading age A numerical summary reflecting a child's ability on READING tests, as compared to established NORMS. (See AGE; TESTS.)

reading power   The ability of a student to comprehend READING matter of a certain level of difficulty, sometimes measured by a test called *Degrees of Reading Power.*

reading readiness test   A type of READINESS TEST employed to help educators assess whether or not a child is ready to learn to read. This is an important assessment because, if not, a child will quickly fall behind the rest of the class academically, since so much other learning depends on the ability to read. Among the areas of development measured by such a test are the child's maturity in using language (listening and speaking), perceptual maturity (the child's ability to distinguish between different line drawings, for example), attention and responsiveness to storytelling, and general background and experience. (For help and further information, see READING.)

Read method   A popular form of natural or prepared CHILDBIRTH, also called the *Dick-Read method.*

rebus approach   Teaching READING by using sentences that combine words with pictures and symbols (such as a drawing of a pig or the symbol "4"), which help the beginning reader by introducing new or unfamiliar words in context.

receptive language   The ability to understand what is heard. (See COMMUNICATION SKILLS AND DISORDERS.)

recessive   In GENETIC INHERITANCE, a gene that produces its effect only when its paired gene is identical or when it is unpaired on an X SEX CHROMOSOME. A recessive gene will not be expressed in the presence of a DOMINANT gene. If a mother contributes to her child a recessive gene for blue eyes, for example, the child will have blue eyes only if the father also contributes a gene for blue eyes. If both parents carry a recessive gene for a GENETIC DISORDER, any child of theirs has a 25-percent chance of inheriting the disorder, and a 50-percent chance of being a healthy CARRIER, someone who carries a defective gene but is unaffected by it and may not even know about it. A recessive defective gene whose effects are blocked by a dominant gene is said to be *masked.* Prospective parents whose family history includes genetic disorders are well advised to consider GENETIC COUNSELING when planning a PREGNANCY and GENETIC SCREENING during a pregnancy. Among the most common recessive disorders are CYSTIC FIBROSIS, PHENYLKETONURIA, sickle-cell ANEMIA, GALACTOSEMIA, Friedreich's ATAXIA, HURLER'S SYNDROME, and most LIPID STORAGE diseases, such as Gaucher's disease and TAY-SACHS DISEASE. (For help and further information, see GENETIC DISORDERS.)

recommended daily allowances (RDAs)   Suggested amounts of essential substances, such as VITAMINS and MINERALS, to be ingested daily to maintain the normal functioning of the body, as recommended by the Food and Nutrition Board of the National Academy of Sciences. Because research on human nutritional requirements is often incomplete or inconsistent, these are only estimates and are updated every five to 10 years on the basis of new research. They are also deliberately set higher than the actual requirement for that nutrient in most individuals, so they will exceed the nutrient requirements of most people. RDAs for men are generally higher than for

women, except for women who are pregnant or BREASTFEEDING. The recommendations are designed to "be adequate to meet the known nutritional needs of practically all healthy persons." They are averages, however, and must be modified for individual circumstances, as the *Surgeon General's Report on Nutrition and Health* notes:

> The fact that most RDA's are intentionally established to exceed the nutrient requirements of most people means that a dietary intake below the RDA is not necessarily inadequate for an individual whose requirement for a nutrient is average or even above average. It also means that the small percent of persons who have unusually high nutrient requirements may not meet nutritional needs even when they consume nutrients at RDA levels. The RDA's are estimates of the nutrient requirements for populations rather than for individuals. In addition, RDA's may need to be modified for people who are ill or injured.

RECOMMENDED DAILY ALLOWANCES, on page 404, lists the RDAs for PROTEIN, 10 vitamins, and six minerals, in categories by body size, gender, and energy consumption, as established in 1980. (Revisions have been proposed but have not, as of this writing, been accepted.)

A second table, ESTIMATES FOR OTHER VITAMINS AND MINERALS, gives proposed ranges considered "safe and adequate" for other nutrients for which research has been so limited that no RDAs have been established. Note the caution that "the toxic level for many TRACE ELEMENTS may be only several times usual intake, [so] the upper levels for the trace elements given in this table should not be habitually exceeded." This is especially important for infants and children, whose bodies are even less able to handle excess amounts of vitamins and minerals than those of adults are and so are subject to poisoning. (For help and further information, see VITAMINS; MINERALS; NUTRITION.)

Other reference source

Recommended Dietary Allowances, 10th edition. Washington, DC: National Academy Press, 1989.

recovery room (RR)   A room near a HOSPITAL's DELIVERY ROOM or operating room, to which patients are taken while they are still under ANESTHESIA. There trained staff monitor the patient's return to consciousness and maintenance of vital signs, with special equipment available should complications occur. From there, patients are taken to their regular hospital room (after childbirth, sometimes called a POSTPARTUM ROOM). To avoid unsettling room shifts before, during, and after CHILDBIRTH, some hospitals have developed all-in-one LABOR/DELIVERY/RECOVERY ROOMS.

recreational therapist   A health professional who tries to ease long HOSPITAL stays for children.

reduction   A procedure used in cases of FRACTURE to restore the bones to their normal position.

Recommended Daily Allowances

	Age (years)	Weight (kg)	Weight (lb)	Height (cm)	Height (in)	Protein (g)	Fat-Soluble Vitamins Vitamin A (μg RE)[a]	Fat-Soluble Vitamins Vitamin D (μg)[b]	Fat-Soluble Vitamins Vitamin E (mg α-TE)[c]
Infants	0.0–0.5	6	13	60	24	kg × 2.2	420	10	3
	0.5–1.0	9	20	71	28	kg × 2.0	400	10	4
Children	1–3	13	29	90	35	23	400	10	5
	4–6	20	44	112	44	30	500	10	6
	7–10	28	62	132	52	34	700	10	7
Males	11–14	45	99	157	62	45	1000	10	8
	15–18	66	145	176	69	56	1000	10	10
	19–22	70	154	177	70	56	1000	7.5	10
	23–50	70	154	178	70	56	1000	5	10
	51+	70	154	178	70	56	1000	5	10
Females	11–14	46	101	157	62	46	800	10	8
	15–18	55	120	163	64	46	800	10	8
	19–22	55	120	163	64	44	800	7.5	8
	23–50	55	120	163	64	44	800	5	8
	51+	55	120	163	64	44	800	5	8
Pregnant						+30	+200	+5	+2
Lactating						+20	+400	+5	+3

The allowances are intended to provide for individual variations among most normal persons as they live in the United States under usual environmental stresses. Diets should be based on a variety of common foods to provide other nutrients for which human requirements have been less well defined.

[a] Retinol equivalents; 1 RE = 1 μg retinol or 6 μg β carotene.

[b] As cholecalciferol; 10 μg cholecalciferol = 4000 IU of vitamin D.

[c] α-tocopherol equivalents; 1 mg *d*-α tocopherol = 1 α-TE.

[d] Niacin equivalent; 1 NE = 1 mg of niacin or 60 mg of dietary tryptophan.

[e] The folacin allowances refer to dietary sources as determined by *Lactobacillus casei* assay after treatment with enzymes (conjugates) to make polyglutamyl forms of the vitamin available to the test organism.

Estimates for Other Vitamins and Minerals

	Age (years)	Vitamins Vitamin K (μg)	Vitamins Biotin (μg)	Vitamins Pantothenic Acid (mg)	Trace Copper (mg)	Trace Manganese (mg)
Infants	0–0.5	12	35	2	0.5–0.7	0.5–0.7
	0.5–1	10–20	50	3	0.7–1.0	0.7–1.0
Children and	1–3	15–30	65	3	1.0–1.5	1.0–1.5
Adolescents	4–6	20–40	85	3–4	1.5–2.0	1.5–2.0
	7–10	30–60	120	4–5	2.0–2.5	2.0–3.0
	11+	50–100	100–200	4–7	2.0–3.0	2.5–5.0
Adults		70–140	100–200	4–7	2.0–3.0	2.5–5.0

Because there is less information on which to base allowances, these figures are not given in the main table of RDA and are provided here in the form of ranges of recommended intakes.

| Water-Soluble Vitamins | | | | | | | Minerals | | | | | |
Vitamin C (mg)	Thiamin (mg)	Riboflavin (mg)	Niacin (mg NE)d	Vitamin B6 (mg)	Folacine (µg)	Vitamin B12 (µg)	Calcium (mg)	Phosphrous (mg)	Magnesium (mg)	Iron (mg)	Zinc (mg)	Iodine (mg)
35	0.3	0.4	6	0.3	30	0.5f	360	240	50	10	3	40
35	0.5	0.6	8	0.6	45	1.5	540	360	70	15	5	50
45	0.7	0.8	9	0.9	100	2.0	800	800	150	15	10	70
45	0.9	1.0	11	1.3	200	2.5	800	800	200	10	10	90
45	1.2	1.4	16	1.6	300	3.0	800	800	250	10	10	120
50	1.4	1.6	18	1.8	400	3.0	1200	1200	350	18	15	150
60	1.4	1.7	18	2.0	400	3.0	1200	1200	400	18	15	150
60	1.5	1.7	19	2.2	400	3.0	800	800	350	10	15	150
60	1.4	1.6	18	2.2	400	3.0	800	800	350	10	15	150
60	1.2	1.4	16	2.2	400	3.0	800	800	350	10	15	150
50	1.1	1.3	15	1.8	400	3.0	1200	1200	300	18	15	150
60	1.1	1.3	14	2.0	400	3.0	1200	1200	300	18	15	150
60	1.1	1.3	14	2.0	400	3.0	800	800	300	18	15	150
60	1.0	1.2	13	2.0	400	3.0	800	800	300	18	15	150
60	1.0	1.2	13	2.0	400	3.0	800	800	300	10	15	150
+20	+0.4	+0.3	+2	+0.6	+400	+1.0	+400	+400	+150	g	+5	+25
+40	+0.5	+0.5	+5	+0.5	+100	+1.0	+400	+400	+150	g	+10	+50

f The recommended daily allowance for vitamin B12 in infants is based on average concentration of the vitamin in human milk. The allowances after weaning are based on energy intake (as recommended by the American Academy of Pediatrics) and consideration of other factors, such as intestinal absorption.

g The increased requirement during pregnancy cannot be met by the iron content of habitual American diets nor by the existing iron stores of many women; therefore, the use of 30–60 mg of supplemental iron is recommended. Iron needs during lactation are not substantially different from those of nonpregnant women, but continued supplementation of the mother for 2–3 months after parturition is advisable to replenish stores depleted by pregnancy.

Source: Food and Nutrition Board, National Academy of Sciences–National Research Council Recommended Daily Dietary Allowances, Revised 1980. "Designed for the maintenance of good nutritional of practically all healthy people in the U.S.A."

| Elementsa | | | | Electrolytes | | |
Fluoride (mg)	Chromium (mg)	Selenium (mg)	Molybdenum (mg)	Sodium (mg)	Potassium (mg)	Choloride (mg)
0.01–0.5	0.01–0.04	0.01–0.04	0.03–0.06	115–350	350–925	275–700
0.2–1.0	0.02–0.06	0.02–0.06	0.04–0.08	250–750	425–1275	400–1200
0.5–1.5	0.02–0.08	0.02–0.08	0.05–0.1	325–975	550–1650	500–1500
1.0–2.5	0.03–0.12	0.03–0.12	0.06–0.15	450–1350	775–2325	700–2100
1.5–2.5	0.05–0.2	0.05–0.2	0.10–0.3	600–1800	1000–3000	925–2775
1.5–2.5	0.05–0.2	0.05–0.2	0.15–0.5	900–2700	1525–4575	1400–4200
1.5–4.0	0.05–0.2	0.05–0.2	0.15–0.5	1100–3300	1875–5625	1700–5100

a Because the toxic levels for many trace elements may be only several times usual intakes, the upper levels for the trace elements given in this table should not be habitually exceeded.

Source: Food and Nutrition Board, National Academy of Sciences-National Research Council. Revised 1980. Estimated Safe and Adequate Daily Intakes of Selected Vitamins and Minerals.

Spitting Up in Babies

Most babies spit up some or even a lot of milk after a feeding. The milk seems to overflow from the baby's mouth. It is often curdled from normal stomach action. This is really not a problem—it is just messy. Babies who spit up grow as fast and strong as those who do not.

There are several tricks to reduce the amount of spitting up. None of them works all the time, and most babies will continue some spitting up even when all of the tricks are tried:

• Burp the baby carefully midway through the feeding, at the end of the feeding, and a few minutes after the feeding.

• Place the baby so that his or her head is higher than the stomach for 10 or 15 minutes after each feeding. This can be done by placing the baby in an infant seat or propping up the head of a cradle or bassinet.

Source: *Infant Care* (1989). Prepared by the Bureau of Maternal and Child Health and Resources Development for the Public Health Service.

---

reflex An involuntary, automatic movement in reaction to a particular event (*stimulus*) that triggers a response from the body's NERVOUS SYSTEM, such as the knee-jerk that follows a sharp tap below the kneecap. Some such SENSORIMOTOR reactions are found only in newborns, generally disappearing in the first few months. Among these so-called *primitive reflexes* are the GRASP REFLEX, TONIC NECK REFLEX, MORO'S REFLEX (STARTLE REFLEX), WALKING or STEPPING REFLEX, and ROOTING REFLEX. Physicians often use various reflexes as SIGNS to indicate the health or illness of a patient, and the primitive reflexes are especially important in judging the early health and development of a baby. Absence or disturbance of one of these reflexes can indicate a problem in the nervous system; for example, LANDAU'S REFLEX can suggest possible CEREBRAL PALSY or MENTAL RETARDATION.

refraction tests A variety of tests used in assessing whether corrective lenses—glasses or contact lenses—are needed. (See EYE AND VISION PROBLEMS.)

Refsum's syndrome (phytanic acid storage disease) A type of LIPID STORAGE DISEASE.

regurgitation The back-flow of fluid, generally referring to the bringing up of food, drink, and perhaps some digestive acids from the stomach to the mouth; sometimes referring to the back-flow of blood in the heart if a valve is defective. Regurgitation from the stomach or esophagus is a less forcible action than VOMITING, and in relation to babies it is often simply called "spitting up." A rare related EATING DISORDER is RUMINATION DISORDER OF INFANCY.

Rehabilitation Act of 1973 A federal law expanding the civil rights of people with handicaps (see HANDICAPPED), Section 504 of which applied to schools and laid the groundwork for the EDUCATION FOR ALL HANDICAPPED CHILDREN ACT OF 1975.

rehydration Restoration of the fluids and essential substances (ELECTROLYTES) normally dissolved in body fluids, to replace those lost during DEHYDRATION.

rejection In relation to a TRANSPLANT, the attacking of the donated organ or tissue by the body's IMMUNE SYSTEM; more widely, it may refer to instances where one or both parents fail to fully accept their roles as parents of a child, often leading to lack of BONDING and MATERNAL DEPRIVATION SYNDROME or FAILURE TO THRIVE.

reliability In relation to TESTS, the degree to which a particular test gives the same scores or readings consistently. For an INTELLIGENCE TEST, reliability would concern whether or not a student got approximately the same score on a different form of the test given at a different time (this is *test–retest reliability*) or whether conditions in the testing situation, variability in the tests, or change in the person giving the test (*interobserver reliability*) would produce widely varying results. For a MEDICAL TEST, reliability primarily concerns how often a test gives accurate results, as opposed to FALSE POSITIVES (suggesting a problem where none exists) or FALSE NEGATIVES (showing no problem when one does exist).

religious school Alternate term for a PRIVATE SCHOOL that is church-related.

REM Abbreviation for rapid eye movement, one of the two main stages of sleep, associated with dreaming (see SLEEPING DISORDERS).

remedial instruction Extra teaching, often tailored to individual needs, aimed at helping students make up deficiencies in knowledge or skills, especially those needed for developing more advanced skills. It is generally short-term additional instruction for students who are otherwise expected to be able to handle coursework in regular classes, as opposed to SPECIAL EDUCATION, which is for HANDICAPPED students who are expected to need longer-term help. Remedial instruction overlaps with COMPENSATORY EDUCATION, which attempts to make up deficiencies caused by a student's special circumstances, such as being socioeconomically disadvantaged.

remedial school A school, often UNGRADED, designed to help students make up for previous academic deficiencies, as for former DROPOUTS returning to school; also called *tutoring school* or *catch-up school*.

remission The lessening or disappearance of the SYMPTOMS and SIGNS of a disease considered chronic, such as PSORIASIS, or progressive, such as MULTIPLE SCLEROSIS. Remission is, of course, the aim of many kinds of therapy, such as the RADIATION therapy used to treat CANCER. But remissions also occur spontaneously and for unknown reasons, even in cancers, and they are even characteristic of some diseases, such as multiple sclerosis. If the remission lasts long enough (the length depending on medical experience with the disease), the disease is considered to be *cured*.

renal failure   Alternate term for kidney failure. (See KIDNEY AND UROLOGICAL DISORDERS.)

renal tubular acidosis   A kind of KIDNEY AND UROLOGICAL DISORDER.

repeat   In EDUCATION, to take again a course that a student has failed to complete satisfactorily, whether through inability to develop the required knowledge and skills, inattention to course work, or other reasons.

Report of Student Answers (ROSA)   A personalized scoring sheet for students, reporting scores for the student's responses on the SCHOLASTIC APTITUDE TEST.

reproductive cycle   Alternate term for MENSTRUAL CYCLE.

required course   A course a student must take to fulfill the requirements of a school and eventually to GRADUATE, as opposed to optional courses, or ELECTIVES.

rescue breathing   Alternate term for ARTIFICIAL RESPIRATION.

resection   The medical term for surgery in which something is removed; in a case of telescoping (INTUSSUSCEPTION), for example, a section of a child's bowel may be cut out to remove an obstruction.

residency requirement   In EDUCATION, a COLLEGE's or university's requirement that a student must be enrolled in the institution for a specified number of years (generally one or two) before being eligible to receive a DEGREE, a requirement waived in EXTERNAL DEGREE PROGRAMS. In a looser sense, the term *residency requirement* sometimes refers to a public college's or university's requirement that a student must have lived in the state for a specified period of time (often one year) to be eligible for the lower TUITION offered to state residents.

resident student   A student whose legal place of residence is in the district served by a school, such as the school district of a local PUBLIC SCHOOL or the state for a state-supported COLLEGE. *Nonresident students* must make special arrangements to attend a school that does not serve their neighborhood; at the college level, they are not eligible for the lower TUITION offered to state residents.

respirator   Alternate name for a VENTILATOR.

respiratory distress syndrome (RDS)   A kind of LUNG AND BREATHING DISORDER in which lungs' air sacs (*alveoli*) lack a substance called *surfactant*, which helps keep the sacs from collapsing after each breath. The disease is most often seen in PREMATURE babies, born after 28 weeks or less of PREGNANCY; it affects boys more severely than girls. There is also a higher risk of RDS if the child's mother has DIABETES MELLITUS, if the delivery was by CESAREAN SECTION, or if the mother was poor and had little or no PRENATAL CARE. It was RDS that killed President John F. Kennedy's two-day-old son in 1963. Among the signs of respiratory distress are rapid breathing (*tachypnea*), blueness (CYANOSIS), abnormally rapid heartbeat (*tachycardia*), grunting and straining of the chest and neck muscles with the effort of breathing, and sometimes lack of breathing altogether (*apnea*). Some other disorders, such as MENINGITIS or low blood sugar (HYPOGLYCEMIA), can present similar symptoms, but RDS is generally diagnosed by chest X-RAYS and BLOOD TESTS.

An RDS baby is often administered oxygen, as through a mask, hood, or tubes; may be given antibiotics and fluids intravenously (PARENTERAL NUTRITION); and is often placed on a VENTILATOR to assist breathing, often with electronic monitoring of pulse, respiration, and heartbeat. Many RDS babies improve over two or three days, but others do not respond to treatment or may develop a variety of related problems, some of which can be fatal, such as malformation of the lungs (*bronchopulmonary dysplasia, or* BPD) or air leak into the chest area around the lungs (PNEUMOTHORAX OR PNEUMOMEDIASTINUM). RDS survivors may also have other associated disorders, such as MENTAL RETARDATION, HYDROCEPHALUS, and sometimes EAR AND HEARING PROBLEMS and EYE AND VISION PROBLEMS. Pregnant women who are at risk for having an RDS baby may wish to consider PRENATAL TESTING, such as ULTRASOUND to assess the maturity of the fetus or AMNIOCENTESIS to check the level of surfactant, especially in cases of possible elective cesarean section, when a low level would suggest letting the fetus mature for longer. (For help and further information, see LUNG AND BREATHING DISORDERS.)

respiratory system   The system that takes oxygen from the air and passes it on to the bloodstream, subject to a variety of LUNG AND BREATHING DISORDERS.

respite care   Care of a person with handicaps, provided to allow the normal CAREGIVER time off to ease strain. As many more children with severe disabilities or illnesses live at home and attend regular schools, where once they might have lived in hospitals or other institutions, their families have had much increased responsibilities and considerable stress. To help relieve this stress, some public and private organizations have made arrangements to provide occasional respite care. (See HANDICAPPED and specific disorders.)

resuscitation   An attempt to restore heartbeat and breathing in a person who is apparently dead or at least has stopped breathing. (See ARTIFICIAL RESPIRATION for a description of procedures.)

retention   In EDUCATION, keeping a student in a GRADE for another school year (especially in ELEMENTARY SCHOOL) because of failure to develop the skills, learn the material, and meet the academic standards of the grade. Because parents, students, and school officials are all—for various reasons—unhappy with retention, many students receive automatic PROMOTION, regardless of their academic performance, which causes serious social problems when students are graduated without necessary skills, some of them being functionally illiterate (see ILLITERACY), sometimes because undiagnosed handicaps, such as LEARNING DISABILITIES or EAR AND HEARING PROBLEMS, prevented learning.

retinitis pigmentosa (RP)   A progressive disease in which the rods of the retina degenerate and become pigmented, causing progressive blindness. (See EYE AND VISION PROBLEMS.)

retinoblastoma A malignant TUMOR that often occurs in the eyes of very young children. (See EYE AND VISION PROBLEMS.)

retinodiencephalic degeneration Alternate name for LAURENCE-MOON-BIEDL SYNDROME.

retinol Alternate name for VITAMIN A.

retinopathy General disease or disorder of the retina in the eye. (See EYE AND VISION PROBLEMS.)

retrognathism A type of MALOCCLUSION in which the jaw and upper front teeth project too far forward.

retrolental fibroplasia A condition in which a mass of scar tissue forms in back of the lens of the eye. (See EYE AND VISION PROBLEMS.)

reversal (transposition) A common type of perceptual mistake involving confusion or shifting of letters and words, often because of RIGHT–LEFT DISORIENTATION or lack of SPATIAL ORIENTATION. Children with LEARNING DISABILITIES, for example, may mistake *tap* for *pat*, or *pat* for *bat*, and may transpose letters within a word, as in *fist* for *sift*.

Reye's syndrome A severe, sometimes fatal, disorder of unknown origin that causes swelling of the brain and accumulation of fats in the liver. It affects primarily children and teenagers, generally as they are recovering from a viral infection, such as influenza, CHICKEN POX (varicella), or EPSTEIN-BARR virus. Early signs, often about a week into a viral illness, include VOMITING, confusion, lethargy, and JAUNDICE, progressing in severe cases to COMA, SEIZURES, disruption of heart rhythm, and cessation of breathing. No specific treatment exists, and Reye's syndrome is a leading cause of DEATH among children beyond infancy, with survivors of serious cases often suffering brain damage. But intensive nursing care—involving steroid drugs to reduce brain swelling, blood TRANSFUSIONS and DIALYSIS to correct problems in body chemistry, and a VENTILATOR to aid breathing—has sharply lowered the MORTALITY RATE, in the most severe cases from 80 percent to well under 50 percent, and in milder cases, down to 10 to 20 percent. Because the disorder seems often to be triggered by aspirin, public health experts recommend acetaminophen instead of aspirin for children with illnesses that are or may be viral.

For help and further information

National Reye's Syndrome Foundation (NRSF)
426 North Lewis
Bryan, OH 43506
419-636-2679, toll-free hotline 800-233-7393
John Freudenberger, President
Organization of families of children who have had Reye's syndrome, health professionals, and others concerned. Gathers and disseminates information through information clearinghouse; operates hotline and counseling line; sponsors research; encourages formation of self-help, mutual-support groups; seeks to encourage government funding of research; publishes various materials, including bimonthly *Washington Reye's Line*, newsletter, and journal.

National Institute of Neurological Disorders and Stroke (NINDS), 301-496-5751. (For full group information, see BRAIN AND BRAIN DISORDERS.)

National Institute of Diabetes and Digestive and Kidney Diseases (NIDDK), 301-496-3583. (For full group information, see DIGESTIVE DISORDERS.)

American Liver Foundation (ALF), 201-857-2626; toll-free number (U.S. except NJ), 800-223-0179. (For full group information, see LIVER PROBLEMS.)

rheumatic fever A once very common childhood disease that causes inflammation in many of the body's tissues and joints and often causes permanent damage to the heart, sometimes apparent only later. It can also affect the NERVOUS SYSTEM, the result being SYDENHAM'S CHOREA, and in severe cases can cause DEATH. Rheumatic fever is associated with infection by *streptococcus* bacteria (as in STREP THROAT), which seems to trigger a kind of AUTOIMMUNE DISORDER in which ANTIBODIES to the strep mistakenly attack the body itself (see IMMUNE SYSTEM). Since the development of antibiotics, rheumatic fever has been far less common in developed countries, though it is still widespread elsewhere. But in the United States, rheumatic fever is on the increase again, possibly because a more virulent strain of strep bacteria has developed and perhaps because antibiotics have failed to work effectively. No IMMUNIZATION is available, nor do any specific tests exist to diagnose rheumatic fever. If a child has a sore throat or fever for more than a day or two, especially if the child has been exposed to strep, public health experts advise that the child be examined by a doctor for the presence of strep. Mild cases may pass in three to four weeks with little effect, but severe cases can last for two to three months, with long-term effects, and may recur. In cases of heart damage, surgery may later be needed.

For help and further information

Council on Cardiovascular Disease in the Young, American Heart Association National Center, 214-373-6300. Publishes *Your Child and Rheumatic Fever* and *Abnormalities of Heart Rhythm—A Guide for Parents.* (For full group information, see HEART AND HEART PROBLEMS.)

National Heart, Lung, and Blood Institute (NHLBI), 301-496-4236. (For full group information, see BLOOD AND BLOOD DISORDERS; HEART AND HEART PROBLEMS; LUNG AND BREATHING DISORDERS.)

National Institute of Allergy and Infectious Diseases (NIAID), 301-496-5717. (For full group information, see ALLERGY.)

National Institute of Child Health and Human Development (NICHD), 301-496-5133. (For full group information, see PREGNANCY.)

Rh incompatibility A mismatch between blood types, in which the blood of one person carries an Rh factor on the red blood cells (Rh-positive) and the other does not (Rh-negative). About 85 percent of the population is Rh-positive. Problems occur when the two types of blood are mixed because the incompatibility causes many of the red blood cells to self-destruct, a process called *hemolysis.* As a result, blood to be used for BLOOD TRANFUSIONS is carefully labeled by type and given only to people of a compatible type, generally being tested on a blood sample beforehand to make sure.

Special problems occur during PREGNANCY when a mother and a father have incompatible blood. If the mother's blood is Rh-negative and the baby's is Rh-positive (from the father), the first pregnancy is often untroubled by incompatability. But that first baby may sensitize the mother to Rh-positive blood, causing her to develop ANTIBODIES to it. Then in later pregnancies, these antibodies may attack and kill the FETUS of any Rh-positive baby, a condition called *erythroblastosis fetalis*. If the baby survives, it may be born with *hemolytic disease of the newborn,* in which large numbers of red blood cells are being destroyed, with resulting buildup of BILIRUBIN in the blood, which can lead to brain damage.

In recent decades, physicians have been able to reduce the incidence of sensitization by giving the mother injections of *immunoglobulin* (see IMMUNE SYSTEM) two or three days before DELIVERY and after MISCARRIAGE, ABORTION, AMNIOCENTESIS, or other such procedures in which fetal blood cells might come into direct contact with the mother's blood cells. If the mother already has been sensitized, the condition of the child is carefully monitored for signs of damage, such as high bilirubin levels. If GESTATION has proceeded far enough, LABOR may be induced to keep the baby from being too severely affected. But if the fetus is too PREMATURE for safe delivery, fetal blood transfusions may be required. After birth, the newborn is carefully monitored and may require special care to counteract the effects of the incompatibility; in severe cases, a BLOOD TRANSFUSION completely replacing the baby's blood (an *exchange transfusion*) may be required. Rh compatibility is routinely checked during PRENATAL CARE, so incidence of these problems has declined sharply.

For help and further information

National Heart, Lung, and Blood Institute (NHLBI), 301-496-4236. (For full group information, see BLOOD AND BLOOD DISORDERS.)

March of Dimes Birth Defects Foundation, 914-428-1700 (local chapters in telephone directory white pages). Publishes information sheet *Rh Disease.* (For full group information, see BIRTH DEFECTS.)

rhinoplasty   A surgical procedure to reconstruct or repair a nose that is deformed due to injury or disease, a kind of PLASTIC SURGERY, or to change its appearance, a kind of COSMETIC SURGERY.

rhythm method   A technique of NATURAL FAMILY PLANNING.

riboflavin   Alternate name for VITAMIN B$_2$.

rickets   A DEFICIENCY DISEASE, in which lack of sufficient CALCIUM and PHOSPHATE results in deformation of a growing child's bones, especially bowing of the legs, flattening of the soft skull and feet, and deformation of the spine, giving a "pot-belly" appearance; in adults the same deficiency is called *osteomalacia*. Often associated with rickets are other BONE DISORDERS, such as SCOLIOSIS and KYPHOSIS, a tendency to FRACTURES, and DEVELOPMENTAL DELAY, as in the MOTOR SKILLS of crawling and WALKING. Rickets is most often caused by lack of VITAMIN D, which is necessary for calcium to be transported to and made into bone, and is generally found among children in underdeveloped countries who have both an unbalanced diet and too little sunlight (a main nonfood source of vitamin D). But rickets can occur in other children as well. PREMATURE babies are vulnerable to the disease, as are children whose families have a restricted diet, such as a VEGETARIAN diet that has not adequately provided for vitamin D. Mothers who are BREASTFEEDING are often advised to give the baby a vitamin D supplement—as breast milk alone is an inadequate source of vitamin D—but only under a doctor's direction, since too much can result in excess calcium, or *hypercalcemia*. ACHONDROPLASIA, a mostly hereditary bone disorder, is sometimes called *fetal rickets*, but its origins are not the same.

For help and further information

National Institute of Diabetes and Digestive and Kidney Diseases (NIDDK), 301-496-3583. (For full group information, see DIGESTIVE DISORDERS.)

National Institute of Arthritis and Musculoskeletal and Skin Diseases (NIAMS), 301-496-8188. (For full group information, see ARTHRITIS; MUSCULAR DYSTROPHY.)

(See also VITAMINS; NUTRITION; BONE DISORDERS.)

right–left disorientation   The inability to consistently distinguish right from left, a perceptual confusion often found in children with LEARNING DISABILITIES, especially those in which DOMINANCE of hand, eye, and foot has not been clearly established. Right–left disorientation can cause great difficulty in READING and working with numbers.

right-handed   A type of HANDEDNESS in which a person relies more heavily on and is more easy and proficient at using the right hand than the left.

Rinne test   A tuning-fork test; a type of HEARING TEST for assessing the kind of hearing loss.

risk factors   Those characteristics or habits that increase the likelihood that a person will develop a certain disease or condition, as SMOKING is a risk factor for CANCER. In relation to PREGNANCY, a woman who has one or more risk factors is said to have a HIGH-RISK PREGNANCY, or to be AT RISK of developing complications. Similarly, a child from a family with a history of CHILD ABUSE AND NEGLECT may be termed *at risk* or a *high-risk child*.

Rocky Mountain spotted fever   An acute disease caused by infection with a bacteria-like microorganism, *Rickettsia rickettsii*, which is transmitted from small woodland animals to humans through the bites of ticks. Originally recognized in the Rocky Mountains (hence the name), it is now found in much of North America, especially along the East Coast. Symptoms generally appear three to twelve days after a bite by an infected tick, often including abrupt and severe fever, chills, headache, muscle pains, coughing, and (about four days after the early symptoms) a rash starting on the wrists, palms, ankles, soles, and forearms, then spreading elsewhere on the body. In more serious cases, complications such as ENCEPHALITIS and pneumonia may develop, in some cases leading to DELIRIUM, COMA, damage to the brain and heart, and DEATH. Before the discovery of antibiotics, one out of every five cases was fatal; the MORTALITY RATE is still 7 percent, though that is generally because treatment is not started quickly enough.

Parents can best protect themselves and their children by dressing in long clothing, with pant legs tucked into socks, in tick-infested areas, such as woods and meadows; by checking themselves on returning from such areas; by checking pets, which can carry ticks into the house; by learning how to properly deal with the type of ticks found in their area; by being aware of the symptoms; and by seeking treatment quickly if Rocky Mountain spotted fever is suspected.

For help and further information

National Institute of Allergy and Infectious Diseases (NIAID), 301-496-5717. (For full group information, see ALLERGY.)

Other reference source

Ticks and What You Can Do About Them, by Roger Drummond. Berkeley, CA: Wilderness, 1990.

Roe v. Wade   A key U.S. Supreme Court decision regarding ABORTION.

Romberg sign   Swaying of the patient when standing with feet together and eyes closed; a SIGN that generally indicates the existence of ATAXIA.

rooming-in   In HOSPITALS, the practice of allowing the MOTHER and newborn (and sometimes the FATHER as well) to stay in the same room, instead of placing the baby in a NURSERY; sometimes the baby remains in the room only during daytime hours, to give the mother more time to recover from the birth. This allows BREASTFEEDING to take place at any time and is valuable for the early BONDING of parent and child. Parents making choices about delivery may want to examine hospital options and rules in this area.

room parent   Alternate term for CLASS PARENT.

root-canal therapy   A dental procedure to clean out infected pulp from a tooth, fill it temporarily until the infection has been cleared up, and then fill the cavity, or root canal, with a neutral filling. The procedure can often save teeth that would otherwise have to be pulled. After root-canal therapy a tooth may turn grayish, but the tooth can be bleached by a DENTIST or covered by a CROWN. Root-canal therapy is often performed by general dentists, but those who specialize in the procedure are called ENDODONTISTS. (For help or further information, see TEETH.)

rooting reflex   The automatic response of a baby when the cheek is touched or stroked, as with a finger, to turn the head to that side and start sucking; a type of "primitive" REFLEX found only in babies and disappearing generally in three to four months but sometimes as late as 12 months. It is this type of reflex that allows the baby to find the nipple in BREASTFEEDING.

Rorschach Psychodiagnostic Test   One of the best-known types of PROJECTIVE TESTS, used with people aged three and up, in which the person is given a series of 10 inkblots, one at a time, and is asked to interpret them. The test is used in evaluations of personality, and the administrator scores the test according to an elaborate system. Variations on this classic inkblot test are also sometimes used. (For help and further information, see TESTS.)

ROSA   Abbreviation for REPORT OF STUDENT ANSWERS.

Rosenthal's syndrome   Alternate name for HEMOPHILIA C.

roseola infantum   An infectious, probably viral, disease common in young children, especially those under two years old, involving an abruptly arriving high FEVER, as high as 105°F, which lasts for four to five days and then drops back to normal, at which time a pink rash spreads over the body, especially the trunk, neck, and thighs, generally lasting from a few hours up to two days. Accompanying symptoms may be sore throat, swollen lymph nodes in the neck, and sometimes CONVULSIONS or SEIZURES. In the absence of a specific therapy, the main treatment is generally to bring the body temperature down, as by giving a sponge bath with lukewarm water or giving acetaminophen (not aspirin, because of its link to REYE'S SYNDROME).

Roswell Chall Auditory Blending Test   An individually administered TEST to assess ability to blend sounds heard orally into recognizable whole words, used with children in grades 2 to 6. Given when problems in AUDITORY SKILLS are suspected, the Roswell Chall test attempts to identify whether a child will have trouble with PHONICS when learning READING. (For help and further information, see TESTS.)

rote learning   Memorization of materials, with no guarantee that any understanding or linking with other knowledge is taking place. (See LEARNING STYLE.)

RP Abbreviation for retinitis pigmentosa. (See EYE AND VISION PROBLEMS.)

RR Abbreviation for RECOVERY ROOM.

rubber Popular name for a CONDOM.

rubella (German measles or **three-day measles)** A highly contagious disease caused by the rubella virus that is spread in droplets through coughing, sneezing, or just talking. Rubella generally causes only mild, temporary symptoms in young children, a low FEVER for a day or so and a rash on the face and neck for two or three days, along with slight discomfort. Teenagers may also get swollen glands in the back of the neck and experience temporary ARTHRITIS, or pain and stiffness in the joints.

However, rubella can cause devastating BIRTH DEFECTS in an unimmunized pregnant woman; perhaps one in four or five affected pregnant women have babies with deformities, while many others have MISCARRIAGES. The last big rubella epidemic in 1964 left some 20,000 babies with severe birth defects, including blindness and other EYE AND VISION PROBLEMS, deafness and other EAR AND HEARING PROBLEMS, abnormally small brains, and MENTAL RETARDATION. Since 1969 a rubella VACCINE has been in use, generally given in a combination MEASLES-MUMPS-RUBELLA VACCINE to infants at about 15 months old. Teenage and adult women who have never had rubella and have not been immunized should take the vaccine at least three months before considering pregnancy. And to prevent the further spread of rubella, so should any child or adult.

For help and further information

National Institute of Allergy and Infectious Diseases (NIAID), 301-496-5717. (For full group information, see ALLERGY.)

National Institute of Child Health and Human Development (NICHD), 301-496-5133. (For full group information, see PREGNANCY.)

(See MEASLES-MUMPS-RUBELLA VACCINE.)

rubella vaccine A type of VACCINE that is normally given in a combination MEASLES-MUMPS-RUBELLA VACCINE.

rubeola Alternate term for MEASLES, as opposed to RUBELLA (German measles).

rumination disorder of infancy A rare type of EATING DISORDER, usually affecting children under age one, that involves REGURGITATION of food from the stomach without the usual involuntary spasms or nausea, the main problem being FAILURE TO THRIVE and MALNUTRITION, leading to retarded growth and development.

rupture of the membranes In PREGNANCY, the breaking of the sac holding the AMNIOTIC FLUID that protects the baby, generally just before the onset of LABOR.

RURESA Abbreviation for Revised UNIFORM RECIPROCAL ENFORCEMENT OF SUPPORT ACT.

Sabin vaccine Alternate name for the ORAL POLIO VACCINE.

safe Popular nickname for a CONDOM.

safety The condition of being kept from harm. (See CHILDPROOFING; ENVIRONMENTAL HAZARDS; EXERCISE; LATCHKEY CHILD; see also SAFETY CHECKLIST: KEEPING BABY SAFE on page 504.)

Salk vaccine Alternate name for the INACTIVATED POLIO VACCINE.

salutatorian In a graduating class, the student with the second-highest academic rank, generally as measured by GRADE AVERAGE, so called because he or she is often asked to give the opening speech, or *salutation*, at GRADUATION ceremonies. The highest-ranked student is the VALEDICTORIAN.

Sandhoff's disease A disorder related to *Tay-Sachs disease*, a type of LIPID STORAGE DISEASE.

sarcoma General term for a kind of MALIGNANT TUMOR, or CANCER, in soft or connective tissues, bone, or muscles, including fibrous body organs, blood vessels, the lymph system, the *meninges* (membrane covering the brain), and cartilage, sometimes associated with RADIATION or BURN scars. Small sarcomas can be cut out and the area treated with radiation therapy, but large sarcomas in the limbs may require amputation. (For help and further information, see TUMOR; CANCER.)

SAT Abbreviation for SCHOLASTIC APTITUDE TEST.

saturated fatty acids A type of FAT mostly from animal sources.

savant syndrome (idiot savant)   Rare disorder in which a person has MENTAL RETARDATION or MENTAL DISORDERS (in centuries past lumped together as "idiocy") but has extraordinary ability in certain distinct areas, usually relating to memory feats or artistic ability. The combination gave the condition its earlier name *idiot savant*, French for "learned idiot." In a classic 1929 description, W.A. White in his *Outlines of Psychiatry* described the syndrome:

> These are rare cases, who, although idiots, still have some special faculty wonderfully developed. It may be music, calculation, memory for some certain variety of facts, etc.
>
> The calculators can name the answer to mathematical problems almost instantly; the musical prodigies often play well and even improvise; one of my cases could instantly name the day of the week for any date for years back.

For help and further information

Extraordinary People: Redefining the "Idiot Savant," by Darold A. Treffert. New York: Harper & Row, 1989.
(See also MENTAL DISORDERS; MENTAL RETARDATION.)

scan   In medicine, one of various techniques to give a picture of the body's internal organs. Some kinds of scans, such as a CT SCAN, ULTRASOUND, and MRI, are not INVASIVE, requiring no INJECTIONS or other intrusions to prepare the body for the test. Many other scans are invasive, requiring the injection of foreign materials into the body to show up on the screen, such as dyed fluid in an ANGIOGRAM or slightly radioactive material in NUCLEAR SCANS. (For help and further information, see MEDICAL TESTS.)

scanning   A rapid READING technique for finding a piece of information in a larger work, such as an index, telephone book, or catalog; a basic LOCATIONAL SKILL.

SCAN team   Abbreviation for Suspected CHILD ABUSE AND NEGLECT team.

scarlatina   Alternate name for SCARLET FEVER.

scarlet fever (scarlatina)   A disease caused by infection with the *streptococcus* bacteria, spread by droplets in the air; so-called because common symptoms include a reddish flush and rash, in addition to sore throat and high FEVER. Once a common and dangerous childhood disease, scarlet fever (like STREP THROAT) can still cause RHEUMATIC FEVER and other serious complications if not recognized and properly treated; but since the development of antibiotics it is relatively rare, and it is usually easily treatable if medication is started promptly.

For help and further information

National Institute of Allergy and Infectious Diseases (NIAID), 301-496-5717. (For full group information, see ALLERGY.)

SCAT   Abbreviation for SCHOOL AND COLLEGE ABILITY TESTS.

schizoid personality disorder   A type of PERSONALITY DISORDER.

schizophrenia   A group of MENTAL DISORDERS that have in common widespread disturbances in thinking, behavior, and emotional reactions, especially lack of relation between thoughts and feelings. It is this split that gives the disorder its popular name, *split personality* (a term also applied to MULTIPLE PERSONALITY DISORDER, where the split is quite different, being between two or more personalities). Often young people with schizophrenia are so disoriented as to be unable to function on a day-to-day basis and need to have SUPERVISION to be sure that the daily necessities of life are met and that they do not come to—or cause—harm.

Schizophrenia is a common form of mental illness that generally appears in ADOLESCENCE or early adulthood, thought to be triggered by the massive hormonal changes in that period. The causes of the various kinds of schizophrenic disorders are unclear. Some genetic component seems to be involved, since the disorder "runs in families," but other factors must play a part, because the disorder sometimes appears in one identical twin but not the other (see MULTIPLE BIRTH). Recent studies have shown that at least some forms of schizophrenia involve some actual physical changes in the brain, notably enlarged VENTRICLES, though how and why they occur is unknown.

Various drugs are used to treat schizophrenia; some of them have dangerous, even life-threatening side effects and must be used with great caution. Parents whose children have schizophrenia face a difficult period, as the disease may last for years, even decades. A substantial portion of young people with schizophrenia, however, recover to a great extent by their early 30s.

For help and further references

American Schizophrenia Association (ASA)
900 North Federal Highway, #330
Boca Raton, FL 33432
407-393-6167
Mary Roddy Haggerty, Executive Director
Organization of health professionals concerned with schizophrenia, seeing it as biochemical disorder, probably inherited. Supports research; seeks to educate public; encourages formation of local self-help groups, called Schizophrenics Anonymous (SA), for people diagnosed as schizophrenics, guided by volunteer professional.

National Institute of Mental Health (NIMH), 301-443-4536. Publishes *Schizophrenia: Questions and Answers*. (For full group information, see MENTAL DISORDERS.)

Other reference sources

Living and Working with Schizophrenia, revised edition, by J.J. Jeffries, E. Plummer, M.V. Seeman, and J.F. Thornton. Cheektowaga, NY: University of Toronto Press, 1990.
Encyclopedia of Schizophrenia, by Richard Noll. New York: Facts on File, 1990.

Surviving Schizophrenia: A Family Manual, by E. Fuller Torrey, M.D. New York: Harper & Row, 1988.

Family Care for Schizophrenia: A Problem-Solving Approach to Mental Illness, by R.H. Falloon, J.L. Boyd, and C.W. McGill. New York: Guilford, 1984.

Schizophrenia: The Epigenetic Puzzle, by I.I. Gotesman and J. Shields. Cambridge: Cambridge University Press, 1982.

(See also MENTAL DISORDERS.)

scholarship Excellence in academic studies; also, and more commonly today, a type of FINANCIAL AID given to a student for use in meeting the costs of attending a COLLEGE or PRIVATE SCHOOL. Scholarships may be awarded on the basis of scholastic excellence alone, or for other reasons, as with an ATHLETIC SCHOLARSHIP to an outstanding player or an award to a minority student by a college that wants a more balanced student body. The dollar amount of the scholarships may depend totally on merit, with the largest amount going to the one with the highest ranking, or on need, as indicated by a MEANS TEST. Scholarships are often contingent, remaining in effect only as long as the student continues to meet a preset standard, such as a B average in college. Some may be voided in other circumstances; for example, many types of federally subsidized financial aid will be suspended or terminated if a student is convicted of possessing or distributing drugs. An *open scholarship* is one for which anyone may apply, while a *closed scholarship* is restricted to certain kinds of applicants, such as those living in a certain state. Unlike loans, scholarships are a type of GRANT that does not have to be repaid. (For help and further information, see FINANCIAL AID.)

Scholastic Aptitude Test (SAT) A series of group-administered ADMISSIONS TESTS required of most HIGH SCHOOL seniors who are applying to COLLEGES and universities, prepared by the EDUCATIONAL TESTING SERVICE (ETS) for the COLLEGE ENTRANCE EXAMINATION BOARD. This precollege hurdle is a six-section, three-hour STANDARDIZED, OBJECTIVE TEST, offered at locations around the country on various dates, covering these main areas:

- *verbal,* in two test sections, with questions involving analogies, reading comprehension, antonyms, and sentence completions.
- *math,* also in two sections, with questions covering arithmetic, algebra, geometry, and quantitative comparisons.
- *Test of Standard Written English* (TSWE), with questions covering usage and sentence corrections, more specifically grammar, sentence structure, and word choice; this section is supposedly used only for class placement, but (contrary to stated intent) it is widely used in college admissions.
- *experimental,* questions being tried out by the ETS and a way of evaluating whether or not the SAT questions are at the same level of difficulty as in the past. This section is not scored, except for ETS internal use.

The verbal and math sections are scored separately, with the raw SCORE for each (the number of questions answered correctly) being converted to a figure on a scale ranging from 200 to 800, in jumps of 10; the scores are also shown as PERCENTILES. The TSWE is scored on a scale from 20 to 60+, and the top score is possible even if a few questions are missed. Several weeks after the test, scores are sent to the schools indicated by the student. Some modest changes in test format are being introduced during the early 1990s.

The related *Preliminary Scholastic Aptitude Test (PSAT)/National Merit Scholarship Qualifying Test (NMSQT)* is offered to high school juniors, originally to give juniors experience but since 1971 as a qualifying test for students hoping to get a National Merit Scholarship. The PSAT/NMSQT contains only two 50-minute sections, math and verbal, the questions often being taken from previous SATs, and the final converted scores range between 20 and 80. In addition, tests on specific subjects are offered, as are tests for college students applying to graduate school. Scores are sent to the schools and scholarship programs indicated.

Ideally, the SAT and similar tests are meant to provide colleges and universities a useful standard of comparison among students coming from widely different backgrounds and schools and graded on very different bases. On a very practical level, they also give students and their parents and counselors some gauge of where they stand among other students in the country, which can help in the process of deciding what colleges students should apply to.

The SAT and related tests have been widely criticized, however, on the basis of both RELIABILITY and VALIDITY. So have colleges and universities, for placing undue emphasis on SAT scores, especially when they are used as CUTOFF SCORES without reference to a student's wider abilities and accomplishments. Many people have also challenged the questions themselves and the ETS/College Board's choice as to the single "correct answer." In New York (and later elsewhere), the TRUTH IN TESTING law forced the College Board to make available to students their answers and a copy of the questions and officially correct answers. Responding still further, the College Board now provides a *Report of Student Answers* (ROSA), personalized scoring sheets informing students of how points for their scores were calculated, and a *Summary of Answers for the PSAT/NMSQT,* giving high school officials a question-by-question analysis of how their students answered questions and how those responses compare to other students around the country.

Despite criticism, such tests are a fact of life, and parents who want to help their children will at least want to get books of sample tests (available from the College Board) and one or more "review" or "strategies" books and possibly consider a review course. Special arrangements can be made for HANDICAPPED children, such as those with LEARNING DISABILITIES, EAR AND HEARING PROBLEMS, and EYE AND VISION PROBLEMS.

For help and further information

The College Board, 212-713-8000. (For full group information, see COLLEGE ENTRANCE EXAMINATION BOARD.)

Other reference sources

Standing Up to the SAT, by John Weiss (president, FAIRTEST/National Center for Fair and Open Testing) and Barbara Beckwith. New York: Prentice Hall/Arco, 1989.

The Case Against the S.A.T., by James Crouse and Dale Trusheim. Chicago: University of Chicago Press, 1988.

None of the Above: Behind the Myth of Scholastic Aptitude, by David Owen. Boston: Houghton Mifflin, 1985.

How to Beat Test Anxiety and Score Higher on the SAT and All Other Exams, by James H. Divine. Hauppauge, NY: Barron's, 1982.

10 SATs: Plus Advice from the College Board on How to Prepare for Them, by The College Board. New York: College Board, 1990.

(See also TESTS.)

school An institution for EDUCATION, including (for students of different ages) PRESCHOOL, ELEMENTARY SCHOOL, MIDDLE SCHOOL, HIGH SCHOOL, and COLLEGE or university.

School and College Ability Tests (SCAT) A set of group-administered TESTS that attempt to measure basic verbal and mathematical abilities for children from grades 3 to 12. The pen-and-pencil test uses analogies in the verbal portion of the test and, in the quantitative part, comparisons demonstrating grasp of basic number skills. Scored by the test administrator or computer, the test yields SCORES for the subtests and an overall score, which can be converted in various ways, including PERCENTILES and STANINES. (For help and further information, see TESTS.)

school of choice Any school other than the neighborhood public school, but generally funded by the public school system, to which parents might send their child. Sometimes the term refers to a wide range of institutions, such as MAGNET SCHOOLS, ALTERNATIVE SCHOOLS, and church-affiliated or other PRIVATE SCHOOLS, including schools for children with SPECIAL NEEDS. Other times it may simply refer to a public school in a different district, to which parents choose to send their children, perhaps one with a more attractive CURRICULUM, focus, or approach. The Department of Education recommends that parents be able to exercise choice in schooling for their children; their CHOOSING A SCHOOL FOR YOUR CHILD excerpt on page 514 includes a checklist for evaluating schools.

Among the advantages cited for school choice are that it:

- offers diversity to suit a wide range of children (not just those from high-income families).
- decentralizes education and gives more power to parents and teachers.

- strengthens schools by fostering competition between them for students and making them accountable to the people they serve.
- will force the closure of poor schools unable to attract students.
- allows parents to have their children in schools near their place of work.

Critics argue that:

- the benefits of choice will accrue only to those families motivated (and probably educated) enough to learn about the options available and select the one best for them.
- the poorest, most disadvantaged children will be left in the least popular, least effective schools.
- the program breaks up the security and convenience of a neighborhood school.
- the money might better be spent on more meaningful reforms.

Over the last few decades, many parents have chosen private schools as a way of maintaining segregation in education. But in recent years, choice among public schools has been increasingly used as a tool for voluntary DESEGREGATION. Indeed, several states experimenting with school choice have by law barred programs that would tend toward segregation; such plans are sometimes called *controlled choice* because they have certain kinds of brakes built in. In Cambridge, Massachusetts, for example, before enrolling their children in school, parents visit a volunteer-staffed information center to find out about the kinds of programs and approaches offered in each of 13 schools. Parents then make first, second, and third choices; the final assignment of schools is made by the district administrators, keeping racial and ethnic balance in mind, but most families get into one of their first three choices.

Early indications are that student achievement levels are higher in school-choice programs, especially when inner-city students go to magnet schools; but the long-term effects, especially on students in the "last-choice" schools, are yet to be decided. (For help and further information, see IF YOUR SCHOOL DISTRICT IS CONSIDERING SCHOOLS OF CHOICE, on page 414; see also CHAPTER 1; PRIVATE SCHOOL; ELEMENTARY SCHOOL; HIGH SCHOOL; and EDUCATION.)

school phobia A general term for the occasional reluctance or refusal of a child to attend school, accompanied often by ANXIETY, nausea, abdominal pain, or headache; also called *school refusal syndrome*. A child may also express resistance by electing to be MUTE. Not really a PHOBIA, in many cases school phobia may simply be a form of SEPARATION ANXIETY and unwillingness to leave home and parents, though in severe cases it may result in SEPARATION ANXIETY DISORDER. But it may also reflect academic or social problems that the child does not want to face. Parents will want to explore carefully the origins of the resistance and help the child deal with whatever problems exist, while seeing that the child returns to school quickly.

If Your School District Is Considering Schools of Choice

The National Coalition of Chapter 1/Title I Parents recommends that, if their school district is considering a school choice plan, parents ask these questions:

- Is free transportation provided?
- In the final school assignment process, do all students have equal chance to be placed in their first choice school, regardless of their previous academic or behavioral record?
- Is the enrollment process simple and are there arrangements to explain them adequately to all parents? More specifically, is there a parent information center in the neighborhood staffed by multilingual counselors?
- Are there enough classroom places for all students who want to exercise choice?
- Do neighborhood schools have the same funding and facilities as magnet schools and other schools with special programs?
- Are parents consulted and their preferences considered in designing school programs?

For help and further information

Coping with Academic Anxiety, by Allen J. Ottens. New York: Rosen, 1984.
(See also EDUCATION.)

school records   Alternate term for STUDENT RECORDS, as covered under the FAMILY EDUCATIONAL RIGHTS AND PRIVACY ACT OF 1976.

Schwannoma   Alternate name for ACOUSTIC NEUROMA.

SCID   Abbreviation for severe combined immunodeficiency disease, in which a child is born lacking all or most defenses of the IMMUNE SYSTEM.

Science Research Associates   Full name of the publisher of the SRA ACHIEVEMENT SERIES.

scoliosis   Abnormal sideways curvature of the spine, in excessive cases becoming almost S-shaped, a type of spinal disorder commonly associated with LORDOSIS or KYPHOSIS (see SPINE AND SPINAL DISORDERS). Scoliosis often appears in childhood or ADOLESCENCE; in infancy it is seen in more boys than girls, but by school age it appears in both sexes. It becomes increasingly obvious as growth occurs, both to the eye and on X-RAYS, and if untreated, it may progress to severe and painful deformity. The malformation can result from unequal leg length, which causes tilting of the body, from TUMORS or injuries, or from diseases such as POLIOMYELITIS, but it is often a GENETIC DISORDER. If detected early, scoliosis can be treated simply by exercises or

ORTHOPEDIC DEVICES, such as shoe lifts to even the leg lengths. But serious and worsening cases may require the use of braces, casts, or surgery, in which bone grafts are used to help force and fuse the spinal vertebrae into a straight line. Children should be checked for scoliosis from early childhood, and if it is detected, the degree of curvature should be checked annually to see that measures being taken are keeping the condition from worsening.

For help and further information
Scoliosis Association (SA)
P.O. Box 51353
Raleigh, NC 27609
919-846-2639
Barbara M. Shulman, President
Organization of people with scoliosis, their families, and concerned others; affiliated with International Federation of Scoliosis Associations. Aims to educate public; encourages screening programs in school; sponsors formation of local mutual-support self-help groups; maintains film library; publishes various materials, including quarterly newsletter *Backtalk, Scoliosis Fact Sheet*, audiovisuals *Scoliosis Screening for Early Detection* and *Watch That Curve*, and bibliography.

National Scoliosis Foundation (NSF)
93 Concord Avenue
P.O. Box 547
Belmont, MA 02178
617-489-0880
Laura B. Gowen, President
Organization of individuals and organizations encouraging screening programs for scoliosis, kyphosis, and lordosis. Seeks to educate public and influence legislation; aids local groups in setting up volunteer screening programs; publishes various print and audiovisual materials, including a semiannual newsletter, *The Spinal Connection*, educational booklets such as *Her Brace Is No Handicap*, brochures such as *In 30 Seconds You Can Change the Shape of Your Child's Life* and *One in Every 10 Persons Has Scoliosis*, and resource lists.

Scoliosis Research Society (SRSO)
222 South Prospect
Park Ridge, IL 60068
312-690-1628
Carole Murphy, Executive Director
Organization of orthopedic surgeons and physicians concerned with spinal deformities, especially scoliosis. Fosters research.

National Institute of Arthritis and Musculoskeletal and Skin Diseases (NIAMS), 301-496-8188. (For full group information, see ARTHRITIS; MUSCULAR DYSTROPHY.)

(See also SPINE AND SPINAL DISORDERS; also HELP FOR SPECIAL CHILDREN on page 578.)

score   In educational testing, a grade or mark indicating the number of correct answers or the number of points awarded for acceptable work. On many OBJECTIVE TESTS, especially STANDARDIZED TESTS, the *raw score* is the actual number of correct answers. Often, however, this is converted into a different kind of score for reporting purposes, such as a PERCENTILE, GRADE-EQUIVALENT, or AGE-EQUIVALENT (EDUCATIONAL AGE). These *converted scores* (sometimes called *scaled scores*) attempt to put the raw score into comparative perspective with large numbers of other students who have taken the test. In the case of ADMISSIONS TESTS, students are sometimes required to score above a certain point, called a CUTOFF SCORE. Scores derived from the results of two or more tests are called *composite scores*.

screening tests Tests given to see if someone has certain characteristics, especially problems. Among the common types are GENETIC SCREENING tests, seeking to identify possible BIRTH DEFECTS or health problems before or during PREGNANCY; NEONATAL SCREENING TESTS, which try to identify medical problems so that they can be treated before doing harm to the developing infant; and DEVELOPMENTAL SCREENING TESTS, used in PRESCHOOL and early school years to identify problems that may adversely affect learning. (For help and further information, see MEDICAL TESTS; TESTS; and the specific types of tests above.)

scrotum The protective sac in which the TESTES are suspended.

scurvy A DEFICIENCY DISEASE caused by lack of VITAMIN C.

SEA Abbreviation for state educational agency, the organization to which federal monies are sent under CHAPTER 1.

sealed records Documents kept confidential by the court, not available for open inspection. In cases of traditional ADOPTION, records are generally open only to the court and the adoption agency, though some laws and other forms of adoption have allowed the records to be somewhat more accessible, such as to the adopted child (on reaching adulthood). Records from JUVENILE COURT also are not made public, being restricted if not actually sealed and sometimes later expunged (see EXPUNGED RECORDS).

seal limbs Alternate term for PHOCOMELIA.

secondary amenorrhea A disorder associated with MENSTRUATION.

secondary-care hospital (Level II) An intermediate-care medical facility offering more sophisticated equipment and laboratories and often more specialized staff than in a community HOSPITAL but less than in a *tertiary-care* (Level III) facility, such as a UNIVERSITY-AFFILIATED FACILITY (UAF). (See HOSPITALS.)

secondary school Alternate term for HIGH SCHOOL.

Secondary School Admission Tests (SSAT) An ADMISSIONS TEST for children in grades 5 to 10, widely used by selective PRIVATE SCHOOLS in deciding whether or not to admit students. Existing in two forms (grades 5 to 7 and 8 to 10), the tests are paper-and-pencil multiple-choice examinations focusing on verbal and mathematical abilities and READING comprehension. Tests are scored by hand or by computer, and the subtest and overall SCORES are compared with NORMS for the student's grade level, then converted in various ways, including into PERCENTILES. Reports of the scores and a booklet on interpreting them

are provided by the publisher, the EDUCATIONAL TESTING SERVICE, which also provides a booklet called *Preparing for the SSAT* for students studying ahead of time. Special testing arrangements can be made for students with physical or visual handicaps (see HANDICAPPED). (For help and further information, see TESTS.)

secondary sex characteristics The external signs of sexual maturity, physical changes that take place in a boy and girl during PUBERTY in response to various HORMONES, such as ESTROGEN in females and TESTOSTERONE in males. Secondary sex characteristics include the growth and development of the PENIS and TESTES in boys and the BREASTS and *labia* (lips of the VULVA) in girls and, in both, the growth of hair in the distribution pattern normal to adults, such as in the pubic area, under the arms, and, in boys, on the face.

secondary tumor A kind of TUMOR started by MALIGNANT cells originating elsewhere in the body, as opposed to a *primary tumor* that originated at the site where found.

Section 504 A portion of the Civil Rights Act for Handicapped Persons, more formally Section 504 of the Rehabilitation Act of 1973, which bars any organization or institution receiving federal funds from discriminating in any way against qualified people with disabilities at the risk of losing those funds. This expansion of the civil rights of people with handicaps applied also to schools and laid the groundwork for the EDUCATION FOR ALL HANDICAPPED CHILDREN ACT OF 1975, which guaranteed public educational services for children with handicaps (see HANDICAPPED).

secular humanism A philosophy that is seen as focusing on the good of humanity over religious belief; used as a pejorative term by many fundamentalist Christians, who see PUBLIC SCHOOLS as teaching secular humanism. As a result, many have founded or placed their children in PRIVATE SCHOOLS with a strongly Christian orientation.

segregation In general, separation of people into groups on the basis of certain characteristics, such as White from Black, male from female, or HANDICAPPED from nonhandicapped. In the past much segregation was generally open, deliberate, and formal, written into law and so called *de jure* (by law). In the schools such legislated segregation was struck down by the landmark Supreme Court case *Brown v. Board of Education* in 1954; subsequent federal civil rights legislation outlawed other kinds of formal discrimination, including some relating to the handicapped and to women. Separation continued, however, as a result of informal social pressures; the result was *de facto* (in fact) segregation, which has similarly been attacked by the courts. One court-mandated approach to segregation in schools has been the controversial BUSING, but more recently many school districts have tried to establish voluntary DESEGREGATION programs, such as those involving SCHOOLS OF CHOICE and MAGNET SCHOOLS. (For help and further information, see DESEGREGATION; SCHOOLS OF CHOICE.)

seizure A sudden period of involuntary, uncontrolled electrical activity in the brain, often accompanied by violent muscular contractions called CONVULSIONS. Most widely known are the wide range of recurrent seizures that result from long-term conditions; these generally fall under the umbrella name of EPILEPSY. (For help and further information about the main types of epileptic seizures, and what to do if a child has one, see EPILEPSY.)

Seizures can also be caused by short-term conditions, such as a reaction to a particular medication or an abrupt high FEVER in a young child. Many children have a seizure at some time in their lives, as from infections such as MENINGITIS or OTITIS MEDIA. The child may lose consciousness and twitch for a few minutes, during which time dangerous objects should be cleared away from the vicinity. To prevent recurrence, parents should attempt to reduce the child's body temperature (see FEVER).

In the past some children who had experienced febrile (fever) seizures were given antiseizure medications to help prevent the development of recurring seizures, or epilepsy. But in the 1980s the National Institutes of Health recommended that such preventive (*prophylactic*) treatment was not necessary unless there was a history of epilepsy in the family, signs of impairment of the NERVOUS SYSTEM, or some special complications in the nature of seizures that might suggest other problems.

selective admissions   A somewhat restricted policy toward ADMISSION to a school.

self-fulfilling prophecy   An event or result caused at least partly by one's belief that it will occur; in relation to children, often meaning that they tend to live up to the expectations that others, especially adults in authority, have of them; sometimes called the PYGMALION EFFECT. In EDUCATION, researchers have clearly established that a teacher's expectations of a child's talents influence how well the child will perform in class; in experiments where children chosen at random were labeled LATE BLOOMERS and their names given to their teachers, those children showed marked improvement.

self-help skills (self-care skills)   Skills that allow a person to take care of his or her own needs, such as feeding, bathing or hygiene, dressing, grooming, and going to the toilet, skills that children learn gradually as they develop independence. In the first year, for example, infants generally learn to eat crackers by themselves, hold a cup with two hands and drink from it with help, and hold out their arms and legs when being dressed; in the next year they usually progress to using a spoon, holding a cup with one hand and drinking from it without help, chewing food, and removing their outer clothes. The CHART OF NORMAL DEVELOPMENT (on page 507) indicates when between birth and age six children first, *on the average*, begin to exhibit the main self-help skills. In TEACHING YOUNG CHILDREN: GUIDELINES AND ACTIVITIES (on page 544), parents will find activities designed to develop children's skills in various areas, including self-help. Children with MENTAL RETARDATION and some other DEVELOPMENTAL DISORDERS will develop self-help skills at a slower pace. Some children with mental retardation, chronic illness, MENTAL DISORDERS, or severe physical handicaps may never be able to care for themselves without some help. Medical and social agencies are assigned to reevaluate their skills periodically through ADOLESCENCE and (if necessary) through adulthood, their aim being to provide therapy and rehabilitation

as seems appropriate to help such people maximize their independent self-help skills. An individual will often function independently in one skill but not another; self-care skills are sometimes graded from zero (for fully independent functioning) to 4 (for complete dependence). For example, someone might need help to get to the toilet and remove and then replace the necessary clothes but might be able to feed him- or herself food brought in on a tray. For people with severe medical problems, self-help skills include the ability to carry out various necessary procedures, such as giving an INSULIN injection or inserting a CATHETER for CLEAN, INTERMITTENT CATHETERIZATION. (For help and further information, see HANDICAPPED; see also HELP FOR SPECIAL CHILDREN on page 578.)

self-mutilation syndrome   A pattern of behavior that involves willful infliction of pain or injury to one's own body but not necessarily intending to commit SUICIDE (though that may result); also known by several other names, including *autoaggression, deliberate self-harm syndrome, symbolic wounding*, and *attempted suicide*. Self-mutilation takes a wide variety of forms, including wrist-cutting, amputation (as of ear or tongue), mutilating GENITALS (including castration or insertion of foreign objects), biting (as of lips or fingers), pulling out hair, gouging out one's eyes, burning, banging one's head against a wall, swallowing harmful substances or objects, and jumping from heights. The syndrome generally begins in late ADOLESCENCE and is associated with BORDERLINE PERSONALITY DISORDER or SCHIZOPHRENIA. Self-mutilation also occurs as part of LESCH-NYHAN SYNDROME, in which a child compulsively bites away his or her lips and fingers.

For help and further information
National Institute of Mental Health (NIMH), 301-443-4515. (For full group information, see MENTAL DISORDERS.)

self-test   In medicine, an alternate term for HOME MEDICAL TEST.

semen   The fluid emitted from the PENIS during EJACULATION at the point of ORGASM. The semen is made up of SPERM (manufactured by the TESTES, matured and stored in the EPIDIDYMIS, and transported via the VAS DEFERENS), fluids from the PROSTATE GLAND, and secretions from the SEMINAL VESICLES.

semen analysis   A common test performed in evaluating INFERTILITY problems.

semester   Originally a period of six months, but in EDUCATION today, two equal periods that often make up the school year, each far short of six months; common alternatives are TRIMESTERS (three equal periods) or QUARTERS (four equal periods).

seminal vesicles   A pair of small structures in males, situated behind the bladder, that form the fluid that makes up most of the SEMEN; this fluid mixes in the EJACULATORY DUCT with SPERM manufactured in the TESTES and fluids from the PROSTATE GLAND.

Stimulating Baby Senses

Your baby, from the moment of birth, is getting in touch with the world. Using her five senses—touch, taste, smell, sight, and hearing—she will begin to learn about her surroundings. Your baby will get her earliest impressions of life from you—from the way you respond to her, the way you look at her, hold her, and talk to her. You are your baby's first important teacher—and student.

You and your baby start to teach and learn from each other and begin to build your special relationship by *stimulating* each other's senses. Here's how it works. When your baby cries, she is telling you that she needs something—food, a diaper change, a burp, or a caress. By trial and error—by offering her various comforts and watching her responses—you soon *learn* what her cries mean. In other words, her cries, facial expressions, and body movements have *stimulated* your ears, eyes, and other senses, and, through this sensory stimulation, you have *learned* something about your baby.

When you respond to your baby—by picking her up, talking to her, or feeding her—you are *stimulating* the growth and development of her sensory organs and the brain structures that make them work. Just as important, you are *teaching* her that someone cares, that the world can be a rewarding place, and that she has some control over the world.

Thus, through the everyday care of your child, you and she are stimulating each other's senses and responding to that stimulation. In so doing, you are learning from each other and are on the way to developing a satisfying relationship—a ''mutual admiration society.'' You are building a solid base of confidence and trust with your child by meeting her needs—a process involving sensory stimulation and appropriate response.

Different Strokes for Different Folks

Each parent and each child has differing needs for contact with people, for the sound of a voice or music, or for things to see and touch. In other words, each needs differing amounts of sensory stimulation. It's important to be aware of both your own and your baby's needs. Some babies are extremely sensitive and cannot take too much stimulation; others seem to need and enjoy more. The same is true of parents. The amount of stimulation that can be tolerated varies from time to time.

For example, you may enjoy company more than your neighbor does. But there may be times when you do not want company at all. You will probably respond differently depending on your needs and mood. So will your baby. She will let you know if she needs or wants company. If she's happy with the attention she is getting, she will respond with coos, gurgles, waving her arms and legs, and, when she is old enough, smiles and laughter.

If your baby's need for stimulation is less than your own, she may not want to be handled, talked to, or have quite as much attention as you would like to give her. She may turn her head or body away from you as if trying to escape, or she may become fussy or just fall asleep as a way of ''tuning out.'' Don't feel hurt or think that you are failing her. It's just her way of letting you know that she has her own individual needs and moods. In fact, she may need you to protect her from well-meaning friends and relatives who are giving her more attention than she wants. When you see her ''escape'' signals, remove her as gracefully as possible from their presence and give her the quiet time she needs.

Continued on page 419

seminiferous tubules   Structures within the TESTES where the SPERM are produced.

semivegetarian   A type of VEGETARIAN diet that excludes red meat but allows some poultry and fish.

sensorineural losses   The type of EAR AND HEARING PROBLEM that involves a malfunction or disorder in the inner ear or the nerves that carry sound to the brain. Sensorineural losses are permanent and more severe than CONDUCTIVE LOSSES; at the present stage of medical knowledge, they cannot be cured or even reduced by a doctor's treatment, but any children with sensorineural losses can be helped greatly by a HEARING AID.

sensory education   In the MONTESSORI METHOD, use of materials designed to enhance a child's use of the various SENSORY MODES or MODALITIES for learning.

sensory modes (modalities)   Any of the five avenues by which someone receives information: seeing (visual), hearing (*auditory*), touching (*tactile*), smelling (*olfactory*), and tasting (*gustatory*), plus the sense of the body's motion (*kinesthetic*, sometimes called *haptic*). According to Piaget's theory, the first stage of a child's COGNITIVE DEVELOPMENT is the *sensory-motor* (or *sensorimotor*) *stage*, during which children gain an awareness of their sense perceptions and use this knowledge in developing MOTOR SKILLS.

Parents, other family members, and caregivers can help children learn about themselves and the world from infancy by exploring the senses (see STIMULATING BABY SENSES, above). Babies who have, for whatever reasons, had too little stimulation of the senses may develop a syndrome called FAILURE TO THRIVE, involving physical and MENTAL RETARDATION. When the sense organs are functioning normally, but the person is unable to interpret the information received, that person is said to have a PERCEPTUAL HANDICAP, a common problem among children with LEARNING DISABILITIES or other DEVELOPMENTAL DISORDERS.

Then, of course, the reverse could be true. Your baby may want more attention and stimulation than you find easy to give. Your baby does need your attention and your encouragement of her efforts to communicate, but she doesn't need it all the time. Other family members and friends, including older children, can talk to, smile at, play with, and rock her on occasion.

It is only in the extreme cases where the lack of stimulation or parental response causes problems for a baby. If, for some reason, a baby doesn't get enough attention, she may show signs of discouragement or depression and she may give up trying to get a response. She may stop smiling, cooing, and waving her arms and legs. When a baby is rarely handled, looked at, or talked to, her development may become retarded. But that is only in extreme cases.

The important thing for you to remember is that you and your baby are unique human beings, each with individual and varying needs for attention and sensory stimulation. Although you try to be aware of your baby's and your own needs—and try to meet them—sometimes you fail. It's impossible for you to know *everything*, and you can't possibly handle *every* situation perfectly. So don't worry about it. If you feel so depressed, tired, or uncomfortable with your baby that you generally avoid holding, talking to, or looking at her, then it is best to seek help from your doctor. You may not be getting the kinds of attention *you* need.

It's Easy

Stimulating your baby is just a natural part of caring for her. It doesn't take great investments of time and effort, and it can be fun for both of you. When you relax and enjoy yourself, your baby will tend to do the same.

Sometimes new parents find it hard to relax because they are so worried about how to handle their infants. Some men, in particular, think they are too clumsy to care for tiny newborns and put off close physical contact until their children are old enough for rough-and-tumble play. As a result, these dads miss a great deal of pleasure, not to mention opportunities for building a close relationship with their children.

Infants do need gentle handling, but they are not china dolls. They enjoy the security of being held in firm, strong hands. Aside from breastfeeding, there is nothing that a mother can do that a father can't. More and more, men are realizing what fathers have been missing, and they are getting into the act by participating in childbirth classes, the actual birth, and the care and feeding of their infants.

Don't worry about spoiling your infant by picking her up or paying too much attention to her. Not that you should walk around with her in your arms all day, but take advantage of her wakeful times and her feedings to build your relationship with her. Look at your baby and give her ample opportunity to look at you. She needs to see the love and pride in your eyes. Talk and sing to her. She loves the soothing sound of your voice and the fun of hearing you respond to her efforts to communicate. And hold her. She needs your firm and tender touch. By stimulating your baby and by responding to her needs, you are getting her off to a good start and probably making life easier for yourself in the future.

Source: *Stimulating Baby Senses*, by Marilyn Sargent, in consultation with National Institute of Mental Health scientists. Washington, DC: Government Printing Office, 1978. Part of the Caring About Kids series, which alternates use of *him* and *her* in its pamphlets; this material uses *she* and *her*, but the material applies to both sexes. For more from this pamphlet, see BOTTLEFEEDING, COMMUNICATION SKILLS AND DISORDERS, MOTOR SKILLS, and VISUAL SKILLS.

For help and further information

Touch, Taste and Smell, revised edition, by Steve Parker. New York: Watts, 1989. For grades 4 to 7.

sensory-motor (sensorimotor) The first stage of children's learning, according to Piaget's theory of COGNITIVE DEVELOPMENT.

SEOG Abbreviation for SUPPLEMENTAL EDUCATIONAL OPPORTUNITY GRANT.

separation anxiety Fear of being divided from home and mother—or whoever is the primary CAREGIVER who bonded with the infant. Whether the threat is real or imagined, separation anxiety is normal among young children, with their cries often causing great anguish to parents. For most, the crying is a means of communication, saying "Don't go!" In many CHILD-CARE situations, however, such cries often dry up once the parent has gone. To ease the process, PSYCHOLOGISTS recommend that parents prepare children beforehand for transitions, familiarizing the child with the place and people with whom he or she will be staying; equally important is to give the child a good dose of one-to-one personal attention on return. Separation anxiety may also be linked to SCHOOL PHOBIA. In some children, ANXIETY grows so great as to constitute SEPARATION ANXIETY DISORDER.

For help and further information

Day-Care Teddy Bear, by True Kelly. New York: Random, 1990.
Mommy's Coming Back, by Madeleine Yates. Nashville, TN: Abingdon, 1988.
Leaving Home, by Arlene Kramer Richards and Irene Willis. New York: Atheneum, 1980. On separation anxiety in children.
(See also BONDING; SEPARATION-INDIVIDUATION.)

separation anxiety disorder A type of MENTAL DISORDER in children or adolescents in which normal SEPARATION ANXIETY becomes elevated to a level of panic (see PANIC ATTACK), so that children fear to leave the house or other familiar areas and even at home often cling persistently to family members to avoid being alone, especially at bedtime. NIGHTMARES and physical and emotional signs of distress are common, as is associated SCHOOL PHOBIA. (For help and further information, see MENTAL DISORDER.)

separation-individuation   The stage during which a child begins to recognize the self as distinct from the MOTHER (or other primary CAREGIVER), after the SYMBIOTIC STAGE, in which the child sees mother and self as one (as in early BONDING). Separation-individuation, once considered to begin around 18 months, when the child usually begins to walk, is now thought to start as early as seven months. Many psychologists believe that it progresses through four phases:

- *differentiation*, or beginning of recognition of separateness of mother and child;
- *practicing*, in which the baby is somewhat oblivious to the mother;
- *rapprochement*, in which the baby once again approaches the mother actively;
- *separation-individuation*, in which the baby becomes fully aware of his or her discrete individuality and identity.

Many psychologists believe that some MENTAL DISORDERS that spring from early childhood, such as IDENTITY DISORDER, SEPARATION ANXIETY DISORDER, PERSONALITY DISORDERS, and borderline PSYCHOSIS, are related to failure of the child to complete satisfactorily the separation-individuation process. (For help and further information, see MENTAL DISORDERS.)

septicemia   A kind of blood poisoning. (See BLOOD AND BLOOD DISORDERS.)

sequential learning   A LEARNING STYLE in which materials are carefully structured so that ever-more-complex tasks build on earlier work.

SESAT   Abbreviation for Stanford Early School Achievement Tests. (See STANFORD ACHIEVEMENT TESTS.)

Seven Sisters   The formerly all-female equivalent of the IVY LEAGUE: Barnard, Bryn Mawr, Mt. Holyoke, Radcliffe, Smith, Vassar, and Wellesley.

severe combined immunodeficiency disease (SCID)   A condition in which a child is born lacking all or most defenses of the IMMUNE SYSTEM.

sex chromosomes   The pair of CHROMOSOMES that determines the sex of an individual, normally with two X chromosomes for a female and an X and a Y chromosome for a male. Traits or disorders associated with genes carried on the X chromosome are called X-LINKED, sex-linked, or sex-limited; among them are COLOR BLINDNESS, HEMOPHILIA, MUSCULAR DYSTROPHY (Duchenne type), and G6PD DEFICIENCY. The smaller Y chromosome carries little genetic information beyond that directly related to male sexual development. Among the CHROMOSOMAL ABNORMALITIES linked with the sex chromosomes are TURNER'S SYNDROME,

KLINEFELTER'S SYNDROME, and FRAGILE X SYNDROME. (For help and further information, see X-LINKED; GENETIC DISORDERS.)

sex education   Teaching children about their own sexuality, its joys and hazards and its place in human life. Traditionally children picked up information about sexuality in bits and pieces, not in any formal way, and only in the rarest circumstances from their parents or any knowledgeable person; in fact, as often as not, what they got was misinformation. In many families and communities, this state of affairs still exists. But the events of the past few decades—the revolution in sexual habits, the enormous increase in ADOLESCENT PREGNANCY, and the spread of SEXUALLY TRANSMITTED DISEASES, including the deadly threat of AIDS—have made it dangerously outmoded.

Some states and communities have responded by establishing sex-education programs, frequently called FAMILY-LIFE EDUCATION, life skills, or health education. Some families have responded, too, by taking responsibility for teaching their children vital knowledge about their own beings. But in many cases, parents still resist any personal involvement in sexual education, while also protesting school and community attempts to fill the gap, as by providing BIRTH-CONTROL information and sometimes protective devices, such as CONDOMS.

Sex-education experts advise that parents who wish to help their children develop responsible attitudes toward their sexuality should respond openly to their questions from early childhood, helping them to understand the role of sexuality in an adult life, and in the process helping them develop the wisdom to make the difficult, sometimes life-or-death sexual decisions that young people must now make.

For help and further information

Sex Information and Education Council of the United States (SIECUS)
32 Washington Place
New York, NY 10003
212-673-3850
Deborah Haffner, Executive Director
Organization of individuals and groups concerned with sex education and health care. Seeks to ensure freedom of information on human sexuality; acts as information clearinghouse; maintains library; publishes various materials, including bimonthly *SIECUS Report*, bibliographies, and books *Winning the Battle for Sex Education* and *Oh NO! What Do I Do Now?*.

American Association of Sex Educators, Counselors, and Therapists
11 Dupont Circle, NW, Suite 220
Washington, DC 20036
202-462-1171
Organization of professionals seeking to set and maintain high standards of training and ethics among sex educators, counselors, and therapists. Provides information to public and professionals; makes referrals; certifies professionals in field; publishes various materials including national directory of certified sex educators and *Journal of Sex Education and Therapy*.

Association of Junior Leagues (AJL), 212-355-4380. Nationwide programs include Adolescent Pregnancy Child Watch and Parent Seminars on Adolescent Sexuality. (For full group information, see ADOLESCENT PREGNANCY.)

National Parents and Teachers Association, 312-787-0977. Publishes materials on teenage sexuality. (For full group information, see EDUCATION.)

Other reference sources

For Parents

Talking to Your Children About Love and Sex, by Leon Somers and Barbara Somers. New York: New American Library, 1989.

Where Babies Come From: Stories to Help Parents Answer Preschoolers' Questions About Sex, by Martin Silverman, M.D., and Harriet Ziefert. New York: Random House, 1989.

A Parent's Guide to Teenage Sexuality, by Jay Gale. New York: Henry Holt, 1989.

Raising a Child Conservatively in a Sexually Permissive World, by Sol Gordon and Judith Gordon. New York: Simon & Schuster, 1989.

The Parent's Guide to Raising Sexually Healthy Children, by Lynn Leight. New York: Rawson Associations, 1988.

How to Help Your Teenager Postpone Sexual Involvement, by Marion Howard. New York: Crossroads/Continuum, 1988.

How To Talk With Your Child About Sexuality, by Planned Parenthood, Faye Wattleton, with Elizabeth Keiffer. Garden City, NY: Doubleday, 1986.

Love and Sex in Plain Language, revised edition, by Eric Johnson. New York: Harper & Row, 1985.

Talking With Your Child About Sex: Questions and Answers for Children from Birth to Puberty, by Mary S. Calderone, M.D., and James W. Ramey. New York: Random House, 1982.

Saying No and Meaning It: A Guide for Parents. New York: National Urban League, 1986.

Straight Talk: Sexuality Education for Parents and Kids, 4–7, by Marilyn Ratner and Susan Chamlin. White Plains, NY: Planned Parenthood of Westchester, 1985.

Training for Life. Tulsa, OK: Margaret Hudson Program for School-Age Parents, 1986. Address: P.O. Drawer 6340, Tulsa, OK 74148, 918-585-8163. Program to train leaders for parent groups, aiming to persuade adolescents to forgo sexual activity until marriage. Encourages adoption as alternative to abortion for pregnant adolescents.

For Young Children

Bellybuttons Are Navels, by Mark Schoen. Buffalo, NY: Prometheus, 1990. On naming body parts and acceptance of the body. For ages 4 to 12.

Love and Sex and Growing Up, revised edition, by Eric W. Johnson. New York: Bantam, 1990. For ages 8 to 12.

Teaching the Truth About Sex: Biblical Sex Education for Today's Youth, by David Lynn and Mike Yaconelli. Grand Rapids, MI: Zondervan, 1990.

Asking about Sex and Growing Up: A Question and Answer Book for Boys and Girls, by Joanna Cole. New York: Morrow, 1988. For ages 8 to 12.

My Body Is Private, by Linda Walvoord Girard. For children 5 to 8. Available from La Leche League International.

For Adolescents

What's Happening to My Body? Book for Girls, new edition, by Lynda Madaras. New York: Newmarket, 1988.

What's Happening to My Body? Book for Boys, new edition, by Lynda Madaras. New York: Newmarket, 1988.

A Young Man's Guide to Sex, by Jay Gale. New York: Holt, Rinehart, Winston, 1984; Los Angeles: Body Press, 1988.

A Young Woman's Guide to Sex, by Jacqueline Voss and Jay Gale. Los Angeles: Body Press, 1988.

Becoming a Woman: Basic Information, Guidance and Attitudes on Sex for Girls, by Valerie R. Dillon. Mystic, CT: Twenty-Third Publications, 1990. From a Christian moral point of view.

Straight From the Heart: How to Talk to Your Teenagers about Love and Sex, by Carol Cassell. New York: Simon & Schuster, 1988.

Girltalk About Guys, by Carol Weston. New York: Harper & Row, 1988. For teenage girls.

Human Sexuality, by Annette Spence; Mario Orlandi and Donald Prue, series editors. New York: Facts on File, 1987.

Changing Bodies, Changing Lives: A Book for Teens on Sex & Relationships, by Ruth Bell, et al. New York: Random House, 1981.

Sexual Abstinence: Making the Right Choice. 1989. Linda Atkinson and Nick Doob, producers and directors. 30-minute video from Human Relations Media, 175 Tompkins Avenue, Pleasantville, NY 10570. For ages 13 to 18.

Background Books

Sexuality Education: A Resource Book, by Carol Cassell and Pamela M. Wilson. New York: Garland, 1989.

Private Parts: A Doctor's Guide to Male Anatomy, by Yosh Taguchi, M.D. Garden City, NY: Doubleday, 1989.

Sex and Morality: Who Is Teaching Our Sex Standards?, by Dr. Ruth Westheimer and Louis Lieberman. San Diego, CA: Harcourt Brace Jovanovich, 1988.

The Sexual Rights of Adolescents: Competence, Vulnerability, and Parental Control, by Hyman Rodman, Susan H. Lewis, and Saralyn B. Griffith. Irvington, NY: Columbia University Press, 1988.

(See also BIRTH CONTROL.)

sexual abuse Relating to young people, one type of CHILD ABUSE AND NEGLECT.

sexually transmitted diseases (STDs) A group of diseases passed between people during sexual intercourse, whether vaginal or anal, or from mother to child during CHILDBIRTH; some can also be spread by hand or mouth contact with the GENITALS of an infected person. In decades past, it was thought that there were only a few sexually transmitted diseases, such as SYPHILIS and GONORRHEA, then called *venereal diseases*. But in recent years, it has been discovered that many more diseases are passed through sexual activity, some of them relatively benign, some of them deadly; collectively, these are all now generally called sexually transmitted diseases.

In its *Introduction to Sexually Transmitted Diseases*, the National Institute of Allergy and Infectious Diseases (NIAID) summarizes what is known about STDs this way:

What are some of the basic facts? It is important to understand at least five key points about all STDs in this country today:

1. STDs affect men and women of all backgrounds and economic levels. They are, however, most prevalent among teenagers and young adults. Nearly one-third of all cases involve teenagers.
2. The incidence of STDs is rising, in part because in the last few decades, young people have become sexually active earlier; sexually active people today are more likely to have more than one sex partner or to change partners frequently. Anyone who has sexual relations is potentially at risk for developing STDs.
3. Many STDs initially cause no symptoms. When symptoms develop, they may be confused with those of other diseases not transmitted through sexual contact. However, even when an STD causes no symptoms, a person who is infected may be able to pass the disease on to a sex partner. That is why many doctors recommend periodic testing for people who have more than one sex partner.
4. Health problems caused by STDs tend to be more severe and more frequent for women than for men.
   • Some STDs can cause pelvic inflammatory disease (PID), a major cause of both infertility and ectopic (tubal) pregnancy. The latter can be fatal to a pregnant woman.
   • STD infections in women may also be associated with cervical cancer. One STD, genital warts, is caused by a virus associated with cervical and other cancers; the relationship between other STDs and cervical cancer is not yet known.
   • STDs can be passed from a mother to her baby before or during birth; some of these congenital infections can be cured easily, but others may cause permanent disability or even death of the infant.
5. When diagnosed and treated early, almost all STDs can be treated effectively. Some organisms, such as certain forms of gonococci, have become resistant to the drugs used to treat them and now require higher doses or newer types of antibiotics. The most serious STD for which no effective treatment or cure now exists is acquired immunodeficiency syndrome (AIDS), a fatal viral infection of the immune system.

Among the 20 or more STDs of special interest to parents, in connection with children or PREGNANCY, are AIDS, CHLAMYDIAL INFECTION, CYTOMEGALOVIRUS INFECTION, GENITAL WARTS, HERPES SIMPLEX, gonorrhea, HEPATITIS, and syphilis. STDs can be avoided completely only by complete sexual abstinence or by both sexual partners having sex only with each other from the start of sexual activity, at whatever age. But there are steps parents and their sexually active children can take to cut down the risk of contracting an STD (see WHAT CAN YOU [OR YOUR CHILD] DO TO AVOID STDs?, on page 423).

For help and further information

National Institute of Allergy and Infectious Diseases (NIAID), 301-496-5717. Publishes brochures *Genital Herpes* and *Sexually Transmitted Diseases*. (For full group information, see ALLERGY.)

American Social Health Association (ASHA)
260 Sheridan Avenue, Suite 307
Palo Alto, CA 94306
415-321-5134, toll-free VD National Hotline 800-227-8922 (US except CA), 800-982-5883 (CA)

Organization seeking to prevent, control, and eliminate veneral diseases. Provides information and makes referrals; operates confidential toll-free hotline for information about STDs; operates Herpes Resource Center; publishes various materials, including quarterlies and brochures.

Other reference sources

General Works

Sexually Transmitted Diseases and Society, Sylvia Cerel Brown, ed. Stanford, CA: Stanford University Press, 1988.

STD: Sexually Transmitted Diseases, by Stephen Zinner. New York: Summit, 1985.

Herpes, AIDS, and Other Sexually Transmitted Diseases, by Derek Llewellyn-Jones. Winchester, MA: Faber & Faber, 1985.

The Truth About STD: The Old Ones—Herpes and Other New Ones—the Primary Causes—the Available Cures, by Allan Chase. New York: Morrow, 1983.

VD: The Silent Epidemic, second edition, by Margaret O. Hyde. New York: McGraw-Hill, 1982.

Sexually Transmitted Diseases: The Facts, by David Barlow. New York: Oxford University Press, 1981.

The Love Diseases, by Paul Redfern. Secaucus, NJ: Citadel, 1981.

For Teenagers

Sexually Transmitted Diseases, by Elaine Landau. Hillside, NJ: Enslow, 1986.

Facts About STD—Sexually Transmitted Diseases, by Sol Gordon. Fayetteville, NY: Ed-U Press, 1983.

What Can You (or Your Child) Do to Avoid STDs?

Although there is no sure way for a sexually active person to avoid exposure to STDs, there are many things that he or she can do to reduce the risk.

A person who has decided to begin a sexual relationship should take the following steps to reduce the risk of developing an STD:

- Be direct and frank about asking a new sex partner whether he or she has an STD, has been exposed to one, or has any unexplained physical symptoms.
- Learn to recognize the physical signs of STDs and inspect a sex partner's body, especially the genital area, for sores, rashes, or discharges.
- Use a condom (rubber) during sexual intercourse and learn to use it correctly. Diaphragms or spermicides (particularly those containing nonoxynol-9), alone or in combination, also may reduce the risk of transmission of some STDs.

Anyone who is sexually active with someone other than a long-term monogamous partner should:

- Have regular checkups for STDs even in the absence of symptoms. These tests can be done during a routine visit to the doctor's office.

- Learn the common symptoms of STDs. Seek medical help immediately if any suspicious symptoms develop, even if they are mild.

Anyone diagnosed as having an STD should:

1. Notify all recent sex partners and urge them to get a checkup.
2. Follow the doctor's orders and complete the full course of medication prescribed. A follow-up test to ensure that the infection has been cured is often an important final step in treatment.
3. Avoid all sexual activity while being treated for an STD.

Sometimes people are too embarrassed or frightened to ask for help or information. Most STDs are readily treated, and the earlier a person seeks treatment and warns sex partners about the disease, the less likely that the disease will do irreparable physical damage, be spread to others, or, in the case of a woman, be passed on to a newborn baby.

Private doctors, local health departments, and family planning clinics have information about STDs. In addition, the American Social Health Association (ASHA) [see below] provides free information and keeps lists of clinics and private doctors who provide treatment for people with STDs.

Source: *An Introduction to Sexually Transmitted Diseases* (1987). Prepared by the National Institute of Allergy and Infectious Diseases, for the Public Health Service.

SGA Abbreviation for small for gestational age. (See GESTATIONAL AGE.)

shaken child syndrome The pattern of injuries, often involving hemorrhaging and swelling of the brain, resulting from violent shaking of a child, common in cases of CHILD ABUSE AND NEGLECT; also called *whiplash-shaken infant syndrome*.

Sheehan's syndrome A disorder found among women who have had massive hemorrhaging associated with CHILDBIRTH. The PITUITARY GLAND may cease to function partially or totally, leading to loss of LACTATION, malfunction of many other glands in the body, and sometimes even DEATH. (For help and further information, see PITUITARY GLAND.)

shock A condition in which blood flow to the body's tissues is so dramatically reduced that blood-starved tissues can be severely damaged, possibly leading to collapse, fainting, COMA, and DEATH. Symptoms of shock include clammy, cold skin; paleness; rapid, weak breathing and pulse; dizziness; and weakness. Emergency medical help should be summoned immediately. Until help arrives, the victim should be wrapped in blankets (with hot water if possible) to maintain body temperature, laid prone on his or her back with feet slightly elevated, and calmly comforted and reassured. Bleeding should be stopped if possible and the breathing passages kept open. No food, drink, or drugs should be given. In a hospital, patients in shock are often given blood, fluids, and/or medications intravenously, as well as oxygen, while the underlying problem is being treated. A danger in any severe injury or illness, shock can result from a variety of causes, including SPINAL-CORD INJURY, injury involving great loss of blood, heart problems blocking the flow of blood or causing extremely low BLOOD PRESSURE (see HEART AND HEART PROBLEMS), BURNS, DEHYDRATION from long-standing DIARRHEA or VOMITING, or poisons. Severe bacterial infection can result in *septic shock syndrome*, including TOXIC SHOCK SYNDROME. A severe allergic reaction (see ALLERGY) to an injected substance, such as a bee's venom or penicillin, is called *anaphylactic shock*.

For help and further information

National Heart, Lung, and Blood Institute (NHLBI), 301-496-4236. (For full group information, see HEART AND HEART PROBLEMS.)

short stature Alternate term for DWARFISM, resulting from a growth disorder.

show In PREGNANCY, the bloody mucus that appears just before the onset of LABOR.

show-and-tell An activity common in PRIMARY SCHOOL, in which children bring to school a thing or story of significance and tell the class about it, an activity designed to enhance various skills, including communication skills (see COMMUNICATION SKILLS AND DISORDERS).

shunt A medical technique that involves insertion of a bypass tube, or *shunt*, to allow fluid to flow freely past an obstruction or narrowing. For example, if a child has HYDROCEPHALUS, or excess fluid in the brain (as when a BRAIN TUMOR blocks the flow of fluid), a shunt may be used to relieve possibly dangerous pressure (see BRAIN AND BRAIN DISORDERS). The procedure carries some risk of introducing infection, causing MENINGITIS or *ventriculitis* (infection of the VENTRICLES, the cavities in the brain where the fluid flows). As a child grows, a new shunt may need to be inserted; a CT SCAN may be used to assess whether the shunt is working properly or needs replacement. One sign that a shunt is malfunctioning can be noisy, difficult breathing, called STRIDOR. (For help and further information, see BRAIN TUMOR; HYDROCEPHALUS.)

shyness A form of STRANGER ANXIETY.

siblings General term for brothers or sisters who share the same two parents, through birth or ADOPTION. Siblings who share only one parent are called HALF-BROTHERS and HALF-SISTERS; STEPBROTHERS and STEPSISTERS are those who have no relation through biology or adoption except that a parent of one is married to a parent of the other. Such various relationships have complicated even further the traditional rivalry between siblings for parental attention, power over each other, or any of the myriad other reasons that children find to fight with each other.

Though sibling rivalry is the bane of many families, child-development experts suggest that the fights can be useful preparation for dealing with others in the wider world. Parents can even turn them to positive advantage if they do not take sides and force a win-or-lose situation but instead help the children learn to resolve the conflict themselves, by stating clearly with them the cause of the conflict, then having the children propose solutions and settle on a solution themselves. Beyond that, parents will, of course, want to assure that no children come to physical harm, and they may want to try some preventive tactics, such as separation, private space, scheduling time with each child, and the like.

When a new baby is expected, parents will have to plan when and how to tell their older children and prepare them for the impending arrival, including the fact that their mother will not be so readily available. Relationships between siblings can become complicated, at birth or later, if one child is HANDI-CAPPED and so requires an inordinate amount of attention.

For help and further information

Sibling Information Network
Connecticut's University Affiliated Program on Developmental Disabilities
University of Connecticut
249 Glenbrook Road, Box U-64
Storrs, CT 06268
203-486-3783
Kathleen Bradley, Coordinator
For families and professionals interested in siblings of handicapped people. Conducts research, gathers information, and refers families to services for such siblings; publishes *Sibling Information Network Newsletter*.

Siblings for Significant Change (SSC)
105 East 22nd Street, 7th Floor
New York, NY 10010
212-420-0776
Gerri Zatlow, Director
For siblings of handicapped persons, their families, and interested professionals. Offers counseling, support, and legal aid to siblings; seeks to educate public as to difficulties faced by families of disabled people; maintains library.

Other reference sources

For Parents

Between Brothers and Sisters: A Celebration of Life's Most Enduring Relationship, by Adele Faber and Elaine Mazlish. New York: Putnam, 1989.

Siblings Without Rivalry: How to Help Your Children Live Together So You Can Live Too, by Adele Faber and Elaine Mazlish. New York: Simon & Schuster, 1988.

He Hit Me First: When Brothers and Sisters Fight, by Louise Bates Ames, Carol Chase Haber, and the Gesell Institute of Human Development. New York: Dembner, 1982; Warner, 1989.

Raising Cain: How to Help Your Children Achieve a Happy Sibling Relationship, by Herbert S. Strean and Lucy Freeman. New York: St. Martin's 1988.

For Kids

The Trouble with Babies, by Angie Sage and Chris Sage. New York: Viking/Kestrel, 1990. For ages 4 to 7.

Sharing, by Nanette Newman. Garden City, NY: Doubleday, 1990.

It's Not Fair!, by Anita Harper. New York: Putnam, 1986. For ages 2 to 4.

A Baby for Max, by Kathryn Lasky. New York: Scribner, 1984. For ages 4 to 8.

A Baby Sister for Frances, by Russell Hoban. New York: Harper & Row, 1976. For ages 4 to 8.

"Hey, What About Me?" Videocassette for siblings of new babies. Available from Kidvidz, 618 Centre Street, Newton, MA, 02158, 617-965-3345.

Living with a Brother or Sister with Special Needs: A Book for Sibs, by Donald J. Meyer, Patricia F. Vadasy, and Rebecca R. Fewell. Available from University of Washington Press, P.O. Box C-50096, Seattle, Washington 98145.

(See also BIRTH ORDER.)

sickle-cell anemia   An inherited form of ANEMIA.

SIDS   Abbreviation for SUDDEN INFANT DEATH SYNDROME.

sight method   Alternate name for the WHOLE-WORD METHOD.

sight vocabulary   Words that a student can read and understand in a READING selection without looking them up, as in a dictionary.

sight word   A word that a student recognizes and understands in a READING selection without needing to sound it out.

sigmoidoscope   A type of ENDOSCOPE used by doctors in visually examining the lower parts of the digestive system. (For help and further information, see DIGESTIVE DISORDERS.)

sign   In medicine, an indication of a disease or disorder that is observable or detectable by a physician; regarded as an objective finding, as opposed to a SYMPTOM, which is a subjective indication noticed by a patient. An observable skin rash or a measurable FEVER is a sign, for example, while the feeling of itching or heat is a symptom. If indications are clear-cut and obvious, they are called HARD SIGNS; if subtle and not so clear-cut, they are called SOFT SIGNS, as in relation to diagnosing LEARNING DISABILITIES or SCHIZOPHRENIA. Among physicians, a sign can also be an observation that fairly conclusively indicates the presence of a particular condition, as BRUDZINSKI'S SIGN indicates MENINGITIS. *Sign* is also sometimes used as synonymous with REFLEX.

sign language   Language that uses expressive gestures and movements of the hands, face, and body to communicate words and concepts. Developed to allow communication with and among people who have EAR AND HEARING PROBLEMS, sign language is a key part of the TOTAL COMMUNICATION approach but is shunned by people who believe that deaf children should not use any form of MANUAL COMMUNICATION. Though sign language can be translated into English for hearing people who do not know sign language, it actually has its own vocabulary and grammar. Various sign language systems are used, including American Sign Language (ASL or Ameslan), Signed English, Seeing Essential English (SEE), and Signing Exact English (See II). (For help and further information, including books on sign language, see EAR AND HEARING PROBLEMS.)

silent STD   A nickname for CHLAMYDIAL INFECTION, the most common of the SEXUALLY TRANSMITTED DISEASES.

simple fracture   A kind of FRACTURE in which two bone pieces are not displaced.

Sjögren-Lahrsson syndrome   A GENETIC DISORDER, of the AUTOSOMAL RECESSIVE type, characterized by MENTAL RETARDATION, ICHTHYOSIS (dry, thickened, darkened, scaly, "fishlike" skin), and spastic PARALYSIS (involuntary contraction of the muscles, resulting in loss of muscle function). Various EYE AND VISION PROBLEMS and communications disorders (see COMMUNICATION SKILLS AND DISORDERS) are sometimes associated with the syndrome, first recognized only in the mid-1950s. Sjögren-Lahrsson syndrome is an AUTOIMMUNE DISORDER, in which the body mistakenly attacks itself, and it is often linked with other autoimmune disorders, such as rheumatoid ARTHRITIS and systemic LUPUS ERYTHEMATOSUS.

For help and further information

Sjögren's Syndrome Foundation (SSF)
29 Gateway Drive
Great Neck, NY 11021
516-487-2243
Elaine K. Harris, President
Organization concerned with helping individuals with Sjögren's syndrome and their families cope with chronic disease. Publishes monthly newsletter *The Moisture Seekers* and *Sjögren's Syndrome Foundation.*

National Institute of Arthritis and Musculoskeletal and Skin Diseases (NIAMS), 301-496-8188. Publishes *NIAMS 1989: Arthritis, Rheumatic Diseases, and Related Disorders* (including Sjögren-Lahrsson syndrome). (For full group information, see ARTHRITIS; MUSCULAR DYSTROPHY.)

(See also IMMUNE SYSTEM; also HELP FOR SPECIAL CHILDREN on page 578.)

skeletal survey   A series of X-RAYS of all of a person's bones to find evidence of old, as well as new, FRACTURES, commonly done in cases of suspected CHILD ABUSE AND NEGLECT.

skewed distribution   A nonstandard form of NORMAL DISTRIBUTION.

skimming   A type of speeded-up READING in which a person gets a general idea of a selection's content without reading word for word.

skin disorders   Problems related to the external covering of the body, a multilayered structure made up of the *epidermis*, the thin outer layer; the *dermis*, the thick inner layer; and *subcutaneous tissue*, which contains fat. Growing through these layers are hair and nails, which are actually special kinds of skin.

Children are subject to a number of disorders that affect the skin, many harmless, some quite dangerous. Among them are ALBINISM (HYPOPIGMENTATION), ALOPECIA, CRADLE CAP, DIAPER RASH, EPIDERMOLYSIS BULLOSA, HEAT RASH, HEMANGIOMAS (birthmarks), HERPES SIMPLEX, NEVUS (moles), MONGOLIAN SPOTS, PSORIASIS, RASH, and VITILIGO. Pregnant women (or women taking BIRTH-CONTROL PILLS) are subject to some special skin disorders, notably HYPERPIGMENTATION.

Skin is a protective covering, but it can also be quite sensitive, as in people who have ALLERGIES; sometimes the tendency of skin to turn red or form crusty patches can be turned to advantage in MEDICAL TESTS, such as the TUBERCULIN SKIN TEST.

For help and further information

National Institute of Arthritis and Musculoskeletal and Skin Diseases (NIAMS), 301-496-8188. (For full group information, see ARTHRITIS; MUSCULAR DYSTROPHY.)

Baby's Skin

Often a baby's skin just isn't as smooth and clear as the advertisements say it is. Almost every baby develops a fine pink or red rash when the skin is irritated by rubbing on bed covers, by spitting up, or by very hot weather. Almost all of these fine pink rashes will go away promptly if the skin is bathed with clean water whenever it is dirty, and washed with mild soap once a day.

When should you worry about a baby's skin? Any pimple or rash that gets bright red and enlarges, or that develops blisters or pus, may be the beginning of an infection that will need medical care. You can soak such a rash with a washcloth or towel wrung out in warm water and keep it clean by washing with mild soap and water twice a day. If it gets worse, or if it doesn't get better in 24 hours, you should call your doctor or clinic.

Any rash that looks like bleeding or bruising in the skin *should be seen by a doctor promptly.*

Source: *Infant Care* (1989). Prepared by the Bureau of Maternal and Child Health and Resources Development, Public Health Service.

Other reference sources

Safe in the Sun, by Mary-Ellen Siegel. New York: Walker, 1990.
Skin Disorders, by Lynne Lamberg. New York: Chelsea House, 1990. For young adults.
Rheumatic and Skin Disease, by Wrynn Smith, Ph.D. New York: Facts on File, 1988. For young adults.
Health Care U.S.A., by Jean Carper. New York: Prentice Hall, 1987. Resource for general and specific health-care information. Lists leading psoriasis specialists and centers for treatment and research, including day-care centers and climatotherapy clinic, and other information.

slapped cheeks disease   Alternate name for ERYTHEMA INFECTIOSUM.

SLE   Abbreviation for systemic lupus erythematosus, the most severe form of LUPUS ERYTHEMATOSUS.

sleep apnea   Brief periods during sleep when breathing ceases, until the brain is alerted to restart breathing. Apnea of up to 15 seconds occurs normally in all ages, but cessation of breathing for over 20 seconds is called *pathologic apnea*; it can result in brain damage and other problems (see BRAIN AND BRAIN DISORDERS).

Most often sleep apnea occurs when the breathing passages are obstructed by relaxation of the soft tissues in the mouth, causing snoring with partial blockage and silence with complete blockage. While such apnea can occur in people of any age, it is especially common in overweight people; in children it is called the CHUBBY PUFFER SYNDROME.

Sleep apnea can also occur with the air passages open if the chest and diaphragm muscles cease to work, presumably because of an irregularity in the brain; this is called *central apnea*. Pathologic apnea may be marked by slowed heartbeat (*bradycardia*), color change (pallor, CYANOSIS or blueness, or sometimes *erythematosis* or redness), and muscular limpness (HYPOTONIA), and sometimes CHOKING or gagging. If these symptoms are marked, they are sometimes labeled an APPARENT LIFE-THREATENING EVENT (ALTE).

Apnea of prematurity (AOP) is very common among PREMATURE babies, occurring among nearly 90 percent of newborns with a GESTATIONAL AGE of under 29 weeks. Premature babies who have not had AOP, or who have "grown out of it," are sometimes called *asymptomatic premature infants*. Infants who have a gestational age of more than 37 weeks are said to show *apnea of infancy (AOI)*. Sleep apnea is often associated with other health disorders, such as RESPIRATORY DISTRESS SYNDROME or pneumonia (see LUNG AND BREATHING DISORDERS), and is thought to be involved in at least some cases of SUDDEN INFANT DEATH SYNDROME.

CARDIAC MONITORS and cardiorespiratory (heart-rate and breathing) monitors are often used with HIGH-RISK BABIES in NEONATAL INTENSIVE CARE UNITS and later at home, to alert parents or other CAREGIVERS that breathing has ceased. The Public Health Service's report on *Infantile Apnea and Home Monitoring* (see HOME MONITORS) stresses the importance of the training and instruction of caregivers so that they will know how to act in cases of apnea (for example, how to attempt resuscitation (using ARTIFICAL RESPIRATION).

For help and further information

National Sudden Infant Death Syndrome Clearinghouse, 703-821-8955. Publishes fact sheets *Facts About Apnea* and *Infantile Apnea and SIDS*. (For full group information, see SUDDEN INFANT DEATH SYNDROME.)

National Heart, Lung, and Blood Institute (NHLBI), Division of Lung Diseases, 301-496-4236. Publishes *Pediatric Respiratory Disorders*. (For full group information, see HEART AND HEART PROBLEMS; LUNG AND BREATHING DISORDERS.)

National Institute of Mental Health (NIMH), 301-443-4515. Publishes materials on sleeping disorders. (For full group information, see MENTAL DISORDERS.)

Other reference sources

Infantile Apnea and Home Monitoring. Washington, DC: Government Printing Office, 1987.
Sleep Apnea Syndromes, C. Guilleminault and W. Dement, eds. New York: Liss, 1978.

sleeping disorders   The state of lessened consciousness, reduced METABOLISM, and limited activity of the skeletal muscles that we call sleep and the problems and disruptions associated with it. Not a single, uniform state, sleep goes through stages, which can be recognized on ELECTROENCEPHALOGRAPHS (EEGs). The two main, alternating stages are named for their primary characteristics: NREM (nonrapid eye movement) and REM (rapid eye movement), during which dreaming occurs. Adults generally start with a period of NREM sleep, which then alternates with short periods of REM sleep throughout the night. Infants, on the other hand, tend to start with REM sleep.

Individual sleeping patterns vary widely, but in general the need for sleep decreases gradually with age. A newborn may sleep as many as 20 hours out of 24. By age one that will have dropped to about 14 hours, by age five to about 12 hours, by adulthood seven to eight hours, and in old age to as little as six hours or less.

Given the amount of our lives spent in sleep and its importance in "knitting up the raveled sleeve of care," it is not surprising that a wide variety of sleep disorders exist. In general, these concern:

- difficulty with going to sleep and staying asleep, or *insomnia*;
- problems with staying awake, such as *narcolepsy*;
- problems with establishing a consistent sleeping/waking schedule, as with jet lag or working rotating shifts; and
- disruptions of sleep patterns, the area in which most childhood sleep disorders fall.

One common kind of sleep disorder found among children is *night terrors* (*pavor nocturnus*), in which a child suddenly sits up in bed, screams or cries piercingly, looks terrified, breathes heavily, and sweats profusely. Later the child will often not remember the brief episode, which takes place during NREM sleep (unlike most dreams). Parents are advised to offer comfort, warmth, and support and not to try to make the child stand up, as that may lead to sleepwalking (which accompanies night terrors in many cases). Night terrors generally occur between ages four and 12, involving boys more often than girls, and gradually disappear as the child grows older. They are not thought to signal any kind of personality disorder.

By contrast, frightening sleep episodes called *nightmares* occur during REM sleep and are often remembered afterward—if not recalled in all of their details, at least remembered with ANXIETY. Nightmares can occur at any age, and recent studies have shown that they are far more common in ADOLESCENCE than was once thought. Scientific evidence has not (so far at least) supported the popular link between nightmares and creativity or genius, nor does the frequency of nightmares seem to signal personality problems; rather, problems with nightmares more often seem linked, recent research indicates, to the anxiety with which a person responds to the nightmare when awake.

Sleepwalking, or *somnambulism*, is also a common sleep disorder among children, affecting perhaps 15 percent of all children between ages five and 12, the Public Health Service estimates. Some may, however, sleepwalk only once or twice in their lives, and most outgrow the disorder. Typically, sleepwalkers sit up, get out of bed, and move around, often in an uncoordinated way. Sometimes they may even dress, go outdoors, eat, and go to the bathroom; they can, in the process, often

Sleeping Babies

Many new parents worry, at first, if their babies are out of their sight. For your peace of mind, you may want to sleep near the crib for the first few nights. But everyone will get more rest if your baby does not sleep in your bedroom. Especially in the first weeks, frequent snorts, gurgles, sneezes, coughs, and irregular breathing will keep you awake wondering what the baby will do next. If you are really needed, your baby will cry loud enough to be heard from nearly everywhere in the house! Even in the smallest apartment, a crib or makeshift crib can be moved to the living room, kitchen, or bathroom when you go to bed for the night.

Try not to let your baby sleep with you. It is almost certain your baby will want to become your constant bedfellow! Neither you nor your partner would want to put up with a wiggling, wet baby for very long.

Your baby shouldn't sleep in a strong draft or breeze. He or she doesn't always need open windows. Air that is fresh enough to breathe during the day is fresh enough to sleep in.

Most babies sleep from 12 to 20 hours during the 24-hour day. Your baby will decide how much to sleep. You won't be able to make your baby sleep any more or less than he or she wants. However, you can arrange to keep your infant awake during the times of the day that are most convenient for you, so that he or she will be more likely to sleep during the night and during morning or afternoon naps. Here are a few other ways, suggested by parents, to try to get the baby's sleeping schedule to fit with your own:

- Make sure that the baby's bed is warm and in a quiet place.
- Taking your baby outside for fresh air may make him or her tired and sleepy.
- A humidifier may make the air in the baby's room more comfortable, and the noise is comforting. Be sure to change the water in the humidifier daily.
- Watch for signs of sleepiness (rubbing his or her nose or eyes, yawning) and put the baby to bed.
- When all else fails, a car ride may help your baby go to sleep.

Sometimes the baby will cry when put down for sleep. Crying may persist. If there is no other reason for crying (such as hunger, wetness, or illness), be patient. Go out of the room, and the baby will usually stop crying after a while.

Source: *Infant Care* (1989). Prepared by the Bureau of Maternal and Child Health and Resources Development for the Public Health Service.

hurt themselves, stumbling over furniture, falling down stairs, going out windows, and the like. Parents need to arrange the environment so as to protect a sleepwalking child, as by locking windows and doors (unless that will cause a fire SAFETY hazard), placing a child's bedroom away from a stairway, or placing a barrier across a stairway or window. In severe cases, doctors can prescribe drugs to help, but sleepwalking is not thought to indicate personality disturbance in children.

Two other common disorders that disrupt sleep are SLEEP APNEA and ENURESIS, or bedwetting (see separate entries).

Parents who have their own sleeping disorders sometimes take sleeping pills, but women should not do so while pregnant, except under a doctor's guidance, as many of them can cause BIRTH DEFECTS. For parents, one of the main problems associated with sleep is getting their child to sleep through the night. (See SLEEPING BABIES on page 427.)

For help and further information

National Institute of Mental Health (NIMH), public affairs, 301-443-4536; publications, 301-443-4513. Publishes "Useful Information On" booklets on topics such as sleep disorders. (For full group information, see MENTAL DISORDERS.)

Association of Sleep Disorders Centers (ASDC)
604 2nd Street, SW
Rochester, MN 55902
Carol C. Westbrook, Executive Director
507-287-6006

Professional organization of specialists in sleep disorders. Encourages high standards and training and ethics; serves as accrediting agency for sleep disorder clinics; publishes various materials, including quarterly newsletter and journal *SLEEP*.

American Narcolepsy Association (ANA)
1139 Bush Street, Suite D
P.O. Box 1187
San Carlos, CA 94070
415-591-7979
William P. Baird, Executive Director

Organization of people suffering from narcolepsy and others interested in sleep disorders, especially sleep apnea. Encourages formation of local mutual-support self-help groups; seeks to educate public and foster more research; provides information and referrals; publishes various materials, including quarterly newsletter *Eye Opener* and *Narcolepsy: A Non-Technical Summary*, *Narcolepsy: A Non-Medical Presentation*, *Sleep Apnea: A Non-Technical Presentation*, and *Keep Us Awake*, booklet accompanying film.

Narcolepsy and Cataplexy Foundation of America (NCFA)
1410 York Avenue, Suite 2D, Mail Box #22
New York, NY 10021
212-628-6315
Helen Dimitroff, Executive Vice President

Organization of people with narcolepsy, their families, and interested others. Gathers and disseminates information to public and professionals; encourages formation of support services; maintains library; publishes various brochures.

Other reference sources

For Parents

Helping Your Child Sleep Through the Night: A Guide for Parents of Children from Infancy to Age Five, by Joanne Cuthbertson and Susie Schevill. Garden City, NY: Doubleday, 1989.

Mommy Says It's Naptime!, by Madeleine Yates. Nashville, TN: Abingdon, 1988.

Solve Your Child's Sleep Problems, by R. Ferber. New York: Simon & Schuster, 1985.

General Works

Sleep: Problems and Solutions, by Quentin Regestein, M.D., et al. New York: Consumer Reports Books, 1989.

Health Care U.S.A., by Jean Carper. New York: Prentice Hall, 1987. Resource for general and specific health-care information, as for such sleep disorders as sleep apnea, narcolepsy, and insomnia; lists major sleep disorder clinics and government-funded sleep disorder treatment or research centers, and other information.

The American Medical Association Guide to Better Sleep, by Lynne Lamberg. New York: Random House, 1984.

A Guide to Better Sleep. Burtonsville, MD: Better Sleep Council, 1984.

The Nightmare, by E. Hartmann. New York: Basic, 1984.

Background Works

Encountering the Monster: Pathways in Children's Dreams, by Denise Beaudet. New York: Crossroad/Continuum, 1990.

The Encyclopedia of Sleep and Sleep Disorders, by Michael Thorpy, M.D., and Jan Yager, Ph.D. New York: Facts on File, 1990.

Sleep Disorders: Diagnosis and Treatment, R. Williams and I. Karacan, eds. New York: Wiley, 1978.

Some Must Watch While Some Must Sleep, by William C. Dement, M.D. New York: Norton, 1978.

For Kids

My Getting-Ready-for-Bed Book, by Harriet Zeifert. Pictures by Mavis Smith. New York: Harper, 1990. For ages 3 to 6.

How to Get Rid of Bad Dreams, by Nancy Hazbry and Roy Condy. New York: Scholastic, 1990. For ages 4 to 6.

Jessica and the Wolf: A Story for Children Who Have Bad Dreams, by Theodore Lobby, illustrated by Tennessee Dixon. New York: Magination, 1990.

Nighty-Nightmare, by James Howe. New York: Avon, 1988. For ages 8 to 12.

Staying Happy and Calm, by Charles Thomas Cayce. Available from A.R.E., 67th St. and Atlantic Ave., P.O. Box 595, Virginia Beach, VA 23451. Part of the Pre-Sleep Series for Children.

Asa's Sweet Dreams. Cassette available from Speaking of Health, 8010 Mountain Road, NE, Albuquerque, NM 87110,

505-265-4033. Part of the Children's Coping series, featuring Asa the elephant.

(See also SLEEP APNEA.)

sleep terrors Alternate name for *night terrors*, a kind of SLEEPING DISORDER.

sleepwalking (somnambulism) A type of SLEEPING DISORDER.

Slingerland Screening Tests for Identifying Children with Specific Learning Disabilities A DIAGNOSTIC ASSESSMENT TEST used to measure the LANGUAGE SKILLS of children in grades 1 to 6; a group-administered, paper-and-pencil test, though some optional parts may be administered individually. The Slingerland tests are widely used to identify children with possible LEARNING DISABILITIES so that they can receive SPECIAL EDUCATION. The main areas covered are visual-motor coordination, visual memory as linked with motor coordination, auditory-visual discrimination, and auditory memory as linked to motor ability, and in some forms also SPATIAL ORIENTATION and ECHOLALIA. (For help and further information, see TESTS; AUDITORY SKILLS; VISUAL SKILLS.)

slit-lamp microscope Basic equipment used to explore the interior of the eye in an eye examination. (See EYE AND VISION PROBLEMS.)

SLS Abbreviation for Supplemental Loans for Students, alternate name for PLUS LOANS.

SMA Abbreviation for spinal muscular atrophies, a group of MOTOR NEURON DISEASES.

small for gestational age (SGA) Referring to an infant who is small and of LOW BIRTH WEIGHT, not because of being PREMATURE but because of slow growth of the FETUS in the UTERUS. By contrast, an infant whose size and stage of development is appropriate to his or her stage of GESTATION, meaning the number of weeks from CONCEPTION, is sometimes referred to as *appropriate for gestational age* (AGA). (See GESTATIONAL AGE.)

smoking, tobacco Inhalation of the fumes of burning tobacco leaves. Long thought soothing and fashionable, smoking has in recent decades been increasingly recognized as a major health hazard. Were it not that tobacco smoking has been part of American history from its earliest days, smoking might well be considered simply another form of SUBSTANCE ABUSE. Like other abused substances, tobacco causes changes in the body; its nicotine produces addiction, with withdrawal symptoms if use ends.

The best-known adverse effect of smoking is increased risk of CANCER, especially of the lungs, but also of the mouth, throat, and esophagus, as well as many internal organs such as the bladder, pancreas, and kidney. Various kinds of LUNG AND BREATHING DISORDERS are also linked with smoking, notably *emphysema* and *bronchitis*. Tobacco smoke, in addition to carrying carcinogens, lessens the body's ability to obtain and use oxygen and is linked with serious heart disease.

Smoking during PREGNANCY poses special risks, with increased likelihood of MISCARRIAGE, PREMATURE DELIVERY, LOW BIRTH WEIGHT, STILLBIRTH, and INFANT MORTALITY. Children of smokers are also more susceptible to ASTHMA and other respiratory diseases (see LUNG AND BREATHING DISORDERS). In recent years, studies have indicated that breathing the smoke from someone else's cigarette—called *passive smoking*—causes many of the same kinds of damage as smoking itself.

Despite these factors, the health warnings on cigarette packages, and the ban on television advertising of smoking, many young people continue to regard smoking as attractive and "grown-up." Some parents and community groups are attempting to make the sale of cigarettes to young people illegal, on the model of alcohol. Once they have started smoking, both young people and adults often have difficulty breaking the habit, though as soon as smoking ends, the body begins in many respects to regenerate itself.

For help and further information

Office on Smoking and Health
U.S. Department of Health and Human Services
Public Health Service
5600 Fishers Lane
Bethesda, MD 20857
301-443-1575
Federal agency that gathers and summarizes scientific evidence on effects of cigarette smoking. Provides information and makes public policy; publishes various materials, including annual review of research findings.

March of Dimes Birth Defects Foundation, 914-428-7100; local chapters in telephone-directory white pages. Publishes *Drugs, Alcohol and Tobacco Abuse During Pregnancy* and *Babies Don't Thrive in Smoke-Filled Wombs*. (For full group information, see BIRTH DEFECTS.)

American Cancer Society, 212-599-8200; toll-free number 800-552-7996. Publishes *Dangers of Smoking, Benefits of Quitting and Relative Risks of Reduced Exposure, Quitter's Guide: A 7-Day Plan to Help You Stop Smoking Cigarettes, Fifty Most-Often-Asked Questions About Smoking*, and *The Decision Is Yours*. (For full group information, see CANCER.)

American Lung Association, 212-315-8700; call telephone white pages for local number. Publishes *Freedom From Smoking© in 20 Days, A Lifetime of Freedom From Smoking©, Help a Friend Stop Smoking, Stop Smoking/Stay Trim*, and videocassette *In Control: A Home Video Freedom From Smoking© Program*. (For full group information, see LUNG AND BREATHING DISORDERS).

National Cancer Institute (NCI), 800-4-CANCER [422-6237]. Publishes *Clearing the Air: A Guide to Quitting Smoking, Why Do You Smoke?* and *You've Kicked the Smoking Habit for Good*. (For full group information, see CANCER.)

National Institute of Diabetes, Digestive, and Kidney Diseases (NIDDK), 301-496-3583. Publishes *Smoking and Your Digestive System*. (For full group information, see DIGESTIVE DISORDERS.)

Stop Teenage Addiction to Tobacco (STAT)
121 Lyman Street, Suite 210
Springfield, MA 01103
413-732-STAT [7828]
Joe B. Tye, Executive Director
Organization of people seeking to stop child smoking. Seeks to educate public and influence legislation; gathers and disseminates information; sponsors educational programs; publishes various materials, including quarterly *Tobacco and Youth Reporter*.

Other reference sources

The Last Puff: Ex-Smokers Share the Secrets of Their Success, by John W. Farquhar and Gene A. Spiller. New York: Norton, 1990.

Health Care U.S.A., by Jean Carper. New York: Prentice Hall, 1987. Resource for general and specific health-care information; lists leading stop-smoking programs and other information.

The American Cancer Society's "Fresh Start": 21 Days to Stop Smoking, by Dee Burton. New York: Pocket, 1986. Video and audio cassette: New York: Simon & Schuster, 1985.

The Scientific Case Against Smoking, by Ruth Winter. New York: Crown, 1980.

For Kids

Know About Smoking, revised edition, by Margaret O. Hyde. New York: Walker, 1990.

Smoking, by Judith Condon. New York: Watts, 1989.

Smoking, by Lila Gano. San Diego, CA: Lucent, 1989.

Why Do People Smoke?, by Pete Sanders. New York: Gloucester, 1989. For grades 3 to 6.

Teen Guide to Pregnancy, Drugs and Smoking, by Jane Hawksley. New York: Watts, 1989.

The Stop Smoking Book for Teens, by Curtis W. Casewit. New York: Messner, 1980.

(See also HELP AGAINST SUBSTANCE ABUSE on page 587.)

Snellen test   Widely used test of distance vision, using a wall chart starting with a "big E," normal vision being 20/20. (See EYE AND VISION PROBLEMS.)

social age   A kind of converted AGE-EQUIVALENT SCORE that results from the VINELAND SOCIAL MATURITY SCALE.

social promotion   Alternate term for automatic PROMOTION.

social skills   The ability to interact normally with others; in infants, this involves first attending to, responding to, and imitating others, gradually working into playing and sharing with others. A CHART OF NORMAL DEVELOPMENT (on page 507) indicates when between birth and age six children first, *on the average*, begin to develop the main social skills.

Children with MENTAL DISORDERS, LEARNING DISABILITIES, and some other DEVELOPMENTAL DISORDERS sometimes have problems with social skills, exhibiting behavior ranging from aggressiveness to withdrawal. They may have difficulty making friends, get overexcited easily, cling excessively, and have strong mood swings. Some may be easily distracted, moving from one place to another without becoming involved in any activity, while others may focus on one activity, refusing to let others join them. Difficulties with social skills often go hand-in-hand with problems in other areas, such as communication skills (see COMMUNICATION SKILLS AND DISORDERS), AUDITORY SKILLS, and VISUAL SKILLS.

Children develop at individual and varying paces, but all children can benefit from activities designed to enhance their natural development, as in imitating speech and body language. In TEACHING YOUNG CHILDREN: GUIDELINES AND ACTIVITIES (on page 544), parents will find activities designed to develop children's skills in various areas, including social skills.

social worker   A professional working with a public or private agency, charged with helping people handle personal, emotional, or social problems, or the effects of medical problems, and seeing that people get the social and other services available to them, often acting as advocate for individuals or families in working with government agencies, schools, clinics, PRESCHOOL programs, and the like. *Psychiatric social workers* specialize in working with people with MENTAL DISORDERS, and some are trained to work as PSYCHOTHERAPISTS. *Medical social workers* counsel people in a HOSPITAL setting, helping them cope with problems posed by severe illness or disability. Social workers often make up part of the team reviewing reports of suspected CHILD ABUSE AND NEGLECT.

sodium   A MINERAL that is extremely important in maintaining water balance and ELECTROLYTE balance in the body and proper functioning of the nerves and muscles. In the kitchen, sodium is usually found as *sodium chloride* (table salt, today often with IODINE added) or *sodium bicarbonate* (baking soda). Most foods contain some sodium, but it is especially abundant in processed foods, ham, cheese, breads and cereals, and meats, fish, and vegetables that have been smoked, pickled, or cured, as well as packed in water treated with water softener. Deficiency is rare in Western countries, except in abnormal circumstances, as with excessive use of diuretic drugs, persistent DIARRHEA or VOMITING, or certain disorders such as CYSTIC FIBROSIS, ADRENAL GLAND problems, or KIDNEY AND UROLOGICAL DISORDERS, the kidneys being the organs that controls the level of sodium in the blood. Too little sodium can cause muscle cramps, weakness, and headache, and severe deficiency can lead to low BLOOD PRESSURE, confusion, and fainting. In the West, excess sodium is far more common, and most dietitians urge restraint in the addition of sodium—and checking manufactured foods for their level of sodium. Too much sodium can lead to hypertension (high BLOOD PRESSURE), EDEMA (water buildup), kidney damage, and heart problems (see HEART AND HEART PROBLEMS). (For help and further information, see MINERALS; NUTRITION.)

soft signs   Observations less clearly indicative of CENTRAL NERVOUS SYSTEM malfunctions than are HARD SIGNS; a term NEUROLOGISTS sometimes use when talking about a child with LEARNING DISABILITIES or other DEVELOPMENTAL DISORDERS. (See SIGNS.)

Starting on Solid Foods

Whenever you decide to start "solids" or spoon foods, here are a few guidelines that will help you:

- *After six months, your baby needs more than breastmilk or formula*. About six to eight breastfeedings or 25 to 32 ounces of formula a day provide enough milk for your baby at this age. Let your baby fill up on other foods.
- *Start slowly*: A few spoonfuls once or twice a day of the same food is enough at first. This food should be very thin (liquid) and smooth. The baby's main nutrition should still come from breastmilk or formula, but spoon-feeding semisolid foods and sips of water and juice from a cup gives both parents and baby a good opportunity to learn about each other. Fathers should try to share in this baby-feeding time.
- *Try just one new food at a time*: Feed the new food every day for several days. Start with simple, pure foods. For example, use pure rice cereal, not mixed cereal; applesauce, not fruit dessert; chicken or turkey, not meat dinner. Some new foods may cause vomiting, diarrhea, or skin rash in a few infants. By starting only one new food every four or five days, and by using simple, single foods, you will know which food is the cause. Once your baby has eaten a food for three or four days without any ill effects, you can use it in the future without worrying.
- *Choose new foods from each of these food groups*:
    Fruits, fruit juices
    Vegetables (including at least one serving of a puréed leafy green vegetable)
    Meat, fish, poultry, egg yolk, cheese
    Bread, cereal, rice, crackers, pasta (wheat products are usually not recommended before eight or nine months of age)
- *Feed your baby a variety of foods*. Once you know which foods your baby can eat, the best way to be sure the baby gets what he or she needs is to be sure you satisfy your baby's appetite for a wide variety of foods. In any two-to-three-day period, in addition to breastmilk or formula, a baby should have several servings (mashed or puréed) from each of the above food groups.
- *Don't feed your baby honey until he or she is one year old*, to avoid the possibility of botulism.

- *Do not give your baby candy, cookies, sugar, sweet desserts, and soft drinks*. They don't provide the nutrients your baby needs, they may spoil the baby's appetite for healthier foods, and they are bad for the baby's teeth.
- *You can tell if a food is not being digested properly if it comes through in bowel movements*. If it does, chop the food more finely or use other foods.
- *When feeding your baby "table food" (that you prepare for the entire family), be sure it doesn't contain chunks or stringy, fibrous parts that can choke a baby*. Don't give your baby small foods such as raisins, grapes, cut-up hot dogs, peanuts, or popcorn, hard foods such as raw vegetables, or sticky foods such as peanut butter—which can cause choking. Watch out for strings on celery and green beans.
- *Encourage your baby to feed him- or herself*. Babies enjoy using their fingers to feed themselves foods such as crackers, bits of bread or toast, bits of cheese or meat, and small bits of soft fruits or vegetables.
- *Let your baby try drinking from a cup at five or six months*. Put just a little liquid (even breastmilk) in the bottom of the cup at first. Then increase the amount as your baby learns to drink out of it.
- *Let your baby help you handle the spoon*. One parent should sit behind the baby so that the baby can hold onto the spoon or the parent's hand and learn the movements needed to eat without help. This may slow you down and make a mess, but your baby will learn to eat without your help sooner. Heavy plastic bibs and washable plastic or newspapers under the high chair will help control the mess.
- *By one year, your baby will probably be able to eat most of what the rest of the family eats*. Someone will still have to mash up some of the vegetables and cut meat, chicken, or fish into tiny bites. You should still avoid the small foods (such as raisins, grapes, chopped hot dogs, peanuts, popcorn) until your child is three or four years old and able to chew and swallow these foods without fear of choking.

Source: *Infant Care* (1989). Prepared by the Bureau of Maternal and Child Health and Resources Development for the Public Health Service.

---

solid foods Nutritious substances other than fluids (such as breast MILK or FORMULA), generally introduced as supplements to infants after four to six months. By this time babies usually have matured enough to be able to sit up with some help and have some control over the head and neck, including tongue and lips. They can also indicate when they do and do not want to eat.

The first solid foods given to infants are hardly "solid" at all, being generally cooked cereals and pureed fruits, vegetables, and meats, also called *spoon foods*. (See STARTING ON SOLID FOODS, above.) The Public Health Service notes that "there is nothing special about the foods that are sold as baby foods except that they are finely strained and convenient," adding that they are "especially expensive for their limited food value." They note that, with a blender or masher (even just a fork), parents can make their own baby foods out of most plain, simple foods prepared for the rest of the family, with the addition of a little water. *The Surgeon General's Report on Nutrition and Health* agrees, noting, "If properly prepared and stored, puréed foods made at home are nutritionally equivalent

---

Eating Patterns in Children

Preschool children are a nutritionally vulnerable group. Their growth rate is slower than it was in infancy and their nutritional needs in relation to body size proportionately reduced. Thus, they often want and eat relatively little food. Food intake can be reduced even further by the increasing independence (expressed as refusals to eat) and immature feeding skills that are characteristic of very young children. Despite these problems, surveys have indicated that, with the exception of a small subgroup, American preschool children are in relatively good nutritional health. Children of lower socioeconomic status are at higher risk of inadequate nutrient intakes (especially iron deficiency) and poorer growth. Although parents have the main responsibility for providing adequate and appropriate food for preschool children, day-care providers supply an increasing proportion of the food that children consume.

Parents continue to be the main influence on the food intake of school-aged children, although an increasing proportion of the diet is consumed in schools, day-care centers, and fast-food restaurants. Between the ages of four and six, children increase the varieties of foods they are willing to eat. Snacks become an important source of calories and nutrients and may contribute as much as one-third of the calories and fat, one-fifth of the protein, and nearly one-half of the carbohydrates 10-year-old children consume. These patterns emphasize the need for parents and schools to provide appropriate meals and snacks and guidance in food choices. Of special concern is the need to encourage appropriate levels of daily physical activity and choice of nutritious snacks that do not promote tooth decay.

The growth spurt of adolescence demands significant increases in calories and nutrient intake to support the rapid growth rate and increased body size. In early adolescence, children still depend on their parents for food, but by the end of adolescence they are largely independent. Irregular eating patterns are common in adolescence, reflecting this growing independence from the family and the teenager's increasingly busy social life and athletic, academic, and vocational activities. Breakfast and lunch are often skipped or eaten on the run. Snacking is characteristic of this age group and contributes significantly to nutrient intake; these snack foods are often higher in calories, fat, and sugar—and lower in vitamins, minerals, and fiber—than foods consumed at family meals. Because lifetime dietary patterns are established during these years, adolescents should be encouraged to choose nutritious foods, to develop good eating habits, and to maintain appropriate levels of physical activity.

Source: *The Surgeon General's Report on Nutrition and Health.* Rocklin, CA: Prima, 1988.

---

to those prepared commercially." They add some cautions, however:

- Do not add salt, butter, fat, sugar, other seasonings, or sauces.
- Use or refrigerate home-prepared baby food immediately (except spinach, beets, and carrots, which should not be stored).
- If you plan to store it for more than 24 hours, try storing it in individual portions (as in an ice cube tray).
- Use only fruits and vegetables from cans specially made for infants; others may contain too much salt, sugar, or possibly lead (see ENVIRONMENTAL HAZARDS).
- Do not heat food (or baby bottles) for your baby in a microwave oven. It heats food unevenly, making some parts cold, some warm, and some hot enough to burn the baby.

Ready-cooked iron-fortified infant cereals are also easy to prepare and should be part of the baby's diet every day until about 18 months of age. By the time the baby is a year old, solid foods should provide more than 50 percent of energy intake.

The whole process of gradually substituting solid foods for BREASTFEEDING or BOTTLEFEEDING is called *weaning.* Though it generally starts during the middle of the first year and is often complete by the end of the first year, some parents and children continue to have breast or bottle as part of the emotional picture well beyond that, though they play a decreasing part nutritionally.

Later the types of foods offered and eaten will follow a more widely varied pattern, depending on family life-style and individual preferences, though working within the guidelines of basic NUTRITION needs and some overall general patterns related to age level and growth. (See EATING PATTERNS IN CHILDREN, above.) A child's appetite, for example, will decrease sharply between ages two and four, as growth needs diminish. Loss of appetite, medically called *anorexia,* can be a sign of a disease, so the parents should watch for any such changes and, if appropriate, see the doctor or clinic. But if the child seems healthy and normal apart from lack of appetite, some doctors advise parents not to try to keep up the child's caloric intake, which can develop into a running battle with the child, but to concentrate on seeing that the child has at least some protein, fruit, and if possible, vegetables to meet basic needs for nutrients. Parents should also recognize that some kinds of food dislikes are based on as-yet-unrecognized mild ALLERGIES or FOOD INTOLERANCES and so should (within reason) respect a child's desire to avoid certain foods.

Children can also develop, anywhere from early in childhood to late in their teens, a variety of DIGESTIVE DISORDERS, METABOLIC DISORDERS (involving inability to break down certain kinds of nutrients in the body), and EATING DISORDERS, such as ANOREXIA NERVOSA and BULIMIA. Children with certain kinds of chronic illnesses, such as DIABETES MELLITUS, may also have eating patterns forced on them by the need to follow special diets.

For help and further information

Poor Eaters: Helping Children Who Refuse to Eat, by Joel Macht. New York: Plenum, 1990.

Solving Your Child's Eating Problems, by Jane Hirschmann and Lela Zaphiropoulos. New York: Fawcett/Columbine, 1990. Formerly titled *Are You Hungry?*.

Parents' Guide to Feeding Your Kids Right: Birth Through Teen Years, by the Children's Television Workshop. New York: Prentice Hall, 1989.

Eat Up, Gemma, by Sarah Hayes. New York: Lothrop, Lee and Shepard, 1988. For ages 2 to 6.

(See also NUTRITION; other specific topics noted above.)

solvent abuse   Inhalation of intoxicating fumes of certain volatile liquids or aerosol sprays, which produces an effect similar to an alcohol- or drug-induced "high." Some of the solvents used are toxic and can harm the air passages, kidneys, liver, and NERVOUS SYSTEM. Of more immediate danger, they can cause COMA and DEATH, either directly by physical effects on the heart or indirectly, as by injuries from a fall or suffocation from lack of oxygen in the plastic bag often used during inhalation. (For an overview of the effects and signs of solvent and other substance abuse, plus organizations, reference works, and recommendations for parents, see HELP AGAINST SUBSTANCE ABUSE on page 587.)

somatic nervous system   The part of the NERVOUS SYSTEM that responds to and provides the brain with information about voluntary movements of the body, as in walking or moving an arm (see BRAIN AND BRAIN DISORDERS).

somnambulism   Alternate name for *sleepwalking*, a type of SLEEPING DISORDER.

sonogram   The moving image created by the ULTRASOUND scanning technique.

sound-symbol association   The ability to recognize sounds and their origins and to recognize that sounds go with letters, a key prerequisite skill for READING.

Spache Diagnostic Reading Scales   Alternate name for DIAGNOSTIC READING SCALES.

Spalding method   A highly structured PHONICS approach to teaching READING at the ELEMENTARY SCHOOL level, sometimes called the *unified phonics method*. (For help and further information, see READING.)

spatial orientation   The ability to understand one's position in space and the relationship between the self and objects nearby, one aspect being FORM CONSTANCY, the ability to recognize an object or shape, regardless of what position or angle it is viewed from. A child with LEARNING DISABILITIES or some other kinds of DEVELOPMENTAL DISORDERS may, for example, be unable to recognize a toy or shape when it is placed in a different position (such as upside down) or fail to recognize a familiar object when it appears in a picture, rather than in three-dimensional form. Spatial orientation is closely linked to both MOTOR SKILLS and VISUAL SKILLS.

spatial relations   The ability to judge the relationship of objects to each other and oneself; closely linked to both MOTOR SKILLS and VISUAL SKILLS. Children with LEARNING DISABILITIES or other DEVELOPMENTAL DISORDERS may have difficulty in judging when they need to duck or crawl under a rope or table, for example, or may consistently try to put an object into too small a box. Children with spatial-relations problems often have trouble putting on clothes, going up and down stairs, fitting lids on boxes, putting keys in locks, riding a tricycle, or coordinating arm movements to throw a ball in the desired direction. Problems in such areas can lead to fear of heights, hesitation of movement, and difficulty in assessing the extent and direction of a movement needed to carry out a task.

special babies   Alternate term for HIGH-RISK BABIES or for children with SPECIAL NEEDS.

special education   The training and teaching of children with SPECIAL NEEDS, those who have mental or physical needs and characteristics that require attention beyond that given to most children, including children with MENTAL RETARDATION or MENTAL DISORDERS, GIFTED CHILDREN, children with physical or LEARNING DISABILITIES, and children whose cultural background (such as different language or socioeconomic disadvantage) requires COMPENSATORY EDUCATION. Materials and methods of instruction in special education programs are adapted to the child's individual needs; for those children designated as HANDICAPPED under the EDUCATION FOR ALL HANDICAPPED CHILDREN ACT OF 1975, the school in cooperation with parents makes up INDIVIDUALIZED EDUCATION PROGRAMS (IEPs). Special education teachers, sometimes called VISITING, *itinerant*, or *resource teachers*, are often employed by school districts or regions to serve several schools, helping to plan long-term and short-term IEPs for such children, working directly with the children and advising the rest of the school staff, as well as the parents. Under SECTION 504 OF THE REHABILITATION ACT OF 1973, children with handicaps or disabilities are supposed to be educated in regular classes wherever possible, an approach called MAINSTREAMING, but where that is not possible, special students are grouped in separate classes, either separately by the type of disability (such as learning disabilities or blindness) or all together as children with exceptional needs. (For help and further information, see EDUCATION; also HELP FOR SPECIAL CHILDREN, on page 578.)

Other reference sources

Concise Encyclopedia of Special Education: A Reference for the Education of the Handicapped and Other Exceptional Children and Adults, by Cecil R. Reynolds and Elaine Fletcher-Janzen. New York: Wiley, 1990.

The Magic Feather: The Truth About "Special Education," by Lori Granger and Bill Granger. New York: Delacorte, 1989.

The Special Education Handbook: A Comprehensive Guide for Parents and Educators, by Kenneth Shore. New York: Teachers College Press, 1986.

Placing Children in Special Education: A Strategy for Equity, K. A. Heller, W. E. Holtzman, and S. Messick, eds. Washington, DC: National Academy Press, 1982.

Special Education Policies: Their History, Implementation, and Finance, Jay G. Chambers and William T. Hartman, eds. Philadelphia: Temple University Press, 1982.

special needs In EDUCATION, designation for a child who cannot be well served by regular school programs and requires SPECIAL EDUCATION or ADAPTED EDUCATION to develop his or her fullest potential. Children with special needs include GIFTED CHILDREN, who have unusual and superior talents, and children with various handicaps (see HANDICAPPED), including those with LEARNING DISABILITIES, MENTAL RETARDATION, and MENTAL DISORDERS, as well as cultural or socioeconomic disadvantages that require COMPENSATORY EDUCATION. (For help and further information, see SPECIAL EDUCATION; also HELP FOR SPECIAL CHILDREN on page 578.)

Special Supplemental Food Program for Women, Infants, and Children (WIC) A program operated under the U.S. Department of Agriculture that is intended to help poor women and children who might otherwise not have sufficient NUTRITION to maintain proper health and functioning. (See NUTRITION.)

specific developmental disorder The psychiatric classification for LEARNING DISABILITIES and communication disorders (see COMMUNICATION SKILLS AND DISORDERS).

Specific Language Disability Tests (Malcomesius Test) A series of tests used as DEVELOPMENTAL SCREENING TESTS for LEARNING DISABILITIES in the area of language. Given individually or in groups, the various subtests attempt to highlight problems in LANGUAGE SKILLS, VISUAL SKILLS, AUDITORY SKILLS, and comprehension. Widely used in schools, the Malcomesius Test is used to screen for children who may need further DIAGNOSTIC ASSESSMENT TESTS or who might benefit from REMEDIAL INSTRUCTION. (For help and further information, see TESTS.)

specific learning disability A kind of LEARNING DISABILITY that affects just one area or kind of skill, in a child who is not experiencing problems in other areas; sometimes called a *specific developmental disorder*. For example, a child may have DYSCALCULIA, difficulty in working with mathematical symbols, but have no difficulties in other areas of learning.

specimen tests General type of MEDICAL TEST that involves taking samples of urine, blood, saliva, stool, and other fluids, waste, and tissue from the body for analysis. The characteristics of normal body substances are well known, so laboratory analysis can indicate if the patient's sample is markedly different from the norm and, if so, in what ways. If blood is removed by inserting a needle into a vein and withdrawing it into a syringe or a CATHETER, the procedure is called *venipuncture*. If a fluid sample is taken from the body using a hollow *aspiration needle*, the procedure is called *centesis*, as in the PRENATAL TEST

called AMNIOCENTESIS. If a tissue sample is taken from the body, often using a similar hollow needle, the procedure is called a BIOPSY. (For help and further information, see MEDICAL TESTS.)

speech disorders Difficulty in actually producing the sounds of the language, often from malfunction in the brain or inability to properly control the muscles needed to produce the sounds. (For help and further information, see COMMUNICATION SKILLS AND DISORDERS.)

speech-language pathologist A specialist who diagnoses and treats communication disorders in children or adults (see COMMUNICATION SKILLS AND DISORDERS), often working in schools with children referred by AUDIOLOGISTS, teachers, or other professionals; also called *speech therapist* or *speech clinician*. After obtaining a full history from parents and teachers, the speech-language pathologist generally meets with a child, frequently in a play setting, to informally observe the child and then gives a variety of tests to assess the child's ability to understand and produce speech. In the course of the SCREENING TESTS, the speech-language pathologist may ask the child to draw pictures, say words, manipulate and name objects, describe pictures, repeat sentences, answer questions, or tell a story. On the basis of the results, the speech-language pathologist designs a program of therapy, which may involve special training programs; referral to another specialist, such as an audiologist, PSYCHOLOGIST, or OTOLARYNGOLOGIST; guidance for parents; and suggestions for teachers of the child.

speechreading (lipreading) A technique for understanding spoken language through visual clues, such as the position of the jaw, lips, and tongue. Commonly used by people who have EAR AND HEARING PROBLEMS, speechreading requires considerable training to learn and even then has limited effectiveness alone, because less than half of the common words in spoken English can be interpreted by lip movements alone. However, speechreading can help enormously to supplement a person's residual hearing. Its value is enhanced when speakers use CUED SPEECH, exaggerating their lip movements and using finger signs for particular sounds that are otherwise easily confused, such as "p" and "b."

speech synthesis Production of speech by a computer from words typed into the computer, usually by a person who has EAR AND HEARING PROBLEMS or speech problems (see COMMUNICATION SKILLS AND DISORDERS).

speech therapist Alternate name for SPEECH-LANGUAGE PATHOLOGIST.

sperm (spermatozoa; singular, **spermatozoon)** The male sex cell, which unites with the female egg (OVUM), normally in the FALLOPIAN TUBES, in the process of FERTILIZATION, to form a fertilized egg, or ZYGOTE. Sperm are manufactured in the TESTES and matured in the EPIDIDYMIS (a "holding area" behind the testes); sperm production is the key sign of male sexual maturity, beginning in PUBERTY.

Normally released by the millions into a woman's VAGINA in SEMEN during EJACULATION as part of sexual intercourse, the sperm must make their way through a formidable series of obstacles:

- *the vagina*, where most sperm are killed by acidic secretions;
- *the* CERVIX, which secretes a hostile mucus, though around the time of OVULATION it is somewhat more hospitable to the sperm's entry. Many sperm also become entrapped in the walls of the cervix;
- *the* UTERUS, a relatively vast expanse to cross, compared to the size of the microscopic sperm;
- *the fallopian tubes*, where yet more mucus-covered walls wait to entrap sperm;
- *the egg*, guarded by two tough outer layers that must be penetrated.

The sperm are equipped with some tools to make their way through this obstacle course. While the vital genetic material is packed into the sperm's head, each sperm develops a tadpole-like tail, to help it "swim upstream" to the egg. Also, under a protective screen, the sperm carries a load of chemicals that, on arrival at the egg, help it to make its way through the egg's protective layers.

The whole journey takes one to a few hours, if all goes well, though the sperm can remain alive and active in the fallopian tube for up to 48 hours. In the end, only a few thousand sperm of the many millions ejaculated survive even to reach the egg. Then one, and only one, can successfully fertilize the egg.

In some cases, the number of sperm in a man's semen (*sperm count*) is too low or the sperm lack sufficient propulsion to make their way through to the egg. Sometimes the acidity of a woman's reproductive organs defeats the sperm. In such instances of reduced fertility or INFERTILITY, other alternatives for fertilization may be tried, including IN VITRO FERTILIZATION, EMBRYO TRANSFER, and ARTIFICIAL INSEMINATION. (For help and further information, see PREGNANCY; INFERTILITY.)

spermatids   Immature SPERM, produced by the TESTES, before they come to maturity in the EPIDYDYMIS.

spermatocele   A SPERM-filled swelling in the EPIDIDYMIS, the sperm "holding area" behind the TESTES. If the spermatocele grows large and painful, surgery may be indicated, though the result may be INFERTILITY on the side operated on.

spermatogonia   The cells in the TESTES that actually produce the SPERM.

sperm bank   A privately run organization that collects SPERM from donors, sometimes paying a fee, and sells it to women or doctors for use in ARTIFICIAL INSEMINATION. Such banks gather full medical histories from the donors, should the mother later wish such information, but the donor's identity is confidential, except where both the donee requests and the donor agrees to reveal it. (For help and further information, see ARTIFICIAL INSEMINATION.)

spermicide   A form of BIRTH CONTROL using various substances—contraceptive foams, creams, jellies, gels, and suppositories—containing ingredients designed to kill SPERM, such as *nonoxynol-9* or *octoxynol*. When used alone, spermicides have a fairly low effectiveness rate as CONTRACEPTIVES, estimated at around 70 to 80 percent by the Food and Drug Administration (FDA). The spermicide needs to be placed in the woman's VAGINA no more than an hour before intercourse, forming both a physical and chemical barrier to sperm, and it must be left in place (that is, not douched) for at least six hours after intercourse. Spermicides can cause allergic reactions in the woman or her sex partner. They are also alleged to cause BIRTH DEFECTS if continued in use after a woman is pregnant (though she may not know it). In one such case, a woman brought a court suit against a spermicide manufacturer for birth defects in her child. The FDA noted: "Although the judge found in favor of the woman and her child, FDA has not found scientific data to support an association between spermicides and birth defects. The agency continues to monitor the situation." If you are considering use of spermicides, you may want to contact the FDA and your doctor or clinic for the most current information. On the plus side, spermicides do somewhat reduce the risk of contracting SEXUALLY TRANSMITTED DISEASES, though they should not be considered any protection against AIDS. (For help and further information, see also BIRTH CONTROL.)

sphingomyelin lipidosis   Alternate name for Niemann-Pick disease, a type of LIPID STORAGE DISEASE.

sphygmomanometer   A device used to measure BLOOD PRESSURE.

spina bifida   Literally, "spine in two parts," a general name for a group of CONGENITAL abnormalities resulting when the membrane-and-tissue-covered "tube" that houses the CENTRAL NERVOUS SYSTEM fails to close completely during an EMBRYO's development. Medically, these disorders are generally called *neural tube defects*. Defects can occur anywhere along the spine but are most common in the lower back. The precise causes of spina bifida are unclear, but both genetic and environmental influences seem to be involved. (See SEARCHING FOR SPINA BIFIDA'S CAUSES on page 437.)

The three main types of spina bifida, from the mildest to the most serious, are:

- *spina bifida occulta*, which involves a small, incomplete closure but no obvious damage to the spinal cord, occurring in perhaps 20 percent or more of the population. In fact, the defect is so minor that many people do not know they have it (hence the name *occulta*, or "hidden"). Externally, the site of the defect may be marked by a dimple, tuft of hair, or TELANGIECTASIA (redness from expanded blood vessels). It is apparently associated with some urinary or bowel problems, as well as weakness and poor circulation in the legs, generally not seen until adulthood.
- *meningocele*, in which the MENINGES, the membrane covering the spinal cord, pushes out through an abnormal opening in the vertebrae. This forms a sac (*-cele*), which appears externally as a bulge, but the spinal cord itself is not damaged and skin covers the sac. A meningocele can often be easily repaired by surgery during the first few days of life.

- *myelomeningocele*, in which nerve and tissue from the spinal cord itself protrudes into the sac, which may or may not be covered externally with skin. This most severe form is what many people call simply *spina bifida*. (To physicians, the meningocele and myelomeningocele together are sometimes called *spina bifida manifesta*, since signs of it are clearly observable.) Among the effects of myelomeningocele may be muscle weakness, loss of sensation, or varying degrees of PARALYSIS below the defect, and loss of bladder and bowel control (INCONTINENCE). A malformation at the base of the brain stem can cause a buildup of the CEREBROSPINAL FLUID that normally circulates within the spinal cord and brain (see BRAIN AND BRAIN DISORDERS). This fluid buildup is called HYDRO-CEPHALUS ("water on the brain"), which needs to be relieved by a SHUNT to avoid neurological damage, including BLINDNESS, DEAFNESS, SEIZURES, and LEARNING DISABILITIES.

Two related neural tube defects include:

- ENCEPHALOCELE, the bulging of part of the brain through a defect in the skull, which may cause brain damage and exposure to infection;
- ANENCEPHALY, the absence of a brain or spinal cord, in which the skull does not close and only a groove appears where the spine should be. Even the most aggressive medical treatment cannot save these babies, and they usually survive only a few hours.

Various GENETIC SCREENING TESTS, including ALPHA FETOPROTEIN, ULTRASOUND, and AMNIOCENTESIS, can be used to try to assess if a FETUS has neural tube defects. Prospective parents may want to seek GENETIC COUNSELING, especially those with any history of such defects in their families.

In the past, most children with myelomeningocele—perhaps 90 percent—died soon after birth, but now surgery performed in the first few days after birth allows many of them to survive. They generally must have a series of operations during their growing years, however, and often need ORTHOPEDIC DEVICES to aid their mobility. With such treatment and encouragement, many of them—the Spina Bifida Association estimates 80 percent—will be able to walk by the time they enter school. In their publication *Spina Bifida: Hope Through Research*, the National Institute of Neurological Diseases and Stroke (NINDS) suggests:

Physicians recommend that a child with spina bifida be encouraged to progress as normally as possible with the development of motor skills. Between six months and one year, all children should sit; by 12 to 18 months, they should begin to crawl and explore their surroundings. Around age 1½ children should be encouraged to stand—even those with high thoracic [chest] damage who will eventually have to use a wheelchair. Standing reduces osteoporosis (a thinning of the bones that results from inactivity and increases the risk of fractures), improves bladder and bowel function, and strengthens the heart and upper body. Parents should also encourage 18-month-olds to walk.

There are a variety of devices to help spina bifida patients attain these developmental milestones. A wheeled device called a chariot, which moves when the sitting child rolls wheels by hand, helps patients who have trouble crawling. Standing appliances provide total body support so that a child can be upright without crutches. The swivel-walker allows a child to shift weight from side to side in a movement that propels the patient forward. A recently developed long-leg brace helps children walk by propelling their legs forward. Mobility varies according to the level of the child's defect.

Many children with myelomeningocele also need special training to learn to manage their bowels and bladder, to prevent possibly serious bladder infections and kidney deteriorations. This special training sometimes involves children learning, from an early age, to insert their own CATHETERS, or tubes to allow passage of urine (for more information, see CLEAN, INTERMITTENT CATHETERIZATION). Courts in various states have ruled that such children should be able to perform such catheterization (or if they are too young, have it performed by the school nurse) in their schools in order to take advantage of SPECIAL EDUCATION services. If CIC proves ineffective, various surgical procedures and medications have proved useful in helping older children achieve urinary continence. Often a combination of special diets and schedules, with medications, are used to achieve bowel continence. These have proved most effective when bowel training is started early in the child's preschool years.

Among other common problems faced by children with spina bifida are lack of sensation, leaving them vulnerable to cuts, BURNS, and resulting infections and sometimes pressure sores that become ulcers. Many also develop spinal disorders such as SCOLIOSIS or KYPHOSIS (see SPINE AND SPINAL DISORDERS), and sometimes EYE AND VISION PROBLEMS, such as STRABISMUS (potentially serious crossed eyes). Many children gain excess weight because of decreased mobility and have some difficulty with fine MOTOR SKILLS. The NINDS estimates that 70 percent of the children have normal IQ; the rest have some MENTAL RETARDATION, generally caused by hydrocephalus, MENINGITIS, or ventriculitis (infection of the VENTRICLES in the brain). Many have some kinds of LEARNING DISABILITIES, such as poor VISUAL-MOTOR INTEGRATION.

Today, children with myelomeningocele attend regular schools. They are covered under the EDUCATION FOR ALL HANDICAPPED CHILDREN ACT OF 1975, which provides that they will have access to educational services in the LEAST RESTRICTIVE ENVIRONMENT they are able to function in.

Apart from these problems, children with spina bifida develop as normal children do, going through the normal sexual changes of PUBERTY, dealing with the trials of ADOLESCENCE, and preparing for adulthood. Many are able to function as sexual adults, though some (especially males) experience problems because of nerve damage. A woman with spina bifida can bear children, though sometimes with difficulty. The NINDS estimates, however, that she has a 4-to-5-percent chance of bearing a child with the same defect.

Parents of children with spina bifida will require a good deal of information and support, much of it being provided by orga-

Searching for Spina Bifida's Cause

The cause of spina bifida is unknown. But scientists have found clues that suggest that a person's genetic makeup may combine with environmental factors to produce this birth defect.

Investigators offer these findings as evidence of spina bifida's genetic connection: parents who have one child with spina bifida have an increased risk of bearing another child with the same problem; more female than male babies are born with spina bifida; and Blacks, Asians, and Ashkenazi Jews have lower rates of spina bifida than do other Whites or Egyptians.

Because spina bifida rates are higher in certain geographic areas than in others, some scientists believe that the environment may somehow contribute to the disease. A higher rate may also reflect increased genetic risk for spina bifida in certain populations. In the United States, where one or two out of 1,000 newborns has spina bifida, more babies with this defect are born in the eastern and southern states than in the West. But the defect is even more common in western Great Britain and Ireland, where about four out of every 1,000 newborns are affected. At one time, eight out of every 1,000 newborns were affected.

Since the highest rates of neural tube defects in Great Britain are found in the poorer areas, scientists suggest that inadequate maternal diet may be an important trigger of spina bifida. Some studies have suggested that spina bifida is more common in babies born to poorly nourished women from lower socioeconomic groups and in babies conceived in winter and early spring, when fresh foods are less available.

Improved maternal nutrition in the United States and Great Britain has been cited as one possible reason for the decline of neural tube defects in the last decade. Recently, British scientists studied how prenatal vitamins affected the occurrence of spina bifida in babies born to women who previously had delivered a child with the disorder. They found that women who took a vitamin supplement with folic acid before conception and during part of pregnancy subsequently had one-seventh the number of babies with spina bifida than a similar group of women who did not take vitamins.

Although certain aspects of this study have been questioned, other scientists suspect that there might be a connection between vitamin and folic-acid deficiencies and spina bifida. Chemicals or drugs that decrease a woman's natural supply of folic acid (a B vitamin found in leafy green vegetables) may trigger the development of spina bifida in her baby. Scientists report that epileptic women who take valproic acid, an anticonvulsant drug that also reduces folic acid, during the first trimester of pregnancy are at moderate risk for having a baby with spina bifida.

Some investigators suggest that spina bifida may occur because the fetus lacks enough zinc. Others speculate that several vitamin shortages could work together to interfere with neural tube development, or that such deficiencies might permit other chemicals to disrupt neural tube development. Research will help determine the precise role of vitamins and other factors—including genetics—in the development of spina bifida.

Source: *Spina Bifida: Hope Through Research* (1986). Prepared for the Public Health Service by the National Institute of Neurological and Communicative Disorders and Stroke.

nizations such as those listed below or under HELP FOR SPECIAL CHILDREN on page 578.

For help and further information

Spina Bifida Association of America (SBAA)
1700 Rockville Pike, Suite 250
Rockville, MD 20852
301-770-SBAA [7222], toll-free number 800-621-3141
Catherine Hartnett, Executive Director
Organization of people with spina bifida, their families, health professionals working with them, and interested others. Encourages formation of local chapters; supports research into causes, treatments, and technical aids; seeks to educate public and strengthen services available; helps arrange adoption of spina bifida children in special circumstances; operates toll-free number; publishes various materials, including newsletter *Insights into Spina Bifida*, books and pamphlets such as *Children with Spina Bifida*, *The Needs of Children with Spina Bifida*, *Introduction to Spina Bifida*, and *Giant Steps for Steven*, informations sheets such as *CIC—The Law* and *The Baby Doe*

Law, as well as audio materials such as *Parents as Advocates for Educational Rights* and video materials such as *The First Year of Life* and *Prenatal Diagnosis and the Genetic Implications of Neural Tube Defects*.

National Institute of Neurological Disorders and Stroke (NINDS), 301-496-5751. Publishes brochure *Spina Bifida*. (For full group information, see BRAIN AND BRAIN DISORDERS.)

Eterna International Foundation for Disabled Children (EIFDC), 312-231-4400. Publishes various materials, including *Spina Bifida Therapy*. (For full group information, see HELP FOR SPECIAL CHILDREN on page 578.)

March of Dimes Birth Defects Foundation, 914-428-7100; local chapters in telephone-directory white pages. Publishes information sheet *Spina Bifida* (For full group information, see BIRTH DEFECTS.)

National Center for Education in Child and Maternal Health (NCEMCH), 202-625-8400. (For full group information, see PREGNANCY.)

Spina Bifida Adoption Referral Program
1955 Florida Drive
Xenia, OH 45385
513-372-2040
Judy Grafstrom, Contact
Organization aiming to facilitate adoption of children with spina bifida. Works with agencies and also directly with birth parents and adoptive parents.

Other reference sources

A Parent's Guide to Spina Bifida, by Beth-Ann Bloom and Edward Seljeskog, M.D. Minneapolis: University of Minnesota Press, 1988.

Health Care U.S.A., by Jean Carper. New York: Prentice Hall, 1987. Resource for general and specific health-care information; lists leading specialists in treating spina bifida and neural tube defects and other information.

Children with Spina Bifida: Early Intervention and Preschool Programming, G. Williamson, ed. Baltimore: Paul H. Brookes, 1987.

spinal-cord injury   Damage to the spine, the column of small circular bones (*vertebrae*) running up the trunk to the neck, and to the spinal cord, the column of nerve tissue that transmits signals to and from the brain, which is housed and usually protected within the spine (see BRAIN AND BRAIN DISORDERS).

The spine is susceptible to injury from various kinds of applied force, mainly:

- *longitudinal compression*, in which vertebrae are crushed together, as in a fall or dive from some height.
- *hinging*, sharp, sudden, extreme bending, as in the "whiplash" a passenger might get in an automobile accident.
- *shearing*, a combination of hinging and sharp twisting of the spinal column, as when someone is hit and spun around in an automobile accident.

As a result of such injuries, vertebrae may be dislocated, fractured, or torn away from the ligaments that bind them together. In severe cases, blood clots or accumulated fluid from swelling may press on the spinal cord, or the spinal cord itself may be damaged or destroyed.

Someone with a possible spinal-cord injury should not be moved unless absolutely necessary until a trained health professional has been able to assess the severity of the injury and the probable danger of further damage. This is especially important in so-called *unstable* cases, in which movement may cause the vertebrae to shift and damage or cut the spinal cord. Then the first order of business is to try to ensure that no further damage is caused, by stabilizing the bones, as through traction or surgical wiring, and minimizing effects such as swelling that can further damage the spinal cord.

Only then can efforts be turned toward rehabilitation. A patient with spinal-cord injury will work closely with PHYSICAL and OCCUPATIONAL THERAPISTS, using carefully tailored exercises to keep the muscles and joints from being badly affected by immobility, while the body slowly tries to heal itself.

Below the point of the injury, nerves—and therefore feeling and movement—will be affected. In the worst case, when the spinal cord has been completely severed, PARALYSIS results, and all ability to feel and move will be lost. Such patients will be almost totally dependent and will require special help (such as use of CATHETERS and enemas) to handle their bodily functions. If the spinal cord has been damaged but not severed, some feeling and motion may remain or may return slowly over a year or so after the accident; in this case the person may feel partial paralysis or weakness (*paresis*).

When the injury is to the neck, paralysis or weakness affects all four limbs and the trunk; this is termed *quadriplegia*. When the injury is below the neck, weakness and paralysis affect the legs and part of the trunk, the condition being called *paraplegia*. If some sensation remains, patients may feel considerable pain as well.

In general, doctors can offer little hope for recovery beyond a year or so after the initial accident. But one promising experimental approach uses computers and electrodes to transmit signals to and from the brain, bypassing the point of the initial injury and allowing some people with spinal-cord injuries to walk in limited settings. New techniques are also being used to hold down swelling and diminish the initial damage, the first eight hours being the most important in limiting the effects of the injury. As a result, some patients with spinal-cord injuries may, in the future, be able to make now-unexpected progress.

For help and further information

National Spinal Cord Injury Association (NSCIA)
149 California Street
Newton, MA 02158
617-964-0521, toll-free number 800-962-9629
Organization of people interested in spinal-cord injuries. Serves as information clearinghouse for public and professionals, especially regarding self-help for patients and families; makes referrals; provides special services such as counseling and drugs at discount; publishes various materials, including quarterly newsletter *Spinal Cord Injury Life*, *Options: Spinal Cord Injury and the Future*, *Handbook for Paraplegics and Quadriplegics*, and *National Resource Directory: An Information Guide for Persons with Spinal Cord Injury and Other Physical Disabilities*.

American Paralysis Association
P.O. Box 187
Short Hills, NJ 07078
201-379-2690, National Spinal Cord Injury Hot Line, 800-526-3456; toll-free number 800-225-0292 (U.S. except NJ)
Organization of people concerned about paralysis, as from spinal-cord injury, head injury, or stroke. Fosters research on treatment and cure; encourages formation of local chapters; publishes various materials, including newsletter on central nervous system and medical journal *Central Nervous System Trauma*.

Spinal Cord Society (SCS)
2410 Lakeview Drive
Fergus Falls, MN 56537
212-739-5252, toll-free hotline 800-328-8253 (U.S. except MN);
    toll-free hotline 800-862-0179 (MN)
Dr. Charles E. Carson, President
Organization of people with spinal-cord injuries, their families,
health professionals, and interested others. Supports research
into possible cures; maintains data bank; operates toll-free hotline; seeks to educate the public; publishes monthly *National
Newsletter*.

American Spinal Injury Association (ASIA)
250 East Superior, Room 619
Chicago, IL 60611
312-908-3425
J. Darrell Shea, M.D., President
Organization of physicians specializing in treating and researching spinal-cord injuries. Encourages research into causes,
cures, and prevention; seeks to educate public and professionals about how to prevent and limit damage from such injuries;
publishes various professional materials.

**National Institute of Neurological Disorders and Stroke
(NINDS)**, 301-496-5751. Publishes *Spinal Cord Injury: Hope
Through Research*. (For full group information, see BRAIN AND
BRAIN DISORDERS.)

Other reference sources

Health Care U.S.A., by Jean Carper. New York: Prentice Hall,
    1987. Resource for general and specific health-care informa-
    tion; lists major spinal-cord injury treatment and research
    centers, key neurologists, and other information.
Spinal Cord Injury: A Guide for Patients and Their Families, by
    Lyn Phillips et al. New York: Raven, 1986.
*Living with Spinal Cord Injury: Questions and Answers for
    Patients, Family and Friends*, by Marjorie Garfunkel and Glen
    Goldfinger; also *Spinal Cord Injury: A Guide for Care*, by
    Glenn Goldfinger and Marcia Hanak. Both available from New
    York University Medical Center, Institute for Rehabilitative
    Medicine, 400 East 34th Street, New York, NY 10016.
*Who Cares: A Handbook on Sex Education and Counseling Ser-
    vices for Disabled People*. Available from The Sex and Disa-
    bility Project, 1828 L Street, NW, Suite 704, Washington, DC
    20036.
Female Sexuality Following Spinal Cord Injury, by E.F. Becker.
    Bloomington, IL: Cheever, 1978. Address: P.O. Box 700,
    Bloomington, IL 61701.
(See also HELP FOR SPECIAL CHILDREN, on page 578.)

spinal muscular atrophies (SMA)   A group of MOTOR NEURON
DISEASES affecting people of various ages and with varying severity.

spine and spinal disorders   Problems with the column of
small, generally cylindrical bones (*vertebrae*) and cartilage that

runs from the head to the pelvis, which supports the head and
trunk and also houses and protects the column of nerve tissue
(*spinal cord*) that transmits signals to and from the brain (see
BRAIN AND BRAIN DISORDERS). The spinal cord (which, with the
brain, makes up the CENTRAL NERVOUS SYSTEM) is enclosed by
three levels of membrane, the *dura mater*, *arachnoid*, and *pia
mater*, collectively called the *meninges*.

The top seven bones in the spinal column, supporting the
head, are the *cervical vertebrae*; the 12 below that are the *thoracic vertebrae*, to which the ribs are attached; the five below
that are the *lumbar vertebrae*, which take most of the strain of
lifting; the five fused vertebrae below that make up the *sacrum*;
and the four fused vertebrae at the bottom are called the *coc-
cyx*.

In young people, the spine may be subject to a number of
disorders, among them SPINA BIFIDA, in which part of the spinal
cord is exposed; OSTEOMYELITIS, in which the bone and BONE
MARROW become infected, as in TUBERCULOSIS; SCOLIOSIS, KYPHO-
SIS, and LORDOSIS, all involving abnormal curvature of the spine;
and SPINAL-CORD INJURY. (For help and further information, see
entries on separate disorders.)

spiral curriculum   A type of CURRICULUM in which a set of
courses are taught over several years, each time with greater
depth and detail.

spirometry   A kind of PULMONARY FUNCTION TEST.

spitting up   Popular term for the backflow of food and fluids
from a baby's stomach. (See REGURGITATION.)

spleen   A central organ in the *lymphatic system*, the network
of vessels and organs that function as filters in the body's
IMMUNE SYSTEM to protect against disease.

SPM   Abbreviation for STANDARD PROGRESSIVE MATRICES.

sponge   Alternate name for a CERVICAL SPONGE.

spoon foods   Alternate term for so-called SOLID FOODS fed to
infants from about six months of age.

sputum analysis   Laboratory analysis of the mucous material
in the air passages, called *sputum* or *phlegm*, which is
increased by infection, ALLERGIES, and ASTHMA. The amount,
color, and makeup of sputum is an aid to diagnosis of LUNG AND
BREATHING DISORDERS, such as TUBERCULOSIS.

SRA Achievement Series   A widely used set of ACHIEVEMENT
TESTS for children in grades K to 12, used in schools to monitor
general academic achievement year by year. As NORM-REFER-
ENCED TESTS, the SRA series allows student SCORES to be compared with national standards. The pencil-and-paper tests cover
READING, mathematics, language, science, social studies, and
sometimes educational ability and use of reference materials.
Various forms at various levels are available, and the tests may
be hand- or computer-scored. (For help and further information, see TESTS.)

SSAT   Abbreviation for SECONDARY SCHOOL ADMISSION TESTS.

Stafford Loans   A federally SUBSIDIZED LOAN program under
which banks, credit unions, other financial institutions, and

sometimes schools lend money to undergraduate and graduate COLLEGE students who have no previous federally subsidized loans; formerly called *Guaranteed Student Loans (GSL)*. Amounts available (as of 1990) vary: up to $2,625 a year for the first two years of undergraduate study; up to $4,000 a year after two years in a bachelor's degree program; and up to $7,500 a year for graduate study. The maximum available for undergraduate study altogether is $17,250 and for undergraduate and graduate study together is $54,750, though in no case can this be more than the actual cost of the education, minus any other FINANCIAL AID the student receives. The student signs a promissory note, and the funds will be lent to the school and then paid either directly to the student or into the school's credit account, less a 5-percent origination fee and up to a 3-percent insurance premium. Interest charged is only 7 to 9 percent, and the repayment period is at least five and up to 10 years. Repayments of at least $50 a month do not begin until six to 12 months after the student either leaves school or drops below half-time, though payments may be further delayed under certain circumstances. (For help and further information, see SUBSIDIZED LOAN.)

stammering   Alternate name for a type of communication disorder (see COMMUNICATION SKILLS AND DISORDERS).

standardized foods   Foods for which the Food and Drug Administration (FDA) has established basic standards for ingredients if the name (such as ketchup or mayonnaise) is to be used. (For help and further information, see FOOD LABELS.)

standardized tests   Tests that have been developed through use on large groups, with the resulting scores being used to establish NORMS for students of specific AGES or GRADES, their main purpose to establish a comparison between a particular student's performance and the average performance of others. For example, if most students in the fourth grade score 75 on a particular ACHIEVEMENT TEST, the norm for fourth-graders is 75. If a third-grader later takes the test and scores 75, her score is better than the average for her grade, and she is said to have an EDUCATIONAL AGE of fourth grade, a comparison called a GRADE-EQUIVALENT. Most widely used, numerically scored tests, such as ACHIEVEMENT TESTS, are developed and standardized on large populations, and the scores tend to be distributed evenly along a *normal distribution* or *bell curve*, like an upturned tulip-shaped bowl, with most scores falling in the middle and many fewer scores at the top and bottom ranges. Such tests generally have written instructions for use. Among professionals, standardized tests are often evaluated on the basis of their RELIABILITY (consistency) and VALIDITY (accuracy in measuring what is intended). (For help and further information, see TESTS.)

Standard Progressive Matrices (SPM or Raven's Coloured Progressive Matrices)

A type of INTELLIGENCE TEST, used with people ages eight to 65, that attempts to assess mental ability without relying on verbal skills, offered either by group or individually. The person is given a series of 60 problems, each a pattern or figure with a missing part, and six possible alternatives from which the person must choose the correct one to complete the pattern. (For help and further information, see TESTS.)

Stanford Achievement Tests

A widely used series of group-administered ACHIEVEMENT TESTS used with children from mid-first grade to ninth grade, available in six grade levels and linked with national NORMS. The two earliest tests (Primary 1 and 2) focus on word study skills, word reading, READING and listening comprehension, spelling, concepts of number, computation, and environment. The next three (Primary 3 and Intermediate 1 and 2) add more language, mathematics applications, science, and social science, dropping word reading and environment. The highest level, Advanced, includes all areas except word study skills. Before mid-first grade and after late ninth grade, schools can use the *Stanford Early School Achievement Tests (SESAT)* and the *Stanford Test of Academic Skills*, respectively, to allow for monitoring of educational progress through the school years. (For help and further information, see TESTS.)

Stanford-Binet Intelligence Test

A widely used, individually administered INTELLIGENCE TEST for people from age two through adulthood; long in existence, it is the test that set the standards in the field. Offered in two forms, giving somewhat different levels of SCORES, the Stanford-Binet tests a wide variety of verbal and nonverbal skills, using tasks similar to those used in the WECHSLER INTELLIGENCE SCALE FOR CHILDREN, REVISED and GESELL PRESCHOOL TEST. However, on the Stanford-Binet, tasks are organized by age levels, based on the average performance of large numbers of children. Then, in evaluating the performance of an individual child, the examiner first finds the *basal age*, the age level at which the child can answer all items correctly, and continues to locate the *ceiling age*, at which the child answers none of the items correctly.

Unlike the Gesell tests, the Stanford-Binet focuses on the result, not on the child's behavior and attitude, though these are noted for the record. And unlike the Wechsler Intelligence Scale for Children, Revised, the Stanford-Binet does not have subdivisions with separate scores. Instead, it results in a single raw SCORE, which is converted to a child's *mental age* (MA), the age in years and months of the average person achieving that raw score on the test; that is then converted by means of a formula to an INTELLIGENCE QUOTIENT (IQ). If a child's CHRONOLOGICAL AGE and mental age are the same, the IQ will be 100; but if the child's mental age is higher, then the IQ will be over 100. Traditionally IQs have been classified as follows:

Gifted	140 and above
Very Superior	130–139
Superior	120–129
Above Average	110–119
Average	90–109
Below Average	80–89
Borderline	70–79
Mild Mental Retardation	60–69
Moderate/Severe Mental Retardation	59 and under

These classifications are still in popular use (and indeed are written into some laws), though the idea of mental age, intelligence quotients, and intelligence tests in general has come under heavy attack. In fact, the above categories are now somewhat outdated, and test professionals more often use statistical measures. But the Stanford-Binet test itself is still widely used, especially as a DIAGNOSTIC ASSESSMENT TEST to identify children who may need SPECIAL EDUCATION. (For help and further information, see INTELLIGENCE TESTS; MENTAL RETARDATION; TESTS.)

stanine A way of ranking test scores, on the same principle as a PERCENTILE, but with nine divisions.

startle reflex Alternate term for MORO'S REFLEX, a type of "primitive" REFLEX found only in babies that disappears in three to four months.

status offense An act that is "criminal" only because it is committed by someone having a particular status, such as a MINOR, and breaks a law applying only to such people. An adolescent who runs away from home or is TRUANT from school is a status offender. By contrast, an act that would be criminal if committed by an adult is, for a JUVENILE, labeled DELINQUENT.

statutory rape A criminal charge against someone for having sexual intercourse with a person under the AGE OF CONSENT, regardless of whether the parties knew each other's ages or who initiated the contact. Statutory rape is so called because it stems from statutes, or laws, and has nothing to do with force or threat of violence, as in other forms of rape.

STDs Abbreviation for SEXUALLY TRANSMITTED DISEASES.

stenosis Abnormal narrowing of a passageway in the body, as between two organs in the digestive system, often requiring surgery. (For help and further information, see DIGESTIVE DISORDERS.)

stepbrother or stepsister SIBLINGS who are not directly related through biology or ADOPTION, except that a parent of one is married to a parent of the other. With modern complicated patterns of divorce and remarriage, many more children are living in a FAMILY with stepbrothers and stepsisters.

stepfamily A FAMILY that includes children who share one parent, not two.

stepping reflex Alternate name for WALKING REFLEX.

stereotypy/habit disorder Psychiatric term for COMFORT HABITS that are so pervasive or extreme they become a clinical problem; a type of MENTAL DISORDER.

sterility Permanent INFERTILITY, as opposed to temporary infertility or impaired fertility (*subfertility*).

sterilization In relation to sexual reproduction, any medical or surgical procedure that is intended to permanently prevent a person from reproducing, including VASECTOMY and TUBAL LIGATION, the intention being to block normal passage of the egg (OVUM) and SPERM. Governments have sometimes used involuntary sterilization to prevent certain people from reproducing, such as those with physical or mental defects. In the United States such practices have been widely challenged, though laws permitting the government to perform involuntary sterilizations are still on the books in many places. Most sterilization today,

however, is voluntary, a permanent form of BIRTH CONTROL for men or women who do not wish to have any more children.

In relation to infections, sterilization also means the destruction of potentially harmful microorganisms by a variety of methods, including use of antiseptics or disinfectants, boiling or steaming (called *autoclaving* when done under high pressure), or RADIATION, including X-RAYS and ultraviolet light. (For help and further information, see also BIRTH CONTROL; VASECTOMY; TUBAL LIGATION.)

steroids, anabolic Compounds related to TESTOSTERONE, the male sex HORMONE, subject to abuse. (See HELP AGAINST SUBSTANCE ABUSE on page 587.)

stillbirth The birth of a FETUS that died before or during DELIVERY, one that was of a GESTATIONAL AGE at which it would have been expected to live, often beyond the 28th week of PREGNANCY and weighing 2.2 pounds (1,000 g); also called *late fetal death*. (Death of a fetus at an earlier stage is called MISCARRIAGE, or *spontaneous abortion*.) In some cases, the cause of death is obvious, such as lack of oxygen because the UMBILICAL CORD is wrapped around the baby's neck or because the PLACENTA malfunctioned; severe malformations or damage to the NERVOUS SYSTEM, such as ANENCEPHALY, SPINA BIFIDA, or HYDROCEPHALUS; RH INCOMPATIBILITY between mother and child; or extremely LOW BIRTH WEIGHT or PREMATURE delivery. In other cases, disorders affecting the mother are responsible—diseases such as DIABETES MELLITUS, RUBELLA, MEASLES, CHICKEN POX, TOXOPLASMOSIS, HERPES SIMPLEX, SYPHILIS, CYTOMEGALOVIRUS, and influenza. But in perhaps a third of the cases of stillbirth, the cause of death is unknown, though doctors (after detecting lack of a heartbeat and delivering the child) are required to examine the child and report cause of death, if known, on a death certificate. (For help and further information, see below; see also DEATH; CHILDBIRTH.)

For help and further information

Association for Recognizing the Life of Stillborns (ARLS), 303-978-9517. (For full group information, see DEATH.)

SHARE (Source of Help in Airing and Resolving Experiences), 618-234-2415 or -2120, ext. 1430. (For full group information, see DEATH.)

Pregnancy and Infant Loss Center (PILC), 612-473-9372. (For full group information, see DEATH.)

Other reference sources

Empty Arms: Coping with Miscarriage, Stillbirth and Infant Death, revised edition, by Sherokee Ilse. Long Lake, MN: Wintergreen, 1990.

Some Babies Die: An Exploration of Stillborn and Neo-natal Death. 54-minute film/video from University of California Extension Media Center, 2176 Shattuck Avenue, Berkeley, CA 94704. For ages 16 to adult.

Surviving Pregnancy Loss, by Rochelle Friedman, M.D., and Bonnie Gradstein. Boston: Little, Brown, 1982.

When Pregnancy Fails: Families Coping with Miscarriage, Stillbirth and Infant Death, by Susan Borg and Judith Lasker. Boston: Beacon, 1981.

Still's disease   Alternate name for juvenile rheumatoid ARTHRITIS.

storage disorder   A type of GENETIC DISORDER, classed as a METABOLIC DISORDER, in which the body lacks certain enzymes necessary to break down compounds, the result being abnormal and damaging accumulations of various substances in body tissues, often seriously affecting the brain. Examples include MUCOPOLYSACCHARIDOSES, LIPID STORAGE DISEASES (*lipidoses*), and *mucolipidoses*.

strabismus   Crossed eyes, often resulting from lack of coordination between the eyes; a kind of EYE AND VISION PROBLEM that may indicate disorders of the brain, such as a BRAIN TUMOR.

stranger anxiety   Popular name for a young child's shrinking from contact with unfamiliar people, a normal response in a child younger than two to 2½ years old. When it develops in older children and becomes disabling shyness, it is generally classified by psychiatrists as AVOIDANT DISORDER OF CHILDHOOD OR ADOLESCENCE.

For help and further information

The Shy Child: A Parent's Guide to Preventing and Overcoming Shyness from Infancy to Adulthood, by Philip G. Zimbardo and Shirley L. Radl. New York: McGraw-Hill, 1981.
Shyness: What It Is, What to Do About It, new edition, by Philip G. Zimbardo. Reading, MA: Addison-Wesley, 1990.
Conquering Shyness: The Battle Anyone Can Win, by Jonathan Cheek. New York: Delacorte, 1990.

streaming   Alternate term for TRACKING.

strep throat   Infection of the throat, tonsils, and sometimes the skin with the bacterium *streptococcus*, the same organism that causes *glomerulonephritis*, a severe kind of KIDNEY AND UROLOGICAL DISORDER, and SCARLET FEVER. Streptococcus is today treatable by antibiotics, but if the infection is not fully cleared up, RHEUMATIC FEVER may result.

stress fracture   A type of FRACTURE that results from overuse.

stretch marks   Darkened streaks on a woman's abdomen, BREASTS, and thighs, often because of enlargement during pregnancy, in which case they are called *striae gravidarum*, but sometimes also during the GROWTH SPURT associated with PUBERTY. The marks later fade but do not disappear completely. They are also sometimes associated with HORMONE DISORDERS.

striae gravidarum   The medical term for the STRETCH MARKS that generally accompany PREGNANCY.

stridor   An abnormal, high-pitched sound that accompanies breathing, usually on intake of breath, because of narrowing or obstruction of the breathing passages, as in CROUP, throat infec- tions, or TUMORS in the throat. Stridor can also result when a child has swallowed an object that has lodged in the throat or as a side effect of a malfunctioning SHUNT, a device placed in a child's head to treat HYDROCEPHALUS. In extreme or emergency cases, a TRACHEOSTOMY, an operation in which a breathing pipe is inserted into the windpipe externally, may be needed.

structural analysis   A type of WORD-ATTACK SKILL necessary for effective, independent READING.

student record (school record)   The cumulative file on a student's progress through a school, including basic identifying information, comments about student and family, some kinds of physical and health information, comments about behavior, notes about DISCIPLINE or counseling given, ATTENDANCE data, scores from various STANDARDIZED TESTS, and courses or classes taken and grades received. When a student transfers to another school or applies for ADMISSION to a COLLEGE, the latter information is summarized for the new school in the form of a TRANSCRIPT. The student record cumulates and is generally kept in the school or system office for immediate reference while the student is enrolled; afterward most of it is maintained as part of the permanent student record. (Some kinds of special confidential reports are kept separately from the main student record.) Student records were once totally under the control of the school, but under the FAMILY EDUCATIONAL RIGHTS AND PRIVACY ACT OF 1974, popularly called the *Buckley Amendment*, schools risk loss of federal funds if they fail to give parents access to the record of students under 18, and the school can by law release the student record to others outside the school only with the parent's authorization; over age 18 the student has control over access to the record and must authorize any access, including that by parents. The law gives the parents the chance to request corrections or clarifications of any misconceptions or skewed comments that may be entered into a child's records and mistakenly be passed on as true; if the request is denied, an appeals procedure is provided. It is important for parents to review the record and attempt to correct it, if necessary, because, long after the people who wrote comments in the record are gone, others will refer to the record in writing recommendations and reports, such as those requested by colleges or employers. (For help and further information, see FAMILY EDUCATIONAL RIGHTS AND PRIVACY ACT OF 1974; EDUCATION.)

student–teacher ratio   The total number of students in a school divided by the number of teachers, the result generally being the average size of the classes in the school. A school with 100 students and four teachers, for example, has a student–teacher ratio of 100 to 4, more generally expressed as 25 to 1, and its average class size is 25. The lower the student–teacher ratio, the more time and attention teachers have for each student, time that is increased if the school also has aides and assistants working with the teacher. Parents evaluating a school for their child should surely check this key ratio (see EDUCATION.)

student tutoring   Alternate term for PEER TUTORING.

study skills A set of PREREQUISITE skills important in a child's being able to learn effectively from a course, including knowing how and when to take notes, being able to organize material, knowing how to approach TESTS, and having the basic LOCATIONAL SKILLS to find the information needed in printed sources. (For help and further information, see EDUCATION; also HELP YOUR CHILD DO BETTER IN SCHOOL on page 526.)

Sturge-Weber syndrome A rare CONGENITAL disorder involving a port-wine stain (HEMANGIOMA) on the face, often on just one side, associated with malformation of blood vessels and CALCIUM deposits in nearby structures, and resulting in conditions such as MENTAL RETARDATION, EYE AND VISION PROBLEMS, and EPILEPSY; also called *Dmitri's disease* or *encephalotrigeminal angiomatosis*. No cure is yet available, though medications can provide some relief from symptoms.

For help and further information

National Institute of Neurological Disorders and Stroke (NINDS), 301-496-5751. (For full group information, see BRAIN AND BRAIN DISORDERS.)

stuttering A type of communication disorder (see COMMUNICATION SKILLS AND DISORDERS).

subcutaneous A type of INJECTION made directly into the tissue beneath the skin, such as the upper arm or thigh, like most common "shots."

subfertility Problems that affect a couple's ability to conceive a desired child but are not permanent and absolute INFERTILITY, or *sterility*, which is far more rare. (For help and further information, see INFERTILITY.)

subject-centered curriculum A type of CURRICULUM that focuses on content, rather than on LEARNING STYLE.

subjective test A type of TEST in which the administrator's handling of the test, observations, discretion, and rapport with the child very much affect the test score; often there are no "right" and "wrong" answers, and the test is designed to pull out information about the individual's thinking, knowledge, and functioning. Examples include individual DEVELOPMENTAL SCREENING TESTS, such as the GESELL PRESCHOOL TEST, and a student's essay for an English class.

subpoena A legal document requiring that a person appear at court at a specified time to testify as a witness. If the person is required to supply certain documents (such as income records in a CHILD SUPPORT case) to the court or to a specified party, the document is sometimes called *subpoena duces tecum* ("bring with you"). A person who fails to honor a subpoena may be considered in CONTEMPT OF COURT.

subsidized loan In EDUCATION, a type of FINANCIAL AID in which a student is given money to help meet the expenses of attending COLLEGE or PRIVATE SCHOOL; unlike SCHOLARSHIPS, loans must be repaid, but federal and other subsidies reduce the interest rate, making these loans very attractive. If taken out in the

student's name, such loans often require no repayment until some months after the student leaves school (at graduation or before). If taken out in a parent's name, payments generally start almost immediately.

To continue receiving financial aid, the student must maintain satisfactory progress, as defined by applicable school and federal guidelines. The loans also may be voided in some circumstances; for example, many types of federally subsidized financial aid will be suspended or terminated if a student is convicted of possessing or distributing drugs.

Among the major federal loan programs are PERKINS LOANS, STAFFORD LOANS, and PLUS LOANS/LOANS FOR STUDENTS. Repayments on these loans may be deferred under certain circumstances. If students have previous loans that are in default—that is, on which payments were not made when due, as when a student has left school for a time and wants to return—they will usually be ineligible for further loans. (For help and further information, see FINANCIAL AID.)

substance abuse A general term encompassing ALCOHOL ABUSE, DRUG ABUSE, SOLVENT ABUSE, and sometimes SMOKING. (For an overview of the effects and signs of substance abuse, plus organizations, reference works, and recommendations for parents, see HELP AGAINST SUBSTANCE ABUSE on page 587.)

subvocalization Forming words with the lips or even whispering them during silent READING, a practice that can significantly slow a student's reading speed but may be useful for those with reading difficulties, such as DYSLEXIA.

sucking An outgrowth of the ROOTING REFLEX, a desire that tends to last beyond such a reflex, sometimes being satisfied by a thumb or finger or by a PACIFIER; a kind of COMFORT HABIT.

Sucking and Pacifiers

Most babies get their thumbs and fingers in their mouths and suck on them. Many seem to find it very enjoyable and do it often. It causes no harm and can be ignored.

Some parents don't like the looks of thumb and finger sucking and substitute a pacifier for the thumb. This is also fine. However, do not use a homemade pacifier (such as the nipple from a baby bottle), one without ventilation holes, or an old pacifier that has cracks, tears, stickiness, or separation. These factors can cause choking. Stop giving the baby the pacifier toward the end of the first year, if you can. Never leave the pacifier on a cord around the baby's neck; the baby can strangle in the cord. And don't substitute the pacifier for the attention, food, or diaper changes that your baby wants and needs when he or she is crying!

Don't use a bottle of formula or juice as a pacifier—your baby's developing teeth can decay from the sugar they contain. [See NURSING BOTTLE SYNDROME.]

Source: *Infant Care* (1989). Prepared by the Bureau of Maternal and Child Health and Resources Development for the Public Health Service.

For many children sucking seems to be both part of the process of exploring their bodies and also a habit that offers comfort, relaxation, and pleasure. (See SUCKING AND PACIFIERS, on page 443.)

Traditionally, it was thought that children sucked their thumbs because they were taken off the breast or bottle too soon; but researchers have found that children still on the breast or bottle also suck their thumbs and sometimes give up both at once, often around age two, though sometimes a good deal later. The consensus seems to be that there is little good—and potential damage to the parent–child relationship—in forcibly trying to stop the thumb-sucking habit. It is now generally thought to do no great harm, unless carried on to age five or six, when (apart from the social stigma) sucking of thumbs or pacifiers can begin to affect the growth of TEETH.

sudden infant death syndrome (SIDS) The abrupt and unexpected DEATH of an infant or young child for which no adequate explanation can be found, either in the child's medical history or in a postmortem examination; also called *crib death*, *cot death*, or *sudden unexplained death syndrome (SUDS)*. SIDS is the leading cause of death among infants over one month old, responsible for approximately 7,000 deaths annually, or about 18 percent of INFANT MORTALITY.

By definition, the causes of SIDS are obscure. There is some evidence that SIDS is associated with SLEEP APNEA and PREMATURITY; certainly a child who has previously had an APPARENT LIFE-THREATENING EVENT (ALTE) is at much elevated risk of SIDS, even when HOME MONITORS are used for the infant during sleep. Somewhat more cases occur in cold weather, and many children lost to SIDS are later found to have had some respiratory symptoms (such as a cold in the nose) before death or to have had some other unexplained symptoms, such as weight loss. Some of these deaths may be due to powerful respiratory infections and others to undetected BIRTH DEFECTS, especially relating to METABOLISM. But most are apparently caused by some interruption of normal heart and breathing rhythms, as in sleep apnea or possibly a problem with the *surfactant*, which normally keeps the lungs' air sacs from collapsing.

Researchers are exploring numerous other factors that may be associated with SIDS, including LOW BIRTH WEIGHT; BOTTLEFEEDING; ADOLESCENT PREGNANCY; SMOKING, DRUG ABUSE, or ANEMIA in the mother; socioeconomic disadvantage; and family history of loss of a previous SIBLING to SIDS. While such research continues and evidence accumulates, prudent prospective parents will want to seek good PRENATAL CARE, avoid smoking and drugs (for these and other reasons), and consider BREASTFEEDING (as it gives the child somewhat better resistance to infection). After the birth, they will want to watch the baby carefully during any minor illness.

In some situations, a NEONATOLOGIST or PEDIATRICIAN may recommend use of a home monitor, to alert parents if the child stops breathing. Home monitors are not wholly reliable, however, sometimes giving a FALSE POSITIVE (indicating a problem where none exists) or a FALSE NEGATIVE (failing to signal that a problem does exist). The Public Health Service's report *Infantile Apnea and Home Monitoring* (for more, see HOME MONITORS) stresses the importance of training and instruction of caregivers so that they will know how to act in cases of apnea, such as how to attempt RESUSCITATION.

For help and further information

National Sudden Infant Death Syndrome Foundation (NSIDSF)
10500 Little Patuxent Parkway, Suite 420
Columbia, MD 21044
301-964-8000, toll-free 24-hour hotline 800-221-SIDS [7437]
Mitchell R Stoller, Executive Vice President
Organization of parents who have lost children to SIDS, medical professionals, and interested others. Encourages formation of mutual-support self-help groups; provides information and referrals; operates 24-hour hotline; publishes various print and audiovisual materials, including newsletter and an information packet, *Facts About Sudden Infant Death Syndrome*.

National Center for the Prevention of Sudden Infant Death Syndrome (NCPSIDS)
330 North Charles Street
Baltimore, MD 21201
301-547-0300, toll-free hotline 800-638-SIDS [7437]
Thomas L. Moran, President
Information clearinghouse for public and professionals on SIDS. Sponsors research; seeks to educate public; provides information and referrals; operates hotline; publishes brochure *Facts on Sudden Infant Death Syndrome*.

National Sudden Infant Death Syndrome Clearinghouse (NSIDSC)
8201 Greensboro Drive, Suite 600
McLean, VA 22102
703-821-8955
Information service, sponsored by the U.S. Department of Health and Human Services, providing information on SIDS to public and professionals; publishes various materials including quarterly *Information Exchange*, *Sudden Infant Death Syndrome: A Review of the Medical Literature, 1974–1979*, directory of SIDS counseling and information programs, and fact sheets: *What Parents Should Know About SIDS*, *What Is SIDS?*, *Facts About Apnea*, *Infantile Apnea and SIDS*, *Parents and the Grieving Process*, and *The Grief of Children*.

International Council for Infant Survival (ICIS)
9178 Nadine River Circle
Fountain Valley, CA 92708
714-856-3522
Chris Elliott, Chairperson
Organization of families who have lost a child to SIDS and other concerned individuals and organizations. Fosters research; gathers and disseminates information on SIDS and home monitoring; offers support to the families; encourages formation of local mutual-support self-help groups; publishes various mate-

rials, including quarterly newsletter, brochure, and research summaries.

National Institute of Child Health and Human Development (NICHD), 301-496-5133. (For full group information, see PREGNANCY.)

National Center for Education in Child and Maternal Health (NCEMCH), 202-625-8400; **National Maternal and Child Health Clearinghouse (NMCHC)**, 202-625-8410. (For full group information, see PREGNANCY.)

Other reference sources

Empty Arms: Coping with Miscarriage, Stillbirth and Infant Death, revised edition, by Sherokee Ilse. Long Lake, MN: Wintergreen, 1990.

The "Discovery" of Sudden Infant Death Syndrome: Lessons in the Practice of Political Medicine, by Abraham B. Bergman, M.D. Seattle: University of Washington Press, 1988.

Health Care U.S.A., by Jean Carper. New York: Prentice Hall, 1987. Resource for general and specific health-care information; lists SIDS information and counseling programs, and other information.

When Pregnancy Fails: Families Coping with Miscarriage, Stillbirth and Infant Death, by Susan Borg and Judith Lasker. Boston: Beacon, 1981.

Surviving Pregnancy Loss, by Rochelle Friedman, M.D., and Bonnie Gradstein. Boston: Little, Brown, 1982.

(See also DEATH; HIGH-RISK BABIES; SLEEPING DISORDERS.)

SUDS Abbreviation for *sudden unexplained death syndrome*, better known as SUDDEN INFANT DEATH SYNDROME (SIDS).

suicide The deliberate killing of oneself, a problem affecting all ages but, most dramatically, adolescents and young adults. In the United States overall, about 2.8 of every 100,000 deaths are suicides, but among 15-to-24-year-olds the rate in the mid-1980s was 12.2 suicides per 100,000, which had tripled over the previous 30 years to become the third most common cause of DEATH in that age group, after accidents and homicide. Since 1977, the Public Health Service reports, more than 5,000 young adults 15 to 25 have committed suicide every year.

Beyond that, many people attempt suicide but fail to kill themselves or are saved by others' intervention. In the whole population perhaps eight to 10 people attempt suicide for every one who completes suicide, but in the 15-to-25 age group, perhaps 25 to 50 people make such attempts for every completed suicide. Uncounted others also have times of *suicide crisis*, when they are obsessed with thoughts of killing themselves, often to the extent of planning a suicide to the tiniest detail, but stop short of an actual attempt. Suicides are less common among children ages five to 14; even so, deliberate self-destructive acts (sometimes leading to DEATH) cause as many as 12,000 children a year to be hospitalized. (See SELF-MUTILATION SYNDROME.)

A large proportion of people who commit suicide—some estimate as high as 90 percent—have some form of MENTAL DISORDER, such as DEPRESSION or SCHIZOPHRENIA, often coupled with ALCOHOL ABUSE or DRUG ABUSE. Beyond that, there are many theories and little solid evidence for why people commit suicide. Many researchers have focused on family history and biochemical imbalances. Among other RISK FACTORS linked with increased likelihood of suicide are CHILD ABUSE AND NEGLECT, personal and social losses (such as a death in the family), serious physical illness, and general social isolation; in older adults, also unemployment, financial problems, and problems of dependence and illness related to aging. Especially among young people, suicides can come in "clusters," where one suicide leads to several more in one small community. This happens so often that many schools and communities have established crisis prevention and intervention programs, attempting to identify those who may be suicidal.

Parents concerned about possible suicide among family or friends should not delude themselves with the popular notion that "people who talk about suicide don't actually kill themselves." In fact, the Public Health Service points out, somewhere between 20 and 50 percent of the people who commit suicide have made attempts before. Though there are no sure-fire ways to identify a potentially suicidal person, they note several warning signs, including:

- previous suicide attempts.
- talk about suicide, often oblique, such as "They won't have to worry about me much longer."
- making arrangements for departure, such as giving away prize possessions or preparing as if for a trip.
- change in behavior or personality, often seen through withdrawal from usual activities, reflecting feelings of hopelessness or worthlessness.
- general depression, often including loss of appetite or weight, change in sleeping patterns, uncommunicativeness, and slowness in speaking, moving, thinking, and acting.

If parents think a family member or friend may be considering suicide, the Public Health Service recommends the following approaches:

- Listen without judging, giving the person an understanding forum in which to try to talk things through.
- Talk specifically about suicidal thoughts, such as: Does he or she have a plan? Has he or she bought a gun? Where is it? Stockpiled pills? Where are they? They note that, "contrary to popular belief, such candor will not give a person dangerous ideas or encourage a suicidal act."
- Evaluate the situation, trying to distinguish between general upset and more serious danger, as when suicide plans *have* been made. If the crisis is acute, *do not leave the person alone.*
- Be supportive, letting the person know you care and trying to break down his or her feelings of isolation.

- Take charge in finding help, without concern about invading the person's privacy. Do not try to handle the problem alone; get professional help immediately. The groups listed below may be sources of help, as may the family doctor, local hospital, mental health clinic, suicide prevention or crisis intervention center, clergy, or police station.
- Make the environment safe, removing from the premises (not just hiding) weapons such as guns, razors, scissors, medication, and other potentially dangerous household items.
- Do not keep suicide talk or threats secret; these are calls for help and call for immediate action.
- Do not challenge, dare, or use verbal shock treatment. They can have tragic effects.
- Make a contract with the person, getting a promise or commitment, preferably in writing, not to make any suicidal attempt until you have talked further.
- Beware of elevated moods and seemingly quick recoveries; sometimes they are illusory, reflecting the relief of finally deciding to commit suicide or reflecting the temporary release of talking to someone, though the underlying problems have not been resolved.

Where warning signs have gone unrecognized or help has been insufficient to prevent a suicide, the aftermath is extremely difficult and painful for everyone involved, not only immediate family but also friends. Groups such as those listed below can help people deal with the grief and pain that can result, including children getting over the loss of a parent or friend and parents getting over the loss of children or a partner. They can also help the survivors learn how to prevent further suicides, which sometimes (especially among young people) come in clusters.

For help and further information

American Association of Suicidology
2459 South Ash Street
Denver, CO 80222
303-692-0985
Julie Perlman, Chief Executive Officer

Organization for medical and social work professionals and others interested in "life-threatening behavior and suicide." Provides information to public and professionals; publishes various materials, including newsletter, directory of suicide prevention and crisis intervention centers, and booklets such as *Suicide in Young People* and *Before It's Too Late: What To Do When Someone You Know Attempts Suicide.*

National Institute of Mental Health, 301-443-4536. Publishes *What To Do When A Friend Is Depressed, A Consumer's Guide to Mental Health Services*, and *Useful Information on Suicide.* (For full group information, see MENTAL DISORDERS.)

National Runaway Switchboard, 800-621-4000. Also functions as **Adolescent Suicide Hotline**. (For full group information, see MISSING CHILDREN.)

The Compassionate Friends (TCF), 312-990-0010. Includes **Survivors After Suicide** group for families and friends. (For full group information, see DEATH.)

Other reference sources

General Works

Youth Suicide Prevention: Lessons from Literature, Sara Munson Deats and Lagretta Tallent Lanker, eds. New York: Plenum, 1989.
Survivors of Suicide, by Rita Robinson. Santa Monica, CA: IBS, 1989.
Children Who Don't Want to Live: The Suicidal Child, by Israel Orbach. San Francisco: Jossey-Bass, 1988.
Suicide: Prevention, Intervention, Postvention, second edition, by Earl A. Grollman. Boston: Beacon, 1988.
Silent Grief: Living in the Wake of Suicide, by Christopher Lukas and Henry M. Seider. New York: Scribner, 1988.
The Encyclopedia of Suicide, by Glen Evans and Norman L. Farberow, Ph.D. New York: Facts on File, 1988.
Health Care, U.S.A., by Jean Carper. New York: Prentice Hall, 1987. Resource for general and specific health-care information; lists centers for treatment or research, specialists in treating depression, suicide prevention centers, and other information.
A Time to Listen: Preventing Youth Suicide, by Patricia Hermes. San Diego, CA: Harcourt Brace Jovanovich, 1987.
A Cry for Help, by Mary Griffin and Carol Felsenthal. Garden City, NY: Doubleday, 1983.

For or By Kids

Teenagers Talk About . . . Suicide, second edition, by Marian Crook. Toronto: NC Press, 1989. Interviews with young people who have considered or tried suicide.
Teen Suicide, by Gail B. Stewart. Mankato, MN: Crestwood, 1988. Part of the Facts About series.
Dead End: A Book About Suicide, by John Langone. Boston: Little, Brown, 1986.
Life Pact. 1988; released 1989. Producer and director, Lee D. Walter. AIMS Media, 6901 Woodley Ave., Van Nuys, CA 91406. 23-minute video or film. Life Pact—an agreement to talk with a specific friend if ever an individual considers suicide.
Power of Choice: Depression and Suicide. 30-minute video available from Live Wire Video Publishers, 3315 Sacramento Street, San Francisco, CA 94118. For ages 13 to adult.
Who Will Cry for Me? Avoiding Suicide. Producers, Joyn Young and David McGoldrick. 50-minute video available from Guidance Associates, Communications Park, Box 3000, Mt. Kisco, NY 10549.

Background Works

Self-Destruction in the Promised Land: A Psychocultural Biology of American Suicide, by Howard I. Kushner. New Brunswick, NJ: Rutgers University Press, 1989.

Terminal Choices: Euthanasia, Suicide, and the Right to Die, by Robert N. Wennberg. Grand Rapids, MI: Eerdmans, 1989.

Suicide and Depression Among Adolescents and Young Adults, Gerald L. Klerman, ed. Washington, DC: American Psychiatric Press, 1986.

People in Crisis: Understanding and Helping, second edition, by L. Hoff. Reading, MA: Addison-Wesley, 1984.

The Psychology of Suicide, by E. Shneidman, N. Faberow, and R. Litman. New York: Aronson, 1983.

sulfatide lipidosis Alternate name for metachromatic leukodystrophy, a type of LIPID STORAGE DISEASE.

sulfur A MINERAL used in several key AMINO ACIDS and therefore vital to the building and maintenance functions of the body, especially in bones, tendons, and connective tissue. Among the main sources of sulfur are wheat germ, dried beans, beef, and clams. Before the advent of penicillin and later antibiotics, drugs containing sulfur (*sulfa drugs*, or *sulfonamides*) were often used to treat infections; they are still used for some kinds of infections, such as urinary-tract infections, and in ointments to treat some SKIN DISORDERS. (For help and further information, see MINERALS; NUTRITION.)

Summary of Answers for the PSAT/NMSQT A report for high school officials on the performance of their students on the PRELIMINARY SCHOLASTIC APTITUDE TEST/NATIONAL MERIT SCHOLARSHIP QUALIFYING TEST.

summative evaluation Alternate term for INFORMAL ASSESSMENT.

supervision In relation to families, the duty of parents or GUARDIANS to protect and guide children who are in their CUSTODY and care. Supervision is part of the PARENTS' RESPONSIBILITIES that run along with the PARENTS' RIGHTS to make basic and important decisions for a child. A parent's failure to provide proper supervision may lead to charges of CHILD ABUSE AND NEGLECT and, in serious cases, to TERMINATION OF PARENTS' RIGHTS and assumption by the state of the task of supervising the child. JUVENILES convicted of DELINQUENT acts or STATUS OFFENSES (such as runaways, TRUANTS, or INCORRIGIBLE children), who are thought to require more supervision than previously provided, may sometimes be placed under court supervision. This may involve PROBATION, or the court may transfer custody to a relative or social agency. Such delinquents are variously called *Children in Need of Supervision* (CHINS), *Juveniles in Need of Supervision* (JINS), *Minors in Need of Supervision* (MINS), or *Persons in Need of Supervision* (PINS).

Supplemental Educational Opportunity Grant (SEOG) A type of GRANT in FINANCIAL AID to help undergraduate students meet the expenses of attending COLLEGE. Grants of up to $4,000, depending on the funds available at each school, are offered to students with exceptional financial need; priority is given to those who have PELL GRANTS. Money is paid directly to the student or credited to the school account. (For help and further information, see FINANCIAL AID.)

Supplemental Loans for Students (SLS) The student form of PLUS LOANS.

suppression amblyopia A serious eye condition that may involve loss of sight in one eye. (See EYE AND VISION PROBLEMS.)

suppressor cells A type of white blood cell (*lymphocyte*) in the IMMUNE SYSTEM.

surrogate family A FAMILY-like network of people chosen as close friends and supporters, often people with shared work, culture, interests, and neighborhoods.

surrogate parenting An arrangement by which a woman agrees to become inseminated by a man, generally through ARTIFICIAL INSEMINATION, bear a child, and then give the baby for ADOPTION to the man and his wife, who is unable to bear children herself. Though physically very simple, surrogate parenting is fraught with legal, emotional, and social pitfalls, including uncertain legal status, social pressures for and against the procedure from various quarters, and feelings of confusion, sadness, and guilt, as the "Baby M" case, for one, amply demonstrated. Laws regarding surrogate arrangements vary widely, and the legal status of agreements among the parties is unclear. For the prospective parents, the major risk is that the surrogate mother will decide not to give the child up for adoption. Though a seemingly simple solution to a situation when the wife is infertile but the husband is not, parents considering this course should explore the ramifications of surrogacy very carefully before making any decision.

For help and further information

Center for Surrogate Parenting (CSP)
8383 Wilshire Boulevard, Suite 750
Beverly Hills, CA 90211
213-655-1974
William Handle, President
Organization of lawyers, physicians, and psychologists working with surrogate parenting. Gathers and disseminates information, as to lawyers handling surrogate parent cases; seeks to influence public policy and legislation; publishes various materials.

National Coalition Against Surrogacy (NCAS)
c/o Foundation on Economic Trends
1130 17th Street, NW, Suite 630
Washington, DC 20036
202-466-2823
Organization of women who have acted as surrogate mothers, lawyers, and others against surrogate parenting. Offers support to women unhappy as surrogate mothers; seeks to influence public policy and legislation against surrogate maternity contracts.

Other reference sources

Birth Power: The Case for Surrogacy, by Carmel Shalev. New Haven, CT: Yale University Press, 1989.

A Mother's Story, by Mary Beth Whitehead with Loretta Schwartz-Nobel. New York: St. Martin's, 1990. Story of the woman who bore "Baby M" as surrogate mother.

Birth Mother: America's First Legal Surrogate Mother Tells the Story of Her Change of Heart, by Elizabeth Kane. San Diego, CA: Harcourt Brace Jovanovich, 1988.

The Case of Baby M: Mary Beth Whitehead and the Facts of Life, by Rochelle Sharpe. New York: Prentice Hall, 1988.

Woman and Child: The Legacy of Baby M, by Phyllis Chesler. New York: Times Books, 1988.

Surrogate Parenting, by Amy Zuckerman. New York: Pharos, 1988.

Surrogate Motherhood: The Ethics of Using Human Beings, by Thomas A. Shannon. New York: Crossroads/Continuum, 1988.

The Surrogate Mother, by Noel P. Keane. New York: Everest House, 1981.

Medicine and the Law, by Neil Grauer. New York: Chelsea House, 1990. Overview of issues including surrogate motherhood and medical malpractice. For grades 7 to 10.

survival skills The skills a person needs to function effectively in an environment, sometimes referring to the skills needed if one were stranded on a desert island or mountainous wilderness but often meaning FUNCTIONAL SKILLS necessary for everyday life.

suspension In EDUCATION, an order for a student to leave a school temporarily, generally for misbehavior. In-school suspension refers to a student's being ordered to leave classes but kept in school elsewhere, as outside a principal's office. Unlike EXPULSION, which is long-term or permanent, suspension is normally lifted in a short time, sometimes after consultation with the student's parents. Various Supreme Court rulings have affected the legal rights of students and schools in cases of suspension and expulsion, as described at right in PROCEDURAL GUIDELINES FOR SUSPENSION AND EXPULSION.

For help and further information

National Committee for Citizens in Education (NCCE), 301-997-9300; toll-free number (U.S. except MD) 800-NET-WORK [638-9675]. Publishes fact sheets on suspension and due process in schools. (For full group information, see EDUCATION.)

swayback Outdated popular name for LORDOSIS.

sweat test MEDICAL TEST that measures concentrations of salt in sweat, abnormally high concentrations of SODIUM and CHLORIDE being a common indicator of CYSTIC FIBROSIS.

sweep-check test Alternate name for the Pure Tone Test, a kind of HEARING TEST.

swimmer's ear Alternate name for otitis externa, inflammation or infection of the outer ear, a common type of EAR AND HEARING PROBLEM.

Sydenham's chorea A pattern of involuntary, quick, jerky movements, called CHOREA, often found in children who have RHEUMATIC FEVER, apparently resulting from *streptococcus* infection in the brain. It generally passes after some weeks, though it may recur in some situations. Sydenham's chorea is relatively rare since the advent of antibiotics.

syllabus An outline of a course offered in a school, often on the COLLEGE level, describing the main topics to be covered, sometimes accompanied by a schedule and listing the works to be assigned or suggested.

symbiotic psychosis Outdated term for AUTISM.

symbiotic stage The early close relationship established between a MOTHER (or other primary CAREGIVER) and child as a result of the BONDING process, in which the baby sees the mother as part of itself and the mother acts as a need-satisfying object to the child. Traditionally, the symbiotic stage was thought to extend from age three to 18 months, to roughly around the time that a child begins to walk; but more recent work suggests that the child begins to see the self and mother as separate entities earlier, perhaps by about seven months, a stage called SEPARATION-INDIVIDUATION.

symbolic wounding Alternate term for SELF-MUTILATION SYNDROME.

symptom In medicine, a subjective indication of illness observed by a patient, as opposed to an objective indication, or SIGN, of disease or disorder observed or detected by a physician. An observable skin rash or a measurable fever is a sign, for example, while the feeling of itching or heat is a symptom.

symptothermal method A technique of NATURAL FAMILY PLANNING.

syndactyly (syndactylism or **syndactylia)** A BIRTH DEFECT in which two or more fingers or (more commonly) toes are joined together, sometimes joined by the skin only but sometimes with bones and skin fused and a single nail. Many forms of syndactyly are inherited, and they affect boys more than girls, but some may be caused by constriction of the FETUS within the UTERUS.

syndrome A group of SIGNS or SYMPTOMS that, when they appear together, indicate the presence of a known condition or disease; literally meaning "running together." Not all syndromes are so called, such as *Tay-Sachs disease* (see LIPID STORAGE DISEASES) or APPARENT LIFE-THREATENING EVENT (ALTE), but many syndromes are tagged as such. Among the many covered in this book are acquired immune deficiency syndrome (AIDS), BATTERED CHILD SYNDROME, CHUBBY PUFFER SYNDROME, congenital varicella syndrome (see CHICKEN POX), CRI DU CHAT (CRY OF THE CAT) SYNDROME, CUSHING'S SYNDROME, DE LANGE SYNDROME, DISPLACED CHILD SYNDROME, DOWN'S SYNDROME,

Procedural Guidelines for Suspension and Expulsion

A school policy may lawfully provide for penalties of varying severity, including suspension and expulsion, to respond to drug-related offenses. The Supreme Court has recently held that because schools "need to be able to impose disciplinary sanctions for a wide range of unanticipated conduct disruptive of the educational process," a school's disciplinary rules need not be so detailed as a criminal code. Nonetheless, it is helpful for school policies to be explicit about the types of offenses that will be punished and about the penalties that may be imposed for each of these (e.g., use, possession, or sale of drugs). State and local law will usually determine the range of sanctions that is permissible. In general, courts will require only that the penalty imposed for drug-related misconduct be rationally related to the severity of the offense.

School officials should not forget that they have jurisdiction to impose punishment for some drug-related offenses that occur off-campus. Depending on state and local laws, schools are often able to punish conduct at off-campus, school-sponsored events as well as off-campus conduct that has a direct and immediate effect on school activities.

Procedural Guidelines

Students facing suspension or expulsion from school are entitled under the U.S. Constitution and most state constitutions to commonsense due process protections of notice and an opportunity to be heard. Because the Supreme Court has recognized that a school's ability to maintain order would be impeded if formal procedures were required every time school authorities sought to discipline a student, the Court has held that the nature and formality of the "hearing" will depend on the severity of the sanction being imposed.

A formal hearing is not required when a school seeks to suspend a student for 10 days or less. The Supreme Court has held that due process in that situation requires only that:

* The school must inform the student, either orally or in writing, of the charges against him or her and of the evidence to support those charges.
* The school must give the student an opportunity to deny the charges and present his or her side of the story.
* As a general rule, this notice and rudimentary hearing should precede a suspension. However, a student whose presence poses a continuing danger to persons or property or an ongoing threat of disrupting the academic process may be immediately removed from school. In such a situation, the notice and rudimentary hearing should follow as soon as possible.

The Supreme Court has also stated that more formal procedures may be required for suspensions longer than 10 days and for expulsions. Although the Court has not established specific procedures to be followed in those situations, other federal courts have set the following guidelines for expulsions. These guidelines would apply to suspensions longer than 10 days as well:

* The student must be notified in writing of the specific charges against him or her which, if proven, would justify expulsion.
* The student should be given the names of the witnesses against him or her and an oral or written report on the facts to which each witness will testify.
* The student should be given the opportunity to present a defense against the charges and to produce witnesses or testimony on his or her behalf.

Many states have laws governing the procedures required for suspensions and expulsions. Because applicable statutes and judicial rulings vary across the country, local school districts may enjoy a greater or lesser degree of flexibility in establishing procedures for suspensions and expulsions.

School officials must also be aware of the special procedures that apply to suspension or expulsion of students with disabilities under federal law and regulations.

Effect of Criminal Proceedings Against a Student

A school may usually pursue disciplinary action against a student regardless of the status of any outside criminal prosecution. That is, federal law does not require the school to await the outcome of the criminal prosecution before initiating proceedings to suspend or expel a student or to impose whatever other penalty is appropriate for the violation of the school's rules. In addition, a school is generally free under federal law to discipline a student when there is evidence that the student has violated a school rule, even if a juvenile court has acquitted (or convicted) the student or if local authorities have declined to prosecute criminal charges stemming from the same incident. Schools may wish to discuss this subject with counsel.

Effect of Expulsion

State and local law will determine the effect of expelling a student from school. Some state laws require the provision of alternative schooling for students below a certain age. In other areas, expulsion may mean the removal from public schools for the balance of the school year or even the permanent denial of access to the public school system.

Source: *What Works: Schools Without Drugs* (1989). U.S. Department of Education.

EATON-LAMBERT SYNDROME, EDWARDS' SYNDROME, FANCONI'S SYN-DROME, FEAR TENSION PAIN SYNDROME, FETAL ALCOHOL SYNDROME, FETAL HYDANTOIN SYNDROME, FLOPPY INFANT SYNDROME, FRAGILE X SYN-DROME, HURLER'S SYNDROME, HUNTER'S SYNDROME, IRRITABLE BOWEL SYNDROME, KLINEFELTER'S SYNDROME, LAURENCE-MOON-BIEDL SYN-DROME, LESCH-NYHAN SYNDROME, LOUIS-BAR SYNDROME, MARFAN SYN-DROME (ARACHNODACTYLY), MATERNAL DEPRIVATION SYNDROME, MENKE'S SYNDROME, MORQUIO'S SYNDROME, NOONAN'S SYNDROME, NURSING BOTTLE SYNDROME, ORGANIC BRAIN SYNDROME, PATAU'S SYN-DROME, PIERRE ROBIN SYNDROME, *premenstrual syndrome* (see MENSTRUATION), REFSUM'S SYNDROME, RESPIRATORY DISTRESS SYN-DROME, REYE'S SYNDROME, ROSENTHAL'S SYNDROME, SAVANT SYN-DROME, SELF-MUTILATION SYNDROME, SHAKEN CHILD SYNDROME, SHEEHAN'S SYNDROME, SJÖGREN-LARSSON SYNDROME, STURGE-WEBER SYNDROME, SUDDEN INFANT DEATH SYNDROME (SIDS), TOURETTE'S SYN-DROME, TOXIC SHOCK SYNDROME, TURNER'S SYNDROME, and VULNERA-BLE CHILD SYNDROME.

synthesis-level thinking   Combining knowledge of several pieces of previously learned information to create ideas new to the thinker; from Benjamin Bloom's description of the various kinds of thinking or learning processes, the other main types being KNOWLEDGE-LEVEL THINKING, COMPREHENSION-LEVEL THINKING, APPLICATION-LEVEL THINKING, ANALYSIS-LEVEL THINKING, and EVALUA-TION-LEVEL THINKING.

synthetic learning   A type of LEARNING STYLE that focuses on the various aspects of a skill or concept first and then on the general concept or rule.

syphilis   A serious progressive disease that, if untreated, can cause MENTAL DISORDERS, BLINDNESS, and DEATH; specifically, infection with the corkscrew-shaped bacterium *Treponema pallidum*, a common SEXUALLY TRANSMITTED DISEASE (STD) and one of the traditional *venereal diseases*. A scourge of humanity for centuries, syphilis is today readily treatable by antibiotics, but cases have recently been on the rise, perhaps partly because the success of the treatment has left many people unaware of the disease's dangers.

The infection is passed through direct contact with an infected person, often through the genital area, mouth, or anus but also through a break in the skin anywhere on the body. A pregnant woman with syphilis can (at least after the fourth month of pregnancy) pass the disease to the FETUS, causing serious BIRTH DEFECTS, such as MENTAL RETARDATION, MENINGITIS, and various deformities; there is also increased risk of MISCAR-RIAGE. The National Institute of Allergy and Infectious Disease (NIAID) reports, however: "The syphilis bacterium is very fragile, and the infection is rarely, if ever, spread by contact with objects such as toilet seats or towels."

Early symptoms, which occur 10 days to three months after exposure, are often very mild—so mild that people often do not seek treatment and meanwhile can pass the infection on to others. The main symptom of the first stage of syphilis (medically called *primary syphilis*) is a usually painless open sore, a *chancre*, often in the genital area but sometimes around the mouth or fingertips; this disappears within a few weeks.

In the second stage, or *secondary syphilis*, about two to 12 weeks after the chancre disappears, a skin rash appears, sometimes only in localized areas, such as the palms or soles of the feet, but sometimes over the whole body. The rash is often accompanied by flulike symptoms, such as low-grade FEVER, headache, fatigue, sore throat, swollen lymph glands, and occasionally hair loss. These symptoms may come and go for one or two years, during which time the person is actively contagious.

After that, the disease enters a so-called *latent* stage. NIAID reports:

> Many people who are not treated will suffer no further consequences of the disease. However, from 15 to 40 percent of those infected go on to develop the complications of late, or *tertiary*, syphilis, in which the bacteria damage the heart, eyes, brain, nervous system, bones, joints, or almost any other part of the body. This stage can last for years, or even for decades. Late syphilis, the final stage, can lead to mental illness, blindness, heart disease, and death.

Syphilis can be diagnosed by its symptoms (though many are similar to those of other STDs), by BLOOD TESTS, and by laboratory identification of the bacteria responsible. Treatment at any stage of the disease, the NIAID reports, will cure it, and within 24 hours of beginning treatment, the patient is no longer contagious. But it cannot reverse damage already done to the body or to the fetus within a pregnant woman. Many doctors recommend that pregnant women be tested for syphilis as a routine part of PRENATAL CARE. (For information on how to avoid infection, see SEXUALLY TRANSMITTED DISEASES.)

For help and further information

National Institute of Allergy and Infectious Diseases (NIAID), 301-496-5717. (For full group information, see ALLERGY.)

American Social Health Association (ASHA), 415-321-5134; toll-free VD National Hotline 800-227-8922 (U.S. except CA); 800-982-5883 (CA).(For full group information, see SEXUALLY TRANSMITTED DISEASES.)

systemic lupus erythematosus (SLE)   The medical name for the most severe form of LUPUS ERYTHEMATOSUS.

systolic pressure   The higher figure in a measurement of BLOOD PRESSURE.

T

tachypnea Abnormally rapid breathing, a common symptom in RESPIRATORY DISTRESS SYNDROME or PERSISTENT FETAL CIRCULATION but sometimes a temporary symptom in otherwise normal infants.

tactile Referring to the sense of touch, often employed in MULTISENSORY approaches to learning, such as VAKT, for children with LEARNING DISABILITIES.

talipes The medical name for the foot-and-ankle deformity commonly called CLUBFOOT.

talking The ability to use communication skills (see COMMUNICATION SKILLS AND DISORDERS).

target child A child who has unusual talents, deficiencies, socioeconomic disadvantage, troubled home situation, or some other special characteristics outlined by a program designed to help children, such as HEAD START, a CHILD ABUSE AND NEGLECT prevention program, or screening for programs under the EDUCATION FOR ALL HANDICAPPED CHILDREN ACT OF 1975 or the GIFTED AND TALENTED CHILDREN'S ACT OF 1978.

target schools Schools selected for special programs, notably to receive federal monies under CHAPTER 1.

task-appropriate General term describing behavior considered well chosen for completion of the task set for a child; a common descriptive phrase used in reports of DEVELOPMENTAL SCREENING TESTS. If the task is drawing a picture, for example, sitting down quietly with crayon and paper would be considered task-appropriate, while walking around the table would not.

TAT Abbreviation for the THEMATIC APPERCEPTION TEST.

Tay-Sachs disease (G_M2 gangliosidosis) A type of LIPID STORAGE DISEASE.

TB Abbreviation for TUBERCULOSIS.

T cells A type of white blood cell (*lymphocyte*) in the IMMUNE SYSTEM.

TDD Abbreviation for TELECOMMUNICATION DEVICES FOR THE DEAF.

Td vaccine The booster vaccine recommended to be given every 10 years to maintain IMMUNIZATION against TETANUS and DIPHTHERIA, the original vaccine generally given as part of the DTP VACCINE.

teacher competency testing An attempt to ensure that teachers meet basic standards, similar to the approach for students in MINIMUM COMPETENCY TESTING.

teeth Bony structures that are rooted in the jaw and cushioned by the gums; they have a coating of enamel and then dentin surrounding living pulp, which includes nerves and blood vessels. Humans get two sets of teeth, the *primary teeth* (also called *baby, milk,* or *deciduous teeth*) that begin appearing in infancy and the *permanent teeth* that start arriving around age six or seven. There are four main types of teeth:

- *incisors*—the shovel-shaped front teeth
- *canines, cuspids,* or *eye teeth*—the long-rooted, pointed teeth at either side of the incisors
- *bicuspids,* or *premolars*—the flat-topped, two-pointed teeth between canines and molars in adults; children have no bicuspids
- *molars*—the large, flat-topped, grinding teeth in the back of the mouth (the third molars, which appear only in adults, are called the *wisdom teeth*).

TEETH—AND WHEN THEY NORMALLY APPEAR (page 452) shows the location of the various types of teeth and when they generally appear, or *erupt*. GENETIC INHERITANCE may alter this schedule, and certain conditions, such as RICKETS or too little production from the THYROID GLAND or PITUITARY GLAND, may slow it down.

During *teething*, the period when the primary teeth appear, the gums over the erupting teeth may become swollen and red, and infants are often irritable and restless; they sometimes like to chew on pacifiers or rubber rings when cutting teeth. Doctors warn against using teething lotions, liquor, or paregoric on gums, for they can be dangerous to the child. Some doctors suggest rubbing a bit of aspirin on the gums to relieve the pain, but that should not be done if the child seems to have any viral illness, since aspirin may trigger some cases of REYE'S SYNDROME. Teething does not in itself cause FEVER and illness, so parents should not assume that signs of illness are caused by it. Children often get the viral illness ROSEOLA during the teething period, but the link between the two is unclear.

Most teeth erupt normally, but some are blocked because the jaw is already overcrowded. Such a blocked tooth is called an IMPACTED TOOTH. This problem mostly affects the last of the permanent teeth to appear, the upper canines, and especially

Teeth—And When They Normally Appear

Primary (Baby) Teeth

Upper Teeth

central incisors	8–12 months
lateral (side) incisors	9–13 months
cuspids (canines)	16–22 months
first molars	13–19 months
second molars	25–33 months

Lower Teeth

second molars	23–31 months
first molars	14–18 months
cuspids (canines)	17–23 months
lateral (side) incisors	10–16 months
central incisors	6–10 months

Permanent Teeth

Upper Teeth

central incisors	7–8 years
lateral (side) incisors	8–9 years
cuspids (canines)	11–12 years
first bicuspids	10–11 years
second bicuspids	10–12 years
first molars	6–7 years
second molars	12–13 years
third molars	17–21 years

Lower Teeth

third molars	17–21 years
second molars	11–13 years
second bicuspids	11–12 years
first molars	6–7 years
first bicuspids	10–12 years
cuspids (canines)	9–10 years
lateral (side) incisors	7–8 years
central incisors	6–7 years

the wisdom teeth. Impacted canines can emerge twisted and out of position, requiring the attention of an ORTHODONTIST; impacted wisdom teeth can often become painful and infected and may need to be extracted. Teeth blocked from eruption by bone or other tissue are sometimes said to be *imbedded*.

The most common dental problem is *caries*, or tooth decay, popularly called *cavities*. Bacteria in the mouth mix with saliva and leftover food to form a deposit on teeth, called *plaque*; as the bacteria break down the food, acid forms, which eats away at the enamel and dentin, literally forming indentations, or cavities. If the cavity is not cleaned out and filled with a neutral substance, the acid will finally attack the pulp, causing pain and often infection and gradually killing the pulp and the tooth. If the pulp becomes infected, or if an *abscess* (a pocket of infection) forms, ROOT CANAL THERAPY may be necessary to clean out the pulp and replace it with a deep filling in an attempt to save the tooth; if all else fails, the tooth will need to be extracted.

Teenagers with BULIMIA have great problems with tooth decay because the stomach acid from frequent vomiting attacks the teeth.

Dental caries can start as soon as teeth appear. Though baby teeth will be replaced, it is still important to prevent tooth decay for the health of the permanent teeth to come. To do this, many dentists recommend that parents:

- be careful about the amount of sugar in the child's food, especially about infants falling asleep with a bottle, which can lead to NURSING BOTTLE SYNDROME;
- clean the infant's teeth with gauze or a clean, damp washcloth after feeding, or at least once a day, and later switch to toothbrushing twice a day, especially at bedtime;
- feed their children a well-balanced diet strong in CALCIUM;
- once children start brushing their own teeth (perhaps in the second year, though some dentists say not until age seven) use DISCLOSING TABLETS to highlight areas missed in brushing;
- get a new toothbrush every three to four months;
- start flossing when the child's teeth fit closely together, around age two or three;
- be sure that the baby is getting sufficient fluoride, if not from the water supply, then from drops or tablets (later from toothpaste or mouthwash).

FLUORIDATION helps to prevent tooth decay by strengthening the enamel coating of the tooth and reducing the amount of acid formed by bacteria in the mouth. It has helped cut the amount of tooth decay by one-half in recent decades.

Other common dental problems include GINGIVITIS, or gum inflammation, and BRUXISM, or tooth grinding. Among the specialists treating dental problems, in addition to the dentist, are the ORTHODONTIST, ENDODONTIST, PERIODONTIST, and ORAL SURGEON.

The National Institute of Dental Research recommends that parents start taking children to the dentist at about the time of their second birthday and then visit the dentist regularly every six months. Modern dentists focus heavily on prevention and stress that the sooner they are able to identify dental problems, such as MALOCCLUSION, or bad bite, the better their chances of treating them successfully. They may also detect inherited GENETIC DISORDERS such as AMELOGENESIS IMPERFECTA.

Cavities in primary teeth must be spotted and filled, to avoid pain for the child and possible loss of the tooth. Lost teeth can cause problems with feeding and speaking. Parents should look for a dentist who is comfortable with and geared to working with very young patients. Pediatric dentists recommend that you prepare young children for a first visit to the dentist by reading a book about the experience (see below), and they stress that the visit should be treated as routine, not an occasion for fear or concern.

Once permanent teeth start arriving, some dentists recommend using a protective sealant to coat the cavity-prone back teeth. If permanent teeth are lost or broken, they must be repaired, as with a CROWN, or replaced; the lack of a tooth can cause the opposite tooth to grow abnormally long or can cause nearby teeth to drift into the empty space, creating malocclusion.

In recent decades, dentists have developed a variety of approaches for restoring discolored or damaged teeth. *Bleaching* several times with a warm peroxide solution can be used to remove some stains, though not the stains caused in children's teeth by the antibiotic tetracycline. *Bonding* is a coating "painted" on teeth that covers stains and may also be used to build up damaged teeth or teeth too wide apart. A *laminate veneer* is a layer of material stuck onto a tooth; it may last somewhat longer than bonding. These new treatments offer alternatives to the use of crowns, in which the whole top of the tooth is replaced; but they are still relatively new, and their long-term durability is unknown.

For help and further information

National Institute of Dental Research (NIDR)
9000 Rockville Pike
Building 31, Room 2C35
Bethesda, MD 20892
301-496-4261
Federal arm, one of the National Institutes of Health, that provides information to public and health professionals related to dental health and disorders. Publishes various materials, including technical reports for specialists and more general brochures (some in Spanish also), such as *Baby Bottle Tooth Decay, Fluoride to Protect Your Children's Teeth, A Healthy Start . . . Fluoride Tablets for Children in Preschool Programs, Fluoride Mouthrinsing in Schools . . . Protection for Children's Teeth, Fluoride Tablets . . . A Healthier Smile for School Children, A Healthy Mouth for You and Your Baby, Tooth Decay, Dental Tips for Diabetics,* and *Periodontal Disease and Diabetes—A Guide for Patients.*

American Dental Association (ADA)
211 East Chicago Avenue
Chicago, IL 60611
312-440-2500, toll-free number 800-621-8099
Thomas J. Ginley, Executive Director
Organization of dental professionals. Seeks to educate public and influence government policy; sponsors research; accredits dental schools; operates toll-free number; publishes various dental health education materials and many professional materials, including *Dentist's Desk Reference* and numerous periodicals.

American Society of Dentistry for Children (ASDC)
211 East Chicago Avenue, Suite 920
Chicago, IL 60611
312-943-1244
Carol Teuscher, Executive Director
Organization of dental professionals specialized in treating children. Sponsors research; publishes various materials, including bimonthly *Journal of Dentistry for Children* and newsletter.

American Association of Pediatric Dentistry (AAPD)
211 East Chicago Avenue, Suite 1036
Chicago, IL 60611

312-337-2169
John A. Bogert, Executive Director
Organization of dentists specializing in treating children. Sponsors research; publishes various materials, including quarterly *Journal of the American Academy of Pediatric Dentistry* and newsletter.

National Foundation of Dentistry for the Handicapped (NFDH), 303-573-0264. (For full group information, see HELP FOR SPECIAL CHILDREN on page 578.)

Other reference sources

The Oral Report: The Consumer's Common Sense Guide to Better Dental Care, by Jerry F. Taintor, D.D.S., with Mary Jane Taintor. New York: Facts on File, 1988.
Taryn Goes to the Dentist, by Jill Krementz. New York: Crown, 1986.
The Berenstain Bears Visit the Dentist, by Stan and Jan Berenstain. New York: Random House, 1981.
Mickey Visits the Dentist, by Ronnie Krauss. New York: Putnam, 1980.

telangiectasia　Increased size and number of blood vessels in the skin, causing redness, especially on the ears and face, sometimes (in hereditary forms) readily susceptible to bleeding. Telangiectasias sometimes occur simply from too much sunlight but are often associated with ALCOHOL ABUSE and with disorders such as a hereditary form of ATAXIA and LUPUS ERYTHEMATOSUS. Some kinds of BIRTHMARKS are a localized form of telangiectasia.

Telecommunication Devices for the Deaf (TDDs or TTYs) Devices that allow deaf or hearing-impaired people to use the telephone by typing on a computer, which then produces digital or print readouts instead of voice transmissions. Some such devices are capable also of SPEECH SYNTHESIS, storing and sending messages, and answering the telephone automatically. Newer forms of the devices can communicate with regular computers, though some earlier ones, using TTY language, cannot. (For help and further information, see EAR AND HEARING PROBLEMS.)

temporary restraining order (TRO)　A court order requiring a person to not carry out threatened acts, such as child abuse or parental kidnapping (see CHILD ABUSE AND NEGLECT; MISSING CHILDREN). A TRO is generally issued after an *ex parte* hearing, in which only one party appears before the judge. After the TRO is in effect, the judge calls for an ORDER TO SHOW CAUSE HEARING to get the other party's side of the question and will then either remove the TRO or make a permanent injunction against action. While a TRO in itself will not stop a potentially violent person, it generally makes the police more likely to intervene.

tender-years doctrine　Popular phrase for the courts' common assumption, from the early 20th century, that the BEST

INTERESTS OF THE CHILD are best served when CUSTODY is awarded to the MOTHER, in case of dispute between the parents.

teratogen   A substance known or thought to cause BIRTH DEFECTS.

teratologist   A medical specialist in the study of BIRTH DEFECTS; from the Greek *teras*, meaning "monster."

term   Alternate name for FULL-TERM, referring to a baby born generally on schedule, rather than PREMATURE; in EDUCATION, also a general term for a major division of the year, during which a course is normally completed, such as a SEMESTER or QUARTER.

termination of parental rights (TPR)   A legal proceeding, often in JUVENILE COURT, that seeks to end PARENTS' RIGHTS to CUSTODY and SUPERVISION of their child, as in some cases of ABANDONMENT or CHILD ABUSE AND NEGLECT. If a TPR proceeding is successful, the child may be placed for ADOPTION without the formal consent of the parents. A BIRTH PARENT placing a child for adoption is agreeing to termination of parental rights, though some forms of adoption modify that somewhat. Sometimes, after TPR, the child may be placed with FOSTER PARENTS temporarily until the parent demonstrates fitness to resume parental rights, as by completing a drug rehabilitation program.

tertiary-care facility   The medical designation for those HOSPITALS with the most sophisticated equipment and specially trained staff, sometimes called *Level III* facilities, including many UNIVERSITY-AFFILIATED FACILITIES (UAFs) with special research and teaching connections. (For help and further information, see HOSPITALS.)

test   A systematic form or procedure designed to measure or assess some ability, skill, aspect, or characteristic of a person, such as MEDICAL TESTS (see separate entry) and various educational and psychological tests. Tests come in a sometimes bewildering variety of shapes and forms and can be described and categorized in many ways.

Many tests for children (as well as adults) come in two main types:

- CRITERION-REFERENCED tests, for which a child either does or does not meet a preset standard, such as being able to complete a given puzzle.
- NORM-REFERENCED tests, in which a child's performance is being compared with the average performance of many other children who have been given the test, sometimes converted to GRADE-EQUIVALENT or AGE-EQUIVALENT scores.

But many other types of tests have no "right" or "wrong" answers, instead being designed to show something about how a child thinks, feels, and functions. Among these are some psychological tests, such as PROJECTIVE TESTS, seeking information on personality and mental condition; *psychomotor tests* that assess the coordination of brain and hands; and MENTAL STATUS EXAMINATIONS, assessing a person's current orientation and mental condition, which merge into the medical area.

Some are *group tests*, designed to be given to a number of children at the same time, with the test administrator not necessarily being specially trained. Others, *individual tests*, are meant to be administered to a child, one-to-one, by a PSYCHOLOGIST, teacher, or other trained person.

There are also OBJECTIVE TESTS, in which scoring does not depend on the administrator's discretion and is often done by use of a key or even by computer. By contrast, in SUBJECTIVE TESTS, the administrator's handling of the test, observations, and discretion much affect the test score.

Many educational tests are STANDARDIZED TESTS, developed by using uniform (standard) procedures on a large population, whose AVERAGE scores become NORMS to which an individual child's score is compared. Others are developed locally, such as a classroom test, tailored to the needs of a particular group but without the statistically supported VALIDITY and RELIABILITY of standardized tests.

Some are *paper-and-pencil tests*, requiring at least the ability to read and write; others are *oral tests*, requiring the student to respond verbally to spoken questions; some are questionnaires called *inventories*, designed to discover information about a child's personality, interests, or attitudes; still others try to circumvent writing, READING, and speaking as much as possible by focusing on doing particular tasks, such as *performance tests* that require a student to put together a puzzle; and some call simply for observing a child's routine behavior, often at play. Tests may employ a variety of such approaches, as with some INTELLIGENCE TESTS.

A test may be given at one sitting or in two or more sittings in a day; a number of tests (a BATTERY) may be given over several days; or a series of tests may be given on completion of various parts of a program, called *phased testing* or *progress testing*. Sometimes tests are paired: one given before instruction (the *pretest*) and the other after (the *posttest*), in an attempt to measure the amount of learning that has taken place.

In a *timed test*, the questions must be completed within a given period; in a *speed test*, the premium is on completing the greatest number of questions in a given amount of time (often set so that few children, if any, will finish the whole test). In some special situations, especially psychological evaluations, observations are made at stated intervals (such as every 10 minutes), a process called *time sampling*.

Though today's parents probably saw an enormous amount of testing in their own lives, their children are seeing even more and starting much earlier. In both medicine and education, researchers have found that the earlier problem conditions are found, the more easily they can be treated. So children today are undergoing a wide range of tests from infancy, whenever any question arises about the normality of a child's development. This is even enshrined into law as, under the EDUCATION FOR ALL HANDICAPPED CHILDREN ACT OF 1975, states are required to try to identify (through programs such as CHILDFIND) any children who might have handicaps that might affect their learning, including LEARNING DISABILITIES. The aim is to find and help these children in the PRESCHOOL YEARS, to give them the SPECIAL EDUCATION and medical services they need so that they will be ready for school.

The whole question of READINESS—having the necessary skills, abilities, and maturity—to benefit from learning has spawned other major groups of tests. At the preschool, KINDERGARTEN, and first-grade levels, READINESS TESTS of all kinds are used to help school officials assess whether a child should be admitted to the school (or advised to wait a year before entering) and if so in what class and with what special help, if any. Highly selective PRESCHOOLS and PRIVATE SCHOOLS use such readiness tests as the GESELL PRESCHOOL TEST more in the nature of an ADMISSION TEST.

In addition, the requirements of the Education for All Handicapped Children Act continue to operate during the school years, and many schools give periodic DEVELOPMENTAL SCREENING TESTS to all students or sometimes only to those who show signs of problems. If the tests indicate that problems do exist, the child will generally be given DIAGNOSTIC ASSESSMENT TESTS, which will more precisely pinpoint the areas of difficulties and will be used to plan a HANDICAPPED child's INDIVIDUALIZED EDUCATION PLAN.

Beyond that, children continue to be barraged by tests of all kinds throughout their school years. In addition to classroom tests, they are periodically given general ACHIEVEMENT TESTS, sometimes called *basic skills tests*. These help the school monitor the child's performance, as well as its own instructional programs, by comparing school scores against national norms. Schools have, in fact, been so harshly criticized for giving automatic PROMOTIONS to students and graduating some who are functionally illiterate (see ILLITERACY) that some districts use graded tests of basic skills that a student must pass to be promoted, an approach called MINIMUM COMPETENCY TESTING.

In the late HIGH SCHOOL years, a child who is planning to go on to COLLEGE faces various college admission tests, such as the SCHOLASTIC APTITUDE TEST and the SCHOOL AND COLLEGE ABILITY TESTS. There are also other testing programs that allow students to get advanced college credit, such as the ADVANCED PLACEMENT PROGRAM, the PROFICIENCY EXAMINATION PROGRAM, and the COLLEGE-LEVEL EXAMINATION PROGRAM.

In this welter of tests, children who are "natural" test-takers have an enormous advantage. So do children who have had a great deal of stimulation and varied experiences at home, especially those from White middle-class, English-speaking, two-parent families. Parents who want to help their children survive in a test-glutted world are advised to help them from a very young age by encouraging the development of their skills and abilities. Some focus on preparing children specifically for testing, an approach sometimes called *hothousing*, analogous to the forcing of flower buds (see *Is Your Child Ready for School?* among the books below). Others focus on more general stimulation; in this regard, parents may find useful TEACHING YOUNG CHILDREN: GUIDELINES AND ACTIVITIES (page 544) useful, as it includes a wide variety of activities to encourage development of children's skills. Also see HELP YOUR CHILD IMPROVE IN TEST-TAKING (page 528). Some children inevitably will resist testing or become anxious about it (see books below), but the best way to lessen the anxiety is to forestall it by building the child's skills and confidence in the early years.

For help and further information

National Committee for Citizens in Education (NCCE), 301-997-9300; toll-free number (U.S. except MD), 800-NETWORK [638-9675]. Publishes *Parents Can Understand Testing*. (For full group information, see EDUCATION.)

Other reference sources

General Works

Is Your Child Ready for School? A Parent's Guide to Preschool and Primary School Entrance Tests, by Jacqueline Robinson. New York: Arco, 1990. (Originally published as *The Baby Boards*, 1988.)

Test Scores and What They Mean, by Howard B. Lyman. Englewood Cliffs, NJ: Prentice-Hall, 1986.

Psychological Testing of Children: A Consumer's Guide, by Stanley Klein. Boston: Exceptional Parent, 1977.

On Test Anxiety and Test-taking

Conquering Test Anxiety, by Neil A. Fiore. New York: Warner, 1987.

Coping with Academic Anxiety, by Allen J. Ottens. New York: Rosen, 1984.

How to Beat Test Anxiety and Score Higher on the SAT and All Other Exams, by James H. Divine. Hauppauge, NY: Barron's, 1982.

Test-Taking Strategies, by Judi Kesselman-Turkel and Franklynn Peterson. Chicago: Contemporary, 1981.

Background Works

Tests: A Comprehensive Reference for Assessments in Psychology, Education, and Business, second edition, Richard C. Sweetland and Daniel J. Keyser, general eds. Kansas City, MO: Test Corporation of America, 1986.

Mental Measurements Yearbook, J.V. Mitchel, ed. Biannual. Lincoln, NE: University of Nebraska Press.

Standards for Educational and Psychological Testing. Washington, DC: American Educational Research Association, American Psychological Association, and National Council on Measurement in Education, 1985.

Essentials of Psychological Testing, fourth edition, by Lee J. Cronbach. New York: Harper & Row, 1984.

Ability Testing: Uses, Consequences, and Controversies, Alexandra K. Wigdoor and Wendell R. Garner, eds. Washington, DC: National Academy, 1982.

Psychological and Educational Assessment of Minority Children, T. Oakland, ed. New York: Brunner/Mazel, 1977.

testes (testicles; singular, testis) The pair of male sexual glands (GONADS) that manufacture the SPERM necessary for reproduction. In a male FETUS, the testes are held inside the abdomen, but by the time of birth they have normally descended into a protective sac, called the *scrotum*, suspended outside the body. The testes are further protected by a fibrous covering called the *tunica albuginea* and nourished by way of the *spermatic cord*. This cord includes arteries, veins, nerves, and other structures, suspended from the abdomen through an opening called the *inguinal ring*. The testes (like the penis) are usually relatively large at birth, soon growing smaller, and then gradually enlarging to adult size during PUBERTY.

Within each testicle are hundreds of coiled, threadlike structures called *seminiferous tubules*, that contain special sperm-generating cells called *spermatogonia*. During puberty, in response to HORMONES from the PITUITARY GLAND, these spermatogonia begin generating sperm, millions each day. Other structures in the testes produce the male hormone TESTOSTERONE.

The spermatogonia actually first produce new cells, called *spermatocytes*. In preparation for possible FERTILIZATION of an egg, each spermatocyte must reduce its genetic contents from 46 chromosomes to 23 strands of DNA, which is done during two divisions, called *meiosis*, the result being four sperm, called *spermatids*. It is in these divisions that some CHROMO-SOMAL ABNORMALITIES can occur, with errors in dividing. It is also here that each sperm is left with the coded SEX CHROMOSOME that will determine the sex of any child that might result from that particular sperm. The woman's egg carries an X sex chromosome. If the sperm also carries an X sex chromosome, then the child will be XX, or female; if the sperm carries a Y sex chromosome, then the child will be XY, or male. The sperm-generating cells keep on generating sperm daily through the man's lifetime, unlike the egg-producing cells in a woman that each produce eggs only once, with eggs maturing only once a month.

The spermatids are sent through small tubes called *vasa efferentia* into a long, coiled tube called the *epididymis*, a "holding area" that lies along the back of the testicles, where they mature. When ready for use, the sperm are moved out of the epididymis into a long tube called the *vas deferens* (part of the spermatic cord) into the PENIS.

A variety of problems can disrupt this complex, sensitive process, including:

1. *undescended testicles (cryptorchidism)*: Sometimes one or both of the testicles fails to drop from inside the abdomen into the scrotum before birth, for several reasons, including hormonal imbalance, fibrous obstruction of the route of descent, or tubes too short to allow full descent. Undescended testicles is a common problem, especially among PREMATURE babies. Sometimes the testicle descends on its own during the boy's first year; if not, doctors may try hormone therapy or a surgical operation called an ORCHIOPEXY to lower the testicle into the scrotum, generally before school age. A testicle that remains in the body will not develop normally and will not be able to produce sperm, the body temperature being too high; it is also associated with an increased risk of CANCER. If both testicles are undescended, the result will be INFER-

TILITY, though not necessarily impotency. Related problems include:
   • *ectopic testicles*, in which testicles descend into the groin or base of the penis, rather than into the scrotum, often corrected by orchiopexy;
   • *failure of one testicle to develop normally*, in which case it may be removed in an ORCHIECTOMY, though the other testicle may be normal.

2. *inflammation of the testes* (ORCHITIS) *or testes and epididymis* (EPIDIDYMO-ORCHITIS): Orchitis most often results from infection with the MUMPS virus, but both the testes and epididymis may become infected by bacteria, often accompanying infection in the PROSTATE GLAND or urinary tract, especially SEXUALLY TRANSMITTED DISEASES, such as CHLAMYDIAL INFECTIONS and GONORRHEA.

3. *swelling or fluid collection in the tissues around the testes*: This can result from a variety of problems, including HYDRO-CELE (a "water sac" in the scrotum), VARICOCELE (swollen veins in the scrotum), or SPERMATOCELE (sperm-filled swelling in the epididymis).

4. *torsion (twisting) of the testis*: The spermatic cord can become twisted, cutting off the blood supply and causing great pain and swelling. The condition more often affects the left side, occurring most commonly during puberty and in the first year of life. Prompt diagnosis, often confirmed by ULTRASOUND, and surgical intervention to untwist the cord normally bring complete recovery. But if the condition is not diagnosed and treated within a few hours, loss of blood supply can cause irreparable damage in the testis (and to its future sperm production), including ATROPHY and gangrene (death of tissue). If that occurs, the affected testis is normally removed, an operation called an ORCHIECTOMY, and the other testis sutured to the scrotum to prevent torsion.

5. CANCER *of the testicles*: Malignancies of the testes are rare, though males who had undescended testicles are at somewhat increased risk. The condition is found mostly in males from puberty to middle years, rarely before puberty or in old age. Testicular cancer is often treated by *orchiectomy* (removal of the affected testicle), RADIATION therapy, and sometimes anticancer drugs. From puberty, young males should be taught to make regular self-examinations (as women make breast self-examinations), feeling their testicles over their entire surface and bringing to the doctor's immediate attention any lump or other abnormality that appears.

Several of these conditions can diminish fertility or cause INFER-TILITY and so require prompt and careful treatment. (For help and further information, see INFERTILITY; PREGNANCY.)

Test of Adolescent Language (TOAL) An individually administered test of the language skills of children in grades 6 to 12, often those suspected of having LEARNING DISABILITIES. Tasks include both paper-and-pencil and oral responses to questions designed to uncover problems in the areas of vocabulary and grammar (syntax), using listening, speaking, READING, and writing, including both receptive and expressive language. SCORES for the various subtests are combined to give an Adolescent Language Quotient (ALQ). (For help and further information, see TESTS.)

Test of Language Development (TOLD)   An individually administered, oral-response test designed to measure the language skills of children, the primary test covering children ages four to nearly nine, and the intermediate one testing children ages 8½ to nearly 13. The test includes seven areas: picture vocabulary, oral vocabulary, grammatic understanding, sentence imitation, grammatic completion, word articulation, and word discrimination. The tests are sometimes used as language ACHIEVEMENT TESTS, but much more often they are used to identify children with language problems, including those with LEARNING DISABILITIES, MENTAL RETARDATION, DEVELOPMENTAL DELAY, and communication disorders (see COMMUNICATION SKILLS AND DISORDERS). (For help and further information, see TESTS.)

testosterone   One of the key male sex HORMONES, produced by the TESTES (and in women, the OVARIES, though only in tiny amounts). Testosterone helps stimulate bone and muscle development and also triggers the appearance of SECONDARY SEX CHARACTERISTICS. Synthetic or animal forms of the hormone are used to treat some kinds of INFERTILITY. As a form of steroid, testosterone is sometimes used by athletes to stimulate growth and development; in women, it leads to development of male characteristics, such as hair growth and voice deepening. More serious effects of testosterone can include liver damage and exacerbation of CANCER in the male reproductive system. (See HELP AGAINST SUBSTANCE ABUSE on page 587.)

Tests of General Educational Development   A series of tests to be passed by someone seeking a GENERAL EQUIVALENCY DIPLOMA (GED).

test-tube fertilization   Alternate term for IN VITRO FERTILIZATION.

tetanus (lockjaw)   A severe disease caused by a bacterium present all around us that enters the body through a break in the skin, especially a deep puncture with a piece of metal. Once in the body, tetanus bacteria produce a powerful toxin, or poison, that attacks the body's NERVOUS SYSTEM. From the first symptoms of headache, irritability, and stiffness in the neck and jaw, the disease progresses to spasms that completely lock the jaw, neck, and limbs, produce rigidity in the abdominal muscles, and cause painful convulsions. Often associated with tetanus are pneumonia (see LUNG AND BREATHING DISORDERS), FRACTURES, and exhaustion from the muscle spasms. Once tetanus takes hold, doctors can use tranquilizers and antispasmodic drugs to treat some of the symptoms, but they cannot treat the underlying disease, which kills four out of 10 people who contract it. Fortunately, a VACCINE exists that is normally given to children as part of a combination DTP VACCINE in a series of five injections between ages two months and six years, with booster shots of TD VACCINE given every 10 years thereafter. (For help and further information, see DTP VACCINE; IMMUNIZATION.)

tetanus vaccine   A type of VACCINE that is normally given first in a combination DTP VACCINE, covering DIPHTHERIA, TETANUS (lockjaw), and PERTUSSIS (whooping cough) and later in booster shots of TD VACCINE.

tetany   Spasms, cramps, or twitching in the muscles, especially of the hands and feet, sometimes with STRIDOR (noisy breathing) as well. Tetany generally results from too little CALCIUM in the body (*hypocalcemia*), often linked with lack of VITAMIN D. In newborns, tetany can result from imbalance in the parathyroid hormone or imbalance in FORMULA and is more common in LOW-BIRTH-WEIGHT babies.

tetralogy of Fallot   A common combination of four CONGENITAL heart defects. (See HEART AND HEART PROBLEMS.)

tetramelia   A type of BIRTH DEFECT in which all four limbs are missing; the more general term for absence of one or more limbs is AMELIA.

thalassemia   An inherited form of ANEMIA.

Thematic Apperception Test (TAT)   A type of PROJECTIVE TEST, given one-to-one by a trained examiner to a person aged 14 to 40, in which the person is shown a series of pictures and asked to make up a story about each. The stories are later analyzed for information about the person's personality and maturity. (For help and further information, see TESTS.)

thiamin   Alternate name for VITAMIN B₁.

Thomsen's disease   Alternate name for MYOTONIA CONGENITA.

three-day measles   Alternate term for RUBELLA.

three R's   Reading, 'riting, and 'rithmetic, the focus of the BACK TO BASICS movement.

thrombocytes   Alternate name for *platelets*, a type of blood cell important in clotting. (See BLOOD AND BLOOD DISORDERS.)

thrombosis   A type of blood disorder involving excess clotting. (See BLOOD AND BLOOD DISORDERS.)

thrush   In medicine, a popular name for the fungal infection CANDIDIASIS.

thymus   A gland in the upper chest that is part of the lymphatic system, the network of vessels and organs that functions as a filter in the body's IMMUNE SYSTEM, protecting against disease.

thyroid gland   A two-lobed gland in the front of the neck that produces several key thyroid HORMONES. These help regulate METABOLISM (the body's biochemical processes), growth and physical development (see GROWTH AND GROWTH DISORDERS), and levels of CALCIUM in the body, often working with hormones from other glands, such as the HYPOTHALAMUS, PITUITARY GLAND, and parathyroid gland. Too little thyroid production leads to a condition known as *hypothyroidism* (or *myxedema*), which in children can cause extremely short stature. Symptoms of hypothyroidism include weight gain, dry skin, hair loss, CONSTIPATION, cold sensitivity, and fatigue. By contrast, too much thyroid hormone, or *hyperthyroidism*, can cause weight loss, DIARRHEA, sweating, heat intolerance, and fatigue.

The thyroid gland is subject to a variety of disorders, including:

- *goiter, or enlargement of the gland,* as from lack of IODINE, hormonal changes during PUBERTY or PREGNANCY, GENETIC DISORDERS, or an unknown cause.
- *absence, abnormal placement, or malfunction of the gland,* often CONGENITAL defects that can lead to severe MENTAL RETARDATION combined with DWARFISM (a condition called *cretinism*).
- TUMORS, which can be benign or MALIGNANT, but generally need to be surgically treated.
- AUTOIMMUNE DISORDERS, in which the body mistakenly attacks its own tissues, including *Graves' disease* and *Hashimoto's thyroiditis*.

Thyroid problems are often diagnosed by BLOOD TESTS that check for the level of hormones, SCANS of the glands, or BIOPSY.

For help and further information

National Institute of Diabetes and Digestive and Kidney Diseases (NIDDK), 301-496-3583. (For full group information, see DIGESTIVE DISORDERS.)

tic disorder   Psychiatric classification for TOURETTE'S SYNDROME.

tinnitus   A type of EAR AND HEARING PROBLEM involving persistent ringing, whistling, buzzing, tinkling, or other annoying noises in the ears. These results from disturbances of the acoustic nerve that transmits to the brain electrical signals unrelated to external sounds, making it a sensorineural problem. The causes of tinnitus are not fully known, but in children it is sometimes associated with trauma, HEAD INJURY affecting the ears, or OTOSCLEROSIS.

For help and further information

American Tinnitus Association (ATA)
P.O. Box 5
Portland, OR 97207
503-248-9985
Gloria E. Reich, Executive Director

Organization of people who suffer from tinnitus, their families, and the health professionals who work with them. Encourages formation of local mutual-support self-help groups; provides information and makes referrals; publishes various materials.

Other reference sources

Tinnitus: Learning to Live With It, by L. Sheppard and A. Hawkridge. Garden City Park, NY: Avery, 1989.
Tinnitus: Facts, Theories, and Treatment. Washington, DC: National Academy of Sciences, 1982.
(See also EAR AND HEARING PROBLEMS.)

tissue typing   The medical technique used in attempting to match organs and tissue for use in TRANSPLANTS; also called *histocompatability testing*. (For help and further information, see IMMUNE SYSTEM.)

Title 18   Short for Title 18, Section 1201A, of the U.S. Code, a law that exempts parents from kidnapping charges regarding their children under 18. (See MISSING CHILDREN.)

Title I of the Elementary and Secondary Education Act of 1965   Originating law of the federal program funding educational programs for students from low-income families, now generally called CHAPTER 1.

TOAL   Abbreviation for TEST OF ADOLESCENT LANGUAGE.

toeing in   Alternate name for METATARSUS VARUS, or pigeon toes.

toeing out   Alternate name for METATARSUS VALGUS, or duck walk.

toilet training   Helping a child learn to control urination and bowel movements. In infants, these functions are not controllable but occur involuntarily. Before children can be toilet-trained, they must first be able to recognize urine and feces as coming from them and to link these events with the physical signals preceding and accompanying them. Children's muscles and nerves must also develop to the point where control of these functions is possible, which normally does not happen until they are about 18 to 20 months old, and the bladder and bowels must grow large enough so that they can store waste for a time, which usually does not occur until about 30 months. In addition, children must have the general communication skills (see COMMUNICATION SKILLS AND DISORDERS) and MOTOR SKILLS to be able to understand and respond to the toilet-training process.

All of these are part of "readiness" for toilet training—and here, experts agree, readiness is all. Children may demonstrate this readiness in a variety of ways. They may, for example, have fewer, more regular bowel movements, sometimes asking to be changed afterward. They may keep their diapers dry for several hours at a time. They may leave the room to urinate or have a bowel movement (in the diaper) privately. They may show an interest in the bathroom and imitate actions of others there.

Parents should be extremely wary of pushing a child into toilet training prematurely, since frustration and resentment are the likely results. Certainly, parents have many pressures to toilet-train early. Quite apart from the obvious chore of changing diapers, many CHILD-CARE centers and PRESCHOOLS will accept children only if they are toilet-trained or will charge extra if a child needs diaper-changing. But for the long-term good of the child and the parent-child relationship, such pressures need to be resisted and in no way communicated to the child. Rather, toilet training is best presented as a positive step, as part of the child's natural growing-up process. Indeed, some children in child-care centers are toilet-trained more easily because they see others using toilets. Similarly, children who are able to see family members (especially of their own sex) using the toilet also seem to learn more readily, by imitation.

Parents will need to decide beforehand whether to use a separate "potty chair" or a special child-size insert into the toilet (with a shield in front for boys, who will urinate sitting down at first, learning stand-up style only later). Parents will also want to plan how to go about toilet training, making sure that they agree between themselves and with the approach taken by child-care workers, because inconsistency (as in the language used or type of response to an "accident") can breed problems. (The books listed below may help; so may some of the general suggestions in TEACHING YOUNG CHILDREN: GUIDELINES AND ACTIVITIES on page 544.) It is often effective to introduce the child to the toilet and its functions (especially flushing, which may intrigue or scare a child) before actually expecting the child to use it. Experts recommend that the start of toilet training be scheduled for a calm period, when the family is not undergoing any particular upheaval (such as a relocation or arrival of a SIBLING) and when one parent can be with the child full-time for a few days.

Parents should also need to understand that toilet training does not occur in a day but rather is a long-term, gradual process that will often take weeks or months. Bowel movements are generally controlled before urination, and full control of daytime urination occurs long before control at night. Accidents will happen, but parents can help in several ways:

- by dressing the child in easy-to-undo clothes, preferably with elastic or Velcro instead of buttons, belts, straps, scarves, and the like.
- by using training pants, especially in the early stages of the process.
- by planning ahead so that a child will not be placed in an impossible position without access to a bathroom (e.g., by using diapers on expeditions where no bathrooms are available) or teaching children how to urinate outdoors where appropriate (as in the woods or by the side of a road).
- by being alert, when outside the home, to where toilets are and responding immediately to a child's request to use one; with children's limited storage capacity and muscular control, seconds count.
- by being supportive of the child's efforts and not treating accidents as tragedies or failures.

With a positive approach at the right time, most children are toilet-trained without great problems, though some children may not develop full nighttime control for years. Usually, this is a form of DEVELOPMENTAL DELAY, and children are clean and dry by the time they enter school. Some school-age children, however, have long-term persistent problems with control of urination, leading to bedwetting, or ENURESIS; or with control of defecation, leading to soiling, or ENCOPRESIS. Because of physical or emotional handicaps (see HANDICAPPED), some children never gain full control over their bodily functions; these need special techniques to handle the resulting INCONTINENCE.

For help and further information

Association for Retarded Citizens (ARC), 817-640-0204. Publishes *Toilet Training for Children with Mental Retardation*. (For full group information, see MENTAL RETARDATION.)

Other reference sources

For Adults

Potty Training Your Baby: A Practical Guide for Easier Toilet Training, by Kathy Van Pelt. Garden City Park, NY: Avery, 1988.

Toilet Learning, by Alison Mack. Boston: Little, Brown, 1978.

Toilet Training in Less Than a Day, by Nathan Azrin and Richard Foxx. New York: Simon & Schuster, 1974.

Toilet Training the Retarded, by Richard M. Foxx and Nathan H. Azrin. Champaign, IL: Research Press, 1973.

For Use With Kids

Annie's Potty, by Judith Caseley. New York: Greenwillow, 1990.

Your New Potty, by Joanna Cole. New York: Morrow, 1989.

Once Upon a Potty, by Alona Frankel. Hauppauge, NY: Barron's, 1984.

Potty Time!, by Anne Civardi. New York: Simon & Schuster, 1988.

Asa's Potty Time. Cassette available from Speaking of Health, 8010 Mountain Road, NE, Albuquerque, NM 87110, 505-265-4033. Part of the Children's Coping series, featuring Asa the elephant.

(See also ENURESIS; ENCOPRESIS; KIDNEY AND UROLOGICAL DISORDERS; DIGESTIVE DISORDERS.)

TOLD Abbreviation for TEST OF LANGUAGE DEVELOPMENT.

tonic-clonic seizure The most striking kind of SEIZURE that goes under the umbrella name of EPILEPSY; also called a *grand mal seizure*.

tonic neck reflex The automatic response of a baby, on turning the head to one side, to stretch out the arm and leg on the same side and to bend the arm and leg on the opposite side; a type of "primitive" REFLEX found only in babies that disappears in the first few months of life.

tonsils Two small organs at the back of the throat that act as filters in the *lymphatic system*, which is the network through which the body's IMMUNE SYSTEM operates. As an infant grows, so do the tonsils, reaching maximum size by about age seven, then gradually shrinking. Once removed routinely in many children, tonsils today are generally left in place unless the child has severe, recurring attacks of *tonsilitis* (inflammation of the tonsils due to infection), a tonsil is abscessed (*quinsy*), or it contains abnormal growths, such as CANCER. The operation itself (*tonsillectomy*) is simple, and recovery from it is brief; ADENOIDS are often removed at the same time.

torsion of the testis Twisting of the spermatic cord, cutting off blood supply to the testis and possibly causing irreparable damage and INFERTILITY if it is not diagnosed and treated within just a few hours. (See TESTES.)

total communication   An approach in which children with EAR AND HEARING PROBLEMS are taught to use any communication skills (see COMMUNICATION SKILLS AND DISORDERS) at their disposal. They are not barred from employing MANUAL COMMUNICATION, such as FINGERSPELLING and AMERICAN SIGN LANGUAGE.

Tourette's syndrome (Gilles de la Tourette syndrome or maladie des tics)   A type of STEREOTYPY/HABIT DISORDER that begins in childhood, generally between ages two and 15, and is characterized first by facial tics and guttural throat noises (vocal tics), progressing to rapid, purposeless, involuntary movements. In more than half of the cases, people with Tourette's syndrome also show compulsive use of foul language (COPROLALIA), repetition of meaningless phrases (ECHOLALIA), increasingly rapid repetition of selected phrases (PALILALIA), compulsive touching, and obsessive doubting (see OBSESSIVE-COMPULSIVE DISORDER). The disorder is rare, affecting only about 100,000 people in the United States, about three-quarters of them male. Its cause is unknown, but it can be treated with lifelong doses of medicines such as haloperidol and the ORPHAN DRUG pimozide.

For help and further information

Tourette Syndrome Association (TSA)
42-40 Bell Boulevard
Bayside, NY 11361
718-224-2999, toll-free number 800-237-0717
Dennis Herschfelder, Executive Director
Organization of people concerned with Tourette's syndrome. Fosters research; offers counseling services; seeks to educate public and health professionals and to influence public policy; publishes various materials, including quarterly newsletter, the audiovisuals *Stop It! I Can't* and *Tourette Syndrome: The Sudden Intruder*, and print publications.

National Institute of Neurological Disorders and Stroke (NINDS), 301-496-5751. (For full group information, see BRAIN AND BRAIN DISORDERS.)

National Institute on Deafness and Other Communication Disorders (NIDCD), 301-496-7243. (For full group information, see COMMUNICATION SKILLS AND DISORDERS.)

National Institute of Mental Health (NIMH), 301-443-4515. (For full group information, see MENTAL DISORDERS.)

Other reference sources

Tourette Syndrome and Human Behavior, by David E. Comings, M.D. Duarte, CA: Hope, 1990.
Ryan: A Mother's Story of Her Hyperactive/Tourette Syndrome Child, by Susan Hughes. Duarte, CA: Hope, 1990.

toxemia of pregnancy   Alternate term for PREECLAMPSIA and ECLAMPSIA.

toxic shock syndrome   A type of SHOCK that results from a severe infection with the bacterium *Staphylococcus aureus*, which produces a poison (toxin) in the body. First recognized in the 1970s in connection with superabsorbent tampons, it is somewhat less common since those brands have been removed from the shelves. Infection today may still be connected with the use of tampons or CONTRACEPTIVE devices (caps, sponges, or diaphragms), especially if left in too long, but it may also result from infection elsewhere in the body. Symptoms include high FEVER, skin rash, clinical shock, and sometimes liver and kidney failure. Even with antibiotic treatment and intravenous therapy, a small percentage of those affected may die of the disease.

For help and further information

National Institute of Allergy and Infectious Diseases (NIAID), 301-496-5717. (For full group information, see ALLERGY.)

National Institute of Child Health and Human Development (NICHD), 301-496-5133. (For full group information, see PREGNANCY.)

Centers for Disease Control (CDC), 404-329-3534. (For full group information, see IMMUNIZATION.)

toxoplasmosis   A disease caused by infection with the protozoa *toxoplasma gondii*, common in many animals and often passed to humans in undercooked meat and from handling cats and their feces. The human body generally fights off the infection with little difficulty, with two major exceptions. A person who has a weakened IMMUNE SYSTEM, such as someone with AIDS or SEVERE COMBINED IMMUNODEFICIENCY (SCID), has trouble fighting the infection, which results in an illness much like INFECTIOUS MONONUCLEOSIS and sometimes causes severe complications, such as inflammation of various sensitive parts of the eye, ENCEPHALITIS, and damage to the heart and lungs. Even more seriously, a pregnant woman who contracts toxoplasmosis, especially early in PREGNANCY, has an increased risk of MISCARRIAGE or STILLBIRTH, or her baby may experience after birth various serious problems such as enlargement of the liver and spleen, HYDROCEPHALUS, EYE AND VISION PROBLEMS, and MENTAL RETARDATION and is at increased risk of dying in infancy. Women who are or may be pregnant should be especially careful to eat only fully cooked meat and, if they have cats, to wash their hands carefully after dealing with their cat and its feces.

For help and further information

National Institute of Allergy and Infectious Diseases (NIAID), 301-496-5717. (For full group information, see ALLERGY.)

TPR   Abbreviation for the legal proceeding of TERMINATION OF PARENTAL RIGHTS.

trace elements Alternate name for elements such as IRON, COPPER, IODINE, ZINC, and FLUORIDE, which are MINERALS needed in only small amounts for proper body functioning; also called MICRONUTRIENTS.

tracheitis Inflammation of the windpipe (*trachea*), a kind of LUNG AND BREATHING DISORDER.

tracheostomy A surgical operation to make an artificial opening in the windpipe (*trachea*), which is then kept open by insertion of a tube. Tracheostomy may be performed as a temporary emergency procedure, as in severe cases of CROUP or CHOKING, or it can be a planned permanent procedure, as when someone is on a VENTILATOR (respirator). (See OSTOMY.)

trachoma A severe bacterial infection of the eye. (See EYE AND VISION PROBLEMS.)

tracking Grouping students into classes based on assessments of their ability and past performance. In an ELEMENTARY or SECONDARY SCHOOL, for example, the result might be an honors or "fast-track" class, a series of middle-range classes for students of descending ability (the number depending on the size of the school), and a "slow-learner" class. Tracking goes under a variety of names, including *ability grouping, streaming, banding*, and *homogeneous grouping*. The main alternative, in which all students are grouped together in an early schoolhouse style, no matter how wide their range of achievement or ability, is called *heterogeneous grouping*.

The main arguments for tracking are that it allows teachers to tailor instruction to the students' needs and abilities, giving extra time and attention to slow learners, providing extra stimulation and challenges to the most academically able students, and avoiding the frustration of the students who are unable to keep up with the academic pace set in a heterogeneous group. Key criticisms of tracking are that it results in LABELING and locks students into a track, with teachers making insufficient efforts to help children shed earlier expectations and grow in new ways. Critics stress that the world itself is a heterogeneous place and all students benefit by working together; and that use of PEER TUTORING can benefit all students. In some places, tracking has also been used—deliberately or otherwise—to maintain de facto SEGREGATION within supposedly desegregated schools. In 1990, the National Education Association, the largest organization of teachers in the United States, came out against tracking.

For help and further information

Keeping Track: How Schools Structure Inequality, by Jeannie Oakes. New Haven, CT: Yale University Press, 1986.

(See also EDUCATION.)

transaminases test Alternate term for aminotransferases test, a kind of LIVER FUNCTION TEST.

transcript The official record of a student's performance at a school, including classes or courses completed, the final grade or evaluation received for each, any diplomas awarded, perhaps comments on the student as a person, and appropriate related information, such as an explanation of the school's grading system. If a student transfers from one school to another or applies for ADMISSION to a COLLEGE, the transcript must be supplied to the new institution. The information included on a transcript is drawn from the STUDENT RECORD.

transitional comfort object Psychologists' name for an object adopted by a young child as a symbol of comfort, safety, and security, often around the first birthday; a kind of COMFORT HABIT, also called *cuddlies*. Like the traditional teddy bear or Linus's "security blanket" in the cartoon "Peanuts," comfort objects are often soft, old, worn, intensely beloved, and taken everywhere by the child, and they are of special importance around sleeptime, during illness, stress, or upset, or when the child is being left with a baby-sitter or going to a HOSPITAL.

translocation A common type of CHROMOSOMAL ABNORMALITY.

transplant The surgical implant of a healthy human organ or tissue to replace one that has failed or is about to fail. The organ often is taken from the body of a person who has died, if the family (or the donor when alive) agrees to make such organs available for transplants. Organs such as the heart and liver are often removed after a determination of BRAIN DEATH but while the donor's heart is still functioning, since it is essential that blood supply be maintained to these organs. Sometimes the transplant tissue, such as skin or BONE MARROW, can come from elsewhere in the patient's own body. In the case of some kinds of transplants, such as kidneys, the organ may be from a close living relative, such as a SIBLING or BIOLOGICAL PARENT. This poses a risk for the relative, since he or she has only one of the important organs left, but it can be a lifesaving gift within a family. Sometimes parents face the difficult decision of whether—and under what circumstances—to approve a transplant from one of their children to another.

The main difficulty with transplants (aside from the shortage of organs for use) is that the body will often reject the transplanted organ. The rejection response is caused when the IMMUNE SYSTEM recognizes the transplant as foreign and attacks it. Only corneal transplants, somewhat sheltered from attack, are less subject to rejection. Scientists try to match transplant tissues so that they are as much alike as possible, using techniques called *tissue typing* or *histocompatibility*. (For more information, see IMMUNOLOGY AND TRANSPLANTS, under IMMUNE SYSTEM). To prevent rejection, a transplant patient must take *immunosuppressive drugs*, such as cyclosporine, to counteract the immune system. At the present stage of medical technology, a transplant patient must plan on taking such drugs for the rest of his or her life. And because suppression of the immune system leaves the body open to attack by various disease organisms, the patient will need careful medical monitoring for life. In addition, transplant patients have been found to be at increased risk for developing certain CANCERS, such as *lymphomas*. But whatever the risks, transplantation has allowed thousands of lives to be saved. (For help and further information, see below; see also BONE-MARROW TRANSPLANT; IMMUNE SYS-

TEM; and specific types of problems, such as HEART AND HEART PROBLEMS.)

For help and further information

Division of Organ Transplantation
Department of Health and Human Services
5608 Fishers Lane
Rockville, MD 20857
301-443-7577
Federal arm charged with overseeing procurement of organs for transplants.

Living Bank
P.O. Box 6725
Houston, TX 77265
800-528-2971
Organ-donor registry. Supplies and encourages filing of donor forms; seeks to educate public; publishes various informative brochures.

National Institute of Allergy and Infectious Diseases (NIAID), 301-496-5717. Publishes *Understanding the Immune System*. (For full group information, see ALLERGY.)

National Institute of Diabetes and Digestive and Kidney Diseases (NIDDK), 301-496-3583. (For full group information, see DIGESTIVE DISORDERS.)

National Heart, Lung, and Blood Institute (NHLBI), 301-496-4236. (For full group information, see BLOOD AND BLOOD DISORDERS; HEART AND HEART PROBLEMS; LUNG AND BREATHING DISORDERS.)

National Association of Patients on Hemodialysis and Transplantation (NAPHT)
211 East 43rd Street
New York, NY 10017
212-867-4486
Susan Kaufer, Executive Director
Organization of and for patients with kidney disease and their families. Provides information; encourages formation of local mutual-support groups; offers special services, such as summer camp for children on dialysis; maintains international directory of dialysis centers; publishes various materials, including a magazine and pamphlets such as *Living with Renal Failure, Renal Failure and Diabetes*, and *Na-K, Sodium-Potassium Counter* (for use in dialysis patient's special diet).

Other reference sources

Many Sleepless Nights: The World of Organ Transplantation, by Lee Gutkind. New York: Norton, 1988.
Taking Heart, by A.C. Greene. New York: Simon & Schuster, 1990. On undergoing a heart-transplant operation.

transposition Alternate term for REVERSAL.

transposition of the great vessels A type of congenital heart defect. (See HEART AND HEART PROBLEMS.)

transverse fracture A type of FRACTURE in which the bones are dislocated sideways.

trauma General term for a physical or psychological wound or injury. (See POST-TRAUMATIC STRESS DISORDER.)

trial-and-error A type of LEARNING STYLE in which a child gains knowledge, skills, and concepts through the experience of daily life, without specific instruction.

trial of labor The medical term for allowing a woman to at least attempt normal VAGINAL BIRTH AFTER CESAREAN (VBAC). (See CESAREAN SECTION.)

trichotillomania A kind of IMPULSE CONTROL DISORDER.

trimester A period of three months. The nine months of PREGNANCY are divided into three trimesters, the first being the most crucial in the development of the child, when exposure to ENVIRONMENTAL HAZARDS or lack of essential VITAMINS and MINERALS leads to many of the grossest BIRTH DEFECTS. In EDUCATION, especially at the COLLEGE level, *trimester* generally refers to a school year divided into three equal parts, instead of two SEMESTERS. (See PREGNANCY for a detailed outline of fetal development by trimesters.)

trisomy A type of CHROMOSOMAL ABNORMALITY in which a person has three copies of a chromosome instead of the normal two. Among the most common types are trisomy 21, or DOWN'S SYNDROME; trisomy 13, or PATAU'S SYNDROME; and trisomy 18, or EDWARDS' SYNDROME.

TRO Abbreviation for TEMPORARY RESTRAINING ORDER.

truant A student who is out of school without a valid excuse on a day when school is considered in session. Such a student is officially regarded as violating laws of COMPULSORY ATTENDANCE and may be contacted by the school's attendance or truant officer.

truth in testing A law that, in New York and by extension some other places, requires that testing agencies offering STANDARDIZED TESTS for college ADMISSION provide students with copies of their answer sheets, along with a copy of the test and identification of the correct answers. On rare occasions students have successfully made a case for ambiguity in question or answer and effective invalidation of a particular test item.

TSWE Abbreviation for Test of Standard Written English, a section of the SCHOLASTIC APTITUDE TEST.

TTY Abbreviation for some forms of TELECOMMUNICATION DEVICES FOR THE DEAF.

tubal ligation A medical procedure for female STERILIZATION that involves the tying (*ligation*) of a woman's FALLOPIAN TUBES so that no egg can pass from the OVARIES into the UTERUS. This is the most common form of CONTRACEPTION for women over 30, according to the National Center for Health Statistics. The oldest type of tubal ligation is the *laparotomy*, often involving a three- to five-inch incision, general ANESTHESIA, a HOSPITAL stay, and recovery of some weeks; today this is generally performed only during some other kind of abdominal surgery or just after birth of the last child. In a *minilaparatomy*, only a one-inch

---

Tubal Ligation: What Are the Risks?

There is a certain amount of discomfort and pain following this operation. Although the complication rate may vary among surgeons and among procedures, the overall complication rate for tubal ligation has been reported to be between 0.1 percent and 15.3 percent. One recent report estimated the serious complications rate for laparoscopy to be 1.7 percent. Very rarely, death occurs during these procedures, often as a complication of general anesthesia.

In addition to complications at the time of surgery, there have been reports of higher rates of hysterectomy later in life for women who have had tubal ligation with electrocautery and higher incidences of premenstrual syndrome (PMS), heavy menstrual bleeding, and irregular cycles. Other investigations, however, have not found these high risks.

Currently under investigation are procedures that may lessen the risks of tubal ligation and enable the operation to be more easily reversible. One of these methods now being studied involves the insertion of silicone plugs into the fallopian tubes that could, at a later date, be removed if the woman wanted more children.

Although some attempts have been made at rejoining the tubes in both men and women, at present these reversal operations have a low success rate; thus, both male and female sterilization must be considered permanent.

Source: *Comparing Contraceptives*, by Judith Levine Willis (1989). Prepared for the Public Health Service by the Food and Drug Administration.

---

incision is used, but general anesthesia is still required. A popular alternative is LAPAROSCOPY, popularly nicknamed *Band-Aid surgery* or *belly-button surgery* because of the small incision near the navel, performed as an outpatient procedure, though still under general anesthesia. A gas is pumped into the abdomen via a needle in the incision, to push the intestines away from the uterus and fallopian tubes. Then, using a lighted flexible tube called a *laparoscope*, inserted through the same or a different incision, the surgeon can cut, clamp, burn (*cauterize*), or otherwise seal the tubes to close them off. Minilaparotomy and laparoscopy have an effectiveness rate as contraceptives of over 99 percent, according to the Public Health Service. In *vaginal tubal ligation*, the incision is made in the VAGINA, but this carries more risk of infection and bleeding and is not so effective. Should a woman change her mind later, surgery can sometimes restore FERTILITY, but this type of sterilization should be regarded as permanent.

tuberculin skin test A type of MEDICAL TEST used to see if a person has IMMUNITY to TUBERCULOSIS. An extract taken from the tuberculosis bacteria is injected into the skin by various methods; if a few days later the skin shows no change, this is a *negative* result, indicating lack of immunity. However, if a circle of skin becomes red, hard, and raised, the test is said to be *positive*, indicating that the person has immunity, either because of previous infection with the disease or because he or she has been effectively immunized by a BCG VACCINE. (For help and further information, see MEDICAL TESTS; TUBERCULOSIS.)

tuberculosis (TB) An infectious bacterial disease that was once a major childhood killer and is still an active threat in many parts of the world, as in inner-city areas with poor NUTRITION and sanitary conditions or among people who have diseases that lower their resistance, such as DIABETES MELLITUS or AIDS. The United States still has some 20,000 new cases of tuberculosis a year, and children are especially at risk if they have contact with anyone, particularly a family member, who has the infection, since it is spread by airborne droplets from sneezes or coughs. Such children are often given a BCG (*bacille Calmette-Guérin*) VACCINE and sometimes preventive antibiotics as well.

Active cases of tuberculosis (or shadows of scars from healed tuberculosis infections) show up on chest X-RAYS, and the bacteria responsible can also be found in the sputum a person coughs up. A TUBERCULIN SKIN TEST also may be used; if positive, it indicates that the person has an active case of tuberculosis—or that the BCG vaccine has produced IMMUNIZATION. Though tuberculosis generally attacks the lungs first, it can (especially if untreated or unresponsive) spread to various parts of the body. In bone and BONE MARROW it produces OSTEOMYELITIS.

For help and further information

National Institute of Allergy and Infectious Diseases (NIAID), 301-496-5717. (For full group information, see ALLERGY.)

Centers for Disease Control (CDC), 404-329-3534. (For full group information, see IMMUNIZATION.)

tuition Money paid for instruction, generally at a school or COLLEGE, not including related expenses such as room and board, books, registration, on-campus health care, and fees for other activities. Schools may reduce or waive tuition for some students, as because of academic excellence, economic need, or minority status; such FINANCIAL AID may be in the form of a SCHOLARSHIP or a GRANT.

tumor General term for any abnormal mass that results from excessive multiplication of cells for unknown, though much examined causes; also called a *neoplasm*. The term *tumor* is sometimes applied in a very general way to any swelling or enlargement due to inflammation.

A tumor is labeled benign if it is not expected to progress to the point of being life-threatening, though a benign tumor can be life-threatening if it affects a vital structure, such as a key part of the brain (see BRAIN TUMOR). Benign tumors grow more slowly and are generally confined, not spreading; though a person may have multiple benign tumors, they each would tend to be distinct. Tumors so confined as to seem surrounded, like a capsule, are called *encapsulated*.

By contrast, a MALIGNANT tumor is progressive, meaning that it is expected to worsen and cause death if untreated or unresponsive to treatment. Malignant tumors grow rapidly, often reach out into other tissues, and may spread (*metastasize*) to other parts of the body, as through the blood (see BLOOD AND BLOOD DISORDERS) or LYMPHATIC SYSTEM. A *primary tumor* is one that arises where it was found; a *secondary* or *metastatic tumor* is one that arose from malignant cells from elsewhere in the body. Even benign tumors need to be monitored, since they can later become malignant.

Tumors are graded according to their severity, especially by their growth rate and their dissimilarity to normal cells. Tumors graded I or II are either benign or mildly malignant, and they grow slowly. Grades III and IV are fully and dangerously malignant. Tumors are given various names, depending on where they originate, whether they are benign or malignant, and their pattern of growth. Among the common general types of tumors are:

- *adenoma*—a tumor that arises from a gland, usually benign but capable of causing various diseases when it results in overproduction of certain HORMONES.
- *carcinoma*—a malignant tumor, or CANCER, that arises from the outer skin, or from skin covering or lining organs (notably the liver and kidneys) or systems (such as the digestive, respiratory, urological, and reproductive systems). Cancers of the BREAST, lungs, stomach, skin, and CERVIX are carcinomas.
- *sarcoma*—a malignant tumor, or cancer, in soft or connective tissues, bone, or muscles, including fibrous body organs, blood vessels, the lymph system, the *meninges* (membrane covering the brain), and cartilage, sometimes associated with RADIATION or BURN scars. Small sarcomas can be cut out and the area treated with RADIATION therapy, but large sarcomas in the limbs may require amputation.
- *glioma*—a tumor arising from within the brain tissue, generally malignant.

The various therapies used in treating tumors are discussed under CANCER. (For help and further information, see BRAIN TUMORS; CANCER.)

tuning-fork test   A type of HEARING TEST for assessing the kind of hearing loss.

tunnel vision   Vision restricted to a narrow span straight ahead, with little *peripheral vision* at the sides. (See EYE AND VISION PROBLEMS.)

Turner's syndrome   A CONGENITAL condition resulting from a CHROMOSOMAL ABNORMALITY, in which a female has not the normal two SEX CHROMOSOMES (XX) but only one. For people with Turner's syndrome, sexual development and MENSTRUATION come late, if at all. Though with HORMONE treatment they may develop SECONDARY SEX CHARACTERISTICS, they are unable to bear children.

People with Turner's syndrome are generally short, are likely to have EAR AND HEARING PROBLEMS and heart problems (see HEART AND HEART PROBLEMS), and have a characteristic webbing of the neck's skin. They sometimes have problems with SPATIAL ORIENTATION, often leading to LEARNING DISABILITIES in mathematics, but have strength in verbal areas; some have MENTAL RETARDATION. Some females (and also some males) with apparently normal sex chromosomes have the characteristics of Turner's syndrome; their condition is called *Noonan's syndrome*.

For help and further information

Turner's Syndrome Society
York University
Administrative Studies Building #006
4700 Keeler Street
Downsview, Ontario M3J 1P3, Canada
416-736-5023
Sandi Hofbauer, Executive Director
Organization for families of children with Turner's syndrome. Provides support for families; gathers and disseminates information; seeks to educate public; publishes various materials, including quarterly newsletter, audiovisual *Turner Syndrome*, and print work *The X's and O's of Turner Syndrome*.

National Institute of Child Health and Human Development (NICHD), 301-496-5133. (For full group information, see PREGNANCY.)

(See also GENETIC DISORDERS.)

tutoring school   Alternate term for REMEDIAL SCHOOL.

21st-century school   A proposal to have before- and after-school CHILD CARE, as well as parenting education, centered in the local public school, a plan put forth by Edward Zigler of Yale University's Bush Center in Child Development and Social Policy. The school, according to Zigler, should coordinate the now highly variable child-care system (including FAMILY DAY CARE) and provide training for CAREGIVERS. Three- and four-year-olds would be cared for in the school setting by trained early-childhood professionals, with a play-oriented CURRICULUM. School-age children up to age 14 would be given before- and after-school care, as needed, and the school itself would operate year-round, a real bonus for working parents. The school would also become a family resource center, providing classes in PRENATAL CARE, parenting skills, and child development. Supporters cite the crisis in reliable child care and the damage to children who have bad child-care experiences or (as in the case of LATCHKEY CHILDREN) who are left unsupervised for substantial periods. Critics say the cost of instituting the "21st-century school" proposals nationwide would be prohibitive and that the present patchwork child-care network at least has the virtue of meeting a wide range of parental needs and desires. They fear a monopoly on child care by a school system that is itself in crisis and has not been notably successful at its main objective: EDUCATION.

tympanostomy   A procedure to solve EAR AND HEARING PROBLEMS that involve chronic buildup of fluid in the middle ear, in which a surgeon inserts a tiny drainage tube in the eardrum.

UAFs   Abbreviation for UNIVERSITY-AFFILIATED FACILITIES.

ulcerative colitis   One of two main types of INFLAMMATORY BOWEL DISEASE (IBD).

ultrasound   Pulses of high-frequency sound waves used in medicine to create a moving image, or *sonogram*, of body tissues on a television monitor. During PREGNANCY, ultrasound is often employed to check the progress of fetal development, identify multiple pregnancy, learn the fetus's sex, identify the position of the FETUS and PLACENTA (should prebirth intervention be necessary), and check for abnormalities, such as ANENCEPHALY or ECTOPIC PREGNANCY, especially if the fetus size is inappropriate for the presumed stage of pregnancy or if family history warrants. Carrying little or no risk to mother or fetus, ultrasound scanning is also used as a guide to physicians in some other GENETIC SCREENING procedures, such as AMNIOCENTESIS and CHORIONIC VILLUS SAMPLING. In newborns, it is sometimes used to peer through gaps in the skull, called FONTANELLES, for brain abnormalities, such as HYDROCEPHALUS or BRAIN TUMORS. In patients of all ages, ultrasound examination can help physicians check for abnormalities in internal tissues, such as those of the liver and gall bladder; special ultrasound examination of the heart is called *echocardiography*. Ultrasound can also help physicians identify possible structural causes of INFERTILITY. (For help and further information, see GENETIC DISORDERS; GENETIC SCREENING; or specific disorders.)

umbilical cord   The hollow, ropelike structure, roughly 1½ to 2 feet long, connecting the FETUS to the PLACENTA, that develops by about the fifth week of PREGNANCY. It supplies oxygen and NUTRITION and takes away waste products by way of two arteries and a vein. During pregnancy, the umbilical cord normally develops numerous twists and turns, even becoming wrapped around the fetus. In some cases this can cause serious problems, as when it becomes wrapped around the fetus's neck; if that happens during DELIVERY, it can often be slipped free. Sometimes a long cord will slip down (*prolapse*) into the mother's CERVIX during LABOR; since that can endanger the flow of oxygen-containing blood, causing HYPOXIA or ANOXIA, a CESAREAN SECTION or sometimes a FOR-

CEPS DELIVERY may be indicated. If the umbilical cord has only one artery, instead of two, the fetus may get insufficient oxygen and nutrition, possibly leading to BIRTH DEFECTS. Shortly after DELIVERY, the umbilical cord is clamped and then cut to about an inch; within days the stump falls off, the remaining scar being called the NAVEL, *umbilicus*, or *belly button*. (For help and further information, see NAVEL; CHILDBIRTH; FETUS.)

umbilical hernia   A pushing out of the abdominal wall because of weakness near the NAVEL, a condition common among infants that also sometimes occurs in women after CHILDBIRTH.

umbilicus   Alternate term for NAVEL.

underachiever   A student whose academic performance is usually well below educators' estimates of his or her potential, especially a student whose scores on STANDARDIZED TESTS of ability are consistently higher than those on ACHIEVEMENT TESTS. Students fail to work up to expected potential for a variety of reasons. A very bright student may be bored and unchallenged by regular schoolwork, in which case ENRICHMENT may be in order; or a student may have specific LEARNING DISABILITIES that hamper learning in one or more ways, despite high general abilities. Students may also "underachieve" because their family or cultural expectations do not tally with those of the school, because of personal or family problems, or because of problems with one or more teachers or aspects of the school situation, such as CORPORAL PUNISHMENT. So-called underachievers may also simply be LATE BLOOMERS, sometimes termed *latent achievers*. (For help and further information, see EDUCATION.)

under-age person   A child who is a MINOR and therefore under the age to be treated legally as an adult, or one who is under the AGE OF CONSENT, being unable to marry without parental or court permission.

underbite   A type of MALOCCLUSION in which the lower jaw and front teeth jut out in front of the upper ones.

undescended testicle   A condition in which one or both testicles fail to drop from inside the abdomen into the SCROTUM before birth; also called *cryptorchidism*. (For help and further information, see TESTES.)

unfit parent   A parent regarded as having a life-style or personal history so harmful to the child as to make the court bar all contact, including VISITATION RIGHTS, as in cases of severe CHILD ABUSE AND NEGLECT or ABANDONMENT.

ungraded (nongraded) class   A class in which students are not grouped according to GRADES (1, 2, 3, etc.) but instead by their level of skill or by category (such as all HANDICAPPED children requiring special services). Many SPECIAL EDUCATION classes are ungraded, as are many adult or continuing education classes. Occasionally, whole schools are run on an ungraded basis, with students being evaluated and frequently reclassified according to their individual progress. In such ALTERNATIVE SCHOOLS, students often pursue INDEPENDENT STUDY and research on projects and courses all or partly of their own selection. Ungraded schools are also particularly attractive for teaching older students, such as former DROPOUTS, who are trying to make up academic deficiencies, as in so-called *remedial, tutoring*, or *catch-up schools*.

Uniform Child Custody Jurisdiction Act (UCCJA)   A statute under which many states have agreed on consistent ways to handle CUSTODY cases. The law was enacted to resolve the many custody dilemmas created when parents and children move from state to state, especially in cases where parents attempt to move from one state to another to obtain a more favorable custody ruling. The UCCJA contains rules for deciding what court has jurisdiction, and it provides that once a decision has been made, other courts will enforce it, or perhaps modify it, rather than making a new and perhaps different decision. In cases of outright parental kidnapping (see MISSING CHILDREN), the UCCJA specifies that the offending parent will be denied custody, except in very special circumstances.

Uniform Parentage Act   A law enacted in some states that attempts to provide common court procedures, definitions, and standards for issues of parentage, especially those involved in establishing the legal FATHER in a PATERNITY SUIT.

Uniform Reciprocal Enforcement of Support Act (URESA)   An act providing the legal basis for enforcing CHILD-SUPPORT payment orders and related actions between parents living in two different states; the revised form of the statute is often called RURESA.

universal birth number   A unique identification number assigned to a newborn by a state's bureau of vital statistics. The digits of the number include the year of birth, the area code of the birth site, and a birth registration number.

universal donor   A person whose blood is of the type O and Rh negative, which can be used for BLOOD TRANSFUSIONS in most other people.

university   An academic institution that offers post-HIGH SCHOOL educational programs and is made up of one or more COLLEGES, GRADUATE schools, and professional schools grouped together, often with a substantial focus on research, in addition to teaching.

university-affiliated facilities (UAFs)   HOSPITALS associated with university research and training facilities, providing highly sophisticated equipment, laboratories, and staff for diagnosis, treatment, and support. Parents with special problems related to PREGNANCY or INFERTILITY, or whose children have serious health problems, are often referred to appropriate UAFs by their PRIMARY HEALTH-CARE PROVIDERS.

unsaturated fatty acids   A type of FAT derived mostly from plant sources.

unsocialized   Description of someone (often a JUVENILE DELINQUENT) whose behavior is disruptive and troublesome, especially flaunting authority. The term implies that the behavior results from lack of or inadequacy of proper role-models from which the juvenile might learn more acceptable kinds of behavior.

unwed father   Term for the presumed biological FATHER if a child's parents are not married and paternity has not been acknowledged or established; legally, sometimes called *putative father*, against whom a PATERNITY SUIT may be brought in some situations.

unwed mother   A MOTHER who is not married at the time she gives birth to a child. Unlike the unwed father, she retains PARENTS' RIGHTS and PARENTS' RESPONSIBILITIES unless she chooses to give them up.

uremia   A condition resulting from permanent and irreversible loss of kidney function, called *end-stage renal disease*. (See KIDNEY AND UROLOGICAL DISORDERS.)

URESA   Abbreviation for UNIFORM RECIPROCAL ENFORCEMENT OF SUPPORT ACT, used to enforce CHILD-SUPPORT payment orders and related actions between parents living in two different states.

urethra   The tube by which urine is carried from the bladder to be excreted. In males, the urethra also carries SEMEN; about nine inches long, it passes from the bladder through the PROSTATE GLAND and through the length of the PENIS. In females, the urethra is only about 1½ inches long, exiting just above the VAGINA. The urethra is quite vulnerable to injury or to inflammation (*urethritis*), as from untreated GONORRHEA, BALANITIS, or other infections. In males, if scarring results, the urethra can become constricted, leading to painful urination, increased likelihood of infections, and possible damage to bladder or kidneys, as well as to painful EJACULATION during sex. Such constriction may need to be corrected—by dilation by a tube inserted through the urethral opening or sometimes by total surgical reconstruction. In females, the urethra is somewhat less vulnerable but more readily carries infection to the bladder and kidneys. CONGENITAL defects involving the urethra include HYPOSPADIAS and EPIS-

PADIAS. (For help and further information, see KIDNEY AND URO-LOGICAL DISORDERS.)

urinalysis A series of tests run on a sample of urine; often considered a kind of KIDNEY FUNCTION TEST, it also tests for a wide variety of other problems and disorders. The urine is first examined for its general characteristics, such as color, acidity (pH), clarity or cloudiness, and concentration. Technicians then use a centrifuge to spin the urine, separating out various substances for analysis, including:

- blood—a possible indication of infection, TUMORS, or kidney stones;
- pus, bacteria, or white blood cells—signs of infection (these may often be further examined in CULTURES);
- protein or protein fragments called *casts*—signs of possible kidney disease or injury;
- bile—sign of possible liver disease;
- crystals—signs of possible METABOLIC DISORDERS;
- GLUCOSE or ketones—signs of possible DIABETES MELLITUS;
- HUMAN CHORIONIC GONADOTROPIN (hCG)—sign of possible PREGNANCY;
- worm eggs—signs of possible parasitic infestation.

(For help and further information, see MEDICAL TESTS.)

urinary ostomy Alternate term for UROSTOMY.

urinary tract infection (UTI) A common kind of KIDNEY AND UROLOGICAL DISORDER affecting children and pregnant women.

urological disorders Problems with the urinary tract. (See KIDNEY AND UROLOGICAL DISORDERS.)

urologist A PHYSICIAN who specializes in diagnosis and treatment of disorders of the urinary tract, including the kidney and bladder in both males and females, and of the male genitals. (See KIDNEY AND UROLOGICAL DISORDERS.)

urostomy (urinary ostomy) A type of OSTOMY that provides a new outlet for the bladder.

uterus A muscular, hollow organ in a woman's lower abdomen, above and behind the bladder, shaped roughly like an upside-down pear, with the FALLOPIAN TUBES lying above and to the right and left. On the bottom of the uterus, the CERVIX, actually the neck of the uterus, leads into the VAGINA. The uterus is the center of the reproductive system; here the fertilized egg implants itself to grow as a FETUS. And here the monthly MENSTRUAL CYCLE centers, with the uterus lining (the *endometrium*) gradually growing in preparation for a fertilized egg and being shed in a menstrual period if none appears. In infant girls, the uterus is tipped backward (*retroverted*); but as a female matures, the uterus normally becomes tipped forward about a quarter-turn from the vagina. Usually weighing only a few ounces, the uterus grows dramatically during pregnancy, some of the growth coming as the endometrium grows thick and develops more blood vessels to supply the fetus through the PLACENTA and some coming from development of powerful muscles that will, during CHILDBIRTH, push the baby through the BIRTH CANAL (the widened cervix and vagina).

Various kinds of disorders of the uterus can affect a woman's ability to reproduce, including:

- *inflammation of the endometrium (endometritis)*: This often results from an infection originating elsewhere, such as the cervix or fallopian tubes; it can also be a complication of CHILDBIRTH, as after a MISCARRIAGE or when not all of the placenta has been expelled after birth.
- TUMORS: A variety of growths can affect the uterus, including many benign TUMORS, such as polyps and fibroid tumors; MALIGNANT tumors of the endometrium; and either benign or malignant growths in the placenta. Women at increased risk of having endometrial cancer are those with long-term high ESTROGEN levels, OBESITY, failure to ovulate, and few or no children; use of the BIRTH-CONTROL PILL lowers the risk.
- *injury*: These mostly result from external causes, such as a badly performed ABORTION or an INTRAUTERINE DEVICE that has damaged the uterus.
- *mispositioning (prolapse)*: Sometimes the uterus can slip out of its normal position, especially when its support ligaments have been stretched and weakened from previous childbirth, though it can also occur in childless women, especially those who are obese. In extreme cases, the uterus slips down so far it can be seen at the opening of the vagina. The bladder and urethra can also be affected. Pelvic floor EXERCISES help strengthen the muscles needed to prevent prolapse after childbirth. In severe cases, the uterus may need to be removed, in an operation called a *hysterectomy*, or a plastic ring called a *pessary* may be inserted to hold the uterus in place.
- *congenital malformation*: Sometimes a uterus develops in an unusual shape, which can predispose a woman to have MAL-PRESENTATION (abnormal birth postion of the fetus) or other problems during delivery. On rare occasions, a uterus is absent altogether, or a woman has two each of the uterus, cervix, and vagina. In some such cases, surgical correction is possible; in others, a normal pregnancy is not possible.

Also associated with the uterus are various problems involving MENSTRUATION. (For help and further information, see PREGNANCY; OVULATION.)

UTI Abbreviation for urinary tract infection, a common kind of KIDNEY AND UROLOGICAL DISORDER affecting children and pregnant women.

V

vaccine   A preparation used in IMMUNIZATION, made up of disease organisms, weakened or killed so that they will not give a person the disease even while their presence causes the body to manufacture ANTIBODIES that will thereafter (for a limited time or a lifetime) protect the person from the disease. The vaccine is usually administered by an INJECTION or taken through the mouth. (For help and further information, see IMMUNIZATION or entries on specific vaccines.)

vacuum extraction   In CHILDBIRTH, use of a suction cup placed on a baby's head and attached to a machine called a *vacuum extractor*, or *ventouse*, to help ease DELIVERY, with the suction timed to the contractions of the UTERUS. Vacuum extraction is used in cases of FETAL DISTRESS—especially early in the delivery or when the mother is unable to push out the baby on her own—as an alternative to FORCEPS DELIVERY. The baby generally has temporary swelling of the scalp following birth. The same kind of machine is also used to perform some kinds of ABORTION, the process then being called *menstrual extraction*. (For help and further information, see CHILDBIRTH.)

vagina   The muscular, expandable canal between a woman's outer GENITALS and the CERVIX that leads to the UTERUS. The vagina is where, during sexual intercourse, the PENIS deposits SPERM for possible FERTILIZATION; it is also the avenue used for the outflow of blood during MENSTRUATION; and during CHILDBIRTH it and the widened cervix become the BIRTH CANAL. In a young girl, the vagina is mostly covered by a membrane called a HYMEN, with an opening in the center that is stretched or torn at the first penetration of the vagina. Partial or complete absence of the vagina (*vaginal atresia*) is a rare CONGENITAL abnormality. Apart from occasional infections, such as from SEXUALLY TRANSMITTED DISEASES, which may involve vaginal discharge or itching, few young people have disorders involving the vagina.

vaginal birth after cesarean (VBAC)   A movement to give women the option of delivering a child in the normal manner, when medically possible, though a previous child was delivered by CESAREAN SECTION.

vaginal mucus method   A technique of NATURAL FAMILY PLANNING.

VAKT (visual, auditory, kinesthetic, tactile)   A highly structured multisensory approach to teaching READING, using not only *auditory* (hearing) and *visual* (seeing) senses, but also *tactile* (touch) and kinesthetic (body motion), in which a child traces a written letter or word while reading it. VAKT approaches are widely used to teach children with LEARNING DISABILITIES, especially DYSLEXIA. With the *Gillingham (Orton-Gillingham) method*, the child learns the sounds of individual letters and is then taught to blend them together into words, using tracing throughout, in a series of five-times-a-week lessons over at least two years. In the *Fernald method*, the child learns to read and spell whole words, first by tracing hand-printed words and learning to reproduce them without referring to the original, then using the word in a sentence or story, and finally reading the word in print. The word is then filed in a "word bank," and the child goes on to learning new words, gradually eliminating the tracing but often speaking and writing the word to "set" it and eventually learning new words by their similarities to words previously learned.

valedictorian   In a graduating class, the student with the highest academic rank, generally as measured by GRADE AVERAGE; so called because he or she is often asked to give a farewell speech, or *valedictory*, at GRADUATION ceremonies. The second-ranked student is the SALUTATORIAN.

validity   In relation to TESTS, the extent to which a test actually measures what it sets out to measure, and so the extent to which it is actually useful or meaningful to use the test results. In educational testing, this is of special concern to parents and a highly controversial question. In INTELLIGENCE TESTS, for example, it is unclear precisely what is being tested, for no one knows for sure what intelligence is and whether and how it would be possible to test it. Professionals often distinguish between different types of validity, including

- *content validity*, which concerns how well the content of the test relates to the test's purpose. To be useful, an ACHIEVEMENT TEST for a particular grade needs to reflect approximately what is actually taught in that grade.
- *predictive validity*, which concerns how well the test scores relate to the future performance they are meant to predict. For example, the SCHOLASTIC ACHIEVEMENT TEST (SAT) is used to predict student success in college, and whether or not it succeeds in doing so (a point much at issue) would be a question of predictive validity. A test's predictive validity may be measured by analysis of the *correlation* between two sets

of figures, such as SAT scores and college GRADE-POINT AVER-AGES; this is generally expressed statistically as a decimal number somewhere between zero correlation (indicating that the SAT correctly predicted GPA scores in no cases) to an ideally perfect 1 (indicating that the SAT correctly predicted GPA in every case).

Two related concerns are *sensitivity*, the ability of the test to correctly identify children with a problem, for example, and *specificity*, a test's ability to correctly indicate which children are not AT RISK. (For help and further information, see TESTS; STANDARDIZED TESTS.)

valvular heart disease   A condition involving abnormal valves in the heart, causing heart "murmur." (See HEART AND HEART PROBLEMS.)

van Bogaert's disease   Alternate name for cerebrotendinous xanthomatosis, a type of LIPID STORAGE DISEASE.

varicella   Alternate name for CHICKEN POX.

varicocele   Swollen (varicose) veins around the TESTES, most often the left testicle. If painful, the condition can be relieved by wearing an athletic supporter or tight briefs, but this can affect fertility. Where pain is great or INFERTILITY is at issue, surgery may be performed to tie off defective veins.

vas deferens   The two tubes by which SPERM leave the EPIDIDY-MIS (the "holding area" behind each of the two TESTES where the sperm mature) to mix with SEMEN and to be released through the EJACULATORY DUCT in ORGASM. It is the vas deferens that are cut during VASECTOMY, a surgical form of STERILIZATION performed on males.

vasectomy   A surgical procedure that is a form of STERILIZA-TION, a permanent form of BIRTH CONTROL for a man who wants to father no more—or no—children. The operation is often performed in a doctor's office under local ANESTHESIA and has an effectiveness rate of 99 percent. The brief procedure involves making two cuts, one on either side of the SCROTUM, and then cutting or clamping the long tubes called the VAS DEFERENS so that no SPERM can pass through them. Some temporary pain and swelling follow the procedure, and sometimes infection can set in. In their flyer *Comparing Contraceptives*, the Public Health Service also reports: "Although there have been reports of adverse effects on the cardiovascular system in animal studies, human studies have shown no differences in cardiovascular problems between men who have had vasectomies and those who haven't. However, about 5 percent of vasectomized men report having psychological problems related to the procedure." Attempts to reverse vasectomies have had a low success rate, so men considering vasectomy should regard the operation as permanent.

For help and further information

Association for Voluntary Surgical Contraception (AVSC), 212-351-2500. (For full group information, see BIRTH CONTROL.)

American Fertility Society (AFS), 205-933-8494. Publishes *Vasectomy: Facts About Male Sterilization* and researches

reversing vasectomies. (For full group information, see INFERTILITY.)

Other reference sources

Understanding Vasectomy, by George C. Denniston, M.D. Atlanta: Peachtree, 1989.
The Vasectomy Book, by Marc Goldstein and Michael Feldberg. Los Angeles: Tarcher, 1982.
(See also STERILIZATION.)

vas efferentia   The tubes by which SPERM leave the testes for the EPIDIDYMIS, the "holding area" where they mature.

VBAC   Abbreviation for vaginal birth after cesarean section. (See CESAREAN SECTION.)

VD   Abbreviation for venereal diseases, now often called SEXUALLY TRANSMITTED DISEASES (STDs).

vegan   Alternate name for a person who follows a so-called strict or pure VEGETARIAN diet.

vegetarian   A type of diet that excludes meat, often poultry and fish, and sometimes also eggs and dairy products. Many peoples of the world follow a largely vegetarian diet, many because of personal poverty and limited regional food resources and some because of religious or philosophical conviction. In the West, some people have also adopted a vegetarian approach to NUTRITION in response to concern about misuse of the world's resources and because of a desire to live a more natural, healthy existence. There are several different types of vegetarian diets, notably:

* *semivegetarian*, which excludes red meat but allows some poultry and fish, plus all other kinds of foods;
* *lacto-ovovegetarian*, which excludes meat, poultry, and fish, but allows eggs, milk, and other dairy products, including cheese;
* *lactovegetarian*, which excludes all animal products except milk and other dairy products, including cheese;
* *vegan*, also called *strict* or *pure vegetarian*, which excludes animal products in any form (including butter and milk for cooking);
* *fruitarian*, which includes only plant products that fall off naturally and do not require destruction of the plant for harvesting, including nuts, beans, peas, corn, cucumbers, tomatoes, berries, and fruits such as apples, pears, and peaches.

Except when most protein is gained from high-fat dairy products and high-CHOLESTEROL eggs, well-balanced, high-fiber vegetarian diets may lower the risk of a number of diseases, including hypertension (high BLOOD PRESSURE), OBESITY, DIABETES MELLITUS (non-insulin-dependent), OSTEOPOROSIS, and DIGESTIVE DISORDERS, including CANCER of the intestines.

The main concern with a vegetarian diet is to get the proper amount and type of PROTEIN, MINERALS, and VITAMINS. Most animal sources of protein contain all of the necessary AMINO ACIDS, but many plant sources contain only some. So people following a vegan or fruitarian diet, especially, must become very familiar with the nutritional content of plant foods and plan to eat them in the proper combinations (such as rice and beans) to get the full range of proteins needed. People following a vegan diet, especially pregnant women, may want to take a vitamin supplement, especially including vitamins B_{12}, C, and D.

For help and further information

North American Vegetarian Society (NAVS)
P.O. Box 72
Dolgeville, NY 13329
518-568-7970
Brian Graff, Secretary
Organization of individuals and groups committed to or interested in vegetarianism. Seeks to educate public; publishes various materials, including quarterly *Vegetarian Voice* and *Facts of Vegetarianism.*

Vegetarian Information Service (VIS)
P.O. Box 5888
Bethesda, MD 20814
301-530-1737
Alex Hershaft, President
Organization devoted to gathering and disseminating information about vegetarianism and its health, social, economic, environmental, and ethical advantages. Seeks to educate public and influence public policy; publishes various materials.

Jewish Vegetarian Society—America (JVS)
P.O. Box 5722
Baltimore, MD 21208
301-486-4948
Izak Luchinsky, Board Chairman
Organization of Jews espousing vegetarianism. Gathers and disseminates information on religious basis for vegetarianism and its health, social, economic, environmental, and ethical advantages, and the negative aspects of meat-eating. Provides information on vegetarian culture, facilities, and services; produces bibliographies and book reviews of related books; maintains hotline; publishes various materials, including monthly newsletter, quarterly *The Jewish Vegetarian*, and *Directory of Vegetarian Restaurants and Hotels*.

American Vegan Society (AVS)
P.O. Box H
Malaga, NJ 08328
609-694-2887
H. Jay Dinshah, President
Organization of people devoted to veganism, involving fully vegetarian diet and no use of animal clothing. Publishes quarterly *Ahimsa* and cookbooks.

(See also NUTRITION.)

venereal diseases (VD)   A group of diseases passed between people during sexual intercourse, today often called SEXUALLY TRANSMITTED DISEASES (STDs).

venereal warts   Alternate medical term for GENITAL WARTS, a SEXUALLY TRANSMITTED DISEASE.

venipuncture   A type of SPECIMEN TEST in which blood is removed by inserting a needle into a vein and withdrawing it into a syringe or a CATHETER; a somewhat INVASIVE kind of MEDICAL TEST, though generally in the West with little risk.

ventilation   Alternate term for ARTIFICIAL RESPIRATION.

ventilator   A machine to assist or totally take over breathing when a person has difficulty or inability in breathing unassisted, as after a severe HEAD INJURY; often called a *respirator* or *life-support machine*. Such machines are generally used in INTENSIVE CARE UNITS of hospitals, often in tandem with electronic monitoring of pulse, respiration, and heartbeat. (For help and further information, see LUNG AND BREATHING DISORDERS.)

ventricles   Cavities or chambers in the body, generally filled with fluid. In the brain, each half of the cerebrum surrounds a ventricle, with two smaller ventricles near the brain stem. Enlargement of the ventricles is found in certain diseases and disorders, such as HYDROCEPHALUS and HUNTINGTON'S CHOREA. In cases of hydrocephalus, a SHUNT is sometimes inserted into the head to bypass a blockage or remove excess CEREBROSPINAL FLUID; on occasion that can cause infection of the ventricles (*ventriculitis*). PREMATURE infants are more than usually susceptible to abnormal, excessive bleeding in the brain ventricles (see INTRAVENTRICULAR HEMORRHAGE; BRAIN AND BRAIN DISORDERS).

In the heart, the name *ventricles* is given to the two lower chambers, which pump the blood they receive from the upper chambers, called *atria*. It is the pumping of the ventricles that we hear as a "heartbeat" and that are graphed by an electrocardiograph when physicians are assessing whether the heart or heartbeat is abnormal (see HEART AND HEART PROBLEMS).

ventricular septal defect (VSD)   A type of CONGENITAL heart defect. (See HEART AND HEART PROBLEMS.)

vertex presentation   An optimal type of FETAL PRESENTATION, in which the FETUS is head first.

very low birth weight (VLBW)   A LOW-BIRTH-WEIGHT baby weighing under 3.3 pounds (1,500 grams) at birth, with sharply increased risk of illnesses and death.

viable   The medical term for an infant who is capable of living, growing, and developing independently. Normally, that means that the infant weighs at least 2.2 pounds (1,000 grams) at birth or has a GESTATIONAL AGE of at least 28 weeks (meaning that the FETUS developed in the UTERUS for at least 28 weeks, the normal number of weeks for GESTATION being 40). A child so PREMATURE would, however, probably need a great deal of special care in the first weeks and months of its life and probably would be placed in a NEONATAL INTENSIVE CARE UNIT (NICU).

vicarious learning   A LEARNING STYLE in which a child gains knowledge, skills, and concepts from the experience of others.

Tips on Making Visitation Work

For Both Parents

- Be flexible and reasonable in making visitation arrangements.
- If the child must travel between parents, agree, as part of your original visitation arrangements, on which parent pays which travel expenses.
- Do not try to pump the children about your ex's activities and friends.
- Do not try to turn the children against your ex.
- Do not use the children to pass messages between you and your ex.
- Do not use the visitation to talk or argue with your ex.
- Do not make unrealistic promises to children or try to outdo your ex by promising something you cannot fulfill.
- Do not undermine the other parent's discipline or feed any tendency for the children to play one parent off against another.
- Understand that children may carry confusion and resentment into visitation and do not try to make such feelings the basis of argument with your ex; if such feelings persist, consider counseling for both child and parents.
- Keep a separate date book purely for visitation arrangements, noting in it any visitation problems, such as failure to keep an appointment or denial of visitation; this can act as a record should there be future dispute over visitation.

For Noncustodial Parents

- Suggest reasonable visiting hours that do not put undue strain on the children or the custodial parent.
- Understand that older children increasingly have their own activities, and take them into account when arranging visitation.
- Pick up children promptly or, if necessary, call as soon as possible to alter arrangements.
- Return children promptly at the agreed-upon time.
- See the children regularly so the children know they can count on you, rather than letting long stretches go by without contact.

- Spend at least some time with the children yourself alone, rather than always involving other relatives or friends or dropping your children off with others.
- Do not insist that a new partner always be present during visitation.
- Try to bring the children into your everyday life and interests, rather than taking the children on a constant whirlwind of outings.
- Do not drink alcohol or use drugs while with the children; apart from the danger to the child, problems in this area can cost you visitation rights.
- See that children are kept reasonably clean and properly cared for, for example, that cuts and scrapes are treated rather than left untended.
- If a child has a rash or some other problem that seems to require a physical examination, protect yourself from possible charges of child abuse and neglect by having a third person present or taking the child to a doctor.
- If you are unable to avoid disagreeable discussion with your ex when picking up the children, try arranging to pick them up elsewhere, as at a friend or relative's house or at school, or have a mutual friend pick them up for you.

For Custodial Parents

- Have children ready when agreed for pickup by your ex or, if necessary, call as soon as possible to alter arrangements.
- Be available at the agreed-upon time for the children's return.
- See that the children are reasonably clean and cared for at the time of visitation.
- Do not drink alcohol or use drugs while with the children; apart from the danger to the child, problems in this area can cause the court to reconsider CUSTODY.

Source: Parents Without Partners and other sources.

Vineland Social Maturity Scale A type of TEST that attempts to assess the development of various SOCIAL SKILLS, SELF-HELP SKILLS, and ADAPTIVE BEHAVIOR of children from infancy to adulthood. Normally a parent, close relative, or other knowledgeable CAREGIVER is interviewed one-to-one about the child's abilities in various areas, such as eating, dressing, communication, movement, and self-direction. The resulting SCORES are converted to an AGE-EQUIVALENT, sometimes called a *social age*. (For help and further information, see TESTS.)

visitation rights The right of a separated, divorced, or otherwise absent parent living elsewhere to see his or her children on some agreed-upon basis; some NONCUSTODIAL PARENTS dislike the implication that they are visitors and prefer the term *parental access*. The ability to visit one's children is a basic PARENTS' RIGHT; the father of a child born to an unmarried mother, if he acknowledges the child as his own or if a PATERNITY SUIT is successful against him, gains visitation rights, though he has no obligation to exercise them. Some states also legally protect GRANDPARENTS' RIGHTS to visit grandchildren, regardless of possible estrangement in the family, and grandparents' organizations have been conducting intensive lobbying to extend recognition of such rights. In some special cases, a person who has no legal responsibility for the child but who is considered the PSYCHOLOGICAL PARENT may also be granted visitation rights.

If a child is placed for ADOPTION, parents generally lose visitation rights, except when the child is being adopted by another family member, such as a stepfather or aunt, or in some forms of *open adoption*. In cases of adoption, grandparents also generally lose visitation rights, though some states protect those rights in special situations, as in adoption by another relative.

Parents can lose visitation rights in some other special situations, as when a parent's life-style is considered so harmful to a child as to make the court bar any parent–child contact or when ABANDONMENT or CHILD ABUSE AND NEGLECT leads to TERMINATION OF PARENTAL RIGHTS. But the court does not usually lightly terminate such rights and more often sets certain conditions on visitation. For example, in cases where a parent has been violent or abusive in the past, the court may require *supervised visitation*, under which the parent and child can meet only with a court-appointed third party present at all times. If the CUSTODIAL PARENT objects to the child visiting overnight with the noncustodial parent and an unmarried partner, the court may sometimes order the child to visit only during the day. If petitioned by one of the parents, the court can also change visitation arrangements, as when a parent begins drinking heavily or decides to openly acknowledge HOMOSEXUALITY; how the court responds to such petitions varies from state to state.

Parents who are separated or divorced but have joint CUSTODY of the child do not—in strict legal terms—have visitation *rights*, because both have custody. But they, like others, have to face the difficult task of arranging visitation schedules. Where separated parents have agreed between themselves as to the terms of custody, they generally are free to arrange visitation schedules, though even with the best of wills it is often very difficult to accommodate the needs of both parents and children. But where custody has been contested and feelings run high, the court sometimes becomes involved in custody and visitation arrangements, setting visitation schedules with the BEST INTERESTS OF THE CHILD in mind, such as every other weekend and part of the summer.

Where shuttling between parents can pose an undue hardship on a child or the custodial parent seems likely to take the child far enough away to effectively deny visitation rights to the other parent, the court may place restrictions on custody. For example, the court may restrict the distance the child may travel, require that the custodial parent continue to live within a certain geographical area, or forbid the custodial parent to move without first giving written notice to the noncustodial parent, allowing time to seek a possible court modification of the visitation arrangements.

Sometimes the court may simply order that visitation be allowed at "reasonable" times and places, leaving the parents to work out the details. Such an arrangement among already-sparring parents is difficult, and experts in family law recommend that parents specify their visitation arrangements at the start, lessening the areas of possible misunderstanding and resentment. More important, specifying visitation rights means that if the custodial parent denies visitation, the noncustodial parent can make a case for violation of a court order. With no arrangements specified, a noncustodial parent has a hard time proving in court that the custodial parent has denied "reasonable visitation."

Denial of visitation rights is often a serious problem. Family-law experts suggest that parents who are having difficulty seeing their children should carefully document their attempts to arrange for visitation, keeping track of each precise meeting time agreed upon and recording every failure to make the child available as agreed, preferably having a third party available to testify that visitation was indeed denied. Sometimes a custodial parent denies visitation in an attempt to obtain overdue CHILD SUPPORT, and conversely some parents withhold child support when denied visitation, but in most states the two are legally quite separate issues. The parent who denies visitation is guilty of CONTEMPT OF COURT for disobeying a court order and may be subject to fines or jail. But in practice, the court is reluctant to jail or fine a custodial parent, since that may harm the child. Some states provide for court-ordered MEDIATION in cases involving visitation disputes; others have special agencies or bureaus to help with visitation enforcement. In a Michigan model, a Friend of the Court system logs lost visitation so that makeup visitations can be arranged.

In extreme cases, where parents have been unable to work out satisfactory visitation arrangements and the state has failed to enforce visitation rights, some parents have resorted to parental kidnapping (see MISSING CHILDREN) to completely bar the other parent's access to the child. Under the CLEAN HANDS DOCTRINE, such parents risk losing all access to their children and generally forfeit any future right to claim custody. (For help and further information, see CUSTODY; MISSING CHILDREN.)

visiting teacher (itinerant teacher) An educator who travels among several schools, providing special instructional services, or who teaches HOMEBOUND STUDENTS.

visual discrimination A key type of VISUAL SKILL.

visual impairment A wide variety of impairments to sight, including but going far wider than legal *blindness*. (See EYE AND VISION PROBLEMS.)

visual memory A key type of VISUAL SKILL.

visual-motor coordination A set of MOTOR SKILLS similar to hand–eye coordination, but involving other parts of the body, as in catching or kicking a ball.

visual-motor integration A key type of VISUAL SKILL that involves synchronizing hand and eye, or body and eye, in motor tasks, such as slicing tomatoes or riding a bicycle; also called *perceptual-motor skills, hand–eye coordination,* or *body–eye coordination.*

visual perception A key type of VISUAL SKILL.

visual skills A set of overlapping skills that involve the eyes, often in combination with MOTOR SKILLS.

Visual perception is the ability to interpret what is seen. Children with LEARNING DISABILITIES or some other DEVELOPMENTAL DISORDERS may have eyes that are physically normal but still have defects that make objects and people appear to change, so they are unable to consistently judge size, shape, location, movement, and color. They are said to have a PERCEPTUAL HANDICAP.

The Eyes Have It!

Researchers have found that a newborn's five senses are more acute than we had realized. For example, it is now known that newborns can focus their eyes and can follow bright moving objects with them. You can enrich your baby's world by placing a *few* interesting things around the crib, carriage, or room—things that she or he may enjoy looking at. For example, hang colorful pictures on the walls, or paste decals on the crib at the baby's eye level, or hang toys from the crib or carriage and mobiles from the ceiling. You may be pleasantly surprised one day to find your baby awake and quietly contemplating some fascinating object nearby.

But *you* are your baby's most important visual stimulus. Scientists have found that newborns actually have visual preferences, preferring to look at *faces* rather than inanimate things. And before long it will be *your* face he or she has learned best and prefers the most. Further, it has been learned that, at four or five months, babies prefer to look at eyes rather than mouths or noses. Encourage development by looking at and holding your baby so that he or she can see your eyes.

Source: *Stimulating Baby Senses*, by Marilyn Sargent, in consultation with National Institute of Mental Health scientists. Washington, DC: Government Printing Office, 1978. Part of the Caring About Kids series. For more from this pamphlet, see BOTTLEFEEDING, COMMUNICATION SKILLS AND DISORDERS, MOTOR SKILLS, and SENSORY MODES.

Such children, for example, have difficulty putting together a puzzle or building with blocks.

Visual discrimination is the ability to look at objects or pictures and recognize if they are the same or different; it is a form of visual AGNOSIA. Children with learning disabilities or other developmental disabilities may show trouble in this area by having difficulty matching blocks, shapes, or line drawings or pointing out which object is unlike the others.

Visual memory is the ability to remember for a short time objects and people in one's environment. Children with learning disabilities or other developmental disabilities may show visual memory problems by, for example, being unable to look at four familiar toys, close their eyes briefly, and then tell which toy has been removed.

Visual tracking is the ability to focus the eyes on one point and move them rhythmically from side to side, up and down, or diagonally, a skill crucial to learning how to read. Children with learning disabilities or other developmental disabilities may show tracking problems by shifting or jerking their eyes while watching activities that involve rhythmic movement, such as the rolling of a ball, a Ping-Pong game, or a child running.

Visual-motor integration is the ability to coordinate eye and hand, or eye and body, to carry out a desired action; this is also called *perceptual-motor skill* and includes *hand–eye coordination*, or *body–eye coordination*. Children with learning disabili-

ties or other developmental disabilities may be unable to make their hands follow signals from their eyes, so they may have trouble copying simple designs and shapes, drawing, cutting and pasting, putting forms in a form board, or putting together a puzzle.

A CHART OF NORMAL DEVELOPMENT (on page 507) indicates when between birth and age six children first, *on the average*, begin to develop the main visual skills. Children develop at individual and varying paces, but all of them can benefit from activities designed to enhance their natural development. In TEACHING YOUNG CHILDREN: GUIDELINES AND ACTIVITIES (on page 544), parents will find activities designed to develop children's skills in various areas. (For help and further information, see EYE AND VISION PROBLEMS.)

visual tracking   A key type of VISUAL SKILL.

vitamin A (retinol)   A VITAMIN important for new cell growth, healthy tissue, and normal vision (especially at night). Signs of deficiency include night-blindness, DIARRHEA, dry skin, XEROPHTHALMIA (abnormally dry eyes), tendency to intestinal infections, and impaired growth. Because vitamin A is a *fat-soluble vitamin*, stored in body fat, overconsumption can have serious consequences, progressing from nausea and blurred vision to headache, loss of hair, dry skin, and irregular MENSTRUATION to impaired growth, enlargement of liver and spleen, bone pain, increased skull pressure mimicking presence of a BRAIN TUMOR and, in pregnant women, BIRTH DEFECTS. (See FETAL RISK FROM VITAMIN A, below.) This condition of overconsumption is called *hypervitaminosis A*.

The body makes vitamin A from various foods containing the yellow pigment *carotene*; these include green and yellow vegetables and yellow fruits, including carrots, leafy green vegetables, sweet potatoes, squash, apricots, and canteloupe. Vitamin A (retinol) itself may be found in liver, egg yolk, and dairy products, where other animals have formed the vitamin A from carotene; it is this form that can lead to hypervitaminosis A if taken in excess. An artificial form of vitamin A is used as a treatment for ACNE, under the name of ACCUTANE. (For help and

Fetal Risk from Vitamin A

Isotretinoin is a vitamin A acid that is known to cause birth defects or developmental disability in 25 percent of children exposed to it in the first trimester of pregnancy. There are case reports of birth defects associated with large doses of vitamin A. Moreover, vitamin A is well known to cause birth defects in laboratory animals. It has been suggested that women who are pregnant or likely to become pregnant should avoid taking supplements containing more than the RDA level for pregnant women.

Source: *The Surgeon General's Report on Nutrition and Health*. Rocklin, CA: Prima, 1988.

further information, see RECOMMENDED DAILY ALLOWANCES; VITA-MINS; ACCUTANE.)

vitamin B₁ (thiamin) A VITAMIN that is important for normal digestion, growth, fertility, LACTATION, nerve-tissue functioning, and CARBOHYDRATE METABOLISM. Lack of vitamin B₁ causes the DEFICIENCY DISEASE called *beriberi*, which involves disrupted functioning of the NERVOUS SYSTEM. Other symptoms include loss of appetite, EDEMA (fluid buildup in the body), heart problems (see HEART AND HEART PROBLEMS), nausea and VOMITING, and spastic muscle contractions. Vitamin B₁ is commonly found in meats such as pork and liver, whole-grain and fortified grain products (including breads, cereals, and pasta), nuts, and beans. No problems of overconsumption are known, because the vitamin is water-soluble, and so any excess is flushed out of the body in urine. (For help and further information, see RECOMMENDED DAILY ALLOWANCES; VITAMINS.)

vitamin B₂ (riboflavin) A VITAMIN that is important in obtaining energy for the body from CARBOHYDRATES and PROTEINS. Vitamin B₂ is commonly found in leafy vegetables, enriched and whole-grain breads, liver, lean meats, eggs, MILK, and cheese. Symptoms of vitamin B₂ deficiency are lip sores and cracks and dim vision. No problems of overconsumption are known, because the vitamin is water-soluble, and so any excess is excreted in urine. (For help and further information, see REC-OMMENDED DAILY ALLOWANCES; VITAMINS.)

vitamin B₆ (pyridoxine, pyridoxal, or pyridoxamine) A VITAMIN that exists in three forms, all important in the body's use of PROTEIN and for the proper growth and maintenance of body functions. Symptoms of deficiency include soreness in the mouth, nausea, dizziness, weight loss, sometimes a type of ANE-MIA, and neurological disorders. Vitamin B₆ is abundant in liver, whole-grain cereals, red meats, green vegetables, and yellow corn. (For help and further information, see RECOMMENDED DAILY ALLOWANCES; VITAMINS.)

vitamin B₁₂ A VITAMIN important to the normal development of red blood cells and to the functioning of all cells, especially in the BONE MARROW, NERVOUS SYSTEM, and intestines. Severe deficiency causes pernicious ANEMIA and neurological disorders, eventually including degeneration of the spinal cord (see SPINE AND SPINAL DISORDERS). Vitamin B₁₂ is abundant in lean meats, organ meats (liver, kidney, and heart), fish, shellfish, MILK, and eggs but is not present in any appreciable amounts in fruit and vegetables. As a result, the Food and Drug Administration recommends that people on a VEGETARIAN diet take vitamin B₁₂ supplements. (For help and further information, see RECOMMENDED DAILY ALLOWANCES; VITAMINS.)

vitamin C (ascorbic acid) A VITAMIN that is important in promoting growth, including formation of TEETH and bones, and repairing tissue, including healing of wounds. As a food additive, vitamin C also acts as a preservative. Lack of the vitamin causes the DEFICIENCY DISEASE called *scurvy*, which involves bleeding, especially noticeable in gums and bruises, weakness, loss of weight, lassitude, and irritability. Vitamin C is abundant in many fruits and vegetables, especially turnip greens, green peppers, kale, broccoli, mustard greens, citrus fruits, strawberries, currants, and tomatoes. The Food and Drug Administration notes: "You can get all the vitamin C your body needs by eating daily a three- to four-ounce serving of any of the foods named." Adults may experience deficiency symptoms briefly when MEGADOSES are discontinued, as may newborns if their mothers took too much vitamin C while pregnant. Though many people believe that large amounts of vitamin C can protect against the common cold, scientific research has so far failed to confirm that this is so. (For help and further information, see RECOMMENDED DAILY ALLOWANCES; VITAMINS.)

vitamin D (calciferol) A VITAMIN existing in several forms, some from plant sources, some from animals, all of which are vital to the absorption of CALCIUM and PHOSPHORUS for bone formation. In the body, vitamin D is converted to a substance that acts something like a HORMONE. Severe lack of the vitamin in children leads to the DEFICIENCY DISEASE called RICKETS, which results in skeletal deformities, including bowed legs, deformed spine, "pot-belly" appearance, and flat feet; in adults, vitamin D deficiency leads to OSTEOMALACIA. Excess vitamin D is stored in the body, and too much of it can cause nausea, weight loss, weakness, excessive urination, and, more seriously, hypertension (see high BLOOD PRESSURE), calcification (hardening) of soft tissues, including the blood vessels and kidneys, and often bone deformities and multiple FRACTURES. Vitamin D is abundant in canned and fresh fish (especially from salt water), egg yolk, and foods fortified with the vitamin, such as MILK and margarine. Such fortified foods are especially important to infants and children with chronic illnesses; others who have normal outside activities usually have enough vitamin D, since it is formed in the skin by ultraviolet rays. (For help and further information, see RECOMMENDED DAILY ALLOWANCES; VITAMINS.)

vitamin E A VITAMIN that acts as an *antioxidant*, to help prevent oxygen from destroying other substances in the body, including other vitamins, such as VITAMIN A. It has been used to treat a rare form of ANEMIA in infants. Research continues on the results of vitamin E deficiency, such as reduction in blood clotting. (See WHAT ABOUT VITAMIN E?, on page 475.) Abundant sources of vitamin E are vegetables oils, beans, eggs, whole grains, liver, fruits, and vegetables. (For help and further information, see RECOMMENDED DAILY ALLOWANCES; VITAMINS.)

vitamin H Outmoded name for BIOTIN.

vitamin K A VITAMIN that exists in several forms—one from plant sources, one from animals and birds, and one made by bacteria in the intestines—all essential to proper clotting of blood. Lack of vitamin K can cause HEMORRHAGE and LIVER PROB-LEMS. The vitamin is abundant in spinach, lettuce, kale, cabbage, cauliflower, liver, and egg yolk. Synthetic forms are also available. Human MILK is low in vitamin K, so the American Academy of Pediatrics Committee on Nutrition has recommended that vitamin K be routinely administered intravenously as part of PARENTERAL NUTRITION to all infants at birth to prevent

What About Vitamin E?

Vitamin E is one of the most talked-about vitamins, and to some extent the exaggerated and unsubstantiated claims made for vitamin E result from a combination of hope and misinterpretation.

The committee on Nutritional Misinformation of the National Academy of Sciences has issued a report on vitamin E. Three statements are quoted here:

Surveys of the U.S. population indicate that adequate amounts of vitamin E are supplied by the usual diet.

Careful studies over a period of years attempting to relate [test animal] symptoms to vitamin E deficiency in human beings have been unproductive.

Self-medication with vitamin E in hope that a more or less serious condition will be alleviated may indeed be hazardous, especially when appropriate diagnosis and treatment may thereby be delayed or avoided.

Source: *Some Facts and Myths of Vitamins* (1988). Prepared by the Food and Drug Administration for the Public Health Service.

bleeding disorders. (For help and further information, see RECOMMENDED DAILY ALLOWANCES; VITAMINS.)

vitamins A group of complex chemical compounds that are vital to the normal functioning of the body. They do not in themselves provide energy or build the body, but they are necessary for the transformation of food into energy to perform those functions. Inadequate amounts of vitamins in the body can have serious consequences, often leading to disorders called DEFICIENCY DISEASES. Vitamins are made up largely of the same elements—carbon, hydrogen, oxygen, and sometimes nitrogen—but they have different chemical arrangements and functions in the body. Before the chemical makeup of vitamins was known, they were called by letters; in some cases (such as vitamin B), it was later found that several different vitamins were involved, so numbers were added as well (as in vitamins B_{12} and B_6). On the other hand, some things originally thought to be vitamins turned out to be inessential and so were dropped from the list, and sometimes different letters were given to vitamins that were later found to be the same. The result is various gaps in lettering and numbering.

The Food and Drug Administration's RECOMMENDED DAILY ALLOWANCES (RDAs) suggest how much of each vitamin a person should have each day, during infancy, early childhood, childhood through adulthood, and PREGNANCY. (See tables under RECOMMENDED DAILY ALLOWANCES.) The amounts listed are those used on FOOD LABELS. (*Note:* The National Academy of Sciences recommends changes in the RDAs that will probably change the FDA's recommendations.) See also VITAMINS FOR PREGNANT AND NURSING WOMEN and VITAMINS FOR GROWING BODIES, on page 476.

Extremely small amounts of vitamins are necessary. Some vitamins are measured in IUs (international units), a scientific measure that indicates minute amounts of biological activity; others are expressed in milligrams (1/1000 of a gram) and micrograms (1/1000 of a milligram). The FDA notes that this means that just one ounce of vitamin B_{12} would supply the daily B_{12} needs of 4,724,921 people.

The FDA stresses the importance of diet, rather than vitamin supplements, to meet vitamin needs, commenting in *Some Facts and Myths of Vitamins:*

A well-balanced diet will usually meet all the body's vitamin needs. So-called average or normal eaters probably never need supplement vitamins, although many think they do. Vitamin deficiency diseases are rarely seen in the U.S. population. People known to have deficient diets require supplemental vitamins, as do those recovering from certain illnesses or vitamin deficiencies.

The FDA recognizes that "many people, nevertheless, believe in being on the 'safe side' and thus take extra vitamins." If you do take vitamin supplements, the FDA notes that no special mix and proportion of vitamins has been shown to have any superiority, nor does timing make any difference (except daily).

Caution: The rule that if a little is good, more is better does *not* apply here. *Megadoses*, or amounts greatly in excess of the RDA for some of these vitamins, can cause serious health problems, BIRTH DEFECTS during pregnancy, and in some cases even DEATH. The FDA puts it bluntly: "Taking excess vitamins is a complete waste, both in money and effect. In fact excess amounts of any of several different vitamins can be harmful." This is especially true of vitamins (notably A, D, E, and K) that are *fat-soluble* and can therefore build up in body fat.

Other vitamins, such as C and B vitamins, are *water-soluble*. In the body, these are used quickly or excreted in urine or perspiration and so must be taken every day. Water-soluble vitamins also break down quickly, and their value can sometime be lost through premature harvesting, poor storage, and overcooking, especially in water. For these kinds of vitamins, generally, the fresher and less-cooked the fruits and vegetables, the greater the amount of the vitamins they contain.

For help and further information

Food and Drug Administration (FDA), 301-443-3170. (For full group information, see NUTRITION; DRUG REACTIONS AND INTERACTIONS.)

Other reference sources

The Vitamin and Mineral Encyclopedia, by Sheldon Saul Hendler, M.D. New York: Simon & Schuster, 1990.

Good Health with Vitamins and Minerals: A Complete Guide to a Lifetime of Safe and Effective Use, by John Gallagher. New York: Summit, 1990.

Drugs, Vitamins, Minerals in Pregnancy, by Ann Karen Henry and Jill Feldhausen. Tucson, AZ: Fisher, 1990.

The People's Guide to Vitamins and Minerals from A to Zinc, revised edition, by Dominick Bosco. Chicago: Contemporary, 1989.

Vitamins for Pregnant and Nursing Women

The RDA for vitamins and minerals for pregnant or lactating women include increased levels above those for non-pregnant women. In healthy women with normal pregnancies, vitamin and mineral needs can usually be met by consuming an adequate diet. With the possible exceptions discussed below, supplements, although usually recommended, have not been associated with measurable health improvements in this population.

American women may have a low intake of dietary folate [VITAMIN B₁₂]. Some European studies have suggested an association of folate deficiency (along with deficiencies of other vitamins) with the development of neural tube defects. These observations stimulated clinical trials in which folate and multivitamin supplements appeared to reduce the risk of neural tube defects in subsequent children born to women who had previously given birth to infants with these defects. These studies, however, were poorly controlled and flawed methodologically. A recent report has found no difference in folate or vitamin B₁₂ concentrations in blood samples from early pregnancy taken from mothers of infants with or without neural tube defects.

Source: *The Surgeon General's Report on Nutrition and Health*. Rocklin, CA: Prima, 1988.

Vitamins for Growing Bodies

Vitamins and the Fetus

Vitamin requirements of the human fetus have not been established. Fat-soluble vitamins cross the placenta by simple diffusion, so maternal dietary intake would be expected to influence fetal levels. Most water-soluble vitamins are transported from the placenta to the fetus by active uptake processes, so fetal blood vitamin concentrations are higher than those in maternal blood. Although specific vitamin deficiencies have been shown to induce reproductive loss and developmental defects in experimental animals, similar data for human fetuses are not available.

Vitamins and Infants

Although infant requirements for micronutrients are not as well defined as those for energy and protein, RDAs have been established for many vitamins and minerals. Full-term infants who obtain breast milk from a well-nourished mother will receive most necessary vitamins, although, under some circumstances, vitamins D and K are exceptions. If breastfed infants have limited exposure to sunlight, vitamin D supplementation may be required to prevent rickets. Human milk is low in vitamin K, and this vitamin should be routinely administered parenterally to all infants at birth to prevent bleeding disorders. Infants fed a commercially available formula that is properly prepared should receive an adequate intake of vitamins.

Vitamins and Children

Inadequate intakes of vitamins and minerals will be reflected in slow growth rates, inadequate mineralization of bones, and very low body reserves of micronutrients. Clinical signs of vitamin deficiency in children are reported infrequently. With the relatively low prevalence of clinical signs of vitamin and mineral deficiency in the general population of children, there is no evidence that supplementation is necessary for this group. Although vitamin and mineral supplements increase the quantity of these nutrients in the diet, they have not been shown to improve biochemical indices of nutrient status in children who are already well nourished. For this reason, recommendations on vitamin and mineral supplementation for children target those at high risk, those from socioeconomically deprived families, and those who have poor appetites or eating habits.

Source: *The Surgeon General's Report on Nutrition and Health*. Rocklin, CA: Prima, 1988.

The Complete Book of Vitamins and Minerals for Health. Emmaus, PA: Rodale, 1988.

(See also NUTRITION; RECOMMENDED DAILY ALLOWANCES; THIAMIN; NIACIN; FOLIC ACID; BIOTIN; PANTOTHENIC ACID; and other specific vitamins.)

vitiligo A SKIN DISORDER in which patches of skin are white and colorless because of lack of skin cells called *melanocytes*, which produce the dark pigment *melanin*. (Another disorder, ALBINISM, results from melanocytes that are present but not functioning properly.) Of unknown origin, vitiligo may appear at any age, though usually in early adulthood. Some suggest that it is an AUTO-IMMUNE DISORDER, while others think that at least some forms are GENETIC DISORDERS. It is sometimes associated with ADDISON'S DISEASE, DIABETES MELLITUS, pernicious ANEMIA, and THYROID GLAND disorders. People with vitiligo are especially susceptible to sunburn. Sometimes pigment reappears in at least some portions of the affected skin. Among the treatments used for vitiligo is *PUVA*, a form of PHOTOTHERAPY combined with medications.

For help and further information

National Institute of Arthritis and Musculoskeletal and Skin Diseases (NIAMS), 301-496-8188. (For full group information, see ARTHRITIS.)

(See also SKIN DISORDERS.)

VLBW Abbreviation for VERY LOW BIRTH WEIGHT, meaning under 3.3 pounds (1,500 grams).

VLDLs Abbreviation for very-low-density lipoproteins, a so-called bad form of CHOLESTEROL.

VMI Abbreviation for DEVELOPMENTAL TEST OF VISUAL-MOTOR INTEGRATION.

vocational curriculum A type of CURRICULUM that focuses on teaching students skills to be used on jobs after graduation.

vocational schools Schools that provide a special CURRICULUM oriented to preparing students for employment after gradua-tion; often a type of MAGNET SCHOOL or SCHOOL OF CHOICE. Though the term has traditionally been used to refer to schools that focused on instruction for non-college-bound students, such as those offering automobile mechanics or printing, schools also may be termed vocational if they give intensive preparation in a subject area that will likely be pursued in college, such as per-forming arts or science. The Department of Education recom-mends that parents exercise choice in finding the right school for their children. Their booklet, *Choosing a School for Your Child*, excerpted on page 514, offers a checklist for evaluating schools. (For help and further information, see EDUCATION.)

Vomiting and Your Baby

Your baby may vomit during a cold or fever or have an ill-ness that may have vomiting, or vomiting and diarrhea, as its only signs.

When your baby vomits, don't give anything to eat or drink for at least *one hour*. Then give ½ ounce of water, sweet juice, or a commercially prepared clear liquid for rehydration. Repeat this half-ounce feeding every 10 to 15 minutes for an hour. Give 1-ounce feedings every 10 to 15 minutes for the next hour, and 2-ounce feedings as often as your baby wants them for the following hour.

If there is no more vomiting, it is OK to give small amounts of breastmilk, formula, cereal, crackers, or toast if your baby is eating solid foods, and then return to regular feeding. If vomiting happens more than two or three times, or your baby seems very sick and weak, you should call your doctor or clinic.

Source: *Infant Care* (1989). Prepared by the Bureau of Maternal and Child Health and Resources Development for the Public Health Service.

---

volvulus The twisting of an organ in the body, such as the intestines or stomach, often causing pain and obstruction and frequently requiring surgical correction. (For help and further information, see DIGESTIVE DISORDERS.)

vomiting Expulsion of the stomach's contents—partially digested food and digestive juices—through the esophagus and the mouth, by contractions of the diaphragm. Vomiting is often involuntary, occurring as a result of irritants in the stomach (as from too much food or alcohol), pressure in the brain (as from HYDROCEPHALUS or a BRAIN TUMOR; see BRAIN AND BRAIN DISORDERS), disturbance of the body's sense of balance (as in some EAR AND HEARING PROBLEMS), or other disorders or imbalances in the body, including APPENDICITIS and various DIGESTIVE and METABOLIC DISORDERS. Vomiting can also be triggered voluntarily, as in

---

Vomiting in Pregnancy

Nausea and vomiting are common complaints during the first month of pregnancy and are usually due to hormonal changes occurring in your body. About half of all pregnant women experience this problem. Nausea may start about the sixth or seventh week but seldom continues beyond the end of the third month. Although often called morning sick-ess, nausea and vomiting may occur at any time of the day. If vomiting is severe and you cannot keep fluids down, report it to your doctor. Never take prescription drugs, over-the-counter medicines, or a home remedy unless rec-ommended by your doctor.

You may find some relief by eating dry cereal, a piece of toast, or a cracker about a half-hour before getting out of bed in the morning. Move slowly when you get up. Let plenty of fresh air into the house to get rid of cooking and other household odors.

Divide your food into five small meals a day rather than three large ones, since keeping food in your stomach seems to control nausea. Avoid greasy and highly spiced foods or any food that disagrees with you. Drinking liquids between meals instead of with your food may help.

The same suggestions may also help with symptoms of heartburn. Heartburn has nothing to do with your heart. It is a burning sensation caused by hormonal changes that slow down your digestive system and by the pressure of the growing uterus against your stomach. Food mixed with stomach acid is pushed up from your stomach and causes the burning, especially after meals. In addition, changing your sleeping position may also help relieve heartburn. Try sleeping with several pillows to raise your head or elevate the head of the bed a few inches. **Note**: Do *not* take baking soda (sodium bicarbonate) to relieve your heartburn. Remember, you should not take medicines unless your doctor recommends them.

Source: *Prenatal Care* (1989). Prepared by the Bureau of Health Care Delivery and Assistance, Division of Maternal and Child Health, for the Public Health Service.

BULIMIA, where it is the "purge" part of the binge–purge syndrome. It is also frequently associated with PREGNANCY, as *morning sickness* (see VOMITING IN PREGNANCY on page 477).

If it persists, vomiting can cause damage and perhaps rupture of the esophagus and, more important, can leave the body short of vital nutrients. For how to handle vomiting in infants, see VOMITING AND YOUR BABY, below. It is important to have the underlying causes discovered and treated, if possible, especially if blood (*hematemesis*) is being vomited as well.

Von Recklinghausen's disease   Alternate name for NEUROFIBROMATOSIS.

voucher system   A program under which school taxes go into a special fund, from which parents are given redeemable coupons called *vouchers* that enable them to "purchase" education (up to specified amount of money) for their children in the school of their choice, whether public or private. Under the present system, many parents whose children attend PRIVATE SCHOOL (approximately one in eight, as of 1985) pay tuition out of their own pockets while also paying school taxes to support the PUBLIC SCHOOLS, a situation proponents of the voucher system think unfair. Critics of the plan believe that parents should instead work to make the public schools responsive to the needs of all students and that the voucher system violates the constitutionally protected separation of church and state, since many of the private schools are religiously oriented or affiliated. The voucher plan has been tried only in limited areas, and often religious-affiliated private schools are not included.

For help and further information

Education Voucher Institute (EVI)
93 Kercheval, Suite 3
Grosse Pointe Farms, MI 48236
313-881-2337
William Coats, Director

Organization of parents and others interested in funding education by giving parents vouchers and letting them choose schools for their children. Serves as information clearinghouse on educational vouchers and tax credits; publishes various materials, including bimonthly newsletter.

(See also EDUCATION.)

VSD   Abbreviation for ventricular septal defect, a type of CONGENITAL heart defect. (See HEART AND HEART PROBLEMS.)

vulnerable child syndrome   The pattern of behavior in which parents of a child who has recovered from a life-threatening illness continue to treat the child as if he or she were still at death's door. In some cases, the parents can create a SELF-FULFILLING PROPHECY; while in others, the child must consciously break out of the "gentle cage" to live a normal life.

vulva (pudendum)   A female's external GENITALS, including the *mons veneris*, the mound of fatty tissue covering the pubic bone; the *clitoris*, the small organ of sexual stimulation (removed in rare female CIRCUMCISION) between the pubic bone and the URETHRA; two sets of folded skin, the outer "lips" (*labia major*) and the inner (*labia minora*); and the opening to the VAGINA, between the urethra and the anus. During CHILDBIRTH, the *perineal tissue* toward the back of the vulva is sometimes surgically cut in an EPISIOTOMY, and the region as a whole may sometimes be anesthetized, using a *pudendal block* (see ANESTHESIA).

A newborn girl's labia and clitoris are rather large at birth due to the effect of the mother's HORMONES but get slightly smaller over the next few weeks. The labia may sometimes be joined at birth but generally separate naturally afterward. A female baby may also have a slight white or pinkish creamy discharge from the vagina in the first few weeks; this is normal and should gradually decline without irritating the skin. But if it becomes worse, if she develops a discharge a week or two after birth, or if there is any bulge or lump in her genitals, she should be examined promptly by a doctor or clinic staff. (See also GENITALS.)

wage attachment   Withholding of money from a person's paycheck to pay off debts, such as to pay CHILD SUPPORT or alimony. In some states, the wage attachment law applies automatically to everyone who has been ordered to pay child support. Sometimes an OBLIGATED PARENT may have wages voluntarily withheld to pay for child support.

WAIS-R   Abbreviation for Wechsler Adult Intelligence Scale–Revised, the adolescent-to-adult version of the WECHSLER INTELLIGENCE SCALE FOR CHILDREN, Revised (WISC-R).

walker   A common type of ORTHOPEDIC DEVICE.

walking   Movement of the body by lifting the feet alternately in a chosen direction, with one foot returning to the ground before the next leaves it, a complicated set of movements controlled by the brain in response to the body's signals about changes in position and balance (as monitored by the inner ear). Newborn infants exhibit a WALKING REFLEX—moving legs when held upright—and walking is one of the main early MOTOR SKILLS learned by a child in the first year or so of life (see CHART OF NORMAL DEVELOPMENT on page 507).

Most babies' legs and feet seem somewhat abnormal to adult eyes (see THOSE FUNNY-LOOKING LEGS, at right), but they generally right themselves during early childhood. Some slight abnormalities remain, but only severe cases will call for correction, by relatively minor surgery. Among the most common leg and foot abnormalities are:

- *metatarsus varus* (*pigeon toes* or *toeing in*), in which the foot and toes point somewhat inward because of rotation of the leg or foot.
- *metatarsus valgus* (*duck walk* or *toeing out*), in which the foot and toes point somewhat outward because of rotation of the leg or foot.
- *genu valgum* (*knock-knees*), in which the legs bend inward, with the knees close together.
- *genu varum* (*bowlegs*), in which the legs bend outward at the knees.

Many other conditions can affect walking, including CLUBFOOT (*talipes*) and PARALYSIS, infections that affect the balancing mechanism in the inner ear, and disorders that affect the muscles or the nerves communicating with the muscles, including MUSCULAR DYSTROPHY, POLIOMYELITIS, MULTIPLE SCLEROSIS, ATAXIA, and CHOREA, some of which are diagnosed partly by a characteristic walk. CONGENITAL DISLOCATION OF THE HIP is sometimes diagnosed first when a child begins to walk, though WELL-BABY EXAMINATIONS include checking the hip. Children with various kinds of ORTHOPEDIC HANDICAPS may need ORTHOPEDIC DEVICES such as crutches or braces to provide some of the support and balance needed for walking.

walking reflex (stepping reflex)   The automatic response of a baby, when held upright with feet touching the ground, to making stepping movements with alternate feet; a type of "primitive" REFLEX found only in babies and disappearing in about two months but reappearing at about six months.

ward   A MINOR child (or sometimes a HANDICAPPED or INCOMPETENT adult) whose CUSTODY and care are legally in the hands of a GUARDIAN rather than a parent. A JUVENILE found to have committed DELINQUENT acts is generally called a ward of the court.

water-breaking   In PREGNANCY, the breaking of the sac holding the AMNIOTIC FLUID that protects the baby, generally just before the onset of LABOR.

Those Funny-Looking Legs

Most babies' legs and feet don't look "normal" until the child has been walking for several years! Their feet seem to turn in or out in the first years of life. By the time they are 12 or 18 months old, their legs look bowed.

Almost all of these funny-looking feet and legs are perfectly normal and will gradually straighten out as babies run, play, and climb. If you can move your baby's foot easily into a "normal"-looking position, and if the foot moves freely when the baby kicks and struggles, it is almost certainly a normal foot that developed a bend or twist while the baby was folded up inside during pregnancy.

You won't cause bowed legs by pulling your baby into a standing position or letting your baby walk or stand "too early." But remember, babies will show you when they are ready to stand or walk—you can't make them do it.

Source: *Infant Care* (1989). Prepared by the Bureau of Maternal and Child Health and Resources Development for the Public Health Service.

---

water loss   Alternate term for DEHYDRATION, in infants a possible medical emergency.

water on the brain   Popular phrase for HYDROCEPHALUS.

weaning   The process of gradually substituting SOLID FOODS for BREASTFEEDING or BOTTLEFEEDING with FORMULA.

Weber's test   One kind of tuning-fork test; a HEARING TEST for assessing the type of hearing loss.

Wechsler Adult Intelligence Scale-Revised (WAIS-R)
The adolescent-to-adult version of the WECHSLER INTELLIGENCE SCALE FOR CHILDREN, REVISED (WISC-R).

Wechsler Intelligence Scale for Children, Revised (WISC-R)
A widely used INTELLIGENCE TEST, administered individually to children ages five to 15, similar in makeup to the WECHSLER PRESCHOOL AND PRIMARY SCALE OF INTELLIGENCE (WPPSI). Among the exceptions are that instead of geometric designs, children are asked to assemble three-dimensional objects (testing SYNTHETIC LEARNING); they are asked to arrange groups of pictures so that they tell simple stories; they must remember and repeat lists of digits; the animal house is replaced by a coding exercise; and mazes is a subtest. Adolescents may also be given the adult version of these tests, *Wechsler Adult Intelligence Scale–Revised (WAIS-R)*. (For help and further information, see WECHSLER PRESCHOOL AND PRIMARY SCALE OF INTELLIGENCE; TESTS.)

Wechsler Preschool and Primary Scale of Intelligence (WPPSI)
A widely used INTELLIGENCE TEST, administered individually to children ages four-and-a-half to six. The WPPSI is divided into verbal and performance tests, each with subtests. In the verbal subtests, the specially trained examiner asks the child about the following subjects:

- *general information*, about the body, money, and food, for example;

- *vocabulary*, definitions of words, starting with simple ones and getting more abstract;
- *arithmetic*, counting, adding, and doing "takeaways";
- *similarities*, such as what you can roll besides a ball or how a pen and pencil are alike;
- *comprehension*, calling for responses to social questions and relation to appropriate behavior;
- *sentences*, having the child repeat progressively longer and more complex sentences.

On the performance side, the child is asked to complete pictures with a missing element, copy geometric designs, use blocks to reproduce designs on a picture card, work through a maze, and make an "animal house" following a model (a timed test). The "animal house" task may be done a second time during the test if the child encountered problems the first time around.

After the test, the examiner totals the SCORES for the various subtests to give separate verbal and performance scores and a total score; all three of these scores are then converted to scaled scores, using special tables. On the basis of the tables, the examiner then assigns a verbal designation to the category in which a child's score falls, such as *average, bright average, superior,* or *very superior* (often considered GIFTED CHILDREN). Examiners do not usually report either numerical INTELLIGENCE QUOTIENTS (IQs) or PERCENTILES. For older children, ages six to 16, the WECHSLER INTELLIGENCE SCALE FOR CHILDREN, REVISED (WISC-R) may be used, while adolescents may be given the *Wechsler Adult Intelligence Scale-Revised (WAIS-R)*.

For help and further information

Is Your Child Ready for School?: A Parent's Guide to Preschool and Primary School Entrance Tests, by Jacqueline Robinson. New York: Arco, 1990. (Originally published as *The Baby Boards*, 1988.) Gives a full description of the Wechsler tests and advice on how to prepare a child for one.

(See also TESTS; INTELLIGENCE TESTS.)

well-baby examination Any of a series of periodic medical examinations of a baby, not because of illness but to try to ensure continuing good health. In well-baby examinations, medical professionals, often physicians but sometimes specially trained nurses, generally:

- check the child's growth and development;
- provide routine IMMUNIZATION;
- perform SCREENING TESTS to try to detect quickly any signs of diseases, especially GENETIC DISORDERS, and begin immediate treatment as appropriate;
- provide guidance to parents in areas such as NUTRITION, SAFETY and accident prevention; and
- prepare parents for what to do for and expect from the child at various stages of growth and development.

The Public Health Service's recommendations for well-baby examinations are given in YOUR BABY'S HEALTH, on page 481.

Wepman Auditory Discrimination Test Alternative name for AUDITORY DISCRIMINATION TEST.

Werdnig-Hoffmann disease Alternate name for infantile (Type 1) spinal muscular atrophy, a type of MOTOR NEURON DISEASE.

wet dream An EJACULATION that occurs during sleep, often among adolescent males; also called a *nocturnal emission*.

wheelchair A common type of ORTHOPEDIC DEVICE. (See ORTHOPEDIC DEVICES for HELPING CHILDREN IN WHEELCHAIRS.)

whiplash-shaken infant syndrome The pattern of injuries, often involving hemorrhaging and swelling of the brain, resulting from the violent shaking of a child, often seen in cases of CHILD ABUSE AND NEGLECT.

whole-language approach A group of methods for teaching READING that stress learning words as complete units, as opposed to the PHONICS METHOD, in which words are broken down into letters associated with sounds. (See WHOLE-WORD METHOD.)

whole-word method An approach to teaching READING that focuses on teaching words as wholes and only later breaking them down into parts; also called the *word-recognition* method or the *sight method*. For many students this works well, especially because the focus is strongly on the meaning and context of the words; but for children who have trouble learning to read, especially those with LEARNING DISABILITIES, some version of the more traditional PHONICS METHOD seems needed, at least as a supplement. Within the English-language community there are several approaches that focus on teaching reading and writing by using the whole words in practical situations; collectively, these are called the *whole-language approach*.

For help and further information

What's Whole in Whole Language, by Ken Goodman. Portsmouth, NH: Heinemann, 1986.
Whole Language: Theory in Use, Judith M. Newman, ed. Portsmouth, NH: Heinemann, 1986.

(See also READING.)

whooping cough Alternate name for PERTUSSIS.

WIC Abbreviation for the SPECIAL SUPPLEMENTAL FOOD PROGRAM FOR WOMEN, INFANTS, AND CHILDREN.

Wide Range Achievement Test-Revised (WRAT-R) A widely used type of ACHIEVEMENT TEST used for ages five to adult, focusing on the basic skills of word recognition (recognizing and naming letters and pronouncing printed words), spelling, and arithmetic, used for educational placement and also for identifying people with possible learning problems. While the READING part must be administered individually, the other parts may be given to groups; large-print editions are available for

Your Baby's Health

You may have chosen a doctor, nurse practitioner or clinic for your baby before he or she was born. [If not, see PEDIATRICIAN.] You will have many questions about your baby that can best be discussed with a person who is a health professional. The doctor or nurse will work with you and explain how you can help your baby grow and develop safely and healthily. Also, your baby should be checked from time to time for normal growth, development, and problems you may not notice. Every child needs certain shots (or "immunizations") and tests to avoid or detect and treat some illnesses. For all of these reasons, you should take your baby to the doctor or clinic several times during the first year.

Going to the doctor or clinic

First, be sure to talk with the doctor who examines your baby in the hospital to find out if all is well. Ask questions and get answers!

Especially with a first baby, you will have more questions in the first days that you and your baby share than at any other time. Books and experienced and trusted friends or family members may be able to answer many of your questions, but don't hesitate to call the doctor, clinic, or hospital staff.

Most doctors and clinics will schedule the first checkup when your baby is between two weeks and one month old and then plan further visits every four to eight weeks for three or four visits and less frequently after that. Your doctor will discuss the schedule with you.

Your conversation with the baby's doctor is the most important part of each visit. The doctor may actually examine your child only three or four times during the first year, but he or she will always want to know how your baby is growing, learning, and developing and whether you have noticed any problems. Between visits to the doctor or clinic, write down your questions and observations so you can be sure to remember them. But if something is pressing, don't wait until the next scheduled visit—call the office. A typical schedule of visits to the doctor or clinic is shown on the following chart:

| | | | | | Age at Visit | | | | |
Procedures During Visit	in Hosp.	1 Mo.	2 Mos.	4 Mos.	6 Mos.	9 Mos.	12 Mos.	15 Mos.	18 Mos.
Discussion & questions	●	●	●	●	●	●	●	●	●
Examination	●	●	●	●	●	●	●	●	●
Measurements of length, weight, head size	●	●	●	●	●	●	●	●	●
DTP shot (diptheria-tetanus-pertussis)			●	●	○			○	○
Oral polio vaccine			●	●	○			○	○
MMR shot (measles, mumps and rubella)								●	
Blood test for anemia						●			
Test for lead exposure						○			
Tuberculin skin test							●		
H. Influenza B. Vaccine									●*

● usually done at this age
○ may be done at this age

(**Note**: Each doctor may have his or her own schedule, but you should expect it to include most of the items listed above. This schedule is only a guide, current as of July 1989, which your doctor or clinic may change to fit your child's needs.)

* Now more commonly done at 15 months.

Keeping records

You should keep a record of your baby's visits to the doctor or clinic. It is important to keep the record up to date in case you change doctors or see someone else when your doctor is not available. You should take your record with you whenever you visit a doctor or clinic so that you can refer to it if you have any questions and update it before you leave the office.

Because a baby's first year is full of change, you might also want to keep a record of significant events in your baby's first year, such as when he or she first said a "word" or first crawled. Saving mementos, photos, and notes in a box or notebook will give you reminders to share with your child later on.

Continued on page 482

When doctors disagree

Sometimes one doctor will give you different advice from that of another, or doctors may actually disagree with each other or with a book.

    For many problems there are many good solutions; a particular book may mention only one. For some other problems, such as an ear infection, each doctor may choose a different medicine—and each may provide relief equally well. In other cases (for example, whether boys should be circumcised), there are real differences of opinion. When two doctors give you conflicting advice—or one doctor gives you advice you do not understand—you should ask for an explanation. Ask questions until you get the information that satisfies you. And if the best step to take is still unclear to you, you may need to ask another doctor for an opinion.

Source: *Infant Care* (1989). Prepared by the Bureau of Maternal and Child Health and Resources Development, Public Health Service.

---

children with EYE AND VISION PROBLEMS. Tests are scored by comparison to NORMS established by AGE. (For help and further information, see TESTS.)

Wilm's tumor (nephroblastoma) A childhood CANCER of the kidney. (See CANCER; KIDNEY AND UROLOGICAL DISORDERS.)

Wilson's disease A rare GENETIC DISORDER in which COPPER accumulates to toxic levels—first in the liver, causing HEPATITIS and then CIRRHOSIS OF THE LIVER, and then in other parts of the body: in the blood, causing hemolytic ANEMIA, and in the brain, causing destruction of tissue and gradually intellectual impairment, tremors, muscle rigidity, DYSARTHRIA, and DEMENTIA. Symptoms of Wilson's disease usually appear in ADOLESCENCE, sometimes earlier; serious damage can be avoided if the disease is recognized quickly and the patient started on a lifelong course of penicillamine. In a related CONGENITAL disorder, *Menkes' syndrome*, the intestines are unable to absorb copper from the digestive system; unusually kinky hair is the main early symptom. Brain degeneration, retarded growth, and early DEATH can result unless the disorder is diagnosed early and copper administered intravenously.

For help and further information

Wilson's Disease Association
P.O. Box 75324
Washington, DC 20013
703-636-3014 or -3003
Carol A. Terry, President

Organization of and for people with Wilson's disease or Menkes' syndrome, and their families. Encourages family-to-family contact for mutual support; provides information to public and professionals; makes referrals; provides some financial aid; publishes quarterly newsletter and brochures *Wilson's Disease: Questions and Answers*.

Foundation for the Study of Wilson's Disease
5447 Palisade Avenue
Bronx, NY 10471

212-430-2091
I. Herbert Scheinberg, M.D., Contact
Organization supporting clinical and laboratory facilities or diagnosing and managing Wilson's disease and related copper and metal metabolic disorders. Seeks to educate public and health professionals as to early diagnosis and appropriate therapy; produces audiovisual and book *Wilson's Disease*.

National Institute of Diabetes and Digestive and Kidney Diseases (NIDDK), 301-496-3583; **National Digestive Disease Information Clearinghouse**, 301-468-6344. (For full group information, see DIGESTIVE DISORDERS.)

National Institute of Child Health and Human Development (NICHD), 301-496-5133. (For full group information, see PREGNANCY.)

National Institute of Neurological Disorders and Stroke (NINDS), 301-496-5751. (For full group information, see BRAIN AND BRAIN DISORDERS.)

(See also LIVER PROBLEMS; METABOLIC DISORDERS.)

WISC-R Abbreviation for WECHSLER INTELLIGENCE SCALE FOR CHILDREN, REVISED.

wisdom teeth The four large third molars, the last of the adult set of permanent TEETH to appear, generally around ages 17 to 21. Sometimes these teeth never erupt at all or become blocked from erupting because the jaw is too small and overcrowded; such teeth are said to be IMPACTED. (See TEETH.)

witch's milk Popular name for the milk sometimes produced by a newborn's enlarged BREASTS in response to the mother's HORMONES.

WJPEB Abbreviation for WOODCOCK-JOHNSON PSYCHOEDUCATIONAL BATTERY.

Wohlfart-Kugelberg-Welander disease Alternate name for juvenile (Type 3) spinal muscular atrophy, a type of MOTOR NEURON DISEASE.

Wolman's disease (acid cholesteryl ester hydrolase deficiency) A type of LIPID STORAGE DISEASE.

womb Alternate name for a woman's UTERUS.

Women, Infants, and Children (WIC) program Short form for SPECIAL SUPPLEMENTAL FOOD PROGRAM FOR WOMEN, INFANTS, AND CHILDREN.

Woodcock-Johnson Psychoeducational Battery (WJPEB) An individually administered test attempting to measure cognitive ability, academic achievement, and interest level in children in grades K to 12. It may be used as a DIAGNOSTIC ASSESSMENT TEST to help diagnose LEARNING DISABILITIES, to help in CURRICULUM planning and class placement, and sometimes for occupational counseling and research. (For help and further information, see TESTS.)

word-attack skills A set of PREREQUISITE skills that are vital to a child's ability to DECODE and understand new or unfamiliar words and therefore to effective, independent READING. Among these word-attack skills are phonics (see PHONICS METHODS), in which the child associates letters with sounds and "sounds out" the word; *structural analysis*, in which the child breaks the word down into meaningful parts, such as "read" and "-ing"; and *content analysis*, in which the child looks at the meaning of the word parts and the context in which they appear.

word blindness Alternate term for ALEXIA, an extreme form of DYSLEXIA, or difficulty in READING.

word-recognition method Alternate name for the WHOLE-WORD METHOD.

work-experience program A type of WORK-STUDY PROGRAM.

work-study program A type of FINANCIAL AID in which students get help in meeting the costs of attending COLLEGE by working part-time, often in programs partly funded by federal money. The main federally funded program in this area is COLLEGE WORK-STUDY. Some colleges have *work-experience* or *cooperative work-study programs*, which are aimed less at providing aid than at giving students additional experience through off-campus work. (For help and further information, see FINANCIAL AID.)

WPPSI Abbreviation for WECHSLER PRESCHOOL AND PRIMARY SCALE OF INTELLIGENCE.

WRAT Abbreviation for WIDE RANGE ACHIEVEMENT TEST.

writing The formation of letters, first taught to children in ELEMENTARY SCHOOL as PRINTING (*manuscript writing*), with each letter formed separately, and later as CURSIVE WRITING, in which letters are joined. The *Palmer method* is the traditional approach to teaching children how to write legibly. Students with problems ENCODING, such as those with LEARNING DISABILITIES, need extra help in learning to write clearly. (For help and further information, see EDUCATION.)

wrongful death A DEATH caused by the wrongful action of someone else. If a person dies wrongfully, usually only a member of the immediate family—such as a parent, child, or spouse—has the right to bring a wrongful-death lawsuit against the party responsible. Others, such as UNWED FATHERS and CO-PARENTS, often have no such right.

xerophthalmia Abnormal dryness of the eyes, a result of severe VITAMIN A deficiency, which can cause serious EYE AND VISION PROBLEMS.

xerostomia A condition called *dry mouth*, resulting from temporary lack of saliva. Often associated with DIABETES MELLITUS, xerostomia may result from infection, some medicines, and RADIATION therapy in the mouth area. Although helped by use of artificial saliva, dry mouth can cause trouble speaking and swallowing and can lead to ulcers in the gums and other dental problems. (For help and further information, see TEETH.)

X-linked (sex-linked or **sex-limited)** Term describing a gene that is located on the X chromosome, one of the two SEX CHROMOSOMES; also a trait or GENETIC DISORDER associated with such a gene. Such traits are RECESSIVE, meaning that the trait will be masked in the presence of a DOMINANT gene. That means that X-linked traits rarely affect women, because both of their X chromosomes must carry the defect; women who have just one abnormal gene are unaffected but are called CARRIERS, because they can pass the trait on to their children. However, men have only one X chromosome (paired with a Y), so any X-linked defect will show itself. Among the most common X-linked genetic disorders are HEMOPHILIA, *agammaglobulinemia* (see IMMUNE SYSTEM), COLOR BLINDNESS, FRAGILE X SYNDROME, MUSCULAR DYSTROPHY (Duchenne type), and spinal ATAXIA. During GENETIC COUNSELING, counselors will gather information from prospective parents or parents-to-be about their medical and genetic history and put that information into the form of a PEDIGREE.

X-Linked Recessive Disorders

Definitions: These recessive genes are on the X chromosomes. For females to be affected, both genes of a given pair must be abnormal. Since males have only one X chromosome, a single abnormal gene will cause the disease to be present.

Characteristics:

- A sex-linked condition does not necessarily appear in every generation.
- On the average, one-half of the male children of carrier females are affected.
- On the average, one-half of the female children of carrier females are carriers.
- Females are only rarely affected.
- There is no male-to-male transmission; affected males are related through unaffected females.

Pedigree Sample

[For information on the symbols, see PEDIGREE.]

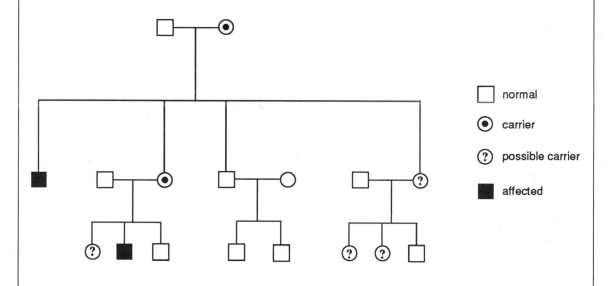

□	normal
◉	carrier
?	possible carrier
■	affected

Source: *Genetic Family History: An Aid to Better Health in Adoptive Children* (1984). Published by the National Center for Education in Maternal and Child Health (NCEMCH), for the Public Health Service's Genetic Diseases Service Branch, Division of Maternal and Child Health, from materials by Catherine A. Reiser from a conference sponsored by Wisconsin Clinical Genetics Center and Waisman Center on Mental Retardation and Human Development, University of Wisconsin–Madison.

(For more information, see X-LINKED RECESSIVE DISORDERS, above; see also GENETIC COUNSELING.)

X-rays In medicine and dentistry, pictures of the body taken by use of RADIATION, in some cases used for treatment. X-rays show what exists beneath the surface of the body and help health professionals identify problems, from IMPACTED TEETH or tooth decay to fractures to TUMORS. Though X-rays should not be over- used, their use in medicine and dentistry generally outweighs their associated risks if they are used appropriately, with lead coverings protecting the vulnerable parts of the body not being photographed. However, X-rays should be used only when vital on a woman during PREGNANCY because of possible danger to the FETUS and only sparingly with children because of possible long- term increase in risk of CANCER, especially of the BREAST.

XX The genetic designation of a female child, referring to the possession of two X SEX CHROMOSOMES, one from the SPERM and one from the egg (OVUM).

XY The genetic designation of a male child, referring to the possession of one X and one Y SEX CHROMOSOME, the X from the egg (OVUM) and the Y from the SPERM.

year-round education An instructional plan in which a school operates through the whole 12 months of the year. Though students attend the same number of days per year, these are arranged differently; for example, a student might be in school for nine weeks and on vacation for three. The three-week blocks of time are staggered so that only three-fourths of the total population is attending school at any one time; that way the school can, in effect, accommodate one-third more students than under the traditional SEMESTER, TRIMESTER, or QUARTER systems. One advantage of year-round education is economic, in that the facilities are used more efficiently and a school district can meet rising student population without building new schools. Also, year-round schooling is thought to have distinct advantages for learning: with only a short period off at the end of each segment, instead of a whole summer at year's end, students forget less and classes need not waste time in review at the beginning of the school year. In families where the parent or parents work, year-round education also has advantages, in that it eliminates the need for CHILD CARE for significant periods and older students do not spend long, fruitless, unsupervised summers. Partly for these reasons, the visionary 21ST CENTURY SCHOOL incorporates year-round education. On the other hand, many people sharply criticize the move away from the traditional school schedule, with its predictable summer vacation; those parents who normally have extensive summer vacation plans are particularly unhappy. So are some families with several children, in cases where the school system has not attempted to coordinate the schedules so that the children in a family are on vacation at the same time. Year-round schooling is relatively new in practice, and its success is yet to be determined.

For help and further information

National Association for Year-Round Education (NAYRE)
c/o Charles Ballinger, Executive Secretary
6401 Linda Vista Road
San Diego, CA 92111
619-292-3679
Organization of schools, parents, and other individuals and groups interested in having year-round education, to improve educational quality, better fit modern living schedules, and use school facilities more efficiently. Maintains library and acts as information clearinghouse; publishes various materials, including annual directory.

A Legislator's Guide to the Year Round School, by Doris M. Ross. Boulder, CO: Education Commission of the States, 1975.

(See also EDUCATION.)

yeshiva An ELEMENTARY SCHOOL for children of the Orthodox Jewish faith; also, an advanced school where Jewish students study the Talmud and rabbinic law in preparation for becoming rabbis.

Z

zinc   A MINERAL needed in the body, though only in trace amounts, in a wide variety of functions, including normal growth and development, especially of the reproductive system, the manufacture of PROTEINS, and the healing of wounds. Zinc is abundant in high-protein foods, such as meat (especially liver), seafood, MILK and other dairy products, nuts, dried beans and peas, and whole-grain or enriched breads and cereals. Deficiency is rare, except in cases of MALNUTRITION; disorders that hinder the body's ability to use zinc (such as MALABSORPTION, CYSTIC FIBROSIS, or CIRRHOSIS OF THE LIVER); or situations involving sharply increased need for zinc, as in cases of BURNS or sickle-cell ANEMIA. Symptoms of zinc deficiency include loss of taste and appetite, slowed growth and sexual maturation in children, slow healing of wounds, and susceptibility to infection and injury. On the other hand, too much zinc, as from taking excessive amounts in mineral supplements, can cause gastrointestinal problems, including nausea, VOMITING, and DIARRHEA, which can also lead to loss of IRON and COPPER. Excess zinc among pregnant women can lead to PREMATURE delivery and STILLBIRTH. (For help and further information, see MINERALS; NUTRITION.)

zygote   The medical name for the fertilized egg (OVUM) up to the time it is implanted in the UTERUS. In relation to MULTIPLE BIRTHS, twins who grew from a single fertilized egg are termed *monozygotic* or *identical*, while those who grew from two separate fertilized eggs are termed *dizygotic*, *nonidentical*, or *fraternal*.

Do Pregnant Women Need Extra Zinc?

The RDA for zinc includes a 5-milligrams-per-day increment during pregnancy over the 15 milligrams per day recommended for nonpregnant women. Zinc deficiency is teratogenic [causes birth defects], and abnormal brain development and behavior have been described in the offspring of zinc-deficient monkeys. Evidence from human populations suggests that the fate of fetal malformations and other poor outcomes of pregnancy may be higher in populations where zinc deficiency has been recognized. However, conflicting reports have also been published, and questions remain about satisfactory measures of zinc status. The role of zinc deficiency in the adverse outcome of human pregnancy remains uncertain at present, and supplements [beyond the 5 milligrams per day over normal] are not recommended.

Source: *The Surgeon General's Report on Nutrition and Health.* Rocklin, CA: Prima, 1988.

Special Help Section

Basic Exercises for During and After Pregnancy

Exercise is very important to you and your baby. If you stay active you will feel better. Outdoor exercise and recreation give you a chance to get sunshine and fresh air. Walking is particularly good, because it strengthens some of the muscles you will use in labor.

If you normally are active in sports, continue to enjoy them. However, it's wise to stop when you get tired. Also, try team activities instead of individual games, and avoid strenuous workouts. Do things with your friends and family—swim in a pool, dance, go on a picnic, and participate in light sports that pose no danger of falling or being bumped. If you are thinking of trying a new sport or exercise, or have been using a specific exercise routine, talk it over with your doctor or someone at your clinic.

Avoid lifting heavy objects and moving furniture while you are pregnant. Stretching will not harm you or your baby, but don't reach for things from a chair or ladder, because you might lose your balance and fall. During the latter part of your pregnancy, you will probably begin to feel awkward, because your balance is affected by your increasing size. At this point you may want to substitute walking for more active sports.

Here are some exercises that are useful for strengthening muscles used in labor and delivery. They are quite simple to do and can be practiced whenever you have an opportunity to sit for a few minutes.

Tailor Sitting

While seated on the floor, bring your feet close to your body and cross your ankles. Maintain this position as long as it is comfortable to do so.

Tailor Press

While seated on the floor, bring the soles of your feet together as close to your body as is comfortable. Place your hands under your knees and press down with your knees while resisting the pressure with your hands. Count slowly to three, then relax. Gradually increase the number of presses until you are doing them ten times, twice each day.

Tailor Stretch

While seated on the floor and keeping your back straight, stretch your legs in front of you with your feet about a foot apart. Allow your feet to flop outward. Stretch your hands forward toward your left foot, then back; toward the center, then back; toward the right foot, then back. Gradually increase the sets of stretches until you are doing ten of them twice a day.

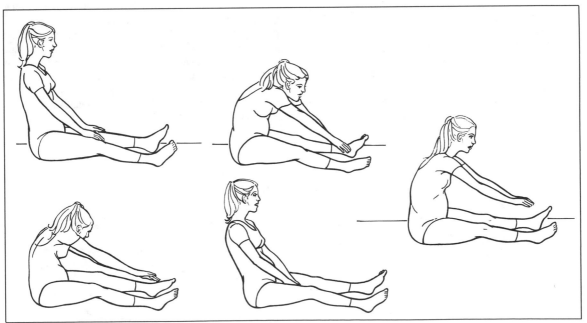

Kegel Exercise

This is sometimes called the Pelvic Floor Exercise, because it is designed to strengthen the muscles in your pelvis. After you have practiced it, you will be able to relax your pelvic muscles for delivery. First, sit down. Then contract the lowest muscles of the pelvis as tightly as you can. Tighten muscles higher in the pelvis until you are contracting the muscles at the top. Counting slowly to 10 helps, tightening additional muscles at each number. Release slowly, as you count back from 10 to 1. You are developing control of the muscles so that you can stop at any point.

These muscles are the same ones you use to stop the flow of urine. To see if you are doing the Kegel exercise correctly, try stopping the flow of urine while you are urinating. Practice the exercise for several minutes two or three times a day.

An alternate method of doing the Kegel exercise is to tighten first the pelvic muscles, then the anal muscle. Hold a few seconds, then release slowly in a reverse order.

Breathing Techniques

There are breathing techniques that you can practice while you are pregnant to help you relax during labor. They also help reduce muscle tension that works against the contractions and causes pain. If you are able to relax, you will be able to use the rest periods between labor contractions to reduce fatigue and build up your energy.

Relaxation. Lie down with your knees bent and feet on the floor. Breathe in once as deeply as possible, then hiss or blow the air out slowly through your mouth. Let yourself completely relax.

Practice Contraction. Pretend that you are having a contraction that lasts about 30 to 45 seconds. At the beginning of the contraction, take a complete breath and blow it out. Then breathe deeply, slowly, and rhythmically through the remainder of the practice contraction. Have your partner or coach go through this technique with you.

Abdominal Breathing. This exercise helps keep the abdominal wall relaxed and keeps the uterus from pressing against the lining of the abdomen. Lie down and place your hands on your abdomen. Breathe in slowly and fully, allowing your abdominal wall to rise gently. Hold this position for four to six heartbeats. Breathe out slowly and smoothly through the mouth, allowing your abdomen to fall. Relax. Repeat four or five times.

You can learn about other breathing techniques in prenatal classes or from your doctor.

Rest

Rest is just as important as exercise during pregnancy. Be sure to get plenty of sleep at night. Most pregnant women need about eight hours of sleep, but your needs may be different. You may also need to rest during the day.

There are some things you can do to keep from getting too tired. If your work requires you to be on your feet most of the day, try to sit down, put your feet up, and close your eyes whenever it is convenient. But if you spend most of your time sitting, get up and walk around for a few minutes every hour. When you are at home, take a nap during the day, especially if you have children who take naps. Plan a short rest period and really relax about the same time every day. When resting, you may find it more comfortable to use an extra pillow as shown in the illustration.

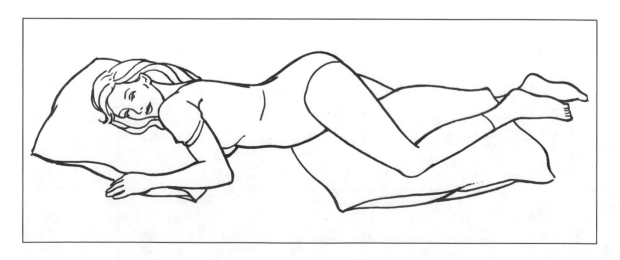

Try to find easier ways to do things, and ask other members of the family to share the workload. Perhaps someone else can help with the grocery shopping, laundry, and housework.

You should also know the best way to get out of bed:

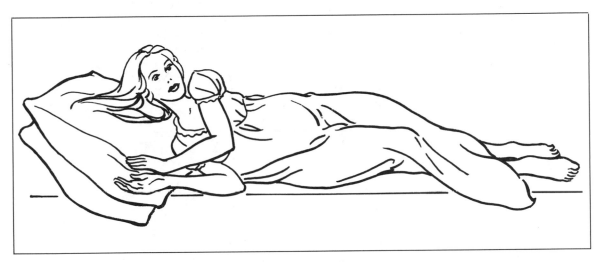

a. Turn onto your side.

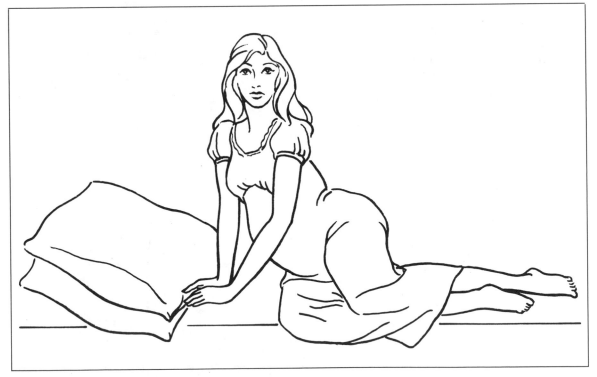

b. While bending your knees, use your arms to raise yourself up.

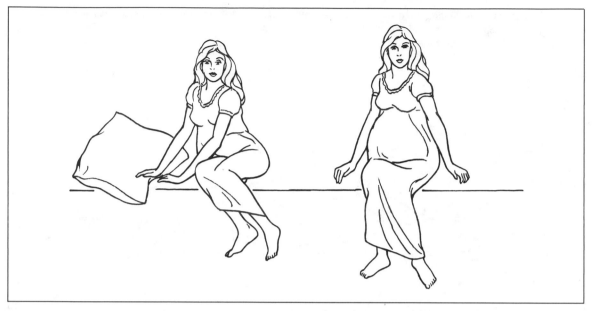

c. Lower your feet to the floor.

d. Sit upright for a few moments and hold onto the side of the bed.

e. Lean forward.

f. Use the muscles in your legs.

Backache

As your pregnancy progresses, your posture changes, because your uterus is growing and pulls on your back muscles. Your pelvic joints also loosen. This may cause backache. To help prevent strain, wear low-heeled supporting shoes. Your doctor may suggest a maternity girdle that gives support without binding.

Good posture is important in preventing backaches. Try not to lift heavy objects, particularly if there is someone around who can lift them for you.

Here are several exercises that should help your back. Ask the nurse or someone at your clinic to help you do the exercises if you are not sure you are doing them correctly.

This squatting exercise helps avoid back strain and strengthens muscles you will use in labor. This position is a good one for reaching low drawers or for lifting a child or an object weighing 15 to 30 pounds:

Holding on to a heavy piece of furniture, squat down on your heels and allow your knees to spread apart. Keep your heels flat on the floor and your toes straight ahead. You may pick up the object from the floor by squatting, holding the object close to your body, and rising slowly, using your leg muscles.

The following exercise, called the "Pelvic Rock," increases the flexibility of your lower back and strengthens your abdominal muscles. It not only relieves backache, but will help improve your posture and appearance. Practice all the versions several times every day. Try walking and standing with your pelvis lifted forward as described below:

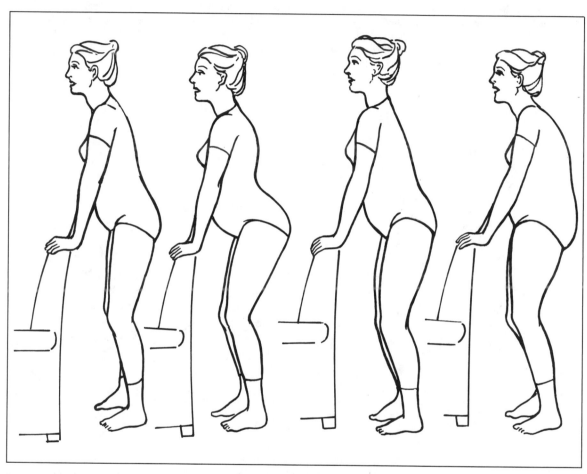

When you practice the pelvic rock standing up, use a sturdy chair. Stand back 2 feet away from the back of the chair and bend slightly forward from your hips. Place your hands on the chair back and keep your elbows straight. Thrust your hips backward and relax your abdominal muscles. You now have a sway back. Bend your knees slightly, then slowly pull your hips forward. Tuck your buttocks under as if someone were pushing you from behind. Repeat.

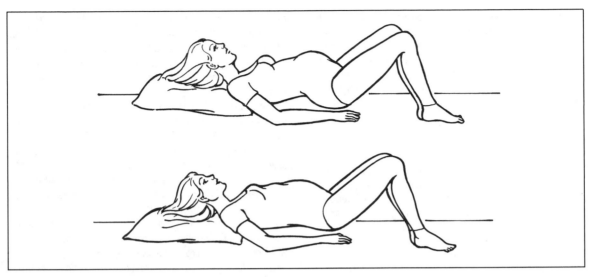

Also practice the pelvic rock lying on your back with your knees bent and feet flat on the floor. Tighten your lower abdominal muscles and the muscles of the buttocks. This elevates your tailbone and presses the small of your back to the floor. Then relax your abdominal and buttock muscles. As you do this, arch your back as high as you can. Rest for a minute, then repeat.

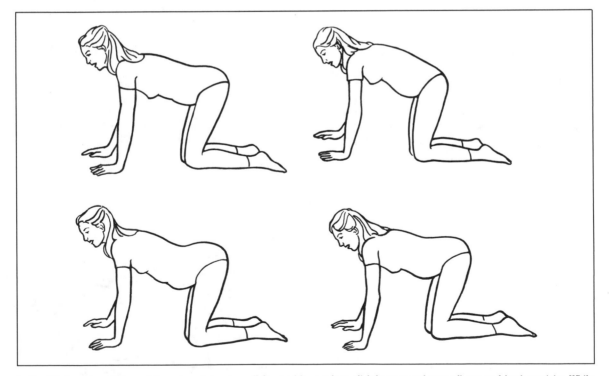

In the third version of the pelvic rock, get down on all fours with your legs slightly apart and your elbows and back straight. While inhaling, arch your back using the muscles in your lower abdomen. As you exhale, slowly relax, allowing your back to sag. Return to the original position. Then repeat.

If you have a problem or pain doing these exercises, tell your doctor, nurse, or teacher.

Many community agencies, hospitals, and clinics offer special exercise classes for pregnant women. Exercises are also a part of most childbirth-preparation classes. Talk to your doctor or nurse about the benefits of such classes and how you can enroll.

Varicose Veins

Varicose or enlarged veins usually occur in your lower legs but may extend into the pelvic area. They are caused by your enlarged uterus, which presses on your abdominal veins and interferes with the return of blood from your legs. Varicose veins usually shrink and disappear during the first few weeks after the baby is born. However, it is wiser to try to avoid varicose veins than to cure them.

You can help avoid varicose veins by not wearing tight garters, stockings, or socks. If at all possible, do not stand in one place for long periods of time. If your job requires you to stand, walk around at break time to improve circulation. If you can, sit down and put your feet up occasionally. Jobs in which you sit most of the day often aggravate varicose veins. Do not sit with your legs crossed or with the pressure of a chair under your knees. If traveling by car, take frequent rest stops and walk around. Support hose may also help you prevent varicose veins.

The illustration below shows a good position to take if you have varicose veins or swelling in your legs. Lie on a bed, couch, or floor and raise your feet and legs in the air, resting your heels against the wall. Take this position for two to five minutes several times a day.

If you have severe varicose veins, you may be advised to wear elastic stockings during the day. Support hose are not as effective as elastic stockings. Put the stockings on before you get out of bed in the morning, before your veins become swollen with blood, and take them off just before you go to bed. Wash them in mild soap after every wearing.

If you have varicose veins around your vaginal area, try to take frequent rest periods. Lie down with a pillow under your buttocks. This position elevates your hips and should give you some relief.

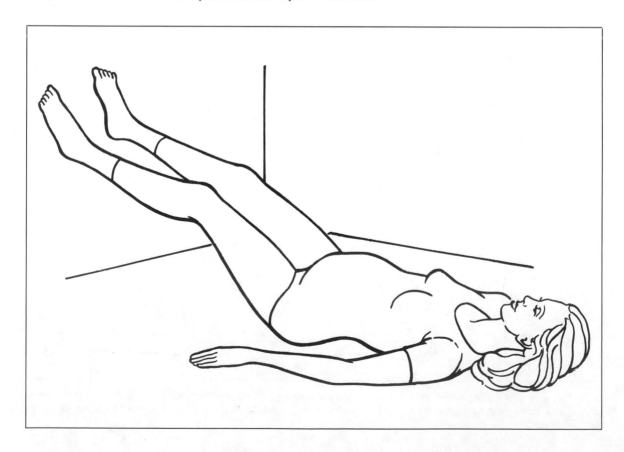

Leg Cramps

Leg cramps are more common during the latter months of your pregnancy and are generally due to presure from the enlarged uterus. They frequently occur in bed. You can often get relief from leg cramps by heat, massage, or stretching the calf muscle. Here are two exercises that may help:

Begin by standing about six inches away from a sturdy chair and holding on to the back of it. Slide the foot of the leg that is cramping as far backward as you can while keeping your heel on the floor. Bend the knee of your other leg as you slide the foot. Hold on to the chair and slide the foot back to the starting position. Repeat.

If you have someone to help you, lie down on the bed or floor and straighten your cramped leg. Have your helper push down against your knee with one hand and push up against the sole of your foot with the other hand so that your foot is at a right angle to your leg. Release and repeat several times. If cramps continue, tell your doctor.

Getting Back into Shape

Getting out of bed and walking around is the first "exercise" you will do after childbirth. Do this as soon as you feel up to it.

With the approval of your doctor or nurse-midwife, exercises may be started 24 hours after a normal delivery. Regular mild exercising will strengthen your muscles and help you get back into shape. Lying on your abdomen will help your uterus return to its normal position. Your doctor or nurse may give you some exercises, or you may want to try some of these.

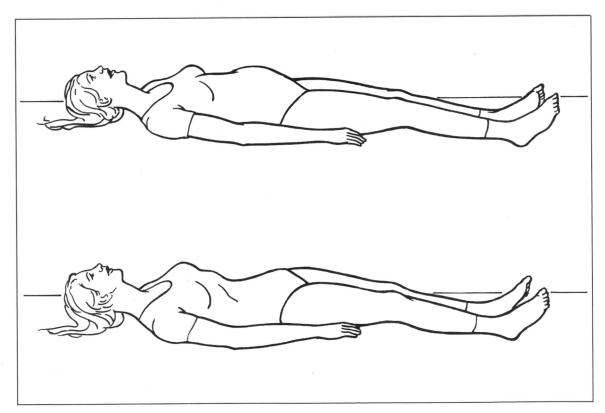

Lie flat. Breathe in deeply from your abdomen. Exhale all the air. Rest. Repeat five times.

Lie flat with your arms out at your sides. With your elbows stiff, raise your arms until they are straight over your head. Bring your palms together. Lower your arms. Rest. Repeat five times.

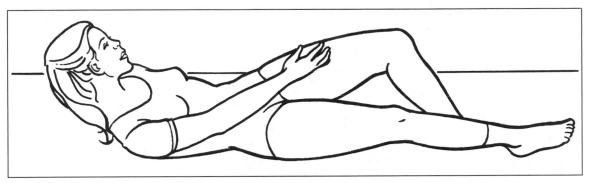

Lie flat with your legs straight. Raise your head and one knee slightly. Reach toward that knee with the opposite hand. Relax, then repeat with the other hand and knee. Repeat the sequence five times.

The following exercises are designed to strengthen your abdominal muscles. You should begin by repeating each exercise about three times and gradually increasing the number as you feel more comfortable.

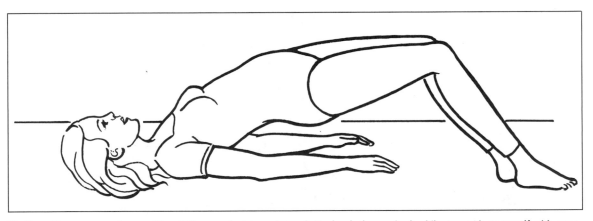

Lie flat with your arms at your sides. Slide your feet toward your buttocks. Arch your back while supporting yourself with arms, shoulders, and feet. Relax.

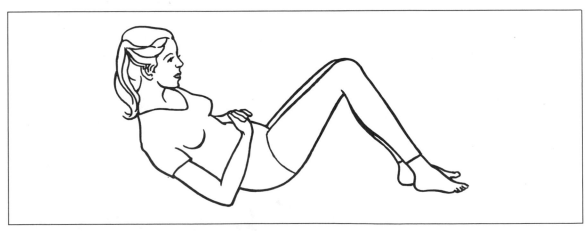

Lie flat with your knees raised. Then lift your head while raising the pelvis and tightening buttock muscles. Relax.

Lie on your back. Raise one knee and pull your thigh down onto your abdomen. Lower your foot to your buttock. Then raise the leg and straighten it. Lower slowly to the floor. Rest and repeat with the other leg.

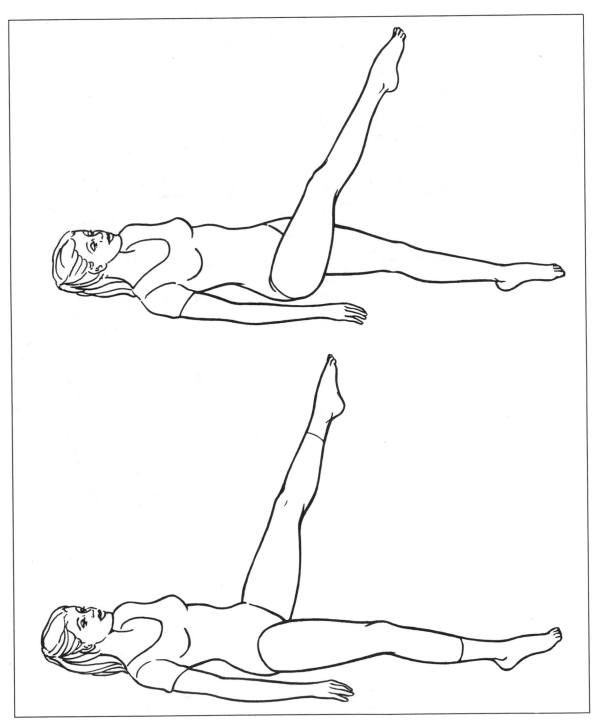

Lie flat on your back with toes extended outward. Raise the left leg using your abdominal muscles. Lower your leg slowly, then repeat with the right leg.

Resting on all fours, arch your back while contracting the muscles in your buttocks and abdomen. Relax, then breathe deeply.

Lie flat on your back as shown. Lift both legs at once using the muscles in your abdomen. Lower your legs slowly.

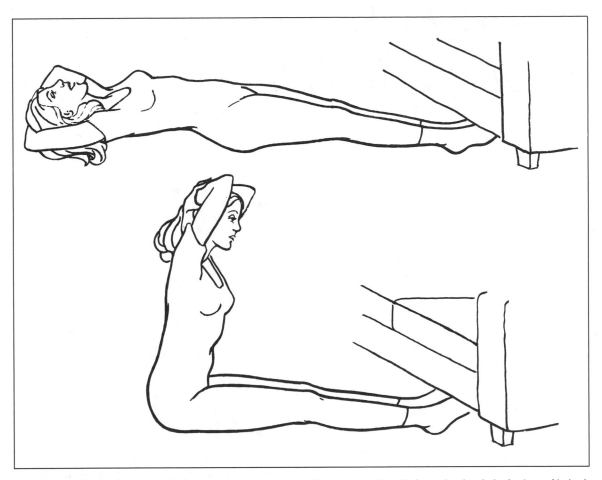

Lie flat on your back using a piece of furniture to brace your feet. Place your hands behind your head and slowly sit up. Lie back slowly using your abdominal muscles.

Source: *Prenatal Care* (1989). Prepared for the Public Health Service by the Health Resources and Services Administration, Bureau of Health Care Delivery and Assistance, Division of Maternal and Child Health.

Safety Checklist: Keeping Baby Safe

SAFETY AND INJURY PREVENTION

Babies born healthy are more likely to get hurt or die from accidents than from any illness. Accidental injuries can cause severe handicaps. You can prevent almost all accidents by knowing what your baby is able to do and making sure it is done in a safe way. Use the following checklists to be sure your home is safe.

Birth To 4 Months

What baby can do:

- Eat, sleep, cry, play, smile
- Roll off a flat surface, wiggle a lot

Babies at this age need complete protection all of the time.

Safety Checklist:

Bath

- Turn thermostat on your hot water heater down to below 120°F.
- Check bath water temperature with your hand to avoid burns.
- Keep one hand on baby at all times in bath. Never leave baby alone in the bath.

Falls

- Never turn your back on a baby who is on a table, bed, or chair.
- Always keep crib sides up.
- If interrupted, put your baby in the crib, under your arm, or on the floor.
- Do not leave baby in an infant seat on a table or counter unattended.

Burns

- Put screens around hot radiators, floor furnaces, stoves, or kerosene heaters.

- Don't let caregivers smoke when they are caring for your baby.
- Don't hold your baby when you are drinking a hot beverage.
- Don't leave a filled coffee or tea cup on a placemat or near a table edge where it could be pulled down.
- Be sure that foods, bottles, and bath water are not too hot. Test before using.
- Avoid heating baby food or formula in a microwave oven—it can get "hot spots."

In Crib, Bassinet, Carriage, or Playpen

- Be sure bars are close enough so that your baby can't slide through or get stuck (2⅜ inches at most).
- Be sure the mattress fits the crib snugly so your baby can't slip between the mattress and the sides of the crib.
- Don't use a pillow.
- Select toys that are too large to swallow and too tough to break, with no small breakable parts and no sharp points or edges.
- Keep pins, buttons, coins, and plastic bags out of reach.
- Never put anything but things a baby can eat or drink in a baby bottle, baby-food jar, or baby's dish. Someone might feed it to the baby.
- Don't use a harness or straps in the crib.
- Toys or mobiles that hang by a string should be out of baby's reach and should never be strung across the crib.

In Motor Vehicles

- Always use your car safety seat in the infant position (semireclining and facing rearward) for your baby when traveling in a motor vehicle.
- The safest place for an infant is in the rear seat of a car, correctly secured into a car safety seat.
- Adults cannot hold on to a baby in even a minor crash. The child is torn from the adult's arm—even if the adult is buckled up.
- Not all models of car safety seats fit all cars. Use a seat that is convenient for you to install; install it in the car according to the instructions and use it each and every time your child rides in the car.

- Safety seats must *always* be anchored to the car with the car's manual lap belt *exactly* as specified by the manufacturer.
- Automatic safety belts are not designed, and should not be used, to install safety seats in a car. For cars without manual lap belts in the front, the safety seat must be installed in the rear.
- Whenever a child safety seat is involved in a crash it must be replaced.
- For the best protection, use the seat only for the length of one child's growth through childhood.
- Never use plastic feeder stands, car beds, pillows, or cushions that are not certified for use in cars.

Other

- Never put a loop of ribbon or cord around your baby's neck to hold a pacifier or for any other reason.
- Do not put necklaces, rings, or bracelets on babies.
- Take all toys and small objects out of the crib or playpen when your baby is asleep or unsupervised.

Supervision

- Don't leave your baby alone with young children or with pets.
- Have the telephone numbers of your physician, the rescue squad, and the poison control center posted near your telephone.

Household

- Teach your older children how and when to call "911," the emergency telephone number.
- Install smoke detectors if you do not already have them. Keep a small fire extinguisher out of children's reach in the kitchen.

4 to 7 Months

What baby can do:

- Move around quickly
- Put things in mouth
- Grasp and pull things

Babies at this age will need more time out of the crib.

Safety checklist:

- Recheck the Birth to 4 Months List.
- Never leave your baby on the floor or bed or in the yard without watching constantly.
- Fence all stairways, top and bottom. Do not use accordion-style expandable baby gates that can strangle.

- Don't tie toys to crib or playpen rails—a baby can strangle in the tapes or string.
- Keep baby's crib away from drapery or venetian blind cords that can strangle.
- Never use a mesh playpen or crib that has holes in the mesh—baby's head can get caught.
- Baby-proof all rooms where the child will play by removing matches, cigarette lighters, cigarette butts, other small objects, breakable objects, sharp objects, and tables or lamps that can be pulled over.
- Cover all unused electric outlets with safety caps or tape.
- Keep all electric cords out of reach.
- Keep high chairs, playpens, and infant seats away from stoves, work counters, radiators, furnaces, kerosene heaters, electrical outlets, electric cords, draperies, and venetian blind cords.
- Always use restraining straps on a high chair and do not leave your baby unattended in one.
- Keep cans, bottles, spray cans, and boxes of all cleansers, detergents, pesticides, bleaches, liquor, and cosmetics out of reach.
- Never put a poisonous household product into a food jar, bottle, or soft drink can. Someone may swallow it or feed it to the baby.
- Do not use old paint that might have been made before February 1978—it could contain lead. If a toy or crib is old and needs repainting, remove the old paint completely (with a chemical—do not sand) and paint it with safe lead-free household paint (check the label). Let it dry thoroughly to avoid fumes.
- If your house is old and has any chipping paint or plaster, repair it (don't sand it) and cover it with wallpaper or safe, new paint. If there is chipped paint or plaster in halls or other places you can't repair, have it tested for lead by the health department. If it contains lead, cover it with wallpaper or fabric, or put furniture in front of it to keep it out of reach.

8 to 12 Months

What baby can do:

- Move fast
- Climb on chairs and stairs
- Open drawers and cupboards
- Open bottles and packages

At this point, your baby needs more opportunity to explore *while you are watching.*

Safety checklist:

- Recheck the Birth to 4 Months List.
- Recheck the 4 to 7 Months List.

- If you use a toy chest or trunk, make sure it has a safety hinge (one that holds the lid open) or remove the lid.
- Baby-proof all cupboards and drawers that can possibly be reached and opened. Remove all small objects and sharp objects, breakables, household products that might poison, plastic bags, and foods that might cause choking (small foods such as nuts, raisins, or popcorn).
- Keep hot foods and beverages and hot pots and pans out of your baby's reach. Turn pot or pan handles toward the back of the stove.
- Don't use a dangling tablecloth; it can be pulled and everything on it can crash on your baby and the floor.
- Keep medicines and household products (such as bleach, oven and drain cleaners, paint solvents, polishes, and waxes) that might poison in a *locked* cabinet. Try to buy items in child-*resistant* containers.
- Never leave your baby alone in the bathtub or wading pool. Babies can drown in only a few inches of water. They can also turn on the faucet and scald themselves.
- Keep young children out of the bathroom unless you are watching. They can drown in a few inches of water (including the toilet or buckets filled with water).

- Be very careful when you or someone else in the family is sick. Medicines are likely to be out of their usual safe place, and your baby may want to imitate you by eating them.
- Keep medicines separate from household products and household products separate from food.
- Never give medicine in the dark. Turn on the light and read the label—EVERY TIME.
- Avoid overexposure to the sun, which can lead to sunburn. Use sunscreens on advice from your doctor or clinic staff.
- Keep diaper pails tightly closed and out of reach.
- Get 1 ounce of Ipecac Syrup from the druggist and keep it on the medicine shelf to treat poisoning. Use as directed.
- Keep a close watch for moving machinery (lawnmowers, cars backing up) when your baby is outdoors.
- The car safety seat can be used in the toddler position with the child sitting up and facing forward when baby is about 20 pounds at about 9 months of age.
- Never leave your baby alone in a child safety seat in a car.
- During hot weather, if your car is parked in the hot sun, cover your child's safety seat with a towel to avoid burning your child.

Source: Infant Care (1989). Prepared for the Public Health Service by the Health Resources and Services Administration, Bureau of Maternal and Child Health and Resources Development.

Chart of Normal Development: Infancy to Six Years of Age

The chart of normal development on the next few pages presents children's achievements from infancy to six years of age in five areas:

- motor skills (gross and fine motor).
- cognitive skills.
- self-help skills.
- social skills.
- communication skills (understanding language and speaking).

In each skill area, the age at which each milestone is reached *on the average* is also presented. This information is useful if you have a child who you suspect is seriously delayed in one or more skill areas.

However, it is important to remember that these milestones are only averages. From the moment of birth, each child is a distinct individual and develops in his or her unique manner. No two children have ever reached all the same developmental milestones at the exact same ages. The examples that follow show what we mean.

By nine months of age, Gi Lin had spent much of her time scooting around on her hands and tummy, making no effort to crawl. After about a week of pulling herself up on chairs and table legs, she let go and started to walk on her own. Gi Lin skipped the crawling stage entirely and scarcely said more than a few sounds until she was 15 months old. But she walked with ease and skill by 9½ months.

Marcus learned to crawl on all fours very early and continued crawling until he was nearly 18 months old, when he started

to walk. However, he said single words and used two-word phrases meaningfully before his first birthday.

Molly worried her parents by saying scarcely a word, although she managed to make her needs known with sounds and gestures. Shortly after her second birthday, Molly suddenly began talking in two- to four-word phrases and sentences. She was never again a quiet child.

All three children were healthy and normal. By the time they were three years old, there were no major differences among them in walking or talking. They had simply developed in their own ways and at their own rates. Some children seem to concentrate on one thing at a time—learning to crawl, to walk, or to talk. Other children develop across areas at a more even rate.

As you read the chart of normal development, remember that children don't read baby books. They don't know they're supposed to be able to point out Daddy when they are a year old, or copy a circle in their third year. And even if they could read the baby books, they probably wouldn't follow them! Age-related development milestones are obtained by averaging out what many children do at various ages. No child is "average" in all areas. Each child is a unique person.

One final word of caution. As children grow, their abilities are shaped by the opportunities they have for learning. For example, although many five-year-olds can repeat songs and rhymes, the child who has not heard songs and rhymes many times cannot be expected to repeat them. All areas of development and learning are influenced by the child's experiences as well as by the abilities he or she is born with.

	Motor Skills		Communication Skills
	Gross Motor Skills	Fine Motor Skills	Understanding Language
0–12 Months	Sits without support. Crawls. Pulls self to standing and stands unaided. Walks with aid. Rolls a ball in imitation of an adult.	Reaches, grasps, puts objects in mouth. Picks things up with thumb and one finger (pincer grasp). Transfers objects from one hand to the other. Drops and picks up toys.	Responds to speech by looking at speaker. Responds differently to aspects of speaker's voice (for example, friendly or unfriendly, male or female). Turns to source of sound. Responds with gesture to "hi," "bye-bye," and "up," when these words are accompanied by appropriate gesture. Stops ongoing action when told "no" (when negative is accompanied by appropriate gesture and tone).
12–24 Months	Walks alone. Walks backward. Picks up toys from floor without falling. Pulls and pushes toys. Seats self in child's chair. Walks up and down stairs (hand-held). Moves to music.	Builds tower of three small blocks. Puts four rings on stick. Places five pegs in pegboard. Turns pages two or three at a time. Scribbles. Turns knobs. Throws small ball. Paints with whole arm movement, shifts hands, makes strokes.	Responds correctly when asked *where* (when question is accompanied by gesture). Understands prepositions *on, in,* and *under.* Follows request to bring familiar object from another room. Understands simple phrases with key words (for example, "Open the door," or "Get the ball"). Follows a series of two simple but related directions.
24–36 Months	Runs forward well. Jumps in place, two feet together. Stands on one foot, with aid. Walks on tiptoe. Kicks ball forward.	Strings four large beads. Turns pages singly. Snips with scissors. Holds crayon with thumb and fingers, not fist. Uses one hand consistently in most activities. Imitates circular, vertical, and horizontal strokes. Paints with some wrist action. Makes dots, lines, and circular strokes. Rolls, pounds, squeezes, and pulls clay.	Points to pictures of common objects when they are named. Can identify objects when told their use. Understands question forms *what* and *where.* Understands negatives *no, not, can't,* and *don't.* Enjoys listening to simple storybooks and requests them again.

Spoken Language	Cognitive Skills	Self-Help Skills	Social Skills
Makes crying and noncrying sounds. Repeats some vowel and consonant sounds (babbles) when alone or when spoken to. Interacts with others by vocalizing after an adult. Communicates meaning through intonation. Attempts to imitate sounds.	Follows moving object with eyes. Recognizes differences among people. Responds to strangers by crying or staring. Responds to and imitates facial expressions of others. Responds to very simple directions (for example, raises arms when someone says, "Come," and turns head when asked, "Where is Daddy?"). Imitates gestures and actions (for example, shakes head no, plays peek-a-boo, waves bye-bye). Puts small objects in and out of a container with intention.	Feeds self a cracker. Holds cup with two hands. Drinks with assistance. Holds out arms and legs while being dressed.	Smiles spontaneously. Responds differently to strangers than to familiar people. Pays attention to own name. Responds to "no." Copies simple actions of others.
Says first meaningful word. Uses single word plus a gesture to ask for objects. Says successive single words to describe an event. Refers to self by name. Uses "my" or "mine" to indicate possession. Has vocabulary of about 50 words for important people, common objects, and the existence, nonexistence, and recurrence of objects and events (for example, "more" and "all gone").	Imitates actions and words of adults. Responds to words or commands with appropriate action (for example: "Stop that." "Get down"). Is able to match two similar objects. Looks at storybook pictures with an adult, naming or pointing to familiar objects on request (for example: "What is that?" "Point to the baby"). Recognizes difference between *you* and *me*. Has very limited attention span. Accomplishes primary learning through own exploration.	Uses spoon, spilling little. Drinks from cup, one hand, unassisted. Chews food. Removes shoes, socks, pants, sweater. Unzips large zipper. Indicates toilet needs.	Recognizes self in mirror or picture. Refers to self by name. Plays by self; initiates own play. Imitates adult behaviors in play. Helps put things away.
Joins vocabulary words together in two-word phrases. Gives first and last name. Asks *what* and *where* questions. Makes negative statements (for example, "Can't open it"). Shows frustration at not being understood.	Responds to simple directions (for example: "Give me the ball and the block." "Get your shoes and socks"). Selects and looks at picture books, names pictured objects, and identifies several objects within one picture. Matches and uses associated objects meaningfully (for example, given cup, saucer, and bead, puts cup and saucer together). Stacks rings on peg in order of size. Recognizes self in mirror, saying *baby* or own name. Can talk briefly about what he or she is doing. Imitates adult actions (for example, housekeeping play). Has limited attention span. Learning is through exploration and adult direction (as in reading of picture stories). Is beginning to understand functional concepts of familiar objects (for example, that a spoon is used for eating) and part/whole concepts (for example, parts of the body).	Uses spoon, spilling little. Gets drink from fountain or faucet unassisted. Opens door by turning handle. Takes off coat. Puts on coat with assistance. Washes and dries hands with assistance.	Plays near other children. Watches other children; joins briefly in their play. Defends own possessions. Begins to play house. Symbolically uses objects, self in play. Participates in simple group activity (for example, sings, claps, dances). Knows gender identity.

Continued on page 510

	Motor Skills		Communication Skills
	Gross Motor Skills	Fine Motor Skills	Understanding Language
36–48 Months	Runs around obstacles. Walks on a line. Balances on one foot for five to ten seconds. Hops on one foot. Pushes, pulls, and steers wheeled toys. Rides (that is, steers and pedals) tricycle. Uses slide without assistance. Jumps over 15-centimeter (6-inch)-high object, landing on both feet together. Throws ball overhead. Catches ball bounced to him or her.	Builds tower of nine small blocks. Drives nails and pegs. Copies circle. Imitates cross. Manipulates clay materials (for example, rolls balls, snakes, cookies).	Begins to understand sentences involving time concepts (for example, "We are going to the zoo tomorrow"). Understands size comparatives such as *big* and *bigger*. Understands relationships expressed by *if . . . then* or *because* sentences. Carries out a series of 2 to 4 related directions. Understands when told, "Let's pretend."
48–60 Months	Walks backward toe–heel. Jumps forward 10 times, without falling. Walks up and down stairs alone, alternating feet. Turns somersault.	Cuts on line continuously. Copies cross. Copies square. Prints a few capital letters.	Follows three unrelated commands in proper order. Understands comparatives like *pretty, prettier,* and *prettiest.* Listens to long stories but often misinterprets the facts. Incorporates verbal directions into play activities. Understands sequencing of events when told them (for example, "First we have to go to the store, then we can make the cake, and tomorrow we will eat it").

Spoken Language	Cognitive Skills	Self-Help Skills	Social Skills
Talks in sentences of 3 or more words, which take the form agent-action-object ("I see the ball") or agent-action-location ("Daddy sits on chair"). Tells about past experiences. Uses "s" on nouns to indicate plurals. Uses "ed" on verbs to indicate past tense. Refers to self using pronouns *I* or *me*. Repeats at least one nursery rhyme and can sing a song. Speech is understandable to strangers, but there are still some sound errors.	Recognizes and matches six colors. Intentionally stacks blocks or rings in order of size. Draws somewhat recognizable picture that is meaningful to child, if not to adult. Names and briefly explains picture. Asks questions for information (*why* and *how* questions requiring simple answers). Knows own age. Knows own last name. Has short attention span. Learns through observing and imitating adults, and by adult instruction and explanation. Is very easily distracted. Has increased understanding of concepts of the functions and groupings of objects (for example, can put doll-house furniture in correct rooms), and part/whole (for example, can identify pictures of hand and foot as parts of body). Begins to be aware of past and present (for example: "Yesterday we went to the park." "Today we go to the library").	Pours well from small pitcher. Spreads soft butter with knife. Buttons and unbuttons large buttons. Washes hands unassisted. Blows nose when reminded. Uses toilet independently.	Joins in play with other children. Begins to interact. Shares toys. Takes turns with assistance. Begins dramatic play, acting out whole scenes (for example, traveling, playing house, pretending to be animals).
Asks when, how, and why questions. Uses modals like *can, will, shall, should,* and *might*. Joins sentences together (for example, "I like chocolate-chip cookies and milk"). Talks about causality by using *because* and *so*. Tells the content of a story but may confuse facts.	Plays with words (creates own rhyming words; says or makes up words having similar sounds). Points to and names four to six colors. Matches pictures of familiar objects (for example, shoe, sock, foot; apple, orange, banana). Draws a person with two to six recognizable parts, such as head, arms, legs. Can name and match drawn parts to own body. Draws, names, and describes recognizable picture. Rote counts to five, imitating adults. Knows own street and town. Has more extended attention span. Learns through observing and listening to adults as well as through exploration. Is easily distracted. Has increased understanding of concepts of function, time, and part/whole relationships. Function or use of objects may be stated in addition to names of objects. Time concepts are expanding. The child can talk about yesterday or last week (a long time ago), about today, and about what will happen tomorrow.	Cuts easy foods with a knife (for example, hamburger patty, tomato slice). Laces shoes.	Plays and interacts with other children. Dramatic play is closer to reality, with attention paid to detail, time, and space. Plays dress-up. Shows interest in exploring sex differences.

Continued on page 512

	Motor Skills		Communication Skills
	Gross Motor Skills	Fine Motor Skills	Understanding Language
60–72 Months	Runs lightly on toes. Walks on balance beam. Can cover 2 meters (6'6") hopping. Skips on alternate feet. Jumps rope. Skates.	Cuts out simple shapes. Copies triangle. Traces diamond. Copies first name. Prints numerals 1 to 5. Colors within lines. Has adult grasp of pencil. Has handedness well established (that is, child is left- or right-handed). Pastes and glues appropriately.	Demonstrates preacademic skills.

Spoken Language	Cognitive Skills	Self-Help Skills	Social Skills
There are few obvious differences between child's grammar and adult's grammar. Still needs to learn such things as subject–verb agreement and some irregular past tense verbs. Can take appropriate turns in a conversation. Gives and receives information. Communicates well with family, friends, or strangers.	Retells story from picture book with reasonable accuracy. Names some letters and numerals. Rote counts to 10. Sorts objects by single characteristics (for example, by color, shape, or size if the difference is obvious). Is beginning to use accurately time concepts of *tomorrow* and *yesterday.* Uses classroom tools (such as scissors and paints) meaningfully and purposefully. Begins to relate clock time to daily schedule. Attention span increases noticeably. Learns through adult instruction. When interested, can ignore distractions. Concepts of function increase as well as understanding of why things happen. Time concepts are expanding into an understanding of the future in terms of major events (for example, "Christmas will come after two weekends").	Dresses self completely. Ties bow. Brushes teeth unassisted. Crosses street safely.	Chooses own friend(s). Plays simple table games. Plays competitive games. Engages with other children in cooperative play involving group decisions, role assignments, and fair play.

Source: *Mainstreaming Preschoolers*, series of books prepared for the Head Start Bureau, Administration of Children, Youth and Family.

Choosing a School for Your Child

THINKING ABOUT YOUR CHILD AND YOUR FAMILY

Start your search for the best school by thinking about what you want a school to do for your child. After all, you know your son or daughter better than anyone else does.

First, think about your child's personality. What is the youngster like? Children who thrive on exploration and responsibility might flourish in an open school or an alternative school. Other students fare better in a traditional school, with closer direction and supervision from the teachers. Both kinds of schools can provide a rich curriculum and a firm foundation; the choice should depend on which situation your child will respond to better.

Another factor is your child's school experience to date. A child who is bored in school may need more challenging work. If your child has had difficulty keeping up, you will want a school with a strong commitment to helping every student learn. The best schools will build on your child's academic strengths and be able to help with any academic difficulties.

How does your child respond to large and small groups? Some youngsters might "fall through the cracks" in a large school; some students do best in the more intimate atmosphere of a small school. Other students can gain from attending a larger school, which can offer a program closely tailored to their needs.

Collecting Information on Available Schools

If you were looking at cars, vacuum cleaners, or refrigerators, you could quickly find information in consumer magazines and other published resources. Investigating schools is not quite so easy; you may have to make phone calls, collect written material from different schools, and look for reports in your local paper to get the information you need. The hard work will be worth your while if you find a school that brings out the best in your child.

If possible, start your investigation a year before you want your child to enroll at a new school. It may take some time to find schools that suit your needs; you will want to obtain written information, visit those schools, make a final choice, and

have time to get your child admitted for the fall. Some schools stop accepting applications as early as January or February.

You will certainly want to know what the school will teach your child. Does it give enough focus to the basics? Is the curriculum enriched with any special programs that would be good for your child? (For comparison, see James Madison Elementary School and High School: A Model Curriculum, on pages 530–43, developed by the U.S. Department of Education.)

Some schools may emphasize specific subjects. Schools of choice are especially likely to stress a special field or topic, such as math and science, performing arts, international commerce, or communications. Religious teaching and moral development are likely to be a part of the focus in church-affiliated schools, and some private schools may provide extra study of the ethnic heritage shared by many of their students.

If a school has a special focus in its curriculum, you should check to be sure that other core subjects and skills are being taught well, too. Asking to see test scores may give you some information; reviewing the curriculum and visiting classes can also help.

School Philosophy

Schools differ in their philosophies. You will want to find out what beliefs guide a school's teaching. What kind of learning does it consider most important? How does it believe students can learn best?

Two schools may have different philosophies and both be excellent for some students. For example, a traditional or back-to-basics school will provide clear standards and structure for the child who needs them, while an open school may allow extra freedom for a child who can use it well.

Many large public school systems offer an alternative school for high school students who are likely to drop out or who have found the regular program unchallenging. Often these schools are deliberately small and informal; they encourage students to feel like "members" who belong to the school community rather than merely attending. Yet a more traditional school with formal classes and wider offerings can bring out the best in most students, provided that school has high standards, clear expectations, and a well-planned program.

Some schools can provide you with written statements of their philosophy. In others, you will have to ask the principal and teachers to describe their goals. Most importantly, visit the school and talk to parents to see if the school's philosophy is working well in practice.

Important School Policies

In addition, you will probably want to know about some other school policies.

1. *Discipline.* The existence of written rules and clear penalties is one sign that a school is working on discipline issues. When you visit the school, you may want to watch carefully to see if those rules are being enforced fairly and firmly.

2. *Homework.* Researchers have found that regular homework can significantly increase student achievement. Find out if the school requires homework and how frequently it is given. Ask if teachers check, grade, and return the homework on a regular basis. Some schools also have hotlines to teachers, after-school clinics, or tutoring programs ready to help kids succeed.

3. *Grades and Feedback.* You will want to know how students' work is judged and how often you will receive report cards on your child's progress. You may also want to ask how else the school gives students feedback on how they are doing and how they can improve. Are there programs to recognize children who do well in school? Are there regular policies for helping children who are having trouble?

Proof of Results

Once you know what a school is trying to do, ask for some indicators about whether it succeeds. Here are some factors you may want to investigate.

1. *Test Scores.* Ask for information on the school's scores over the last few years. The school district or the school should be able to provide these to you. If the scores have been going down in recent years, you will want to ask the school's principal why this is so.

If you are told that a school's scores are above the national average, be careful. A recent research report pointed out that "no state is below average on any of the six major nationally normed, commercially available tests." In other words, every state, and most districts, may be able to show you test results showing that their schools are above average. How is this possible? It may be that education has improved since the "national averages" were determined, but it may also be that the test designers set the norms too low at the start or that schools are "teaching to the test."

The principal should be willing to share information about test scores. If an administrator refuses to give you information about test results, think very carefully about placing your child in that school.

2. *Attendance Rates.* Another important measure is attendance. Parents should ask about attendance of both students and teachers. A school with a more than 10-percent absence rate for either may have some serious problems.

3. *Turnover and Graduation Rates.* You may want to find out how stable the student body is: How many students leave the school in a year? How many of those move or transfer? How many drop out? For high schools, graduation rates provide one indication of whether schools are providing an education their students value. On the other hand, remember that a diploma alone does not tell you what those students learned; gather other information to tell you whether a school's graduates got a sound education while enrolled there.

4. *Postgraduation Activities.* Some schools conduct surveys to determine how many students find jobs, join the military, or seek postsecondary education. Generally, high schools in affluent areas have a high percentage of graduates attending colleges and universities. However, some urban schools in poor neighborhoods pride themselves on encouraging students to continue their formal education. You may want to pay special attention to a school that sends many graduates from less wealthy homes on to colleges, universities, and technical training and business schools.

5. *Special Achievements.* Has the school had special successes in recent years? A school you are considering may have received an award for excellence, initiated an important new program, or dramatically improved its students' achievement. Staff members may have been recognized for superior teaching. Successes like these tell you what a school does well, and they may also show that the principal, teachers, and families at that school work together for good education.

School Facilities

Research indicates that fancy facilities do not always lead to higher achievement. Be sure to bear this in mind when you look into a school's resources. But a library and classroom books are always important. Children need to read many good books in order to learn independently and build their reading skills; textbooks are not enough. If a school does not have a wide variety of interesting books readily available to its students, that is a serious weakness.

VISITING A SCHOOL

Be sure to visit any school before you finally decide to send your child there. Make an appointment before you visit, calling the principal's office or, if the school has one, the admissions office. You will want to tour the school during regular school hours. If possible, you will want to visit a few classes. To get a real feeling for how the school usually operates, avoid visiting during the first or last week of a school term.

You will also want some scheduled time to talk to the principal and some teachers about the school. Ask for an appointment that will let you do all these things. Attending an open house, PTA meeting, or other school function could also give you valuable information about the attitudes of staff, students, and parents.

Things to Look For

As you walk around a school or visit some classrooms, you should ask yourself questions like the following: Do I feel comfortable walking into the school? How do the adults talk to children? Are they friendly or harsh? Are the children clearly interested in what they are doing? Is the overall atmosphere one that allows students to work hard and learn? Do pupils seem to have opportunity for quiet reading as well as group activities?

Are there some areas of the school or some classrooms the tour guide avoids? Does the school display examples of excellent student work? Is the building tidy and well maintained?

In general, schools where students do best are clean, orderly, pleasant places. Staff members in good schools respect each other, their students, and their parents. They speak enthusiastically of the children. Teachers are clearly interested in the subjects they teach. Students are friendly and respectful, and you can tell that they are busy learning. Parents should hesitate before placing children in schools that do not have these characteristics.

A visit also lets you double check some of the information you may have collected earlier. Does the library appear both well stocked and well used? Do the disciplinary rules you read about really seem to be enforced? Do any special programs you were interested in appear to be working well?

Checklist

(Make a photocopy for each school you consider.)

In looking at available schools, you may want to use the checklist below as a guide. During your school visit, you can confirm what you heard or read earlier. Once you select a school, you will want to double check the admissions information you collected to make sure you meet all the requirements.

Curriculum

1. Thorough coverage of basic subjects? ☐ Yes ☐ No

If no, which subjects are not covered completely?

_____

2. A special focus or theme to the curriculum? ☐ Yes ☐ No

What is it?

_____

3. Elective offerings (if appropriate)

_____

_____

4. Extracurricular programs to enhance learning and character development

_____

_____

_____

Philosophy

5. Emphasis on a particular approach to teaching and learning _____

6. Belief that every child can learn?   ☐ Yes ☐ No

7. Encouragement of attributes of good character?   ☐ Yes ☐ No

Important Policies

8. Discipline _____

9. Drugs _____

10. Homework: How much per subject? _____

11. Homework hotlines?   ☐ Yes ☐ No

12. Tutoring?   ☐ Yes ☐ No

If yes, by whom? _____

13. Grades, feedback, and recognition: How often? _____

What type? _____

14. Teacher opportunities and incentives _____

Proof of Results

15. Standardized test scores: Current _____ Past _____

16. Attendance rate: Students_____

Teachers _____

17. Graduation rate _____

18. How many leave school in a year? _____

Why?_____

19. Special achievements or honors for the school _____

School Resources

20. Staff backgrounds and qualifications _____

21. Library?   ☐ Yes ☐ No

22. Classroom books for independent reading?   ☐ Yes ☐ No

23. Auditorium or other meeting room?   ☐ Yes ☐ No

24. Physical education facilities?   ☐ Yes ☐ No

If yes, what type? If no, what alternatives?

Parent and Community Involvement

25. Parent volunteers in school?   ☐ Yes ☐ No

Doing what? _____

Continued on page 518

26. Teachers enlist parent cooperation on home learning? ☐ Yes ☐ No

If yes, how? _____

_____

27. Other community members involved in school? ☐ Yes ☐ No

28. Partnerships with local businesses or other institutions

_____

_____

Reputation

29. Views of parents with children in the school

_____

_____

_____

30. Views of friends and neighbors

_____

_____

_____

31. Views of community leaders

_____

_____

_____

Special Questions for Private and Church-affiliated Schools

Financial obligations

32. Tuition $_____

33. Other fees $_____

34. Uniforms? ☐ Yes ☐ No

35. Book purchases? ☐ Yes ☐ No

36. Required participation in fundraising? ☐ Yes ☐ No

Financial assistance

37. Scholarships up to what percent of tuition? _____

38. Loans _____

39. Reduced fees if more than one child enrolls _____

40. State aid available to families _____

41. Apply how and when? _____

_____

Other

42. School's age and financial status _____

_____

43. Religious instruction and activities _____

_____

Admissions Requirements and Procedures

For a public, church-affiliated, or other private school of choice

44. List of materials to submit (application form, transcript, test scores, references, etc.)

_____

_____

_____

45. Interview required?   ☐ Yes ☐ No

Date _____ Time _____

46. Date school will decide _____

47. How will school select students?

_____

_____

For other public schools

48. Borders of the attendance area the school usually serves

_____

49. Does state law give you a right to transfer your child to another public school?   ☐ Yes ☐ No

50. Tuition or other charges for transferring students $_____

51. Facts considered important in deciding whether to grant a request for a transfer

_____

_____

52. When will a decision be made on transfer requests? _____

53. Names of district officials who can permit a child to transfer to a school outside that child's attendance area

_____

_____

_____

Source: *Choosing a School for Your Child* (1989). Prepared by the U.S. Department of Education. (See original for fuller discussion.)

Help Your Child Become a Good Reader

Your child, like most children, will learn how to read. Whether the child will read and read fluently depends partly on you.

Children who read well come from homes in which there are plenty of books, magazines, and newspapers and in which everyone reads—parents, brothers, and sisters. Their parents encourage reading and make time for it; it's clear that the family enjoys reading.

Children who read well have parents who:

- read aloud to them.
- talk to them about their ideas and experiences.
- take them places.
- let them watch television but limit it.
- take an interest in their reading progress.

If you want your child to read well and with understanding—to get "hooked on books"—begin early to lay the right foundation.

You need not be a professional teacher yourself. You do need to care and to take every opportunity to help your child learn about the written language.

INFLUENCES

Certain things influence children's success and interest in reading. They are:

Wide knowledge. The more knowledge children acquire at home, the greater their chances to become successful readers. Children who go on trips, walk in parks, and visit museums and zoos get good background knowledge for school reading.

Thoughtful talking. The way in which you talk to your child about things makes a big difference. Talking can increase the child's supply of concepts and vocabulary. It's not enough to ask a question. ("What do you think is under the windshield wiper?") Ask a question that makes the child think. ("Why do you think there's a slip of paper under the windshield wiper?") Thought-provoking questions stimulate the curiosity needed for success in reading. *The content and style of the language you use with your child will influence the child's school achievement in reading.*

Talk about events. Encourage children to think about past and future events. Don't allow conversation to focus entirely on ongoing events, for example, the clothes the child is putting on or the food that is being eaten for dinner.

Ask your children to describe something in which you did not participate—for instance, a visit to a friend's home. This gives children a chance to use their memories, reflect on experience, learn to describe people and events, and tell complete stories.

Children who hold lengthy conversations at home learn to reflect on experience and to construct meaning from events. This is part of their learning to read and understanding what they read.

As mentioned earlier, have lots of reading materials around your home. Let your children see you reading and enjoying it.

THINGS TO DO

Read aloud. This is the single most important thing you can do for your children. It's especially important in the preschool years, *but don't stop reading aloud to children after they learn to read.* Reading aloud forms an important bond between you and your children.

When reading aloud, keep certain things in mind. For instance, preschoolers enjoy hearing the same story over and over again. Books that repeat phrases, such as *This Is The House That Jack Built,* are special favorites and give very young children an opportunity to participate by reading the repetitive parts with you. This lets children know that they can read and that reading can be fun.

Begin reading to a child when the child is a year old or even younger. Read from simple picture books. Cardboard pages are fairly easy for a toddler to turn and this exercise will help a child learn how to take care of books.

Talk to your children about the stories you read. Help toddlers learn to identify letters and words. Talk about the meaning of words. Talk about your favorite children's books and read them aloud. Ask what your children think about the stories and why they think that.

Ask questions about a story that make children think. Avoid asking questions that can be answered with "yes" or "no." For instance, if you're reading your son a story about a dog, don't ask if he likes dogs but which dogs he likes best and why.

Let these questions carry over to other areas of the child's life. Encourage the child to discuss daily activities. If your daughter spent the day with the babysitter, ask what they did and how or why they did it. Always ask questions that require children to use their memories and reflect on their experiences. Talking about experiences helps a child learn about concepts and helps build vocabulary. These abilities help your child to become a good reader.

If you're reading to an older child or to several children, consider wonderful classics like *The Call of the Wild, The Adventures of Huckleberry Finn,* and *The Red Badge of Courage.*

Do relate episodes in stories to real-life events. If you've been reading *Huckleberry Finn* to your children, discuss the friendship between Huck and Jim and compare it with your children's friendships.

Teach alphabet letters. It's never too soon to begin teaching a youngster to recognize letters of the alphabet. Point out letters on signs, food cans, and cereal boxes, in stories, and in books. For example, when reading *The Three Bears,* point out the letter "T" in the story, then ask your child to pick out the letter "T" from alphabet blocks. And all children love to find the letters in their names!

Provide a place to read. Make sure that your child has a comfortable, quiet, well-lighted place to read or play with reading materials.

Materials. Have plenty of paper, pencils, chalkboards, and crayons for your child to use in drawing and writing. Writing helps children learn the relationships between letters and sounds. If the child is too young to write with a pencil, use magnetic boards and letters.

Records and tapes. You can borrow records and tapes from the library that have follow-along books for young children. They add variety to reading activities.

Television. If your child likes to watch "Sesame Street," "Mister Rogers," or any other educational TV program, help relate the TV lesson to other situations. For example, if the show focuses on the letter "B," have your child give you examples of other words beginning with "B." Have the child show you a toy that begins with that letter, such as a ball or a bear.

Many parents worry that TV may adversely affect a child's reading skills. Research shows that watching for a reasonable amount of time—no more than 10 hours weekly—is all right and may even help a child learn. In fact, the dramatization of a novel or an animated production of a favorite story may inspire a child to read the book or story.

Computers. Many companies are developing reading programs for home computers. At present, however, there's little solid information about the impact of computers on children's reading. One thing we do know: simply placing children in front of computer terminals with reading software programs won't teach them to read.

Make a scrapbook. Encourage your child to make scrapbooks. This activity can help the child to identify words and letters. Have a preschooler make an alphabet scrapbook using an old notebook or sheets of cardboard tied with a shoestring. One day the child could work on "A" and cut pictures from magazines beginning with "A"—apple, airplane, automobile. The next day the child could work on "B."

An older child may enjoy keeping a scrapbook about a hobby, a favorite singer, or a sport.

Help prepare for phonics. Help prepare a young child for learning phonics (the relationship between letters and sounds), as phonics will be an important part of reading lessons in the first and second grades. Label objects in the child's bedroom—clock, dresser, chair, curtain, window, toys, etc.—to help the child relate the sound of the word to the written word. Teach the child rhymes and alphabet songs. Encourage scribbling and tracing letters on paper.

Talk about school. You can increase children's reading success by helping them look forward to school as a happy place. Always talk about school in a pleasant, positive way.

Monitor performance. It's important to keep tabs on children's school performance and make sure that they do their homework correctly. Visit teachers and observe classrooms periodically.

Visit the library. Make weekly trips to the library. Show your child the variety of things to read: books on hobbies, animals, crafts, sports, famous people, etc.

Having a reading hour. Let your child know how important reading is by suggesting reading as a leisure-time activity, or setting aside an established "reading hour" every night, perhaps just before bedtime.

Stay involved. Stay interested and involved in your child's growth as a reader. Encourage your child to read to you. Praise the child's progress. Try to give the child a feeling of "can do" confidence—that's what reading is all about!

To order a descriptive list of the best books published in the past year for preschool through middle-school-age children, send $1.00 to Books for Children, Consumer Information Center, Department 109N, Pueblo, CO 81002.

Source: Office of Educational Research and Improvement, U.S. Department of Education.

Help Your Child Learn to Write Well

Should you help your child with writing? Yes, if you want your child to:

- do well in school.
- enjoy self-expression.
- become more self-reliant.

You know how important writing will be to your child's life. It will be important from first grade through college and throughout adulthood. Writing is:

Practical. Most of us make lists, jot down reminders, and write notes and instructions at least occasionally.

Job-related. Professional and white-collar workers write frequently—preparing memos, letters, briefing papers, sales reports, articles, research reports, proposals, and the like. Most workers do some writing on the job.

Stimulating. Writing helps to provoke thoughts and to organize them logically and concisely.

Social. Most of us write thank-you notes and letters to friends at least now and then.

Therapeutic. It can be helpful to express feelings in writing that cannot be expressed so easily by speaking.

Unfortunately, many schools are unable to give children sufficient instruction in writing. There are various reasons: teachers aren't trained to teach writing skills, writing classes may be too large, it's often difficult to measure writing skills, etc.

Study after study shows that students' writing lacks clarity, coherence, and organization. Only a few students can write persuasive essays or competent business letters. As many as one out of four have serious writing difficulties. And students say they like writing less and less as they go through school.

That's why the Office of Educational Research and Improvement (OERI) suggests that you help your child with writing. OERI believes you, a parent, can make a big difference. You can use helping strategies that are simple and fun. You can use them to help your child learn to write well—and to enjoy doing it! This chapter tells you how.

THINGS TO KNOW

Writing is more than putting words on paper. It's a final stage in the complex process of communicating that begins with *thinking.* Writing is an especially important stage in communication, the intent being to leave no room for doubt. Has any country ratified a verbal treaty?

One of the first means of communication for your child is through drawing. Do encourage the child to draw and to discuss his or her drawings. Ask questions: "What is the boy doing? Does the house look like ours? Can you tell a story about this picture?"

Most children's basic speech patterns are formed by the time they enter school. By that time children speak clearly, recognize most letters of the alphabet, and may try to write. Show an interest in, and ask questions about, the things your child says, draws, and may try to write. Writing well requires:

Clear thinking. Sometimes the child needs to have his or her memory refreshed about a past event in order to write about it.

Sufficient time. Children may have "stories in their heads" but need time to think them through and write them down. School class periods are often not long enough.

Reading. Reading can stimulate a child to write about his or her own family or school life. If your child reads good books, he or she will be a better writer.

A meaningful task. A child needs meaningful, not artificial, writing tasks. You'll find suggestions for such tasks in the section "Things To Do."

Interest. All the time in the world won't help if there is nothing to write, nothing to say. Some of the reasons for writing include sending messages, keeping records, expressing feelings, and relaying information.

Practice. And more practice.

Revising. Students need experience in revising their work—i.e., seeing what they can do to make it clearer, more descriptive, more concise, etc.

POINTERS FOR PARENTS

In helping your child to learn to write well, remember that your goal is to make writing easier and more enjoyable.

Provide a place. It's important for a child to have a good place to write—a desk or table with a smooth, flat surface and good lighting.

Have the materials. Provide plenty of paper—lined and unlined—and things to write with, including pencils, pens, and crayons.

Allow time. Help your child spend time thinking about a writing project or exercise. Good writers do a great deal of thinking. Your child may dawdle, sharpen a pencil, get papers ready, or look up the spelling of a word. Be patient—your child may be thinking.

Respond. Do respond to the ideas your child expresses verbally or in writing. Make it clear that you are interested in the true function of writing, which is to convey ideas. This means focusing on *what* the child has written, not *how* it was written. It's usually wise to ignore minor errors, particularly at the stage when your child is just getting ideas together.

Don't you write it! Don't write a paper for your child that will be turned in as his or her work. Never rewrite a child's work. Meeting a writing deadline, taking responsibility for the finished product, and feeling ownership of it are important parts of writing well.

Praise. Take a positive approach and say something good about your child's writing. Is it accurate? Descriptive? Thoughtful? Interesting? Does it say someting?

THINGS TO DO

Make it real. Your child needs to do real writing. It's more important for the child to write a letter to a relative than it is to write a one-line note on a greeting card. Encourage the child to write to relatives and friends. Perhaps your child would enjoy corresponding with a pen pal.

Suggest note-taking. Encourage your child to take notes on trips or outings and to describe what he or she saw. This could include a description of nature walks, a boat ride, a car trip, or other events that lend themselves to note-taking.

Brainstorm. Talk with your child as much as possible about his or her impressions and encourage the child to describe people and events to you. If the child's description is especially accurate and colorful, say so.

Encourage keeping a journal. This is excellent writing practice as well as a good outlet for venting feelings. Encourage your child to write about things that happen at home and school, about people he or she likes or dislikes and why, or about things to remember or what the child wants to do. Especially encourage your child to write about personal feelings—pleasures as well as disappointments. If the child wants to share the journal with you, read the entries and discuss them—especially the child's ideas and perceptions.

Write together. Have your child help you with letters, even such routine ones as ordering items from an advertisement or writing to a business firm. This helps the child to see firsthand that writing is important to adults and truly useful.

Use games. There are numerous games and puzzles that can help a child to increase vocabulary and become more fluent in speaking and writing. Remember, building a vocabulary builds confidence. Try crossword puzzles, word games, anagrams, and cryptograms designed especially for children. Flash cards are good, too, and they're easy to make at home.

Suggest making lists. Most children like to make lists just as they like to count. Encourage this. Making lists is good practice and helps a child to become more organized. Boys and girls might make lists of their records, tapes, baseball cards, dolls, furniture in a room, etc. They could include items they want. It's also good practice to make lists of things to do, schoolwork, dates for tests, social events, and other reminders.

Encourage copying. If a child likes a particular song, suggest learning the words by writing them down—replaying the song on your stereo or tape player, or jotting down the words whenever the song is played on a radio program. Also encourage copying favorite poems or quotations from books and plays.

Source: Office of Educational Research and Improvement, U.S. Department of Education.

Help Your Child Learn Math

Your child probably loves games, and puzzles, too. That's why it's helpful to connect the games and puzzles played at home with the math taught in school.

You can help make "the math connection" so that your child will find it easier to learn and like math.

What to do?

The Office of Educational Research and Improvement (OERI) believes the most important thing you can do is to reinforce the math lessons your child receives in school. You needn't be a teacher or a mathematical genius. Just use the "helping" strategies described in this chapter.

These strategies are best for helping first-, second-, and third-graders, but they may be useful also for an older child who has difficulty with math.

IT COMES NATURALLY!

Math is learned naturally by the inventive, curious mind. Preschoolers are easy and confident with numbers. They love to count and use counting in a number of ways. By the time they enter kindergarten, they have many practical—but informal—math skills. For example:

- They can deal comfortably with situations requiring an idea of what is largest, smallest, tallest, longest, inside, outside, closest, farthest, and the like.
- They can do simple addition and subtraction by counting and looking at actual objects—apples, pencils, books, etc.
- They can estimate proportions for groups of objects—for example, they can tell that a group of 10 marbles is closer in size to a group of 12 marbles than a group of 12 is to 20.
- They can correctly count to 10 and beyond, and many can count to 14 or more.

However, they do not have an adult's understanding of what numbers mean, and they are easily distracted by irrelevant detail. So don't be surprised if a preschooler fails to see that the number of marbles in a row doesn't increase when the row is spread out . . . or decrease when the marbles are crowded together.

Essentials

Three things are essential for a child to learn math and all three are things you can help reinforce:

Understanding. The child must understand the steps involved in working and solving a math problem. If the child's ability to solve problems is based solely on memorization without understanding, the ability won't carry over from one problem to another.

Practice. This means practicing the base skills—addition, subtraction, multiplication, division, fractions, and decimals—so that the child can learn and remember them and then use them correctly.

Seeing patterns. Children need to see patterns and regularity in math and ways of organizing mathematical information. Math builds and extends simple ideas into more general concepts.

Good problem-solvers have certain things in common. They are quick to understand the important features of a problem, they approach a problem with confidence, and they can transfer their learning from one problem to another. When they get an answer to a problem, they know whether the answer is reasonable because they estimate well.

Counting

Counting is a mixed blessing. It's essential for learning addition and subtraction. It becomes a detriment only for children who rely on it too heavily—especially, on fingercounting—so that they never adopt more efficient ways of doing math. (For one thing, they are slower than other students and can't work as many problems.)

What is counting? It's not just reciting a string of numbers. It includes such things as matching objects and arriving at totals. Research has identified six stages that a child must go through in counting, beginning with rote-counting (1,2,3,4, etc.) and becoming progressively more sophisticated (for example, counting up 7 from 44 to 51 or counting back 3 from 12 to get 9). Following this, the child is ready for open addition problems such as $13 + ? = 19$.

To help your child develop confidence in counting, use concrete objects and examples. Drop 5 marbles in a jar and have the child count as you drop additional marbles in the jar: 6, 7,

8, 9, etc. Use rhymes and songs like the one that begins "One, two, buckle my shoe . . . ."

If the child has trouble keeping a mental tally when counting from one number to another, suggest reciting the first number in a soft voice and the next numbers in a progressively louder voice.

Use familiar, repetitious situations to reinforce counting. Encourage the child to count with the secondhand as it sweeps around the clock. Count the dishes on the table. Count the number of cookies in a box . . . the bikes in a bike rack . . . the leaves on a plant.

Have the child touch each object as it is counted. Arrange the objects in various positions—in lines, in rows, in circles, and randomly. This will assist the child's understanding of numbers.

Estimating & Measuring

Estimation is one of the cornerstones of math. It can enrich counting, measurement, and problem-solving abilities. A child who can make a good estimate of the answer to a problem clearly understands the problem. Children who can estimate are able to reject unreasonable answers and know when they are "in the ballpark."

Despite the importance of estimation, few schools stress it. Those schools that use estimation in teaching arithmetic generally don't introduce it soon enough. Yet even children in kindergarten can correctly estimate relative sizes and proportions.

You can help your child develop estimation skills by helping him or her practice rounding numbers to the nearest 1, 10, or 100. This is a strategic step in acquiring this skill.

Practice estimation with your child. "How many marbles do you think are in the jar?" "Who is taller, your father or mother?" "Which is wider—the door or the table?"

Measurement is also essential, and many children are weak in this area. You can help your child with measurement by making comparisons. Ask if the child has "too much" or "too little" of something and if an object is "too short" or "too long." A typical comparison might be: "Which will require more paper to cover, the bulletin board or the door?"

Help your child practice measuring things that are longer than the measuring instrument, such as a meter stick. Include measurements that involve fractions other than one-half.

Make a floor plan of your house or apartment with your child's help. Have the child take the measurements with a tape measure while you write down the dimensions.

Time is among the things to be measured. Discuss time with your child rather than "telling time": "It takes Mother 45 minutes to get to work. When should she leave the house to get to the office by 9:00? When should she leave the office in order to get home by 6:30?"

Age is another measurement. Ask how old the child is in months . . . weeks . . . days . . . hours . . . minutes. (Many experts suggest practicing exercises of this kind with a calculator.)

Correcting Mistakes

Find out what kinds of mistakes your child makes in arithmetic. Use an arithmetic book to find easier problems of the same type, and have the child rework those problems. Make sure your child understands a simpler problem before going to a more difficult one.

Ask the child to describe how to work a problem, step by step. Doing this may help the child to identify the error. While the child is doing this, look for patterns in errors, because one misunderstanding may cause others like it.

If a child consistently makes a subtraction error ($25 - 16 = 19$) and you are not sure whether this is from carelessness or lack of understanding, use objects to work with the child. Place 25 marbles in a jar and ask the child to remove 16. Make sure that the child checks the subtraction with addition ($19 + 16 = ?$).

If your child has difficulty with word problems, remind him or her to concentrate on the information that is essential to solving the problem. Sometimes a problem includes irrelevant information that confuses the child.

Do's and Don'ts

Do ask your child's teacher about the kinds of help that you as a parent can provide. Your role is to reinforce and help your child practice the things taught at school.

Do encourage a child to restate what a mathematical word problem is all about—the information it gives and the information it asks for. Putting it in the child's own words will help clarify it.

Do make sure that "home" math has a noticeable problem-solving flavor. It should contain a challenge or question that must be answered. ("How many nickels do you have in your bank? How many do you need to buy an ice-cream cone?")

Do use objects that your child can touch, handle, and move. Researchers call these things "manipulatives," and they can be any familiar object such as soft toys, blocks, marbles, drinking straws, fruit, etc.

Do reward your child with praise for the correct answers. This helps build the child's confidence in problem-solving.

Don't tell your child that some people are "no good" in math. Never tell your child you are "no good" in math, no matter how low your opinion is of your own skills!

Don't think that girls aren't as good in math as boys.

Source: Office of Educational Research and Improvement, U.S. Department of Education.

Help Your Child Do Better in School

Some children do well in school. They learn quickly and remember facts; they "catch on."

Some don't do so well. They have trouble paying attention. Their grades are poor. Yet they may be as smart as—or smarter than—their successful classmates.

Why the difference in performance?

It may not be a question of I.Q. but of *behavior* and *attitude*. Research has shown that these qualities affect success in the classroom.

Successful students behave in certain ways. They have the "right" attitude. They're motivated, . . . they pay attention, . . . they're relaxed, . . . they ignore distractions that might interfere with learning. And, when they need help with schoolwork, they know how to get it.

None of those things are *inborn,* but they can be learned. And you, as a parent, can help a child learn them.

The Office of Educational Research and Improvement (OERI) offers four steps children can take to become better students. They are for children of all grades. They will sound simple, because they are. But they can make a world of difference to your youngsters.

You can teach your children strategies for the four steps:

- Paying attention
- Keeping interested in schoolwork
- Learning and remembering
- Studying

Paying Attention

Children can learn the knack of paying attention. Never threaten or order them to "pay attention" in school, as it won't work! Some simple techniques will.

Using self-talk and positive images. Children can use words or phrases to help control attention. For example, they can tell themselves to keep their eyes on the blackboard while the teacher is writing on it to explain a problem. You can help them practice positive self-talk at home in various situations: when playing a game, helping around the house, or working at a hobby.

Help them stop negative self-talk ("It's hopeless") and to be positive about themselves, to say, "I can do it." Positive self-talk might include the slogan "Quitters don't win and winners don't quit."

No more negative images, either! Children can and must learn to see themselves doing well in school. Tell them to picture themselves answering questions correctly in class and feeling good about knowing the answers. Spend time talking with them about their successes, as well as their difficulties.

Asking questions. This helps children focus their attention while studying. When reading about World War II, students might ask themselves "Which countries were our friends and allies? Which were Germany's? Which countries did Germany occupy?"

You can suggest general questions to a child, such as: "What is this paragraph about? Who did what and why? Is the main point true or false?" Asking questions can grab *wandering* attention.

Setting specific study goals. Your children can set goals that will help improve attention. Ask them to study a lesson until they can tell you the main point of the paragraph, solve a specific math problem, or know specific names, dates, and places mentioned in the text. Discuss each goal. Remember that many small goals, one after another, are better than a single large one.

Keeping Interested

Learning is a joint effort. Everyone must help if students are to learn. Teachers are responsible for teaching and parents for parenting, but students must realize that no one else can do their learning for them.

Children must *believe* that the hours they spend studying and the effort they put into it make the difference between success and failure. Some youngsters believe other things control success or failure—teachers, basic intelligence, or luck. They ignore their own responsibility.

You can help your children accept the fact that their efforts *do* make a difference. The next time they bring home test results, written comments, or report cards, discuss the reasons *why* they did well or poorly. Help them relate their efforts to the result.

Do reward a child for improvement. Your praise is music to your child's ears. You might consider treats or trips or privileges for special achievements. Do stress the benefits of doing well in school. Some benefits are immediate, such as having more free time, and some are long-term, such as getting a scholarship or an interesting job.

Remembering

OERI research has shown that a child's success in school is determined not just by intelligence but by the *strategies* he or she uses to master many facts and ideas.

Understanding a subject doesn't just happen. It takes work. It requires taking an interest in the subject and relating new information to familiar information.

Besides teaching the strategies for paying attention, you can help your child use various strategies to remember. You can decide how best to adapt a particular strategy.

Here are the strategies:

Making inferences. Encourage your children to try to draw conclusions from the material they are studying. When they are reading about an invention—perhaps the telephone—they could consider what people would do without telephones.

Building bridges. It helps children to build a bridge between the new and the old—between new information and things they already know. They should look for similarities between the new and the familiar. For example, a child studying our court system could relate the judge's role in settling disputes to his or her own experience with arguments and disagreements.

Finding the main ideas. As students listen or read, they must frequently ask themselves, "What's the point being made here?" By constantly looking for the main idea, they concentrate on learning the important material. This also helps to keep them actively engaged in studying.

Categorizing information. Many school activities involve learning and remembering large amounts of information. Sometimes there are long lists of names and dates. When there are many items of information to learn, students should group them in categories. Students in beginning music classes don't try to remember the names and characteristics of every musical instrument, but group them: percussion, woodwinds, strings, and brass. Your children should try this technique in subjects ranging from geography to English to math.

Studying

Your children need a place to study. Whether you live in a one-bedroom apartment or a sprawling ranchhouse, you can set aside a study area. It can be a desk in a bedroom or the kitchen table, but it must be fairly quiet with good light.

Children also need a *time for studying.* Help your children create schedules. If they set aside time for chores, work, fun, and study on a weekly basis, they can make better use of their time. These schedules should be flexible enough to allow trade-offs and shifts when necessary.

Previewing material. Encourage children to begin an assignment by previewing the material—for example, by reading the introduction to a chapter, the headings, and summary. This is like looking at a road map. Here they create a mental "map" of what is ahead. They complete the "map's" details when they read the chapter.

Reading and thinking. When reading a chapter, they should try to fit details into their mental "map." This is the time to use the attention-grabbing strategies—self-talk, positive images, and questions. It helps if they pause before each new section to "test" their understanding. Using the strategies for learning and remembering, they can ask: "What conclusions can I draw from this? How should I categorize the information? Do I see analogies? What are the main ideas?"

Taking notes. Children can't remember everything they read. It will help them, though, to take notes of the main points. These notes serve as a summary of the most important points. The act of taking them and reviewing them will help the student to categorize the material, understand, and remember it. And the notes will help in preparing for tests.

Self-testing. Children should test themselves to see what they know and don't know. They can then apply their study time more efficiently to the sections on which they are weakest. You can help by making up test questions, for example, "What are the chief food products of the country being studied? Why? Do we use these in our home?"

Preparing for tests. Encourage your children to prepare for tests by spacing studying over days or weeks. They should make sure they understand the material and relate it to what they already know. They should review it more than once. "Cramming" the night before is not a good idea, and it is important to get a good night's sleep.

Source: Office of Educational Research and Improvement, U.S. Department of Education.

Help Your Child Improve in Test-Taking

Test. It's a loaded word. Important . . . something to care about . . . something that can mean so much we get apprehensive thinking about it.

Tests are important, especially to schoolchildren. A test may measure a basic skill. It can affect a year's grade. Or, if it measures the ability to learn, it can affect a child's placement in school. So it's important to do well on tests.

Besides, the ability to do well on tests can help throughout life in such things as getting a driver's license, trying out for sports, or getting a job. Without this ability, a person can be severely handicapped.

Your child can develop this ability. And you can help the child do it. Just try the simple techniques developed through Office of Educational Research and Improvement (OERI) research. This chapter tells you how.

WHY TEST?

It's helpful for a child to understand why schools give tests, and to know the different kinds of tests.

Tests are a yardstick. Schools use them to measure, and then improve, education. Some tell schools that they need to strengthen courses or change teaching techniques. Other tests compare students by school, school district, or city. All tests determine how well *your child* is doing. And that's very important.

Most of the tests your child will take are "teacher-made." That is, teachers design them. These tests are associated with the grades on report cards. They help measure a student's progress—telling the teacher and the student whether he or she is keeping up with the class, needs extra help, or, perhaps, is far ahead of other students.

Now and then your child will take "standardized" tests. These use the same standards to measure student performance across the country. Everyone takes the same test according to the same rules. This makes it possible to measure each student's performance against that of others. The group with whom a student's performance is compared is a "norm group" and consists of many students of the same age or grade who took the same test.

Ask the School

It could be useful for you to know the school's policies and practices on giving standardized tests and the use of test scores. Ask your child's teacher or guidance counselor about the kinds of tests your child will take during the year—and the schedule for testing.

One other thing: some schools give students practice in taking tests. This helps to make sure that they are familiar with directions and test format. Find out whether your child's school gives "test-taking practice" on a regular basis or will provide such practice if your child needs it.

Avoid Test Anxiety

It's good to be concerned about taking a test. It's not good to get "test anxiety." This is excessive worry about doing well on a test and it can mean disaster for a student.

Students who suffer from test anxiety tend to worry about success in school, especially doing well on tests. They worry about the future and are extremely self-critical. Instead of feeling challenged by the prospect of success, they become afraid of failure. This makes them anxious about tests and their own abilities. Ultimately, they become so worked up that they feel incompetent about the subject matter or the test.

It doesn't help to tell the child to relax, to think about something else, or to stop worrying. But there are ways to reduce test anxiety. Encourage your child to do these things:

- Space studying over days or weeks. (Real learning occurs through studying that takes place over a period of time.) Understand the information and relate it to what is already known. Review it more than once. (By doing this, the student should feel prepared at exam time.)
- Don't "cram" the night before—cramming increases anxiety, which interferes with clear thinking. Get a good night's sleep. Rest, exercise, and eating well are as important to test-taking as they are to other schoolwork.
- Read the directions carefully when the teacher hands out the test. If you don't understand them, ask the teacher to explain.

- Look quickly at the entire examination to see what types of questions are included (multiple choice, matching, true/false, essay) and, if possible, the number of points for each. This will help you pace yourself.
- In taking an essay exam, read all the questions first and use the margin for noting phrases that relate to the answers. These phases will help in writing the essay answer.
- If you don't know the answer to a question, skip it and go on. Don't waste time worrying about it. Mark it so you can identify it as unanswered. If you have time at the end of the exam, return to the unanswered question(s).

Do's and Don'ts

You can be a great help to your children if you will observe these do's and don'ts about tests and testing:

- Don't be too anxious about a child's test scores. Placing too much emphasis on test scores can upset a child.
- Do encourage children. Praise them for the things they do well. If they feel good about themselves, they will do their best. Children who are afraid of failing are more likely to become anxious when taking tests and more likely to make mistakes.
- Don't judge a child on the basis of a single test score. Test scores are not perfect measures of what a child can do. There are many other things that might influence a test score. For example, a child can be affected by the way he or she is feeling, the setting in the classroom, and the attitude of the teacher. Remember, also, that one test is simply one test.
- Meet with your child's teacher as often as possible to discuss his or her progress. Ask the teacher to suggest activities for you and your child to do at home to help prepare for tests and improve your child's understanding of schoolwork. Parents and teachers should work together to benefit students.
- Make sure your child attends school regularly. Remember, tests do reflect children's overall achievement. The more effort and energy a child puts into learning, the more likely he or she will do well on tests.

- Provide a quiet, comfortable place for studying at home.
- Make sure that your child is well rested on school days and especially the day of a test. Children who are tired are less able to pay attention in class or to handle the demands of a test.
- Give your child a well-rounded diet. A healthy body leads to a healthy, active mind. Most schools provide free breakfast and lunch for economically disadvantaged students. If you believe your child qualifies, talk to the school principal.
- Provide books and magazines for your youngster to read at home. By reading new materials, a child will learn new words that might appear on a test. Ask your child's school about a suggested outside reading list or get suggestions from the public library.

After the Test

It's important for children to review test results. This is especially true when they take teacher-made tests. They can learn from a graded exam paper. It will show where they had difficulty and, perhaps, why. This is especially important for classes where the material builds from one section to the next, as in math. Students who have not mastered the basics of math will be unable to work with fractions, square roots, beginning algebra, and so on.

Discuss the wrong answers with your children and find out why they answered as they did. Sometimes a child misunderstands the way a question is worded or misinterprets what was asked. The child may have known the correct answer but failed to express it effectively.

It's important, too, for children to see how well they used their time on the test and whether guessing was a good idea. This helps them to change what they do on the next test, if necessary.

You and the child should read and discuss all comments written by the teacher. If there are any comments that aren't clear, the child should ask the teacher to explain.

Source: Office of Educational Research and Improvement, U.S. Department of Education.

James Madison
Elementary School:
A Model Curriculum

The Program in Brief: A Plan for Kindergarten through Grade 8

SUBJECT	KINDERGARTEN THROUGH GRADE 3	GRADES 4 THROUGH 6	GRADES 7 AND 8
ENGLISH	INTRODUCTION TO READING AND WRITING (phonics, silent and oral reading, basic rules of grammar and spelling, vocabulary, writing and penmanship, elementary composition, and library skills)	INTRODUCTION TO CRITICAL READING (children's literature, independent reading and book reports; more advanced grammar, spelling and vocabulary; and composition skills)	Grade 7: SURVEY OF ELEMENTARY GRAMMAR AND COMPOSITION Grade 8: SURVEY OF ELEMENTARY LITERARY ANALYSIS
SOCIAL STUDIES	INTRODUCTION TO HISTORY, GEOGRAPHY, AND CIVICS (significant Americans, explorers; native Americans; American holidays, customs, and symbols; citizenship; and landscape, climate, and mapwork)	Grade 4: U.S. HISTORY TO CIVIL WAR Grade 5: U.S. HISTORY SINCE 1865 Grade 6: WORLD HISTORY TO THE MIDDLE AGES	Grade 7: WORLD HISTORY FROM THE MIDDLE AGES TO 1900 Grade 8: WORLD GEOGRAPHY and U.S. CONSTITUTIONAL GOVERNMENT
MATHEMATICS	INTRODUCTION TO MATHEMATICS (numbers, basic operations; fractions and decimals; rounding, geometric shapes; measurement of length, area, and volume; bar graphs; and estimation and elementary statistics)	INTERMEDIATE ARITHMETIC AND GEOMETRY (number theory; negative numbers, percentages, and exponents; line graphs; the Pythagorean theorem; and basic probability)	*Two from among the following one-year courses:* GENERAL MATH, PRE-ALGEBRA, and ALGEBRA
SCIENCE	INTRODUCTION TO SCIENCE (plants and animals, the food chain, the solar system, rocks and minerals, weather, magnets, energy and motion, properties of matter, and simple experiments)	Grade 4: EARTH SCIENCE AND OTHER TOPICS Grade 5: LIFE SCIENCE AND OTHER TOPICS Grade 6: PHYSICAL SCIENCE AND OTHER TOPICS	Grade 7: BIOLOGY Grade 8: CHEMISTRY AND PHYSICS
FOREIGN LANGUAGE	[OPTIONAL]	INTRODUCTION TO FOREIGN LANGUAGE (basic vocabulary, grammar, reading, writing, conversation, and cultural material)	FORMAL LANGUAGE STUDY *Two years strongly recommended*
FINE ARTS	MUSIC AND VISUAL ART (songs, recordings, musical sounds and instruments, painting, craftmaking, and visual effects)	MUSIC AND VISUAL ART (great composers, musical styles and forms, elementary music theory, great painters, interpretation of art, and creative projects)	MUSIC APPRECIATION and ART APPRECIATION *One semester of each required*
PHYSICAL EDUCATION/HEALTH	PHYSICAL EDUCATION AND HEALTH (body control, fitness, sports, games, and exercises, sportsmanship, safety, hygiene, nutrition, and drug prevention education)	PHYSICAL EDUCATION AND HEALTH (team and individual sports, first aid, drug prevention education, and appropriate sex education)	PHYSICAL EDUCATION AND HEALTH (strategy in team sports, gymnastics, aerobics, self-assessment for health, drug prevention education, and appropriate sex education)

SUBJECT DESCRIPTIONS

English

Kindergarten

Preparation for reading and writing. Elementary phonics is introduced and letter–sound associations are emphasized. A significant part of each day is devoted to teacher-directed storytime, which stimulates students' interest in reading and gives them an opportunity to experience and discuss various forms of imaginative literature: fables, fairy tales, poems, short stories, and nursery rhymes. Teachers' transcriptions of student stories provide first experiences with the process of writing. Students are introduced to the school library, where they learn its layout and rules and the proper care of books.

Grade 1

Phonics instruction continues, integrated with a carefully designed program of reading and writing. Students build vocabulary while they read—silently and aloud—a variety of stories, poetry, fairy tales, folk tales, and legends. Grammar is introduced: nouns, verbs, and their agreement; elementary rules of punctuation and capitalization; and simple sentence structure. Instruction in writing begins and includes attention to the alphabet, handwriting, spelling, syllabification, and the reinforcement of grammatical lessons through short writing assignments (sentences, story summaries, and creative and descriptive exercises). Students visit the library regularly and borrow books for independent reading.

Grade 2

Phonics instruction is completed and students begin to read silently for longer periods of time. Group reading of imaginative literature emphasizes the development of interpretive skills: making generalizations, drawing inferences, and determining character motivation and plot sequence. Vocabulary and spelling work is done both in the context of readings and in isolation. Instruction in grammar covers word order, pronouns and their antecedents, adjectives, contractions, and possessives. Cursive writing is introduced, and student writing assignments include stories, poems, letters, and simple book reports. Children have frequent opportunities to share their reading and writing with classmates. During library visits, students learn to identify books by their titles, authors, and illustrators.

Grade 3

Students expand vocabulary and comprehension skills while they read and discuss various literary forms: fables, legends, poems, plays, and nonfiction articles. Reading work includes exercise in choral speaking to allow children to refine their oral language abilities. Grammatical instruction covers subject and predicate rules and the function of adverbs. Attention to spelling and penmanship continues. Lessons in writing emphasize formal process (outlining, drafting, revising, and editing) and more advanced compositional skills: word selection (synonyms, antonyms, and homonyms); detailing; and paragraphing. Independent reading and writing are a significant part of each day. At the library, students learn basic reference skills with tables of contents, indexes, atlases, dictionaries, encyclopedias, and the card catalog.

Grade 4

An introduction to critical reading, with selections from classic children's literature: adventure and animal stories, fables, legends, myths, and tall tales. Students identify story structure, examine cause–effect relationships, and distinguish fact from fiction. Topics in grammar include compound subjects and predicates, and verb tenses. Spelling work introduces etymology as a tool. Students continue to refine handwriting and vocabulary. Writing assignments emphasize the construction of introductions and conclusions in creative and expository composition and introduce more advanced techniques like summarization and dialogue. Independent reading and writing are a significant part of each day. Students use library visits to prepare written and oral book reports.

Grade 5

A continued introduction to critical reading, with selections from a variety of new and familiar genres and styles: short stories, essays, plays, short novels, and biographies. Students investigate plot and characterization in detail, interpret figurative speech and conditional statements, and distinguish stated and implied main ideas. Grammatical lessons include inverted word order, direct and indirect objects, conjunctions, prepositions, and prepositional phrases. Written work emphasizes research skills and revision, and students are expected fully to apply their knowledge of grammar, spelling, and vocabulary to final drafts. Speaking exercises require students to deliver a short original talk before their classmates. Independent reading and writing are a significant part of each day. Students continue to use library visits to prepare written and oral book reports.

Grade 6

A review of reading skills developed in the early grades, and an introduction to classical mythology and simple lyric, narrative, and dramatic poetry. Reading selections serve as subjects for a variety of writing assignments, including short essays, narratives, letters, and book reviews. Speaking exercises require students to memorize and recite selected short poems. Students hone library skills (bibliographies and note-taking) during preparation of a research project. Topics in grammar include irregular verbs and the subjunctive mood. Independent reading and writing are a significant part of each day.

Grade 7

A thorough survey of elementary grammar and composition. Students diagram sentences; review the parts of speech and the structure of sentences; learn the active and passive voices; and study verbals (infinitives, participles, and gerunds), independent clauses, and subordinate clauses. Readings in literature serve as models of good writing and as subjects for students' own frequent writing exercises, including short essays, book reviews, and a research paper. Instruction in composition covers topic sentences, supporting ideas, transitions, varied sentence structure, conclusions, and the development of individual style. Students are given continued experience in classroom speaking and use of the library.

Grade 8

A survey of elementary literary analysis. Students read, discuss, and interpret a careful selection of novels, short stories, essays, plays, and poetry. Classwork emphasizes close reading of each work for theme, style, point of view, plot, setting, character, mood, irony, and imagery. Readings serve as models of fine composition and as subjects for writing assignments that stress a mastery of elementary vocabulary, grammar, usage, mechanics, description, persuasion, narration, and exposition. Students are given continued experience in classroom speaking and use of the library.

Social Studies: History, Geography, and Civics

Kindergarten

Preparation for history, geography, and civics. Historical understanding is encouraged by a focus on important holidays and the individuals or groups they celebrate. Geography lessons begin with identification of home and school address and routes between the two, and include the names of community, state, and nation. Students are taught elementary concepts of distance and direction, the globe as a model of the Earth, and simple map-making exercises. Initial citizenship education concerns the importance of school rules; the value of honesty, fair play, hard work, and the Golden Rule; the meaning and importance of the American flag; memorization and understanding of the Pledge of Allegiance; and identification of the President, the White House, and the nation's capital in Washington.

Grade 1

Historical instruction includes attention to American customs through study of traditional and patriotic songs, legends, and folk tales; lessons about daily life in the American past; and a

unit on the beliefs, traditions, and geography of a foreign country. Other lessons in geography teach students to give and follow simple directions; to identify common landforms; and to trace initial connections among landscape, climate, land use, transportation, and commerce. Civics instruction encourages good character through stories about moral problems and their solutions; develops individual responsibility through assignment of classroom chores; identifies familiar American symbols (the bald eagle, the Liberty Bell, the Statue of Liberty, the Capitol, and Uncle Sam); and briefly describes the Constitution and Bill of Rights.

Grade 2

Students expand their understanding of the past through study of the lives and accomplishments of important American leaders (e.g., George Washington, James Madison, Abraham Lincoln, Susan B. Anthony, and Martin Luther King, Jr.) and famous scientists and inventors (e.g., Benjamin Franklin, the Wright Brothers, Henry Ford, Thomas Edison, Alexander Graham Bell, and George Washington Carver). Timelines are used to promote a more concrete understanding of past, present, and future. Where appropriate, students explore their own family backgrounds and discuss the customs, beliefs, and geography of their ancestors' homelands. Further geography instruction teaches students to recognize cardinal directions, map symbols, and physical and cultural distinctions among urban, suburban, and rural areas. Civics instruction focuses on the duties and privileges of citizenship, and voting and elections.

Grade 3

History lessons explore the culture, beliefs, and daily life of selected Native American peoples. Students learn about Columbus, the impact of European settlers' arrival, the influence of Native American traditions on contemporary society, and the location of major Indian tribes and settlements on maps. Additional instruction in geography focuses on the travels and adventures of such significant explorers as Marco Polo, the Vikings, Sir Francis Drake, Balboa, Daniel Boone, Henry Hudson, Lewis and Clark, and Admiral Peary. As they trace the explorers' paths, students refine their map- and globe-reading skills, identifying latitude, longitude, the equator, the continents, the oceans, the hemispheres, and the poles. Civics instruction examines the Massachusetts and Virginia settlements and their ideas about religious tolerance and local government.

Grade 4

Major topics in American history and culture from early settlement to the Civil War, taught through story and textbook readings. Students study the French, Dutch, Spanish, and English settlers; daily life in the colonies; the Declaration of Independence and the American Revolution; the Constitutional Convention; the Louisiana Purchase and westward expansion; the growth of canals and railroads; and the sectional differences preceding the Civil War. Where possible, local and state developments are highlighted. Map work identifies the 13 colonies and follows westward migration and national expansion to the Pacific. Civics covers the functions of the three branches of government, the two-party system, and constitutional issues surrounding slavery.

Grade 5

Major topics in American history and culture from the Civil War to the present, taught through story and textbook readings. Students study events leading to the Civil War; slavery and abolition; the war itself; Reconstruction; the industrial revolution; urbanization and immigration; World War I; the Great Depression and the New Deal; World War II; the Cold War; the civil rights movement; and the war in Vietnam. Where possible, local and state developments are highlighted. Students commit the 50 states and their capitals to memory. Map work identifies Union, border, and Confederate states; traces major military campaigns; and describes source countries of 19th-century immigration. Civics lessons address major constitutional issues and amendments and examine democracy and its adversaries in the 20th century.

Grade 6

Major topics in world history and geography from prehistoric times to the Middle Ages, taught through story and textbook readings. Students study early man; ancient civilizations of the Near East, India, and China; classical Greece and Rome; the growth of Judaism and Christianity; the Byzantine Empire; Charlemagne; the rise of Islam; and early civilizations in Latin America and Africa. Map work traces the growth and decline of civilizations in the ancient world and follows the sea and land trade routes that facilitated the spread of civilization and contact among cultures. Work in civics explores the roots of democracy in the Greek city-state and their contemporary application to American government.

Grade 7

Major topics in world history and geography from the Middle Ages to 1900, through story and textbook readings. Students study feudal Europe, the Renaissance, the Reformation, the scientific revolution, exploration and colonialism, the Enlightenment, the French Revolution, parliamentary democracy in England, the industrial revolution, and the emergence of modern European states. Map work charts the expansion and decline of empires and follows the development of national political boundaries in Europe, Asia, Africa, and South America. Work in civics explores contributions to democracy made by European political thought, and its contemporary application to American government.

Grade 8

Students take both of the following half-year courses:

American Constitutional Government. Study of the U.S. Constitution and discussions of the political structures and principles it establishes: separation of powers, checks and balances, and republican government; duties of congressional representatives and their terms of office; the legislative process; congressional authority and its limits; national elections and the electoral college; the president and vice-president, their terms of office, and their responsibilities; the system of federal courts, due process, and judicial review; and provision for amendments.

World Geography. Students identify, analyze, and compare physical and cultural characteristics of major world regions and major countries in each. Attention is given to international boundaries; capitals and principal cities; major landforms and bodies of water; climate, weather, and natural resources; transportation and communication; commerce and economy; population growth, decline, and shift; major races, languages, cultures, and religions; agriculture; and politics and government.

Mathematics

Kindergarten

Students use woodblocks and other manipulatives to develop number sense and to count and compare the sizes of sets. They solve story problems that introduce simple addition and subtraction, classify objects, identify simple geometric shapes, and learn how to tell time.

Grade 1

Students learn to count, count back, and skip count; estimate and compare the sizes of sets; recognize geometric shapes in a variety of positions; measure and compare lengths; read simple bar graphs; and solve story problems that involve addition and subtraction of one- and two-digit numbers, and are introduced to concepts of simple multiplication and division.

Grade 2

Students learn place value by grouping physical objects; round numbers to the nearest tens and hundreds; master simple addition and subtraction facts; estimate solutions to large-number addition and subtraction problems; solve story problems that involve multiplication and division facts; discuss coins and the money system; and are introduced to fractions. In geometry, students recognize properties of two- and three-dimensional shapes; classify models of plane and solid figures; and learn about edges, sides, and angles.

Grade 3

Students master the multiplication table; develop computational proficiency with two- and three-digit addition and subtraction, two- and three-digit by single-digit multiplication, and division with single-digit divisors; and solve story problems that involve whole number operations, fractions, mixed numbers, and decimals. Manipulatives are used throughout to extend concepts of place value to other bases; to add and subtract decimals; and to find equivalent fractions. In geometry and measurement, students learn units of length, area, volume, weight, and time; measure area and volume using squares and cubes; and interpret bar and picture graphs with units greater than one. Class projects involve the collection, display, and analysis of data and include simple experiments in probability.

Grade 4

Students solve story problems that reinforce whole number operations and fraction and decimal concepts; use estimation and rounding to divide large numbers by two- and three-digit divisors; interpret line graphs; compute mean, median, and mode; and, where and when possible, organize and display graphs and data on computers. In geometry, topics include symmetry, congruence, and parallel and perpendicular lines; acute, right, and obtuse angles; and more advanced characteristics of polygons.

Grade 5

Students explore prime numbers, factors, multiples, the number line, negative numbers, and the concept of infinity; learn percentages and ratios using physical materials and representational models; identify and convert equivalent fractions and decimals; and study more complex probability problems using "hand-on" experiments. In geometry, students estimate angles and make protractor measurements; draw, measure, and compare triangles and quadrilaterals; and, where and when possible, use computer graphing software to model two- and three-dimensional shapes.

Grade 6

Students learn arithmetic and geometric series; the associative, commutative, and distributive properties of numerical expressions; exponents; square and cube root concepts; and basic functional relationships. Story problems involve percentages, ratios, negative numbers, and simple equations with variables. In geometry, topics include the relations among length, area, and volume; features of circles, cylinders, spheres, and cones; the Pythagorean theorem and the angle-sum theorem; and model construction of the regular polyhedra.

Grades 7 and 8

Students take two of the following three full-year courses in sequence, beginning where appropriate with either General Math or Pre-Algebra:

General Math. A thorough review of basic topics in arithmetic and geometry, and their various applications.

Pre-Algebra. Students learn rational and negative exponents, scientific notation, Euclid's algorithm, factorization of linear expressions, and basic principles of formal logic. Story problems involve fractions and decimals; ratio, proportion, and percentage; the order of operations; and linear equations and inequalities. The Cartesian plane is introduced and used to solve problems of location and distance.

Algebra. Students solve quadratic equations by factoring, completing the square, and applying the quadratic formula, and they use substitution and matrices to solve systems of linear equations. Algebraic modeling is used to explore problems of exponential growth and decay. In context of the Cartesian plane, students learn ideas about functions, absolute value, range, and domain; interpret graphs and their relations to corresponding equations; and analyze the effects of parameter changes on graphs of functions. Story problems relate quadratic and linear equations to geometric concepts. Problems in logic are solved using Venn diagrams.

Science

Kindergarten

An introduction to science, with an emphasis on the observation of familiar, everyday things. Students identify common plants and animals; sense organs and their functions; simple topographical features (e.g., mountains, valleys, oceans, and rivers); the sun, Earth, and moon; heat and cold; light and shadow; common colors; and groupings of like objects. Instruction should encourage hands-on discovery and exploration of objects and phenomena.

Grade 1

Topics may include the characteristics and habitats of animals; pet care; the parts and growth patterns of plants; differences between day and night; common weather conditions and climate; properties of water and air; and forms and sources of energy. Students handle and observe growing plants; monitor and record facts of their development; and perform simple experiments involving variations in water, soil, and sunlight, predicting results and testing their hypotheses.

Grade 2

Topics may include seasonal changes and life cycles in various organisms; how seeds mature into plants; differences between vertebrates and invertebrates; the Earth's orbit and its effect on the seasons; the effect of the moon on tides; basic ideas about magnets and magnetism; forces of motion; and simple machines and their inventors. Students construct their own magnetic compasses, use them to determine general directions, and participate in orienteering games and exercises.

Grade 3

Topics may include the growth stages of animals; the food chain; simple rocks and minerals; basic physical and chemical properties of matter, the solar system, planets, moons, stars, and galaxies; important events and achievements in the history of space exploration; and electricity and electric charges. Students collect, compare, classify, and record the shape, size, weight, and texture of different rock and mineral samples.

Grade 4

A special emphasis on the earth sciences. Topics may include rock formation; glaciers; the process of erosion; the creation of fossil fuels; the atmosphere and weather forecasting; and stages of the water cycle (rain, evaporation, and clouds). Additional topics from the life and physical sciences may include the life cycle and behavior of social insects; important bones and muscles of the human body; distinguishing features of comets, asteroids, and meteors; heat as a form of energy; and the idea of heat transfer. Through news reports and, where possible, their own observations and measurements, students monitor changes in local rainfall, temperature, barometric pressure, sunrise and sunset, humidity, and wind speed and direction, and learn simple techniques of weather prediction.

Grade 5

A special emphasis on the life sciences. Topics may include the reproduction of plants and flowers; the process of photosynthesis; the basic structures and functions of the human body; food groups and nutrition; and the evolutionary history of the Earth, including fossils, dinosaurs, and other prehistoric life. Additional topics from the earth and physical sciences may include geological change over time, problems of pollution and conservation, and complex machines and the concept of work. Students examine cross-sections of celery stems and tree tunks, grow mold on bread, observe mushroom spores by making spore prints on paper, compare different types of algae, and investigate water movement through plant and flower roots.

Grade 6

A special emphasis on the physical sciences. Topics may include the atomic theory of matter; states of matter (solid, liquid, and gas); conservation of matter; relations among weight, volume, and density; and simple optics, including telescopes. Additional topics from the life and earth sciences may include the structure of the Earth's crust and plate tectonics; distinctions between living and nonliving things; and instinct and learning in animals. Students explore, record, and graph boiling and freezing points of common substances; examine light filtered through a prism; and observe the reflection and refraction of light rays by mirrors and through lenses.

Grade 7

A broad study of biology as it applies to cells, organisms, and larger life systems. Topics may include the structure of cells; the functions of cellular organelles; elementary concepts in genetics and the role of DNA; embryology and fetal development; the function, structure, and interaction of various organ systems; classification of bacteria, fungi, plants, and animals; the structure of communities within ecological systems; and the major ecological systems of the Earth. Laboratory exercises include observation with microscopes and simple animal dissections.

Grade 8

A broad study of chemistry and physics designed to familiarize students with further atomic and macroscopic properties of matter. Topics may include the metric system of measurement; elementary particles and atomic structure; the periodic table; the structure of molecules; compounds, solutions, and mixtures; chemical reactions; Newton's first law; potential and kinetic energy; cells, batteries, and electricity; and the motion and octaves of sound waves. Students generate and observe simple chemical reactions, isolate various substances from solutions and mixtures, and measure the effects of different weights on the arc of a pendulum, synthesizing previous laboratory work into formal principles of scientific method and procedure (hypothesis formation, identification of necessary tools and materials, testing and retesting, data collection and analysis, and concluding written reports).

Foreign Language

Grades 4 through 6

An introduction to one foreign language, with a strong initial emphasis on pronunciation, intonation, conversation and dialogue, and vocabulary building. Grammar begins with simple verbs and sentence structure. Students read and write short passages. Attention is paid to elementary cultural material from countries in which the language is national or widespread, including children's games, folk songs for choral singing, fairy tales, legends, and simple arts and crafts.

Grades 7 and 8

Two full-year elective courses of formal language instruction, building on previously acquired skills. Together these courses cover material studied in the first year of high school foreign language: more advanced vocabulary, grammar, syntax, and constructions; extended conversation; selections of foreign literature; writing assignments; elementary translations; and frequent cultural lessons.

Fine Arts

Kindergarten through Grade 3

An introduction to basic ideas and skills in music and art. Music lessons familiarize students with rhythm and melody through classroom songs, recordings, and experiments with simple percussion instruments; teach students to identify musical instruments by their shape and composition; and introduce distinctions among pitch, volume, and timbre in musical sound. Art lessons include exercises in painting, drawing, and craftmaking; instruction in shape, color, form, texture, and the visual effects they create; examples of sculpture, painting, photography, design, and architecture that illustrate these effects; and first attempts to identify and describe content in works of art. Where and when possible, field trips are made to museum art exhibits and concerts.

Grades 4 through 6

Continued study of music and art. Music lessons familiarize students with the lives and works of selected great composers; teach them to recognize different musical styles and forms; introduce recordings of music from other countries and cultures; demonstrate how sounds are made and notes are played on various musical instruments; and begin a hands-on investigation of elementary theory—including such ideas as harmony, tempo, key, and simple notation—as applied to music heard and studied in class. Art lessons familiarize students with selected great painters, sculptors, architects, and photographers; refine their ability to look at art and interpret it; and provide classroom opportunities for work on creative projects in a variety of media, with emphasis on elements present in the works of art they have viewed—perspective, proportion, scale, symmetry, motion, color, and light. Where and when possible, field trips are made to museum art exhibits and concerts.

Grades 7 and 8

Students take both of the following two half-year courses in the theory, history, and practice of music and art:

Art Appreciation. An introduction to major developments in the Western visual arts, from prehistoric drawings to the present day. Classroom activities include short readings that expand the vocabulary of art history, biography, and criticism; examinations of a small number of works in detail through film, slides, or museum trips; and instruction in techniques of drawing, color-mixing, and painting.

Music Appreciation. An introduction to major developments in Western music, from earliest surviving examples to the present day. Classroom activities include short readings that expand the vocabulary of music history, biography, and criticism; examinations of a small number of works in detail through recordings, classroom performance, or concert trips; and instruction in elementary techniques of composition and instrumentation.

Physical Education/Health

Kindergarten through Grade 3

A general program on physical and health education. Physical education activities cover body control (rhythm, flexibility, agility, balance, direction, speed, and intensity); simple sports skills (running, jumping, throwing, catching, and kicking); and basic games and exercises (rope jumping, footraces, dances, and gymnastics). Instruction should encourage fitness, respect for rules, sportsmanship, safety, and use and care of sports equipment. Topics in health include hygiene; nutrition; parts of the body and ideas about growth; disease prevention; first aid and safety; the dangers of alcohol, tobacco, and illegal drugs; and rest and exercise.

Grades 4 through 6

A general program of physical and health education. Physical education activities apply previously learned skills to common team and individual sports; teach the terminology and rules associated with each game; introduce further dances and gymnastic exercises; and continue to emphasize fitness, respect for rules, sportsmanship, safety, and use and care of sports equipment. Topics in health include hygiene; nutrition; disease prevention; first aid and safety; peer resistance and individual responsibility in connection with alcohol, tobacco, and illegal drugs; and rest and exercise. Lessons about sexual maturation—taught according to community standards and with parental involvement and approval—should provide basic information about physiological and psychological changes associated with puberty; conception, pregnancy, and childbirth; and the importance of the family.

Grades 7 and 8

A general program of physical and health education. Physical education activities refine strategy, skills, and understanding of rules in selected team and individual sports; introduce further dance and gymnastic exercises for coordination and aerobics; and continue to emphasize fitness, respect for rules, sportsmanship, safety, and use and care of sports equipment. Topics in health include hygiene; nutrition; identification and prevention of common, chronic, and communicable diseases; first aid, safety, and emergency medical care; the dangers of alcohol, tobacco, and illegal drugs to individuals and society; rest and exercise; and self-assessment of weight, blood pressure, and other indicators of general health. Sex education—taught according to community standards and with parental involvement and approval—should provide basic information about the biological "facts of life" in an open, serious, and moral context, emphasizing responsibility, awareness of emotional and medical considerations, and the importance of the family.

Source: James Madison Elementary School: A Curriculum for American Students (1988). U.S. Department of Education.

James Madison High School: A Model Curriculum

The Program in Brief: A Four-Year Plan

SUBJECT	1st YEAR	2nd YEAR	3rd YEAR	4th YEAR
ENGLISH	Introduction to Literature	American Literature	British Literature	Introduction to World Literature
SOCIAL STUDIES	Western Civilization	American History	Principles of American Democracy *(1 sem.)* and American Democracy & the World *(1 sem.)*	
MATHEMATICS	Three Years Required from among the Following Courses: Algebra I, Plane & Solid Geometry, Algebra II & Trigonometry, Statistics & Probability *(1 sem.)*, Pre-Calculus *(1 sem.)*, and Calculus AB or BC			
SCIENCE	Three Years Required from among the Following Courses: Astronomy/Geology, Biology, Chemistry, and Physics or Principles of Technology			
FOREIGN LANGUAGE	Two Years Required in a Single Language from among Offerings Determined by Local Jurisdictions			
PHYSICAL EDUCATION/HEALTH	Physical Education/Health 9	Physical Education/Health 10		
FINE ARTS	Art History *(1 sem.)* Music History *(1 sem.)*			

This chart describes the James Madison High School curriculum. For each core subject, it shows the number of years required and the names of courses that fulfill them. Each course is two semesters long, except as indicated.

In certain core subjects (English, social studies, and physical education/health), all students are obliged to take particular courses in a set sequence. In other core subjects (mathematics, science, foreign language, and fine arts), the selection of courses and/or their sequence is more flexible. This flexibility permits adjustments for individual student interests, needs, or abilities, and it provides room throughout the four-year pro-gram for elective, supplemental, or locally mandated study within or outside the seven core subjects.

The shaded area above represents room for such classes in a four-year schedule of seven-period days.

Enough Time in the Day? Sample Student Schedules

There are more than 15,000 public school districts in the United States. Roughly half of them organize secondary education around a six-period school day, which permits 48 semester-units of course work over four years. The other half follow a seven-period day, which permits 56 semester-units. Applied to either schedule, the 36 semester-units required by the James Madison High School program leave open at least 25 percent of available class time for supplemental, elective, or locally required study. That's a lot. It should be enough.

Consider the following sample student schedules, based on the more restrictive six-period day. Each of these students fully satisfies James Madison High School requirements. In addition, Student A takes an extra year of physical education/health and studies typing, word processing, bookkeeping, psychology, technical writing, and graphic arts. Student B takes an additional year of math and science and plays in the school band. Student C takes two extra years of a foreign language, a fourth year of math and science, a studio arts class, and computer science. The James Madison High School program prevents none of these students from fully pursuing individual interests, and it should also permit any school or school system substantial flexibility for course design and scheduling.

Student A

9th Grade

Introduction to Literature
Western Civilization
Algebra I
Spanish I
P.E./Health
Typing/Word Processing (*elective*)

10th Grade

American Literature
American History
Astronomy/Geology
Spanish II
P.E./Health
Bookkeeping (*elective*)

11th Grade

British Literature
Principles of American Democracy (*1 sem.*)
American Democracy and the World (*1 sem.*)
Plane and Solid Geometry
Biology
P.E./Health (*elective*)
Psychology (*elective*)

12th Grade

Introduction to World Literature
Algebra II and Trigonometry
Principles of Technology
Art History/Music History
Technical Writing (*elective*)
Graphic Arts (*elective*)

Student B

9th Grade

Introduction to Literature
Western Civilization
Algebra I
Astronomy/Geology
P.E./Health
Band (*elective*)

10th Grade

American Literature
American History
Plane and Solid Geometry
Biology
P.E./Health
Band (*elective*)

11th Grade

British Literature
Principles of American Democracy (*1 sem.*)
American Democracy and the World (*1 sem.*)
Algebra II and Trigonometry
Chemistry
French I
Band (*elective*)

12th Grade

Introduction to World Literature
Statistics and Probability (*1 sem., elective*)
Pre-calculus (*1 sem., elective*)
Physics (*elective*)
French II
Art History/Music History
Band (*elective*)

Continued on page 540

Student C

9th Grade

Introduction to Literature
Western Civilization
Plane and Solid Geometry
Astronomy/Geology
Latin I
P.E./Health

11th Grade

British Literature
Principles of American Democracy (*1 sem.*)
American Democracy and the World (*1 sem.*)
Statistics and Probability (*1 sem.*)
Pre-calculus (*1 sem.*)
Chemistry
Latin III (*elective*)
Art History/Music History

10th Grade

American Literature
American History
Algebra II and Trigonometry
Biology
Latin II
P.E./Health

12th Grade

Introduction to World Literature
Calculus AB (*elective*)
Physics (*elective*)
Latin IV (*elective*)
Computer Science (*elective*)
Painting and Drawing (*elective*)

COURSE DESCRIPTIONS

English

Introduction to Literature (9th grade)

The syllabus is limited to allow close reading and is confined to recognized masterworks of Western literature. A good selection might include a few books of Homer's *Odyssey*, parts of the Bible, sonnets and plays of Shakespeare, *Huckleberry Finn*, and a Dickens novel. These readings serve as models of good writing and as subjects for students' own writing exercises, which are emphasized throughout. Students review grammar and then study sentence and paragraph structure. They learn how to craft a strong thesis; how to write a cogent, coherent, and concise essay to support it; and how to revise and edit their own work, in consultation with their teacher. Also, students are given periodic practice delivering oral reports in class. *One year, required.*

American Literature (10th grade)

Students read a careful selection of American fiction, drama, and poetry. A good syllabus designed to spotlight the distinctive American achievement in literature might include Franklin, Irving, Hawthorne, Poe, Whitman, Twain, Melville, Dickinson, Faulkner, Wharton, Hemingway, O'Neill, Fitzgerald, Frost, Ralph Ellison, and Robert Penn Warren. Regular writing assignments are made and continued emphasis is placed on clarity, precision, and frequent revision. Students are given increasing experience in classroom speaking. *One year, required.*

British Literature (11th grade)

Students examine a broad selection of British fiction, drama, and poetry. A good syllabus might include Chaucer, Shakespeare, Donne, Milton, Swift, Blake, Wordsworth, Keats, Austen, the Brontës, Dickens, George Eliot, Hardy, Conrad, T.S. Eliot, and Shaw. Regular writing assignments are made and continued emphasis is placed on clarity, precision, and frequent revision. Students are given continued experience in classroom speaking. *One year, required.*

Introduction to World Literature (12th grade)

Students read a careful selection of European and non-Western fiction, drama, and poetry in translation. A good syllabus might include a small number of works by authors from classical Greece and Rome (Sophocles and Virgil); a more generous selection from noted authors of Europe and Russia (e.g., Dante, Cervantes, Molière, Balzac, Chekhov, Dostoevsky, Zola, Mann, and Ibsen); and depending on the instructor's knowledge and interest, a small number of works from Japan, China, the Near East, Africa, or Latin America. Regular writing assignments are made throughout, and a senior research paper is required. Students' work in classroom speaking continues, culminating in a substantial prepared talk before their classmates. *One year, required.*

Social Studies: History, Geography, and Civics

Western Civilization (9th grade)

A general survey history of Western civilization from its beginnings through the early 20th century. Includes a brief review of classical Greece and Rome; the development of Judaism and Christianity; Medieval Europe; the rise of Islam; the Renaissance; the Reformation; the age of commerce, colonies, and discovery; the Enlightenment; the American and French Revolutions; the industrial revolution in England; nationalist and unification movements in 19th-century Europe; Western imperialism; and great power conflicts before World War I. Knowledge of geography should be emphasized. Writing assignments are made throughout. Where possible, students also discuss literary and artistic developments. *One year, required.*

American History (10th grade)

A general survey history of the United States from European discovery through the present. Includes attention to colonial America; the American Revolution and the rise of American political thought; the Federalist and Republican eras; westward expansion; Jacksonian democracy; manifest destiny; slavery; the Civil War; Reconstruction; the Gilded Age; immigration; America as a world power; the Progressive era; American participation in World War II; and domestic issues since 1945. Knowledge of geography should be emphasized. Writing assignments are made throughout. *One year, required.*

Principles of American Democracy (11th grade, 1st semester)

Fundamentals of American government and political philosophy. Includes attention to the structural development of the modern federal and state governments; the idea of federalism; the rise of the party system; electoral, legislative, and judicial processes; the presidency; and the history of major constitutional questions, especially as treated by the Supreme Court. Includes detailed study of the intellectual roots of the American Revolution and Declaration of Independence, the Philadelphia Convention and the Constitution, and readings from *The Federalist*, the Gettysburg Address, Martin Luther King, Jr.'s "Letter From Birmingham Jail," and other speeches and essays by American statesmen. Writing assignments are made throughout, and a research paper is required. *One semester, required.*

American Democracy and the World (11th grade, 2nd semester)

American democracy and its rivals in the 20th century. Topics covered may include World War I; revolution in Russia; the rise of totalitarianism; World War II; the postwar reconstruction of Europe; the Soviet Union as a world power; the United Nations; Israel in the Middle East; NATO, the cold war, the Truman Doctrine, and containment of communism; the Warsaw Pact and the partition of Europe; the Korean War; the Sino-Soviet rift; the Berlin blockade and airlift; the Cuban missile crisis; Vietnam; detente and arms control; the United States and the Soviet Union in the Third World; democracy as a goal of American security, trade, and foreign aid policy; and political condi-

tions today in Europe, the Middle East, Africa, Latin America, Asia, and the Soviet Union. Writing assignments are made throughout, including a research paper. Students should become familiar with the contemporary world map and changing political boundaries since 1945. *One semester, required.*

Mathematics

Algebra I

An introduction to elementary algebra. Topics addressed include sets, variables, functions and relations, graphing, factorization of polynomials, simple systems of linear equations/inequalities, rational exponents, and simple quadratic equations. *One year.*

Plane and Solid Geometry

An introduction to geometry. Includes treatment of basic geometric theorems, with emphasis on writing proofs; calculation of area for regular polygons, and of surface area and volume for simple solids; and introduction to conic sections (analytic geometry). *One year. Prerequisite: Algebra I.*

Algebra II and Trigonometry

Principles of algebra, continued. Includes attention to properties of special functions (the natural logarithm, the exponential function, trigonometric functions and their inverses); the binomial theorem and complex numbers; polar and spherical coordinates; addition and multiplication of matrices; calculation of determinants; and elementary row and column operations. *One year. Prerequisite: Plane and Solid Geometry.*

Statistics and Probability

An introduction to statistical tools, including standard deviations, means, and medians; measures of central tendency; sampling techniques; techniques of data analysis and statistical decision-making; and permutations, combinations, and other aspects of elementary probability theory. *One semester. Prerequisite: Algebra II and Trigonometry.*

Pre-calculus

A preparation for calculus. Includes treatment of vector operations, parametric equations, Taylor expansions, limits, and continuity; graphs of polynomials and rational functions; the definition of a derivative; the derivative of polynomials as a measure of rate of change, and the integral of polynomials as a measure of the area under their graphs; and the Fundamental Theorem of Calculus. *One semester. Prerequisite: Algebra II and Trigonometry.*

Calculus AB

An introduction to elementary calculus. Includes treatment of Simpson's Rule and the Trapezoidal Rule; integration and differentiation of special functions; rate-of-change problems; the Mean Value Theorem, the Inverse Function Theorem, and the Implicit Function Theorem; special integration techniques (integration by parts, substitution of variables, and trigonometric substitution); volume integrals; the shell method and the disk method; and L'Hopital's Rule. *One year. Prerequisite: Pre-calculus.*

Calculus BC

A more demanding introduction to calculus. The topics of Calculus AB are covered (as above), followed by improper integrals; vector-valued functions; elementary linear differential equations; infinite sequences and series, including power series and Taylor series; convergence, divergence, and uniform convergence; remainder theorems; convergence tests; and integration and differentiation of series. *One year. Prerequisite: Pre-calculus.*

Science

Astronomy/Geology

An introduction to the heavens and the Earth. First-semester topics addressed may include the structure and history of the universe; the life cycle of stars (red giants, white dwarfs, neutron stars, supernovae, and black holes); meteorites, comets, and asteroids; quasars and pulsars; and the sun, the planets in our solar system, and their satellites. Second-semester topics include the history and structure of the Earth; plate tectonics, continental shift, volcanos, and earthquakes; the geologic cycle; rocks, minerals, and their formation; and composition and circulation of the atmosphere and oceans. *One year.*

Biology

A basic survey of biological science. Topics addressed may include cellular structure and function; molecular biology; metabolism (anaerobic and aerobic respiration); mitosis and meiosis; photosynthesis and elementary plant biology; genetics (structure, function, and production of nucleic acids and proteins); physiological structure and function, with special emphasis on biological feedback and endocrine control; evolution, adaptation, and reproduction; and neurology (neural structure and the transmission of nervous impulses). *One year.*

Chemistry

A survey of basic chemistry. Topics addressed may include the structure of the atom and nuclear energy; chemical periodicity; chemical bonding, acids, bases, and salts; solutions, colloids, and suspensions; chemical kinetics; pressure and temperature in chemical reactions; balancing equations; equilibria; states of matter; elementary thermodynamics; phase diagrams; reduction and oxidation reactions (electrochemistry); basic organic chemistry (compounds, polymers); and environmental chemistry. *One year.*

Physics

A survey of basic physics. Topics addressed may include classical mechanics (Newton's laws, harmonic motion, reference frames, work and energy, and rotational dynamics); optics; acoustics; special relativity; an introduction to quantum behavior; electricity and magnetism (charge, potential, electric and magnetic fields, circuit theory, and Maxwell's equations); and waves. *One year.*

Principles of Technology

An introduction to the design of buildings, bridges, machines, and electrical circuits. Topics chosen from structural, electrical, and mechanical engineering may include force, shear, bending, vibration, deflection, buckling, properties of building materials, resonance, elementary circuit components and theory, diodes, transistors, amplifiers, logic elements, digital circuits, work, energy, momentum, power, moments, torque, and heat transfer. Students perform a variety of hands-on experiments (e.g., constructing model bridges designed to carry as much weight as possible, creating simple electrical circuits, and building small motors). *One year.*

Foreign Language

First Year

Includes basic vocabulary and pronunciation, basic grammar and constructions, elementary readings and translations, and basic cultural material. Oral communication is emphasized.

Second Year

Includes a review of grammar and introduction of more sophisticated constructions and vocabulary; idiomatic expressions; further reading, translation, and writing exercises; and more advanced cultural material. Speaking and comprehension skills are given continued stress.

Third Year

Emphasizes advanced oral expression, with continued study of grammar, vocabulary, and idiom. Includes readings from foreign periodicals and literature, advanced dictations and translation, and short essays.

Fourth Year

An introduction to literary study, with analysis and discussion of major works in the original and attention to larger historical themes. Includes additional exposure to grammatical structures and vocabulary, and frequent translation and written work.

Fifth Year

A continued study of literature and conversation that allows students to perfect their oral and written skills.

Fine Arts

Art History

An analytic study of representative masterpieces from key periods in the history of Western art, including classical Greece and Rome, Gothic architecture, the Renaissance, and the Baroque, Neoclassic, Romantic, Realist, Impressionist, Postimpressionist, and Modern periods. Where appropriate, American developments are highlighted. Focus is on recognition and appreciation of elements of design in painting, architecture, and sculpture, and on the relation of artistic style to larger historical and cultural themes. *One semester, required.*

Music History

An analytic study of representative masterpieces from dominant trends and periods in the history of Western music, from early religious and secular traditions through the Renaissance, Baroque, Classical, Romantic, and post-Romantic periods. Where appropriate, American developments (e.g., jazz) are highlighted. Focus is on recognition and appreciation of selected musical forms (e.g., sonata-allegro, the symphony, opera, and fugue), with an introduction to compositional elements like instrumentation, rhythm, and harmony and counterpoint. *One semester, required.*

Physical Education/Health

Physical Education/Health (9th and 10th grades)

Students participate in team and individual sports. Emphasis is on fitness, coordination, and sportsmanship. One quarter of each year's class is devoted to health education, which over the two-year period covers nutrition and first aid (e.g., cardiopulmonary resuscitation and the Heimlich maneuver), instruction about the dangers of alcohol and drugs, and sex education. *Two years, required.*

Source: *James Madison High School: A Curriculum for American Students* (1987). U.S. Department of Education.

Teaching Young Children: Guidelines and Activities

GUIDELINES FOR TEACHING

As a parent, you are your child's first and foremost teacher. All young children learn by having different experiences and by trying things out. This means that your child—like all children, including those with handicaps—needs to be involved as much as possible in daily activities at home. In helping prepare dinner, for example, tasks such as peeling and cutting carrots or mixing the cookie dough provide practice in fine-motor and visual-motor skills. Any activity the child can be involved in can go a long way toward helping him or her build self-confidence and competence.

You will probably have to make some additional effort to help your child become actively involved in daily events. Once the child starts preschool and school, work out with the teacher what you can realistically do, but recognize that extra effort is necessary.

Activities at home should be as enjoyable as possible for the child and for the family. Don't overburden yourself or your child. Ask the teacher to suggest things that can easily be built into the daily routine. If the suggestions are very hard to carry out, they may not get done.

On the other hand, if you are willing to take a more active teaching role at home, ask for extra suggestions for things you can do. Talk with the teacher about what you like to do with your child and about what the child likes to do at home. Those activities can all be learning opportunities.

If you would like some specific activities to do at home with your child, look over the activities given later on for building particular skills. Remember, however, that you need not be a formal teacher for your child. Often the best way to help the child is to be loving and helpful and to use the daily routine as a way to teach him or her.

Using the Daily Routine

All of the things that you do at home can be used to help a child, including one with special needs, learn more about the world. For example, you can describe what you're doing when you set the table, make the bed, or water the plants. You can point out and name colors in the house and outside. You can name your child's pieces of clothing. You can give the child simple chores, like putting the napkins by each plate, passing the cookies, or putting clothes in the laundry basket. Don't expect the job to be done perfectly the first time, or even the second. With patience and affection you can help your child learn and improve.

Be consistent in what you ask your child to do. If it is reasonable to expect a child to hang pajamas on a hook in the morning, then you should expect the child to do this every morning.

Expensive toys or materials aren't needed to help children learn. The kinds of things that are in all homes—pots and pans, socks, spoons, and magazine pictures—are all good teaching aids. Pots and pans can be used as rhythm instruments, can be stacked or nested, or can be sorted. Socks can be matched by color, counted, and folded together. Pictures can be named or used to tell stories.

Most handicapped children need more, not less, stimulation from people around them. A good and simple way to achieve this is for you and other members of the family to talk to the child about what you're doing as you do it and to listen to and encourage the child to talk. It is very important to talk and listen to a learning-disabled child.

Confusion and failure can result if you shower the child with too many activities. As you work with your child, you will recognize when he or she has had enough. You can help the child's teachers recognize this limit, too.

Fostering Independence

Help your child become as independent as possible. It's tempting for all of us to do things for children that they could do on their own, since we do them faster and better. But it is very important for children—including and perhaps especially handicapped children—to learn to do as much as they can by themselves. Independence helps children feel good about themselves and improves their ability to get along with others.

- If your child has clumsy or uncoordinated body movements, you may worry that he or she could get hurt by all that tripping and falling. You may even feel that you should put the child in a playpen or crib to protect him or her from bumps and bruises. Doing so, however, is a disservice to the child, who learns best about the world by exploring it firsthand. Try to "childproof" your home so that exploration is less dangerous for a child who isn't too steady on his or her feet.

- If your child is fearful about toileting, you may worry that he or she may have frequent "accidents" at preschool. You may even feel that you should put the child back into diapers. Doing so, however, is a disservice to the child, who learns best about the world and daily routines by participating firsthand. You might ask the teacher to suggest ways in which you can make toileting less fearful for your child so that eventually he or she can perform this routine without assistance.

- If your hearing-impaired child cannot yet speak clearly, you may worry that he or she won't be able to play outside with the neighborhood children or go on an errand for you. But keeping the child in the house and never giving responsibilities is not allowing him or her to improve abilities or to learn by doing. You might ask the teacher to suggest some simple duties to assign at home or some ways to encourage the child to get along with neighborhood playmates.

Praise and Encouragement

All of us—children as well as adults—benefit from honest praise. Praise teachers and aides honestly for their efforts with your child, and ask them for feedback on your work with the child. Remember also to praise your child's achievements. For some children, even small tasks can take a lot of time to master. Every achievement—from learning to sit still to managing to eat independently, from learning to handle food appropriately to spending a whole evening with a babysitter without continually crying or acting destructively—represents real progress and deserves real praise.

Also, praise the child for trying, even if failure or mistakes result. Continued effort is essential for children with special needs, who have many obstacles to overcome. Repeated, steady praise will help the child to keep trying.

It is important, however, that your praise be honest and that your child has done something to earn it. Children with disabilities, just like other children, are very good at recognizing insincerity. If you praise your child at times when he or she has not been trying or has not mastered something, the youngster will be confused and will not understand what your expectations are.

Preparing Your Child

You can help both your child and the staff by preparing the child for any preschool program. Just before the start of class, bring your child to the center or school. Introduce yourself and the child to the teacher and other staff members. Encourage your child to explore the classroom and to play with some of the materials. Try to make sure that the child has a good time during this visit.

Some children are frightened at first about leaving home, while others will be excited about meeting other children and learning new things. Sometimes a child will have both these feelings at the same time. You and the teacher may want to discuss whether it would be helpful to your child if you remained in the classroom during the first few days. At some point your child will have to feel comfortable in the classroom without your being there. Feeling at ease without a parent's presence takes more time for some children than for others. This is especially true of some retarded children, who function like much younger children.

A little bit of home at preschool and a little bit of preschool at home go a long way toward helping children feel comfortable and secure. Perhaps you can hang some pictures at home that your child did at school, or your youngster could be sent to class with a favorite toy or familiar object from home to increase his or her feelings of security.

Try to have your child arrive in class on time. Let the teacher know of important events at home that might influence the child's behavior in class. These special events may be happy times (such as birthdays, a family visitor, or a trip) or unhappy ones (such as death, illness, or disruption in the family routine).

Understanding Skill Areas

You may feel that you need help from the teacher in understanding the skill areas—such as language skills, motor skills, social skills, or self-help skills—in which your child has serious weaknesses. Don't hesitate to approach the teacher for this help or for help in figuring out ways to use daily home activities to help build on the child's strengths and work on his or her problems.

Ask the teacher to share assessment or evaluation results with you. Everyone involved should understand how the child is functioning and share pleasure at his or her progress. Try to talk frequently with the teacher in terms of specific skills. Exchange suggestions. If your child is living with both parents, both of you should try to get involved in conferences and conversations. Each parent may have a different perspective.

Ask to see for yourself what the teacher does and how he or she does it in the classroom. You might even want to try practicing skills with your child in the classroom. Sometimes it is better for you to work with a child other than your own. In either case, such an activity will give you practice and an opportunity to exchange ideas with the teacher. Describe to the teacher an average day at home, in order to learn how you can use these everyday events to work on the skills with which your child is having problems.

Below are some general and specific teaching guidelines that may be useful to both parents and teachers, and following that are sets of teaching activities to be used with three-to-five-year-olds. These activities, and the skills they are intended to teach and strengthen, apply to all children—nonhandicapped as well as handicapped. You know your child's strengths and weaknesses best and can choose from among these activities those that will best suit the child's needs and interests.

GENERAL TEACHING GUIDELINES

There are many good ways to teach. Because of your personality, temperament, and values, you will have developed your own individual teaching style, which is reflected in the activities you choose and the ways you interact with children. Good teaching techniques are often the same for the education of any child, whether handicapped or not. It is best not to change your natural teaching style if your child has a learning problem. Doing so will only serve to make you and the child uncomfortable.

With children who have learning problems, such as learning disabilities or mental retardation, you will want to apply your teaching skills consciously, using those skills that most effectively serve the needs of the child. You would do much the same for every child; but since a child with a handicap has problems that seriously interfere with overall performance, he or she requires extra consideration. Below are some basic principles that you probably already know and use with all children. They are particularly useful in working with children who have handicaps.

For Parents of Children with Handicaps

Some parents and teachers are nervous and worried about teaching a handicapped child. This is a common reaction in the beginning. As a result, they sometimes start out thinking of the child as a "disabled child." As they spend time with, watch, play with, hug, and love the child, they usually find that they have begun to think of the child as a "child with a disability," and soon they think of him or her as a "child," plain and simple.

You may not always understand the behavior of a disabled or disturbed child. Your efforts working with the child may not all be successful—this is to be expected. You may feel frustrated and guilty. If something goes wrong, try to figure out what happened, and keep it in mind for the next time.

Don't expect miracles. No one can or should expect you to cure a child, or to make the child into the fastest puzzle-doer or the best runner or climber. Sometimes, even with the very best help from parents, teachers, the staff, and specialists, a child just doesn't make as much progress as was hoped.

Setting Limits

Some limits must be put on children to protect their physical safety. Safety limits are usually clear-cut: for example, "We walk in the store" or "Look both ways before crossing the street." State safety limits simply and frequently, and demonstrate them when necessary. Enforce them consistently, so that children will learn that they must be followed.

Children also need limits to help them control their behavior. Unlike safety limits, behavioral limits require you to make some judgments about what is appropriate and what is not. Each of us has a range of child behavior that we accept or can tolerate in our homes. (Some parents don't mind a lot of noise or a messy paint area, for example, while others can't stand this.)

Whatever behavioral limits you set, be consistent in enforcing them. If the limits keep changing, the children will never know what you expect and will not learn what you are trying to teach. Praise children for their efforts, and try to ignore borderline but tolerable behavior. Let the children know that you accept and respect them, whatever the quality of their performance. As a result, the children will not feel personally threatened by failure. They will approach learning without fear.

Before setting a behavioral limit, look carefully at the behavior you are concerned with, and ask yourself the following questions.

How does it affect other people?

Does the behavior disrupt other people? If it does not disturb them, then perhaps it is something you may want to learn to live with.

For example, Carol may need to have people repeat directions and demonstrate for her several times before she understands what is being said. This may be much more annoying to you than to everyone else, but it is important that she be able to ask for repetition. It is her way of coping with her auditory memory problem.

Can the child help it?

Does the child have control over the behavior? For example, Arthur may just stand and stare, no matter how many times you repeat a direction. Saying it louder or repeating directions may be fruitless. In order to understand the direction, Arthur needs to have you model or demonstrate the task. This means you must adapt to the child's behavior. Concentrating on the child's needs rather than on the behavior may help *you* change.

Is a change justified?

Do you have a good reason for wanting to change the child's behavior? What is your educational reason for wanting to alter the behavior? In other words, make sure the behavior change is good for the child, not just more convenient for you.

Lou is a child who has a hard time keeping still for long. Helping him learn to stay and work at the puzzle table is important, because he won't be able to learn the skills that puzzles can teach him if he is running around the room. On the other hand, it's not important that Lou *sit* at the table. He may need to move around the table as he works on the puzzle, but he can still learn this way. There would be no educational reason for asking him to sit still.

Can you think of substitute behavior?

What behavior do you want the child to substitute for the unacceptable behavior? One good way to help children change undesirable behavior is to teach them a good substitute. A child who hits other children can be taught to express anger with words, such as "Stop it!" "I'm mad!" "That hurt!" "Go away!" or "Don't hit me!" As children learn to control their environment with words, they begin to rely less on other behaviors like hitting or crying. Other alternatives you might teach are to stalk away from the anger-producing situation or to hit a punching bag. Make sure that the new behavior competes with the undesirable one. Laura can't hit Rudy and stalk away from him at the same time, so stalking away would be a successful technique for her.

Pacing

Plan your day—or whatever portion of it you have set aside to be together—so that the activities are varied. Alternate between active and quiet activities, between organized projects and free play. Teach new skills by building on a child's strengths. Present a new skill first in familiar contexts, along with some skills the child already has. This lessens the child's uncertainty and frustration.

A child with learning disabilities, emotional disturbance, or mental retardation is especially sensitive to the pace of the day. Some such children tire easily and may need more quiet times than nonhandicapped children. This doesn't necessarily mean a nap—often 10 minutes alone in a quiet corner is enough. Also, the child's attention span may need training and strengthening, especially if he or she isn't used to preschool. If a child's attention span is short, make the activities short, too. You can lengthen them as the child learns to pay attention for longer stretches of time.

Finally, plan to leave extra time for a child who needs more than one turn to understand or to do something. Providing time for that extra turn or two can mean the difference between success and failure. Some children with learning disabilities may need extra time to settle down after recess or active games. Giving such children a minute or two to "switch channels" may prevent overflow energy from interfering with the next activity.

Children Helping Children

No child, handicapped or nonhandicapped, is good at everything or bad at everything. All children should have the opportunity to give help to their siblings, friends, and classmates and to receive help from them, especially to learn a new skill by seeing someone else perform it correctly. This interaction is called "peer modeling." There is great benefit in using children as models for each other. This is especially true for children with special needs, who are sometimes isolated at home from other children.

Try to plan and organize learning situations with other children so peer modeling can occur. In areas where a handicapped child is weak, another child (a peer) who has the skill can act as a model. Likewise, in areas where a handicapped child excels, she or he might be paired with a less skilled child. Young children are often eager to serve as helpers for each other. This experience has a bonus: it helps them develop positive attitudes about handicapped people and encourages appropriate behaviors. Ways in which nonhandicapped children can help in mainstreaming a handicapped child include:

- helping a confused child organize his or her materials by handing the child the scissors or the glue from the shelf.
- assisting a poorly coordinated child at playground games.
- taking the hand of a child who has spatial-relations problems when walking to the bus.
- alerting a child whose attention wanders that it is time to go out to the playground.
- repeating to a child verbal directions given by an adult, if the child doesn't seem to understand what to do.
- showing a child who has difficulty following directions what to do.
- introducing a child to the physical setting of a new classroom, such as by showing where the bathroom is.
- providing a child with opportunities to practice newly learned skills.
- helping a child with a spatial-relations problem find the cubby area each day.
- calling the name of a child with hearing impairment, several times if needed, to ask him or her to join a game.
- demonstrating to a hearing-impaired child when to clap, move feet, or stand up during a group game.

Peer helpers should be used often, and this includes using a handicapped child in areas where he or she excels. In this way, all the children will learn that they each have areas of strength and weakness. They will also learn that the need to receive help does not mean that they are failures or are less worthy than those who offer help.

You may find that there is a nonhandicapped child in your child's class or play group who is unusually responsible and enjoys being a big brother or big sister to a child with learning problems. This is fine, but make sure that you are not relying so much on your helper that he or she becomes a substitute teacher or does more for a learning-disabled child than is needed.

Breaking Down Skills

Every skill is really composed of many subskills—there is no such thing as a one-step activity. Skills such as tying shoes, cutting a circle with scissors, doing a somersault, stringing beads, copying shapes from a model, walking on a balance beam, listening to a story, or learning to count consist of many subskills.

Some children can master a new skill very quickly with little help from you. These are children who already know the subskills and can use them in performing the new skill. Handicapped children, however, don't have some of the subskills necessary and need to be taught them before they can succeed at the overall activity. Children with mental retardation or emotional disturbance have this problem in all skill areas.

For these children, you can break down the activity into subskills that can be learned at their current skill level:

- If you want to teach a child to hop, check to see if he or she can balance on one foot. Such balancing is a subskill of hopping and must be mastered first.
- If you want to teach a child to ask for what he or she wants at the table at lunch time, you should make sure that the child can name the different things he or she might have to ask for. You might cut out pictures of various foods and have the child learn their names first.
- If you want to teach a child to share a toy, you should make sure that the child knows the meaning of "my turn" and "your turn," has the ability to wait and delay gratification while another child uses the toy, and is willing to share the toy with another child.
- If you are trying to teach a child to throw a ball to another child, the first child must understand the concept of exchange, must be able to get the attention of the child to whom he or she is throwing the ball, and must possess the fine and gross motor skills necessary to throw the ball.
- If you want to teach a child to name animals, check first to see if he or she can point to the correct animals when you name them. Understanding a word usually occurs before a child can say it.

Since breaking down skills into small parts is especially important with learning-disabled and mentally retarded children, we give further detailed examples of how to do it later, in "Activities for Teaching Key Skills to Children."

Sequencing Activities

In addition to sequencing skills within an activity, sequence a series of activities. Start with simple activities and gradually increase the level of difficulty as a child learns.

- An obstacle course can be designed to include two or three activities, such as walking on a balance beam, crawling through a tunnel, or climbing over a bench. After a child has mastered each of these steps, add a new activity to challenge him or her, with a success factor built in.
- Children can begin to learn about traffic lights by hearing a story about one and by coloring a picture of one with red, yellow, and green crayons. Then you can play a game of "Red Light, Green Light" with them. The next step might be to set up a maze, complete with handmade traffic signals, and have each child go through the maze as the light changes. (You can make the light change by inserting red, yellow, or green cards at different times.) Finally, you will want to go outside and have the children practice the real thing.
- Shana wanted to use a tricycle that Amani was using. She rushed over, began pulling the tricycle, and screamed at Amani, "Get off! Get off!" To help Shana learn a more appropriate way of expressing her desire to use the tricycle, you might sequence the activity as follows:

  1. Hold Shana's hand (for restraint), and try to explain the meaning of "my turn" and "your turn."
  2. Give Shana a concrete way of knowing when it is her turn, such as "when Amani has finished riding" or "when all the sand on this little timer is at the bottom."
  3. When it is Shana's turn, demonstrate to her how to go about getting the tricycle. For example, say to Shana, "Tell Amani that his time is up and you would like to take your turn now."

By sequencing these activities from simple to more complex, you have helped the child to generalize and have reinforced the concepts you are teaching.

Be sure to demonstrate to a child how the skills learned in one activity can be use in others. A child with learning problems may need to repeat a subskill, a skill, or an activity several times with your help and several more times without it before moving on to new activities at a more difficult level.

Physical Contact and Guidance

Use physical contact to help a child; to ensure safety; to provide guidance, support, and encouragement; and to limit space. Express your affectionate feelings with a pat or a hug. Guard against using physical contact to punish a child.

Physical contact is especially important for a child with learning problems, who may learn best by being "moved through" an activity one or more times, until independent participation is possible. Put your hand over Sandy's and show her the swirling movements of fingerpainting. Put the scissors in Barry's hand and put your hand over his, or use four-hole scissors (scissors for two people to use together) so that he can feel the motions of cutting.

Using physical guidance as you move Sandy through the motions of fingerpainting and as you help Barry with the scissors is a temporary technique that allows them to be successful on their own. In this sense, physical guidance is like the training wheels on a two-wheel bike. The success children have with your help makes them more willing to try again, and the structured practice helps them learn more quickly. After a while, your help, just like the training wheels, will no longer be needed.

Physical contact can also be especially helpful for a hearing-impaired child who may not have understood your spoken directions or your words of praise. Your directions ("Put the dirt in the flower pot") take on more meaning if you repeat them while guiding the child's hands in performing the task. Your compliments ("Good for you! You heard your name!") may be understood primarily through a smile and a friendly pat on the back as you speak.

Some emotionally disturbed children shy away from physical contact. Be patient. It may take time to build trust and develop the ability to accept affection. You can use physical contact and guidance to ensure safety in various ways, from offering your hand as support when the child is walking a balance beam to rigorously holding and restraining a child who is out of control and threatening to hurt himself or herself or others. Such physical restraint may be helpful when a child is truly out of control and when scolding only seems to make matters worse—provoking another outburst or making the child feel absolutely miserable. You should use restraint as little as possible, and only as a last resort. Physical restraint should be done in a matter-of-fact way, showing concern but not anger. After restraining a child you should spend some time with him or her until the child has regained composure. This kind of restraint is time-consuming and requires a firm understanding of the child's underlying problems, not just of the behavior you are trying to control.

Avoiding Overdependence

It is sometimes hard to be accurate and realistic about what children are capable of doing for themselves. In the case of many children with special needs, it is all too easy to assume that they are more helpless than they really are. Seeing that they cannot do some things may make us think that they cannot do others.

Some parents overprotect their children, especially handicapped children, to make up for all the extra problems that the children have to deal with. Some children therefore go to Head Start or other preschool programs expecting that everything will be done for them, simply because this is what they are used to.

Overprotecting a child is a trap that you don't have to get caught in. You have to ask yourself: "Is this really impossible for the child? Could the child do it alone with more time? Could the child do it with more help from me?" Think hard, and be honest. It is tempting to do things for a slow child because you can do them faster and better. But if you're always the one who zips the zipper, sets out the paintbrushes, finishes the puzzle, does the talking, and turns the book right-side up, the child won't have a chance to try to learn to do these things.

Being extra patient and giving extra encouragement to children who try to do things on their own will pay off many times in the future. You can help children think of themselves as able, not unable. When they grow up, they will be in the habit of expecting as much from themselves as they are really capable of.

SPECIFIC TEACHING TECHNIQUES

This section suggests specific teaching techniques that you can use to help children learn better. All of these techniques will be helpful in working with children, especially those with disabilities or learning problems. It includes techniques for improving self-concept, tips to keep in mind, the techniques of task analysis and behavior modification, advice on how to handle transition times, and ways to help with language problems.

Improving Self-Concept

Self-concept is a term used to describe how a person feels about himself or herself. Children's self-concept is affected by the expectations of the people who are important to them. For example, if Jackie's parents and teachers think it is important to eat neatly, she will enjoy their approval, and feel proud of herself, when she keeps her milk in the cup and her food on the plate. On the other hand, if Bobby's attempts to build a sandcastle are met with constant criticism, he is likely to lose interest in the activity, as well as feel incapable, frustrated, and humiliated. Children who believe that they are capable of fulfilling the expectations of the people who are important to them develop a positive self-concept, or a sense of worth in themselves. This sense of worth in turn encourages them to try new things and again be successful. They begin to feel capable when they are praised and valued for the good things they do. For this reason, social skills, gross motor skills, and all the other skills have to be thought about in connection with children's self-concept.

"Do the other children like me?" "Am I big and strong?" "Can I climb to the top of the jungle gym?" "Is my father proud of me?" Children ask themselves these kinds of questions often. Those who can answer "yes" are likely to have a positive self-concept—they find the world a friendly and delightful place, and they are eager to try out new things. Children who answer "no" are likely to have a negative self-concept—the world is an unpleasant place where new experiences mean new failures. Since failing is so painful, these children may tend to avoid the new experiences, because they foresee getting hurt by them.

Children with a negative self-concept can react in a number of ways. They seem to need your attention very often. They may be withdrawn and quiet and may refuse to play with other children. They may be frightened, insecure, and timid. They may be resentful and sullen. They may cry a lot. They may misbehave, disrupt activities, or annoy or try to hurt other children.

Although poor self-concept is damaging, it is a special problem for children with handicaps: their handicaps mean that they can't yet do some things that other children their age can. Mildly and moderately retarded children, for example, are very well aware that in some ways they don't "measure up" to other children. An anxious child may realize that he or she is uncomfortable in situations where other children join right in. A hyperactive child may be aware that he or she is the one who always spills water at the table. These feelings can cause children to feel less valued or worthy than other children. This is why children who are retarded, disturbed, or disabled are very much in need of successes. With successful experiences, these children will feel better about themselves.

The two most essential supports a parent or teacher can provide for a child—any child—to nurture a positive self-concept are:

- helping a child to experience many successes in varied activities.
- letting a child know that he or she is valued for his or her own self.

Below are some guidelines you can follow to help children develop a better self-concept.

Think positively about the child. As you think about and plan your work with a child, focus on the child's *strengths*. Believe that the child's behavior can be improved upon and changed, and recognize that your attitude toward him or her plays an important role in what and how the child learns and in how the child feels about himself or herself.

Help others to think positively about the child. Family and school staff want to feel that they play a significant role in the child's learning. When you communicate to them your appreciation for the child and his or her efforts and progress, they are more likely to appreciate the child's efforts and accomplishments. Children are more likely to try new, more challenging experiences when met with encouragement and praise from a variety of sources.

Help other children to think more positively about a disturbed, disabled, or retarded child, too. Encourage them to include the child in their play. Design activities so that this can be done. Teach children by your example to treat others fairly and kindly, and encourage them to help a disturbed, disabled, or retarded child learn necessary skills or behavior by being helpers or friends.

Work positively with the child. All children need to be shown that they are cared about and that what and how they do things *does* matter. Praise *progress*, no matter how small; praise the effort a child puts forth even though the results may not meet your (or the child's) expectations. Be positive, even about failures. You can encourage success by saying, for example, "You tried very hard. With such good practice, I'm sure you'll learn how to do that soon." Be tender, accepting, loving,

and patient. Use words and gestures to express your supportiveness. As children begin to feel better about themselves and more self-confident in their abilities, you may begin to see that they can manage by themselves more often. Just knowing that they are performing well helps them feel good about themselves. However, building a positive self-concept is a slow process and you may need to be patient. Some children will continue to depend on praise while others will gradually internalize your esteem for them and will feel genuinely self-confident. There are some other steps you can take to help children develop a better self-concept:

- Be patient when it is necessary to show a child how to do something many times.
- Don't talk about a child's problems in front of him or her.
- Concentrate on a child's strengths, not weaknesses. Use those strengths to the child's best advantage.
- Fit the activity to the child, so that it is challenging but not overwhelming.
- Be consistent about what you expect from a child.
- Make the child responsible for a part of the daily routine, and praise his or her reliability.
- Never allow other children to make fun of a child.
- Include each child as fully as possible in all activities; isolation hurts.
- Give each child the opportunity to show off a little, such as by displaying drawings. When a child is proud of something, show it to others.

Teaching Tips

1. *Make it simple.* When you are explaining something, make your directions simple. Use only a few words. Speak slowly and clearly, especially to children who have language or auditory problems. Be sure they are paying attention.

Show a child who has visual and/or motor problems how to do a particular task. Physically move the child through the task so that he or she begins to "feel" what to do.

- If you are teaching Susie how to draw a circle, put your hand over hers and move the crayon in a circular motion.
- If you are teaching John how to jump, lift him off the ground with you as you jump, to show him how it feels.
- If you are teaching Molly, an anxious child, how to use the sand table, gently guide her hand through the sand to show her how it feels.

Stand or sit close to a child during a task, so you can help when needed. (But help only when needed!) For example, sit by a child with spatial-relations problems during a task such as putting together a puzzle, so that you can help him or her judge relationships among the puzzle pieces.

Reduce clutter and noise, especially for children who are distractible or who have poor discrimination skills. Use materials that are clear and plain, with bold lines, especially if visual discrimination is a problem, so that the child can recognize similarities and differences among the materials. Avoid materials that have confusing backgrounds or crowded pages.

2. *Make it short.* Some children are very active, and they may be easily distracted or have difficulty following directions. It will be hard for them to sit and listen. When a child isn't paying attention, make sure that the activity isn't too hard. Most of us quit trying when we don't understand what to do. Children also have problems when the activity is too long, even when it is simple. Be sensitive to when a child has had enough.

3. *Keep it organized.* Help children learn better by providing an environment that is structured and well organized. When your child is at home with you, plan each day so that it is balanced between quiet times and active times. Discuss the routine with your child or children. As you finish each activity, explain what comes next. You might even post a picture schedule to show the order and kinds of activities. Where appropriate, follow the same routine each day, so the children can anticipate the next activity.

Give clear directions, but only one at a time, especially for children with language and/or auditory problems. Show the children how to do what you are describing.

Don't change activities abruptly. Let the children know that it will be time to stop "when the bell rings," "when the lights go off and on," or "when you hear the music." This allows them to get ready for the shift and can help prevent tears and tantrums.

4. *Teach it.* Many children often seem to learn without being taught. They observe lots of things they see around them and soon recognize and know them: colors, cars, rhymes, and numbers. But children with learning problems often have to be taught things that other children learn on their own. For example, most children learn simple concepts such as *top* without specific teaching. But some children must be carefully taught the difference between "the top of the table" and "the top of the desk."

When you notice that a child is having problems learning in particular areas, you will need to try different teaching approaches until you find one that works for that child.

Children who are distractible, who have a short attention span, or who have frequent conflicts with other children may occasionally need a quiet place to work. A small, screened-off area or a separate room can make learning easier for such children.

Children with auditory, language, motor, or cognitive problems and mentally retarded or emotionally disturbed children can often learn better through demonstrations rather than through words. Don't just tell them how to do something—show them how.

Give the children lots of practice. Repeat the same activity at home and on the playground. Each time you do an activity, help the children remember when they did it before. For example, "We are going to hold hands just like we did during our trip to the zoo."

Point things out and describe them. For example: "Look at the big, soft pillow." "Miyeko's jacket is blue." "Herman's jacket is brown." Or "Look at how that lady is taking big, giant steps. Now she is taking little, baby steps. Can you take a big step and a little step?"

Teach in small steps and don't go too fast, but expect a little more from the children each day. Remind them of their successes and encourage them to try their best.

5. *Make it meaningful.* Select activities that give a child a reasonable chance for success. Ingredients for success are self-confidence, motivation, and mastery. When children think they can do a task, enjoy the challenge it provides, and have the necessary skills, they are likely to become involved and gain a sense of accomplishment.

Show an active interest in the child's accomplishments. Many children enjoy sharing their successes with each other—even showing off a bit. Others are more self-conscious. They are pleased with their success in a quiet way and appreciate a friendly acknowledgment without much fanfare.

Be sure to show respect for the child's work. Take the time to display a painting attractively and put the child's name on his or her work. Find a safe place to keep what he or she makes. Remind the child to share his or her accomplishments with friends and family. Such respectful care for the work of disturbed, disabled, or retarded children is particularly important.

6. *Keep experimenting.* If you try all of the above techniques and a child is still having difficulty mastering the task at hand, keep experimenting until you find a way that works. There are countless ways of teaching a task. Some children can perform a motor task, for example, better if they talk their way through it as they are doing it: "First I put the ball in here, then I turn the knob." Others may need several demonstrations of a task, followed by being physically moved through it by someone. Analyzing the task will also help you to pinpoint those steps that are most troublesome for a child. Once the task has been broken down into steps, there are many ways you can try to teach each step until the child masters it.

Task Analysis

Task analysis is a teaching technique you may already know about. It is an extremely useful technique for working with all children, but especially children who are disabled, disturbed, or retarded. The technique calls for breaking down a task (activity) into small, sequential steps and teaching each step one at a time until the child can do the entire task. For example, if Mara is having trouble learning to put her T-shirt on, you can break the task down into the following smaller steps:

1. Lay the shirt flat on a table with the label side up and the bottom toward the child.

2. Put both arms inside the shirt.

3. Move both arms along the sides of the shirt to the armholes. Push arms through the armholes.

4. Lift the shirt up so the neck hole is on top of the head.

5. Pull the neck hole down over the head.

6. Pull the bottom of the shirt down from the armpits to the chest.

7. Pull the bottom of the shirt down from the chest to the waist.

When you consider how many motions it takes to put on a shirt, it's no wonder that some children find it a complicated task. Going through this type of analysis can help you be patient with a child, who knows perfectly well when a task is complicated!

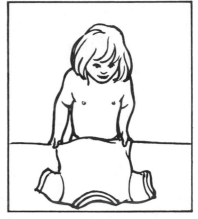

1.

2.

3.

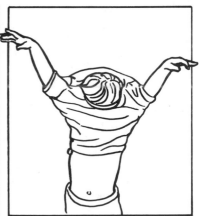

4.

5.

6.

7.

Often the easiest way to teach most skills, including self-help skills, is to teach the last step first. This technique is called *backward chaining*. The satisfaction in doing something, either putting on a shirt or completing a puzzle, is greatest as the last step is finished. Backward chaining not only makes it more likely that children will succeed at doing something, it also lets them see the result of their effort immediately and be pleased at their accomplishment. On the other hand, if you teach children how to put on a shirt by starting with the first step, for example, they will have a long wait before the final successful moment. And some of them might not have the patience to wait that long for success.

Mara's father taught her how to put on her shirt using backward chaining. He first helped her get her shirt almost all the way on, but taught her to do the last step by herself—to pull the shirt down from her chest to her waist. As soon as she could do that, he congratulated her and taught her the next-to-last step—to pull it down from her armpits to her chest. Each time she learned a step, he congratulated her and taught her the one just before. This way, Mara got lots of practice, was successful, felt proud of herself, and learned to do more each day.

In using task analysis with learning-disabled children, you may need to involve a variety of sensory modes (visual, auditory, motor, and so on), as you progress from step to step. For example, if Kathy doesn't understand when you say, "Put both arms inside the shirt," try using another sensory mode. Add the visual mode by demonstrating how to put both arms inside the shirt. If this fails, add Kathy's motor skills by putting your arms over hers and moving her through the task. By figuring out which sensory modes are easiest for a particular child, you can capitalize on the child's strengths as you go through each step of a task.

Behavior Modification

Behavior modification is a teaching technique that relies on an old principle: when we are rewarded for something we do, we are more likely to do it again. Psychologists call this *positive reinforcement*. For example, if you tell Sasha that his shirt is beautiful, he is more likely to wear it again.

Rewarding children for effort and accomplishment keeps them working and learning, according to the principles of behavior modification. You probably reward children often and without special effort. For example, when they have worked very hard, you probably praise their efforts, smile, or give them a friendly pat. But what is rewarding and motivating for one child may not be rewarding and motivating for another. With some children, you may need to make a special effort to figure out what is most motivating to them. To do this, you have to closely observe the individual child and consider what you do that makes that child work harder and behave in desirable ways. Sometimes rewarding children for effort or accomplishment by allowing them to listen to a favorite record, giving them extra time to play with a favorite toy, or giving them the privilege of feeding the fish or watering the plants can motivate them.

To motivate children, the reward must be something they want and must be given right after they make an effort or accomplish a task. While you want to give children time to practice what they have learned, you want to be sure that you encourage them to learn more. And to learn more, children need to do a little bit more or a little bit better.

On the other hand, when we are punished for something we do, for example, are criticized for how we colored a drawing, the unpleasantness tends to make us want to stop doing it. Punishment, however, can have the opposite effect from what you intend. The attention from being scolded, for example, is a kind of positive reinforcement for children who don't get enough attention. They are therefore encouraged to repeat the undesirable behavior, not to stop it. This is why ignoring undesirable behavior (along with modeling the desirable behavior) sometimes works better than punishing children. Modeling involves describing the correct behavior of one child ("Billy is sitting on his mat so he'll be all ready to listen to the story") and then praising the other children when they exhibit that desired behavior. When children are no longer rewarded with a parent's attention by scolding or criticizing them, they are less likely to continue the problem behavior.

Although punishment is not useful for changing most kinds of undesirable behavior, there are times when you have to stop a child, with a firm "no" or a gentle scolding, to protect the safety of the child or another child. You obviously have to stop a child right away from running out into a heavily traveled street or from hitting another child.

You will find that one good way to prevent dangerous or undesirable behavior is to teach children appropriate behavior instead. Of course, physical punishment in any form does not belong in a preschool classroom.

Handling Transition Times

The hardest times for many parents, teachers, and children are the times between activities. For children with mental retardation, learning disabilities, or emotional disturbance, these unstructured times can be disastrous. Without careful management, the time can become confusing for a child, sometimes resulting in misbehavior.

When a group of children must move from one area to another, it helps to divide them into smaller groups or pairs (buddies). This cuts down on the milling around and sets a smoother tone for the next activity.

To prepare children for a change in activity, tell them a few minutes ahead of time that they will have to stop when the bell rings, when they hear the music, or when the lights go off and on. This winding-down time is especially important for many mentally retarded, learning disabled, or emotionally disturbed children. Eric, a moderately retarded child, couldn't cope with sudden changes. If he was told to stop immediately, with no warning, he would throw himself onto the floor and bang his head. But when he was told a few minutes in advance that it was almost time to stop, he was able to shift gears and stop even his favorite activities without a tantrum.

HELPING WITH LANGUAGE PROBLEMS

Children sometimes have problems talking and understanding speech, especially children with mental retardation or learning disabilities. If you had a child who was old enough to tie her shoes but didn't yet know how, you would do more than give her twenty pairs of shoes to tie—you would teach her how to tie shoes. In the same way, children who have not yet learned the speech or language skills that other children have learned clearly need more help than just hearing people talk. If that were enough, they would have learned in the first place. The next few pages contain several suggestions for helping retarded, disturbed, or disabled children to communicate better.

Be a Good Listener

It is difficult to practice talking if there is no one listening to you. Children with a language problem need to be listened to and rewarded for trying to talk. It really helps them when they realize that adults will stop and listen seriously to what they are saying.

Sometimes, children with speech problems are hard to understand. Usually, as you listen to them more and more, you begin to develop an ear for what they are saying. As parents, you can often help teachers to understand your child; they might ask you for help.

It is also important that you help other children understand what a retarded child is saying. It often happens, however, that the children understand the child better than you do at first!

Talk About What You Are Doing

Children's earliest speech is about the present—what is happening now. While you do things with the children, talk about them. For example, if you were helping the children make pretzels, you might make comments such as these:

We need to put the flour in the bowl. Hamilton is pouring it in. Mary, can you hold the bowl for him? Okay, the flour is all in. Who can add the sugar? Good, now the sugar's in. Jennifer is putting in the salt.

Give Directions Simply

Children with language problems sometimes don't do what you ask them to do because they don't understand what you want.

Help them learn to follow directions by taking the following steps:

- Get their attention.
- Talk to them in language that is appropriate to their level of language development. Children tend to understand more than they can speak. For example, if the children speak in two- or three-word sentences, tell them what to do in three- or four-word sentences.
- While you are talking, use motions to show them what to do. If they still don't understand, take them through the directions step by step, using your hands to move their bodies.

Use What the Children Already Know

It is easiest to learn something new if it is paired with something familiar when you teach it. For example, if a child uses single words and you want him or her to begin to use two words together, put together two single words the child already knows to make a two-word phrase.

Sylvia has never used more than one word at a time. She knows the words "more" and "juice." Each day at snack time you might ask, "Sylvia, do you want more juice?" One day she may reply, "More juice." Then you can say, "Good! You want more juice." Sylvia has spoken her first two-word phrase.

Similarly, Gita has trouble find the right word at the right time. You know that she has a special interest in the woodworking area and has learned the names of the tools through association. If you ask her "What do you pound with?" Gita may reply "hammer." Then you can say, "Right! You pound with a hammer." Help a child develop associations in an interesting and familiar area to facilitate the child's overall language development.

Repeat Words Correctly

Repeating what children say with a correction is called "modeling." It allows children to hear the right way of saying something without making a big deal about their mistakes. If Leon says, "I want more duce," you can reply, "Yes, you want more *juice*." If Merry says, "I did painted today," you can reply, "You did a painting today? How nice!"

Expand on What Children Say

Expansion is like modeling, because it also involves repeating what a child has said. But instead of just saying what the children have said, you add something more—you "expand" the phrase. This not only shows them that you understand what they have said, it also suggests new information they might add. When Paul says, "Susie is hiding," you might say, "Yes, Susie is hiding behind the box." When Alice says "I goed to the beach yesterday," you might say "That's right, you went to the beach yesterday with your mother and brother."

Get the Children Talking

Many retarded, disturbed, or disabled children with language and speech problems don't talk unless they are encouraged to do so. It is sometimes hard to talk very much to children who don't answer very much. But in order to speed up their speech and language development, it is important to get these children talking, to keep them talking, and to listen to them. The following suggestions may help these children to talk more.

- Talk to the children while they are doing something. They are more likely to talk at these times, because their hands are busy and they are less self-conscious.
- Encourage the children to show you their special things and to take them to class; arrange with the teacher to give them time to share these special things with the rest of the class.
- Encourage the children to talk about how they feel. Being able to tell a friend that you are angry may cut down on the need to hit your friend. In the same way, being able to say "I like you" has its special rewards.
- Let the children do as many different things as possible; it gives them more to talk about.
- Teach the children how to give important information, such as their names and addresses. They will probably have to learn such information bit by bit.
- Teach the children a short rhyme or song they can perform for others. Being able to put on a show can really build children's confidence in their speaking ability.
- Include activities and words that are meaningful to the children. They have all heard the word "milk" but they may never have heard of "eggnog."
- Ask the children open-ended rather than yes/no questions. "What are you going to buy with that nickel?" is better than, "Are you going to buy sugarless gum with that nickel?" Even for children whose choices *have* to be limited, you can build in choice as well as language. For example, say, "Are you going to play with the blocks or in the house?"
- Listen when a child talks. Few people talk for very long if no one wants to listen to them.

ACTIVITIES FOR TEACHING KEY SKILLS TO CHILDREN

All preschoolers need experience and practice in the following skill areas:

- self-help
- gross motor
- visual
- auditory
- fine motor
- communication
- cognitive
- social

Many of these skills lay the foundation for future success in learning. A child's attitude toward preschool and learning is closely related to his or her success in learning these basic skills. Through observation and assessment, parents and teachers can obtain information about how the child is functioning in each skill area listed. [Checklists like those found under COMMUNICATION SKILLS AND DISORDERS, EAR AND HEARING PROBLEMS, EYE AND VISION PROBLEMS, LEARNING DISABILITIES, or MENTAL RETARDATION can help.] This information can help parents and teachers to individualize instruction to help that child in difficult areas.

The next few pages list by skill area examples of activities that you can use to help a child improve his or her performance in these specific skills. The lists are followed by some routine activities that can be used to teach skills.

Self-Help Skills and Self-Concept

Self-help skills are those that enable children to take care of themselves in areas such as dressing, eating, and personal hygiene. Success in these areas can help to form a foundation for a positive self-concept. Self-help skills and the development of a positive self-concept can be promoted in activities such as:

- housekeeping activities.
- dress-up play, dressing dolls.
- cooking activities.
- preparing snacks, including preparation and cleanup.
- buttoning, snapping, and lacing clothes.
- body-image activities, such as tracing children's bodies on paper.
- drawing self-portraits.
- making *My Book About Me*.

Gross Motor Skills

Gross motor skills involve the large muscles used to move the arms, legs, torso, hands, and feet. These skills can be improved in activities such as:

- balance-beam or walking-board activities. (For example, draw a line on the floor with masking tape. The children can pretend they are circus performers walking the tightrope.)
- crawling through tunnels. (Large packing boxes with both ends open make great tunnels.)
- climbing activities.
- jumping, hopping, and skipping games.
- walking on tip-toes.
- throwing, kicking, and lifting things.
- movement games like the "Hokie-Pokie," "Twister," or "Head, Shoulders, Knees, and Toes."
- obstacle course.
- "Simon Says."
- music activities that involve marching and clapping.
- movement exploration activities, such as rolling down a hill in the park.

Fine Motor Skills

Fine motor skills involve the small muscles used to move the fingers and wrists. These skills can be improved in activities such as:

- puzzles, games, and manipulative activities.
- peg-board and form-board activities.
- buttoning, lacing, and snapping clothes.
- stringing and sorting beads.
- cutting and pasting tasks.
- coloring.
- tracing.
- stencil and template activities.
- dot-to-dot exercises.
- copying tasks—horizontal and vertical lines, and circles.
- hanging clothespins on a clothesline.

Communication Skills

Communication skills include receptive language and expressive language. Receptive language involves the ability to understand what is heard, while expressive language involves the ability to express yourself using words. Both receptive and expressive skills can be improved by using the activities listed below. In a naming activity, for example, if you want to concentrate on receptive language, you can do most of the talking. If you say to a child, "Find the yellow truck," the child can indicate that he or she understands by pointing at the yellow truck. If, on the other hand, you want to concentrate on expressive language, let the child do most of the talking. You can tell the child, "Find the yellow truck," then ask the child to tell you where he or she found it.

- Naming activities ("Find the _____.")
- Matching spoken words with pictures
- Describing exercises using pictures or objects as cues ("Tell me about the _____.")
- Describing exercises using pictures in a series ("Tell me a story using these pictures.")
- Circle-time activities such as "Show and Tell"
- Games that call for following directions, such as "Simon Says"
- Sentence-completion games ("I eat with a _____." "I draw with a _____." "You are wearing a _____ dress.")
- Imitation games such as "Say What I Say" or "Do What I Do" (You might have children imitate movements of the tongue or lips for actions such as blowing.)
- Puppet play
- Acting games (dramatizations)
- "What Did We See" activities, to follow a field trip

Visual Skills

Visual skills include discrimination, tracking, memory, and visual-motor integration. Visual discrimination is the ability to look at objects or pictures and recognize whether they are alike or different. Visual tracking (following something with the eyes) involves focusing the eyes on one point and moving them rhythmically from side to side, up or down, or diagonally. The next subskill, visual memory, is the ability to coordinate vision with the movements of the body or of parts of the body (for example, hand–eye coordination).

Visual discrimination, tracking, memory, and visual-motor integration skills can be improved in the activities listed below. Depending on how you structure the activity, you can emphasize any one of these subskills. The first activity (matching blocks by color) will involve visual discrimination no matter how you structure it. If you want to build in visual tracking, you can line up the blocks in a long row so that the child will have to focus on one block and move his or her eyes from side to side to find blocks that are the same color. To turn this into a visual-memory activity, you can show a child two blocks, conceal them, and then ask the child to look at a row of four blocks to pick out two that are the same color as the ones you are hiding. To use the matching activity to concentrate on visual-motor skills, show the child a piece of paper with squares drawn in the same size and color as the blocks. Have the child place each block on the appropriate square.

- Matching blocks by color, or line drawings by simple shapes
- Placing forms in a form board
- Sorting activities
- Hiding activities (For example, have children find objects in the room and/or in pictures. Then hide these objects so that they are still partially visible, and ask the children to find them again.)
- Discrimination activities using pictures, geometric shapes, and textured materials
- Field trips, such as a walk in a park (When children see a bird they can look for the size, the color, the type of beak, or the type of feathers.)
- Remembering what was seen on a field trip for discussion
- Tracking exercises (For example, have the children follow a pointer or flashlight as you move it up, down, left, and right.)
- Memory games using objects that look and feel different
- Visual-motor integration activities (See the activities listed earlier under "Fine Motor Skills.")

Auditory Skills

Auditory skills include the subskills of discrimination, memory, and localization. Auditory discrimination is the ability to tell the difference between sounds. Auditory memory is the ability to remember what you hear for even a short period of time.

Localization is the ability to locate where a sound is coming from.

These skills can be improved in the activities listed below. Again, depending on how you structure the activities you can use them to teach any of these subskills. For example, if you concentrate on asking a child to tell you which sounds are the same and which are different, you are teaching auditory discrimination. If you ask the child to tell you where in the room different sounds are coming from, you are emphasizing localization. If you have the child listen to three different everyday sounds and then ask him or her which sound came first, you are helping the child to practice auditory memory.

- Recognition, discrimination, and localization activities using everyday sounds such as water running, doors shutting, or dogs barking ("Can you recognize these sounds?" "Tell me which sounds are the same and which are different." "Where are the sounds coming from?")
- Using musical instruments to teach sound discrimination and localization: high notes, low notes, short sounds, long sounds
- Guessing games using the voices of adults and children ("Can you guess who's talking?" "Where in the room are they?")
- Discrimination exercises using tapes and records
- Remembering games with child blindfolded ("How many times did I clap?"); remembering games with two, three, or four instructions ("Pick up the blue book, put it on the table, and open the door.")
- Sentence-completion games ("What did you hear at the circus? What did you hear first? Next?")
- Learning the words to songs
- Games that call for following directions, such as "Simon Says" or running an obstacle course
- Games that call for auditory memory, such as "Pass the Secret" or "Telephone"
- Remembering what was heard on a field trip

Cognitive Skills

Cognitive skills are those that relate to how children understand and organize their world. They include reasoning, storing and remembering information, recognizing relationships and differences, classifying things, comparing and contrasting, problem solving, and more. Language skills and cognitive skills overlap each other.

Cognitive skills can be improved in activities such as:

- adjective concept games. ("Find the big truck." "Point to the long table.")
- picture identification games using action words. ("Find the picture with the girl sitting. Find the one with the girl running.")

- picture-identification games using prepositions. ("Find the picture with the ball on the table. Find the one with the ball under the table.")
- color-concept activities, such as matching and sorting by color.
- puzzles and form boards.
- number-concept games, such as matching numbers, counting objects, naming numbers, and matching numbers to groups of objects.
- activities for matching, sorting, and selecting colors, numbers, or pictures.
- sequencing games using picture cards.
- science activities to teach general information (for example, teaching children about the different forms of water: steam, liquid, and ice).
- water play to learn about such concepts as buoyancy (whether things float or sink).

Social Skills

Social skills are those involved in interacting and getting along with others and forming relationships with other children and adults. Such skills involve learning to communicate, understand, and get along with others. They can be improved in activities such as:

- story reading.
- snack time.
- group playground activities.
- cooking with a group.
- group music games, such as singing and moving to music.
- circle time.
- participating in preparation and cleanup for daily activities.
- pretending games, such as playing house and dress-up.
- water play and sand play.
- field trips.

ACTIVITIES FOR YOUNG CHILDREN

This section shows how the teaching techniques discussed earlier and the activities listed by skill area can be integrated into a few typical preschool activities.

Games, Puzzles, and Manipulative Activities

These activities include playing with peg boards, picture cards, tinker toys, and stencils. Such activities can help children improve their:

- visual discrimination.
- fine motor coordination.
- hand–eye coordination.

- understanding of spatial relationships.
- sense of position in space.
- depth perception (near/far).
- ability to follow a sequence (the order of steps involved in a task).
- ability to follow directions.

Preparation. Although these activities are generally done independently by one child or by a small group of children, some special preparation can be helpful. Materials should be carefully boxed or arranged in clearly designated areas on low shelves. (Some materials may have to be stored out of children's reach, for example, games with small parts that could easily be lost.) Provide an assortment of materials. You might have one shelf area for "hard" games that need an adult's or older child's help, one for "easy" things to do alone, and a "special shelf" for new materials. Make these differences clear so that the children can develop independence in making their choices.

Tips. Take time to observe the child's style of approaching activities and his or her activity preferences. Such observations can help you to decide what kind of assistance the child may need.

If a child is having trouble discriminating between puzzle pieces, shapes, and so on, encourage him or her to touch and feel the pieces.

If a child is particularly distractible, he or she may need a separate work space, an area free from distracting objects, such as a table that is free of other materials.

If a child is reluctant to leave an activity that he or she has mastered, try to interest the child in a new or different activity. Give guidance and reassurance as necessary.

For an aimless or restless child, structure time by using a timer. Make it clear what the activity is and how much time can be allotted to it.

For a retarded child, choose simple three-piece puzzles of animals or objects that the child can recognize. Find a quiet spot for the child to work on the puzzles, with just you. Show the child the puzzle. Name the pieces, as you point to them ("the red one," "the long one," "the round one"). Show the child how to fit a piece in. Give the child that piece and tell him or her to "put it in." If the child can't do it, put your hand over his or her hand and put the piece in. Keep helping the child, gradually letting him or her do more without assistance.

Introduce puzzles to a child with retardation one at a time. It is best not to start a new puzzle until the child has mastered the last one. Don't be surprised if the child would rather twist, mouth, or feel the puzzle's pieces and holes than fit the pieces in.

Story Reading

Story-reading activities can help children improve their:

- ability to pay attention.
- listening skills.
- speech development (pointing to pictures, naming pictures).
- language development (understanding the story, learning new words).
- ability to sequence (retelling the story).
- memory and recall (reviewing familiar or similar experiences).
- social skills.
- ability to express feelings and ideas.

Preparation. Plan ahead of time which book you are going to read. In selecting a story, consider what concepts can be taught, what new words can be learned, or what memory and speech skills can be taught. Try to find a story that ties in with something else you have been doing or are going to do that day in the classroom. For example, if your child has a new pet turtle, you may want to read Dr. Seuss's *Yertle the Turtle.* Big, bright, colorful pictures, pop-up illustrations, and touchable books will help a child with learning problems stay interested and tuned in.

Tips. Prepare the child or children for a quiet activity by helping them relax (talk softly, play quiet music, and so on). Let them get comfortable on mats, pillows, or rugs. Make sure that everyone can see the book and pictures. Tell the children a little about the story and what to watch for. Read the story using different voices for different characters. Vary the loudness and softness of your voice. Change the speed a little, but don't read so fast that children can't follow. Show the pictures as you go along, giving children time to look, touch, and feel the illustrations. Let children comment on the story.

There are many opportunities for building cognitive and communication skills through the use of interesting stories and follow-up discussions. Stimulate the children's thinking with questions like the following:

"How would you have felt if . . .?"
"What do you think the Fairy Godmother meant when she said . . .?"
"How else could Johnny have helped . . .?"
"When did the three bears realize . . .?"
"Who found . . .?"

People listen in all kinds of positions. It's okay if a child wants to lean on you, lie down, or listen from under the table.

If a child wanders away, don't make a big deal about it. You may want to draw the child back by asking him or her to point to something, or having the child help you turn pages.

Use short stories; children especially like rhyming words and nonsense sounds in rhythm.

Many parents and teachers find it helpful to make up a story for a child who has a particular worry. Often it helps to change the sex or age of the story character so that the experience does not seem so personal to the child. You may find that the child wants to hear a particular story or detail of a story over and over ("Tell about when it got dark."). Such a story is worth writing down for the child to keep.

Snack Time

Snack-time activities can help children improve their:

- speech and language development (naming foods, asking for what they want).
- ability to use various senses (tasting, smelling, and discovering different textures of food).
- social skills.
- fine motor coordination (grasping utensils, hand–eye coordination).
- cognitive skills (learning about different food groups, quantity, and so on).
- self-help skills (setting the table, serving food, clearing the table, and table manners).

Preparation. Have the snack, plates, glasses, napkins, and anything else you need clean and ready. Allow children to take turns setting the table, passing the snack, and cleaning up. Show the child with learning problems how to do each task, and give help when needed. Have the snack at the same time every day so that children can anticipate it. If there is something that is hard to portion out (like raisins or peanuts), divide it ahead of time and give each child a small paper cup full.

Tips. Use snack time as a social time to share, talk, and take turns and to encourage self-feeding skills for children who are just learning to eat independently.

Use a routine for cleanup. If necessary, show a child how to pour and pick up plates to avoid spills and crashes. Have a sponge ready for those accidental spills.

Some children have special worries about routines like snack time. Be reliable: provide food when you say you will, remain seated if you promised that you would, and see that each child gets his or her fair share. It may be helpful to allow a child who is constantly worried about there not being enough food to go around to sit near you or the person in charge of, for example, the juice pitcher. It may also be helpful to let this child know in advance that "seconds" are available or that there is a limit on cookies.

Snack time is a good time to teach all kinds of concepts. Talk about colors of different juices and of cups and pitchers. Begin teaching number concepts ("how many cups," "how many napkins") and begin to apply what the children may know about numbers and sets. This is also a good time to teach manners (such as "May I please . . . ?").

Playground

Playground activities can help children improve their:

- muscle coordination.
- body awareness.
- rhythm.
- balance.
- ability to follow directions.

- language development ("Step on the circle." "Jump off the step." "Pick up the ball." "Stand beside the tree.").
- hand–eye coordination.
- socialization with other children.

Preparation. Playground or gym time should be a planned part of every day. The equipment that you need for the activity (such as balls, hoops, beanbags, parachute, or records) should be ready and in good shape. Time spent on the playground should allow for free play as well as planned games and activities. The activities should emphasize cooperative play whenever possible.

Tips. Give verbal directions and show the children what to do. Stay close to children with retardation until you are sure they understand. Be sure you have planned the transition from one activity to the next.

Some children can get too excited during free play. If this happens, invite the child to play with you (catch, kickball, or animal walks). If a child consistently overreacts during free play, you might consider making up a plan for the child that leaves out free play for a while.

Beanbags are easier to catch than balls. Provide them to ensure a child's success at catching.

Rather than have the children choose sides in games, divide them by the colors of their shirts, or by separating them into two equal groups. It hurts not to be chosen for a team.

End every activity in a way that makes starting the next one easier. For example, end a race by having all children sit down when their turn is over.

Be sure that the play area is safe: fenced, with no glass, and small enough to be well supervised.

Obstacle Course

An obstacle course helps children improve their:

- muscle coordination.
- body awareness.
- balance.
- socialization with other children.
- ability to follow directions.
- language development ("Go under the table," "Jump over the pillow," "Wiggle through the tire").

Preparation. Set up a simple obstacle course inside a large room or on the playground. Chairs, tables with blankets over them, rubber tires, and cloth tunnels can be put together to make an obstacle course. Make the first one easy so that everyone can do it alone or with little help. Check the course for safety to make sure that a tumble won't hurt anyone.

Tips. Show the children how to go through the course by doing it yourself, as much as you can, or by having a child demonstrate it for the others. As the children go through the course, describe what they are doing. ("Susan is going under the chair, through the tunnel, and over the chair.") Let children take several turns for fun and practice.

Make sure the children go through it one at a time, so they can take it at their own pace.

Sorting

Sorting activities help children work on:

- concept formation (classification).
- receptive language (understanding description of objects: "Put the red cars here and the blue cars there").
- hand–eye coordination.
- socialization.

Preparation. Have the materials to be sorted ready, such as pots and pans or different-colored toys.

Tips. Explain and demonstrate the activity. Once the child understands, let him or her take several turns. Give help as needed. When the child finishes, check the work. Ask the child to tell you what he or she did. Praise efforts and successes.

Start with objects that differ from each other in only one way. For example, you might have ten small trucks—five blue and five red. When you are sure that the child knows how to sort these, you can make the game harder.

Using pictures rather than objects is one way to make the activity harder. Another way is to increase the number of things and the ways in which they are different. For example, put all of the small, blue circles together and all of the large, green circles together.

Having the children sort by functional categories makes the activity still harder. For example, "Put all of the things we could ride in together"; "Put all of the things we could eat together."

Be sure the objects for sorting are interesting. Make sure the materials are safe; you may want to laminate many of them. And finally, choose objects that are easy to handle and that won't bounce or roll away.

SUMMARY

Every activity described above provides practice in at least two skill areas, which means that the child will be helped in several ways at once. You can determine which skill areas to work on from your own observations and from your discussions with the child's teachers or handicap specialists. Remember that these activities are only examples—you know and do many more than these. Think about the skills involved in other activities at home or in school. Water play, blocks, dress-up, puppet play, and coloring all involve many skill areas.

Source: Mainstreaming Preschoolers, a series of books for both teachers and parents of children involved in the Head Start program; though the focus of the original materials (prepared for the Administration for Children, Youth and Families) was on three-to-five-year-olds with various minor-to-major disabilities, the general guidelines and activities apply to all children. Material from several books has been merged and modified somewhat for use by parents or child-care workers.

Guides to Children's Reading

Here is a selection of guides to children's reading, some intended for parents, others aimed at librarians and teachers, but all useful to anyone looking for books for children of different ages, needs, and interests. In addition, following this section is a list of MEDAL-WINNING CHILDREN'S BOOKS. Many books for children on specific topics, such as sleeping disorders or learning disabilities, are also given under those topics in the A-to-Z portion of the book.

Periodical sources of the best current books

Notable Children's Books. Annual list of best new children's books; available for 30¢ from American Library Association, 50 East Huron Street, Chicago, IL 60611. (Many state and local libraries also prepare such lists.)

Books for Children. Annual list of best new books, preschool to junior-high ages, selected by Library of Congress committee; available for $1 from Consumer Information Center, Department 116V, Pueblo, CO 81009.

The Horn Book. Journal, published six times a year, with reviews, articles, and special features about best new books for children and young adults. Subscription available from The Horn Book, Inc., 31 St. James Avenue, Boston, MA 02116-4167.

Children's books in general

Choosing Books for Children: A Commonsense Guide, revised edition, by Betsy Hearne. New York: Dell/Delacorte, 1990.

Picture Books for Children, third edition, by Patricia J. Cianciolo. Chicago, IL: ALA Books, 1990.

Best Books for Children: Preschool Through Grade 6, fourth edition, by John T. Gillespie and Corinne J. Naden. New York: Bowker, 1990.

Mother Goose Comes First: An Annotated Guide to the Best Books and Recordings for Your Preschool Child, by Lois Winkel and Sue Kimmel. New York: Henry Holt, 1990.

Reading for the Love of It: Best Books for Young Readers, by Michele Landsberg. New York: Prentice Hall, 1989.

Books for Children to Read Alone™: A Guide for Parents and Librarians, by George Wilson and Joyce Moss. New York: Bowker, 1989. Books for children 4 to 8.

Adventuring with Books: A Booklist for Pre-K–Grade 6, edited by Mary Jett-Simpson. NCTE, 1989.

Books Kids Love. 42-minute video introducing parents to 50 recommended books for children of various ages. Available from Winward, P.O. Box 50, BL190, Amherst, NY 14226.

Beginning with Excellence: An Adult Guide to Great Children's Reading. Three 3-hour cassettes, available from Sound Advantage Audio Publishers, 61 Walk Hill Street, Boston, MA 02130. Book people recommend good books for children.

Choosing Books for Kids: Choosing the Right Book for the Right Child at the Right Time, by Barbara Brenner, Betty D. Boegehold, and Joanne Oppenheim, The Bank Street College of Education. New York: Ballantine, 1988.

The New York Times Parent's Guide to the Best Books for Children, by Eden Ross Lipson. New York: Times Books, 1988.

For babies

Sweet Sleep: A Collection of Lullabies and Cradle Songs, by Christopher Headington. New York: Clarkson N. Potter, 1990. For all ages.

Nursery Treasury: A Collection of Baby Games, Rhymes and Lullabies, compiled by Sally Emerson. Illustrated by Moira and Colin Maclean. Garden City, NY: Doubleday, 1988.

Baby's Bedtime Book, by Kay Chorao. New York: Dutton, 1984. Cassette (with Judy Collins singing)–book package (1989) available from E.P. Dutton, Order Department, P.O. Box 120, Bergenfield, NJ 07261.

The Baby's Story Book, by Kay Chorao. New York: Dutton, 1984. Cassette (with Arlo Gurthrie reading)–book package (1989) available from E.P. Dutton, Order Department, P.O. Box 120, Bergenfield, NJ 07261.

Babies Need Books, by Dorothy Butler. New York: Atheneum, 1980. Books for ages starting from infancy.

On storytelling and reading aloud

The Boy Who Would Be a Helicopter: The Uses of Storytelling in the Classroom, by Vivian Gussin Paley. Cambridge, MA: Harvard University Press, 1990.

American Children's Folklore: A Book of Rhymes, Games, Jokes, Stories, and Camp Legends for Parents, Grandparents, Teachers, Counselors, and All Adults Who Were Once Children, by Simon Bronner. Little Rock, AK: August House, 1989.

The New Read-Aloud Handbook, by Jim Trelease. New York: Penguin, 1989.

Storytelling™: Art and Technique, by Augusta Baker and Ellin Greene. New York: Bowker, 1989. Books for children 3 to 13.

The Read-Aloud Treasury: Favorite Nursery Rhymes, Poems, Stories, and More for the Very Young, compiled by Joanna Cole and Stephanie Calmenson. Illustrated by Ann Schweninger. Garden City, NY: Doubleday, 1988.

For Reading Out Loud! A Guide to Sharing Books with Children, 2nd edition, by Margaret M. Kimmel and Elizabeth Segel. New York: Delacorte, 1988.

Twice Upon a Time: Stories to Tell, Retell, Act Out, and Write About, by Judy Sierra and Robert Kaminski. Bronx, New York: H.W. Wilson, 1989.

On specific areas of interest or concern

Science and Technology in Fact and Fiction: A Guide to Children's Books, by DayAnn M. Kennedy, et al. New York: Bowker, 1990.

Science and Technology in Fact and Fiction: A Guide to Young Adult Books, by DayAnn M. Kennedy, et al. New York: Bowker, 1990.

The Bookfinder 4: When Kids Need Books: Annotations of Books Published 1983 Through 1986, by Sharon Spredemann Dreyer. Circle Pines, MN: American Guidance Service, 1989. Series of books matching needs and problems of young people, with *Bookfinder 1* covering pre-1974 books, *Bookfinder 2* books published 1975–78, and *Bookfinder 3* covering 1979–82. Books for ages 2 to 15.

Literature for Young People on War and Peace: An Annotated Bibliography, by Harry Eiss, comp. Westport, CT: Greenwood, 1989.

Books for the Gifted Child: Volume 2, by Paula Hauser and Gail A. Nelson. New York: Bowker, 1988. Current books for ages 3 to 13, since the closing date of Vol. 1.

Books for the Gifted Child, Volume 1, by Barbara H. Baskin and Karen Harris. New York: Bowker, 1980.

Eye-Openers! How to Choose and Use Children's Books about Real People, Places and Things, by Beverly Kobrin. New York: Penguin, 1988.

Values in Selected Children's Books of Fiction and Fantasy, by Carolyn W. Field and Jacqueline Schachter Weiss. Hamden, CT: Shoe String, 1987. Books for preschool to eighth grade.

Helping Children Cope: Mastering Stress Through Books and Stories, by Joan Fassler. New York: Free Press, 1978.

Books to Help Children Cope with Separation and Loss, by Joane E. Bernstein. New York: Bowker, 1977.

Background works

Don't Tell the Grownups: Subversive Children's Literature, by Alison Lurie. Boston: Little, Brown, 1990.

From Wonder to Wisdom: Using Stories to Help Children Grow, by Charles A. Smith. New York: New American Library, 1989.

Rose, Where Did You Get That Red? Teaching Great Poetry to Children, by Kenneth Koch. New York: Vintage, 1989.

Children's Literature in the Elementary School, 4th edition, by Charlotte Huck, et al. New York: Henry Holt, 1987.

Introducing Books to Children, 2nd edition, by Aidan Chambers. Boston, MA: Horn Books, 1983.

The Way of the Storyteller, by Ruth Sawyer. New York: Penguin, 1976.

Choosing videos and computer programs for children

Only the Best: The Guide to Highest-Rated Educational Software, Preschool–Grade 12. New York: Bowker, annual and cumulative editions.

Choosing the Best in Children's Videos. Producers: Joshua M. Greene and Susan Lazarus. Director: Shiva Kumar. Video offering samples of children's programs, available from ALA Video, 50 East Huron Street, Chicago, IL 60611.

Parents' Choice Magazine Guide to Videocassettes for Children, by Diana Huss Green and the editors of Consumer Reports Books. New York: Consumer Reports Books, 1989.

Medal-Winning Children's Books

Newbery Medal Winners

1990 *Number the Stars,* by Lois Lowry. (Houghton Mifflin)

1989 *Joyful Noise: Poems for Two Voices,* by Paul Fleischman. (Harper)

1988 *Lincoln: A Photobiography,* by Russell Freedman. (Houghton Mifflin)

1987 *The Whipping Boy,* by Sid Fleischman. (Greenwillow)

1986 *Sarah, Plain and Tall,* by Patricia MacLachlan. (Harper)

1985 *The Hero and the Crown,* by Robin McKinley. (Greenwillow)

1984 *Dear Mr. Henshaw,* by Beverly Cleary. (Morrow)

1983 *Dicey's Song,* by Cynthia Voigt. (Atheneum)

1982 *A Visit to William Blake's Inn: Poems for Innocent and Experienced Travelers,* by Nancy Willard. (Harcourt)

1981 *Jacob Have I Loved,* by Katherine Paterson. (Crowell)

1980 *A Gathering of Days,* by Joan W. Blos. (Scribner)

1979 *The Westing Game,* by Ellen Raskin. (Dutton)

1978 *Bridge to Terabithia,* by Katherine Paterson. (Crowell)

1977 *Roll of Thunder, Hear My Cry,* by Mildred D. Taylor. (Dial)

1976 *The Grey King,* by Susan Cooper. (Atheneum)

1975 *M. C. Higgins, the Great,* by Virginia Hamilton. (Macmillan)

1974 *The Slave Dancer,* by Paula Fox. (Bradbury)

1973 *Julie of the Wolves,* by Jean Craighead George. (Harper)

1972 *Mrs. Frisby and the Rats of NIMH,* by Robert C. O'Brien. (Atheneum)

1971 *Summer of the Swans,* by Betsy Byars. (Viking)

1970 *Sounder,* by William H. Armstrong. (Harper)

1969 *The High King,* by Lloyd Alexander (Holt)

1968 *From the Mixed-Up Files of Mrs. Basil E. Frankweiler,* by E. L. Konigsburg. (Atheneum)

1967 *Up a Road Slowly,* by Irene Hunt. (Follett)

1966 *I, Juan de Pareja,* by Elizabeth Borton de Trevino. (Farrar, Straus)

1965 *Shadow of a Bull,* by Maia Wojciechowska. (Atheneum)

1964 *It's Like This,* Cat, by Emily Neville. (Harper)

1963 *A Wrinkle in Time,* by Madeleine L'Engle. (Farrar, Straus)

1962 *The Bronze Bow,* by Elizabeth George Speare. (Houghton Mifflin)

1961 *Island of the Blue Dolphins,* by Scott O'Dell. (Houghton Mifflin)

1960 *Onion John,* by Joseph Krumgold (Crowell)

1959 *The Witch of Blackbird Pond,* by Elizabeth George Speare. (Houghton Mifflin)

1958 *Rifles for Watie,* by Harold Keith. (Crowell)

1957 *Miracles on Maple Hill,* by Virginia Sorensen. (Harcourt)

1956 *Carry on, Mr. Bowditch,* by Jean Lee Latham. (Houghton Mifflin)

1955 *The Wheel of the School,* by Meindert De Jong. (Harper)

1954 *... And Now Miguel,* by Joseph Krumgold. (Crowell)

1953 *Secret of the Andes,* by Ann Nolan Clark. (Viking)

1952 *Ginger Pye,* by Eleanor Estes. (Harcourt)

1951 *Amos Fortune, Free Man,* by Elizabeth Yates. (Dutton)

1950 *The Door in the Wall,* by Marguerite de Angeli. (Doubleday)

1949 *King of the Wind,* by Marguerite Henry. (Rand McNally)

1948 *The Twenty-One Balloons,* by William Pène du Bois. (Viking)

1947 *Miss Hickory,* by Carolyn Bailey. (Viking)

1946 *Strawberry Girl,* by Lois Lenski. (Lippincott)

1945 *Rabbit Hill,* by Robert Lawson. (Viking)

1944 *Johnny Tremain,* by Esther Forbes. (Houghton Mifflin)

1943 *Adam of the Road,* by Elizabeth Gray. (Viking)

1942 *The Matchlock Gun,* by Walter Edmonds. (Dodd)

1941 *Call It Courage,* by Armstrong Sperry. (Macmillan)

1940 *Daniel Boone,* by James Daugherty. (Viking)

1939 *Thimble Summer,* by Elizabeth Enright. (Holt, Rinehart)

1938 *The White Stag,* by Kate Seredy. (Viking)

1937 *Roller Skates,* by Ruth Sawyer. (Viking)

1936 *Caddie Woodlawn,* by Carol Brink. (Macmillan)

1935 *Dobry,* by Monica Shannon. (Viking)

1934 *Invincible Louisa,* by Cornelia Meigs. (Little, Brown)

1933 *Young Fu of the Upper Yangtze,* by Elizabeth Lewis. (Winston)

1932 *Waterless Mountain,* by Laura Armer. (Longmans)

1931 *The Cat Who Went to Heaven,* by Elizabeth Coatsworth. (Macmillan)

1930 *Hitty, Her First Hundred Years,* by Rachel Field. (Macmillan)

1929 *The Trumpeter of Krakow,* by Eric P. Kelly. (Macmillan)

1928 *Gay Neck, the Story of a Pigeon,* by Dhan Mukerji. (Dutton)

1927 *Smoky, the Cowhorse,* by Will James. (Scribner)

1926 *Shen of the Sea,* by Arthur Chrisman. (Dutton)

1925 *Tales from Silver Lands,* by Charles Finger. (Doubleday)

1924 *The Dark Frigate,* by Charles Hawes. (Atlantic/Little)

1923 *The Voyages of Doctor Dolittle,* by Hugh Lofting. (Lippincott)

1922 *The Story of Mankind,* by Henrik Van Loon. (Liveright)

Caldecott Medal Winners

1990 *Lon Po Po: A Red Riding Hood Story from China,* by Ed Young. (Philomel)

1989 *Song and Dance Man,* by Karen Ackerman, illustrated by Stephen Gammell. (Knopf)

1988 *Own Moon,* by Jane Yolen, illustrated by John Schoenherr. (Philomel)

1987 *Hey, Al,* by Arthur Yorinks, illustrated by Richard Egielski. (Farrar, Straus)

1986 *The Polar Express,* by Chris Van Allsburg. (Houghton Mifflin)

1985 *Saint George and the Dragon,* retold by Margaret Hodges, illustrated by Trina Schart Hyman. (Little, Brown)

1984 *The Glorious Flight: Across the Channel with Louis Blériot,* by Alice and Martin Provensen. (Viking)

1983 *Shadow,* by Blaise Cendrars, translated and illustrated by Marcia Brown. (Scribner)

1982 *Jumanji,* by Chris Van Allsburg. (Houghton Mifflin)

1981 *Fables,* by Arnold Lobel. (Harper)

1980 *Ox-Cart Man,* by Donald Hall, illustrated by Barbara Cooney. (Viking)

1979 *The Girl Who Loved Wild Horses,* by Paul Goble. (Bradbury)

1978 *Noah's Ark,* by Peter Spier. (Doubleday)

1977 *Ashanti to Zulu,* by Margaret Musgrove, illustrated by Leo and Diane Dillon. (Dial)

1976 *Why Mosquitos Buzz in People's Ears,* retold by Verna Aardema, illustrated by Leo and Diane Dillon. (Dial)

1975 *Arrow to the Sun,* by Gerald McDermott. (Viking)

1974 *Duffy and the Devil,* retold by Harve Zemach, illustrated by Margot Zemach. (Farrar, Straus)

1973 *The Funny Little Woman,* by Lafcadio Hearn, retold by Arlene Mosel, illustrated by Blair Lent. (Dutton)

1972 *One Fine Day,* by Nonny Hogrogian. (Macmillan)

1971 *A Story A Story,* by Gail E. Haley. (Atheneum)

1970 *Sylvester and the Magic Pebble,* by William Steig. (Windmill)

1969 *The Fool of the World and the Flying Ship,* retold by Arthur Ransome, illustrated by Uri Shulevitz. (Farrar, Straus)

1968 *Drummer Hoff,* adapted by Barbara Emberley, illustrated by Ed Emberley. (Prentice-Hall)

1967 *Sam, Bangs & Moonshine,* by Evaline Ness. (Holt)

1966 *Always Room for One More,* by Sorche Nic Leodhas, illustrated by Nonny Hogrogian. (Holt)

1965 *May I Bring a Friend?* by Beatrice Schenk de Regniers, illustrated by Beni Montresor. (Atheneum)

1964 *Where the Wild Things Are,* by Maurice Sendak. (Harper)

1963 *The Snowy Day,* by Ezra Jack Keats. (Viking)

1962 *Once a Mouse,* by Marcia Brown. (Scribner)

1961 *Baboushka and the Three Kings,* by Ruth Robbins, illustrated by Nicolas Sidjakov. (Parnassus)

1960 *Nine Days to Christmas,* by Marie Hall Ets and Aurora Labastida. (Viking)

1959 *Chanticleer and the Fox,* by Barbara Cooney. (Crowell)

1958 *Time of Wonder,* by Robert McCloskey. (Viking)

1957 *A Tree Is Nice,* by Janice Udry, illustrated by Marc Simont. (Harper)

1956 *Frog Went A-Courtin',* retold by John Langstaff, illustrated by Feodor Rojankovsky. (Harcourt)

1955 *Cinderella,* illustrated and retold from Perrault by Marcia Brown. (Scribner)

1954 *Madeline's Rescue,* by Ludwig Bemelmans. (Viking)

1953 *The Biggest Bear,* by Lynd Ward. (Houghton Mifflin)

1952 *Finders Keepers,* by Will Lipkind, illustrated by Nicolas Mordvinoff. (Harcourt)

1951 *The Egg Tree,* by Katherine Milhous. (Scribner)

1950 *Song of the Swallows,* by Leo Politi. (Scribner)

1949 *The Big Snow,* by Berta and Elmer Hader. (Macmillan)

1948 *White Snow, Bright Snow,* by Alvin Tresselt, illustrated by Roger Duvoisin. (Lothrop)

1947 *The Little Island,* by Golden MacDonald, illustrated by Leonard Weisgard. (Doubleday)

1946 *The Rooster Crows,* by Maude and Miska Petersham. (Macmillan)

1945 *Prayer for a Child,* by Rachel Field, illustrated by Elizabeth Orton Jones. (Macmillan)

1944 *Many Moons,* by James Thurber, illustrated by Louis Slobodkin. (Harcourt)

1943 *The Little House,* by Virginia Lee Burton. (Houghton Mifflin)

1942 *Make Way for Ducklings,* by Robert McCloskey. (Viking)

1941 *They Were Strong and Good,* by Robert Lawson. (Viking)

1940 *Abraham Lincoln,* by Ingri and Edgar Parin d'Aulaire. (Doubleday)

1939 *Mei Li,* by Thomas Handforth. (Doubleday)

1938 *Animals of the Bible,* by Helen Dean Fish, illustrated by Dorothy P. Lathrop. (Lippincott)

Parent's Bookshelf

Here is a sampling of recent books (with an occasional older classic) on parenting in general and on some special concerns, such as single parents, divorce's effect on children, or caring for a new baby. These are drawn from the flood of books that are published every year on one or another aspect of parenting. Libraries and bookstores will have (or can get) these and other titles on topics of interest to parents. For new books being published, parents may want to subscribe to one or more parenting magazines and perhaps join one of the several children's book clubs.

Some children's books on family life and activities are included below; for guides to books for children, see GUIDES TO CHILDREN'S READING (on page 561), followed by MEDAL-WINNING CHILDREN'S BOOKS. For books on specific topics, such as learning disabilities or Down's syndrome, for both parents and children, see those entries in the A-to-Z section of this book.

General works on parenting

Experts Advise Parents: A Guide to Raising Loving, Responsible Children, Eileen Shiff, ed. New York: Delacorte, 1990.

Compassionate Child-Rearing: An In-Depth Approach to Optimal Parenting, by Robert W. Firestone. New York: Plenum, 1990.

The Essential Partnership: How Parents and Children Can Meet the Emotional Challenges of Infancy and Childhood, by Stanley Greenspan, M.D., and Nancy Thorndike Greenspan. New York: Viking, 1989; Penguin, 1990.

Meeting Your Child's Hidden Needs, by Bruce Narramore. Old Tappan, NJ: Revell, 1990.

You Can Postpone Anything But Love, by Randall Colton Rolfe. New York: Warner, 1990.

Children of Fast-Track Parents: Raising Self-Sufficient and Confident Children in an Achievement-Oriented World, by Andrée Aelion Brooks. New York: Penguin, 1990.

The Anxious Parent, by Michael Schwartzman with Judith Sachs. New York: Simon & Schuster, 1990.

You and Your Child, expanded edition with study guide, by Charles R. Swindoll. Nashville, TN: Thomas Nelson, 1990.

The Family Contract: A Parent's Bill of Rights, by Howard Leftin. Summit, NJ: PIA, 1990.

The Power of Positive Parenting, by Dr. William Mitchell and Dr. Charles Paul Conn. New York: Wynwood, 1989.

The Parent–Child Connection, by Dr. Arnold Rincover. New York: Pocket, 1989.

The Parents' Guide to Dirty Tricks: How to Con, Hoodwink, and Outsmart Your Kids, by Bill Dodds. Deephaven, MN: Meadowbrook, 1989.

Growing Up Happy: Captain Kangaroo Tells Yesterday's Children How to Nurture Their Own, by Bob Keeshan. Garden City, NY: Doubleday, 1989.

Love and Power—Parent and Child: How to Raise Competent, Confident Children, by Glenn Austin, M.D. Rolling Hills Estates, CA: Robert Erdman, 1989.

Know Your Child: An Authoritative Guide for Today's Parents, by Stella Chess and Alexander Thomas. New York: Basic, 1989.

50/50 Parenting: Sharing Family Rewards and Responsibilities, by Gayle Kimball. Lexington, MA: Lexington, 1989.

Surviving Your Baby and Child: How to Raise a Child and Live to Tell About It, by Victor Langer. New York: Collier/Macmillan, 1989.

The Secret of a Happy Family: How to Find Freedom, Fulfillment and Love Together, by Steve Biddulph and Shaaron Biddulph. Garden City, NY: Doubleday, 1989.

Raising Positive Kids in a Negative World, by Zig Ziglar. New York: Ballantine, 1989.

How's Your Family? A Guide to Identifying Your Family's Strengths and Weaknesses, by Jerry M. Lewis, M.D. New York: Brunner/Mazel, 1989.

Predictive Parenting: What to Say When You Talk to Your Kids, by Shad Helmstetter. New York: Morrow, 1989.

Dr. Spock On Parenting: Sensible Advice for Today, by Dr. Benjamin Spock. New York: Simon & Schuster, 1988.

Straight Answers to Parents' Questions from Louise Bates Ames, Associate Director of the Gesell Institute of Child Development. New York: Crown, 1988.

A Good Enough Parent: A Book on Child-Rearing, by Bruno Bettelheim. New York: Vintage, 1988.

The Competent Child: An Approach to Psychotherapy and Preventive Mental Health, by Joseph M. Strayhorn. New York: Guilford, 1988.

Confident Parenting, by Mel Silberman. New York: Warner, 1988.

101 Ways to Tell Your Child "I Love You," by Vicki Lansky. Chicago: Contemporary, 1988.

Winning with Kids: How to Negotiate with Your Baby Bully, Kid Tyrant, Loner, Saint, Underdog or Winner So They Love Themselves and You Too, by Tessa Albert Warschaw and Victoria Secunda. New York: Bantam, 1988.

The Growing Years: The Cornell Medical Center's Guide to Your Child's Emotional Development from Birth to Adolescence, by the New York Hospital-Cornell Medical Center with Mark Rubenstein, M.D. New York: Atheneum, 1988.

Six Weeks to Better Parenting, by Caryl Waller Krueger. Nashville, TN: Abingdon, 1988.

Bradshaw On: The Family: A Revolutionary Way of Self-Discovery, by John Bradshaw. Pompano Beach, FL: Health Communications, 1988.

The Self-Confident Child, by Jean Yoder and William Proctor. New York: Facts on File, 1988.

Raising Your Family Naturally, by Joy Gross and Karen Freifeld. Secaucus, NJ: Lyle Stuart, 1988.

How to Talk So Kids Will Listen and Listen So Kids Will Talk, by Adele Faber and Elaine Mazlish. New York: Avon, 1982; Chicago: Nightingale-Conant, 1988.

Quality Parenting: How to Transform the Everyday Moments We Spend with Our Children into Special, Meaningful Time, by Linda Albert and Michael Popkin. New York: Random House, 1987.

I Only Want What's Best for You: A Parent's Guide to Raising Emotionally Healthy Children, by Judith R. Brown. New York: St. Martin's, 1986.

On Becoming a Family: The Growth of Attachment, by T. Berry Brazelton. New York: Delacorte/Seymour Lawrence, 1981.

On parenting infants

The Baby Kit: Everything You Need to Know About Caring for Your Newborn, by Penelope Leach. New York: Simon & Schuster, 1990.

I Wish Someone Had Told Me: Comfort, Support, and Advice for New Moms from More Than 60 Real-Life Mothers, by Nina Barrett. New York: Simon & Schuster/Fireside, 1990.

Taking Care of Your New Baby: A Guide to the First Month of Parenting, by Jeanne Watson Driscoll and Marsha Walker. Garden City Park, NY: Avery, 1990.

The Crying Baby, by Sheila Kitzinger. New York: Penguin, 1990.

The Superbaby Syndrome: Escaping the Dangers of Hurrying Your Child, by Jean Grasso Fitzpatrick. Orlando, FL: Harcourt Brace Jovanovich, 1990.

Taking Care of Your New Baby: A Guide to Infant Care, by Jeanne Driscoll and Marsha Walker. Garden City Park, NY: Avery, 1989.

Day-By-Day Baby Care, by Dr. Miriam Stoppard. New York: Ballantine, 1989.

Your Baby: The First Twelve Months, by William Sears, M.D. Hauppauge, NY: Barron's, 1989.

The World of the Baby: A Celebration of Infancy Through the Ages, by Georgina O'Hara. Garden City, NY: Doubleday, 1989.

First-Year Baby Care, revised edition, by Paula Kelly, M.D. Deephaven, MN: Meadowbrook, 1989.

The Great American Baby Almanac: A Complete Compendium of Facts, Fancies, and Traditions, by Irena Chalmers. New York: Viking, 1989.

What to Expect the First Year, by Arlene Eisenberg, Heidi E. Murkoff, and Sandee E. Hathaway. New York: Workman, 1988.

Old-Fashioned Baby Care: A Parents' Guide to Burping, Bathing, Feeding, Changing, Playing with & Loving Your New Baby, by Mama Ruby Wright with Carrie Carmichael. New York: Prentice Hall, 1988.

What Every Baby Knows, by T. Berry Brazelton. New York: Ballantine, 1988.

Your Newborn Baby: Everything You Need to Know, featuring Joan Lunden, by Michael Krauss with Sue Castle. New York: Warner, 1988.

Bringing Out the Best in Your Baby, by Art Ulene and Steven Shelov. New York: Collier/Macmillan, 1988.

In Celebration of Babies, by Carol Tannenhauser and Cheryl Moch. New York: Ballantine, 1988.

A Present to the Newborn: A Book for Parents and All Those Whose Lives Touch the Lives of Children, by Emily Hunter Slingluff. Washington, DC: Acropolis, 1988.

The World of the Newborn, by Daphne Maurer and Charles Maurer. New York: Basic, 1988.

Baby Hints, by Chris Casson Madden. New York: Fawcett, 1988.

Baby's First Year, by Phyllis Hoffman. New York: Harper & Row, 1988.

Baby and Child Care, revised edition, by Benjamin Spock and Michael B. Rothenberg. New York: Pocket, 1985.

Activities with babies

Our Baby: A Book of Records and Memories, with pictures by Michael Hague. New York: Arcade/Little, Brown, 1990.

Baby's First Year: A Beatrix Potter Gift Set, illustrated by Beatrix Potter. New York: Frederick Warne/Penguin, 1990.

Baby Time: A Grownup's Handbook to Use with Baby, by Laurie Krasny Brown. Illustrated by Marc Brown. New York: Knopf, 1989.

Infant Massage: A Handbook for Loving Parents, revised edition, by Vimala Schneider McClure. New York: Bantam, 1989.

Baby Massage, by Amelia D. Auckett. New York: Newmarket, 1989.

Good Times with Baby, by Lulu Delacre. New York: Grosset & Dunlap, 1989.

Baby Peek-a-Boo Album, by Debra Meryl. New York: Grosset & Dunlap, 1989.

Baby Time, by Laurie Krasny Brown. New York: Knopf, 1989. Baby-care advice for parents *and* children.

Baby Games, by Elaine Martin. Philadelphia: Running Press, 1988.

Baby name books

What's in a Name? The Heroes and Heroines Baby Name Book, by Nancy Heffernan and Louis Judson. Rocklin, CA: Prima, 1990.

The Baby Name Countdown: Meanings and Popularity Ratings for 50,000 Names, by Janet Schwegel. New York: Paragon, 1990.

The Worst Baby Name Book, by Bob Glickman. Kansas City, MO: Andrews and McMeel, 1990.

The Great Beginnings Baby Name Book: Illustrious Names from the Arts, History, Literature, Sports, Mythology, and Cultures Around the World, by Sara L. Whitter. Chicago: Contemporary, 1989.

What People Will Think of Your Baby's Name, by Bruce Lansky and Barry Sinrod. Deephaven, MN: Meadowbrook, 1989.

The Ultimate Baby Name Book, by the editors of Consumer Guide.® New York: New American Library, 1989.

What to Name Your Jewish Baby, by Anita Diamant. New York: Summit, 1989.

Buying for babies and older children

The Childwise Catalog, revised edition, by Jack Gillis and Mary Ellen Fise. New York: Harper & Row/Perennial, 1990.

Guide to Baby Products, 2nd edition, by Sandy Jones, et al. New York: Consumer Reports Books, 1989.

Buying the Best for Your Baby, by Tom Biracree and Nancy Biracree. New York: Dodd, Mead, 1988.

On kids' rooms and parties

Nursery Design: Creating a Perfect Environment for Your Child, by Barbara Aria. Photographs by Andrew Bordwin. New York: Bantam, 1990.

It's My Party, by Laurine Croasdale and Carole Davis. Minneapolis, MN: Meadowbrook, 1990. Theme parties for kids.

Children's Parties: Planning Unique and Unforgettable Parties for Your Child, by Barbara Radcliffe Rogers and Juliette Rogers. Los Angeles: Price Stern Sloan, 1990.

Nursery Style: Creating Beautiful Rooms for Children, by Annie Sloan and Felicity Bryan. Chicago: Contemporary, 1989.

Baby Rooms: Creating the Perfect Space for Your Baby to Grow In, by Warren Shoulberg. Los Angeles: Price Stern Sloan, 1989.

In My Room: Designing for and with Children, by Antonio F. Torrice and Ro Logrippo. New York: Ballantine, 1989.

Children's Rooms & Play Yards. Menlo Park, CA: Sunset, 1988.

A Piece of Cake: Fun and Easy Theme Parties for Children, by Gwenn Boechler, Shirley Charlton, and Alice Trader Wayne. Garden City, NY: Doubleday, 1988.

On parenting young children

Everyday Parenting: The First Five Years, by Robin Goldstein with Janet Gallant. New York: Penguin, 1990.

The Inner Child: Understanding Your Child's Emotional Growth in the First Six Years of Life, by H. Paul Gabriel and Robert Wool. New York: Times Books, 1990.

Your Baby and Child: From Birth to Age Five, revised edition, by Penelope Leach. New York: Schocken, 1989.

Toddlers and Parents: A Declaration of Independence, revised edition, by T. Berry Brazelton. New York: Delacorte, 1989.

Your One-Year-Old: The Fun-loving, Funny 12-to-24-month Old, by Louise Bates Ames, et al. New York: Delacorte, 1982.

Your Two-Year-Old: Terrible or Tender, by Louise Bates Ames and Frances L. Ilg. New York: Dell, 1980.

Your Three-Year-Old: Friend or Enemy, by Louise Bates Ames and Frances L. Ilg. New York: Dell, 1980.

Your Four-Year-Old: Wild & Wonderful, by Louise Bates Ames and Frances L. Ilg. New York: Dell, 1980.

Your Five-Year-Old: Sunny & Serene, by Louise Bates Ames and Frances L. Ilg. New York: Dell, 1981.

Your Six-Year-Old: Loving and Defiant, by Louise Bates Ames, et al. New York: Dell, 1981.

Your Seven-Year-Old: Life in a Minor Key, by Louise Bates Ames and Carol C. Haber. New York: Delacorte, 1985.

Your Eight-Year-Old: Lively and Outgoing, by Louise Bates Ames and Carol Chase Haber. New York: Delacorte, 1990.

Your Nine-Year-Old: Thoughtful and Mysterious, by Louise Bates Ames and Carol Chase Haber. New York: Delacorte, 1990.

Your Ten- to Fourteen-Year-Old, by Louise Bates Ames, Frances L. Ilg, M.D., and Sidney M. Baker. New York: Delacorte, 1988.

The Mother's Almanac II: Your Child from Six to Twelve: The Most Complete Book Ever Written on the Joys, Challenges, and Changes of the School Years, by Marguerite Kelly. Garden City, NY: Doubleday, 1989.

The Preschool Years: Family Strategies That Work From Experts and Parents, by Ellen Galinsky and Judy David. New York: Times Books, 1988.

When Your Child Needs You: A Parents' Guide Through the Early Years, by Eleanor Weisberger. Bethesda, MD: Adler & Adler, 1987.

Dr. Balter's Child Sense: Understanding and Handling the Common Problems of Infancy and Early Childhood, by Lawrence Balter with Anita Shreve. New York: Poseidon, 1985.

To Listen to a Child: Understanding the Normal Problems of Growing Up, by T. Berry Brazelton. Reading, MA: Addison-Wesley, 1984.

The Well Child Book, Book 1: Birth–18 Months, Book 2: 18–36 Months, by Mike Samuels and Nancy Samuels. Illustrated by Wendy Frost. New York: Summit, 1982.

You and Your Small Wonder, by Marler B. Karnes. Circle Pines, MN: American Guidance Service, 1982.

Welcoming Your 2nd Baby, revised edition, by Vicki Lansky. New York: Avon, 1987.

Traveling With Your Baby, by Vicki Lansky. New York: Avon, 1985.

The Parents' Book of Facts: Child Development from Birth to Age Five, by Tom and Nancy Biracree. New York: Facts on File, 1989.

On children's moral and social views

Free to Be . . . A Family: A Book About All Kinds of Belonging, by Marlo Thomas and Friends. New York: Bantam, 1990.

Free to Be . . . You and Me: A Different Kind of Book for Children and Adults to Enjoy Together, conceived by Marlo Thomas, developed and edited by Carole Hart, Letty Cottin Pogrebin, Mary Rodgers, and Marlo Thomas. New York: Bantam, 1990.

Spiritual Parenting, by David L. Carroll. New York: Paragon House, 1990. On communicating moral and spiritual values.

Who's Calling the Shots? How to Respond Effectively to Children's Fascination with War Play and War Toys, by Nancy Carlsson-Paige and Diane Levin. Philadelphia: New Society, 1990.

Do I Have to Say Hello? Aunt Delia's Manners Quiz for Kids and Their Grown-ups, by Delia Ephron. New York: Viking, 1989.

Raising Kids on Purpose, by Gwen Weising. Old Tappan, NJ: Fleming Revell, 1989. On communicating parental values to children.

When Children Ask About God, by Rabbi Harold S. Kushner. New York: Schocken, 1989.

Why Kids Lie: How Parents Can Encourage Truthfulness, by Paul Ekman. New York: Scribner, 1989.

How to Raise Good Children: Encouraging Moral Growth, by Laurel Hughes. Nashville, TN: Abingdon, 1988.

Why Good Parents Have Bad Kids: How to Make Sure that Your Child Grows Up Right, by E. Kent Hayes. Garden City, NY: Doubleday, 1988.

Parenting for Peace and Justice: Ten Years Later, revised and updated edition, by Kathleen McGinnis and James McGinnis. Maryknoll, NY: Orbis, 1990.

The Moral Child: Nurturing Children's Natural Moral Growth, by William Damon. New York: Free Press/Macmillan, 1990.

Raising Wise Children: How to Teach Your Child to Think, by Carolyn Kohlenberger and Noel Wescombe. Portland, OR: Multnomah, 1990.

Building Your Child's Faith, by Alice Chapin. Nashville, TN: Thomas Nelson, 1990.

The Delicate Balance: Love and Authority in Torah Parenting, by Sarah Radcliffe. Spring Valley, NY: Philipp Feldheim, 1990.

Children and Prejudice: The Development of Ethnic Awareness and Identity, by Frances Aboud. New York: Basil Blackwell, 1988.

Watermelons Not War!: A Support Book for Parents in the Nuclear Age, by Kate Cloud, et al. Philadelphia, PA: New Society, 1984.

Right from the Start: A Guide to Nonsexist Child Rearing, by Selma Greenberg. Boston: Houghton Mifflin, 1978.

On parenting adolescents

Teen Is a Four-Letter Word: A Survival Kit for Parents, second edition, by Joan Wester Anderson. Crozet, Va: Betterway, 1990.

I'm On Your Side: Resolving Conflict Between Parents and Teenagers, by Jane Nelsen and Lynn Lott. Rocklin, CA: Prima, 1990.

You and Your Adolescent: A Parent's Guide to Ages 12 to 20, by Laurence Steinberg and Ann Levine. New York: Harper & Row, 1990.

A Parent's Guide to Adolescence: Understanding Your Teenager, by David R. Miller. Denver: Accent, 1989.

My Teenager Is Driving Me Crazy, by Joyce L. Vedral. New York: Ballantine, 1989.

How to Stop the Battle with Your Teenager: A Practical Guide to Solving Everyday Problems, by Don Fleming and Laurel J. Schmidt. New York: Prentice Hall, 1989.

Teenage Years—A Parent's Survival Guide, by Beverly Guhl. Tucson, AZ: Fisher, 1989.

Secret of a Good Life With Your Teenager, by Angela B. McBride. Tucson, AZ: Fisher, 1989.

Dear Teenager, by Norma Swanson. Nashville, TN: Thomas Nelson, 1989.

Parents' Work Is Never Done: Helping Children from 16–30 Grow Toward Psychological Well-Being, by Margaret Neely and James Haines. Far Hills, NJ: New Horizon, 1989.

Adolescence: What's A Parent to Do?, by Richard D. Parsons. Mahwah, NJ: Paulist Press, 1988.

Teenagers: When to Worry and What to Do, by Douglas Powell. Garden City, NY: Doubleday, 1988.

Stop Struggling with Your Teen, by Evonne Weinhaus and Karen Friedman. New York: Penguin, 1988.

Apprenticeship for Adulthood: Preparing Youth for the Future, by Stephen F. Hamilton. New York: Free Press, 1989.

When Teenagers Work: The Psychological and Social Costs of Adolescent Employment, by Ellen Greenberger and Laurence Steinberg. New York: Basic, 1988.

I Wish My Parents Understood: The Nonkin/TeenAge Relationships Survey, by Lesley Jan Nonkin. New York: Freundlich, 1985.

Adolescent Relations with Mothers, Fathers, and Friends, by James Youniss and Jacqueline Smollar. Chicago: University of Chicago Press, 1985.

The Changing Legal World of Adolescence, by Franklin E. Zimring. New York: Free Press, 1982.

(For books on adolescence *for* adolescents, see ADOLESCENCE in the A-to-Z section.)

On fathering

How to Dad, by John Boswell and Ron Barrett. New York: Delacorte, 1990.

Dads Say the Dumbest Things!, by Bruce Lansky and K.L. Jones. Minneapolis, MN: Meadowbrook, 1990.

Daddy's Home! Reflections of a Family Man, by Steven Schnur. New York: Crown, 1990.

Just Between Father and Son, by James Wilder. Downers Grove, IL: Inter Varsity Press, 1990.

Finding Our Fathers: How a Man's Life Is Shaped by His Relationship with His Father, by Samuel Osherson. New York: Fawcett/Columbine, 1990.

Between Father and Child: How to Become the Kind of Father You Want to Be, by Dr. Ronald Levant and John Kelly. New York: Viking, 1989.

Divorced Father: Coping with Problems, Creating Solutions, by Gerald A. Hill. Crozet, VA: Betterway, 1989.

The Birth of a Father: New Fathers Talk About Pregnancy, Childbirth, and the First Three Months, by Cecilia Worth. New York: McGraw-Hill, 1988.

The Nurturing Father, by Kyle D. Pruett. New York: Warner, 1988.

On Being a Father, by Frank Ferrara. New York: Doubleday/Dolphin, 1985. Fathers after divorce.

Father/Son Book, by Joel D. Joseph. Bethesda, MD: National, 1985. Guide to activities for fathers and sons up to age 6.

Dimensions of Fatherhood, by Shirley Hanson and Frederick Bozett, eds. Beverly Hills, CA: Sage Publications, 1985. Scholarly research report.

Single Fathers, by Geoffrey L. Greif. Lexington, MA: Lexington, 1985. Study of 1,100 single fathers.

Fatherhood U.S.A.: The First National Guide to Programs, Services, and Resources for and about Fathers, by Debra G. Klinman and Rhiana Kohl. New York: Garland, 1984.

Divorced Fathers: Reconstructing a Quality Life, by Thomas Oakland. New York: Human Sciences, 1984.

Saturday Parent: A Book for Separated Families, by Peter Rowlands. New York: Continuum, 1980.

On mothering

Motherhood. Philadelphia: Running Press, 1990.

Motherhood: What It Does to Your Mind, by Jane Price. Winchester, MA: Unwin Hyman, 1989.

Mother's First Year: A Coping Guide for Recent and Prospective Mothers, by Hanns G. Pieper. Crozet, VA: Betterway, 1989.

The Mother's Survival Guide, by Shirley R. Radl. Dallas, TX: Steve Davis, 1989.

The Dictionary According to Mommy, by Joyce Armor. Deephaven, MN: Meadowbrook, 1989.

Too Long a Child: The Mother–Daughter Dyad, by Nini Herman. Irvington, NY: Columbia University Press, 1989.

Babies and Their Mothers, by D.W. Winnicott. Reading, MA: Addison-Wesley, 1988.

After Having a Baby, by Diana Bert, Katherine Dusay, Susan Keel, Mary Oeiand, and Jan Yanehiro. New York: Dell, 1988.

Mothers: A Celebration in Prose, Poetry and Photographs of Mothers and Motherhood, by Alexandra Towle, ed. New York: Simon & Schuster, 1988.

The Motherhood Report: How Women Feel about Being Mothers, by Louis Genevie and Eva Margolis. New York: Macmillan, 1987.

Absentee Mothers, by Patricia Paskowicz. New York: Universe, 1982; also Totowa, NJ: Allanheld, Osmun, 1982.

The Critical Importance of Mothering, by Elliott Barker. Available from La Leche League International.

Pronatalism: The Myth of Mom and Apple Pie, by Ellen Peck and Judith Senderowitz. New York: Crowell, 1974.

Becoming a Stepfamily: Stages of Development in Remarried Families, by Frank Cardelle. New York: Gardner, 1989.

Intermarriage: The Challenge of Living with Differences, by Susan Weidman Schneider. New York: Free Press, 1989.

Stepfathers: Struggles and Solutions, by Charles Somervill. Louisville, KY: Westminster/John Knox, 1989.

Remarriage and Blended Families, by Stephen R. Treat. New York: Pilgrim, 1988.

What's Happening to the American Family, revised edition, by Sar A. Levitan, Richard S. Belous, and Frank Gallo. Baltimore, MD: Johns Hopkins, 1988.

Changing Families: A Guide for Kids and Grown-ups, by David Fassler, M.D., Michele Lash, and Sally B. Ives. Burlington, VT: Waterfront, 1988.

Stepfathering, by Mark Bruce Rosin. New York: Ballantine, 1988.

The Good Stepmother: A Practical Guide, by Karen Savage and Patricia Adams. New York: Crown, 1988.

Happily Intermarried: Authoritative Advice for a Joyous Jewish-Christian Marriage, by Rabbi Roy A. Rosenberg, Father Peter Meehan, and Reverend John Wade Payne. New York: Macmillan, 1988.

Last-Chance Children: Growing Up With Older Parents, by Monica Morris. Irvington, NY: Columbia University Press, 1988. Pros, cons, and long-term effects.

Stepfathering: Stepfathers' Advice on Creating a New Family, by Mark Bruce Rosin. New York: Simon & Schuster, 1987.

The Rainbow Effect: Interracial Families, by Kathlyn Gay. New York: Franklin Watts, 1987.

Raising Your Jewish/Christian Child: How Interfaith Parents Can Give Children the Best of Both Heritages, by Lee F. Gruzen. New York: Dodd, Mead, 1987; paperback New York: Newmarket, 1990.

Stepfamilies: Making Them Work, by Erna Paris. New York: Avon, 1984.

Nontraditional Families: Parenting and Child Development, Michael E. Lamb, ed. Hillsdale, NJ: Erlbaum, 1982.

Raising Other People's Kids, by Evelyn Felker. Grand Rapids, MI: William B. Erdman, 1981.

On stepfamilies and nontraditional families, for kids

Sam Is My Half Brother, by Lizi Boyd. New York: Viking, 1990. For ages 4 to 6.

Stepfamilies, by Marilyn Bailey. New York: Crestwood/Macmillan, 1990. Part of the Facts About series.

Stepfamilies, by Elizabeth Hodder. New York: Watts/Gloucester, 1990. For young readers.

Heather Has Two Mommies, by Lesléa Newman. Northampton, MA: In Other Words, 1990. For ages 3 to 5.

Martha's New Daddy, by Danielle Steel. New York: Delacorte, 1989. For ages 4 to 7.

Mommy Never Went to Hebrew School, by Mindy Avra Portnoy. Brooklyn, NY: Kane/Miller, 1989.

Living in Two Worlds, by Maxine B. Rosenberg. New York: Lothrop, Lee & Shepard, 1986. For young readers.

The Not-So-Wicked Stepmother, by Lizi Boyd. New York: Penguin, 1987. For ages 4 to 6.

About divorce and children

Second Chances: Men, Women, and Children a Decade After Divorce, by Judith Wallerstein and Sandra Blakeslee. Boston: Houghton Mifflin, 1990.

Vicki Lansky's Divorce Book for Parents: Helping Your Kids Cope with Divorce and Its Aftermath, by Vicki Lansky. New York: New American Library, 1989.

Long-Distance Parenting: A Guide for Divorced Parents, by Miriam Galper Cohen. New York: New American Library, 1989.

Growing Up With Divorce: Helping Your Child Avoid Immediate and Later Emotional Problems, by Neil Kalter. New York: Free Press, 1989.

Divorced Families: Meeting the Challenge of Divorce and Remarriage, by Constance R. Ahrons and Roy H. Rodgers. New York: Norton, 1989.

Helping Children of Divorce: A Handbook for Parents and Teachers, by Susan Arnsberg Diamond. New York: Schocken, 1985.

The Divorce Revolution: The Unexpected Social and Economic Consequences for Women and Children in America, by Lenore J. Weitzman. New York: Free Press, 1985.

On Being a Father, by Frank Ferrara. New York: Doubleday/Dolphin, 1985. Fathers after divorce.

On divorce, for kids

When Your Parents Get a Divorce, by Ann Banks. New York: Puffin/Penguin, 1990. For ages 8 to 12.

Divorce, by Angela Grunsell. New York: Gloucester, 1990. For ages 7 to 10.

Divorce, by Caroline Evensen Lazo. New York: Crestwood, 1990. Part of the Facts About series.

Growing Up with Divorce: Helping Your Child Avoid Immediate and Later Emotional Problems, by Neil Kalter. New York: Free Press, 1989.

Where Is Daddy? The Story of a Divorce, by Beth Goff. Boston, MA: Beacon, 1988. For young children

How It Feels When Parents Divorce, by Jill Krementz. New York: Knopf, 1984.

Growing Up Divorced, by Linda Francke. New York: Simon & Schuster, 1983.

You're Divorced but Your Children Aren't, by T. Roger Duncan and Darlene Duncan. Englewood Cliffs, NJ: Prentice-Hall, 1979.

(See also CUSTODY; CHILD SUPPORT in the A-to-Z section.)

On single parenting

The Single Mother's Book: A Practical Guide to Managing Your Children, Career, Home, Finances, and Everything Else, by Joan Anderson. Atlanta: Peachtree, 1990.

My Kind of Family: A Book for Kids in Single-Parent Homes, by Michele Lash, Sally Ives Loughridge, and David Fassler. Burlington, VT: Waterfront, 1990.

This Is Me and My Single Parent: A Discovery Workbook for Children and Single Parents, by Marla D. Evans. New York: Magination, 1989.

Single Mothers Raising Sons, by Bobbie Reed. Nashville, TN: Thomas Nelson, 1988.

The Single Mother's Handbook, by Elizabeth Greywold. New York: Morrow, 1984.

How to Become a Single Parent: A Guide for Single People Considering Adoption or Natural Parenthood Alone, by Josephine Curto. Englewood Cliffs, NJ: Prentice Hall, 1983.

Single-Parent Families, by Marilyn Bailey. New York: Crestwood, 1990. For young readers.

On working parents

Making It Work: Finding the Time and Energy for Your Career, Marriage, Children, and Self, by Victoria Houston. Chicago: Contemporary, 1990.

Working Parent/Happy Child: You Can Balance Job and Family, by Caryl Waller Krueger. Nashville, TN: Abingdon, 1990.

Answers to the Mommy Track: How Wives and Mothers in Business Reach the Top and Balance Their Lives, by Trudi Ferguson. Far Hills, NJ: New Horizon, 1990.

The Phantom Spouse: Helping Your Family Survive Business Travel or Relocation, by Denise V. Lang. Crozet, VA: Betterway, 1990.

Tips for Working Parents: Creative Solutions to Everyday Problems, by Kathleen McBride. Pownal, VT: Storey/Garden Way, 1989.

The Second Shift: Working Parents and the Revolution at Home, by Arlie Hochschild. New York: Viking, 1989.

Sequencing: A New Solution for Women Who Want Marriage, Career, and Family, by Arlene Rossen Cardozo. New York: Collier/Macmillan, 1989.

Remaking Motherhood: How Working Mothers Are Shaping Our Children's Future, by Anita Shreve. New York: Fawcett, 1988.

Time Out for Motherhood: A Guide to the Financial, Emotional, and Career Aspects of Having a Baby, by Lucy Scott and Meredith Joan Angwin. Los Angeles: Tarcher, 1988.

The Working Parent Dilemma: How to Balance the Responsibilities of Children and Careers, by Earl Grollman and Gerri L. Sweder. Boston, MA: Beacon, 1988.

The Woman Who Works, The Parent Who Cares: A Revolutionary Program for Raising Your Child, by Sirgay Sanger, M.D., and John Kelly. New York: Harper & Row, 1988.

Don't Call Mommy at Work Today Unless the House Is on Fire, by Mary McBride and Veronica McBride. Deephaven, MN: Meadowbrook, 1988.

The Working Mother's Complete Handbook, revised edition, by Gloria Norris and Jo Ann Miller. New York: New American Library, 1984.

On grandparenting

The Grandparent Book: A Guide to Changes in Birth and Child Rearing, by Linda B. White, M.D. Gateway, 1990.

Congratulations! You're Going to Be a Grandmother, by Lanie Carter. New York: Pocket, 1990.

Funny, You Don't Look Like a Grandmother, by Lois Wyse. New York: Avon, 1990.

Grandparenting: Understanding Today's Children, by David Elkind. Glenview, IL: Scott, Foresman, 1989.

Grandparenting for the Nineties: Parenting Is Forever, by Robert Aldrich, M.D. and Glenn Austin, M.D. Rolling Hills Estates, CA: Robert Erdman, 1989.

A Survival Manual for New Grandparents, by Linda B. White, M.D. San Francisco: Gateway, 1989.

The New American Grandparent: A Place in the Family, A Life Apart, by Andrew J. Cherlin. New York: Basic, 1988.

Between Parents and Grandparents, by Arthur Kornhaber. New York: St. Martin's, 1986.

How to Grandparent, by Fitzhugh Dodson and Paula Reuben. New York: Harper and Row, 1981.

On handling family problems

Who's in Charge Here? Overcoming Power Struggles with Your Kids, by Robert G. Barnes, Jr. Irving, TX: Word, 1990.

A Guide to a Happier Family: Overcoming the Anger, Frustration, and Boredom that Destroy Family Life, by Andrew Schwebel, et al. Los Angeles: Tarcher, 1990.

When Parents Love Too Much: What Happens When Parents Won't Let Go, by Laurie Asher and Mitch Meyerson. New York: Morrow, 1990.

Living with the Active Alert Child: Groundbreaking Strategies for Parents, by Linda S. Budd. New York: Prentice Hall, 1990. For dealing with the seemingly uncontrollable child.

Endangered Brains, by Jane Healy. New York: Simon & Schuster, 1990. On the shaping of the brain by environment.

Fixing Your Frazzled Family, by Dean Feldmeyer. Loveland, CO: Group Publishing, 1990.

Families: Crisis and Caring, by T. Berry Brazelton, M.D. Reading, MA: Addison-Wesley; New York: Ballantine, 1990.

Stop the Violence: Overcoming Self-Destruction, by Nelson George with the National Urban League. New York: Pantheon, 1990.

Helping Your Kids Handle Stress, by H. Norman Wright. San Bernardino, CA: Here's Life, 1990.

Family Passages, by Glenn H. Asquith, Jr. Nashville, TN: Broadman, 1990. On dealing with family crises.

The Co-Dependent Parent: A Recovery Program to Help You Stop Enabling Your Child's Worst Behavior, by Barbara Cottman Becnel. Chicago: Lowell House/Contemporary, 1990.

Adult Children Raising Children: Ending the Cycle of Co-Dependency for Your Children, by Randy Rolfe. Deerfield Beach, FL: Health Communications, 1990.

How to Stay Lovers While Raising Your Children: A Burned-Out Parents' Guide to Sex, by Anne Mayer. Los Angeles: Price Stern Sloan, 1990.

Go Ask Your Mother: Family Life and Other Impossible Situations, by Thomas Trowbridge III. New York: Morrow, 1990.

Kids Out of Control, by Alan Cohen. Summit, NJ: PIA, 1989.

The Difficult Child, revised edition, by Stanley Turecki, M.D., and Leslie Tonner. New York: Bantam, 1989.

The Too Precious Child, by Lynne H. Williams, M.D., Henry S. Berman, M.D., and Louisa Rose. New York: Warner, 1989.

Families At Risk: Treating the Multi-Problem Family, by Katherine M. Wood and Ludwig L. Geismar. New York: Human Sciences, 1989.

Kids Who Have Too Much: "Does Your Child Really Need the Best of Everything?" by Dr. Ralph Minear and William Proctor. Nashville, TN: Thomas Nelson, 1989.

When Families Fight: How to Handle Conflict with Those You Love, by Jeffrey Rubin and Carol Rubin. New York: Morrow, 1988.

Relief for Hurting Parents: What to Do and How to Think When You're Having Trouble With Your Kids, by Buddy Scott. Nashville, TN: Thomas Nelson, 1989.

A Guide to a Happier Family: Rewriting Your Family Drama to Overcome the Anger, Frustration and Boredom That Destroy Family Life, by Andrew Schwebel, et al. Los Angeles: Tarcher, 1989. By a family of therapists.

When Your Child Grows Up Too Fast, by Alan Yellin and Penelope B. Grenoble. Chicago, IL: Contemporary, 1988.

The Hurried Child: Growing Up Too Fast Too Soon, revised edition, by David Elkind. Reading, MA: Addison-Wesley, 1988.

Adult Children: The Secrets of Dysfunctional Families, by John Friel and Linda Friel. Pompano Beach, FL: Health Communications, 1988.

Stress, Coping, and Development in Children, by Norman Garmezy and Michael Rutter. Baltimore, MD: Johns Hopkins University Press, 1988.

Your Prodigal Child: Hope and Comfort for Hurting Parents, by D. James Kennedy. Nashville, TN: Thomas Nelson, 1988.

High Risk: Children Without a Conscience, by Ken Magid and Carole A. McKelvey. New York: Bantam, 1988.

America's Troubled Children, edited by Jeanne Burr. New York: Facts on File, 1980.

Children Without Childhood, by Marie Winn. New York: Pantheon, 1983. On lack of parental authority and premature thrusting of children into adult situations.

On children and social problems

A Parent's Guide to Teens and Cults, by Richard Altesman and Larry E. Dumont. Summit, NJ: PIA, 1990.

Cults: What Parents Should Know, by Joan Carol Ross and Michael D. Langone. New York: Carol Communications/Lyle Stuart, 1989.

Homeless Children, by Karen O'Connor. San Diego: Lucent, 1989.

The Cult Movement, by Joan Johnson. New York: Franklin Watts, 1984.

All God's Children: The Cult Experience—Salvation or Slavery?, by Carroll Stoner and Jo Anne Parke. Radnor, PA: Chilton, 1977.

On family and social problems, for kids

When Andy's Father Went to Prison, by Martha Whitmore Hickman. Niles, IL: Whitman, 1990. For ages 7 to 10.

Teenage Violence, by Elaine Landau. New York: Messner, 1990. For ages 12 and up.

Violence and Drugs, by Gilda Berger. New York: Watts, 1990.

Gangs, by Renardo Barden. New York: Crestwood, 1990.

The Homeless, by Laurie Beckelman. New York: Crestwood, 1990.

Bullying, by Angela Grunsell. New York: Gloucester, 1990. For ages 7 to 10.

Discrimination, by Gail Stewart. New York: Crestwood, 1990.

Shake Off the Dust, by Jay Strack. Nashville, TN: Thomas Nelson, 1988.

Background books

A Lasting Relationship: Parents and Children over Three Centuries, by Linda Pollock. Hanover, NH: University Press of New England, 1990.

The State of the World's Children 1990, by James P. Grant, ed. New York: Oxford, 1990.

Babies Remember Birth: And Other Extraordinary Scientific Discoveries About the Mind and Personality of Your Newborn, by David Chamberlain. New York: Ballantine, 1990.

The Encyclopedia of Marriage, Divorce and the Family, by Margaret DiCanio, Ph.D. New York: Facts on File, 1989.

In Defense of Children: Understanding the Rights, Needs and Interests of the Child, by Thomas A. Nazario. New York: Scribner, 1988.

Growing with Your Children, by Herbert Kohl. Boston: Little, Brown, 1978.

On parent–child relations, for kids

We're Very Good Friends, My Father and I, by P.K. Hallinan. Nashville, TN: Ideals, 1990. For ages 3 to 5.

We're Very Good Friends, My Mother and I, by P.K. Hallinan. Nashville, TN: Ideals, 1990. For ages 3 to 5.

Weird Parents, by Audrey Wood. New York: Dial, 1990. For young readers.

Coping with Family Expectations, by Margaret Hill. New York: Rosen, 1990. For adolescents. On understanding and dealing with others' expectations.

Coping with Overprotective Parents, by Margot Webb. New York: Rosen, 1990. For adolescents.

Straight Talk about Parents, by Elizabeth A. Ryan. New York: Facts on File, 1990. For young adults.

The Emotional Incest Syndrome: What to Do When a Parent's Love Controls Your Life, by Patricia Love with Jo Robinson. New York: Bantam, 1990.

Dear Dad, Love Laurie, by Susan Beth Pfeffer. New York: Scholastic, 1990. For ages 8 to 12.

When Grownups Drive You Crazy, by Eda Le Shan. New York: Macmillan, 1988.

Medical books on kids' health

The Columbia University College of Physicians and Surgeons Complete Guide to Early Child Care, Genell Subak-Sharpe, editorial director. New York: Crown, 1990.

The Parents' Guide to Baby and Child Medical Care, revised edition, Terril H. Hart, M.D., ed. Deephaven, MN: Meadowbrook, 1990.

Healthy Kids for Life, by Charles Kuntzleman. New York: Simon & Schuster, 1990.

Healthier Children, by Barbara Kahan. New Canaan, CT: Keats, 1990.

Taking Care of Your Child: A Parent's Guide to Medical Care, 3rd edition, by Robert H. Pantell, M.D., James F. Fries., M.D., and Donald M. Vickery, M.D. Reading, MA: Addison-Wesley, 1990.

Natural Medicine for Children: Drug-free Healthcare for Children, by Dr. Julian Scott. New York: Morrow, 1990.

Consumer Health Information Source Book, 3rd edition, Alan M. Rees and Catherine Hoffman, eds. Phoenix, AZ: Oryx, 1990.

One Children's Place: A Profile of Pediatric Medicine, by Lee Gutkin. New York: Grove Weidenfeld, 1990.

Childhood Emergencies—What to Do: A Quick Reference Guide, by Project Care for Children. Palo Alto, CA: Bull, 1989.

The Growing Years: The New York Hospital–Cornell Medical Center Guide to Your Child's Emotional Development from Birth to Adolescence, by Mark Rubinstein, M.D. New York: Simon & Schuster, 1989.

The Mothercare Guide to Child Health: Keeping Children Healthy /A–Z of Illnesses/Coping with Emergencies, by Penny Stanway, M.D. New York: Prentice Hall, 1989.

The New American Encyclopedia of Children's Health, by Robert Hoeckleman, M.D., and David Baum, M.D. New York: New American Library, 1989.

Complete Guide to Pediatric Symptoms, Illness & Medications, by H. Winter Griffith. Los Angeles: Body Press, 1989.

Health Questions Your Children Ask, by Cory SerVaas, M.D. Nashville, TN: Thomas Nelson, 1989.

The Available Pediatrician, by Ann Parker, M.D., and Ralph Berberich, M.D. New York: Pantheon, 1988.

Should I Call the Doctor? A Comprehensive Guide to Understanding Your Child's Illnesses and Injuries, by Christine A. Nelson and Susan C. Pescar. New York: Warner, 1986.

Baby and Child A to Z Medical Handbook: Parents' Easy Reference Guide to Children's Illnesses, Symptoms and Treatment, by Dr. Miriam Stoppard. Tucson, AZ: HP Books/Body Press, 1986.

Childhood Symptoms: Every Parent's Guide to Childhood Illnesses, by Edward R. Brace and John P. Pacanowski. New York: Harper & Row, 1985.

The Encyclopedia of Baby & Child Care, by Lendon H. Smith, M.D. New York: Warner, 1980; updated reprint of 1972 Prentice Hall work.

General home medical books

The American Medical Association Handbook of First Aid and Emergency Care. New York: Random House, 1990.

The Doctors Book of Home Remedies. Emmaus, PA: Rodale, 1990.

Everywoman's Health: The Complete Guide to Body and Mind by 18 Woman Doctors, 4th edition, Douglas S. Thompson, consulting ed. New York: Prentice Hall, 1990.

The Black Women's Health Book: Speaking for Ourselves, Evelyn C. White, ed. Seattle, WA: Seal, 1990.

Woman: Your Body, Your Health, by Josleen Wilson. Orlando, FL: Harcourt Brace Jovanovich/Harvest, 1990.

The New Handbook of Health and Preventive Medicine, by Kurt Butler with Lynn Rayner, M.D., and John V. Mickey, M.D. Buffalo, NY: Prometheus, 1990.

Take Care of Yourself: Your Own Master Plan for Maintaining Health and Preventing Illness, 4th edition, by James F. Fries., M.D., and Donald M. Vickery, M.D. Reading, MA: Addison-Wesley, 1990.

Columbia University College of Physicians and Surgeons Complete Home Medical Guide, revised edition, Genell Subak-Sharpe, ed. New York: Crown, 1989.

American Medical Association Encyclopedia of Medicine, Charles B. Clayman, ed. New York: Random House, 1989.

Complete Guide to Symptoms, Illness & Surgery, revised edition, by H. Winter Griffith. Los Angeles: Body Press, 1989.

Encyclopedia of Alternative Health Care, by Kristin Olsen. New York: Pocket, 1989.

Making Medical Decisions, by Thomas Scully, M.D., and Celia Scully. New York: Fireside, 1989.

The New American Medical Dictionary and Health Manual, 5th edition, by Robert E. Rothenberg, M.D. New York: New American Library, 1988.

Where Does It Hurt? A Guide to Symptoms and Illnesses, by Susan C. Pescar and Christine A. Nelson, M.D. New York: Facts on File, 1983; Ballantine, 1985.

The Manual of Natural Therapy: A Succinct Catalog of Complementary Treatments, by Moshe Olshevsky, C.A., B.A., Ph.D., Shlomo Noy, M.D., and Mouricio Zwang, Ph.D., with Robert E. Burger. New York: Facts on File, 1989.

When a Loved One Is Ill: How to Take Better Care of Your Loved One, Your Family, and Yourself, by Leonard Felder. New York: New American Library, 1990.

A Doctor's Prescription for Getting the Best Medical Care, by Kurt Link, M.D. New York: Dembner, 1990.

American Medical Association Family Medical Guide, by Jeffrey R.M. Kunz, M.D., and Asher J. Finkel, M.D. New York: Random House, 1987.

The Merck Manual of Diagnosis and Therapy, 15th edition, Robert Berkow, editor-in-chief. Rahway, NJ: Merck, Sharpe & Dohme Research Laboratories, 1987. Very detailed, highly technical professional manual.

General works on drugs and medications

The Pill Book Guide to Children's Medications, by Michael Mitchell, M.D. New York: Bantam, 1990.

The Complete Guide to Prescription and Non-Prescription Drugs, 7th edition, by H. Winter Griffith, M.D. Los Angeles: Body Press, 1990.

The Pill Book, 4th edition, by Harold M. Silverman. New York: Bantam, 1990.

The Intelligent Consumer's Pharmacy: The Complete User's Guide to Drugs, Vitamins and Other Chemical Products, by

Ellen Hodgson Brown and Lynn Paige Walker. New York: Carroll & Graf, 1990.

The Essential Guide to Psychiatric Drugs, by Jack M. Gorman. New York: St. Martin's, 1990.

Psychiatric Drugs: A Consumer's Guide, by Stuart Yudofsky, M.D., Robert E. Hales, M.D., and Tom Ferguson, M.D. New York: Grove Weidenfeld, 1990.

The Essential Guide to Prescription Drugs 1990, by James W. Long, M.D. New York: Harper & Row, 1989.

Drug Information for the Consumer, by authority of the United States Pharmacopeial Convention. New York: Consumer Reports Books, 1989.

The American Medical Association Guide to Prescription and Over-the-Counter Drugs: Brand Name Drugs, Generic Drugs, Vitamins, Minerals and Food Additives, by the American Medical Association. New York: Random House, 1988.

The Pharmacist's Guide to the Misused and Abused Drugs in America: Prescription Drugs·Over-the-Counter Drugs·Designer Drugs, by Ken Liska. New York: Macmillan, 1988.

The New Consumer Drug Digest, by The American Society of Hospital Pharmacists. New York: Facts on File, 1985.

On consumer advocacy in health

Your Medical Rights: How to Become an Empowered Consumer, by Charles B. Inlander and Eugene Pavalon. Boston: Little, Brown, 1990.

A Doctor's Prescription: For Getting the Best Medical Care, by Kurt Link, M.D. New York: Dembner, 1990.

Medical Choices, Medical Chances: How Patients, Families and Physicians Can Cope with Uncertainty, by Harold Bursztain, Richard I. Feinbloom, Robert M. Hamm, and Archie Brodsky. New York: Routledge, 1990.

Taking Charge of Your Medical Fate, by Lawrence Horowitz, M.D. New York: Random House, 1988. Encourages patients (including parents) to become active in obtaining the best medical treatment; approach credited by Edward Kennedy for saving his son's life.

The Doctor Book: A Nuts & Bolts Guide to Patient Power, by Wesley J. Smith. Los Angeles: Price Stern Sloan, 1988.

The Consumer's Guide to Medical Care, 3rd edition. Donald M. Vickery, M.D., and James F. Frieds, M.D., eds. Reading, MA: Addison-Wesley, 1988.

The New Medical Marketplace: A Physician's Guide to the Health Care Revolution, by Anne Stoline, et al. Baltimore, MD: Johns Hopkins University Press, 1988.

Communicating With Your Doctor, by J. Alfred Jones, M.D., and Gerald M. Phillips. Carbondale, IL: Illinois University Press, 1988.

On general health, for kids

Dinosaurs Alive and Well: A Guide to Good Health, by Laurie Krasny Brown and Marc Brown. Boston: Joy Street/Little, Brown, 1990. For ages 4 to 8.

Medical Dilemmas, by Margaret Hyde and Elizabeth Forsyth. New York: Putnam, 1990. For ages 12 and up.

Double-Dip Feelings: A Book to Help Children Understand Emotions, by Barbara Cain. New York: Magination, 1990. For ages 4 to 10.

How & Why: A Kid's Book About the Body, by Catherine O'Neill. Illustrations by Loel Barr. New York: Consumer Reports Books, 1988.

Maintaining Good Health, by Mario Orlandi, Donald Prue, and Annette Spence. New York: Facts on File, 1989.

On sports

Going the Distance—How to Excel as an Athlete in College—and Graduate, by Stephen Figler and Howard Figler. Princeton, NJ: Peterson's, 1990.

Violence and Sports, by Gilda Berger. New York: Watts, 1990. For grades 9 to 12.

A Parent's Guide to Coaching Soccer, by John P. McCarthy. Crozet, VA: Betterway, 1990.

Little League's Official How-to-Play Baseball Book, by Peter Kreutzer and Ted Kerley. Garden City, NY: Doubleday, 1990.

Parents' Complete Guide to Youth Sports, by Ronald E. Smith, Frank L. Small, and Nathan J. Smith. Costa Mesa, CA: HDL Communications, 1989.

The Winning Edge: A Complete Guide to Intercollegiate Athletic Programs, by Frances Killpatrick and James Killpatrick. Alexandria, VA: Octameron, 1989.

A Parent's Guide to Coaching Baseball, by John P. McCarthy. Crozet, VA: Betterway, 1989.

Dying to Win: The Athlete's Guide to Safe & Unsafe Drugs in Sports, by Michael J. Asken. Washington, DC: Acropolis, 1988.

Barron's Sports Injuries Handbook: Prevention, Diagnosis, Treatment, by J.P.R. Williams, M.D., cons. ed., James Wilson-MacDonald, M.D., and Colin Fergusson, M.D. Hauppauge, NY: Barron's, 1988.

The Sports-Confident Child, by Chris Hopper. New York: Pantheon, 1988.

Moms & Dads·Kids & Sports, by Pat McInally. New York: Scribner, 1988.

The First Book of Football, by John Madden. New York: Crown, 1988.

Our Soccer League, by Chuck Solomon. New York: Crown, 1988.

Parenting Your Superstar: How to Help Your Child Get the Most Out of Sports, by Robert J. Rotella and Linda K. Bunker. Champaign, IL: Leisure, 1987.

Peterson's Athlete's Game Plan for College and Career, by Stephen Figler and Howard Figler. Princeton, NJ: Peterson's, 1984.

Kidsports: A Survival Guide for Parents, by Nathan J. Smith, Ronald E. Smith, and Frank L. Smoll. Reading, MA: Addison-Wesley, 1983.

On other leisure activities

The World's Best Street and Yard Games, by Glen Vecchione. New York: Sterling, 1990.

Summer Options for Teenagers, by Cindy Ware. New York: Prentice Hall/Arco, 1990. For grades 5 and up.

The Parent's Guide to Getting the Most Out of Television: How Use TV to Your Child's Advantage, by Dorothy G. Singer, Jerome L. Singer, and Diana M. Zuckerman. Washington, DC: Acropolis, 1990.

What Would We Do Without You?: A Guide to Volunteer Activities for Kids, by Kathy Henderson. Crozet, VA: Betterway, 1990. For ages 12 to adult.

Who Touched the Remote Control? Television and Christian Choices for Children and Adults Who Care About Children. New York: Friendship, 1990.

The Electronic Lifeline: A Media Exploration for Youth, by Linda Woods Peterson. New York: Friendship, 1990.

School's Out—Now What? by Joan Bergstrom. Berkeley, CA: Ten Speed, 1990.

All the Best Contests for Kids 1990–1991, by Joan Bergstrom and Craig Bergstrom. Berkeley, CA: Ten Speed, 1990.

The Teenage Entrepreneur's Guide: 50 Money-Making Business Ideas, second edition, by Sarah Riehm. Chicago: Surrey, 1990.

Free Stuff for Kids, revised 1990 edition, by the Free Stuff Editors. Deephaven, MN: Meadowbrook, 1989.

50 Simple Things Kids Can Do to Save the Earth, by The Earth Works Group. Kansas City, MO: Andrews and McMeel, 1990.

1990–91 Directory of American Youth Organizations: A Guide to Over 400 Clubs, Groups, Troops, Teams, Societies, Lodges, and More for Young People, by Judith B. Erickson. Minneapolis, MN: Free Spirit, 1989.

Sharing Time: A Big Person/Little Person Project Book, by Kathy Leichliter Millter. Blue Ridge Summit, PA: TAB, 1989.

The Self-Respecting Child: Development Through Spontaneous Play, by Alison Stallibrass. Reading, MA: Addison-Wesley, 1989.

101 Amusing Ways to Develop Your Child's Thinking Skills and Creativity, by Sarina Simon. Chicago: Contemporary, 1989.

Child's Play: 200 Instant Crafts and Activities for Preschoolers, by Leslie Hamilton. New York: Crown, 1989.

The Parent's Book of Ballet, by Angela Whitehill and William Noble. Pennington, NJ: Princeton Book Company, 1989.

The Centering Book: Awareness Activities for Children and Adults to Relax the Body and Mind, by Gay Hendricks and Russel Wills. New York: Prentice Hall, 1989.

The Second Centering Book: More Awareness Activities for Children and Adults to Relax the Body and Mind, by Gay Hendricks and Thomas B. Roberts. New York: Prentice Hall, 1989.

The Joyful Child: A Sourcebook of Activities and Ideas for Releasing Children's Natural Joy, by Peggy Jenkins. Tucson, AZ: Harbinger House, 1989.

Where's My Other Sock? How to Get Organized and Drive Your Parents Crazy, by Claudine Wirths and Mary Bowman-Kruhm. New York: Crowell, 1989. For ages 10 and up.

Peterson's Summer Opportunities for Kids and Teenagers. Princeton, NJ: Peterson's, annual.

1001 Things to Do With Your Kids, by Caryl Waller Krueger. Nashville, TN: Abingdon, 1988.

Joy in a Woolly Coat: Living With, Loving and Letting Go of Treasured Animal Friends, by Julie Adams Church. Tiburon, CA: HJ Kramer, 1988.

How to Shoot Your Kids on Home Video: Moviemaking for the Whole Family, by David Hajdu. New York: Newmarket, 1988.

The Quality Time Almanac: A Sourcebook of Ideas and Activities for Parents and Kids, by St. Clair Adams Sullivan, with illustrations by the author. Garden City, NY: Doubleday, 1986.

The Pleasure of Their Company: How to Have More Fun With Your Children, prepared by the Bank Street College of Education, William H. Hooks, ed. Radnor, PA: Chilton, 1981.

On business, legal, and social matters

The Baby's Budget Book: Financial Planning for New Parents, by Randolph W. Farmer and Robert V. Ling. Carrollton, TX: Shadetree, 1990.

Insurance & Alternatives for Uninsurables. Boise, ID: Kessinger, 1990.

The Living Together Kit: A Detailed Guide to Help Unmarried Couples Deal with Legal Realities, revised edition, by Toni Ihara and Ralph Warner. Berkeley, CA: Nolo, 1990.

Choosing the Right Health Care Plan, by Henry Berman, M.D., and Louisa Rose. New York: Consumer Reports Books, 1989.

What's Wrong with Your Life Insurance, by Norman F. Dacey. New York: Macmillan, 1989.

The Encyclopedia of Marriage, Divorce, and the Family, by Margaret DiCanio, New York: Facts on File, 1989.

Making Cents: Every Kid's Guide to Money, by Elizabeth Wilkinson. Boston: Little, Brown, 1989.

Health Insurance Made Simple, by Kathleen Hogue, Cheryl Jensen, and Kathy Urban, M.D. New York: Walker, 1988.

The Parents' Guide: Money Sense, Teach Your Child About Money, by Harwood Nichols. Washington, DC: Acropolis, 1988.

Money Matters for Parents and Their Kids, by Ron Blue and Judy Blue. Nashville, TN: Thomas Nelson, 1988.

What Children Can Tell Us: Eliciting, Interpreting, and Evaluating Information from Children, by James Garbarino, Frances M. Stott, and the faculty of the Erikson Institute. San Francisco: Jossey-Bass, 1989.

The Parents' Guide to Helping Their Teenagers Find the Right Careers, by Charles J. Shields. New York: College Board, 1988.

Family Law Dictionary: Marriage, Divorce, Children & Living Together, by Robin D. Leonard and Stephen R. Elias. Berkeley, CA: Nolo, 1988.

Legal Guide to Marriage, Divorce, Custody & Living Together, by Steven Sack. Tucson, AZ: Fisher, 1989.

Help for Special Children

Here are some key organizations and reference works that give general help, information, programs, and services to special children—those with long-term handicaps, long-term disorders, or other exceptional needs—and to the families and professionals concerned with them. In Help for Special Children we focus on resources that apply generally to many children (and adults) who are handicapped, disabled, chronically ill, or terminally ill. Organizations and resources relating to many specific disorders are provided elsewhere, in the A-to-Z portion of the book under the name of the disability or disorder, such as SPINA BIFIDA, CEREBRAL PALSY, MENTAL RETARDATION, and MENTAL DISORDERS. For a quick reference guide and index see HOTLINES, HELPLINES, AND HELPING ORGANIZATIONS, on page 601.

ORGANIZATIONS OFFERING HELP AND INFORMATION

General Organizations for Special Children

National Information Center for Children and Youth with Handicaps (NICHCY)
P.O. Box 1492
Washington, DC 20013
703-893-6061
Carol Valdivieso, Project Director

Organization working with individual parents of disabled children. Offers information about rights to education and special services available for handicapped children; helps parents work with public and private agencies to meet disabled children's needs; publishes various materials, including fact sheets on various disabilities and resources available.

Association for the Care of Children's Health (ACCH)
3615 Wisconsin Avenue NW
Washington, DC 20016
202-244-1801
Beverly H. Johnson, Executive Director

Organization of health professionals who work in pediatric care. Publishes various materials, including *Organizing and Maintaining Support Groups for Parents of Children with Chronic Illness and Handicapping Conditions, When Your Child Has a Life-Threatening Illness, Understanding Your Health Care Options: A Guide for Families Who Have Children with Special Health*

Needs, New Directions for Exceptional Parenting, Your Child with Special Needs at Home and in the Community, and *Parent Resource Directory*.

Eterna International Foundation for Disabled Children (EIFDC)
P.O. Box 1344
Oak Brook, IL 60522
312-231-4400
Stephen B. Parrish, President

Organization of medical and social professionals and others involved in caring for and educating disabled or chronically ill children. Gathers information and conducts research on how best to treat such children, acting as clearinghouse for others; arranges for adoption of handicapped infants when parents are unable to care for them; publishes various materials, including *Special Education Bulletin and Review, Spina Bifida Therapy, Trisomy 21*, and *Parenting Studies*.

Federation for Children with Special Needs
95 Berkeley Street, Suite 104
Boston, MA 02116
617-482-2915
Martha H. Ziegler, Executive Director

Organization for parents of children with special needs. Publishes various materials, including *Newsline*.

Children In Hospitals (CIH)
31 Wilshire Park
Needham, MA 02192
617-482-2915
Barbara Popper, Executive Director

Organization of parents, health professionals, and others interested in hospitalized children. Encourages flexible parental visiting policies in hospitals; provides support, information, and referrals; publishes various materials, including quarterly newsletter and *CIH Consumer Directory of Hospitals*.

SKIP (Sick Kids need Involved People)
216 Newport Drive
Severna Park, MD 21146
301-621-7830
Karen A. Shannon, Executive Director

Organization of parents, health professionals, and groups concerned with home care for chronically ill or handicapped children. Offers support and referrals; seeks to educate public and change government policies; publishes various materials, including quarterly newsletter and annual *Parent Handbook.*

General Organizations and Government Agencies

National Easter Seal Society
2023 West Ogden Avenue
Chicago, IL 60612
312-243-8400 (voice); 312-243-8880 (TDD); toll-free number 800-221-6827
John R. Garrison, Executive Director

National network of societies to aid people with disabilities of any kind, including problems stemming from cerebral palsy, epilepsy, multiple sclerosis, communication disorders, spina bifida, arthritis, learning disabilities, heart disease, developmental disabilities, or accidents. Provides information about disabilities and services available to the handicapped; operates local rehabilitation centers and other programs for disabled people; seeks to influence public policy and legislation, especially in provision of services for disabled people; provides information and referrals; publishes many materials, including quarterly newsletter *Communicator, Camps for Children With Disabilities, Self-Help Clothing for Children Who Have Physical Disabilities, Choosing and Using a Wheelchair, Using Everything You've Got,* and *Reflections on Managing Disability,* as well as *Are You Listening to What Your Child May Not Be Saying?, A Speech Pathologist Talks to the Parents of a Nonverbal Child,* and *First Aid for Aphasics.*

National Rehabilitation Information Center (NARIC)
8455 Colesville Road, Suite 935
Silver Spring, MD 20910
301-588-9284
Toll-free number, voice/TDD, 800-346-2742
Mark Odum, Director

Clearinghouse for information on products, services, research, and resources for disabled people. Provides information and makes referrals; maintains databases REHABDATA (on special topics) and ABLEDATA (commercially available technical aids); publishes various materials.

Administration on Developmental Disabilities
Office of Human Development Services
U.S. Department of Health and Human Services, Room 348-F
200 Independence Avenue, SW
Washington, DC 20201
202-245-2890

Federal arm charged with overseeing and providing public information on developmental disabilities.

Disabled in Action National (DIA)
P.O. Box 1273
New York, NY 10009

718-261-3737
Frieda Zames, Coordinator

Organization of and for people with disabilities, aimed at achieving full access of handicapped people to all phases of society, including education, transportation, employment, and housing; seeks to influence public policy and legislation. Publishes various materials, including *Disabled in Action Speaks.*

American Association of University Affiliated Programs for Persons with Developmental Disabilities (AAUAP)
8630 Fenton Street, Suite 410
Silver Spring, MD 20910
301-588-8252
William E. Jones, Executive Director

Network of federally supported centers—University Affiliated Facilities (UAFs) or University Affiliated Programs (UAPs)—for assessment and treatment of developmental disabilities; some centers have specific focus, some treat whole range of problems. Provides referrals for public and professionals.

National Association for Home Care (NAHC)
519 C Street, NE, Stanton Park
Washington, DC 20002
202-547-7424
Val J. Halamandaris, President

Organization of health professionals and others interested in improving home health-care services.

Information Center for Individuals with Disabilities (ICID)
Fort Point Place, 27-43 Wormwood Street
Boston, MA 022210
617-727-5540 (voice/TDD)
Toll-free number (MA only; voice and TDD) 800-462-5015
Lee Rachel Segal, Executive Officer

Information exchange for people with disabilities; computerized database provides information on all areas of activity and on hundreds of public and private agencies for the handicapped. Operates toll-free number; publishes various materials, including monthly fact sheets.

TASH: The Association for Persons with Severe Handicaps
7010 Roosevelt Way, NE
Seattle, WA 98115
206-523-8446
Liz Lindley, Executive Director

Organization for parents, professionals, and other people interested in improving the quality of life for people with severe handicaps. Endorses education from infancy through adulthood; gathers and disseminates information; operates referral service. Publishes monthly newsletter and other materials.

Gazette International Networking Institute (GINI)
4502 Maryland Avenue
St. Louis, MO 63108
314-361-0475
Gini Laurie, Chairwoman

Organization for severely disabled people, such as polio victims or those who have spinal-cord injuries or use ventilators, and also their families, friends, and the professionals who work with them. Aims to act as communication network and clearinghouse for information on severe disabilities and all aspects of life, especially ways to achieve independent living; maintains library and holds conferences. Publishes various materials, including *Polio Network News* and *Rehabilitation Gazette*.

Accent on Information (AI)
P.O. Box 700
Gillum Road and High Drive
Bloomington, IL 61701
309-378-2961
Raymond C. Cheever, Publisher

Computerized service designed to help handicapped people get information on problems, products, and services available to them. Company offering service also publishes magazine for handicapped, *Accent on Living*, and other materials.

Access for the Handicapped (AH)
5014 42nd Street, NW
Washington, DC 20016
202-966-5500
Harold W. Snider, President

Organization serving the handicapped, seeking to widen access and opportunities. Acts in interest of handicapped vis-á-vis government and public policy; conducts research, does training, and develops aids, sometimes under government contract; offers special programs for children; publishes various materials, including computerized Braille transcription service.

People First International (PFI)
P.O. Box 12642
Salem, OR 97309
503-362-0336
Mike Easterly, Executive Officer

Organization seeking to enhance advocacy and independent skills for mentally retarded and developmentally disabled people. Aids and advises local groups; publishes various materials, including book *We Are People First* and movie *People First*.

PRIDE Foundation — Promote Real Independence for the Disabled and Elderly
71 Plaza Court
Groton, CT 06340

203-445-1448
Evelyn S. Kennedy, Executive Director

Organization to help disabled and elderly people dress and care for themselves at home independently, through such items as specially designed clothes and technical aids; provides training for handicapped people. Disseminates information to other interested groups; publishes various materials, including *Dressing with Pride: Clothing Changes for Special Needs*.

American Amputee Foundation (AAF)
Box 55218
Little Rock, AR 72225
501-666-2523
Jack M. East, Executive Director

Organization for amputees and their families. Helps ease adjustment after amputation and initial emergency aid; provides access to other legal, technical, and rehabilitative services available; publishes various materials, including *Ability Magazine*.

National Organization on Disability (NOD)
910 16th Street, NW, Suite 600
Washington, DC 20006
202-293-5690 (voice); 202-293-5968 (TTD)
Alan A. Reich, President

National Information Center for Health Related Services
The Center for Developmental Disabilities
University of South Carolina
1244 Blossom Street
Columbia, SC 29208
803-777-4435; toll-free number 800-922-9234

On Access to Education, Culture, and Library Services

PACER Center (Parent Advocacy Coalition for Educational Rights)
4826 Chicago Avenue South
Minneapolis, MN 55417
612-827-2966 (Voice & TTY)

Parent training coalition of and for parents of disabled students, focusing on rights to education. Publishes various materials, including resource booklets *Parents Can Be the Key* and *Unlocking Doors: A Guide to Effective Communication*.

Council for Exceptional Children (CEC)
1920 Association Drive
Reston, VA 22091
703-620-3660
Jeptha V. Greer, Executive Director

ERIC Clearinghouse on Handicapped and Gifted Children
CEC Information Center

703-620-3660
Fred Weintraub, Associate Director

Organization of educators working with children with special needs; includes 17 special education divisions, including Division on Physically Handicapped (DPH). Seeks to educate public and influence legislation and public policy; encourages research and increased services; operates federally funded ERIC information clearinghouse; publishes various materials, including professional journals, and works such as *Reflections on Growing Up Disabled, College Planning for Gifted Students,* and *Not All Wagons Are Red: The Exceptional Child's Early Years.*

National Library Services for the Blind and Physically Handicapped

Library of Congress
1291 Taylor Street, NW
Washington, DC 20542
202-287-5100
Toll-free number (U.S. except DC) 800-424-8567
Frank Kurt Cylke, Director

Federal services providing general-interest books, magazines, and other publications on record or tape to people certified as having reading disabilities from whatever cause. Makes available special playing equipment; materials distributed postage-free in both directions from nationwide network of libraries; publishes free information package for children or adults.

National Association of Private Schools for Exceptional Children (NAPSEC)

2021 K Street, NW, Suite 315
Washington, DC 20006
202-296-1800
Susan B. Nelson, Executive Director

Organization of private schools with programs for children with special needs. Provides information and referrals to parents; publishes directory of member schools.

Human Resources Center (HRC)

I. U. Willets Road
Albertson, NY 11507
516-747-5400
Dr. Edwin Martin, Jr., President

Organization providing various special programs for handicapped people, including Human Resources School for severely disabled, otherwise homebound students, K–12. Maintains library and seeks to educate public through tours and seminars; spreads information on model programs to other groups; publishes print and audiovisual materials.

HEATH (Higher Education and the Handicapped) Resource Center

National Clearinghouse on Postsecondary Education for Handicapped Individuals
One Dupont Circle, Suite 800
Washington, DC 20036

202-939-9320
Rhona Hartman, Director

Organization of college-level educators, counselors, and administrators, seeking to help handicapped people obtain post-secondary education. Offers information for handicapped students about services and adaptations available on campus; encourages colleges to offer scholarships; publishes various materials, including newsletter, fact sheet, annual *Resource Directory*, and state-by-state lists of agencies for the handicapped. Partly funded by U.S. Department of Education.

Scholastic Aptitude Test (SAT)

Admissions Testing Program for Handicapped Students
CN 6603
Princeton, NJ 08541
Contact: Dr. Catherine Nelson
609-734-5068

Major testing organization that offers special testing arrangements for students documented to have learning disabilities, visual or hearing disabilties, or dyslexia, including untimed tests or additional time, tests in large type or braille, tests on tape cassette or read to student, scribe, or interpreter, and rest breaks.

Very Special Arts (VSA)

John F. Kennedy Center for the Performing Arts
Education Office
Washington, DC 20566
202-662-8899 (voice)
202-662-8898 (TTD)
Eugene Maillard, Chief Executive Officer

International agency designed to provide rich arts experiences and educational programs to disabled people, working with public and private groups. Publishes newsletter and other publications.

On Legal Problems

Disability Rights Education and Defense Fund

2212 Sixth Street
Berkeley, CA 94710
415-644-2555
Robert J. Funk, Director

Organization aimed at enhancing the rights and freedoms of the handicapped, including the rights of disabled children to public education. Seeks to influence public policy and legislation; studies special needs of disabled women and girls; offers information, advice, and assistance; publishes various materials, including *Disability Rights Review*.

Center on Human Policy (CHP)

c/o Syracuse University
200 Huntington Hall, 2nd Floor
Syracuse, NY 13244

315-423-3851
Steven Taylor, Director

Organization for parents of and professionals working with handicapped people, especially the severely physically and emotionally disabled, including autistic children and bilingual disabled children. Aims to bring physically or emotionally disabled people into the mainsteam as much as possible; provides information on rights, regulations, laws, and programs related to the handicapped; attempts to influence public policy and legislation; advises local groups and agencies, through Human Policy Press (address: P.O. Box 127, University Station, Syracuse, NY 13210); publishes many materials, focusing on fullest possible integration of people with severe disabilities, including mental retardation, into community life.

National Health Lawyers Association (NHLA)
522 21st Street, NW, Suite 120
Washington, DC 20006
202-833-1100
David J. Greenburg, Executive Director

Interdisciplinary organization of attorneys and health professionals working health-related legal areas, such as hospital law, health insurance, long-term care, health contract, and health maintenance organizations. Maintains library of information on health and the law; publishes various materials, including monthly *Health Law Digest* and *Health Lawyers News Report*, quarterly register, and annual digest index.

Center for Law and Education, 617-495-4666. (For full group information, see EDUCATION.)

Children's Defense Fund (CDF), 202-628-8787. (For full group information, see INDIVIDUALIZED EDUCATION PLAN.)

Mental Disability Legal Resource Center (MDLRC), American Bar Association, 202-331-2240. (For full group information, see MENTAL DISORDERS.)

National Center for Youth Law (NCYL), 415-543-3307. (For full group information, see CHILD ABUSE AND NEGLECT.)

On Recreational Programs

National Therapeutic Recreation Society
3101 Park Center Drive, 12th Floor
Alexandria, VA 22302
703-820-4940
Dean Tice, Executive Director

Organization of people who specialize in organization therapeutic recreational programs for the handicapped. Provides information and referrals; an arm of the National Recreation and Park Association.

Special Olympics International
1350 New York Avenue, NW, Suite 500
Washington, DC 20005

202-628-3630
Sargent Shriver, President

Organization promoting competitive sports and physical fitness for children and adults with handicaps.

Mobility International U.S.A. (MIUSA)
P.O. Box 3551
Eugene, OR 97403
503-343-1284 (voice and TDD)
Susan Sygall, Executive Director

For handicapped people and the organizations that service them. Provides information facilitating international education and recreational exchange programs, including stays with foreign families; offers work-study programs for young and adult disabled people; publishes various materials, including *Over the Rainbow* newsletter and *Community Service and Travel for Persons with Disabilities: A Guide to International Educational Exchange*.

National Advisory Committee on Scouting for the Handicapped (NACOSH)
1325 Walnut Hill Lane
Irving, TX 75038
214-580-2127
Ben H. Love, Chief Scout Executive

Arm of the Boy Scouts of America dedicated to developing scouting program for handicapped young people, coordinating with other organizations for the handicapped. Seeks also to sensitize other scouts to the special needs of the handicapped; publishes various materials, including newsletter, resource manual *Scouting for the Handicapped*, pamphlet *Scouting for the Emotionally Disturbed*, manual for deaf scouts, and materials in braille.

Special Recreation, Inc. (SRI)
362 Koser Avenue
Iowa City, IA 52240
319-337-7578
John A. Nesbit, President

For disabled individuals, their families, related professionals, and others interested in expanding recreational opportunities for the handicapped. Gathers and disseminates information about special programs and services, working with public and private groups; maintains library; publishes various materials.

Blind Outdoor Leisure Development
533 East Main Street
Aspen, CO 81611
303-925-8922

Organization funded by donations to provide recreational vacations for the blind, with guides and instructors provided by local clubs. Offers outdoor sports including skiing, golfing, skating, swimming, and camping.

Amputees in Motion (AIM)

P.O. Box 2703
Escondido, CA 92025
619-454-9300
Paul Scalice, President

Organization for amputees and their families. Aims to help adults and children reestablish active life, including sports and recreation, in which it offers special training and competitions; provides information on technical aids, such as driving attachments and special sports equipment; serves as information resource on services and benefits available to amputees; publishes newsletter.

National Association of Sports for Cerebral Palsy (NASCP), (212-481-6300). (For full group information, see CEREBRAL PALSY.)

On Wishes for Terminally or Chronically Ill Children

Make-a-Wish Foundation of America (MWFA)

4601 North 16th Street, Suite 205
Phoenix, AZ 85016
602-234-0960
Jean K. Elder, Executive Director

Organization funded by donations dedicated to granting a wish to terminally ill children, with special attention paid to the child's family.

Brass Ring Society (BRS), Inc.

314 South Main Street
Ottawa, Kansas 66067
913-242-1666, toll-free number 800-666-9474
Ray Esposito, President

Organization funded by donations dedicated to granting a wish to terminally ill children. Mobilizes airlines and other services to help in doing so; publishes bimonthly *Carousel*.

Children's Wish Foundation International (CWFI)

32 Perimeter Center East, NE, Suite 100
Atlanta, GA 30346
404-393-WISH [9474]; toll-free number 800-323-9474
Arthur Stein, President

Organization dedicated to granting a wish to terminally ill children. Publishes newsletters and other materials.

Starlight Foundation (SF)

10100 Santa Monica Boulevard, Suite 785
Los Angeles, CA 90067
213-208-5885
Carol Brown, Executive Director

Organization funded by donations dedicated to granting a wish to terminally or chronically ill children.

Sunshine Foundation (SF)

4010 Levick Street
Philadelphia, PA 19135
215-335-2622
Bill Sample, President

Organization funded by donations dedicated to granting a wish to terminally or chronically ill children, often providing a vacation for children and their families.

A Wish with Wings

P.O. Box 110418
Arlington, TX 76007
817-469-9474
Pat Skaggs, President

Organization funded by donations dedicated to granting a wish to children with life-threatening illnesses.

On Other Special Programs or Services

New England Assistance Dog Service (NEADS)

P.O. Box 213
West Boylston, MA 01583
508-835-3304
Sheila O'Brien, Executive Director

Organization that trains guide dogs for hearing-impaired people and service dogs for those physically handicapped. Publishes quarterly newsletter.

National Institute for Rehabilitation Engineering

97 Decker Road
Butler, NJ 07405
201-838-2500

Nonprofit organization of handicapped people, engineering and medical professionals, and others interested in providing equipment to increase independence of the handicapped. Evaluates equipment, modifies or custom-makes equipment, and trains others in its use; sets fees on ability to pay; provides rebuilt used equipment to needy handicapped people.

Canine Companions for Independence (CCI)

6901 Harrisburg Pike
Orient, OH 43146
614-871-2554

For physically handicapped individuals, veterinarians, dog trainers, and other interested parties. Provides dogs to help qualified disabled individuals live more independently, as by helping them up after a fall or opening doors; publishes newsletter *Support Line*.

National Foundation of Dentistry for the Handicapped (NFDH)

1600 Stout Street, Suite 1420
Denver, CO 80202

303-573-0264

Larry Coffee, Executive Director

Organization of dental professionals concerned with special children.

On Information and Services for Families of Special Children

Parents Helping Parents (PHP)

535 Race Street, Suite 220

San Jose, CA 95126

408-288-5010

Florene Poyadue, Executive Director

"Special children's family resource center," organization of parents, professionals, and lay counselors concerned with children with special needs. Encourages formation of mutual-support, self-help groups; publishes various materials on handicaps, including bibliographies and information packets.

Sibling Information Network, Connecticut's University Affiliated Program on Developmental Disabilities, 203-486-3783. (For full group information, see SIBLINGS.)

Siblings for Significant Change (SSC), 212-420-0776. (For full group information, see SIBLINGS.)

La Leche League International (LLLI), 312-455-7730. Publishes *A Special Kind of Parenting: Meeting the Needs of Handicapped Children*. (For full group information, see BREASTFEEDING.)

Other Reference Sources

General Works

The Exceptional Parent Magazine, published eight times a year, for parents of special children. Address: 1170 Commonwealth Avenue, 3rd Floor, Boston, MA 02134. For subscription orders: P.O. Box 3000, Department EP, Denville, NJ 07834; toll-free number 800-247-8080.

Parenting Plus: Raising Children with Special Health Needs, by Peggy Finston, M.D. New York: Dutton, 1990.

Building a New Dream: A Family Guide to Coping with Chronic Illness and Disability, by Janet R. Maurer and Patricia D. Strasberg. Reading, MA: Addison-Wesley, 1989.

The Special Child: A Source Book for Parents of Children with Developmental Disabilities, by Siegfried M. Pueschel, James C. Bernier, and Leslie E. Weidenman. Baltimore: Paul H. Brookes, 1988.

Exceptional Children and Youth, E. Meyen and T. Skirtic, eds. Denver: Love Publications, 1988.

Mainstreaming Preschoolers: Children with Orthopedic Handicaps: A Guide for Teachers, Parents, and Others Who Work with Orthopedically Handicapped Preschoolers, by Shari Stokes Kieran, et al. (1986). Prepared for the Department

of Health and Human Services by the Administration for Children, Youth and Families, Head Start Bureau. Discusses how orthopedic handicaps affect 3-to-5-year-olds and their learning, with suggestions for teaching activities to enhance their skills.

Mainstreaming Preschoolers: Children with Health Impairment: A Guide for Teachers, Parents, and Others Who Work with Health Impaired Preschoolers, by Alfred Healy, et al. (1979). Prepared for the Department of Health and Human Services by the Administration for Children, Youth and Families, Head Start Bureau. Discusses how health impairment affects 3-to-5-year-olds and their learning, with suggestions for teaching activities to enhance their skills. (For other titles in this series, see EYE AND VISION PROBLEMS, EAR AND HEARING PROBLEMS, LEARNING DISABILITIES, MENTAL RETARDATION, and MENTAL DISORDERS.)

We Are Not Alone: Learning to Live with Chronic Illness, by Sefra Pitzele. Minneapolis, MN: Thompson, 1985.

Handicapped Infants and Children: A Handbook for Parents and Professionals, by Carol Tingye-Michaelis. Baltimore: University Park Press, 1983.

Care of the Neurologically Handicapped Child: A Book for Parents and Professionals, by A.L. Prensky and H.S. Pulkens. New York: Oxford University Press, 1982.

Hope for the Families: New Directions for Parents of Persons with Retardation and Other Disabilities, by R. Perske. Nashville, TN: Abingdon, 1981.

Yes They Can: A Handbook for Effectively Parenting the Handicapped. Irvine, CA: Reality Productions Publications, 1981. Address: P.O. Box 18452, Irvine, CA 92713.

On Families of Special Children

After the Tears: Parents Talk About Raising a Child with a Disability, by Robin Simons. San Diego: Harcourt, Brace, Jovanovich, 1987.

A Difference in the Family: Living with a Disabled Child, Helen Featherstone. New York: Penguin, 1981.

Coping with Prolonged Health Impairment in Your Child, by A. T. McCollum. Boston, MA: Little, Brown, 1975.

Living with a Brother or Sister with Special Needs: A Book for Sibs, by Donald J. Meyer, Patricia F. Vadasy, and Rebecca R. Fewell. Available (for $10.95 plus $2 shipping) from University of Washington Press, P.O. Box C-50096, Seattle, WA 98145.

On Mobility and Medical Questions

Health Care U.S.A., by Jean Carper. New York: Prentice Hall, 1987. Resource for general and specific health-care information, including sections on mental retardation, developmental disabilities, and learning disabilities. Lists key rehabilitation centers specializing in infant and early childhood development, government-supported university-affiliated facilities (UAFs) for learning disabilities and UAF-associated specialists, mental retardation research centers, special schools for dyslexic children, leading physical rehabilitation centers, leading brain-injury centers, and government-funded rehabilitation research and training centers, rehabilitation engineering centers (RECs), sources of products and services for the handicapped, sports organizations for the disabled, and other information.

Holistic Health Care for Children with Developmental Disabilities, by Una Haynes. Baltimore: University Park, 1983.

Making Toys for Handicapped Children: A Guide for Parents and Teachers, by Roy McConkey and Dorothy Jeffree. Englewood Cliffs, NJ: Prentice Hall, 1983.

Easy to Make Aids for Your Handicapped Child: A Guide for Parents and Teachers, by Don Caston. Englewood Cliffs, NJ: Prentice Hall, 1982.

A Handbook for the Disabled: Ideas and Inventions for Easier Living, by S. Lunt. New York: Scribner, 1982.

Access: The Guide to a Better Life for Disabled Americans, by Lilly Bruck. New York: Random House, 1978.

On Legal, Educational, and Social Questions

Disability and the Family: A Guide to Decisions for Adulthood, by H. Rutherford Turnbull, Ann P. Turnbull, Jean Ann Summers, and Constance Roeder-Gordon. Baltimore: Paul H. Brookes, 1989. Planning for adulthood of disabled children.

Insurance & Alternatives for Uninsurables, by Roger A. Kessinger. New York: Kessinger Publishing, distributed by Quality Books, 1989.

Transition from School to Work: New Challenges for Youth with Severe Disabilities. Baltimore: Paul H. Brookes, 1988.

Educating Children with Multiple Disabilities: A Transdisciplinary Approach, F. Orelove and D. Sobsey. Baltimore: Paul H. Brookes, 1987.

Systematic Instruction of Persons with Severe Handicaps, 3rd edition, M. E. Snell, ed. Columbus, OH: Merrill, 1987.

Alternatives: A Family Guide to Legal and Financial Planning for the Disabled, by Mark L. Russell. Available from First Publications, P.O. Box 1832, Evanston, IL 60204.

Legal Rights Primer for the Handicapped: In and Out of the Classroom, by Joseph Roberts and Bonnie Hawk. Novato, CA: Academic Therapy Publications, 1980. Address: 20 Commercial Boulevard, Novato, CA 94947.

Colleges That Enable: A Guide to Support Services Offered to Physically Disabled Students on 40 U.S. Campuses, by Prudence K. Tweed and Jason C. Tweed. New York: Park Avenue Press, distributed by Quality Books, 1989.

Who Cares: A Handbook on Sex Education and Counseling Services for Disabled People. Available from The Sex and Disability Project, 1828 L Street, NW, Suite 704, Washington, DC 20036.

Teaching Individuals with Physical and Multiple Disabilities, by J. L. Bigge. Columbus, OH: Charles E. Merrill, 1982.

Educating the Chronically Ill Child, by Susan B. Kleinberg. Rockville, MD: Aspen, 1982.

Educating the Severely Physically Handicapped, by J. Umbreit and P. Cardullas. Columbus, OH: Special Press, 1980.

Teaching and Learning Strategies for Physically Handicapped Students, by M.L. Calhoun and M. Hawisher. Baltimore: University Park, 1979.

Program Guide for Infants and Toddlers with Neuromotor and Other Developmental Disabilities, Frances Connor, Gordon Williamson, and John M. Siepp, eds. New York: Teachers College Press/Harper and Row, 1978.

Background Works

An Exposure of the Heart, by Rebeca Busselle. New York: Penguin, 1990. About a year spent observing in an institution for the developmentally disabled.

Ordinary Families, Special Children: A Systems Approach to Childhood Disability, by Milton Seligman and Rosalyn Benjamin Darling. New York: Guilford, 1989. On the effect of a child's disability on others in the family.

Supported Employment for Persons with Disabilities, Paul Wehman and John Kregel, eds. New York: Human Sciences, 1989.

Living with Chronic Illness: Days of Patience and Passion, by Cheri Register. New York: Free Press/Macmillan, 1987.

Faith, Hope and Luck, a Sociological Study of Children Growing up with a Lifethreatening Illness, by Charles Waddell. Washington, DC: University Press of America, 1983.

Children Who Are Different: Meeting the Challenges of Birth Defects in Society, by Rosalyn Benjamin Darling and Jon Darling. St. Louis: Mosby, 1982.

Families Against Society: A Study of Reactions to Children with Birth Defects, by Rosalyn Benjamin Darling. Beverly Hills, CA: Sage, 1979.

Disabled? Yes. Defeated? NO: Resources for the Disabled and their Families, Friends and Therapists, by Kathleen Cruzic. Englewood Cliffs, NJ: Prentice Hall, 1982.

When Bad Things Happen to Good People, by Harold S. Kushner. New York: Avon, 1981.

A Reader's Guide: For Parents of Children with Mental, Physical, or Emotional Disabilities, by Coralie B. Moore and Kathryn Gorham Morton, with Joni B. Mills. Prepared for the Public Health Service by Family and Community Services, Montgomery County (Maryland) Association for Retarded Citizens. (1979). Though now dated, many earlier works listed are still useful.

For Special Kids

How It Feels to Fight for Your Life, by Jill Krementz. Boston: Joy Street/Little, Brown, 1989. Young people talk about dealing with life-threatening medical problems.

My Friend Leslie, by Maxine B. Rosenberg. New York: Lothrop, Lee & Shepard, 1989. For young readers.

Mental and Emotional Disabilities, by Jean Dick. Mankato, MN: Crestwood, 1989. Part of the Facts About series.

The Physically Disabled, by Connie Baron. Mankato, MN: Crestwood, 1989. Part of the Facts About series.

Finding a Way: Living with Exceptional Brothers and Sisters, by Maxine B. Rosenberg. New York: Lothrop, Lee & Shepard, 1988.

A Service Dog Goes to School: The Story of a Dog Trained to Help the Disabled, by Elizabeth Simpson Smith. New York: Morrow, 1988. For ages 6 to 9.

Born Different: The Amazing Stories of Some Very Special People, by Frederick Drimmer. New York: Atheneum, 1988.

Help Against Substance Abuse

Here are some key organizations and reference works that can give information and help to parents and children facing drug or alcohol abuse—or trying to prevent it. Following that is some resource material on different kinds of drugs and alcohol, their characteristics and effects, signs of use and abuse, and some suggestions about what parents can do.

ORGANIZATIONS OFFERING HELP AND INFORMATION

On Substance Abuse in General

National Clearinghouse for Alcohol and Drug Abuse Information (NCADI)
P.O. Box 2345
5600 Fishers Lane, Room 10A-43
Rockville, MD 20857
301-443-6500
Address for mail orders:
P.O. Box 416
Kensington, MD 20795

Federally supported alcohol and drug-abuse information clearinghouse. Provides information to public and professionals; advises on setting up local parent–peer groups to counter drug use; publishes various materials, including newsletters *Prevention Pipeline: An Alcohol and Drug Awareness Service* and *The Challenge* on successful school-based drug prevention programs; data reports on drug and alcohol use and abuse; materials for parents and community leaders, such as *Parents, Peers and Pot II: Parents in Action; Parents: What You Can Do About Drug Abuse; For Parents Only, Adolescent Drug Abuse: Analyses of Treatment Research, National Trends in Drug Use and Related Factors Among American High School Students, 1975–1986, Strategies for Controlling Drug Use, Drug Prevention Curricula: A Guide to Selection and Presentation*, and *Adolescent Peer Pressure Theory, Correlates and Program Implications for Drug Abuse Prevention*; flyers and pamphlets such as *The Fact Is . . . You Can Prevent Alcohol and Other Drug Problems Among Elementary School Children, Team Up for Drug Prevention with America's*

Young Athletes, Communities: What You Can Do About Drug and Alcohol Abuse, Are You a Drug Quiz Whiz?, Alcohol and Youth, When Cocaine Affects Someone You Love, The Fact Is Big Lies Promote Cocaine and Crack Use, and *Alcohol and Birth Defects*; fact sheets on specific topics, such as hallucinogens and PCP, marijuana, inhalants, opiates, pencyclidine, sedative-hypnotics, and stimulants and cocaine; reprint of article for teens, "When Your Parent Drinks Too Much"; and kits for and special reports on children of alcoholics.

Alcohol, Drug Abuse, and Mental Health Administration (ADAMHA)
Parklawn Building
5600 Fishers Lane
Rockville, MD 20857
301-443-6780

Federal arm overseeing and providing public information on drug and alcohol use and abuse. Conducts research and provides information; publishes many materials.

National Institute on Drug Abuse (NIDA) Hotline (9 A.M.–3 A.M. M–F; Noon–3 A.M. Sat–Sun), 800-662-HELP [4357]; in Spanish, 800-66A-YUDA [662-9832]. Federal organization offering drug treatment information and referrals.

Fair Oaks Hospital Hotline, 800-COCAINE; treatment referrals only; no counseling.

Food and Drug Administration, 301-295-8012. (For full group information, see DRUG REACTIONS AND INTERACTIONS.)

National PRIDE (Parents' Resource Institute for Drug Education)
The Hurt Building
50 Hurt Plaza, Suite 210
Atlanta, GA 30303
404-577-4500; toll-free hotline 800-67-PRIDE [677-7433]
Thomas J. Gleason, Executive Officer

Organization for individuals and groups of parents, community leaders, and professionals. Encourages formation of community-based groups to counter drug use; gathers and distributes data on drugs and their effects; seeks to influence public policy and legislation; sponsors annual International Drug Conference; operates toll-free number for drug information and referral

587

services; publishes newsletter and other materials, including pamphlet *What Parents Must Learn*.

Cottage Program International (CPI)
736 South 500 East
Salt Lake City, UT 84102
801-532-5185; toll-free number 800-752-6102
Bernell Boswell, Executive Director

Organization focusing on use of behavior modification in prevention and treatment of alcohol and drug abuse. Trained volunteers aid families, schools, and other organizations in running substance-abuse prevention programs; publishes training programs and other materials.

National Council on Alcoholism and Drug Dependency (NCADD)
12 West 21st Street, 7th Floor
New York, NY 10010
212-206-6770; toll-free number 800-NCA-CALL [622-2255]
Thomas Seessel, Executive Director

Network of volunteer organizations fighting alcoholism and other drug addictions. Provides information for public, makes referrals; publishes various print and audiovisual materials, including *What Every Teenager Should Know About Alcohol* and newsletter *The Amethyst*.

Narcotic Educational Foundation of America (NEFA)
5055 Sunset Boulevard
Los Angeles, CA 90027
213-663-5171
Henry B. Hall, Executive Director

Organization dedicated to educating young people and adults about hazards of drug abuse. Gathers research data and maintains library; produces film and print materials, including *Student Warning-Reference Sheets* about drugs.

Solvent Abuse Foundation for Education (SAFE)
750 17th Street, NW, Suite 250
Washington, DC 20006
202-332-7233
Hugh F. Young, President

Information clearinghouse for public and professionals on solvent-abuse resources.

National Association for Prenatal Addiction Research and Education (NAPARE)
11 East Hubbard Street, Suite 200
Chicago, IL 60611
312-329-2512
Ira Chasnoff, M.D., President

Organization concerned with prenatal addiction. Supports research; operates clinic; seeks to educate public and act as information clearinghouse; publishes monthly *NAPARE Update*.

Special Substance-Abuse Programs

Alcoholics Anonymous World Services (AA)
P.O. Box 459, Grand Central Station
New York, NY 10163
212-686-1100 (see telephone-directory white pages or information for local number)

For recovering alcoholics, both adults and teenagers; an international, nondenominational network of wholly independent mutual-support groups aimed at helping individuals achieve sobriety. Publishes numerous books and other materials, including *A Message for Teenagers*, book *Alcoholics Anonymous*, and monthly *AA Grapevine*.

Drugs Anonymous (DA)
P.O. Box 473, Ansonia Station
New York, NY 10023
212-784-0700
Mary Lou Phippen, Secretary

Network of mutual-support self-help groups of drug abusers, modeled on Alcoholics Anonymous (see separate entry). Offers Pil-Anon Family Program for families of drug abusers (formerly Pills Anonymous).

Narcotics Anonymous (NA)
P.O. Box 9999
Van Nuys, CA 91409
818-780-3951 (see telephone directory or information for local numbers, including hotlines in major cities)
Bob Stone, Director

Network of mutual-support self-help groups for recovering narcotic addicts, modeled on Alcoholics Anonymous (see separate entry). Operates hotlines; publishes various materials, including *NA Way Magazine* and book *Narcotics Anonymous*.

Toughlove, 215-348-7090; toll-free number 800-333-1069. (For full group information, see DISCIPLINE.)

Hazelden Foundation (HF)
Box 11
Center City, MN 55012
612-257-4010; toll-free number for treatment programs, U.S. except MN and AK, 800-262-5010; toll-free numbers for publications, U.S. except MN and AK, 800-328-9000; MN, 800-257-0070.

Organization offering treatment and rehabilitation for people addicted to alcohol or drugs. Wide range of services include Hazelden's Pioneer House Program for teenagers and young adults, group home for young male drug addicts, family programs, such as that of Hazelden Renewal Center, and outpatient or aftercare programs. Trains professionals counselors and gathers and maintains research data on abuse problems; publishes many books and other materials.

Straight, Inc. (SI)

P.O. Box 21686
St. Petersburg, FL 33742
813-576-8929
Mel J. Riddile, Executive Director

Rehabilitation program for drug abusers and their families, involving a year-long course of structured therapy under trained professionals and rehabilitated drug abusers, while also relying on approaches developed by Alcoholics Anonymous. Produces various print and video materials.

Johnson Institute

7151 Metro Boulevard
Minneapolis, MN 55435
612-341-0435, toll-free number, business hours, U.S. except MN 800-231-5165; toll-free number, MN, 800-247-0484
Vernon Johnson, founder and president emeritus

Organization seeking to aid individuals, groups, schools, hospitals, and other institutions in the prevention and treatment of and recovery from chemical dependence, from alcohol or other substances. Provides training and consultation to professionals in the field; operates toll-free numbers; publishes numerous print and audiovisual materials, including books such as *Everything You Need to Know About Chemical Dependence: Vernon Johnson's Complete Guide for Families, Parenting for Prevention: How to Raise a Child to Say No to Alcohol/Drugs: For Parents, Teachers and Other Concerned Adults, Choices & Consequences: What to Do When a Teenager Uses Alcohol/Drugs: A Step-By-Step System That Really Works, Can I Handle Alcohol/Drugs? A Self-Assessment Guide for Youth, Family Secrets That Keep Us Sick, Intervention: How to Help Someone Who Doesn't Want Help, A Step-by-Step Guide for Families and Friends of Chemically Dependent Persons, Children in Recovery: Healing the Parent-Child Relationship in Alcohol-Addictive Families, From Peer Pressure to Peer Support: Alcohol/Drug Prevention Through Group Process: A Curriculum For Grades 7–12, Children Are People, Inc. Prevention Curriculum for Grades K–6, Cocaine and Crack: What You Need to Know, Facing Shame: Families in Recovery*, and *Solving Alcohol/Drug Problems in Your School: Why Student Assistance Programs Work*; booklets such as *Alcohol and Adolescents: Identifying and Managing the Problems, Drinking and Driving: New Directions, Drinking and Pregnancy: Preventing Fetal Alcohol Syndrome, Breaking Away: Saying Good-bye to Alcohol/Drugs: A Guide to Help Teenagers Stop Using Chemicals; Chemical Dependence and Recovery: A Family Affair, Recovery of Chemically Dependent Families, The Family Enablers, How It Feels to Be Chemically Dependent, Why Haven't I Been Able to Help?, Alcoholism and Depression*, and *Alcohol and Anxiety*; films and videocassettes such as *Enabling: Masking Reality, Intervention: Facing Reality, Co-Dependence: The Joy of Recovery, Choices and Consequences: Intervention with Youth in Trouble with Alcohol/Drugs, The Enablers, Where's Shelley?* (for children aged 9 to 11); and book or booklet/film or cassette sets such as *Different Like Me* (one for teenage children of alcoholics, one for ages 5 to 10) and *A Story About Feelings* (coloring book and film for children aged 5 to 8).

Families Anonymous (FA)

P.O. Box 528
Van Nuys, CA 91408
818-989-7841

Network of mutual-support self-help groups for family and friends of drug abusers or those with related emotional problems; modeled after Al-Anon (see separate entry) and its relationship to Alcoholics Anonymous (see separate entry). Helps new groups get started and provides telephone referrals; publishes various materials, including newsletter, *A Guide for the Family of the Drug Abuser*, and *A Father Faces Drug Abuse*.

On Anti-Substance-Abuse Programs for Parents and Community Leaders

American Council for Drug Education (ACDE)

204 Monroe Street, Suite 110
Rockville, MD 20852
301-294-0600
Lee I. Dogoloff, Executive Director

Organizations of individuals and groups, including professionals and parents, concerned about drug abuse. Distributes information on drugs; publishes print and audiovisual materials, including newsletter *The Drug Educator* and multimedia drug education program *Building Drug-Free Schools*.

Families in Action

2296 Henderson Mill Road, Suite 204
Atlanta, GA 30345
404-934-6364
Sue Rusche, Executive Director

For parents and others interested in preventing drug abuse among children and adolescents. Aims to educate public and change social climate; supports passage of laws banning drug paraphernalia; gathers and distributes information on drug use; conducts education and training programs; publishes various materials, including quarterly *Drug Abuse Update* and *How to Form a Families Action Group in Your Community*.

U.S. Department of Education

Drug-Free Schools Staff
400 Maryland Avenue, SW
Washington, DC 20202
202-732-4599

Special federal program helping local school districts and education agencies develop and coordinate alcohol and drug-abuse prevention and education programs. Provides technical assistance and training, through five regional centers:

Northeast Regional Center for Drug-Free Schools and Communities
12 Overton Avenue
Sayville, NY 11782
516-589-7022

Serves Connecticut, Delaware, Maine, Maryland, Massachusetts, New Hampshire, New Jersey, New York, Ohio, Pennsylvania, Rhode Island, and Vermont.

Southeast Regional Center for Drug-Free Schools and Communities
The Hurt Building
50 Hurt Plaza, Suite 210
Atlanta, GA 30303
404-688-9277

Serves Alabama, District of Columbia, Florida, Georgia, Kentucky, North Carolina, South Carolina, Tennessee, Virginia, West Virginia, Virgin Islands, and Puerto Rico.

Midwest Regional Center for Drug-Free Schools and Communities
2001 North Claybourn, Suite 302
Chicago, IL 60614
312-883-8888

Serves Indiana, Illinois, Iowa, Michigan, Minnesota, Missouri, Nebraska, North Dakota, South Dakota, and Wisconsin.

Southwest Regional Center for Drug-Free Schools and Communities
555 Constitution Avenue
Norman, OK 73037
405-325-1454; toll-free number (except OK) 800-234-7972

Serves Arizona, Arkansas, Colorado, Kansas, Louisiana, Mississippi, New Mexico, Oklahoma, Texas, and Utah.

Western Regional Center for Drug-Free Schools and Communities
101 Southwest Main Street, Suite 500
Portland, OR 97204
503-275-9479; toll-free number (except OR) 800-547-6339

Serves Alaska, California, Hawaii, Idaho, Montana, Nevada, Oregon, Washington, Wyoming, American Samoa, Guam, Northern Mariana Islands, and Republic of Palau.

National Federation of Parents for Drug-Free Youth (NFP)
1423 North Jefferson
Springfield, MO 65802

417-836-3709
Ruby Smith, Networker

Nationwide network of parent groups concerned about the hazards of drug abuse. Seeks to educate young people and parents and encourages formation of anti-drug-use parent groups; supports laws banning drug paraphernalia; opposes legalization of marijuana; publishes various materials, including starter kit for parent groups.

ACTION Drug Prevention Program
806 Connecticut Avenue, NW, Suite M-606
Washington, DC 20525
202-634-9757

Federal volunteer agency encouraging and sponsoring development of groups or networks of drug prevention programs at all levels aimed at young people.

National Woman's Christian Temperance Union (WCTU)
1730 Chicago Avenue
Evanston, IL 60201
312-864-1396
Mrs. Kermit Edgar, President

Network of women's groups seeking total abolition of alcohol. Seeks to educate public as to dangers of alcohol. Sponsors abstinence training camps for young people; gathers and disseminates research data on various topics, including teenage drinking, narcotics, and alcohol as cause of traffic accidents; maintains library; makes video materials available to schools and churches for training programs; publishes various materials, including monthly children's magazine *Young Crusader*.

Organizations Against Drunk Driving

Mothers Against Drunk Driving (MADD)
669 Airport Freeway, Suite 310
Hurst, TX 76053
817-268-MADD [6233]
D.E. Schaet, Executive Director

Organization of families of drunk-driving victims and others interested in the problem. Seeks to educate public and government agencies as to need for stronger penalties; refers survivors to bereavement groups and aids them in negotiating through the judicial system; maintains library; publishes various materials, including newsletter.

RID-United States of America (Remove Intoxicated Drivers)
P.O. Box 520
Schenectady, NY 12301

Victims National Hotline, 518-372-0034
Doris Aiken, President

Organization of individuals and groups seeking to keep drunk drivers off the highways. Seeks to educate public and influence public policy and legislation; offers emotional support for drunk-driving victims and their families, and practical aid for negotiating through the judicial system; operates national hotline; maintains library; monitors court treatment of drunk drivers; publishes various materials, including newsletter and *Victims Aid Network*.

Students Against Driving Drunk (SADD)
P.O. Box 800
Marlboro, MA 01752
617-481-3568
Robert Anastas, Executive Officer

Organization of students and interested adults. Encourages students to work against drunk driving; seeks stronger penalties for intoxicated drivers; seeks to educate public and influence public policy and legislation; publishes various materials, including quarterly *SADD in Your School*.

National Safety Council (NSC), 312-527-4800. Publishes *Designated Driver Program* and booklets on drinking and driving, such as *Will You Make It Home Tonight?* and *R. O. A. D. Risks, Odds, and Decisions.* (For full group information, see EXERCISE.)

Citizens for Safe Drivers Against Drunk Drivers/Chronic Offenders
7401 MacKenzie Court
Bethesda, MD 20817
301-469-6282
Ken Nathanson, President

Organization of families of drunk-driving crash victims, traffic experts, and interested others. Seeks to strengthen drunk-driving penalties, licensing regulations, and use of U.S. Department of Transportation's national register of drivers whose licenses have been revoked; serves as support network for victims' families and general information clearinghouse; publishes newsletter.

Programs for Families and Friends of Alcoholics

Al-Anon Family Group Headquarters (AAFGH)
1372 Broadway
New York, NY 10018
212-302-7240 (see Alcoholics Anonymous in white pages for local number)
Susan Handley, Public Information Coordinator

For family and friends of alcoholics; a network of mutual-support groups paralleling Alcoholics Anonymous, with Alateen groups especially for children 12 to 20. Aims to help people deal with the problems resulting from another's drinking; pub-

lishes numerous books and other materials, including *Alcoholism: The Family Disease.*

Children of Alcoholics Foundation (CAF)
200 Park Avenue, 31st Floor
New York, NY 10166
212-949-1404
Peter Goldberg, Secretary

Organization focusing on research on and public dissemination of the effects on children of alcohol and substance abuse in the family, as on the parent–child relationship and child abuse. Publishes various reports.

National Association for Children of Alcoholics (NACOA)
31706 Coast Highway, Suite 201
South Laguna, CA 92677
714-499-3889
Gerald S. Myers, Executive Director

Organization for professionals and others interested in helping children of alcoholics (COAs), and the children themselves. Acts as information clearinghouse and provides referrals for children needing treatment; aims to strengthen social services for COAs, through education, research, legislation, and development of support networks; publishes newsletter and other materials, including *Children of Alcoholics Handbook* and *Children of Alcoholics in the Schools.*

Other Reference Sources

General Works

The Recovery Resource Book: The Best Available Information on Addictions and Co-Dependence, by Barbara Yoder. New York: Simon & Schuster/Fireside, 1990.

The 800-COCAINE Book of Drug and Alcohol Recovery, by James Cocores, M.D. New York: Villard, 1990.

Desperate to Be Needed: Freeing the Family from Chemical Codependency, by Janet Ohlemacher. Grand Rapids, MI: Zondervan, 1990. For victims of drug and alcohol abuse.

Growing Out of an Alcoholic Family, by Karen Sandvig. Ventura, CA: Regal, 1990.

Relationships in Recovery: Healing Strategies for Couples and Families, by Emily Marlin. New York: Harper, 1990.

Cocaine Kids: The Inside Story of a Teenage Drug Ring, by Terry Williams. Reading, MA: Addison-Wesley, 1990.

Growing Up Drug Free: A Parent's Guide to Prevention, U.S. Department of Education. 52-page handbook available free in single copies from Growing Up Drug Free, Pueblo, CO 81009.

Freeing Someone You Love from Alcohol and Other Drugs, by Ronald L. Rogers and Chandler Scott McMullin. Los Angeles: Price Stern Sloan, 1989.

Parents Who Help Their Children Overcome Drugs, by Barbara Cottman Becnel. Chicago: Contemporary, 1989.

Rx for Recovery: The Medical and Health Guide for Alcoholics, Addicts, and Their Families, by Jeffrey Weisberg, M.D., and Gene Hawes. New York: Watts, 1989; Ivy/Ballantine; 1990.

Driving the Drunk Off the Road, by Sandy Golden. Old Tappan, NJ: Revell, 1990.

Facing Shame: Families in Recovery, by Merle A. Fossum and Marilyn J. Mason. New York: Norton, 1989.

You Are What You Drink: The Authoritative Report on What Alcohol Does to Your Mind, Body and Longevity, by Allan Luks and Joseph Barbato. New York: Villard, 1989.

Adult Children of Alcoholics Remember: True Stories of Abuse and Recovery, E. Nelson Hayes, ed. New York: Crown, 1989.

Help to Get Help: When Someone Else's Drinking or Drugging Is Hurting You, by John O'Neill and Pat O'Neill. Austin: Texas Monthly Press, 1989.

Hooked on Life: How to Totally Recover from Addictions and Dependency, by Tim Timmons and Steve Arterburn. Nashville, TN: Thomas Nelson, 1989.

Living on the Edge: A Guide to Intervention for Families with Drug and Alcohol Problems, by Katherine Ketcham and Ginny Lyford Gustafson. New York: Bantam, 1989.

Drugs, Alcohol, and Your Children: A Parent's Survival Manual, by Geraldine Youcha and Judith S. Seixas. New York: Crown, 1989.

Kick the Drug Habit: The Basic Guide, 3rd edition, by Clifton J. Alexander. Tuscon, AZ: Antler, 1989.

Parents Who Help Their Children Overcome Drugs, by Barbara Cottman Becnel. Los Angeles: Lowell House, distributed by Contemporary Books, 1989.

Peterson's Drug and Alcohol Programs and Policies at Four-Year Colleges, Janet Carney Schneider and Bunny Porter-Shirley, eds. Princeton, NJ: Peterson's, 1989.

Ecstasy: The MDMA Story, by Bruce Eisner. Berkeley, CA: Ronin, 1989.

Drug-proof Your Kids: A Prevention Guide & an Intervention Plan, by Stephen Arterburn and Jim Burns. Pomona, CA: Focus on the Family, distributed by Word, 1989. From a Christian perspective.

Kids and Drugs: A Handbook for Parents and Professionals, by Joyce Tobias. Annandale, VA: PANDAA Press, 1986. Address: 4111 Watkins Trail, Annandale, VA 22003, 703-750-9285.

Unhooked: Staying Sober and Drug-Free, by James Christopher. Buffalo: Prometheus, 1989.

Peer Pressure Reversal, by Sharon Scott. Amherst, MA: Human Resource Development Press, 1985.

Kids and Drugs: A Parent's Handbook of Drug Abuse, Prevention and Treatment, by Jason D. Baron. New York: Perigee, 1984.

Getting Tough on Gateway Drugs: A Guide for the Family, by Robert L. DuPont, Jr., M.D. Washington, DC: American Psychiatric Press, 1984.

Managing the "Drugs" In Your Life: A Personal and Family Guide to the Responsible Use of Drugs, Alcohol, Medicine, by Stephen J. Levy. New York: McGraw-Hill, 1983.

Getting Off the Hook, by Meg Patterson. Wheaton, IL: Harold Shaw, 1983.

Stopping Valium, by Eve Bargmann. New York: Warner, 1983.

Daytop Village, by Barry Sugarman. New York: Irvington, 1983.

Toughlove, by Phyllis York and David York. New York: Doubleday, 1982; Bantam, 1984.

Steering Clear: Helping Your Child Through the High-Risk Drug Years, by Dorothy Cretcher. Minneapolis: Winstone, 1982.

If Your Child Is Drinking . . . , by Randy Meyers Wolfson and Virginia DeLuca. New York: Warner, 1981.

Background Works

Encyclopedia of Drug Abuse, second edition, by Robert O'Brien and Sidney Cohen, M.D. New York: Facts on File, 1990.

Compact Paperback Library of the Encyclopedia of Psychoactive Drugs, including individual volumes: *The Addictive Personality; Amphetamines; Barbiturates; Celebrity Drug Use; Cocaine; Drinking; Driving & Drugs; Drugs & Pregnancy; Drugs & Sports; Drugs & Women; Heroin; Marijuana;* and *Teenage Depression and Suicide*. New York: Chelsea House, 1989.

Cocaine: An Annotated Bibliography, by Carlton E. Turner, et al. Jackson, MS: University Press of Mississippi, 1989.

Health Care U.S.A., by Jean Carper. New York: Prentice Hall, 1987. Resource for general and specific health-care information; lists major drug treatment programs for teenagers, state alcoholism and drug-abuse agencies, centers for research, and other information.

Children of Alcoholism: A Survivor's Manual, by Judith S. Seixas and Geraldine Youcha. New York: Crown, 1985.

The Courage to Change: Hope and Help for Alcoholics and Their Families, by Dennis Wholey. Boston: Houghton Mifflin, 1984.

Adult Children of Alcoholics, by Janet Geringer Woititz. Pompano Beach: FL: Health Communications, 1983.

The Natural History of Alcoholism, by G.E. Vaillant. Cambridge, MA: Harvard University Press, 1983.

Addiction: Its Causes, Problems, and Treatment, by G. Berger. New York: Watts, 1982.

Encyclopedia of Alcoholism, by Robert O'Brien and Morris Chaetz, M.D. New York: Facts on File, 1982.

Alcohol Addiction and Chronic Alcoholism, by E.M. Jellinek. Salem, NH: Ayer, 1981.

Alcohol Problems and Alcoholism: A Comprehensive Survey, by James Royce. New York: Free Press, 1981.

The Addicted Society, by J. Fort. New York: Grove, 1981.

The Pleasure Addicts: The Addictive Process—Food, Sex, Drugs, Alcohol, Work, and More, by Lawrence Hatterer. New York: Barnes, 1980.

The Invisible Alcoholics: Women and Alcohol Abuse in America, by Marian Sandmaier. New York: McGraw-Hill, 1980.

For Kids

Drug Abuse A–Z, by Gilda Berger and Melvin Berger. Hillside, NJ: Enslow, 1990. For grades 7 to 12.

Focus on Drugs and the Brain, by David Friedman. Frederick, MD: Twenty-First Century, 1990. For ages 8 to 12.

Focus on Alcohol, by Catherine O'Neill. Frederick, MD: Twenty-First Century, 1990. For ages 8 to 12.

Focus on Marijuana, by Paula Klevan Zeller. Frederick, MD: Twenty-First Century, 1990. For ages 8 to 12.

Focus on Cocaine and Crack, by Jeffrey Shulman. Frederick, MD: Twenty-First Century, 1990. For ages 8 to 12.

Focus on Nicotine and Caffeine, by Robert Perry. Frederick, MD: Twenty-First Century, 1990. For ages 8 to 12.

Focus on Marijuana, by Paula Klevan Zeller. Frederick, MD: Twenty-First Century, 1990. For ages 8 to 12.

Focus on Cocaine and Crack, by Jeffrey Shulman. Frederick, MD: Twenty-First Century, 1990. For ages 8 to 12.

Focus on Nicotine and Caffeine, by Robert Perry. Frederick, MD: Twenty-First Century, 1990. For ages 8 to 12.

Everything You Need to Know About an Alcoholic Parent, by Nancy Shuker. New York: Rosen, 1990. Part of a large-format, large-type series for teenagers (grades 7 to 12) with reading difficulties.

Coping with an Alcoholic Parent, by Kay Marie Porterfield. New York: Rosen, 1990. For adolescents.

Crack and Cocaine, by Mary C. Turck. New York: Crestwood, 1990. Part of the Facts About series.

Drinking and Driving, by Andy Hjelmeland. New York: Crestwood, 1990. Part of the Facts About series.

Crack: The New Drug Epidemic, by Gilda Berger. New York: Watts, 1989. For young readers.

Living with a Parent Who Takes Drugs, by Judith S. Seixas. New York: Greenwillow/Morrow, 1989.

The Don't Spoil Your Body Book, by Claire Rayner. Hauppauge, NY: Barron's, 1989. For ages 8 and up.

The Brain: What It Is, What It Does, by Ruth Dowling Bruun and Bertel Bruun, illustrated by Peter Bruun. New York: Greenwillow, 1989. For children grades 2 to 3; includes material on how drugs and alcohol affect the brain.

Making Up Your Mind About Drugs, by Gilda Berger. New York: Lodestar, 1988. For ages 9 to 11.

Breaking the Connection: How Young People Achieve Drug-free Lives, by Essie Lee. New York: Messner, 1988.

Not My Family: Sharing the Truth About Alcoholism, by Maxine B. Rosenberg. New York: Bradbury, 1988. For ages 9 to 12.

Stimulants and Hallucinogens, by Judy Monroe. Mankato, MN: Crestwood, 1988. Part of the Facts About series.

Alcohol and Tobacco, by Mary C. Turck. Mankato, MN: Crestwood, 1988. Part of the Facts About series.

Prescription Drugs, by Judy Monroe. Mankato, MN: Crestwood, 1988. Part of the Facts About series.

Crack and Cocaine, by David Brown. New York: Watts, 1987.

PCP: The Dangerous Angel, by Marilyn Carroll. New York: Chelsea House, 1985.

When Your Parent Drinks Too Much: A Book for Teenagers, by Eric Ryerson. New York: Facts On File, 1985.

RESOURCE MATERIALS ON SUBSTANCE ABUSE

Following are an overview of signs of drug use, some suggestions of what parents might do to lessen the likelihood that a child will succumb to substance abuse, and descriptions of specific types of drugs and their effects.

Signs of Drug Use

Changing patterns of performance, appearance, and behavior may signal use of drugs. The items in the first category listed below provide direct evidence of drug use; the items in the other categories offer signs that may indicate drug use. Adults should watch for extreme changes in children's behavior, changes that together form a pattern associated with drug use.

Signs of Drugs and Drug Paraphernalia

- Possession of drug-related paraphernalia such as pipes, rolling papers, small decongestant bottles, eye drops, or small butane torches.
- Possession of drugs or evidence of drugs, such as pills, white powder, small glass vials, or hypodermic needles; peculiar plants or butts, seeds, or leaves in ashtrays or in clothing pockets.
- Odor of drugs, smell of incense or other "cover-up" scents.

Identification with Drug Culture

- Drug-related magazines, slogans on clothing.
- Conversation and jokes that are preoccupied with drugs.
- Hostility in discussing drugs.
- Collection of beer cans.

Signs of Physical Deterioration

- Memory lapses, short attention span, difficulty in concentrating.
- Poor physical coordination, slurred or incoherent speech.
- Unhealthy appearance, indifference to hygiene and grooming.
- Bloodshot eyes, dilated pupils.

Dramatic Changes in School Performance

- Marked downturn in student's grades—not just from C's to F's, but from A's to B's and C's; assignments not completed.
- Increased absenteeism or tardiness.

Changes in Behavior

- Chronic dishonesty (lying, stealing, cheating); trouble with the police.
- Changes in friends; evasiveness in talking about new ones.
- Possession of large amounts of money.
- Increasing and inappropriate anger, hostility, irritability, secretiveness.
- Reduced motivation, energy, self-discipline, self-esteem.
- Diminished interest in extracurricular activities and hobbies.

Instilling Responsibility

Recommendation #1:

Teach standards of right and wrong and demonstrate these standards through personal example.

Children who are brought up to value individual responsiblity and self-discipline and to have a clear sense of right and wrong are less likely to try drugs than those who are not. Parents can help to instill these values by:

- Setting a good example for children and not using drugs themselves.
- Explaining to their children at an early age that drug use is wrong, harmful, and unlawful, and reinforcing this teaching throughout adolescence.
- Encouraging self-discipline by giving children regular duties and holding them accountable for their actions.
- Establishing standards of behavior concerning drugs, drinking, dating, curfews, and unsupervised activities, and enforcing them consistently and fairly.
- Encouraging their children to stand by their convictions when pressured to use drugs.

Recommendation #2:

Help children to resist peer pressure to use alcohol and other drugs by supervising their activities, knowing who their friends are, and talking with them about their interests and problems.

When parents take an active interest in their children's behavior, they provide the guidance and support children need to resist drugs. Parents can do this by:

- Knowing their children's whereabouts, activities, and friends.
- Working to maintain and improve family communications and listening to their children.
- Being able to discuss drugs knowledgeably. It is far better for children to obtain their information from their parents than from their peers or on the street.
- Communicating regularly with the parents of their children's friends and sharing their knowledge about drugs with other parents.
- Being selective about their children's viewing of television and movies that portray drug use as glamorous or exciting.

In addition, parents can work with the school in its efforts to fight drugs by:

- Encouraging the development of a school policy with a clear no-use message.
- Supporting administrators who are tough on drugs.
- Assisting the school in monitoring students' attendance and planning and chaperoning school-sponsored activities.
- Communicating regularly with the school regarding their children's behavior.

Recommendation #3:

Be knowledgeable about drugs and signs of drug use. When symptoms are observed, respond promptly.

Parents are in the best position to recognize early signs of drug use in their children. To inform and involve themselves, parents should take the following steps:

- Learn about the extent of the drug problem in their community and in their children's schools.
- Learn how to recognize signs of drug use.
- Meet with parents of their children's friends or classmates about the drug problem at their school. Establish a means of sharing information to determine which children are using drugs and who is supplying them.

Parents who suspect their children are using drugs often must deal with their emotions of anger, resentment, and guilt. Frequently they deny the evidence and postpone confronting their children. Yet, the earlier a drug problem is detected and faced, the less difficult it is to overcome. If parents suspect that their children are using drugs, they should take the following steps:

- Devise a plan of action. Consult with school officials and other parents.
- Discuss their suspicions with their children in a calm, objective manner. Do not confront a child while he or she is under the influence of alcohol or other drugs.
- Impose disciplinary measures that help remove the child from those circumstances where drug use might occur.
- Seek advice and assistance from drug treatment professionals and from a parent group.

SPECIFIC DRUGS AND THEIR EFFECTS

Alcohol

Effects

Alcohol consumption causes a number of marked changes in behavior. Even low doses significantly impair the judgment and coordination required to drive a car safely, increasing the likelihood that the driver will be involved in an accident. Low to moderate doses of alcohol also increase the incidence of a variety of aggressive acts, including spouse and child abuse. Moderate to high doses of alcohol cause marked impairments in higher mental functions, severely altering a person's ability to learn and remember information. Very high doses cause respiratory depression and death. If combined with other depressants of the central nervous system, much lower doses of alcohol will produce the effects just described.

Repeated use of alcohol can lead to dependence. Sudden cessation of alcohol intake is likely to produce withdrawal symptoms, including severe anxiety, tremors, hallucinations, and convulsions. Alcohol withdrawal can be life-threatening. Long-term consumption of large quantities of alcohol, particularly when combined with poor nutrition, can also lead to permanent damage to vital organs such as the brain and the liver.

Mothers who drink alcohol during pregnancy may give birth to infants with fetal alcohol syndrome. These infants have irreversible physical abnormalities and mental retardation. In addition, research indicates that children of alcoholic parents are at greater risk than other youngsters of becoming alcoholics.

Cannabis

Effects

All forms of cannabis have negative physical and mental effects. Several regularly observed physical effects of cannabis are a substantial increase in the heart rate, bloodshot eyes, a dry mouth and throat, and increased appetite.

Use of cannabis may impair or reduce short-term memory and comprehension, alter sense of time, and reduce ability to perform tasks requiring concentration and coordination, such as driving a car. Research also shows that students do not retain knowledge when they are "high." Motivation and cognition may be altered, making the acquisition of new information difficult. Marijuana can also produce paranoia and psychosis.

Because users often inhale the unfiltered smoke deeply and then hold it in their lungs as long as possible, marijuana is damaging to the lungs and pulmonary system. Marijuana smoke contains more cancer-causing agents than tobacco smoke.

Long-term users of cannabis may develop psychological dependence and require more of the drug to get the same effect. The drug can become the center of their lives.

Cannabis

Type	What is it called?	What does it look like?	How is it used?
Marijuana	Pot Grass Weed Reefer Dope Mary Jane Sinsemilla Acapulco gold Thai sticks	Dried parsley mixed with stems that may include seeds	Eaten Smoked
Tetrahydrocannabinol	TCH	Soft gelatin capsules	Taken orally
Hashish	Hash	Brown or black cakes or balls	Eaten Smoked
Hashish oil	Hash oil	Concentrated syrupy liquid varying in color from clear to black	Smoked—mixed with tobacco

Inhalants

Effects

The immediate negative effects of inhalants include nausea, sneezing, coughing, nosebleeds, fatigue, lack of coordination, and loss of appetite. Solvents and aerosol sprays also decrease the heart and respiratory rates and impair judgment. Amyl and butyl nitrate cause rapid pulse, headaches, and involuntary passing of urine and feces. Long-term use may result in hepatitis or brain damage.

Deeply inhaling the vapors, or using large amounts over a short time, may result in disorientation, violent behavior, unconsciousness, or death. High concentrations of inhalants can cause suffocation by displacing the oxygen in the lungs or by depressing the central nervous system to the point that breathing stops.

Long-term use can cause weight loss, fatigue, electrolyte imbalance, and muscle fatigue. Repeated sniffing of concentrated vapors over time can permanently damage the nervous system.

(See table on next page.)

Inhalants

Type	What is it called?	What does it look like?	How is it used?
Nitrous Oxide	Laughing gas Whippets	Propellant for whipped cream in aerosal spray can Small 8-gram metal cylinder sold with a balloon or pipe (buzz bomb)	Vapors inhaled
Amyl Nitrite	Poppers Snappers	Clear yellowish liquid in ampules	Vapors inhaled
Butyl Nitrite	Rush Bold Locker room Bullet Climax	Packed in small bottles	Vapors inhaled
Chlorohydrocarbons	Aerosol sprays	Aerosol paint cans Containers of cleaning fluid	Vapors inhaled
Hydrocarbons	Solvents	Cans of aerosol propellants, gasoline, glue, paint thinner	Vapors inhaled

Cocaine

Effects

Cocaine stimulates the central nervous system. Its immediate effects include dilated pupils and elevated blood pressure, heart rate, respiratory rate, and body temperature. Occasional use can cause a stuffy or runny nose, while chronic use can ulcerate the mucous membrane of the nose. Injecting cocaine with contaminated equipment can cause AIDS, hepatitis, and other diseases. Preparation of freebase, which involves the use of volatile solvents, can result in death or injury from fire or explosion. Cocaine can produce psychological and physical dependency, a feeling that the user cannot function without the drug. In addition, tolerance develops rapidly.

Crack or freebase rock is extremely addictive, and its effects are felt within 10 seconds. The physical effects include dilated pupils, increased pulse rate, elevated blood pressure, insomnia, loss of appetite, tactile hallucinations, paranoia, and seizures.

The use of cocaine can cause death by cardiac arrest or respiratory failure.

Cocaine

Type	What is it called?	What does it look like?	How is it used?
Cocaine	Coke Snow Flake White Blow Nose candy Big C Snowbirds Lady	White crystalline powder, often diluted with other ingredients	Inhaled through nasal passages
Crack	Freebase rocks Rock	Light brown or beige pellets—or crystalline rocks that resemble coagulated soap; often packaged in small vials	Smoked

Other Stimulants

Effects

Stimulants can cause increased heart and respiratory rates, elevated blood pressure, dilated pupils, and decreased appetite. In addition, users may experience sweating, headache, blurred vision, dizziness, sleeplessness, and anxiety. Extremely high doses can cause a rapid or irregular heartbeat, tremors, loss of coordination, and even physical collapse. An amphetamine injection creates a sudden increase in blood pressure that can result in stroke, very high fever, or heart failure.

In addition to the physical effects, users report feeling restless, anxious, and moody. Higher doses intensify the effects. Persons who use large amounts of amphetamines over a long period of time can develop amphetamine psychosis that includes hallucinations, delusions, and paranoia. These symptoms usually disappear when drug use ceases.

Other Stimulants

Type	What is it called?	What does it look like?	How is it used?
Amphetamines	Speed Uppers Ups Black beauties Pep pills Copilots Bumblebees Hearts Benzedrine Dexedrine Footballs Biphetamine	Capsules Pills Tablets	Taken orally Injected Inhaled through nasal passages
Methamphetamines	Crank Crystal meth Crystal methadrine Speed	White powder Pills A rock that resembles a block of paraffin	Taken orally Injected Inhaled through nasal passages
Additional stimulants	Ritalin Cylert Preludin Didrex Pre-State Voranil Tenuate Tepanil Pondimin Sandrex Plegine Ionamin	Pills Capsules Tablets	Taken orally Injected

Depressants

Effects

The effects of depressants are in many ways similar to the effects of alcohol. Small amounts can produce calmness and relaxed muscles, but somewhat larger doses can cause slurred speech, staggering gait, and altered perception. Very large doses can cause respiratory depression, coma, and death. The combination of depressants and alcohol can multiply the effects of the drugs, thereby multiplying the risks.

The use of depressants can cause both physical and psychological dependence. Regular use over time may result in tolerance to the drug, leading the user to increase the quantity consumed. When regular users suddenly stop taking large doses, they may develop withdrawal symptoms ranging from restlessness, insomnia, and anxiety to convulsions and death.

Babies born to mothers who abuse depressants during pregnancy may be physically dependent on the drugs and show withdrawal symptoms shortly after they are born. Birth defects and behavioral problems also may result.

Depressants

Type	What is it called?	What does it look like?	How is it used?
Barbiturates	Downers Barbs Blue devils Red devils Yellow jacket Yellows Nembutal Seconal Amytal Tuinals	Red, yellow, blue, or red-and-blue capsules	Taken orally

Methaqualone	Quaaludes Ludes Sopors	Tablets	Taken orally
Tranquilizers	Valium Librium Equanil Miltown Serax Tranxene	Tablets Capsules	Taken orally

Hallucinogens

Effects

Phencyclidine (PCP) interrupts the functions of the neocortex, the section of the brain that controls the intellect and keeps instincts in check. Because the drugs blocks pain receptors, violent PCP episodes may result in self-inflicted injuries.

The effects of PCP vary, but users frequently report a sense of distance and estrangement. Time and body movement are slowed down. Muscular coordination worsens and senses are dulled. Speech is blocked and incoherent.

Chronic users of PCP report persistent memory problems and speech difficulties. Some of these effects may last 6 months to a year following prolonged daily use. Mood disorders—depression, anxiety, and violent behavior—also occur. In later stages of chronic use, users often exhibit paranoid and violent behavior and experience hallucinations.

Large doses may produce convulsions and coma, as well as heart and lung failure.

Lysergic acid (LSD), mescaline, and psilocybin cause illusions and hallucinations. The physical effects may include dilated pupils, elevated body temperature, increased heart rate and blood pressure, loss of appetite, sleeplessness, and tremors.

Sensations and feelings may change rapidly. It is common to have a bad psychological reaction to LSD, mescaline, and psilocybin. The user may experience panic, confusion, suspicion, anxiety, and loss of control. Delayed effects, or flashbacks, can occur even after use has ceased.

Hallucinogens

Type	What is it called?	What does it look like?	How is it used?
Phencyclidine	PCP Angel dust Loveboat Lovely Hog Killer weed	Liquid Capsules White crystalline powder Pills	Taken orally Injected Smoked—can be sprayed on cigarettes, parsley, and marijuana
Lysergic acid diethylamide	LSD Acid Green or red dragon White lightning Blue heaven Sugar cubes Microdot	Brightly colored tablets Impregnated blotter paper Thin squares of gelatin Clear liquid	Taken orally Licked off paper Gelatin and liquid can be put in the eyes
Mescaline and Peyote	Mesc Buttons Cactus	Hard brown discs Tablets Capsules	Discs—chewed, swallowed, or smoked Tablets and capsules—taken orally
Psilocybin	Magic mushrooms 'shrooms	Fresh or dried mushrooms	Chewed and swallowed

Narcotics

Effects

Narcotics initially produce a feeling of euphoria that often is followed by drowsiness, nausea, and vomiting. Users also may experience constricted pupils, watery eyes, and itching. An overdose may produce slow and shallow breathing, clammy skin, convulsions, coma, and possible death.

Tolerance to narcotics develops rapidly and dependence is likely. The use of contaminated syringes may result in disease such as AIDS, endocarditis, and hepatitis. Addiction in pregnant women can lead to premature, stillborn, or addicted infants who experience severe withdrawal symptoms.

Narcotics

Type	What is it called?	What does it look like?	How is it used?
Heroin	Smack Horse Brown sugar Junk Mud Big H Black Tar	Powder, white to dark brown Tarlike substance	Injected Inhaled through nasal passages Smoked
Methadone	Dolophine Methadose Amidone	Solution	Taken orally Injected
Codeine	Epririn compound with codeine Tylenol with codeine Codeine Codeine in cough medicines	Dark liquid varying in thickness Capsules Tablets	Taken orally Injected
Morphine	Pectoral syrup	White crystals Hypodermic tablets Injectable solutions	Injected Taken orally Smoked
Meperidine	Pethidien Demerol Mepergan	White powder Solution Tablets	Taken orally Injected
Opium	Paregoric Dover's powder Parepectolin	Dark brown chunks Powder	Smoked Eaten
Other narcotics	Perocet Percodan Tussionex Fentanyl Darvon Talwin Lomotil	Tablets Capsules Liquid	Taken orally Injected

Designer Drugs

Effects

Illegal drugs are defined in terms of their chemical formulas. To circumvent these legal restrictions, underground chemists modify the molecular structure of certain illegal drugs to produce analogs known as "designer drugs." These drugs can be several hundred times stronger than the drugs they are designed to imitate.

Many of the so-called drugs are related to amphetamines and have mild stimulant properties but are mostly euphoriants. They can produce severe neurochemical damage to the brain.

The narcotic analogs can cause symptoms such as those seen in Parkinson's disease: uncontrollable tremors, drooling, impaired speech, paralysis, and irreversible brain damage. Analogs of amphetamines and methamphetamines cause nausea, blurred vision, chills or sweating, and faintness. Psychological effects include anxiety, depression, and paranoia. As little as one dose can cause brain damage. The analogs of phencyclidine cause illusions, hallucinations, and impaired perception.

Designer Drugs

Type	What is it called?	What does it look like?	How is it used?
Analogs of Fentanyl (Narcotic)	Synthetic Heroin China White	White powder identically resembling heroin	Inhaled through nasal passages Injected
Analogs of Meperidine (Narcotic)	Synthetic Heroin MPTP (New Heroin) MPPP	White Powder	Inhaled through nasal passages Injected
Analogs of Amphetamines and Methamphetamines (Hallucinogens)	MDMA (Ecstasy, XTC, Adam, Essence) MDM STP PMA 2, 5-DMA TMA DOM DOB EVE	White powder Tablets Capsules	Taken orally Injected Inhaled through nasal passages
Analogs of Phencyclidine (PCP)	PCPy PCE	White powder	Taken orally Injected Smoked

Anabolic Steroids

Anabolic steroids are a group of powerful compounds closely related to the male sex hormone testosterone. Developed in the 1930s, steroids are seldom prescribed by physicians today. Current legitimate medical uses are limited to certain kinds of anemia, severe burns, and some types of breast cancer.

Taken in combination with a program of muscle-building exercise and diet, steroids may contribute to increases in body weight and muscular strength. Because of these properties, athletes in a variety of sports have used steroids since the 1950s, hoping to inhance performance. Today, they are being joined by increasing numbers of young people seeking to accelerate their physical development.

Steroid users subject themselves to more than 70 side effects ranging in severity from liver cancer to acne and including psychological as well as physical reactions. The liver and cardiovascular and reproductive systems are most seriously affected by steroid use. In males, use can cause withered testicles, sterility, and impotence. In females, irreversible masculine traits can develop along with breast reduction and sterility. Psychological effects in both sexes include very aggressive behavior known as "roid rage" and depression. While some side effects appear quickly, others, such as heart attacks and strokes, may not show up for years.

Signs of steroid use include quick weight and muscle gains (if steroids are being used in conjunction with a weight training program); behavioral changes, particularly increased aggressiveness and combativeness; jaundice; purple or red spots on the body; swelling of feet or lower legs; trembling; unexplained darkening of the skin; and persistent unpleasant breath odor.

Steroids are produced in tablet or capsule form for oral ingestion, or as a liquid for intramuscular injection.

Source: *What Works: Schools Without Drugs* (1989). U.S. Department of Education.

Hotlines, Helplines, and Helping Organizations: A Quick Reference Guide and Index

Below is a quick reference guide and index to the organizations mentioned in this book, along with their hotlines, helplines, and regular telephone numbers. If you want only the telephone number, just look up the name of the hotline or organization. If you want to know more about the organization, turn to the page number indicated in italics following the entry for fuller description and information, as well as other useful organizations.

If you do not know the name of the organization, look in the A-to-Z section of the book for the topic that concerns you, such as LEARNING DISABILITIES or PRENATAL CARE. There you will find a write-up on the topic, followed by organizations and reference works relating to it. You can also call one of the general numbers listed below.

General Hotlines and Helplines

Federal Information Center, for referral to the proper government agency for your question, 800-347-1997 9 A.M.-10:30 P.M. EST).

National Institutes of Health, for referral to the government organization dealing with specific health questions, 301-496-4000.

National Health Information Clearinghouse, for referrals to other hotlines or helplines, 800-336-4797.

Toll-free Number Directory, AT&T directory, 800-555-1212.

Specific Hotlines, Helplines, and Helping Organizations

AASK America (Aid to Adoption of Special Kids), 415-543-2275; toll-free number, 800-23A-ASK1 [232-2751]. *13*

Immune Deficiency Foundation (IDF), 301-461-3127. *259*

IMPACC, abbreviation for INTESTINAL MULTIPLE POLYPOSIS AND COLORECTAL CANCER. *73*

Information Center for Individuals with Disabilities (ICID), voice/TDD 617-727-5540; toll-free number, MA only, voice/TDD 800-462-5015. *579*

Institute for Childhood Resources (INICR), 415-864-1169. *375*

Inter-National Association for Widowed People (IAWP), 217-787-0886. *135*

International Association of Parents and Professionals for Safe Alternatives in Childbirth (NAPSAC), 314-238-2010. *92*

International Childbirth Education Association (ICEA), 612-854-8660. *92*

International Council for Infant Survival (ICIS), 714-856-3522. *444*

International Foundation for Stutterers (IFS), 201-359-6469. *117*

International Hearing Dog, Inc. (IHDI), 303-287-EARS [3277], voice/TTY. *164*

International Institute for Visually Impaired, 0-7 (IIVI, 0-7), 517-332-2666. *196*

International Nanny Association, 512-454-6462. *95*

International Reading Association (IRA), 302-731-1600. *401*

International Social Service, American Branch (ISS/AB), 212-532-5858. *12*

International Society for Prevention of Child Abuse and Neglect (ISPCAN), 303-321-3963. *88*

International Soundex Reunion Registry (ISRR), 702-882-6270. *14*

Interracial Family Alliance (IFA), 713-454-5018. *201*

Intestinal Multiple Polyposis and Colorectal Cancer (IMPACC), 301-791-7526. *73*

Institute for Responsive Education (IRE), 617-353-3309. *173*

Jewish Vegetarian Society—America (JVS), 301-486-4948. *470*

Johnson Institute, 612-341-0435; toll-free numbers, U.S. except MN, 800-231-5165; MN, 800-247-0484. *589*

Joint Custody Association (JCA), 213-475-5352. *128*

Joslin Diabetes Center (JDC), 617-732-2400. *144*

Juvenile Diabetes Foundation International (JDFI), 212-889-7575. *144*

Keller (Helen) National Center for Deaf-Blind Youths and Adults, 516-944-8900. *163*

Lactaid Hotline, 800-257-8650. *66*

La Leche League International (LLLI), 312-455-7730. *66*

Lambda Legal Defense and Education Fund (LLDEF), 212-995-8585. *249*

Latin America Parents Association (LAPA), 516-795-7427. *12*

Laubach Literacy Action (LLA), 315-422-9121. *401*

Lefthanders International (LHI), 913-234-2177. *232*

Lesbian Mothers National Defense Fund (LMNDF), 206-325-2643. *249*

Lesbian Rights Project (LRP), 415-621-0674. *249*

Leukemia Society of America, 212-573-8484. *293*

Library of Congress, National Library Services for the Blind and Physically Handicapped, 202-287-5100; toll-free number 800-424-8567. *581*

Literacy Hotline, CETA Services, Contact Literacy Center, 800-228-8813. *257*

Little People of America, 415-589-0695 *230*

Living Bank, 800-528-2971. *462*

Lung Line, National Jewish Hospital/National Asthma Center, 800-222-LUNG [5864], 8–5 MT, M–F. *37*

Lupus Foundation of America (LFA), 202-328-4550; toll-free number, U.S. except DC, 800-558-0121 for printed material. *299*

Make-a-Wish Foundation of America (MWFA), 602-234-0960. *583*

Malignant Hyperthermia Association of the United States (MHAUS), 203-655-3007; Medic Alert Hotline 209-634-4917. *302*

March of Dimes Birth Defects Foundation (MDBDF), 914-428-7100; local chapters in telephone-directory white pages. *52, 219.* March of Dimes National Registry for MPS/ML Disorders (MPS/ML Registry), 312-341-1370. *332*

Maternity Center Association (MCA), 212-369-7300. *304*

Mended Hearts (MH), c/o American Heart Association, 214-750-5442. *239*

Mental Disability Legal Resource Center (MDLRC), American Bar Association, 202-331-2240. *314*

Mental Retardation Association of America (MRAA), 801-571-8011. *319*

Missing Children . . . Help Center (MCHC), 813-623-5437; toll-free hotline 800-USA-KIDS [872-5437]. *326*

Missing Children of America (MCA), 907-248-7300. *326*

ML (Mucolipidoses) IV Foundation, 914-425-0639. *332*

Mobility International U.S.A. (MIUSA), voice/TDD, 503-343-1284. *584*

Mothers Against Drunk Driving (MADD), 817-268-MADD [6233]. *590*

Mothers at Home, 703-352-2292. *329*

Mothers of AIDS Patients, 619-544-0430.   *18*

Mothers Without Custody (MWOC), 713-840-1622.   *129*

MPS/ML Registry (March of Dimes National Registry for MPS/ML Disorders), 312-341-1370.   *332*

Mucolipidoses (ML) IV Foundation, 914-425-0639.   *332*

Muscular Dystrophy Association (MDA), 212-586-0808.   *337*

Myasthenia Gravis Foundation (MG), 914-328-1717.   *337*

NAACP Legal Defense and Educational Fund (LDF), 212-219-1900.   *174*

NACOSH, abbreviation for NATIONAL ADVISORY COMMITTEE ON SCOUTING FOR THE HANDICAPPED.   *582*

NAEYC, abbreviation for NATIONAL ASSOCIATION FOR THE EDUCATION OF YOUNG CHILDREN.   *388*

NAPSAC, shorthand for INTERNATIONAL ASSOCIATION OF PARENTS AND PROFESSIONALS FOR SAFE ALTERNATIVES IN CHILDBIRTH.   *92*

NAPSEC, abbreviation for NATIONAL ASSOCIATION OF PRIVATE SCHOOLS FOR EXCEPTIONAL CHILDREN.   *581*

Narcolepsy and Cataplexy Foundation of America (NCFA), 212-628-6315.   *428*

Narcotic Educational Foundation of America (NEFA), 213-663-5171.   *588*

Narcotics Anonymous (NA), 818-780-3951; see telephone directory or information for local numbers, including hotlines in major cities.   *588*

National Abortion Federation (NAF), 202-667-5881; Abortion Referral Hotline, U.S. except DC, 800-772-9100.   *2*

National Abortion Rights Action League (NARAL), 202-371-0779.   *2*

National Adoption Exchange, 215-925-0200.   *12*

National Advisory Committee on Scouting for the Handicapped (NACOSH), 214-580-2127.   *582*

National AIDS Hotline, 800-342-AIDS [2437].   *18*

National AIDS Information Clearinghouse, 301-762-5111.   *18*

National Alliance for the Mentally Ill (NAMI), 703-524-7600.   *314*

National Alopecia Areata Foundation (NAAF), 415-456-4644.   *22*

National Anorexic Aid Society (NAAS), 614-436-1112.   *28*

National Association for Children of Alcoholics (NACOA), 714-499-3889.   *591*

National Association for Creative Children and Adults (NACCA), 513-631-1777.   *224*

National Association for Down's Syndrome (NADS), 312-325-9112.   *153*

National Association for Family Day Care (NAFDC), 801-268-9148.   *95*

National Association for Gifted Children (NAGC), 612-784-3475.   *223*

National Association for Hearing and Speech Action (NAHSA), American Speech-Language-Hearing Association, 301-897-8682, voice/TDD, MD, AK, and HI call collect; toll-free number, voice/TDD, U.S. except MD, AK, and HI, 800-638-TALK [8255].   *116, 162*

National Association for Home Care (NAHC), 202-547-7424.   *579*

National Association for Legal Support of Alternative Schools (NALSAS), 505-471-6928.   *23*

National Association for Parents of the Visually Impaired (NAPVI), 315-245-3442; toll-free number 800-562-6265.   *196*

National Association for Prenatal Addiction Research and Education (NAPARE), 312-329-2512.   *588*

National Association for Sickle Cell Diseases (NASCD), 213-936-7205; toll-free number, U.S. except CA, 800-321-8453.   *25*

National Association for the Advancement of Colored People (NAACP), Legal Defense and Educational Fund (LDF), 212-219-1900.   *174*

National Association for the Dually Diagnosed (NADD), 914-331-4336.   *319*

National Association for the Education of Young Children (NAEYC), 202-232-8777; toll-free number 800-424-2460.   *388*

National Association for Visually Handicapped (NAVH), 212-889-3141.   *197*

National Association for Year-Round Education (NAYRE), 619-292-3679.   *485*

National Association of Anorexia Nervosa and Associated Disorders, Hotline, 708-831-3438.   *28*

National Association of Childbearing Centers (NACC), 215-234-8068.   *304*

National Association of Childbirth Education (NACE), 714-686-0422.   *93*

National Association of Hebrew Day School PTA's, 212-406-4190.   *173*

National Association of Independent Schools (NAIS), 617-723-6900.   *391*

National Association of Patients on Hemodialysis and Transplantation (NAPHT), 212-867-4486.   *146, 462*

National Association of People with AIDS, 202-429-2856.   *19*

National Association of Private, Nontraditional Schools and Colleges (NAPNSC), 303-243-5441.   *391*

National Association of Private Schools for Exceptional Children (NAPSEC), 202-296-1800.   *581*

National Association of Psychiatric Treatment Centers for Children (NAPTCC), 202-638-1991.   *314*